Scholastic
Children's
Dictionary

By the Editors of Scholastic Inc.

New York   Toronto   London   Auckland   Sydney

Photo credits: Unless otherwise credited, photography by Mark Mason Studio. NYPL: 2, General Motors: 3, Archive Photos: 4, Atomic Energy Commission: 33, U.S. Fish & Wildlife Service: 39, No credit: 43, 144, 154, 528, Rhoda Sidney: 50, Gabe Palmer: 53, National Oceanic and Atmospheric Administration: 67, UPI: 69, 150, Leo Keeler/Animals Animals: 71, SuperStock: 87, 112, 113, 115, 120, 125, 130, 134, 142, 176, 180, 185, 201, 203, 227, 228, 230, 233, 236, 239, 253, 256, 265, 266, 272, 275, 276, 286, 287, 288, 291, 299, 303, 310, 311, 312, 316, 319, 323, 341, 343, 349, 354, 372, 390, 392, 396, 397, 400, 405, 413, 422, 423, 434, 448, 449, 450, 456, 458, 474, 477, 479, 487, 488, 492, 504, 521, 527, 533, 535, 542, 547, 550, 556, 565, 566, 575, 581, 586, 590, 597, 600, 602, 603, 604, 607, 630, 632, Historical Society of Pennsylvania: 98, Anne Stentiford: 132, AP/Wide World: 133, 187, 394, 424, 508, Gamma Liaison Int'l: 136, 155, UN photo: 139, American Dental Association: 141, Tony Stone Images: 165, Don Normark/West Stock: 167, NASA: cover, 168, 216, 274, John Gruen: 283, Rubio/West Stock: 362, Gail Shumway/FPG Int'l: 406, Morris M. Macy: 408, Dean Siracusa/FPG Int'l: 415, FPG Int'l: 417, Alan Kearney/FPG Int'l: 418, Ralph Wetmore II/Tony Stone Images: 421, U.S. Geological Survey: 421, Jon Levy/Gamma Liaison: 441, Berenice Abbott/Museum of the City of New York: 446, Kaluzny-Thatchet/Tony Stone Images: 491, David S. Waitz: cover, *i*, 495, Philip Gendreau: 497, EPA-Documerica: 500, Popperfoto/Archive Photos: 507, Lambert/Archive Photos: 519, U.S. Postal Service: 520, Quentin Reynolds/American Heritage Library: 567, Dan Nelken: 591.

Art credits: Unless otherwise credited, illustrations by Sean Wilkinson, Gerald Wood, Nicholas Hewetson, Ian Jackson, Peter Dennis, Michelle Ross, Chris Shields, Kuo Kang Chen, David Goldston, Dan Courtney, Andrew Beckett, Hans Jenssen, Nick Gibbard, Maurice Pledger, David Wright, Chris Lyon, Isabel Bowring, Peter Geissler, Aziz Khan, Steven Kirk, Jason Lewis, Peter Goodwin, Louise Nixon, Malcolm McGregor. Laura Cornell: 6, Justin Novak: 16, 183, Phil Scheuer: 36, Jared Lee: 42, Lloyd Birmingham: 76, Barbara Gray: 138, Steve Henry: 140, 442, Chris Reed: 144, 161, Kate Keller: 158, Dawn Adelman: 166, Virginia L. Dustin: 261, Mel Pickering/Two-Can Publishing, Ltd., & Scholastic Inc.: 549, Dream Maker Software, 636-643.

Library of Congress Cataloging-in-Publication Data

Scholastic Children's Dictionary.
p. cm.
Includes index.
ISBN 0-590-25271-2
1. English Language—Dictionaries, Juvenile. [1. English Language—Dictionaries.]   I. Scholastic Inc.
PE 1628.5.S3 1996
423—dc20   95–26237
                                              CIP
                                              AC

First Edition by Usborne Publishing Ltd.

12 11 10 9 8 7 6 5 4 3 2 1   6 7 8 9/9 0 1/0
Printed in the U.S.A.
First Scholastic printing, August 1996

Contents

Dictionary Staff

Publisher	Peggy Intrator
Editorial Director	Wendy Barish
Editor in Chief	Sue Macy
Lexicographic Consultant	Joanne Sher Grumet, Ph.D.
Editors	Jacqueline B. Glasthal Sheila Wolinsky
Managing Editors	Nancy Laties Feresten Pamela Nelson Manuela Soares
Copy Editors	Karen Booth Susan McCloskey
Proofreaders	Juanita Galuska Sarah L. Jordan
Contributing Editors	Judy Gitenstein Iris Rosoff
Design Director	Elliot Kreloff
Production Manager	Judith A.V. Harlan
Designer	Joan Gazdik Gillner
Design Assistant	Virginia L. Dustin
Cover Designer	Tilman Reitzle
Manufacturing Coordinator	Heather Service
Photo Research Manager	Grace How
Photo Researchers	Dylan Crossgrove Thea Day Heather Miller Anne Nakasone
Data Inputters	Veronica A. Gazdik Noreen Morin Michele A. Young
Database Designer	David Small, Apple Centre Oxford

The publisher would like to thank American Reference Publishing, Inc., for its invaluable contribution during the initial stages of the preparation of this book.

Advisory Board

General Consultant
Anne Soukhanov
Bedford, Virginia

Library Advisors
Jane Claes, M.L.S.
Library Media Specialist
Irving School District
Carrollton, Texas

Pat Scales, M.L.S.
Library Media Specialist
Greenville Middle School
Greenville, South Carolina

Language Arts Advisor
Linda F. Davis, M.A.
Deputy Superintendent
Division of Program Development and
    Instructional Support Services
San Francisco Unified School District
San Francisco, California

Child Development Consultant
Adele Brodkin, Ph.D.
Clinical Associate Professor
Division of Child and Adolescent Psychiatry
UMDNJ—New Jersey Medical School
Newark, New Jersey

Science Advisor
Ken R. Mechling, Ph.D.
Professor of Biology and Science Education
Clarion University
Clarion, Pennsylvania

Mathematics Advisor
Joseph Payne, Ph.D.
Professor Emeritus of Mathematics
University of Michigan
Ann Arbor, Michigan

Technology Advisors
Tom Boudrot, Ed.D.
Director of Technology
The Edison Project
New York, New York

Stephen M. Tomecek
Executive Director
Science Plus
Hyde Park, New York

Pronunciation Guide

There are no strange symbols in this dictionary's pronunciation system. Instead, letters and letter combinations are used to stand for different sounds. To make our system as clear as possible, we have included more than one way to pronounce some sounds. These alternatives are indented, below. For example, the s- sound is given the pronunciation symbol (s) at the beginning of a word or syllable, as in (**see**) for the word **see**, but the symbol (ss) at the end of a word or syllable, as in (**layss**) for the word **lace**.

Pronunciations are not listed for some entries that consist of two or more words, such as **acid rain**, or words that are hyphenated, such as **mix-up**. The pronunciations for those words are found elsewhere in the dictionary. **Acid rain**, for example, has pronunciations indicated at the entries for **acid** and **rain**, and the words in **mix-up** are pronounced at **mix** and **up**.

Many words contain two or more syllables. In most cases, those words have one syllable that gets greater stress than any other syllable. This accented syllable is marked in boldface letters, as in (**ak**-shuhn) for the word **action**. Some words also have a syllable with a second or lighter stress. This second accented syllable is marked in italic, as in (**koh**-kuh-*nuht*) for **coconut**.

The symbol (uh) is used for both the accented vowel in the word **cup** and for almost all unaccented syllables in words, as in (uh-**bout**) for the word **about**. Here are the letters and letter combinations that stand for each sound in this dictionary.

Vowels

a	m**a**d, p**a**t
ah	f**a**ther
air	f**air**, c**are**
ar	d**ar**k
ay	p**ay**, accl**ai**m
	(a-*consonant*-e) m**ade**, n**ape**
aw	r**aw**, c**au**ght
e	m**e**t, m**e**n
ee	b**ee**t
i	b**i**t, acc**i**dent
ihr	f**ear**, **here**
eye	**i**ron, rabb**i**
	(i-*consonant*-e) f**ile**, r**ipe**
	(*consonant*-ye) r**ye**, l**ie**, m**y**
o	c**o**t, d**o**t
oh	f**oe**, d**ou**gh
	(o-*consonant*-e) al**one**, st**one**
oo	p**oo**l, r**u**de
or	c**or**n, m**or**e
oi	b**oi**l, t**oy**
ou	h**ow**, **ou**ch
u	p**u**t, b**oo**k
uh	b**u**n, nati**o**n, comm**a**
ur	b**ur**n, work**er**
yoo	m**u**sic, p**u**re

Consonants

b	**b**ad, so**b**
ch	**ch**ip, di**tch**
d	**d**ip, re**d**
f	**f**un, cu**ff**, laug**h**
g	**g**et, be**g**
h	**h**am
j	**j**am, e**dg**e
k	**k**eep, sa**ck**
l	**l**ap, te**ll**
m	**m**an, lam**b**
n	**n**ow, te**n**, **gn**at, **kn**ow
ng	si**ng**
p	**p**an, si**p**
r	**r**ib, pou**r**
s	**s**et
ss	mi**ss**, ra**c**e, ye**s**
sh	**sh**ip, ra**sh**
t	**t**ub, ra**t**
th	**th**in, ba**th**
TH	**th**is, ba**th**e
v	**v**an, hi**v**e
w	**w**ell, **wh**ale
y	**y**ell
z	**z**ip, ha**s**, tho**s**e
zh	mea**s**ure

Overview

A dictionary is a reference book that gives all kinds of information about words. This dictionary is your guidebook to the English language. You can refer to it to find out what a word means, check its spelling or pronunciation, or figure out how to use it in a sentence. Special features such as Word History boxes reveal the origins of some words, and Synonym boxes suggest similar words to help you add variety to your writing and your speech. On these two pages, we've highlighted some of the other features of this book.

"About This Letter" Boxes appear on the opening page of each new letter. In each one, you will find a fact about that letter or a spelling tip for words containing that letter's sound.

Guide Words tell you the first and last main entry words that appear on a page.

Thumb-Index Tabs help you scan the side of the book to find the section that you are looking for. For example, since "I" is the ninth letter in the alphabet, you can locate it by opening the book at the ninth red tab from the top.

Entries are listed in alphabetical order. Many words have several different meanings and uses that are listed under different numbers within the entry. Some entries have illustrations or photographs.

Main Entry Words are set in bold (dark) type and jut out a bit from the meanings. The dictionary was designed this way to make it easy for you to find the words you look up.

Word History and Other Boxes. Word History, Prefix, Suffix, Synonym, and Language Note boxes appear throughout this dictionary. These boxes give you extra information about the origin or usage of a word or word part.

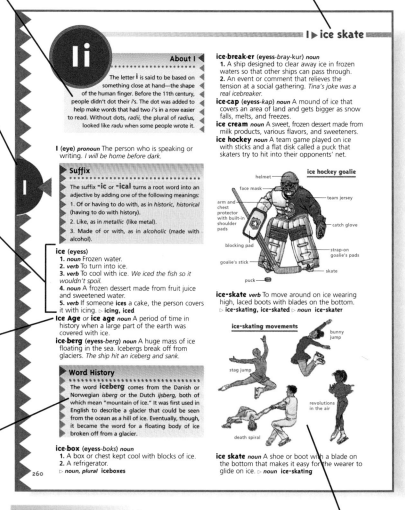

Ii

About I

The letter **i** is said to be based on something close at hand—the shape of the human finger. Before the 11th century, people didn't dot their *i*'s. The dot was added to help make words that had two *i*'s in a row easier to read. Without dots, *radii*, the plural of *radius*, looked like *radu* when some people wrote it.

I (eye) *pronoun* The person who is speaking or writing. *I will be home before dark.*

Suffix

The suffix **-ic** or **-ical** turns a root word into an adjective by adding one of the following meanings:
1. Of or having to do with, as in *historic, historical* (having to do with history).
2. Like, as in *metallic* (like metal).
3. Made of or with, as in *alcoholic* (made with alcohol).

ice (eyess)
1. *noun* Frozen water.
2. *verb* To turn into ice.
3. *verb* To cool with ice. *We iced the fish so it wouldn't spoil.*
4. *noun* A frozen dessert made from fruit juice and sweetened water.
5. *verb* If someone **ices** a cake, the person covers it with icing. ▷ **icing, iced**

Ice Age or **ice age** *noun* A period of time in history when a large part of the earth was covered with ice.

ice·berg (eyess-berg) *noun* A huge mass of ice floating in the sea. Icebergs break off from glaciers. *The ship hit an iceberg and sank.*

Word History

The word **iceberg** comes from the Danish or Norwegian *isberg* or the Dutch *ijsberg*, both of which mean "mountain of ice." It was first used in English to describe a glacier that could be seen from the ocean as a hill of ice. Eventually, though, it became the word for a floating body of ice broken off from a glacier.

ice·box (eyess-boks) *noun*
1. A box or chest kept cool with blocks of ice.
2. A refrigerator.
▷ *noun, plural* **iceboxes**

260

I ▶ ice skate

ice·break·er (eyess-bray-kur) *noun*
1. A ship designed to clear away ice in frozen waters so that other ships can pass through.
2. An event or comment that relieves the tension at a social gathering. *Tina's joke was a real icebreaker.*

ice·cap (eyess-kap) *noun* A mound of ice that covers an area of land and gets bigger as snow falls, melts, and freezes.

ice cream *noun* A sweet, frozen dessert made from milk products, various flavors, and sweeteners.

ice hockey *noun* A team game played on ice with sticks and a flat disk called a puck that skaters try to hit into their opponents' net.

ice hockey goalie

helmet
face mask
arm and chest protector with built-in shoulder pads
catch glove
team jersey
blocking pad
goalie's stick
strap-on goalie's pads
skate
puck

ice-skate *verb* To move around on ice wearing high, laced boots with blades on the bottom. ▷ **ice-skating, ice-skated** ▷ *noun* **ice-skater**

ice-skating movements

bunny jump
stag jump
revolutions in the air
death spiral

ice skate *noun* A shoe or boot with a blade on the bottom that makes it easy for the wearer to glide on ice. ▷ *noun* **ice-skating**

Labeled Illustrations show you the details of objects defined in main entries. Some of the labels in the illustrations are entry words, and others are not. The labels that are not entry words are listed in the Index of Picture Labels on pages 647 and 648.

Dictionary Entries Close Up

Syllable Breaks are indicated by small dots in most main entry words. Entries made up of two separate words or two words and a hyphen are not broken into syllables. To find their syllable breaks, look up each part of the term separately. For example, to find the syllable breaks for *table manners*, look up *table* and *manners*.

Numbers appear at the beginning of each meaning when a word has more than one meaning. The most frequently used meanings generally appear first.

Usage Guides tell you that a meaning of a word is informal or slang. Informal words are used in everyday speech but not usually in formal speech or in writing. Many slang terms or meanings are very popular only for a short period of time. Like informal words, they are not appropriate in formal writing such as term papers and essays.

Pronunciations, given in parentheses, follow most main entry words. The "Pronunciation Guide" on page v explains which letters represent each sound. If the pronunciation of a word changes depending on its meaning, the appropriate pronunciation appears with the appropriate meaning.

Definitions tell the meanings of words. When the main entry word is used within the definition, it is printed in **boldface**. In the rare cases that a definition includes a word that is not in the dictionary, that word appears in *italics*.

---

mouth·piece (mouth-*peess*) *noun*
1. The part of a telephone that you talk into.
2. The part of a musical instrument that you blow over or into. *See* **bagpipes, recorder, saxophone.**
3. *(informal)* Someone who acts as a spokesperson for an individual or a group.

---

prog·ress
1. (pruh-**gress**) *verb* To move forward or to improve. *How are you progressing with your fitness program?* ▷ **progresses, progressing, progressed**
2. (**prog**-ruhss) *noun* A forward movement or improvement. *The teacher saw some progress in the student's work.*
3. (**prog**-ruhss) If something is **in progress,** it is happening. *Road construction will be in progress all this week.*

---

rap (rap)
1. *verb* To hit something sharply and quickly. *Bettina rapped on the window.* ▷ *noun* **rap**
2. *noun* A type of song in which the words are spoken in a rhythmical way to a musical background. ▷ *noun* **rapper** ▷ *verb* **rap**
3. *verb* (*slang*) To talk.
Rap sounds like **wrap.**
▷ *verb* **rapping, rapped**

Part of Speech labels usually appear on the first lines of entries. However, if a word's part of speech changes from one meaning to the next, the part of speech label starts each new meaning. When a meaning shows the word as part of a common phrase or idiom, no part of speech is given.

Cross References tell you where to turn in the dictionary for a picture of, or more information about, the main entry word.

Sample Sentences appear in italics after some of the meanings. These sentences show the word used in context. Captions, or sentences that explain what is shown in photographs and illustrations, also appear in italics.

Related Words and Word Forms appear at the end of an entry or at the end of a meaning. This dictionary also lists irregular plural forms with entry words that are nouns, -er and -est forms with adjectives, and -ed, -ing, and irregular forms with verbs.

Homophones, words that sound alike but have different spellings and meanings, are listed toward the ends of definitions.

Initials, Acronyms, and Abbreviations

An **initial** is a letter, usually followed by a period, that takes the place of a whole word.
An **acronym** is a group of initials that forms another word or phrase.
An **abbreviation** is a shortened form of a word, followed by a period.

A.A. = Alcoholics Anonymous
A.C.L.U. = American Civil Liberties Union
AM = amplitude modulation
anon. = anonymous
A.S.A.P. = as soon as possible
A.S.P.C.A. = American Society for the Prevention of Cruelty to Animals
Aug. = August
AWOL = absent without official leave
B.B.B. = Better Business Bureau
C = Celsius
C.E.O. = chief executive officer
CIA = Central Intelligence Agency
Co. = company
C.O.D. = cash on delivery
Corp. = corporation
D.A. = district attorney
dB = decibel
D.C. = District of Columbia
D.D.S. = Doctor of Dental Science
Dec. = December
Dept. = department
D.O.B. = date of birth
D.V.M. = Doctor of Veterinary Medicine
EMT = emergency medical technician
EPA = Environmental Protection Agency
ERA = Equal Rights Amendment
ESL = English as a Second Language
F = Fahrenheit
FBI = Federal Bureau of Investigation
Feb. = February
FM = frequency modulation
Fri. = Friday
F.Y.I. = for your information
GCF = greatest common factor
GIGO = garbage in, garbage out

G.O.P. = Grand Old Party (Republican party)
HQ = headquarters
HST = Hawaiian standard time
Inc. = incorporated
IRS = Internal Revenue Service
Jan. = January
Jr. = junior
K.K.K. = Ku Klux Klan
LCD = lowest (or least) common denominator
LCM = lowest (or least) common multiple
MADD = Mothers Against Drunk Driving
MC = master of ceremonies
M.D. = Medicinae Doctor (Latin for "doctor of medicine")
MIA = missing in action
min. = minute
misc. = miscellaneous
Mon. = Monday
NAACP = National Association for the Advancement of Colored People
NASA = National Aeronautics and Space Administration
N.B.A. = National Basketball Association
N.F.L. = National Football League
N.H.L. = National Hockey League
Nov. = November
NOW = National Organization for Women
Oct. = October
OPEC = Organization of Petroleum Exporting Countries
P.A. = public address
P.O. = Post Office
POW = prisoner of war
P.T.A. = Parent-Teacher Association

R and R = rest and recreation
R.N. = registered nurse
R.S.V.P. = répondez s'il vous plait (French for "please respond")
RV = recreational vehicle
SADD = Students Against Drunk Driving
SALT = Strategic Arms Limitation Talks
S.A.S.E. = self-addressed stamped envelope
Sat. = Saturday
sec. = second
Sept. = September
SIDS = sudden infant death syndrome
Sr. = senior
S.R.O. = standing room only
Sun. = Sunday
S.W.A.K. = sealed with a kiss
T or tbsp. = tablespoon
tsp. = teaspoon
T.B.A. = to be announced
T.G.I.F. = thank God it's Friday
Thurs. = Thursday
TM = trademark
Tues. = Tuesday
U.N. = United Nations
UNESCO = United Nations Educational, Scientific, and Cultural Organization
UNICEF = United Nations International Children's Education Fund
UPC = Universal Product Code
U.S.A. = United States of America
VISTA = Volunteers in Service to America
WAC = Women's Army Corps
Wed. = Wednesday
w/o = without

Aa

Each letter in our alphabet started as a drawing of an animal, object, or person. **A** probably was first drawn upside down like a V, with a bar across the middle. It may have stood for the horns of an ox, since farmers used to guide oxen by a rope attached to a bar across their horns.

a (uh *or* a) *indefinite article*
1. Any. *Pick a card.*
2. One. *I have a car.*
3. Per. *They travelled two hundred miles a day during the trip.*

aard·vark (ard-*vark*) *noun* An African mammal with a long, sticky tongue that it uses to search for insects.

aardvark

▶ Word History

The **aardvark** owes its name to the Afrikaans language, which is spoken in South Africa, where these animals are found. In this language, *aard* means "earth" and *vark* means "pig." Aardvark was therefore the perfect term for this piglike animal that digs in the ground (or earth) to hunt for ants and termites.

ab·a·cus (ab-uh-kuhss) *noun* A frame with sliding beads on wires, used for adding, subtracting, multiplying, and dividing. ▷ *noun, plural* **abacuses** *or* **abaci** (ab-uh-sye *or* ab-uh-kye)

ab·a·lo·ne (*ab*-uh-**loh**-nee) *noun* A large sea snail with a flat shell whose meat people eat and whose shell lining is shiny like a pearl.

a·ban·don (uh-ban-duhn) *verb*
1. To leave forever. *Abandon ship!*
2. To give up. *Never abandon hope!*
▷ *verb* **abandoning, abandoned**

a·ban·doned (uh-ban-duhnd) *adjective* Deserted, or no longer used. *The house was abandoned many years ago.*

a·bate (uh-bayt) *verb* To become less intense. *Once the storm abated, we went outside to see if there was any damage.* ▷ **abating, abated**

ab·bey (ab-ee) *noun* A group of buildings where monks or nuns live and work.

ab·bre·vi·ate (uh-**bree**-vee-*ate*) *verb* To make something shorter, such as a word. *When you abbreviate a word, you leave out some of the letters and sometimes add a period.* ▷ **abbreviating, abbreviated** ▷ *adjective* **abbreviated**

ab·bre·vi·a·tion (uh-*bree*-vee-ay-shuhn) *noun* A short way of writing a word. *Rd. is an abbreviation of road.*

ab·di·cate (ab-di-kate) *verb* To give up power. *When the queen abdicated the throne, her son became king.* ▷ **abdicating, abdicated** ▷ *noun* **abdication**

ab·do·men (ab-duh-muhn) *noun*
1. The part of your body between your chest and hips.
2. The back section of an insect's body. *See* **beetle.**

ab·duct (ab-dukt) *verb* To kidnap someone. ▷ **abducting, abducted** ▷ *noun* **abduction**

ab·hor (ab-hor) *verb* To hate someone or something. *Alix abhors romantic movies.* ▷ **abhorring, abhorred** ▷ *adjective* **abhorrent**

a·bide (uh-bide) *verb*
1. To stay or live somewhere. *We no longer abide in New York.*
2. If you **cannot abide** something, you cannot comply with it. *I cannot abide that decision.* ▷ *verb* **abiding, abided** *or* **abode** (uh-**bohd**)

a·bil·i·ty (uh-**bil**-i-tee) *noun*
1. The power to do something. *I know I have the ability to do better.*
2. Skill. *Pablo has great ability in art.* ▷ *noun, plural* **abilities**

a·blaze (uh-blaze) *adjective* On fire.

a·ble (ay-buhl) *adjective*
1. If you are **able** to do something, you can do it.
2. Skillful or talented. *We picked the most able players for the team.* ▷ *adjective* **abler, ablest** ▷ *adverb* **ably**

▶ Suffix

The suffix **-able** turns a root word into an adjective by adding one of the following meanings to the root word:
1. Capable of or able to, as in *a breakable toy* (capable of breaking).
2. Likely to, as in *an agreeable kid* (likely to agree).
3. Worthy of or deserving, as in *a lovable kitten* (worthy of love).

able-bod·ied (bod-eed) *adjective* Someone who is **able-bodied** has a strong, healthy body.

ab·nor·mal (ab-nor-muhl) *adjective* Unusual, or not normal. ▷ *noun* **abnormality** (ab-nor-**mal**-i-tee)

1

a·board (uh-bord) *adverb* On or into a train, ship, or aircraft. *Climb aboard!* ▷ *preposition* **aboard**

a·bode (uh-bode) *noun* A home.

a·bol·ish (uh-bol-ish) *verb* To put an end to something officially. *The 13th Amendment to the U.S. Constitution abolished slavery.* ▷ **abolishes, abolishing, abolished** ▷ *noun* **abolition**

a·bo·li·tion·ist (ab-uh-lish-uh-nist) *noun* Someone who worked to abolish slavery before the Civil War. *Frederick Douglass escaped a life of slavery and became a leading abolitionist.*

Frederick Douglass

a·bom·i·na·ble (uh-**bom**-uh-nuh-buhl) *adjective* Horrible, or disgusting. *Vera's room was an abominable mess before she cleaned it.* ▷ *adverb* **abominably**

Ab·o·rig·i·ne (ab-uh-rij-uh-nee) *noun* One of the native peoples of Australia who have lived there since before the Europeans arrived. *This picture shows Aborigines performing a traditional dance.* ▷ *adjective* **Aboriginal**

Aborigines

a·bort (uh-bort) *verb* To stop something from happening in the early stages. *The pilot was forced to abort the takeoff of our airplane because of bad weather and treacherous flying conditions on our route.* ▷ **aborting, aborted** ▷ *adjective* **abortive**

a·bound (uh-bound) *verb* To have a large amount of something. *The forest abounds with wildlife.* ▷ **abounding, abounded**

a·bout (uh-bout)
1. *preposition* On a particular subject. *Tell me about your vacation.*
2. *adverb* Almost, or more or less. *My dad's about 40 years old.*

a·bove (uh-buhv) *preposition*
1. Higher up than, or over. *The balloon was flying high above the clouds.*
2. More than, as in *above average.*

a·bove·board (uh-buhv-bord) *adjective* If an action is **aboveboard,** it is completely honest and legal.

ab·ra·sive (uh-bray-siv) *adjective*
1. Rough and grinding. *Sandpaper has an abrasive surface.* ▷ *noun* **abrasive**
2. Rude. *Roger has an abrasive manner.*

a·breast (uh-brest) *adverb* Side by side. *We walked three abreast.*

a·bridged (uh-brijd) *adjective* Shortened, as in *an abridged novel.* ▷ *verb* **abridge**

a·broad (uh-brawd) *adverb* In or to another country. In the United States, *abroad* usually means "overseas." *We are going abroad this fall.*

a·brupt (uh-brupt) *adjective*
1. Sudden and unexpected. *The car came to an abrupt halt.*
2. Rude and overly quick, as in *an abrupt reply.*
▷ *adverb* **abruptly**

ab·scess (ab-sess) *noun* A painful swelling full of a yellow substance called pus. ▷ *noun, plural* **abscesses**

ab·scond (ab-skond) *verb* To go away suddenly and secretly, usually after doing something wrong. ▷ **absconding, absconded**

ab·sent (ab-suhnt) *adjective* Not present. ▷ *noun* **absence,** *noun* **absentee,** *noun* **absenteeism**

absent-mind·ed (mine-duhd) *adjective* If you are **absent-minded,** you are forgetful and do not think about what you are doing. ▷ *adverb* **absent-mindedly**

ab·so·lute (ab-suh-loot) *adjective*
1. Complete, or total. *Ben looks like an absolute idiot in that hat.*
2. Without any limit. *The dictator had absolute power.*
▷ *adverb* **absolutely**

ab·solve (ab-zolv) *verb* To pardon someone or free the person from blame. ▷ **absolving, absolved** ▷ *noun* **absolution**

ab·sorb (ab-zorb) *verb*
1. To soak up liquid. *The sponge absorbed the juice.*
2. To take in information. *The students absorbed all the facts.*
3. If something **absorbs** you, it takes up all your attention.
▷ *verb* **absorbing,** **absorbed**

ab·sorb·ent (ab-zor-buhnt) *adjective* Something that soaks up liquid, such as a washcloth, towel, or sponge, is **absorbent.**

ab·sorp·tion (ab-zorp-shuhn) *noun* The process of soaking up liquid, heat, or light.

ab·stain (ab-stayn) *verb* To stop yourself from doing something. *The prisoners abstained from eating until their demands were met.*
▷ **abstaining, abstained** ▷ *noun* **abstention**

ab·stract (ab-strakt *or* ab-**strakt**) *adjective*
1. Based on ideas rather than things. *Abstract paintings show impressions rather than what people or objects actually look like.*
2. Hard to understand. *Your explanation of atoms and electrons is too abstract for me.*

ab·surd (ab-**surd** *or* ab-**zurd**) *adjective* Silly, or ridiculous. *Wearing a bathing suit in winter is an absurd idea.* ▷ **absurder, absurdest** ▷ *noun* **absurdity** ▷ *adverb* **absurdly**

a·bun·dant (uh-**bun**-duhnt) *adjective* If there is an **abundant** supply of something, there is plenty of it. ▷ *noun* **abundance** ▷ *adverb* **abundantly**

a·buse
1. (uh-**byooss**) *noun* Rude or unkind words.
2. (uh-**byooz**) *verb* To treat a person or creature cruelly. ▷ **abusing, abused** ▷ *noun* **abuser**
3. (uh-**byooss**) *noun* Wrong or harmful use of something or treatment of someone, as in *alcohol abuse* or *child abuse.* ▷ *verb* **abuse** (uh-**byooz**)
▷ *adjective* **abusive**

a·bys·mal (uh-**biz**-muhl) *adjective* Very bad, or terrible. *Todd's handwriting is abysmal.* ▷ *adverb* **abysmally**

a·byss (uh-**biss**) *noun* A very deep hole that seems to have no bottom. ▷ *noun, plural* **abysses**

a·ca·cia (uh-**kay**-shuh) *noun* A small tree or shrub that has feathery leaves and pleasant-smelling white or yellow flowers and grows in warm parts of the world.

ac·a·dem·ic (ak-uh-**dem**-ik)
1. *adjective* To do with study and learning. *Anna loves sports but hates academic work.* ▷ *adverb* **academically**
2. *noun* Someone who teaches in a university or college or someone who does research.

a·cad·e·my (uh-**kad**-uh-mee) *noun*
1. A private junior high, middle school, or high school.
2. A school that teaches special subjects, as in *a military academy.*
▷ *noun, plural* **academies**

ac·cel·er·ate (ak-**sel**-uh-*rate*) *verb* To get faster and faster. *The car accelerated.* ▷ **accelerating, accelerated** ▷ *noun* **acceleration**

ac·cent (ak-sent) *noun*
1. The way that you pronounce words. *Helmut speaks with a German accent.* ▷ *verb* **accent**
2. Some languages use an **accent mark** over, under, or next to a letter to show how it is pronounced, as in *café.*

ac·cen·tu·ate (ak-**sen**-choo-*ate*) *verb* To emphasize or draw attention to something. *Mascara accentuates eyelashes.* ▷ **accentuating, accentuated**

ac·cept (ak-**sept**) *verb*
1. To take something that you are offered.
2. To agree to something. *Manny won't accept our plan.*
▷ *verb* **accepting, accepted** ▷ *noun* **acceptance**
▷ *adjective* **acceptable**

ac·cess (ak-**sess**)
1. *noun* A way to enter, or an approach to a place. *Only someone with a pass is allowed access to the beach.* ▷ *noun, plural* **accesses** ▷ *adjective* **accessible**
2. *verb* To get information from a computer. *Orlando accessed the database.* ▷ **accesses, accessing, accessed**

ac·ces·so·ry (ak-**sess**-uh-ree) *noun*
1. An extra part for something, as in *computer accessories.*
2. Something, such as a belt or a scarf, that goes with your clothes.
3. An **accessory** to a crime is someone who helps another person commit a crime or helps cover up a crime by not reporting it.
▷ *noun, plural* **accessories**

ac·ci·dent (ak-si-duhnt) *noun* Something that takes place unexpectedly and that often involves people being hurt. *Crash tests such as this one show how a car might be affected in accidents at different driving speeds.* ▷ *adjective* **accidental** ▷ *adverb* **accidentally**

accident

ac·claim (uh-**klaym**) *noun* Praise. ▷ *verb* **acclaim**

ac·cli·ma·tize (uh-**klye**-muh-*tize*) *verb* To get used to a different climate or to new surroundings. ▷ **acclimatizing, acclimatized** ▷ *noun* **acclimatization**

ac·com·mo·date (uh-**kom**-uh-*date*) *verb*
1. To help out or reply to a request. *When we asked for no salt, the cook was able to accommodate us.*
2. To provide with a place to stay. *The hotel has just enough rooms to accommodate our convention.*
▷ *verb* **accommodating, accommodated**

ac·com·pa·ny (uh-**kum**-puh-nee) *verb*
1. To go somewhere with someone.
2. To support a musician or singer by playing along on a musical instrument. ▷ *noun* **accompaniment**, *noun* **accompanist**
▷ *verb* **accompanies, accompanying, accompanied**

ac·com·plice (uh-kom-pliss) *noun* Someone who helps another person commit a crime.

ac·com·plish (uh-kom-plish) *verb* To do something successfully. ▷ **accomplishes, accomplishing, accomplished** ▷ *noun* **accomplishment**

ac·com·plished (uh-kom-plisht) *adjective* Skillful, as in *an accomplished musician.*

ac·cord (uh-kord) *noun*
1. Peaceful agreement.
2. If you do something **of your own accord,** you do it without being asked.

according to *preposition*
1. As someone has said or written. *According to the schedule, a bus stops here every half hour.*
2. In a way that is suitable. *You'll be paid according to the amount of work that you do.*
▷ *adverb* **accordingly**

ac·cor·di·on (uh-kor-dee-uhn)
noun A musical instrument that you squeeze to make sound and play by pressing keys and buttons. *Orchestra leader Lawrence Welk was a famous accordion player.* See **instrument.**

accordion

ac·cost (uh-kost) *verb* To approach someone and talk to the person, usually in an annoying or hostile way. ▷ **accosting, accosted**

ac·count (uh-kount)
1. *noun* A description of something that has happened, as in *an account of the accident.*
2. *noun* An arrangement to keep money in a bank, as in *a checking or savings account.*
3. accounts *noun, plural* Records of money earned and spent.
4. *verb* If you **account for** something, you explain it. ▷ **accounting, accounted** ▷ *adjective* **accountable**

ac·count·ant (uh-koun-tuhnt) *noun* An expert in money matters and keeping accounts. ▷ *noun* **accountancy**

ac·cu·mu·late (uh-kyoo-myuh-late) *verb* To collect things or let them pile up. ▷ **accumulating, accumulated** ▷ *noun* **accumulation**

ac·cu·rate (ak-yuh-ruht) *adjective* Exactly correct. ▷ *noun* **accuracy** ▷ *adverb* **accurately**

ac·cuse (uh-kyooz) *verb* To say that someone has done something wrong. ▷ **accusing, accused** ▷ *noun* **accusation,** *noun* **accuser**

ac·cus·tomed (uh-kuss-tuhmd) *adjective*
1. Usual, as in *my accustomed seat.*
2. When you are **accustomed to** something, you are used to it.

ace (ayss) *noun*
1. A playing card with only one symbol on it. In most card games, the ace has the highest value.
2. A serve in tennis that is not returned, or even touched, by the other player.

ache (ake) *noun* A dull pain that goes on and on. ▷ *verb* **ache**

a·chieve (uh-cheev) *verb* To do something successfully, especially after a lot of effort. ▷ **achieving, achieved** ▷ *noun* **achievement,** *noun* **achiever**

ac·id (ass-id)
1. *noun* A substance with a sour taste that will react with a base to form a salt. Acids turn blue litmus paper red. Strong acids can burn your skin.
2. *adjective* Sour, or bitter. ▷ *adjective* **acidic**

acid rain *noun* Rain that is polluted by acid in the atmosphere and damages the environment. *The diagram shows how fumes containing acids from factories, car exhausts, etc., travel until they meet damp air, then fall as acid rain.*

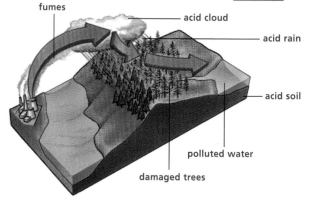

acid rain

fumes
acid cloud
acid rain
acid soil
polluted water
damaged trees

ac·knowl·edge (ak-nol-ij) *verb*
1. To admit to something. *I acknowledged that I could have run faster.*
2. To show that you have seen and recognized somebody. *Terri walked by without acknowledging me.*
3. To let the sender know that you have received a letter or package.
▷ *verb* **acknowledging, acknowledged** ▷ *noun* **acknowledgment**

ac·ne (ak-nee) *noun* A skin condition that results from clogging up or blocking the oil glands in the skin. This causes inflammation and red pimples on the face, back, or chest.

a·corn (ay-korn) *noun* The seed of an oak tree.

a·cou·stic (uh-koo-stik)
1. *adjective* To do with sound or hearing.
2. **acoustics** *noun, plural* If a place has good **acoustics,** you can hear sounds and music very clearly inside it.

acoustic guitar *noun* A guitar that does not need an electronic amplifier.

acoustic guitar

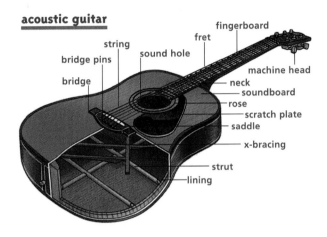

- fingerboard
- fret
- string
- sound hole
- bridge pins
- bridge
- machine head
- neck
- soundboard
- rose
- scratch plate
- saddle
- x-bracing
- strut
- lining

ac·quain·tance (uh-kwayn-tuhnss) *noun* Someone you have met but do not know very well.

ac·quire (uh-kwire) *verb*
1. To obtain or get something.
2. If something is an **acquired taste,** you grow to like it slowly. *For some people, olives are an acquired taste.*
▷ *verb* **acquiring, acquired**

ac·quit (uh-kwit) *verb* To find someone not guilty of a crime.
▷ **acquitting, acquitted** ▷ *noun* **acquittal**

a·cre (ay-kur) *noun* A measurement of area equal to 43,560 square feet. An acre is almost the size of a standard football field. ▷ *noun* **acreage**

ac·ro·bat (ak-ruh-bat) *noun* A person who performs exciting gymnastic acts that require great skill. Acrobats often work with a circus.

ac·ro·bat·ics (ak-ruh-bat-iks) *noun, plural* Difficult gymnastic acts, often performed in the air or on a high wire. *The picture shows a "human column," an example of acrobatics.*
▷ *adjective* **acrobatic**

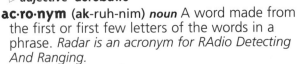

acrobatics

ac·ro·nym (ak-ruh-nim) *noun* A word made from the first or first few letters of the words in a phrase. *Radar is an acronym for RAdio Detecting And Ranging.*

a·cross (uh-kross) *preposition*
1. From one side of to the other side of. *We ran across the field.*
2. On the other side of. *Emma lives across the street from me.*

a·cryl·ic (uh-kril-ik) *noun* A chemical substance used to make fibers and paints.

act (akt)
1. *verb* To do something. *We must act now to save the rain forests.* ▷ *noun* **act**
2. *verb* To perform in a play, movie, etc.
3. *verb* To have an effect. *This drug acts quickly.*
4. *noun* A short performance, as in *a comedy act.*
5. *noun* One of the parts of a play.
6. *noun* A bill that has been passed by Congress. If signed by the president, it becomes law.
▷ *verb* **acting, acted**

ac·tion (ak-shuhn) *noun*
1. Something that you do to achieve a result. *Sonia's quick action prevented a serious accident.*
2. When you **take action,** you do something for a purpose.

ac·ti·vate (ak-tuh-vate) *verb* To turn on, or to cause to work. *Smoke activates a smoke alarm.*
▷ **activating, activated** ▷ *noun* **activator**

ac·tive (ak-tiv) *adjective*
1. Energetic and busy, as in *an active social life.*
2. The subject of an active verb does the action, rather than having something done to it. *In the sentence "I kicked the ball," the verb is active, but in "The ball was kicked," the verb is passive.*

ac·tiv·i·ty (ak-tiv-uh-tee) *noun*
1. Action, or movement. *The playground was full of activity.*
2. Something that you do for pleasure, as in *a rainy-day activity.*
▷ *noun, plural* **activities**

ac·tor (ak-tur) *noun* A person who performs in the theater, movies, television, etc.

ac·tress (ak-triss) *noun* A girl or a woman who performs the theater, movies, television, etc.

ac·tu·al (ak-choo-uhl) *adjective* Real, or true. *A fire drill prepares you for an actual fire.* ▷ *adverb* **actually**

ac·u·punc·ture (ak-yoo-pungk-chur) *noun* A way of treating illness by pricking parts of the body with small needles.

a·cute (uh-kyoot) *adjective*
1. Sharp, or severe, as in *an acute pain.*
2. Able to detect things easily, as in *an acute sense of smell.* ▷ *noun* **acuteness** ▷ *adverb* **acutely**
3. An **acute** angle is an angle of less than 90 degrees.
▷ *adjective* **acuter, acutest**

A.D. (ay dee) The initials of the Latin phrase *Anno Domini*, which means "in the year of the Lord." A.D. is used to show that a date comes after the birth of Jesus. *Astronomer Nicolaus Copernicus died in A.D. 1543.*

ad (ad) *noun* A short term for **advertisement** or **advertising**, as in *ad agency.*

ad·age (ad-ij) *noun* An old saying that people generally believe is true. *"Time heals all wounds" is an example of an adage.*

a·dapt (uh-**dapt**) *verb*
1. To make something suitable for a different purpose. *We have adapted our garage into a family room.*
2. To change because you are in a new situation. *It can be hard to adapt to life in a foreign country.*
▷ *verb* **adapting, adapted** ▷ *adjective* **adaptable**

ad·ap·ta·tion (ad-ap-tay-shuhn) *noun*
1. The act of adjusting.
2. A change that a living thing goes through so it fits in better with its environment. *A turtle's hard shell is an adaptation that helps keep it safe from predators.*

a·dapt·er *or* **a·dap·tor** (uh-**dap**-tur) *noun* A device that connects two parts that are of slightly different shapes or sizes. *Sam found that he needed an adapter when he tried to hook up his CD player to his old stereo.*

add (ad) *verb*
1. To find the sum of two or more numbers.
2. To put one thing with another. *Add the eggs to the flour.*
▷ *verb* **adding, added**

ad·dend (ad-end) *noun* Any number that is added to another to form a sum. In the equation 6 + 4 = 10, the addends are 6 and 4.

ad·der (ad-ur) *noun*
1. A small, poisonous European snake, sometimes called a viper, as in the *common adder, below.*
2. A harmless North American snake that hisses and swells up its head when annoyed.

common adder

(male)

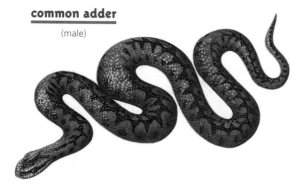

ad·dict (ad-ikt) *noun* A person who cannot give up doing or using something, as in *a drug addict.* ▷ *noun* **addiction** ▷ *adjective* **addicted**

ad·dic·tive (uh-dik-tiv) *adjective* If something, such as a drug, is **addictive,** people find it very hard to give it up. *Smoking is addictive.*

ad·di·tion (uh-dish-uhn) *noun*
1. In math, **addition** is the adding together of two or more numbers to come up with a sum.
2. A part of a building that is added on to the original. *Our home is so much bigger now with the new addition.*
3. Anything or anyone new. *We have a new addition to our family.*

ad·di·tion·al (uh-dish-uh-nuhl) *adjective* Extra, or more. *I have to do additional research before I write my report.*

ad·di·tive (ad-uh-tiv) *noun* Something added to a substance to change it in some way. *The additives in American cheese keep it from spoiling.*

ad·dress (uh-dress *or* ad-ress)
1. *noun* The street, number, etc., of a business or residence.
2. *verb* To write an address on a letter, card, or package. *Remember to address the envelope.*
3. *verb* To give a speech to. *Morgan addressed the group on the subject of racial equality.* ▷ *noun* **address**
4. *verb* When you **address** a problem, you tackle it or deal with it.
▷ *verb* **addresses, addressing, addressed** ▷ *noun* **addressee** (ad-ress-ee)

addressing an envelope

The President
The White House
Washington, DC 20500

ad·e·noid (ad-uh-*noyd*) *noun* A spongy lump of flesh at the back of your nose that can become swollen, making it hard to breathe.

a·dept (uh-dept) *adjective* Able to do something well. *My dad is quite adept at cooking.*

ad·e·quate (ad-uh-kwit) *adjective* Just enough, or good enough. ▷ *adverb* **adequately**

ad·here (ad-hihr) *verb*
1. To stick very tightly to something. *This glue adheres permanently.*

2. To stick with an idea or plan. *Drew adhered to his promise to visit his grandmother every week.* ▷ *verb* **adhering, adhered**

ad·he·sive (ad-**hee**-siv) *noun* A substance, such as glue, that makes things stick together. ▷ *adjective* **adhesive**

a·di·os (ah-dee-**ohss**) *interjection* The Spanish word for good-bye.

ad·ja·cent (uh-**jay**-suhnt) *adjective* Close or next to something or someone. *Our families live on adjacent streets.*

ad·jec·tive (**aj**-ik-tiv) *noun* A word that describes a noun or pronoun. *In the phrase "A tall, handsome stranger," "tall" and "handsome" are adjectives.*

ad·journ (uh-**jurn**) *verb* To close or end something, especially a court session or government meeting. *After several hours of testimony, court adjourned for the day.* ▷ **adjourning, adjourned**

ad·just (uh-**juhst**) *verb*
1. To move or change something slightly. *Evan adjusted the picture on the wall.* ▷ *adjective* **adjustable**
2. To get used to something new and different. ▷ *verb* **adjusting, adjusted** ▷ *noun* **adjustment**

ad lib (ad lib) *verb* To speak in public without preparing first. *Some comedians like to ad lib onstage.* ▷ **ad libbing, ad libbed** ▷ *adverb* **ad lib**

ad·min·is·ter (ad-**min**-uh-stur) *verb*
1. To govern or control something. *Pat administers the English department at the high school.* ▷ *noun* **administrator**
2. To give something to someone. *The nurse administered the medicine.*
▷ *verb* **administering, administered** ▷ *noun* **administration**

ad·mi·ral (**ad**-muh-ruhl) *noun* An officer who ranks above a vice admiral in the navy or coast guard.

ad·mire (ad-**mire**) *verb*
1. To like and respect someone. *I admire my teacher.*
2. To look at something and enjoy it. *Anna admired the painting.*
▷ *verb* **admiring, admired** ▷ *noun* **admiration**

ad·mit (ad-**mit**) *verb*
1. To confess to something, or agree that something is true, often reluctantly. *Sonia admitted that she had taken the missing cookies.*
2. To allow someone or something to enter. *Albert admitted his friends to his secret hiding place*
▷ *verb* **admitting, admitted** ▷ *noun* **admission**, *noun* **admittance**

ad·mon·ish (ad-**mon**-ish) *verb* To warn or advise someone of his or her faults. ▷ **admonishes,**

admonishing, admonished ▷ *noun* **admonishment**

a·do·be (uh-**doh**-bee) *noun*
1. A brick made of clay mixed with straw and dried in the sun.
2. A building made with these bricks. *Adobes are often found in Mexico and the southwestern United States.*

> ### ▶ Word History
> •
> **Adobe** is a Spanish word for a popular building material in Mexico and the southwestern United States with a long history that begins in Egypt. The ancient Egyptians were the first to build with bricks made of straw and dried mud. The Arabic word for these bricks, pronounced *at-toob*, made its way to Europe. Spanish explorers brought a version of the word to the New World, and it was taken into English.

ad·o·les·cent (ad-uh-**less**-uhnt) *noun* A young person who is more grown-up than a child but is not yet an adult. ▷ *noun* **adolescence** ▷ *adjective* **adolescent**

a·dopt (uh-**dopt**) *verb*
1. When adults **adopt** a child, they take the child into their family and become his or her legal parents. ▷ *adjective* **adopted**
2. To accept an idea or a way of doing things. *The mayor adopted a tough approach to crime.*
▷ *verb* **adopting, adopted** ▷ *noun* **adoption**

a·dor·a·ble (uh-**dor**-uh-buhl) *adjective* Very sweet and lovable. *What an adorable kitten!*

a·dore (uh-**dor**) *verb* To be very fond of someone or something. *I adore ice cream.* ▷ **adoring, adored** ▷ *noun* **adoration** (a-dor-**ay**-shuhn)

a·dorned (uh-**dornd**) *adjective* Decorated. *I made a cake adorned with roses.* ▷ *verb* **adorn**

ad·ren·a·line (uh-**dren**-uh-lin) *noun*
1. A chemical produced by your body when you are excited, frightened, or angry.
2. Adrenalin is a trademark for a manufactured substance that speeds up a person's heartbeat, decreases tiredness, and increases energy.

a·drift (uh-**drift**) *adverb* Drifting or floating freely through water or air. *The raft with the survivors floated adrift in the ocean until a rescue ship arrived.* ▷ *adjective* **adrift**

a·dult (uh-**duhlt** *or* ah-**duhlt**) *noun* A fully grown person or animal. ▷ *noun* **adulthood** ▷ *adjective* **adult**

a·dul·ter·ate (uh-**dul**-tuh-*rate*) *verb* To spoil something by adding something less good to it. ▷ **adulterating, adulterated**

A

ad·vance (ad-vanss)
1. *verb* To move forward, or to make progress.
▷ *noun* **advancement**
2. *adjective* Happening before something else, as in *advance warning*.
3. *verb* To lend money. *My mom advanced me $5 on my allowance.* ▷ *noun* **advance**
4. *noun* A movement forward made by a group of soldiers.
▷ *verb* **advancing, advanced**

ad·vanced (ad-vanst) *adjective*
1. If something has reached an **advanced** stage, it is nearly finished or fully developed.
2. **Advanced** work is not elementary or easy, as in *advanced math.*

ad·van·tage (ad-van-tij)
1. *noun* Something that helps you or is useful to you. ▷ *adjective* **advantageous** (*ad-vuhn-tay-juhss*)
2. *noun* The first point in a tennis game after the score of deuce.
3. If you **take advantage of** a person or situation, you use it for your own benefit.

ad·vent (ad-vent) *noun*
1. The beginning of something important, as in *the advent of the computer age.*
2. **Advent** The period leading up to Christmas in the Christian church's year.

ad·ven·ture (ad-ven-chur) *noun* An exciting or dangerous experience. ▷ *adjective* **adventurous**

ad·verb (ad-verb) *noun* A word usually used to describe a verb or adjective. Adverbs tell how, when, where, how often, or how much something happens. *"Slowly," "late," and "soon" are all adverbs.*

ad·ver·sar·y (ad-ver-ser-ee) *noun* Someone who fights or argues against you. ▷ *noun, plural* **adversaries**

ad·verse (ad-verss) *adjective* Unfavorable, or difficult, as in *adverse weather conditions.*
▷ *adverb* **adversely**

ad·ver·si·ty (ad-vur-suh-tee) *noun* Hardship, or misfortune. *The pioneers in covered wagons showed great courage in the face of adversity.*
▷ *noun, plural* **adversities**

ad·ver·tise (ad-ver-tize) *verb* To give information about something that you want to sell. *Bob used handouts to advertise his show.* ▷ **advertising, advertised** ▷ *noun* **advertiser**

ad·ver·tise·ment (*ad-ver-tize-muhnt or ad-vuhr-tiss-muhnt*) *noun* A public notice, usually published in the press or broadcast over the air, that calls attention to something, such as a product or an event.

ad·vice (ad-vice) *noun* A suggestion about what someone should do. *Grace gave me good advice on how to fix my bike.*

ad·vis·a·ble (ad-vye-zuh-buhl) *adjective* If something is **advisable,** it is sensible and worth doing. ▷ *adverb* **advisably**

ad·vise (ad-vize) *verb* To give someone information or suggestions. *Tom advised me to stay at home until rush hour was over.* ▷ **advising, advised** ▷ *noun* **adviser,** *noun* **advisor** ▷ *adjective* **advisory**

ad·vo·cate
1. *verb* (ad-vuh-kate) To support or call for an idea or a plan. *I would never advocate violence.*
▷ **advocating, advocated**
2. *noun* (ad-vuh-kit) A person who supports an idea or plan, as in *a women's rights advocate.*

aer·i·al (air-ee-uhl)
1. *noun* A piece of wire that receives television or radio signals.
2. *adjective* Happening in the air, as in *aerial refueling.*

aer·o·bat·ics (*air-uh-bat-iks*) *noun, plural* Skillful or dangerous movements performed by aircraft in the sky. *The picture shows a plane performing the positive flick roll, an example of aerobatics.*
▷ *adjective* **aerobatic**

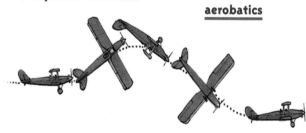

aerobatics

▶ **Language Note**

Aero- is a type of *combining form,* a word part that combines with other words or word parts to form new terms. *Aero-* means "air" or "atmosphere." *Aerospace* is the earth's atmosphere and outer space. *Aerobics* are exercises that cause your breathing (or intake of air) and heart rate to increase temporarily.

---

aer·o·bics (air-oh-biks) *noun, plural* Energetic exercises that strengthen the heart and improve respiration. Aerobics are often performed to music. ▷ *adjective* **aerobic**

aerobics

aer·o·dy·nam·ic (*air*-oh-**dye**-nam-mik) *adjective* Designed to move through the air very easily and quickly. *The streamlined shape of this motorcycle makes it aerodynamic.*

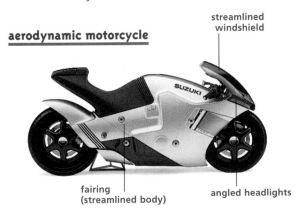

aerodynamic motorcycle

streamlined windshield

fairing (streamlined body)

angled headlights

aer·o·nau·tics (*air*-uh-**naw**-tiks) *noun* The science and practice of designing, building, and fixing aircraft. ▷ *adjective* **aeronautical**

aer·o·sol (**air**-uh-sol) *noun*
1. A mass of tiny solid or liquid particles suspended in air or another gas. *Smoke is a natural aerosol.*
2. A product, such as a deodorant or insecticide, that is sold in a pressurized container. When you press the nozzle, the substance comes out in a spray.
▷ *adjective* **aerosol**

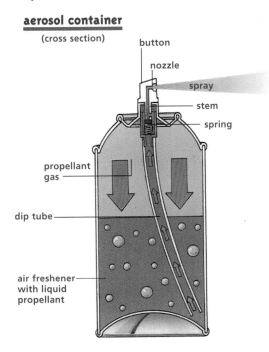

aerosol container

(cross section)

button

nozzle

spray

stem

spring

propellant gas

dip tube

air freshener with liquid propellant

aer·o·space (air-oh-**spayss**)
1. *noun* The earth's atmosphere and all the space beyond it.
2. *adjective* To do with the science and technology of jet flight or space travel. *Claude's mom works in the aerospace industry.*

af·fa·ble (**af**-uh-buhl) *adjective* Friendly, or pleasant. *Joy attracted many friends with her affable manner.*

af·fair (uh-**fair**)
1. *noun* A special event. *We hired a caterer to organize the affair.*
2. **affairs** *noun, plural* Matters connected with private or public life, as in *personal affairs* or *business affairs.*

af·fect (uh-**fekt**) *verb* To influence or change someone or something. *Jason's accident affected him badly.* ▷ **affecting, affected**

af·fect·ed (uh-**fek**-tid) *adjective* False and unnatural. *Jemma's affected voice makes her sound like she's acting.*

af·fec·tion (uh-**fek**-shuhn) *noun* A great liking for someone or something.

af·fec·tion·ate (uh-**fek**-shuh-nuht) *adjective* Very loving. ▷ *adverb* **affectionately**

af·fil·i·ate (uh-**fil**-ee-*ate*) *verb* To join or connect closely with something. *Our softball league is affiliated with the league in the next town.*
▷ **affiliating, affiliated** ▷ *noun* **affiliate** (uh-**fil**-ee-it)

af·fin·i·ty (uh-**fin**-i-tee) *noun* If you have an **affinity** for something, you like it and feel a natural attraction to it. ▷ *noun, plural* **affinities**

af·firm·a·tive (uh-**fur**-muh-tiv) *adjective* Giving the answer "yes," or stating that something is true. *When his teacher asked if he had done his homework, Nate gave an affirmative reply.*

affirmative action *noun* A program that promotes increased opportunities for minorities and women in order to make up for past discrimination.

af·flic·tion (uh-**flik**-shuhn) *noun* Illness, or suffering. ▷ *verb* **afflict**

af·flu·ent (**af**-loo-uhnt) *adjective* If you are **affluent**, you have plenty of money. ▷ *noun* **affluence**

af·ford (uh-**ford**) *verb*
1. If you can **afford** something, you have enough money to buy it.
2. To have enough time or ability to do something. *I'm so far ahead in the race, I can afford to slow down.*
▷ *verb* **affording, afforded**

af·ghan (**af**-gan) *noun* A crocheted or knitted blanket.

a·float (uh-**flote**) *adjective* Floating on water.

A

a·fraid (uh-**frayd**) *adjective*
1. Frightened, or worried.
2. Sorry. *I'm afraid I can't come to your party.*

> ### Synonyms: afraid
> ●
>
> **Afraid** means feeling great fear of something. It may be happening right now: *I'm afraid the wind is going to blow the roof off the house.* It may be something in the future that you're always worried about: *I'm afraid to sleep without a hall light on.* Afraid is not used before nouns.
>
> **Frightened** means very afraid, and is used before nouns or after the verb be: *The passengers were frightened when the bus stalled on the railroad tracks. The frightened children waited for their teacher.*
>
> **Scared** is used when something causes someone to be frightened or afraid: *The horror movie scared some of the little kids.*
>
> **Terrified** means really scared, to the point where you have trouble even breathing normally or thinking straight: *When the earthquake struck, people in the street were terrified.*
>
> **Alarmed** means scared suddenly by something that you were not expecting: *He was alarmed at being awakened so late at night by loud noises.*

a·fresh (uh-**fresh**) *adverb* When you start **afresh**, you begin something again.

Af·ri·can American (af-ruh-kuhn) *noun* Someone who was born in the United States or who became a U.S. citizen and can trace his or her ancestors back to Africa. ▷ *adjective* **African-American**

Af·ro (af-roh) *noun* An African-American hairstyle dating back to the 1960s with tight curls in a full, rounded shape.

aft (aft) *adverb* Toward the back of a ship or an airplane.

af·ter (af-tur) *preposition*
1. Later than, as in *after lunch.*
2. Following behind. *The puppy ran after her.*
3. Trying to catch someone or something. *The police are after him.*

af·ter·noon (af-tur-**noon**) *noun* The time of day between noon and evening.

af·ter·wards (af-tur-*werdz*) *adverb* Later.

a·gain (uh-**gen**) *adverb* One more time. *Say it again, Sam.*

a·gainst (uh-**genst**) *preposition*
1. Next to and touching. *Put your ear against the wall.*
2. Competing with. *It's the Chicago Bears against the Miami Dolphins tonight.*
3. Opposed to. *I'm against killing whales.*

ag·ate (ag-it) *noun* A hard, semiprecious stone with bands of color. *The picture shows a piece of agate that has been cut in half and polished.*

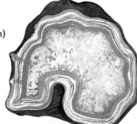

agate
(cross section)

age (aje)
1. *noun* The number of years that someone has lived or that something has existed. *Elsie lived to the age of 97.*
2. *noun* A period of time in history, as in *the Stone Age.*
3. *verb* To become or seem older. *Donna has aged since I saw her last.* ▷ **aging** or **ageing, aged**
4. When you **come of age,** you become an adult in the eyes of the law.

a·ged *adjective*
1. (ayjd) Being a particular number of years old. *Anyone aged 12 can join our club.*
2. (ay-jid) Someone who is **aged** is very old.
▷ *noun, plural* **the aged**

age·ism (aje-iz-uhm) *noun* Prejudice or discrimination because of age. ▷ *adjective* **ageist**

a·gen·cy (ay-juhn-see) *noun* An office or a business that provides a service to the public. *Instead of calling the airline directly, he went to a travel agency.* ▷ *noun, plural* **agencies**

a·gen·da (uh-jen-duh) *noun* A list of things that need to be done or discussed.

a·gent (ay-juhnt) *noun*
1. Someone who arranges things for other people, as in *a travel agent.*
2. A spy, as in *a secret agent.*

ag·gra·vate (ag-ruh-*vate*) *verb*
1. To make something even worse. *He aggravated his cold by swimming in the lake.*
2. To annoy someone. *Stop aggravating me!*
▷ *verb* **aggravating, aggravated** ▷ *noun* **aggravation** ▷ *adjective* **aggravating**

ag·gre·gate (ag-ri-guht) *noun* A total created by adding together lots of smaller amounts. *The aggregate of our scores was 75 percent.*

ag·gres·sion (uh-gresh-uhn) *noun* Fierce or threatening behavior. ▷ *adjective* **aggressive** ▷ *adverb* **aggressively**

a·ghast (uh-gast) *adjective* Shocked and dismayed.

ag·ile (aj-il *or* aj-ile) *adjective*
1. If you are **agile**, you can move fast and easily.
2. Someone with an **agile** mind can think quickly and cleverly.
▷ *noun* **agility**

ag·ing (ay-jing) *adjective* Growing older, as in *an aging population.*

A

ag·i·tate (aj-uh-*tate*) *verb*
1. To make someone nervous and worried.
▷ *noun* **agitation** ▷ *adjective* **agitated**
2. To stir or shake up. *Washing machines clean by agitating clothes.*
▷ *verb* **agitating, agitated**

ag·nos·tic (ag-*nos*-tik) *noun* Someone who believes that it is impossible to prove if God exists. ▷ *adjective* **agnostic**

a·go (uh-*goh*) *adverb* Before now, or in the past, as in *three days ago.*

ag·o·ny (ag-uh-nee) *noun* Great pain or suffering. *After he fell, David screamed in agony.*
▷ *noun, plural* **agonies** ▷ *adjective* **agonizing**

a·gree (uh-*gree*) *verb*
1. To say yes to something. *I agreed to his plan.*
2. To share the same opinions. *Dan and I always agree on politics.*
3. If something **agrees with** you, it suits you, or is good for you.
▷ *verb* **agreeing, agreed**

a·gree·a·ble (uh-*gree*-uh-buhl) *adjective*
1. Pleasing or likable. *Ken is an agreeable person.*
2. Willing or ready to say yes. *If you are agreeable, we will meet an hour before the show.*

a·gree·ment (uh-*gree*-muhnt) *noun*
1. If you are **in agreement** with someone, you think the same way about a particular topic.
2. An arrangement. *The strike ended when the workers and owners signed an agreement on salary levels.*

ag·ri·cul·ture (ag-ruh-*kul*-chur) *noun* Farming. *This picture of agriculture in the Middle Ages shows laborers using scythes to mow a field.*
▷ *adjective* **agricultural** *See* **farm.**

medieval farming

a·ground (uh-*ground*) *adverb* If a boat runs **aground,** it gets stuck on the bottom in shallow water.

a·head (uh-*hed*) *adverb*
1. In front. *She is ahead of me in line.*
2. In the future. *You must think ahead.*

a·hoy (uh-*hoi*) *interjection* An exclamation used by sailors to call other ships or attract attention.

"Ahoy there!" is another way of saying *"Hello there!"* or *"You there!"*

AI Short for **artificial intelligence**.

aid (ayd)
1. *verb* To help someone. *We aided the earthquake victims.* ▷ **aiding, aided** ▷ *noun* **aid**
2. *noun* Money or equipment for people in need, as in *foreign aid.*

aide (ayd) *noun* A person who works along with others to help them do their jobs. *Kevin worked as a nurse's aide.*

AIDS (aydz) *noun*
A fatal illness in which the body's ability to protect itself against disease is destroyed. AIDS stands for *Acquired Immune Deficiency Syndrome*.

AIDS virus
(magnified)

ai·ki·do (eye-kee-doh) *noun* A Japanese art of self-defense in which you use wrist, joint, and elbow grips to stop or throw your opponent.

ai·le·ron (ay-luh-*ron*) *noun* A hinged piece on an aircraft wing, used to control balance. *See* **aircraft.**

ail·ment (ayl-muhnt) *noun* An illness, though not usually a serious one.

aim (aym) *verb*
1. To hit, throw, or shoot something in a particular direction. *Ellen aimed the ball at Darren's glove.*
2. To intend to achieve something. *I aim to become a chef.*
▷ *verb* **aiming, aimed** ▷ *noun* **aim**

aim·less (aym-luhss) *adjective* Without direction or purpose. ▷ *adverb* **aimlessly**

ain't (aynt) *contraction* (informal) A short form of *am not, is not, are not, has not,* or *have not.*

> ## Language Note
> ●
> Although **ain't** sometimes is used in casual speech, it is not considered proper English. Ain't definitely should not be used in formal speech or writing.

air (air)
1. *noun* The invisible mixture of gases around you that you need to breathe.
2. *verb* To let air into a room. ▷ **airing, aired**
3. *noun* An appearance, or a manner. *Wanda has an air of mystery.*

air conditioning *noun* A system for keeping the air inside cool and clean when it is hot outside.

air·craft (air-*kraft*) *noun* A vehicle that can fly. *The picture shows a Boeing 747 aircraft, known as a jumbo jet because of its enormous size. It can carry up to 500 passengers and cruises at about 600 miles (965 kilometers) per hour.* ▷ *noun, plural* **aircraft**

long-haul passenger aircraft

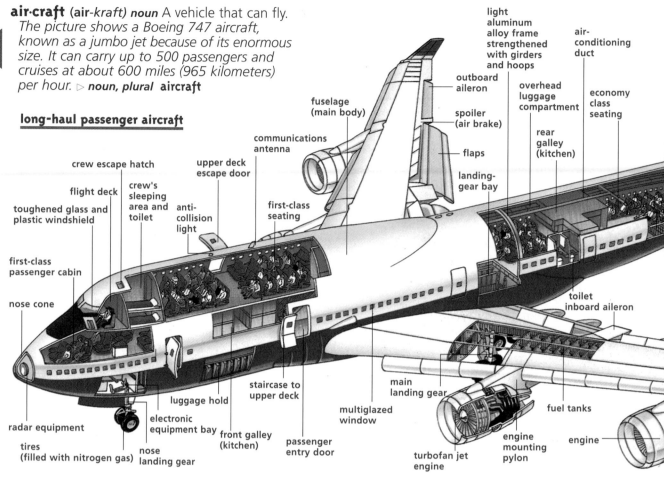

light aluminum alloy frame strengthened with girders and hoops

air-conditioning duct

outboard aileron

overhead luggage compartment

economy class seating

fuselage (main body)

spoiler (air brake)

rear galley (kitchen)

communications antenna

flaps

crew escape hatch

upper deck escape door

landing-gear bay

flight deck

crew's sleeping area and toilet

first-class seating

toughened glass and plastic windshield

anti-collision light

first-class passenger cabin

toilet

inboard aileron

nose cone

radar equipment

tires (filled with nitrogen gas)

nose landing gear

luggage hold

electronic equipment bay

staircase to upper deck

front galley (kitchen)

passenger entry door

multiglazed window

main landing gear

fuel tanks

turbofan jet engine

engine mounting pylon

engine

aircraft car·ri·er (ka-ree-ur) *noun* A warship with a large, flat deck where aircraft take off and land.

air·field (air-*feeld*) *noun*
1. A large area that includes a runway for airplanes to take off and land.
2. An airport.

air force *noun* The part of a country's fighting force that can attack or defend from the air.

air·line (air-*line*) *noun* A company that owns and flies aircraft, carrying passengers and freight by air.

air·mail (air-*mayl*) *noun* A postal service by which letters, packages, etc., are carried by aircraft.

air·plane (air-*plane*) *noun* A machine with wings and an engine that flies through the air. *See* **aircraft.**

air·port (air-*port*) *noun* A place where aircraft take off and land and where people get on and off them.

air pressure *noun* The density or weight of the air, which is greater near the earth than it is at high altitudes. *The change in air pressure in the plane made the passengers' ears pop.*

air·ship (air-*ship*) *noun*
A large air balloon with engines and a passenger compartment hanging underneath it. Blimps and zeppelins are airships. *This zeppelin was built in Germany in 1910.*

airship

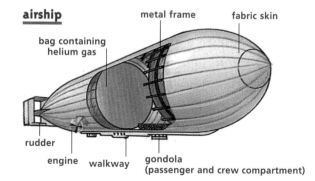

metal frame

fabric skin

bag containing helium gas

rudder

engine   walkway

gondola (passenger and crew compartment)

air·sick (air-*sik*) *adjective* If you are **airsick,** you feel ill while flying in a plane, with symptoms that include nausea and dizziness.

air·tight (air-*tite*) *adjective* If a container is **airtight,** it is so well sealed that no air can get in or out.

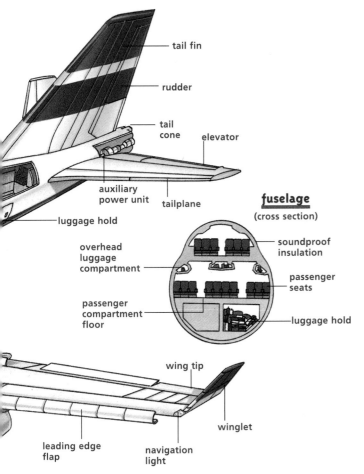

tail fin

rudder

tail cone

elevator

auxiliary power unit

tailplane

luggage hold

fuselage (cross section)

overhead luggage compartment

soundproof insulation

passenger seats

passenger compartment floor

luggage hold

wing tip

winglet

leading edge flap

navigation light

air·y (air-ee) *adjective*
1. An **airy** room is full of fresh air.
2. Lighthearted, or casual. *Judy gave an airy wave.*
▷ *adjective* **airier, airiest** ▷ *adverb* **airily**

aisle (ile) *noun* The passage that runs between the rows of seats in a theater, house of worship, aircraft, etc. **Aisle** sounds like **isle** or **I'll.**

a·jar (uh-jar) *adjective* If a door is **ajar**, it is partly open. ▷ *adverb* **ajar**

a·kim·bo (uh-kim-boh) *adjective* If you have your arms **akimbo**, your hands or knuckles are on your hips and your elbows are turned outward. *He stood with arms akimbo.* ▷ *adverb* **akimbo**

▶ **Word History**
• •
Eight hundred years ago, *in kene bowe* was the English phrase for "in a sharp bend." People mispronounced the phrase and ran the words together, but the meaning stuck. Today, when you stand with arms **akimbo**, your hands are on your hips and your elbows are "in a sharp bend" outward.

a·kin (uh-kin) *adjective*
1. Belonging to the same family. *Lions are akin to tigers and leopards.*
2. Similar. *In Cory's mind, saying you don't like the Dodgers is akin to saying you don't like baseball.*

a·la·bas·ter (al-uh-*bass*-tur)
1. *noun* A smooth, white piece of stone, often used to make sculpture.
2. *adjective* Smooth, pale, and almost see-through. *The model has reddish hair and alabaster skin.*

a·larm (uh-larm)
1. *noun* A device with a bell, buzzer, or siren that wakes people or warns them of danger.
2. *noun* A sudden fear that something bad will happen. *Don't worry, there's no cause for alarm!*
3. *verb* To make someone afraid that something bad might happen. *I don't want to alarm you, but I can smell smoke.* ▷ **alarming, alarmed**
▷ *adjective* **alarming** ▷ *adverb* **alarmingly**

alarm clock *noun* A type of clock that can be set to ring or buzz at a particular time.

a·las (uh-lass) *interjection* Unfortunately, or sadly. *I'd love to come, but alas, I can't.*

al·ba·tross (al-buh-*tross*) *noun*
1. A large seabird with webbed feet and long wings that can fly for a long time.
2. If something is an **albatross around your neck,** it is a burden.
▷ *noun, plural* **albatrosses**

al·bi·no (al-bye-noh) *noun* A person or animal born without any natural coloring in the skin, hair, or eyes.

al·bum (al-buhm) *noun*
1. A book in which you keep photographs, stamps, etc.
2. A collection of music recorded on a CD, tape, or record.

al·co·hol (al-kuh-*hol*) *noun*
1. A colorless liquid found in drinks such as wine, whiskey, and beer that can make people drunk.
2. A liquid used in making medicines, chemicals, and fuels.

al·co·hol·ic (*al*-kuh-hol-ik)
1. *adjective* Containing alcohol.
2. *noun* An **alcoholic** has a disease that makes it difficult not to drink alcohol even when drinking hurts his or her body, mind, or ability to function. ▷ *noun* **alcoholism**

al·cove (al-kove) *noun* A part of a room that is set back from the main area.

al·der (awl-dur) *noun* A tree or bush with rough bark and jagged leaves that grows in cool, moist places.

ale (ayl) *noun* An alcoholic drink that is similar to beer but has a more bitter taste.

A

a·lert (uh-**lurt**)
1. *adjective* If you are **alert,** you pay attention to what is happening and are ready for action.
2. *verb* To warn someone that there might be danger. *Alert the fire department!* ▷ **alerting, alerted**
3. *noun* A warning of danger, as in *a nuclear alert.*

al·fal·fa (al-**fal**-fuh) *noun* A type of grain that is used mostly as feed for farm animals.

al·gae (al-**jee**) *noun, plural* Small plants without roots or stems that grow in water or on damp surfaces.

al·ge·bra (al-**juh**-bruh) *noun* A type of mathematics in which symbols and letters are used to represent unknown numbers; for example, $2x + y = 7$.

a·li·as (ay-lee-uhss) *noun* A false name, especially one used by a criminal. ▷ *noun, plural* **aliases**

al·i·bi (al-i-*bye*) *noun* A claim that a person accused of a crime was somewhere else when the crime was committed. *Alec says he has an alibi for the time of the robbery; he was at the movies.*

al·ien (ay-lee-uhn *or* ay-lyuhn)
1. *noun* A creature from another planet.
2. *noun* A foreigner.
3. *adjective* Different and strange. *Jenna found her new school very alien.*

a·lign (uh-**line**) *verb* To put a series of things in a straight line. *The members of the marching band were aligned in six rows across the field.*
▷ **aligning, aligned** ▷ *noun* **alignment**

a·like (uh-**like**)
1. *adjective* Looking or acting the same.
2. *adverb* In a similar way. *All the children were treated alike.*

al·i·men·ta·ry canal (al-uh-men-tuh-ree) *noun* The path that food follows as it is digested by the body. It includes the esophagus, stomach, small intestine, and large intestine.

a·live (uh-**live**) *adjective*
1. Living. *You must water the plants to keep them alive.*
2. Full of life. *Mytra's eyes were alive with excitement.*

al·ka·li (al-kuh-*lye*) *noun* A strong base, such as lye or ammonia, that dissolves in water and reacts with an acid to form a salt. Strong alkalis can burn your skin. ▷ *adjective* **alkaline** (al-kuh-*line*)

all (awl)
1. *adjective* **All** of a group or thing is the whole of it. *All the candy was gone in 30 seconds.*
2. *pronoun* Everyone. *All must pay taxes on time.*
3. *adverb* Completely. *When you are all dressed, we can leave.*
4. *adverb* For each side. *The score was four all after nine innings.*
5. *noun* Everything. *Is this all you want me to do?* **All** sounds like **awl.**

Al·lah (al-uh) *noun* The Muslim name for God.

al·lege (uh-**lej**) *verb* To say that something is true without offering proof. *The news story alleged that the official had taken a bribe.* ▷ **alleging, alleged**

al·leged (uh-**lejd** *or* uh-**lej**-uhd) *adjective* If a newspaper reports that someone is an **alleged** jewel thief, he or she has been accused of stealing but has not yet been convicted.
▷ *adverb* **allegedly**

al·le·giance (uh-**lee**-junss) *noun* Loyal support for someone or something.

al·ler·gic (uh-**lur**-jik) *adjective* If you are **allergic** to something, it causes you to sneeze, develop a rash, or have another unpleasant reaction. People can be allergic to dust, pollen, foods, and other things. ▷ *noun* **allergy** (al-er-jee)

al·ley (al-ee) *noun*
1. A narrow passageway between or behind buildings or backyards.
2. bowling alley A long, narrow lane down which you roll bowling balls. Also the building where you go to bowl.
▷ *noun, plural* **alleys**

al·li·ance (uh-**lye**-uhnss) *noun* A friendly agreement to work together.

al·lied (al-**ide**) *adjective*
1. People or groups that join together for a common cause are **allied.** *The allied troops forced the enemy back across the border.*
2. Similar or related. *She'll take biology, chemistry, and other allied subjects.*

al·li·ga·tor (al-i-*gay*-tuhr) *noun* A large reptile with strong jaws and very sharp teeth, related to the crocodile. Alligators live in parts of North and South America and China.

alligator

> ## Word History
> •
> Spanish explorers had never seen an **alligator** before they came to the New World. When they encountered one, they thought it looked like a very large lizard. They called it *el lagarto,* Spanish for "lizard." Later, when English settlers heard *el lagarto* spoken fast, they spelled what they heard as alligator.

al·lit·er·a·tion (uh-lit-uh-ray-shuhn) *noun*
Repeated use of the same sound at the beginning of a group of words; for example, "The gruesome ghost gave a ghastly groan."
▷ *adjective* **alliterative**

al·lo·cate (al-uh-kate) *verb* To decide that something should be used for a particular purpose. *We allocated half the money to charity.*
▷ **allocating, allocated** ▷ *noun* **allocation**

al·lot (uh-lot) *verb*
1. To give out something in equal shares or parts. *The teacher allotted eight crayons to each child.*
2. To set aside for a particular purpose. *The teacher allotted 20 minutes for the test.*
▷ *verb* **allotting, allotted** ▷ *noun* **allotment**

al·low (uh-lou) *verb* To let someone have or do something. *My mom allows me to stay up until 10 o'clock.* ▷ **allowing, allowed**

al·low·ance (uh-lou-uhnss) *noun* Money given to someone regularly.

al·loy (al-oi) *noun* A mixture of two or more metals.

all right
1. *adjective* Good enough, or acceptable. *The band at the party was all right.*
2. *adjective* Not hurt, or not ill. *Bernette fell off her horse, but she's all right now.*
3. *adverb* You say **all right** when you agree to do something.

al·lude (uh-lood) *verb* To hint at or mention briefly. *Brenda alluded to an argument she had with her brother.* ▷ **alluding, alluded**

al·ly (al-eye) *noun* A person or country that gives support to another. ▷ *noun, plural* **allies**

al·ma·nac (awl-muh-nak) *noun* A book published once a year with facts and statistics about a large variety of subjects. The *Farmer's Almanac* is a type of almanac that focuses on weather projections, tides, and full moons for the year.

al·might·y (awl-mye-tee) *adjective*
1. Possessing total power.
2. Very big, as in *an almighty crash.*

al·mond (ah-muhnd *or* ahl-muhnd) *noun* A sweet, oval-shaped nut that is used in cooking or baking or eaten alone. *See* **hull**.

al·most (awl-most) *adverb* Very nearly.

al·oe (a-loh) *noun* An African plant whose juice can be used to help heal burns and cuts. Aloe is often used in creams to soften skin.

a·loft (uh-loft) *adjective* High up in the air. *The plane was aloft moments after speeding down the runway.* ▷ *adverb* **aloft**

a·lo·ha (uh-loh-ha) *interjection* In Hawaiian, a term used to say hello or good-bye.

a·lone (uh-lone) *adjective* Without anyone else. *Ed stayed home alone.* ▷ *adverb* **alone**

a·long (uh-lawng) *preposition*
1. Following the length or direction of. *We drove along the street.*
2. all along All the time. *I knew all along that Jonah was lying.*

a·loof (uh-loof)
1. *adverb* When you remain **aloof** from someone or something, you keep yourself apart and don't get involved. *Akimi always seems to remain aloof from her classmates.*
2. *adjective* Distant or not friendly. *Because of his aloof manner, some of Mr. Harding's students don't like him.*

a·loud (uh-loud) *adverb* In a voice that other people can hear, as in *reading aloud.*

al·pac·a (al-pak-uh) *noun* A South American animal that is related to the camel and the llama. It has long, silky wool that is used to make clothing. ▷ *noun, plural* **alpacas**

al·pha·bet (al-fuh-bet) *noun* All the letters of a language arranged in order. *The first six letters of the Greek alphabet are shown here.* ▷ *adjective* **alphabetical**

Greek alphabet

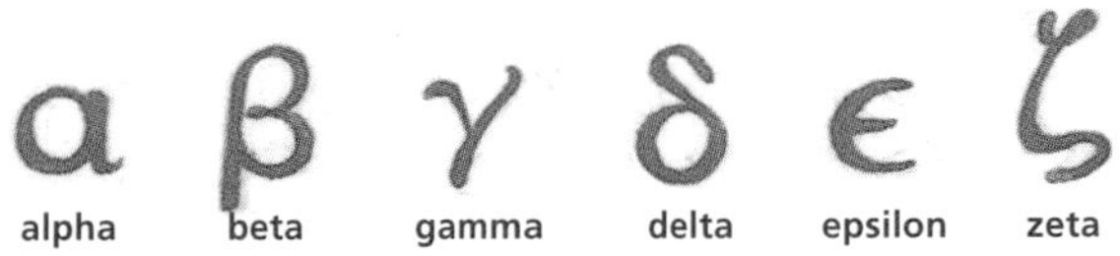

α β γ δ ε ζ
alpha beta gamma delta epsilon zeta

al·pha·bet·ize (al-fah-buh-tize) *verb* To arrange a series of things so that they follow the order of the letters of the alphabet, from *A* to *Z*. *The words in this dictionary have been alphabetized.*
▷ **alphabetizing, alphabetized**

al·read·y (awl-red-ee) *adverb* Before now. *I've n that movie already.*

al·so (awl-soh) *adverb* As well.

al·tar (awl-tur) *noun* A large table in a house of worship, used for religious ceremonies.

al·ter (awl-tur) *verb* To change something. *We've altered our plans.* ▷ **altering, altered** ▷ *noun* **alteration**

alternate ▶ ambivalent

al·ter·nate
1. *adjective* (awl-tur-nit) If something happens on **alternate** days, it happens every second day.
2. *verb* (awl-tuhr-nate) To take turns. *Mom and dad alternate in driving us to school.*
▷ **alternating, alternated**

al·ter·na·tive (awl-tur-nuh-tiv)
1. *noun* Something that you can choose to have or do instead of something else. ▷ *adjective* **alternative** ▷ *adverb* **alternatively**
2. *adjective* Different from what is usual, as in *alternative medicine.*

alternative energy *noun* Energy from natural sources that are renewable and don't harm the environment, such as the sun, ocean waves, and wind. *See* **solar energy, wind turbine.**

al·though (awl-THoh) *conjunction*
1. In spite of the fact that. *Although it was raining, we all enjoyed ourselves.*
2. But. *Lulu is only nine, although she seems older.*

al·tim·e·ter (al-tim-uh-tur) *noun* An instrument that measures how high something is above the ground. Airplane pilots use altimeters when they fly. *See* **hang glider.**

al·ti·tude (al-ti-tood) *noun* The height of something above the ground. *This plane can fly at very high altitudes.*

al·to (al-toh) *noun*
1. A singing voice that is high for a male and low for a female.
2. A singer with an alto voice.

al·to·geth·er (awl-tuh-ge-THur) *adverb*
1. In total. *Tonya has seven hats altogether.*
2. Completely, or entirely. *What I told you wasn't altogether true.*
3. On the whole. *Altogether, it was a good party.*

a·lu·mi·num (uh-loo-mi-nuhm) *noun* A light, silver-colored metal.

al·ways (awl-waze) *adverb* If something is **always** happening, it happens all the time or very many times.

A.M. (ay em) The initials of the Latin phrase *ante meridiem,* which means "before midday." *I get up at 7 A.M.*

am·a·teur (am-uh-chur *or* am-uh-tur) *noun* Someone who takes part in a sport or other activity for pleasure rather than

for money. *When it comes to skiing, she is an amateur.* ▷ *adjective* **amateur**

a·maze (uh-maze) *verb* To make someone feel very surprised. ▷ **amazing, amazed** ▷ *noun* **amazement** ▷ *adjective* **amazing** ▷ *adverb* **amazingly**

am·bas·sa·dor (am-bass-uh-dur) *noun* The top person sent by a government to represent it in another country. *Eugenie Moore Anderson was the first American woman to become an ambassador. She was the U.S. ambassador to Denmark from 1949 through 1953.*

am·ber (am-bur) *noun*
1. A yellowish brown substance formed from fossilized tree sap and used for making ornaments and jewelry. *This piece of amber contains an insect that was trapped in the sap before it hardened and fossilized.*
2. A yellowish brown color. ▷ *adjective* **amber**

amber

am·bi·dex·trous (am-bi-dek-struhss) *adjective* If you are **ambidextrous,** you can use both hands equally well, especially for writing.

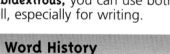
aluminum can

> ## Word History
> In Latin, *ambi-* means "both" and *dexter* means "right-handed." So if you are **ambidextrous,** it is as if you had two right hands. Since most people can use one hand better than the other (and for many people it is the right hand), ambidextrous means you are able to use both hands equally well. The word *dexterity,* which means "skill in using your hands," comes from the same Latin root.

am·big·u·ous (am-big-yoo-uhss) *adjective* If something is **ambiguous,** it can be understood in more than one way. *Conrad gave an ambiguous answer—he could mean yes or no.* ▷ *noun* **ambiguity** (am-buh-gyoo-uh-tee) ▷ *adverb* **ambiguously**

am·bi·tion (am-bish-uhn) *noun*
1. Something you really want to do. *My ambition is to be president.*
2. A strong wish to be successful. *Pedro is driven by ambition.* ▷ *adjective* **ambitious**

am·biv·a·lent (am-biv-uh-luhnt) *adjective* If you feel **ambivalent** about something, you have two different opinions about it at the same time. ▷ *noun* **ambivalence**

am·ble (am-buhl) *verb* To walk slowly because you are not in a hurry. ▷ **ambling, ambled**

am·bu·lance (am-byuh-luhnss) *noun* A vehicle that takes ill or injured people to the hospital.

am·bush (am-bush) *verb* To hide and then attack someone. ▷ **ambushes, ambushing, ambushed** ▷ *noun* **ambush**

a·men (ay-men *or* ah-men) *interjection*
1. People say **amen** after a prayer to mean "May it be so."
2. **Amen** also shows agreement with a statement. *Whitney was so right about why she was the best person for the job that all I could say was "Amen."*

a·mend (uh-mend)
1. *verb* To change a legal document or a law. *In 1951, Congress amended the U.S. Constitution so that it limits a president's time in office to two elected terms.* ▷ **amending, amended**
2. *noun, plural* When you make **amends,** you do something to make up for a wrong or a mistake.

a·mend·ment (uh-mend-muhnt) *noun* A change that is made to a law or a legal document. *The first 10 amendments to the Constitution are known as the Bill of Rights.*

A·mer·i·can (uh-mer-uh-kuhn)
1. *adjective* To do with the United States, as in *American government.*
2. *adjective* To do with North, Central, or South America, as in *the American continents.*
3. *noun* Someone born or living in the United States.
4. *noun* Someone born or living in either North, Central, or South America.

American Indian *noun* One of the original inhabitants of North, Central, or South America, or a descendant. American Indians are sometimes called **Native Americans.** ▷ *adjective* **American Indian**

am·e·thyst (am-uh-thist) *noun*
1. A type of quartz crystal that is purple or violet and often is used as a gemstone in jewelry.
2. A shade of purple.

a·mi·a·ble (ay-mee-uh-bul) *adjective* Friendly and easygoing. *Sue's amiable boss was pleasant even when things went wrong.*

a·mi·go (uh-mee-goh) *noun* The Spanish word for "male friend." The Spanish word for "female friend" is **amiga** (uh-mee-guh).

am·mo·nia (uh-moh-nyuh) *noun* A gas or solution with a strong smell. Some cleaning liquids contain ammonia.

am·mu·ni·tion (am-yuh-nish-uhn) *noun*
1. Things that can be fired from weapons, such as bullets or arrows.
2. Information that you can use against somebody else.

am·ne·sia (am-nee-zhuh) *noun* A partial or total loss of memory that can be temporary or permanent. *The blow to the head that he received in the accident gave him amnesia.*

am·nes·ty (am-nuh-stee) *noun*
1. An official promise by a government to release prisoners and pardon crimes. *The government granted amnesty to all war protesters.*
2. A chance to hand in something you should not possess, without being punished. *The city will offer amnesty to anyone who turns in an illegal handgun.* ▷ *noun, plural* **amnesties**

a·moe·ba (uh-mee-buh) *noun* A microscopic creature made of only one cell. *The diagram shows the parts of an amoeba.* ▷ *noun, plural* **amoebas** *or* **amoebae** (uh-mee-bee)

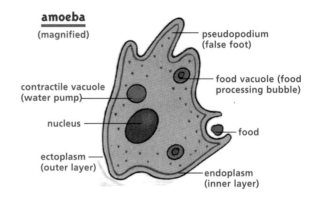

amoeba (magnified): pseudopodium (false foot), food vacuole (food processing bubble), food, endoplasm (inner layer), ectoplasm (outer layer), nucleus, contractile vacuole (water pump)

a·mong *or* **a·mongst** (uh-mung *or* uh-mungst) *preposition*
1. In the middle of, or surrounded by. *Kerry felt safe because she was among friends.*
2. If you share something **among** several people, you divide it between them.

a·mount (uh-mount)
1. *noun* The **amount** of something is how much of it there is.
2. *verb* If something **amounts to** a total, it adds up to that total. ▷ **amounting, amounted**

amp (amp) *noun* A unit used to measure the strength of an electrical current. Amp is short for *ampere* (am-pihr).

am·phi·bi·an (am-fib-ee-uhn) *noun*
1. A cold-blooded animal with a backbone that lives in water and breathes with gills when young. As an adult, it develops lungs and lives on land. Frogs, toads, and salamanders are amphibians.
2. A vehicle that can travel on land and in water.
▷ *adjective* **amphibious**

am·phi·the·a·ter (am-fi-*thee*-uh-tur) *noun* A large, open-air building with rows of seats in a high circle around an arena. In ancient Roman times, amphitheaters were used for public entertainment, such as gladiator and animal fights. *The picture shows a famous Roman amphitheater.*

The Colosseum, Rome, Italy

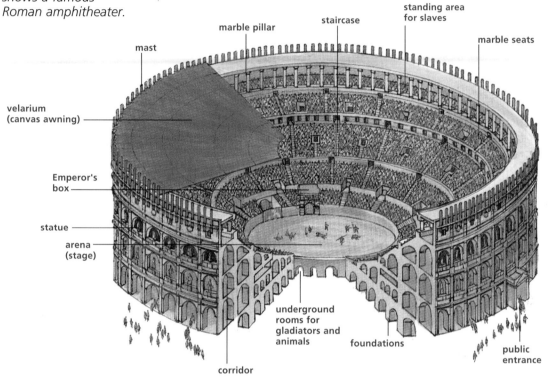

mast

marble pillar

staircase

standing area for slaves

marble seats

velarium (canvas awning)

Emperor's box

statue

arena (stage)

underground rooms for gladiators and animals

foundations

public entrance

corridor

am·ple (am-puhl) *adjective*
1. More than enough. *There was ample food for everyone.* ▷ *adverb* **amply**
2. Large. *The car has an ample trunk.*
▷ *adjective* **ampler, amplest**

am·pli·fi·er (am-pluh-fye-ur) *noun* A piece of equipment that makes sound louder. ▷ *noun* **amplification** *See* **speaker.**

am·pli·fy (am-pli-*fye*) *verb* To make something louder or stronger. *He amplified his voice with a microphone.* ▷ **amplifies, amplifying, amplified**

am·pu·tate (am-pyuh-*tate*) *verb* To cut off someone's arm, leg, finger, etc., usually because it is damaged or diseased. ▷ **amputating, amputated** ▷ *noun* **amputation**

a·muse (uh-**myooz**) *verb*
1. To make someone laugh or smile. *Your jokes amuse me.* ▷ *adjective* **amusing**
2. To keep someone happy and stop him or her from being bored. *Ken's new chemistry set amused him for hours.*
▷ *verb* **amusing, amused** ▷ *noun* **amusement**

amusement park *noun* A place where people pay to go on rides, play games of skill, and enjoy other forms of entertainment.

an (uhn *or* an) *indefinite article* A form of **a** used before a word that is pronounced with a vowel as its first sound, as in *an onion.*

an·a·con·da (an-uh-**kon**-duh) *noun* A very long, nonpoisonous South American snake that wraps itself tightly around its prey to kill it.

an·a·gram (an-uh-gram) *noun* A word or phrase made by rearranging the letters in another word or phrase. *"Stop" is an anagram of "post."*

an·a·log (an-uh-log) *adjective* Using moving parts to show changing information. *An analog clock uses hour and minute hands to show the time. A digital clock uses only numbers.*

an·a·lyze (an-uh-lize) *verb* To examine something carefully in order to understand it. *Let's analyze the problem before we act.* ▷ **analyzing, analyzed** ▷ *noun* **analysis** (uh-**nal**-uh-siss) ▷ *adjective* **analytical**

an·ar·chy (an-ur-kee) *noun* A situation with no order and no one in control. ▷ *noun* **anarchist**

A

a·nat·o·my (uh-**nat**-uh-mee) *noun*
1. The **anatomy** of a person or an animal is the structure of its body.
2. The scientific study of the structure of living things.
▷ *noun, plural* **anatomies** ▷ *adjective* **anatomical** (*an*-uh-**tom**-i-kuhl)

anatomy of a frog

(female)

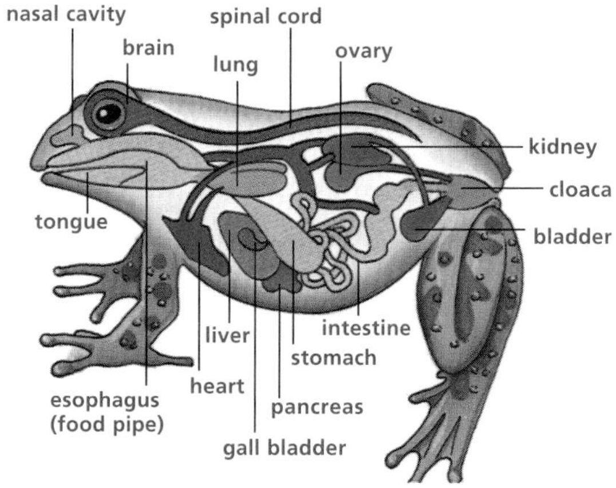

nasal cavity
brain
spinal cord
lung
ovary
kidney
cloaca
bladder
tongue
liver
intestine
stomach
heart
pancreas
esophagus
(food pipe)
gall bladder

an·ces·tor (an-**sess**-tur) *noun* Your **ancestors** are members of your family who lived a long time ago, usually before your grandparents. ▷ *noun* **ancestry** ▷ *adjective* **ancestral**

an·chor (**ang**-kur) *noun* A heavy metal hook that is lowered from a ship or boat to stop it from drifting. *See* **ship.**

an·chor·per·son (**ang**-kur-*pur*-suhn) *noun* The main person who reports the news on a television news show.

an·cho·vy (an-**choh**-vee) *noun* A small, edible fish. Anchovies have a salty taste. ▷ *noun, plural* **anchovies**

an·cient (**ayn**-shunt) *adjective*
1. Very old. *Our textbooks are ancient.*
2. Belonging to a time long ago, as in *an ancient monument* or *ancient Rome.*

and (and) *conjunction*
1. As well as. *The dog wagged his tail and barked.*
2. Added to, or plus. *Five and one make six.*
3. As a result. *My mom got a new job, and we had to move.*
4. *(informal)* To. *Try and do the best you can.*

an·droid (**an**-droid) *noun* A robot that acts and looks like a human being. ▷ *adjective* **android**

an·ec·dote (**an**-ik-dote) *noun* A short, often funny story about something that has happened.
▷ *adjective* **anecdotal**

a·ne·mic (uh-**nee**-mik) *adjective* If you are **anemic,** you feel weak and become easily tired because

your blood does not contain enough iron.
▷ *noun* **anemia**

an·e·mom·et·er (an-i-**mom**-uh-tur) *noun* A scientific instrument used to measure the wind's speed.

a·nem·o·ne (uh-**nem**-uh-nee) *noun* A plant with purple, red, white, or pink flowers.

an·es·thet·ic (an-iss-**thet**-ik) *noun* A drug or a gas given to people before an operation to prevent them from feeling pain.

a·nes·the·tist (uh-**ness**-thuh-tist) *noun* A medical professional who specializes in giving people drugs or gas to prevent pain during operations.

a·new (uh-**noo**) *adverb* Again, or once more. *The heavy rain ruined our hike, so we returned to camp and the next day we began anew.*

an·gel (**ayn**-juhl) *noun*
1. In religion, a messenger of God.
2. A very kind, gentle person.
▷ *adjective* **angelic**

an·ger (**ang**-gur) *noun* The strong feeling of being very annoyed.

an·gle (**ang**-guhl) *noun*
1. The figure formed by two lines that start at the same point. Angles are measured in degrees.
2. A way of looking at something. *Jesse approached the problem from a different angle.*
3. If something is **at an angle,** it is sloping and not straight.

an·gling (**ang**-gling) *noun* The sport of fishing with a fishing rod rather than a net. *The picture shows equipment used for freshwater angling.*
▷ *noun* **angler** ▷ *verb* **angle**

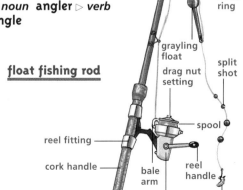

line
rod ring
carbon fiber rod
float ring
grayling float
split shot
drag nut setting
spool
reel handle
bait on hook
reel fitting
cork handle
bale arm
fixed spool reel

float fishing rod

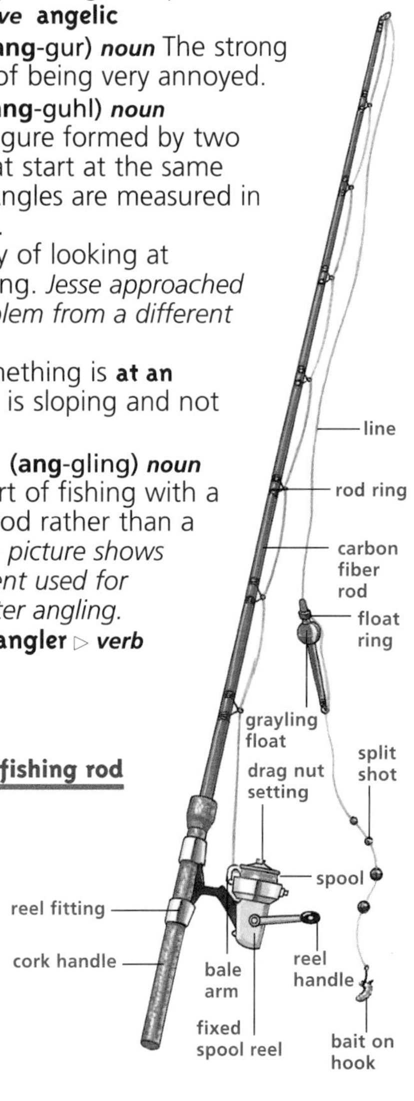

an·go·ra (ang-**gor**-uh) *noun*
1. A long-haired variety of rabbit, goat, or cat.
2. Fluffy wool made from the hair of angora rabbits or goats mixed with sheep's wool.

angora rabbits

an·gry (**ang**-gree) *adjective* If you are **angry**, you feel that you want to argue or fight with someone. ▷ **angrier, angriest** ▷ *adverb* **angrily**

an·guish (**ang**-gwish) *noun* A strong feeling of misery or distress. ▷ *adjective* **anguished**

an·gu·lar (**ang**-gyu-lur) *adjective* Something that is **angular** has straight lines and sharp turns or corners. *Jamie had a thin, angular face.*

an·i·mal (**an**-uh-muhl) *noun* Any living creature that can breathe and move about.

animal rights *noun* A movement for the fair and humane treatment of animals. Some of the people who support animal rights object to the wearing of fur coats and the use of animals for scientific experiments. ▷ *adjective* **animal rights**

an·i·mat·ed (**an**-i-may-tid) *adjective*
1. Lively, as in *an animated conversation.* ▷ *noun* **animation** ▷ *adverb* **animatedly**
2. An **animated film** is made by projecting a series of drawings very quickly, one after the other, so that the characters in the drawings seem to move. *Artists provide hundreds of thousands of drawings, such as these, to make an animated film.* ▷ *noun* **animation**, *noun* **animator** ▷ *verb* **animate**

animation sequence

an·i·mos·i·ty (an-i-**moss**-uh-tee) *noun* A strong dislike for someone.

an·i·seed (**an**-i-*seed*) *noun* A strong-smelling seed of the herb anise. It's used as a spice in candy and drinks.

an·kle (**ang**-kuhl) *noun* The joint that connects your foot to your leg.

an·nex
1. (an-**eks** *or* **an**-eks) *verb* When one country **annexes** another, it takes control of it by force. ▷ **annexes, annexing, annexed**

2. (**an**-eks) *noun* An extra building that is joined onto or placed near a main building. ▷ *noun* **annexation**

an·ni·hi·late (uh-**nye**-uh-late) *verb* To destroy something completely. ▷ **annihilating, annihilated** ▷ *noun* **annihilation**

an·ni·ver·sa·ry (an-uh-**vur**-suh-ree) *noun* A date that people remember because something important happened on that date in the past, as in *a wedding anniversary.* ▷ *noun, plural* **anniversaries**

an·no·tate (**an**-oh-tate) *verb* To write notes explaining a piece of writing. ▷ **annotating, annotated** ▷ *noun* **annotation** ▷ *adjective* **annotated**

an·nounce (uh-**nounss**) *verb* To say something officially or publicly. *Abe announced his retirement.* ▷ **announcing, announced** ▷ *noun* **announcement**

an·nounc·er (uh-**noun**-sur) *noun*
1. Someone who introduces programs on television or radio.
2. Someone who describes the action during a sports event.

an·noy (uh-**noi**) *verb* To make someone lose patience or feel angry. *It really annoys me when a car alarm rings for half an hour.* ▷ **annoying, annoyed** ▷ *noun* **annoyance** ▷ *adjective* **annoying** ▷ *adverb* **annoyingly**

an·nu·al (**an**-yoo-uhl)
1. *adjective* Happening once every year or over a period of one year, as in *the annual Labor Day parade* or *an annual magazine subscription.* ▷ *adverb* **annually**
2. *noun* A book published once a year.
3. *noun* A plant that lives for only one year. *Most sunflowers are annuals.*

a·noint (uh-**noint**) *verb* To honor someone during a religious ceremony by rubbing oil on his or her head. *The archbishop anointed the new queen.* ▷ **anointing, anointed**

a·non·y·mous (uh-**non**-uh-muhss) *adjective* Written, done, or given by a person whose name is not known or made public, as in *an anonymous letter.* ▷ *noun* **anonymity** (an-o-**nim**-i-tee) ▷ *adverb* **anonymously**

an·o·rak (**an**-uh-rak) *noun* A pullover jacket with a hood.

an·o·rex·ic (an-uh-**rek**-sik) *adjective* When people are **anorexic**, they think they are too fat, so they eat very little and become dangerously thin. ▷ *noun* **anorexic**, *noun* **anorexia** (an-uh-**rek**-see-uh)

an·oth·er (uh-**nuTH**-ur)
1. *adjective* One more of the same kind of thing. *Have another apple.*
2. *pronoun* A different one. *I didn't like the red dress, so I chose another.*

an·swer (an-sur)
1. *verb* To say or write something as a reply, as in *to answer a question.* ▷ *noun* **answer**
2. *noun* The solution to a problem. *Is there an answer to world poverty?*
3. *verb* If you **answer back,** you make a rude reply.
4. If someone **has a lot to answer for,** he or she has caused a lot of trouble.
▷ *verb* **answering, answered**

an·swer·a·ble (an-sur-uh-buhl) *adjective*
Responsible. *Each leader is answerable for the safety of her group.*

answering machine *noun* A machine connected to or built into a telephone that records messages from people who telephone while you are out.

ant (ant) *noun* A small insect that lives in a large group called a colony. Ants are very strong for their size. They can carry 27 times their own weight. *See* **desert, insect.**

an·tag·o·nize (an-tag-uh-nize) *verb* If you **antagonize** a person or an animal, you make it very angry. ▷ **antagonizing, antagonized** ▷ *noun* **antagonism, *noun*** **antagonist**

Ant·arc·tic (ant-ark-tik) *noun* The area around the South Pole. ▷ *adjective*
Antarctic *See* **polar.**

ant·eat·er
(ant-ee-tur) *noun*
A South American mammal with a very long tongue that it uses to search for ants and other small insects.

giant anteater

an·te·ced·ent (*an*-tuh-see-duhnt) *noun*
In grammar, the word or phrase to which a pronoun refers. In *Ramón cooked the burger and then ate it,* the **antecedent** of *it* is *the burger.*

an·te·lope (an-tuh-lope) *noun* An animal that looks like a large deer and runs very fast. Antelopes have long horns without branches and are found in Africa and parts of Asia.

an·ten·na (an-ten-uh) *noun*
1. A feeler on the head of an insect. *See* **beetle.**
2. A wire that receives radio and television signals. *See* **car, satellite.**
▷ *noun, plural* **antennas** *or* **antennae** (an-ten-ee)

an·them (an-thuhm) *noun* A religious or national song, often sung by a choir, as in *a national anthem.*

an·ther (an-thur) *noun* The part of a flower at the tip of the stamen that contains its pollen. *See* **flower.**

an·thol·o·gy (an-thol-uh-jee) *noun* A collection of poems or stories by different writers that are all printed in the same book. ▷ *noun, plural* **anthologies**

an·thra·cite (an-thruh-*site*) *noun* A type of shiny, hard coal that doesn't give off much smoke when it is burned.

an·thro·pol·o·gy (*an*-thruh-**pol**-uh-jee) *noun* The study of the beliefs and ways of life of different people around the world. ▷ *noun* **anthropologist**

an·ti·bi·ot·ic (*an*-ti-bye-ot-ik) *noun* A drug, such as penicillin, that kills bacteria and is used to cure infections and diseases.

> **Prefix**
> •
> The prefix **anti-** adds one of these meanings to a root word:
> 1. Against, as in *antisocial* (against society) or *antiwar* (against war).
> 2. Preventing or working against, as in *antiperspirant* (something that works against perspiration) or *antidote* (something that works against poison).
>
> When a word begins with a capital letter, the prefix anti- is added with a hyphen, as in *anti-Nazi* or *anti-American.*

an·ti·bod·y (an-ti-*bod*-ee) *noun* Your blood makes **antibodies** to fight against infection and disease. ▷ *noun, plural* **antibodies**

an·tic·i·pate (an-**tiss**-i-*pate*) *verb* To expect something to happen and be prepared for it. *The police anticipated trouble after the long, bitter court trial.* ▷ **anticipating, anticipated** ▷ *noun* **anticipation**

an·ti·cli·max (*an*-ti-**klye**-maks) *noun* If something is an **anticlimax,** it is not as exciting as you had expected. *After the fun of getting ready, the party was an anticlimax.* ▷ *noun, plural* **anticlimaxes**

an·ti·dote (an-ti-dote) *noun* Something that stops a poison from working.

an·ti·freeze (an-tee-*freez*) *noun* A chemical substance that is added to liquid to stop it from freezing. Antifreeze is mixed with the water in a car's radiator to keep the car running in cold weather.

an·ti·per·spi·rant (*an*-tee-**pur**-spuh-ruhnt) *noun* A substance that you put on your skin to stop you from sweating too much.

an·tique (an-teek)
1. *noun* A very old object that is valuable because it is rare or beautiful.
2. *adjective* Very old, as in *antique jewelry.*

an·ti·sep·tic (an-ti-sep-tik) *noun* A substance that kills germs and prevents infection by stopping the growth of germs.

an·ti·so·cial (an-tee-soh-shuhl) *adjective*
1. If somebody is **antisocial,** he or she does not enjoy being with others.
2. When people behave in an **antisocial** way, they do something that upsets or harms other people.

ant·ler (ant-lur) *noun*
One of the two large, branching, bony structures on the head of a deer, moose, or elk. These animals grow and shed new antlers each year. *The diagram shows a new antler.*

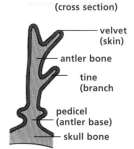

stag's antler
(cross section)

- velvet (skin)
- antler bone
- tine (branch)
- pedicel (antler base)
- skull bone

▶ Word History

● ●

When the Romans watched a stag, or male deer, bending his head to drink water, they noticed that his antler looked like a branch in front of his eyes. So they named it *ramum ante ocularis,* "the branch before the eyes." The Latin *ante ocularis* developed into the French *antoillier,* which became antler later on in English.

an·to·nym (an-toh-nim) *noun* A word that means the opposite of another word. **Hot** and **cold** are antonyms; so are **weak** and **strong; up** and **down; over** and **under.**

anx·i·e·ty (ang-zye-uh-tee) *noun* A feeling of worry or fear. ▷ *noun, plural* **anxieties**

anx·ious (angk-shuhss) *adjective*
1. Worried. *Mom gets anxious when I'm late.* ▷ *adverb* **anxiously**
2. Very eager to do something. *Kareem is anxious to do well on his exams.*

an·y (en-ee)
1. *adjective* One or more. *Do you have any brothers or sisters?*
2. *adjective* Every. *Any teacher would be proud to have you as a student.*
3. *pronoun* A way of suggesting people or things without naming them. *She'd like to team up with any of them for the debate.*
4. *adverb* At all. *Do you feel any better?*

an·y·bod·y (en-ee-bod-ee) *pronoun* Any person.

an·y·how (en-ee-hou) *adverb* In any case. *I didn't want to come anyhow.*

an·y·more (en-ee-mor) *adverb* Now, or from now on. *I won't bother you anymore.*

an·y·one (en-ee-wuhn) *pronoun* Any person.

an·y·place (en-ee-playss) *adverb* Anywhere. *Your glasses could be anyplace.*

an·y·thing (en-ee-thing)
1. *pronoun* Any thing or item of any kind. *I'm not fussy; I'll eat anything.*
2. *adverb* At all. *You aren't anything like Sue.*

an·y·time (en-ee-time) *adverb* At any hour or date, or whenever. *Since my parents own a pizza parlor, I can eat pizza anytime I want.*

an·y·way (en-ee-way) *adverb* In any case. *I never liked him anyway.*

an·y·where (en-ee-wair) *adverb* In or to any place. *I'd follow Jason anywhere.*

a·or·ta (ay-or-tuh) *noun* The main tube that carries blood away from the heart to the rest of the body, except the lungs. *See* **circulation, heart.**

A·pach·e (uh-pa-chee) *noun* One of a group of American Indians that lives primarily in the southwestern United States. ▷ *noun, plural* **Apache** *or* **Apaches**

a·part (uh-part) *adverb* If two people or things are **apart,** they are separated from each other.

a·part·heid (uh-part-hate *or* uh-part-hite) *noun* A political policy in which people of different races are kept apart from each other.

a·part·ment (uh-part-muhnt) *noun* A set of rooms to live in, usually on one floor of a building.

ap·a·thet·ic (ap-uh-thet-ik) *adjective* If you are **apathetic,** you do not care about anything or want to do anything. ▷ *noun* **apathy**

ape (ape)
1. *noun* A large animal related to a monkey, but with no tail. Gorillas, gibbons, orangutans, and chimpanzees are kinds of apes. *The picture shows a chimpanzee poking a stick into a termite mound to find food.*

chimpanzee

2. *verb* To copy the way another person behaves or speaks. *Are you aping me?* ▷ **aping, aped**

ap·er·ture (ap-ur-chur) *noun* A hole behind a camera lens that can be opened or closed to control the amount of light that shines onto the film. *See* **photography.**

a·pex (ay-peks) *noun* The highest point of something, as in *the apex of a mountain.* ▷ *noun, plural* **apexes**

a·phid (ay-fid) *noun* A tiny insect that feeds by sucking the juices from plants.

a·piece (uh-**peess**) *adverb* Each. *The apples are 50 cents apiece.*

a·pol·o·gize (uh-**pol**-uh-jize) *verb* To say that you are sorry about something. ▷ **apologizing, apologized** ▷ *noun* **apology** ▷ *adjective* **apologetic**

a·pos·tle (uh-**poss**-uhl) *noun*
1. A close follower of another person or cause.
2. In Christianity, one of the 12 men chosen by Jesus to spread his teaching, plus St. Paul. *This picture of the apostle Matthew was made in the seventh century.*

apostle

a·pos·tro·phe (uh-**poss**-truh-fee) *noun* A punctuation mark (') used to show ownership; for example, "Jane's bag," or to show that letters have been left out; for example, "can't."

ap·pall·ing (uh-**paw**-ling) *adjective* Horrifying and shocking. ▷ *adverb* **appallingly**

ap·pa·rat·us (ap-uh-**rat**-uhss) *noun*
1. Equipment used for performing sports, especially gymnastics.
2. Equipment or machines used to do a job or laboratory experiment.
▷ *noun, plural* **apparatus** *or* **apparatuses**

laboratory apparatus

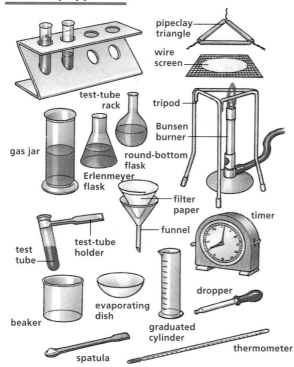

pipeclay triangle
wire screen
test-tube rack
tripod
Bunsen burner
gas jar
round-bottom flask
Erlenmeyer flask
filter paper
timer
funnel
test tube
test-tube holder
dropper
evaporating dish
beaker
graduated cylinder
thermometer
spatula

ap·par·el (uh-**pa**-ruhl) *noun* Clothing. *This store sells women's apparel.*

ap·par·ent (uh-**pa**-ruhnt) *adjective*
1. Obvious, or clear. *Bill's guilt was apparent to us.*
2. Seeming real or true. *Claudia's apparent confidence is really an act.*
▷ *adverb* **apparently**

ap·peal (uh-**peel**) *verb*
1. To ask for something urgently. *We appealed to the doctor for help.*
2. To ask for a decision made by a court of law to be changed. ▷ *noun* **appeal**
3. If something **appeals to** you, you like it or find it interesting.
▷ *verb* **appealing, appealed**

ap·pear (uh-**pihr**) *verb*
1. To come into view. *Suddenly, clouds appeared.*
2. To seem. *Dylan appears to be happy.*
▷ *verb* **appearing, appeared** ▷ *noun* **appearance**

ap·pease (uh-**peez**) *verb*
1. To make someone content or calm. *My brother and I appeased our mother by doing our homework before dinner.*
2. To give someone what is needed, or to satisfy someone. *All I need to appease my hunger is one home-cooked meal.*
▷ *verb* **appeasing, appeased**

ap·pen·di·ci·tis (uh-*pen*-duh-**sye**-tiss) *noun* A person with **appendicitis** has an infected appendix and is in pain.

ap·pen·dix (uh-**pen**-diks) *noun*
1. A small, closed tube leading from the large intestine. *See* **digestion.**
2. Extra information at the end of a book.
▷ *noun, plural* **appendixes** *or* **appendices** (uh-**pen**-di-seez)

ap·pe·tite (ap-uh-*tite*) *noun*
1. Desire for food.
2. Great enjoyment of something. *Heather has a real appetite for work.*

ap·pe·tiz·ing (ap-uh-*tye*-zing) *adjective* Food that is **appetizing** looks and smells good to eat.

ap·plaud (uh-**plawd**) *verb* To show that you like something, usually by clapping your hands.
▷ **applauding, applauded** ▷ *noun* **applause**

ap·ple (ap-uhl) *noun* A round, usually crisp fruit. *See* **fruit.**

ap·pli·ance (uh-**plye**-uhnss) *noun* A machine designed to do a particular job. *Our kitchen is full of modern appliances.*

ap·pli·cant (ap-luh-kuhnt) *noun* Someone who has written formally asking for something, such as a job, a loan, or entrance to a school.

ap·pli·ca·tion (ap-luh-**kay**-shuhn) *noun*
1. A written request for something, such as a job, as in *a job application.*
2. A way of using something. *Our computer system has many different applications.*

A

ap·ply (uh-**plye**) *verb*
1. To bring something into direct contact with something else, as in *to apply makeup.*
2. To ask for something in writing, as in *to apply for a loan.*
3. To be relevant. *These rules don't apply to us.*
4. If you **apply yourself** to something, you work hard at it.
▷ *verb* **applies, applying, applied**

ap·point (uh-**point**) *verb*
1. To choose someone for a job.
2. To arrange something officially. *We've already appointed a time for the conference.*
▷ *verb* **appointing, appointed**

ap·point·ment (uh-**point**-muhnt) *noun*
1. The act of naming or choosing someone for a job. *The mayor will announce the appointment of the new school superintendent tomorrow.*
2. The job itself. *She was thrilled to receive the appointment as company vice president.*
3. The arrangement to meet someone at a certain time, as in *a dentist appointment.*

ap·praise (uh-**praze**) *verb* To decide on something's value by inspecting it closely. *I want a jeweler to appraise my grandfather's pocket watch before I try to sell it.* ▷ **appraising, appraised**

ap·pre·cia·ble (uh-**pree**-shuh-buhl) *adjective* Enough to be noticed. *The company has lost an appreciable amount of money.*

ap·pre·ci·ate (uh-**pree**-shee-*ate*) *verb*
1. To enjoy or value somebody or something.
▷ *adjective* **appreciative** ▷ *adverb* **appreciatively**
2. To understand something. *I appreciate your point of view.*
3. To increase in worth. *The value of this stamp has appreciated since I bought it for my collection.*
▷ *verb* **appreciating, appreciated** ▷ *noun* **appreciation**

ap·pre·hend (ap-ri-**hend**) *verb*
1. To capture and arrest someone. *Thanks to a tip, the police apprehended the bank robber.*
2. To understand, or to capture the meaning of something. *He motioned vaguely with his hand, but I couldn't apprehend what he meant by that.*
▷ *verb* **apprehending, apprehended**

ap·pre·hen·sive (ap-ri-**hen**-siv) *adjective* Worried and slightly afraid. *Dolores was apprehensive about making her speech.* ▷ *noun* **apprehension**
▷ *adverb* **apprehensively**

ap·pren·tice (uh-**pren**-tiss) *noun* Someone who learns a trade or craft by working with a skilled person. ▷ *noun* **apprenticeship**

ap·proach (uh-**prohch**) *verb*
1. To move nearer. *A big storm is approaching.*
2. If you **approach** somebody, you go up to the person and talk to him or her.
3. When you **approach** a problem, you think of ways of tackling it.
▷ *verb* **approaches, approaching, approached**
▷ *noun* **approach**

ap·proach·a·ble (uh-**proh**-chuh-buhl) *adjective* If people are **approachable,** they are friendly and easy to talk to.

ap·pro·pri·ate
1. (uh-**proh**-pree-uht) *adjective* Suitable, or right, as in *appropriate attire.* ▷ *adverb* **appropriately**
2. (uh-**proh**-pree-*ate*) *verb* To take something that is not yours. ▷ *verb* **appropriating, appropriated**

ap·prove (uh-**proov**) *verb*
1. If you **approve of** someone or something, you think that he or she is acceptable or good.
2. To officially accept a plan or an idea. *Congress approved the transportation bill.*
▷ *verb* **approving, approved** ▷ *noun* **approval**

ap·prox·i·mate (uh-**prok**-si-muht) *adjective* More or less accurate or correct, as in *an approximate price.* ▷ *noun* **approximation** ▷ *adverb* **approximately**

a·pri·cot (**ay**-pri-*kot* or **ap**-ri-*kot*) *noun* A small, soft fruit with an orange skin. *See* **fruit.**

A·pril (**ay**-pruhl) *noun* The fourth month on the calendar, after March and before May. April has 30 days.

April Fools' Day April 1, a day when it is customary to play practical jokes on people.

a·pron (**ay**-pruhn) *noun*
1. An article of clothing that you wear to protect your clothes when you are cooking, painting, etc.
2. The part of a stage in front of the curtain.

apt (apt) *adjective*
1. Very suitable, as in *an apt reply.*
2. Quick to learn things, as in *an apt student.*
3. If you are **apt** to do something, you are likely to do it.

ap·ti·tude (**ap**-ti-tood) *noun* A natural ability to do something well, as in *an aptitude for drawing.*

Aq·ua-Lung (ak-wuh-*lung*) *noun* Trademark for a breathing apparatus for diving. An Aqua-Lung consists of an air tank with a tube leading to a mouthpiece.

a·quar·i·um (uh-kwair-ee-uhm) *noun* A glass tank in which you can keep fish. *The picture shows an aquarium for tropical freshwater fish.* ▷ **noun, plural aquariums** *or* **aquaria** (uh-kwair-ee-uh)

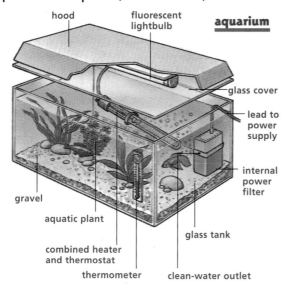

aquarium

hood
fluorescent lightbulb
glass cover
lead to power supply
internal power filter
gravel
aquatic plant
glass tank
combined heater and thermostat
thermometer
clean-water outlet

a·quat·ic (uh-**kwat**-ik *or* uh-**kwot**-ik) *adjective*
1. Living or growing in water, as in *aquatic plants.*
2. Performed in or on water, as in *aquatic sports.*

aq·ue·duct (ak-wuh-*duhkt*) *noun* A large bridge built to carry water across a valley. *The Roman aqueduct shown here was built in France in A.D.14.*

aqueduct

Ar·a·bic (a-ruh-bik) *noun* A language spoken by many people in the Middle East and North Africa.

Arabic numerals *noun, plural* The figures 0, 1, 2, 3, 4, 5, 6, 7, 8, and 9 that we use today. These numerals were first taught to Europeans by Arab scholars.

ar·a·ble (a-ruh-buhl) *adjective* Arable land is fit for growing crops.

ar·bi·trar·y (ar-buh-*trer*-ee) *adjective* Based on personal feelings or opinions rather than on law or logic. *His decision to walk to school instead of taking the free school bus was completely arbitrary.*

ar·bi·trate (ar-bi-*trate*) *verb* To help two sides reach an agreement in a dispute. ▷ **arbitrating, arbitrated** ▷ *noun* **arbitration,** *noun* **arbitrator**

ar·bor (ar-bur) *noun*
1. A place that is surrounded by trees, shrubs, vines, or other plants. *Our house has a grape arbor that forms a covered passageway from the back door to the garden.*
2. Arbor Day is a day in spring that is set aside for planting trees. The actual date varies.

arc (ark) *noun*
1. A curved line.
2. In math, an **arc** is a curved line between two points. *See* **circle.**
Arc sounds like **ark.**

ar·cade (ar-kade) *noun*
1. A row of arches in a building.
2. penny arcade A covered area with machines for amusement, such as pinball games, that you pay to use.
3. shopping arcade A covered passageway with stores or stalls.

arch (arch)
1. *noun* A curved structure. Arches often help support a building or bridge. *The picture shows four different types of arches.*
2. *verb* To curve. *The cat arched its back and spat.* ▷ **arches, arching, arched** ▷ *adjective* **arched**
3. *adjective* Main or chief. *Joe is my arch enemy.*

arches

Roman
Islamic horseshoe
Gothic pointed
Gothic ogee

ar·chae·o·lo·gy *or* **archeology** (ar-kee-ol-uh-jee) *noun* If you study **archaeology,** you learn about the past by digging up old buildings and objects and examining them carefully. ▷ *noun* **archeologist** ▷ *adjective* **archeological**

ar·cha·ic (ar-kay-ik) *adjective* Very old-fashioned and not used anymore, as in *archaic customs.*

arch·bish·op (arch-bish-uhp) *noun* The supervisor of bishops in some Christian denominations.

ar·che·o·lo·gy *See* **archaeology.**

arch·er·y (ar-chuh-ree) *noun* The sport of shooting at targets using a bow and arrow. ▷ *noun* **archer**

ar·chi·pel·a·go (*ar*-kuh-pel-uh-goh) *noun* A group of small islands.

ar·chi·tect (ar-ki-tekt) *noun* Someone who designs buildings and checks that they are built properly.

architecture

ar·chi·tec·ture (ar-ki-tek-chur) *noun*
1. The activity of designing buildings.
2. The style in which buildings are designed.
The selection of buildings here shows how different styles of architecture have been used for places of worship throughout the world as well as for a range of modern buildings.
▷ *adjective* **architectural** *See also* **building.**

pyramid
(The Great Pyramids, Giza, Egypt)

Greek temple
(The Parthenon, Athens, Greece)

architecture

pagoda
(Soochow Lake, China)

Gothic cathedral
(Salisbury, England)

Shinto shrine
(Izumo, Japan)

Byzantine cathedral
(St Basil's, Moscow, Russia)

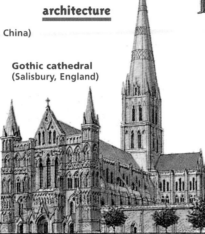

communications tower
(CN Tower, Toronto, Canada)

mosque
(The Blue Mosque, Istanbul, Turkey)

skyscraper
(Empire State Building, New York) — Total height: 1,454 feet

— TV tower

master FM antenna

— 102nd floor observatory (1,250 feet up)

— 86th floor observatory (1,050 feet up)

Inside:
- 60 miles of water pipe
- 73 elevators operating in 7 miles of shafts
- 3,500 miles of telephone and telegraph wire
- 6,500 windows
- 1,860 steps from street to 102nd floor

opera house
(Sydney, Australia)

museum entrance
(Louvre Museum, Paris, France)

Hindu temple
(Khajuraho, India)

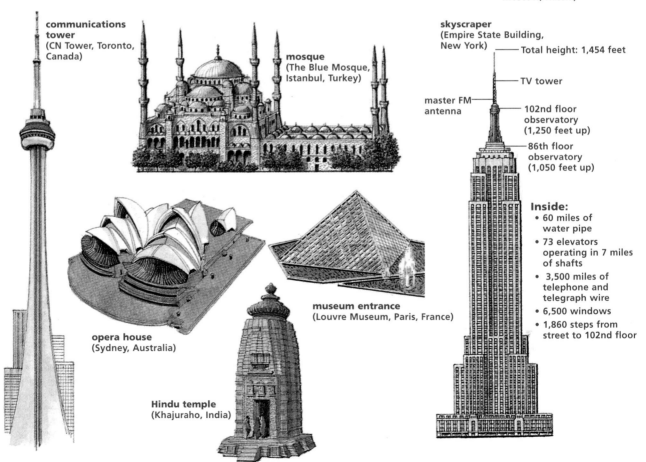

A

arc·tic (ark-tik)
1. *adjective* Extremely cold and wintry, as in *arctic weather conditions.*
2. The Arctic *noun* The frozen area around the North Pole. ▷ *adjective* **Arctic** *See* **polar.**

ar·dent (ar-duhnt) *adjective* If you are **ardent** about something, you feel very strongly about it, as in *an ardent supporter of animal rights.* ▷ *adverb* **ardently**

ar·du·ous (ar-joo-uhss) *adjective* Very difficult and demanding a lot of effort, as in *an arduous task.*

ar·e·a (air-ee-uh) *noun*
1. The amount of surface within a given boundary, measured in square units.
2. A part of a place, as in *a poor area of town.*

area code *noun* A three-digit number that indicates the telephone service area in which you live. When telephoning from one area to another, you dial 1 plus the area code, followed by the seven-digit local number.

a·re·na (uh-ree-nuh) *noun* A large area that is used for sports or entertainment. *See* **amphitheater, track and field.**

aren't (arnt *or* ar-ent) *contraction* A short form of *are not. You aren't going to like this.*

ar·gue (ar-gyoo) *verb*
1. To give your opinion about something. *Sean argued that whaling was cruel.* ▷ *noun* **argument**
2. To disagree with someone forcefully.
▷ *adjective* **argumentative** (*ar*-gyoo-**men**-tuh-tiv)
▷ *verb* **arguing, argued**

ar·id (a-rid) *adjective* Land that is **arid** is extremely dry because very little rain has fallen on it.

a·rise (uh-rize) *verb*
1. To get up.
2. To come into being. *A problem arose.*
▷ *verb* **arising, arose** (uh-**rohz**), **arisen** (uh-**riz**-in)

a·ris·to·crat (uh-**riss**-tuh-krat) *noun* A member of a group of people thought to be the best in some way, usually based on how much money they have, how well-known they are, or how much they are respected. In history, a member of the highest social rank, or nobility. ▷ *noun* **aristocracy** (a-ruh-**stok**-ruh-see) ▷ *adjective* **aristocratic**

a·rith·me·tic (uh-**rith**-muh-tik) *noun* The science of numbers and computation. Addition, subtraction, multiplication, and division are the four basic operations of arithmetic.

ark (ark) *noun*
1. In the Bible, a boat built by Noah to carry his family and two of every kind of animal during the great flood.
2. In a synagogue, the cabinet in which the Torah scrolls are kept. *The rabbi told everyone to stand as he opened the ark.*
Ark sounds like **arc.**

arm (arm)
1. *noun* The part of your body between your shoulder and your hand.
2. *verb* If a country **arms** itself, it gets ready for war by taking up weapons. ▷ **arming, armed**
3. arms *noun, plural* Weapons.

ar·ma·da (ar-mah-duh) *noun* A large group of warships.

ar·ma·dil·lo (ar-muh-dil-oh) *noun* A mammal covered by hard, bony plates. *The nine-banded armadillo, shown here, is found in North and South America.*

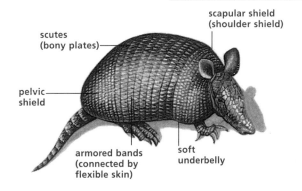

nine-banded armadillo

scapular shield (shoulder shield)
scutes (bony plates)
pelvic shield
armored bands (connected by flexible skin)
soft underbelly

Word History
• •

Like the alligator, the **armadillo** was an unknown creature to the Spanish explorers of North America. Since they had no name for this bony, armor-covered mammal, they called it armadillo, Spanish for "the little armored one." Many words with the root *arma-* or *arm-*, such as *armada, armor,* and *army,* come from the Latin word for weapons.

ar·ma·ments (ar-muh-muhnts) *noun, plural* Weapons and other equipment used for fighting wars.

arm·chair (arm-*chair*) *noun* A comfortable chair with supports for your arms.

armed forces *noun, plural* All of the branches of a country's military. In the United States, the armed forces include the Army, Navy, Air Force, Marine Corps, and Coast Guard.

ar·mis·tice (arm-iss-tiss) *noun* A temporary agreement to stop fighting a war.

ar·mor (ar-mur) *noun*
1. Metal covering worn by soldiers to protect them in battle. *See* **knight.**
2. Strong metal protection for tanks and other military vehicles.
3. Protective scales, spines, etc., that cover some animals, such as an armadillo. *See* **armadillo.**

A

armored vehicle *noun*
A tank or other military vehicle with a strong metal covering. *This armored vehicle is used for carrying troops.*

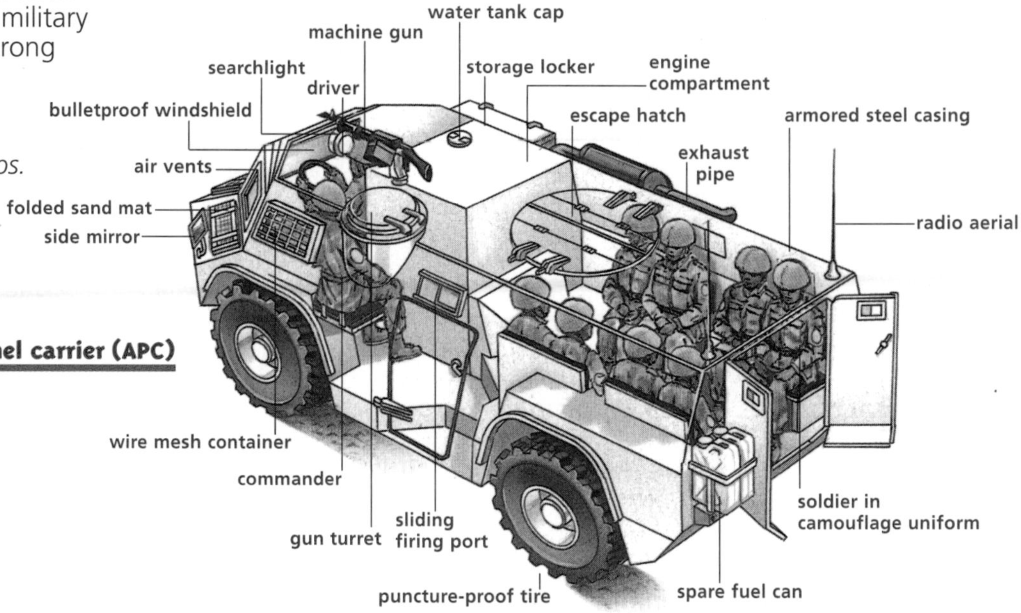

water tank cap
machine gun
searchlight
driver
storage locker
engine compartment
bulletproof windshield
escape hatch
armored steel casing
exhaust pipe
air vents
armored steel casing
folded sand mat
radio aerial
side mirror

armored personnel carrier (APC)

wire mesh container
commander
sliding firing port
gun turret
soldier in camouflage uniform
puncture-proof tire
spare fuel can

ar·mor·y (ar-mur-ee) *noun* A place where weapons are stored or soldiers are trained.
▷ *noun, plural* **armories**

arm·pit (arm-*pit*) *noun* The area under your arm where it joins your shoulder.

ar·my (ar-mee) *noun* A large group of people trained to fight on land. ▷ *noun, plural* **armies**

a·ro·ma (uh-roh-muh) *noun* A smell that is usually pleasant. ▷ *adjective* **aromatic** (a-ruh-mat-ik)

a·round (uh-round)
1. *preposition* Surrounding. *He tied a rope around the tree.*
2. *adverb* In many different parts of a place. *We traveled around a lot.*
3. *adverb* More or less. *There were around 30 of us at the party.*

a·rouse (uh-rouz) *verb*
1. To stir up a feeling. *Miguel's questions aroused my curiosity.*
2. To wake up someone.
▷ *verb* **arousing, aroused** ▷ *noun* **arousal**

ar·range (uh-raynj) *verb*
1. To make plans for something to happen. *After Mom left, Dad and I arranged her surprise party.*
2. To place things so that they look attractive, as in *to arrange flowers.*
3. To change a piece of music slightly, so that it can be played on different instruments, as in *to arrange music.*
4. If you have an **arranged marriage,** your parents choose a husband or wife for you.
▷ *verb* **arranging, arranged** ▷ *noun* **arrangement**

ar·ray (uh-ray) *noun*
1. A large number of things. *She was excited by the array of delicious foods.*
2. An orderly arrangement. *The soldiers marched in battle array.*
▷ *verb* **array**

ar·rest (uh-rest) *verb*
1. To stop and hold someone by the power of law.
2. To stop something from developing or happening anymore.
▷ *verb* **arresting, arrested** ▷ *noun* **arrest**

ar·ri·val (uh-rye-vuhl) *noun*
1. The act of getting to a place. *She eagerly awaited his arrival at the airport.*
2. Someone or something that has gotten to a place. *The museum displayed its newest arrival, the 500-year-old skeleton of a horse.*

ar·rive (uh-rive) *verb*
1. To reach a place. *We arrived home early.*
2. To come. *At last, my birthday arrived.*
▷ *verb* **arriving, arrived**

ar·ro·gant (a-ruh-guhnt) *adjective* Conceited and too proud. ▷ *noun* **arrogance** ▷ *adverb* **arrogantly**

ar·row (a-roh) *noun*
1. A pointed stick shot from a bow.
2. A sign (→) showing a direction on maps, road signs, etc.

ar·row·head (a-roh-*hed*) *noun* The sharp tip of an arrow. *While he was digging in his backyard, Malcolm found two old American Indian arrowheads that were made of stone.*

ar·se·nal (ar-suh-nuhl) *noun* A place where

A

weapons and ammunition are made or stored.

ar·se·nic (ar-suh-nik) *noun* A chemical element that usually appears as a gray-white powder and is poisonous if swallowed.

ar·son (ar-suhn) *noun* If someone commits **arson,** he or she deliberately and wrongly sets fire to something. ▷ *noun* **arsonist**

art (art)
1. *noun* The skill of creating something beautiful by drawing, painting, or making things with your hands.
2. *noun* Something that requires a lot of skill, as in *the art of Chinese cooking.*
3. the arts *noun, plural* Forms of entertainment, such as music, theater, and film.

ar·ter·y (ar-tuh-ree) *noun*
1. One of the tubes that carry blood from your heart to all the other parts of your body. *See* **circulation.**
2. A main road.
▷ *noun, plural* **arteries** ▷ *adjective* **arterial**

ar·thri·tis (ar-thrye-tiss) *noun* A disease that makes people's joints swollen and painful.
▷ *adjective* **arthritic**

ar·thro·pod (ar-thruh-pod) *noun* An animal without a backbone that has a hard outer skeleton and three or more pairs of legs that can bend. Insects, spiders, lobsters, and shrimp are all arthropods.

ar·ti·cle (ar-ti-kuhl) *noun*
1. An object, or a thing, as in *an article of clothing.*
2. A piece of writing published in a newspaper or magazine.
3. A word, such as *a, an,* or *the,* that goes in front of a noun.

ar·tic·u·late (ar-tik-yuh-luht) *adjective* If you are **articulate,** you can express yourself clearly in words. ▷ *verb* **articulate** (ar-tik-yuh-late)
▷ *adverb* **articulately**

ar·ti·fact (art-uh-fakt) *noun* An object made or changed by human beings, especially a tool or weapon used in the past. *We saw wooden bowls, leather pouches, and other artifacts at the museum.*

ar·ti·fi·cial (ar-ti-fish-uhl) *adjective* False, not real, or not natural, as in *artificial flowers.* ▷ *adverb* **artificially**

artificial intelligence *noun* The science of making computers do things that previously needed human intelligence, such as understanding language. Abbreviated AI.

artificial respiration *noun* A method of starting breathing after it has stopped by forcing air into and out of somebody's lungs. *The lifeguard performed artificial respiration and saved the boy's life.*

ar·til·ler·y (ar-til-uh-ree) *noun*
1. Large, powerful guns that are mounted on wheels or tracks.
2. The part of an army that uses large guns.

ar·ti·san (ar-tuh-zuhn) *noun* Someone who is skilled at working with his or her hands at a particular craft. Carpenters and quiltmakers are artisans.

art·ist (ar-tist) *noun* Someone very skilled at painting, making things, or performing in the arts. *This picture shows materials used by painters.*
▷ *adjective* **artistic** ▷ *adverb* **artistically**

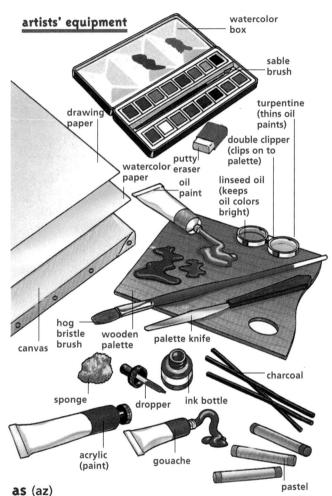

artists' equipment

watercolor box
sable brush
turpentine (thins oil paints)
double clipper (clips on to palette)
linseed oil (keeps oil colors bright)
drawing paper
watercolor paper
putty eraser
oil paint
hog bristle brush
wooden palette
palette knife
canvas
charcoal
sponge
dropper
ink bottle
acrylic (paint)
gouache
pastel

as (az)
1. *conjunction* In comparison with. *Are you as good a basketball player as Angela is?*
2. *adverb* To the same degree. *I like my answer better because yours is not as good.*
3. *conjunction* In the same way that. *Raise your hand as I do.*
4. *conjunction* While or when. *Todd petted the cat as she lay on his lap.*
5. *conjunction* Since or because. *As you seemed to enjoy the roller coaster, we should go on it again.*
6. *preposition* In the manner of, or in the role of. *As your mother, I know what's best for you.*

as·bes·tos (ass-bess-tuhss) *noun* A grayish mineral whose fibers can be woven into a fireproof fabric. Asbestos is rarely used today, even though it was once a popular building material, because breathing its fibers is now known to cause serious illness.

as·cend (uh-send) *verb* To move or go up. *The plane began to ascend.* ▷ **ascending, ascended** ▷ *noun* **ascent**

ash (ash) *noun*
1. The powder that remains after something has been burned.
2. A tree with long, thin leaves.
▷ *noun, plural* **ashes**

a·shamed (uh-shamed) *adjective* If you are **ashamed,** you feel embarrassed and guilty.

a·shore (uh-shor) *adverb* On or to the shore or land. *The strong tide washed the raft ashore.*

A·sian American (ay-zhuhn) *noun* Someone who was born in the United States or became a U.S. citizen and can trace his or her ancestors back to Asia. ▷ *adjective* **Asian-American**

a·side (uh-side)
1. *adverb* To one side, or out of the way. *Elena pushed her brother aside.*
2. *noun* A remark made quietly so that not everyone can hear it. *In an aside, Marc told Carrie that he wanted to leave the party.*

ask (ask) *verb*
1. To make a request or put a question to someone. *Jill asked her sister to turn down the radio.*
2. To invite someone to do something. *Martin asked Brenda to go to the movies.*
▷ *verb* **asking, asked**

a·skew (uh-skyoo) *adverb* Crooked, or off center. *Sam liked to wear his hat askew.* ▷ *adjective* **askew**

a·sleep (uh-sleep) *adjective* Sleeping. *The baby is asleep.*

as·par·a·gus (uh-spar-uh-guhss) *noun* A green plant whose spear-shaped stalks can be cooked and eaten as a vegetable. *See* **vegetable.**

as·pect (ass-pekt) *noun* One feature or characteristic of something. *Adam enjoys most aspects of school life.*

as·pen (ass-puhn) *noun* A kind of poplar tree with white wood that is used to make paper. Aspens are well-known for their leaves, which flutter in the slightest breeze.

as·phalt (ass-fawlt) *noun* A black, tarlike substance that is mixed with sand and gravel and then rolled flat to make roads.

as·phyx·i·ate (ass-fik-see-*ate*) *verb* To suffocate. ▷ **asphyxiating, asphyxiated** ▷ *noun* **asphyxiation**

as·pi·ra·tion (ass-pi-ray-shuhn) *noun* A strong desire to do something great or important. *Jewelle's aspiration is to become a famous actress.* ▷ *verb* **aspire**

as·pi·rin (ass-pi-rin) *noun* A drug that relieves pain and reduces fever.

ass (ass) *noun*
1. A donkey.
2. *(informal)* A silly or stupid person.
▷ *noun, plural* **asses**

as·sas·si·nate (uh-sass-uh-nate) *verb* To murder someone who is well-known or important, such as a president. ▷ **assassinating, assassinated** ▷ *noun* **assassin,** *noun* **assassination**

as·sault (uh-sawlt) *verb* To attack someone or something violently. ▷ **assaulting, assaulted** ▷ *noun* **assault**

as·sem·ble (uh-sem-buhl) *verb*
1. To gather together in one place. *The whole school assembled in the hall.*
2. To put all the parts of something together. *Follow the instructions to assemble this model.*
▷ *verb* **assembling, assembled**

as·sem·bly (uh-sem-blee) *noun*
1. A meeting of lots of people.
2. assembly line An arrangement of machines and workers in a factory, where work passes from one person or machine to the next until it is complete.

as·sent (uh-sent) *verb* To agree to something. ▷ **assenting, assented** ▷ *noun* **assent**

as·sert (uh-surt) *verb* If you **assert yourself,** you behave in a strong, confident way so that people take notice of you. ▷ **asserting, asserted**

as·ser·tive (uh-sur-tiv) *adjective* If you are **assertive,** you are able to stand up for yourself and tell other people what you think or want. ▷ *noun* **assertiveness** ▷ *adverb* **assertively**

as·sess (uh-sess) *verb* To judge how good or bad something is. ▷ **assesses, assessing, assessed** ▷ *noun* **assessment,** *noun* **assessor**

as·set (ass-et) *noun* Something or somebody who is helpful or useful. *Ian is a great asset to our team.*

as·sign·ment (uh-sine-muhnt) *noun* A specific job that is given to somebody. ▷ *verb* **assign**

as·sist·ance (uh-siss-tuhnss) *noun* If someone gives you **assistance,** he or she does something to help you or to make things easier for you. ▷ *verb* **assist**

as·sist·ant (uh-siss-tuhnt) *noun* A person who helps someone else do a task or job.

as·so·ci·a·tion (uh-*soh*-see-ay-shuhn) *noun*
1. An organization, a club, or a society.
2. A connection that you make in your mind

between thoughts and feelings and a person or thing. *Our vacation cabin has many happy associations for me.* ▷ *verb* **associate**

as·so·nance (ass-uh-nuhnss) *noun* Repeated use of the same vowel sound in words that are close together; for example, "How now, brown cow?"

as·sort·ment (uh-sort-muhnt) *noun* A mixture of different things. ▷ *adjective* **assorted**

as·sume (uh-soom) *verb*
1. To suppose that something is true, without checking it. *I assume that you're right.* ▷ *noun* **assumption** (uh-suhmp-shuhn)
2. If you **assume** responsibility for something, you agree to look after it.
3. An **assumed name** is a false name.
▷ *verb* **assuming, assumed**

as·sur·ance (uh-shur-uhnss) *noun*
1. A firm promise.
2. **Self-assurance** is confidence in yourself and in what you can do.

as·sure (uh-shur) *verb*
1. To promise something, or say something positively. *Annie assured me of her support.*
2. If you **assure yourself** about something, you make certain of it.
▷ *verb* **assuring, assured**

as·ter (ass-tur) *noun* A plant with flowers that have white, pink, yellow, or purple petals around a yellow center. Asters resemble daisies.

as·ter·isk (ass-tuh-risk) *noun* The mark (*) used in printing and writing to tell readers to look elsewhere on the page for more information.

as·ter·oid (ass-tuh-roid) *noun* A very small planet that travels around the sun.

asth·ma (az-muh) *noun* If you have **asthma,** you have a condition that sometimes causes you to wheeze and have difficulty breathing. ▷ *noun* **asthmatic** (az-mat-ik) ▷ *adjective* **asthmatic**

as·ton·ish (uh-ston-ish) *verb* To make someone feel very surprised. *Kelly astonished me with her kindness.* ▷ **astonishes, astonishing, astonished** ▷ *noun* **astonishment** ▷ *adjective* **astonishing** ▷ *adverb* **astonishingly**

as·tound (uh-stound) *verb* To amaze or astonish someone. *Dad astounded us by bringing home a puppy.* ▷ **astounding, astounded**

a·stray (uh-stray) *adverb*
1. If something has gone **astray,** it has been lost.
2. If someone **leads you astray,** the person encourages you to do something wrong.

a·stride (uh-stride) *preposition* If you sit **astride** something, such as a horse or a bicycle, you sit with a leg on either side of it.

as·trol·o·gy (uh-strol-uh-jee) *noun* The study of how the positions of stars and planets

supposedly affect people's lives. ▷ *noun* **astrologer** ▷ *adjective* **astrological** (ass-truh-loj-i-kuhl)

as·tro·naut (ass-truh-*nawt*) *noun* Someone who travels in space. *The picture shows an astronaut operating a manned maneuvering unit (MMU), which is used for moving around outside a spaceship.*

astronaut with manned maneuvering unit

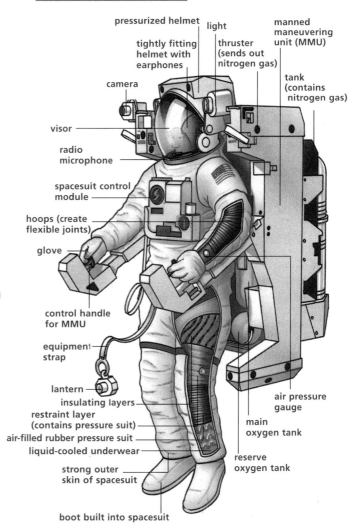

pressurized helmet
light
manned maneuvering unit (MMU)
tightly fitting helmet with earphones
thruster (sends out nitrogen gas)
tank (contains nitrogen gas)
camera
visor
radio microphone
spacesuit control module
hoops (create flexible joints)
glove
control handle for MMU
equipment strap
lantern
insulating layers
restraint layer (contains pressure suit)
air-filled rubber pressure suit
liquid-cooled underwear
strong outer skin of spacesuit
air pressure gauge
main oxygen tank
reserve oxygen tank
boot built into spacesuit

Language Note

Both **astro-** and **naut** are combining forms. (See *aero-* for more on this type of vocabulary builder.) In Greek, *astro-* means "star" and *naut* means "sailor." An astronaut "sails" among the stars. *Astronomy* and *nautical* also use these combining forms.

A

as·tro·nom·i·cal
(*ass*-truh-**nom**-uh-kuhl)
adjective
1. To do with astronomy. *The astronomical instrument shown here dates from the 16th century and was used to work out the positions of the stars.*
2. Very large, as in *an astronomical amount of money.*
▷ *adverb*
astronomically

astronomical sphere

as·tron·o·my
(uh-**stron**-uh-mee) *noun* The study of stars, planets, and space. ▷ *noun* **astronomer**

as·tute
(uh-**stoot**) *adjective* If someone is **astute,** he or she understands situations and people clearly and quickly.

a·sun·der
(uh-**sun**-dur) *adverb* In or into pieces, as in *torn asunder.*

a·sy·lum
(uh-**sye**-luhm) *noun*
1. Protection given by a country to people escaping from danger in their own country.
2. A hospital for people who are mentally ill and cannot live independently.

a·sym·met·ri·cal
(ay-si-**met**-ruh-kuhl) *adjective* A shape that is **asymmetrical** cannot be divided so both pieces match exactly in shape and size.

at
(at) *preposition*
1. In a place or position. *We were at the movies.*
2. Describing a time. *We'll meet at noon.*
3. In the direction of. *Look at all those books!*
4. In a state or condition of. *The two countries were at war.*
5. In the amount or price of. *The store sells apples at $1.00 per pound.*

a·the·ist
(**ay**-thee-ist) *noun* Someone who does not believe that there is a God. ▷ *noun* **atheism**

ath·lete
(**ath**-leet) *noun* Someone who is trained in or very good at sports or games that require strength, speed, and/or skill. ▷ *adjective* **athletic** (ath-**let**-ik)

athlete's foot
noun An itchy rash that can develop on your feet and between your toes. Athlete's foot is caused by a fungus and is usually treated by applying special creams or ointments to the rash.

ath·let·ics
(ath-**let**-iks) *noun, plural*
1. Competitive sports that involve running, jumping, or throwing. *See* **track and field.**
2. All competitive sports. ▷ *adjective* **athletic**

at·las
(**at**-luhss) *noun* A book of maps.

▶ Word History
In Greek mythology, Atlas was a man who was punished for taking part in a revolt against the gods. As his punishment, he was forced to stand on a mountain, holding the heavens apart from the earth. Pioneer mapmaker Gerardus Mercator used a drawing of Atlas holding a globe for the cover of a book of maps he published in the 1500s. So many other mapmakers copied his cover idea that a collection of maps became known as an **atlas**.

at·mos·phere
(**at**-muhss-fihr) *noun*
1. The mixture of gases that surrounds a planet. *The layers of the earth's atmosphere are shown in this diagram.*
2. The air in a particular place. *The atmosphere in some of our cities is very polluted.*
3. A mood or feeling created by a place or a work of art. *I didn't like the atmosphere in the old house.*
▷ *adjective* **atmospheric**

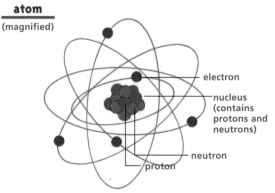
layers of the atmosphere

- **ionosphere** above 30 miles
- **stratosphere** up to 30 miles (50 km)
- **ozone layer** 12 to 30 miles (20 to 48 km)
- **troposphere** up to 7 miles (11 km)

at·oll
(**a**-tol) *noun* A chain of tiny coral islands that forms a ring around a lagoon.

at·om
(**at**-uhm) *noun*
The tiniest part of a substance that has all the properties of that substance. Everything is made up of atoms. *The diagram shows the main parts of an atom.*

atom (magnified)

- electron
- nucleus (contains protons and neutrons)
- neutron
- proton

a·tom·ic (uh-**tom**-ik) *adjective*
1. To do with atoms, as in *atomic research.*
2. Using the power created when atoms are split. *The Nautilus was a submarine powered by atomic energy.*

atomic bomb

atomic bomb

noun A powerful bomb that explodes with great force, heat, and bright light. The explosion results from the energy that is released by splitting atoms. It destroys large areas and leaves behind dangerous radiation. *The picture shows an atomic bomb test explosion.*

atomic energy *noun* The energy released when atoms are split apart or forced together. Atomic energy is also called nuclear energy. It can be used to power submarines, heat homes, and treat certain diseases.

a·tone (uh-**tone**) *verb* If you **atone** for something, you make up for it. *Kate atoned for her lateness by working extra hard.* ▷ **atoning, atoned**

a·tri·um (ay-tree-uhm) *noun*
1. Either of two sections of the heart that receive blood from the veins. *See* **heart.**
2. A patio or courtyard around which a building is built.
▷*noun, plural* **atriums** *or* **atria** (ay-tree-uh)

a·tro·cious (uh-**troh**-shuhss) *adjective* Very cruel, or terrible, as in *an atrocious accident.*

a·troc·i·ty (uh-**tross**-uh-tee) *noun* A very wicked or cruel act, often involving killing. ▷ *noun, plural* **atrocities**

at·tach (uh-**tach**) *verb*
1. To join or fix one thing to another.
2. If you are **attached to** someone, you are very fond of that person.
▷ *verb* **attaches, attaching, attached** ▷ *noun* **attachment**

at·tack (uh-**tak**)
1. *verb* To try to hurt someone or something.
2. *verb* To criticize someone strongly.
3. *verb* To try to defeat an enemy or capture a place where the enemy is. *The troops attacked the castle.*
4. *noun* A sudden period of illness, as in *a bad attack of flu.*
▷ *verb* **attacking, attacked** ▷ *noun* **attack,** *noun* **attacker**

at·tain·ment (uh-**tayn**-muhnt) *noun* An achievement. ▷ *verb* **attain** ▷ *adjective* **attainable**

at·tempt (uh-**tempt**) *verb* To try to do something. *I attempted to swim across the big lake.* ▷ **attempting, attempted** ▷ *noun* **attempt**

at·tend (uh-**tend**) *verb*
1. To be present in a place or at an event. *Thousands of people attended the concert.* ▷ *noun* **attendance**
2. If you **attend to** something, you deal with it. ▷ *verb* **attending, attended**

at·ten·dant (uh-**ten**-duhnt) *noun* Someone who looks after a person or place, as in *a parking lot attendant.*

at·ten·tion (uh-**ten**-shuhn) *noun*
1. Concentration and careful thought, as in *attention to detail.*
2. If you **pay attention,** you concentrate on something.
3. If something needs **attention,** it needs you to do something to it.
4. When soldiers **stand at attention,** they stand up straight, with their feet together and their arms by their sides.

at·ten·tive (uh-**ten**-tiv) *adjective* If you are **attentive,** you are alert and are paying close attention to something or someone. *The class suddenly became attentive when the teacher announced there would be a test.* ▷ *adverb* **attentively**

at·test (uh-**test**) *verb*
1. To declare that something is true. *My father can attest to all the work I put into this project.*
2. To be proof of something. *This wonderful song attests to your talent as a musician.*
▷ *verb* **attesting, attested**

at·tic (**at**-ik) *noun* A space in a building just under the roof.

at·tire (uh-**tire**) *noun* Clothing. *We wore formal attire to the graduation.* ▷ *verb* **attire**

at·ti·tude (**at**-i-tood) *noun*
1. Your opinions and feelings about someone or something. *Theo has a positive attitude toward his work.*
2. The position in which you are standing or sitting.

at·tor·ney (uh-**tur**-nee) *noun* A lawyer. *The attorney argued her case before the court.*

at·tract (uh-**trakt**) *verb*
1. If something **attracts** you, you are interested in it.
2. If a person **attracts** you, you like him or her.
3. If something **attracts** objects or people to itself, it pulls them toward itself. *Magnets attract iron and steel.*
▷ *verb* **attracting, attracted** ▷ *noun* **attraction**

at·trac·tive (uh-**trak**-tiv) *adjective*
1. Pleasant or pretty to look at. *Kelly has a very attractive smile.*
2. Interesting, or exciting, as in *an attractive idea.*
▷ *noun* **attractiveness** ▷ *adverb* **attractively**

at·trib·ute
1. (**at**-ruh-*byoot*) *noun* A quality or characteristic that belongs to or describes a person or thing. *Kindness is her greatest attribute.*
2. (uh-**trib**-yoot) *verb* When you **attribute** something to someone, you give him or her credit for it. *The author attributed her success to her ninth-grade English teacher.* ▷ **attributing, attributed**

au·burn (**aw**-burn) *noun* A reddish brown color.
▷ *adjective* **auburn**

auc·tion (**awk**-shuhn) *noun* A sale where goods are sold to the person who offers the most money for them. ▷ *noun* **auctioneer** (*awk*-shuh-**neer**)

au·di·ble (**aw**-duh-buhl) *adjective* Loud enough to be heard. *Although she was whispering, her words were audible across the room.*

au·di·ence (**aw**-dee-uhnss) *noun*
1. The people who watch or listen to a performance, speech, or movie.
2. A formal meeting with an important or powerful person, as in *an audience with the Pope.*

au·di·o (**aw**-dee-oh)
1. *adjective* To do with how sound is heard, recorded, and played back. *My uncle gave me his old audio equipment, including a CD player, a tape deck, and speakers.*
2. *noun* Sound, especially the sound portion of a television or motion picture. *Before he finished the film, the director wanted to record the audio one more time.*

au·di·o·tape (**aw**-daw-dee-oh-*tape*) *noun* Magnetic tape that records sound. *The library has audiotapes of all the mayor's speeches.*

au·di·o·vis·u·al (*aw*-dee-oh-**vizh**-oo-uhl) *adjective* **Audiovisual** equipment uses sound and pictures, often to teach people something.

au·di·tion (aw-**dish**-uhn) *noun* A short performance by an actor, singer, musician, or dancer to see whether he or she is suitable for a part in a play, concert, etc. ▷ *verb* **audition**

au·di·to·ri·um (aw-di-**tor**-ee-uhm) *noun* A building or large room where people gather for meetings, plays, concerts, or other events. *Assemblies are always held in the school auditorium.*

aug·ment (awg-**ment**) *verb* You **augment** something when you add to it or make it larger. *She augmented her allowance by delivering newspapers every morning.* ▷ **augmenting, augmented**

Au·gust (**aw**-guhst) *noun* The eighth month on the calendar, after July and before September. August has 31 days.

> ### ▶ Word History
> **August** is named after the first emperor of ancient Rome, Augustus Caesar. Originally, the month of August was supposed to have only 30 days, but Augustus Caesar protested. July, named after his uncle, Julius Caesar, had 31 days, and Augustus thought his month should be just as long. To please the emperor, calendar makers stole one day from February to give August 31 days in all.

aunt (ant *or* ahnt) *noun* The sister of your father or mother, or the wife of your uncle.

au pair (oh pair) *noun* A young person from another country who lives with a family and helps them, in order to learn that country's language.

au·ral (**or**-uhl) *adjective* To do with listening. *My piano exam includes an aural test.* **Aural** sounds like **oral.**

au·ri·cle (**or**-uh-kuhl) *noun*
1. The outer part of the ear.
2. Either of two sections of the heart that receive blood from the veins. Also called **atrium.**

au·ro·ra bo·re·al·is (uh-**ror**-uh *bor*-ee-**al**-iss) *noun* Colorful bands of flashing lights that sometimes can be seen at night, especially near the Arctic Circle. Also called the **northern lights.**

aus·tere (aw-**stihr**) *adjective* Severe or cold in manner or appearance. *The austere room had only a lamp, a table, and four wooden chairs.*

aus·ter·i·ty (aw-**stair**-uh-tee) *noun* A way of living without extras or comforts. *My folks say I can't get a new bicycle this year because they are emphasizing austerity; they want to save money for a new house.* ▷ *noun, plural* **austerities**

au·then·tic (aw-**then**-tik) *adjective* Real, or genuine. *The store sells authentic jewelry from Arizona.*

au·thor (**aw**-thur) *noun* The writer of a book, play, article, or poem. ▷ *noun* **authorship**

au·thor·i·ta·tive (uh-**thor**-uh-tay-tiv) *adjective*
1. Official, or coming from someone who has the power to give orders. *His teacher spoke in an authoritative manner.*
2. Expert. *They believed the story because it came from an authoritative source.*

au·thor·i·ty (uh-**thor**-uh-tee) *noun*
1. The right to do something or to tell other people what to do. *The detectives have authority to search the house.*

2. A group of people with power in a certain area. *The Transportation Authority is adding new bus routes.*

3. Someone who knows a lot about a particular subject. *Jodi is an authority on computers.*
▷ *noun, plural* **authorities**

au·thor·ize (aw-thuh-*rize*) *verb* To give official permission for something to happen.
▷ **authorizing, authorized** ▷ *noun* **authorization**

au·tis·tic (aw-tiss-tik) *adjective* People who are **autistic** have a condition that causes them to have trouble communicating and forming relationships with people. They may have difficulty with language.▷ *noun* **autism**

au·to·bi·og·ra·phy (*aw*-toh-bye-og-ruh-fee) *noun* A book in which the author tells the story of his or her life. ▷ *noun, plural* **autobiographies**
▷ *adjective* **autobiographical**

au·to·graph (aw-tuh-*graf*) *noun* A person's handwritten signature.

au·to·mat·ic (aw-tuh-mat-ik) *adjective*
1. An **automatic** machine can perform its functions without anyone operating it.
2. An **automatic** action happens without your thinking about it.
▷ *adverb* **automatically**

au·to·ma·tion (aw-tuh-**may**-shuhn) *noun* The use of machines rather than people to do jobs, especially in factories. ▷ *verb* **automate**

au·to·mo·bile (aw-tuh-muh-*beel*) *noun* A passenger vehicle that usually has four wheels and is powered by an engine. *See* **car, race car.**

au·top·sy (aw-top-see) *noun* An examination performed on a dead person to find the cause of death. *The police waited for the results of the autopsy before charging the suspect with murder.* ▷ *noun, plural* **autopsies**

au·tumn (aw-tuhm) *noun* The season between summer and winter, from late September to late December in the Northern Hemisphere. It is also called **fall.** ▷ *adjective* **autumnal** (aw-**tuhm**-nuhl)

aux·il·ia·ry (awg-zil-yur-ee) *adjective* Helping, or giving extra support. *An auxiliary verb is a verb that helps to complete the meaning of the main verb.* ▷ *noun* **auxiliary**

a·vail·a·ble (uh-**vay**-luh-buhl) *adjective*
1. Ready to be used or bought. *The new toys will be available in stores next week.*
2. Not busy, and therefore free to talk to people.
▷ *noun* **availability**

av·a·lanche (av-uh-lanch) *noun* A large mass of snow, ice, or earth that suddenly moves down the side of a mountain.

av·e·nue (av-uh-noo) *noun* A wide road in a town or city.

av·er·age (av-uh-rij)
1. *noun* In math, you find an **average** by adding a group of figures together and then dividing the sum by the number of figures you have added. *The average of 2, 5, and 14 is 7.* ▷ *verb* **average**
2. *adjective* Usual, or ordinary. *John is of average height and has black hair.*

a·vert (uh-**vurt**) *verb* To turn away from something or avoid it. *Make sure to avert your eyes from the sun during an eclipse.* ▷ **averting, averted** ▷ *noun* **aversion** (uh-vur-zhuhn)

a·vi·ar·y (ay-vee-*air*-ee) *noun* A large cage or other enclosed area for birds. ▷ *noun, plural* **aviaries**

a·vi·a·tion (*ay*-vee-ay-shuhn) *noun* The science of building and flying aircraft. *The great age of aviation began in 1903, when Orville Wright first left the ground in the Flyer.* ▷ *noun* **aviator**

The Wright Flyer

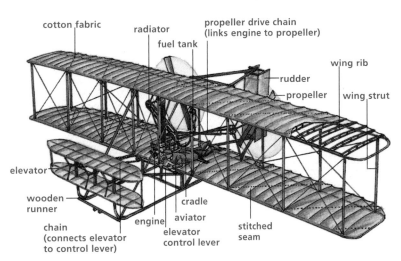

cotton fabric — radiator — fuel tank — propeller drive chain (links engine to propeller) — wing rib — rudder — propeller — wing strut — elevator — wooden runner — chain (connects elevator to control lever) — engine — aviator — cradle — elevator control lever — stitched seam

av·id (av-id) *adjective* Very eager or committed. *She's an avid golfer.* ▷ *adverb* **avidly**

av·o·ca·do (av-uh-kah-doh) *noun* A green or black pear-shaped fruit with a tough skin and a creamy, light green pulp. ▷ *noun, plural* **avocados**

av·o·ca·tion (a-voh-kay-shun) *noun* If you have an **avocation,** you have a hobby or pastime that is different from your regular job. *Photography is our teacher's avocation.*

a·void (uh-**void**) *verb*
1. To stay away from a person or place. *Julio tried to avoid Jackie after their argument.*
2. To try to prevent something from happening. *We must avoid making that mistake again.*
▷ *verb* **avoiding, avoided** ▷ *noun* **avoidance**
▷ *adjective* **avoidable**

a·wait (uh-**wayt**) *verb* To wait for or expect someone or something. ▷ **awaiting, awaited**

a·wake (uh-**wake**)
1. *adjective* Not asleep. *I'm wide awake.*
2. *verb* To wake up. ▷ **awaking, awoke** (uh-**wohk**), **awoken** (uh-**woh**-ken)
▷ *noun* **awakening**

a·ward (uh-**word**) *verb* To give someone something officially, such as a prize. ▷ **awarding, awarded** ▷ *noun* **award**

a·ware (uh-**wair**) *adjective* If you are **aware** of something, you know that it exists. ▷ *noun* **awareness**

a·way (uh-**way**)
1. *adverb* Moving from a place, person, or thing. *Toshi ran away from me.*
2. *adverb* Distant from a place. *We live three miles away.*
3. *adverb* Not at home, or not present.
4. *adverb* In a safe place. *Put your money away.*
5. *adjective* An **away** game in sports is one you play at your opponent's home field or court.

awe (aw) *noun* A feeling of admiration and respect, mixed with a little fear. *Nikki is in awe of her drama teacher.* ▷ *adjective* **awesome** (aw-*suhm*)

aw·ful (aw-fuhl) *adjective*
1. Terrible, or horrible. *Failing that test was awful!*
2. (*informal*) Very great. *Mom spent an awful lot of money on my birthday present.* ▷ *adverb* **awfully**

▶ **Synonyms: awful**
••••••••••••••••••••••••••••••••••

Awful is a word used very often to describe anything or anyone that is unpleasant, unlikable, or nasty. Besides those words, there are some other words you can use to describe things, situations, or people that you dislike. Sometimes, of course, awful fits: *The reception on our old TV set is just awful.*

Terrible can mean very unpleasant, damaging, or having serious results: *The storm last week was terrible. The gymnast broke her leg during a terrible fall off the balance beam.*

Dreadful means really bad or dangerous: *Her cold was so dreadful we were afraid it would turn into pneumonia.*

Horrible can describe something so awful that you can hardly stand to look at it or be around it: *The hero of the story was turned into a horrible monster by an evil witch.*

Ghastly can mean so bad that you can hardly face up to the situation: *It was ghastly for the little girl to be lost all night on the mountain.*

awk·ward (awk-wurd) *adjective*
1. Difficult or embarrassing. *In an awkward*

moment, I forgot my teacher's name while introducing him to my parents.
2. Not able to relax and talk to people easily. ▷ *noun* **awkwardness** ▷ *adverb* **awkwardly**

awl (awl) *noun* A sharp metal tool for making holes in leather or wood. **Awl** sounds like **all**.

aw·ning (aw-ning) *noun* A piece of cloth, metal, or wood that is fastened to the top of a window or to the front roof of a building to shade it from sun and help keep out rain. *People gathered under the store's awning when the rain started to fall.*

a store with an awning

ax *or* **axe** (aks)
1. *noun* A tool with a sharp blade on the end of a handle, used for chopping wood. ▷ *noun, plural* **axes**
2. *verb* To bring something to an end. *Two hundred jobs will be axed.* ▷ **axing, axed**

ax·is (ak-siss) *noun*
1. An imaginary line through the middle of an object, around which that object spins, as in *the earth's axis.*
2. A line at the side or the bottom of a graph.
▷ *noun, plural* **axes** (ak-seez)

ax·le (ak-suhl) *noun* A rod in the center of a wheel, around which the wheel turns.

aye (eye) *noun* A vote of "yes." *The opposite of aye is nay.* ▷ *adverb* **aye**

a·za·lea (uh-zayl-yuh) *noun* A shrub with funnel-shaped pink, orange, or white flowers and dark green leaves.

Az·tec (az-tek) *noun* A member of a Mexican Indian people who built a great civilization before the conquest of Mexico by Cortés in the 16th century. ▷ *adjective* **Aztec**

az·ure (azh-ur) *noun* A deep, clear blue, such as the color of a cloudless sky or deep, still water. ▷ *adjective* **azure**

B

About B ◀

Spelling Hint: Words that begin with a *bye* sound are spelled *bi* or *by*. Examples: bike, bind, bypass, bystander.

bab·ble (bab-uhl) *verb*
1. To talk in an excited way, without making any sense. *Bob tends to babble when he gets excited.*
2. To make sounds like a baby.
▷ *verb* **babbling, babbled**

ba·boon (ba-boon) *noun* A large monkey that lives in Africa. Baboons have long, doglike snouts and large teeth.

olive baboons

ba·by (bay-bee) *noun* A newly born or very young child or animal.
▷ *noun, plural* **babies**
▷ *adjective* **babyish**

baby boom *noun* A noticeable increase in the number of babies born in a nation, as in *the United States baby boom* between 1946 and 1964. ▷ *noun* **baby boomer**

baby·sit·ter (sit-ur) *noun* Someone who is paid to stay with and look after children. ▷ *verb* **baby-sit**

baby tooth *noun* A first tooth in infants and baby mammals. Baby teeth fall out and are replaced by permanent teeth. ▷ *noun, plural* **baby teeth**

bach·e·lor (bach-uh-lur) *noun* A man who has never been married.

back (bak)
1. *noun* The rear part of your body between your neck and the end of your spine.
2. *noun* The opposite end or side from the front, as in *the back of the room.* ▷ *adjective* **back**
3. *adverb* Where someone or something was before. *Why did she come back after being away for so long?*
4. *verb* To support someone. *We all back the mayor's reelection.* ▷ *noun* **backer**
5. **back down** *verb* To stop arguing for something.
6. **back out** *verb* To decide not to do something that you had agreed to do.
▷ *verb* **backing, backed**

back·board (bak-bord) *noun* The wood or plastic surface attached to a basketball hoop and net.

back·bone (bak-bohn) *noun* A set of connected bones that run down the middle of the back. The backbone is also called the **spine** and the **spinal column.** *See* **skeleton.**

back·fire (bak-fire) *verb*
1. If an action **backfires,** it does not work out as you planned it.
2. If a car **backfires,** there is a small explosion inside its exhaust pipe.
▷ *verb* **backfiring, backfired**

back·ground (bak-ground) *noun*
1. The part of a picture that is behind the main subject. *The portrait of George Washington has an American flag in the background.*
2. A person's past experience. *We check the background of everyone we hire.*
▷ *adjective* **background**

back·hand (bak-hand) *noun* A stroke in tennis that you play with your arm across your body and the back of your hand facing outward. *The sequence shows how to play a backhand.*

backhand stroke

back·hoe (bak-hoh) *noun* A digging machine that has a bucket with teeth. The bucket is pulled down and backward through the earth.

back·pack (bak-pak)
1. *noun* A large bag that you carry on your back when you are walking or climbing.
2. *verb* If you **backpack,** you go on a long walk or hike carrying a backpack.

back·stroke (bak-stroke) *noun* A style of swimming in which you lie on your back.

back·ward (bak-wurd) *or* **back·wards** (bak-wurdz) *adverb*
1. In the reverse direction. *Eric stepped backward.*
2. In the opposite to the usual way. *Say the alphabet backward.* ▷ *adjective* **backward**

back·yard (bak-yard) *noun* An open area behind a house.

ba·con (bay-kuhn) *noun* Smoked or salted meat from the back or sides of a pig.

bac·te·ri·a (bak-**tihr**-ee-uh) *noun, plural*
Microscopic living things that exist all around you and inside you. Many bacteria are useful, but some cause disease. *The diagram shows a simplified bacterium cell, magnified millions of times.* ▷ *noun, singular* **bacterium** (bak-**tihr**-ee-uhm)

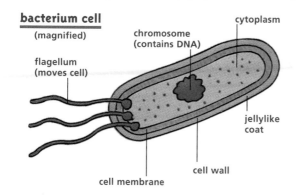

bacterium cell
(magnified)
cytoplasm
chromosome (contains DNA)
flagellum (moves cell)
jellylike coat
cell wall
cell membrane

bad (bad) *adjective*
1. Not good, as in *bad news.*
2. Serious, as in *a bad mistake.*
3. Not fit to eat. *This fish has gone bad.*
4. Sorry. *I feel bad that you didn't enjoy the film.*
▷ *adjective* **worse, worst**

Synonyms: bad

Bad, like **awful,** can describe anything that is not good. Food, ideas, the weather—almost anything you can imagine or have an opinion about—can be bad or awful: *It was a bad idea to leave my bicycle unlocked while I returned the library book. I thought that was a bad movie. We were caught in an awful storm on the way home from school.*

Naughty refers to some action or activity that is bad and a bit mischievous. Naughty usually describes the disobedient actions of young children: *My little sister was being very naughty when she pulled the kitten's tail.*

Serious can describe something bad enough to have very unpleasant effects or results: *A serious disagreement led to the end of their friendship.*

Poor can mean "inferior" or "lacking in quality": *My eyesight is so poor that I need to wear glasses all the time.*

Wrong means "incorrect" or "not good in a moral sense": *She gave a wrong answer. It is wrong to take something that does not belong to you.*

Rotten and **spoiled** describe something that has changed from good to bad and often refers to food: *The apples were so old that they had become rotten.*

badge (baj) *noun* A small sign with a picture, name, or message on it that you pin to your clothes.

badg·er (**baj**-ur)
1. *noun* A mammal with a gray body and a black and white head that lives in a burrow and comes out at night to eat.
2. *verb* To keep asking someone to do something. *Karen kept badgering me to let her come with us.* ▷ **badgering, badgered**

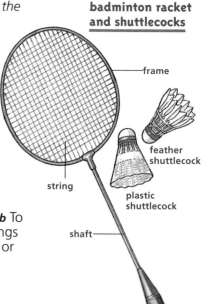

badger's burrow
sow (female badger)
cubs on bedding of dry grass and leaves
burrow entrance
chamber
tunnel

bad·ly (**bad**-lee) *adverb*
1. Urgently. *I want it badly.*
2. Not well, or not skillfully. *Mr. Isaacs plays the piano badly.*

bad·min·ton (**bad**-min-tuhn) *noun* A game similar to tennis in which players use rackets to hit a shuttlecock back and forth over a high net.

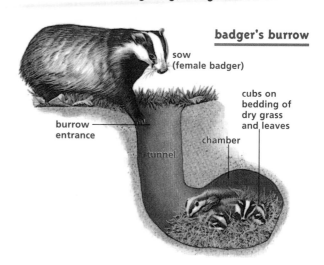

badminton racket and shuttlecocks
frame
feather shuttlecock
string
plastic shuttlecock
shaft

bad·mouth (**bad**-*mouth*) *verb* To say negative things about someone or something.
▷ **badmouthing, badmouthed**

baf·fle (**baf**-uhl) *verb* To puzzle or confuse someone. *Your actions baffle me.* ▷ **baffling, baffled**
▷ *adjective* **baffling**

bag (bag) *noun* A usually flexible container for carrying things. ▷ *verb* **bag**

ba·gel (bay-guhl) *noun* A round, chewy roll with a hole in the middle. A bagel looks like a doughnut but is made of bread.

bag·gage (bag-ij) *noun* Travelers' suitcases, bags, and trunks.

bag·gy (bag-ee) *adjective* Hanging in loose folds, as in *baggy shorts*. ▷ **baggier, baggiest**

bag·pipes (bag-*pipes*) *noun, plural* A musical instrument. To play the bagpipes, you blow air through a pipe into a bag and squeeze it out through the drones and the chanter.

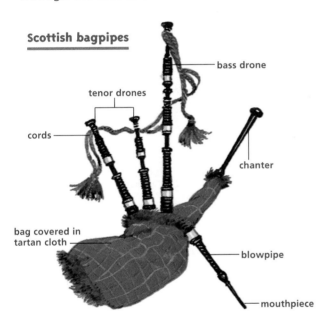

Scottish bagpipes

bass drone

tenor drones

cords

chanter

bag covered in tartan cloth

blowpipe

mouthpiece

bail (bayl) *noun* A sum of money paid to a court to allow someone accused of a crime to be set free until his or her trial. *Keith was released on bail.*

bail·iff (bay-lif) *noun* A law officer who has charge of prisoners in court.

bail out *verb*
1. To jump out of an aircraft using a parachute.
2. To scoop water out of a boat.
3. If you **bail someone out,** you pay his or her bail or help him or her out of a difficult situation.
▷ *verb* **bailing out, bailed out**

bait (bayt) *noun* A small amount of food used to attract a fish or an animal so you can catch it. *See* **angling.**

baize (bayz) *noun* A feltlike material that is usually green and is used for covering card tables, pool tables, and billiard tables.

bake (bayk) *verb*
1. To cook food in an oven, especially bread or cake. *Kyle baked a cake for dessert.* ▷ *noun* **baker,** *noun* **bakery**
2. To heat something in order to make it hard. *Bake the clay pot in a kiln before glazing it.*
▷ *verb* **baking, baked**

bak·ing powder (bayk-ing) *noun* A white powder used in baking to make dough or batter rise.

baking soda *noun* A white powder used to make dough rise, or to soothe an upset stomach. Also called **sodium bicarbonate.**

bal·ance (bal-uhnss)
1. *noun* Your **balance** is your ability to keep steady and not fall over.
2. *verb* If you **balance** something, you keep it steady and do not let it fall. *The waiter balanced the dishes on the trays.*
3. *verb* When two things **balance** in a pair of scales, they weigh the same and do not tip the scales either way.
4. *noun* An instrument used for weighing things.
5. *noun* Remainder. *After a sunny morning, the balance of the day was cloudy.*
▷ *verb* **balancing, balanced**

bal·co·ny (bal-kuh-nee) *noun*
1. A platform with railings on the outside of a building, usually on an upper level.
2. The upstairs seating in a theater.

bald (bawld) *adjective*
1. Someone who is **bald** has very little or no hair on his or her head. ▷ *noun* **baldness**
▷ *adjective* **balding**
2. Without any natural covering. *The lawn was bald where the trash barrels had covered it.*
▷ *adjective* **balder, baldest**

bald eagle *noun* An eagle with a brown body and a white head that appears bald from a distance. The bald eagle is the national symbol of the United States.

bald eagle

B

B

bale (bale)

1. *noun* A large bundle of things, such as straw or hay, that is tied tightly together. *The bales of hay were stacked in the barn.*

2. *verb* To put hay or some other substance into a tightly packed bundle. *The farmer spent the last week baling hay for the winter.* See **farm.**

▷ **baling, baled**

ball (bawl) *noun*

1. A round object used in games.

2. Something made into a round shape, as in *a ball of wool.*

3. A formal party where people dance.

4. In baseball, a pitch that a batter does not swing at and that does not cross home plate between the batter's shoulders and knees.

5. *(informal)* If you are **on the ball,** you are quick at understanding things.

Ball sounds like **bawl.**

bal·lad (bal-uhd) *noun* A song or poem that tells a story.

bal·last (bal-uhst) *noun*

1. Heavy material, such as water or sand, that is carried by a ship to make it more stable.

2. **ballast tank** A large tank in a submarine that is filled with water to make the submarine sink or with air to make it come to the surface.

ball bearings *noun, plural* Small metal balls used to help parts of machinery move more smoothly against each other.

bal·le·ri·na (bal-uh-ree-nuh) *noun* A female ballet dancer.

bal·let (bal-lay *or* bal-lay) *noun*

1. A style of dance with set movements.

2. A performance that uses dance and music, often to tell a story. *The pictures show three ballet movements.*

grand jeté

ballet movements

arabesque

pirouette

bal·lis·tics (buh-liss-tiks) *noun* The science and study of missiles that are fired from guns.

▷ *adjective* **ballistic**

bal·loon (buh-loon) *noun*

1. A small bag made of thin rubber that is blown up and used as a decoration.

2. A **hot-air balloon** is an aircraft consisting of a very large bag filled with hot air or gas, with a basket for carrying passengers.

hot-air balloon

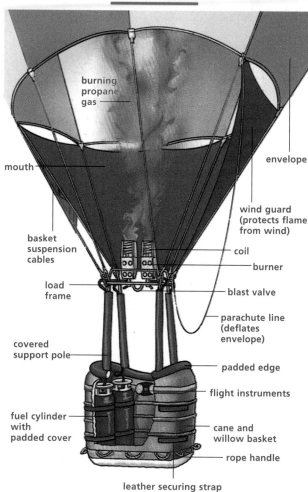

burning propane gas

mouth

envelope

wind guard (protects flame from wind)

basket suspension cables

coil

burner

load frame

blast valve

parachute line (deflates envelope)

covered support pole

padded edge

flight instruments

fuel cylinder with padded cover

cane and willow basket

rope handle

leather securing strap

bal·lot (bal-uht) *noun*

1. A secret way of voting, such as on a machine or on a slip of paper.

2. **ballot box** A box with a slit in the top into which votes are put.

ball·point (bawl-*point*) *noun* A pen with a tiny ball at its tip that lets ink flow as you write.

ball·room (bawl-*room*) *noun* A very large room where parties and dances are held.

bal·sa (bawl-suh) *noun* A very light wood used for making models. *The model airplane is made out of balsa.*

bal·sam fir (bawl-suhm) *noun* A type of fragrant evergreen tree found in North America.

bam·boo (bam-boo) *noun* A tropical plant with a hard, hollow stem, often used for making furniture.

ban (ban) *verb* To forbid something. *Ball games are banned in this park.* ▷ **banning, banned** ▷ *noun* **ban**

ba·nan·a (buh-na-nuh) *noun* A tropical fruit that is long, curved, and yellow.

banana tree

unripe bananas

flower

band (band)
1. *noun* A narrow ring of rubber, paper, or other material that is put around something, sometimes to hold it together.
2. *noun* A group of people who play music together.
3. *noun* A group of people who do something together, as in *a band of robbers.*
4. *noun* A stripe of color or material. *The bird has a band of blue on its wings.*
5. *verb* When people **band** together, they join together in a group in order to do something. ▷ **banding, banded**

band·age (ban-dij) *noun* A piece of cloth or material that is wrapped around an injured part of the body to protect it. ▷ *verb* **bandage**

ban·dan·na (ban-dan-uh) *noun* A large, brightly colored handkerchief. *The cowboy wore a bandanna around his neck.*

ban·dit (ban-dit) *noun* An armed robber, usually a member of a gang.

bang (bang)
1. *noun* A sudden loud noise. *The picture fell off the wall with a bang.*
2. *verb* To knock hard against something. *The musician banged the cymbals together.* ▷ **banging, banged**

bang·le (bang-guhl) *noun* A band of metal, plastic, etc., worn as jewelry around the wrist.

bangs (bangz) *noun, plural* The hair that hangs over your forehead.

ban·ish (ban-ish) *verb* To send someone away from a place and order the person not to return. ▷ **banishing, banished** ▷ *noun* **banishment**

ban·is·ter (ban-iss-tur) *noun* A railing that runs along the side of a flight of stairs.

ban·jo (ban-joh) *noun* A musical instrument similar to a guitar, with a small, round body and a long neck. ▷ *noun, plural* **banjos** or **banjoes**

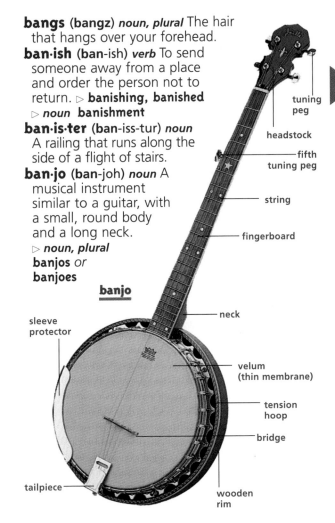

banjo

tuning peg

headstock

fifth tuning peg

string

fingerboard

neck

sleeve protector

velum (thin membrane)

tension hoop

bridge

tailpiece

wooden rim

bank (bangk)
1. *noun* A place where people keep their money. Banks also lend money and offer other financial services. ▷ *noun* **banker** ▷ *verb* **bank**
2. *noun* The land along the side of a river or a canal. *The banks of the river were covered with wildflowers.*
3. *noun* A place where something is collected and stored, as in *a blood bank.*
4. If you **bank on** something, you rely on it. *I'm banking on the weather being good tomorrow.*

Word History

Bank originally meant a "mound of earth" in English. In other Germanic languages it could also mean a "bench or table." In medieval Italy, the word was borrowed by moneylenders to refer to the narrow benches, or *bancas*, where they worked. The French borrowed the word and changed it to *banque*. This form was the source of the English word bank, as in *savings bank*.

B

bank·rupt (bangk-*ruhpt*) *adjective* If people or companies are **bankrupt,** they cannot pay their debts. ▷ *noun* **bankruptcy** ▷ *verb* **bankrupt**

ban·ner (ban-ur) *noun* A long piece of material with writing, pictures, or designs on it, hung from a pole or displayed at sporting events or parades.

sports fans with a banner

ban·quet (bang-kwit) *noun* A formal meal for a large number of people, usually on a special occasion.

ban·ter (ban-tur) *verb* To tease someone in a friendly way. *The Democrats and Republicans bantered before the opening session of Congress.* ▷ **bantering, bantered** ▷ *noun* **banter**

bap·tize (bap-tize) *verb* To pour water on someone's head or to immerse someone in water, as a sign that he or she has become a Christian. ▷ **baptizing, baptized** ▷ *noun* **baptism**

bar (bar)
1. *noun* A long stick of metal, as in *an iron bar.*
2. *noun* A long, flat block of something hard, as in *a chocolate bar.*
3. *noun* A place where drinks, especially alcoholic drinks, are sold.
4. *noun* One of the groups of notes into which a piece of music is divided.
5. *verb* To block someone, or to keep someone out. *The police barred the reporters from the courtroom.* ▷ **barring, barred**

bar·bar·i·an (bar-bair-ee-uhn) *noun* Anyone who is savage or uncivilized.

bar·bar·ic (bar-ba-rik) *adjective* Very cruel. *The animals were kept in barbaric conditions.*

bar·be·cue (bar-buh-kyoo) *noun*
1. A charcoal grill used for cooking meat and other food outdoors. ▷ *verb* **barbecue**
2. An outdoor meal or party in which food is cooked using a barbecue.

barbed wire (barbd) *noun* Wire with small spikes along it, used for fences.

bar·ber (bar-bur) *noun* Someone who cuts hair and trims or shaves beards.

bar code *noun* A band of thick and thin lines printed on goods sold in stores. When read electronically, the bar code gives the price and other information about the product.

bare (bair)
1. *adjective* Wearing no clothes, or not covered. *Although it was cold, Tim went out with his head bare.*
2. *adjective* Empty. *The cupboard was bare.*
3. *verb* To uncover or reveal something. *The dog bared its teeth. Eileen bared her secret thoughts.* ▷ **baring, bared**
4. *adjective* Plain and simple. *Just give me the bare facts.*
Bare sounds like **bear.**
▷ *adjective* **barer, barest**

bare·back (bair-*bak*) *adverb* If you ride a horse **bareback,** you do not use a saddle. ▷ *adjective* **bareback**

bare·faced (bair-*fayst*) *adjective* Open and not disguised, as in *a barefaced lie.*

bare·foot (bair-*fut*) *adjective* Without shoes or socks. ▷ *adverb* **barefoot**

bare·ly (bair-lee) *adverb* Hardly, or almost not. *Terry was so scared he could barely speak.*

bar·gain (bar-guhn)
1. *noun* Something that you buy for less than the usual price.
2. *verb* When you **bargain** with someone, you discuss the price of something or the terms of an agreement. ▷ **bargaining, bargained**

barge (barj)
1. *noun* A long boat with a flat bottom, used on canals.
2. *verb* If you **barge** into a room, you enter it rudely or abruptly. ▷ **barging, barged**

bar graph *noun* A chart that shows the comparison of information by the lengths of rectangular bars.

bar·i·tone (ba-ruh-*tone*) *noun*
1. The second-lowest singing voice for a man. ▷ *adjective* **baritone**
2. A singer with such a voice.

bar·i·um (bair-ee-uhm) *noun* A silver-colored chemical element used in paints and ceramics to make them white. When a patient drinks a liquid containing barium, the digestive system can be seen better in X-rays.

bark (bark)
1. *verb* When a dog **barks,** it makes a short, loud sound. ▷ *noun* **bark**
2. *noun* The hard covering on the outside of a tree.

3. *verb* To shout at someone gruffly. *"Attention!" barked the sergeant.*
▷ *verb* **barking, barked**

> ### Word History
>
> The noun **bark** refers to two different things, and each meaning has its own history. The sound a dog makes comes from an Old English word for that sound, *barca*. The Scandinavians gave us the other definition, from the word *borke*, which means "the outer covering of a tree."

bar·ley (bar-lee) *noun* A common cereal plant. *See* **grain.**

bar mitz·vah (bar mits-vuh) *noun* A ceremony and celebration that takes place on or close to a Jewish boy's 13th birthday, after which he can take part in his religion as an adult.

barn (barn) *noun* A farm building where crops, animals, and equipment are kept.

bar·na·cle (bar-nuh-kuhl) *noun* A small shellfish that attaches itself firmly to the sides of boats, rocks, and other shellfish. *See* **scallop.**

barn·yard (bahrn-*yard*) *noun* The area near a barn, usually surrounded by a fence.

ba·rom·e·ter (buh-rom-uh-tur) *noun* An instrument that measures changes in air pressure and shows how the weather is going to change.

bar·on (ba-ruhn) *noun* A nobleman of the lowest rank. ▷ *adjective* **baronial** (ba-rohn-ee-uhl)

bar·on·ess (ba-ruhn-iss) *noun* A noblewoman of the lowest rank. ▷ *noun, plural* **baronesses**

bar·racks (ba-ruhks) *noun, plural* The building or buildings where soldiers live.

bar·ra·cu·da (ba-ruh-koo-duh) *noun* A fish with a long, narrow body and many sharp teeth.

bar·rage (buh-rahzh) *noun*
1. Concentrated gunfire. *The fort was hit with a barrage just after dawn.*
2. A large amount of something that all comes at the same time, as in *a barrage of complaints.*

barometer

bar·rel (ba-ruhl) *noun*
1. A large container that has curved sides and a flat top and bottom.
2. The long part of a gun that looks like a tube.
3. If someone has you **over a barrel,** he or she has made you powerless.

bar·ren (ba-ruhn) *adjective* If land is **barren,** farmers cannot grow crops on it.

bar·rette (buh-ret) *noun* A plastic or metal clip used to hold the hair in place.

bar·ri·cade (ba-ruh-*kade*)
1. *noun* A barrier to stop people from getting past a certain point.
2. *verb* If people **barricade** themselves into a place, they build walls or put up obstacles to stop other people from reaching them.
▷ **barricading, barricaded**

bar·ri·er (ba-ree-ur) *noun*
1. A bar, fence, or wall that prevents people, traffic, or other things from going past it.
2. Anything that prevents you from communicating properly with someone else, as in *a language barrier.*

bar·ring (bar-ing) *preposition* Except for. *We'll be there, barring an accident.*

bar·ri·o (ba-ree-oh) *noun* A neighborhood where Spanish is the main language. Barrio means "neighborhood" in Spanish.

bar·row (ba-roh) *noun* A mound of earth made to cover a grave in prehistoric times.

bar·ten·der (bar-*ten*-dur) *noun* Someone who mixes and serves drinks at a bar or tavern.

bar·ter (bar-tur) *verb* To trade by exchanging food or other goods or services, rather than by using money. *The explorers bartered food for clothing with the island natives.* ▷ **bartering, bartered** ▷ *noun* **barter**

base (bayss)
1. *noun* The lowest part of something, or the part that it stands on, as in *the base of a lamp.*
2. *verb* To use something as the starting point for something else. *The film is based on a true story.* ▷ **basing, based**
3. *noun* The place from which a business, an army, etc., is controlled, as in *a base of operations.*
4. *noun* In baseball, a **base** is one of the four corners of the diamond to which you must run in order to score. *See* **baseball.**
5. *noun* In chemistry, a **base** is a substance that will react with an acid to form a salt. *Bases turn red litmus paper blue.*
6. *noun* In mathematics, a **base** is the starting point for a counting system. For example, ten is the base of the decimal system.
7. *adjective* Selfish or mean, as in *a base trick.*
▷ **baser, basest**

base·ball (bayss-*bawl*) *noun*
1. A game played with a bat and ball and two teams of nine players each. *The picture shows a baseball field and some equipment used in the game.*
2. The ball used in this game.

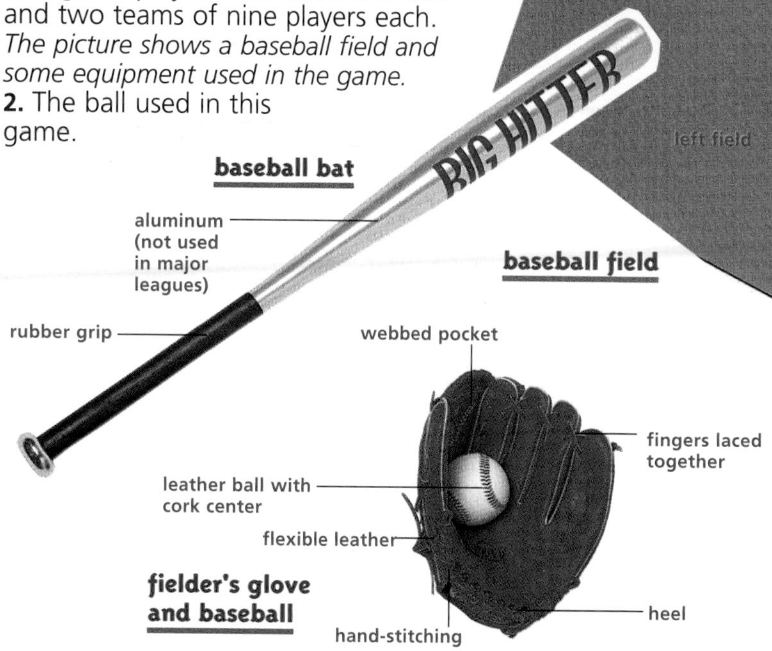

baseball bat

aluminum (not used in major leagues)

rubber grip

baseball field

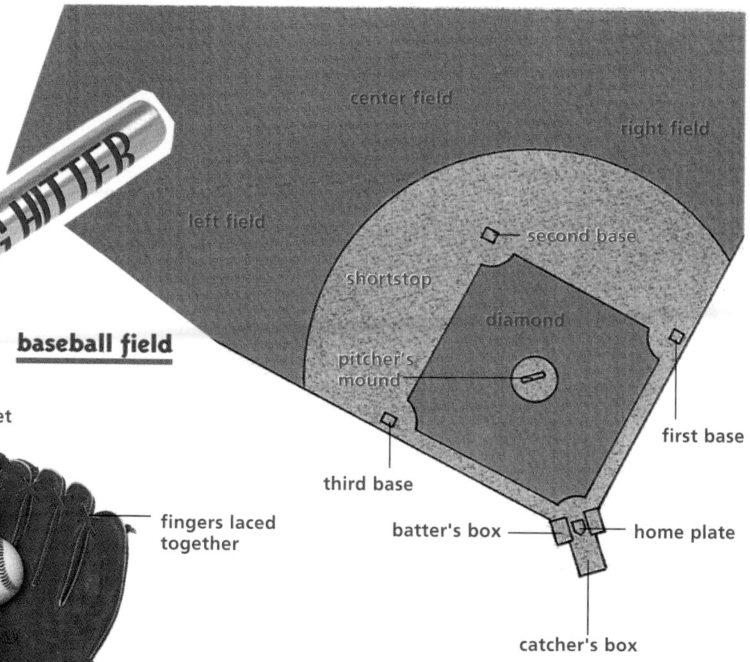

center field

right field

left field

second base

shortstop

diamond

pitcher's mound

first base

third base

batter's box

home plate

catcher's box

webbed pocket

fingers laced together

leather ball with cork center

flexible leather

fielder's glove and baseball

hand-stitching

heel

base·ment (bayss-muhnt) *noun* An area or room in a building below ground level.

bash (bash)
1. *verb* To hit something hard. *Dawn accidentally bashed her head against the wall.* ▷ **bashes, bashing, bashed**
2. *noun* (informal) A very large party. *The seniors had a big bash at the end of the school year.*

bash·ful (bash-fuhl) *adjective* Shy. ▷ *adverb* **bashfully**

BA·SIC (bay-sik) *noun* A computer programming language that is easy to learn. BASIC is an acronym for *Beginner's All-purpose Symbolic Instruction Code.*

ba·sic (bay-sik)
1. *adjective* Essential and fundamental.
2. **basics** *noun, plural* The most important things to know about a subject. *The new teacher covered the basics in math and English.*

ba·sin (bay-suhn) *noun*
1. A large bowl used for washing, usually fixed to a wall.
2. An area of land around a river from which water drains into the river.

ba·sis (bay-siss) *noun* The idea or reason behind something, as in *the basis of a plan.*

bask (bask) *verb*
1. To lie or sit in the sunshine and enjoy it.
2. If you **bask in** someone's praise, admiration, etc., you enjoy it.
▷ *verb* **basking, basked**

bas·ket (bass-kit) *noun* A container, often with handles, made of cane, wire, etc.

bas·ket·ball (bass-kit-*bawl*) *noun*
1. A game played by two teams of five players each that try to score points by throwing a ball through a high net at the end of a court. *The picture sequence shows a basketball player running, jumping, and shooting.*
2. The large, round ball used in this game.

basketball

bass *noun*
1. (bayss) The lowest singing voice for a man.
2. (bayss) A singer with such a voice.
3. (bayss) A stringed instrument that makes a low sound, as in *a bass guitar.*
4. (bass) Any of several freshwater or saltwater fish found in North America.
▷ *noun, plural* **bass** or **basses**

B

bass drum *noun* A very large drum that makes a deep, loud noise.

bas·soon (buh-soon) *noun* A musical instrument with keys, holes, and a small curved mouthpiece. The bassoon makes a very deep sound. *See* **orchestra, woodwind.**

baste (bayst) *verb*
1. To pour juices from the pan over food while it is cooking in an oven.
2. To sew something with loose stitches to hold it in place temporarily.
▷ *verb* **basting, basted**

bat (bat)
1. *noun* A small, flying mammal that comes out at night to feed. Bats find their way around by making squeaks. These noises send back echoes that are picked up by their sensitive ears.
2. *noun* A piece of wood or aluminum used for hitting the ball in baseball and softball. *See* **baseball.**
3. *verb* To take a turn at trying to hit the ball and score a run or runs in baseball or softball. *It's Eddie's turn to bat.* ▷ **batting, batted**

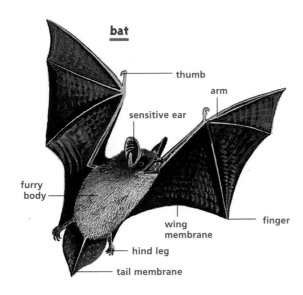

bat

thumb
arm
sensitive ear
furry body
wing membrane
finger
hind leg
tail membrane

batch (bach) *noun* A group of things that arrive together or are made together, as in *a batch of cookies.* ▷ *noun, plural* **batches**

bath (bath) *noun*
1. The act of washing something in water.
2. The water used in bathing, as in *a warm bath.*
3. A bathroom. *The house has two baths.*

bathe (bayTH) *verb*
1. To take a bath.
2. To give someone a bath, as in *to bathe a baby.*
3. To go swimming. ▷ *noun* **bather**
▷ *verb* **bathing, bathed**

bathing suit *noun* A piece of clothing that people wear to go swimming; a swimsuit.

bath·robe (bath-robe) *noun* A long, loose piece of clothing that people wear after bathing or while relaxing.

bath·room (bath-room or bath-rum) *noun* A room that contains a sink and a toilet and often a bathtub or a shower.

bath·tub (bath-tuhb) *noun* A large, open container for water in which you sit and wash your whole body.

ba·tik (buh-teek) *noun* A method of printing designs on cloth, started in Indonesia. Parts of the cloth are covered with wax so that when it is put into the dye these parts are not colored.

bat mitz·vah (baht mits-vuh) *noun* A ceremony and celebration that takes place on or close to a Jewish girl's 13th birthday, after which she can take part in her religion as an adult. Also called **bas mitzvah (bahss mits-**vuh).

ba·ton (buh-ton) *noun*
1. A short, thin stick used by a conductor to beat time for an orchestra.
2. A short stick passed from one runner to another in a relay race.

bat·tal·ion (buh-tal-yun) *noun* A large unit of soldiers.

bat·ter (bat-ur)
1. *verb* To injure someone by hitting him or her over and over. ▷ **battering, battered** ▷ *noun* **battering** ▷ *adjective* **battered**
2. *noun* A mixture consisting mainly of milk, eggs, and flour used to make cakes or other baked goods or used to coat food that you fry.
3. *noun* The player whose turn it is to bat in baseball or softball.

battering ram
noun A heavy wooden beam, sometimes protected by a hut on wheels, that is rammed against an enemy's walls or gates. *Battering rams were used in ancient times and in the Middle Ages.*

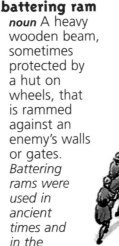

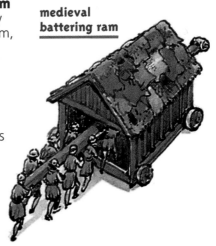

medieval battering ram

bat·ter·y (bat-uh-ree) *noun*
1. A container filled with chemicals that produces electrical power. *See* **car.**
2. A group of machines, devices, or heavy guns that are all used together. *The winning pitcher faced a battery of microphones.* ▷ *noun, plural* **batteries**

battery

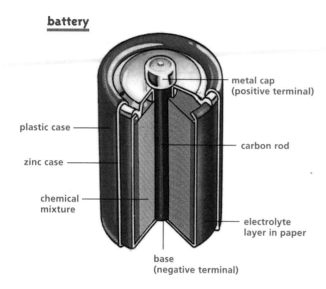

metal cap
(positive terminal)

plastic case

zinc case

carbon rod

chemical
mixture

electrolyte
layer in paper

base
(negative terminal)

bat·tle (bat-uhl) *noun*
1. A fight between two armies.
2. A struggle with someone.
▷ *verb* **battle**

bat·tle·ground (bat-uhl-*ground*) *noun* A field or an area where a battle is fought.

bat·tle·ship (bat-uhl-*ship*) *noun* A warship armed with powerful guns.

bawl (bawl) *verb*
1. To cry out loud like a baby.
2. To shout in a harsh voice. *"Get that dog out of my yard!" bawled Mr. Jones.*
3. When you **bawl** someone **out,** you scold him or her.
Bawl sounds like **ball.**
▷ *verb* **bawling, bawled**

bay (bay) *noun*
1. A portion of the ocean that is partly enclosed by land.
2. If you keep someone or something **at bay,** you fight it off. *Angela managed to keep her fears at bay.*
3. bay window A window that sticks out from the wall of a house. *See* **building.**

bay·o·net (bay-uh-net) *noun* A long knife that can be fastened to the end of a rifle.

bay·ou (bye-oo) *noun* A stream that runs slowly through a swamp and leads to or from a lake or river. Bayous are most common in Louisiana and Mississippi.

ba·zaar (buh-zar) *noun*
1. A sale held to raise money for charity.
2. A street market.

B.C. (bee cee) The initials of the phrase "before Christ." B.C. is used to show that a date comes before the birth of Jesus. *Caesar died in 44 B.C.*

be (bee) *verb*
1. To exist. *There **is** time left to play.*
2. To happen. *The start of our vacation **was** last week.*
3. To take up space. *The cat **was** on the couch.*
4. To come or go. *I've **been** to the store many times today.*
5. To stay or continue. *They've **been** in class for over an hour.*
6. Be can connect the subject of a sentence to a noun, adjective, or pronoun. *Roses **are** white, red, pink, and many other colors.*
7. Be can support the main verb in a sentence. *We **are** eating dinner together tonight.*
Be sounds like **bee.**

▶ **Language Note**

Be is a word that takes different forms, depending upon the tense and the person to whom it refers.

	First Person	Second Person	Third Person
Present Tense			
Singular	**am**	**are**	**is**
Plural	**are**	**are**	**are**
Present Participle	**being**	**being**	**being**
Past Tense			
Singular	**was**	**were**	**was**
Plural	**were**	**were**	**were**
Past Participle	**been**	**been**	**been**

beach (beech) *noun* A strip of sand or pebbles where land meets water. **Beach** sounds like **beech.** ▷ *noun, plural* **beaches**

bea·con (bee-kuhn) *noun* A light or fire used as a signal or warning.

bead (beed) *noun*
1. A small piece of glass, wood, or plastic with a hole through the middle that can be threaded onto a string.
2. A drop of liquid. *There were beads of water on the table.*

bea·gle (bee-guhl) *noun* A medium-sized dog with short legs, long ears, and a smooth coat. Beagles are often kept as pets or used as hunting dogs.

beak (beek) *noun* The hard, horny part of a bird's mouth.

beak·er (bee-kur) *noun* A plastic or glass jar with a spout for pouring, used in chemistry. *See* **apparatus.**

beam (beem)
1. *noun* A ray or band of light from a flashlight, a car headlight, or the sun.
2. *noun* A long, thick piece of wood, concrete, or metal used to support the roof or floors of a building.
3. *verb* To shine. *The sun beamed across the water.*
4. *verb* To smile widely. *Greg beamed when he saw the "A" on his report.*
▷ *verb* **beaming, beamed**

bean (been)
1. *noun* **Beans** are large seeds or pods that you can eat or that can be used to make a drink, as in *baked beans* and *coffee beans.*
2. *verb* To hit someone on the head with something you throw, such as a baseball.
▷ **beaning, beaned**

bear (bair)

grizzly bear

1. *verb* To support or carry something. *Is the ice thick enough to bear my weight?*
2. *verb* When a tree or plant **bears** fruit, flowers, or leaves, it produces them.
3. *verb* If you cannot **bear** something, you cannot put up with it, either because it upsets you or because you do not like it at all. *Some people can't bear loud music.* ▷ *adjective* **bearable**
4. *verb* If you **bear** a resemblance to someone, you look somewhat like the person.
5. *noun* A large, heavy mammal with thick fur. *The picture shows a young male grizzly bear catching a salmon.*
Bear sounds like **bare.**
▷ *verb* **bearing, bore** (bor), **borne** (born)

beard (bihrd) *noun* The hair on a man's chin and cheeks. ▷ *adjective* **bearded**

bear·ing (bair-ing) *noun*
1. The way someone acts, stands, or walks. *That handsome man has the bearing of an athlete.*
2. A connection to something else. *The weather will have no bearing on our plans.*
3. In machinery, a part that allows moving parts to work with as little friction as possible. *The bearings around the axle were completely worn away.*
4. *noun, plural* Your **bearings** are your sense of direction in relation to where things are. *The hikers lost their bearings in the dense woods and spent hours walking in circles.*

beast (beest) *noun*
1. A wild animal.
2. A horrible or unkind person. ▷ *noun* **beastliness** ▷ *adjective* **beastly**

beat (beet)
1. *verb* To hit someone or something many times. ▷ *noun* **beating**
2. *verb* To defeat someone in a game or contest. *Steve beat me at chess.*
3. *noun* The regular rhythm of a piece of music or of your heart.
4. *verb* In cooking, if you **beat** a mixture, you stir it up quickly with a machine, spoon, or fork.
5. *noun* A regular route, as in *a police officer's beat.*
Beat sounds like **beet.**
▷ *verb* **beating, beat, beaten** (beet-in)

beau·ti·ful (byoo-ti-fuhl) *adjective* Very pleasant to look at or listen to. ▷ *noun* **beauty** (byoo-tee) ▷ *verb* **beautify** (byoo-ti-fye) ▷ *adverb* **beautifully**

bea·ver (bee-vur) *noun* An animal similar to a large rat with a wide, flat tail that lives both on land and in water. By gnawing down trees, beavers build dams across streams to create safe areas for their lodges.

beaver's dam and lodge

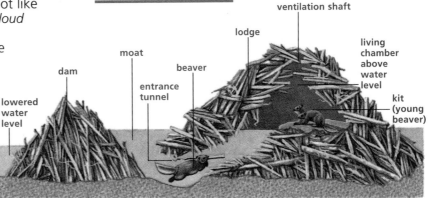

ventilation shaft
lodge
living chamber above water level
moat
beaver
kit (young beaver)
dam
entrance tunnel
lowered water level

be·cause (bi-**kawz**) *conjunction* For the reason that. *I came because I wanted to see you.*

beck·on (**bek**-uhn) *verb* To make a sign to someone, asking the person to come. *Jack beckoned us to follow him.* ▷ **beckoning, beckoned**

be·come (bi-**kuhm**) *verb*
1. To start to be. *When did you become suspicious?*
2. To suit, or to look good on. *That haircut becomes you.*
▷ *verb* **becoming, became** (bi-**kaym**)

be·com·ing (bi-**kuhm**-ing) *adjective* Flattering or attractive. *That dress is quite becoming on you.*

bed (bed) *noun*
1. A piece of furniture that you sleep on. ▷ *verb* **bed**
2. A place in a garden where flowers are planted.
3. The bottom of a body of water, as in *an ocean bed.*

> ### ▶ Word History
> Our beds today are a lot more comfortable than when the word **bed** came into use. The word goes back to the root *bhedh,* meaning "to dig." In the old Germanic languages, which became English, German, and Swedish, the word was *bedde* or *betti,* which meant both "a garden plot" and "a sleeping place." It suggests that early people slept in "beds" dug out of the ground.

bed·ding (**bed**-ing) *noun* Sheets, blankets, comforters, quilts, etc.

be·drag·gled (bi-**drag**-uhld) *adjective* Wet, limp, or soiled; messy. *Caught in a rainstorm, the bedraggled hikers finally got home.*

bed·rid·den (**bed**-rid-uhn) *adjective* If you are **bedridden,** you must stay in bed, usually because of illness.

bed·rock (**bed**-rok) *noun* The solid layer of rock under the soil and loose rock.

bed·room (**bed**-room or **bed**-rum) *noun* A room used for sleeping.

bed·side (**bed**-side)
1. *noun* The area next to a bed. *Grandmother rushed to Grandfather's bedside.*
2. *adjective* To do with something that sits by a bed. *She laid her book on the bedside table.*

bed·spread (**bed**-spred) *noun* A decorative quilt or other cover for a bed.

bed·time (**bed**-time) *noun* The time when someone usually goes to bed. *My regular bedtime is nine o'clock, but on weekends it's ten o'clock.*

bee (bee) *noun* A flying insect with four wings that collects pollen to make honey. *A bee lets other bees know where food is by performing a "dance" in which it waggles its abdomen a certain number of times. Also see* **hive, honeycomb, insect.**

bee dance

watching bee · dance direction · dancing bee · waggling abdomen

beech (beech) *noun* A tree with smooth, gray bark and small nuts that are eaten as food. **Beech** sounds like **beach.** ▷ *noun, plural* **beeches**

beef (beef) *noun* The meat from a steer, bull, or cow.

bee·hive (bee-**hive**) *noun* A nest or house for a swarm of bees. *See* **hive.**

beep (beep) *noun* A short, high sound, as made by a horn or machine. ▷ *noun* **beeper** ▷ *verb* **beep** ▷ *adjective* **beeping**

beer (bihr) *noun* An alcoholic drink made from malt, barley, and hops.

bees·wax (beez-**waks**) *noun* A waxy substance produced and used by bees to make their honeycombs. Beeswax is used to make candles, crayons, and furniture polish.

beet (beet) *noun* A dark red root vegetable. **Beet** sounds like **beat.** *See* **vegetable.**

bee·tle (bee-**tuhl**) *noun* An insect with two pairs of wings. A pair of hard wings in front protects a pair of soft flying wings that are folded underneath. *See* **insect.**

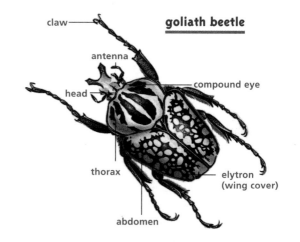

goliath beetle

claw · antenna · head · compound eye · thorax · abdomen · elytron (wing cover)

be·fall (bi-fawl) *verb* To happen to someone. *He wondered what fate would befall him if he opened the door to the abandoned house.*
▷ **befalling, befell, befallen**

be·fore (bi-for)
1. *preposition* Sooner, or earlier than, as in *the time before last.*
2. *preposition* In front of. *The criminal stood before the judge.*
3. *adverb* Earlier. *I've been here before.*
4. *conjunction* Rather than. *I would starve before I would eat at that restaurant.*

be·fore·hand (bi-for-hand) *adverb* Ahead of time. *If you decide to come over, let me know beforehand.* ▷ *adjective* **beforehand**

be·friend (bi-frend) *verb* To make friends with someone. *She finds it easy to befriend people.*
▷ **befriending, befriended**

beg (beg) *verb*
1. To ask someone in the street for help, especially for money or food. ▷ *noun* **beggar**
2. To plead with someone to do something. *Emily begged Tom to come to her party.*
▷ *verb* **begging, begged**

be·gin (bi-gin) *verb* To start. ▷ **beginning, began** (bi-gan)**, begun** (bi-guhn) ▷ *noun* **beginner,** *noun* **beginning**

be·go·ni·a (bi-goh-nyuh) *noun* A tropical plant with white, yellow, red, purple, or pink flowers.

be·half (bi-haf) *noun* If you do something **on behalf** of someone else, you do it for that person or in his or her place. *On behalf of my family, I'd like to thank you all for coming.*

be·have (bi-hayv) *verb*
1. To act properly. *I wish you would behave yourself!*
2. To do and say things in a particular way. *Matthew behaved very strangely.*
▷ *verb* **behaving, behaved** ▷ *noun* **behavior** (bi-hayv-yuhr)

be·head (bi-hed) *verb* To chop off someone's head. *During the French Revolution, people were beheaded on the guillotine.* ▷ **beheading, beheaded**

be·hind (bi-hinde)
1. *preposition* On the other side, or toward the back of something. *Look behind the curtain.*
2. *preposition* Further back, or in a lower position. *Enrique finished the race behind me.*
3. *preposition* Later than, as in *behind schedule.*
4. *preposition* In support of. *The striking ballplayers stood behind their leaders.*
5. *adverb* Not making good progress. *I'm behind in my work.*

be·hold (bi-hohld) *verb* To look at something with great interest, or to see. *The sun setting over the ocean is a beautiful sight to behold.*
▷ **beholding, beheld**

beige (bayzh) *noun* A pale brown color.
▷ *adjective* **beige**

be·ing (bee-ing) *noun*
1. The state of existing.
2. A person or creature that is alive.

be·lat·ed (bi-lay-tuhd) *adjective* Delayed, or late. *I missed my friend's birthday, so I had to send a belated card.* ▷ *adverb* **belatedly**

belch (belch) *verb*
1. To let out gases from your stomach through your mouth with a loud noise. ▷ *noun* **belch**
2. To send out fire and smoke. *The volcano belched ashes and lava.*
▷ *verb* **belches, belching, belched**

bel·fry (bel-free) *noun* The tower, or room in a tower, where a large bell is hung. ▷ *noun, plural* **belfries**

be·lieve (bi-leev) *verb*
1. To feel sure that something is true. *Twana believed her cousin's story.* ▷ *noun* **belief** (bi-leef)
▷ *adjective* **believable**
2. To support someone or something. *I believe in rights for children.*
▷ *verb* **believing, believed** ▷ *noun* **believer**

bell (bel) *noun*
1. An instrument that makes a ringing sound. Bells are often cone-shaped and have clappers hanging inside them.
2. *(informal)* If something **rings a bell,** you think you have heard it somewhere before.
3. Something that is shaped like a bell, especially on a musical instrument. See **brass.**

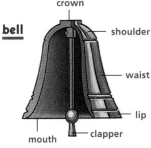

bel·lig·er·ent (buh-lij-ur-uhnt) *adjective*
1. Eager to fight, or hostile. *Sam has a belligerent attitude; he's always ready for a fight.*
2. Warlike, as in *belligerent nations.*
▷ *adverb* **belligerently**

bel·low (bel-oh)
1. *verb* To shout or to roar. *He bellowed in pain.*
▷ **bellowing, bellowed** ▷ *noun* **bellow**
2. bellows *noun, plural* An instrument or a device whose sides are squeezed to pump air into something such as an organ or a fire.

bel·ly (bel-ee) *noun*
1. The stomach, or the part of a human's or animal's body that contains the stomach and intestines.
2. belly flop A dive into water in which you hit the water hard with the front of your body.
▷ *noun, plural* **bellies**

belly button *noun* The navel; a hollow or raised dimple in the center of your stomach where your umbilical cord was attached to your mother before you were born.

be·long (bi-long) *verb*
1. If something **belongs** to you, you own it. ▷ *noun, plural* **belongings**
2. If you **belong** to a group, you are a member of it.
3. If something **belongs** somewhere, that is its proper place. ▷ *verb* **belonging, belonged**

be·lov·ed (bi-luhv-id)
1. *adjective* Greatly loved or dear to someone's heart. *I was so sad when my beloved pet died.*
2. *noun* Someone who is greatly loved. *I wrote a letter to my beloved.*

be·low (bi-loh)
1. *preposition* Lower than. *The temperature today is below freezing.*
2. *adverb* In or to a lower place than. *The sun sank below the horizon.*

belt (belt)
1. *noun* A strip of leather or other material that you wear around your waist. ▷ *verb* **belt**
2. *noun* A moving band of rubber used for transporting objects or for driving machinery, as in *a conveyor belt*.
3. *verb* (informal) To hit someone hard. ▷ **belting, belted**
4. *noun* An area or strip, as in *the corn belt*.

bench (bench) *noun*
1. A long, narrow seat for several people, usually made of wood or plastic.
2. A table in a workshop or laboratory, as in *a carpenter's bench*.
3. The place where a judge sits in a court of law. Judges ask lawyers to "approach the bench" to discuss issues in private during a trial. *The picture shows the judge's seat in a courtroom.*

the bench

bend (bend) *verb*
1. If you **bend** or **bend over,** you lean forward from your waist.

2. If something **bends,** it changes direction by turning to one side. *The road bends to the left.* ▷ *noun* **bend**
3. To change the shape of something so that it is no longer straight. *Bend your arm.*
▷ *verb* **bending, bent** (bent)

be·neath (bi-neeth) *preposition*
1. Lower than, or not worthy of. *It's beneath my dignity to talk to her.*
2. Underneath. *We hid beneath the bed.* ▷ *adverb* **beneath**

ben·e·fi·cial (ben-uh-fish-uhl) *adjective* Something that is **beneficial** is good for you. ▷ *adverb* **beneficially**

ben·e·fit (ben-uh-fit)
1. *verb* If you **benefit** from something, you get an advantage from it or are helped by it. *We really benefited from our vacation.* ▷ **benefiting, benefited** ▷ *noun* **benefit**
2. benefits *noun, plural* Money paid by a government, employer, or insurance company to people in time of need, as in *unemployment benefits.*

be·nev·o·lent (buh-nev-uh-luhnt) *adjective* Kind and helpful. ▷ *noun* **benevolence** ▷ *adverb* **benevolently**

be·nign (bi-nine) *adjective* Harmless. *The lump on my mother's leg was benign.*

bent (bent) *adjective*
1. Crooked or curved.
2. Determined. *Doug was bent on going home.*

be·queath (bi-kweeth) *verb* To leave something to somebody in a will. *My uncle bequeathed a farm to my parents.* ▷ **bequeathing, bequeathed** ▷ *noun* **bequest** (bi-kwest)

be·reaved (bi-reevd) *adjective* A **bereaved** person feels sad because someone very close to him or her has died. ▷ *noun* **bereavement**

be·ret (buh-ray) *noun* A round, flat cap made of felt, wool, or some other soft material.

ber·ry (ber-ee) *noun* A small, often brightly colored fruit found on bushes or trees. **Berry** sounds like **bury.** ▷ *noun, plural* **berries**

berth (burth)
1. *noun* A bed in a ship, a train, or an airplane.
2. *noun* A place in a harbor where a boat is tied up.
3. *verb* When a boat **berths,** it comes into a harbor and is tied up. ▷ **berthing, berthed Berth** sounds like **birth.**

be·seech (bi-seech) *verb* To ask someone in a very serious way; to beg. *He beseeched the judge to allow his son to go free.* ▷ **beseeching, besought** (bi-sawt)**, beseeched**

be·set (bi-set) *verb* To attack on all sides. *I was beset by difficulties.* ▷ **besetting, beset**

be·side (bi-side) *preposition*
1. Next to. *Walk beside me.*
2. Apart from. *Your excuse is beside the point.*
3. If you are **beside yourself,** you are overcome with emotion. *George is beside himself with rage.*

be·sides (bi-sidez)
1. *preposition* As well as, or apart from. *Who went to the game besides Jim?*
2. *adverb* Also, or in addition to this. *I hate boats and, besides, I can't swim.*

be·siege (bi-seej) *verb*
1. To surround a place to make it surrender. *Enemy troops are besieging the castle.*
2. To crowd around. *Screaming fans besieged the rock star.*
▷ *verb* **besieging, besieged**

best (best) *adjective*
1. Better than everything else.
2. When you **do your best,** you try as hard as you can to do something.
3. **best man** The friend or relative of a bridegroom who helps him at his wedding.
▷ *noun* **best** ▷ *verb* **best** ▷ *adverb* **best**

be·stow (bi-stoh) *verb* To give someone a gift or a prize. *The gym teacher bestowed the blue ribbon on the winner of the race.* ▷ **bestowing, bestowed**

bet (bet) *verb*
1. To risk a sum of money on the result of something, such as a horse race. If you guess the result correctly, you win some money; if not, you lose money. ▷ *noun* **bet,** *noun* **betting**
2. If you **bet** someone that he or she cannot do something, you dare the person to do it. *I bet you can't climb that tree!*
3. *(informal)* If you **bet** that someone will do something, you predict that he or she will do it. *I bet Jeremy will trip over that cat.*
▷ *verb* **betting, bet**

be·tray (bi-tray) *verb*
1. If you **betray** someone, you are not loyal to that person or do something to hurt him or her. ▷ *noun* **betrayal**
2. If you **betray** your feelings, you are not able to keep them hidden.
▷ *verb* **betraying, betrayed**

bet·ter (bet-ur)
1. *adjective* More suitable, or higher in quality, as in *a better job.*
2. *adjective* No longer ill or hurting. *Jenny is much better today.*
3. **better off** Richer, or in an improved condition. *The family is better off now that they have moved.*
4. *adverb* More efficiently, more completely, or more suitably. *The new car runs better than the old one.*
▷ *verb* **better**

be·tween (bi-tween) *preposition*
1. If something is **between** two things, it has them on either side of it. *The car is parked between two trucks.*
2. From one to the other of. *We threw the ball between us.*
3. Somewhere within the limits of. *Peter left between three and four o'clock.*
4. By comparing. *Please choose between the boots and the sneakers.*

bev·er·age (bev-rij) *noun* A drink.

be·ware (bi-wair) *verb* If a person or a sign tells you to **beware of** something, it warns you to look out for something dangerous or harmful.

be·wil·der (bi-wil-dur) *verb* To confuse someone. *The instructions to the game completely bewilder me.* ▷ **bewildering, bewildered** ▷ *noun* **bewilderment** ▷ *adjective* **bewildered**

be·witch (bi-wich) *verb* To cast a spell on.
▷ **bewitching, bewitched**

be·yond (bi-yond) *preposition*
1. On the far side of something. *We couldn't see beyond the bushes.* ▷ *adverb* **beyond**
2. If something is **beyond** you, you cannot understand it. *How you can get your room so messy is beyond me.*

bi·ased (bye-uhst) *adjective* Prejudiced, or favoring one person or point of view more than another. *Tim thinks the referee is biased against our team.* ▷ *noun* **bias** ▷ *verb* **bias**

> **Prefix**
> •
> The prefix **bi-** adds one of the following meanings to a root word:
> 1. Twice every, as in *bimonthly* (twice every month).
> 2. Having two, as in *bicuspid* (a tooth having two points).

bi·ath·lon (bye-ath-lon) *noun* A sport in which the participants carry a rifle as they ski on a course and stop to shoot at targets along the way.

Bi·ble (bye-buhl) *noun*
1. The sacred book of the Christian religion that contains the Old and New Testaments.
2. The sacred book in the Jewish religion consisting of the Old Testament.

bib·li·og·ra·phy (bib-lee-og-ruh-fee) *noun* A list of writings on a subject. ▷ *noun, plural* **bibliographies** ▷ *adjective* **bibliographical** (bib-lee-uh-graf-i-kuhl)

bi·ceps (bye-seps) *noun, plural* The large muscle on the front of your arm between your shoulder and inner elbow. *See* **muscle.**

bick·er (bik-ur) *verb* To argue about small things. *Some days my brother and I bicker over who has to take out the garbage.* ▷ **bickering, bickered**

bi·coast·al (bye-kohss-tuhl) *adjective* Living and working on both the east and west coasts of the United States. *Hugo's family is bicoastal; his parents live in California and he and his brother live in New York.*

bi·cus·pid (bye-kuss-pid) *noun* A tooth with two points located just beside the front sets of upper and lower teeth.

bi·cy·cle (bye-si-kuhl) *noun* A vehicle with two wheels that you ride by steering with handlebars and by pedaling. *This mountain bike is a type of bicycle that was specially developed for cycling on dirt.* ▷ *verb* **bicycle**

mountain bike, tools, and accessories

padded, fingerless gloves · saddle · gear shifters · grip · handlebars · handlebar stem · rear brake lever · crossbar or top tube · brake cable · head tube · gear cable · rear safety reflector · bridge cable · seat post · seat tube · down tube · front safety reflector · cantilever brakes · seat stay · water bottle · safety helmet · toe strap · rear light · fork · hub · front light · pedal · crank · reflecting belt · spoke reflector · socket wrench · gear protector · chain stay · front derailleur · pump · puncture repair kit · rear derailleur · pump connector · link extractor · small screwdriver · tire levers · adjustable wrench · bicycle grease · spoke nipple tool · allen keys

wheel
inner tube · tire valve · dust cap · nipple · spoke · rim · rubber tire · tire tread

derailleur gear system
chain · front derailleur · clamp bolt · freewheel sprocket · chain ring · gear cable · rear derailleur · tooth · tension wheel · crank · axle

bid (bid)
1. *verb* To offer a certain amount of money for something, as at an auction. *We bid $50.00 for the trunk.* ▷ *noun* **bid,** *noun* **bidder**
2. *verb* To order someone to do something. *The teacher bid the class to be quiet.*
3. *verb* To say, as in *to bid someone hello.*
4. *noun* An attempt to do or win something. *Elvis made a bid for fame.*
▷ *verb* **bidding, bid** *or* **bade** (bayd)

bide (bide) *verb* To wait for the right moment. *I will have to bide my time until I ask for a higher allowance.* ▷ **biding, bided**

bi·en·ni·al (bye-en-ee-uhl)
1. *adjective* Happening every two years or over a period of two years.
2. *noun* A plant that lives for two years.

bi·fo·cals (bye-*foh*-kuhlz) *noun, plural* Glasses or lenses that have two sections, for seeing up close and farther away.

big (big) *adjective*
1. Large in size. *What a big car!*
2. Of great importance. *I couldn't wait to hear the big news.*
▷ *adjective* **bigger, biggest**

▶ **Synonyms: big**
· ·

▶ **Big** can describe things, people, ideas, or anything else that has great size or importance: *An elephant is a big animal. Choosing a career is a big decision.*

▶ **Large** is often used in place of big and refers to anything greater than normal size or quantity: *My mom runs a large business with a lot of employees.*

▶ **Immense** describes something so big that you can hardly measure or comprehend it: *An immense snowstorm blanketed several states with deep snow.*

▶ **Enormous,** like immense, means extremely big or large: *He gave me an enormous hug.*

▶ **Huge** means very large in scope or a very large amount: *My parents took me out for a huge meal at my favorite restaurant.*

▶ **Vast** means extending for great distances: *The farmer grew vast fields of corn.*

---

big·horn (big-*horn*) *noun* A type of sheep with large, rounded horns, found in the western mountains of North America.

big·ot (big-uht) *noun* Someone who has a strong and unreasonable dislike for a certain other group of people, especially people of a different race, nationality, or religion. ▷ *noun* **bigotry**
▷ *adjective* **bigoted**

bike (bike)
1. *noun* A bicycle, or a motorcycle.
2. *verb* To ride a bicycle or motorcycle. *Malcolm and I biked to the mall.* ▷ **biking, biked** ▷ *noun* **biker**

bi·ki·ni (bi-kee-nee) *noun* A two-piece bathing suit worn by women and girls.

bile (bile) *noun* A green liquid that is made by the liver and helps digest food.

bi·lin·gual (bye-ling-gwuhl) *adjective* If someone is **bilingual,** the person can speak two languages well.

bill (bil) *noun*
1. A piece of paper telling you how much money you owe for something that you have bought. ▷ *verb* **bill**
2. A written plan for a new law, to be debated in Congress.
3. The beak of a bird.
4. A piece of paper money, as in *a ten-dollar bill.*

bill·board (bil-*bord*) *noun* A large outdoor sign used to advertise products or services.

billboard

bill·fold (bil-*fohld*) *noun* A small folding wallet for paper money.

bil·liards (bil-yurdz) *noun, plural* A game in which you use a stick, called a cue, to hit balls around a table.

bil·lion (bil-yuhn) *noun* One thousand times one million, written 1,000,000,000. ▷ *adjective* **billion**

bil·low (bil-oh)
1. *verb* When a curtain, sail, or sheet **billows,** it is pushed outward by the wind.
2. *verb* If smoke or fog **billows,** it rises up in large clouds.
3. *noun* A large ocean wave.
▷ *verb* **billowing, billowed**

bin (bin) *noun* A large covered container or box for storing things, as in *a trash bin.*

bi·na·ry (bye-nuh-ree *or* bye-ner-ee) *adjective*
1. Made up of two parts or units.
2. In mathematics, the **binary** number system uses only two digits, 1 and 0.

bind (binde) *verb*
1. To tie something up.
2. To wrap a piece of material tightly around something, as in *to bind a wound.*
3. If you **bind** a book, you fasten its pages together and put a cover on it. ▷ *noun* **binding**
4. To oblige. *This contract binds you to do this job for the next year.* ▷ *adjective* **binding**
▷ *verb* **binding, bound** (bound)

bind·er (bine-dur) *noun* A detachable cover used for holding papers.

binge (binj)
1. *verb* To overdo some activity such as eating or drinking. ▷ **bingeing** *or* **binging, binged**
2. *noun* A period of overdoing something; a spree.

bin·go (bing-goh) *noun* A game in which you cross out numbers on a card as they are called out.

bin·oc·u·lars (buh-**nok**-yuh-lurz) *noun, plural* An instrument that you look through with both eyes to make distant things seem nearer.

bi·o·de·grad·a·ble (*bye*-oh-di-**gray**-duh-buhl) *adjective* Something that is **biodegradable** can be broken down naturally by bacteria. *Biodegradable packaging helps to reduce waste and pollution.*

bi·o·di·ver·si·ty (*bye*-oh-duh-**vurs**-it-ee) *noun* The condition of nature in which a wide variety of species live in a single area.

bi·og·ra·phy (bye-**og**-ruh-fee) *noun* A book that tells someone's life story. ▷ *noun, plural* **biographies** ▷ *noun* **biographer** ▷ *adjective* **biographical** (bye-*oh*-**graf**-i-kuhl)

bi·ol·o·gy (bye-**ol**-uh-jee) *noun* The scientific study of living things. ▷ *noun* **biologist** ▷ *adjective* **biological** (bye-oh-**log**-i-kuhl) ▷ *adverb* **biologically**

bi·on·ic (bye-**on**-ik) *adjective*
1. To do with mechanical parts designed to replace limbs or other parts of the body. *The man's bionic arm worked with signals from his brain.*
2. To do with superhuman strength.
▷ *noun, plural* **bionics**

bi·o·rhythm (**bye**-oh-*riTH*-uhm) *noun* The natural rhythm of the human body.

bi·plane (**bye**-*plane*) *noun* An airplane with two sets of wings, one above the other.

birch (burch) *noun* A type of tree with hard wood and smooth bark that peels off easily in long strips.

bird (burd) *noun* A warm-blooded creature with two legs, wings, feathers, and a beak. All birds lay eggs and most birds can fly. *There are about 8,600 different species of birds alive today. Shown here is a sampling of birds from around the world. The picture of an orange chat on the right shows the main parts of a bird's body.*

birds

swift
turtledove
king penguin
sparkling violet-eared hummingbird
Indian hornbill
red and green macaw
red-bellied trogon
waxwing
red and yellow barbet
ostrich
short-eared owl
white-cheeked turaco
spotted tinamou

wing
secondary feathers
ear coverts
beak
nape
crown
throat
breast
belly
claw
toe
primary feathers
flank
scaly leg
under-tail coverts
thigh
tail

orange chat

sooty-capped puffbird

greater roadrunner

hoopoe

red-throated bee-eater

white-backed mousebird

whooping crane

Canada goose

painted buttonquail

red grouse

mallee fowl

B

birth (burth) *noun*
1. The event of being born.
2. The beginning of something, as in *the birth of television.*
3. When a woman **gives birth,** she has a baby. **Birth** sounds like **berth.**

birth·day (burth-*day*) *noun* The day that someone was born, or the yearly celebration in its honor.

birth·mark (burth-*mark*) *noun* A mark on the skin that was there from birth.

birth·place (burth-*playss*) *noun* The place where someone was born, or where something began. *Springfield, Massachusetts, is the birthplace of the game of basketball.*

birth·right (burth-*rite*) *noun* A right or an object given to someone because the person is born into a specific family or group.

bis·cuit (biss-kit) *noun* A small, round bread, often made with baking soda.

bi·sect (bye-*sekt*) *verb* To divide a line, an angle, or a shape into two equal parts. ▷ **bisecting, bisected** ▷ *noun* **bisection**

bish·op (bish-uhp) *noun*
1. A senior priest in the Christian church who is in charge of priests and churches in a large area called a **diocese.**
2. A chess piece that can move diagonally across the board. *The picture shows a bishop from a 12th-century Viking chess set. See* **chess.**

bishop chess piece

bi·son (bye-suhn) *noun* A large animal with a big, shaggy head, a humped back, and short horns, found in North America; a buffalo. *See* **buffalo.** ▷ *noun, plural* **bison**

bit (bit) *noun*
1. A small piece or amount of something.
2. The smallest unit of information in a computer's memory.
3. The metal bar that goes in a horse's mouth and is attached to the reins. *See* **tack.**
4. The end part of a drill. *See* **drill.**

bite (bite) *verb*
1. To close your teeth around something. *Lindsay bit into the apple.*
2. If an insect or snake **bites** you, it makes a wound in your skin with its stinger or its teeth. **Bite** sounds like **byte.**
▷ *verb* **biting, bit** (bit), **bitten** (bit-in) ▷ *noun* **bite**

bit·ter (bit-ur) *adjective*
1. Tasting sharp and harsh, like aspirin.
2. If you feel **bitter,** you are upset and angry about something.
3. If the weather is **bitter,** it is very cold.
▷ *adjective* **bitterest** ▷ *noun* **bitterness**

bi·zarre (bi-zar) *adjective* Very strange or odd. *No one could explain her bizarre behavior.*

blab·ber·mouth (blab-ur-*mouth*) *noun* (informal) Someone who talks too much or who can't keep a secret.

black (blak) *noun* The color of coal or of the sky at night. ▷ *adjective* **black**

black·ber·ry (blak-*ber*-ee) *noun* A small, juicy, black fruit that grows on brambles. *See* **bramble, fruit.** ▷ *noun, plural* **blackberries**

black·bird (blak-*burd*) *noun* One of a large number of birds with black feathers. Crows and grackles are types of blackbirds.

black·board (blak-*bord*) *noun* A hard, smooth surface, often made of slate, that people write on with chalk.

black eye *noun* A bruise on the skin around the eye, caused by broken blood vessels.

Black·foot (blak-*fut*) *noun* One of a group of American Indians that lives principally in Montana and in the Canadian provinces of Alberta and Saskatchewan. *See* **Apache.** ▷ *noun, plural* **Blackfoot** or **Blackfeet**

black hole *noun* The area in space around a collapsed star whose gravity sucks in everything around it, even light.

black·mail (blak-*mayl*) *noun* The crime of threatening to reveal a secret about someone unless the person pays a sum of money or grants a favor. ▷ *verb* **blackmail**

black·out (blak-*out*) *noun*
1. If someone has a **blackout,** he or she becomes unconscious for a short time.
2. If a town or city suffers a **blackout,** the lights go off because the electricity has failed.
▷ *verb* **black out**

black·smith (blak-*smith*) *noun* Someone who makes and fits horseshoes and mends things made of iron.

black·top (blak-*top*) *noun* Asphalt that covers many roadways, parking lots, and playgrounds.

blad·der (blad-ur) *noun* The organ where waste liquid is stored before it leaves your body. *See* **organ.**

blade (blayd) *noun*
1. The cutting part on a knife, sword, dagger, etc.
2. The long, thin part of an oar or propeller.
3. A single piece of grass.
4. The metal runner on an ice skate.

blame (blaym) *verb* If you **blame** someone for something, you say that it is his or her fault.
▷ **blaming, blamed** ▷ *noun* **blame**

bland (bland) *adjective* Mild and rather dull, as in *bland food.* ▷ **blander, blandest**

blank (blangk)
1. *adjective* If something is **blank,** it has nothing on it, as in *a blank cassette.* ▷ **blanker, blankest**
2. *noun* An empty line or space. *Fill in the blanks.*
3. *noun* A cartridge for a gun that makes a noise but does not fire a bullet.
4. If you **go blank,** you suddenly cannot think of anything.
5. **blank verse** A type of poetry that does not rhyme. *"So through the darkness and the cold we flew," by Wordsworth, is an example of blank verse.*

blan·ket (blang-kit) *noun*
1. A thick cover for a bed.
2. A thick covering of something, such as snow or flowers. ▷ *verb* **blanket**

blare (blair) *verb* To make a very loud and unpleasant noise. *His radio has been blaring all day.* ▷ **blaring, blared**

blas·phe·my (blass-fuh-mee) *noun* The act of saying offensive things about God or a religion. ▷ *verb* **blaspheme** (blass-feem) ▷ *adjective* **blasphemous** (blass-fuh-muhss)

blast (blast)
1. *noun* A loud noise or an explosion.
2. *noun* A sudden rush of air.
3. *verb* To blow up with explosives. ▷ **blasting, blasted**
4. When a rocket or spaceship **blasts off,** it leaves the ground.

blast·off (blast-*awf*) *noun* The launching into space of a rocket, missile, or spaceship.

bla·tant (blay-tuhnt) *adjective* Obvious and shameless. *Mike grinned as he told a blatant lie.* ▷ *adverb* **blatantly**

blaze (blayz)
1. *verb* To burn fiercely. ▷ **blazing, blazed**
2. *noun* A large fire.

blaz·er (blay-zur) *noun* An informal jacket.

bleach (bleech)
1. *noun* A chemical that takes color, dirt, and stains out of materials.
2. *verb* To make something cleaner or lighter in color by using a bleach or the sun. *When I go to the beach, my brown hair is bleached by the sun.* ▷ **bleaching, bleached**

bleach·ers (blee-churz) *noun, plural* Raised seats or benches arranged in rows. Bleachers are usually found in stadiums or along a parade route.

bleak (bleek) *adjective*
1. A **bleak** place is cold, empty, and depressing.

2. Without hope. *The future looks really bleak.*
▷ *adjective* **bleaker, bleakest**

bleat (bleet) *noun* The cry made by a sheep or goat. ▷ *verb* **bleat**

bleed (bleed) *verb*
1. To lose blood.
2. If your heart **bleeds** for someone, you feel sorrow or pity for the person.
▷ *verb* **bleeding, bled** (bled) ▷ *adjective* **bleeding**

bleep (bleep) *verb* To make a short, high sound.
▷ **bleeping, bleeped** ▷ *noun* **bleep**

blem·ish (blem-ish) *noun* A mark or spot that makes something less than perfect; a flaw.
▷ *verb* **blemish**

blend (blend) *verb* To mix two or more things together. ▷ **blending, blended** ▷ *noun* **blend**

blend·er (blen-dur) *noun* An electrical machine that grinds and mixes food.

bless (bless) *verb*
1. To make sacred. *The priest blessed our new home.*
2. To ask God to look after someone or something.
3. You say **bless you** when a person sneezes, or as a way of thanking someone.
▷ *verb* **blesses, blessing, blessed** ▷ *noun* **blessing**

blight (blite) *noun*
1. A disease that destroys plants.
2. Something that can hurt or destroy the health or beauty of something. *The dilapidated house was a blight on the neighborhood.*

blimp (blimp) *noun* An airship, or dirigible, whose body does not have a rigid frame.

blind (blinde)
1. *adjective* Someone who is **blind** cannot see.
▷ *noun* **blindness**
2. *adjective* A **blind** corner is so sharp that drivers cannot see around it.
3. *noun* A covering for a window that can be pulled down over it or across it.
4. A driver's **blind spot** is the area slightly behind the vehicle that cannot be seen either in the side or rear mirror.
5. *verb* To cause to lose judgment. *Donna's friendship with Marcus blinded her to his faults.*
▷ **blinding, blinded**

blind·fold (blinde-fohld)
1. *verb* To cover someone's eyes with a strip of material so that he or she cannot see.
▷ **blindfolding, blindfolded**
2. *noun* Something that is put over the eyes and tied around the head, designed to keep the wearer from seeing anything.

blink (blingk) *verb*
1. To move your eyelids up and down very quickly. *You blink all the time without realizing it.*

2. To flash on and off. *The light blinked all night.*
▷ *verb* **blinking, blinked** ▷ *noun* **blink**

bliss (bliss) *noun* Great happiness. *It was bliss to be home again.* ▷ *adjective* **blissful** ▷ *adverb* **blissfully**

blis·ter (bliss-tur) *noun* A sore bubble of skin, filled with liquid, that is caused by something burning the skin or rubbing against it. ▷ *verb* **blister**

bliz·zard (bliz-urd) *noun* A heavy snowstorm.

bloat·ed (bloh-tid) *adjective* Swollen, often as a result of eating too much.

blob (blob) *noun* A small lump of something soft, wet, or thick; a drop. *A blob of paint fell on the canvas because I had too much paint on my brush.*

block (blok)
1. *noun* A piece of something hard, as in *a block of wood.*
2. *verb* To stop something from getting past or from happening. ▷ **blocking, blocked** ▷ *noun* **block**
3. *noun* The distance or area from one street to another.
4. *noun* The area or section in a city surrounded by four streets.

block·ade (blok-ade) *noun* A closing off of an area to keep people or supplies from going in or out.

blond (blond) *noun* A person with golden or pale yellow hair. A girl or woman with such hair is usually referred to as a *blonde.* ▷ *adjective* **blond**

blood (bluhd) *noun* The red liquid that is pumped through your body by your heart. *Blood is made up of red cells, white cells, and platelets, all floating in plasma.*

human blood
(magnified)

red blood cell
nucleus
white blood cell
platelet
plasma

blood bank *noun* A place where blood is donated and stored. Hospitals use this stored blood to replace blood lost by someone during an operation or in an accident.

blood donor *noun* A person who lets some blood be taken out of his or her body to be stored and given to somebody else.

blood·hound (bluhd-*hound*) *noun* A large dog with a wrinkled face, drooping ears, and a very good sense of smell.

blood·shed (bluhd-*shed*) *noun* The killing that happens in a battle or war. *We must try to prevent further bloodshed.*

blood·shot (bluhd-*shot*) *adjective* Red and irritated, as in *bloodshot eyes.*

blood·stream (bluhd-*streem*) *noun* Blood circulating through the body.

blood·thirst·y (bluhd-*thur*-stee) *adjective* Someone who is **bloodthirsty** enjoys violence or killing.

blood vessel *noun* One of the narrow tubes in your body through which your blood flows.

blood·y (bluhd-ee) *adjective*
1. Full of blood, or covered with blood. *The bandage soon became bloody.*
2. Violent, or showing blood. *That horror film was too bloody for me.*
▷ *adjective* **bloodier, bloodiest**

bloom (bloom)
1. *noun* A flower on a plant.
2. *verb* When a plant **blooms,** its flowers appear.
3. *verb* To flourish. *Her career has really bloomed.*
▷ *verb* **blooming, bloomed** ▷ *adjective* **blooming**

blos·som (bloss-uhm)
1. *noun* A flower on a fruit tree or other plant, as in *apple blossoms.*
2. *verb* To grow or to improve. *Tina has blossomed into a wonderful dancer.* ▷ **blossoming, blossomed**

blot (blot)
1. *noun* A stain of ink, paint, etc.
2. *verb* To dry by soaking up excess liquid. *She blotted her lips with a tissue.* ▷ **blotting, blotted**

blotch (bloch) *noun* An area of reddened skin, or a stain. ▷ *noun, plural* **blotches** ▷ *adjective* **blotchy**

blot·ter (blot-ur) *noun* A pad or piece of thick paper that absorbs extra ink.

blouse (blouss) *noun* A loose shirt worn by women and girls.

blow (bloh)
1. *verb* To make air come out of your mouth.
2. *verb* To move in the wind. *The leaves were blowing around.*
3. *noun* A punch or hit on the body. *The boxer suffered many blows to the ribs.*
4. *noun* A shock or a disappointment. *Not getting the job was a great blow to Greg.*
5. blow up *verb* To destroy something with an explosion.
▷ *verb* **blowing, blew** (bloo), **blown** (blohn)

blow·torch (bloh-*torch*) *noun* A small torch with an intense flame that is used to melt metal or take off paint. ▷ *noun, plural* **blowtorches**

blub·ber (bluh-bur)
1. *noun* The fat under the skin of a whale or seal.
2. *verb* To cry noisily. *Katie blubbered through the whole movie.* ▷ **blubbering, blubbered**

blue (bloo)
1. *noun* The color of the sky on a sunny day. ▷ *adjective* **blue**
2. *adjective* Sad and depressed. *Winter makes me blue.* ▷ **bluer, bluest**
3. out of the blue Suddenly and unexpectedly.

blue·ber·ry (bloo-*ber*-ee) *noun* A round, dark blue berry that grows on bushes. ▷ *noun, plural* **blueberries**

blue·bird (bloo-*burd*) *noun* A small songbird that has blue feathers on its back and wings. It is found in North America.

blue·fish (bloo-*fish*) *noun* A silver-blue ocean fish. ▷ *noun, plural* **bluefish** or **bluefishes**

blue·grass (bloo-*grass*) *noun*
1. A grass with a slightly blue tinge, used for lawns and for cattle and horse feed.
2. A type of country music. ▷ *adjective* **bluegrass**

blue jay (jay) *noun* A blue and white bird with a crest of feathers that is found in North America.

blue jeans *noun, plural* Pants made of blue denim; dungarees.

blue·print (bloo-*print*) *noun* A detailed plan for a project or an idea.

blues (blooz) *noun, plural*
1. A type of slow, sad jazz music first sung by African Americans.
2. Low spirits. *Since her best friend moved, Orlene has had the blues.*

blue whale *noun* A type of whale that can weigh up to 100 tons.

bluff (bluhf)
1. *verb* To pretend to be in a stronger position than you really are or to know more about something than you really do. *Nat says he's going to win, but I think he's bluffing.* ▷ **bluffing, bluffed** ▷ *noun* **bluff**
2. If you **call someone's bluff,** you challenge the person to do what he or she says he or she can do.

blun·der (bluhn-dur)
1. *noun* A stupid mistake.
2. *verb* To make a stupid mistake.
3. *verb* To move in an awkward and clumsy way, usually because you cannot see where you are going. *The troops blundered their way through the dense fog.*
▷ *verb* **blundering, blundered**

blunt (bluhnt)
1. *adjective* Not sharp, as in *a blunt instrument.*
2. *verb* To make or become less sharp.
▷ **blunting, blunted**

3. *adjective* Direct and straightforward in what you say.
▷ *adjective* **blunter, bluntest** ▷ *noun* **bluntness**
▷ *adverb* **bluntly**

blur (blur)
1. *verb* To make something smeared and unclear. ▷ **blurring, blurred**
2. *noun* A shape that is unclear because it has no outline or is moving too fast.
▷ *adjective* **blurred**

blurb (blurb) *noun* A short piece written about a person or a product in order to get people interested in buying it.

blurt (blurt) *verb* If you **blurt** something out, you say it suddenly, without thinking. ▷ **blurting, blurted**

blush (bluhsh) *verb* When you **blush,** your face turns red because you are embarrassed or ashamed. ▷ **blushes, blushing, blushed** ▷ *noun* **blush**

blus·ter (bluhss-tur) *verb*
1. To blow in gusts. *The wind blustered all day.* ▷ *adjective* **blustery**
2. To act or speak in an aggressive and overconfident way.
▷ *verb* **blustering, blustered** ▷ *noun* **bluster**

bo·a con·stric·tor (boh-uh kuhn-strik-tur) *noun* A large, nonpoisonous tropical snake that kills its prey by coiling around it and squeezing.
▷ *noun, plural* **boa constrictors**

boar (bor) *noun*   **wild boar**
1. A male pig.
2. A type of wild pig.
Boar sounds like **bore.**

board (bord)
1. *noun* A flat piece of wood or a stiff card, as in *a cutting board.*
2. *verb* To get on a train, an airplane, a bus, or a ship.
▷ **boarding, boarded**
3. *noun* The **board** of a company is the group of people who control it.
4. *noun* Meals provided to paying guests. *The college fee includes room and board.*

board·er (bor-dur) *noun* A person who pays to live somewhere and receive meals.

boarding school *noun* A school that students may live in during the school year.

boast (bohst) *verb*
1. To talk proudly about what you can do or what you own in order to impress people.
2. If a place **boasts** something good, it possesses it. *New Orleans boasts many fine restaurants.*
▷ *verb* **boasting, boasted** ▷ *noun* **boast** ▷ *adjective* **boastful** ▷ *adverb* **boastfully**

boat (bote) *noun*
1. A vehicle used for traveling on water. *The boat shown here is a motorboat.* ▷ *verb* **boat**
2. If people are **in the same boat,** they are all in the same situation.

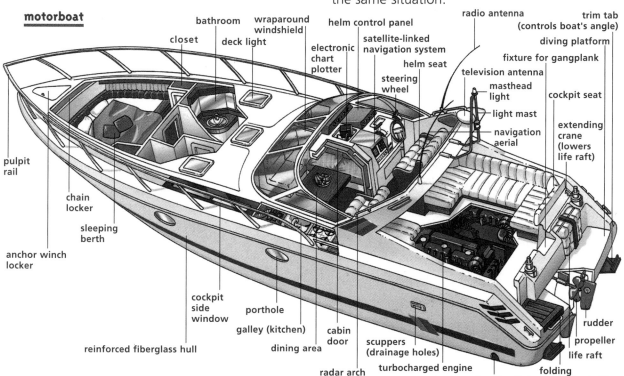

motorboat

pulpit rail — chain locker — sleeping berth — anchor winch locker — closet — bathroom — deck light — wraparound windshield — helm control panel — electronic chart plotter — satellite-linked navigation system — steering wheel — helm seat — radio antenna — trim tab (controls boat's angle) — diving platform — fixture for gangplank — television antenna — masthead light — light mast — navigation aerial — cockpit seat — extending crane (lowers life raft) — cockpit side window — porthole — galley (kitchen) — cabin door — scuppers (drainage holes) — rudder — propeller — life raft — folding swimming ladder — reinforced fiberglass hull — dining area — radar arch — turbocharged engine — engine exhaust outlet

boat·house (boht-*houss*) *noun* A building where small boats are sheltered or stored.

boat people *noun, plural* People who are forced to leave their country in boats, usually because of a war.

bob (bob)
1. *verb* To keep moving up and down on water. ▷ **bobbing, bobbed**
2. *noun* A short haircut in which the hair is all one length. ▷ *verb* **bob**

bob·bin (bob-in) *noun* A spool inside a sewing machine or on a loom that holds the thread. *See* **lace.**

bob·by pin (bob-ee) *noun* A piece of bent wire with sides that press together to hold hair in place.

bob·cat (bob-*kat*) *noun* A small, wild cat with reddish brown fur, black spots, and a short tail. A bobcat is a type of lynx.

bob·o·link (bob-uh-*link*) *noun* A North and South American songbird that lives in fields.

bob·sled (bob-*sled*) *noun* A sled with a steering wheel and brakes, used for racing down a steep, ice-covered run. ▷ *verb* **bobsled**

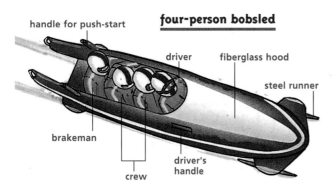

four-person bobsled

handle for push-start
driver
fiberglass hood
steel runner
brakeman
driver's handle
crew

bob·white (bob-wite) *noun* A common North American songbird with a reddish brown body and white, black, and tan markings. A bobwhite is a type of quail. Its call sounds like its name. ▷ *noun, plural* **bobwhite** or **bobwhites**

bode (bohd) *verb* To be a sign of something. *The fact that it was raining when we woke up did not bode well for our trip.* ▷ **boding, boded**

bod·y (bod-ee) *noun*
1. All the parts that a person or an animal is made of, as in *the human body.*
2. The main part of something, especially a car or an aircraft.
3. A dead person. *The detectives have found another body.*
4. A group of people working together, as in *the student body.*

5. A separate mass of matter, as in *a heavenly body.*

bod·y·guard (bod-ee-*gard*) *noun* A man or woman who protects someone.

bog (bog)
1. *noun* An area of wet, spongy land. ▷ *adjective* **boggy**
2. *verb* To make or become stuck. *The talks bogged down and no agreement was reached.* ▷ **bogging, bogged**

bo·gus (boh-guhss) *adjective* False. *Bill gave a bogus name to the police.*

boil (boil)
1. *verb* To heat a liquid until it starts to bubble and give off steam. ▷ *noun* **boil** ▷ *adjective* **boiling**
2. *verb* To cook something in boiling water.
3. *noun* An infected lump under the skin.
▷ *verb* **boiling, boiled**

boil·er (boi-lur) *noun* A tank that heats water for a house or other building.

boiling point *noun* The temperature at which a liquid that has been heated turns to a gas. The boiling point of water is 212 degrees Fahrenheit or 100 degrees Celsius.

bois·ter·ous (boi-stur-uhss) *adjective* If you are **boisterous,** you behave in a wild and noisy way. ▷ *noun* **boisterousness** ▷ *adverb* **boisterously**

bold (bohld) *adjective*
1. Someone who is **bold** is very confident and shows no fear of danger. ▷ *noun* **boldness**
2. Bold colors stand out clearly.
▷ *adjective* **bolder, boldest** ▷ *adverb* **boldly**

boll wee·vil (bohl wee-vuhl) *noun* A beetle that lays eggs in cotton plants.

bol·ster (bohl-stur)
1. *verb* To support someone or something. *Your phone call has bolstered my courage.* ▷ **bolstering, bolstered**
2. *noun* A long pillow.

bolt (bohlt)
1. *noun* A metal bar that slides into place and locks something. ▷ *verb* **bolt**
2. *noun* A strong metal pin with spiral grooves, used with a metal nut to hold things together.
3. *verb* To run away suddenly. *If you scare the rabbit, it will bolt from the garden.* ▷ **bolting, bolted**
4. *noun* A flash of lightning or crack of thunder.
5. *noun* A roll of something, such as cloth.

bomb (bom)
1. *noun* A container filled with explosives, used in war or to blow up buildings, vehicles, etc.
2. *verb* To attack a place with bombs.
▷ **bombing, bombed**

bom·bard (bom-bahrd) *verb*
1. To attack a place with heavy gunfire.

2. If you **bombard** someone with questions, you ask the person lots of questions in a short time. ▷ *verb* **bombarding, bombarded** ▷ *noun* **bombardment**

bomb·er (bom-ur) *noun*
1. A large airplane that drops bombs on targets.
2. Someone who sets off bombs.

bomb·shell (bom-*shel*) *noun*
1. A bomb.
2. Something that shocks and surprises you.

bo·na fide (bone-uh *fide*) *adjective*
1. Genuine or sincere, as in *a bona fide friendship*.
2. In good faith, or without fraud, as in *a bona fide agreement*.

bond (bond)
1. *noun* A close friendship or connection with someone. *A special bond developed between the boys.*
2. *verb* When you **bond** two things, you cause them to stick together. *I used glue to bond the airplane model to the base.* ▷ **bonding, bonded** ▷ *noun* **bond**
3. bonds *noun, plural* Ropes, chains, etc., used to tie someone up.

bond·age (bon-dij) *noun* If people are held in **bondage,** they are held against their will or kept as slaves.

bone (bohn) *noun* One of the hard, white parts that make up the skeleton of a person or an animal. *The picture shows the human thighbone.*

human thighbone

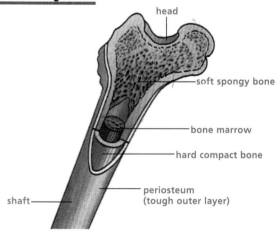

bon·fire (bon-*fire*) *noun* A large outdoor fire.
bon·go drum (bong-goh) *noun* Either of a pair of small connected drums, held between the knees and struck with the fingers.
bon·net (bon-it) *noun* A baby's or woman's hat, tied with strings under the chin.

bon·sai (bon-sye)
noun A miniature tree or shrub, grown in a pot for decoration. ▷ *noun, plural* **bonsai**

bonsai
(needle juniper)

bo·nus (boh-nuhss)
noun
1. An extra reward that you get for doing something well.
2. A good thing that is more than you expected. *It's a bonus to have a library so close to our new house.*
▷ *noun, plural* **bonuses** ▷ *adjective* **bonus**

bon·y (boh-nee) *adjective*
1. Extremely thin or full of bones. *In spite of her large appetite, Gloria was a bony child.*
2. Made of bone. *The skeleton is a bony structure.*

boo·by trap (boo-bee) *noun* A hidden trap or explosive device that is set off when someone or something touches it. ▷ *verb* **booby-trap**

book (buk)
1. *noun* A set of pages that are bound together in a cover.
2. *verb* To arrange for something ahead of time. *We've booked a vacation in Mexico.* ▷ **booking, booked** ▷ *noun* **booking**

hardback book

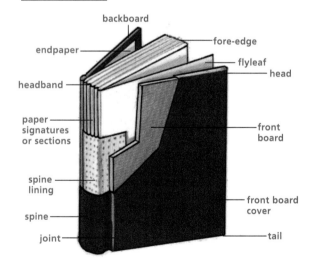

book·case (buk-*kayss*) *noun* A cabinet or piece of furniture with shelves that hold books.
book·keep·er (buk-*kee*-pur) *noun* Someone who keeps financial records for a business. ▷ *noun* **bookkeeping**

B

book·let (buk-luht) *noun* A book with a paper cover and a small number of pages.

book·mark (buk-*mark*) *noun* A piece of ribbon, paper, or other material used to mark a place in a book.

book·mo·bile (buk-muh-beel) *noun* A van or truck that is used as a small, mobile library.

book·worm (buk-*wurm*) *noun* Someone who loves reading books.

boom (boom)
1. *noun* A very loud, deep sound, such as an explosion.
2. *verb* To speak in a loud, deep voice. *"Sit down!" the guard boomed at us.* ▷ **booming, boomed**
3. *noun* A rapid increase in something, as in *a building boom.*
4. If you **lower the boom** on someone, you punish the person.

boo·mer·ang (boo-muh-rang) *noun* A curved stick that can be thrown through the air so that it returns to the thrower. *Boomerangs were invented by Aboriginal hunters in Australia.*

Aboriginal boomerang

boon (boon) *noun* Something that makes life easier. *Our dishwasher is a real boon.*

boost (boost)
1. *verb* To lift someone or something by pushing from below.
2. *verb* To increase the power or amount of something, as in *to boost profits.*
3. *noun* If something gives you a **boost,** it cheers you up.
▷ *noun* **boost** ▷ *verb* **boosting, boosted**

boost·er (boo-stur) *noun*
1. A rocket that gives extra power to a spacecraft. *See* **space shuttle.**
2. A **booster shot** is an injection of a drug given to increase the effect of an earlier injection.

boot (boot)
1. *noun* A heavy shoe that covers your ankle and sometimes part of your leg.
2. *verb* When you **boot up** a computer, you turn it on and get it ready to work.
3. *verb* To misplay a ground ball in baseball.
4. *verb* To kick the ball in football.
▷ *verb* **booting, booted**

booth (booth) *noun*
1. A temporary display area that is used to sell or show a product. *We sold a lot of cakes at our booth at the fair.*
2. A small enclosed place, such as *a voting booth, a ticket booth,* or *a telephone booth.*

boo·ty (boo-tee) *noun* Valuable objects that are taken away by force, as by an army after a battle.

bor·der (bor-dur)
1. *noun* The dividing line between one country or region and another.
2. *verb* If two countries **border** one another, their boundaries meet. ▷ **bordering, bordered**
3. *noun* A decorative strip around the edge of something.

bore (bor)
1. *verb* If something or someone **bores** you, you find the thing or person very dull and not interesting. ▷ *noun* **bore,** *noun* **boredom**
2. *verb* To make a hole in something with a drill. *This machine can bore into solid rock.*
3. *noun* The hole inside a gun barrel.
Bore sounds like **boar.**
▷ *verb* **boring, bored**

born (born) *adjective*
1. Brought into life. *Our kittens were born two weeks ago.*
2. Naturally gifted at something. *He's a born entertainer.*

bor·ough (bur-oh) *noun*
1. In some states, a town or village that has its own local government.
2. One of the five political divisions of New York City.
Borough sounds like **burro** and **burrow.**

bor·row (bor-oh) *verb* To use something that belongs to someone else, with permission.
▷ **borrowing, borrowed**

bos·om (buz-uhm *or* boo-zuhm)
1. *noun* The front part of a person's chest.
2. *adjective* Close and dear. *Joe and Jack are bosom buddies.*

boss (bawss)
1. *noun* Someone in charge of a company, or someone for whom people work. ▷ *noun, plural* **bosses** ▷ *verb* **boss**
2. **boss around** *verb* To keep telling somebody what to do. ▷ **bosses, bossing, bossed**

> ## Word History
> •
>
> While working people today would not want to call their employer "master," that is pretty much what they are doing when they say **boss.** The word, from the Dutch *baas,* was a term of respect for an older relative. When Dutch settlers came to America, they used the word as a term of respect instead of *master.* Other settlers thought the foreign word seemed less negative than *master,* and they started using it, too.

bos·sy (bawss-ee) *adjective* A **bossy** person likes telling other people what to do. ▷ **bossier, bossiest** ▷ *noun* **bossiness**

bot·a·ny (bot-uh-nee) *noun* The scientific study of plants. *The picture shows a painting from an 18th-century book on botany.* ▷ *noun* **botanist** ▷ *adjective* **botanical** (buh-tan-i-kuhl)

botanical drawing

both (bohth)
1. *pronoun* Two things or people. *You should both come in now.*
2. *adjective* Referring to the one and the other. *Use both your eyes.*
3. *conjunction* Equally, or as well. *The movie was both scary and funny.*

both·er (boTH-ur)
1. *verb* If something **bothers** you, it disturbs or annoys you.
2. *noun* Something that annoys you. *Cleaning up is such a bother.*
3. *verb* To make an effort to do something. *At least Chaka bothered to come to the meeting.*
▷ *verb* **bothering, bothered**

bot·tle (bot-uhl)
1. *noun* A glass or plastic container with a narrow neck and mouth and no handle.
2. *verb* To put things into bottles.
3. *verb* If you **bottle up** your feelings, you keep them to yourself.
▷ *verb* **bottling, bottled**

bot·tle·neck (bot-uhl-nek) *noun* A narrow part of a road that causes traffic jams.

bot·tom (bot-uhm) *noun*
1. The lowest part of something, as in *the bottom of the sea.* ▷ *adjective* **bottom**
2. The part of your body that you sit on.
3. The most basic part of something. *He'll get to the bottom of this.*

bough (bou) *noun* A thick branch on a tree.

boul·der (bohl-dur) *noun* A large, rounded rock.

bou·le·vard (bul-uh-vard) *noun* A wide city street that often has grass, trees, or flowers planted down the middle or along either side.

bounce (bounss)
1. *verb* To spring back after hitting something.
▷ **bouncing, bounced** ▷ *noun* **bounce**
2. *noun* If someone has lots of **bounce**, he or she is very cheerful.

▷ *adjective* **bouncy**

bound (bound)
1. *verb* To move forward quickly with leaps and jumps. ▷ **bounding, bounded** ▷ *noun* **bound**
2. *adjective* If something is **bound** to happen, it will certainly or almost certainly take place.
3. If a place is **out of bounds**, you are not allowed to go there. In sports, **out of bounds** means out of the field of play.

bound·a·ry (boun-duh-ree) *noun* The line, fence, etc., that separates one area from another.
▷ *noun, plural* **boundaries**

boun·ti·ful (boun-tuh-fuhl) *adjective* More than enough; generous; plentiful. *We had a bountiful feast on Thanksgiving.*

boun·ty (boun-tee) *noun*
1. Goodness or generosity. *We all benefited from nature's bounty at the Thanksgiving feast.*
2. A reward offered for the capture of a criminal or a harmful animal.

bou·quet (boh-kay) *or* (boo-kay) *noun* A bunch of picked or cut flowers.

bout (bout) *noun*
1. An attack or a spell. *I was out of school for a week with a bout of the flu.*
2. A boxing match. *Last night there were three bouts at the gym.*

bou·tique (boo-teek) *noun* A small shop that sells fashionable clothes or other specialty items.

bow
1. (bou) *verb* To bend low as a sign of respect or to accept applause. ▷ **bowing, bowed** ▷ *noun* **bow**
2. (boh) *noun* A knot with loops.
3. (bou) *noun* The front of a ship.
4. (boh) *noun* A long, flat piece of wood with strings stretched along it, used for playing stringed instruments. *See* **strings.**
5. (boh) *noun* A curved piece of wood with a stretched string attached to it, used for shooting arrows. *This archer from a famous tapestry draws his bow, ready to shoot, and holds some spare arrows in his hand.*

medieval archer

bow·els (boulz) *noun, plural* Intestines.

bowl (bohl)
1. *noun* A deep dish. *This porcelain dragon bowl was made in China in the 16th century.*
2. *verb* When you **bowl,** you roll a heavy ball down an alley to knock over wooden pins. ▷ **bowling, bowled** ▷ *noun* **bowler**
3. When something **bowls you over,** it greatly surprises you.

Chinese dragon bowl

bow·leg·ged (boh-*leg*-id) *adjective* If someone is **bowlegged,** he or she has legs that are curved outward so that the knees do not touch when the ankles are together.

bowl·ing (boh-ling) *noun* A game played by rolling a heavy ball down an alley at wooden pins.

bow tie *noun* A necktie in the shape of a bow, often worn on formal occasions.

box (boks)
1. *noun* A container, especially one with four flat sides. ▷ *verb* **box**
2. *verb* To fight with your fists as a sport. ▷ *noun* **boxer,** *noun* **boxing**
3. *verb* If you **box** someone **in,** you surround the person so that he or she cannot escape.
▷ *noun, plural* **boxes** ▷ *verb* **boxes, boxing, boxed**

box·car (boks-*kar*) *noun* An enclosed railway car with a sliding door on one side to load and unload freight.

box office *noun* The ticket office at a theater.

boy (boi) *noun* A male child. ▷ *adjective* **boyish**

boy·cott (boi-kot) *verb* To refuse to buy something or to take part in something as a way of making a protest. ▷ **boycotting, boycotted** ▷ *noun* **boycott**

boy·friend (boi-*frend*) *noun*
1. The man or boy with whom someone is having a romantic relationship.
2. A male friend.

bra (brah) *noun* An undergarment that covers and supports a woman's breasts. Bra is short for *brassiere.*

brace (brayss)
1. *noun* An object fastened to another object to support it. ▷ *verb* **brace**
2. braces *noun, plural* A device with wires worn inside your mouth to straighten your teeth.
3. *verb* If you **brace** yourself, you prepare yourself for a shock or for the force of something hitting you. ▷ **bracing, braced**

brace·let (brayss-lit) *noun* A band worn around the wrist as a piece of jewelry.

brack·et (brak-it) *noun*
1. A support, made of metal or wood, used to hold up a shelf or cupboard.
2. A grouping. *This game is intended for your age bracket and is in my price bracket.*
3. *noun, plural* **Brackets** are the two symbols [ ] that are used to separate some material from the main written text. ▷ *verb* **bracket**

brag (brag) *verb* To talk in a boastful way about how good you are at something. ▷ **bragging, bragged**

braid (brayd) *noun* A piece of hair or other material that has been divided into three or more parts and woven together. ▷ *verb* **braid**

Braille (brayl) *noun* A system of writing and printing for blind people. Braille uses raised dots that are read by feeling with the fingertips. *This picture shows what the word* Braille *looks like when it is printed in Braille. See Appendix.*

B R A I L L E

brain (brayn) *noun*
1. The organ inside your head that controls your body and allows you to think and have feelings.
2. Your mind or intelligence.

human brain

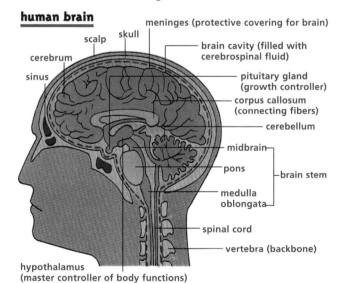

scalp
skull
meninges (protective covering for brain)
cerebrum
brain cavity (filled with cerebrospinal fluid)
sinus
pituitary gland (growth controller)
corpus callosum (connecting fibers)
cerebellum
midbrain
pons
brain stem
medulla oblongata
spinal cord
vertebra (backbone)
hypothalamus (master controller of body functions)

brain·child (brayn-*child*) *noun* The result of someone's creative work or thought. *It was Jan's brainchild to build the playground out of old tires.*

brain·storm (brayn-*storm*)
1. *verb* When people **brainstorm,** they get together to share ideas on a topic or to solve a problem. ▷ **brainstorming, brainstormed** ▷ *noun* **brainstorming**
2. *noun* A sudden idea.

brain·wash (brayn-*wahsh*) *verb* To make someone accept and believe something by saying it over and over again. *The guards brainwashed the captured pilot into believing that his government had started the war.*
▷ **brainwashes, brainwashing, brainwashed**
▷ *noun* **brainwashing**

brain·y (bray-nee) *adjective* Clever, or intelligent.
▷ **brainier, brainiest**

brake (brayk)
1. *noun* A device to slow down or stop a vehicle.
2. *verb* To slow down or stop by using a brake.
▷ **braking, braked**
Brake sounds like **break.**

brake·man (brake-muhn) *noun*
1. A worker on a train who helps the conductor. Originally, the brakeman worked the brakes on the train. ▷ *noun, plural* **brakemen**
2. The end person on a bobsled team who operates the brakes. *See* **bobsled.**

bram·ble (bram-buhl) *noun* A thorny bush or shrub. Blackberries grow on a type of bramble.

bran (bran) *noun* The outer covering of wheat or other grains that is sifted out when flour is made. Bran is used in baked goods and cereals.

branch (branch)
1. *noun* A part of a tree that grows out of its trunk like an arm.
2. *verb* When a road, river, etc., **branches,** it splits into two or more parts that go in different directions. ▷ *noun* **branch**
3. *noun* A **branch** of a company or organization is one of its stores, offices, etc., in a particular area.
4. *verb* If you **branch out,** you start doing something new.
▷ *noun, plural* **branches** ▷ *verb* **branches, branching, branched**

brand (brand)
1. *noun* A particular make of a product, as in *a brand of toothpaste.*
2. *verb* If someone **brands** an animal, the person burns a mark onto its skin to show that the animal belongs to him or her. ▷ *noun* **brand**
3. *verb* To call by a shameful name. *The politician was branded a liar.*
▷ *verb* **branding, branded**

bran·dish (bran-dish) *verb* To hold up something, such as a weapon, and wave it around.
▷ **brandishes, brandishing, brandished**

brand-new *adjective* Never used before; completely new, or recently purchased. *His skates are brand-new.*

brand·y (bran-dee) *noun* A strong alcoholic drink made from wine.

brass (brass)
1. *noun* A yellow metal made from copper and zinc.
2. *adjective* The **brass** section in an orchestra contains musical instruments that are made of brass and usually have a funnel-shaped mouthpiece. *The picture shows the main instruments in an orchestra's brass section.*

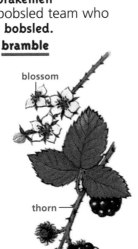

bramble
blossom
thorn
blackberry

cornet

mouthpiece
first valve
trumpet
second valve
third valve
valve casing
first valve slide
brace
second valve slide
finger hook
third valve slide
water key
finger support
tuning slide
bell

tuba

French horn
coiled tubing

trombone
weight (balances slide)
slide

brass rubbing *noun* A copy of a picture carved on a brass plate. Brass rubbings are made by rubbing with a wax crayon on a piece of paper placed over the plate. *This brass rubbing is taken from the tomb of a 15th-century knight.*

brass rubbing

brat (brat) *noun* An unpleasant or spoiled child who misbehaves or has bad manners.

bra·va·do (bruh-**vah**-doh) *noun* If you are full of **bravado,** you pretend to be braver and more confident than you really are.

brave (brave)
1. *adjective* If you are **brave,** you show courage and are willing to do difficult things. ▷ **braver, bravest** ▷ *noun* **bravery** ▷ *adverb* **bravely**
2. *verb* If you **brave** something unpleasant and difficult, you face it with determination.
▷ **braving, braved**
3. *noun* In history, an American Indian warrior.

> ### ▶ Synonyms: brave
> ·
> **Brave** describes someone who is unafraid to face danger: *The brave woman leaped into the water to save the drowning boy.*
>
> **Courageous** refers to a person who faces danger repeatedly or for an extended time: *The courageous rescue workers searched the collapsed building despite the risks.*
>
> **Bold** refers to someone or something that is fearless and daring: *It was a bold move for Dorothy to speak to the Wizard of Oz.*
>
> **Fearless** describes someone who does brave deeds or takes great risks: *The fearless performer walked on the tightrope high above the floor of the circus tent.*
>
> **Heroic** refers to people or actions that are much more than brave: *The sergeant received many medals for his heroic deeds during the war.*
>
> **Valiant** describes someone with great courage or something requiring it: *It took a valiant effort to carry the injured hiker down the mountain.*

bra·vo (brah-**voh** *or* **brah**-voh) *interjection* Well done!

brawl (brawl) *noun* A rough fight. ▷ *verb* **brawl**

bray (bray) *verb*
1. When a donkey **brays,** it makes a loud, harsh noise. ▷ *noun* **bray**
2. When a person **brays,** he or she makes a harsh noise like a donkey.
▷ *verb* **braying, brayed**

braz·en (**bray**-zuhn) *adjective*
1. Shameless. *His brazen boasting made him unpopular at work.* ▷ *adverb* **brazenly**
2. Harsh sounding, or loud.

breach (breech)
1. *verb* To break through something; to make a hole in something. ▷ **breaches, breaching, breached**
2. *noun* A failure to live up to a law or promise, as in *a breach of contract.*
3. *noun* A break in a relationship. *It's sad to have a breach between friends.*
▷ *noun, plural* **breaches**

bread (bred) *noun*
1. A baked food made from flour, water, and often yeast.
2. *(slang)* Money.

breadth (bredth) *noun*
1. The distance from one side of something to the other.
2. A wide range. *José has great breadth of experience in caring for animals.*

bread·win·ner (**bred**-*win*-ur) *noun* Someone who earns money for a family.

break (brayk)
1. *verb* To damage something so that it is in pieces or no longer works. ▷ *noun* **break,** *noun* **breakage** ▷ *adjective* **breakable,** *adjective* **broken**
2. *noun* A rest from working or studying.
3. *verb* To stop, as in *to break a bad habit.*
4. *verb* To do better than, as in *to break a record.*
5. *verb* If someone **breaks** the rules or the law, the person does something that is not allowed.
6. *verb* **break in** To get into a building by force.
7. *verb* **break out** To begin suddenly. *Fighting broke out in the streets.*
▷ *verb* **breaking, broke** (brohk), **broken** (**brohk**-in)

break dancing *noun* A very energetic and acrobatic form of dance in which dancers touch the ground with their hands, heads, etc. ▷ *noun* **break-dancer** ▷ *verb* **break-dance**

break·down (**brayk**-down) *noun*
1. If you have a **breakdown** while you are traveling, your vehicle stops moving because something has gone wrong.
2. If someone has a **breakdown,** the person is so worried or depressed about something that he or she becomes ill.

break·er (**bray**-kur) *noun* A big sea wave that breaks into foam when it reaches the shore.

break·fast (brek-fuhst) *noun* The first meal of the day.

break-in (brake-*in*) *noun* The act of forcibly entering a building or house in order to steal things.

break·through (brayk-*throo*) *noun* An important step toward achieving something. ▷ *adjective* **breakthrough**

break·wa·ter (brayk-*wah*-tur) *noun* A wall built to protect a harbor or beach from the force of ocean waves. *In this picture, the breakwater is on the right, between the water and the pavement.*

breakwater

breast (brest) *noun*
1. One of the glands in a female mammal that can produce milk to feed her young.
2. A man's or a woman's chest. *He beat his breast in sorrow.*

breast·bone (brest-*bohn*) *noun* The flat bone in your chest that is attached to your ribs.

breast·stroke (brest-*stroke*) *noun* A style of swimming face down in which you move your arms forward and out from your chest and kick your legs like a frog.

breath (breth) *noun*
1. The air that you take into your lungs and breathe out again.
2. If you are **out of breath,** you have difficulty breathing.
3. When you say something **under your breath,** you say it very quietly.

breathe (breeTH) *verb*
1. To take air in and out of your lungs. *I breathed deeply when I left the classroom and got out into the fresh air.*
2. To whisper. *Don't breathe a word to anyone.*
▷ *verb* **breathing, breathed**

breath·er (bree-THur) *noun* A short rest. *I want to take a breather before I climb back up that ladder and continue painting the house.*

breath·less (breth-liss) *adjective*
1. Out of breath.
2. Very fast. *The instructor kept us exercising at a breathless pace.*

breath·tak·ing (breth-*tay*-king) *adjective* Very beautiful or impressive. *The view of the sunset from the cliff yesterday was breathtaking.*
▷ *adverb* **breathtakingly**

breech·es (brich-iz) *noun, plural* Knee-length pants that are tight at the bottom.

breed (breed)
1. *verb* To keep animals or plants so that you can produce more of them and control their quality. ▷ *noun* **breeder**
2. *verb* When animals **breed,** they mate and produce young.
3. *noun* A particular type of animal, as in *a popular breed of dog.*
▷ *verb* **breeding, bred** (bred)

breeze (breez)
1. *noun* A gentle wind. ▷ *adjective* **breezy**
2. *verb* To move quickly and easily. *Once we passed the city, the traffic breezed along.*
▷ **breezing, breezed**

brew (broo) *verb*
1. To make tea or coffee.
2. To make beer.
3. If something is **brewing,** it is about to start. *There's trouble brewing at home.*
▷ *verb* **brewing, brewed** ▷ *noun* **brew**

brew·er·y (broo-ur-ee) *noun* A place where beer is made. ▷ *noun, plural* **breweries**

bri·ar (brye-ur) *See* **brier.**

bribe (bribe)
1. *noun* Money or a gift that you offer to someone to persuade the person to do something for you, especially something wrong.
2. *verb* To offer someone a bribe. ▷ **bribing, bribed** ▷ *noun* **bribery**

bric-a-brac (brik-uh-*brak*) *noun, plural* Various objects that are used as ornaments. *The bookcase is full of bric-a-brac.*

brick (brik) *noun* A block of hard-baked clay, used for building.

bride (bride) *noun* A woman who is about to get married or has just gotten married. ▷ *adjective* **bridal**

bride·groom (bride-*groom*) *noun* A man who is about to get married or has just gotten married.

brides·maid (bridez-*mayd*) *noun* A girl or woman who helps a bride on her wedding day.

bridge (brij)
1. *noun* A structure built over a river, railway, etc., so that people or vehicles can get to the other side. ▷ *verb* **bridge**
2. *noun* A card game for four players.
3. *noun* The bony part of your nose between your eyes.
4. If something **bridges a gap**, it provides a connection between two different things.
5. *noun* An upright piece of wood on a guitar, violin, etc., over which the strings are stretched. *See* **guitar, strings.**

bridges

suspension bridge

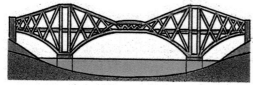

cantilever bridge

beam bridge

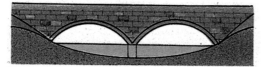

arch bridge

bri·dle (brye-duhl) *noun* The straps that fit around a horse's head and mouth and are used to control it. *See* **tack.** ▷ *verb* **bridle**
bridle path *noun* A track or path for riding or walking horses.
brief (breef)
1. *adjective* Lasting only a short time, as in *a brief visit.*
2. *adjective* Using only a few words. *Be as brief as you can.*
3. *verb* To give someone information so that the person can carry out a task. *The sales manager briefed her staff on the new products.* ▷ **briefing, briefed**

4. *noun* An outline of the main information and arguments of a legal case.
▷ *adjective* **briefer, briefest** ▷ *adverb* **briefly**
brief·case (breef-*kayss*) *noun* A bag with a handle, used for carrying papers.
bri·er (brye-ur) *noun* A prickly twig or the shrub on which it grows.
brig (brig) *noun*
1. A military prison, usually on a ship. *The sailor was thrown in the brig.*
2. A sailing ship with two masts and square sails.
bri·gade (bri-gayd) *noun*
1. A unit of an army.
2. An organized group of workers, as in *the fire brigade.*
brig·and (bri-gund) *noun* (old-fashioned) A member of a gang of robbers.
bright (brite) *adjective*
1. A **bright** light or color is strong and can be seen clearly. ▷ *adverb* **brightly**
2. Smart.
▷ *adjective* **brighter, brightest** ▷ *noun* **brightness**
bril·liant (bril-yuhnt) *adjective*
1. Shining very brightly, as in *a brilliant diamond.*
2. Very smart.
3. Splendid, or terrific, as in *a brilliant performance.*
▷ *noun* **brilliance** ▷ *adverb* **brilliantly**
brim (brim) *noun*
1. The wide part that sticks out around the bottom of a hat.
2. The edge of a cup or glass. *The glass is filled to the brim.*
brine (brine) *noun* Salty water.
bring (bring) *verb*
1. To take something or someone with you. *Bring a friend.*
2. To make something happen or appear. *Clouds often bring rain.*
3. To sell for. *My coin collection should bring a good price.*
4. If a company **brings out** a product, it starts selling it.
5. **bring up** To look after and guide a child as he or she grows up.
▷ *verb* **bringing, brought** (brawt)
brink (bringk) *noun*
1. The edge of something, such as a cliff or the bank of a river.
2. If you are **on the brink** of something, you are just about to do it. *Rachel is on the brink of leaving.*
brisk (brisk) *adjective* Quick and energetic, as in *a brisk walk.* ▷ **brisker, briskest** ▷ *adverb* **briskly**

bris·tle (briss-uhl)
1. *noun* One of the long, wiry hairs used to make brushes.
2. **bristles** *noun, plural* The short, stiff hairs that start to grow on a man's chin if he does not shave.
3. *verb* To show anger. *I bristled when Nick asked if I would leave the room.* ▷ **bristling, bristled**
▷ *adjective* **bristly**

brit·tle (brit-uhl) *adjective* Easily snapped or broken. *Dried flowers can be very brittle.*
▷ **brittler, brittlest**

broach (brohch) *verb* When you **broach** a subject with someone, you start to talk or ask about it.
▷ **broaches, broaching, broached**

broad (brawd) *adjective*
1. Wide. *Broadway is the city's broadest street.*
2. Covering the most important points, but not the details. *Give me a broad outline of the story.*
▷ *adjective* **broader, broadest** ▷ *adverb* **broadly**

broad·cast (brawd-kast)
1. *verb* To send out a program on television or radio. ▷ **broadcasting, broadcasted** ▷ *noun* **broadcaster,** *noun* **broadcasting**
2. *noun* A television or radio program.

broad·en (brawd-uhn) *verb* To make something broader or more liberal. *The principal broadened the dress code rules.* ▷ **broadening, broadened**

broad·mind·ed (minde-id) *adjective* If you are **broad-minded,** you are open to new ideas and other people's views.

bro·cade (broh-kayd) *noun* Fabric woven with a raised overall pattern.

broc·co·li (brok-uh-lee) *noun* A green vegetable with rounded heads on stalks. *See* **vegetable.**

bro·chure (broh-shur) *noun* A booklet, usually with pictures, that gives information about a product or service, as in *a vacation brochure.*

broil·er (broi-lur) *noun* The part of a stove that heats food from above.

broke (brohk) *adjective* (informal) If you are **broke,** you have no money.

bron·chi·al tubes (brong-kee-uhl) *noun, plural* Small tubes in your lungs through which air passes. *See* **respiration.**

bron·chi·tis (brong-kye-tiss) *noun* An illness of the throat and lungs that makes you cough a lot.

bron·co (brong-ko) *noun* A type of wild horse found in the western United States. ▷ *noun, plural* **broncos**

bron·to·saur·us (bron-tuh-sor-uhss) *noun* A large, plant-eating dinosaur with a long neck and tail and a small head, from the Jurassic period. The brontosaurus is now called an apatosaurus.

bronze (bronz) *noun*
1. A hard, reddish brown metal that is a mixture of copper and tin.
2. A reddish brown color. ▷ *adjective* **bronze**
▷ *verb* **bronze**

Bronze Age *noun* A period of history, before the introduction of iron, when bronze was commonly used to make tools and weapons. Different parts of the world experienced a Bronze Age at different times.

brooch (brohch *or* brooch) *noun* A piece of jewelry that can be pinned to your clothes. *The brooch shown here was made in 10th-century Ireland.*

Tara brooch

brood (brood)
1. *verb* To keep worrying or thinking about something. *Juan was brooding about his problems.*
▷ **brooding, brooded**
2. *noun* A family of young birds.
3. *noun* All the children in one family.

brook (bruk) *noun* A small stream.

broom (broom) *noun* A large brush with a long handle, used for sweeping floors.

broth (brawth) *noun* The clear liquid that remains after meat or vegetables have been cooked.

broth·er (bruhTH-ur) *noun* A boy or man who has the same parents as another person.
▷ *adjective* **brotherly**

The Wright brothers

Wilbur Wright   Orville Wright

broth·er·hood (bruhTH-ur-hud) *noun*
1. Warm feelings and good will among people.
2. A group that works or lives together in a brotherly way.

brother-in-law *noun* Someone's **brother-in-law** is the brother of his or her spouse or the husband of his or her sister. ▷ *noun, plural* **brothers-in-law**

brow (brou) *noun*
1. Forehead, as in *a wrinkled brow.*
2. The top of a hill.

brow·beat (brou-*beet*) *verb* If you **browbeat** someone, you bully the person in an argument.
▷ **browbeating, browbeat, browbeaten**

brown (broun)
1. *noun* The color of wood, chocolate, leather, or coffee. ▷ *adjective* **brown**
2. *verb* To make something brown, as by cooking it. *I browned the chopped meat in a pan.*
▷ **browning, browned**

brown·ie (brou-nee) *noun* A small, flat chocolate cake, usually with nuts in it.

brown·out (broun-*out*) *noun* A partial loss of electrical power that causes the lights to dim. *When we all turned on our air conditioners, it caused a brownout.*

browse (brouz) *verb* To look casually at something. *Max browsed through the newspaper.* ▷ **browsing, browsed**

bruise (brooz) *noun* A dark mark that you get on your skin when you fall or are hit by something.
▷ *verb* **bruise** ▷ *adjective* **bruised**

bru·nette (broo-net) *noun* A person with dark brown hair. ▷ *adjective* **brunette**

brush (bruhsh)
1. *noun* An object with bristles and a handle, used for sweeping, painting, or smoothing hair.
2. *verb* To use a brush.
3. *verb* To touch something lightly. *The runner brushed his opponent as he passed him.*
4. *noun* An area of land where small trees and shrubs grow.
▷ *noun, plural* **brushes** ▷ *verb* **brushes, brushing, brushed**

Brus·sels sprout (bruss-uhlz sprout) *noun* A vegetable that looks like a small head of cabbage. *See* **vegetable.** ▷ *noun, plural* **Brussels sprouts**

bru·tal (broo-tuhl) *adjective* Cruel and violent. *The final battle of the war was a very brutal one.*
▷ *noun* **brutality** (broo-tal-i-tee) ▷ *adverb* **brutally**

brute (broot)
1. *noun* A rough and violent person.
2. If you do something by **brute force,** you use a lot of strength instead of skill or intelligence.

bub·ble (buh-buhl)
1. *noun* One of the tiny balls of gas in fizzy drinks, boiling water, etc.
2. *verb* To make bubbles. *The water bubbled in the saucepan.* ▷ **bubbling, bubbled**

bub·bly (buhb-lee) *adjective*
1. If a liquid is **bubbly,** it is full of balls of gas.
2. If a person is **bubbly,** he or she is very lively and talkative.

buc·ca·neer (buhk-uh-nihr) *noun* A pirate. *The picture shows a 17th-century buccaneer.*

buccaneer

buck (buhk)
1. *noun* A male deer, antelope, or rabbit.
2. *verb* If a horse **bucks,** it jumps in the air with its head down and all four feet off the ground.
3. If you **pass the buck,** you pass on the responsibility for something to someone else.
4. *noun* (slang) A dollar.
5. *verb* To work against. *We bucked the rules and won the right to have pets in our apartment building.*
▷ *verb* **bucking, bucked**

buck·et (buh-kit) *noun* A plastic, wooden, or metal container with a handle, used for carrying liquids or other things.

buck·le (buhk-uhl)
1. *noun* A metal fastening on shoes, belts, or straps. *The elaborate buckle shown here was made by artisans in the 7th century A.D.* ▷ *verb* **buckle**

buckle

2. *verb* To crumple. *The runner's legs buckled under him and he fell.*
3. When someone **buckles down,** he or she works very hard.
▷ *verb* **buckling, buckled**

buck·skin (buhk-*skin*) *noun* A strong, soft material made from the skin of a deer or sheep.

buck·tooth (buhk-tooth) *noun* A longer front tooth that sticks out. ▷ *noun, plural* **buckteeth**

buck·wheat (buhk-weet) *noun* A plant with small seeds, used as cattle feed or made into flour.

bud (buhd) *noun* A small shoot on a plant that grows into a leaf or flower. *See* **plant.**
▷ *verb* **bud**

Bud·dha (boo-duh) *noun*
Buddha
1. The name given to Siddhartha Gautama, the Indian teacher who founded the religion of Buddhism.
2. A statue or picture of Buddha.

70

Bud·dhism (boo-diz-uhm) *noun* A religion based on the teachings of Buddha and practiced mainly in eastern and central Asia. Buddhists believe that you should not become too attached to material things and that you live many lives in different bodies. ▷ *noun* **Buddhist** ▷ *adjective* **Buddhist**

bud·ding (buhd-ing) *adjective* In the early stages of maturity, or gaining skill. *She is a budding artist.*

bud·dy (buhd-ee) *noun* A close friend; a pal. *He and his uncle were real buddies.* ▷ *noun, plural* **buddies**

budge (buhj) *verb* If you cannot **budge** something, you are not able to move it. ▷ **budging, budged**

budg·et (buhj-it)
1. *noun* A plan for how money will be earned and spent. ▷ *adjective* **budgetary**
2. *verb* If you **budget** your money, you plan how you will spend it. ▷ **budgeting, budgeted**

buff (buhf)
1. *noun* A pale, yellow-brown color. ▷ *adjective* **buff**
2. *noun* (informal) Someone who knows a lot about a particular subject. *Barry is a great film buff.*
3. *verb* To polish something. *He buffed his car every Saturday.* ▷ **buffing, buffed**

buf·fa·lo (buhf-uh-loh) *noun*
1. A type of ox with heavy horns found in Europe, Africa, and Asia.
2. A bison.
▷ *noun, plural* **buffaloes** *or* **buffalos** *or* **buffalo**

American bison

buff·er (buhf-ur) *noun* Something that softens a blow. *The padding on the outfield wall serves as a buffer when players run into it.* ▷ *verb* **buffer**

buf·fet
1. (buh-fit) *verb* To strike and shake something or someone. *The wind buffeted the trees.*
▷ **buffeting, buffeted**

2. (buf-ay) *noun* A meal in which many foods are laid out on a table and people serve themselves.
3. (buf-ay) *noun* A piece of furniture with a flat top for serving food and drawers for storing dishes and silverware.

bug (buhg)
1. *noun* An insect.
2. *noun* A minor illness caused by germs, as in *a stomach bug.*
3. *noun* An error in a computer program or system that prevents it from working properly.
4. *verb* If someone **bugs** a room, the person hides microphones there so that he or she can listen to what people are saying. ▷ *noun* **bug**
5. *verb* (informal) If people or things **bug** you, they annoy you.
▷ *verb* **bugging, bugged**

bug·gy (buhg-ee) *noun*
1. A light carriage with two wheels pulled by a horse. *This buggy dates from the 1800s and has seats for three passengers.*
2. A baby carriage.
▷ *noun, plural* **buggies**

hooded buggy

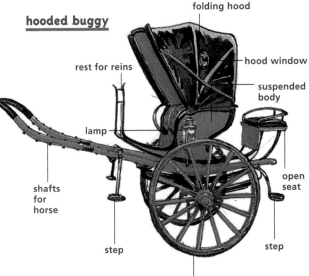

folding hood

hood window

suspended body

open seat

step

rubber tire

step

shafts for horse

lamp

rest for reins

bu·gle (byoo-guhl) *noun* A musical instrument shaped like a trumpet but without keys. Bugles are often used in the army to send signals to the troops. ▷ *noun* **bugler**

build (bild)
1. *verb* To make something by putting different parts together.
2. *noun* The size and shape of a person's body. *Theo has quite a large build.*
3. **build up** *verb* To increase or make stronger. *The traffic to the beach started to build up at noon.*
▷ *verb* **building, built** (bilt)

build·ing (bil-ding) *noun* A structure with walls and a roof. *This picture of a modern house shows the different parts of a building.*

built-in *adjective* Built as a permanent part of something. *My brother's room has built-in shelves to hold his toys and books.*

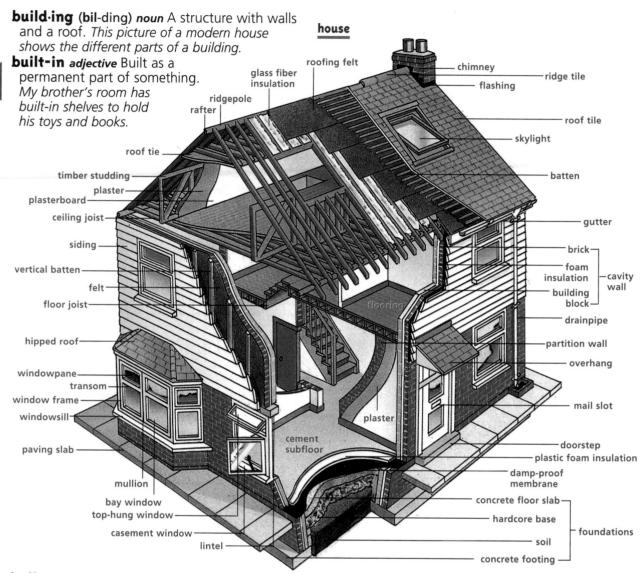

house

roofing felt
chimney
ridge tile
flashing
glass fiber insulation
ridgepole
rafter
roof tile
skylight
roof tie
timber studding
batten
plaster
plasterboard
ceiling joist
gutter
siding
brick
vertical batten
foam insulation
felt
building block
floor joist
cavity wall
drainpipe
hipped roof
partition wall
windowpane
overhang
transom
window frame
windowsill
mail slot
paving slab
plaster
doorstep
cement subfloor
plastic foam insulation
mullion
damp-proof membrane
bay window
concrete floor slab
top-hung window
hardcore base
casement window
foundations
lintel
soil
concrete footing

bulb (buhlb) *noun*
1. The onion-shaped underground plant part from which some plants grow. Tulips and lilies grow from bulbs.
2. The glass part of an electric light or flashlight that lights up when you switch it on. *When you switch on a light, an electric current travels along the connecting wires inside the bulb and makes the filament glow white-hot.*

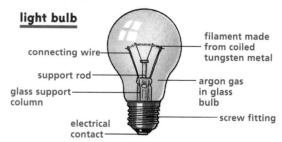

light bulb

connecting wire
filament made from coiled tungsten metal
support rod
argon gas in glass bulb
glass support column
electrical contact
screw fitting

bulge (buhlj) *verb* To swell out like a lump. *Ralph's knapsack bulged with presents.*
▷ **bulging, bulged** ▷ *noun* **bulge**

bulk (buhlk) *noun*
1. Large size. *We were surprised by the bulk of the dresser.*
2. The **bulk** of something is the main part of it.
3. When you buy **in bulk**, you buy in large quantities.

bulk·y (buhl-kee) *adjective*
1. Large and difficult to handle, as in *a bulky package.*
2. Taking up a lot of space, as in *a bulky sweater.* ▷ *adjective* **bulkier, bulkiest**

bull (bul) *noun*
1. The male of the cattle family.
2. A male elephant, seal, moose, or whale.

B

bull·dog (bul-*dawg*) *noun* A strong dog with a round head, powerful jaws, and short legs.

bull·doz·er (bul-*doh*-zur) *noun* A powerful tractor with a wide blade at the front, used for moving earth and rocks.

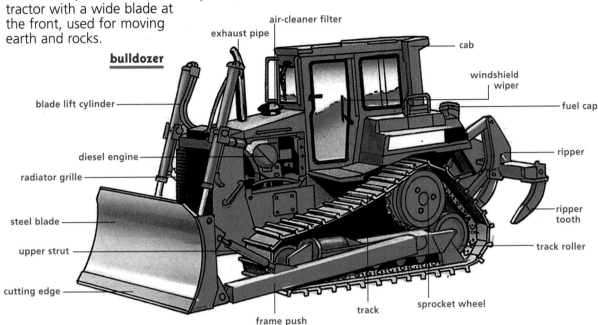

bulldozer

air-cleaner filter
exhaust pipe
cab
windshield wiper
fuel cap
blade lift cylinder
diesel engine
radiator grille
ripper
steel blade
upper strut
ripper tooth
cutting edge
track roller
frame push
track
sprocket wheel

bul·let (bul-it) *noun* A small, pointed metal object fired from a gun.

bul·le·tin (bul-uh-tuhn) *noun* A short, important news report on television or the radio.

bul·let·proof (bul-uht-*proof*) *adjective* Something that is **bulletproof** is made to protect people from bullets, as in *bulletproof glass.*

bull·fight (bul-*fite*) *noun* A public entertainment in which people fight against bulls. ▷ *noun* **bullfighter**

bull·frog (bul-*frawg*) *noun* A large frog with a deep croak.

bul·lion (bul-yuhn) *noun* Gold or silver shaped into bars.

bull's-eye *noun* The center of a target that is usually round and is used for archery or darts.

bul·ly (bul-ee) *verb* To frighten or pick on people who are weaker than you. ▷ **bullies, bullying, bullied** ▷ *noun* **bully**

bum·ble·bee (buhm-buhl-*bee*) *noun* A large, hairy bee with yellow and black stripes that hums when it flies. *See* **insect.**

bump (buhmp)
1. *verb* To knock into something. *I bumped into the bookcase as I was hurrying into the room.* ▷ *noun* **bump**
2. *noun* A heavy knock or collision.
3. *noun* A round lump or swelling.
4. *verb* If you **bump into** someone, you meet the person by chance.

5. *verb* To move with jolts and jerks. *The cart bumped along the dirt road.*
▷ *verb* **bumping, bumped**

bump·er (buhm-pur)
1. *noun* The heavy metal bar on the front or back of a car or truck that helps protect the vehicle in an accident. *See* **car, helicopter.**
2. *adjective* Very large. *The gardener had a bumper crop of corn this year.*

bump·tious (buhmp-shuhss) *adjective* Loud and conceited.

bump·y (buhm-pee) *adjective* Very uneven, as in *a bumpy road.* ▷ **bumpier, bumpiest**

bun (buhn) *noun*
1. A small, round cake or roll.
2. Hair fastened in a round shape at the back of the head.

bunch (buhnch) *noun* A group of people or things. ▷ *noun, plural* **bunches** ▷ *verb* **bunch**

bun·dle (buhn-duhl) *verb*
1. To tie or wrap things together. ▷ *noun* **bundle**
2. To hurry someone. *We bundled the children off to the movies.*
▷ *verb* **bundling, bundled**

bun·ga·low (buhng-guh-loh) *noun* A small house, usually with only one floor.

bun·gee jumping (buhn-jee) *noun* A sport in which someone jumps from a high place and is stopped from hitting the ground by a long elastic cord attached to his or her legs.

bun·gle (buhng-guhl) *verb* To do something badly or clumsily. *Because the electrician bungled the repair job, all the lights went out.* ▷ **bungling, bungled**

bunk (buhngk) *noun*
1. A narrow bed.
2. bunk bed A bed stacked on top of or below another.
▷ *verb* **bunk**

bun·ker (buhngk-ur) *noun*
1. An underground shelter from bomb attacks and gunfire.
2. A large, sand-filled hollow on a golf course.

bun·ny (buhn-ee) *noun* A rabbit. ▷ *noun, plural* **bunnies**

bunt (buhnt) *verb* To tap a baseball lightly with a bat, so that the ball doesn't go very far. ▷ **bunting, bunted**

bun·ting (buhn-ting) *noun*
1. A light cloth used for making flags.
2. Small flags joined by a string and used for decorations.

buoy (boi *or* boo-ee) *noun* A floating marker in the ocean or in a river. *Buoys often warn ships of danger.*

buoy·ant (boi-uhnt *or* boo-yuhnt) *adjective*
1. Able to keep afloat. ▷ *noun* **buoyancy**
2. Cheerful, as in *a buoyant personality.*
▷ *adverb* **buoyantly**

bur *or* **burr** (bur) *noun*
1. A prickly pod that sticks to the clothing of people or the fur of animals.
2. The bush that produces these pods.

bur·den (bur-duhn)
1. *noun* A heavy load that someone has to carry.
2. *verb* To weigh someone down with something heavy. *We burdened Dad with all our bags and suitcases.* ▷ **burdening, burdened**
3. *noun* A serious task or responsibility.
▷ *adjective* **burdensome**

bu·reau (byur-oh) *noun*
1. A chest of drawers.
2. An office that provides information or some other service, as in *a travel bureau.*

buoy
top mark
lantern
radar reflector
waterline
float
shackle for mooring line
tail

burg·er (bur-gur) *noun* A round, flat piece of cooked meat, usually served on a bun. Burger is short for **hamburger.**

bur·glar (burg-lur) *noun* Someone who breaks into a building and steals things. ▷ *noun* **burglary**

bur·i·al (ber-ee-uhl) *noun* The placing of a dead body in the earth or sea.

bur·lap (bur-lap) *noun* A tough, coarse material used to make bags that will hold heavy objects during shipping. *We put the potatoes in a burlap bag and then onto the truck.*

bur·ly (bur-lee) *adjective* Husky; strong and with large muscles. *The burly teenager was able to subdue the criminal until the police arrived.*
▷ **burlier, burliest**

burn (burn)
1. *verb* To hurt or damage someone or something by means of heat, a chemical, or radiation.
2. *noun* A sore area on the skin or a mark on something, caused by burning.
3. *verb* To feel very hot. *Erica is burning with fever.*
4. *verb* To feel strong emotion. *I burned with anger when I found out what Jackie did.*
▷ *verb* **burning, burned** *or* **burnt (burnt)**
▷ *adjective* **burnt**

burn·er (bur-nur) *noun* The circular, flat area on a stove where flame or heat is used to cook things. *The water didn't boil because the burner wasn't working.*

burp (burp) *verb* To make a noise in your throat because gases have been forced up from your stomach, usually after eating and drinking.
▷ **burping, burped** ▷ *noun* **burp**

bur·ro (bur-oh) *noun* A small donkey. **Burro** sounds like **borough** and **burrow.** ▷ *noun, plural* **burros**

bur·row (bur-oh)
1. *noun* A tunnel or hole in the ground made or used by a rabbit or other animal.
2. *verb* To dig or live in such a tunnel or hole.
▷ **burrowing, burrowed**
Burrow sounds like **borough** and **burro.**

bur·sar (bur-sur) *noun* A person whose job is to manage finances.

burst (burst)
1. *verb* To explode or break apart suddenly. *The balloon burst.*
2. *noun* A short, concentrated outbreak of something, such as speed, gunfire, or applause.
3. *verb* To start doing something suddenly. *Teresa burst into tears.*
4. *verb* To be very full. *The suitcase is bursting with clothes.*
▷ *verb* **bursting, burst**

bur·y (ber-ee) *verb*
1. To put a dead body into a grave.
2. To hide something in the ground or under a pile of things.
Bury sounds like **berry.**
▷ *verb* **buries, burying, buried**

bus (buhss) *noun* A large vehicle used for carrying passengers. ▷ *noun, plural* **buses** ▷ *verb* **bus**

bush (bush) *noun*
1. A large plant with many branches.
2. If you **beat around the bush,** you talk a lot but don't come to the point.
▷ *noun, plural* **bushes**

bush·el (bush-uhl) *noun* A unit of dry measure that tells how much a container holds. A bushel equals 32 quarts.

bush·whack (bush-*wak*) *verb*
1. To make a path, usually in the jungle, by cutting away at the underbrush with a machete or other sharp tool.
2. To ambush someone from a hiding place.
▷ *verb* **bushwhacking, bushwhacked** ▷ *noun* **bushwhacker**

bush·y (bush-ee) *adjective* Thick and spreading, as in *bushy eyebrows.* ▷ **bushier, bushiest**

busi·ness (biz-niss) *noun*
1. The buying and selling of goods and services. *Our company does a lot of business with Japan.*
2. The type of work that someone does. *Hank's in the music business.*
3. A company that makes or sells things or provides a service.
4. If something is **none of your business,** it has nothing to do with you.
▷ *noun, plural* **businesses**

busi·ness·like (biz-niss-*like*) *adjective* Efficient and practical.

bust (buhst)
1. *noun* A sculpture of a person's head and shoulders. *This marble bust is of the ancient Roman scientist Galen.*
2. *verb* To break something. ▷ **busting, busted** *or* **bust** ▷ *adjective* **bust** *or* **busted**

bus·tle (buh-suhl) *verb* To rush around being busy. ▷ **bustling, bustled** ▷ *noun* **bustle**

bus·y (biz-ee) *adjective*
1. If you are **busy,** you have a lot of things to do. ▷ *verb* **busy** ▷ *adverb* **busily**

marble bust

2. A **busy** place has a lot of people in it and is full of activity.
3. In use. *Your phone has been busy all morning.*
▷ *adjective* **busier, busiest**

bus·y·bod·y (biz-ee-*bod*-ee) *noun* Someone who likes to know other people's business. *At first we thought he was sincerely interested in us, but now we know he's just a busybody.* ▷ *noun, plural* **busybodies**

but (buht)
1. *conjunction* On the other hand. *He may be large, but he's not strong.*
2. *preposition* Other than. *There is no road to riches but hard work.*
3. *preposition* With the exception of. *We've chosen everyone but him.*
4. *adverb* Only, or just. *The train left but a minute ago.*
But sounds like **butt.**

butch·er (buch-ur) *noun* Someone who prepares and sells meat.

but·ler (buht-lur) *noun* The chief male servant in a house.

butt (buht)
1. *noun* Someone whom people make fun of.
2. *verb* To hit with the head or horns. *The goat butted the fence.* ▷ **butting, butted**
3. *noun* The thicker end, as in *a rifle butt.*
Butt sounds like **but.**

butte (byoot) *noun* A large mountain with steep sides and a flat top that stands by itself, mostly found in the western United States.

but·ter (buht-ur) *noun* A yellow fat made from cream, used in cooking and for spreading on bread. *This picture shows a 19th-century woman using a plunger churn to turn cream into butter.*

butter-making

but·ter·cup (buht-ur-*kuhp*) *noun* A small, yellow wildflower. *See* **plant.**

but·ter·fly (buht-ur-*flye*) *noun* A thin insect with large, often brightly colored wings. *See* **caterpillar.** ▷ *noun, plural* **butterflies**

butterflies

great purple
hairstreak

purple
tip

clouded
yellow

Adonis
blue

peacock

high brown
fritillary

forewing

head

antenna

hindwing

thorax

tongue

leg

but·ter·milk (buht-ur-*milk*) *noun* The sour liquid left over after butter has been churned from cream.

but·ter·scotch (buht-ur-*skoch*) *noun* A flavor or candy made by mixing brown sugar, butter, and vanilla extract.

but·tock (buht-uhk) *noun* The back of your hip that forms the fleshy part on which you sit.

but·ton (buht-uhn) *noun*
1. A round piece of plastic, metal, etc., that is sewn onto clothing and used as a fastener. ▷ *verb* **button**
2. A small knob on a machine that you turn or press to make it work.

but·ton·hole (buht-uhn-*hole*) *noun* The small hole that you push a button through in order to close a garment.

buy (bye)
1. *verb* To get something by paying money for it. ▷ **buying, bought (bawt)** ▷ *noun* **buyer**
2. *noun* A bargain. *The shirt was a good buy.* **Buy** sounds like **by.**

buzz (buhz) *verb* To make a noise like a bee or a wasp. ▷ **buzzes, buzzing, buzzed** ▷ *noun* **buzz,** *noun* **buzzer**

buz·zard (buz-urd) *noun* A large bird of prey, similar to a vulture, with a hooked beak and long, sharp claws.

by (bye)
1. *preposition* Next to, or beside, as in *a phone by the door.*
2. *adverb* Near, or close at hand. *They just stood by and laughed.*
3. *preposition* Through the work of. *It was painted by my father.*
4. *preposition* Through the means of. *We went home by bus.*
5. *preposition* Beyond, or past. *They drove by the accident.*
6. *adverb* Past. *Time goes by slowly.*
7. by and by After a while; soon. *We'll do the work by and by.*
By sounds like **buy.**

by·gone (bye-*gon*) *adjective* Past or former. *Grandma had memories of bygone days.*

by·pass (bye-*pass*)
1. *noun* A main road that goes around a town rather than through it. ▷ *noun, plural* **bypasses**
2. *verb* To avoid something by going around it. ▷ **bypasses, bypassing, bypassed** ▷ *adjective* **bypass**

by-product (bye-*prod*-uhkt) *noun* Something that is left over after you make or do something. *Sawdust is a by-product of sawing lumber.*

by·stand·er (bye-*stan*-dur) *noun* Someone who is at a place where something happens to someone else; a spectator. *She was a bystander when the accident occurred.*

byte (bite) *noun* A unit of information that is contained in a computer's memory. **Byte** sounds like **bite.**

Byz·an·tine (biz-uhn-teen) *adjective*
1. To do with Byzantium (biz-**an**-tee-uhm), the ancient eastern Roman Empire.
2. In the style of art or architecture used in the Byzantine Empire, especially in the 5th and 6th centuries. Byzantine buildings have large domes and rounded arches and are highly decorated, often with mosaics.

Cc

Spelling Hint: Some words that are spelled with the letter *c* are pronounced with a *k*- sound. Examples: cab, cable. Some are pronounced with an *s*- sound. Examples: cigar, cite.

cab (kab) *noun*
1. A car that takes people from one place to another for a fee. *We took a cab home because we were carrying a lot of packages.*
2. The driver's area of a large truck or machine, such as a bulldozer. *See* **bulldozer, tractor, truck.**

cab·bage (kab-ij) *noun* A large vegetable with green or purple leaves shaped into a round head. *See* **vegetable.**

cab·in (kab-in) *noun*
1. A small, simple house, often built of wood.
2. A private room for passengers or members of the crew to sleep in on a ship.
3. A section of an airplane for the passengers, crew, or cargo.

cab·i·net (kab-in-it) *noun*
1. A piece of furniture with shelves or drawers.
2. A group of advisors for the head of a government.

ca·ble (kay-buhl) *noun*
1. A thick wire or rope.
2. A tight bundle of wires used for carrying electricity, television signals, etc.
3. A message sent by an underwater cable.
▷ *verb* **cable**
4. **cable car** A vehicle pulled along by a moving cable, used for carrying people along city streets or up mountains.
5. **cable television** A television service in which signals from broadcasting stations are sent by cable to the homes of paying customers.

ca·boose (kuh-booss) *noun* The last car on a freight train, used by the crew.

ca·ca·o (kuh-kaw) *noun* An evergreen tree found in warm climates that produces a seed from which cocoa and chocolate are made.

cack·le (kak-uhl) *verb* To laugh in a sharp, loud way. *The audience cackled all through the stand-up comedy performance.* ▷ **cackling, cackled** ▷ *noun* **cackle**

ca·coph·o·ny (kuh-ka-fuh-*nee*) *noun* A harsh, unpleasant sound or combination of sounds. *We heard a cacophony coming from the parade.* ▷ *noun, plural* **cacophonies** ▷ *adjective* **cacophonous**

cac·tus (kak-tuhss) *noun* A plant with a thick trunk and sharp spikes in place of leaves that grows in hot, dry areas. ▷ *noun, plural* **cacti** (kak-tye) *or* **cactuses**

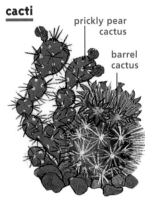

cacti

prickly pear cactus

barrel cactus

CAD (see ay dee) *noun* Short for **computer-aided design.**

ca·det (kuh-det) *noun* A young person who is training to become a member of the armed forces or a police force.

ca·fé (kaf-ay) *noun* A small restaurant.

caf·e·te·ri·a (kaf-uh-tihr-ee-uh) *noun* A self-service restaurant.

caf·feine (kaf-een *or* kaf-een) *noun* A chemical found in tea, coffee, and some soft drinks that acts as a stimulant.

caf·tan (kaf-tuhn) *noun* An ankle-length, loose piece of clothing with long sleeves, often worn by men in Arabic countries.

cage (kayj) *noun* A container in which birds or other kinds of animals are kept, made of wires or bars. ▷ *verb* **cage** ▷ *adjective* **caged**

ca·gey (kay-jee) *adjective* Cautious or wary.

ca·jole (kuh-johl) *verb* To persuade someone to do something by flattering or coaxing the person. *Don't think you can cajole me into taking you to dinner.* ▷ **cajoling, cajoled**

Ca·jun (kay-juhn)
1. *noun* Someone who is a descendant of the French-speaking people who left eastern Canada for Louisiana in the 1700s.
2. *adjective* To do with a style of spicy cooking invented by the Cajuns, as in *Cajun rice.*

cake (kayk)
1. *noun* A sweet food made by baking flour, butter, eggs, and sugar together.
2. *noun* A shaped mass of something, as in *a cake of soap.*
3. *adjective* If you are **caked** in something, you are covered with it.

ca·lam·i·ty (kuh-lam-it-ee) *noun* A terrible disaster. ▷ *noun, plural* **calamities** ▷ *adjective* **calamitous**

cal·ci·um (kal-see-uhm) *noun* A soft, silver-white chemical element found in teeth and bones.

cal·cu·late (kal-kyuh-late) *verb* To work out by using arithmetic. *Andy calculated that it would take two hours to get there by car.* ▷ **calculating, calculated** ▷ *noun* **calculation**

C

cal·cu·lat·ing (kal-kyuh-*lay*-ting) *adjective* A **calculating** person schemes to make sure things work out the way he or she wants.

cal·cu·la·tor (kal-kyuh-*lay*-tur) *noun* An electronic machine used for figuring out math problems. *This picture shows the face, circuit board, and case of a pocket calculator.*

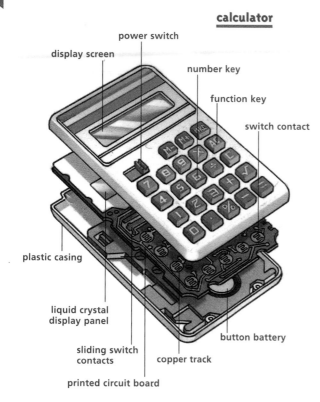

calculator

power switch
display screen
number key
function key
switch contact
plastic casing
liquid crystal display panel
button battery
sliding switch contacts
copper track
printed circuit board

cal·en·dar (kal-uhn-dur) *noun* A chart showing all the days, weeks, and months in a year.

calf (kaf) *noun*
1. A young cow, seal, elephant, giraffe, or whale.
2. The fleshy part at the back of your leg, below your knee.
▷ *noun, plural* **calves**

cal·i·co (kal-i-koh)
1. *noun* Plain cotton cloth printed with a colorful pattern, as in *a dress made of calico.* ▷ *noun, plural* **calicoes** or **calicos** ▷ *adjective* **calico**
2. *adjective* Having spotted colors, as in *a calico cat.*

call (kawl) *verb*
1. To give someone or something a name.
2. To shout something out, especially someone's name.
3. To telephone someone. ▷ *noun* **caller**
4. If you **call on** someone, you visit the person.
5. If something is **called off,** it is canceled.

6. call collect To reverse telephone charges from the person who is making the call to the person who is receiving it.
▷ *verb* **calling, called** ▷ *noun* **call**

cal·lig·ra·phy (kuh-**lig**-ruh-fee) *noun* The art of beautiful handwriting. *The picture shows a dip pen and the word* calligraphy *written in this handwriting.*

calligraphy

cal·lous (kal-uhss) *adjective* Having no tender feelings; cruel. ▷ *noun* **callousness** ▷ *adverb* **callously**

calm (kahm)
1. *adjective* Peaceful and not troubled. ▷ **calmer, calmest** ▷ *noun* **calmness** ▷ *adverb* **calmly**
2. *verb* To soothe. *The music calmed her nerves.* ▷ **calming, calmed**
3. *noun* Peacefulness.
4. *noun* A lack of wind or motion.

cal·o·rie (kal-uh-ree) *noun* A measurement of the amount of energy that a food gives you.

ca·lyp·so (kuh-**lip**-soh) *noun* A style of Caribbean music with a strong rhythm.

cam·cord·er (kam-*kor*-dur) *noun* A video camera with a sound recorder that you can carry around with you. *When light from the camcorder lens reaches the image-sensing chip, an electrical signal is created. This signal travels through electrical circuits to the record-playback head, which records magnetic patterns onto the videotape and also stores the sound.*

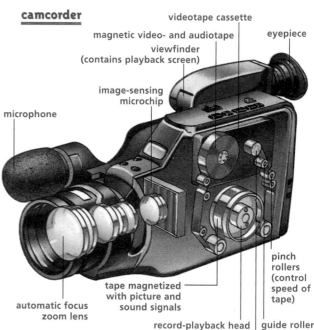

camcorder

videotape cassette
magnetic video- and audiotape
eyepiece
viewfinder (contains playback screen)
image-sensing microchip
microphone
pinch rollers (control speed of tape)
tape magnetized with picture and sound signals
automatic focus zoom lens
record-playback head
guide roller
take-up spool

cam·el (kam-uhl) *noun* A mammal with one or two humps on its back. Camels are used for carrying people and goods across the desert. *The two types of camel are shown here.*

camels

Bactrian camel

dromedary or Arabian camel

cam·e·o (kam-ee-oh) *noun*
1. A piece of colored stone with a figure carved into it.
2. A small character part taken in a play or a movie, usually by a famous actor.

cameo

cam·er·a (kam-ur-uh) *noun*
1. A machine for taking photographs or making films. *See* **photography.**
2. A device for transmitting images of a television broadcast.

cam·er·a·per·son (kam-ur-uh-*per*-suhn) *noun* Someone whose job is to use a camera to make films and television programs.

cam·ou·flage (kam-uh-flahzh)
1. *noun* Coloring or covering that makes animals, people, and objects look like their surroundings. *The praying mantis uses camouflage to hide from its prey.*
2. *verb* To disguise something so that it blends in with its surroundings.
▷ **camouflaging, camouflaged**

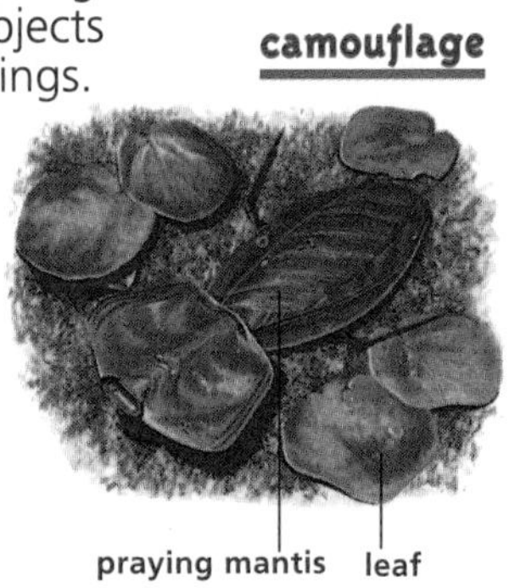

camouflage

praying mantis   leaf

camp (kamp)
1. *noun* An outdoor area, usually with tents or cabins, where people stay for a while.
2. *verb* To live or stay in a camp. ▷ **camping, camped** ▷ *noun* **camping**

cam·paign (kam-payn) *noun* A series of actions organized over a period of time in order to achieve or win something, as in *an election campaign.* ▷ *verb* **campaign**

camp·er (kam-pur) *noun*
1. Someone who stays or vacations at a camp.
2. A large vehicle in which you can sleep and cook meals.

camp·fire (kamp-*fire*) *noun* A fire lit at the site of a camp for warmth and for cooking.

camp·us (kam-puhss) *noun* The land and buildings of a school, college, or university.

can (kan)
1. *verb* To be able to. *Ian can speak French.*
2. *verb* (*informal*) To be allowed to do something. *You can stay out until dark.*
3. *noun* A metal container.
4. *verb* To put in a jar or can; to preserve.
▷ **canning, canned** ▷ *adjective* **canned**
▷ *verb* **could**

ca·nal (kuh-nal) *noun* A channel that is dug across land. Canals connect bodies of water so that ships can travel between them.

ca·nar·y (kuh-nair-ee) *noun*
1. A bright yellow bird noted for its singing ability. ▷ *noun, plural* **canaries**
2. A bright yellow color.

can·cel (kan-suhl) *verb*
1. If someone **cancels** something that has been arranged, he or she has decided that it is not going to happen.
2. cancel out If two things **cancel** each other **out,** they stop the effect of one another. *Using the dishwasher canceled out our attempts to save water.*
3. If you **cancel** a postage stamp, you mark it so that it cannot be used again.
▷ *verb* **canceling, canceled** ▷ *noun* **cancel**

can·cer (kan-sur) *noun* A serious disease in which some cells in the body grow faster than normal cells and destroy healthy organs and tissues.
▷ *adjective* **cancerous**

can·did (kan-did) *adjective* Honest and open in what you are saying. *If you want my candid opinion, I think you look silly in that hat.* ▷ *noun* **candor** ▷ *adverb* **candidly**

can·di·date (kan-duh-date) *noun* Someone who is applying for a job or running in an election.
▷ *noun* **candidacy**

Word History

Candidate comes from the Latin word *candidatus,* meaning "a person standing for public office." *Candidatus* comes from the Latin word *candidus,* meaning "white." In ancient Rome, candidates wore bleached white togas to the public forum as a symbol of political purity.

can·dle (kan-duhl) *noun* A stick of wax or tallow with a string or wick running through it that you burn to give light. ▷ *noun* **candlelight**

79

C

can·dy (kan-dee)
1. *noun* A small piece of food made with sugar or syrup and often chocolate, nuts, or other flavorings. ▷ *noun, plural* **candies**
2. *verb* To coat with sugar, as in *to candy yams.* ▷ **candies, candying, candied** ▷ *adjective* **candied**

> ### Word History
> The word **candy** came into English by way of French and Italian from the Arabic *qandi*. The word had its origins in India, however, where it meant "sugar." The first meaning of candy in English was of candy made from pure sugar, and in "sugar candy" it still has that sense. But today candy is made from syrup as well and may contain other flavorings or ingredients. The verb *to candy* retains the original sense of coating with sugar.

cane (kane)
1. *noun* The woody, sometimes hollow, stem of a plant such as bamboo or sugarcane.
2. *noun* A plant or grass having such a woody, jointed stem.
3. *noun* A stick, especially a walking stick or a stick used for beating someone.
4. *verb* To beat someone with a cane or a stick as a punishment. ▷ **caning, caned**

ca·nine (kay-nine)
1. *adjective* To do with dogs. ▷ *noun* **canine**
2. *noun* One of the pointed teeth on each side of your upper and lower jaws. There are four canines. *See* **teeth.**

can·ni·bal (kan-uh-buhl) *noun* Someone who eats human flesh. ▷ *noun* **cannibalism**

can·non (kan-uhn) *noun* A heavy gun that fires large metal balls. *The picture shows an 18th-century cannon.*

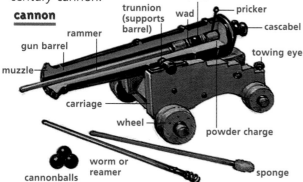

cannon
shot
trunnion (supports barrel)
wad
pricker
rammer
cascabel
gun barrel
towing eye
muzzle
carriage
wheel
powder charge
worm or reamer
sponge
cannonballs

ca·noe (kuh-noo) *noun* A narrow boat that you move through the water by paddling.

can·o·py (kan-uh-pee) *noun*
1. A piece of cloth or other material suspended as a cover over an entrance, bed, etc.
2. A shelter over something. *The trees formed a*

canopy over the forest floor.
3. A cover over an airplane cockpit. *See* **glider, helicopter.**
▷ *noun, plural* **canopies**

can't (kant) *contraction* A short form of *cannot.*

can·ta·loupe (kan-tuh-lope) *noun* A melon with a rough skin and sweet, juicy, orange fruit.

can·teen (kan-teen) *noun* A small portable metal container for holding water or other liquids.

can·ter (kan-tur) *verb* When a horse **canters,** it runs at a speed between a trot and a gallop.
▷ **cantering, cantered** ▷ *noun* **canter**

can·vas (kan-vuhss) *noun*
1. A type of coarse, strong cloth used for tents, sails, and clothing.
2. A surface for painting made from canvas cloth stretched over a wooden frame. *Artists paint on canvas.* ▷ *noun, plural* **canvases**

can·vass (kan-vuhss) *verb* To ask people for their opinions or votes. ▷ **canvasses, canvassing, canvassed** ▷ *noun* **canvasser**

can·yon (kan-yuhn) *noun* A deep, narrow river valley with steep sides.

cap (kap) *noun*
1. A soft, flat hat with a peak at the front.
2. The top of a bottle, jar, or pen. ▷ *verb* **cap**
3. A small amount of explosive on a piece of paper that makes a bang when fired in a toy gun.

ca·pa·ble (kay-puh-buhl) *adjective*
1. If you are **capable** of doing something, you are able to do it. *Stephanie is capable of winning the competition.* ▷ *noun* **capability**
2. Adept and skillful. *Michael is a capable tennis player.* ▷ *adverb* **capably**

ca·pac·i·ty (kuh-pass-uh-tee) *noun*
1. The amount that a container can hold.
2. An ability to do something. *Steve has the capacity to absorb facts very quickly.*
3. A role or job. *In Linda's capacity as president, she has the final say.*
▷ *noun, plural* **capacities**

cape (kape) *noun*
1. A sleeveless coat that you wear over your shoulders.
2. A part of the coastline that sticks out into the sea. *The map shows Cape Cod, Massachusetts.*

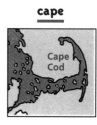

cape
Cape Cod

ca·per (kay-pur) *noun*
1. A trick or prank.
2. *(slang)* A criminal act, as in *a bank caper.*

cap·il·lar·y (kap-uh-ler-ee) *noun* A small tube in your body that carries blood between the arteries and veins. ▷ *noun, plural* **capillaries**

cap·i·tal (kap-uh-tuhl) *noun*
1. A large letter. *You begin a sentence with a capital.*

2. The city in a country or state where the government is based.

3. An amount of money used to start a business.

4. capital punishment Punishment by death.

▷ *adjective* **capital**

cap·i·tal·ism (kap-uh-tuh-*liz*-uhm) *noun* A way of organizing a country's economy so that all the land, houses, factories, etc., belong to private individuals rather than the government. ▷ *noun* **capitalist** ▷ *adjective* **capitalist**

Cap·lets (kap-luhts) *noun, plural* Trademark for medicine tablets shaped like capsules.

cap·puc·ci·no (*kap*-uh-**chee**-noh) *noun* Coffee made with frothy milk and often flavored with cinnamon.

ca·pri·cious (kuh-**prish**-uhss) *adjective* Someone who is **capricious** is unpredictable and tends to change his or her mind without any obvious reason.

cap·size (kap-size) *verb* If a boat or ship **capsizes**, it turns over in the water. ▷ **capsizing, capsized**

cap·sule (kap-suhl) *noun*

1. A small container you can swallow that holds one dose of medicine.

2. The part of a rocket or spacecraft in which the crew travels.

cap·tain (kap-tuhn) *noun*

1. The person in charge of a ship or an aircraft.

2. The leader of a sports team.

3. An officer in the armed forces.

▷ *verb* **captain**

cap·tion (kap-shuhn) *noun* A short title or description printed below a cartoon, drawing, or photograph.

cap·ti·vate (kap-ti-vate) *verb* To delight someone. *Kimiko captivated us with her singing.*

▷ **captivating, captivated**

cap·tive (kap-tiv) *noun* A person or an animal that has been taken prisoner. ▷ *noun* **captivity** ▷ *adjective* **captive**

cap·ture (kap-chur) *verb*

1. To take a person, an animal, or a place by force.

2. To attract and hold. *The book captured my attention.*

▷ *verb* **capturing, captured** ▷ *noun* **capture**

car (kar) *noun*

1. A type of passenger motor vehicle.

2. A vehicle on wheels that carries passengers and freight, such as a unit of a train.

3. The part of an elevator or balloon that carries people or freight.

C

▶ Word History

Car comes from the Latin *carrus,* meaning "chariot." The word was dying out in English until the late 19th century, when Americans borrowed a term from Dutch, *carre,* which referred to a wheeled vehicle for carrying people and things. Americans used the word to refer to railway carriages as well as to the compartment of passenger or freight elevators. In the late 19th century, *motorcar* was the term for the new invention of the day, and that was later shortened to car.

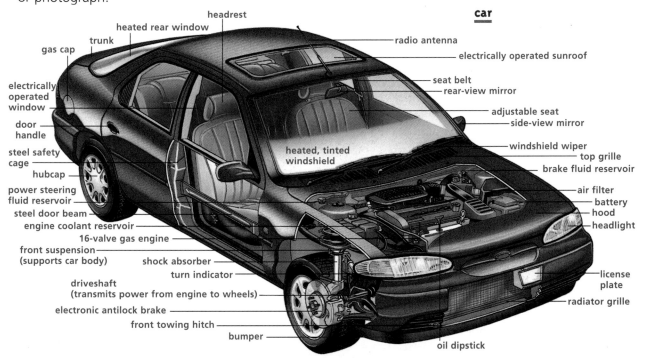

car

headrest
heated rear window
trunk
gas cap
radio antenna
electrically operated sunroof
electrically operated window
seat belt
rear-view mirror
door handle
adjustable seat
side-view mirror
steel safety cage
heated, tinted windshield
windshield wiper
top grille
brake fluid reservoir
hubcap
power steering fluid reservoir
air filter
battery
hood
steel door beam
headlight
engine coolant reservoir
16-valve gas engine
front suspension (supports car body)
shock absorber
turn indicator
driveshaft (transmits power from engine to wheels)
license plate
electronic antilock brake
radiator grille
front towing hitch
bumper
oil dipstick

C

car·a·mel (ka-ruh-muhl *or* kar-muhl) *noun*
1. Burnt sugar.
2. A candy made from burnt sugar, butter, and milk.
3. A light brown color.
▷ *adjective* **caramel**

car·at (ka-ruht) *noun* A unit for measuring the weight of precious gems and metals. **Carat** sounds like **carrot.**

car·a·van (ka-ruh-*van*)
noun A group of people or vehicles traveling together.

desert caravan

car·bo·hy·drate (*kar*-boh-**hye**-drate) *noun* One of the substances in foods such as bread, rice, and potatoes that give you energy. Carbohydrates are made up of carbon, hydrogen, and oxygen and are produced by green plants.

car·bon (kar-buhn) *noun*
1. A chemical element found in coal and diamonds and in all plants and animals.
2. **carbon di·ox·ide** (dye-**ok**-side) A gas that is a mixture of carbon and oxygen, with no color or odor. People and animals breathe this gas out, while plants absorb it during the day.
3. **carbon mon·ox·ide** (muh-**nok**-side) A poisonous gas produced by the engines of vehicles.

car·bu·re·tor (kar-buh-ray-tur) *noun* The part of an engine where air and gasoline mix.

car·cass (kar-kuhss) *noun* The body of a dead animal. ▷ *noun, plural* **carcasses**

card (kard) *noun*
1. Stiff paper.
2. A folded piece of card sent on birthdays and special occasions.
3. One of a set of rectangular pieces of card, used in games such as poker and bridge. *The cards shown here were made in France in the 18th century.*

playing cards

card·board (kard-bord) *noun* Very thick, stiff paper used for making boxes and other things.

car·di·ac (kar-dee-ak) *adjective* To do with the heart.

car·di·gan (kar-duh-guhn) *noun* A knitted sweater that fastens down the front.

car·di·nal (kar-duh-nuhl)
1. *noun* A songbird with black coloring around the beak and a crest of feathers on its head. The male is bright red.
2. *noun* One of the officials in the Roman Catholic church, ranking just below the pope in importance.
3. *adjective* Most important, as in *a cardinal rule.*

care (kair)
1. *verb* If you **care** about something, you are very concerned about what happens to it.
▷ **caring, cared** ▷ *noun* **care** ▷ *adjective* **caring**
2. *noun* Concern or attention. *They did their work with care.*
3. If you **take care of** someone, you look after him or her.
4. *noun* A worry or a fear. *I haven't a care in the world.*

ca·reer (kuh-**rihr**) *noun* The work or the series of jobs that a person has, usually in the same profession, as in *a career in teaching.*

care·free (kair-*free*) *adjective* Someone who is **carefree** has no worries.

care·ful (kair-fuhl) *adjective* Someone who is **careful** takes trouble over what he or she is doing and does not take risks. ▷ *adverb* **carefully**

> ### Synonyms: careful
>
> **Careful** means paying close attention when you are doing something, so that you avoid mistakes or injuries: *I was careful when I walked across the icy street.*
>
> **Painstaking** means taking great care while you are doing something: *Scientists conduct painstaking research to make sure their findings are accurate.*
>
> **Thorough** means doing something completely without missing anything: *After the smoke cleared, the firefighters made a thorough search of the house to make sure nothing was left burning.*
>
> **Exact** means doing something correctly and carefully, with much attention to detail: *The carpenter made exact measurements of the space where the bookcase will go.*
>
> **Accurate** means truthful and exact, without any mistake: *The police spoke to everyone in the building to get an accurate description of the intruder.*

care·giv·er (kair-*giv*-ur) *noun* Someone who takes care of children or very sick people.

care·less (kair-luhss) *adjective* Someone who is **careless** does not take much trouble over things and often makes mistakes. ▷ *noun* **carelessness** ▷ *adverb* **carelessly**

ca·ress (kuh-ress) *verb* To touch gently.
▷ caresses, caressing, caressed ▷ *noun* caress

care·tak·er (kair-*tay*-kur) *noun* Someone whose job is to look after a building, property, or other people.

car·fare (kar-*fair*) *noun* The money used to pay for a ride on a bus, subway, etc.

car·go (kar-goh) *noun* Freight that is carried by a ship or an aircraft. ▷ *noun, plural* cargoes

Ca·rib·be·an (kuh-rib-ee-uhn *or* ka-ri-bee-uhn) *noun* The sea near the Atlantic Ocean, between North and South America. The Caribbean is dotted with many small islands. ▷ *adjective* Caribbean

car·i·bou (ka-ri-boo) *noun* A large North American mammal of the deer family. Caribou are related to reindeer. ▷ *noun, plural* caribou *or* caribous

car·i·ca·ture (ka-ri-kuh-chur) *noun* An exaggerated drawing of someone.

car·jack (kar-*jak*) *verb* To steal a car by threat of force against the driver. ▷ carjacking, carjacked ▷ *noun* carjacking

car·na·tion (kar-nay-shuhn) *noun*
1. A fragrant flower, usually pink, white, or red.
2. A pink color.

car·ni·val (kar-nuh-vuhl) *noun* A public celebration, often with rides, games, and parades.

car·ni·vore (kar-nuh-*vor*) *noun* An animal that eats meat.

car·niv·o·rous (kar-niv-ur-uhss) *adjective* Eating meat. Wolves, lions, dogs, and cats are carnivorous animals.

car·ob (kar-ruhb) *noun*
1. An evergreen tree whose beans are used to make a food something like chocolate.
2. A food similar to chocolate.

car·ol (kar-ruhl) *noun* A joyful song, especially one that people sing at Christmas. ▷ *verb* carol

carp (karp)
1. *noun* A large fish that lives in fresh water and is used as food. ▷ *noun, plural* carp *or* carps
2. *verb* To find fault with someone or something. *Instead of carping about the mess in the kitchen, let's just clean it up.* ▷ carping, carped

car·pen·ter (kahr-puhn-tur) *noun* Someone who works with wood or builds and repairs the wooden parts of buildings. ▷ *noun* carpentry

car·pet (kar-pit) *noun*
1. A thick floor covering made of a woven fabric.
2. A thick layer of something, as in *a carpet of flowers*.
▷ *verb* carpet

car pool *noun*
1. A system in which a group of people travel together, often taking turns driving their own cars.
2. A group of people involved in such a system.

car·riage (ka-rij) *noun*
1. A vehicle with wheels, sometimes pulled by horses.
2. Your **carriage** is the way you stand, sit, and walk.

car·rot (kar-ruht) *noun*
1. An orange root vegetable. *See* vegetable.
2. If someone holds out a **carrot** to you, the person promises you something nice in order to persuade you to do something.
Carrot sounds like **carat**.

car·ry (ka-ree) *verb*
1. To hold onto something and take it somewhere. *Please carry this tray inside.*
2. If a sound **carries,** it can be heard some distance away.
3. To offer something for sale. *The store carries my favorite brand of jeans.*
4. To continue or to extend. *You carried your complaining a bit too far.*
5. To sing, as in *to carry a tune.*
6. When you **carry on** with something, you continue to do it.
7. If you **carry out** a plan or an idea, you put it into practice.
▷ *verb* carries, carrying, carried

car·sick (kar-*sik*) *adjective* Having a dizzy, nauseated feeling from the motion of a moving vehicle such as a car, train, or bus.

cart (kart) *noun*
1. A small wagon with two wheels, often pulled by an animal.
2. A light wagon that is pushed by someone and used to carry heavy items such as groceries.

car·ti·lage (kar-tuh-lij) *noun* A strong, elastic tissue that connects bones in human beings and animals. The outside of your ear is also mostly cartilage.

car·tog·ra·phy (kar-tog-ruh-fee) *noun* The art of making maps. ▷ *noun* cartographer

car·ton (kar-tuhn) *noun* A cardboard or plastic box or container used for holding or shipping goods.

car·toon (kar-toon) *noun*
1. A short, animated film.
2. A funny drawing or series of drawings.
▷ *noun* cartoonist

car·tridge (kar-trij) *noun*
1. A container that holds a bullet or pellets and the explosive that fires them.
2. Any small container that holds something, as in *an ink cartridge for a fountain pen.*

cart·wheel (kart-*weel*) *noun* A circular, sideways handstand.

carve (karv) *verb*
1. To cut slices from a piece of meat.
2. To cut a shape out of a piece of wood, stone, or other substance.
▷ *verb* carving, carved ▷ *noun* carver, *noun* carving

83

cas·cade (kass-kade)
1. *noun* A waterfall.
2. *noun* Anything arranged in a downward pattern, such as streamers or flowers in a bouquet.
3. *verb* To fall like water over rocks. ▷ **cascading, cascaded**

case (kayss) *noun*
1. An example of something. *This is a case of deliberate disobedience!*
2. A trial in a court of law.
3. A crime that the police are investigating.
4. A box or container that holds something, as in *a camera case.*

cash (kash)
1. *noun* Money in the form of bills and coins.
2. *verb* If someone **cashes** a check, the person exchanges it for money.
3. *verb* If you **cash in** on something, you take advantage of it.
▷ *verb* **cashes, cashing, cashed**

cash·ew (kash-oo) *noun* A sweet nut that is shaped like a bean. Cashews grow on evergreen trees in tropical countries.

cash·ier (ka-shihr) *noun* Someone who takes in or pays out money in a store or bank.

cash machine *noun* A machine usually found outside a bank that allows customers to take out or put in money, using a special card; also called an ATM, which stands for *automatic teller machine.*

cask (kask) *noun* A large, wooden barrel, usually used to make and store wine.

cas·ket (kass-kit) *noun*
1. A long, wooden or metal container into which a dead person is placed for burial; a coffin.
2. A jewelry box.

cas·se·role (kass-uh-role) *noun*
1. A dish with a lid that is used for cooking and serving.
2. Food that is cooked in such a dish.

cas·sette (ka-**set** *or* kuh-**set**) *noun* A flat, plastic box that contains recording tape, used to record and play sound or sound and pictures. *See* **tape.**

cast (kast)
1. *noun* The actors in a play, movie, or television program.
2. *noun* A hard plaster covering that supports a broken arm or leg.
3. *verb* When people who fish **cast** their fishing lines or nets, they throw them into the water.
▷ *noun* **cast**
4. *verb* When you **cast** a ballot in an election, you formally include your vote.
5. *verb* To form something by pouring soft material into a mold. *The sculptor cast the statue in bronze.*
▷ *verb* **casting, cast**

cast·a·way (kass-tuh-*way*) *noun* Someone left on a deserted island after a shipwreck.

cast iron *noun* A hard and brittle form of iron made by melting iron with other metals. The mixture is poured into a mold to make something.

cas·tle (kass-uhl) *noun*
1. A large building, often surrounded by a wall and a moat. In the Middle Ages, noble families stayed in castles and soldiers defended them

castle keep
(tower)

man-at-arms
four-poster bed
turret
parapet
arrow loop
(slit for shooting
arrows through)
lord's bedchamber
crenellation
merlon
crenel
stables
garderobe
(toilet)
toilet
chute
forge
kitchen
blacksmith
knife
grinder
storeroom
inner bailey
entrance

from attack. *The picture shows a medieval castle's keep or tower and a ground plan of the castle. See also* **portcullis.**
2. A piece used in chess, also known as a rook, that moves in straight lines across the board. *See* **chess.**

cas·u·al (kazh-oo-uhl) *adjective*
1. Not formal, as in *casual dress.*
2. Not planned, as in *a casual meeting.*
▷ *adverb* **casually**

castle

(ground plan)

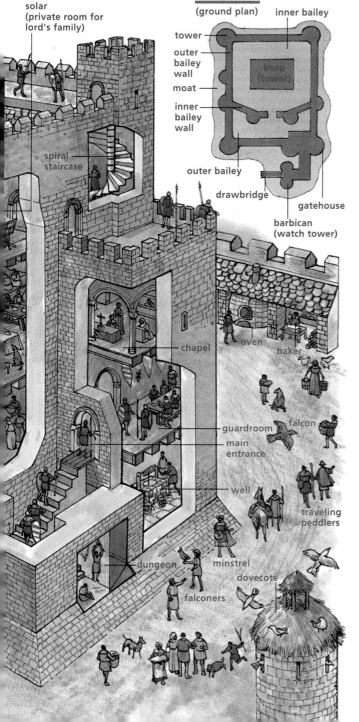

solar (private room for lord's family)

inner bailey

tower

outer bailey wall

keep (tower)

moat

inner bailey wall

spiral staircase

outer bailey

drawbridge

gatehouse

barbican (watch tower)

chapel

oven

baker

guardroom

main entrance

falcon

well

traveling peddlers

dungeon

minstrel

dovecote

falconers

cas·u·al·ty (kazh-oo-uhl-tee) *noun* Someone who is injured or killed in an accident, a disaster, or a war.
▷ *noun, plural* **casualties**

cat (kat) *noun*
1. A small, furry animal with sharp claws and whiskers, often kept as a pet. *The picture shows four breeds of cat.*
2. Any member of the cat family, including lions, tigers, and cheetahs.

cats

silver classic tabby

Persian

Abyssinian

seal-point Siamese

cat·a·log *or* **cat·a·logue** (kat-uh-log) *noun*
1. A book or pamphlet listing things you can buy from a company or works of art in an exhibition.
2. A list of all the books in a library.
▷ *verb* **catalog** *or* **catalogue**

cat·a·lyst (kat-uh-list) *noun*
1. A substance that causes or speeds up a chemical reaction, without itself changing.
2. A person or thing that causes something to happen.

cat·a·ma·ran (*kat*-uh-muh-**ran**) *noun* A boat with two hulls that are joined together.

cat·a·pult (kat-uh-*puhlt*) *noun*
1. A hydraulic device used to launch airplanes from the deck of a ship.
2. A weapon, similar to a large slingshot, used in the past for firing rocks over castle walls.
▷ *verb* **catapult**

cat·a·ract (kat-uh-*rakt*) *noun*
1. A cloudy film that sometimes grows on the lens of a person's eye, causing blindness or partial blindness.
2. A steep waterfall.

ca·tas·tro·phe (kuh-**tass**-truh-fee) *noun* A terrible and sudden disaster. ▷ *adjective* **catastrophic** (kat-uh-**strof**-ik)

cat·bird (kat-*burd*) *noun* A gray North American songbird with a call that sounds like a cat meowing.

catch (kach)
1. *verb* To grab hold of something moving through the air, as in *to catch a ball.* ▷ *noun* **catch**
2. *verb* To get something or someone you are chasing. *The police caught the thieves.*
3. *verb* If you **catch** a bus or train, you get on it.
4. *verb* If you **catch** someone doing something wrong, you see him or her doing it.
5. *noun* A fastening on a door, box, etc.
6. *noun* A game in which two or more people throw a ball to one another.
7. *verb* To attend or to watch. *I want to catch the ball game on TV tonight.*
8. *verb* If something **catches on,** it becomes very popular.
▷ *noun, plural* **catches** ▷ *verb* **catches, catching, caught** (kawt)

catch·er (ka-chur) *noun* Someone who catches; the baseball player behind home plate who catches the balls thrown by the pitcher.

cat·e·gor·i·cal (*kat*-uh-gor-i-kuhl) *adjective* Clear and plain. *Elena's reply was a categorical "No."*
▷ *adverb* **categorically**

cat·e·go·ry (kat-uh-*gor*-ee) *noun* A class or group of things that has something in common.
▷ *noun, plural* **categories**

ca·ter (kay-tur) *verb*
1. To provide food for a lot of people, as at a large party. ▷ *noun* **caterer,** *noun* **catering**
2. To provide people with the things they need. *This restaurant caters to vegetarians.*
▷ *verb* **catering, catered**

cat·er·pil·lar (kat-ur-pil-ur) *noun* A larva that changes into a butterfly or moth. It looks like a worm and is sometimes hairy. *The picture shows the main parts of a swallowtail caterpillar and the life cycle of a swallowtail butterfly.*

caterpillar to butterfly

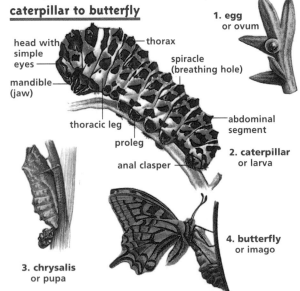

head with simple eyes
thorax
mandible (jaw)
spiracle (breathing hole)
thoracic leg
proleg
anal clasper
abdominal segment
1. egg or ovum
2. caterpillar or larva
4. butterfly or imago
3. chrysalis or pupa

cat·fish (kat-*fish*) *noun* A freshwater fish with long tendrils around its mouth that look like cat whiskers. *See* **tropical fish.**

ca·the·dral (kuh-thee-druhl) *noun* A large and important church with a bishop or an archbishop as its main priest. *The picture shows Chartres cathedral in France.*

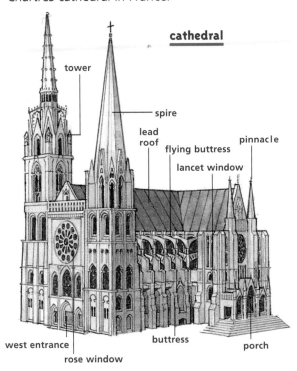

cathedral

tower
spire
lead roof
flying buttress
pinnacle
lancet window
west entrance
rose window
buttress
porch

cath·ode-ray tube (kath-ode) *noun* A glass tube with no air inside it, through which rays travel to produce an image on a screen. *See* **television.**

Cath·o·lic (kath-uh-lik) *noun* A member of the Roman Catholic church. ▷ *noun* **Catholicism**
▷ *adjective* **Catholic**

CAT scan (kat) *noun* An X-ray image made by computer from a series of cross-sectional images, resulting in a single three-dimensional image. CAT is an acronym for *Computerized Axial Tomography*

cat·sup (kat-suhp *or* kech-uhp) *See* **ketchup.**

cat·tail (kat-*tayl*) *noun* A tall, thin plant with long, brown, furry pods at the top and narrow leaves. Cattails grow in large groups in marshes.

cat·tle (kat-uhl) *noun, plural* Cows, bulls, and steers that are raised for food or for their hides.

Cau·ca·sian (kaw-kay-zhuhn) *noun* A member of a race of peoples with light or tan skin. It refers to many people from Europe, America, northern Africa, India, and other regions. ▷ *adjective* **Caucasian**

caul·dron (kawl-druhn) *noun* A large, rounded cooking pot.

C

cau·li·flow·er (kaw-luh-*flou*-ur) *noun* A vegetable with a large, rounded, white head surrounded by leaves. *See* **vegetable.**

caulk (kawk)
1. *noun* A waterproof paste that is applied to edges that need to be watertight.
2. *verb* To apply a waterproof material to something in order to prevent water from leaking in or out. ▷ **caulking, caulked**

cause (kawz)
1. *verb* To make something happen. *Be careful, or you'll cause an accident!* ▷ **causing, caused**
2. *noun* The reason that something happens.
3. *noun* An aim or a principle for which people fight, raise money, etc.

cause·way (kawz-*way*) *noun* A raised road built across water or low ground.

cau·tion (kaw-shun)
1. *noun* Carefulness or watchfulness. *Exercise caution when crossing the street, please.*
2. *verb* To warn about something or someone. *Mom cautioned us not to hitchhike.* ▷ **cautioning, cautioned**

cau·tious (kaw-shuhss) *adjective* If you are **cautious,** you try hard to avoid mistakes or danger. ▷ *noun* **caution** ▷ *adverb* **cautiously**

cav·al·ry (kav-uhl-ree) *noun*
1. Soldiers who fight on horseback.
2. Soldiers who fight in armored vehicles.
▷ *noun, plural* **cavalries**

cave (kayv)
1. *noun* A large hole underground or in the side of a hill or cliff.
2. *verb* If something **caves in,** it collapses.
▷ **caving, caved**

cave-in *noun* The collapse of a structure such as a mine or tunnel. *Search crews worked all night after the cave-in at the mine.*

cave·man (kayv-*man*) *noun* A man who lived in a cave in prehistoric times. ▷ *noun, plural* **cavemen**

cave painting *noun* A picture painted by a cave dweller on a cave wall in prehistoric times. *This cave painting of a bison was discovered in northern Spain.*

cave painting

cav·ern (kav-ern) *noun* A large cave. ▷ *adjective* **cavernous**

cave·wom·an (kayv-*wum*-uhn) *noun* A woman who lived in a cave in prehistoric times. ▷ *noun, plural* **cavewomen**

cav·i·ty (kav-uh-tee) *noun* A hole or hollow space in something solid, such as a tooth. ▷ *noun, plural* **cavities**

CB (see bee) *noun* A radio system that people use to talk to each other over short distances. The initials stand for *citizens band.*

CD (see dee) Short for *compact disk.*

CD-ROM (see dee rom) *noun* A compact disk that produces text and pictures that can be read by a computer. The initials stand for *compact disk read only memory.*

cease (seess) *verb* To stop. ▷ **ceasing, ceased**

cease-fire *noun* A period during a war when both sides agree to stop fighting.

ce·dar (see-dur) *noun* A type of evergreen tree with leaves shaped like needles and red bark, often used for making closet or trunk linings. ▷ *adjective* **cedar**

cedar

ceil·ing (see-ling) *noun*
1. The upper surface inside a room.
2. The upper limit that something can reach, as in *a price ceiling.*

cel·e·brate (sel-uh-brate) *verb* To do something enjoyable on a special occasion, such as having a party. ▷ **celebrating, celebrated** ▷ *adjective* **celebratory** (sel-uh-bra-*tor*-ee)

cel·e·bra·tion (sel-uh-bray-shuhn) *noun* A joyous ceremony or gathering, usually to mark a major event. *We held a huge celebration on the last day of school.*

ce·leb·ri·ty (suh-leb-ruh-tee) *noun* A famous person, especially an entertainer or a movie star. ▷ *noun, plural* **celebrities**

cel·e·ry (sel-uh-ree) *noun* A vegetable with white or green crisp stalks, often eaten raw in salads. *See* **vegetable.**

ce·les·tial (suh-less-chuhl) *adjective* To do with the sky or the heavens. ▷ *adverb* **celestially**

cell (sel) *noun*
1. A room in a prison or a police station for locking up people.
2. A basic, microscopic part of an animal or a plant.
Cell sounds like **sell.**

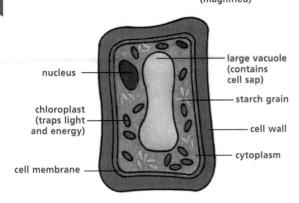

plant cell
(magnified)

nucleus

chloroplast
(traps light
and energy)

cell membrane

large vacuole
(contains
cell sap)

starch grain

cell wall

cytoplasm

cel·lar (sel-ur) *noun* A room below ground level in a house, often used for storage.

cel·lo (chel-oh) *noun* A large stringed instrument that rests on the floor. It is played with a bow like a violin but is held between the knees. The cello has a deep, resonant sound. *See* **orchestra, strings.**

cel·lo·phane (sel-uh-fayn) *noun* Clear plastic material made from cellulose and used to wrap food and make clear tape.

cel·lu·lar (sel-yuh-lur) *adjective*
1. Made out of or to do with cells, as in *cellular tissue.*
2. To do with a telephone system in which portable phones use signals sent over radio channels.

cel·lu·loid (sel-yuh-loid) *noun*
1. A substance similar to plastic once used to make motion picture film.
2. Motion picture film.
▷ *adjective* **celluloid**

cel·lu·lose (sel-yuh-lohss) *noun* The substance from which the cell walls of plants are made. Cellulose is used to make paper, cloth, and plastics.

Cel·si·us (sel-see-uhss) *adjective* A measurement of temperature using a scale on which water boils at 100 degrees and freezes at 0 degrees. It is also called **centigrade.**

ce·ment (suh-ment) *noun*
1. A gray powder made from crushed limestone that is used in building and that becomes hard when you mix it with water and let it dry. Cement is used to make concrete.
2. A substance that joins two things together.
▷ *verb* **cement**

cem·e·ter·y (sem-uh-ter-ee) *noun* A place where

dead people are buried. ▷ *noun, plural* **cemeteries**

cen·sor (sen-sur)
1. *verb* To remove parts of a book, film, play, etc., thought to be harmful or offensive to the public. ▷ **censoring, censored** ▷ *noun* **censorship**
2. *noun* Someone whose job is to examine books, films, plays, etc., for objectionable parts.

cen·sus (sen-suhss) *noun* An official count of all the people living in a country or district.

cent (sent) *noun* A unit of money in the United States, Canada, Australia, and New Zealand. One hundred cents are equal to one dollar. **Cent** sounds like **scent** and **sent.**

cen·taur (sen-tor) *noun* A creature found in Greek and Roman myths that has the body and legs of a horse but the chest, arms, and head of a man.

cen·ten·ar·y (sen-ten-uh-ree) *noun* The 100th anniversary of something. ▷ *noun, plural* **centenaries** ▷ *adjective* **centenary**

cen·ten·ni·al (sen-ten-ee-uhl) *noun* The 100th-year celebration of an event. ▷ *adjective* **centennial**

cen·ter (sen-tur)
1. *noun* The middle of something.
2. *noun* A place where people go to do a particular activity, as in *an arts center.*
3. *verb* To concentrate on something. *The campaign centers on the problems of the elderly.* ▷ **centering, centered**
4. **center of gravity** *noun* The point on an object at which it can balance.

cen·ti·grade (sen-tuh-grayd) *adjective See* **Celsius.**

cen·ti·me·ter (sent-uh-*mee*-tur) *noun* A unit of length in the metric system. A centimeter is equal to $\frac{1}{100}$ of a meter. A pencil is approximately one centimeter wide.

cen·ti·pede (sen-ti-peed)
noun A small creature with a very long body and lots of legs. *The tropical giant centipede shown here is eight inches long.*

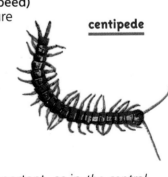

centipede

cen·tral (sen-truhl)
1. *adjective* In the middle. ▷ *adverb* **centrally**
2. *adjective* Most important, as in *the central problem.*
3. **central heating** *noun* A system for heating a building in which water or air is heated in one place and then carried in pipes all over the building.

cen·tri·fu·gal (sen-**trif**-yuh-guhl) *adjective* To do with a physical force that causes a body rotating around a center to move away from the center.

cen·trip·e·tal (sen-**trip**-uh-tuhl) *adjective* To do with the physical force that pulls a body toward a center it is rotating around.

cen·tu·ri·on (sen-**tur**-ee-uhn) *noun* An officer in the ancient Roman army who was in command of 100 soldiers.

centurion

- plumed helmet
- chain mail corselet
- dagger
- double-pleated kilt
- bronze greave (shin plate)
- woolen cloak
- decorated belt
- sword
- twisted vine rod

cen·tu·ry (sen-**chuh**-ree) *noun* A period of 100 years. ▷ *noun, plural* **centuries**

ce·ram·ics (suh-**ram**-iks)
1. *noun* The craft of making objects out of clay.
2. *noun, plural* Objects made of clay.
▷ *adjective* **ceramic**

ce·re·al (**sihr**-ee-uhl) *noun*
1. A grain crop grown for food, such as wheat, corn, rice, oats, and barley.
2. A breakfast food usually made from grain and eaten with milk.
Cereal sounds like **serial**.

cer·e·mo·ny (**ser**-uh-*moh*-nee) *noun* Formal actions, words, and often music performed to mark an important occasion, as in *a wedding ceremony*. ▷ *noun, plural* **ceremonies** ▷ *adjective* **ceremonial** ▷ *adverb* **ceremonially**

cer·tain (**sur**-tuhn) *adjective*
1. If you are **certain** about something, you are sure of it. *Ray was certain he had mailed the letter.* ▷ *noun* **certainty** ▷ *adverb* **certainly**
2. Particular. *The store is open at certain times.*

cer·tif·i·cate (sur-**tif**-uh-kit) *noun* A piece of paper that officially states that something is a fact. *A birth certificate states when and where you were born.*

CFC (see ef see) Short for **chlorofluorocarbon.**

chafe (chayf) *verb*
1. To make something raw or sore by rubbing. *The elastic chafed her wrists.*
2. To annoy. *The extra homework chafed.*
▷ *verb* **chafing, chafed**

chain (chayn) *noun*
1. A series of metal rings, called links, joined together.
2. A series of connected things, as in *a chain of events.*
3. chain store One of a group of stores in different towns that is owned by the same company and sells similar products.
▷ *verb* **chain**

chair (chair)
1. *noun* A piece of furniture that you sit on, with a seat, legs, and a back.
2. *noun* A chairman or a chairwoman.
3. *verb* To take charge of a meeting. ▷ **chairing, chaired**

chair·lift (**chair**-*lift*) *noun* A line of chairs attached to a moving cable, used for carrying people up mountains, usually to ski.

chair·man (**chair**-*man*) *noun* Someone, especially a man, who is in charge of a committee, company, or department in a school. ▷ *noun, plural* **chairmen**

chair·per·son (**chair**-*pur*-suhn) *noun* A chairman or a chairwoman.

chair·woman (**chair**-*wum*-uhn) *noun* A woman who is in charge of a committee, company, or department in a school. ▷ *noun, plural* **chairwomen**

cha·let (**shal**-ay *or* shal-**ay**) *noun* A small, wooden house with a sloping roof.

chalk (chawk) *noun*
1. A soft, white rock.
2. A stick of this material, used for writing on blackboards. ▷ *verb* **chalk**

chalk·board (**chawk**-*bord*) *noun* A hard, smooth, slate surface on which chalk is used; a blackboard.

chal·lenge (**chal**-uhnj)
1. *noun* Something difficult that requires extra work or effort to do. ▷ *adjective* **challenging**
2. *verb* If you **challenge** someone, you invite the person to fight or to try to do something.
3. *verb* If you **challenge** something, you question whether it is right or not. ▷ *noun* **challenge**
▷ *verb* **challenging, challenged**

C

cham·ber (chaym-bur) *noun*
1. A large room.
2. An enclosed space in a machine or an animal's body, as in *the four chambers of the human heart.*
3. **chamber music** Classical music for a small number of instruments.

cha·me·le·on (kuh-mee-lee-uhn) *noun* A lizard that can change color, sometimes matching its surroundings.

chameleon

cham·pagne (sham-payn) *noun* A fine white wine that has small bubbles.

cham·pi·on (cham-pee-uhn)
1. *noun* The winner of a competition or a tournament. ▷ *noun* **championship**
2. *verb* If someone **champions** a cause, he or she supports it. ▷ **championing, championed** ▷ *noun* **champion**

cham·pi·on·ship (cham-pee-uhn-ship) *noun* A contest or final game of a series that determines which team or player will be the overall winner.

chance (chanss) *noun*
1. The possibility of something happening. *We have a chance to win the championship.*
2. An opportunity to do something. *Warren has the chance to learn to ski.*
3. If you **take a chance,** you try something even though it is risky.
4. If something happens **by chance,** it happens accidentally.

chan·cel·lor (chan-suh-lur) *noun* A title for the leader of a country or a university.

chan·de·lier (shan-duh-lihr) *noun* A light fixture that hangs from the ceiling and is usually lit by many small lights. *We have a crystal chandelier over our dining room table.*

▶ **Word History**
. . . .
▶ The word **chandelier** was originally a French
▶ word meaning "something to hold candles," from
▶ the French word for candle, *chandelle*. Chandeliers
▶ today hold electric lights instead of candles.

change (chaynj)
1. *verb* To become different or to make different. *We changed the furniture in the living room.* ▷ *noun* **change**
2. *noun* If you pay more money than something costs, the money you get back is called **change**.
3. *noun* Coins rather than bills. *I have a dollar's worth of change in my pocket.*
4. *verb* To exchange. *Kia and I changed seats so we could share books with people who didn't have them.*
▷ *verb* **changing, changed**

chan·nel (chan-uhl) *noun*
1. A narrow stretch of water between two areas of land.
2. A television or radio station. *Our TV set receives over 100 channels.*

chant (chant) *verb* To say or sing a phrase over and over again. ▷ **chanting, chanted** ▷ *noun* **chant**

Cha·nu·kah (hah-nuh-kuh) *See* **Hanukkah.**

cha·os (kay-oss) *noun* Total confusion. ▷ *adjective* **chaotic** (kay-ot-ik) ▷ *adverb* **chaotically**

chap (chap)
1. *verb* To become rough or dry to the point of cracking, especially skin. *The hot sun chapped her lips.* ▷ **chapping, chapped** ▷ *adjective* **chapped**
2. *noun* A man or boy; a fellow.

chap·el (chap-uhl) *noun*
1. A small church.
2. A small, separate section of a large church or synagogue.
3. A place in a college, prison, etc., where religious services are held.

chap·lain (chap-lin) *noun* A priest, minister, or rabbi who works in the military, or in a school or prison. A chaplain leads religious services and counsels people.

chaps (chaps) *noun, plural* Leather leggings that fit over jeans or other pants and protect the legs of people riding on horseback.

chap·ter (chap-tur) *noun*
1. One of the parts into which a book is divided.
2. A branch of an organization. *Sonja is a member of the local chapter of the National Organization for Women.*

char·ac·ter (ka-rik-tur) *noun*
1. Your **character** is what sort of person you are.
2. One of the people in a story, book, play, movie, or television program.
3. A letter, figure, or other mark used in printing. All the letters of the alphabet are characters.

char·ac·ter·is·tic (*ka*-rik-tuh-**riss**-tik)
1. *noun* A typical quality or feature. *Curly hair is a characteristic of our family.*
2. *adjective* Typical. *Sandy worked with characteristic efficiency.*
▷ *adverb* **characteristically**

char·ac·ter·ize (ka-rik-tuh-rize) *verb*
1. To describe the individual qualities of something or someone. *He characterized my story as childish.*
2. To mark or identify the important qualities of someone or something.
▷ *verb* **characterizing, characterized**

char·coal (char-kole) *noun* A form of carbon made from incompletely burned wood. Charcoal is used in drawing pencils and as barbecue fuel.

charge (charj)
1. *verb* To ask someone to pay a particular price for something. *The store charges $3.00 a day to rent a video.*
2. *noun* The cost or price.
3. *verb* To rush at in order to attack. *The soldiers charged the fort.*
4. *noun* An attack.
5. *verb* To put off paying for something by using a credit card or signing an agreement. *We charged the dinner on Felix's credit card.*
6. *verb* To accuse. *Jana's boss charged her with spending too much time on the telephone.*
7. *noun* An accusation or statement of blame, as in *a charge of murder.*
8. *verb* When you **charge** a battery, you pass an electric current through it so that it stores electricity.
9. If someone is **in charge** of something, he or she has to manage it or take control of it.
▷ *verb* **charging, charged**

char·i·ot (cha-ree-uht) *noun* A small vehicle pulled by a horse, used in ancient times in battles or for racing. *The picture shows a Roman chariot.*

Roman chariot

cha·ris·ma (kuh-**riz**-muh) *noun* A powerful personal appeal that attracts a great number of people, as in *the charisma of a popular politician.*
▷ *adjective* **charismatic** (ka-riz-**mat**-ik)

char·i·ty (cha-ruh-tee) *noun*
1. An organization that raises money to help people in need.
2. Money or other help that is given to people in need.
▷ *noun, plural* **charities** ▷ *adjective* **charitable**

charm (charm)
1. *noun* If someone has **charm,** he or she behaves in a pleasing and attractive way. ▷ *noun* **charmer**
2. *verb* To please someone and make the person like you. ▷ **charming, charmed**
3. *noun* A small object that some people believe will bring them good luck. *This ancient Egyptian charm represents a sacred eye.*

Egyptian charm

charm·ing (charm-ing)
adjective Attractive, full of charm, or delightful.

chart (chart)
1. *noun* A drawing that shows information in the form of a table, graph, or picture.
2. *noun* A map of the stars or the oceans.
3. *verb* To show information in the form of a chart. ▷ **charting, charted**

char·ter (char-tur)
1. *noun* A formal document that states the rights or duties of a group of people.
2. *verb* To hire a bus, plane, etc., for private use. *The school chartered a bus for its annual trip.*
▷ **chartering, chartered**

chase (chayss) *verb* To run after someone in order to catch the person or make him or her go away. ▷ **chasing, chased** ▷ *noun* **chase**

chasm (kaz-uhm) *noun* A deep crack in the surface of the earth.

chas·sis (chass-ee *or* shass-ee) *noun* The frame on which the body of a vehicle is built. ▷ *noun, plural* **chassis**

chat (chat) *verb* To talk in a friendly and informal way. ▷ **chatting, chatted** ▷ *noun* **chat**

châ·teau (sha-toh)
noun A castle or large country house in France. *The picture shows a château in the Loire valley in France.*
▷ *noun, plural* **châteaux** (sha-**toh** *or* sha-**tohz**)

château

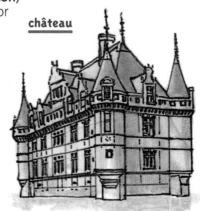

chat·ter (chat-ur) *verb*
1. To talk about unimportant things. ▷ *noun* **chatter**
2. When your teeth **chatter,** they knock together because you are cold.
▷ *verb* **chattering, chattered**

chauf·feur (shoh-fur) *noun* Someone whose job is to drive a car for somebody else. ▷ *verb* **chauffeur**

chau·vin·ist (shoh-vuh-nist) *noun* Someone who is overly proud of his or her nationality, gender, ethnic background, etc. ▷ *noun* **chauvinism**
▷ *adjective* **chauvinistic**

cheap (cheep) *adjective*
1. Not costing or worth very much. ▷ *noun* **cheapness** ▷ *adverb* **cheaply**
2. Unkind and mean. *That was a cheap trick you played on me.*
▷ *adjective* **cheaper, cheapest**

cheat (cheet)
1. *verb* To act dishonestly in order to win a game or get what you want. ▷ **cheating, cheated**
2. *noun* A person who acts dishonestly.

check (chek)
1. *verb* To look at something in order to make sure that it is all right.
2. *verb* To stop something from moving or growing. *We must check inflation.*
3. *noun* A pattern of squares of different colors.
▷ *adjective* **checked**
4. *noun* A printed piece of paper on which someone writes to tell the bank to pay money from his or her account.
5. *noun* A mark (✓) used to show that a thing has been looked at or verified. ▷ *verb* **check**
6. *verb* If you **check in,** you register for a room at a motel or hotel.
7. *verb* If you **check out,** you pay your bill at a motel or hotel and leave.
8. *verb* If you **check** your coat in a public place, you leave it with someone whose job is to guard it.
▷ *verb* **checking, checked**

check·ers (chek-urz) *noun* A game for two people with 12 round pieces each, played on a board marked with squares of alternating colors.

check·out (chek-out) *noun* The place in a supermarket where you pay for your purchases.

check·up (chek-uhp) *noun* A medical examination to make sure that there is nothing wrong with you.

cheek (cheek) *noun*
1. Either side of your face below your eyes.
2. Rude and disrespectful behavior or speech.
▷ *adjective* **cheeky** ▷ *adverb* **cheekily**

cheer (chihr)
1. *verb* To shout encouragement or approval.
2. *noun* A shout of encouragement.
3. *verb* If you **cheer up,** you begin to feel better.
4. *noun* Happiness.
5. If you **are of good cheer,** you are happy.
▷ *verb* **cheering, cheered**

cheer·ful (chihr-fuhl) *adjective* Happy and lively.
▷ *noun* **cheerfulness** ▷ *adverb* **cheerfully**

cheese (cheez) *noun* A food made from the solid parts of milk after the milk has turned sour.

chee·tah (chee-tuh) *noun* A wild cat with a spotted coat that is found in Africa and southern Asia. Cheetahs can run faster than any other land animal in short bursts.

cheetah

chef (shef) *noun* The chief cook in a restaurant.

chem·i·cal (kem-uh-kuhl)
1. *noun* A substance used in chemistry, as in *dangerous chemicals.*
2. *adjective* To do with or made by chemistry, as in *a chemical reaction.* ▷ *adverb* **chemically**

chem·ist (kem-ist) *noun* A person trained in chemistry.

chem·is·try (kem-is-tree) *noun* The scientific study of substances, what they are composed of, and the ways in which they react with each other.

che·mo·ther·a·py (*kee-moh-ther-uh-pee*) *noun* The use of chemicals to kill diseased cells in cancer patients. ▷ *noun* **chemotherapist**

cher·ish (cher-ish) *verb* To care for someone or something in a kind and loving way. ▷ **cherishes, cherishing, cherished**

Cher·o·kee (cher-uh-kee) *noun* A member of an American Indian nation that lives primarily in Oklahoma and North Carolina.

cher·ry (cher-ee) *noun*
1. A small, sweet, red fruit with a pit inside. *See* **fruit.** ▷ *noun, plural* **cherries**
2. A bright red color.

chess (chess) *noun* A game for two people with 16 pieces each, played on a board marked with squares of alternating colors. *See* **bishop**.

chess game

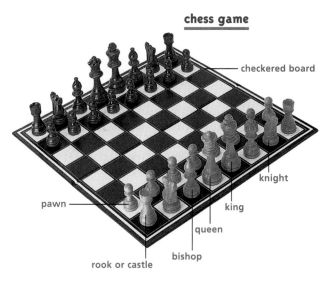

- checkered board
- knight
- pawn
- king
- queen
- bishop
- rook or castle

chest (chest) *noun*
1. The front part of your body between your neck and waist.
2. A large, strong box.

chest·nut (chess-*nuht*) *noun*
1. A large, reddish brown nut that grows in a prickly case.
2. A tree that produces chestnuts.
3. A reddish brown color.
▷ *adjective* **chestnut**

chest of drawers *noun* A piece of furniture with drawers, usually used for storing clothes.
▷ *noun, plural* **chests of drawers**

chew (choo) *verb* To grind food between your teeth. ▷ **chewing, chewed**

chewing gum *noun* A sweet, flavored substance that you chew for a long time but do not swallow.

Chey·enne (shye-en) *noun* A member of an American Indian nation that lives primarily in Montana and Oklahoma.

Chi·ca·na (chi-kah-nuh) *noun*
1. An American girl or woman born of Mexican parents; a Mexican American.
2. A Mexican woman living and working in the United States.
▷ *noun, plural* **Chicanas**

Chi·ca·no (chi-kah-noh) *noun*
1. An American boy or man born of Mexican parents; a Mexican American.
2. A Mexican man living and working in the United States.
▷ *noun, plural* **Chicanos**

chick (chik) *noun* A very young bird, especially a very young chicken, or a small lobster.

chick·a·dee (chik-uh-dee) *noun* One of a group of small birds with a black head and throat, gray wings, and white feathers on its underside. The call of the chickadee sounds like its name.

chick·en (chik-uhn) *noun*
1. A common type of fowl that is raised on farms for its meat and eggs.
2. The meat from this bird, used as food, as in *roast chicken*.
3. *(slang)* Someone who is too scared to do something.

chicken

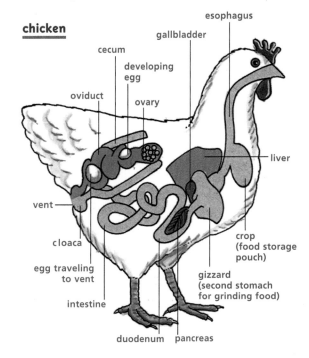

- esophagus
- gallbladder
- cecum
- developing egg
- oviduct
- ovary
- liver
- vent
- cloaca
- crop (food storage pouch)
- egg traveling to vent
- gizzard (second stomach for grinding food)
- intestine
- duodenum
- pancreas

chicken pox (poks) *noun* A common, contagious disease, especially among children, that causes red, itchy spots on the skin.

chick·pea (chick-*pea*) *noun* The edible seed of a plant originally grown in Asia. Chickpeas resemble peas in size and shape.

chide (chide) *verb* To scold or to find fault with someone. *My mother chided me for playing in the dirt.* ▷ **chiding, chided**

chief (cheef)
1. *noun* The leader of a group of people, as in *a chief of police*.
2. *adjective* Main, or most important. *A teacher's chief objective is to educate students.* ▷ *adverb* **chiefly**

chief·tain (cheef-tuhn) *noun* The chief or leader of a tribe, clan, or community.

chig·ger (chig-ur) *noun* A tiny insect that burrows under the skin, causing a rash and severe itching.

child (childe) *noun*
  1. A young boy or girl.
  2. A son or daughter. *The McKinleys have one child.*
  ▷ *noun, plural* **children** (chil-drin)

child·birth (childe-*burth*) *noun* The act or process of giving birth to a baby.

child·hood (childe-hud) *noun* The time when you are a child. *Marco had a happy childhood.*

child·ish (chile-dish) *adjective* Immature and silly, as in *childish behavior.* ▷ *noun* **childishness** ▷ *adverb* **childishly**

chill (chil)
  1. *verb* To make something cold. *If we chill the water, we won't need to use ice.* ▷ **chilling, chilled**
  2. *noun* A feeling of slight coldness. *There is a chill in the air.* ▷ *adjective* **chilly**
  3. *noun* A shiver you feel in your body, often related to fear. *I felt a chill go up my spine.* ▷ *adjective* **chilling**
  4. *adjective* Cool or cold. *A chill wind made us huddle together.* ▷ **chillier, chilliest**

chime (chime) *verb* When a bell or clock **chimes,** it makes a ringing sound. ▷ **chiming, chimed** ▷ *noun* **chime**

chim·ney (chim-nee) *noun* An upright pipe or hollow structure that carries smoke away from a fire. See **building.**

chim·pan·zee (*chim*-pan-zee *or* chim-**pan**-zee) *noun* A small ape with dark fur that comes from Africa. See **ape.**

chin (chin) *noun* The part of your face below your mouth.

chi·na (chye-nuh) *noun*
  1. Very thin, delicate pottery.
  2. Cups, plates, and dishes made of china. See **bowl.**

chin·chil·la (chin-chil-uh) *noun* A small South American rodent with silvery-gray fur.

chink (chingk) *noun* A narrow opening. *There was a chink in the old wall.*

chip (chip)
  1. *noun* A small piece of something that is cut or broken off.
  2. *verb* To break a small piece off something. *He chipped a tooth while eating.* ▷ *noun* **chip**
  3. If you have a **chip on your shoulder,** you feel angry because you think you have been treated unfairly.
  4. *verb* If you **chip in** with others to buy something, you give some money for it.
  5. *noun* A very thin slice of potato cooked in oil.
  6. *noun* A tiny piece of silicon with electronic circuits printed on it, used in computers and electronic equipment. *The magnified silicon chip*

shown here is small enough to fit on your fingernail.
  ▷ *verb* **chipping, chipped**

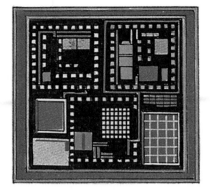

silicon chip
(magnified)

chip·munk (chip-*muhnk*) *noun* A small animal related to the squirrel that is found in North America. Chipmunks have brown fur and dark stripes on their backs and tails.

Chip·pe·wa (chip-uh-wah) *See* **Ojibwa.**

chi·ro·prac·tor (kye-roh-prak-tur) *noun* A person who treats back pain and other illnesses by adjusting the spine.

chirp (churp)
  1. *noun* The twittering sound a bird makes; the high sound an insect makes.
  2. *verb* To make such a sound. *My alarm clock chirps every morning at 7.* ▷ **chirping, chirped**

chis·el (chiz-uhl)
  1. *noun* A tool with a flat, sharp end used to cut or shape wood, stone, or metal.
  2. *verb* To chip away at something and form it into a desired shape. *The artist chiseled the stone until she had finished the sculpture.* ▷ **chiseling, chiseled**

chiv·al·ry (shiv-uhl-ree) *noun*
  1. Very polite and helpful behavior, especially by a man toward a woman.
  2. A code of noble and polite behavior that was expected of a medieval knight.
  ▷ *adjective* **chivalrous**

chlo·rine (klor-een) *noun* A gas with a strong smell that is added to water to kill harmful germs. ▷ *verb* **chlorinate** (klor-i-*nate*)

chlo·ro·fluor·o·car·bon (*klor*-oh-**flur**-oh-*kar*-buhn) *noun* Any of several gases containing carbon, chlorine, and fluorine that are suspected of damaging the earth's ozone layer. Chlorofluorocarbons were used in refrigerators and aerosol cans, but their use has been phased out since the 1980s. Also called CFC.

chlo·ro·phyll (klor-uh-fil) *noun* The green substance in plants that uses light to manufacture food from carbon dioxide and water.

choc·o·late (chok-uh-lit *or* chok-lit) *noun* A food, especially a candy, made from beans that grow on the tropical cacao tree. *The picture shows a cacao pod and some dried and roasted beans that can be ground up to make chocolate.* ▷ *adjective* **chocolate,** *adjective* **chocolaty**

cacao pod and beans

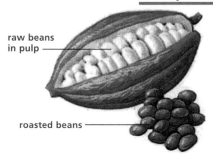

raw beans
in pulp

roasted beans

Choc·taw (chok-taw) *noun* A member of an American Indian nation that lives primarily in Oklahoma, Mississippi, and Louisiana. ▷ *noun, plural* **Choctaw** *or* **Choctaws**

choice (choiss)
1. *noun* The thing or person that has been selected. *Vinh was a good choice as team captain.*
2. *noun* All the things that you can choose from. *This menu offers a very wide choice.*
3. *noun* The chance to choose. *I have the choice of taking Spanish or French at school next year.*
4. *adjective* Of very good quality, as in *choice fruits and vegetables.*

choir (kwire) *noun* A group of people who sing together.

choke (chohk) *verb*
1. To struggle to breathe because something is blocking your breathing passages.
2. To cause someone to stop breathing by squeezing his or her neck.
3. To block something. *Leaves had choked the stream.*
4. To hold back. *Her father choked back his anger.*
▷ *verb* **choking, choked**

chol·e·ra (kol-ur-uh) *noun* A dangerous disease that causes severe sickness and diarrhea.

cho·les·ter·ol (kuh-less-tuh-*rol*) *noun* A fatty substance that humans and animals need to digest food and produce certain vitamins and hormones. Too much cholesterol in the blood can increase the possibility of heart disease.

choose (chooz) *verb*
1. To pick out one person or thing from several.
2. If you **choose** to do something, you decide to do it.
▷ *verb* **choosing, chose** (chohz)**, chosen** (chohz-in)

chop (chop)
1. *verb* To cut something with a knife or an axe. ▷ **chopping, chopped** ▷ *noun* **chop**
2. *noun* A small piece of lamb, veal, or pork with a rib bone attached.

chop·py (chop-ee) *adjective*
1. When the sea is **choppy,** it is quite rough.
2. A **choppy** sentence is expressed in a jerky, unclear style.
▷ *adjective* **choppier, choppiest**

chop·sticks (chop-*stiks*) *noun, plural* Narrow sticks for eating food, used primarily by people in Asian countries.

cho·ral (kor-uhl) *adjective* Sung by a choir, as in *choral music.* **Choral** sounds like **coral.**

chord (kord) *noun*
1. A combination of musical notes played at the same time. *See* **notation.**
2. A straight line that joins two points on a curve. *See* **circle.**
Chord sounds like **cord.**

chore (chor) *noun* A job that has to be done regularly, such as washing dishes or cleaning.

cho·re·og·ra·pher (*kor*-ee-og-ruh-fur) *noun* Someone who arranges dance steps and movements for a ballet or show. ▷ *noun* **choreography** ▷ *verb* **choreograph** (kor-ee-uh-*graph*)

cho·rus (kor-uhss) *noun*
1. The part of a song that is repeated after each verse.
2. A large group of people who sing or speak together. ▷ *noun, plural* **choruses**

chow·der (chou-dur) *noun* A thick soup made with clams or fish and vegetables.

Christ (kriste) *noun* Jesus, the figure that Christians worship as the son of God. *This mosaic of Christ was made in the 12th century.*

Christ

chris·ten·ing (kriss-uhn-ing) *noun* A ceremony in which a baby is given a name and accepted into the Christian religion. ▷ *verb* **christen**

Chris·ti·an·i·ty (*kriss*-chee-an-uh-tee) *noun* The religion based on the life and teachings of Jesus. Christians believe that Jesus is the son of God and that he died so that, after death, their souls would go to heaven. ▷ *noun* **Christian** ▷ *adjective* **Christian**

Christ·mas (kriss-muhss) *noun* The Christian festival on December 25 that celebrates the birth of Jesus. ▷ *noun, plural* **Christmases**

chro·ma·to·gra·phy (kroh-muh-**tog**-ruh-fee) **noun** The process of separating parts of a mixture by letting it travel through a material that absorbs each part at a different rate. *You can use chromatography to separate ink into chemicals of different colors.*

chro·mo·some (kroh-muh-*sohm*) **noun** The part of a cell that carries the genes that give living things their special characteristics. Chromosomes determine your hair color, eye color, size, etc., which you inherit from your parents.

chron·ic (**kron**-ik) **adjective** If something is **chronic,** it does not get better for a long time. *My grandfather has chronic bronchitis.* ▷ **adverb** **chronically**

chron·i·cle (**kron**-uh-kuhl) **verb** To record historical events in a careful, detailed way. ▷ **chronicling, chronicled** ▷ **noun** **chronicle**

chron·o·log·i·cal (kron-uh-**loj**-uh-kuhl) **adjective** Arranged in the order in which events happened. ▷ **noun** **chronology** (kruh-**nol**-uh-jee) ▷ **adverb** **chronologically**

chrys·a·lis (**kriss**-uh-liss) **noun** A butterfly at the stage of development between a caterpillar and an adult. A chrysalis is covered by a hard outer shell. *See* **caterpillar.** ▷ **noun, plural** **chrysalises**

chry·san·the·mum (kruh-**san**-thuh-muhm) **noun** A flower of various shapes and colors that has many usually small petals.

chub·by (**chuhb**-ee) **adjective** Slightly fat or plump. ▷ **chubbier, chubbiest**

chuck·le (**chuh**-kuhl) **verb** To laugh quietly. ▷ **chuckling, chuckled** ▷ **noun** **chuckle**

chuck·wag·on (**chuhk**-*wag*-uhn) **noun** A covered wagon that serves as a portable kitchen.

chug (**chuhg**) **verb** To make a heavy, regular, thumping sound while moving along. *The truck chugged slowly up the hill.* ▷ **chugging, chugged**

chum (**chuhm**) **noun** A friend, buddy, or pal.

chunk (**chuhngk**) **noun** A thick piece of something.

chunk·y (**chuhng**-kee) **adjective**
1. Full of chunks or pieces. *He likes smooth peanut butter; I like it chunky.*
2. Short and solid in build; stocky. *Jonathan was chunky as a kid but became a tall, lean adult.*
▷ **adjective** **chunkier, chunkiest**

church (**church**) **noun**
1. A building used by Christians for worship.
2. A group of Christians.
3. Christian religious services.
▷ **noun, plural** **churches**

churn (**churn**)
1. **noun** A machine or device in which milk is made into butter. *See* **butter.** ▷ **verb** **churn**

2. **verb** To move roughly. *The tractor churned the mud up.* ▷ **churning, churned**

chute (**shoot**) **noun** A narrow, tilted passage for goods, garbage, laundry, grain, or coal. **Chute** sounds like **shoot.**

chut·ney (**chut**-nee) **noun** A relish of vegetables, fruit, and spices.

ci·der (**sye**-dur) **noun** A beverage made by pressing apples.

ci·gar (si-**gar**) **noun** A thick, brown roll of tobacco that people smoke.

cig·a·rette or **cig·a·ret** (sig-uh-**ret**) **noun** A thin roll of tobacco covered with paper that people smoke.

cin·der (**sin**-dur) **noun** A small piece of wood or coal that has been partly burned.

cin·e·ma (**sin**-uh-muh) **noun**
1. A movie theater.
2. The film industry. ▷ **adjective** **cinematic**

cin·na·mon (**sin**-uh-muhn) **noun**
1. A spice that comes from the inner bark of a tropical tree. *See* **spice.**
2. A light reddish brown color. *The cat's fur is best described as cinnamon.*

cir·ca (**sur**-kuh) **preposition** The Latin word for "about." You can also write circa as "c." or "ca." *George Washington was born circa 1730.*

cir·cle (**sur**-kuhl)
1. **noun** A flat, perfectly round shape. *The diagrams below show parts of a circle and other geometric terms connected with circles.* ▷ **adjective** **circular** (**sur**-kyuh-lur)
2. **verb** To draw or make a circle around something. *Circle the correct answer. The plane circled the airport before coming in to land.* ▷ **circling, circled**
3. **noun** A group of people who all know each other. *Enrique has a wide circle of friends.*

parts of a circle

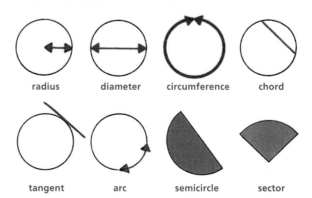

| radius | diameter | circumference | chord |
| tangent | arc | semicircle | sector |

cir·cuit (sur-kit) *noun*
1. A circular route.
2. The complete path that an electrical current can flow around.

circuit breaker *noun* A device that switches the electricity off when there is too much current in the system.

cir·cu·late (sur-kyuh-late) *verb*
1. To move in a circle or pattern. *If I turn on the fan, it will circulate the air in the room.*
2. To follow a course from place to place or person to person. *She circulated at the party and talked to every person there.*
▷ *verb* **circulating, circulated**

cir·cu·la·tion (*sur*-kyuh-**lay**-shuhn) *noun*
1. The movement of blood in blood vessels through the body. *Blood travels from the heart in arteries and returns to the heart in veins. It then travels to the lungs to collect oxygen before returning to the heart to be pumped around again. See also* **organ.**
▷ *adjective* **circulatory** (sur-kyuh-luh-*tor*-ee)
2. The number of copies of a newspaper, magazine, etc., that are bought each day, week, etc.

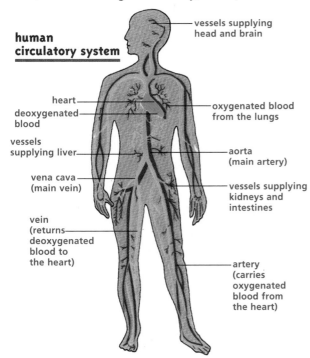

human circulatory system

vessels supplying head and brain

heart
deoxygenated blood

oxygenated blood from the lungs

vessels supplying liver

aorta (main artery)

vena cava (main vein)

vessels supplying kidneys and intestines

vein (returns deoxygenated blood to the heart)

artery (carries oxygenated blood from the heart)

cir·cum·fer·ence (sur-kuhm-fur-uhnss) *noun*
1. The outer edge of a circle or the length of this edge. *See* **circle.**
2. The distance around something. *We walked around the whole circumference of the ranch.*

cir·cum·spect (sur-kuhm-*spekt*) *adjective*
Cautious or careful, as in *a circumspect reply.*
▷ *noun* **circumspection** ▷ *adverb* **circumspectly**

cir·cum·stance (sur-kuhm-stanss) *noun* The **circumstances** of an event are the facts or conditions that are connected to it. *Laura took her exam under very difficult circumstances.*

cir·cus (sur-kuhss) *noun* A traveling show in which clowns, acrobats, and animals perform.
▷ *noun, plural* **circuses**

cis·tern (siss-turn) *noun* A reservoir or tank for storing water.

cite (site) *verb*
1. To quote from a written work. *My essay cited lines from the book* Black Beauty.
2. To give someone a commendation or medal. *He was cited for bravery for rescuing the baby from the pool.*
3. To use a thing or an event as proof of an argument. *He cited her many lies as proof of her poor character.*
▷ *verb* **citing, cited**
Cite sounds like **site** and **sight.**

cit·i·zen (sit-i-zuhn) *noun*
1. A member of a particular country who has the right to live there.
2. A resident of a particular town or city.

cit·i·zen·ship (sit-uh-zuhn-ship) *noun* The rights, privileges, and duties that come with being a citizen of a certain country.

cit·rus fruit (sit-ruhss) *noun* An acidic, juicy fruit such as an orange, a lemon, or a grapefruit.

cit·y (sit-ee) *noun* A very large or important town.
▷ *noun, plural* **cities**

> ### ▶ Word History
> •
> **City** comes to us from the older French word *cité.* Its Latin root is *civitas,* meaning "an organized community." You can see this same Latin root in the words *civilian* and *civilization.*

civ·ic (siv-ik) *adjective* To do with a city or the people who live in it, as in *civic pride.*

civ·ics (siv-iks) *noun* The study of being a good citizen of a community or country.

civ·il (siv-il)
1. *adjective* To do with the government or people of a country, rather than its army or religion, as in *civil service.*
2. *adjective* Polite. ▷ *noun* **civility** (si-vil-i-tee)
3. **civil rights** *noun, plural* The individual rights that all members of a society have to freedom and equal treatment under the law.
4. **civil servant** *noun* Someone who works in a government department.

ci·vil·ian (si-vil-yuhn) *noun* Someone who is not a member of the armed forces.

97

civ·i·li·za·tion (siv-i-luh-**zay**-shuhn) *noun*
1. An advanced stage of human organization, technology, and culture.
2. A highly developed and organized society, as in *the ancient civilizations of Greece and Rome.*

civ·i·lize (**siv**-i-lize) *verb*
1. To improve someone's manners and education.
2. To improve a society so that it is better organized and its people have a higher standard of living.
▷ *verb* **civilizing, civilized** ▷ *adjective* **civilized**

civil war *noun*
1. A war between different groups of people within the same country.
2. Civil War The U.S. war between the Confederacy, or southern states, and the Union, or northern states, that lasted from 1861–1865. *This painting by Frederick F. Cavada shows the Battle of Fredericksburg on December 15, 1862.*

Civil War battle

clad (klad) *verb* A past tense and past participle of **clothe.** *She was clad only in a light jacket and caught a cold.*

claim (klaym) *verb*
1. To say that something belongs to you or that you have a right to have it. *My sister claims credit for convincing Mom to take us to the circus.*
2. To say that something is true. *José claims he can beat me.*
▷ *verb* **claiming, claimed** ▷ *noun* **claim**

clam (klam) *noun* A shellfish with two tightly closed shells that are hinged together. The soft meat inside the shells can be eaten.

clam·bake (klam-bake) *noun* A party, often held at the beach, where clams are cooked on heated stones.

clamb·er (klam-bur) *verb* To climb quickly and awkwardly by using the hands and feet. *The hikers clambered up the rocky cliff.* ▷ **clambering, clambered**

clam·my (klam-ee) *adjective* Unpleasantly damp, as in *clammy hands.* ▷ **clammier, clammiest**

clam·or (klam-ur) *verb* To demand something noisily. *The children clamored for food.*
▷ **clamoring, clamored** ▷ *noun* **clamor**

clamp (klamp)
1. *noun* A tool for holding things firmly in place.
2. *verb* To fasten something with a clamp.
3. *verb* When you **clamp down** on something, you control it more firmly. *The police have clamped down on illegal parking.*
▷ *verb* **clamping, clamped**

clan (klan) *noun* A large group of families, especially in Scotland, who believe they all are descended from a common ancestor.

clap (klap)
1. *verb* To hit your hands together to show that you have enjoyed something or to get someone's attention. ▷ **clapping, clapped** ▷ *noun* **clap**
2. *noun* A loud bang of thunder.

clar·i·fy (kla-ruh-fye) *verb* To make something clear. ▷ **clarifies, clarifying, clarified** ▷ *noun* **clarification**

clar·i·net (klair-uh-net) *noun* A long, hollow woodwind instrument. A clarinet is played by blowing into a mouthpiece and pressing keys or covering holes with the fingers to change the pitch. *See* **orchestra.**

clar·i·ty (kla-ruh-tee) *noun* Clearness.

clash (klash) *verb*
1. To fight or argue vehemently.
2. If colors **clash,** they look unpleasant together.
3. To make a loud, crashing noise. *The cymbals clashed.*
▷ *verb* **clashes, clashing, clashed** ▷ *noun* **clash**

clasp (klasp)
1. *verb* To hold firmly and tightly. *Dawn clasped Gary's hand as they approached the cave.*
▷ **clasping, clasped**
2. *noun* A small fastener. *Inéz couldn't close her suitcase because the clasp was broken.*

class (klass) *noun*
1. A group of people who are taught together, as in *a fifth grade class.*
2. A group of people or things that are similar, as in *a class of automobiles.*
3. A group of people in society with a similar way of life or range of income, as in *the middle class.*
4. (*informal*) Attractiveness and style. *That outfit has class.*
▷ *noun, plural* **classes**

clas·sic (klass-ik)
1. *adjective* Of very good quality and likely to remain popular for a long time, as in *a classic movie.*
2. *adjective* Typical. *This pair of sandals is a classic example of summer shoes.*

3. classics *noun, plural* The languages and literature of ancient Greece and Rome.

clas·si·cal (klass-uh-kuhl) *adjective*
1. In the style of ancient Greece or Rome, as in *classical architecture.*
2. Traditional or accepted.
3. Classical music is timeless, serious music in the European tradition, such as opera, chamber music, and symphony.

clas·si·fied (klass-uh-fide) *adjective*
1. Declared secret by the government, as in *classified information.*
2. A **classified** advertisement in a newspaper is a small ad for a job or item on sale listed in columns according to the subject.

clas·si·fy (klass-uh-fye) *verb* To put things into groups according to their characteristics.
▷ **classifies, classifying, classified** ▷ *noun* **classification**

class·mate (klass-*mate*) *noun* Someone who is in the same class as another.

class·room (klass-*room*) *noun* A room in a school in which classes take place.

clas·sy (klass-ee) *adjective (informal)* Attractive and stylish.

clat·ter (klat-ur) *verb* When things **clatter,** they bang together noisily. ▷ **clattering, clattered**
▷ *noun* **clatter**

clause (klawz) *noun*
1. A group of words that contains a subject and a predicate and forms a sentence or one part of a sentence. *The sentence "She ran away when she saw the fire" is made up of two clauses: "She ran away" and "when she saw the fire."*
2. One section of a formal legal document.

claus·tro·pho·bi·a (*klawss*-truh-**foh**-bee-uh) *noun* The fear of being in small, enclosed places. ▷ *adjective* **claustrophobic**

claw (klaw)
1. *noun* A hard, curved nail on the foot of an animal or a bird.
2. *verb* To scratch with nails or claws. *The lion clawed at the bars of the cage.* ▷ **clawing, clawed**

clay (klay) *noun* A kind of earth that can be shaped when wet and baked to make bricks or pottery.

clean (kleen)
1. *adjective* Not dirty or messy. ▷ *noun* **cleanness**
▷ *adverb* **cleanly**
2. *adjective* Fair, or obeying the rules. *The politician ran a clean campaign.*
3. *verb* To remove the dirt from something.
▷ **cleaning, cleaned**
▷ *noun* **cleaner** ▷ *adjective* **cleaner, cleanest**

clean·li·ness (klen-lee-niss) *noun* Cleanness. *Cleanliness is important for good health.*

cleanse (klenz) *verb* To make something clean or pure. ▷ **cleansing, cleansed**

cleans·er (klen-zur) *noun* A powder or liquid used to clean or scrub things.

clear (klihr)
1. *adjective* Easy to see through.
2. *verb* To make or become bright. *The sky cleared.*
3. *adjective* Bright; not dark or cloudy, as in *clear skies.*
4. *adjective* Easy to understand, as in *clear instructions.*
5. *verb* To remove things that are covering or blocking a place. *Clear the table.*
6. *verb* To jump over something without touching it. *The horse cleared all the fences.*
7. *verb* To declare that someone is not guilty of a crime. *The jury cleared her of all charges.*
8. *adjective* Free from worry or guilt, as in *a clear conscience.*
9. *adverb* In a clear way; distinctly. *Say it loud and clear.*
▷ *verb* **clearing, cleared** ▷ *noun* **clearness**
▷ *adjective* **clearer, clearest** ▷ *adverb* **clearly**

clear·ance (klihr-uhnss) *noun*
1. The act of clearing.
2. Permission to do something.
3. The space between two objects such that neither object will touch the other. *There was no clearance between the truck and the roof of the tunnel.*

clear·ing (klihr-ing) *noun* An area of a forest or woods from which trees have been removed.

clef (klef) *noun* A symbol written at the beginning of a line of music to show the pitch of the notes, as in *bass clef; treble clef.* See **notation**.

cleft (kleft) *noun*
1. A split or division. *Moss grew in a cleft in the rock.*
2. An indentation something like a dimple. *Uncle Max has a cleft in his chin.*

clench (klench) *verb* To hold or squeeze something tightly. ▷ **clenches, clenching, clenched**

cler·gy (klur-jee) *noun* A group of people trained to conduct religious services, such as priests, ministers, and rabbis. ▷ *noun, plural* **clergies**

cl·er·i·cal (kler-i-kuhl) *adjective*
1. To do with the clergy.
2. Clerical work is general office work, such as filing.

clerk (klurk) *noun*
1. A salesperson in a store.
2. Someone who keeps records in an office, a bank, or a law court.

C

clev·er (klev-ur) *adjective*
1. Able to understand things or do things quickly and easily. *Ann is a clever math student.*
2. Intelligently and carefully thought out, as in *a clever plan.*
▷ *adjective* **cleverer, cleverest** ▷ *noun* **cleverness**
▷ *adverb* **cleverly**

cli·ché (klee-shay) *noun* An idea or a phrase that is used so often that it no longer has very much meaning. *"We're all in the same boat" is a cliché.*

click (klik) *verb*
1. To make a short, sharp sound. ▷ *noun* **click**
2. *(informal)* If an idea **clicks,** it suddenly becomes clear to you.
▷ *verb* **clicking, clicked**

cli·ent (klye-uhnt) *noun* Someone who uses the services of a professional person such as a lawyer or an accountant.

cliff (klif) *noun* A high, steep rock face. *From the cliff, we could see the valley below.*

cliff·hang·er (hang-ur) *noun* A story, movie, or television program presented in several parts that is exciting because each part ends at a moment of suspense.

cli·mate (klye-mit) *noun*
1. The usual weather in a place, as in *a warm climate.* ▷ *adjective* **climatic** (klye-mat-ik)
2. The general situation or mood at a particular time, as in *a positive climate for change.*

cli·max (klye-maks) *noun* The most exciting part of a story or an event, usually happening near the end. ▷ *noun, plural* **climaxes**

climb (klime)
1. *verb* To move upward. ▷ *noun* **climber**
2. *noun* An upward movement or slope.
3. *verb* To go in various directions using your hands to support and help you. *We climbed down the stairs.*
▷ *verb* **climbing, climbed**

clinch (klinch) *verb* To settle a matter once and for all. ▷ *verb* **clinches, clinching, clinched**

cling (kling) *verb* To stick to or hold on to something or someone very tightly. ▷ **clinging, clung** (kluhng)

clin·ic (klin-ik) *noun* A room or building where people can go for medical treatment or advice, as in *a dental clinic* or *an emergency clinic.*

clip (klip)
1. *verb* To attach things together with a small fastener.
2. *noun* A small metal or plastic fastener.
3. *verb* To trim something, as in *to clip the hedges.*
4. *noun* A short piece of a movie or television program shown by itself.
▷ *verb* **clipping, clipped**

clip art *noun* Images or pictures that are stored on disk in a computer for use in illustrating a document.

clip·board (klip-bord) *noun* A board with a clip at the top for holding papers.

clip·per (klip-ur) *noun*
1. A tool that clips something, such as hedges or fingernails.
2. A fast sailing ship with three masts, built in the United States in the 1800s and used to carry cargo.

clip·ping (klip-ing) *noun* Something clipped or cut from something else, as in *a magazine clipping* or *grass clippings.*

clique (kleek) *noun* A small group of people who are very friendly with each other and do not easily accept others into their group. ▷ *adjective* **cliquish**

cloak (klohk) *noun*
1. A loose coat with no sleeves that you wrap around your shoulders and fasten at the neck.
2. cloakroom (klohk-room) A room where you can hang coats and store umbrellas, hats, and bags.

clob·ber (klob-ur) *verb (slang)* To hit someone or something hard. ▷ **clobbering, clobbered**

clock (klok)
1. *noun* An instrument that tells the time. *The picture shows the main working parts of a spring-driven clock. When you wind the clock, you tighten the mainspring, which unwinds very slowly. Energy from the mainspring is transferred to the hour and minute hands by a series of wheels. The escape wheel keeps the clock ticking regularly.*
2. *verb* To measure the time or speed of something, as in *to clock a race.*

spring-driven clock

balance — hairspring — platform — escape wheel — minute-hand square — intermediate wheel — minute hand — center post — hour wheel — great wheel — hour hand — mainspring — barrel

clock·wise (klok-wize) *adverb* In the direction that the hands of a clock move. *We ran clockwise around the track.* ▷ *adjective* **clockwise**

clock·work (klok-wurk) *noun*
1. A mechanism with gears, springs, and wheels that makes things such as clocks and toys work. ▷ *adjective* **clockwork**
2. If things go **like clockwork,** there are no problems.

clod (klod) *noun*
1. A lump of earth or clay.
2. A dull or awkward person.

clog (klog)
1. *verb* To block something. *Some leaves had clogged the drain.* ▷ **clogging, clogged**
2. *noun* A heavy wooden shoe, often worn in the Netherlands.

clois·ter (kloi-stur) *noun*
1. A place where nuns and monks live; a convent or monastery.
2. A covered walk with columns along the wall of a convent, monastery, or other building.

Dutch clogs

clone (klohn) *verb* To grow a plant or an animal from the cells of a parent plant or animal so that it is identical to the parent. ▷ **cloning, cloned** ▷ *noun* **clone**

close
1. (klohz) *verb* To shut something. *Please close the window.*
2. (klohz) *verb* To end something. *The police have closed the investigation.* ▷ *noun* **close**
3. (klohss) *adverb* Near. *Stay close to me!* ▷ *adjective* **close**
4. (klohss) *adjective* Careful. *Keep a close watch on the children.* ▷ *adverb* **closely**
5. (klohss) *adjective* When the weather is **close,** it is very hot and humid.
6. (klohss) *adjective* Almost even. *The race was close, but Jeremy won.*
▷ *verb* **closing, closed** ▷ *adjective* **closer, closest, adjective closed** ▷ *adverb* **closer, closest**

closed-circuit television *noun* A television system that shows images or pictures to a limited number of television screens.

clos·et (kloz-it) *noun* A small room used for storing things, especially clothes.

close-up (klohss) *noun* A very detailed view of something, especially a camera shot taken at close range. *The actress applied fresh makeup before posing for her close-up.* ▷ *adjective* **close-up**

clot (klot) *verb* When a liquid, such as blood, **clots,** it becomes thicker and more solid. ▷ **clotting, clotted** ▷ *noun* **clot**

cloth (kloth *or* klawth) *noun*
1. Material made from wool, cotton, etc.
2. A small piece of material used for cleaning or some other purpose.

clothe (klohTH) *verb* To dress or provide with clothing. *The woman clothed her baby in expensive dresses.* ▷ **clothing, clothed**

clothes (klohz) *noun, plural* Things that you wear; for example, shirts, pants, and dresses.

clothes·pin (klohz-pin) *noun* A wood or plastic clip used to hold freshly washed or wet clothes on a line while they dry.

cloth·ing (kloh-THing) *noun* Garments worn to cover the body; clothes.

cloud (kloud)
1. *noun* A white or gray mass of water drops or ice crystals suspended in the air. *The picture shows different types of clouds and their approximate levels in the sky.*
2. *noun* A mass of smoke or dust.
3. *verb* If something **clouds over,** it becomes less easy to see through. ▷ **clouding, clouded**

cloud·burst (kloud-burst) *noun* A sudden, heavy rain shower.

cloud·y (kloud-ee) *adjective*
1. Covered with clouds.
2. Not clear. *The water looked cloudy, so it did not seem safe to drink.*
▷ *adjective* **cloudier, cloudiest**

clouds

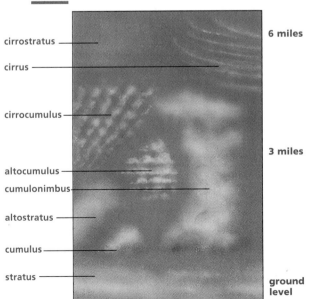

6 miles
cirrostratus
cirrus
cirrocumulus
3 miles
altocumulus
cumulonimbus
altostratus
cumulus
stratus
ground level

C

clove (klove) *noun*
1. The dried flower bud of a tropical tree, used whole or ground up as a spice in cooking. *See* **spice.**
2. One of the sections of a bulb of garlic.

clo·ver (kloh-vur) *noun* A small plant with pink or white flowers and leaves usually divided into three parts. *Clovers with four leaves are rare and are believed to be lucky.*

clown (kloun)
1. *noun* An entertainer who wears funny clothes, has a painted face, and tries to make people laugh.
2. *noun* Someone who does silly or foolish things.
3. *verb* To do silly things in order to make people laugh. *Antonia is always clowning around.*
▷ **clowning, clowned**

club (kluhb) *noun*
1. A group of people who meet regularly to enjoy a common interest.
2. The place where a group meets to share a common interest.
3. A stick with a metal or wooden head used in the game of golf. *See* **golf.**
4. A thick, heavy stick used as a weapon. ▷ *verb* **club**
5. **clubs** *noun, plural* One of the four suits in a deck of cards, with a black symbol having three leaves.

clue (kloo) *noun* Something that helps you find an answer to a question or a mystery.

clump (kluhmp)
1. *noun* A group of trees, other plants, or dirt.
2. *verb* To walk slowly, with clumsy, noisy footsteps. *Kumar clumped up the stairs and woke everyone up.* ▷ **clumping, clumped** ▷ *noun* **clump**

clum·sy (kluhm-zee) *adjective* Careless and awkward in the way that you move or behave. *Grace felt particularly clumsy after dropping an entire stack of dishes.* ▷ **clumsier, clumsiest** ▷ *noun* **clumsiness** ▷ *adverb* **clumsily**

clus·ter (kluhss-tur) *verb* To stand or grow close together. *The flowers clustered around the tree.* ▷ **clustering, clustered** ▷ *noun* **cluster**

clutch (kluhch)
1. *verb* To hold onto something tightly. *Kevin's knuckles were white from clutching his baseball bat so tightly.*
▷ **clutches, clutching, clutched** ▷ *noun* **clutch**
2. *noun* The pedal or lever of some cars and other vehicles that you press to change gears in a motor.

clut·ter (kluht-ur) *verb* To fill up a place and make it messy. ▷ **cluttering, cluttered** ▷ *noun* **clutter**

co. Short for **company.**

coach (kohch)
1. *verb* To train someone in a subject or a sport. *My brother coaches our school basketball team.*
▷ **coaches, coaching, coached** ▷ *noun* **coach**
2. *noun* A large carriage pulled by horses. *See* **stagecoach.**
3. *noun* A section of passenger seats on a bus, a train, or an airplane that are less expensive than first class.
4. *noun* A bus or railroad passenger car.
▷ *noun, plural* **coaches**

> **Word History**
> •
> Before cars and planes, the fastest way around was by **coach**—either pulled by horses or powered by steam. The word comes from *Kocs,* the name of a village in Hungary where such carriages originated. Some language specialists believe that the word has come to mean "tutor" or "trainer" because the coach was an instructor who brought his pupils along in the fastest way possible.

coal (kohl) *noun*
1. A black mineral formed from the remains of ancient plants. Coal is mined underground and burned as a fuel.
2. A small piece of coal.
3. A piece of burned wood.

co·a·li·tion (koh-uh-lish-uhn) *noun* When two or more groups form a **coalition,** they join together for a common purpose.

coarse (korss) *adjective*
1. If something is **coarse,** it has a rough texture or surface.
2. If a person is **coarse,** he or she is rude and has bad manners.
3. Having large particles; not fine. *I like to cook with coarse salt.*
Coarse sounds like **course.**
▷ *adjective* **coarser, coarsest** ▷ *noun* **coarseness** ▷ *adverb* **coarsely**

coast (kohst)
1. *noun* The land that is next to the sea.
▷ *adjective* **coastal**
2. *verb* To move along in a car or other vehicle without using any power.
3. *verb* To make progress without much effort. *Sam coasted through his exams.*
▷ *verb* **coasting, coasted**

coast guard (kohst *gard*) *noun* The branch of a nation's armed forces that watches the sea for ships in danger and protects the coastline.

coast·line (kohst-*line*) *noun* The place where the land and the ocean meet; the outline of the coast.

coat (koht)
1. *noun* A piece of clothing that you wear over other clothes to keep you warm.
2. *noun* An animal's fur or wool.
3. *noun* A thin layer. *There was a coat of ice on the trees.*
4. *verb* To cover a surface with a thin layer of something. ▷ **coating, coated**

coat·ing (koht-ing) *noun* A layer that is covering something, as in *a coating of dust.*

coat of arms *noun* A design in the shape of a shield that is used as the special sign of a family, a city, or an organization. ▷ *noun, plural* **coats of arms**

Royal coat of arms

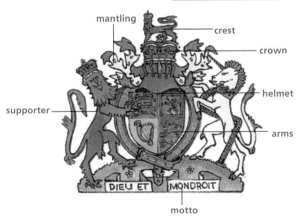

mantling
crest
crown
helmet
supporter
arms
DIEU ET MONDROIT
motto

coax (kohks) *verb* To persuade someone gently and patiently to do something. *We've coaxed Jacqui into staying for supper.* ▷ **coaxes, coaxing, coaxed** ▷ *adjective* **coaxing** ▷ *adverb* **coaxingly**

cob (kob) *noun* The center part of an ear of corn on which the kernels grow.

co·balt (koh-bahlt) *noun*
1. A silver-white chemical element used to make alloys and paints.
2. A deep blue color. ▷ *adjective* **cobalt**

cob·bler (kob-lur) *noun*
1. Someone who makes or repairs shoes.
2. A dessert made of fruit, with a top crust.

cob·ble·stone (kob-uhl-*stone*) *noun* A flat, round gray rock once used to pave roads and driveways. ▷ *adjective* **cobbled**

co·bra (koh-bruh) *noun* A large, poisonous snake that when excited rears up and spreads its skin so that its head and neck look like a hood. It can be as long as seven feet.

cob·web (kob-*web*) *noun* A very fine net of sticky threads made by a spider to catch flies and other insects.

co·caine (koh-kayn) *noun* A powerful drug used medically to block pain. Cocaine is dangerous and is used illegally by some people.

cock (kok)
1. *noun* A fully grown male chicken.
2. *noun* A male bird.
3. *verb* To turn up to one side. *When she heard her name, Chana cocked her head.* ▷ **cocking, cocked**

cock·a·too (kok-uh-too) *noun* A white parrot with a crest of feathers, found in Asia and Australia.

cock·er spaniel (kok-ur) *noun* A popular breed of small dog, with a long, silky coat and long ears.

cock·le (kok-uhl) *noun* An edible shellfish shaped like a heart.

cock·pit (kok-*pit*) *noun* The area in the front of a plane or boat where the pilot sits. *See* **rescue.**

cock·roach (kok-*rohch*) *noun* A brown or black insect that lives in warm, dark places and is a household pest. *See* **insect.**

cock·tail (kok-*tayl*) *noun*
1. A drink made by mixing several different kinds of liquids together. Cocktails are usually alcoholic.
2. Seafood or fruit served at the start of a meal, as in *a shrimp cocktail.*

cock·y (kok-ee) *adjective* (*informal*) Too sure of oneself; self-confident to the point of being unpleasant. *Hannah was accused of acting a bit too cocky when she started bragging about her perfect report card.* ▷ **cockier, cockiest**

co·coa (koh-koh) *noun*
1. A brown powder made from the roasted beans of the cacao tree and used to make chocolate. *See* **chocolate.**
2. A hot drink made with cocoa powder, sugar, and milk or water.

co·co·nut (koh-kuh-*nuht*) *noun* A very large nut with a hard, hairy shell and sweet, white meat that is often shredded for use as food.

co·coon (kuh-**koon**) *noun* A covering made from silky threads produced by some animals to protect themselves or their eggs.

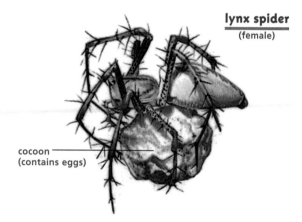

lynx spider
(female)

cocoon
(contains eggs)

C.O.D. (**cee oh dee**) An abbreviation meaning *cash on delivery;* a way to send packages so that the receiver must pay for the merchandise when it is delivered.

cod (kod) *noun* A fish that is found in the northern Atlantic Ocean and that has white meat that you can eat. ▷ *noun, plural* **cod**

code (kode) *noun*
1. A system of words, letters, symbols, or numbers used instead of ordinary words to send messages or store information, as in *a secret code.* ▷ *verb* **code** ▷ *adjective* **coded**
2. A set of rules, as in *a safety code.*

co·ed·u·ca·tion (*koh*-ej-uh-**kay**-shuhn) *noun* The system of teaching boys and girls together in the same school. ▷ *adjective* **coeducational**

co·erce (koh-**urss**) *verb* To force someone to do something. ▷ **coercing, coerced** ▷ *noun* **coercion**

cof·fee (**kaw**-fee *or* **kof**-ee) *noun*
1. A hot drink made from the roasted and ground beans of the coffee shrub.
2. Ground coffee beans used to make coffee.

cof·fin (**kawf**-in) *noun* A long container into which a dead person is placed for burial.

cog (kog) *noun*
1. One of the teeth on the edge of a wheel that turns machinery.
2. **cog·wheel** (**kog**-*weel*) A wheel with teeth that turns machinery. See **gear.**

co·her·ent (koh-**hihr**-uhnt) *adjective* Clear and logical, as in *a coherent argument.*

coil (koil)
1. *verb* To wind something around and around into a series of loops. *The sailor coiled the rope neatly.*
2. *noun* A loop or series of loops.

3. *verb* To wind or wrap around something. *The snake coiled around Evan's leg.*
▷ *verb* **coiling, coiled**

coin (koin)
1. *noun* A small piece of metal stamped with a design and used as money. ▷ *verb* **coin**
2. *verb* To invent a new word or a new meaning of a word.
▷ **coining, coined**
▷ *noun* **coinage**

ancient Chinese coins

co·in·cide (koh-in-**side**) *verb* If two things **coincide,** they happen at the same time.
▷ **coinciding, coincided**

co·in·ci·dence (koh-**in**-si-duhnss) *noun* A chance happening or meeting. ▷ *adjective* **coincidental** (*koh*-in-si-**den**-tuhl) ▷ *adverb* **coincidentally**

col·an·der (**kol**-uhn-dur) *noun* A kitchen utensil with holes, used for draining liquid off foods.

cold (kohld)
1. *adjective* Having a low temperature. ▷ *noun* **cold**
2. *noun* A common mild illness that causes sneezes, a sore throat, and sometimes a cough and a slight fever.
3. *adjective* Unfriendly. *My attempt to be friendly was met with a cold stare.* ▷ *noun* **coldness**
▷ *adverb* **coldly** ▷ *adjective* **colder, coldest**

▶ **Synonyms: cold**

Cold describes anything that is not as warm as you expect it to be or that is not as warm as your body temperature: *It seemed warm in the sun and cold in the shade.*

Chilly means cold enough to be unpleasant: *She wrapped her coat tightly around her in the chilly evening air.*

Icy means covered with ice, or extremely cold to the touch: *During the snowstorm, the windshield became icy.* Icy can also refer to an attitude that is distant and hostile: *He looked at his enemy with an icy stare.*

Freezing means so cold that you are really uncomfortable: *With the heat turned down, we were freezing when we got up this morning.*

Frozen, in its original sense, means at or below the freezing point of 32 degrees Fahrenheit, as in *frozen yogurt.* In another sense it can mean extremely cold: *My hands are frozen.*

cold-blood·ed (bluhd-id) *adjective*
1. Cold-blooded animals have body temperatures that change according to the temperature of their surroundings. *Reptiles and fish are cold-blooded.*
2. A **cold-blooded** act is done deliberately and cruelly.

cole·slaw (kohl-*slaw*) *noun* A salad made up of shredded cabbage mixed with a dressing of vinegar and other ingredients.

col·i·se·um (kol-i-see-uhm) *noun* A large stadium or auditorium for sports or other events.

col·lab·o·rate (kuh-lab-uh-rate) *verb* To work together to do something. ▷ **collaborating, collaborated** ▷ *noun* **collaboration,** *noun* **collaborator**

col·lage (kuh-lahzh) *noun* A picture made by fixing different things onto a surface, such as pieces of cloth onto paper.

col·lapse (kuh-laps) *verb*
1. To fall down suddenly from weakness or illness. *The apartment building collapsed after the earthquake. The dancer collapsed after the performance.*
2. To fail suddenly and completely. *The bank collapsed because of the president's actions.*
▷ *verb* **collapsing, collapsed** ▷ *noun* **collapse**

col·lar (kol-ur)
1. *noun* The part of a shirt, blouse, coat, etc., that fits around your neck and is usually folded down.
2. *noun* A thin band of material worn around the neck of a dog or cat.
3. *verb* To catch someone. *The police officer collared the pickpocket.* ▷ **collaring, collared**

col·lards (kol-urdz) *noun, plural* The green leaves of a vegetable related to cabbage, popular in the southern United States.

col·league (kol-eeg) *noun* Someone who works with you.

col·lect (kuh-lekt) *verb*
1. To gather things together.
2. To ask for payment for something bought or delivered.
▷ *verb* **collecting, collected**

col·lec·tion (kuh-lek-shuhn) *noun*
1. A group of things gathered over a long time, as in *a shell collection.*
2. If you **take up a collection** for something, you gather money for it.

col·lege (kol-ij) *noun* A place of higher learning where students can continue to study after they have finished high school.

col·lide (kuh-lide) *verb* To crash together forcefully, often at high speed. *The cars collided.*
▷ **colliding, collided** ▷ *noun* **collision**

col·lie (kol-ee) *noun* A breed of large dog with a long nose, a narrow head, and a thick coat. *See* **dog.**

col·lier·y (kol-yur-ee) *noun* A coal mine. ▷ *noun, plural* **collieries**

col·lo·qui·al (kuh-loh-kwee-uhl) *adjective* **Colloquial** language is used in everyday informal conversation.

co·lon (koh-luhn) *noun*
1. The punctuation mark (:) used to introduce a list of things.
2. The part of your large intestine where partially digested food is broken down by bacteria and has water removed from it. *See* **digestion.**

colo·nel (kur-nuhl) *noun* An officer in the army, air force, or Marine Corps ranking below a general.

col·o·nist (kol-uh-nist) *noun* Someone who lives in a newly settled area.

col·o·nize (kol-uh-nize) *verb* To establish a new colony in. ▷ **colonizing, colonized**

col·o·ny (kol-uh-nee) *noun*
1. A group of people who leave their country to settle in a new area.
2. A territory that has been settled by people from another country and is controlled by that country. ▷ *adjective* **colonial** (kuh-loh-nee-uhl)
3. A large group of insects that live together, as in *a colony of ants.*
▷ *noun, plural* **colonies**

col·or (kuhl-ur)
1. *noun* A property of an object that reflects light of a certain wavelength. The eye perceives such light as being red, yellow, blue, etc.
▷ *adjective* **colorful,** *adjective* **colorless**
2. *verb* To make something red, yellow, black, etc. *Timmy colored the flower red.* ▷ **coloring, colored**
3. *noun* The appearance of a person's skin. *You have good color since you returned from the beach.*
4. *adjective* If you are **color-blind,** you are unable to see the difference between certain colors. *You may not be able to see the number in this pattern if you are color-blind.*

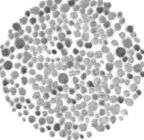

color-blindness test

col·or·ing (kuhl-ur-ing) *noun*
1. The way in which something is colored.
2. Something used to color something else.

col·or·ize (kuhl-ur-ize) *verb* To add color, usually to motion pictures, using a computer.
▷ **colorizing, colorized** ▷ *noun* **colorization**

co·los·sal (kuh-**loss**-uhl) *adjective* Extremely large.

colt (kohlt) *noun* A young horse, donkey, or zebra, especially a male.

col·um·bine (**kol**-uhm-bine) *noun* A tall flower with long, narrow petals.

Co·lum·bus Day (kuh-**luhm**-buhss) *noun* A holiday, the second Monday in October, celebrating Christopher Columbus's arrival in North America in 1492.

col·umn (**kol**-uhm) *noun*
1. A tall, upright pillar that helps support a building or statue. *The picture below shows three styles of Greek columns.*
2. A row of numbers or words running down a page.
3. A piece of writing by the same person, or on the same subject, that appears regularly in a newspaper or magazine. ▷ *noun* **columnist**

Greek columns

| Doric | Ionic | Corinthian |

co·ma (**koh**-muh) *noun* A state of deep unconsciousness from which it is very hard to wake up.

comb (kohm)
1. *noun* A flat piece of metal or plastic with a row of teeth, used for making your hair smooth and neat.
2. *verb* To use a comb to make your hair smooth and neat.
3. *verb* To search a place thoroughly.
4. *noun* The brightly colored crest on the head of a rooster or a related bird.
▷ *verb* **combing, combed**

com·bat (**kom**-bat)
1. *noun* Fighting between people or armies.
2. *verb* To fight against something. *Regular brushing helps combat tooth decay.* ▷ **combating, combated** or **combatting, combatted**

com·bine (kuhm-**bine**) *verb* To join or mix two or more things together. ▷ **combining, combined** ▷ *noun* **combination**

com·bus·ti·ble (kuhm-**buhss**-tuh-buhl) *adjective* Capable of catching fire. *Dry leaves are combustible.*

com·bus·tion (kuhm-**buss**-chuhn) *noun* The process of catching fire and burning.

come (kuhm) *verb*
1. To move toward a place. *I saw Louise come into the garden.*
2. To arrive. *Derrick was waiting for his friends to come.*
3. If you **come from** a particular place, you were born in that place.
4. If something **comes about,** it happens.
5. If you **come across** something, you find it by chance.
6. If you **come down with** something, you become sick with it.
7. If you **come into** money, you inherit it.
8. If you **come to,** you become conscious again.
▷ *verb* **coming, came** (kaym), **come**

co·me·di·an (kuh-**mee**-dee-uhn) *noun* An entertainer who tells jokes and funny stories to make people laugh.

com·e·dy (**kom**-uh-dee) *noun*
1. A funny play or film.
2. Anything that makes people laugh. *Mark's first attempt at skating was a comedy.*
▷ *noun, plural* **comedies**

com·et (**kom**-it) *noun* A bright heavenly body with a long tail of light. A comet travels around the sun in a long, slow path.

▶ **Word History**

Comet comes from a Greek word meaning "long-haired star," because the tail of the comet looks like flowing hair.

com·fort (**kuhm**-furt)
1. *verb* To make someone feel less worried or upset. *We comforted the lost child.* ▷ **comforting, comforted** ▷ *adjective* **comforting** ▷ *adverb* **comfortingly**
2. *noun* The feeling of being relaxed and free from pain or worries.
3. *noun* Something that makes your life more pleasant and enjoyable, as in *the comforts of home.*

com·fort·a·ble (**kuhm**-fur-tuh-buhl) *adjective*
1. If you are **comfortable,** you feel relaxed in your body or your mind.
2. If something is **comfortable,** it allows you to relax and feel pleasure, as in *a comfortable chair.*
▷ *adverb* **comfortably**

com·ic (**kom**-ik)
1. *noun* Someone who tells jokes and funny stories.
2. *adjective* Funny or amusing.
3. **comics** *noun, plural* A group of comic strips.

com·i·cal (**kom**-i-kuhl) *adjective* Causing amusement or laughter. ▷ *adverb* **comically**

comic book *noun* A booklet with stories told in cartoons.

comic strip *noun* A story told in a sequence of panels or cartoons, found in a newspaper or comic book.

com·ma (kom-uh) *noun* The punctuation mark (,) used for separating parts of a sentence or words in a list.

com·mand (kuh-mand)
1. *verb* To order someone to do something.
2. *verb* To have control over a group of people in the armed forces. ▷ *noun* **commander**
3. *noun* Your **command** of something is your knowledge of it and your skill in using it. *Alexis has a good command of Russian.*
▷ *verb* **commanding, commanded** ▷ *noun* **command**

com·mand·ment (kuh-mand-muhnt) *noun* A law or order from someone in power.

com·mem·o·rate (kuh-mem-uh-rate) *verb* When you **commemorate** an event or the life of an important person, you do something special to honor and remember it. ▷ **commemorating, commemorated** ▷ *noun* **commemoration** ▷ *adjective* **commemorative**

com·mence (kuh-menss) *verb* To begin something. ▷ **commencing, commenced**

com·mence·ment (kuh-menss-ment) *noun*
1. The start or beginning of something.
2. Graduation day, or a graduation ceremony.

com·mend (kuh-mend) *verb* To praise. *The mayor commended us for raising money for the earthquake victims.* ▷ **commending, commended** ▷ *noun* **commendation** ▷ *adjective* **commendable**

com·ment (kom-ent)
1. *noun* A remark or note that expresses your opinion or gives an explanation.
2. *verb* If you **comment** on something, you give an explanation or an opinion about it.
▷ **commenting, commented**

com·men·tar·y (kom-uhn-*ter*-ee) *noun*
1. A description of and comments about an event, as in *political commentary.* ▷ *noun* **commentator**
2. Something that serves as an example or an illustration. *The team's failure to win a game is a sad commentary on its lack of practice.*
▷ *noun, plural* **commentaries**

com·merce (kom-urss) *noun* The buying and selling of things in order to make money.

com·mer·cial (kuh-mur-shuhl)
1. *adjective* To do with buying and selling things, as in *commercial activities.*
2. *noun* A television or radio advertisement.
3. *adjective* Having profit as a main aim, as in *a commercial idea.*

com·mer·cial·ized (kuh-mur-shuh-lized) *adjective* If something is **commercialized,** it has been changed in order to make a profit. ▷ *noun* **commercialization**

com·mis·er·ate (kuh-miz-ur-ate) *verb* To share someone else's sadness or disappointment. *We commiserated with Amy over her bad luck.* ▷ **commiserating, commiserated** ▷ *noun* **commiseration**

com·mis·sion (kuh-mish-uhn)
1. *noun* A group of people who meet to solve a particular problem or do certain tasks.
2. *noun* Money for work done.
3. *noun* A written order giving rank in the armed services. *After completing college, he received a commission in the navy.*
4. *noun* The act of committing. *She received a commendation for her commission of charitable acts.*
5. *noun* Working order or condition. *When I have a cold, I'm totally out of commission.*
6. *verb* To give someone the power to do something. *An architect was commissioned to design a new room for the house.*
7. *verb* To put a ship into service.
▷ *verb* **commissioning, commissioned**

com·mit (kuh-mit) *verb*
1. To do something wrong or illegal, as in *to commit murder.*
2. If you **commit** yourself to something, you promise that you will do it or support it.
▷ *verb* **committing, committed** ▷ *noun* **commitment** ▷ *adjective* **committed**

com·mit·tee (kuh-mit-ee) *noun* A group of people chosen to discuss things and make decisions for a larger group.

com·mod·i·ty (kuh-mod-uh-tee) *noun* A product that is bought and sold. ▷ *noun, plural* **commodities**

com·mon (kom-uhn) *adjective*
1. Existing in large numbers.
2. Happening often, as in *a common problem.*
3. Ordinary and not special in any way.
4. Shared by two or more people or things. *This feature is common to both cars.*
▷ *adjective* **commoner, commonest**

common denominator *noun*
1. A denominator shared by several fractions. In the fractions $\frac{1}{4}$ and $\frac{3}{4}$, the common denominator is the number 4.
2. A trait or belief held in common by many people. *Freedom of speech is the common denominator in most democracies.*

Common Market *noun* Former name for the **European Economic Community,** a European trade group.

common noun *noun* A noun that refers to a class of people, places, or things and is generally not spelled with a capital. The words *boy* and *island* are common nouns in the sentence *The boy lives on an island.* See **proper noun.**

com·mon·place (kom-uhn-*playss*) *adjective* Ordinary, or not new. *Computers are commonplace in most offices today.*

C

common sense *noun* Common sense is the ability to think and behave sensibly.

com·mon·wealth (kom-uhn-*welth*) *noun*
1. A nation or state that is governed by the people who live there.
2. The people who live in and make up a nation.

com·mo·tion (kuh-moh-shuhn) *noun* A lot of noisy, excited activity.

com·mu·nal (kuh-*myoo*-nuhl) *adjective* Shared by several people, as in *a communal bathroom*.
▷ *adverb* **communally**

com·mune (kom-yoon) *noun* A group of people who live together and share things with each other.

com·mu·ni·ca·ble (kuh-*myoo*-nuh-kuh-buhl) *adjective* Easily passed from one person to another. *The common cold is a communicable disease.*

com·mu·ni·cate (kuh-*myoo*-nuh-kate) *verb* To share information, ideas, or feelings with another person by talking, writing, etc.
▷ **communicating, communicated** ▷ *noun* **communication** ▷ *adjective* **communicative** (kuh-*myoo*-nuh-kuh-tiv)

Com·mun·ion (kuh-*myoo*-nyuhn) *noun* A Christian service in which people eat bread and drink wine or grape juice to remember the last meal of Jesus.

com·mu·ni·qué (kuh-*myoo*-nuh-kay) *noun* An official report or statement.

com·mun·ism or **Com·mun·ism** (kom-yuh-*niz*-uhm) *noun* A way of organizing a country so that all the land, houses, factories, etc., belong to the government or community, and the profits are shared by all. ▷ *noun* **communist** ▷ *adjective* **communist**

Communist party *noun* The main political party of the former Soviet Union, which advocated the principles of communism.

com·mu·ni·ty (kuh-*myoo*-nuh-tee) *noun* A group of people who live in the same area or who have something in common with each other.
▷ *noun, plural* **communities**

com·mut·er (kuh-*myoo*-tur) *noun* Someone who travels a relatively long distance to work or school each day, usually by car, bus, or train.
▷ *verb* **commute**

com·pact
1. (kuhm-*pakt*) *adjective* Designed to take up very little space. ▷ *noun* **compactness**
2. (kom-pakt) *noun* A small, flat case containing face powder and a mirror.
3. (kom-pakt) *noun* An agreement between people or groups.

compact disk *noun* A disk with music or information stored on it that can be read by using a laser beam. *The picture inset shows the thin metal layer inside the plastic disk, with its pattern of pits and flat areas, which is read by a laser beam as the disk rotates.*

compact disk

compact disk
(magnified view from below)

flat
pit
aluminum layer
laser beam

com·pan·ion (kuhm-pan-yuhn) *noun*
1. Someone with whom you spend time; a friend.
2. A person hired to spend time with another person.
▷ *noun* **companionship**

com·pa·ny (kuhm-puh-nee) *noun*
1. A group of people who work together to produce or sell products or services.
2. One or more guests. *We have company this weekend.*
3. An army unit under the command of a captain.
4. A group of performers, as in *a ballet company.*
5. Companionship. *I was grateful for my cousin's company last week.*
▷ *noun, plural* **companies**

com·par·a·tive (kuhm-pa-ruh-tiv) *adjective*
1. Judged against other similar things. *This year's play was a comparative success.* ▷ *adverb* **comparatively**
2. **Comparative** forms of adjectives and adverbs are used when you compare two things or actions. *"Older" is the comparative form of "old"; "more quickly" is the comparative form of "quickly."* ▷ *noun* **comparative**

com·pare (kuhm-pair) *verb*
1. To judge one thing against another and notice similarities and differences. ▷ *noun* **comparison**
2. To be as good as something or somebody else. *Our team compares with any in the area.*
▷ *verb* **comparing, compared**

com·part·ment (kuhm-part-muhnt) *noun* A separate part of a container, used for keeping certain things, as in *a wallet compartment.*

com·pass (kuhm-puhss) *noun*
1. An instrument for finding directions, with a magnetic needle that always points north. *You can use a compass such as the one below to follow a route on a map.*
2. An instrument that has two legs connected by a flexible joint, used for drawing circles. *See* **geometry.**
▷ *noun, plural* **compasses**

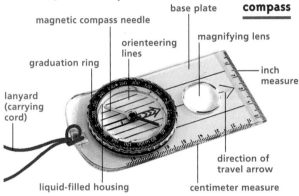

base plate　　**compass**

magnetic compass needle

orienteering lines

magnifying lens

graduation ring

inch measure

lanyard (carrying cord)

direction of travel arrow

liquid-filled housing

centimeter measure

com·pas·sion (kuhm-pash-uhn) *noun* A feeling of sympathy for and a desire to help someone who is suffering. ▷ *adjective* **compassionate** ▷ *adverb* **compassionately**

com·pat·i·ble (kuhm-pat-uh-buhl) *adjective* If people or objects are **compatible,** they can live together or be used together without difficulty. ▷ *noun* **compatibility**

com·pel (kuhm-pel) *verb* To make someone do something by giving him or her orders or by using force. ▷ **compelling, compelled**

com·pen·sate (kom-puhn-sate) *verb*
1. To make up for something. *Nothing can compensate for my suffering.*
2. To pay. *Phil was compensated for baby-sitting.*
▷ *noun* **compensation** ▷ *verb* **compensating, compensated**

com·pete (kuhm-peet) *verb* To try hard to outdo others at a task, race, or contest. *I want to compete in a marathon someday.* ▷ **competing, competed**

com·pe·tent (kom-puh-tuhnt) *adjective* If you are **competent** at something, you have the skill or ability to do it well. ▷ *noun* **competence** ▷ *adverb* **competently**

com·pe·ti·tion (kom-puh-tish-uhn) *noun*
1. A situation in which two or more people are trying to get the same thing. *There was a lot of competition for awards at school.*
2. A contest of some kind, as in *a swimming competition.* ▷ *noun* **competitor** (kuhm-pet-i-tur)

com·pet·i·tive (kuhm-pet-uh-tiv) *adjective*
1. A **competitive** sport or game is one in which the players try to win.
2. Very eager to win.
3. If a store offers **competitive** prices, its prices are at least as low as in most other stores.

com·pile (kuhm-pile) *verb* If you **compile** a list, you bring together many pieces of information. ▷ **compiling, compiled** ▷ *noun* **compilation** (kom-puh-lay-shun)

com·pla·cent (kuhm-play-suhnt) *adjective* Overly satisfied or happy with one's situation in life.

com·plain (kuhm-playn) *verb*
1. To say that you are unhappy about something. *Bev always complains about the heat in the summer.*
2. To report, or to make an accusation. *We complained to the police about the robbery.*
▷ **complaining, complained**

com·plaint (kuhm-playnt) *noun*
1. A statement saying that you are unhappy about something.
2. A cause for complaining, such as an illness. *Arthritis is a common complaint in Miguel's family.*
3. A formal charge against someone.

com·ple·ment (kom-pluh-muhnt) *noun* Something that completes something or makes a thing whole and perfect. *Dessert is the perfect complement to a good meal.* **Complement** sounds like **compliment.**

com·plete (kuhm-pleet)
1. *adjective* If something is **complete,** it has all the parts that are needed or wanted, as in *a complete deck of cards.*
2. *verb* To finish something. ▷ **completing, completed** ▷ *noun* **completion**
3. *adjective* In every way. *The news was a complete surprise.* ▷ *adverb* **completely**

com·plex
1. (kuhm-pleks *or* kom-pleks) *adjective* Very complicated, as in *complex instructions.* ▷ *noun* **complexity**
2. (kuhm-pleks *or* kom-pleks) *adjective* Having a large number of parts. *A computer is a complex mechanism.*
3. (kom-pleks) *noun* A set of strong feelings that you cannot control or forget about and that causes problems for you.
4. (kom-pleks) *noun* A group of buildings that are close together and are used for a particular purpose, as in *a sports complex.*
▷ *noun, plural* **complexes**

com·plex·ion (kuhm-plek-shuhn) *noun* The color and look of the skin, especially that on your face.

com·pli·cat·ed (kom-pli-kay-tid) *adjective* Something that is **complicated** contains lots of different parts or ideas and so is difficult to use or understand. ▷ *noun* **complication** ▷ *verb* **complicate**

com·pli·ment (kom-pluh-ment) *verb* When you **compliment** someone, you tell the person that you admire him or her or think that he or she has done something well. **Compliment** sounds like **complement.** ▷ **complimenting, complimented** ▷ *noun* **compliment**

com·pli·men·ta·ry (kom-pli-**men**-tuh-ree) *adjective*
1. If someone is **complimentary** about a person or thing, the person praises it. *Jason was complimentary about my new dress.*
2. Free or without cost, as in *complimentary tickets.*

com·ply (kuhm-**plye**) *verb* To act in agreement with rules or requests. *We complied with Mother's request to stay inside while it was raining.* ▷ **complies, complying, complied**

com·po·nent (kuhm-**poh**-nuhnt) *noun* A part of a machine or system.

com·pose (kuhm-**poze**) *verb*
1. To write a piece of music, a poem, etc. ▷ *noun* **composer**
2. If something is **composed** of certain things, it is made from those things. ▷ *verb* **composing, composed**

com·pos·ite (kuhm-**poz**-it) *adjective* Made up of many parts from different sources. *The police used a composite sketch to catch the burglar.*

com·po·si·tion (kom-puh-**zish**-uhn) *noun*
1. The combining of parts to form a whole. *The composition of the painting was very balanced.*
2. What something is made of. *Today we learned about the composition of the moon.*
3. Something that is created, especially a written work. *My composition on Benjamin Franklin is due tomorrow.*

com·post (kom-pohst) *noun* A mixture of rotted leaves, vegetables, manure, etc., that is added to soil to make it richer.

com·po·sure (kuhm-**poh**-zhur) *noun* A calm state; self-control. *After the firecracker exploded, it took me a few minutes to regain my composure.*

com·pound
1. (kom-pound) *noun* An area of land, usually fenced in.
2. (kom-pound) *noun* Something formed by combining two or more parts.
3. (kom-pound) *adjective* Having two or more parts.
4. (kom-pound) *verb* To add to, as in *to compound the problem.* ▷ **compounding, compounded**

com·pre·hend (kom-pri-**hend**) *verb* To understand. *That math problem was hard to comprehend.* ▷ **comprehending, comprehended**

com·pre·hen·sion (kom-pri-**hen**-shuhn) *noun* Understanding, or the power to understand.

com·pre·hen·sive (kom-pri-**hen**-siv) *adjective* Complete and inclusive, as in *a comprehensive list of supplies.* ▷ *adverb* **comprehensively**

com·press
1. (kuhm-**press**) *verb* To press or to squeeze something so that it will fit into a small space. ▷ **compresses, compressing, compressed** ▷ *noun* **compression**
2. (kom-press) *noun* A small cloth pad placed on a part of the body for warmth, cold, or pressure. ▷ *noun, plural* **compresses**

com·prise (kuhm-**prize**) *verb* To include or to contain. *The class comprises 25 students.* ▷ **comprising, comprised**

com·pro·mise (kom-pruh-mize)
1. *verb* To agree to accept something that is not exactly what you wanted. ▷ **compromising, compromised**
2. *noun* An agreement that is reached after people with opposing views each give up some of their demands.

com·pul·so·ry (kuhm-**puhl**-suh-ree) *adjective* If something is **compulsory,** there is a law or rule that says you must do it.

com·pute (kuhm-**pyoot**) *verb* To find an answer by using mathematics; to calculate. ▷ *noun* **computation**

com·put·er (kuhm-**pyoo**-tur) *noun* An electronic machine that can store and retrieve large amounts of information and do very quick and complicated calculations. ▷ *noun* **computing**

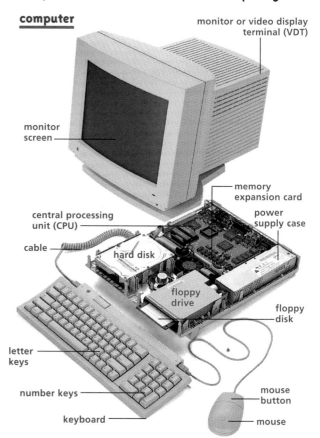

computer

monitor or video display terminal (VDT)

monitor screen

central processing unit (CPU)

cable

hard disk

memory expansion card

power supply case

floppy drive

floppy disk

letter keys

number keys

keyboard

mouse button

mouse

computer-aided design *noun* The process of using plans and drawings displayed on a computer screen to develop vehicles, buildings, etc. It is sometimes shortened to CAD.

computer graphics *noun, plural* The pictures or images that can be made on a computer.

computer language *noun* The words and symbols used in computer programs that tell the computer how to perform certain processes. *BASIC is a popular computer language.*

computer science *noun* The study of computers and how they work.

com·rade (kom-rad) *noun*
1. A good friend or a colleague. ▷ *noun* **comradeship**
2. A companion in combat, as in *comrades in arms.*

con·cave (kon-kayv *or* kong-kayv) *adjective* Curved inward, like the inside surface of a dish. See **lens.**

con·ceal (kuhn-seel) *verb* To hide something. ▷ **concealing, concealed** ▷ *noun* **concealment**

con·cede (kuhn-seed) *verb* To admit something unwillingly. *Eventually, Natalie conceded that she was wrong.* ▷ **conceding, conceded**

con·ceit·ed (kuhn-see-tid) *adjective* If you are **conceited,** you are too proud of yourself and what you can do. ▷ *noun* **conceit**

con·ceive (kuhn-seev) *verb*
1. To come up with an idea. *Hiroshi conceived an excellent plan.*
2. To become pregnant.
▷ *verb* **conceiving, conceived**

con·cen·trate (kon-suhn-trate) *verb*
1. To focus your thoughts and attention on something. *Beverly concentrated on learning her lines for the play.*
2. To come together in one place. *The shoppers concentrated at the new store.*
3. To make a liquid thicker and stronger by removing water from it.
▷ *verb* **concentrating, concentrated** ▷ *noun* **concentrate,** *noun* **concentration** ▷ *adjective* **concentrated**

con·cen·tric (kuhn-sen-trik) *adjective* Concentric circles all have their center at the same point.

con·cept (kon-sept) *noun* A general idea or understanding of something. *Leo has a very vague concept of history.*

con·cep·tion (kuhn-sep-shuhn) *noun*
1. A general idea. *Do you have any conception of what it's like to be homeless?*
2. The process of becoming pregnant.

con·cern (kuhn-surn) *verb*
1. To involve someone or be of interest to him

or her. *These plans concern you.*
2. To be about a particular subject. *This project concerns local history.*
3. To worry. *Your health concerns all of us.*
▷ *verb* **concerning, concerned** ▷ *noun* **concern**

con·cerned (kuhn-surnd) *adjective* If you are **concerned** about something, you are anxious and worried about it.

con·cern·ing (kuhn-sern-ing) *preposition* Having to do with; about. *The call is concerning the lost dog.*

con·cert (kon-surt) *noun* A performance by musicians or singers.

con·cer·to (kuhn-cher-toh) *noun* A piece of music for one or more solo instruments playing with an orchestra. ▷ *noun, plural* **concertos** *or* **concerti** (kuhn-chur-tee)

con·cess·ion (kuhn-sesh-uhn) *noun*
1. An agreement to allow something that would not normally be permitted. *As a special concession, you may stay up late.*
2. Permission to sell something, especially food, granted by a governing body to the seller. *My dad has the concession to sell candy at the carnival this year.*

conch (kongk *or* konch) *noun*
1. A marine animal that lives in a spiral shell.
2. The shell of this animal.

con·cise (kuhn-sisse) *adjective* Saying a lot in a few words. ▷ *adverb* **concisely**

con·clude (kuhn-klood) *verb*
1. To arrive at a decision or realization based on the facts that you have. *When I saw my book sitting on a shelf in Bill's room, I concluded that he must have taken it.*
2. To finish or end something. *We concluded the meeting after we discussed the plans for the party.*
▷ *verb* **concluding, concluded** ▷ *noun* **conclusion**

con·coct (kon-kokt *or* kuhn-kokt) *verb*
1. To create something by mixing several different things together. ▷ *noun* **concoction**
2. If you **concoct** an excuse, you invent it.
▷ *verb* **concocting, concocted**

con·cord (kon-kord) *noun*
1. A state of harmony and peace, especially between two people or groups.
2. A treaty or an agreement.

con·crete (kon-kreet *or* kon-kreet)
1. *noun* A building material made from a mixture of sand, gravel, cement, and water.
2. *adjective* Real or definite. *The detectives need some concrete evidence.*

con·cur (kuhn-kur) *verb* To agree. *I concur that something must be done about the problem of pollution.* ▷ **concurring, concurred**

con·cus·sion (kuhn-**kush**-uhn) *noun* An injury to the brain caused by a heavy blow to the head. A concussion can result in unconsciousness, dizziness, or sickness. ▷ *adjective* **concussed**

con·demn (kuhn-**dem**) *verb*
1. To say very strongly that you do not approve of something. *Martin Luther King, Jr., condemned all violence.* ▷ *noun* **condemnation** (kon-dem-**nay**-shuhn)
2. To force someone to suffer something unpleasant. *The murderer was condemned to death.*
3. To state that something is unsafe. *The city condemned the old building.*
▷ *verb* **condemning, condemned**

con·den·sa·tion *noun* (kon-den-**say**-shuhn)
1. The act or process of condensing something.
2. Something that has been condensed. *Ivan read the condensation of the novel.*

con·dense (kuhn-**denss**) *verb*
1. When a gas **condenses,** it turns into a liquid, usually as a result of cooling.
2. To make a piece of writing shorter by taking out unnecessary parts.
3. To make something thicker by boiling away liquid.
▷ *verb* **condensing, condensed** ▷ *adjective* **condensed**

con·de·scend·ing (kon-di-**sen**-ding) *adjective* If you are **condescending,** you behave as though you are better or more important than other people. ▷ *noun* **condescension** ▷ *verb* **condescend**

con·di·tion (kuhn-**dish**-uhn)
1. *noun* The general state of a person, an animal, or a thing. *The house was in terrible condition.*
2. *noun* General health or physical fitness. *Runners try to stay in good condition.*
3. *verb* To get into good health. *Physical exercise conditions your body.*
4. *noun* A medical problem that continues over a long period of time, as in *a heart condition.*
5. *noun* Something that is needed before another thing can happen or be allowed. *One condition of having a bike is that you always lock it up.*
6. *verb* To train someone to believe certain things or to behave in certain ways. *We conditioned our dog to roll over when we say "Roll!"* ▷ *noun* **conditioning**
▷ *verb* **conditioning, conditioned**

con·di·tion·al (kuhn-**dish**-uh-nuhl) *adjective* Requiring something else to happen first. *Making the team was conditional on getting passing grades.* ▷ *adverb* **conditionally**

con·di·tion·er (kuhn-**dish**-uh-nur) *noun* A thick liquid that you rub into your hair after washing it to make it strong and shiny.

con·do·lence (kuhn-**doh**-luhnss) *noun* An expression of sympathy for a person who is upset because a friend or relative has just died.

con·do·min·i·um (kon-duh-**min**-ee-uhm) *noun* An apartment house or other development in which each unit is owned by the person who lives in it.

con·dor (kon-dur) *noun* A large vulture. Condors are the largest flying birds in the Western Hemisphere.

condor

con·duct
1. (kuhn-**duhkt**) *verb* To organize something and carry it out. *The police conducted the murder inquiry.*
2. (kuhn-**duhkt**) *verb* To stand in front of a group of musicians and direct their playing.
3. (kuhn-**duhkt**) *verb* If something **conducts** heat, electricity, or sound, it allows it to pass through. *Copper and aluminum conduct electricity.* ▷ *noun* **conduction**
4. (kon-duhkt) *noun* Behavior. ▷ *verb* **conduct** (kuhn-**duhkt**)
▷ *verb* **conducting, conducted**

con·duc·tor (kuhn-**duhk**-tur) *noun*
1. Someone who stands in front of a group of musicians and directs it as it plays.
2. Someone who collects railroad fares.
3. A substance that allows heat, electricity, or sound to travel through it. *Metal is a good conductor of heat.*

cone (kohn) *noun*
1. An object or a shape with a round base and a point at the top. *See* **shape.** ▷ *adjective* **conical** (kon-i-kuhl)
2. The hard, woody fruit of a pine or fir tree.

con·fed·er·a·cy (kuhn-**fed**-ur-uh-see) *noun*
1. A union of states, provinces, tribes, towns, or people with a common goal.

2. The Confederacy The group of 11 states that declared it was independent from the rest of the United States just before the Civil War.
▷ *noun, plural* **confederacies**

con·fed·er·ate (kuhn-*fed*-ur-uht)
1. *adjective* Belonging to a confederacy or union.
2. Confederate *adjective* Having to do with the Confederacy before and during the Civil War.
3. *noun* Someone who bands together with others for a common purpose.

con·fed·er·a·tion (kuhn-*fed*-er-ay-shun) *noun* A union or confederacy.

con·fer (kuhn-*fur*) *verb*
1. To give someone something, such as a gift, an honor, or a reward. *The high school conferred a diploma on each of its graduates.*
2. To hold a meeting with someone; to seek someone's advice. *I conferred with Dad on what to do about the bully at school.*
▷ *verb* **conferring, conferred**

con·fer·ence (kon-fur-uhnss *or* kon-fruhnss) *noun* A formal meeting for discussing ideas and opinions.

con·fess (kuhn-*fess*) *verb* To admit that you have done something wrong. ▷ **confesses, confessing, confessed** ▷ *noun* **confession**

con·fet·ti (kuhn-*fet*-ee) *noun, plural* Small pieces of colored paper that are thrown over the bride and groom after a wedding or at parades, carnivals, and other celebrations.

con·fide (kuhn-*fide*) *verb* If you **confide** in someone, you tell the person a secret.
▷ **confiding, confided**

con·fi·dent (kon-fuh-duhnt) *adjective*
1. Having a strong belief in your own abilities. *Tawanda is a confident swimmer.*
2. Certain that things will happen in the way you want. *I am confident that I will pass the test.*
▷ *noun* **confidence** ▷ *adverb* **confidently**

con·fi·den·tial (*kon*-fuh-*den*-shuhl) *adjective* Secret. ▷ *adverb* **confidentially**

con·fine (kuhn-*fine*) *verb*
1. To keep within certain bounds; to limit. *He confined his remarks to the subject at hand.*
2. To shut or keep in or prevent from leaving a place. *The prisoner was confined to her cell.*
▷ *verb* **confining, confined** ▷ *noun* **confinement**

con·firm (kuhn-*furm*) *verb*
1. To say that something is definitely true or will definitely happen.
2. When someone is **confirmed,** the person is accepted as a full member of a church or synagogue in a special ceremony.
▷ *verb* **confirming, confirmed** ▷ *noun* **confirmation**

con·fis·cate (kon-fuh-skate) *verb* To take something away from someone as a punishment or because that thing is not allowed. *The teacher confiscated the students' comic books.* ▷ **confiscating, confiscated** ▷ *noun* **confiscation**

con·flict
1. (*kon*-flict) *noun* A serious disagreement.
2. (*kon*-flict) *noun* A war or a period of fighting.
3. (kuhn-*flict*) *verb* To clash or to disagree. *Todd's ideas always conflict with mine.* ▷ **conflicting, conflicted**

con·form (kuhn-*form*) *verb*
1. If you **conform,** you behave in the same way as everyone else or in a way that is expected of you. ▷ *noun* **conformist,** *noun* **conformity**
2. If something **conforms** to a rule or law, it does what the rule or law requires. *All these toys conform to strict safety regulations.*
▷ *verb* **conforming, conformed**

con·front (kuhn-*fruhnt*) *verb*
1. To meet or face someone in a threatening or accusing way. *The police confronted the protesters.* ▷ *noun* **confrontation**
2. To come face to face with something. *Herman confronted his fear of dogs by helping his cousin train her new puppy.*
▷ *verb* **confronting, confronted**

Con·fu·cius (kuhn-*fyoo*-shuhss) *noun* A Chinese philosopher who lived from 551 to 479 B.C. His teachings are called Confucianism, an important system of ethics. *The painting shows a 17th-century portrait of Confucius by a Chinese artist.*
▷ *adjective* **Confucian**

Confucius

con·fuse (kuhn-*fyooz*) *verb*
1. If someone or something **confuses** you, you do not understand it or know what to do.
▷ *adjective* **confusing,** *adjective* **confused**
2. To mistake one thing for another. *I confused Roy with his twin brother.*
▷ *verb* **confusing, confused** ▷ *noun* **confusion**

con·geal (kuhn-*jeel*) *verb* When a liquid **congeals,** it becomes thick or solid. ▷ **congealing, congealed**

con·ges·ted (kuhn-*jess*-tid) *adjective* Blocked up and not allowing movement, as in *congested roads; congested sinuses.* ▷ *noun* **congestion**

con·grat·u·late (kuhn-*grach*-uh-late) *verb* To tell someone that you are pleased because something good has happened to the person or he or she has done something well.
▷ **congratulating, congratulated** ▷ *noun* **congratulation**

C

congregate ▶ consider

con·gre·gate (kon-gri-gate) *verb* To gather together for a common activity. *The athletes congregated for the track meet.* ▷ **congregating, congregated**

> ### Word History
> **Congregate** comes from the Latin verb *congregare*, meaning "to flock together," as animals or birds do. It is applied to people who come together for a purpose. The same Latin root is found in the word *segregate*, which means to go from the flock, or to separate.

con·gre·ga·tion (kong-gruh-gay-shuhn) *noun* A group of people gathered together for worship.

Con·gress (kong-griss) *noun* The government body of the United States that makes laws, made up of the Senate and the House of Representatives. ▷ *adjective* **congressional**

con·gru·ent (kuhn-groo-ent) *adjective* Equal in shape or size, as in *congruent triangles.*

con·i·fer (kon-uh-fur *or* koh-nuh-fur) *noun* An evergreen tree that produces cones. ▷ *adjective* **coniferous** (kuh-nif-ur-uhss)

con·junc·tion (kuhn-juhngk-shuhn) *noun* A word that connects words, phrases, or sentences. The words *and, but,* and *if* are all conjunctions.

con·jur·er *or* **con·jur·or** (kon-juh-rur) *noun* A person who performs magic tricks to entertain people. ▷ *noun* **conjuring** ▷ *verb* **conjure**

con·nect (kuh-nekt) *verb* To join together two or more things, ideas, or places. ▷ **connecting, connected**

con·nec·tion (kuh-nek-shuhn) *noun*
1. A link between objects, people, ideas, etc.
2. A train, plane, or bus scheduled so that people getting off other trains, planes, or buses can use it to continue their journey.
3. **connections** *noun, plural* People you know, especially people who might be useful to you in your career.

con·nois·seur (kon-uh-sur) *noun* Someone who knows a lot about a subject and appreciates things that are of good quality.

con·quer (kong-kur) *verb* To defeat and take control of an enemy. ▷ **conquering, conquered** ▷ *noun* **conqueror**

con·quest (kon-kwest) *noun*
1. Something that is won, such as land, treasure, or buildings.
2. The act of conquering.

con·science (kon-shuhnss) *noun* Your knowledge of what is right and wrong that makes you feel guilty when you have done something wrong.

con·sci·en·tious (kon-shee-en-shuhss) *adjective*
1. If you are **conscientious,** you make sure that you do things well and thoroughly. ▷ *adverb* **conscientiously**
2. A **conscientious objector** is someone who refuses to fight in a war because he or she believes that it is wrong to fight and kill.

con·scious (kon-shuhss) *adjective*
1. Awake and able to think and perceive.
2. Aware of something. *I slowly became conscious that everyone was looking at me.*
3. Deliberate. *I've made a conscious effort to improve.*
▷ *noun* **consciousness** ▷ *adverb* **consciously**

con·sec·u·tive (kuhn-sek-yuh-tiv) *adjective* Happening or following one after the other. *Marcia was away for four consecutive days.* ▷ *adverb* **consecutively**

con·sen·sus (kuhn-sen-suhss) *noun* An agreement among all the people in a discussion or meeting. *We reached a consensus on having a holiday party.*

con·sent (kuhn-sent) *verb* If you **consent** to something, you agree to it. ▷ **consenting, consented** ▷ *noun* **consent**

con·se·quence (kon-suh-kwenss) *noun* The result of an action. ▷ *adjective* **consequent** ▷ *adverb* **consequently**

con·ser·va·tion (kon-sur-vay-shuhn) *noun* The protection of valuable things, especially forests, wildlife, and natural resources. ▷ *noun* **conservationist**

con·serv·a·tive (kuhn-sur-vuh-tiv)
1. *adjective* Moderate, cautious, and not extreme. *Marcus is a very conservative dresser.*
2. *noun* Someone who opposes radical change and likes things to stay as they are or used to be.
▷ *adjective* **conservatively**

con·serv·a·to·ry (kuhn-sur-vuh-tor-ee) *noun*
1. A school for music or the arts.
2. A greenhouse, or a glass room attached to a house and used for growing plants.
▷ *noun, plural* **conservatories**

con·serve (kuhn-surv) *verb* To save something from loss, decay, or waste; to preserve. *We try to turn out the lights when we leave a room to conserve energy.* ▷ **conserving, conserved**

con·sid·er (kuhn-sid-ur) *verb*
1. To think about something carefully before deciding what to do.
2. To believe that something is true. *Shelley considers school to be a waste of time.*
3. To take something into account. *We must consider Danny's feelings.*
▷ *verb* **considering, considered**

114

con·sid·er·a·ble (kuhn-**sid**-uh-ruh-buhl) *adjective*
A **considerable** amount is a fairly large amount.
▷ *adverb* **considerably**

con·sid·er·ate (kuhn-**sid**-uh-rit) *adjective* If you
are **considerate,** you think about other people's
needs and feelings when you do something.
▷ *adverb* **considerately**

con·sid·er·a·tion (kuhn-sid-uh-**ray**-shuhn) *noun*
1. If you show **consideration,** you show you care
about other people's needs and feelings.
2. Careful thought that you give to something
before making a decision. *After much
consideration, I decided to stop taking piano lessons.*
3. A fact that needs to be taken into account
before a decision can be made. *Safety should be
a consideration when we plan the playground.*

con·sign·ment (kuhn-**sine**-muhnt) *noun* A
number of things that are delivered together.

con·sist (kùhn-**sist**) *verb* If something **consists** of
different things, it is made up of those things.
▷ **consisting, consisted**

con·sis·tent (kuhn-**siss**-tuhnt) *adjective* If you are
consistent, you always behave in the same way
or support the same ideas or principles. ▷ *noun*
consistency ▷ *adverb* **consistently**

con·sole
1. (kuhn-**sole**) *verb* To cheer up or comfort
someone. ▷ **consoling, consoled** ▷ *noun*
consolation (*kon*-suh-**lay**-shun)
2. (**kon**-sole) *noun* A cabinet for a television,
radio, etc., designed to stand on the floor.

con·sol·i·date (kuhn-**sol**-uh-date) *verb* To bring
several different parts together into one. *We
consolidated our two reports.* ▷ **consolidating,
consolidated** ▷ *noun* **consolidation**

con·so·nant (**kon**-suh-nuhnt) *noun* A speech
sound that is not a vowel. Consonants
are represented by the written letters *b,
m, r,* etc.

con·spic·u·ous (kuhn-**spik**-yoo-uhss) *adjective*
Something that is **conspicuous** stands out and
can be seen easily. ▷ *adverb* **conspicuously**

con·spir·a·cy (kuhn-**spihr**-uh-see) *noun* A secret,
illegal plan made by two or more people.
▷ *noun, plural* **conspiracies** ▷ *noun* **conspirator**
▷ *verb* **conspire** (kuhn-**spire**) ▷ *adjective*
conspiratorial (kuhn-*spihr*-uh-**tor**-ee-uhl)

con·sta·ble (**kon**-stuh-buhl) *noun* A police officer,
especially in a rural area of Great Britain.

con·stant (**kon**-stuhnt) *adjective*
1. Happening all the time and never stopping. *The
traffic creates constant noise.* ▷ *adverb* **constantly**
2. Staying at the same rate or level all the time,
as in *a constant speed.*

con·stel·la·tion (*kon*-stuh-**lay**-shuhn) *noun* A
group of stars that forms a shape or pattern.

con·sti·pat·ed (**kon**-sti-*pay*-tid) *adjective* If
someone is **constipated,** the person cannot
move his or her bowels frequently or easily.
▷ *noun* **constipation**

con·stit·u·ent (kuhn-**stich**-oo-uhnt) *noun* A voter
represented by an elected official. *The senator
went home to speak to his constituents.*

con·sti·tute (**kon**-stuh-toot) *verb*
1. To form or to compose; to make up. *Two
halves constitute a whole.*
2. To set up or form legally, as in *to constitute a
set of laws.*
▷ *verb* **constituting, constituted**

con·sti·tu·tion (*kon*-stuh-**too**-shuhn) *noun*
1. The system of laws in a country that state the
rights of the people and the powers of the
government.
2. Constitution The written document containing
the governmental principles by which the United
States is governed. It went into effect in 1789.
3. Your general health and strength.
▷ *adjective* **constitutional**

con·straint (kuhn-**straynt**) *noun* Something that
limits what you are able or allowed to do.
▷ *verb* **constrain**

con·strict (kuhn-**strikt**) *verb* To slow or stop a
natural flow; to squeeze. ▷ **constricting, constricted**

con·struct (kuhn-**struhkt**) *verb* To build or make
something. ▷ **constructing, constructed** ▷ *noun*
construction

constructing a house

con·struc·tive (kuhn-**struhk**-tiv) *adjective* Helpful
and useful, as in *constructive criticism.* ▷ *adverb*
constructively

con·sul (**kon**-suhl) *noun* Someone appointed by
the government of a country to live and work in
another country. A consul's job is to protect fellow
citizens who are working or traveling abroad.

con·sult (kuhn-**suhlt**) *verb*
1. To go to a person for advice. *If you need help
with your taxes, you should consult an
accountant.* ▷ *noun* **consultation**
2. If you **consult** a book or map, you use it to
find information.
▷ *verb* **consulting, consulted**

con·sul·tant (kuhn-suhl-tuhnt) *noun* A person with a lot of knowledge and experience who gives professional advice to others.

con·sume (kuhn-soom) *verb*
1. To eat or drink something. *We consumed a gallon of ice cream.*
2. To use something up. *School consumes most of my time.*
3. If a fire **consumes** something, it destroys it.
▷ *verb* **consuming, consumed** ▷ *noun* **consumption**

con·sum·er (kuhn-soo-mur) *noun* Someone who buys and uses products and services.

con·tact (kon-takt)
1. *noun* When things are in **contact,** they touch each other.
2. *noun* If you are in **contact** with someone, you write or talk to the person.
3. *verb* To get in touch with someone.
▷ **contacting, contacted**

contact lens *noun* A small plastic lens that fits closely over your eyeball to improve your eyesight. ▷ *noun, plural* **contact lenses**

con·ta·gious (kuhn-tay-juhss) *adjective* A **contagious** disease can be spread by direct contact with someone or something already infected with it. *Chicken pox and the flu are contagious diseases.*

con·tain (kuhn-tayn) *verb*
1. When an object **contains** something, it holds that thing inside itself, or that thing forms a part of it. *This book contains many stories.*
2. To keep an emotion under control. *I tried to contain my laughter.*
▷ *verb* **containing, contained**

con·tain·er (kuhn-tayn-er) *noun* A box, jar, barrel, etc., that is used to hold something.

con·tam·i·nat·ed (kuhn-tam-uh-nay-tid) *adjective* If something is **contaminated,** it has been made dirty or unfit for use, as in *contaminated drinking water.* ▷ *noun* **contamination** ▷ *verb* **contaminate**

con·tem·plate (kon-tuhm-plate) *verb*
1. To think seriously about something. *Matthew contemplated leaving college.*
2. To look at something thoughtfully. *Augusta contemplated the view.*
▷ *verb* **contemplating, contemplated** ▷ *noun* **contemplation**

con·tem·po·rar·y (kuhn-tem-puh-rer-ee)
1. *adjective* Up-to-date or modern.
2. *adjective* If an event is **contemporary** with another event, it happened at about the same time. *The entrances of Alaska and Hawaii into statehood were contemporary events.*
3. *noun* A **contemporary** is a person of about the same age as you. ▷ *noun, plural* **contemporaries**

con·tempt (kuhn-tempt) *noun* Total lack of respect. ▷ *adjective* **contemptuous** ▷ *adverb* **contemptuously**

con·tend (kuhn-tend) *verb*
1. To compete. *The two teams contended for the league championship.* ▷ *noun* **contender**
2. To argue. *I contend that you were wrong to cancel your plans at the last moment.*
3. To try to deal with a difficulty. *Lucy has had a lot to contend with since her parents divorced.*
▷ *verb* **contending, contended**

con·tent (kuhn-tent)
1. *adjective* Happy and satisfied. ▷ *noun* **content, noun** **contentment** ▷ *adjective* **contented** ▷ *adverb* **contentedly**
2. *verb* If you **content yourself** with something, you are satisfied with it. ▷ **contenting, contented**

con·tents (kon-tentss) *noun, plural* The things that are inside something or that make it up.

con·test
1. (kon-test) *noun* A competition.
2. (kuhn-test) *verb* To compete or fight for something. ▷ *noun* **contestant**
3. (kuhn-test) *verb* To claim that something is wrong. *Tony contested the judge's decision.*
▷ *verb* **contesting, contested**

con·text (kon-tekst) *noun*
1. The **context** of a word or phrase is the language around it that helps you understand its meaning.
2. If you put an event or an action **in context,** you take into account all the things that affect it.

con·ti·nent (kon-tuh-nuhnt) *noun*
1. One of the seven large land masses of the earth. They are Asia, Africa, Europe, North America, South America, Australia, and Antarctica.
2. the Continent The mainland of Europe.
▷ *adjective* **continental**

continents

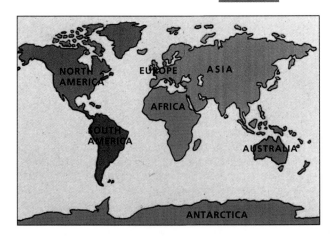

NORTH AMERICA
EUROPE
ASIA
AFRICA
SOUTH AMERICA
AUSTRALIA
ANTARCTICA

C

continental shelf *noun* A shallow, gently sloping area of the sea floor near a coastline.

con·tin·u·al (kuhn-tin-yoo-uhl) *adjective*
1. Happening again and again; frequent.
2. Happening without a pause; continuous.
▷ *adverb* **continually**

con·tin·ue (kuhn-tin-yoo) *verb* To go on doing something. *We'll continue working until we've finished our report.* ▷ **continuing, continued**
▷ *noun* **continuation**

con·tin·u·ous (kuhn-tin-yoo-uhss) *adjective* When something is **continuous,** it does not stop, as in *a continuous noise.* ▷ *adverb* **continuously**

con·tort (kuhn-tort) *verb* To twist something out of its usual shape. ▷ **contorting, contorted** ▷ *noun* **contortion** ▷ *adjective* **contorted**

con·tour (kon-toor) *noun* The outline of a curving figure or object.

con·tract
1. (kon-trakt) *noun* A legal agreement between people or companies stating the terms by which one will work for the other or sell to the other.
2. (kuhn-trakt) *verb* To become smaller.
3. (kuhn-trakt) *verb* To get. *He contracted chicken pox from his sister.*
▷ *verb* **contracting, contracted**

con·trac·tion (kuhn-trak-shuhn) *noun*
1. A shortening of something. *We were happy about the contraction of the school day.*
2. Two words combined with an apostrophe, such as *can't, wouldn't, I'd, won't.*

con·tra·dict (kon-truh-dikt) *verb* To say the opposite of what has been said. ▷ **contradicting, contradicted** ▷ *noun* **contradiction**

con·tra·dic·tor·y (kon-truh-dik-tur-ee) *adjective* Opposite, contrary, or not consistent. *I find it contradictory that you're concerned about the environment but you don't recycle your bottles and cans.*

con·trap·tion (kuhn-trap-shuhn) *noun* A strange or odd device or machine.

con·trar·y *adjective*
1. (kon-trer-ee) Opposite. *John and Denise have contrary views on politics; he is liberal, while she is conservative.* ▷ *noun* **contrary**
2. (kuhn-trair-ee) Deliberately stubborn and difficult. *Brian is the most contrary boy I ever met.*

con·trast (kuhn-trast) *verb*
1. To be very different from something else. *Claude's views contrast strongly with mine.*
2. To identify the differences between things.
▷ *verb* **contrasting, contrasted** ▷ *noun* **contrast** (kon-trast)

con·tri·bute (kuhn-trib-yoot) *verb*
1. To give help or money to a person or an organization.

2. To write for a magazine or newspaper.
▷ *verb* **contributing, contributed** ▷ *noun* **contribution,** *noun* **contributor**

con·trive (kuhn-trive) *verb*
1. To form an intelligent plan; to scheme. *The criminals contrived to kidnap someone.*
2. To make something up.
▷ *verb* **contriving, contrived**

con·trol (kuhn-trohl)
1. *verb* To make something or someone do what you want. ▷ *noun* **control**
2. *noun* Power or authority over people or a situation.
3. *noun, plural* The **controls** of a machine are the levers and switches that make it work.
4. *verb* To hold back. *Please control your anger.*
▷ *verb* **controlling, controlled**

con·tro·ver·sial (kon-truh-vur-shuhl) *adjective* If something is **controversial,** it causes a lot of argument. ▷ *noun* **controversy**

con·va·les·cence (kon-vuh-less-uhnss) *noun* The time during which someone recovers from an illness. ▷ *verb* **convalesce**

con·va·les·cent (kon-vuh-less-uhnt)
1. *noun* A person recovering from an illness.
2. *adjective* To do with a person recovering from an illness or with a period of convalescence.

con·vec·tion (kuhn-vek-shuhn) *noun* The movement of heat through liquids and gases. *The diagram shows how convection currents are created when a liquid is heated.*

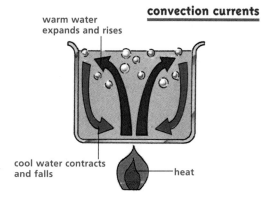

convection currents

warm water expands and rises

cool water contracts and falls

heat

con·vene (kuhn-veen) *verb* To gather together. *The meeting convened at 8 o'clock.* ▷ **convening, convened**

con·ven·ience (kuhn-vee-nyuhnss)
1. *noun* Something that is useful and easy to use. *The cottage has been equipped with all the modern conveniences.* ▷ *adjective* **convenient** ▷ *adverb* **conveniently**
2. *adjective* **Convenience food** is food that is quick and easy to prepare, such as a frozen dinner.

con·ven·ient (kuhn-vee-nyuhnt) *adjective* If something is **convenient**, it is useful or easy to use. *The No. 4 bus is very convenient for me since it stops right near my house.* ▷ *adverb* **conveniently**

con·vent (kon-vent) *noun* A building where nuns live and work.

con·ven·tion (kuhn-ven-shuhn) *noun*
1. A large gathering of people who have the same interests, such as a political meeting where party candidates are chosen.
2. A custom or accepted way to behave.

con·ven·tion·al (kuhn-ven-shuh-nuhl) *adjective* A **conventional** person does things in a traditional or accepted way. ▷ *adverb* **conventionally**

con·verge (kuhn-verj) *verb* To come together and form a single unit. ▷ **converging, converged**

con·ver·sa·tion (kon-vur-say-shuhn) *noun* If you have a **conversation** with someone, you talk with the person for a while.

con·verse
1. (kon-vurss) *verb* To talk with someone.
▷ **conversing, conversed**
2. (kon-vurss) *noun* The opposite. ▷ *adverb* **conversely**

con·vert
1. (kuhn-vurt) *verb* To make something into something else. *We've converted our loft into a bedroom.* ▷ **converting, converted**
2. (kon-vert) *noun* A person who has changed his or her religion or other beliefs.
▷ *noun* **conversion**

con·vert·i·ble (kuhn-vur-tuh-buhl)
1. *adjective* Able to be changed into something else. *Our convertible couch becomes a bed at night.*
2. *noun* A car with a top that can be put down or removed.

con·vex (kon-veks *or* kuhn-veks) *adjective* Curved outward, like the outer side of a ball. *See* **lens.**

con·vey (kuhn-vay) *verb*
1. To carry or take from one place to another. *Taxis conveyed the visitors to the auditorium.*
2. To tell or to communicate. *She conveyed the good news about her grades.*
▷ *verb* **conveying, conveyed**

con·vey·or belt (kuhn-vay-ur) *noun* A moving belt that carries objects from one place to another in a factory.

con·vict
1. (kuhn-vikt) *verb* To find or prove that someone is guilty of a crime. *The suspect was convicted of stealing a police car.* ▷ **convicting, convicted**
2. (kon-vikt) *noun* Someone who is in prison because he or she has committed a crime.

con·vic·tion (kuhn-vik-shuhn) *noun*
1. A strong belief in something.
2. If you have a **conviction** for a crime, you have been found guilty of committing it.

con·vince (kuhn-vinss) *verb* If you **convince** somebody, you make the person believe you. *We convinced Hal that he should go on the stage.*
▷ **convincing, convinced** ▷ *adjective* **convincing**
▷ *adverb* **convincingly**

con·voy (kon-voi) *noun* A group of ships, military vehicles, trucks, etc., traveling together for convenience or safety.

con·vul·sion (kuhn-vul-shuhn) *noun* An involuntary jerking movement of the muscles or the whole body; a spasm.

cook (kuk)
1. *verb* To prepare and heat food for a meal.
▷ **cooking, cooked** ▷ *noun* **cooking**
2. *noun* Someone whose job is to prepare food.

cook·book (kuk-buk) *noun* A book filled with recipes, cooking directions, and information about food.

cook·ie (kuk-ee) *noun* A small, sweetened, usually flat cake.

cool (kool)
1. *adjective* Rather cold. ▷ *noun* **coolness**
2. *verb* To lower the temperature of something.
▷ **cooling, cooled**
3. *adjective* Unfriendly and distant. *Chico met my news with a cool stare.* ▷ *adverb* **coolly** *or* **cooly**
4. *adjective* (informal) Fashionable and trendy. *Grace wore a cool T-shirt.*
▷ *adjective* **cooler, coolest**

coop (koop) *noun* A small building or pen used to house chickens, rabbits, or other small animals.

co-op (koh-op) *noun* A store, society, or building in which the members own shares in the organization.

co·op·er·ate (koh-op-uh-rate) *verb* To work together. ▷ **cooperating, cooperated** ▷ *noun* **cooperation**

co·op·er·a·tive (koh-op-ur-uh-tiv)
1. *adjective* If you are **cooperative,** you work well with other people. ▷ *noun* **cooperativeness**
2. *noun* A business owned by all the people who work in it.

co·or·di·nate
1. (koh-or-duh-nate) *verb* To organize activities or people so that they all work together.
▷ **coordinating, coordinated** ▷ *noun* **coordination,** *noun* **coordinator**
2. (koh-or-duh-nit) *noun* One of a set of numbers used to show the position of a point on a line, graph, or map.

co·or·di·nat·ed (koh-or-duh-nay-tid) *adjective* If you are **coordinated,** you have good control in moving your arms and legs.

cope (kope) *verb* To deal with something successfully. ▷ **coping, coped**

cop·per (kop-ur) *noun*
1. A reddish brown metal that conducts heat and electricity well. *See* **mineral.**
2. A reddish brown color. ▷ *adjective* **copper,** *adjective* **coppery**

cop·per·head (kop-ur-*hed*) *noun* A poisonous snake with a light brown body and dark brown markings. Copperheads are found in the eastern part of the United States.

cop·y (kop-ee)
1. *verb* To do the same as someone else.
2. *noun* A **copy** of something is made to look or sound exactly the same as the original.
3. *verb* To make a copy of something.
▷ *noun, plural* **copies** ▷ *verb* **copies, copying, copied**

cop·y·right (kop-ee-rite) *noun* The right to produce, publish, or sell a song, book, etc., such that others must obtain permission to copy or perform the material.

cor·al (kor-uhl) *noun*
1. A substance found underwater, made up of the skeletons of tiny sea creatures. *The picture shows two kinds of coral.*
2. A pink-red color.

coral

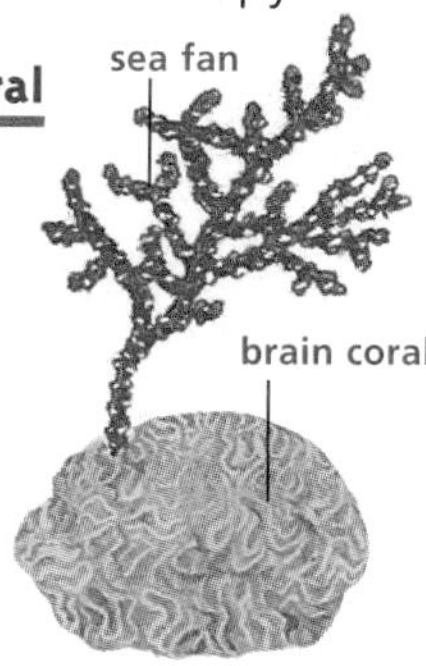

sea fan

brain coral

coral reef *noun* A reef made of coral and other materials that have solidified into rock.

coral snake *noun* A poisonous snake with red, black, and yellow bands on its body.

cord (kord) *noun*
1. A length of string or rope.
2. Covered wire that connects an electrical appliance to an outlet.
3. A pile of cut wood four feet wide, four feet high, and eight feet long.
Cord sounds like **chord.**

cor·dial (kor-juhl) *adjective* Friendly, as in *a cordial visit.* ▷ *adverb* **cordially**

cor·don (kord-uhn) *noun* A line of people or objects used to control crowds. *A police cordon blocked the street.* ▷ *verb* **cordon**

cor·du·roy (kor-duh-roi) *noun* A heavy cotton material with many rows of close ribs.

core (kor) *noun*
1. The hard center part of an apple, pear, etc., which often contains seeds. ▷ *verb* **core**
2. The intensely hot, most inner part of the earth. *See* **earth.**
3. The most important part of something. *The core of the idea was to build a new bridge.*
4. The place in a nuclear reactor where fission occurs.

cork (kork) *noun* Soft bark used as a stopper in bottles or to make mats, etc. ▷ *verb* **cork**

cork·screw (kork-*skroo*)
1. *noun* A tool for pulling corks out of bottles.
2. *adjective* Spiraling or turning in circles, as in *corkscrew pasta.*

corn (korn) *noun*
1. The sweet seeds that grow in rows on the large ears of a tall grass plant, eaten as a vegetable.
2. A small patch of hard skin on your foot.

cor·ne·a (kor-nee-uh) *noun* The transparent outer layer of the eyeball. The cornea covers the iris and pupil. *See* **eye.**

cor·ner (kor-nur)
1. *noun* The place where two sides of something meet. *A square has four corners.* ▷ *adjective* **corner**
2. *verb* To get a person or an animal into a situation or position that is a trap. ▷ **cornering, cornered**

cor·net (kor-net) *noun* A brass musical instrument that is similar to but shorter than a trumpet. *See* **brass.**

corn·meal (korn-*meel*) *noun* Ground corn.

corn·row (korn-*roh*) *noun* A flat braid arranged close to the scalp. *She wore her hair in cornrows.* ▷ *verb* **cornrow**

cor·o·nar·y (kor-uh-ner-ee)
1. *adjective* To do with the heart, as in *a coronary disease.*
2. *noun* A heart attack. ▷ *noun, plural* **coronaries**

cor·o·na·tion (kor-uh-nay-shun) *noun* The ceremony in which a king or queen is crowned.

cor·o·ner (kor-uh-nur) *noun* A medical official who investigates sudden or unnatural deaths.

cor·po·ral (kor-pur-uhl) *noun* A soldier who ranks below a sergeant.

corporal punishment *noun* Physical punishment, such as spanking.

cor·po·ra·tion (kor-puh-ray-shuhn) *noun* A group of people who are allowed by law to run a company, college, or town as a single person. Like an individual, a corporation can enter into contracts and buy and sell property.

corps (kor) *noun*
1. A group of people acting together or doing the same thing.
2. A company of military officers and enlisted personnel. ▷ *noun, plural* **corps** (kors)

corpse (korps) *noun* A dead body, especially of a human.

cor·pus·cle (kor-puhss-uhl) *noun* A red or white blood cell.

cor·ral (kuh-ral)
1. *noun* A fenced area that holds horses, cattle, or other animals.
2. *verb* To gather people, animals, or things in an enclosed area. *She corralled the whole family in the kitchen.* ▷ **corralling, corralled**

C

C

cor·rect (kuh-rekt)
  1. *adjective* True, or right. ▷ *adverb* **correctly**
  2. *verb* To make something right. *Please correct your spelling.* ▷ **correcting, corrected** ▷ *noun* **correction**

cor·res·pond (kor-uh-spond) *verb*
  1. When you **correspond** with someone, you write letters to each other.
  2. If two things **correspond,** they match in some way. *Your skills correspond to our needs.*
  ▷ *verb* **corresponding, corresponded** ▷ *noun* **correspondence**

cor·res·pond·ent (kor-uh-spon-duhnt) *noun*
  1. Someone who reports for television, radio, or newspapers about a special subject or place, as in *a war correspondent.*
  2. Someone who writes letters.

cor·ri·dor (kor-uh-dur) *noun* A long hallway or passage in a building or train.

cor·rode (kuh-rode) *verb* To destroy or eat away at something little by little. *Water corrodes metal and makes it rust.* ▷ **corroding, corroded** ▷ *noun* **corrosion** ▷ *adjective* **corrosive**

cor·ru·gat·ed (kor-uh-gay-tid) *adjective* Shaped into ridges or ripples, as in *corrugated iron.*

cor·rupt (kuh-ruhpt)
  1. *verb* To make someone bad or dishonest. *Some people think that power corrupts.*
  ▷ **corrupting, corrupted** ▷ *adjective* **corrupt**
  2. *adjective* If computer data is **corrupt,** it contains errors. ▷ *verb* **corrupt**

cor·sage (kor-sahj) *noun* A small flower bouquet worn on clothing or strapped to the wrist.

cos·met·ic (koz-met-ik)
  1. cosmetics *noun, plural* Beauty products such as lipstick and mascara.
  2. *adjective* Done to change the way a person or thing looks, as in *cosmetic surgery.*

cos·mic (koz-mik) *adjective* To do with the universe, as in *cosmic laws.* ▷ *adverb* **cosmically**

cos·mo·naut (koz-muh-nawt) *noun* A Russian astronaut.

cos·mo·pol·i·tan (koz-muh-pol-uh-tuhn) *adjective* If you are **cosmopolitan,** you feel at home in more than one country. ▷ *noun* **cosmopolitan**

cos·mos (koz-muhss) *noun* The universe.

cost (kost *or* kawst)
  1. *verb* To have a certain price. *How much does this cost?*
  2. *verb* To make someone give up or lose something. *The battle cost many lives.*
  3. cost of living *noun* The amount of money you need to spend on food, housing, clothing, etc. *The cost of living is usually higher in a city than in the country.*
  ▷ *noun* **cost** ▷ *verb* **costing, cost**

co-star (koh-star) *noun* An actor who appears in a movie, play, or television show with another actor of equal importance. ▷ *verb* **co-star**

cost·ly (kost-lee) *adjective* Expensive, as in *costly gifts.* ▷ **costlier, costliest**

cos·tume (koss-toom) *noun*
  1. Clothes worn by actors or people dressing in disguise.
  2. Clothes worn by people at a particular time or in a particular place. *These pictures show the traditional costumes of tribal chiefs in Ghana, Africa, and young women in Tokyo, Japan.*

traditional costumes

cot (kot) *noun* A small, narrow bed that can be folded up and put away.

cot·tage (kot-ij) *noun* A small house, especially in a beach or country setting. *See* **thatch.**

cottage cheese *noun* Soft, white cheese made from curdled skim milk.

cot·ton (kot-uhn) *noun*
  1. Cloth made from the fluffy white fibers surrounding the seed pods of a certain plant.
  2. The plant that produces such fibers.
  3. Thread from these fibers, used for sewing.
  ▷ *adjective* **cotton**

cotton plant

raw cotton

boll

cot·ton·mouth (kot-uhn-mouth) *noun* A poisonous snake that lives near water and in swamps in the southeastern part of the United States. It is also called a water moccasin.

cot·ton·tail (kot-uhn-*tale*) *noun* A rabbit with a short, fluffy, white tail.

couch (kouch) *noun*
1. A long, soft piece of furniture that two or more people can sit on at the same time.
▷ *noun, plural* **couches**
2. couch potato (*informal*) Someone who spends most of his or her time watching television rather than being active.

cou·gar (koo-gur) *noun* A member of the cat family with a small head, long legs, and a strong body. Cougars lived in the mountains of North and South America, but are now mostly extinct; also called **mountain lions**, **panthers**, or **pumas**.

cough (kawf)
1. *verb* To make a sudden, harsh noise as you force air out of your lungs. ▷ **coughing, coughed**
▷ *noun* **cough**
2. *noun* An illness that makes you cough.

could (kud) *verb* Past tense of **can.**

could·n't (kud-uhnt) *contraction* A short form of *could not. Jesse couldn't write his report until he went to the library and did some research.*

coun·cil (koun-suhl) *noun* A group of people chosen to look after the interests of a town, a county, or an organization, as in *the city council.*
Council sounds like **counsel.**

coun·sel (koun-suhl)
1. *verb* To listen to people's problems and give advice. *My mom counseled me on how to study for the test.* ▷ **counseling, counseled**
2. *noun* Advice.
Counsel sounds like **council.**
▷ *noun* **counseling**

coun·sel·or (koun-suh-lur) *noun*
1. Someone trained to help with problems or give advice. *He felt better after seeing the school counselor.*
2. A lawyer.

count (kount) *verb*
1. To say numbers in order. ▷ *noun* **counting**
2. To work out how many there are of something. *I counted the planes as they took off.*
▷ *noun* **count**
3. To be worth something. *In our family, everyone's opinion counts.*
4. If you can **count on** something or someone, you rely on that thing or person.
5. To think of as. *We count ourselves lucky to have survived the earthquake.*
▷ *verb* **counting, counted**

count·down (kount-*down*) *noun* A backward counting from a certain number down to zero, as at a missile launch.

coun·ter (koun-tur)
1. *noun* A long, flat surface, as in *a counter in a department store.*
2. *noun* A small, flat, round playing piece used in some games or to do math.
3. *adjective* Opposite. *Your opinion is counter to mine.* ▷ *adverb* **counter**

coun·ter·act (*koun*-tur-akt) *verb* To act against something so that it is less effective. *You should do some exercise to counteract the effects of overeating.* ▷ **counteracting, counteracted**

coun·ter·clock·wise (*koun*-tur-klok-wize) *adverb* In a direction opposite to the hands of a clock. *I opened the top of the jar by turning it counterclockwise.* ▷ *adjective* **counterclockwise**

coun·ter·feit (koun-tur-fit) *adjective* Something that has been made to look like the real thing but is a fake, as in *counterfeit money.* ▷ *noun* **counterfeit** ▷ *verb* **counterfeit**

coun·ter·part (koun-tur-*part*) *noun*
1. Someone or something that closely resembles another in some way.
2. One of two parts that complete each other.

count·less (kount-liss) *adjective* So many that you cannot count them. *We had countless arguments.*

coun·try (kuhn-tree) *noun*
1. A part of the world with its own borders and government.
2. Undeveloped land away from towns or cities. ▷ *adjective* **country**
3. The people of a nation. *He asked the country's forgiveness.*
▷ *noun, plural* **countries**

coun·try·side (kuhn-tree-*side*) *noun* Undeveloped land away from towns or cities.

coun·ty (koun-tee) *noun* A division or part of a state with its own local government. ▷ *noun, plural* **counties** ▷ *adjective* **county**

cou·ple (kuhp-uhl) *noun*
1. Two of something.
2. Two people paired together.

cou·pon (koo-pon) *noun*
1. A small piece of paper that gives you a discount on something.
2. A small form that you fill out to get information about something.

cour·age (kur-ij) *noun* Bravery, or fearlessness. ▷ *adjective* **courageous** (kuh-ray-juhss) ▷ *adverb* **courageously**

cour·i·er (kur-ee-ur *or* koor-ee-ur) *noun* Someone who carries messages or parcels for somebody else.

course (korss) *noun*
1. A part of a meal served by itself.
2. A series of lessons.
3. An area where a sport is played, as in *a golf course.*
4. A route. *The ship followed a straight course from Florida to Bermuda.*
Course sounds like **coarse.**

court (kort)
1. *noun* A place where legal cases are heard and decided.
2. *noun* An area where games such as basketball, tennis, and racquetball are played.
3. *noun* A place closed in by walls or buildings.
4. *verb* To try to win the love of someone, especially so as to marry.
5. *verb* To try to attract. *Politicians court voters at election time.*
6. *verb* To tempt. *Don't court disaster.*
▷ *verb* **courting, courted**

cour·te·ous (kur-tee-uhss) *adjective* Polite and respectful. ▷ *noun* **courteousness** ▷ *adverb* **courteously**

cour·te·sy (kur-tuh-see)
1. *noun* Behaving in a way that shows good manners and behavior. *He showed her the greatest courtesy on their date.*
2. *noun* A thoughtful act; a favor. *His work on weekends was a courtesy to his grandmother.*
▷ *noun, plural* **courtesies**

court·house (kort-houss) *noun* A building where trials and government business are conducted.

court·ship (kort-ship) *noun* Attempts by one person to win the love and affection of another.

court·yard (kort-yard) *noun* An open area surrounded by walls; a court.

cous·in (kuhz-uhn) *noun* Your **cousin** is the child of your uncle or aunt.

cove (kove) *noun* A small, sheltered inlet along a coast.

cov·er (kuhv-ur) *verb*
1. To put something over something else. *Cover the table with a cloth.* ▷ *noun* **cover**
2. To teach or study something thoroughly. *Have you covered that topic?* ▷ *noun* **coverage**
3. To travel a certain distance. *We covered 20 miles before sunset.*
4. To include or to provide for. *Does your insurance cover storm damage?*
▷ *verb* **covering, covered**

covered wagon *noun* A large, wooden wagon with a canvas cover spread over metal hoops, used by pioneers crossing the country during the United States' westward expansion.

cov·et (kuhv-it) *verb* To want something very much that belongs to someone else. ▷ **coveting, coveted**

cow (kou) *noun*
1. An adult female of cattle, raised especially for her milk. *See* **cud.**
2. An adult female of some other large mammals, including seals and whales.

cow·ard (kou-urd) *noun* Someone who is easily scared and runs away from frightening situations. ▷ *adjective* **cowardly**

cow·ard·ice (kou-ur-diss) *noun* Lack of bravery.

cow·boy (kou-boi) *noun* A man or boy who herds and looks after cattle. *See* **rodeo.**

cow·girl (kou-gurl) *noun* A woman or girl who herds and looks after cattle.

cow·hand (kou-hand) *noun* Someone who works on a ranch.

cow·hide (kou-hide) *noun* The skin of a cow, used to make leather goods.

cox·swain (kok-suhn) *noun* Someone who steers a small boat that is rowed and gives orders to its crew.

coy·o·te (kye-oh-tee *or* kye-oht) *noun* An animal that looks like a small wolf and is native to the western United States. ▷ *noun, plural* **coyote** *or* **coyotes**

co·zy (koh-zee) *adjective* Comfortable or snug. *The cottage was small but cozy.* ▷ **cozier, coziest** ▷ *noun* **coziness** ▷ *adverb* **cozily**

CPR *noun* (see pee ar) A method of reviving heart attack victims using mouth-to-mouth breathing and rhythmical compressing of the chest. CPR stands for *CardioPulmonary Resuscitation.*

crab (krab) *noun* A creature that lives in water and has a hard shell, eight legs, and two claws, or pincers.

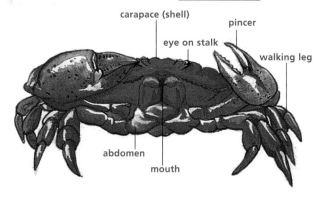

furrowed crab

carapace (shell)
pincer
eye on stalk
walking leg
abdomen
mouth

crab apple *noun* A small, sour apple used to make jelly.

crack (krak)
1. *verb* To break or split, often with a loud, sharp noise. ▷ *noun* **crack**
2. *verb* To find the answer to something. *At last, we cracked the problem.*
3. *noun* A break or a narrow opening. *We opened the window a crack.*
4. *noun* (informal) A nasty or sarcastic remark.
5. *noun* (slang) A form of the drug cocaine.
6. (informal) When you **take a crack at** something, you try to do it.
▷ *verb* **cracking, cracked**

crack·er (krak-ur) *noun* A thin, plain biscuit or wafer.

crack·le (krak-uhl) *verb* To make a lot of quick, sharp sounds. *The dry twigs crackled underfoot.*
▷ **crackling, crackled** ▷ *noun* **crackle**

cra·dle (kray-duhl)
1. *noun* A small bed for a young baby.
2. *verb* To hold something or someone in or as if in a cradle. *Rachel cradled the kitten in her arms.*
▷ **cradling, cradled**
3. *noun* The place where something starts, as in *the cradle of democracy.*

craft (kraft) *noun*
1. Work or a hobby in which you make things with your hands. *Woodwork, pottery, and needlework are all crafts.* ▷ *verb* **craft**
2. A vehicle such as a boat, spaceship, or plane.

crafts·per·son (krafts-per-suhn) *noun* Someone skilled at making things with his or her hands.
▷ *noun, plural* **craftsmen** ▷ *noun* **craftsmanship**

craft·y (kraf-tee) *adjective* A **crafty** person is skilled at tricking other people. ▷ **craftier, craftiest** ▷ *adverb* **craftily**

crag (krag) *noun* A steep, sharp rock or cliff.
▷ *adjective* **craggy**

cram (kram) *verb*
1. To fit things into a small space. *I crammed all my clothes into a backpack.*
2. To study very hard over a short period of time, as in *to cram for an exam.*
▷ *verb* **cramming, crammed**

cramp (kramp)
1. *noun* Pain caused by a muscle tightening suddenly. ▷ *verb* **cramp**
2. *verb* (informal) If someone or something **cramps your style,** it does not allow you to express yourself freely. ▷ **cramping, cramped**
3. *noun, plural* **Cramps** are sharp pains in your abdomen.

cramped (krampt) *adjective* If a place is **cramped,** there is not enough room in it for everyone or everything.

cran·ber·ry (kran-ber-ee) *noun* A small, red, tart berry that grows on low bushes in bogs and in swamps. *See* **fruit.**

crane (krane)
1. *noun* A large wading bird with long legs and a long neck and bill.
2. *noun* A machine with a long arm used to lift and move heavy objects.
3. *verb* To stretch your neck so that you can see over or around something better. ▷ **craning, craned**

crane

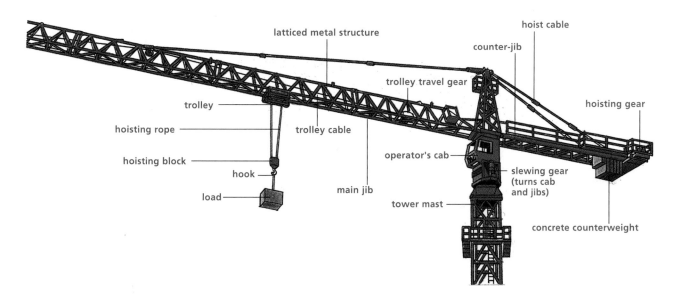

hoist cable
latticed metal structure
counter-jib
trolley travel gear
hoisting gear
trolley
hoisting rope
trolley cable
operator's cab
hoisting block
slewing gear (turns cab and jibs)
hook
main jib
load
tower mast
concrete counterweight

C

crank (krangk)
1. *noun* A handle that is attached at a right angle to a shaft and is turned to make a machine work. *See* **bicycle.**
2. *verb* To start something, such as an old-fashioned car, by turning a crank. ▷ **cranking, cranked**
3. *noun* (*informal*) Someone with strange ideas. *A crank called the radio station at least once a day.* ▷ *adjective* **crank**

crank·y (krang-kee) *adjective* Acting in an annoyed way; grouchy. *The baby gets cranky before her nap.* ▷ *adjective* **crankier, crankiest**

crash (krash)
1. *verb* To make a loud noise like thunder. ▷ *noun* **crash**
2. *noun* An accident in which a vehicle hits something at high speed. *See* **accident.** ▷ *verb* **crash** ▷ *noun, plural* **crashes**
3. *verb* When a computer system or program **crashes,** it fails completely.
▷ *verb* **crashes, crashing, crashed**

crate (krate) *noun* A large, usually wooden box, as in *a crate of oranges.* ▷ *verb* **crate**

cra·ter (kray-tur) *noun*
1. The mouth of a volcano or geyser. *See* **volcano.**
2. A large hole in the ground caused by something such as a bomb or meteorite.

crave (krave) *verb* To want something desperately. ▷ **craving, craved** ▷ *noun* **craving**

crawl (krawl)
1. *verb* To move on your hands and knees.
2. *verb* To move slowly. *Traffic crawled during the morning rush hour.*
3. *noun* A style of swimming face down in which you use your arms in turn while kicking your legs.
▷ *noun* **crawl** ▷ *verb* **crawling, crawled**

cray·fish (kray-*fish*) *noun* A small animal related to the lobster that lives in fresh water and is used for food. ▷ *noun, plural* **crayfish** *or* **crayfishes**

cray·on (kray-uhn *or* kray-on)
1. *noun* A colored wax stick used for drawing and coloring.
2. *verb* To draw or color with a crayon.
▷ **crayoning, crayoned**

craze (kraze) *noun* A very popular fashion or pastime that usually does not stay popular very long. *Squeezing lots of people into telephone booths was a craze in the 1950s.*

cra·zy (kray-zee) *adjective*
1. Insane or foolish.
2. (*informal*) Very enthusiastic. *Josh is crazy about football.*
▷ *adjective* **crazier, craziest** ▷ *noun* **craziness**
▷ *adverb* **crazily**

creak (kreek) *verb* To make a squeaky, grating noise. **Creak** sounds like **creek.** ▷ **creaking, creaked** ▷ *noun* **creak** ▷ *adjective* **creaky** ▷ *adverb* **creakily**

cream (kreem) *noun*
1. A thick, fatty liquid found in whole milk. When cream is churned, butter forms. ▷ *verb* **cream**
2. A thick, smooth substance like cream that you put on your skin, as in *hand cream.*
3. A yellow-white color, or the color of cream.
▷ *adjective* **cream**
4. The best part, as in *the cream of the crop.*
▷ *noun* **creaminess** ▷ *adjective* **creamy**

crease (kreess) *verb* To make lines or folds in something, especially fabric or paper. ▷ **creasing, creased** ▷ *noun* **crease**

cre·ate (kree-ate) *verb* To make or design something. ▷ **creating, created** ▷ *noun* **creator**

cre·a·tion (kree-ay-shuhn) *noun*
1. Something that has been made.
2. The act of making something.

cre·a·tive (kree-ay-tiv) *adjective* If you are **creative,** you use your imagination and are good at thinking of new ideas. ▷ *noun* **creativity** ▷ *adverb* **creatively**

crea·ture (kree-chur) *noun* A living being, human or animal.

crèche (kresh) *noun* A model of the baby Jesus with his parents, visitors, animals, etc., in the stable where he was born.

cre·den·tials (kri-den-shuhlz) *noun, plural* Written proof of someone's background, experience, or certification, such as a diploma or certificate.

cred·i·ble (kred-uh-buhl) *adjective* Believable, as in *a credible witness.* ▷ *noun* **credibility**

cred·it (kred-it) *noun*
1. If you buy something **on credit,** you pay for it later.
2. The balance in your favor in an account. *I have a credit of $36.00 at the store because I returned a blouse that I bought.*
3. Praise or acknowledgement. *No one gave me credit for my hard work.*
4. *noun, plural* The **credits** at the end of a movie or television program tell you who made it.
▷ *verb* **credit**

credit card *noun* A small, plastic card used in stores and restaurants to pay for products. Later, a bill is sent by the credit card company for all purchases made that month.

creed (kreed) *noun* A system of beliefs; a guiding belief.

creek (kreek) *noun* A small stream, usually one that is larger than a brook and smaller than a river. **Creek** sounds like **creak.**

creep (kreep)
1. *verb* To move very slowly and quietly. ▷ *noun* creep
2. *verb* To crawl along the ground.
3. *noun* (*slang*) An unpleasant person.
4. (*informal*) If something or someone **gives you the creeps,** that thing or person is unpleasant and frightening.
▷ *noun* **creep** ▷ *verb* **creeping, crept (krept)**
▷ *adjective* **creepy**

cre·mate (kree-mate) *verb* To burn a dead body to ashes. ▷ **cremating, cremated** ▷ *noun* **cremation**

Cre·ole (kree-ohl)
1. *noun* Someone of European descent born in the West Indies or South America.
2. *noun* Someone of French or Spanish descent living in Louisiana or Texas.
3. *noun* The French language spoken in Louisiana and Haiti.
4. creole or **Creole** *adjective* Prepared with a spicy sauce of tomatoes, peppers, okra, etc.

crepe (krape) *noun* A very thin pancake that is sometimes rolled up around a filling.

crepe paper *noun* A thin paper with a crinkled texture, often used as a party decoration.

cres·cent (kress-uhnt) *noun* A curved shape similar to that of the moon when it is just a sliver in the sky.

crest (krest)
1. *noun* The top of something such as a wave or a hill.
2. *noun* A comb or tuft of feathers on a bird's head. ▷ *adjective* **crested**
3. *verb* To reach the highest point. *The wave crested at eight feet high.* ▷ **cresting, crested**
4. *noun* Part of a coat of arms. *See* **coat of arms.**

crev·ice (krev-iss) *noun* A crack or split in something, such as a rock.

crew (kroo) *noun* A team of people who work together on a ship, an aircraft, or a specific job.

crib (krib)
1. *noun* A small bed for a baby.
2. *noun* A small farm building in which grain is stored.
3. *verb* (*informal*) To copy someone else's work and pretend it is your own. ▷ **cribbing, cribbed**

crick·et (krik-it) *noun*
1. A jumping insect similar to a grasshopper. *The field cricket, shown here, is one of the most familiar insects in North America.*

field cricket

2. An outdoor game played by two teams of 11 players with smooth, flat bats; a small, hard ball; and two wickets. It is popular in England.

crime (krime) *noun* Something that is against the law.

crim·i·nal (krim-uh-nuhl)
1. *noun* Someone who commits a crime.
2. *adjective* To do with crime, as in *a criminal investigation.* ▷ *adverb* **criminally**

crim·son (krim-zuhn) *noun* A deep red color.
▷ *adjective* **crimson**

crin·kle (kring-kuhl) *verb*
1. To wrinkle or to crumple. ▷ *adjective* **crinkled**
2. To make a soft, slight, rustling sound.
▷ *verb* **crinkling, crinkled** ▷ *noun* **crinkle**

crip·ple (krip-uhl)
1. *noun* Someone who is not able to walk normally due to disease or injury. ▷ *verb* **cripple**
2. *verb* To stop someone or something from moving or working properly. *The company was crippled by strikes.* ▷ **crippling, crippled**
▷ *adjective* **crippled**

cri·sis (krye-siss) *noun*
1. A time of danger and difficulty.
2. A turning point or decision point.
▷ *noun, plural* **crises** (krye-seez)

crisp (krisp) *adjective*
1. Firm and easily broken, as in *a crisp piece of toast.* ▷ *adjective* **crispy**
2. Fresh, dry, and cool, as in *a crisp winter morning.*
▷ *adverb* **crisply** ▷ *adjective* **crisper, crispest**

criss·cross (kriss-*krawss*) *verb* To form or move in a pattern of intersecting lines. ▷ **crisscrossing, crisscrossed** ▷ *noun* **crisscross** ▷ *adjective* **crisscross**

crit·ic (krit-ik) *noun*
1. Someone who finds something wrong with people or things.
2. Someone whose job is to write a review of a book, movie, play, television program, etc.

crit·i·cal (krit-uh-kuhl) *adjective*
1. If you are **critical** of something, you find fault with it.
2. Dangerous or serious, as in *a critical operation.*
▷ *adverb* **critically**

crit·i·cize (krit-uh-size) *verb*
1. To tell someone what he or she has done wrong.
2. To point out the good and bad parts in a book, movie, play, television program, etc.
▷ *verb* **criticizing, criticized** ▷ *noun* **criticism**

croak (krohk) *verb*
1. When a frog **croaks,** it makes a deep, hoarse sound.
2. If you **croak,** you speak with a deep, hoarse voice. ▷ *adjective* **croaky**
3. (*slang*) To die.
▷ *verb* **croaking, croaked** ▷ *noun* **croak**

cro·chet (croh-shay) *verb* To make a kind of needlework from thread or yarn using a hooked needle. ▷ **crocheting, crocheted** ▷ *noun* **crochet,** *noun* **crocheting**

crock·er·y (krok-ur-ee) *noun* Pottery that you use for food, such as plates, cups, and saucers.

croc·o·dile (krok-uh-dile) *noun* A large, scaly reptile with short legs and strong jaws, related to the alligator.

crocodile

▶ **Word History**

• •

Crocodile comes from the Greek word *krokodilos,* meaning "lizard," because it looks like a very large lizard.

cro·cus (kroh-kuhss) *noun* A small plant with purple, yellow, or white flowers and thin leaves like blades of grass. Crocuses bloom early in the spring. ▷ *noun, plural* **crocuses, crocus** *or* **croci**

crook (kruk) *noun*
1. A bent or curved part of something, as in *the crook of your arm.* ▷ *verb* **crook**
2. A dishonest person or a criminal.
3. A long stick with a hook at one end used by shepherds.

crook·ed (kruk-id) *adjective*
1. Not straight, as in *a crooked path.*
2. Dishonest, as in *a crooked deal.*

crop (krop)
1. *noun* A plant grown in large amounts, usually for food. *Potatoes and wheat are crops.*
2. *noun* The amount of food produced in a single harvest, as in *a big tomato crop.*
3. *verb* If an animal **crops** grass, it eats the top part of it.
4. *verb* To cut off or remove the tops or edges from something, as in *to crop a photograph.*
5. *noun* The pouch in a bird's gullet where food is stored and softened before being digested. *See* **chicken.**
▷ *verb* **cropping, cropped**

cro·quet (kroh-kay) *noun* An outdoor game played by hitting wooden balls with sticks through wire hoops that are stuck into the ground.

cross (krawss)
1. *verb* To go from one side to the other. *We crossed the street.*
2. *adjective* Angry and not pleased.
3. *noun* The shape x is a **cross.** So is +.
4. *noun* An upright post with a horizontal bar that crosses it, or a pendant shaped this way. The cross is the symbol of Christianity.
5. *verb* To draw a line through. *Be sure to cross your* t*'s.*
6. *verb* To intersect. *Elm Street crosses Broadway.*
7. *verb* If someone **crosses** you, the person opposes you.
8. *verb* To make the sign of a cross on. *I crossed my heart.*
▷ *verb* **crosses, crossing, crossed**

cross·bow (krawss-boh) *noun* A weapon with a bow mounted across a piece of wood. Crossbows were first used in the Middle Ages.

cross-country *adjective* A **cross-country** race is run through the countryside instead of on a track.

cross-examine *verb* To question somebody very closely. ▷ **cross-examining, cross-examined** ▷ *noun* **cross-examination**

cross-eyed *adjective* Having eyes that turn inward, toward each other, so that they are difficult to focus and the person cannot see clearly.

cross-reference *noun* A mention in one part of a book that tells you where to find more information in another part. A cross-reference can be in the index or in the text of the book.

cross·roads (krawss-rohdz)
1. A place where one road crosses another.
2. A point where an important decision must be made.
▷ *noun, plural* **crossroads**

cross section *noun*
1. A diagram that shows the inside of something, as if it had been cut through.
2. A **cross section** of the public is a selection of different types of people. ▷ *adjective* **cross-sectional**

cross·walk (krawss-wawk) *noun* A place where pedestrians can safely cross a street, often marked with painted lines.

cross·word puzzle (krawss-wurd) *noun* A puzzle in which you answer clues in order to fill blank squares with words, writing one letter in each square.

crotch (krotch) *noun* The area of the body below the abdomen and between the legs.

crouch (krouch) *verb* When you **crouch,** you bend your legs and lower your body. ▷ **crouches, crouching, crouched** ▷ *noun* **crouch**

croup (kroop) *noun* A children's disease that causes frequent coughing and difficulty in breathing.

crow (kroh)
1. *noun* A large, black bird.
2. *verb* When a rooster **crows,** it makes a loud, crying noise. ▷ *noun* **crow**
3. *verb* To boast about something. *Ricky crowed about the A on his report card.*
▷ *verb* **crowing, crowed**

crow·bar (kroh-*bar*) *noun* A heavy steel or iron bar with a flat end that can be used to lift heavy things or as a lever to pry something open.

crowd (kroud)
1. *noun* A lot of people packed together.
▷ *adjective* **crowded**
2. *verb* If you **crowd** someone, you do not give the person enough room. ▷ **crowding, crowded**

crown (kroun)
1. *noun* A headdress worn by a king or queen made from gold or silver and jewels.
2. *verb* To make someone king or queen by placing a crown on his or her head.
3. *noun* The top of something. *The ball hit him on the crown of his head.*
4. *verb* To declare someone to be the winner. *The referee crowned Sonya the marathon champion.*
5. *noun* A wreath or headdress given to the winner of a competition.
▷ *noun* **crowning** ▷ *verb* **crowning, crowned**

crow's nest *noun* A small platform used for a lookout, found on top of the mast of a sailing ship.

cru·cial (kroo-shuhl) *adjective* Extremely important or vital. *The congresswoman's support is crucial if you want the bill to pass.* ▷ *adverb* **crucially**

crude (krood) *adjective*
1. Rough and poorly made. *The crude material irritated my skin.*
2. A **crude** joke is rude and in poor taste. ▷ *noun* **crudity**
▷ *adjective* **cruder, crudest** ▷ *adverb* **crudely**

cru·el (kroo-uhl) *adjective* A **cruel** person deliberately causes pain to others or is happy to see them suffer. ▷ **crueler, cruelest** ▷ *noun* **cruelty** ▷ *adverb* **cruelly**

cruise (krooz)
1. *noun* If you go on a **cruise,** you take a vacation on a ship that docks at several places.
▷ *verb* **cruise**
2. *verb* To travel smoothly and easily. *We cruised down the highway.* ▷ **cruising, cruised**

cruis·er (kroo-zur) *noun*
1. A boat with a cabin that is used for short cruises. *See* **boat.**

2. A warship that is faster than a battleship and has fewer guns.

crumb (kruhm) *noun* A tiny piece of bread or cake.

crum·ble (kruhm-buhl) *verb* To break into small pieces. ▷ **crumbling, crumbled** ▷ *adjective* **crumbly**

crum·ple (kruhm-puhl) *verb*
1. If you **crumple** a piece of paper, you crush it into wrinkles and folds.
2. To collapse.
▷ *verb* **crumpling, crumpled** ▷ *adjective* **crumpled**

crunch (kruhnch) *verb* If you **crunch** something, you crush or chew it noisily. *Ali crunched his carrot.* ▷ **crunches, crunching, crunched** ▷ *noun* **crunch** ▷ *adjective* **crunchy**

cru·sade (kroo-sade) *noun*
1. A battle or fight for which someone feels a great deal of emotion. *He was on a crusade against crime in the neighborhood.*
2. One of the battles fought in the 11th, 12th, and 13th centuries by European Christians attempting to capture Biblical lands from the Muslims.

crush (kruhsh)
1. *verb* To squash something under a heavy weight.
2. *noun* If you have a **crush** on someone, you have strong, romantic feelings toward him or her.
3. *verb* To put down or to dash. *My hopes were crushed when I didn't make the team.*
▷ *verb* **crushes, crushing, crushed**

crust (kruhst) *noun*
1. The crisp, outer layer of bread or pastry.
▷ *adjective* **crusty**
2. The earth's **crust** is its hard outer layer. *See* **earth.**

crus·ta·cean (kruhss-tay-shuhn) *noun* A sea creature that has an outer skeleton, such as a crab, lobster, or shrimp.

crutch (kruhch) *noun* A long stick with a padded top, used to help support someone with a leg injury. ▷ *noun, plural* **crutches**

cry (krye) *verb*
1. To weep tears.
2. To shout out.
▷ *verb* **cries, crying, cried** ▷ *noun* **cry**

crys·tal (kriss-tuhl) *noun*
1. A clear or nearly clear mineral or rock, such as quartz. *See* **quartz.**
2. A body that forms a pattern of many flat surfaces when it becomes a solid. Salt and snowflakes are crystals.
3. Glass of superior quality, used to make fine glasses for drinking, vases, etc. ▷ *adjective* **crystal,** *adjective* **crystalline** (kriss-tuh-lin)

C

crys·tal·lize (kriss-tuh-lize) *verb*
1. To form crystals
2. To take form. *After several minutes, the idea crystallized in her mind.*
▷ *verb* **crystallizing, crystallized**

cub (kuhb) *noun* A young lion, wolf, bear, etc.

cube (kyoob)
1. *noun* A three-dimensional shape with six square faces. Dice are cubes. *See* **shape.**
▷ *verb* **cube** ▷ *adjective* **cubic**
2. *verb* To multiply a number by itself twice. *The number 4 cubed is 4 x 4 x 4. It is written 4^3.*
▷ **cubing, cubed** ▷ *noun* **cube**

cu·bi·cle (kyoo-buh-kuhl) *noun* A small office or area surrounded by partitions.

cu·bit (kyoo-bit) *noun* An ancient form of measurement based on the length of the forearm, measured from the elbow to the tip of the middle finger (usually 17 to 22 inches).

cuck·oo (koo-koo)
1. *noun* A bird with a distinct call, long tail, and the odd habit of laying eggs in other birds' nests. ▷ *noun, plural* **cuckoos**
2. *adjective* (*informal*) Silly, or acting in a scatterbrained manner.

cu·cum·ber (kyoo-kuhm-bur) *noun* A long, green vegetable with a soft center filled with seeds. *See* **vegetable.**

cud (kuhd) *noun* Food that has not been digested that cows bring up from the first part of their stomachs to chew again. *Grass is*

formed into balls of cud in the rumen and then returned to the mouth for chewing and passed into the reticulum. The pulp can then be digested.

cud·dle (kudh-uhl) *verb* To hold someone closely and lovingly in your arms. ▷ **cuddling, cuddled**

cue (kyoo) *noun*
1. The signal to say some lines or do some specific thing in a play.
2. Any signal to do something.
3. A long stick used to hit the ball in billiards and pool.
Cue sounds like **queue.** ▷ *verb* **cue**

cuff (kuhf) *noun*
1. The folded part of the sleeve of a shirt or blouse that goes around your wrist.
2. The band at the bottom of a trouser leg.
3. If you speak **off the cuff,** you give a speech or an answer without preparing it first.

cui·sine (kwi-zeen) *noun* A style or manner of cooking or presenting food.

cul-de-sac (kuhl-duh-sak) *noun* A road that is closed at one end; a dead end.

cul·mi·nate (kuhl-mi-nate) *verb* To reach the highest or final point. *The athlete's career culminated in winning the gold medal.*
▷ **culminating, culminated** ▷ *noun* **culmination**

cul·prit (kuhl-prit) *noun* A person who is guilty of doing something wrong or of committing a crime.

cult (kuhlt) *noun*
1. A particular form of religious worship.
2. A strong, almost religious devotion to a person, a thing, an idea, or a way of life, as in *a cult of sun lovers.*
3. A **cult hero** is someone who is very popular with his or her devoted followers.

cul·ti·vate (kuhl-tuh-vate) *verb*
1. If you **cultivate** land, you grow crops on it.
2. To develop by studying. *Doug wants to cultivate an appreciation for opera.*
▷ *verb* **cultivating, cultivated** ▷ *noun* **cultivation**

cul·ture (kuhl-chur) *noun*
1. An appreciation for the arts, such as music, literature, painting, etc.
2. The **culture** of a group of people is their way of life, ideas, customs, and traditions.
▷ *adjective* **cultural**

cul·tured (kuhl-churd) *adjective* Well-educated or refined.

cum·ber·some (kum-bur-suhm) *adjective* Heavy or bulky and difficult to move around. *The couch is too cumbersome to move across the room.*

cun·ning (kuhn-ing) *adjective* A **cunning** person is clever at tricking people. ▷ *noun* **cunning**
▷ *adverb* **cunningly**

digestive system of a cow

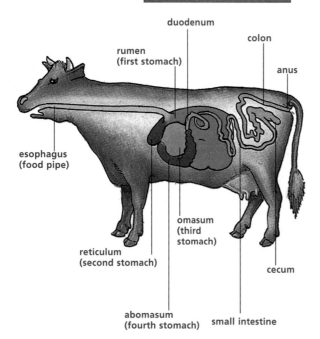

duodenum

colon

rumen
(first stomach)

anus

esophagus
(food pipe)

omasum
(third stomach)

reticulum
(second stomach)

cecum

abomasum
(fourth stomach)

small intestine

cup (kuhp) *noun*
1. A small container for holding liquids, often with a handle.
2. A unit of measurement equal to eight fluid ounces.
3. Any ornament shaped like a cup. *I won a silver cup as first prize.*

cup·board (kuhb-urd) *noun* A cabinet or closet for storing dishes, food, etc.

cup·cake (kuhp-*kake*) *noun* A small, round cake made in a baking pan that has individual cups.

cup·ful (kuhp-ful) *noun*
1. The amount a cup can hold.
2. An amount equal to eight fluid ounces; half a pint.

cu·ra·tor (kyoo-ray-tur *or* kyoo-**ray**-tur) *noun* The person in charge of a museum or an art gallery.

curb (kurb)
1. *noun* A raised border along the edge of a paved street.
2. *verb* To control or hold back something. *I curbed my desire for another cookie.* ▷ **curbing, curbed**

curd (kurd) *noun* The solid part of sour milk, often used to make cheese.

cur·dle (kur-duhl) *verb* When milk **curdles,** it goes sour and breaks up into curds and whey. ▷ **curdling, curdled** ▷ *adjective* **curdled**

cure (kyur)
1. *verb* To make someone better when he or she has been sick. ▷ **curing, cured**
2. *noun* A drug or course of treatment that makes someone better.

cur·few (kur-fyoo) *noun* A rule or an order that prevents people from traveling around freely, especially after dark.

▶ **Word History**
. . . .

Curfew comes from the medieval law that fires be put out at a specific hour at night, probably to lessen the risk of a general fire in the town. In French the term was *couvre-feu,* a combination of *couvrir,* "to cover," and *feu,* "fire."

---

cu·ri·ous (kyur-ee-uhss) *adjective*
1. Eager to find out.
2. Strange, as in *a curious creature.*
▷ *noun* **curiosity** (*kyur*-ee-**ahss**-i-tee) ▷ *adverb* **curiously**

curl (kurl)
1. *noun* A curved lock of hair.
2. *verb* To bend or move into a spiral shape.
▷ **curling, curled**

cur·ly (kur-lee) *adjective* Having curls; twisted.
▷ **curlier, curliest**

cur·rant (kur-uhnt) *noun*
1. A small raisin used in cooking and baking.
2. A small, sour berry, used in making jelly.
Currant sounds like **current.**

cur·ren·cy (kur-uhn-see) *noun* The form of money used in a country. ▷ *noun, plural* **currencies**

cur·rent (kur-uhnt)
1. *noun* The movement of water in a river or an ocean, or of electricity through a wire.
2. *adjective* Happening now. ▷ *adverb* **currently**
Current sounds like **currant.**

current affairs *noun, plural* Important events that are happening now and are often discussed on television or in newspapers.

cur·ric·u·lum (kuh-rik-yuh-luhm) *noun* A program of study for a school or college, as in *the science curriculum.* ▷ *noun, plural* **curricula** (kuh-rik-yuh-luh)

cur·ry (kuh-ree) *noun*
1. A powder with a hot, pungent taste, made from grinding various spices.
2. A dish made with curry and meat, fish, or vegetables. ▷ *noun, plural* **curries** ▷ *adjective* **curried**

curse (kurss)
1. *noun* An evil spell intended to harm someone. ▷ *verb* **curse**
2. *verb* To swear. ▷ **cursing, cursed**

cur·sor (kur-sur) *noun* A small indicator, often a flashing rectangle, that shows your position on a computer screen.

curt (kurt) *adjective* Short and abrupt; delivered in a rude manner, as in *a curt answer.* ▷ **curter, curtest**

cur·tain (kurt-uhn) *noun* A piece of fabric pulled across a window or stage to cover it.

curt·sy (kurt-see) *verb* To bend slightly at the knee, with one leg crossed behind the other. Women and girls curtsy, while men and boys bow, to show respect or to accept applause. ▷ **curtsies, curtsying, curtsied** ▷ *noun* **curtsy**

curve (kurv)
1. *verb* To bend or turn gently and continuously. *The path curved toward the cottage.* ▷ **curving, curved**
2. *noun* A continuous bend in something.
3. A **curve ball** is a baseball or softball pitch that spins away from a straight path as it approaches the batter.
▷ *adjective* **curved,** *adjective* **curvy**

cush·ion (kush-uhn)
1. *noun* A type of pillow used to make chairs or sofas more comfortable.
2. *verb* To soften the effect of something. *The mattress cushioned her fall.* ▷ **cushioning, cushioned** ▷ *noun* **cushion**

C

cus·tard (kuhss-turd) *noun* A sweet, yellow dessert made from milk, eggs, and sugar.

cus·to·di·an (kuhss-toh-dee-uhn) *noun*
1. Someone who takes care of someone.
2. A person whose job is to clean and maintain a large building or institution, as in *a school custodian*.

cus·to·dy (kuhss-tuh-dee) *noun*
1. If someone has **custody** of a child, he or she has the legal right to look after the child.
2. If someone is taken into **custody,** he or she is arrested by the police.
▷ *noun, plural* **custodies** ▷ *adjective* **custodial** (kuhss-**toh**-dee-uhl)

cus·tom (kuhss-tuhm) *noun*
1. A tradition in a culture or society. *Playing tricks on people on the first day of April is a custom in the United States and in many European countries.*
2. Something that you do regularly, as in *a family custom*.
3. **customs** *noun, plural* A checkpoint at a country's borders, ports, or airports where officials make sure that you are not carrying anything illegal.

cus·tom·ar·y (kuss-tuh-*mer*-ee) *adjective* Happening regularly by habit or custom; usual. *It's customary for me to sleep late on Saturday.*

cus·tom·er (kuhss-tuh-mur) *noun* A store's **customers** are the people who buy things from it.

cus·tom·ize (kuhss-tuh-mize) *verb* To change something to suit an individual's needs, as in *to customize a car*. ▷ **customizing, customized**

cut (kuht)
1. *verb* To use a sharp instrument, such as scissors or a knife, to divide, shorten, or shape something.
2. *verb* To reduce something. *The store is cutting its prices.*
3. *noun* A skin wound.
4. *verb* To shorten or trim, as in *to cut the grass*.
5. *verb* To stop or interrupt. *The storm cut the power last night.*
6. *verb* If you are **cut off** from other people, you are isolated from them.
7. *verb* If you **cut down** on something such as caffeine, you have it less often.
8. *verb* If a person or an organization **cuts back,** it reduces the amount of money that it spends.
9. If you **cut and paste** words or images on a computer document, you move them from one place to another.
▷ *noun* **cutback,** *noun* **cut** ▷ *verb* **cutting, cut**

cute (kyoot) *adjective* Charming, pretty, or attractive. ▷ **cuter, cutest**

cu·ti·cle (kyoo-tuh-kuhl) *noun* The tough layer of dead skin around the edges of a fingernail or a toenail.

cut·le·ry (kuht-luh-ree) *noun* Knives, forks, and spoons.

cut·ting (kuht-ing)
1. *noun* A small part of a plant taken off to put in the ground and grow a new plant.
2. *adjective* If you make a **cutting** remark, you say something hurtful.

cy·ber·space (sye-bur-*spayss*) *noun*
1. The total communications universe available to computer networks.
2. The environment of virtual reality.

cy·cle (sye-kuhl)
1. *verb* To ride a bicycle. ▷ **cycling, cycled** ▷ *noun* **cyclist**
2. *noun* A bicycle. *See* **bicycle.**
3. *noun* A series of events that are repeated over and over again, as in *the cycle of the seasons*.

cy·clone (sye-klone) *noun* A storm with very strong, destructive winds that blow around a quiet center; a tornado.

cyclone

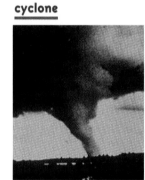

cyg·net (sig-nit) *noun* A young swan. *See* **swan.**

cyl·in·der (sil-uhn-dur) *noun*
1. A shape with flat, circular ends and sides shaped like the outside of a tube. *Most drink cans are cylinders. See* **shape.** ▷ *adjective* **cylindrical**
2. A chamber in an engine that is shaped like a tube. *See* **engine.**

cym·bal (sim-buhl) *noun* A musical instrument made of brass and shaped like a plate. It is played by striking it with a stick or another cymbal. **Cymbal** sounds like **symbol.**

cyn·i·cal (sin-uh-kuhl) *adjective* Someone who is **cynical** always expects the worst to happen and thinks that anything people do is for selfish reasons. ▷ *noun* **cynic,** *noun* **cynicism** ▷ *adverb* **cynically**

cy·press (sye-pruhss) *noun* An evergreen tree with small, dark green leaves that resemble scales. ▷ *noun, plural* **cypresses**

cyst (sist) *noun* A small sac of tissue inside the skin that fills with fluid and is sometimes removed by surgery.

cy·to·plasm (sye-tuh-*plaz*-uhm) *noun* The contents of a cell, apart from its nucleus. *See* **cell.**

czar or **tsar** (zar) *noun* An emperor of Russia before the revolution of 1917.

cza·ri·na or **tsa·ri·na** (zar-ee-nuh) *noun* A former empress of Russia or wife of a czar.

About D ◄

Spelling Hint: Words that begin with a *dye* sound are spelled *di* or *dy*. Examples: die, dice, dynamic, dynamo, dynasty.

dab (dab)
1. *verb* To touch a surface gently with something soft. *She dabbed her eyes with a handkerchief.*
2. *verb* To apply. *He dabbed some ointment on the wound.*
3. *noun* A little bit, as in *a dab of mustard.*
▷ *verb* **dabbing, dabbed**

dab·ble (dab-uhl) *verb*
1. If you **dabble** in something, you do not do it very seriously or very thoroughly. ▷ *noun* **dabbler**
2. To dip something playfully in and out of water. *The children dabbled their fingers in the pool.*
▷ *verb* **dabbling, dabbled**

dachs·hund (dahks-*hunt*) *noun* A breed of dog with a long body, brown or red hair, very short legs, and drooping ears.

dad (dad) *or* **dad·dy** (dad-ee) *noun* (informal) Father.

daddy-long·legs (long-*legz*) *noun* An animal that looks like a spider but has a small, rounded body and very long, spindly legs. ▷ *noun, plural* **daddy-longlegs**

daf·fo·dil (daf-uh-dil) *noun* A plant that has yellow, bell-like flowers and long, narrow leaves.

daft (daft) *adjective* (informal) Silly or foolish, as in *a daft idea.* ▷ **dafter, daftest**

dag·ger (dag-ur) *noun* A short, pointed weapon that is used for stabbing. *The dagger shown here was made around 4000 B.C.*

dagger and sheath

dai·ly (day-lee) *adjective* Produced or happening every day, as in *a daily newspaper.* ▷ *noun* **daily** ▷ *adverb* **daily**

dain·ty (dayn-tee) *adjective* Small and delicate. *The tablecloth had a dainty design around the edges.* ▷ **daintier, daintiest** ▷ *noun* **daintiness** ▷ *adverb* **daintily**

dair·y (dair-ee)
1. *noun* A place where milk is bottled and milk products, such as cheese and yogurt, are made. ▷ *noun, plural* **dairies**
2. *adjective* If something is a **dairy** product, it is made with milk.

dais (day-iss) *noun* A raised platform at the end of a meeting room or banquet hall, used to seat special guests or to speak from. *The professor lectured from the dais.* ▷ *noun, plural* **daises**

dai·sy (day-zee) *noun* A flower with white, pink, or yellow petals and a yellow center. ▷ *noun, plural* **daisies**

dale (dayl) *noun* A valley. *Our hike took us over hill and dale.*

dal·ma·tian (dal-may-shuhn) *noun* A breed of large dog with a white coat and black or brown spots. Dalmatians are often mascots at firehouses. *See* **dog.**

dam (dam) *noun* A strong barrier built across a stream or river to hold back water. *See* **beaver.**

dam·age (dam-ij)
1. *verb* To harm something. *The fire damaged the museum.* ▷ **damaging, damaged**
2. *noun* The harm that something does, as in *flood damage.*
3. **damages** *noun, plural* Money given to individuals by a court of law to try to make up for an injury or a loss that they have suffered. *The jury awarded the accident victims $12 million in damages.*
▷ *adjective* **damaging**

damp (damp) *adjective* Slightly wet, or moist. *Halloween was a damp and chilly day.* ▷ **damper, dampest** ▷ *noun* **dampness**

damp·en (dam-puhn) *verb*
1. To make something moist or slightly wet. *The nurse dampened a cloth and wiped the patient's forehead.*
2. To make dull or depressed. *The sad news dampened our spirits.*
▷ *verb* **dampening, dampened**

dam·sel (dam-zuhl) *noun* A young woman. *This story is about a damsel in distress.*

dance (danss)
1. *verb* To move in time to music. *The girls and boys danced at the party.* ▷ **dancing, danced**
2. *noun* A place or event where people dance.
3. *noun* A particular set of steps, such as a waltz, square dance, etc.
▷ *noun* **dancer,** *noun* **dancing**

dan·de·li·on (dan-duh-*lye*-uhn) *noun* A plant with bright yellow flowers that is often found on lawns. Dandelion leaves can be eaten in salads.

D

dan·druff (dan-druhf) *noun* Small, white flakes of dead skin from the scalp, sometimes found in hair.

dan·dy (dan-dee)
1. *noun* A **dandy** is a man who pays too much attention to his appearance or clothing. ▷ *noun, plural* **dandies**
2. *adjective* Great, or fine. *My mom just bought a dandy new car.* ▷ **dandier, dandiest**

dan·ger (dayn-jur)
1. *noun* A situation that is not safe.
2. *noun* Something or someone that may cause harm or injury. *Icy roads are a danger to drivers.*

danger sign

dan·ger·ous (dayn-jur-uhss) *adjective* Likely to cause harm or injury; not safe; risky. *The road was dangerous in snow.* ▷ *adverb* **dangerously**

dan·gle (dang-guhl) *verb* To swing or hang down loosely. *The rope dangled from the tree limb.* ▷ **dangling, dangled**

dank (dangk) *adjective* Unpleasantly wet or damp, as in *a dank cellar.* ▷ **danker, dankest**

dap·pled (dap-uhld) *adjective* Marked with spots or patches of light and dark, as in *a dappled pony.*

dare (dair) *verb*
1. To challenge someone to do something. *My sister dared me to ski down the steepest slope.*
2. To be brave enough to do something. *Do you dare to dive into the river?*
▷ *verb* **daring, dared** ▷ *noun* **dare**
▷ *adjective* **daring** ▷ *adverb* **daringly**

dare·dev·il (dair-dev-il) *noun* Someone who takes risks and does dangerous things. *My brother is a daredevil on his bicycle.*

dark (dark)
1. *adjective* Without light, as in *a dark night.*
2. *adjective* Containing more black than white, as in *dark blue.*
3. *noun* Nightfall. *I'm not allowed out after dark.*
4. *noun* Lack or absense of light. *We got lost in the dark.*
5. *adjective* Bad, or evil, as in *a dark secret.*
6. *adjective* Gloomy, or dismal.
▷ *adjective* **darker, darkest** ▷ *noun* **darkness**

Synonyms: dark

Dark means having very little light: *It was too dark in the basement to find the shelf holding the tools.*

Dim means darkened enough to make it difficult to see things clearly, or to make out exactly what you are seeing: *In the dim light of his closet, Bobby thought he saw a monster.*

Shadowy means darkened by shadows, so that what you see is not clear: *We could just make out the thief's shadowy form in the moonlight as she ran across the lawn.*

Gloomy means dark and unpleasant, especially describing people, things, or conditions that make you sad: *The gloomy weather caused our usually happy spirits to fall.*

Murky means very dark or dim, especially when caused by something thick, smoky, or foggy: *The water of the lake was murky because of the muddy bottom.*

dark·en (dar-kuhn) *verb* To make or become darker. *I darkened the room by pulling down the shade.* ▷ **darkening, darkened** ▷ *adjective* **darkened**

dark·room (dark-room) *noun* A room with special equipment and chemicals where you can develop photographs.

dar·ling (dar-ling)
1. *noun* Someone who is dearly loved.
2. *adjective* Beloved, or cherished, as in *my darling daughter.*
3. *adjective* Charming, or adorable. *My aunt says our new house is "just darling."*

darn (darn) *verb* To fix or mend a hole in a piece of cloth by sewing back and forth across it. *Mario darned the hole in his pocket.* ▷ **darning, darned** ▷ *noun* **darning**

dart (dart)
1. *noun* A pointed object that you throw at a target in the game of darts.
2. **darts** *noun* A game in which players score points by throwing darts at a target that usually has concentric circles and a bull's-eye in the center.
3. *verb* To move suddenly and quickly. *The cat darted out into the traffic.* ▷ **darting, darted**
4. *noun* A kind of pleat in a piece of clothing that makes it fit better.

dart

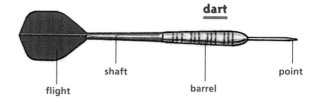

flight   shaft   barrel   point

dash (dash)
1. *noun* A very small amount of something. *Add a dash of salt.*
2. *noun* A horizontal line (—) used as a punctuation mark to show a pause in a sentence. *The whale was huge—and it was only a baby.*
3. *verb* To move quickly. *I dashed to the phone.*
4. *noun* A short race, as in *a 50-yard dash.*
5. *verb* To destroy or crush. *Kendra's broken leg dashed her plans of going skiing.*
▷ *noun, plural* **dashes** ▷ *verb* **dashes, dashing, dashed**

dash·board (dash-*bord*) *noun* The instrument panel of a car or truck where the gauges and warning lights are located.

da·ta (day-tuh) *noun* Information, or facts. *The scientists examined all the data.*

> ▶ **Language Note**
> ●
>
> **Data** is used with a singular verb to mean "information": *The data was put into the computer.* However, data was originally a plural noun and was used with a plural verb. It is still used that way to mean "facts": *The data were incorrect.* In this sense, the singular form is **da·tum** (day-tuhm), meaning a single fact or statistic.

da·ta·base (day-tuh-*bayss*) *noun* The information that is organized and stored in a computer.

date (dayt)
1. *noun* A particular day, month, or year.
2. *noun* An appointment to meet someone, especially a girlfriend or boyfriend. *They made a date to go to the movies.*
3. *verb* To go out with on a date. *Barbie and Ken have been dating for years.*
4. *verb* If something **dates** from a certain time, it was made then. *This vase dates from the 19th century.*
5. *noun* A sticky, brown fruit with a long, thin pit inside it.
6. *adjective* If something is **dated** or **out of date,** it is no longer fashionable.
7. If something is **up to date,** it is modern.
▷ *verb* **dating, dated**

daub (dawb) *verb* To smear or coat with a substance such as plaster, paint, or mud.
▷ **daubing, daubed**

daugh·ter (daw-tur) *noun* Someone's **daughter** is his or her female child.

daughter-in-law *noun* Someone's **daughter-in-law** is his or her son's wife. ▷ *noun, plural* **daughters-in-law**

daunt (dawnt) *verb* If something **daunts** you, it frightens and discourages you. *I am daunted by the size of that hill.* ▷ **daunting, daunted**

daw·dle (daw-duhl) *verb* To do something slowly, or to waste time. *Jenny dawdled over her breakfast.* ▷ **dawdling, dawdled** ▷ *noun* **dawdler**

dawn (dawn)
1. *noun* The beginning of the day; sunrise.
2. *noun* The start of something new, as in *the dawn of a new age.*
3. *verb* If something **dawns** on you, you begin to understand it. *It finally dawned on me that Jane was really smart.* ▷ **dawning, dawned**

day (day) *noun*
1. A 24-hour period, from midnight to midnight.
2. The period of light between sunrise and sunset.
3. The part of the day spent at work, as in *a five-day work schedule.*
4. A certain period of time. *Not everyone wears the fashion of the day.*

day·break (day-*brayk*) *noun* Dawn, or the time when the first rays of sunlight appear.

day care *noun*
1. Care given by adults to young children away from their homes during the day.
2. The place where care is provided.
▷ *adjective* **day-care**

children at day care

day·dream (day-*dreem*)
1. *noun* A pleasant dream you have while you are awake. *In Iris's daydream, she was president.*
2. *verb* To let your mind wander. *Ron daydreams whenever he listens to that music.* ▷ **daydreaming, daydreamed** ▷ *noun* **daydreamer**

day·light (day-*lite*) *noun* The light of the sun during daytime hours. *We rushed to finish the hike while it was still daylight.*

day·time (day-*time*) *noun* The hours of daylight, from dawn till dusk.

daze (dayz)
1. *noun* If you are in a **daze,** you are stunned and unable to think clearly.
2. *verb* To confuse or bewilder someone. *Getting hit by the snowball dazed me.* ▷ **dazing, dazed**

D

daz·zle (daz-uhl) *verb*
1. To blind someone for a short time with a bright light. *The spotlight dazzled Willie.*
2. To amaze someone. *Hiroko dazzled the audience with her playing.*
▷ *verb* **dazzling, dazzled** ▷ *adjective* **dazzling**

Prefix

The prefix **de-** adds one of these meanings to a root word:

1. Take away or remove, as in *defrost* (take away frost) or *detach* (remove something).

2. Undo or do the opposite of, as in *decode* (undo a code) or *desegregate* (undo segregation).

dea·con (dee-kuhn) *noun* In the Christian church, a person who helps a minister or preacher.

dead (ded)
1. *adjective* No longer alive.
2. *adjective* Without activity or excitement. *This town is dead after 6 P.M.*
3. *adverb* Completely, as in *dead tired.*
4. the dead *noun, plural* All those who are no longer alive. *We said a prayer for the dead at the cemetery.*

dead·en (ded-uhn) *verb* To weaken or make less sharp. *Some people pat cold tea on sunburned skin to deaden the pain.* ▷ **deadening, deadened**

dead end
1. *noun* A street that is closed to traffic at one end.
2. dead-end *adjective* Leading nowhere. *Pete is worried that he has a dead-end job.*

dead end sign

dead·line (ded-line) *noun* A time by which a piece of work or a job must be finished. *The deadline for the assignment is Monday.*

dead·lock (ded-lok) *noun* A situation where nothing can be agreed upon. *The players and team owner arrived at a deadlock.*

dead·ly (ded-lee) *adjective*
1. Capable of killing, or likely to kill, as in *a deadly explosion.*
2. Aiming to kill or destroy someone, as in *deadly enemies.*
▷ *adjective* **deadlier, deadliest**

deaf (def) *adjective*
1. If someone is **deaf,** he or she cannot hear anything or can hear very little. ▷ **deafer, deafest**
2. If you are **deaf to** something, you choose not to hear it. *Mom was deaf to my excuses.*
▷ *noun* **deafness**

deaf·en·ing (def-uh-ning) *adjective* Very loud, as in *a deafening crash.* ▷ *adverb* **deafeningly**

deal (deel)
1. *verb* To cover a subject or an area. *Does that book deal with dogs?*
2. *verb* To do business. *That store deals in baseball cards.*
3. *noun* An agreement. *Yoko made a deal with her brother.*
4. *verb* To give or to deliver, as in *to deal the cards* or *to deal a blow.*
5. *verb* When you **deal with** something, you take some sort of action about it. *Their parents dealt with the situation.*
▷ *verb* **dealing, dealt** (delt)

deal·er (dee-lur) *noun*
1. Someone who buys and sells things. *My uncle is an antiques dealer.*
2. Someone who gives out cards during a card game.

dear (dihr)
1. *adjective* Highly valued or much loved, as in *a dear friend.*
2. *noun* A kind or sweet person. *You are a dear to help me out.*
3. *adjective* You use the word **dear** when you write to someone, as in *Dear Sir.*
4. *adjective* Expensive. *The coat is quite dear.*
Dear sounds like **deer.**
▷ *adjective* **dearer, dearest** ▷ *adverb* **dearly**

death (deth) *noun*
1. The end of life.
2. The destruction or end of something. *Many people thought television would cause the death of radio.*

death·ly (deth-lee) *adjective* Very pale, or very quiet. *Carl's face turned deathly white.*

death·trap (deth-trap) *noun* A place or a vehicle that is very dangerous. *The old car was a deathtrap.*

de·bate (di-**bate**)
1. *noun* A discussion between sides with different views. *The candidates held a debate before the election.*
2. *verb* To consider or discuss something. *The family debated where to go on their vacation.*
▷ **debating, debated** ▷ *adjective* **debatable**

deb·it (**deb**-it)
1. *noun* An entry of money that is owed. *My account shows a small debit.*
2. *verb* If a bank **debits** your account, the bank removes a certain amount of money from the account. ▷ **debiting, debited**

de·bris (duh-**bree**) *noun* The scattered pieces of something that has been broken or destroyed. *The debris from the plane crash was all over the field.*

debt (det) *noun*
1. An amount of money or something else that you owe. *I will pay all my debts this month.*
2. If you are **in debt** to someone, you owe the person money or a favor.

> ### ▶ Word History
> •
> If you ever forget the silent "b" when you spell **debt,** you can blame the language experts of the 16th century. Debt comes from the French word *dette,* but those experts thought it came from the Latin *debitum.* They chose debt as the official spelling, with the *b* from Latin, even though people continued to leave out the *b* when they said the word.

debt·or (**det**-ur) *noun* Someone who owes money. *The department store is giving all debtors an extra month to pay their credit card bills.*

de·bug (dee-**buhg**) *verb*
1. To remove the defects or errors in a computer program.
2. To remove secret listening devices from a place. *The FBI debugged the office.*
▷ *verb* **debugging, debugged**

de·but (**day**-byoo *or* day-**byoo**)
1. *noun* A first public appearance, as in *an acting debut.*
2. *verb* To perform something for the first time. *The dance company will debut the ballet tonight.*
▷ **debuting, debuted**

dec·ade (**dek**-ayd) *noun* A period of 10 years.

de·caf·fein·at·ed (dee-**kaf**-uh-nay-tid) *adjective* If a drink, such as coffee or tea, is **decaffeinated,** it has had most of its caffeine removed. ▷ *verb* **decaffeinate**

de·cal (**dee**-kal) *noun* A picture or label on specially treated paper that can be transferred to glass, metal, or other hard surfaces. *Kyle's suitcase is covered with decals from every state he's visited.*

de·cant·er (di-**kan**-tur) *noun* A fancy glass bottle with a stopper, used to hold and serve liquids, especially wine.

de·cap·i·tate (di-**kap**-uh-*tate*) *verb* To remove the head of a person or creature. ▷ **decapitating, decapitated** ▷ *noun* **decapitation**

de·cath·lon (di-**kath**-lon) *noun* A track-and-field contest made up of 10 athletic events.

de·cay (di-**kay**)
1. *verb* To rot or break down. *Leaves decay to make soil.*
2. *verb* To decline in quality. *His health has decayed over the years.*
3. *noun* The breaking down of plant or animal matter by natural causes, as in *tooth decay.*
4. *noun* A decline in quality.
▷ *verb* **decaying, decayed**

de·ceased (di-**seest**) *adjective* Dead. *The library is named after our deceased mayor.*

de·ceit (di-**seet**) *noun* The act of lying to or deceiving someone.

de·ceit·ful (di-**seet**-fuhl) *adjective* If someone is **deceitful,** that person might lie to you or deceive you. ▷ *adverb* **deceitfully**

de·ceive (di-**seev**) *verb* If someone **deceives** you, that person tricks you into believing something that is not true. ▷ **deceiving, deceived**

De·cem·ber (di-**sem**-bur) *noun* The 12th month on the calendar. December follows November and has 31 days.

> ### ▶ Word History
> •
> Since **December** comes from the Latin word *decem,* or *ten,* you might expect it to be the 10th month of the year. That was the case 2,000 years ago. Then the Romans introduced a new calendar, adding more months to their old calendar. That's how December, the "10th month," became the 12th.

de·cent (**dee**-suhnt) *adjective*
1. Good or satisfactory, as in *decent quality.*
2. Respectable and proper, as in *decent behavior.*
3. Thoughtful or kind. *It was decent of them to take the girls home.*
▷ *noun* **decency** ▷ *adverb* **decently**

de·cep·tion (di-**sep**-shuhn) *noun* A trick that makes people believe something that is not true; a lie.

de·cep·tive (di-**sep**-tiv) *adjective* Misleading, or not telling the true situation. *Her smile was deceptive.* ▷ *adverb* **deceptively**

dec·i·bel (dess-uh-bel) *noun* A unit for measuring the volume of sounds. *The quietest sound the human ear can hear measures 0 decibels.*

de·cide (di-side) *verb*
1. To make up your mind about something. *They decided to stay.*
2. To settle something. *The vote was decided by a show of hands.*
▷ *verb* **deciding, decided**

de·cid·u·ous (di-sij-oo-uhss) *adjective* Trees that are **deciduous** shed their leaves every year. *Beeches and maples are deciduous trees.*

dec·i·mal (dess-uh-muhl)
1. *adjective* A **decimal** system is a system of counting and computation that has 10 as its base.
2. *noun* A fraction, or a whole number and a fraction, written with a decimal point. *The numbers 0.5, 6.37, and 8.254 are all decimals.*

decimal point *noun* A period used in a number to show that all the numbers to its right are less than 1. The number 3.14 combines the whole number 3 and the fraction .14, or 14 hundredths.

de·ci·pher (di-sye-fur) *verb* To figure out something that is written in code or is hard to understand. *I can't decipher Jim's handwriting.*
▷ **deciphering, deciphered** ▷ *adjective* **decipherable**

de·ci·sion (di-sizh-uhn) *noun* If you make a **decision,** you make up your mind about something.

de·ci·sive (di-sye-siv) *adjective* If you are **decisive,** you make choices quickly and easily. ▷ *adverb* **decisively**

deck (dek) *noun*
1. The floor of a boat or ship.
2. A platform with railings on the outside of a building.
3. A full set of playing cards.

a house with a deck

dec·la·ra·tion (dek-luh-ray-shuhn) *noun* The act of announcing something, or the announcement made, as in *a declaration of war.*

Declaration of Independence *noun* A document declaring the freedom of the 13 American colonies from British rule. It was adopted on July 4, 1776.

de·clare (di-klair) *verb*
1. To say something firmly. *Justin declared that he would never eat meat again.*
2. To announce something formally. *The government declared that the war was over.*
▷ *verb* **declaring, declared**

de·cline (di-kline) *verb*
1. To turn something down or refuse something. *I'm sorry we have to decline your invitation.*
2. To get worse, or to get smaller. *Tawanda's health began to decline. The population of our town is declining.*
3. To bend or slope downward. *The road declines and ends at the dock.*
▷ *verb* **declining, declined** ▷ *noun* **decline**

de·code (dee-kode) *verb* To turn something that is written in code into ordinary language. *The detective decoded the message.* ▷ **decoding, decoded** ▷ *noun* **decoder**

de·com·pose (dee-kuhm-poze) *verb* To rot or decay. *The leaves were decomposing.*
▷ **decomposing, decomposed** ▷ *noun* **decomposition,** *noun* **decomposer**

de·con·ges·tant (dee-kuhn-jess-tuhnt) *noun* A drug or treatment that unblocks your nose, chest, etc., when you have a cold. ▷ *noun* **decongestion** ▷ *verb* **decongest**

de·con·tam·i·nate (dee-kuhn-tam-uh-nate) *verb* To remove radioactive or other harmful substances from something or someplace. *After the accident, the lab had to be decontaminated.*
▷ **decontaminating, decontaminated** ▷ *noun* **decontamination**

dec·o·rate (dek-uh-rate) *verb*
1. If you **decorate** something, you add things to it to make it prettier. ▷ *noun* **decorator** ▷ *adjective* **decorative** (dek-ur-uh-tiv)
2. To give a medal or badge to someone. *She was decorated for her bravery in the war.*
▷ *verb* **decorating, decorated** ▷ *noun* **decorating,** *noun* **decoration**

de·cou·page (day-koo-pahzh) *noun* The art of decorating a surface by pasting on pieces of paper and then covering the whole object with layers of varnish.

de·coy (dee-koi)
1. *noun* A carved model of a bird used by hunters to attract real birds.
2. *noun* Someone who lures a person into a trap or draws attention away from something.
3. (di-koi *or* dee-koi) *verb* To lure someone or something into a trap. *Let's try to decoy the mouse*

into the trap with cheese. ▷ **decoying, decoyed**

de·crease (dee-kreess *or* di-**kreess**)
1. *verb* To become less, smaller, or fewer. *If I sit down, the pain decreases.* ▷ **decreasing, decreased** ▷ *adjective* **decreasing** ▷ *adverb* **decreasingly**
2. *noun* A loss, or the amount by which something grows less, as in *a decrease in your allowance.*

de·cree (di-**kree**)
1. *verb* To give an order or proclaim officially. *The governor decreed a new state holiday.*
▷ **decreeing, decreed**
2. *noun* An official decision or order, as in *a divorce decree.*

de·crep·it (di-**krep**-it) *adjective* Weakened by old age or too much use, as in *a decrepit building.*

ded·i·cate (**ded**-uh-kate) *verb*
1. If you **dedicate** yourself to something, you give a lot of time and energy to it.
2. If you **dedicate** a book to someone, you put that person's name at the front of it, usually to say thanks or show appreciation.
▷ *verb* **dedicating, dedicated**

ded·i·ca·tion (*ded*-uh-**kay**-shun) *noun*
1. Devotion or concentration of effort. *They worked with much dedication.*
2. The inscription written in a book.
3. The opening of a new bridge, hospital, etc., with a special ceremony.

de·duce (di-**dooss**) *verb* To figure something out from clues or from what you know already. *Mohammed deduced the solution to the mystery.*
▷ **deducing, deduced**

de·duct (di-**duhkt**) *verb* To take away or subtract something. *Lizzie deducted the cost of the skates from the total bill.* ▷ **deducting, deducted**
▷ *adjective* **deductible**

de·duc·tion (di-**duhk**-shuhn) *noun*
1. An amount that is taken away or subtracted from a larger amount. *The deduction on all items was 50 percent.*
2. Something that is figured out from clues, as in *a logical deduction.*

deed (deed) *noun*
1. Something that is done, as in *a good deed.*
2. A legal document saying who owns a house or a piece of land.

deep (deep) *adjective*
1. Going a long way down, as in *a deep well.*
2. Very intense and strong, as in *deep sorrow.*
3. Very low in pitch, as in *a deep voice.*
4. Not easy to understand. *That lecture was too deep for me.*
▷ *adjective* **deeper, deepest** ▷ *noun* **deep** ▷ *verb* **deepen** ▷ *adverb* **deeply**

deep-sea *adjective* Living or happening in the deeper part of an ocean. *Some deep-sea creatures, such as this viperfish, make their own light from luminous cells.*

viperfish

deer (dihr) *noun* An animal with hooves that runs very fast and eats plants. Male deer grow bony, branching antlers. **Deer** sounds like **dear**. *See* **antler**. ▷ *noun, plural* **deer**

de·face (di-**fayss**) *verb* To spoil the way something looks by writing on it, scratching it, etc. *The men defaced the poster.* ▷ **defacing, defaced**

de·feat (di-**feet**)
1. *verb* To beat someone in a war or a competition. ▷ **defeating, defeated**
2. *noun* If you suffer a **defeat**, you are beaten.

de·fect
1. (**dee**-fekt *or* di-**fekt**) *noun* A fault or weakness in something or someone. ▷ *adjective* **defective**
2. (di-**fekt**) *verb* To leave your country or political party and join another one. *The politician defected to the other party.* ▷ **defecting, defected**
▷ *noun* **defector**, *noun* **defection**

de·fend (di-**fend**) *verb*
1. To protect something or someone from harm. *The bear defended her cub.*
2. To support someone or some idea by arguing. *The strikers defended their action.*
3. To try to stop points being scored in football, hockey, soccer, basketball, etc. *The goalkeeper defended the goal well.*
▷ *verb* **defending, defended** ▷ *noun* **defense**, *noun* **defender**

de·fend·ant (di-**fen**-duhnt) *noun* The person in a court case who has been accused of a crime or who is being sued. *After the jury found the defendant not guilty, she was released.*

de·fen·sive (di-**fen**-siv) *adjective*
1. Serving to defend yourself or others, as in *defensive action* or *defensive plans.*
2. If you are **defensive** or **on the defensive**, you feel and act as if you are being attacked or criticized. ▷ *noun* **defensiveness** ▷ *adverb* **defensively**

137

de·fer (di-**fur**) *verb*
1. To put something off until later. *The field trip will be deferred until next term.*
2. To give in to another's wishes or opinions. *Maria deferred to her older sister.*
▷ *verb* **deferring, deferred** ▷ *noun* **deferment**

de·fi·ant (di-**fye**-uhnt) *adjective* If you are **defiant,** you stand up to someone or to some organization and refuse to obey. *When Jed was told to clean his room, he became defiant.*
▷ *noun* **defiance** ▷ *adverb* **defiantly**

de·fi·cient (di-**fish**-uhnt) *adjective* Lacking something necessary. *Their diet is deficient in vitamins.* ▷ *noun* **deficiency**

def·i·cit (**def**-uh-sit) *noun*
1. If a **deficit** exists, more money has been spent than has come in.
2. A lessening in quality or amount.

de·fine (di-**fine**) *verb* To explain or describe something exactly. ▷ **defining, defined** ▷ *noun* **definer**

def·i·nite (**def**-uh-nit) *adjective*
1. Certain. *Do we have a definite date for the trip?* ▷ *adverb* **definitely**
2. Clear, as in *a definite writing style.*

definite article *noun* The term for the article *the.* A definite article is used before a noun when the noun refers to something specific.

def·i·ni·tion (def-uh-**nish**-uhn) *noun* An explanation of the meaning of a word or phrase.

de·flate (di-**flate**) *verb*
1. To let the air out of something such as a tire or a balloon.
2. To reduce in size or importance. *The critic's bad review deflated the actor's ego.*
▷ *verb* **deflating, deflated** ▷ *noun* **deflation**

de·flect (di-**flekt**) *verb* To make something go in a different direction. ▷ **deflecting, deflected**
▷ *noun* **deflection**

de·for·est·a·tion (di-for-uh-**stay**-shuhn) *noun* The cutting down of forests.

de·formed (di-**formd**) *adjective* Twisted, bent, or disfigured. ▷ *noun* **deformity** ▷ *verb* **deform**

de·fraud (di-**frawd**) *verb* To cheat someone out of something that belongs to him or her, such as money or property, as in *to defraud the government of taxes.* ▷ **defrauding, defrauded**

de·frost (di-**frawst**) *verb*
1. To completely thaw out an item that is frozen, as in *to defrost a steak.*
2. To remove ice from something, such as a refrigerator or freezer.
▷ *verb* **defrosting, defrosted**

deft (deft) *adjective* Skillful, quick, and neat. *Anne's deft fingers moved gracefully across the keyboard.* ▷ **defter, deftest** ▷ *noun* **deftness**

▷ *adverb* **deftly**

de·fuse (dee-**fyooz**) *verb*
1. When someone **defuses** a bomb, he or she makes it safe so it cannot explode.
2. If a situation is **defused,** it is made calmer.
▷ *verb* **defusing, defused**

de·fy (di-**fye**) *verb*
1. If you **defy** a person or a rule, you refuse to obey.
2. To challenge or dare someone to do something. *I defy you to swim across the lake.*
▷ *verb* **defies, defying, defied**

de·gen·er·ate (di-**gen**-uh-rate) *verb* To become worse or inferior in quality. *After a few minutes, our discussion degenerated into an argument.*
▷ **degenerating, degenerated**

de·grad·ing (di-**gray**-ding) *adjective* If a situation or an activity is **degrading,** it makes you feel worthless or disgraced. ▷ *noun* **degradation** (deg-ruh-**day**-shuhn) ▷ *verb* **degrade**

de·gree (di-**gree**) *noun*
1. A step in a series.
2. A unit for measuring temperature. The symbol for a degree is °, as in *85° Fahrenheit.*
3. A unit for measuring arcs and angles. *One degree equals $\frac{1}{360}$ of a circle.*
4. A title given by a college or university, as in *a degree in medicine.*

thermometer

degrees Fahrenheit

de·hy·drat·ed (dee-**hye**-dray-tid) *adjective*
1. Dehydrated food has had the water removed from it.
2. If you are **dehydrated,** you do not have enough water in your body.
▷ *noun* **dehydration** ▷ *verb* **dehydrate**

de·i·ty (**dee**-uh-tee) *noun*
1. A god or a goddess.
2. the Diety God.
▷ *noun, plural* **deities**

de·ject·ed (di-**jek**-tid) *adjective* Sad and depressed. *Meo felt dejected when she failed the test.* ▷ *noun* **dejection** ▷ *adverb* **dejectedly**

de·lay (di-lay) *verb*
1. To be late. *Don't delay or we'll miss the bus!*
2. To make someone or something late. *The accident delayed Joe's arrival.*
3. To put something off until later. *Tamika delayed doing her homework until the last minute.*
▷ *verb* **delaying, delayed** ▷ *noun* **delay**

del·e·gate
1. (del-uh-gate) *verb* To give someone responsibility for doing a part of your job. *Joey delegated some of his chores to his brother.*
▷ **delegating, delegated**
2. (del-uh-guht) *noun* Someone who represents other people at a meeting. *At the United Nations, delegates from close to 200 countries meet to discuss world problems.*

United Nations delegates

del·e·ga·tion (del-uh-gay-shuhn) *noun* A group of people that represents an organization or a government at meetings. *The U.S. delegation was the first to arrive at the peace talks.*

de·lete (di-leet) *verb* To remove something from a piece of writing or computer text. *Delete the last two sentences.* ▷ **deleting, deleted** ▷ *noun* **deletion**

de·lib·er·ate
1. (duh-lib-ur-uht) *adjective* Planned or intended.
▷ *adverb* **deliberately**
2. (duh-lib-ur-uht) *adjective* Careful and slow. *She walked with deliberate steps on the icy sidewalk.*
3. (duh-lib-uh-rate) *verb* To consider something carefully. *Dad deliberated before punishing me.*
▷ **deliberating, deliberated**
▷ *noun* **deliberation**

del·i·cate (del-uh-kuht) *adjective*
1. Very pleasant to the senses, as in *a delicate flavor.*
2. Finely made or sensitive, as in *a delicate instrument.*
3. If a person is **delicate,** he or she is not very strong and can easily become ill.
▷ *adverb* **delicately**

del·i·ca·tes·sen (del-uh-kuh-tess-uhn) *noun* A store that sells different kinds of food already prepared.

de·li·cious (di-lish-uhss) *adjective* Very pleasing to taste or smell. *That apple pie was delicious!*
▷ *adverb* **deliciously**

de·light (di-lite)
1. *noun* Great pleasure. *The trip was a delight.*
▷ *adjective* **delightful** ▷ *adverb* **delightfully**
2. *verb* If something **delights** you, it pleases you very much. ▷ **delighting, delighted** ▷ *adjective* **delighted**

de·lin·quent (di-ling-kwuhnt)
1. *noun* A person who is often in trouble with the police. ▷ *adjective* **delinquent**
2. *adjective* Overdue for payment, as in *a delinquent account.*
▷ *noun* **delinquency**

de·lir·i·ous (di-lihr-ee-uhss) *adjective* If you are **delirious,** you cannot think straight either because you have a high fever or you are extremely happy. ▷ *adverb* **deliriously**

de·liv·er (di-liv-ur) *verb*
1. To take something to someone. *A messenger was sent to deliver the package.*
2. To say. *The teacher delivered an exciting talk.*
3. When someone **delivers** a baby, he or she helps it to be born.
4. To rescue someone from something. *Deliver us from evil.* ▷ *noun* **deliverance**
▷ *verb* **delivering, delivered** ▷ *noun* **delivery**

del·ta (del-tuh) *noun*
1. An area of land shaped like a triangle where a river deposits mud, sand, or pebbles as it enters the sea. *See* **river.**
2. The fourth letter of the Greek alphabet. *See* **alphabet.**

del·uge (del-yooj)
1. *noun* Heavy rain, or a flood.
2. *verb* If a river or storm **deluges** a place, it floods it.
3. *verb* If people **deluge** you with letters, presents, etc., they send you lots of them.
▷ *noun* **deluge**
▷ *verb* **deluging, deluged**

de·lu·sion (di-loo-zhuhn) *noun* A false idea or a hallucination. ▷ *verb* **delude**

139

de·mand (di-mand)
1. *verb* To claim something, or to ask for something firmly. *We demand justice!*
2. *verb* To require. *Archery demands a steady arm.*
3. *noun* If there is a **demand** for something, many people want it.
▷ *verb* **demanding, demanded**

de·mand·ing (di-man-ding) *adjective* Requiring a lot of time, attention, or effort. *Cecilia's job was very demanding.*

de·mer·it (di-mer-it) *noun* A mark against someone, usually given for doing something wrong. *Students with three demerits for lateness had to meet with the principal.*

dem·o (dem-oh) *noun (informal)* A recording made to demonstrate a new performer or piece of music.

de·moc·ra·cy (di-mok-ruh-see) *noun*
1. A way of governing a country in which the people choose their leaders in elections.
2. A country that has an elected government. *The United States is a democracy.* ▷ *noun, plural* **democracies**

dem·o·crat (dem-uh-krat) *noun*
1. Someone who agrees with the system of democracy.
2. Democrat A member of the Democratic Party.

dem·o·crat·ic (dem-uh-krat-ik) *adjective*
1. To do with or in favor of democracy.
2. A **democratic** system is one where all people have equal rights. ▷ *adverb* **democratically**

Democratic Party *noun* One of the main political parties in the United States. *In the 19th century, artist Thomas Nast chose the donkey as the symbol of the Democratic Party.*

symbol of the Democratic Party

de·mo·graph·ics (dee-moh-**gra**-fiks) *noun, plural* Population statistics, including data on age and income. Companies often use demographics to decide how and where to sell their products.
▷ *adjective* **demographic**

de·mol·ish (di-mol-ish) *verb* To knock down or destroy something. *The builders demolished the old school.* ▷ **demolishes, demolishing, demolished** ▷ *noun* **demolition** (dem-oh-**lish**-uhn)

de·mon (dee-muhn) *noun*
1. A devil, or an evil spirit.
2. If you work **like a demon,** you are very energetic.
▷ *adjective* **demonic** (dee-**mon**-ik)

dem·on·strate (dem-uhn-strate) *verb*
1. To show other people how to do something or use something. *Alice demonstrated how to use the computer.*
2. To show something clearly. *Alex demonstrated how angry he felt by stamping his foot.*
3. To join together with other people to protest something. *The students demonstrated against the budget cuts to the library.*
▷ *verb* **demonstrating, demonstrated** ▷ *noun* **demonstration**

dem·on·stra·tive (duh-**mon**-struh-tiv) *adjective* Showing affection freely; affectionate. *The demonstrative child hugged and kissed her baby brother.*

de·mor·al·ized (di-**mor**-uh-lized) *adjective* If you are **demoralized,** you feel depressed and hopeless.

den (den) *noun*
1. The home of a wild animal, such as a lion.
2. A small, comfortable room where you can work or play.

den·im (den-im) *noun* Strong cotton material used to make jeans and other articles of clothing. ▷ *adjective* **denim**

de·nom·i·na·tion (di-nom-uh-**nay**-shuhn) *noun*
1. An organized religion. *There are many Protestant denominations.*
2. A value or unit in a system of measurement. *When I cashed my birthday check, I asked for the money in denominations of 5 and 10.*

de·nom·i·na·tor (di-**nom**-uh-nay-tur) *noun* In fractions, the **denominator** is the number under the line that shows how many equal parts the whole number can be divided into. *In the fraction $\frac{7}{8}$, 8 is the denominator.*

de·note (di-note) *verb*
1. To show or be a sign of something. *The Rx after a store's name denotes a pharmacy.*
2. To mean. *The word* bird *denotes a creature with two legs, wings, feathers, and a beak.*
▷ *verb* **denoting, denoted** ▷ *noun* **denotation**

de·nounce (di-nounss) *verb* To say in public that someone has done something wrong. *The mayor was denounced in the paper for his crime.*
▷ **denouncing, denounced**

dense (denss) *adjective*
1. Crowded, or thick, as in *dense fog.*
2. *(informal)* Slow to understand. *Josie was dense when it came to doing arithmetic.*
▷ *adjective* **denser, densest** ▷ *noun* **denseness**
▷ *adverb* **densely**

den·si·ty (den-si-tee) *noun*
1. The **density** of an object is how heavy or light it is for its size. Density is measured by dividing an object's mass by its volume.
2. The amount of something per unit. *The population density was greater in the North.*

dent (dent) *verb* To damage something by making a hollow in it. *Lester dented his new bike.* ▷ **denting, dented** ▷ *noun* **dent**

den·tal (den-tuhl) *adjective* To do with your teeth, as in *dental hygiene.*

den·tist (den-tist) *noun* Someone who is trained to examine, clean, and treat teeth. ▷ *noun* **dentistry**

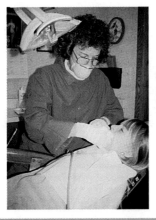

visiting the dentist

Word History

. . . .

Dentist, the English word for tooth doctor, actually comes from French. *Dent* is the French word for tooth.

den·ture (den-chur) *noun*
1. A device that fits into someone's mouth, with a false tooth or false teeth attached to it.
2. dentures *noun, plural* A set of false teeth.

de·ny (di-nye) *verb*
1. To say that something is not true. *Laura denied that she had taken the cookies.*
2. To stop someone from having something or going somewhere. *The guards denied us entry to the hall.*
▷ *verb* **denies, denying, denied** ▷ *noun* **denial**

de·o·dor·ant (dee-oh-duh-ruhnt) *noun* A substance used to cover up or get rid of unpleasant smells.

de·part (di-part) *verb*
1. To leave, especially to go on a journey.
2. To change a course of action. *The actor departed from the writer's script.*
▷ *verb* **departing, departed** ▷ *noun* **departure**

de·part·ment (di-part-muhnt) *noun* A part of a store, hospital, university, etc., that has a particular function or purpose. ▷ *adjective* **departmental**

department store *noun* A large store with sections or departments for the different kinds of things sold.

de·pend (di-pend) *verb*
1. To rely on someone or something. *We're depending on your help.* ▷ *adjective* **dependable**
2. If a thing **depends on** something else, it is determined or influenced by it. *The result will depend on the skill of our team.*
▷ *verb* **depending, depended** ▷ *noun* **dependence**

de·pend·ent (di-pen-duhnt)
1. *noun* A person who is looked after and supported by somebody else. *Joe's parents have four dependents—Joe, his brother, and his two sisters.*
2. *adjective* Depending on or controlled by something or someone else.
3. A **dependent clause** is a part of a sentence that cannot stand on its own. *"When he goes" is a dependent clause in the sentence "He will take his coat when he goes."* See **independent clause.**

de·pict (di-pikt) *verb* To show something in a picture or by using words. *Paolo's painting depicts a purple alien.* ▷ **depicting, depicted**

de·plete (di-pleet) *verb* To empty, or to use up. *The long strike depleted our savings.* ▷ **depleting, depleted** ▷ *noun* **depletion** (di-plee-shuhn)

de·plor·a·ble (di-plor-uh-buhl) *adjective* Very bad, as in *deplorable conditions.* ▷ *verb* **deplore** ▷ *adverb* **deplorably**

de·port (di-port) *verb* To send people back to their own country. *The terrorists were deported to face trial at home.* ▷ **deporting, deported** ▷ *noun* **deportation**

de·port·ment (di-port-muhnt) *noun* The way that you behave. *Their deportment was excellent.*

de·pose (di-poze) *verb*
1. If kings or queens are **deposed,** they have their power taken from them.
2. To declare under oath or in writing.
▷ *verb* **deposing, deposed** ▷ *noun* **deposition** (dep-uh-zish-uhn)

de·pos·it (di-poz-it)
1. *noun* A sum of money given as the first part of a payment or as a promise to pay for something.
2. *noun* A natural layer of rock, sand, or minerals found in the ground.
3. *verb* To place, or to lay down. *Dad deposited several packages on the table.*
4. *verb* To put money into a bank account. *George deposited $120 in his account.*
▷ *verb* **depositing, deposited**

de·pot (dee-poh) *noun* A bus station or railroad station.

de·pre·ci·ate (di-pree-shee-ate) *verb* To lose value. *Cars depreciate as they grow older.*
▷ **depreciating, depreciated** ▷ *noun* **depreciation**

de·pressed (di-prest) *adjective* If you feel **depressed,** you feel sad or gloomy. ▷ *adjective* **depressing** ▷ *verb* **depress**

de·pres·sion (di-presh-uhn) *noun*
1. Sadness or gloominess.
2. A time when businesses do badly and many people become poor. *Many people lose their jobs during a depression.*
3. A hollow place. *Juanita's body made a depression in the sand.*

de·prive (di-prive) *verb* To prevent a person from having something, or to take a thing away from someone. *Amanda was deprived of watching television.* ▷ **depriving, deprived** ▷ *noun* **deprivation** (*dep*-ri-**vay**-shuhn) ▷ *adjective* **deprived**

depth (depth) *noun*
1. Deepness, or a measurement of deepness.
2. If you study something **in depth,** you study it thoroughly.
3. If you are **out of your depth,** you cannot understand what is going on.

dep·u·ty (dep-yuh-tee) *noun* A person who helps or acts for somebody else, as in *a sheriff's deputy.* ▷ *noun, plural* **deputies** ▷ *verb* **deputize**

de·ranged (di-**raynjd**) *adjective* Insane. *The criminal was deranged.*

der·by (dur-bee) *noun*
1. A stiff hat with a narrow brim and a round top.
2. A race or contest, especially one involving horses. *The Kentucky Derby usually takes place the first Saturday in May.*
▷ *noun, plural* **derbies**

der·e·lict (der-uh-likt)
1. *adjective* Neglected and in ruins. *The house was in a derelict state.*
2. *noun* A wandering homeless person.

de·rive (di-rive) *verb*
1. To take or receive something. *Eva derives a lot of pleasure from her work.*

2. If a word is **derived** from another word, it has developed from it. *The word* dictionary *is derived from the Latin word* dictio, *meaning "word" or "phrase."*
▷ *verb* **deriving, derived** ▷ *noun* **derivation** (der-i-**vay**-shuhn)

der·rick (der-ik) *noun*
1. A tall crane with a long, movable arm that can raise or lower heavy objects.
2. A tall framework that holds the machines used to drill oil wells. *See* **oil rig.**

oil derricks at dusk

de·scend (di-send) *verb*
1. To climb down or go down to a lower level. *To get downstairs, you will need to descend the staircase.*
2. If you are **descended** from someone, you belong to a later generation of the same family.
▷ *verb* **descending, descended** ▷ *noun* **descent**

de·scend·ant (di-send-uhnt) *noun* Your **descendants** are your children, their children, and so on into the future.

de·scribe (di-skribe) *verb* To create a picture of something in words. *I described my new haircut to my friend during our phone conversation.*
▷ **describing, described** ▷ *noun* **description** (di-**skrip**-shuhn) ▷ *adjective* **descriptive** (di-**skrip**-tiv)

de·seg·re·gate (dee-seg-ruh-gate) *verb* To do away with the practice of separating people of different races in schools, restaurants, and other public places. *A 1954 ruling by the U.S. Supreme Court required towns with separate schools for blacks and whites to desegregate.*
▷ **desegregating, desegregated** ▷ *noun* **desegregation**

des·ert

1. (di-**zurt**) *verb* To abandon someone or something, or to run away from the army. *The cat deserted its kittens.*
▷ **deserting, deserted**
▷ *noun* **deserter,** *noun* **desertion**
2. (**dez**-urt) *noun* A dry, often sandy area where hardly any plants grow because there is so little rain. *The map shows the main deserts of the world and is surrounded by examples of desert wildlife.*
▷ *adjective* **desert**

fennec fox
(North Africa and Middle East)

Sturt's desert pea
(Australia)

honey-pot ant
(Australia)

deserts and desert wildlife

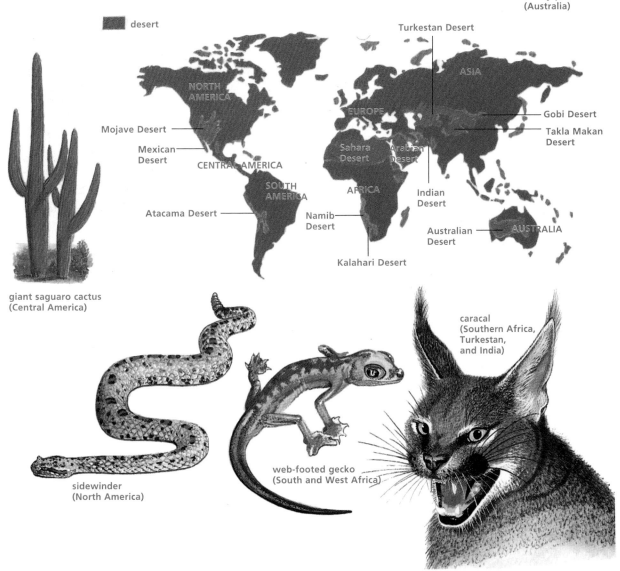

■ desert

Turkestan Desert

NORTH AMERICA

ASIA

EUROPE

Gobi Desert

Mojave Desert

Takla Makan Desert

Mexican Desert

CENTRAL AMERICA

Sahara Desert

Arabian Desert

SOUTH AMERICA

AFRICA

Indian Desert

Atacama Desert

Namib Desert

Australian Desert

AUSTRALIA

Kalahari Desert

giant saguaro cactus
(Central America)

caracal
(Southern Africa, Turkestan, and India)

sidewinder
(North America)

web-footed gecko
(South and West Africa)

143

de·serve (di-**zurv**) *verb* To earn something because of the way you behave. *Angelica deserves a reward for her hard work.*
▷ **deserving, deserved** ▷ *adjective* **deserving**

de·sign (di-**zine**)
1. *verb* To draw something that could be built or made. *The architect designed a new house.*
▷ **designing, designed** ▷ *noun* **designer**
2. *noun* The shape or style of something. *The floor design had diamonds and squares.*

des·ig·nate (**dez**-ig-nate) *verb*
1. To name or mark something. *On many maps, stars designate state capitals.*
2. To call or name something. *Writers have designated the time we live in as the "Modern Age."*
3. To choose someone for an office or duty. *Shawna was designated captain of the soccer team.*
▷ *verb* **designating, designated** ▷ *noun* **designation**

designated hitter *noun* In baseball, a player who is named at the start of the game to bat in the pitcher's place without causing the pitcher to be taken out of the game.

de·sire (di-**zire**) *noun* A strong wish or need for something or someone. *Clifford had a burning desire to run in the marathon.* ▷ *verb* **desire** ▷ *adjective* **desirable**

desk (desk) *noun* A table, often with drawers, used for working at or writing on.

desk

desk·top publishing (**desk**-top) *noun* The process of writing, editing, and designing a book or a newsletter on a computer so that the pages are ready to be printed.

des·o·late (**dess**-uh-luht) *adjective*
1. Deserted or uninhabited, as in *a desolate village.*
2. Sad and lonely. *After my friend left, I felt desolate.*
▷ *noun* **desolation** ▷ *adverb* **desolately**

de·spair (di-**spair**) *verb* To lose hope completely. *Harry despaired of getting home on time.*
▷ **despairing, despaired** ▷ *noun* **despair**
▷ *adjective* **despairing** ▷ *adverb* **despairingly**

des·per·a·do (dess-puh-**rah**-doh) *noun* A bold, reckless criminal; a bandit. *In the movie, the desperado gave up his criminal career after he fell in love.* ▷ *noun, plural* **desperadoes** or **desperados**

des·per·ate (**dess**-pur-it) *adjective*
1. If you are **desperate,** you will do anything to change your situation. ▷ *noun* **desperation**
2. Dangerous or difficult, as in *a desperate act.*
▷ *adverb* **desperately**

de·spise (di-**spize**) *verb* If you **despise** something or someone, you dislike that thing or that person greatly. ▷ **despising, despised** ▷ *adjective* **despicable**

de·spite (di-**spite**) *preposition* In spite of. *Alejandro won the race, despite falling off his bike.*

de·spond·ent (di-**spon**-duhnt) *adjective* Miserable and depressed. *Bob was despondent after he lost the game.* ▷ *adverb* **despondently**

des·sert
(di-**zurt**)
noun A food, such as ice cream, fruit, or cake, usually served at the end of a meal.

a special dessert

des·ti·na·tion (dess-tuh-**nay**-shuhn) *noun* The place that a person or vehicle is traveling to. *The plane's destination was Miami.*

des·tined (**dess**-tuhnd) *adjective*
1. Having a certain fate. *Carolyn is destined to become a great teacher.*
2. Bound for a certain place. *That cruise ship is destined for the Caribbean.*

des·ti·ny (**dess**-tuh-nee) *noun* Your **destiny** is your fate or the future events in your life.
▷ *noun, plural* **destinies**

des·ti·tute (**dess**-tuh-toot) *adjective* A **destitute** person lacks food, shelter, and clothing. ▷ *noun* **destitution**

de·stroy (di-**stroi**) *verb* To ruin something or someone completely. ▷ **destroying, destroyed** ▷ *noun* **destruction** (di-**struhk**-shuhn)

de·stroy·er (di-**stroi**-ur) *noun* A small, very fast warship that uses guns, missiles, and torpedoes to protect other ships from submarines.

de·struc·tive (di-**struhk**-tiv) *adjective* Causing lots of damage and unhappiness. ▷ *adverb* **destructively**

de·tach (di-tach) *verb* To separate one part of something from the rest of it. *We detached the trailer from our car.* ▷ **detaches, detaching, detached** ▷ *adjective* **detachable**

de·tached (di-tacht) *adjective*
1. If you are **detached,** you are able to stand back from a situation and not get too involved in it. ▷ *noun* **detachment**
2. If a house is **detached,** it is separate and not connected to another building.

de·tail (di-tayl *or* dee-tayl) *noun*
1. A small part of a whole item, as in *as in a detail of a painting.*
2. The treatment of something item by item. *Jee's stories are full of detail.* ▷ *adjective* **detailed**
3. *noun, plural* If you ask for **details** about something, you want information about it. ▷ *verb* **detail**

de·tain (di-tayn) *verb* To hold somebody back when he or she wants to go. *The police detained two men for questioning.* ▷ **detaining, detained**

de·tect (di-tekt) *verb* To notice or discover something. *I detected a strange smell in the house.* ▷ **detecting, detected** ▷ *noun* **detection** ▷ *adjective* **detectable**

de·tec·tive (di-tek-tiv) *noun* One who investigates crimes, usually for or with the police.

de·tec·tor (di-tek-tur) *noun* A machine used to reveal the presence of something, such as smoke, metal, or radioactivity, as in *a smoke detector.*

de·ten·tion (di-ten-shuhn) *noun*
1. A punishment in which a student has to report early to or stay after school.
2. If people are held **in detention,** they are kept as prisoners until their trial date.

de·ter (di-tur) *verb* To prevent or discourage something. *The snow deterred us from going to the play.* ▷ **deterring, deterred**

de·ter·gent (di-tur-juhnt) *noun* Liquid or powder used for cleaning things.

de·te·ri·o·rate (di-tihr-ee-uh-rate) *verb* To get worse. *The weather deteriorated throughout the day.* ▷ **deteriorating, deteriorated** ▷ *noun* **deterioration**

de·ter·mine (di-tur-min) *verb*
1. To have an effect on. *The war determined their fate.*
2. To make a discovery or to find out. *I determined that the witness was lying.*
3. If you **determine** the solution to a problem, you are able to settle or resolve it.

de·ter·mined (di-tur-mind) *adjective* If you are **determined** to do something, you have made a firm decision to do it. ▷ *noun* **determination** ▷ *adverb* **determinedly**

de·ter·rent (di-tur-uhnt) *noun* A thing that stops something else from happening. *Burglar alarms are effective deterrents against crime.*

de·test (di-test) *verb* If you **detest** something or somebody, you dislike that thing or person very much. ▷ **detesting, detested** ▷ *adjective* **detestable**

det·o·nate (det-uh-nate) *verb* To set off an explosion. *The heat of the fire detonated the gunpowder.* ▷ **detonating, detonated** ▷ *noun* **detonator**

de·tour (dee-toor) *noun* A longer alternative route usually taken when the direct route is closed for repairs.

de·tract (di-trakt) *verb* To take away something enjoyable or valuable. *The rain detracted from the pleasure of our walk.* ▷ **detracting, detracted**

det·ri·men·tal (det-ri-men-tuhl) *adjective* Harmful. *Smoking is detrimental to your health.* ▷ *noun* **detriment**

deuce (dooss) *noun*
1. In tennis, the score of **deuce** means that there is a tie and both players have 40 points.
2. In card games, a card marked 2.

de·val·ue (dee-val-yoo) *verb* To reduce the value of a currency in relation to another currency or to gold. ▷ **devaluing, devalued** ▷ *noun* **devaluation**

dev·as·tat·ed (dev-uh-stay-tid) *adjective*
1. Very badly damaged, or destroyed. *The area was devastated by floods.* ▷ *noun* **devastation**
2. Shocked and distressed. *I was devastated by the dreadful news.*
▷ *adjective* **devastating** ▷ *verb* **devastate**

de·vel·op (di-vel-uhp) *verb*
1. To grow. *The boys' friendship developed slowly.*
2. To build on something, or to make something grow. *The writer developed his short story into a novel.*
3. When film is **developed,** it is treated with chemicals to bring out the pictures that have been taken.
▷ *verb* **developing, developed** ▷ *noun* **developer, noun development**

de·vi·ate (dee-vee-ate) *verb* To do something differently from the usual way. *The mail carrier deviated from her everyday route.* ▷ **deviating, deviated** ▷ *noun* **deviation**

de·vice (di-visse) *noun*
1. A piece of equipment that does a particular job. *The computer is a device with many functions.*
2. If you are **left to your own devices,** you can do what you want.

dev·il (dev-uhl) *noun*
1. **Devil** or **devil** In many religions, the primary spirit of evil.
2. If you call someone a **devil,** you mean that the person is full of mischief or is wicked.
▷ *adjective* **devilish**

de·vi·ous (dee-vee-uhss) *adjective* Devious people keep their thoughts and actions secret and cannot be trusted. ▷ *noun* **deviousness** ▷ *adverb* **deviously**

de·vise (di-vize) *verb* To think something up, or to invent something. *Let's devise a way to escape.* ▷ **devising, devised**

de·void (di-void) *adjective* Without something, or empty of something. *The house was devoid of furniture.*

de·vote (di-voht) *verb* To give your time, effort, or attention to some purpose. *He devoted his life to helping the poor.* ▷ **devoting, devoted**

de·vot·ed (di-voh-tid) *adjective* Loyal and loving. ▷ *noun* **devotion** ▷ *adverb* **devotedly**

de·vour (di-vour) *verb* To eat something quickly and hungrily. *Geena devoured her lunch.* ▷ **devouring, devoured**

de·vout (di-vout) *adjective* Deeply religious, as in *devout church members.* ▷ *noun* **devoutness** ▷ *adverb* **devoutly**

dew (doo) *noun* Moisture in the form of small drops that collects overnight on cool surfaces outside. **Dew** sounds like **do** and **due.** ▷ *adjective* **dewy**

dew·lap (doo-*lap*) *noun* The loose skin that hangs under an animal's chin or neck. *See* **lizard.**

dex·ter·i·ty (dek-ster-uh-tee) *noun* Skill, especially in using your hands. *This paint job requires great dexterity.* ▷ *adjective* **dexterous**

di·a·be·tes (dye-uh-bee-tuhss *or* dye-uh-bee-teez) *noun* A disease in which there is too much sugar in the blood. ▷ *adjective* **diabetic** (dye-uh-bet-ik)

di·a·bol·ic (dye-uh-bol-ik) *adjective*
1. Extremely wicked, as in *a diabolic plan.*
2. To do with the devil. ▷ *adjective* **diabolical** ▷ *adverb* **diabolically**

di·ag·nose (dye-uhg-nohss) *verb* To determine what disease a patient has or what the cause of a problem is. *The mechanic diagnosed the car's problem as a dead battery.* ▷ **diagnosing, diagnosed** ▷ *noun* **diagnosis**

di·ag·o·nal (dye-ag-uh-nuhl) *adjective* A **diagonal** line is a straight line joining opposite corners of a square or rectangle. ▷ *noun* **diagonal** ▷ *adverb* **diagonally**

di·a·gram (dye-uh-gram) *noun* A drawing or plan that explains something. ▷ *adjective* **diagrammatic**

di·al (dye-uhl)
1. *noun* The face on a clock, watch, or other measuring instrument.
2. *noun* A disk on certain devices, such as a television set or telephone, that is moved to operate the device.
3. *verb* To enter a telephone number by pressing buttons or, on older phones, turning a dial. ▷ **dialing, dialed**

di·a·lect (dye-uh-lekt) *noun* A way a language is spoken in a particular place or among a particular group of people. *Many dialects were spoken in the mountain region.*

di·a·logue (dye-uh-lawg) *noun* Conversation, especially in a play, movie, television program, or book. *The movie's dialogue was silly.*

dial tone *noun* The sound that you should hear when you first pick up a telephone receiver.

di·am·e·ter (dye-am-uh-tur) *noun* A straight line through the center of a circle, from one side to another. *See* **circle.**

di·a·mond (dye-muhnd *or* dye-uh-muhnd) *noun*
1. A very hard, clear, precious stone.
2. A shape with four equal sides, like a square standing on one of its corners.
3. **diamonds** *noun, plural* One of the four suits in a deck of cards.
4. The area of a baseball field enclosed by first, second, and third base, plus home plate.

di·a·per (dye-pur *or* dye-uh-pur) *noun* A piece of soft, absorbent clothing worn as underwear by babies and young children.

di·a·phragm (dye-uh-fram) *noun* The wall of muscle between your chest and your abdomen. *See* **respiration.**

di·ar·rhe·a (*dye-uh-ree-uh*) *noun* A condition in which normally solid waste becomes runny and frequent.

di·a·ry (dye-uh-ree) *noun* A book in which people write down things that happen each day, either to use as a record or to plan ahead. ▷ *noun, plural* **diaries**

dice (disse)
1. *noun, plural* Cubes with a different number of dots on each face, used in games. The singular of *dice* is *die,* although some people use *dice* as the singular.
2. *verb* To cut something, such as vegetables, into cubes, as in *to dice the carrots.* ▷ **dicing, diced** ▷ *adjective* **diced**

dice

dic·tate (dik-tate) *verb*
1. To talk aloud so that someone can write down what you say. *The supervisor dictated a long letter to her assistant.* ▷ *noun* **dictation**

2. To control. *Our parents dictate the amount of spending money we get.*
▷ *verb* **dictating, dictated**

dic·ta·tor (dik-tay-tur) *noun* Someone who has complete control of a country, often ruling it unjustly. ▷ *noun* **dictatorship**

dic·tion·ar·y (dik-shuh-ner-ee) *noun* A book such as this one that lists words in a language in alphabetical order and explains what they mean. ▷ *noun, plural* **dictionaries**

did·n't (did-uhnt) *contraction* A short form of *did not. I didn't think you would remember to call me this evening.*

die (dye)
1. *verb* To stop living, or to come to an end. *The sound of the train's whistle died in the distance.*
2. *verb* If you are **dying** to do something, you really want to do it.
3. *noun* The singular form of the word *dice.*
Die sounds like **dye.**
▷ *verb* **dying, died**

die·sel (dee-zuhl) *noun* A fuel used in diesel engines that is heavier than gasoline.

diesel engine *noun* A type of engine that burns fuel oil using heat produced by compressing air. By contrast, a gasoline engine uses an electric spark to start the burning process.

▶ **Word History**
· ·

Diesel engines owe their name to their inventor, Dr. Rudolph Diesel. This engineer developed his heavy-duty engine in Germany from 1892 through 1897 and spent the rest of his life perfecting it.

---

di·et (dye-uht)
1. *noun* Your **diet** is what you usually eat.
▷ *adjective* **dietary**
2. *noun* A prescribed or selected eating plan, usually for losing weight.
3. *verb* When you **diet,** you choose what you eat in order to lose weight, gain weight, or improve your health. ▷ **dieting, dieted** ▷ *noun* **dieter**

dif·fer·ence (dif-ur-uhnss or dif-ruhnss) *noun*
1. The way in which things are not like each other. *What's the difference between margarine and butter?* ▷ *verb* **differ**
2. The **difference** between two numbers is the amount by which one is less or more than the other. *The difference between 5 and 2 is 3.*

dif·fer·ent (dif-ur-uhnt or dif-ruhnt) *adjective* Not the same. *Jill's opinion is different from mine.*
▷ *adverb* **differently**

dif·fi·cult (dif-uh-*kuhlt*) *adjective*
1. Not easy, as in *a difficult exam.*
2. A **difficult** person is not easy to get along with.

dif·fi·cul·ty (dif-uh-*kuhl*-tee) *noun* A problem. *There were many difficulties to resolve before we could get started.* ▷ *noun, plural* **difficulties**

dig (dig)
1. *verb* To use a shovel or spade to move earth.
2. *verb* To look very hard for information. *Dig up all the facts.*
3. *noun* A push or a poke, as in *a dig in the ribs.*
4. *noun* An unkind remark. *That was a nasty dig.*
5. *noun* An archaeological excavation. *Denise was on a dig in Egypt.*
▷ *verb* **digging, dug** (duhg)

di·gest
1. (dye-jest) *verb* To break down food in the organs of digestion so that it can be absorbed into the blood and used by the body.
▷ **digesting, digested**
2. (dye-jest) *noun* A shortened form of a book or other written work, or a collection of such shortened forms. *I read a digest of that article.*

di·ges·tion (duh-jess-chuhn) *noun* The process of breaking down food in the stomach and other organs so that it can be absorbed into the blood. *This diagram shows the main organs used in human digestion. See also* **organ.** ▷ *adjective* **digestive**

human digestive system

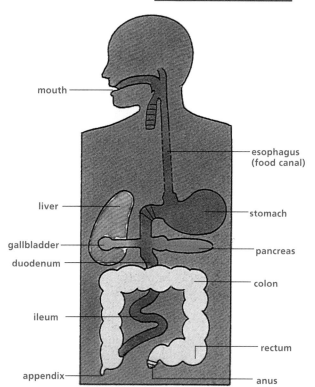

mouth
esophagus (food canal)
liver
stomach
gallbladder
pancreas
duodenum
colon
ileum
rectum
appendix
anus

dig·it (dij-it) *noun*
1. Any one of the Arabic numerals from 1 to 9, and sometimes 0. *There are 7 digits in my phone number.*
2. A finger or toe.

dig·it·al (dij-uh-tuhl) *adjective* A **digital** display shows time, speed, etc., in numerals.

dig·i·tize (dij-uh-tize) *verb* To convert or change data or graphic images to digital form, usable by a computer. ▷ **digitizing, digitized**

dig·ni·fied (dig-nuh-fide) *adjective* Calm, proud, and in control; noble; stately. *The tennis player accepted defeat in a dignified manner.*

dig·ni·ty (dig-nuh-tee) *noun* A person who has **dignity** has a quality or manner that makes him or her worthy of honor or respect.

dike (dike) *noun* A high wall or dam that is built to hold back water and prevent flooding.

di·lap·i·dat·ed (duh-lap-uh-day-tid) *adjective* Shabby and falling to pieces, as in *a dilapidated old barn.* ▷ *noun* **dilapidation**

di·lem·ma (duh-lem-uh) *noun* If you are **in a dilemma,** you have to make a choice between two difficult alternatives.

dil·i·gent (dil-uh-juhnt) *adjective* Working hard and carefully. *Maria was diligent about doing her homework before watching television.* ▷ *noun* **diligence** ▷ *adverb* **diligently**

di·lute (duh-lute *or* dye-lute) *verb* When you **dilute** something, you make it weaker by adding water or other liquid. ▷ **diluting, diluted** ▷ *noun* **dilution**

dim (dim)
1. *adjective* Somewhat dark, as in *a dim corner of the room.*
2. *adjective* Formless, or hard to see. *When I turned the corner, I could see the dim outline of a building in the fog.*
3. *verb* To make less bright. *The teacher dimmed the lights so he could show the movie.* ▷ **dimming, dimmed**

dime (dime) *noun* A small coin of the United States and Canada that is worth 10 cents. *There are 10 dimes in a dollar.*

di·men·sion (duh-men-shuhn) *noun* The **dimensions** of an object are its measurements or its size. All objects have three dimensions: length, width, and height. ▷ *adjective* **dimensional**

di·min·ish (duh-min-ish) *verb* If something **diminishes,** it becomes smaller or weaker. *The long drought diminished our water supply.* ▷ **diminishes, diminishing, diminished**

di·min·u·tive (duh-min-yuh-tiv) *adjective* Tiny, or very small. *Although she is a diminutive woman, her strong singing voice can fill an auditorium.*

dim·ple (dim-puhl) *noun* A small hollow in a person's cheek or chin. ▷ *adjective* **dimpled**

din (din) *noun* A great deal of noise. *We could not hear each other over the din of the crowd.*

dine (dine) *verb* To have a meal, especially dinner, in a formal way. *We dined by candlelight.* ▷ **dining, dined**

din·er (dye-nur) *noun*
1. A person eating in a restaurant, hotel, etc.
2. A restaurant with a long counter and small eating areas or booths.

di·nette (dye-net) *noun*
1. A small space, usually off the kitchen, for eating meals.
2. A **dinette set** is a table and chairs used for eating in such an area.

ding·bat (ding-*bat*) *noun*
1. *(slang)* Someone who is scatterbrained or a fool.
2. In printing, a symbol other than letters and numbers. *The symbols $, &, and @ are dingbats.*

din·ghy (ding-ee) *noun* A small, open boat. ▷ *noun, plural* **dinghies**

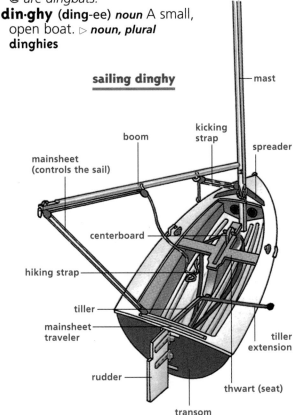

sailing dinghy

mast — boom — kicking strap — spreader — mainsheet (controls the sail) — centerboard — hiking strap — tiller — mainsheet traveler — rudder — tiller extension — thwart (seat) — transom

din·gy (din-jee) *adjective* Dull and dirty, as in *a dingy room.* ▷ **dingier, dingiest**

dining room *noun* A room where meals are served. *Our cousins met us for lunch in the hotel dining room.*

din·ner (din-ur) *noun*
1. The main meal of the day.
2. A formal banquet. *The president gave a dinner for the queen of England.*

di·no·saur (dye-nuh-sor) *noun* Any of a group of large reptiles that lived on land in prehistoric times. *The picture shows a range of dinosaurs and the periods when they existed.*

■ Triassic 248-213 million years ago
■ Jurassic 213-144 million years ago
■ Cretaceous 144-65 million years ago

dinosaurs

■ staurikosaurus
■ plateosaurus
■ triceratops
■ parasaurolophus
■ velociraptor
■ kentrosaurus
■ brachiosaurus
■ deinonychus
■ spinosaurus
■ stegosaurus
■ pachycephalosaurus
■ tyrannosaurus rex

di·o·cese (dye-uh-siss *or* dye-uh-seess) *noun* A church district that is presided over by a bishop.
▷ *noun, plural* **dioceses** (dye-uh-seess *or* dye-uh-siss-iz)

dip (dip)
1. *verb* To put something briefly into a liquid. *Dip your brush in the water.*
2. *verb* To slope downward. *The road ahead dipped sharply.* ▷ *noun* **dip**
3. *noun* If you **take a dip,** you go for a short swim.
4. *noun* A thick, tasty sauce into which you dip raw vegetables, chips, etc.
▷ *verb* **dipping, dipped**

di·plo·ma (duh-ploh-muh) *noun* A certificate from a school showing that you have finished a course of study.

dip·lo·mat (dip-luh-mat) *noun* A person who represents his or her country's government in a foreign country.

dip·lo·mat·ic (dip-luh-mat-ik) *adjective*
1. To do with being a diplomat, as in *the diplomatic service.*
2. If you are **diplomatic,** you are tactful and good at dealing with people. ▷ *noun* **diplomacy** (di-ploh-muh-see)

149

dip·per (dip-ur) *noun* A cup with a long handle used to scoop liquid out of a large container. *The Big Dipper and the Little Dipper are two constellations whose stars form the shape of a dipper.*

dire (dire) *adjective* Dreadful or urgent, as in *dire need.* ▷ **direr, direst**

di·rect (duh-**rekt** *or* dye-**rekt**)
1. *adjective* In a straight line, or by the shortest route. *The arrow traveled in a direct path.*
2. *verb* To supervise people, especially in a play, movie, or television program. *Jennifer directed her classmates in the school play.*
3. *verb* To tell someone the way to go. *Please direct me to the hotel.*
4. *adjective* If someone is **direct,** he or she has a very straightforward manner.
▷ *verb* **directing, directed** ▷ *adverb* **directly**

di·rec·tion (duh-**rek**-shuhn) *noun*
1. The way that someone or something is moving or pointing. *We traveled in the direction of the lake.*
2. Guidance or supervision. *Luís learned to ski under the direction of a famous pro.*
3. directions *noun, plural* Instructions. *Follow the directions carefully.*

di·rec·tor (duh-**rek**-tur) *noun*
1. The person in charge of making a play, a movie, or a radio or television program.
2. One of a group of people responsible for directing the affairs of a company.

di·rec·to·ry (duh-**rek**-tuh-ree) *noun* A book that gives addresses, phone numbers, etc., in alphabetical order. ▷ *noun, plural* **directories**

di·ri·gi·ble (dihr-uh-juh-buhl) *noun* An aircraft that is shaped like a cigar, filled with a gas that makes it rise, and powered by a motor. *This photograph shows the giant dirigible U.S.S. Macon on a 1933 flight over New York City.*

dirigible

dirt (durt) *noun*
1. Earth, or soil. *We loosened the dirt in our garden to get ready for planting.*
2. Mud, dust, and other unclean substances. *My brother paid me $5.00 to wash the dirt off his car.*

dir·ty (durt-ee) *adjective*
1. Not clean.
2. Unfair, as in *a dirty trick.*
3. Showing bad feeling toward someone, as in *dirty looks.*
▷ *adjective* **dirtier, dirtiest**

> ## Synonyms: dirty
>
> **Dirty** means not clean. It can refer to people or things: *We all got really dirty when we played soccer on the muddy field. Dirty clothes go in a pile near the washing machine.*
>
> **Filthy** is a much stronger word that means dirty to the extreme: *When we moved into the apartment, it was so filthy that we didn't know where to begin cleaning it.*
>
> **Foul** describes something that not only is dirty but also smells that way: *The refrigerator was foul with the smell of spoiled milk.*
>
> **Smudged** means smeared or a little bit dirty: *Her arm was smudged with charcoal after she cleaned the barbecue grill.*
>
> **Soiled** means stained or dirty. It especially refers to clothing: *He changed the baby's soiled diaper.*

dis (diss) *verb* (slang) To show disrespect for someone. *I didn't mean to dis you when I said you couldn't dance.* ▷ *verb* **disses, dissing, dissed**

> ## Prefix
>
> The prefix **dis-** adds one of these meanings to a root word:
>
> **1.** Not or opposite, as in *disagree* (to not agree) or *disinfect* (to do the opposite of infect).
>
> **2.** Lack of, as in *disbelief* (lack of belief) or *disrespect* (lack of respect).

dis·a·ble (diss-ay-buhl) *verb* To take away the ability to do something. *A dead battery disabled the car.* ▷ **disabling, disabled**

dis·a·bled (diss-ay-buhld) *adjective* People who are **disabled** are restricted in what they can do, usually because of an illness or injury or from a condition present from birth. ▷ *noun* **disability**

dis·ad·van·tage (diss-uhd-**van**-tij) *noun*
1. Something that causes a problem or makes life more difficult. *Being too heavy is a disadvantage for a dancer.*
2. Loss or damage. *It is to our disadvantage if our team arrives at the game late.*
3. disadvantaged *adjective* People who are **disadvantaged** are very poor and lack many opportunities.

dis·a·gree (diss-uh-**gree**) *verb*
1. If you **disagree** with someone, you have different opinions. ▷ *noun* **disagreement**
2. To cause discomfort. *Peppers disagree with me.*
▷ *verb* **disagreeing, disagreed**

dis·ap·pear (diss-uh-**pihr**) *verb* To go out of sight. ▷ **disappearing, disappeared** ▷ *noun* **disappearance**

dis·ap·point (diss-uh-**point**) *verb* To let someone down by failing to do what he or she expected. *George's grades will disappoint his parents.*
▷ **disappointing, disappointed** ▷ *noun* **disappointment** ▷ *adjective* **disappointed,** *adjective* **disappointing**

dis·ap·prove (diss-uh-**proov**) *verb* If you **disapprove** of something, you do not think it is a good thing. ▷ **disapproving, disapproved** ▷ *noun* **disapproval**

dis·arm (diss-**arm**) *verb*
1. To take weapons away from somebody.
2. If a country **disarms,** it gives up its weapons. ▷ *noun* **disarmament**
3. If someone **disarms** you, the person makes you feel friendly or forget your suspicions.
▷ *adjective* **disarming**
▷ *verb* **disarming, disarmed**

dis·as·ter (duh-**zass**-tur) *noun*
1. An event that causes great damage, loss, or suffering, such as a flood or a serious train wreck.
2. If something is a **disaster,** it turns out completely wrong.
▷ *adjective* **disastrous** ▷ *adverb* **disastrously**

dis·be·lief (diss-bi-**leef**) *noun* Refusal to believe something. *My story was greeted with total disbelief.*

dis·be·lieve (diss-bi-**leev**) *verb* If you **disbelieve** something, you do not think it is true.
▷ **disbelieving, disbelieved**

disc (disk) *noun* Another spelling of **disk.**

dis·card (diss-**kard**) *verb* To throw something away. *Peter discarded all his old toys.*
▷ **discarding, discarded**

dis·charge (diss-**charj**) *verb*
1. To tell someone officially that he or she can go or leave. *The doctor has discharged me from the hospital.*
2. To release a substance into the open. *The factory discharged chemicals into the river.*

▷ *verb* **discharging, discharged** ▷ *noun* **discharge** (diss-*charj*)

dis·ci·ple (duh-**sye**-puhl) *noun* Someone who follows the teachings of a leader.

dis·ci·pline (diss-uh-plin) *noun*
1. Control over the way that you or other people behave. *My aunt thinks my brother is too wild and needs more discipline.* ▷ *verb* **discipline** ▷ *adjective* **disciplinary**
2. An area of study. *Science and history are both disciplines.*

disc jockey *noun* Someone who plays music on the radio or at a party or club. ▷ *noun, plural* **disc jockeys**

dis·close (diss-**klohz**) *verb* To reveal something. *André promised not to disclose where his parents hid his brother's birthday present.* ▷ *noun* **disclosure** (diss-**kloh**-zhur)

dis·co (diss-koh)
1. *noun* A club where music is played for dancing. ▷ *noun, plural* **discos**
2. *adjective* A type of music played at clubs.

dis·com·fort (diss-**kuhm**-furt) *noun* A feeling of pain or uneasiness that keeps you from relaxing. *The dentist said I might feel some discomfort when I got home.*

dis·con·nect (diss-kuh-**nekt**) *verb*
1. To separate things that are joined together.
2. If something such as the electrical supply or a telephone line is **disconnected,** it is cut off.
▷ *verb* **disconnecting, disconnected** ▷ *noun* **disconnection**

dis·con·tent·ed (diss-kuhn-**ten**-tid) *adjective* Not satisfied. *Elizabeth was discontented with her boring part-time job.* ▷ *noun* **discontent** ▷ *adverb* **discontentedly**

dis·con·tin·ue (diss-kuhn-**tin**-yoo) *verb* To stop something that is done regularly. *We discontinued the newspaper delivery while we were away.* ▷ **discontinuing, discontinued**

dis·cord (diss-kord) *noun*
1. Disagreement between two or more people.
2. A mixture of musical notes that sounds unpleasant. ▷ *adjective* **discordant** (diss-**kord**-uhnt)

dis·count (diss-kount) *noun*
1. A price cut.
2. A **discount store** sells things at reduced prices.

dis·cour·age (diss-**kur**-ij)
1. *verb* If you **discourage** people from doing something, you persuade them not to do it. *My parents discouraged me from leaving school.*
▷ **discouraging, discouraged**
2. *adjective* If you are **discouraged,** you lose your enthusiasm or confidence. *Jon was discouraged after failing the driving test.*
▷ *noun* **discouragement**

dis·cov·er (diss-kuh-vur) *verb*
1. To find something. *We discovered the treasure as we were exploring the attic.*
2. To find out about something. *I soon discovered that Li was lying.*
▷ *verb* **discovering, discovered** ▷ *noun* **discovery,** *noun* **discoverer**

dis·creet (diss-kreet) *adjective* If you are **discreet,** you know the right thing to say and can be trusted to keep a secret. ▷ *noun* **discretion** (diss-kre-shuhn) ▷ *adverb* **discreetly**

dis·crim·i·nate (diss-krim-uh-nate) *verb*
1. If you **discriminate** against people, you are prejudiced against them and treat them unfairly. ▷ **discriminating, discriminated** ▷ *adjective* **discriminatory**
2. To recognize differences between things or people. *We must discriminate good behavior from bad.* ▷ *adjective* **discriminating**

dis·crim·i·na·tion (*diss*-krim-i-**nay**-shuhn) *noun*
1. Prejudice or unjust behavior to others based on differences in age, race, gender, etc.
2. The ability to recognize small differences.

dis·cus (diss-kuhss) *noun* A large heavy disk that is thrown in a track-and-field event. *This statue shows an ancient Greek athlete throwing the discus.* ▷ *noun, plural* **discuses**

discus thrower

dis·cuss (diss-kuhss) *verb* To talk over something. *Can we meet to discuss the new plans?* ▷ **discusses, discussing, discussed** ▷ *noun* **discussion**

dis·ease (duh-zeez) *noun*
1. A specific illness. *Measles is an infectious disease.*
2. Sickness in general. *Disease spread throughout the city.* ▷ *adjective* **diseased**

dis·fig·ure (diss-fig-yur) *verb* To spoil the way something looks. *Doctor Kubrik specializes in helping people who have been disfigured in accidents.* ▷ **disfiguring, disfigured** ▷ *noun* **disfigurement** ▷ *adjective* **disfigured**

dis·grace (diss-grayss)
1. *verb* If you **disgrace** yourself, you do something that other people disapprove of and that makes you feel ashamed. ▷ **disgracing, disgraced**
2. *noun* If something is a **disgrace,** it causes shame or disapproval. ▷ *adjective* **disgraceful**

dis·grun·tled (diss-grunt-uhld) *adjective* Unhappy, or dissatisfied. *The boss tried to reason with the disgruntled employees.*

dis·guise (diss-gize)
1. *verb* To hide something. *Steve tried to disguise his boredom.* ▷ **disguising, disguised**
2. *noun* If you put on a **disguise,** you dress in a way that hides your identity.

dis·gust·ing (diss-guhss-ting) *adjective* Very unpleasant and offensive to others. *The room had a disgusting smell.* ▷ *noun* **disgust** ▷ *verb* **disgust** ▷ *adverb* **disgustingly**

dish (dish)
1. *noun* A container, such as a plate or bowl, used for serving food.
2. *noun* Food made in a certain way, as in *a chicken dish.*
3. *verb* If you **dish up** food, you put or serve it in a dish. ▷ **dishes, dishing, dished** ▷ *noun, plural* **dishes**

di·shev·eled (di-shev-uhld) *adjective* Very messy. *Hector's clothes were always disheveled.*

dis·hon·est (diss-on-ist) *adjective* Not honest or fair. *It is dishonest to cheat.* ▷ *noun* **dishonesty** ▷ *adverb* **dishonestly**

dis·hon·or (diss-on-ur) *verb* To bring shame or disgrace upon yourself or others. *The football player said he would rather lose a game than dishonor his team by cheating.* ▷ **dishonoring, dishonored** ▷ *noun* **dishonor** ▷ *adjective* **dishonorable**

dish·wash·er (dish-*wah*-shur) *noun*
1. A machine for washing dishes.
2. Someone whose job is to wash dishes.

dis·il·lu·sion (diss-i-loo-zhuhn) *verb* If you **disillusion** someone, you destroy his or her mistaken ideas or unrealistic hopes about something. *Sam disillusioned his brother about camp.* ▷ **disillusioning, disillusioned** ▷ *noun* **disillusionment**

dis·in·fect·ant (diss-in-fek-tuhnt) *noun* A chemical used to kill germs, as on a cut or on a household surface. ▷ *verb* **disinfect**

dis·in·te·grate (diss-in-tuh-grate) *verb*
1. To break into small pieces. *The walnut shell disintegrated when I hit it with a hammer.*
2. To break up. *Emily is sad because her parents' marriage is disintegrating.*
▷ *verb* **disintegrating, disintegrated** ▷ *noun* **disintegration**

dis·in·ter·est·ed (diss-in-tuh-*ress*-tid) *adjective* Impartial, or without personal feelings for either side of a contest or an argument. *We need a disinterested person to act as referee for our swimming race.*

dis·joint·ed (diss-join-tid) *adjective* Not connected, or not flowing smoothly. *Her speech was long and disjointed.*

disk *or* **disc** (disk) *noun*
1. A flat, circular object. *A Frisbee is a disk.*
2. A piece of plastic, used for recording music or computer information, as in *a floppy disk.*

disk drive *noun* The part of a computer that reads information from, or saves information onto, a disk.

dis·like (diss-like) *verb* If you **dislike** someone or something, you have a feeling of displeasure about that person or thing. ▷ **disliking, disliked** ▷ *noun* **dislike**

dis·lo·cate (diss-loh-kate *or* diss-loh-*kate*) *verb* If you **dislocate** a bone, it comes out of its usual place, as in *to dislocate a shoulder.* ▷ **dislocating, dislocated** ▷ *noun* **dislocation** ▷ *adjective* **dislocated**

dis·lodge (diss-loj) *verb* To force something out of position. *She used a shovel to dislodge the boulder.* ▷ **dislodging, dislodged**

dis·mal (diz-muhl) *adjective*
1. Gloomy and sad.
2. Dreadful, as in *a dismal failure.*

dis·man·tle (diss-man-tuhl) *verb* To take something apart, as in *to dismantle a store display.* ▷ **dismantling, dismantled**

dis·mayed (diss-made) *adjective* If you are **dismayed,** you are upset and worried about something. ▷ *noun* **dismay**

dis·miss (diss-miss) *verb*
1. To allow to leave. *Our teacher dismissed us from class early.*
2. To fire someone from a job. *The airline dismissed 500 workers.*
3. To put something out of your mind. *I've dismissed the idea of having a party.*
▷ *verb* **dismisses, dismissing, dismissed** ▷ *noun* **dismissal**

dis·mount (diss-mount) *verb* If you **dismount** from something, you get off it. *Arnold dismounted from the pony and landed on his feet.* ▷ **dismounting, dismounted** ▷ *noun* **dismount**

dis·o·be·di·ent (diss-uh-bee-dee-uhnt) *adjective* If you are **disobedient,** you do not do as you are told. ▷ *noun* **disobedience** ▷ *adverb* **disobediently**

dis·o·bey (diss-oh-bay) *verb* To go against the rules or someone's wishes. *My mother told me to do my homework after school, but I disobeyed her and was punished.* ▷ **disobeying, disobeyed**

dis·or·der·ly (diss-or-dur-lee) *adjective*
1. Untidy and disorganized, as in *a disorderly desk.*
2. A **disorderly** mob of people is uncontrolled and possibly violent.
▷ *noun* **disorderliness,** *noun* **disorder**

dis·or·gan·i·zed (diss-or-guh-nized) *adjective* Confused and not in order. *John is so disorganized that he can never find anything in his room.* ▷ *noun* **disorganization**

dis·own (diss-ohn) *verb* If you **disown** someone, you refuse to accept the person as a relative any longer. *The criminal's parents disowned him.* ▷ **disowning, disowned**

dis·patch (diss-pach)
1. *noun* A message or a report. *Four dispatches reached the newspaper at the same time.* ▷ *noun, plural* **dispatches**
2. *verb* To send something or somebody off. *We dispatched a messenger to their office.*
▷ **dispatches, dispatching, dispatched**

dis·pel (diss-pel) *verb* To put an end to something, as in *to dispel a rumor.* ▷ **dispelling, dispelled**

dis·pen·sa·ry (di-spen-suh-ree) *noun* A place where medicines are prepared and given out. ▷ *noun, plural* **dispensaries** ▷ *verb* **dispense**

dis·perse (diss-purss) *verb* To scatter. *The police dispersed the crowd.* ▷ **dispersing, dispersed** ▷ *noun* **dispersal**

dis·place (diss-playss) *verb*
1. To move someone or something from its usual place. *The earthquake displaced many people.*
2. To take the place of something or somebody else. *When you sit in a bathtub, you displace some water.*
▷ *verb* **displacing, displaced** ▷ *noun* **displacement**

dis·play (diss-play)
1. *verb* To show something. *Jo displayed surprise as she read my note.* ▷ **displaying, displayed**
2. *noun* A public show or exhibition. *The library had a display of rare manuscripts.*
3. *noun* A screen or panel on electronic equipment that shows information, as in *the video display terminal of a computer.*
4. *noun* Special behavior by an animal to attract a mate.

dis·please (diss-pleez) *verb* If you **displease** someone, you annoy the person or cause him or her to be dissatisfied. *Loud music displeases my parents.* ▷ **displeasing, displeased** ▷ *noun* **displeasure** (diss-plezh-ur) ▷ *adjective* **displeased**

dis·pos·a·ble (diss-poh-zuh-buhl) *adjective* Made to be thrown away after use, as in *disposable diapers.* ▷ *verb* **dispose**

dis·pos·al (diss-poze-uhl) *noun*
1. The act of throwing away or recycling something. *During the camping trip, each person was responsible for the proper disposal of his or her trash.*
2. A **garbage disposal** is a small machine under a sink that grinds up leftover food and sends it into the sewer system.

D

dis·po·si·tion (diss-puh-**zish**-uhn) *noun*
1. A person's general attitude or temperament. *Julie has a pleasant disposition.*
2. A tendency or inclination to behave a certain way. *Aaron doesn't have the disposition to lie.*

dis·prove (diss-**proov**) *verb* If you **disprove** something, you show that it cannot be true. ▷ **disproving, disproved**

dis·pute (diss-**pyoot**)
1. *noun* A disagreement.
2. *verb* If you **dispute** what someone says, you say that you think it is wrong. ▷ **disputing, disputed**

dis·qual·i·fy (diss-**kwol**-uh-fye) *verb* To prevent someone from taking part in an activity, often because the person has broken a rule. ▷ **disqualifies, disqualifying, disqualified** ▷ *noun* **disqualification**

dis·re·gard (diss-ri-**gard**) *verb* To take no notice of someone or something. ▷ **disregarding, disregarded** ▷ *noun* **disregard**

dis·rep·u·ta·ble (diss-**rep**-yuh-tuh-buhl) *adjective* If someone or something is **disreputable,** that person or thing has a bad reputation. ▷ *noun* **disrepute** (diss-ri-**pyoot**)

dis·res·pect (diss-ri-**spekt**) *noun* A lack of respect, or rudeness. ▷ *adjective* **disrespectful** ▷ *adverb* **disrespectfully**

dis·rupt (diss-**ruhpt**) *verb* To disturb or break up something that is happening. *Josh disrupted the meeting by shouting out loud.* ▷ **disrupting, disrupted** ▷ *noun* **disruption** ▷ *adjective* **disruptive**

dis·sat·is·fied (diss-**sat**-uhss-fide) *adjective* Unhappy or discontented. ▷ *noun* **dissatisfaction** ▷ *verb* **dissatisfy**

dis·sect (di-**sekt** *or* dye-**sekt**) *verb*
1. To cut apart an animal or a human body so as to examine it. *The picture shows a screen from Operation Frog, a computer program in which you dissect a frog.*
2. To examine and analyze something very carefully, as in *to dissect an argument.*
▷ *verb* **dissecting, dissected** ▷ *noun* **dissection**

dissecting a frog

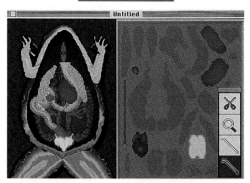

dis·sent (di-**sent**)
1. *verb* To disagree with an idea or opinion. *No one dissented when my class voted to adopt a stray dog.* ▷ **dissenting, dissented**
2. *noun* Disagreement with an opinion or idea. *There was dissent over the new contract among the members of the labor union.*
▷ *noun* **dissension**

dis·si·dent (diss-uh-**duhnt**) *noun* Someone who disagrees with the laws of a country or an organization, as in *a political dissident.* ▷ *noun* **dissidence**

dis·solve (di-**zolv**) *verb*
1. To seem to disappear when mixed with liquid. *Does this tablet dissolve in water?*
2. If a partnership is **dissolved,** it is officially ended.
▷ *verb* **dissolving, dissolved** ▷ *noun* **dissolution** (diss-uh-**loo**-shuhn)

dis·tance (diss-**tuhnss**) *noun*
1. The amount of space between two places.
2. If you see something **in the distance,** it is far away.
3. If you **keep your distance** from somebody, you keep away from the person.

dis·tant (diss-**tuhnt**) *adjective*
1. Not close in space or time, as in *a distant land* or *the distant future.*
2. Not closely related, as in *a distant cousin.*
3. Not warm or friendly. *She sometimes has a distant attitude toward her friends.*

dis·taste (diss-**tayst**) *noun* A feeling of not liking. *I have a distaste for violent movies.*

dis·taste·ful (diss-**tayst**-fuhl) *adjective* Unpleasant or not to a person's taste; offensive. *I find that remark distasteful.*

dis·tem·per (diss-**temp**-ur) *noun* An often deadly disease common among dogs and some other animals. It is caused by a virus and has symptoms including fever and loss of appetite.

dis·till (di-**stil**) *verb* To purify a liquid by heating it until it turns into a gas and then letting the gas cool to form a liquid again. ▷ **distilling, distilled** ▷ *noun* **distillation,** *noun* **distiller** ▷ *adjective* **distilled**

dis·tinct (diss-**tingkt**) *adjective*
1. Very clear. *Pascale has a distinct French accent.* ▷ *adverb* **distinctly**
2. Clearly different. *The original recording is quite distinct from the cheap copies.*

dis·tinc·tion (diss-**tingk**-shuhn) *noun*
1. A clear difference.
2. Excellence, as in *an actor of distinction.*
3. Something that makes an object or a person unusual or different. *Gloria has the distinction of being the best player on the soccer team.*

dis·tinc·tive (diss-**tingk**-tiv) *adjective* Making a person or thing different from all others. *Carrie has a very distinctive taste in clothes.*

dis·tin·guish (diss-**ting**-gwish) *verb*
1. To tell the difference between things. *Can you distinguish between a frog and a toad?*
2. To see or hear clearly. *We were able to distinguish their faces in the crowd.*
▷ *verb* **distinguishes, distinguishing, distinguished** ▷ *adjective* **distinguishable**

dis·tin·guished (diss-**ting**-gwisht) *adjective* A **distinguished** person is noted for the important things that he or she has done.

dis·tort (diss-**tort**) *verb*
1. To twist something out of shape.
2. To change the facts in order to mislead someone. *The magazine article distorted the real story about the politician.*
▷ *verb* **distorting, distorted** ▷ *noun* **distortion**
▷ *adjective* **distorted**

dis·tract (diss-**trakt**) *verb* If someone or something **distracts** you, that person or thing weakens your concentration on what you are doing. ▷ **distracting, distracted** ▷ *noun* **distraction**

dis·tress (diss-**tress**) *noun*
1. A feeling of great pain or sadness. *The letter about your aunt's car accident caused me great distress.* ▷ *verb* **distress** ▷ *adjective* **distressed,** *adjective* **distressing**
2. in distress In need of help. *The ship was in distress.*

dis·trib·ute (diss-**trib**-yoot) *verb*
1. To give things out. *Louie distributed the candy among his friends*
2. To deliver products to various places.
▷ *verb* **distributing, distributed** ▷ *noun* **distribution** (diss-tri-**byoo**-shuhn)

dis·trib·u·tor (diss-**trib**-yuh-tur) *noun*
1. A person or company that delivers products to various places.
2. The part of a car engine that sends electricity from the ignition system to the spark plugs.

dis·trict (diss-**trikt**) *noun* An area or a region.

dis·trust (diss-**trust**) *verb* If you **distrust** someone, you think that the person may do you harm.
▷ **distrusting, distrusted** ▷ *noun* **distrust**
▷ *adjective* **distrustful** ▷ *adverb* **distrustfully**

dis·turb (diss-**turb**) *verb*
1. To interrupt somebody when he or she is doing something.
2. To worry or upset someone. ▷ *adjective* **disturbing**
▷ *verb* **disturbing, disturbed**

dis·use (diss-**yooss**) *noun* If something is in **disuse**, it is no longer used. ▷ *adjective* **disused**

ditch (dich)
1. *noun* A long, narrow trench that drains water away. *The photograph shows a ditch that was dug so that a pipeline (shown in blue) could be laid.* ▷ *noun, plural* **ditches**
2. *verb* If a pilot **ditches** a plane, he or she makes an emergency landing in water.
3. *verb* (slang) If one person **ditches** another, he or she leaves the person suddenly. *Jodie ditched her boyfriend last week.*
▷ *verb* **ditches, ditching, ditched**

ditch

dit·to (**dit**-oh) *noun* **Ditto** marks (") are used in lists to show that what is written above is repeated on the line with the marks. ▷ *noun, plural* **dittos**

dive (dive) *verb*
1. To plunge with your head first into water with your arms stretched out in front of you.
2. To drop down suddenly. *The kite dived to the ground.*
▷ *verb* **diving, dived** *or* **dove** (dohv) ▷ *noun* **dive**

div·er (**dye**-vur) *noun*
1. Someone who dives underwater.
2. Someone who uses breathing apparatus to swim or explore underwater. *See* **scuba diving**.

di·verse (duh-**vurss** *or* dye-**vurss**) *adjective* Varied or assorted. *Hal has a diverse collection of friends.*

di·ver·sion (duh-**vur**-zhuhn *or* dye-**vur**-zhuhn) *noun* Something that takes your mind off other things. *Dad's favorite diversion is riding his bicycle.*

di·ver·si·ty (di-**vur**-suh-tee) *noun* A variety. *The people in the room represented a diversity of backgrounds and experiences.*

di·vert (duh-**vurt** *or* dye-**vurt**) *verb*
1. If someone **diverts** the traffic, he or she makes it take a different route.
2. When you **divert** someone's attention from something, you stop the person from thinking about it.
▷ *verb* **diverting, diverted** ▷ *adjective* **diverting**

D

di·vide (duh-**vide**) *verb*
1. To split into parts.
2. In math, if you **divide** one number by a second number, you figure out how many times the second number will go into the first. *Twelve divided by 4 is 3, or 12 ÷ 4 = 3.*
3. To share something. *Let's divide the food between us.*
4. To split into opposing groups. *The judges were divided in their choice for the winner.*
▷ *verb* **dividing, divided**

div·i·dend (div-i-*dend*) *noun*
1. In a division problem, the number that is divided. *In the problem 12 divided by 3, the dividend is 12.*
2. A share of the money earned by an investment or a business.

di·vine (duh-**vine**)
1. *adjective* To do with or from God or a god, as in *divine worship* or *divine love.*
2. *verb* To discover something by instinct, magic, or guessing. *Eddie divined that the treasure was buried beneath the old oak tree.* ▷ **divining, divined**
3. *adjective* Wonderful. *Our dinner was divine.*

diving board *noun* A long wooden or plastic board that juts out over the deep end of a swimming pool, allowing people to jump or dive into the water.

di·vis·i·ble (di-**viz**-uh-buhl) *adjective* Able to be divided. *Nine is evenly divisible only by itself, 3, and 1. Dividing 9 by any other number leaves a remainder.*

di·vi·sion (di-**vizh**-uhn) *noun*
1. The act of dividing one number by another, as in *long division.*
2. One of the parts into which something large has been divided, as in *the research division of a chemical company.*
3. Part of an army made up of several regiments.
4. Something that separates.

di·vi·sor (di-**vye**-zur) *noun* In a division problem, the number that you divide by. *In the problem 12 divided by 3, the divisor is 3.*

di·vorce (di-**vorss**)
1. *noun* The ending of a marriage by a court of law. ▷ *verb* **divorce**
2. *verb* Totally separated from something. *I divorced myself from the argument.* ▷ **divorcing, divorced**
▷ *adjective* **divorced**

di·vulge (di-**vulj**) *verb* To reveal information that was secret or unknown. *The author divulged the identity of the murderer in the last chapter.*
▷ **divulging, divulged**

diz·zy (**diz**-ee) *adjective*
1. If you are **dizzy,** you feel very unsteady on your feet, and your head seems to be spinning.
2. Bewildered and confused. *Having so many choices made me feel dizzy.*
▷ *adjective* **dizzier, dizziest,** *adjective* **dizzying**

DJ (dee *jay*) *noun* Short for **disc jockey.**

DNA (dee en ay) *noun*
The molecule that carries the genetic code that gives living things their special characteristics. The letters stand for *DeoxyriboNucleic Acid. The diagram shows the linked strands of DNA that separate as a cell divides to produce two identical new cells.*

DNA

do (doo) *verb*
1. To perform an action. *Dad was doing the washing.*
2. To complete. *Please do your homework!*
3. To be acceptable. *It's a small house, but it will do.*
4. To get along. *Raynelle is doing well at college.*
5. To behave or act in a certain way. *Do as you're told.*
6. To create. *You did a great presentation.*
7. To bring about an effect. *Yelling will do nothing to change my mind.*
Do sounds like **dew** and **due.**
▷ *verb* **does** (duhz), **doing, did** (did), **done** (duhn)

Do·ber·man pin·scher (doh-bur-muhn **pin**-chur) *noun* A breed of dog with a long head; a large, muscular body; and a short, black or brown coat.

doc·ile (**doss**-uhl) *adjective* Calm and easy to manage or train, as in *a docile pet.*

dock (dok) *noun* A place where ships load and unload cargo. ▷ *verb* **dock**

doc·tor (**dok**-tur) *noun*
1. Someone trained and licensed to treat sick and injured people. *Fortunately, there was a doctor nearby when Dad became ill.*
2. Someone who has the highest degree given by universities.

doc·trine (**dok**-trin) *noun* A belief or teaching of a religion or other group of people. *Conservative political doctrine calls for lower taxes and less government involvement in people's lives.*

doc·u·dra·ma (dok-yuh-*drah*-muh) *noun* A television show, movie, or play that presents a retelling of actual events, especially recent events surrounded by scandal or controversy.

doc·u·ment (**dok**-yuh-muhnt) *noun* A piece of paper containing important information. *Be sure to bring documents, such as your birth certificate, when you go to get your passport.* ▷ *verb* **document** (dok-yuh-ment)

doc·u·men·ta·ry (dok-yuh-**men**-tuh-ree) *noun* A movie or television program made about real situations and people. ▷ *noun, plural* **documentaries**

do·dec·a·he·dron (doh-*dek*-uh-**hee**-dron) *noun* A solid shape with 12 faces. *See* **shape.**

dodge (doj) *verb*
1. To avoid something or somebody by moving quickly, as in *to dodge a thrown ball.*
2. To avoid. *Kirsty dodged our question about where she bought the sweater.*
▷ *verb* **dodging, dodged** ▷ *noun* **dodge**

do·do (**doh**-doh) *noun*
1. An extinct bird that had a large body and wings so small it was unable to fly. Dodos lived on an island in the Indian Ocean. *See* **extinct.**
2. *(slang)* A stupid person.
▷ *noun, plural* **dodos** *or* **dodoes**

doe (doh) *noun* A female deer; the female of any mammal where the male is called a buck. **Doe** sounds like **dough.**

does·n't (**duhz**-uhnt) *contraction* A short form of *does not. My mother doesn't like me to chew gum.*

doff (dof) *verb*
1. If you **doff** a coat, jacket, or another article of clothing, you remove it.
2. If you **doff your hat** or **cap,** you tip it as a sign of greeting.
▷ *verb* **doffing, doffed**

dog (dawg *or* dog)
1. *noun* A domestic mammal with four legs that is often kept as a pet or as a work animal. Dogs are related to wolves, coyotes, and foxes.
2. *verb* To follow someone closely. *The child dogged the baby-sitter all morning.* ▷ **dogging, dogged**

Word History

Dog is a word original to English, rather than coming from another language. At first, the word *hund,* or *hound,* was used to refer to all breeds of dogs, and *dogge* referred only to one large, powerful breed. Over time, however, *dog* came to mean all breeds, and *hound* started to apply only to hunting dogs.

▶ D

dog·mat·ic (dawg-**mat**-ik) *adjective* If you are **dogmatic,** you insist very strongly that you are right about things.

dog·wood (**dawg**-*wud*) *noun* A tree or shrub that has small, green flowers surrounded by pink or white leaves that look like petals.

doi·ly (**doi**-lee) *noun* A small piece of lace or cut paper placed under a plate or other item as a decoration or on furniture to protect it. ▷ *noun, plural* **doilies**

do-it-yourself *adjective* To do with home improvements, repairs, or projects that you do yourself.

dole (dohl) *verb* If you **dole out** something, such as food or money, you give it out in small quantities. ▷ **doling, doled**

doll (dol) *noun* A small model of a human being used as a child's toy.

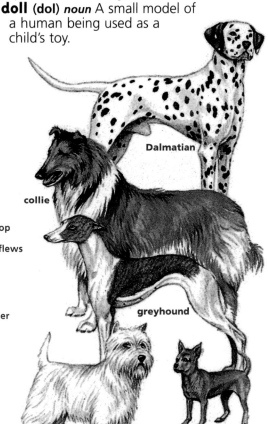

Dalmatian

collie

greyhound

Chihuahua

West Highland white terrier

dogs

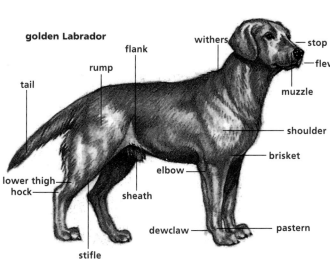

golden Labrador

tail

rump

flank

withers

stop

flews

muzzle

shoulder

brisket

elbow

lower thigh

hock

sheath

stifle

dewclaw

pastern

dol·lar (dol-ur) *noun* The main unit of money in the United States, Canada, Australia, and New Zealand.

dol·phin (dol-fin) *noun* An intelligent water mammal with a long snout, related to whales, but smaller.

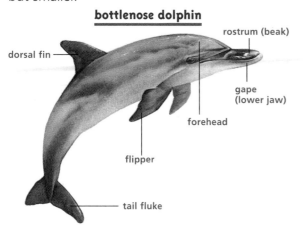

bottlenose dolphin

rostrum (beak)

dorsal fin

gape (lower jaw)

forehead

flipper

tail fluke

dome (dohm) *noun* A roof shaped like half of a sphere.

do·mes·tic (duh-mess-tik) *adjective*
1. To do with the home, as in *domestic chores*.
2. Domestic animals are no longer wild but are kept for food, as work animals, or as pets.
3. To do with your own country, as in *the domestic market*.

do·mes·ti·cate (duh-mess-tuh-kate) *verb* To tame something so it can live with or be used by human beings. *The settlers got milk from the wild goats that they had domesticated.*
▷ **domesticating, domesticated** ▷ *adjective* **domesticated**

dom·i·nant (dom-uh-nuhnt) *adjective* Most influential or powerful. *Our country plays a dominant role in the world's economy.*

dom·i·nate (dom-uh-nate) *verb*
1. To control, or to rule. ▷ *noun* **domination**
2. To be the main feature of a situation. *The castle dominates the view.*
▷ *verb* **dominating, dominated**

do·min·ion (duh-min-yuhn) *noun*
1. A large area of land controlled by a single ruler or government. *Canada was once a British dominion.*
2. Power to rule over something. *The captain has dominion over his ship.*

dom·i·no (dom-uh-noh) *noun*
1. A small rectangular tile that is divided into two halves that are blank or contain dots.
2. dominoes A game played with a number of these tiles. ▷ *noun, plural* **dominoes**

don (don) *verb* If you **don** clothing, you put it on.

She donned a jacket because the weather had turned chilly. ▷ **donning, donned**

do·nate (doh-nate) *verb* To give something as a present. *The company donated a portion of its profits to charity.* ▷ **donating, donated** ▷ *noun* **donation**

don·key (dong-kee) *noun* A mammal with long ears, related to the horse, but smaller.

do·nor (doh-nur) *noun*
1. Someone who gives something, usually to an organization or a charity.
2. Someone who agrees to give his or her body, or a part of it, to medical science to help sick people. *I volunteered to be a blood donor.*

don't (dohnt) *contraction* A short form of *do not*. *I don't know what my parents are getting me for my birthday.*

do·nut (doh-nuht) *See* **doughnut.**

doo·dle (doo-duhl) *verb* To draw absentmindedly while you are concentrating on something else. ▷ **doodling, doodled** ▷ *noun* **doodle**

doom (doom) *noun* If you meet your **doom**, you suffer a terrible fate, usually ending in death. ▷ *verb* **doom** ▷ *adjective* **doomed**

door (dor) *noun*
1. A barrier that opens and closes at the entrance or exit of a building, room, etc.
2. A house or a building. *My friend lives three doors away.*

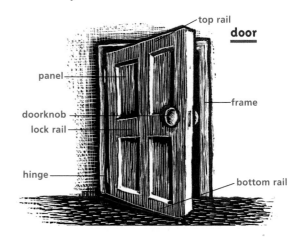

top rail

door

panel

frame

doorknob

lock rail

hinge

bottom rail

door·bell (dor-*bel*) *noun* A bell or buzzer outside a door that is rung by someone who wants the door to be opened.

door·knob (dor-*nob*) *noun* A handle that you turn to open a door.

door·step (dor-*step*) *noun* A step or steps on the outside doorway of a building.

door·way (dor-*way*) *noun* An area between two rooms, or between the inside and outside of a building, that can be closed by a door.

dope (dohp) *noun*
1. *(informal)* A stupid person.
2. *(informal)* An illegal or addictive drug.
3. A thick varnish.

dor·mant (dor-muhnt) *adjective*
1. Animals become **dormant** when they hibernate. They show no signs of action, as if they were asleep.
2. A **dormant** volcano is not active at present but could erupt again.
3. When plants or seeds are **dormant,** they are alive but not growing.

dor·mi·to·ry (dor-muh-tor-ee) *noun* A building with many separate sleeping rooms, as in *a college dormitory.* ▷ *noun, plural* **dormitories**

dor·mouse (dor-*mouss*) *noun* A European, African, or Asian rodent that looks like a small squirrel, with black or gray fur and a furry tail. ▷ *noun, plural* **dormice** (dor-*misse*)

DOS (doss) *noun* A system of commands and codes that make it possible to run and use a computer. DOS stands for *Disk Operating System.*

dose (dohss) *noun*
1. A prescribed amount of medicine.
2. A small amount, especially of something unpleasant, as in *a dose of hard work.*

dot (dot)
1. *noun* A small, round point. ▷ *verb* **dot**
2. *verb* To be here and there around an area. *Trees dotted the hills.* ▷ **dotting, dotted**

dote (doht) *verb* To pay too much attention to, or to show too much fondness for. *She doted on her granddaughter.* ▷ **doting, doted**

dou·ble (duh-buhl)
1. *adjective* Twice the amount, the number, or the strength.
2. *adverb* Twice as much. *It cost us double.*
3. *verb* To make something twice as big.
4. *noun* If you have a **double,** there is another person who looks just like you.
5. **doubles** *noun, plural* When you play **doubles** in badminton, tennis, etc., there are two players on each side.
6. *noun* A hit in baseball that allows the player to get to second base.
7. *verb* To bend or fold in two.
8. *verb* To serve more than one purpose. *The dining room table doubles as a desk.* ▷ *verb* **doubling, doubled**

double-cross *verb* When you **double-cross** someone, you betray him or her. ▷ **double-crosses, double-crossing, double-crossed** ▷ *noun* **double cross**

double-head·er (hed-ur) *noun* Two baseball games played one right after the other. ▷ *noun, plural* **double-headers**

doubt (dout)
1. *noun* Uncertainty.
2. *verb* If you **doubt** something, you are uncertain about it. *I doubt we will reach home before dark.* ▷ **doubting, doubted** ▷ *adjective* **doubtful** ▷ *adverb* **doubtfully**

dough (doh) *noun*
1. A thick, sticky mixture of flour, water, etc., used to make bread, cookies, muffins, and other foods.
2. *(slang)* Money.
Dough sounds like **doe.**

dough·nut (doh-nuht) *noun* A cake fried in fat. A doughnut is round and usually has a hole in the middle. Also spelled **donut.**

dove (duhv) *noun* A plump bird that makes a gentle cooing sound. *The dove is often used as a symbol of peace.*

down (doun)
1. *preposition* From a higher to a lower place. *Emma ran down the hill.* ▷ *adjective* **downward** (doun-wurd) ▷ *adverb* **downward** *or* **downwards**
2. *noun* The soft feathers of a bird. ▷ *adjective* **downy**
3. *adjective* If you feel **down,** you feel sad or depressed.
4. *noun* In football, one of a series of four attempts to advance the ball ten yards.
5. *adverb* To a lower place or condition. *Push the button down.*
6. *preposition* In a direction lower or farther away, as in *down the ladder* or *down the road.*

down·cast (down-*kast*) *adjective* Very sad.

down·load (doun-*lohd*) *verb* To transfer information from a computer or network to a disk or the memory of another computer. ▷ **downloading, downloaded**

down·pour (doun-*por*) *noun* A very heavy rain.

down·right (doun-*rite*)
1. *adjective* Total, or complete. *It's a downright shame that you have to leave so soon.*
2. *adverb* Absolutely, or completely. *Your reasons for not going to the concert with us are downright silly.*

downs (dounz) *noun, plural* An area of rolling hills, especially in England.

down·size (doun-*size*) *verb* To reduce the size of something, such as the scale of an automobile or the number of employees in a company. ▷ **downsizing, downsized**

down·stairs
1. (doun-stairz) *adverb* Down the stairs or to a lower floor. *The ball bounced downstairs.*
2. *adjective* (doun-stairz) On a lower level of a house. *Jasper is in the downstairs playroom.* ▷ *noun* **downstairs**

down·stream (doun-streem) *adverb* In the direction of the flowing current in a river or stream. *We stopped rowing and let the boat float downstream.* ▷ *adjective* **downstream**

Down syndrome *noun* A genetic condition in which a person is born mentally retarded and with eyes that appear to slant, a broad skull, and shorter fingers than normal. Also called *Down's syndrome.*

down·town (doun-toun) *adverb* To or in a city's main business district. *My mom took us downtown to our favorite restaurant.* ▷ *adjective* **downtown**

dow·ry (dou-ree) *noun* The money or property that women in some cultures bring with them when they marry. ▷ *noun, plural* **dowries**

doze (dohz) *verb* To sleep lightly for a short time. *Uncle Arthur has dozed off again.* ▷ **dozing, dozed** ▷ *noun* **doze**

doz·en (duhz-uhn) *noun* A group of 12.

Dr. Short for **Doctor.**

drab (drab) *adjective* Very dull and dreary. *Sonia wore a drab, gray dress.* ▷ *noun* **drabness**

draft (draft)
1. *noun* A flow of cold air. ▷ *adjective* **drafty**
2. *adjective* Drawn out of a barrel or keg, as in *draft beer.*
3. *verb* When you **draft** something, such as a letter, you make a first rough copy of it.
4. *verb* If someone is **drafted,** the person is made to join the armed forces.
▷ *noun* **draft** ▷ *verb* **drafting, drafted**

drag (drag)
1. *verb* To pull something along the ground.
2. *verb* If something **drags,** it seems to go slowly. *The lesson really dragged.*
3. *noun* (informal) If something is a **drag,** it is boring.
▷ *verb* **dragging, dragged**

drag·on (drag-uhn) *noun* A mythical monster that breathes fire. *In China, people create colorful dragons that dance in New Year processions.*

Chinese dragon

drag·on·fly (drag-uhn-*flye*) *noun* A large insect with two sets of wings and a long, slender body. *See* **insect.**

drain (drayn)
1. *verb* To remove the liquid from something.
2. *noun* A pipe or channel that takes away water or sewage.
3. *verb* To tire, or to use up. *Building the new house drained our savings.*
▷ *verb* **draining, drained**

drain·age (dray-nij) *noun* The act or process of removing liquid from an area. *We have poor drainage in our backyard.*

drained (draynd) *adjective* If you feel **drained,** you have no energy left.

dra·ma (drah-muh) *noun*
1. A play.
2. If you study **drama,** you learn about acting and the theater.
3. Something that affects people seriously.

dra·mat·ic (druh-mat-ik) *adjective*
1. To do with acting and the theater.
2. Very noticeable, as in *a dramatic change.*
3. If someone is being **dramatic,** the person is making too much fuss about something.
▷ *adverb* **dramatically**

dram·a·tist (dram-uh-tist) *noun* Someone who writes plays.

dram·a·tize (dram-uh-tize) *verb*
1. To adapt a story into a play.
2. If you **dramatize** an event, you make it seem more exciting than it really was.
▷ *verb* **dramatizing, dramatized**

drape (drayp) *noun*
1. A piece of material placed across a window or stage to cover it. *We have drapes in the den.*
▷ *noun* **drapery**
2. *verb* To cover with a loosely hanging cloth. *I draped a sweater over my arms.*

dras·tic (drass-tik) *adjective* If you do something **drastic,** you take sudden, severe, or violent action. ▷ *adverb* **drastically**

draw (draw)
1. *verb* To make a picture with a pencil, pen, etc.
▷ *noun* **drawing**
2. *verb* To pull something. *The wagon was drawn by horses.*
3. *verb* To attract, as in *to draw a crowd.*
4. *verb* To figure out by using your power of reason, as in *to draw conclusions.*
5. *verb* To inhale, as in *to draw a deep breath.*
6. *noun* If a competition ends in a **draw,** both sides are even.
▷ *verb* **drawing, drew (droo), drawn (drawn)**

draw·back (draw-*bak*) *noun* A problem or disadvantage.

draw·bridge (draw-*brij*) *noun* A bridge that can be raised or moved to let boats pass underneath. *See* **portcullis.**

draw·er (dror) *noun* A sliding box in a piece of furniture, used for storing things.

drawing room *noun* A formal room where guests are entertained.

drawl (drawl)
1. *verb* To speak in a slow manner, stretching out the vowel sounds. *Tyler looked at each person in the room as he drawled his answer.*
▷ **drawling, drawled**
2. *noun* A slow manner of speaking. *Listening to Cindy's southern drawl brought back memories of my vacation in Georgia.*

draw·string (draw-*string*) *noun* A string or cord that closes or tightens a bag or piece of clothing when you pull the ends. *I like these sweatpants because they have a drawstring around the waist.*

dread (dred) *verb* If you **dread** something, you are very afraid of it. ▷ **dreading, dreaded** ▷ *noun* **dread** ▷ *adjective* **dreaded**

dread·ful (dred-fuhl) *adjective*
1. Very frightening; awful, as in *a dreadful storm.*
2. Very bad, as in *a dreadful movie.*
▷ *adverb* **dreadfully**

dread·locks (dred-loks) *noun, plural* A hairstyle in which the hair is grown long and worn in thick, ropelike strands.

dream (dreem) *verb*
1. To imagine events while you are asleep.
2. If you **dream** of doing something, you really want to do it.
▷ *verb* **dreaming, dreamed** *or* **dreamt** (dremt)
▷ *noun* **dream,** *noun* **dreamer**

dream·y (dree-mee) *adjective*
1. If you are **dreamy,** you are always daydreaming.
2. Vague or soft, as in *dreamy music.*
▷ *adjective* **dreamier, dreamiest** ▷ *adverb* **dreamily**

drear·y (drihr-ee) *adjective* Dull and miserable.
▷ **drearier, dreariest** ▷ *adverb* **drearily**

dredge (drej) *verb* To scrape sand, mud, etc., from the bottom of a river or harbor.
▷ **dredging, dredged** ▷ *noun* **dredger**

dregs (dregz) *noun, plural* The solid bits that drop to the bottom of some liquids, such as coffee.

drench (drench) *verb* To make something completely wet. ▷ **drenches, drenching, drenched**

dress (dress)
1. *verb* To put clothes on.
2. *noun* A piece of clothing worn by women and girls that covers the body from shoulders to legs.

▷ *noun, plural* **dresses**
3. *noun* Clothes in general, as in *formal dress.*
4. *verb* If you **dress a wound,** you put an ointment on it and bandage it.
▷ *verb* **dresses, dressing, dressed**

dress·er (dress-ur) *noun* A piece of furniture with drawers, used for storing clothes.

dresser

dress·ing (dress-ing) *noun*
1. A covering for a wound.
2. A type of sauce for salads.
3. A mixture used to stuff a chicken or turkey before it is roasted.

dressing table *noun* A piece of bedroom furniture, often with a mirror and drawers.

dress rehearsal *noun* The last rehearsal of a play, in full costume.

drib·ble (drib-uhl) *verb*
1. To let liquid trickle from your mouth.
2. When you **dribble** in basketball, you bounce the ball while running, keeping it under your control.
▷ *verb* **dribbling, dribbled**

drift (drift)
1. *verb* When something **drifts,** it moves wherever the water or wind takes it.
2. *verb* To move or act without any sense of purpose. *Don spent the whole day just drifting around.* ▷ *noun* **drifter**
3. *noun* A pile of sand or snow created by the wind.
4. If you **get someone's drift,** you understand what the person is saying.
▷ *verb* **drifting, drifted**

drift·wood (drift-*wud*) *noun* Wood that floats ashore or is floating on water.

D

drill ▶ drop

drill (dril)
1. noun A tool used for making holes.
2. verb To use a drill.
3. verb To teach someone how to do something by having the person do it over and over again.
▷ **noun** drill
▷ **verb** drilling, drilled

drink (dringk)
1. noun A liquid that you swallow.
2. verb To swallow liquid. ▷ **drinking, drank** (drangk)**, drunk** (druhngk)
3. noun An alcoholic liquid.
▷ **noun** drinker

drip (drip)
1. verb When a liquid **drips,** it falls slowly, drop by drop. ▷ **dripping, dripped** ▷ **noun** drip
2. noun (informal) A silly and boring person.

drip·pings (drip-ingz) **noun, plural** Fat and liquid or juice obtained from meat while it is cooking, which can often be used again.

drive (drive)
1. verb To operate and control a vehicle. ▷ **noun** driver, **noun** driving
2. verb To carry someone somewhere in a vehicle. *She drove Lou to the mall to do some shopping.* ▷ **noun** drive
3. verb To hit something hard and far. *Jerry drove the golf ball over the hill.*
4. verb To force someone into a desperate state. *Losing his bicycle drove Matt to despair.*
5. noun A private road leading to a house.
6. noun Energy and determination. *Jenny will succeed because she has a lot of drive.*
7. noun An organized campaign to do something.
▷ **verb** driving, drove, driven (driv-in)

drive-in **adjective** Designed so that customers may be served or entertained in their cars. *Between 1947 and 1950, 2,000 drive-in movie theaters opened in the United States.* ▷ **noun** drive-in

driv·el (driv-uhl) **noun** If someone talks **drivel,** what he or she says is nonsense.

drive·way (drive-way) **noun** A private road that leads from the street to a house or garage.

driz·zle (driz-uhl) **noun** Light rain. ▷ **verb** drizzle

drom·e·dar·y (drom-uh-der-ee) **noun** A camel

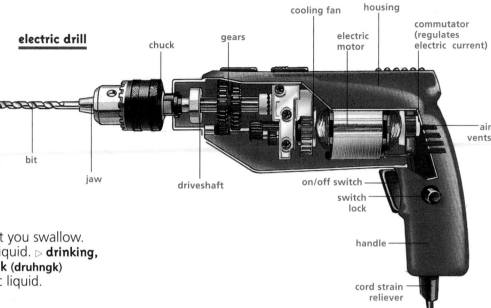

electric drill

chuck · gears · cooling fan · housing · electric motor · commutator (regulates electric current) · air vents · bit · jaw · driveshaft · on/off switch · switch lock · handle · cord strain reliever

with one hump, found in the Middle East and northern Africa. *See* **camel.** ▷ **noun, plural** dromedaries

drone (drohn)
1. verb To make a steady, dull sound.
2. verb To talk in a dull, monotonous way. *Sam droned on about his skill at racquetball.*
3. noun A male insect such as a bee whose function is to mate with the queen. *See* **honeycomb.** ▷ **verb** droning, droned

drool (drool) **verb**
1. To let saliva trickle from your mouth.
2. If you **drool over** something, you really like it and want it.
▷ **verb** drooling, drooled

droop (droop) **verb**
1. To hang down, or to sag. ▷ **adjective** drooping
2. When people **droop,** they run out of energy.
▷ **verb** drooping, drooped

drop (drop)
1. verb To let something fall. *Nancy dropped her bag on the sofa.*
2. verb To fall down. *The acrobat dropped to the floor.* ▷ **noun** drop
3. noun A small quantity of liquid, as in *a drop of water.*
4. noun Any small amount, as in *a drop of kindness.*
5. verb If you **drop out,** you stop doing something. ▷ **noun** dropout

6. *verb* When players are **dropped,** they are not kept on a team.

7. A drop in the bucket is a very small amount.

8. *noun* A small piece of candy or medication for the throat, as in *lemon drops* and *cough drops.*

9. *verb* To leave out. *Drop the letter "e" when you add "ing" to the word* write.

10. drop off *verb* To deliver. *I will drop off the present on my way home from the store.*

11. drop by *verb* To pay a short visit. *Let's drop by Grandma's house.*

▷ *verb* **dropping, dropped**

drought (drout) *noun* A long spell of very dry weather.

drove (drove)

1. *noun* A large herd of animals being moved as a group. *After the fire, the rangers moved a drove of mountain goats to the western end of the national park.*

2. *noun* A large crowd of people. *Fans showed up in droves.*

3. *verb* Past tense of *drive.*

drown (droun) *verb*

1. To die from lack of air when under water or another liquid.

2. drown out To make a louder noise than something else. *The noise of the power drill drowned out my singing.*

▷ *verb* **drowning, drowned**

drow·sy (drou-zee) *adjective* Sleepy. *This medicine may make you feel drowsy.* ▷ **drowsier, drowsiest**

▷ *noun* **drowsiness** ▷ *verb* **drowse** ▷ *adverb* **drowsily**

drudg·er·y (druhj-ur-ee) *noun* Difficult, boring, or unpleasant work, as in *household drudgery.*

drug (druhg)

1. *noun* A substance, either natural or synthetic, used to treat illness.

2. *noun* A chemical substance that people take because of its effect on them. Drugs are dangerous and usually cause addiction.

3. *verb* To make someone unconscious by giving him or her a drug. ▷ **drugging, drugged** ▷ *adjective* **drugged**

4. drug addict *noun* Someone who cannot give up using drugs.

drug·gist (druhg-ist) *noun* A person who is trained to prepare and sell drug prescriptions; a pharmacist.

drug·store (druhg-stor) *noun* A store where medicines and other items are sold.

drum (druhm)

1. *noun* A musical instrument with a hollow body covered with a stretched skin that makes a loud noise when you hit it.

2. *verb* To beat a drum or other surface with drumsticks or with your fingers. *Joe drummed his fingers on the table.* ▷ **drumming, drummed** ▷ *noun* **drummer**

3. *noun* A container shaped like a drum. *Oil is stored in drums.*

D

drum kit

crash cymbal

tom-tom holder

tom-tom

tom-tom

ride cymbal

hi-hat cymbal

snare drum

cymbal stand

snare drum stand

bass drum

floor tom-tom

pedal

pedal

drum·stick (druhm-*stik*) *noun*
  1. A stick used to hit a drum.
  2. The leg portion of a chicken, turkey, etc.

drunk (druhngk)
  1. *adjective* If people are **drunk,** they have had too much alcohol to drink and cannot control their actions or emotions.
  2. *noun* A person who often gets drunk. ▷ *noun* **drunkard** ▷ *adjective* **drunken**
  3. *verb* Past participle of **drink.**

dry (drye)
  1. *verb* To take the moisture out of something. ▷ **dries, drying, dried**
  2. *adjective* Not wet.
  3. *adjective* Dull and boring, as in *a dry speech.*
  4. *adjective* Without butter or margarine, as in *dry toast.*
  ▷ *adjective* **drier, driest** ▷ *adverb* **drily**

dry cell *noun* A container in which chemicals that produce electricity are stored in paste form so that they cannot spill. Dry cells are used in toys and other small appliances.

dry-clean *verb* To clean clothes with special chemicals in order to remove stains. ▷ **dry-cleaning, dry-cleaned** ▷ *noun* **dry cleaner**

dry·er (drye-ur) *noun* A machine that dries something. *We just bought a new clothes dryer.*

dry goods *noun, plural* Fabric, clothing, and related materials, such as threads and ribbons.

du·al (doo-uhl) *adjective*
  1. Double. *When I learned to drive, my instructor used a dual-control car.*
  2. Made up of two parts.
  Dual sounds like **duel.**

du·bi·ous (doo-bee-uhss) *adjective* If you are **dubious** about something, you are not sure about it. ▷ *adverb* **dubiously**

du·chess (duhch-iss) *noun* The wife or widow of a duke, or a woman with the rank that is equal to that of a duke.

duck (duhk)
  1. *noun* A bird with webbed feet that swims and feeds in water.
  2. *verb* To bend low to avoid something.
  3. *verb* To avoid or to evade. *The celebrity ducked the newspaper reporters.*
  ▷ *verb* **ducking, ducked**

ducks

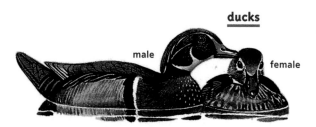

male   female

duct (duhkt) *noun* A tube that carries air or liquid from one place to another, as in *air conditioning ducts.*

dud (duhd) *noun* Something that does not work as it should. ▷ *adjective* **dud**

due (doo) *adjective*
  1. If someone or something is **due,** it is expected to arrive or happen.
  2. Suitable. *Please handle these books with due care.* ▷ *adverb* **duly**
  3. If something happens **due to** something else, it happens because of it.
  4. Owed. *The amount that is due is shown on your bill.*
  Due sounds like **dew** and **do.**

du·el (doo-uhl) *noun* A fight between two people using swords or guns, fought according to strict rules. **Duel** sounds like **dual.**

du·et (doo-et) *noun* A piece of music that is played or a song that is sung by two people.

dug·out (duhg-out) *noun*
  1. A long, low shelter where baseball players sit when they are not at bat or in the field.
  2. A rough shelter dug out of the ground or in the side of a hill.
  3. A canoe made from the outer portion of a large log.

duke (dook) *noun* A nobleman. In Britain, a duke holds the rank just below that of a prince.

dull (duhl) *adjective*
  1. Not bright; dim. *The lamp shed a dull light.*
  2. Not perceptive or intelligent.
  3. Boring.
  4. Not shiny, as in *a dull finish.*
  5. Not sharp, as in *a dull blade.*
  6. Slow or sluggish. *Trading was dull in the stock market today.*
  ▷ *adjective* **duller, dullest** ▷ *verb* **dull** ▷ *adverb* **dully**

dumb (duhm) *adjective*
  1. Not able to speak.
  2. Stupid.
  ▷ *adjective* **dumber, dumbest**

dumb·bell (duhm-bel) *noun*
  1. A short bar with heavy weights at each end, used to exercise and strengthen the muscles.
  2. (slang) A stupid person.

dumb·found·ed (duhm-found-id) *adjective* So amazed that you cannot speak.

dum·my (duhm-ee) *noun*
  1. An imitation person or object, as in *a crash-test dummy.*
  2. (informal) A stupid person.
  ▷ *noun, plural* **dummies**

dump (duhmp)
  1. *verb* To put something down thoughtlessly or

roughly. *Keith dumped his sports equipment in the hall.*

2. *noun* A place where unwanted things can be left, as in *a garbage dump.*

3. *verb* (informal) To end a friendship with someone. *Jeremy dumped Peg last weekend.*
▷ *verb* **dumping, dumped**

dune (doon) *noun* A sand hill made by the wind near the ocean or a large lake or in a desert. *The photograph shows the Mesquite Flat Dunes at the Death Valley National Monument in southeastern California.*

dunes

dun·ga·ree (*duhng*-guh-ree) *noun*
1. Blue denim; a heavy cotton cloth used to make work clothes.
2. dungarees *noun, plural* Blue jeans.

dun·geon (duhn-juhn) *noun* A prison, usually underground. *See* **castle.**

du·pli·cate
1. (doo-pluh-*kate*) *verb* To make an exact copy of something. ▷ **duplicating, duplicated** ▷ *noun* **duplication,** *noun* **duplicator**
2. (doo-pluh-kit) *noun* An exact copy.

du·ra·ble (dur-uh-buhl) *adjective* Tough and lasting for a long time, as in *a durable material.* ▷ *noun* **durability**

du·ra·tion (du-ray-shuhn) *noun* The period of time during which something lasts. *I sat next to my dad for the duration of our trip.*

dur·ing (du-ring) *preposition* Within a particular time. *Please call during the morning.*

dusk (duhsk) *noun* The time of day after sunset when it is nearly dark.

dust (duhst)
1. *noun* Tiny particles of dirt, fluff, etc., that gather on surfaces or in the air.
2. *verb* To remove dirt from surfaces. ▷ **dusting, dusted** ▷ *noun* **duster**

dust·bin (duhst-*bin*) *noun* A large container for rubbish.

du·ti·ful (doo-ti-fuhl) *adjective* If you are **dutiful,** you are obedient and aware of what you should or must do. *He was a dutiful son, so he went to his parents' house for dinner every Sunday.*
▷ *adverb* **dutifully**

du·ty (doo-tee) *noun*
1. A thing a person must do or ought to do. *It is a soldier's duty to obey orders.*
2. Tax charged on goods brought into a country.
3. If you are **on duty,** you are at work.
▷ *noun, plural* **duties**

dwarf (dworf)
1. *noun* A very small person, animal, or plant.
▷ *noun, plural* **dwarfs** *or* **dwarves** (dworvz)
▷ *adjective* **dwarf**
2. *verb* To make something else seem very small. *The skyscraper dwarfed all the buildings around it.*
▷ **dwarfing, dwarfed**

dwell (dwel) *verb* To live in a place. ▷ **dwelling, dwelt** (dwelt) *or* **dwelled**

dwell·ing (dwel-ing) *noun* The place where someone lives, such as a house or an apartment.

dwin·dle (dwin-duhl) *verb* To become smaller or less. *The number of pandas is dwindling.*
▷ **dwindling, dwindled**

dye (dye)
1. *noun* A substance used to change the color of something.
2. *verb* If someone **dyes** something, he or she changes its color by soaking it in dye. ▷ **dying, dyed** ▷ *adjective* **dyed**
Dye sounds like **die.**

dy·nam·ic (dye-nam-ik) *adjective* If someone is **dynamic,** he or she is very energetic and good at getting things done. ▷ *noun* **dynamism**

dy·na·mite (dye-nuh-mite) *noun* A very powerful explosive.

dy·na·mo (dye-nuh-moh) *noun*
1. A machine for converting the power of a turning wheel into electricity; a generator. *Dynamo is short for dynamoelectric.*
2. A forceful person who works very hard.
▷ *noun, plural* **dynamos**

dy·nas·ty (dye-nuh-stee) *noun*
1. A series of rulers belonging to the same family, as in *the Ming dynasty.*
2. A group or family that succeeds for a long time. *The New York Yankees were a baseball dynasty; from 1947 through 1962, the team won 10 World Series.* ▷ *noun, plural* **dynasties**

dys·lex·i·a (diss-lek-see-uh) *noun* If someone has **dyslexia,** the person finds reading extremely difficult. He or she may often see letters and symbols in the wrong order or in mirror image. Another word for *reading disorders.* ▷ *adjective* **dyslexic**

D

Ee

About E

E is the most commonly used letter in the English language. In order of use, e is followed by t and then by a, i, s, o, n, h, r, d, l, u, c, m, f, w, y, p, g, b, v, k, j, q, x, and z.

E

each (eech)
1. adjective Every one of two or more. *The building has an emergency exit on each floor.*
2. pronoun Every one. *Each went her separate way.*
3. adverb Apiece. *The tickets now cost $8.00 each!*

ea·ger (ee-gur) **adjective** Very interested in doing something; enthusiastic. *Gail was eager to start her new job.* ▷ **noun eagerness** ▷ **adverb eagerly**

ea·gle (ee-guhl) **noun** A large bird of prey that often nests on mountains.

ear (ihr) **noun**
1. The part of the body used for hearing. *Sound waves travel down the ear canal and hit the eardrum, making it vibrate. These vibrations are transferred to the cochlea, where they are changed to electrical signals and sent to the brain.*
2. The outer part of the ear, formed of skin and cartilage.
3. The part of some plants on which grain or seeds grow, as in *an ear of corn.*

human ear

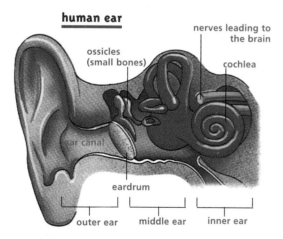

nerves leading to the brain
ossicles (small bones)
cochlea
ear canal
eardrum
outer ear   middle ear   inner ear

ear·ache (ihr-ake) **noun** A pain inside the ear.
ear·drum (ihr-druhm) **noun** A membrane inside the ear that vibrates as sound strikes it. See **ear.**
ear·ly (ur-lee)
1. adverb At or near the beginning. *We had a brief shower early this morning.*
2. adjective Before the usual time. *We got up at sunrise so we would have an early start.*

3. adjective Near the beginning of a period of time, as in *an early-20th-century house.*
▷ **adjective earlier, earliest**

ear·muffs (ihr-muhfss)
noun, plural Pads that fit over the ears to keep them warm in cold weather. *The girl in this cartoon is wearing earmuffs.*

girl wearing earmuffs

earn (urn) **verb**
1. To receive payment for work done. *Emilio earns a decent salary.* ▷ **noun earner** ▷ **noun, plural earnings**
2. To work to achieve a result. *You have earned your reward.*
Earn sounds like **urn.**
▷ **verb earning, earned**

ear·nest (ur-nist) **adjective** Serious and eager. *Beverly showed that she was an earnest worker by showing up early at her job every day.* ▷ **adverb earnestly**

ear·ring (ihr-ing) **noun** A piece of jewelry worn on or through the ear.

earth (urth) **noun**
1. The planet on which we live. Earth is the third planet from the sun, between Venus and Mars. In cases where it is described as a part of the solar system, Earth is often capitalized. *The diagram below shows the different layers of Earth.*
2. Soil. *Some plants grow best in very moist earth.*
3. The ground; dry land. *The earth shook as a large truck rumbled by.*
4. If someone is **down to earth,** he or she does not pretend to be someone important.
▷ **adjective earthly**

Earth

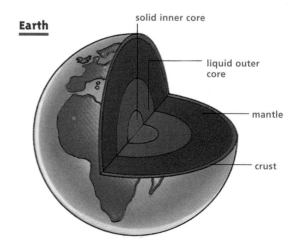

solid inner core
liquid outer core
mantle
crust

earth·quake (urth-*kwayk*) *noun* A sudden, violent shaking of the earth, caused by a shifting of the earth's crust. *See* **fault, quake.**

earth·worm (urth-*wurm*) *noun* A gray, pink, red, or brown worm that digs through the ground and eats the nutrients in dirt. *Earthworms do not have eyes, ears, or lungs.*

earthworm

ease (eez)
1. *noun* Freedom from hard work, pain, or discomfort. *After working for many years, she retired and led a life of ease.*
2. *noun* A calm state of mind. *The principal's friendly manner put the new student at ease.*
3. *verb* To make less difficult. *Mitch eased Suzanne's load by typing the paper for her.*
4. *verb* To lessen, as in *to ease a person's fear.*
5. *verb* To maneuver something into a tight space. *I eased the big truck into the warehouse.*
▷ *verb* **easing, eased**

ea·sel (ee-zuhl) *noun* A folding wooden stand used to support a painting, sign, etc.

east (eest)
1. *noun* One of the four main points of the compass. *The sun rises in the east.* ▷ *adverb* **east**
2. East *noun* Any area or region lying in this direction.
3. the East *noun* In the United States, the states lying along the Atlantic coast, especially those east of the Allegheny Mountains and north of Maryland.
4. *adjective* To do with or existing in the east, as in *the east side of the city.* ▷ *adjective* **eastern**
▷ *adjective* **Eastern**

Eas·ter (ee-stur) *noun* The Christian holiday on which people celebrate the resurrection of Jesus.

Eastern Hemisphere *noun* The half of the world east of the Atlantic Ocean. It includes Europe, Africa, Asia, and Australia.

eas·y (ee-zee) *adjective*
1. If something is **easy,** it does not require much effort, ability, or training. ▷ *noun* **easiness**
▷ *adverb* **easily**
2. Comfortable and relaxing, as in *an easy chair.*
3. Not strict or hard to please, as in *an easy teacher.*
▷ *adjective* **easier, easiest**

eat (eet) *verb*
1. To take in food through your mouth. *Do you always eat three meals a day?*
2. To have a meal. *We ate lunch early yesterday.*
3. If something is being **eaten away,** it is being destroyed slowly.
▷ *verb* **eating, ate** (ayt), **eaten** (ee-tin)

> **Synonyms: eat**
>
> **Eat** is the general word that means to take food or nourishment into the body: *When everyone had arrived, we sat down to eat.* There are quite a few words that describe the different ways a person can eat.
>
> **Consume** can mean to eat a large amount of something or to eat something completely: *After hiking all morning, we consumed the food we had brought with us and then headed home.*
>
> **Devour** can mean to eat quickly and greedily and is often used to describe the way animals eat: *The wild beast devoured its prey.*
>
> **Feast** means to eat as if you were at a feast or celebration where there is more than enough for everyone: *At Thanksgiving dinner, we feasted on turkey with all the trimmings.*
>
> **Nibble** means to eat by taking tiny bites: *She only nibbled at her lunch because she was not really hungry.*

eaves (eevz) *noun, plural* The part of a roof that hangs over the side of a building.

eaves·drop (eevz-*drop*) *verb* To listen in secret to someone's conversation. *It is not polite to eavesdrop.* ▷ **eavesdropping, eavesdropped**
▷ *noun* **eavesdropper**

ebb (eb) *verb*
1. When the tide **ebbs,** it goes down and back out to sea. ▷ *noun* **ebb**
2. To fade or to get weaker. *The wounded tiger's strength ebbed.*
▷ *verb* **ebbing, ebbed**

eb·on·y (eb-uh-nee) *noun*
1. A very hard, black wood. *The black piano keys are made of ebony.*
2. A deep black color.
▷ *adjective* **ebony**

ec·cen·tric (ek-sen-trik)
1. *adjective* Acting odd or strange, but in a harmless or charming way. *My eccentric aunt cleans her house in the middle of the night.*
▷ *adverb* **eccentrically**
2. *noun* Someone with odd habits.

ech·o (ek-oh) *verb* When a sound **echoes**, it repeats because its sound waves have met a large surface and have bounced back. ▷ **echoes, echoing, echoed** ▷ *noun* **echo**

e·clec·tic (i-klek-tik) *adjective* If you have **eclectic** taste, you like a wide range of things. *I have eclectic taste in books because I like everything from horror novels to biographies and romances.*

e·clipse (i-klips)
1. *noun* In an **eclipse of the moon,** the earth comes between the sun and the moon so that all or part of the moon's light is blocked out.
2. *noun* In an **eclipse of the sun,** the moon comes between the sun and the earth so that all or part of the sun's light is blocked out.
3. *verb* To do a great deal better than, as in *eclipse other teams.* ▷ **eclipsing, eclipsed** ▷ *verb* **eclipse**

an eclipse of the sun

e·col·o·gy (ee-kol-uh-jee) *noun*
1. The study of the relationship between plants, animals, and their environment.
2. The study of how human activity affects the earth. This is also known as human ecology. ▷ *noun* **ecologist** ▷ *adjective* **ecological** (ek-uh-loj-i-kuhl) ▷ *adverb* **ecologically**

ec·o·nom·i·cal (ee-kuh-nom-uh-kuhl *or* ek-uh-nom-uh-kuhl) *adjective* Not wasteful. *Our car is very economical on gasoline.* ▷ *adverb* **economically**

ec·o·nom·ics (ee-kuh-nom-iks *or* ek-uh-nom-iks) *noun* The study of the way money, goods, and services are made and used in a society; the study of wealth. ▷ *noun* **economist** (ee-kon-i-mist) ▷ *adjective* **economic**

e·con·o·mize (i-kon-uh-mize) *verb* To cut down on spending in order to save money. ▷ **economizing, economized**

e·con·o·my (i-kon-uh-mee) *noun*
1. The way a country runs its industry, trade, and finance.
2. The careful use of money and other things to cut down on waste. *We'll have enough food for everyone if we practice economy.* ▷ *noun, plural* **economies**

ec·o·sys·tem (ee-koh-*siss*-tuhm *or* ek-oh-*siss*-tuhm) *noun* A community of animals and plants, interacting with their environment. *If part of an ecosystem is destroyed, other parts may be affected.*

ec·sta·sy (ek-stuh-see) *noun* A feeling of great happiness; extreme joy. ▷ *noun, plural* **ecstasies** ▷ *adjective* **ecstatic** ▷ *adverb* **ecstatically**

ec·ze·ma (ek-suh-muh *or* eg-zee-muh) *noun* A skin disease that makes the skin dry, rough, and itchy.

> **Suffix**
> •
> The suffix **-ed** makes one of these changes to a root word:
> **1.** Forms the past tense and past participle of regular verbs, as in *waited, drafted, mowed.*
> **2.** Turns a noun into an adjective, as in *left-handed, bowlegged.*

ed·dy (ed-ee) *noun* A circular current in water or air. ▷ *noun, plural* **eddies** ▷ *verb* **eddy** ▷ *adjective* **eddying**

edge (ej)
1. *noun* A boundary.
2. *verb* To move very slowly and carefully. *We edged our way along the cliff.* ▷ **edging, edged**
3. *noun* The sharp side of a cutting tool, as in *a razor's edge.*
4. *noun* An advantage. *The fastest runner has a big edge in a race.*
5. If you are **on edge,** you are nervous or anxious. ▷ *adjective* **edgy**

edge·wise (ej-wize) *adverb*
1. Sideways.
2. If you cannot **get a word in edgewise** in a discussion, other people do not give you a chance to speak.

ed·i·ble (ed-uh-buhl) *adjective* Able to be eaten. *Pick only the edible mushrooms!*

ed·it (ed-it) *verb*
1. To check a piece of writing for spelling, grammatical, stylistic, and factual mistakes and shorten it if it is too long.
2. To cut and rearrange pieces of film, audiotape, or videotape to make a movie, television program, etc. ▷ *verb* **editing, edited**

e·di·tion (i-dish-uhn) *noun*
1. The form or version of a book or newspaper that is printed at a particular time, as in *a new paperback edition.*
2. The number of copies of a newspaper, magazine, or book that are printed at the same time.

ed·i·tor (ed-uh-tur) *noun*
1. Someone who checks the contents of a book and gets it ready to be published.
2. The person in charge of a newspaper or a magazine.

ed·i·to·ri·al (ed-uh-tor-ee-uhl)
1. *adjective* To do with putting together a publication, as in *an editorial department.*
2. *noun* An article or a statement that reflects the opinions of a newspaper or magazine editor or the managers of a television or radio station.

ed·u·cate (ej-u-kate) *verb*
1. To give knowledge or a skill. *I want to be a teacher and educate young children.*
2. To send someone to school, as in *to educate a child.*
▷ *verb* **educating, educated** ▷ *noun* **educator**

ed·u·ca·tion (ej-uh-kay-shuhn) *noun*
1. The process of gaining or giving knowledge and skills.
2. The knowledge, skills, and abilities gained from schooling.
▷ *adjective* **educational**

eel (eel) *noun* A long, snakelike fish. *The electric eel stuns its prey with a strong electric shock.*

ee·rie (ihr-ee) *adjective* Strange and frightening, as in *an eerie sight.* ▷ **eerier, eeriest** ▷ *adverb* **eerily**

electric eel

ef·fect (uh-fekt)
1. *noun* The result or consequence of something, as in *the effect of the explosion.*
2. *noun* Influence, or the power to make something happen. *Praise had a great effect on her behavior.*
3. *noun* When something **goes into effect,** it starts to happen.
4. *verb* To cause to happen, as in *to effect a change.* ▷ **effecting, effected**

ef·fec·tive (uh-fek-tiv) *adjective*
1. Working very well, or getting the job done. *The medicine was effective.* ▷ *adverb* **effectively**
2. In force. *The law becomes effective next week.*

ef·fer·ves·cent (ef-ur-vess-uhnt) *adjective*
1. An **effervescent** liquid is very bubbly.
2. An **effervescent** person is very lively.
▷ *noun* **effervescence**

ef·fi·cient (uh-fish-uhnt) *adjective* If people or things are **efficient,** they work very well and do not waste time or energy. ▷ *noun* **efficiency**
▷ *adverb* **efficiently**

ef·flu·ent (ef-loo-uhnt) *noun*
1. Something that flows out. ▷ *adjective* **effluent**
2. Waste water and sewage.

ef·fort (ef-urt) *noun* If you make an **effort,** you try hard.

e.g. (eee jee) The initials of the Latin phrase *exempli gratia,* which means "for example."

egg (eg) *noun*
1. An oval or round object with a covering or shell, produced by female birds, reptiles, and fish, in which their young develop. *See* **chicken.**
2. A cell created within the body of a woman or female animal that, when fertilized, grows into a new individual.

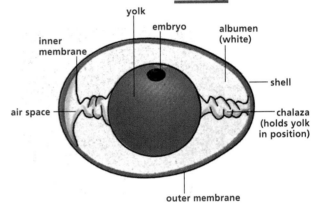
hen's egg
yolk, embryo, albumen (white), inner membrane, air space, shell, chalaza (holds yolk in position), outer membrane

egg·plant (eg-plant) *noun* A large purple vegetable shaped like a pear. *See* **vegetable.**

e·go·cen·tric (ee-goh-sen-trik) *adjective* If you are **egocentric,** you are far more interested in yourself than in others. ▷ *noun* **egocentricity**

e·gret (ee-grit) *noun* A tall heron with white feathers.

ei·der (eye-dur) *noun* A sea duck that lives in northern waters.

ei·der·down (eye-dur-doun) *noun*
1. The soft feathers of an eider duck.
2. A warm comforter filled with eiderdown.

eight (ate) *noun* The whole number, written 8, that comes after seven and before nine.
▷ *adjective* **eight**

ei·ther (ee-THur *or* eye-THur)
1. *conjunction* **Either** can be used to indicate a choice. *You can either stay or go.*
2. *pronoun* One of two. *Take either of them.*
3. *adverb* Also, or similarly. *If Tom's not going, I won't either.*
4. *adjective* One or the other of two, as in *either glove.*
5. *adjective* Each of two. *Maria and Frank sat on either side of the car.*

e·ject (i-jekt) *verb*
1. To push something out. *Press this button to eject the tape.*
2. To throw someone out. *We had to eject an especially rowdy student from our meeting.*
3. When fighter pilots **eject** in an emergency, they are hurled out of the cockpit by a special seat.
▷ *verb* **ejecting, ejected**

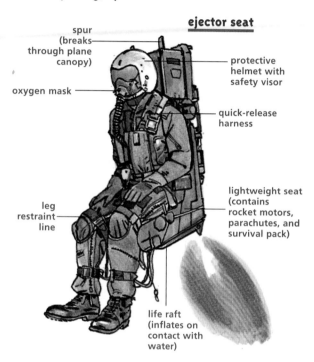

ejector seat

spur (breaks through plane canopy)

oxygen mask

protective helmet with safety visor

quick-release harness

leg restraint line

lightweight seat (contains rocket motors, parachutes, and survival pack)

life raft (inflates on contact with water)

e·lab·o·rate
1. (i-lab-ur-it) *adjective* Complicated and detailed, as in *an elaborate pattern.* ▷ *adverb* **elaborately**
2. (i-lab-uh-rate) *verb* To give more details. *Please elaborate on your plans.* ▷ **elaborating, elaborated**

e·lapse (i-laps) *verb* When time **elapses,** it passes. ▷ **elapsing, elapsed**

e·las·tic (i-lass-tik) *noun* A rubbery material that stretches. ▷ *noun* **elasticity** ▷ *adjective* **elastic**

e·lat·ed (i-lay-tid) *adjective* Very pleased and excited. *Julia was elated about her promotion.* ▷ *noun* **elation**

el·bow (el-boh) *noun* The joint that connects the upper and lower parts of your arm.

el·der (el-dur) *adjective* Older. *My elder sister drove me to school today.*

el·der·ly (el-dur-lee) *adjective* Old. *The elderly man was 90 when he won the dance contest.*

el·dest (el-duhst) *adjective* The oldest in a group, as in *my eldest child.*

e·lect (i-lekt) *verb* To choose someone or decide something by voting. ▷ **electing, elected**

e·lec·tion (i-lek-shuhn) *noun* The act or process of choosing someone or deciding something by voting. *She won the election by only 15 votes.*

electric eel *noun* A long, snakelike fish that can give off electric shocks to protect itself and stun its prey. *See* **eel.**

e·lec·tri·cian (i-lek-**trish**-uhn) *noun* Someone who installs electrical systems and fixes electrical equipment.

e·lec·tric·i·ty (i-lek-**triss**-uh-tee) *noun*
1. A form of energy caused by the motion of electrons and protons. It can be produced by rotating a magnet within a coil of wire.
▷ *adjective* **electric,** *adjective* **electrical**
2. Electrical power or an electric current.

▶ **Word History**
· ·
In ancient times, a Greek philosopher named Thales noticed that rubbing amber—a dark yellow substance from pine trees—caused it to attract other materials such as bits of straw or splinters of wood. In the 17th century, the English scientist William Gilbert experimented with amber, too. When he wrote about his experiments, he used the word **electricity** to describe what was happening. The root of electricity is the Latin word *electrum,* which came from the Greek word *ēlektron,* meaning "amber." The root lives on in the words *electron, electronic,* and in many other English words beginning with the prefix *electro-.*

e·lec·tro·cute (i-lek-truh-*kyoot*) *verb* To injure or kill yourself or someone else with a severe electric shock. ▷ **electrocuting, electrocuted** ▷ *noun* **electrocution**

e·lec·trode (i-lek-trode) *noun* A point through which an electric current can flow into or out of a device or substance. *See* **spark plug.**

e·lec·tro·lyte (i-lek-truh-*lite*) *noun* A soluble substance that conducts electricity.

e·lec·tro·mag·net (i-*lek*-troh-**mag**-nit) *noun* A temporary magnet formed when electricity flows through a coil of wire. ▷ *adjective* **electromagnetic**

e·lec·tron (i-lek-tron) *noun* A tiny particle that moves around the nucleus of an atom. Electrons carry a negative electrical charge. *See* **atom.**

e·lec·tron·ic (i-lek-tron-ik) *adjective* Electronic devices are powered by minute amounts of electricity produced by electrons. They contain transistors, silicon chips, or valves that control an electric current. *Computers, televisions, and radios are all electronic.* ▷ *adverb* **electronically**

E

electronic mail *See* **E-mail.**

e·lec·tron·ics (i-lek-tron-iks) *noun*
1. The scientific study of the behavior of electrons.
2. The technology that makes electronic machines work.

el·e·gant (el-uh-guhnt) *adjective* Graceful and stylish, as in *an elegant wedding.* ▷ *noun* **elegance** ▷ *adverb* **elegantly**

el·e·ment (el-uh-muhnt) *noun*
1. One of the simple, basic parts of something. *Claude taught me the elements of cooking.*
2. In chemistry, an **element** is a substance that cannot be split into a simpler substance. *Oxygen, copper, and carbon are elements.*
3. A wire or coil in an electric heater or toaster that heats up when electricity passes through it. *See* **iron.**
4. **the elements** *noun, plural* The weather.

el·e·men·ta·ry (el-uh-men-tuh-ree) *adjective* Simple or basic, as in *elementary arithmetic.*

elementary school *noun* A school that children attend from kindergarten through sixth or eighth grade.

el·e·phant (el-uh-fuhnt) *noun* A large mammal with a long trunk and ivory tusks that lives in Africa and India.

elephants

African elephant

Indian elephant

el·e·vate (el-uh-vate) *verb*
1. To lift something up. *If we can elevate those shelves, we'll have more space underneath them.*
2. To promote someone to an important job or status. *Abe was elevated to the rank of colonel.*
▷ *verb* **elevating, elevated** ▷ *adjective* **elevated**

el·e·va·tion (el-uh-vay-shuhn) *noun*
1. A high place or a hill.
2. The height above sea level.

el·e·va·tor (el-uh-vay-tur) *noun*
1. A machine that carries people or goods up and down between different levels of a building.
2. A very large, hollow building used for storing grain after it is harvested.
3. A movable part of an airplane tail assembly used to change the angle of flight of an aircraft. *See* **aircraft.**

e·lev·en (i-lev-uhn) *noun* The whole number, written 11, that comes after ten and before twelve. ▷ *adjective* **eleven**

> ▶ **Word History**
> ●
> Counting has often been based on the decimal system—the number 10— throughout history. That fact becomes very clear when we look at the origin of the word **eleven.** The ancient Germanic root of eleven means "one left over after counting ten." *Twelve* means "two left over after counting ten."

elf (elf) *noun* A small, magical, mischievous person described in legends and fairy tales. ▷ *noun, plural* **elves** (elvz) ▷ *adjective* **elfin**

el·i·gi·ble (el-uh-juh-buhl) *adjective*
1. If you are **eligible** for something, such as a job, you have the right qualifications for it.
2. An **eligible** man or woman is a suitable person for someone to marry.
▷ *noun* **eligibility**

e·lim·i·nate (i-lim-uh-nate) *verb*
1. To leave out, or to get rid of. *Let's try to eliminate pollution from the planet.*
2. To remove from a competition by a defeat. *Our team was eliminated from the tournament.*
▷ *verb* **eliminating, eliminated** ▷ *noun* **elimination**

e·lite (i-leet *or* ay-leet) *noun* A group of people who have special advantages and privileges. ▷ *noun* **elitism** ▷ *adjective* **elite**

elk (elk) *noun* A type of large deer similar to, but smaller than, the moose.

el·lipse (i-lips) *noun* An oval shape. ▷ *adjective* **elliptical**

elm (elm) *noun* A tall tree with spreading branches.

el·o·cu·tion (el-uh-kyoo-shuhn) *noun* The art of speaking clearly and effectively.

e·lon·gate (i-lawng-gate)
1. *verb* To make something longer or more stretched out. ▷ **elongating, elongated**
2. **elongated** *adjective* Long and thin.

e·lope (i-lope) *verb* When a man and woman **elope**, they run away to get married without others knowing about it. ▷ **eloping, eloped** ▷ *noun* **elopement**

el·o·quent (el-uh-kwuhnt) *adjective* An **eloquent** person expresses him- or herself smoothly and clearly. ▷ *noun* **eloquence** ▷ *adverb* **eloquently**

else (elss) *adverb*
1. Other, or different. *They have gone somewhere else.*
2. More. *Please let me know if you need anything else.*

else·where (elss-wair) *adverb* Somewhere else. *Trudy was so annoyed by the store's prices, she decided to do her shopping elsewhere.*

e·lude (i-lude) *verb* To escape or get away from someone. *I eluded my friends during our game of tag.* ▷ **eluding, eluded**

e·lu·sive (i-loo-siv) *adjective* Very hard to find or catch. *Farmer Jones was finally able to outwit the elusive rabbit.* ▷ *noun* **elusiveness** ▷ *adverb* **elusively**

E-mail (ee-mayl) *noun* Electronic messages that are sent between computer terminals linked by phone lines. Short for *electronic mail. It's much faster to send a message via E-mail than through the postal system.* ▷ *verb* **E-mail** ▷ *adjective* **E-mail**

e·man·ci·pate (i-man-si-pate) *verb* To free a person or group from slavery or control. *In 1863, Abraham Lincoln signed a proclamation emancipating the slaves.* ▷ **emancipating, emancipated** ▷ *noun* **emancipation**

em·bank·ment (em-bangk-muhnt) *noun*
1. A long, low, earthen structure built to carry a railroad, road, etc.
2. A high bank at the sides of a river built to keep it from flooding.

em·bar·go (em-bar-goh) *noun* An official order forbidding something from happening, especially trade. ▷ *noun, plural* **embargoes**

em·bark (em-bark) *verb*
1. To go on board a ship or an airplane, ready for a journey.
2. To start something that will take a long time to finish. *Tanya has embarked on a massive art project.*
▷ *verb* **embarking, embarked**

em·bar·rass (em-ba-ruhss) *verb* If something **embarrasses** you, it makes you feel awkward and uncomfortable. *Ron's poor behavior embarrassed his family.* ▷ **embarrasses, embarrassing, embarrassed** ▷ *noun* **embarrassment** ▷ *adjective* **embarrassing,** *adjective* **embarrassed**

em·bas·sy (em-buh-see) *noun* The official place in a foreign country where an ambassador lives and works. ▷ *noun, plural* **embassies**

em·bers (em-burz) *noun, plural* The hot, glowing remains of a fire.

em·bez·zle (em-bez-uhl) *verb* To steal money secretly from the organization that you work for. *Steve embezzled thousands of dollars before he was caught.* ▷ **embezzling, embezzled** ▷ *noun* **embezzler,** *noun* **embezzlement**

em·blem (em-bluhm) *noun* A symbol or a sign. *The emblem of our club is a spider.*

em·boss (em-boss) *verb* To create raised lettering or designs on a flat piece of paper or metal. *The fancy stationery was embossed with his initials.* ▷ **embosses, embossing, embossed**

em·brace (em-brayss) *verb*
1. To hug. *The couple embraced before they parted.* ▷ *noun* **embrace**
2. To take up eagerly; to welcome. *Alicia embraced the chance to work at a shelter.*
3. To include. *The book embraces all points of view.*
4. To cherish or to love. *I embrace you with all my heart.*
▷ *verb* **embracing, embraced**

em·broi·der (em-broi-dur) *verb* To sew a picture or a design onto cloth. ▷ **embroidering, embroidered** ▷ *noun* **embroiderer,** *noun* **embroidery**

embroidery stitches

backstitch

French knots

running stitch

cross-stitch

feather stitch

chain stitch

blanket stitch

double cross-stitch

satin stitch

em·bry·o (em-bree-oh) *noun*
1. A fetus in its earliest stage of development.

2. A plant in its first stage of development, contained within a seed.
▷ *noun, plural* **embryos**

em·er·ald (em-ur-uhld) *noun*
1. A bright green precious stone.
2. A bright green color.
▷ *adjective* **emerald**

e·merge (i-murj) *verb*
1. If you **emerge** from somewhere, you come out into the open.
2. To become known. *News is emerging of a serious avalanche in the mountains.*
▷ *verb* **emerging, emerged** ▷ *noun* **emergence**

e·mer·gen·cy (i-mur-juhn-see) *noun* A sudden and dangerous situation that must be dealt with quickly. ▷ *noun, plural* **emergencies**

em·er·y (em-ur-ee) *noun* A mineral used for grinding or polishing. *She filed her nails with a board made of emery.*

em·i·grate (em-uh-grate) *verb* To leave your own country in order to live in another one. *During the famine, many families decided to emigrate.*
▷ **emigrating, emigrated** ▷ *noun* **emigrant,** *noun* **emigration**

em·i·nent (em-uh-nuhnt) *adjective* Well-known and respected, as in *an eminent professor.*
▷ *noun* **eminence** ▷ *adverb* **eminently**

e·mis·sion (i-mish-uhn) *noun*
1. The release of something such as chemicals into the atmosphere.
2. emissions *noun, plural* Substances released into the air.

e·mit (i-mit) *verb* To release or send out something such as heat, light, or sound. *The spaceship emitted a strange sound.* ▷ **emitting, emitted**

e·mo·tion (i-moh-shuhn) *noun* A strong feeling, such as happiness, love, anger, or grief.

e·mo·tion·al (i-moh-shuh-nuhl) *adjective*
1. To do with your feelings, as in *emotional problems.*
2. When someone becomes **emotional,** the person shows his or her feelings.
▷ *adverb* **emotionally**

em·per·or (em-pur-ur) *noun* The male ruler of an empire.

em·pha·sis (em-fuh-siss) *noun* Importance given to something. *Because my sister was becoming a teenager, we put special emphasis on her birthday.* ▷ *noun, plural* **emphases** (em-fuh-*seez*)

em·pha·size (em-fuh-size) *verb* If you **emphasize** something, you make it stand out clearly because you think it is important.
▷ **emphasizing, emphasized** ▷ *adjective* **emphatic** (em-fat-ik)

em·pire (em-pire) *noun*
1. A group of countries that have the same ruler, as in *the Roman Empire.*
2. A country that is ruled over by an emperor or empress. *In 221 B.C., Ch'in Shih Huang Ti became the first emperor of the newly formed Chinese empire.*
3. A large group of companies controlled by one person, as in *a communications empire.*

em·ploy (em-ploi) *verb*
1. To pay someone to work for you. *A large factory on the edge of town employs most of the people who live here.* ▷ *noun* **employer,** *noun* **employment**
2. To use something. *You can employ a blender to beat the eggs.*
▷ *verb* **employing, employed**

em·ploy·ee (em-ploi-ee *or* em-ploi-ee) *noun* A person who works for and is paid by another person or business.

em·press (em-priss) *noun* The female ruler of an empire, or the wife of an emperor.

em·pty (emp-tee)
1. *adjective* If a container is **empty,** there is nothing inside it.
2. *verb* To take the contents out of a container. *Eva emptied the box of crayons onto the table.*
▷ **empties, emptying, emptied**
3. *noun* An empty bottle or can. ▷ *noun, plural* **empties**
4. *adjective* Without meaning or purpose, as in *an empty promise.*
▷ *noun* **emptiness** ▷ *adjective* **emptier, emptiest**

e·mu (ee-myoo) *noun* A large bird from Australia that is related to the ostrich. It runs fast but does not fly.

e·mul·sion (i-muhl-shuhn) *noun*
1. A mixture of two liquids in which the particles of one liquid mix with the other liquid but do not dissolve. *When oil and vinegar are mixed, they form an emulsion.*
2. A light-sensitive chemical coating on camera film.

en·a·ble (en-ay-buhl) *verb* To make it possible for someone to do something. *Telescopes enable people to see the stars more clearly.* ▷ **enabling, enabled** ▷ *noun* **enabler**

e·nam·el (i-nam-uhl) *noun*
1. A shiny substance similar to glass that is used to coat and protect metal, pottery, and other materials.
2. Paint that dries to a hard, shiny surface.
3. The hard, white surface of your teeth. *See* **tooth.**
▷ *verb* **enamel** ▷ *adjective* **enameled**

E

en·chant (en-chant) *verb* To delight or charm someone. *Ron enchanted us as he described his trip to Spain.* ▷ **enchanting, enchanted**

en·chant·ed (en-chan-tid) *adjective* A place or thing that is **enchanted** has been put under a magic spell or seems magical, as in *an enchanted castle.*

en·chant·ing (en-chan-ting) *adjective* Delightful and charming. ▷ *adverb* **enchantingly**

en·close (en-kloze) *verb*
1. To put a fence or a wall around an area.
2. To put something in with a letter or a package that you are sending.
▷ *verb* **enclosing, enclosed** ▷ *adjective* **enclosed**

en·clo·sure (en-kloh-zhur) *noun*
1. An area closed in by a fence, walls, etc.
2. Something put in with a letter or a package.

en·com·pass (en-kuhm-puhss) *verb*
1. To form a circle around something. *A fence encompasses the yard behind my house.*
2. To include something. *Our history lesson will encompass the Civil War period.*
▷ *verb* **encompasses, encompassing, encompassed**

en·core (ong-kor *or* on-kor)
1. *noun* An extra song or musical selection added to the end of a performance because the audience has been cheering for more or applauding so much.
2. *interjection* Again, please!

en·coun·ter (en-koun-tur) *noun* An unexpected or difficult meeting. ▷ *verb* **encounter**

en·cour·age (en-kur-ij) *verb* To give someone confidence by praising or supporting the person. *The teacher encouraged us to do our best.*
▷ **encouraging, encouraged** ▷ *noun* **encouragement** ▷ *adjective* **encouraging** ▷ *adverb* **encouragingly**

en·cy·clo·pe·di·a (en-sye-kloh-pee-dee-uh) *noun* A book or set of books with information about many different subjects, usually arranged in alphabetical order. ▷ *adjective* **encyclopedic**

end (end)
1. *noun* The last part of something.
2. *noun* One of the two points farthest from the middle of an object.
3. *verb* To finish. *The party ended after all the birthday cake was gone.* ▷ **ending, ended**

en·dan·ger (en-dayn-jur) *verb* To put in a dangerous situation; to threaten. *Pollution can endanger wildlife.* ▷ **endangering, endangered** ▷ *adjective* **endangered**

endangered species *noun* A species or type of plant or animal that is in danger of becoming extinct. *Like many other animals, the orangutan is an endangered species because its habitat is being destroyed.*

en·deav·or (en-dev-ur)
1. *verb* To try very hard to do something. *I will endeavor to finish reading the whole book in one day.* ▷ **endeavoring, endeavored**
2. *noun* A serious attempt or effort. *Her endeavor to win the presidency won her much praise.*

end·less (end-liss) *adjective* Something **endless** has no end or seems to have no end. ▷ *adverb* **endlessly**

en·dor·phin (en-dor-fuhn) *noun* A substance created by the brain that reduces pain.

en·dorse (en-dorss) *verb*
1. To support or approve of someone or something. *I strongly endorse your plan to attend medical school.*
2. To sign one's name on the reverse side of an official document. *You'll have to endorse the check before you can cash it.*
▷ *verb* **endorsing, endorsed** ▷ *noun* **endorsement**

en·dow (en-dou) *verb*
1. If you are **endowed** with a gift or a talent, you are given it or enriched by it.
2. To give money or property. *The college was endowed by a wealthy graduate.*
▷ *verb* **endowing, endowed** ▷ *noun* **endowment**

en·dure (en-dur) *verb*
1. If you **endure** something unpleasant or painful, you put up with it.
2. If something **endures,** it lasts for a long time.
▷ *verb* **enduring, endured** ▷ *adjective* **enduring**
▷ *noun* **endurance**

en·e·my (en-uh-mee) *noun*
1. Someone who hates and wants to harm or destroy another.
2. The country or army that you are fighting against in a war.
▷ *noun, plural* **enemies**

en·er·get·ic (en-ur-jet-ik) *adjective* Strong and active, as in *an energetic workout.* ▷ *adverb* **energetically**

en·er·gy (en-ur-jee) *noun*
1. The strength to do active things without getting tired.
2. Power from coal, electricity, or other sources that makes machines work and produces heat.
3. In physics, **energy** is the ability of something to do work. It is measured in **joules.**

en·force (en-forss) *verb* To make sure that a law or rule is obeyed. *Police officers enforce the traffic laws by using radar traps.* ▷ **enforcing, enforced** ▷ *noun* **enforcement**

en·gaged (en-gayjd) *adjective*
1. If two people are **engaged,** they have decided that they will get married.
2. If someone is **engaged** in doing something, the person is busy and occupied doing it.
▷ *noun* **engagement**

en·gine (en-juhn) *noun*
1. A machine that changes an energy source such as gasoline into movement. *In the gasoline engine shown here, electrical sparks from the spark plugs ignite the compressed gasoline vapor and air mixture in the cylinders. The mixture burns rapidly and pushes the pistons down in turn. The fast-moving pistons turn the crankshaft, which drives the car. See also* **jet engine.**
2. The front part of a train that pulls the cars. *See* **steam locomotive.**

▶ **Word History**

The word **enemy** actually has a lot in common with its opposite, *friend.* It comes from the Latin root, *amicus,* which means "friend." Enemy in Latin is *inimicus,* combining the prefix *in-,* meaning "not," and *amicus.* Enemy is a good example of how a negative prefix can reverse the meaning of a word.

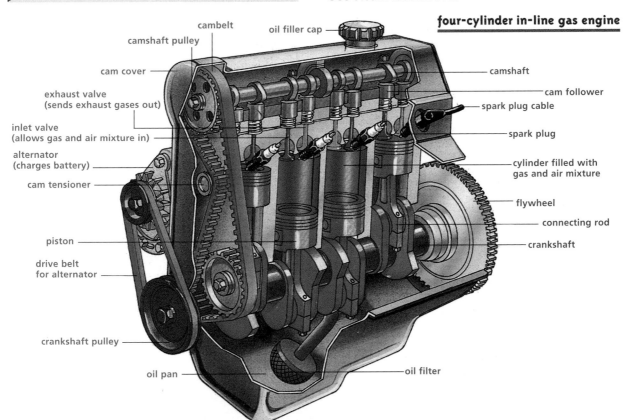

four-cylinder in-line gas engine

- cambelt
- oil filler cap
- camshaft pulley
- cam cover
- camshaft
- exhaust valve (sends exhaust gases out)
- cam follower
- spark plug cable
- inlet valve (allows gas and air mixture in)
- spark plug
- alternator (charges battery)
- cylinder filled with gas and air mixture
- cam tensioner
- flywheel
- connecting rod
- piston
- crankshaft
- drive belt for alternator
- crankshaft pulley
- oil pan
- oil filter

en·gi·neer (en-juh-nihr)
1. noun Someone who is trained to design and build machines, vehicles, bridges, roads, or other structures. ▷ **noun engineering**
2. verb To make something happen by using a clever plan. *Don engineered a meeting between the two rivals.* ▷ **engineering, engineered**

Eng·lish (ing-glish)
1. adjective From England, or to do with England.
2. noun The main language spoken in the United States, Canada, Great Britain, Australia, and many other countries.
3. adjective To do with the English language.

en·grave (en-grayv) **verb** To cut a design or letters into a metal, wood, or glass surface. *The tools shown here can be used to engrave a picture in metal.* ▷ **engraving, engraved** ▷ **noun engraver, noun engraving** ▷ **adjective engraved**

engraving tools

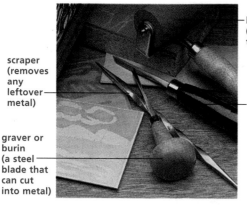

scraper (removes any leftover metal)

graver or burin (a steel blade that can cut into metal)

brayer (distributes the ink)

burnisher (smoothes any rough edges)

en·grossed (en-grohst) **adjective** If you are **engrossed** in something, you give it all your attention. ▷ **adjective engrossing**

en·gulf (en-guhlf) **verb** To cover or swallow up someone or something. *A huge wave engulfed the swimmers.* ▷ **engulfing, engulfed**

en·hance (en-hanss) **verb** To make something better or greater. *She enhanced her ability to help her sick father by learning first aid.* ▷ **enhancing, enhanced** ▷ **noun enhancement**

e·nig·ma (i-nig-muh) **noun** A mystery or a puzzle. *Life is an enigma.* ▷ **adjective enigmatic**

en·joy (en-joi) **verb**
1. To get pleasure from doing something.
2. To have the benefit of. *We enjoyed a mild winter last year.*
▷ **verb enjoying, enjoyed** ▷ **noun enjoyment** ▷ **adjective enjoyable** ▷ **adverb enjoyably**

en·large (en-larj) **verb** To make bigger. *We want to enlarge this photo.* ▷ **enlarging, enlarged** ▷ **noun enlarger, noun enlargement**

en·light·en (en-lite-uhn) **verb** To teach or give understanding to. *The doctor enlightened us about the need for a healthy diet.* ▷ **enlightening, enlightened** ▷ **noun enlightenment**

en·list (en-list) **verb**
1. To join or get someone to join the army, navy, or one of the other armed forces.
2. If you **enlist** someone's help, you get the person to assist you.
▷ **verb enlisting, enlisted**

e·nor·mous (i-nor-muhss) **adjective** Extremely large. ▷ **noun enormity, noun enormousness** ▷ **adverb enormously**

e·nough (i-nuf) **adjective** As much as is needed. *There were enough apples to feed everyone in our group.* ▷ **noun enough** ▷ **pronoun enough** ▷ **adverb enough**

en·rage (en-rayj) **verb** To make someone angry. *Kim's nasty comments enraged me.* ▷ **enraging, enraged**

en·rich (en-rich) **verb**
1. To make richer. *Leah and Paul were enriched by their appearance on the game show.*
2. To improve the quality of something by adding good things to it. *The dairy enriches their milk with vitamins.*
3. To fertilize. *You can enrich soil with compost.*
▷ **verb enriches, enriching, enriched** ▷ **noun enrichment** ▷ **adjective enriching, adjective enriched**

en·roll (en-rohl) **verb** When you **enroll** in a club, class, or school, you put your name on a list because you want to join. ▷ **enrolling, enrolled** ▷ **noun enrollment**

en route (on root) **adverb** On the way. *Many people claim that Washington slept here en route to Philadelphia.* ▷ **adjective en route**

en·sem·ble (on-som-buhl) **noun** A group of musicians or actors who perform together.

en·sue (en-soo) **verb** To happen next. *A furious argument ensued.* ▷ **ensuing, ensued** ▷ **adjective ensuing**

en·sure (en-shur) **verb** To make certain that something happens. *Please ensure that the door is locked.* ▷ **ensuring, ensured**

en·tan·gle (en-tang-guhl) **verb**
1. To become twisted or trapped. *My hair was so messy it became entangled in my brush.*
2. To get into a difficult situation. *She was entangled in a dangerous scheme.*
▷ **verb entangling, entangled** ▷ **noun entanglement**

en·ter (en-tur) **verb**
1. To go into a place.
2. To sign up for a competition, a race, or an exam.
3. To type information into a computer or write it in a book.
▷ **verb entering, entered**

en·ter·prise (en-tur-*prize*) *noun* Something that you do or plan to do that is very important, dangerous, or difficult. Explorations, research, and starting up a business are all enterprises.

en·ter·pris·ing (en-tur-*prize*-ing) *adjective* Someone who is **enterprising** has a lot of good ideas and is brave enough to try things that are new and difficult.

en·ter·tain (en-tur-tayn) *verb*
1. To amuse and interest someone. ▷ *noun* **entertainer,** *noun* **entertainment** ▷ *adjective* **entertaining**
2. To invite people to your home for a party, a visit, or a meal, as in *to entertain friends.*
▷ *verb* **entertaining, entertained**

en·thrall (en-thrawl) *verb* To excite or charm someone. *A good actress is able to enthrall an audience with her performance.* ▷ **enthralling, enthralled**

en·thu·si·asm (en-thoo-zee-*az*-uhm) *noun* Great excitement or interest. *Tony's speech filled his supporters with enthusiasm.*

en·thu·si·as·tic (en-*thoo*-zee-ass-tik) *adjective* If you are **enthusiastic** about something, you are very excited about it or interested in it. ▷ *noun* **enthusiast** ▷ *adverb* **enthusiastically**

en·tice (en-tisse) *verb* To tempt someone to do something. ▷ **enticing, enticed** ▷ *noun* **enticement** ▷ *adjective* **enticing**

en·tire (en-tire) *adjective* Whole. ▷ *adverb* **entirely**

en·ti·tle (en-tye-tuhl) *verb*
1. To give a right or a privilege to someone. *My library card entitles me to borrow books as well as audio- and videotapes.* ▷ *noun* **entitlement**
2. To put a name on a book or other work. *He entitled his essay "My Summer Vacation."*
▷ *verb* **entitling, entitled**

en·trance
1. (en-truhnss) *noun* The way into a place.
2. (en-transs) *verb* To give someone a feeling of wonder and pleasure. ▷ **entrancing, entranced**
▷ *adjective* **entrancing**

en·trant (en-truhnt) *noun* Someone who takes part in a contest, competition, or race.

en·tre·pre·neur (*on*-truh-pruh-**nur**) *noun* Someone who starts businesses and is good at finding new ways to make money. ▷ *adjective* **entrepreneurial**

en·trust (en-truhst) *verb* If you **entrust** someone with something valuable or important, you give it to the person to look after for you.
▷ **entrusting, entrusted**

en·try (en-tree) *noun*
1. A way into a place.
2. A picture, a story, an answer, etc., that you send in to a competition.
3. A piece of information in a dictionary, diary, computer, etc.
▷ *noun, plural* **entries**

e·nun·ci·ate (i-nuhn-see-ate) *verb* To speak or pronounce words. *The opera singer enunciated her words so clearly that the audience could follow the story.* ▷ **enunciating, enunciated** ▷ *noun* **enunciation**

en·vel·op (en-vel-uhp) *verb* To cover or surround something completely. *The house was soon enveloped in flames.* ▷ **enveloping, enveloped**

en·ve·lope (en-vuh-lope *or* on-vuh-lope) *noun* A paper container for a letter or anything flat that is to be mailed. *See* **address.**

en·vi·a·ble (en-vee-uh-buhl) *adjective* Very desirable or much wanted. *Marcella has an enviable job with the company.*

en·vi·ous (en-vee-uhss) *adjective* If you are **envious,** you wish that you could have something that someone else has. ▷ *adverb* **enviously**

en·vi·ron·ment (en-vye-ruhn-muhnt) *noun*
1. All the things that influence your life, such as the area where you live, your family, and the things that happen to you. *Some children never have a secure home environment.*
2. The natural world of the land, sea, and air. *We must protect the environment.*
▷ *noun* **environmentalist** ▷ *adjective* **environmental** ▷ *adverb* **environmentally**

environmentally friendly *adjective* Products are **environmentally friendly** if they are made of substances that do not damage the natural environment and if they are reusable or can be recycled easily.

en·vy (en-vee) *verb* When you **envy** someone, you wish that you could have something that the person has or do something that he or she has done. ▷ **envies, envying, envied** ▷ *noun* **envy**

en·zyme (en-zime) *noun* A protein in the bodies of humans and animals that causes chemical reactions to occur. *Enzymes help digest food.*

e·on (ee-on) *noun* A very long period of time. *The universe has existed for eons.*

ep·ic (ep-ik)
1. *noun* A long story, poem, or movie about heroic adventures and great battles. An epic is usually historical in subject matter.
2. *adjective* Heroic or impressive, as in *an epic voyage of exploration.*
3. *adjective* Very large. *The spaceship was of epic proportions.*

ep·i·cen·ter (ep-uh-*sent*-ur) *noun* The area directly above the place where an earthquake occurs. *The people at an earthquake's epicenter are in the greatest danger.*

ep·i·dem·ic (ep-uh-dem-ik) *noun* When there is an **epidemic,** an infectious disease spreads quickly through a population.

ep·i·gram (ep-uh-*gram*) *noun* A short, witty saying. ▷ *adjective* **epigrammatic**

ep·i·lep·sy (ep-uh-*lep*-see) *noun* A disease of the brain that causes a person to have sudden blackouts or convulsions. ▷ *noun* **epileptic** ▷ *adjective* **epileptic**

ep·i·logue (ep-uh-*log*) *noun* A short speech or piece of writing added to the end of a play, story, or poem.

ep·i·sode (ep-uh-*sode*) *noun*
1. An event or set of events in your life. *I don't want to talk about that embarrassing episode!*
2. One of the programs in a television or radio series.

ep·i·taph (ep-uh-*taf*) *noun* A short description of someone who has died, written on the person's gravestone.

e·poch (ep-uhk) *noun* A period of history marked by important events. *The second part of the 20th century is sometimes described as the epoch of space travel.*

e·qual (ee-kwuhl)
1. *adjective* The same as something else in size, value, or amount. *Two pints are equal to one quart.* ▷ *adverb* **equally**
2. *adjective* The same for each member of a group, as in *equal housing opportunities.*
3. *noun* A person of equal ability or position, or a thing of equal quality, as in *a jury of one's equals.*
4. *verb* If you **equal** what someone else has done, you do as well as that person. ▷ **equaling, equaled**

e·qual·i·ty (i-kwol-uh-tee) *noun* The same rights for everyone.

e·qua·tion (i-kway-zhuhn *or* i-kway-shuhn) *noun* A mathematical statement that one set of numbers or values is equal to another set of numbers or values. For example, $4 \times 4 = 16$ and $3x + 2y = 13$ are equations.

e·qua·tor (i-kway-tur) *noun* An imaginary line around the middle of the earth, halfway between the North and South Poles. *The equator is marked by a red line on this picture.* ▷ *adjective* **equatorial** (ek-wuh-*tor*-ee-uhl)

equator

e·ques·tri·an (i-kwess-tree-uhn) *adjective* To do with horseback riding. *A great many equestrian events were held during the course of the rodeo.* ▷ *noun* **equestrian**

e·qui·lat·er·al (ee-kwuh-lat-ur-uhl) *adjective* Having sides of equal length. *In an equilateral triangle, the three angles, as well as the three sides, are all equal. See **shape.***

e·qui·lib·ri·um (ee-kwuh-lib-ree-uhm) *noun* Balance. *It is difficult to keep your equilibrium while standing on one foot.*

e·qui·nox (ee-kwuh-*noks*) *noun* One of the two days in the year when day and night last exactly the same length of time all over the world. ▷ *noun, plural* **equinoxes**

e·quip (i-kwip) *verb* To provide with the things that are needed. *My classroom is equipped with chairs, desks, a chalkboard, and books.* ▷ **equipping, equipped**

e·quip·ment (i-kwip-muhnt) *noun* The tools and machines needed for a particular purpose.

e·quiv·a·lent (i-kwiv-uh-luhnt) *adjective* If one thing is **equivalent** to another, it is the same as the other in amount, value, or importance. ▷ *noun* **equivalent,** *noun* **equivalence**

> ## ▶ Suffix
> •
>
> There are two suffixes **-er** in English. The first adds one of the following meanings to a root word:
>
> **1.** One who, as in *baker* (one who bakes).
>
> **2.** A person who lives in or comes from a place, as in *highlander, mainlander.*
>
> The second **-er** suffix adds the meaning "more" to a root adjective or adverb, as in *warmer* (more warm), *thinner* (more thin), *slower* (more slow).

e·ra (ihr-uh) *noun* A period of time in history.

e·rad·i·cate (i-rad-uh-kate) *verb* To get rid of something completely, especially something bad such as disease, crime, or poverty. *Doctors work to eradicate cancer.* ▷ **eradicating, eradicated** ▷ *noun* **eradication,** *noun* **eradicator**

e·rase (i-rayss) *verb*
1. To rub something out with an eraser.
2. To wipe out something stored in a computer or recorded on a tape.
3. To get rid of completely. *Erase that thought from your mind.*
▷ *verb* **erasing, erased** ▷ *noun* **erasure**

e·ras·er (i-ray-sur) *noun* Something used for rubbing off pencil or pen marks from paper, or chalk marks from a blackboard, etc.

e·rect (i-rekt)
1. *adjective* Standing upright. ▷ *adverb* **erectly**
2. *verb* To put up a structure. *This building was erected in 1982.* ▷ **erecting, erected**
▷ *noun* **erection**

er·mine (ur-muhn) *noun* A kind of weasel. Its brown fur turns white in winter.

e·rode (i-rode) *verb* When something is **eroded,** it is gradually worn away by water or wind.
▷ **eroding, eroded**

e·ro·sion (i-roh-zhuhn) *noun* The gradual wearing away of a substance by water or wind, as in *soil erosion.*

er·rand (er-uhnd) *noun* If someone sends you on an **errand,** the person asks you to take a message or to deliver or pick up something.

er·rat·ic (i-rat-ik) *adjective* If something is **erratic,** it does not follow a regular pattern, as in *erratic behavior.* ▷ *adverb* **erratically**

er·ror (er-ur) *noun* A mistake.

e·rupt (i-ruhpt) *verb*
1. When a volcano **erupts,** it throws out rocks, hot ashes, and lava with great force. ▷ *noun* **eruption**
2. To start happening suddenly. *Fighting erupted on the streets.*
3. If someone **erupts,** the person suddenly becomes very angry.
▷ *verb* **erupting, erupted**

es·ca·la·tor (ess-kuh-lay-tur) *noun* A moving staircase. *This diagram of an escalator shows how a moving belt of stairs is controlled by a drive belt that is driven by a drive wheel.*

es·cape (ess-kape)
1. *verb* To break free from a place where you have been kept against your will.
2. *noun* The act of breaking free from a place.
3. *noun* A way of escaping. *The bridge was their escape from the burning city.*
4. *verb* To avoid something. *We escaped the rush hour traffic.*
5. *verb* To leak out. *Gas was escaping from the pipe.*
▷ *verb* **escaping, escaped**

es·cort (ess-kort) *verb* To accompany someone, especially to protect the person. ▷ **escorting, escorted** ▷ *noun* **escort** (ess-kort)

Es·ki·mo (ess-kuh-moh) *noun* A member of a group of native peoples of the Arctic, the area around the North Pole. *See* **Inuit.** ▷ *noun, plural* **Eskimo** *or* **Eskimos**

e·soph·a·gus (i-sof-uh-guhss) *noun* The tube that carries food from the throat to the stomach. *See* **anatomy, digestion.**

E

escalator

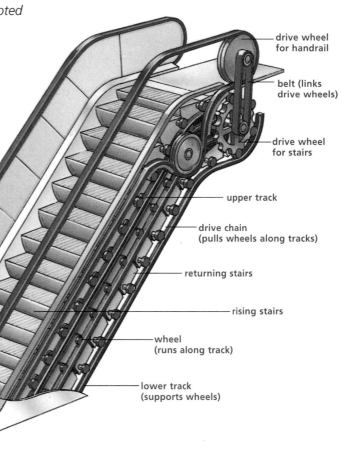

drive wheel for handrail

belt (links drive wheels)

drive wheel for stairs

upper track

drive chain (pulls wheels along tracks)

returning stairs

rising stairs

wheel (runs along track)

lower track (supports wheels)

moving handrail

es·pe·cial·ly (ess-pesh-uh-lee) *adverb*
1. More than usually; particularly. *Cathy is especially good at singing.*
2. Mainly. *Alex loves sports, especially tennis.*

Es·pe·ran·to (ess-puh-ron-toh) *noun* A language invented in the 19th century and intended to be a world language.

es·pi·o·nage (ess-pee-uh-*nahzh*) *noun* The act of spying or the work of a spy in trying to gain national or economic secret information.

es·say (ess-ay) *noun* A piece of writing about a particular subject.

es·sence (ess-uhnss) *noun*
1. The most important quality of something that makes it what it is. *The essence of friendship is loyalty.*
2. A plant substance used to make perfume.

es·sen·tial (i-sen-shuhl)
1. *adjective* Vital and important. *It is essential that you read the instructions before you begin.*
2. *noun* Something you really need and cannot do without. *I carry only essentials when I travel.*
▷ *adverb* **essentially**

> ### Suffix
> ●
>
> The suffix **-est** means "*most*" when added to a root adjective or adverb, as in *hottest* (most hot), *biggest* (most big), *slowest* (most slow).
>
> Sometimes the final consonant in the root word is doubled before the -*est* suffix is added. Always look up the word if you're not sure how to spell it.

es·tab·lish (ess-tab-lish) *verb*
1. To set up a business, a society, or an organization. ▷ *noun* **establishment**
2. To settle somewhere. *We established ourselves in our new house.*
3. To confirm that something is true or correct. *The detectives established that the crime took place at night.*
▷ *verb* **establishes, establishing, established**

es·tate (ess-tate) *noun*
1. A large area of land, usually with a house on it.
2. All the money, property, and other assets that someone leaves behind when he or she dies.

es·teem (ess-teem) *noun* If you hold someone in **esteem,** you respect and admire the person.
▷ *verb* **esteem** ▷ *adjective* **esteemed**

es·ti·mate
1. (ess-ti-muht) *noun* A rough guess or calculation about an amount, distance, cost, etc, as in *an estimate of the room's length.*
2. (ess-ti-mate) *verb* To form an opinion about something. *Leon estimated that his younger*

brother was old enough to join the club.
▷ **estimating, estimated** ▷ *noun* **estimator**

es·tu·ar·y (ess-chu-er-ee) *noun* The wide part of a river where it joins a sea. ▷ *noun, plural* **estuaries**

etc. (et set-uh-ruh) An abbreviation of the Latin phrase *et cetera*, which means "and the rest." *Etc.* is used at the end of a list to mean that the list is not complete.

etch (ech) *verb* To engrave or draw on metal or glass, using a sharp object and acid to cut through the surface. ▷ **etches, etching, etched**
▷ *adjective* **etched**

etch *noun* A picture or print that is made from an etched plate.

e·ter·nal (i-tur-nuhl) *adjective* Lasting forever.
▷ *adverb* **eternally**

e·ter·ni·ty (i-tur-nuh-tee) *noun*
1. Time without beginning or end.
2. A seemingly endless time period. *Jean waited an eternity for the bus.*
▷ *noun, plural* **eternities**

e·ther (ee-thur) *noun* A clear liquid with a strong smell. Ether is used to put a person to sleep before an operation.

eth·nic (eth-nik) *adjective* To do with a group of people sharing the same national origins, language, or culture. *The United States is home to many ethnic groups.* ▷ *adverb* **ethnically**

et·i·quette (et-uh-ket) *noun* Rules of polite behavior, such as the proper way to introduce people to each other or to eat. *It is proper etiquette to put your napkin on your lap when eating.*

é·tude (ay-tood) *noun* A piece of music designed to teach a particular technique. *Playing the étude over and over helped the pianist learn the musical scales.*

et·y·mol·o·gy (et-uh-mol-uh-jee) *noun* The history of a word, tracing it back to its earlier form and meaning and including changes it has undergone along the way. *Each Word History in this dictionary is an etymology.* ▷ *noun, plural* **etymologies**

eu·ca·lyp·tus (yoo-kuh-lip-tuhss) *noun*
A fragrant evergreen tree that grows in dry climates. *Koala bears, such as this one, often live in eucalyptus trees and feed on their leaves.*
▷ *noun, plural* **eucalyptuses**

koala bear feeding on eucalyptus

Eu·ro·pe·an (*yu*-ruh-pee-uhn) *adjective* From Europe or to do with Europe. ▷ *noun* **European**

European Economic Community *noun* A group of European countries that have joined together to encourage trade among them.

eu·tha·na·sia (*yoo*-thuh-**nay**-zhuh) *noun* The ending of a life so as to release an animal or a person from an incurable disease or intolerable suffering.

e·vac·u·ate (i-**vak**-yoo-ate) *verb* To move away from an area because it is dangerous there. *Everybody evacuate the building, please!* ▷ **evacuating, evacuated** ▷ *noun* **evacuation**

e·vade (i-vade) *verb*
1. To keep away from someone, or to keep out of someone's way.
2. To avoid something that you should do or respond to. *Shaun keeps evading the question.* ▷ *verb* **evading, evaded** ▷ *noun* **evasion** ▷ *adjective* **evasive**

e·val·u·ate (i-**val**-yoo-*ate*) *verb* To decide how good or how valuable something is after thinking carefully about it. ▷ **evaluating, evaluated** ▷ *noun* **evaluation,** *noun* **evaluator**

e·van·gel·i·cal (ev-uhn-**jel**-uh-kuhl) *adjective* An **evangelical** Christian tells people about the Christian gospel. ▷ *noun* **evangelism** (ee-van-jel-izm) ▷ *noun* **evangelist** (ee-van-jel-ist)

e·vap·o·rate (i-**vap**-uh-rate) *verb*
1. When a liquid **evaporates,** it changes into a vapor or gas. ▷ *noun* **evaporation**
2. To become less and then disappear completely. *Neal's confidence evaporated when he walked into the crowded party.* ▷ *verb* **evaporating, evaporated**

eve (eev) *noun* The evening or day before an important or special day, as in *New Year's Eve.*

e·ven (ee-vuhn)
1. *adjective* Staying about the same, as in *an even speed* or *an even temperature.*
2. *adjective* An **even** number can be divided exactly by two.
3. *adjective* Equal, as in *an even score.*
4. *adjective* Smooth and level, as in *an even surface.*
5. *verb* If you **even** something, you make it smooth, level, or equal. ▷ **evening, evened**
6. *adverb* Indeed. *Even if it takes all day, I'll complete the race.*
7. *adverb* Surprisingly. *We all enjoyed the movie, even Sarah.* ▷ *adverb* **evenly**

eve·ning (eev-ning) *noun* The time of day between the late afternoon and the early part of the night.

e·vent (i-vent) *noun*
1. Something that happens, especially something interesting or important. ▷ *adjective* **eventful**
2. One of the activities, such as a race, that is held during a sports competition.

e·ven·tu·al (i-ven-choo-uhl) *adjective* Final, or happening at the end. *Bad behavior led to his eventual suspension.*

e·ven·tu·al·ly (i-ven-choo-uh-lee) *adverb* Finally or at last. *Eventually we fell asleep.*

ev·er (ev-ur) *adverb*
1. At any time. *Have you ever tried hang gliding?*
2. All the time, as in *ever grateful.*
3. In any way. *How can I ever repay you for your kindness?*

ev·er·glade (ev-ur-*glade*) *noun* An area of swampy land with tall grasses and many slow streams.

ev·er·green (ev-ur-*green*) *noun* A bush or tree that has green leaves throughout the year. ▷ *adjective* **evergreen**

ev·er·last·ing (ev-ur-**lass**-ting) *adjective* Lasting forever or for a very long time.

eve·ry (ev-ree) *adjective* Each of the people or things in a group, as in *every day of the week.*

eve·ry·bod·y (ev-ree-*buh*-dee) *pronoun* Each and every person.

eve·ry·day (ev-ree-*day*) *adjective*
1. Happening every day, as in *everyday events.*
2. All right for ordinary days, as in *everyday clothing.*

eve·ry·one (ev-ree-*wuhn*) *pronoun* Every person; everybody.

eve·ry·thing (ev-ree-*thing*) *pronoun*
1. Each and every thing.
2. A very important thing. *Love is everything to me.*

eve·ry·where (ev-ree-wair) *adverb* In all places. *Last night, there was fog everywhere.*

e·vict (i-vikt) *verb* To force someone to move out of a home, building, or occupied land. ▷ **evicting, evicted** ▷ *noun* **eviction**

ev·i·dence (ev-uh-duhnss) *noun* Information and facts that help prove something or make you believe that something is true.

ev·i·dent (ev-uh-duhnt) *adjective* Clear and obvious. *It is evident that you don't believe what I'm saying.* ▷ *adverb* **evidently**

e·vil (ee-vuhl) *adjective* Wicked and cruel. ▷ *noun* **evil**

ev·o·lu·tion (ev-uh-loo-shuhn) *noun*
1. The gradual change of living things over thousands of years.
2. Gradual change into a different form. ▷ *adjective* **evolutionary**

e·volve (i-volv) *verb*
1. To change slowly, sometimes over many years. *Dogs and wolves evolved from a common ancestor.*
2. To develop an idea or a plan by making small changes. *My grandmother evolved the perfect cake recipe by trying many different ingredients.*
▷ *verb* **evolving, evolved**

ewe (yoo) *noun* A female sheep. **Ewe** sounds like **you** and **yew.**

> ### Prefix
> ●
> The prefix **ex-** adds the following meaning when added to a root word: "former," as in *ex-senator.* It is always followed by a hyphen.

ex·act (eg-zakt) *adjective* Perfectly correct and accurate. *The cashier handed me exact change.*
▷ *noun* **exactness** ▷ *adverb* **exactly**

ex·ag·ger·ate (eg-zaj-uh-rate) *verb* To make something seem bigger, better, more important, etc., than it really is. *Ted exaggerated his abilities at tennis.* ▷ **exaggerating, exaggerated** ▷ *noun* **exaggeration** ▷ *adjective* **exaggerated**

ex·am (eg-zam) *noun* An official test that you take to show how much you know about a subject. Exam is short for examination.

ex·am·i·na·tion (eg-zam-uh-nay-shuhn) *noun*
1. See **exam.**
2. A careful check or inspection, as in *a medical examination.*

ex·am·ine (eg-zam-uhn) *verb*
1. To look carefully at something. *The detectives examined the evidence.*
2. When doctors **examine** you, they check your body carefully to see if anything is wrong with you.
▷ *verb* **examining, examined** ▷ *noun* **examiner**

ex·am·ple (eg-zam-puhl) *noun*
1. Something typical of a larger group of things. *The whale is an example of a mammal.*
2. A model for others to follow. *Sandra is a good example for the rest of the class.*
3. A question or a problem, given with its answer. *The example on the board should help you with your homework.*
4. If you **make an example** of someone, you punish the person as a warning to others.

ex·as·per·ate (eg-zass-puh-rate) *verb* If someone or something **exasperates** you, you become very annoyed. ▷ **exasperating, exasperated** ▷ *noun* **exasperation** ▷ *adjective* **exasperating,** *adjective* **exasperated**

ex·ca·vate (ek-skuh-vate) *verb* To dig in the earth, either to put up a building or to search for ancient remains. ▷ **excavating, excavated** ▷ *noun* **excavation,** *noun* **excavator**

ex·ceed (ek-seed) *verb*
1. To be greater or better than something else. *Last month's vacation exceeded my wildest dreams.*
2. To do more than is allowed or expected. *Drivers who exceed the speed limit will be fined.*
▷ *verb* **exceeding, exceeded**

ex·cel (ek-sel) *verb* If you **excel** at something, you do it extremely well. *George excels at ice-skating.*
▷ **excelling, excelled**

ex·cel·lent (ek-suh-luhnt) *adjective* Very good. *My teacher told me that I did an excellent job on my essay.* ▷ *noun* **excellence** ▷ *adverb* **excellently**

ex·cept (ek-sept)
1. *preposition* Apart from. *Everyone except Hannah went home.*
2. *conjunction* But for the fact that. *I would have won the race except I tripped and fell down.*

ex·cep·tion (ek-sep-shuhn) *noun*
1. Something that is not included in a general rule or statement. *Julian dislikes most school subjects, with just a few exceptions.*
2. If someone **takes exception** to something, the person is offended or annoyed by it.

ex·cep·tion·al (ek-sep-shuh-nuhl) *adjective* Outstanding or rare. *Belle shows exceptional talent in drawing.*

ex·cerpt (ek-surpt) *noun* A short piece taken from a longer piece of writing, music, or film. *The speaker read an excerpt from my poem at the recital.* ▷ *verb* **excerpt** (ek-surpt)

ex·cess (ek-sess *or* ek-sess) *noun*
1. Too much of something. *The sponge soaked up the excess when the water overflowed.*
▷ *adjective* **excess**
2. in excess of More than.
3. If you do something **to excess,** you do it too much.
▷ *noun, plural* **excesses**

ex·ces·sive (ek-sess-iv) *adjective* Too much. *Archie always eats an excessive amount.* ▷ *adverb* **excessively**

ex·change (eks-chaynj)
1. *verb* To give one thing and receive another. *We exchanged presents. They exchanged glances.* ▷ **exchanging, exchanged** ▷ *noun* **exchange**
2. *noun* A place where people meet to buy and sell things such as stock, merchandise, etc., as in *a stock exchange.*
3. exchange rate *noun* A comparison of the worth of currency in different countries. You use the exchange rate to calculate how much money you will get when you exchange one currency for another.

ex·cite (ek-site) *verb* If something **excites** you, it makes you eager and interested. ▷ **exciting, excited** ▷ *noun* **excitement** ▷ *adjective* **exciting,** *adjective* **excited**

ex·claim (ek-sklaym) *verb* To say something suddenly or with force, especially because you are surprised or excited. *"You are so lucky," exclaimed my friend Teresa when I won first prize at the carnival.* ▷ **exclaiming, exclaimed** ▷ *noun* **exclamation** (ek-skluh-may-shuhn)

exclamation mark *noun* The punctuation mark (!) used after an expression of surprise, excitement, or another strong feeling.

ex·clude (ek-sklood) *verb*
1. If you **exclude** something, you leave it out. *The list excludes prices.* ▷ *preposition* **excluding**
2. To keep someone from joining or taking part in something.
▷ *verb* **excluding, excluded** ▷ *noun* **exclusion**

ex·clu·sive (ek-skloo-siv)
1. *adjective* If a group or club is **exclusive,** only certain people are welcome to join it.
2. *adjective* Complete or whole. *You have my exclusive attention.*
3. *noun* A story that appears in one place only. *The soccer player promised the newspaper an exclusive on how she prepares for a big game.*

ex·crete (ek-skreet) *verb* To pass waste matter out of the body. ▷ **excreting, excreted** ▷ *noun* **excretion** ▷ *adjective* **excretory** (ek-skruh-tor-ee)

ex·cru·ci·at·ing (ek-skroo-shee-ay-ting) *adjective* Extremely painful, as in *an excruciating headache.* ▷ *adverb* **excruciatingly**

ex·cur·sion (ek-skur-zhuhn) *noun*
1. A short journey, often to a place of interest.
2. A trip on a train, plane, bus, etc., at a reduced fare.

ex·cuse
1. *noun* (ek-skyooss) A reason you give to explain why you have done something wrong.
2. *verb* (ek-skyooz) To give someone permission not to do something. *The teacher excused Lydia from gym because of her injured toe.*
3. *verb* (ek-skyooz) If you **excuse** someone for doing something, you forgive the person.
▷ *verb* **excusing, excused** ▷ *adjective* **excusable**

ex·e·cute (ek-suh-kyoot) *verb*
1. If you **execute** a plan or an order, you put it into action.
2. To kill someone as a punishment for a crime.
▷ *verb* **executing, executed** ▷ *noun* **execution**

ex·ec·u·tive (eg-zek-yuh-tiv)
1. *noun* Someone who has a senior job in a company and is involved in planning its future.
▷ *adjective* **executive**
2. *adjective* To do with the branch of

government that executes the laws of the United States or any state.

ex·empt (eg-zempt) *adjective* If you are **exempt** from something, you do not have to take part in it. ▷ *noun* **exemption** ▷ *verb* **exempt**

ex·er·cise (ek-sur-size)
1. *noun* Physical activity that you do to keep fit and healthy. *This boy is doing exercises that will strengthen his biceps and his back.*
2. *verb* To make your body work hard through vigorous activity, such as sports, in order to keep fit and healthy.

exercise

3. *noun* A piece of work that you do in order to practice a skill, as in *piano exercises.*
4. *verb* To put into practice. *Every eligible citizen can exercise his or her right to vote.*
▷ *verb* **exercising, exercised**

ex·ert (eg-zurt) *verb* To make an effort to do something. *Philip exerted himself to get his book report done on time.* ▷ **exerting, exerted** ▷ *noun* **exertion**

ex·hale (eks-hale) *verb* To breathe out. ▷ **exhaling, exhaled** ▷ *noun* **exhalation**

ex·haust (eg-zawst)
1. *verb* If something **exhausts** you, it makes you very tired. ▷ *noun* **exhaustion** ▷ *adjective* **exhausting,** *adjective* **exhausted**
2. *verb* To use something up completely. *The explorers had almost exhausted their food supplies.*
3. *noun* The waste gases produced by the engine of a motor vehicle.
4. *noun* The pipe found at the back of a motor vehicle from which waste gases from the engine escape.
▷ *verb* **exhausting, exhausted**

ex·hib·it (eg-zib-it) *verb* To show something to the public. ▷ **exhibiting, exhibited** ▷ *noun* **exhibit,** *noun* **exhibitor**

ex·hi·bi·tion (ek-suh-bish-uhn) *noun* A public display of works of art, historical objects, etc.

ex·hil·a·rat·ing (eg-zil-uh-ray-ting) *adjective* Very exciting and thrilling, as in *an exhilarating ride on the roller coaster.* ▷ *noun* **exhilaration** ▷ *verb* **exhilarate**

ex·ile (eg-zile *or* ek-sile) *verb* To send someone away from his or her own country and order the person not to return. *The king was exiled from his homeland after the country was conquered by a new ruler.* ▷ **exiling, exiled** ▷ *noun* **exile**

ex·ist (eg-zist) *verb*
1. To live, or to have reality. *Do unicorns really exist?*
2. To have just enough food to stay alive. *We existed on berries and water.*
▷ *verb* **existing, existed** ▷ *noun* **existence**

ex·it (eg-zit *or* ek-sit)
1. *verb* To leave or to go out. *As I exited the movie theatre, I ran into some friends who were waiting to see the next show.* ▷ **exiting, exited** ▷ *noun* **exit**
2. *noun* The way out of a place.

ex·o·dus (ek-suh-duhss) *noun* A departure of a large number of people at one time.

ex·o·skel·e·ton (eks-oh-skel-uht-uhn) *noun* A bony structure on the outside of an animal, such as the shell of a lobster or a crab.

ex·o·tic (eg-zot-ik) *adjective*
1. Strange and fascinating, as in *an exotic perfume.*
2. From a faraway country, as in *an exotic plant.*

ex·pand (ek-spand) *verb* To increase in size.
▷ **expanding, expanded** ▷ *noun* **expansion**
▷ *adjective* **expandable**

ex·panse (ek-spanss) *noun* A broad, open area. *A vast expanse of desert stretched ahead.*

ex·pect (ek-spekt) *verb*
1. To wait for someone to arrive. *We're expecting visitors.*
2. To think that something ought to happen. *Aunt Jane expects you to behave perfectly.* ▷ *noun* **expectation**
3. If a woman is **expecting**, she is pregnant.
▷ *verb* **expecting, expected**

ex·pe·di·tion (ek-spuh-dish-uhn) *noun*
1. A long journey for a special purpose, such as exploring.
2. A short trip to do something enjoyable, as in *a shopping expedition.*

ex·pel (ek-spel) *verb*
1. If someone is **expelled** from a school, the person has to leave because he or she has behaved badly.
2. To send or force something out. *You expel air from your lungs when you exhale.*
▷ *verb* **expelling, expelled** ▷ *noun* **expulsion** (ek-**spuhl**-shuhn)

ex·pend·i·ture (ek-spen-duh-chur) *noun*
1. The spending or using up of time, money, or materials in order to do something.
2. The amount of money that a person, company, or country spends.

ex·pense (ek-spenss) *noun*
1. The spending of money, time, energy, etc. *Never mind the expense!*
2. Money spent on a particular job or task, as in *business expenses.*

ex·pen·sive (ek-spen-siv) *adjective* Costing a lot of money. ▷ *adverb* **expensively**

ex·pe·ri·ence (ek-spihr-ee-uhnss)
1. *noun* Something that happens to you.
2. *verb* If you **experience** something, it happens to you. ▷ **experiencing, experienced**
3. *noun* The knowledge and skill that you gain by doing something. *Do you have any experience in using computers?* ▷ *adjective* **experienced**

ex·per·i·ment (ek-sper-uh-ment)
1. *noun* A scientific test to try out a theory or to see the effect of something. ▷ *verb* **experiment**
2. *verb* To try something new. ▷ **experimenting, experimented** ▷ *noun* **experiment**

ex·per·i·men·tal (ek-*sper*-uh-men-tuhl) *adjective* If something is **experimental,** it has not yet been tested thoroughly.

ex·pert (ek-spurt) *noun* Someone who is very skilled at something or knows a lot about a particular subject. ▷ *adjective* **expert** (ek-spurt *or* ek-spurt)

ex·pire (ek-spire) *verb*
1. When a ticket, license, etc., **expires,** it reaches the end of the time when it can be used.
▷ *noun* **expiration**
2. To die.
▷ *verb* **expiring, expired**

ex·plain (ek-splayn) *verb*
1. To make something clear so that it is easier to understand. ▷ *adjective* **explanatory** (ek-**splan**-uh-*tor*-ee)
2. To give a reason for something. *Please explain why you are so late.*
▷ *verb* **explaining, explained** ▷ *noun* **explanation** (ek-spluh-**nay**-shuhn)

ex·plic·it (ek-spliss-it) *adjective* Very clearly stated. *The skydiving instructor gave his students explicit instructions on how to open their parachutes.*

ex·plode (ek-splode) *verb* If something **explodes,** it blows apart with a loud bang and great force.
▷ **exploding, exploded**

ex·ploit
1. (ek-sploit) *noun* A brave or daring deed.
2. (ek-sploit) *verb* To treat someone unfairly, usually by not paying the person enough for his or her work. ▷ **exploiting, exploited** ▷ *noun* **exploitation**

ex·plo·ra·tion (ek-spluh-ray-shuhn) *noun* The act of looking into or studying something or someplace unknown.

ex·plore (ek-splor) *verb*
1. To travel in order to discover what a place is like. ▷ *noun* **explorer**
2. If you **explore** an idea or a possibility, you discuss it or think about it carefully.
▷ *verb* **exploring, explored** ▷ *adjective* **exploratory**

ex·plo·sion (ek-sploh-zhuhn) *noun*
1. A sudden and noisy release of energy.
2. A sudden increase or growth, as in *a population explosion.*

ex·plo·sive (ek-sploh-siv)
1. *noun* A substance that can blow up.
2. *adjective* Able or likely to explode. ▷ *adverb* **explosively**
3. *adjective* If a situation is **explosive,** it is very dangerous.

ex·po·nent (ek-spoh-nuhnt) *noun* A number placed next to and above another to show how many times that number is to be multiplied by itself. *In 4^3, 3 is the exponent.*

ex·port
1. *verb* (ek-**sport** *or* **ek**-sport) To send products to another country to be sold there. ▷ **exporting, exported**
2. *noun* (**ek**-sport) The act of selling something to another country, or a product thus sold. *Our company sells exports to Europe.*
▷ *noun* **exporter**

ex·pose (ek-spoze) *verb*
1. To uncover something so it can be seen.
2. To reveal the truth about someone or something. ▷ *noun* **exposé**
3. To let light fall on photographic film.
4. To leave without protection. *When the tent fell in, we were exposed to the storm.*
▷ *verb* **exposing, exposed**

ex·po·sure (ek-spoh-zhur) *noun*
1. The harmful effect of severe weather on someone's body. *The survivors of the shipwreck were suffering from exposure.*
2. A piece of film that produces a photograph when it is exposed to light. *This film has 36 exposures.*
3. The length of time that a photographic film is exposed to the light.

ex·press (ek-spress)
1. *verb* To show what you feel or think by saying, doing, or writing something. *I express my deepest feelings in my diary.* ▷ **expresses, expressing, expressed**
2. *noun* A fast train or bus that stops at only a few stations. ▷ *noun, plural* **expresses**
3. *adjective* Very fast, as in *express delivery.*

ex·pres·sion (ek-spresh-uhn) *noun*
1. A phrase that has a particular meaning, as in *the expression "lock, stock, and barrel."*
2. The look on someone's face, as in *a puzzled expression.*
3. The act of showing your feelings, as in *the expression of our concern.*

ex·pres·sive (ek-spress-iv) *adjective* Filled with meaning or feeling. *The mime's expressive eyes allowed him to communicate sadness without using words.* ▷ *adverb* **expressively**

ex·press·way (ek-spress-*way*) *noun* A wide highway on which cars, trucks, etc., can go long distances without traffic lights or stop signs.

expressway

ex·quis·ite (ek-swiz-it *or* ek-swi-zit) *adjective* Very beautiful and delicate, as in *an exquisite piece of embroidery.* ▷ *adverb* **exquisitely**

ex·tend (ek-stend) *verb*
1. To make something longer or bigger. *The frog extended its tongue, catching the beetle.*
2. To stretch out. *Our yard extends to the lake.*
3. To offer, as in *to extend help to flood victims.*
▷ *verb* **extending, extended** ▷ *noun* **extension**

ex·ten·sive (ek-sten-siv) *adjective*
1. Spreading over a wide area.
2. Including a lot of things, as in *an extensive choice of desserts.*

ex·tent (ek-stent) *noun* The size, level, or scale of something. *What is the extent of the damage?*

ex·te·ri·or (ek-stihr-ee-ur) *noun* The outside of something, especially a building. ▷ *adjective* **exterior**

ex·ter·mi·nate (ek-stur-muh-nate) *verb* To kill large numbers of people or animals.
▷ **exterminating, exterminated** ▷ *noun* **extermination,** *noun* **exterminator**

ex·ter·nal (ek-stur-nuhl) *adjective* On the outside.
▷ *adverb* **externally**

E

E

ex·tinct (ek-stingkt) *adjective*
1. If a type of animal or plant is **extinct**, it has died out. *The dodo was a large bird that became extinct in the 18th century.* ▷ *noun* **extinction**
2. If a volcano is **extinct**, it has stopped erupting.

dodo

ex·tin·guish (ek-sting-gwish) *verb*
1. To put out a flame, a fire, or a light. ▷ *noun* **extinguisher**
2. To put an end to a feeling or a belief. *Nothing could extinguish Romeo's love for Juliet.*
▷ *verb* **extinguishes, extinguishing, extinguished**

ex·tra (ek-struh)
1. *adjective* More than the usual amount, as in *an extra helping of potatoes.*
2. *adverb* Extremely, or more than usual, as in *extra large.*
3. *noun* Something that is added to the usual or the normal. *Extras on the new car included an alarm system and air conditioning.*

ex·tract
1. (ek-strakt) *verb* To take or pull something out. ▷ **extracting, extracted** ▷ *noun* **extraction**
2. (ek-strakt) *noun* A short section taken from a book, speech, piece of music, etc.

ex·traor·di·nar·y (ek-stror-duh-*ner*-ee) *adjective* Very unusual or remarkable, as in *an extraordinary skill.* ▷ *adverb* **extraordinarily**

ex·tra·ter·res·tri·al (ek-struh-tuh-ress-tree-uhl)
1. *adjective* Coming from outer space, as in *extraterrestrial messages in a science fiction story.*
2. *noun* A creature from outer space.

ex·trav·a·gance (ek-strav-uh-guhnss) *noun* A very large outlay of money. *Buying a diamond necklace is an extravagance.*

ex·trav·a·gant (ek-strav-uh-guhnt) *adjective* If you are **extravagant**, you spend too much money or are wasteful in the way you use things. ▷ *adverb* **extravagantly**

ex·treme (ek-streem)
1. *adjective* Very great, as in *extreme happiness.* ▷ *adverb* **extremely**
2. *adjective* Farthest. *We reached the extreme edge of the woods.*
3. *noun* One of two ends or opposites, as in *extremes of love and hate.*

ex·trem·i·ty (ek-strem-i-tee) *noun*
1. The extreme point or end of something.
2. Your **extremities** are your hands and feet.
▷ *noun, plural* **extremities**

ex·tro·vert (ek-struh-vurt) *noun* Someone who enjoys being with other people and is lively and talkative. ▷ *adjective* **extrovert**, *adjective* **extroverted**

ex·u·ber·ant (eg-zoo-bur-uhnt) *adjective* Very cheerful and lively, as in *an exuberant mood.*
▷ *noun* **exuberance** ▷ *adverb* **exuberantly**

eye (eye)
1. *noun* One of the two organs in your head that you use to see with.
2. *noun* The small hole in a needle.
3. If you **have an eye for** something, you can judge how good it is. *Sue has an eye for bargains.*
4. *verb* To look carefully at someone or something. *Bert eyed his opponent suspiciously.*
▷ **eyeing, eyed**
5. *noun* The calm, clear zone at the very center of a hurricane.

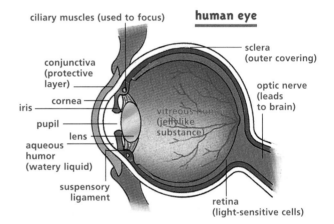

human eye

ciliary muscles (used to focus)
conjunctiva (protective layer)
iris
cornea
pupil
lens
aqueous humor (watery liquid)
suspensory ligament
sclera (outer covering)
optic nerve (leads to brain)
vitreous humor (jellylike substance)
retina (light-sensitive cells)

eye·ball (eye-*bawl*)
1. *noun* The globe or spherical part of the eye.
2. *verb* To take a close look at something. *The baseball player eyeballed the distance to the back fence before she hit the ball.* ▷ **eyeballing, eyeballed**

eye·brow (eye-*brou*) *noun* The line of hair that grows above each of your eyes.

eye·glass·es (eye-*glass*-uhz) *noun, plural* A pair of lenses in a frame that helps a person see better.

eye·lash (eye-*lash*) *noun* One of the short, curved hairs that grows on the edge of eyelids. ▷ *noun, plural* **eyelashes**

eye·lid (eye-*lid*) *noun* The upper or lower fold of skin that covers the eye when it is closed.

eye·sight (eye-*site*) *noun* The ability to see.

eye·tooth (eye-*tooth*) *noun* A pointed tooth found on the front of the upper jaw. Each person has two eyeteeth. ▷ *noun, plural* **eyeteeth**

eye·wit·ness (eye-wit-niss) *noun* Someone who has seen something take place and can describe what happened. ▷ *noun, plural* **eyewitnesses**

Ff

Spelling Hint: Some words that begin with an *f* sound are spelled *ph*. Examples: phonograph, phosphorescence, phrase, physician.

fa·ble (fay-buhl) *noun*
1. A story that teaches a lesson. Fables often have animal characters that talk and act like people.
2. A lie or an untrue story.

fab·ric (fab-rik) *noun* Cloth or material.

fab·u·lous (fab-yuh-luhss) *adjective*
1. Wonderful or marvelous. ▷ *adverb* **fabulously**
2. Amazing or hard to believe. *I wrote a story about dragons and other fabulous creatures.*

face (fayss)
1. *noun* The front of your head, from your forehead to your chin. ▷ *adjective* **facial**
2. *noun* An expression or look on the face. *The clown made a silly face.*
3. *noun* The front, outer, or upper surface of something, as in *a mountain face* or *a clock face.*
4. *verb* To look toward something. *Our apartment faces the park.* ▷ *adjective* **facing**
5. *verb* To deal with something boldly or bravely. *Robin faced many dangers.*
▷ *verb* **facing, faced**

fac·et (fass-it) *noun*
1. A flat, polished surface of a cut gem.
2. A part or side of something. *Grandpa is enjoying this new facet of his life.*

fa·cil·i·tate (fuh-sil-uh-tate) *verb* To make something easier. *A computer can facilitate the task of writing a report.* ▷ **facilitating, facilitated**
▷ *noun* **facilitator**

fa·cil·i·ty (fuh-sil-uh-tee) *noun*
1. The ability to do something easily or skillfully. *Daisy has a facility for drawing.*
2. A service provided for people to use and enjoy, such as a sports recreation center, park, etc. *The ice skating facility has a snack bar.*
▷ *noun, plural* **facilities**

fact (fakt) *noun*
1. A piece of information that is true. ▷ *adjective* **factual** ▷ *adverb* **factually**
2. in fact Actually.

fac·tor (fak-tur) *noun*
1. One of the things that help produce a result. *Randy's speed was a factor in his winning the race.*
2. A whole number that can be divided exactly into a larger number. *The numbers 1, 2, 3, 4, 6, and 12 are factors of 12.*
▷ *verb* **factor**

fac·to·ry (fak-tuh-ree) *noun* A building where products, such as cars or chemicals, are made in large numbers, often using machines. A factory is also called a **plant.** ▷ *noun, plural* **factories**

fac·ul·ty (fak-uhl-tee) *noun*
1. A group of teachers and professors at a school, college, or university, as in *the history faculty.*
2. One of the powers of the body or mind, such as memory, reason, sight, or speech.
3. A unique talent or ability. *Someone with perfect pitch has a faculty for music.*
▷ *noun, plural* **faculties**

fad (fad) *noun*
Something that is very popular for a short time. *In the late 1950s, crowding a lot of people into a phone booth was a fad.*

a fad in the 1950s

fade (fayd) *verb*
1. To become paler in color.
2. To lose freshness. *The flowers are beginning to fade.*
3. To become gradually weaker. *Hope is fading among the survivors.*
▷ *verb* **fading, faded**

Fahr·en·heit (fa-ren-*hite*) *adjective* A measurement of temperature using a scale on which water boils at 212 degrees and freezes at 32 degrees.

fail (fayl) *verb*
1. If you **fail** to do something, you do not do it.
2. If you **fail** an exam or a test, you do not pass it.
3. To disappoint. *Luís failed his friends when he broke his promise.*
4. To break down or stop working. *Fortunately, no one was hurt when the brakes in the car failed.*
5. To lose power or strength. *My grandfather's hearing is failing.*
6. To go bankrupt.
7. without fail Definitely, or every single time.
▷ *verb* **failing, failed**

fail·ure (fayl-yur) *noun*
1. Someone or something that is not successful.
2. Lack of favorable results. *Failure will not be accepted.*
3. A weakening or loss of ability, as in *heart failure.*
4. Neglect. *Failure to do your homework will result in bad grades.*

F

faint (faynt)
1. *adjective* Not clear or strong. *We barely heard the faint sound.*
2. *adjective* Dizzy and weak.
3. *verb* To become dizzy and lose consciousness for a short time. ▷ **fainting, fainted** ▷ *noun* **faint**
4. *adjective* A **faint** chance is a very slight one.
5. **faint-hearted** (hart-id) *adjective* Timid and not at all confident.
Faint sounds like **feint.**
▷ *noun* **faintness** ▷ *adjective* **fainter, faintest**
▷ *adverb* **faintly**

fair (fair)
1. *adjective* Reasonable and just, as in *fair treatment.* ▷ *noun* **fairness** ▷ *adverb* **fairly**
2. *adjective* **Fair** hair is light yellow.
3. *adjective* Neither good nor bad. *Greg is just a fair student.* ▷ *adverb* **fairly**
4. *adjective* **Fair** weather is clear and sunny.
5. *noun* An outdoor show of farm products and animals, often with entertainment, amusements, and rides.
6. *adverb* By the rules. *Play fair!* ▷ *adverb* **fairer, fairest**
Fair sounds like **fare.**
▷ *adjective* **fairer, fairest**

fair·ground (fair-*ground*) *noun* A large outdoor area where fairs are held.

fair·y (fair-ee) *noun*
1. A magical creature such as a tiny person with wings, found in fairy tales.
2. **fairy tale** A children's story about magic, fairies, giants, witches, etc.
▷ *noun, plural* **fairies**

faith (fayth) *noun*
1. Trust and confidence in someone or something. *Our coach has lots of faith in our team.*
2. Belief in God.
3. A religion.

faith·ful (fayth-fuhl) *adjective* Loyal and trustworthy. ▷ *noun* **faithfulness** ▷ *adverb* **faithfully**

fake (fayk)
1. *verb* To pretend that something is genuine. *Mia faked a headache.* ▷ **faking, faked**
2. *noun* Someone or something that is not what it seems to be. *This painting is not by Picasso, but it's a clever fake.*
3. *verb* To make a fake of something. *John faked his boss's signature.*
▷ *noun* **faker** ▷ *adjective* **fake**

fa·la·fel (fuh-lah-fuhl) *noun* A spicy mixture of ground vegetables, such as chickpeas, that is shaped into a ball or a patty and fried.

fal·con (fawl-kuhn *or* fal-kuhn) *noun* A bird of prey with long wings and hooked claws that catches small birds in flight. Falcons can be trained to return with their prey to their owner.
▷ *noun* **falconry,** *noun* **falconer**

falcon

fall (fawl)
1. *verb* To drop down to the ground. *Snow falls.*
2. *verb* To decrease or become lower. *The temperature has fallen.*
3. *verb* To become. *After a while, Ellen fell asleep.*
4. *verb* To happen. *Night fell quickly.*
5. *noun* The season between summer and winter, when it gets colder, the days get shorter, and the leaves fall from the trees.
6. *verb* To be defeated, captured, or overthrown. *The town fell to the enemy after a long battle.*
7. *verb* If two people **fall out,** they quarrel with each other.
8. *verb* If something **falls through,** it fails to happen.
▷ *verb* **falling, fell** (fel), **fallen** (fawl-in) ▷ *noun* **fall**

fall·out (fawl-*out*) *noun*
1. Radioactive dust from a nuclear explosion.
2. The result of an action. *A politician who takes a strong stand on an issue will have to face some fallout.*

fal·low (fal-oh) *adjective* Land that is **fallow** has not been planted with crops. It remains out of use so that its nutrients can be restored.

false (fawlss) *adjective*
1. Not true or correct, as in *false information.*
▷ *adverb* **falsely**
2. Not faithful or loyal. *Liars make false friends.*
3. Not real, as in *false eyelashes.*

false·hood (fawlss-hud) *noun* A lie.

fal·ter (fawl-tur) *verb*
1. To act or move in an unsteady way.
2. To pause while speaking because you are unsure or confused. *Audrey faltered during her oral report when she looked up and saw the principal.*
▷ *verb* **faltering, faltered**

fame (faym) *noun* Being well-known. *The young actor longed for fame.* ▷ *adjective* **famed**

fa·mil·iar (fuh-mil-yur) *adjective*
1. If something is **familiar,** it is well-known or easily recognized, as in *a familiar saying.*
2. If you are **familiar** with something, you know it well. *Joanne is familiar with all of Shakespeare's plays.*

3. Friendly. *Luckily, we are on familiar terms with our neighbors.*

fam·i·ly (fam-uh-lee) *noun*
1. A group of people related to one another, especially parents or guardians and their children.
2. A group of related animals or plants. *The leopard and the jaguar are members of the cat family.*
3. family tree A chart that shows how the members of a family are related over many generations.
▷ *noun, plural* **families**

fam·ine (fam-uhn) *noun* A serious lack of food.

fam·ished (fam-isht) *adjective* If you are **famished,** you are very hungry.

fa·mous (fay-muhss) *adjective* If you are **famous,** you are well-known to many people.

fan (fan) *noun*
1. A person who is very interested in or enthusiastic about something.
2. A machine or an object that you use to blow or wave air on to you in order to keep cool.
▷ *verb* **fan**

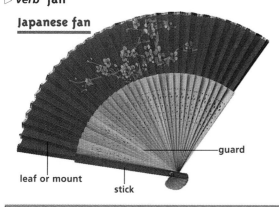

Japanese fan

— **guard**

leaf or mount

stick

> **Word History**
> •
> When someone loves a sport or other entertainment a lot, he or she is a **fan**. The word fan is a shortened form of *fanatic,* which comes from the Latin word *fanaticus,* meaning "frantic." *Fanatic* now means having intense feeling for something.

fa·nat·ic (fuh-nat-ik) *noun* Someone who is wildly enthusiastic about a belief, a cause, or an interest. *Lee is a football fanatic and never misses a game.* ▷ *adjective* **fanatical** ▷ *adverb* **fanatically**

fan·cy (fan-see)
1. *adjective* Highly decorated or elaborate.
▷ **fancier, fanciest**
2. *noun* Imagination. *Ogres and trolls are creatures of fancy.*
3. *noun* A great liking. *My aunt has a fancy for big hats.*

4. *verb* To imagine. *He fancied himself a great soccer player.* ▷ **fancies, fancying, fancied**
▷ *noun, plural* **fancies**

fang (fang) *noun* A long, pointed tooth.

fan·ny pack (fan-ee) *noun* A small bag on a belt. It is worn around the waist and used to carry personal items.

fan·tas·tic (fan-tass-tik) *adjective*
1. Too strange to be believable.
2. Terrific or wonderful.
▷ *adverb* **fantastically**

fan·ta·sy (fan-tuh-see *or* fan-tuh-zee) *noun*
1. Something you imagine happening that is not likely to happen in real life. ▷ *verb* **fantasize**
2. A story with very strange characters, places, or events.
▷ *noun, plural* **fantasies**

fan·zine (fan-zeen) *noun* A magazine prepared by and for people who like the same thing, such as science fiction or fantasy stories.

far (far)
1. *adverb* A great distance. *Have you traveled far?*
2. *adverb* Very much. *It is far better to enjoy winter than to be impatient for spring.*
3. *adjective* Distant or not near. *Kim was waving from the far side of the river.*
▷ *adjective and adverb* **farther, farthest** *or* **further, furthest**

far·a·way (far-uh-way) *adjective*
1. Distant or remote. *As a young boy, Columbus dreamed of visiting faraway lands.*
2. Dreamy or lost in thought. *I could tell she wasn't listening to me because she had a faraway look in her eyes.*

farce (farss) *noun*
1. A funny play in which there are many silly misunderstandings.
2. A ridiculous situation. ▷ *adjective* **farcical**

fare (fair)
1. *noun* The cost of traveling on a bus, subway, train, plane, etc.
2. *verb* To get along. *How did they fare on their trip?*
Fare sounds like **fair.**

Far East *noun* The countries in eastern Asia, such as China, Japan, and Korea.

fare·well (fair-wel) *interjection* Good-bye and good luck. *Farewell, Hector! Have a good trip!*
▷ *noun* **farewell**

far-fetched *adjective* Hard to believe.

farm (farm)
1. *verb* To grow crops and raise animals.
▷ **farming, farmed** ▷ *noun* **farmer,** *noun* **farming**
2. *noun* An area of land with buildings on it used for growing crops or raising animals.
▷ *adjective* **farm**

F

far·sight·ed (far-site-uhd) *adjective*
 1. Able to see things in the distance more clearly than things that are close.
 2. Able to imagine and plan for the future. *Farsighted people save their money for difficult times.*

far·ther (far-THur)
 1. *adjective and adverb* A comparative of **far.**
 2. *adverb* At greater distance than something else. *While my broken ankle was healing, I tried to walk farther each day.*
 3. *adjective* More distant or remote. *The park is on the farther side of the lake.*

fas·ci·nate (fass-uh-nate) *verb* To attract and hold the attention of. ▷ **fascinating, fascinated** ▷ *noun* **fascination**

fas·cism (fash-iz-uhm) *noun* A form of government in which a dictator and the dictator's political party have complete power over a country. ▷ *noun* **fascist**

fash·ion (fash-uhn)
 1. *noun* A style of clothing that is popular at a certain time. ▷ *adjective* **fashionable**
 2. *noun* A way of doing things. *During the fire drill, we left the building in an orderly fashion.*
 3. *verb* To make or shape something. *Dad fashioned a bird out of folded paper.*
 ▷ **fashioning, fashioned**

fast (fast)
 1. *adjective* Moving in a hurry, or quick. ▷ *adverb* **fast**
 2. *verb* To give up eating food for a time. *Muslims fast during Ramadan.* ▷ **fasting, fasted** ▷ *noun* **fast**
 3. *adjective* **Fast** colors or dyes do not run or fade when you wash them.
 4. *adjective* Ahead of the right time. *My watch is five minutes fast.*
 ▷ *adjective* **faster, fastest**

> ### Synonyms: fast
>
> **Fast** means "moving in a hurry" and can be used as an adjective or an adverb. Adjective: *She's a fast runner.* Adverb: *She runs fast.* The examples below show synonyms that are adjectives.
>
> **Speedy** means "having great quickness": *He's a speedy runner.* It also can mean "happening faster than usual," as in *a speedy trial.*
>
> **Hasty** means "speedy" but implies carelessness: *My hasty decision did not allow me to weigh all the possibilities.*
>
> **Rapid** means "moving forward quickly": *I am making rapid progress in learning Spanish.*
>
> **Quick** means "very fast" and often refers to mental abilities: *Kia has a quick mind and comes up with good solutions to problems.*
>
> **Swift** means "quick to respond" and often refers to physical speed: *Ben's swift action saved the dog from being hit by a car.*

women's fashions from the 20th century

| 1900s | 1910s | 1920s | 1930s | 1940s | 1950s | 1960s |

fas·ten (fass-uhn) *verb* To tie, attach, or close firmly. *Please fasten your seatbelt before the plane takes off.* ▷ **fastening, fastened** ▷ *noun* **fastening**

fas·ten·er (fass-uhn-ur) *noun* An object such as a button, buckle, or clip that is used to hold things together.

fast food *noun* Food such as hamburgers, fried chicken, and pizza that is prepared and served quickly by restaurants.

fat (fat)
1. *adjective* Heavy or plump. ▷ *noun* **fatness** ▷ *verb* **fatten**
2. *noun* An oily substance found in the body tissues of animals and some plants. Fats are found in foods such as meat, milk, nuts, and avocados. They give you energy and are stored in your body to keep you warm. ▷ *adjective* **fatty**
3. *adjective* Big or thick, as in *a fat dictionary.* ▷ *adjective* **fatter, fattest**

fa·tal (fay-tuhl) *adjective*
1. Causing death, as in *a fatal accident.* ▷ *adverb* **fatally**
2. Likely to have very bad or harmful results, as in *a fatal mistake.*

fa·tal·i·ty (fay-**tal**-uh-tee *or* fuh-**tal**-uh-tee) *noun* A death caused by an accident, a war, or other form of violence. ▷ *noun, plural* **fatalities**

fate (fayt) *noun*
1. The force that some people believe controls events and decides what happens to people. *The daredevil was sure that fate was on his side.*
2. Your **fate** is what will happen to you.

fate·ful (fayt-fuhl) *adjective* Important because it has a strong and usually unpleasant effect on future events. *I remember the fateful day I first met the class bully.* ▷ *adverb* **fatefully**

fa·ther (fah-THur) *noun*
1. A male parent. ▷ *noun* **fatherhood** ▷ *adjective* **fatherly**
2. A priest.

father-in-law *noun* Someone's **father-in-law** is the father of his or her spouse. ▷ *noun, plural* **fathers-in-law**

Father's Day *noun* A holiday that honors fathers, celebrated on the third Sunday in June.

fath·om (faTH-uhm)
1. *noun* A unit for measuring the depth of water. One fathom equals six feet.
2. *verb* If you cannot **fathom** something, you cannot understand it. ▷ **fathoming, fathomed**

fa·tigue (fuh-**teeg**) *noun* Great tiredness. ▷ *verb* **fatigue**

fau·cet (faw-sit) *noun* A device with a valve used to turn the flow of a liquid on or off.

fault (fawlt)
1. *noun* If something is your **fault,** you are to blame for it.
2. *noun* Something wrong that keeps another thing from being perfect. *The car broke down because of a fault in the engine.*
3. *noun* A weakness in someone's character. *Everyone has some faults.*
4. *verb* To criticize or find a mistake in something. *I can't fault your plan.* ▷ **faulting, faulted**
5. *noun* A large crack in the earth's surface that can cause earthquakes. *The picture shows a strike-slip fault, like the San Andreas fault in California, where parts of the earth's crust have pulled in opposite directions.*

strike-slip fault

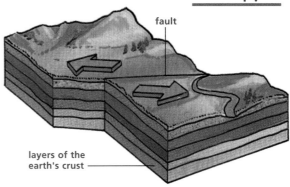

fault

layers of the earth's crust

fau·na (faw-nuh) *noun* The animal life of a particular area.

fa·vor (fay-vur)
1. *noun* Something helpful or kind that you do for someone.
2. *verb* To like one thing or person best. *Dad always favors Johnny!*
3. *verb* To look like someone else. *Hank favors his grandfather.*
4. *noun* A small gift. *All of the children at my birthday party received crayons, coloring books, and other favors.*
5. If you are **in favor of** something, you agree with it or support it.
▷ *verb* **favoring, favored**

fa·vor·a·ble (fay-vur-uh-buhl) *adjective*
1. Helpful. *The favorable winds helped our sailboat get to shore quickly.*
2. Approving, as in *a favorable review.*
3. Pleasing, as in *a favorable impression.*

fa·vor·ite (fay-vuh-rit) *noun*
1. The person or thing that you like best.
2. The person, team, or animal that is expected to win a race.
▷ *adjective* **favorite**

F

fa·vor·it·ism (fay-vur-i-*tiz*-uhm) *noun* Unfair advantage shown to one person more than others.

fawn (fawn) *noun*
1. A young deer.
2. A light brown color. ▷ *adjective* **fawn**

fax (faks) *noun* A copy of a letter, document, etc., sent along a telephone line using a special machine. Fax is short for *facsimile*. ▷ ***noun, plural* faxes** ▷ ***verb* fax**

fear (fihr)
1. *noun* The feeling you have when you are in danger or you expect something bad to happen. ▷ *adjective* **fearful**
2. *verb* To be afraid of something or someone.
3. *verb* To be worried about something. *I fear we're going to be late again.*
▷ *verb* **fearing, feared**

fear·less (fihr-liss) *adjective* Very brave and not afraid, as in *a fearless knight*. ▷ *adverb* **fearlessly**

fear·some (fihr-suhm) *adjective* Frightening, as in *a fearsome monster*.

fea·si·ble (fee-zuh-buhl) *adjective* If something is **feasible,** it can be done. ▷ *noun* **feasibility**
▷ *adverb* **feasibly**

feast (feest) *noun* A large, fancy meal for a lot of people on a special occasion. ▷ *verb* **feast**

feat (feet) *noun* An achievement that shows great courage, strength, or skill.

feath·er (feTH-ur) *noun* One of the light, fluffy parts that cover a bird's body. *See* **bird.**
▷ *adjective* **feathered,** *adjective* **feathery**

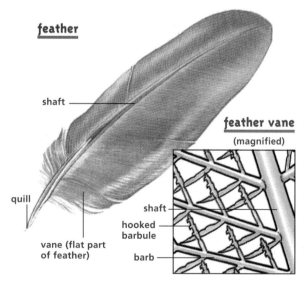

feather

shaft

feather vane
(magnified)

quill

shaft

hooked
barbule

vane (flat part
of feather)

barb

fea·ture (fee-chur) *noun*
1. An important part or quality of something. *My new computer has several useful features.*
▷ *verb* **feature**

2. Your **features** are the different parts of your face.
3. A full-length movie.
4. A newspaper article or part of a television program that deals with a particular subject.

Feb·ru·ar·y (feb-roo-er-ee *or* feb-yoo-er-ee) *noun* The second month on the calendar, after January and before March. February has 28 days except in a leap year, when it has 29.

> **Word History**
> •
> The month of **February** gets its name from the Latin word for a feast of purification, *februa*, held every year on February 15 in ancient Rome.

fed·er·al (fed-ur-uhl) *adjective* In a **federal** government, several states are united under and controlled by one central power or authority. However, each state also has its own government and can make its own laws. *The United States has a federal government.* ▷ *noun* **federalism,** *noun* **federalist**

fed·er·a·tion (fed-uh-ray-shuhn) *noun* A union of states, nations, or other groups joined together by an agreement.

fed up *adjective* (*informal*) If you are **fed up,** you are annoyed, bored, or disgusted about something.

fee (fee) *noun* The amount of money that someone charges for a service.

fee·ble (fee-buhl) *adjective* Very weak. ▷ **feebler, feeblest**

feed (feed)
1. *verb* To give food to a person or an animal.
2. *verb* When animals **feed,** they eat.
3. *noun* Food for animals.
4. *verb* To supply, or to put in. *We fed the telephone with quarters.*
▷ *verb* **feeding, fed (fed)**

feed·back (feed-bak) *noun*
1. Comments and reactions to something. *I'd like some feedback on these ideas.*
2. The loud, piercing noise made when sounds produced by an amplifier go back into it.

feel (feel) *verb*
1. To touch something with your fingers, or to experience something touching you. *Jess felt the sun on her face.* ▷ *noun* **feel**
2. To have a certain emotion or sensation. *I feel sleepy.*
3. To think or to have an opinion. *Barney felt that he had been badly treated.*
4. To seem to be. *Your shirt feels damp.*
▷ *verb* **feeling, felt (felt)** ▷ *noun* **feeling**

feign (fayn) *verb* To pretend. *Bob feigned surprise when he opened the present.* ▷ **feigning, feigned**

feint (faynt) *noun* A blow or movement meant to take attention away from the real point of attack. *The troops made a feint on one side of the island before they actually attacked the other side.* **Feint** sounds like **faint.** ▷ *verb* **feint**

feist·y (fye-stee) *adjective*
1. Easily angered or likely to quarrel. *The feisty coach was ready to argue with the referee about any of his decisions.*
2. Very lively or frisky. *You seem to be rather feisty today!*

fe·line (fee-line)
1. *adjective* To do with cats.
2. *noun* Any animal of the cat family.
3. *adjective* Like a cat. *The dancer moved with feline grace.*

fell (fel) *verb* To cut something down or to make something fall. *The gardener felled the tree. The wrestler felled his opponent.* ▷ **felling, felled**

fel·low (fel-oh)
1. *noun* A man or a boy.
2. *adjective* Belonging to the same class or group. *I like my fellow students.* ▷ *noun* **fellow**

fel·on (fel-uhn) *noun* Someone who has committed a serious crime, such as murder or burglary. ▷ *noun* **felony**

felt (felt) *noun* A thick cloth made of wool or other fibers that are pressed together in layers.

fe·male (fee-male) *noun* A person or an animal of the sex that can give birth to young animals or lay eggs. ▷ *adjective* **female**

▶ Word History
● ●

The word **female** comes to us from French *femelle,* from the Latin word *femella,* "girl." The Latin word could also refer to a female animal. The form of the English word shifted from *femelle* to female under the influence of the English word *male,* so that now the words for the genders seem as though they have the same root.

fem·i·nine (fem-uh-nuhn) *adjective*
1. To do with women.
2. Someone who is **feminine** has qualities that are supposed to be typical of women. ▷ *noun* **femininity**

fem·i·nist (fem-uh-nist) *noun* Someone who believes strongly that women ought to have the same opportunities and rights that men have. ▷ *noun* **feminism** ▷ *adjective* **feminist**

fence (fenss)
1. *noun* A structure, often made of wood or wire, used to surround, protect, or mark off an area. ▷ *verb* **fence**
2. *verb* To fight with long, thin swords, or foils, as a sport. ▷ **fencing, fenced** ▷ *noun* **fencer**
3. If you are **on the fence,** you are undecided about which side to take in an argument.

fenc·ing (fen-sing) *noun*
1. The sport of fighting with long, thin swords called foils.
2. Fences, or the material used to make them.

fencing
mask
foil

fend (fend) *verb*
1. If you **fend** for yourself, you take care of yourself.
2. If you **fend off** someone who is attacking you, you defend yourself.
▷ *verb* **fending, fended**

fend·er (fen-dur) *noun* A metal cover over the wheel of a car or bicycle that protects the wheel against damage and reduces splashing.

fe·ral (fihr-uhl) *adjective* To do with or like wild animals.

fer·ment (fur-ment) *verb* When a drink, such as beer or wine, **ferments,** a chemical change takes place that makes the sugar in it turn into alcohol. ▷ **fermenting, fermented** ▷ *noun* **fermentation**

fern (furn) *noun* A plant with feathery leaves, or fronds, and no flowers. Ferns usually grow in damp places. They reproduce by spores instead of seeds.

fern frond
spore cases on underside of frond

fe·ro·cious (fuh-roh-shuhss) *adjective* Very fierce and savage, as in *a ferocious lion.* ▷ *noun* **ferocity** (fuh-rah-si-tee) ▷ *adverb* **ferociously**

fer·ret (fer-it)
1. *noun* A long, thin animal that is related to the weasel.
2. *verb* To search. *He ferreted through his drawer and found his other sock.* ▷ **ferreting, ferreted**

Fer·ris wheel (fer-iss) *noun* A large, spinning wheel with seats hung on its side, used as a ride in a carnival or amusement park.

fer·ry (fer-ee)
1. *noun* A boat or ship that regularly carries people across a stretch of water. ▷ *noun, plural* **ferries**
2. *verb* To carry people or things from one place to another. ▷ **ferries, ferrying, ferried**

fer·tile (fur-tuhl) *adjective*
1. Land that is **fertile** is good for growing lots of crops and plants.
2. Able to have babies.
3. Having a lot of ideas, as in *a fertile imagination.*
▷ *noun* **fertility**

fer·ti·lize (fur-tuh-lize) *verb*
1. To put a substance such as manure on land to make it richer and to make crops grow better. ▷ *noun* **fertilizer**
2. To begin reproduction in an egg or a plant by causing sperm to join with the egg or pollen to come into contact with the reproductive part of the plant.
▷ *verb* **fertilizing, fertilized** ▷ *noun* **fertilization**

fer·vent (fur-vuhnt) *adjective* Showing strong or intense feeling. *Susan B. Anthony was a fervent feminist.* ▷ *noun* **fervor** ▷ *adverb* **fervently**

fes·ti·val (fess-tuh-vuhl) *noun*
1. A celebration or holiday.
2. An organized set of artistic or musical events, often held at the same time each year. *My parents saw many plays at the Shakespeare festival.*

fes·tive (fess-tiv) *adjective* Cheerful and lively, as in *a festive mood.*

fes·tiv·i·ty (fess-tiv-uh-tee) *noun* An activity that is part of a celebration. ▷ *noun, plural* **festivities**

fes·toon (fess-toon) *verb* To cover something with flowers, ribbons, or other decorations.
▷ **festooning, festooned**

fetch (fech) *verb*
1. To go after and bring back something or somebody.
2. To be sold for a particular price. *That lamp should fetch a good price.*
▷ *verb* **fetches, fetching, fetched**

fetch·ing (fech-ing) *adjective* Attractive or pretty.

fet·tuc·ci·ne (fet-uh-**chee**-nee) *noun* A narrow strip of pasta that is shaped like a ribbon.
▷ *noun, plural* **fettuccini** (fet-uh-**chee**-nee)

fe·tus (fee-tuhss) *noun* A baby or an animal before it is born, at the stage when it is developing in its mother's womb. *See* **pregnant.**

feud (fyood) *noun* A bitter quarrel between two people, families, or groups that lasts for a long time. ▷ *verb* **feud**

feu·dal·ism (fyoo-duh-li-zuhm) *noun* The medieval system in which people were given land and protection by the owner of the land, or lord, and in return worked and fought for him. *This diagram shows how feudalism worked, with the king at the head of the system and people at every level of society owing loyalty to the lord above them.* ▷ *adjective* **feudal**

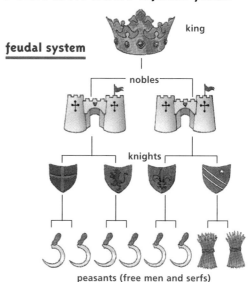

feudal system
king
nobles
knights
peasants (free men and serfs)

fe·ver (fee-vur) *noun*
1. A body temperature that is higher than normal. Most people have a fever if their temperature is more than 98.6 degrees Fahrenheit.
2. Great excitement or activity.
▷ *adjective* **feverish**

few (fyoo) *adjective* Not many. ▷ *noun* **few**

fez (fez) *noun* A round, red felt cap with no brim. Fezzes are worn by men, mainly in the Middle East. ▷ *noun, plural* **fezzes**

fi·an·cé (fee-ahn-**say** *or* fee-ahn-say) *noun* If a man and woman are engaged to be married, he is her **fiancé.**

fi·an·cée (fee-ahn-**say** *or* fee-ahn-say) *noun* If a man and woman are engaged to be married, she is his **fiancée.**

fi·as·co (fee-ass-koh) *noun* A complete failure. *The tennis game turned into a fiasco when it began to rain.* ▷ *noun, plural* **fiascoes**

fib (fib) *verb* To tell a small lie. ▷ **fibbing, fibbed**
▷ *noun* **fib,** *noun* **fibber**

fi·ber (fye-bur) *noun*
1. A long, thin thread of material such as cotton, wool, hemp, or nylon.
2. A part of foods such as bran, fruits, and vegetables that passes through the body but is not digested. Fiber helps food move through the intestines. ▷ *adjective* **fibrous**

fi·ber·glass (fye-bur-*glass*) *noun* A strong insulating material made from fine threads of glass, used in buildings, cars, boats, etc.

fiber op·tics (op-tiks) *noun, plural* Bundles of extremely thin glass or plastic tubes, or fibers through which light passes. Fiber optics are used in medical operations and for sending telephone signals.

fick·le (fik-uhl) *adjective* Someone who is **fickle** changes his or her mind often. ▷ *noun* **fickleness**

fic·tion (fik-shuhn) *noun* Stories about characters and events that are not real. *My favorite fiction stories are ones that include talking animals.*
▷ *adjective* **fictional**, *adjective* **fictitious** (fik-tish-uhss)

fid·dle (fid-uhl)
1. *noun* (informal) A violin. ▷ *noun* **fiddler**
2. *verb* To touch or play nervously with something, as in *to fiddle with a pencil.*
3. *verb* To waste. *Oscar fiddled the whole morning away doing nothing.*
▷ *verb* **fiddling, fiddled**

fidg·et (fij-it) *verb* To keep moving because you are bored, nervous, or uneasy. *Barney sat in his seat fidgeting after he finished the test.*
▷ **fidgeting, fidgeted** ▷ *adjective* **fidgety**

field (feeld)
1. *noun* A piece of open land, sometimes used for growing crops or playing sports.
2. *verb* In baseball, to catch or stop a ball that has been hit. *Barbara fielded the ball perfectly, and the batter was out.* ▷ **fielding, fielded**
3. *noun* An area of study or interest. *Robin is an expert in the field of ornithology.*

field·er (feel-dur) *noun* A baseball player who has a position in the outfield.

field goal *noun*
1. In football, a play in which the ball is kicked from the field, scoring three points.
2. In basketball, a basket made when the ball is in play, scoring two or three points.

field hockey *noun* A team game played on a rectangular field using curved sticks and a small ball. Players attempt to hit the ball along the ground and into the opposition's goal.

field trip *noun* If you go on a **field trip,** you travel somewhere with a group to see things and learn.

fiend (feend) *noun*
1. An evil spirit.
2. An evil or cruel person.
▷ *adjective* **fiendish** ▷ *adverb* **fiendishly**

> **Word History**
> The word **fiend** comes from a root word meaning "hate" or "foe." In Old English it could refer to an enemy or the Devil. Today it refers to a devilish spirit or an evil person.

fierce (fihrss) *adjective*
1. Violent or dangerous. *Many animals can become fierce if they are trapped.*
2. Very strong or extreme. *The fierce wind blew down many trees.*
▷ *adjective* **fiercer, fiercest** ▷ *noun* **fierceness**
▷ *adverb* **fiercely**

fier·y (fye-ree *or* fye-uh-ree) *adjective*
1. Like fire, or to do with fire.
2. Very emotional, as in *a fiery speech.*
▷ *adjective* **fierier, fieriest**

fi·es·ta (fee-ess-tuh) *noun* A holiday or religious festival, especially in Spain and Latin America.

fife (fife) *noun* A small instrument, similar to a flute, that has a high pitch and is often played with drums in a band.

fifth (fifth)
1. *adjective* That which comes after fourth and before sixth.
2. *noun* One part of something that has been divided into five equal parts, written $\frac{1}{5}$.

fig (fig) *noun* A small, sweet fruit with tiny seeds, often eaten dried.

fight (fite)
1. *noun* A battle between animals, persons, or groups in which each side tries to hurt the other. ▷ *verb* **fight**
2. *verb* To have an argument or a quarrel.
▷ **fighting, fought** (fawt) ▷ *noun* **fight**
3. *noun* A hard struggle to gain a goal. *The speaker invited us to join the fight against poverty.*
▷ *noun* **fighter**

fig·ure (fig-yur)
1. *noun* A written number.
2. figures *noun, plural* Arithmetic. *She's very good at figures.*
3. *noun* An amount given in numbers, as in *a population figure.*
4. *noun* A shape or an outline. *We saw a shadowy figure in the doorway.*
5. *noun* A person's shape. *Marilyn has a slim figure.*
6. *noun* A well-known person, as in *a public figure.*
7. figure out *verb* To understand or solve something. ▷ **figuring, figured**

F

fig·ure·head (fig-yur-*hed*) *noun*
1. Someone who holds an important position or office but has no real power.
2. A carved statue found on the bow of a ship. *See* **ship.**

figure of speech *noun* An expression, such as a metaphor, in which words are used in a poetic way. Authors often use figures of speech to make their writing more colorful. "He is as strong as an ox" is a figure of speech that means "He is very strong." ▷ *noun, plural* **figures of speech**

fil·a·ment (fil-uh-muhnt) *noun* A very fine wire or thread. In a light bulb, the filament is a fine thread of tungsten that glows and produces light. *See* **bulb.**

file (file)
1. *noun* A box or folder for papers or documents.
2. *verb* To put papers or documents away in a file. ▷ **filing, filed**
3. *noun* A tool used to make things smooth. *See* **woodwork.** ▷ *verb* **file**
4. *noun* A set of data held in a computer. *I called up the file on my computer.*
5. *noun* A line of people one behind the other. *We marched in single file.*

fill (fil) *verb*
1. To make or become full.
2. To take up the whole space of. *The crowd filled the gym.*
3. To stop or plug up, as in *to fill a hole.*
4. If you **fill in** a form, you answer all the questions on it.
5. If you **fill in** for someone, you do the person's job while he or she is away.
▷ *verb* **filling, filled**

fil·let (fil-**ay** *or* fil-ay) *noun* A piece of meat or fish with the bones taken out. ▷ *verb* **fillet**

fill·ing (fil-ing) *noun*
1. A substance that a dentist puts into holes in your teeth to prevent more decay.
2. The food inside a sandwich, pie, cake, etc.

fil·ly (fil-ee) *noun* A young female horse. ▷ *noun, plural* **fillies**

film (film)
1. *noun* A very thin layer of something, as in *a film of dirt.*
2. *noun* A roll of thin plastic that you put in a camera so you can take photographs or motion pictures.
3. *verb* To record something with a camera or a camcorder. ▷ **filming, filmed**
4. *noun* A movie.

fil·ter (fil-tur)
1. *noun* A device that cleans liquids or gases as they pass through it. *See* **aquarium.**
2. *verb* To put something through a filter.
3. *verb* To go through very slowly or sparsely. *Sunlight filtered through the clouds.*
▷ *verb* **filtering, filtered**

filth (filth) *noun*
1. Dirt.
2. Foul or obscene language.
▷ *noun* **filthiness** ▷ *adjective* **filthy**

fin (fin) *noun*
1. A part on the body of a fish shaped like a flap that is used for moving and steering through the water. *See* **fish.**
2. A small, triangular structure on an airplane, boat, etc., used to help with steering. *See* **aircraft.**
3. One of two long, flat attachments worn on the feet to help you swim underwater. *See* **scuba diving.**

fi·nal (fye-nuhl)
1. *adjective* Last. *This is your final chance.* ▷ *adverb* **finally**
2. *adjective* Not to be changed or discussed. *His decision was final.*
3. *noun* The last and usually most important examination in a school term.

fi·na·le (fuh-nal-ee) *noun* The last part of a show or piece of music.

fi·nal·ist (fye-nuh-list) *noun* Someone who has reached the last part of a competition.

fi·nal·ize (fye-nuh-lize) *verb* To finish making arrangements. *Are the dates for your trip finalized yet?* ▷ **finalizing, finalized**

▶ **Language Note**

Finalize is a term with a controversial past. It means to put something in final form and dates back to the 1920s. Since then, many writers and language experts have strongly objected to its use. Finalize was widely used among government and military employees, but many writers felt the word had no place in elegant speech or formal writing. After presidents Eisenhower and Kennedy made it part of their vocabularies, though, the word slowly entered general use.

---

fi·nance (fuh-nanss *or* fye-nanss)
1. *noun* The management and use of money by businesses, banks, and governments. ▷ *adjective* **financial** ▷ *adverb* **financially**
2. *verb* To provide money for something.
▷ **financing, financed**
3. **finances** *noun, plural* The amount of money that an individual or a company has. *Our finances are rather low at the moment.*

finch (finch) *noun* A small songbird with a strong, thick bill used for cracking seeds.
▷ *noun, plural* **finches**

find (finde)
1. *verb* To discover or come across something. *I found a penny on my way to school today.*
2. *verb* To come to and state a decision. *The jury found the defendant not guilty.*
3. find out *verb* To learn about something or someone. *Today in school we found out why earthquakes occur.*
4. *noun* A valuable or important discovery. *The discovery of the king's tomb was a great archeological find.*
▷ *verb* **finding, found** (found)

finding *noun* One of the results of an investigation or a study.

fine (fine)
1. *adjective* Very good or excellent, as in *a fine painting.*
2. *adjective* Not cloudy or rainy, as in *a fine day.*
3. *adjective* Thin or delicate.
4. *noun* A sum of money paid as a punishment for doing something wrong. ▷ *verb* **fine**
▷ *noun* **fineness** ▷ *adjective* **finer, finest**

fin·ger (fing-gur)
1. *noun* One of the long parts of your hands that you can move.
2. *verb* To touch something lightly with your fingers. *Ted fingered the fishing rod longingly.*
▷ **fingering, fingered**

fin·ger·nail (fing-gur-*nale*) *noun* The hard layer of material at the tip of each finger.

fin·ger·print (fing-gur-*print*) *noun* The print made by the pattern of curved ridges on the tips of your fingers.

fin·ick·y (fin-uh-kee) *adjective* Fussy, especially about food, as in *a finicky eater.*

fin·ish (fin-ish)
1. *verb* To end or complete something. *I'm not allowed to watch television until I finish my homework.* ▷ **finishes, finishing, finished**
2. *noun* The end of something, such as a race.
3. *noun* A coating on the surface of metal, wood, etc. *The floor has a nice finish.* ▷ *verb* **finish**
▷ *noun, plural* **finishes**

fi·nite (fye-nite) *adjective* Limited, or with an end. *The lifetime of a person is finite.*

fiord (fyord) *noun* See **fjord.**

fir (fur) *noun* A pointed evergreen tree with thin, flat needles and cones that grow erect on the branches. **Fir** sounds like **fur.**

fire (fire)
1. *noun* Flames, heat, and light produced by burning.
2. *verb* To shoot a gun or other weapon. ▷ *noun* **fire**

3. *noun* Strong emotion. *Martin Luther King, Jr.'s, speeches were full of fire.*
4. *verb* To dismiss someone from his or her job. *Pete was fired from his job because he always showed up late for work.*
▷ *verb* **firing, fired**

fire·arm (fire-*arm*) *noun* A weapon that shoots bullets. Rifles, pistols, and shotguns are firearms.

fire·crack·er (fire-*krak*-ur) *noun* A paper tube containing gunpowder and a fuse. Firecrackers make a loud popping noise when they explode.

fire engine *noun* A large truck that carries powerful pumps, hoses, ladders, and firefighters to a fire.

fire escape *noun* A set of metal stairs on the outside of a building, designed to allow people to escape in case of fire.

fire extinguisher *noun* A metal container with chemicals and water inside it that you use to put out a fire. *When you squeeze the handle of a foam-and-water fire extinguisher, the piercer punctures the canister and releases carbon dioxide gas. The gas pushes on the surface of the water and detergent mixture, forcing it up the tube, through the hose, and out of the spray nozzle in a jet of foam and water.*

F

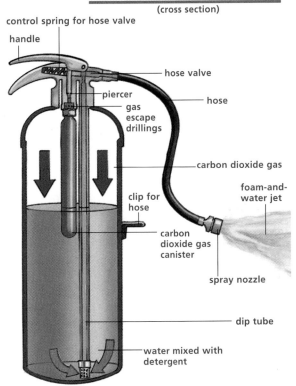

foam-and-water fire extinguisher
(cross section)

control spring for hose valve
handle
hose valve
piercer
hose
gas escape drillings
carbon dioxide gas
foam-and-water jet
clip for hose
carbon dioxide gas canister
spray nozzle
dip tube
water mixed with detergent

F

fire·fight·er (fire-*fite*-ur) *noun* Someone who is trained to put out fires.

fire·fly (fire-*flye*) *noun* A small beetle that flies at night and gives off flashes of chemically produced light from the rear part of its body. Also called **lightning bug.** *See* **insect.** ▷ *noun, plural* **fireflies**

fire·house (fire-*houss*) *noun* A building where fire engines are kept and where firefighters wait until they are needed to put out fires.

fire·man (fire-muhn) *noun* A male firefighter. ▷ *noun, plural* **firemen**

fire·place (fire-*playss*) *noun* A structure, usually made of brick or stone, in which a fire can burn safely.

fire·proof (fire-*proof*) *adjective* If something is **fireproof,** it is made from material that will not burn easily.

fire·side (fire-*side*) *noun* The area around a fireplace.

fire station *noun* Another term for **firehouse.**

fire·trap (fire-*trap*) *noun* A building that is likely to catch on fire, or one that would be hard to escape from if it caught fire.

fire·wood (fire-*wud*) *noun* Logs or other pieces of wood that are burned as fuel.

fire·works (fire-*wurks*) *noun, plural* Devices that make very loud noises and colorful lights when they are burned or exploded.

firm (furm)
1. *adjective* Strong and solid, as in *a firm mattress.*
2. *adjective* Definite and not easily changed, as in *a firm belief.*
3. *adjective* Steady, as in *a firm voice.*
4. *noun* A business or a company.
▷ *adjective* **firmer, firmest** ▷ *adverb* **firmly**

first (furst)
1. *adjective* That which comes before second.
2. *noun* A person or thing that acts or happens earliest. *Seth was the first to leave the party.*
3. *adjective* Earliest in time. *Rob took the first bus.*
4. *adverb* Before something else. *Ginny always gets to school first.*
5. *adjective* Best, or most important, as in *the first team.*

first aid *noun* Emergency care given to an injured or sick person before he or she is examined by a doctor.

first class
1. *noun* The most expensive level of service offered to travelers on trains, ships, and airplanes. *First class was crowded with salespeople.*
2. *noun* A level of mail service used for letters, postcards, and bills that usually is faster than other levels of service, except for express delivery.
3. first-class *adjective* Of the highest quality. *He was considered a first-class detective.*
▷ *adjective* **first-class** ▷ *adverb* **first-class**

first·hand (furst-hand) *adjective* Direct from the original source. *Ian gave a firsthand account of the accident.* ▷ *adverb* **firsthand**

first-rate *adjective* Excellent. *This diner makes first-rate sandwiches.*

fish (fish)
1. *noun* A cold-blooded animal that lives in water and has scales, fins, and gills. *The picture shows a female perch. See also* **gill.** ▷ *noun, plural* **fish** *or* **fishes**
2. *verb* To try to catch fish. *See* **angling.** ▷ *noun* **fishing**
3. *verb* If you **fish** for information, you try to discover something in a sly or indirect way.
▷ *verb* **fishes, fishing, fished**

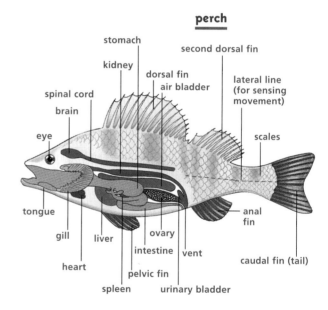

perch

stomach
kidney
second dorsal fin
dorsal fin
air bladder
lateral line (for sensing movement)
spinal cord
brain
eye
scales
tongue
anal fin
gill
liver
ovary
intestine
vent
caudal fin (tail)
heart
pelvic fin
spleen
urinary bladder

fish·er·man (fish-ur-muhn) *noun* Someone who catches fish for a job or as a sport. ▷ *noun, plural* **fishermen**

fish·er·y (fish-ur-ee) *noun*
1. A place where fish are bred commercially.
2. A place where fish are caught.
▷ *noun, plural* **fisheries**

fishing rod *noun* A long, flexible pole used with a hook, line, and reel to catch fish. *See* **angling.**

fish·y (fish-ee) *adjective*
1. Tasting or smelling of fish.
2. *(informal)* Unlikely or suspicious, as in *a fishy story.*
▷ *adjective* **fishier, fishiest**

fis·sion (fish-uhn) *noun*
1. The act of splitting into parts, as in *cell fission.*
2. nuclear fission *noun* The splitting of the nucleus of an atom, which creates energy.

fist (fist) *noun* A tightly closed hand.

fit (fit)
1. *verb* To be the right size or shape. *This skirt doesn't fit.*
2. *verb* To be right for, as in *fit for a king.*
3. *adjective* Healthy and strong. ▷ *noun* **fitness**
4. *noun* A sudden attack of something that cannot be controlled, as in *a fit of giggles.*
5. *adjective* Good enough, as in *fit to eat.*
▷ *verb* **fitting, fitted,** *or* **fit** ▷ *adjective* **fitter, fittest**

fit·ting (fit-ing)
1. *adjective* Right or suitable. *Many people think it is fitting to wear dark colors at funerals.*
2. *noun* A small metal or plastic part that connects things, as in *pipe fittings.*

five (five) *noun* The whole number, written 5, that comes after four and before six. ▷ *adjective* **five**

fix (fiks)
1. *verb* To repair something.
2. *verb* To decide on something. *Shall we fix a date for the party?*
3. *verb* To get something ready to eat. *It's time to fix lunch.*
4. *verb* To place or fasten firmly. *We fixed the pegs for the tent in the ground.*
5. *noun* If you are in a **fix,** you are in an awkward or difficult situation. ▷ *noun, plural* **fixes**
▷ *verb* **fixes, fixing, fixed**

fix·a·tion (fik-**say**-shuhn) *noun* An overly strong attachment to a person, idea, or thing. *Jonathan has a fixation about football.* ▷ *verb* **fixate** (fik-sate)

fix·ture (fiks-chur) *noun* Something that is fixed firmly and permanently in place. *A sink is a bathroom fixture.*

fizz (fiz) *verb* To bubble and hiss. ▷ **fizzes, fizzing, fizzed** ▷ *adjective* **fizzy**

fiz·zle (fiz-uhl) *verb*
1. To make a hissing or sputtering sound.
2. *(informal)* To fail or die out, especially after a good start. *All our plans fizzled out.*
▷ *verb* **fizzling, fizzled**

fjord (fyord) *noun* A long, narrow inlet of the ocean between high cliffs. Fjords were formed by glaciers during the Ice Age.

flab (flab) *noun* Extra fat on your body. ▷ *noun* **flabbiness** ▷ *adjective* **flabby**

flab·ber·gast·ed (flab-ur-*gass*-tid) *adjective* *(informal)* Stunned and surprised.

flac·cid (flass-id *or* flak-sid) *adjective* Soft and limp, as in *flaccid muscles.*

flag (flag)
1. *noun* A piece of cloth with a pattern on it that is a symbol of a country, an organization, etc.
2. *verb* To stop, or to signal. *We flagged down the police officer.* ▷ **flagging, flagged**

international flags

United Nations

Olympic Games

International Red Cross

Flag Day *noun* A holiday that celebrates the day in 1777 when the Stars and Stripes became the official flag of the United States. It is celebrated on June 14.

flag·pole (flag-*pohl*) *noun* A tall pole made of wood or metal for raising and flying a flag.

flair (flair) *noun* Natural skill or ability. *Raymond has a flair for cooking.* **Flair** sounds like **flare.**

flak (flak) *noun*
1. Shots fired against aircraft.
2. *(informal)* Opposition and criticism. *The mayor's idea received much flak from the newspapers.*

flake (flayk)
1. *noun* A small, thin piece of something. *Flakes of paint fell off the door.* ▷ *adjective* **flaky**
2. *verb* If something **flakes,** small, thin pieces of it peel off. ▷ **flaking, flaked**

flam·boy·ant (flam-boi-uhnt) *adjective* Bold, showy, or brightly colored, as in *a flamboyant shirt.*

flame (flaym)
1. *noun* A tongue of heat and light given off by a fire. ▷ *adjective* **flaming**
2. flame-colored *adjective* Deep orange-red.

fla·min·go (fluh-**ming**-goh) *noun* A pink bird with a long neck, long legs, and webbed feet.
▷ *noun, plural* **flamingos** *or* **flamingoes**

flamingos

flam·ma·ble (flam-uh-buhl) *adjective* Likely to catch fire.

F

flank (flangk)
1. *noun* The side of an animal, between its ribs and hips.
2. *verb* To guard or be at the side of something or someone. *The king was flanked by attendants.*
▷ **flanking, flanked**
3. *noun* The far left or right side of a group of soldiers, a fort, or a naval fleet.

flan·nel (flan-uhl) *noun* A soft, woven cloth, usually made of cotton or wool.

flap (flap)
1. *verb* To move up and down. *The bird flapped its wings.*
2. *verb* To swing loosely. *The sail flapped in the breeze.*
3. *noun* A hanging part attached on the side of something, as in *the flap of an envelope.*
4. *noun* A hinged part on an airplane wing, used to control the way the plane rises and falls. *See* **aircraft.**
▷ *verb* **flapping, flapped**

flap·jack (flap-*jak*) *noun* A pancake.

flare (flair) *verb*
1. To burn with a sudden, very bright light.
2. To break out in sudden or violent feeling. *Tempers flared during the argument.*
3. To spread out in a bell shape at the bottom. *Her blue skirt flared out above her bright red shoes.*
4. If something **flares up,** it suddenly becomes stronger or more violent.
Flare sounds like **flair.**
▷ *verb* **flaring, flared**

flash (flash)
1. *noun* A short burst of light, as in *a flash of lightning.*
2. *noun* A very brief period of time. *He was there in a flash.*
3. *verb* To move rapidly. *A car flashed by.*
▷ **flashes, flashing, flashed**
4. *noun* A sudden outburst, as in *a flash of anger.*
5. *noun* A brief report of very recent or important news.
▷ *noun, plural* **flashes**

flash·back (flash-*bak*) *noun*
1. A part of a book or movie that tells you what happened earlier in the story.
2. A sudden memory of something that happened and was forgotten.

flash·light (flash-*lite*) *noun* A portable light that is powered by a battery.

flash·y (flash-ee) *adjective* If something is **flashy,** it is showy and very bright. *Todd wears flashy clothes.* ▷ **flashier, flashiest**

flask (flask) *noun*
1. A small, flat bottle made to be carried in the pocket.

2. A bottle with a narrow neck used in science laboratories. *See* **apparatus.**

flat (flat) *adjective*
1. Smooth and even, as in *flat land.*
2. Lying or stretched at full length. *He was lying flat on his back.*
3. Not very deep or thick, as in *a flat tray.*
4. Very definite, as in *a flat refusal.*
5. Emptied of air, as in *a flat tire.*
6. Dull or lifeless, as in *a flat performance.*
7. In music, a **flat** note is lower in pitch than the usual note. *B flat is a semitone lower than B.*
8. In a musical score, a **flat** sign shows that the next note is flat. *See* **notation.**
▷ *adjective* **flatter, flattest** ▷ *noun* **flat** ▷ *verb* **flatten**

flat·bed (flat-*bed*) *noun* A truck with a large, flat cargo area in the back, designed to carry a heavy load.

flat·car (flat-*kar*) *noun* A railroad car that has no roof or sides and is used to carry freight.

flat·fish (flat-*fish*) *noun* A fish with a flat body and both eyes on its upper side, such as halibut, sole, or flounder. ▷ *noun, plural* **flatfish** *or* **flatfishes**

flat·ter (flat-ur)
1. *verb* To praise too much or insincerely, especially when you want a favor. ▷ **flattering, flattered** ▷ *noun* **flatterer,** *noun* **flattery**
2. *adjective* If something, such as a piece of clothing, is **flattering,** it makes you look good.

flaunt (flawnt) *verb* To show off in order to impress others. *The duchess flaunted her diamonds.* ▷ **flaunting, flaunted**

fla·vor (flay-vur)
1. *noun* Taste. ▷ *adjective* **flavored,** *adjective* **flavorless**
2. *verb* To add taste to food. *Flavor the stew with pepper.* ▷ **flavoring, flavored** ▷ *noun* **flavoring**

flaw (flaw) *noun* A fault or a weakness.
▷ *adjective* **flawed,** *adjective* **flawless**

flax (flaks) *noun*
1. A plant with blue flowers and long leaves that produces oil and fiber.
2. The fiber of the flax, which can be woven into thread that is used to make linen.

flea (flee) *noun*
1. A small, wingless insect that lives on the blood of people and other animals.
2. flea market An indoor or outdoor market selling old clothes and other secondhand items.
Flea sounds like **flee.**

flea
(magnified)

fleck (flek) *noun* A spot or tiny patch of something. *A fleck of soot landed on Carl's white shirt.* ▷ *adjective* **flecked**

fledg·ling (flej-ling) *noun* A young bird.

flee (flee) *verb* To run away from danger.
Flee sounds like **flea.** ▷ **fleeing, fled** (fled)

fleece (fleess)
1. *noun* A sheep's woolly coat. ▷ *adjective* **fleecy**
2. *verb* To rob someone, especially in a tricky way. ▷ **fleecing, fleeced**

fleet (fleet)
1. *noun* A group of warships under one command.
2. *noun* A number of ships, planes, or cars that form a group, as in *a fleet of taxis.*
3. *adjective* Swift or fast.

fleet·ing (fleet-ing) *adjective* Not lasting long, as in *a fleeting glance.* ▷ *adverb* **fleetingly**

flesh (flesh) *noun*
1. The soft part of your body that covers your bones. Flesh is made up of fat and muscle.
2. The meat of an animal, or the part of a fruit or vegetable that you can eat. ▷ *adjective* **fleshy**

flex (fleks) *verb* To bend or stretch something. *Tarzan flexed his muscles.* ▷ **flexes, flexing, flexed**

flex·i·ble (flek-suh-buhl) *adjective*
1. Able to bend. *Rubber is flexible.*
2. Able to change. *Francis is flexible about Saturday's arrangements.*
▷ *noun* **flexibility** ▷ *adverb* **flexibly**

flex·time (fleks-time) *noun* A system of adjusting the hours of work so that employees may select their own starting and finishing times.

flick (flik) *verb* To move with a quick, sudden movement. *Pete flicked a pea off the table.*
▷ **flicking, flicked** ▷ *noun* **flick**

flick·er (flik-ur) *verb* If something **flickers,** it moves unsteadily. *The flame flickered in the wind.* ▷ **flickering, flickered** ▷ *noun* **flicker**

flight (flite) *noun*
1. The act or manner of flying, or the ability to fly. *The flight of the kite was very graceful.*
2. A journey by aircraft.
3. A set of stairs or steps between floors or landings of a building.
4. If you **take flight,** you run away.

flight attendant *noun* Someone who helps passengers and serves food and beverages on an airplane.

flim·sy (flim-zee) *adjective* Thin, or weak, as in *flimsy material.* ▷ **flimsier, flimsiest** ▷ *noun* **flimsiness** ▷ *adverb* **flimsily**

flinch (flinch) *verb* To make a quick movement away from the source of a pain or fear. *Diane flinched as the nurse approached with a needle.*
▷ **flinches, flinching, flinched** ▷ *noun* **flinch**

fling (fling) *verb* To throw something violently.
▷ **flinging, flung** (fluhng)

flint (flint) *noun* A very hard, gray stone that makes sparks when steel is struck against it.

flip (flip)
1. *verb* To toss or move something quickly. *Ramón flipped the pancakes.*
2. *noun* A somersault.
3. *verb* (*informal*) If someone **flips,** he or she suddenly becomes angry or delighted.
▷ *verb* **flipping, flipped**

flip·pant (flip-uhnt) *adjective* Lacking respect or seriousness, as in *a flippant comment.* ▷ *noun* **flippancy** ▷ *adverb* **flippantly**

flip·per (flip-ur) *noun*
1. One of the broad, flat limbs of a sea creature such as a seal or a dolphin that help it swim. *See* **dolphin.**
2. One of the two long, flat rubber attachments that you wear on your feet to help you swim.

flirt (flurt) *verb*
1. If you **flirt** with someone, you play at being in love with that person. ▷ *noun* **flirt**
2. If you **flirt** with an idea, you consider it, but not very seriously.
▷ *verb* **flirting, flirted**

float (floht)
1. *verb* To rest on water or air.
2. *verb* To move lightly and easily.
3. *noun* A small floating object attached to the end of a fishing line that holds the line up. *See* **angling.**
4. *noun* A decorated truck or flat platform that forms part of a parade.
▷ *verb* **floating, floated**

flock (flok)
1. *noun* A group of animals of one kind that live, travel, or feed together.
2. *verb* To gather in a crowd. *Hundreds of fans flocked to see the band.* ▷ **flocking, flocked**

flock of sheep

flog (flog) *verb* To beat with a whip or a stick.
▷ **flogging, flogged** ▷ *noun* **flogging**

F

flood (fluhd) *verb*
1. When something, such as a river, **floods,** it overflows with water beyond its normal limits.
2. To overwhelm, or to come in large amounts. *The charity was flooded with offers of help.*
▷ *verb* **flooding, flooded** ▷ *noun* **flood**

flood·light (fluhd-*lite*) *noun* A lamp that produces a broad and very bright beam of light.

flood plain *noun* An area of low land near a stream or river that becomes flooded during heavy rains.

floor (flor)
1. *noun* The flat surface that you walk or stand on inside a building. ▷ *noun* **flooring**
2. *noun* A story in a building. *The skyscraper has over 40 floors.*
3. *verb* (informal) To surprise. *Maria was floored by the news.* ▷ **flooring, floored**

flop (flop) *verb*
1. To fall or drop heavily. *Sarah flopped into a chair.*
2. To flap or move about. *The kite flopped about in the breeze.* ▷ *adjective* **floppy**
3. (informal) To fail. *The play flopped.* ▷ *noun* **flop**
▷ *verb* **flopping, flopped**

floppy disk *noun* A small, thin piece of flexible plastic coated with magnetic particles used for storing information from a computer. *See* **computer.**

flo·ra (flor-uh) *noun* The plant life of a particular area, as in *desert flora.*

flo·ral (flor-uhl) *adjective* Of, relating to, or showing flowers, as in *a floral arrangement* or *floral curtains.*

flo·rist (flor-ist) *noun* Someone who sells flowers and plants.

floss (flawss *or* floss) *noun* A thin strand of thread used to clean between the teeth. Also called *dental floss.*

flot·sam (flot-suhm) *noun* Objects from a shipwreck that float in the sea or are washed up on the shore.

floun·der (floun-dur)
1. *verb* To struggle through water, snow, mud, etc.
2. *verb* To have difficulties coping with something. *Bill is floundering with his science project.*
3. *noun* A flat ocean fish used for food.
▷ *verb* **floundering, floundered**

flour (flou-ur) *noun* Ground wheat or other grain that you use for baking. **Flour** sounds like **flower.**
▷ *adjective* **floury**

flour·ish (flur-ish) *verb*
1. To grow and succeed. *Our garden flourished.*
2. To wave something around in order to show it off. *Jan flourished her medal.* ▷ *noun* **flourish**
▷ *verb* **flourishes, flourishing, flourished**

flout (flout) *verb* If you **flout** the rules, you break them deliberately. ▷ **flouting, flouted**

flow (floh) *verb* To move along smoothly, like a river. ▷ **flowing, flowed** ▷ *noun* **flow**

flow·chart (floh-*chart*) *noun* A diagram that shows how something develops and progresses, step by step.

flow·er (flou-ur)
1. *noun* The colored part of a plant that produces seeds or fruit.
2. *verb* To produce flowers. ▷ **flowering, flowered**
3. *noun* A plant that has flowers.
Flour sounds like **flower.**

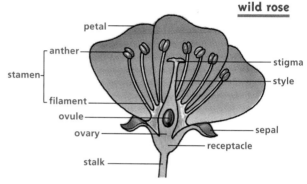

wild rose

petal
anther
stamen
filament
ovule
ovary
stalk
stigma
style
sepal
receptacle

flu (floo) *noun* An illness that is like a bad cold, with fever and muscle pains. Flu is short for influenza. It is caused by a virus.

fluc·tu·ate (fluhk-choo-ate) *verb* To change back and forth or up and down. *Gasoline prices keep fluctuating.* ▷ **fluctuating, fluctuated** ▷ *noun* **fluctuation**

flue (floo) *noun* A hollow part or passage, such as the pipe inside a chimney that carries smoke away from a fire. *See* **termite.**

flu·ent (floo-uhnt) *adjective* Able to speak smoothly and clearly, especially in another language. *John is fluent in French.* ▷ *noun* **fluency** ▷ *adverb* **fluently**

fluff (fluhf)
1. *noun* A light, soft, downy substance.
2. *verb* When a bird **fluffs** its feathers, it shakes them out.
3. *verb* To make a mistake in speaking or reading something. *He fluffed his lines in the play.*
▷ *verb* **fluffing, fluffed**

fluff·y (fluhf-ee) *adjective*
1. Light and airy, as in *a fluffy pillow.*
2. Covered with soft, fine hair or feathers, as in *a fluffy rabbit.*
▷ *adjective* **fluffier, fluffiest**

flu·id (floo-id)
1. *noun* A flowing substance, either a liquid or a gas. *Water, oil, and nitrogen are fluids.*
2. *adjective* Flowing, or liquid. ▷ *noun* **fluidity**

fluke (flook) *noun*
1. A lucky accident.
2. Part of the tail of a sea creature such as a whale or dolphin. *See* **dolphin.**

fluo·res·cent (flu-ress-uhnt) *adjective*
1. Giving out a bright light by using a certain type of energy, such as ultraviolet light or X rays, as in *fluorescent lighting.* ▷ *noun* **fluorescence**
2. A **fluorescent** color is so bright that it seems to give out light when a light is shone on it.

fluor·i·date (flawr-uh-date) *verb* To add fluoride in order to fight decay in teeth. *The city plans to fluoridate its water supply.* ▷ **fluoridating, fluoridated**

fluor·ide (flawr-ide) *noun* A chemical compound put in toothpaste and water to prevent tooth decay.

fluo·rine (flawr-een) *noun* A green or yellow gaseous element that easily combines with other elements to form compounds.

flur·ry (flur-ee) *noun*
1. A confusion or a commotion, as in *a flurry of activity.*
2. A brief snow shower.
▷ *noun, plural* **flurries**

flush (fluhsh)
1. *verb* To turn red or to blush. *I flushed with embarrassment.*
2. *verb* To flood something with water as a way of cleaning it. ▷ *noun* **flush**
3. *adjective* Exactly even. *The door was flush with the wall.*
▷ *verb* **flushes, flushing, flushed**

flushed (fluhsht) *adjective* If you are **flushed,** your face has become red. ▷ *noun* **flush**

flus·ter (fluhss-tur) *verb* To confuse or rush someone. ▷ **flustering, flustered**

flute (floot) *noun* A long, cylindrical musical instrument played by blowing air across a hole at one end and fingering keys to change notes. *See* **orchestra, woodwind.**

flut·ter (fluht-ur)
1. *verb* To wave or flap rapidly. *The flag fluttered in the breeze.* ▷ **fluttering, fluttered**
2. *noun* If you are in a **flutter** about something, you are excited and nervous about it.

fly (flye)
1. *verb* To travel through the air.
2. *noun* An insect with two wings. *See* **insect.**
3. *noun* A flap on trousers covering a zipper or buttons.
4. *verb* To move or pass quickly. *Time just flew by.*
5. *noun* A baseball hit high in the air.
▷ *noun, plural* **flies** ▷ *verb* **flies, flying, flew** (floo), **flown** (flohn)

fly·catch·er (flye-*kach*-ur) *noun* A songbird that feeds on insects caught in the air.

fly fishing *noun* A type of fishing using fake flies made from fur, feathers, etc., attached to a hook that the fish swallows. *Shown below are a variety of flies used by anglers in the United States.*

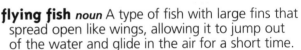

flying fish *noun* A type of fish with large fins that spread open like wings, allowing it to jump out of the water and glide in the air for a short time.

flying saucer *noun* Any of various flying objects shaped like disks, reportedly seen by some people and believed to be spacecraft from other planets.

foal (fohl)
1. *noun* A young horse, donkey, or zebra.
2. *verb* To give birth to a young horse or similar animal. ▷ **foaling, foaled**

foam (fohm)
1. *noun* A mass of small bubbles.
2. *verb* To make bubbles. ▷ **foaming, foamed**

foam rubber *noun* A soft, spongy material often used to stuff toys and furniture.

fo·cus (foh-kuhss)
1. *noun* The point where rays of light meet after being bent by a lens. ▷ *verb* **focus**
2. *verb* To adjust your eyes or a camera lens so that you can see something clearly. *I focused my camera carefully before I took the picture.*
3. *verb* To concentrate on something or somebody. *Let's focus on your problems.*
4. *noun* The center of activity, interest, or attention. *The focus of the town meeting was new taxes.*
▷ *noun, plural* **focuses** or **foci** (foh-sye) ▷ *verb* **focuses, focusing, focused** ▷ *adjective* **focal**

fod·der (fod-ur) *noun* Food for cattle and horses.

foe (foh) *noun* An enemy.

fog (fog *or* fawg) *noun*
1. A very thick mist of water vapor in the air.
2. A daze or a state of confusion.
▷ *verb* **fog, fogging, fogged** ▷ *adjective* **foggy**

fog·horn (fog-*horn*) *noun* A loud horn used to warn ships in foggy weather.

foil (foil)
1. *noun* Thin, silvery sheets of metal.
2. *verb* To prevent someone from doing something. *The police foiled the robbers' plot.* ▷ **foiling, foiled**
3. *noun* A long, thin sword used in fencing. *See* **fencing.**

fold (fohld)
1. *verb* To bend something over on itself. *Henry folded the sheets.*
2. *noun* A line or crease made by folding.
3. *verb* To bring together, or to bend close to the body, as in *to fold one's arms.*
4. *noun* A small, enclosed area for sheep.
5. *verb* If a company **folds,** it collapses.
▷ *verb* **folding, folded**

fold·er (fohl-dur) *noun* A cardboard holder used for keeping papers.

fo·li·age (foh-lee-ij) *noun* Leaves.

folk (fohk)
1. *noun* People. *Do you know the folks in this neighborhood?* ▷ *noun, plural* **folk** or **folks**
2. **folks** *noun, plural* Family members, especially parents. *These are my folks.*
3. *adjective* Traditional and belonging to ordinary people, as in *folk music.*

folk dance *noun* A kind of dance that is native to a particular area or group.

folk·lore (fohk-*lor*) *noun* The stories, customs, and beliefs of ordinary people that are passed down to their children.

folk music *noun* Traditional music of an area that is often handed down from one generation to the next.

folk singer *noun* Someone who sings folk music.

folk song *noun* A traditional song with music and words, usually with a simple melody.

folk·tale (fohk-*tale*) *noun* A story that is passed down orally from generation to generation.

fol·low (fol-oh) *verb*
1. To be guided by someone or something. *Harvey always follows the latest trends.*
2. To go behind someone. *The police car followed us.*
3. To come after. *December follows November.*
4. To obey, as in *to follow orders.*
5. If you **follow up** on something, you return to something that you started.
▷ *verb* **following, followed** ▷ *noun* **follower**

following
1. *preposition* Next, after, or coming after.

Following the dinner, there will be a dance.
2. *adjective* Next in time or order of occurrence, as in *the following year.*
3. *noun* If someone has a **following,** the person has many supporters or admirers.

fol·ly (fol-ee) *noun* Foolishness. *It's folly to think you can go out in this hurricane.* ▷ *noun, plural* **follies**

fond (fond) *adjective* If you are **fond** of something, you like it very much. ▷ **fonder, fondest** ▷ *noun* **fondness** ▷ *adverb* **fondly**

fon·dle (fon-duhl) *verb* To touch or stroke lovingly or tenderly. *Nancy fondled the kitten.* ▷ **fondling, fondled**

font (font) *noun*
1. A large, stone bowl used in a church to hold the water for baptisms.
2. A set of type of one size and style. *See* **type.**

food (food) *noun* Substances that people, animals, and plants eat to stay alive and grow.

food chain *noun* An ordered arrangement of animals and plants in which each feeds on the one below it in the chain. *Shown here is one example of a food chain.*

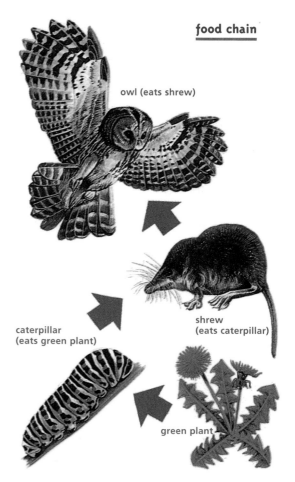

food chain

owl (eats shrew)

shrew (eats caterpillar)

caterpillar (eats green plant)

green plant

food pro·ces·sor (pross-ess-ur) *noun* A machine that cuts up, purees, or liquefies food.

food web *noun* The complex network of food chains in an ecosystem.

fool (fool)
1. *noun* A person who lacks good sense.
2. *verb* To trick someone. ▷ **fooling, fooled**

fool·ish (fool-ish) *adjective* Not showing good sense; not wise. ▷ *noun* **foolishness**

fool·proof (fool-*proof*) *adjective* Something that is **foolproof** is very simple to use and cannot easily go wrong.

foot (fut) *noun*
1. The part of your body at the end of your leg.
2. The bottom or lower end of something, as in *the foot of the bed*.
3. A unit of length that equals 12 inches.
4. If you **put your foot down,** you insist on something and act firmly.
▷ *noun, plural* **feet** (feet)

foot·ball (fut-*bal*) *noun*
1. A game played by two teams of 11 players each on a long field with goals at each end. Each team tries to score points by getting the ball across the opponent's goal line. *The picture shows a football player with part of his uniform cut away.*
2. The ball used in this game.

football player

shoulder pad
football
helmet
face mask
chin strap
wrist pad
chest protector
jersey
hip pad
towel
pants
thigh pad
knee pad
elastic tape (protects ankle)
sock
cleated shoe

foot·hill (fut-*hil*) *noun* A low hill at the base of a mountain or mountain range.

foot·ing (fut-ing) *noun*
1. A secure place on which to stand.
2. In architecture, the **footing** of a building is the bottom of its foundation. *See* **building.**

foot·lights (fut-*lites*) *noun, plural* Lights arranged along the front floor of a stage that allow the audience to see the actors.

foot·note (fut-*noht*) *noun* A note at the bottom of a page that explains something in the text.

foot·print (fut-*print*) *noun* A mark made by a foot or shoe.

foot·step (fut-*step*) *noun*
1. The act of placing the foot on the ground or floor.
2. The sound that the foot makes when it hits the ground or floor.

for (for)
1. *preposition* Intended to be used on or with. *These markers are for posters.*
2. *preposition* Meeting the needs of. *I take vitamins for my health.*
3. *preposition* Over the time or distance of. *We marched for miles.*
4. *preposition* Due to. *She has to travel for her job.*
5. *preposition* In honor of, or on behalf of. *He picked the flowers for me.*
6. *preposition* Worth the amount of. *I bought a pack of gum for 50 cents.*
7. *preposition* Intended for, or sent to. *This is for you.*
8. *preposition* In place of. *In the recipe, we substituted honey for sugar.*
9. *conjunction* Because. *We must rejoice, for life is good.*

for·age (for-ij)
1. *noun* Hay, grain, and other food for horses, cattle, and similar animals.
2. *verb* To go in search of food. *The outlaws foraged for berries in the woods.* ▷ **foraging, foraged**

for·bid (fur-bid) *verb* To order someone not to do something. ▷ **forbidding, forbade** (fur-*bayd*), **forbidden** (fur-bid-in) ▷ *adjective* **forbidden**

for·bid·ding (fur-bid-ing) *adjective* Looking unfriendly or dangerous. *At night, the alley was forbidding.* ▷ *adverb* **forbiddingly**

force (forss)
1. *noun* Strength or power. *The batter hit the ball with great force.* ▷ *adjective* **forceful** ▷ *adverb* **forcefully**
2. *verb* If you **force** someone to do something, you make the person do it. ▷ **forcing, forced**
3. *noun* In physics, a **force** is any action that changes the shape or the movement of an object.
4. *noun* An army or other team of people who work together, as in *the police force*.

F

F

for·ceps (for-seps) *noun, plural* Tongs used for grasping, holding, or pulling, especially by dentists or surgeons.

ford (ford)
1. *noun* A shallow part of a stream or river where you can cross.
2. *verb* To cross at a ford. ▷ **fording, forded**

▶ Prefix
• •
The prefix **fore-** adds one of the following meanings to a root word:
1. Before or ahead of time, as in *forecast* (tell what will happen before it actually does).
2. The front or in front of, as in *forearm* (the front of your arm).

fore·arm (for-arm) *noun* The part of your arm from your wrist to your elbow.

fore·cast (for-kast) *verb* To say what you think will happen in the future. *The radio announcer forecasts rain for tomorrow.* ▷ **forecasting, forecast** or **forecasted** ▷ *noun* **forecast,** *noun* **forecaster**

fore·fa·ther (for-*fah*-THur) *noun* An ancestor.

fore·fin·ger (for-*fing*-gur) *noun* The finger used for pointing; the index finger.

fore·gone (for-*gon*) *adjective* Decided in advance. *It was a foregone conclusion.*

fore·ground (for-*ground*) *noun* The part of a picture that is or seems to be nearest to the person looking at it. *This painting has a cottage in the foreground.*

fore·head (for-id *or* for-hed) *noun* The top part of your face between your hair and your eyes.

for·eign (for-uhn) *adjective*
1. To do with or coming from another country. ▷ *noun* **foreigner**
2. If something is **foreign** to you, it is strange or unnatural.

fore·leg (for-*leg*) *noun* One of the front legs of an animal with four legs.

fore·man (for-muhn) *noun*
1. Someone who leads a group of people who work together.
2. The lead man or woman on a jury.
▷ *noun, plural* **foremen**

fore·most (for-*mohst*) *adjective* First in rank, position, or importance.

fo·ren·sic (fuh-**ren**-sik) *adjective* Using science to help investigate or solve crimes. A forensic investigation uses fingerprints, blood tests, handwriting analysis, etc.

fore·per·son (for-*pur*-suhn) *noun* A foreman or a forewoman.

fore·run·ner (for-*ruhn*-ur) *noun*
1. Someone who has come before, such as an ancestor or a predecessor.

2. A sign of something to come. *The groundhog is a forerunner of spring.*

fore·see (for-see) *verb* To expect or predict that something will happen. ▷ **foreseeing, foresaw, foreseen** ▷ *adjective* **foreseeable**

fore·sight (for-*site*) *noun* The ability to see into or plan for the future. *Lacking foresight, we didn't bring our umbrellas.*

for·est (for-ist *or* fo-rist) *noun* A large area thickly covered with trees and plants. ▷ *adjective* **forested**

forest ranger *noun* A person who manages and protects the land in a forest.

fore·tell (for-tel) *verb* To forecast or predict something. ▷ **foretelling, foretold**

for·ev·er (fur-ev-ur) *adverb*
1. For all time. *No one can expect to live forever.*
2. Always or continually. *Matt is forever asking questions.*

fore·wom·an (for-wum-an) *noun*
1. A woman who leads a group of people who work together.
2. The lead woman on a jury.
▷ *noun, plural* **forewomen**

for·feit (for-fit)
1. *noun* A penalty for something not done or badly done.
2. *verb* To give up the right to something. *If you are convicted of a crime, you might forfeit your right to vote.* ▷ *noun* **forfeiture** ▷ **forfeiting, forfeited**

forge (forj)
1. *verb* To make illegal copies of paintings, money, etc. ▷ *noun* **forger,** *noun* **forgery**
2. *verb* If you **forge ahead,** you move forward or make progress.
3. *verb* To make or to form. *The senators forged an agreement.*
4. *noun* A blacksmith's shop.
▷ *verb* **forging, forged**

for·get (fur-get) *verb* If you **forget** something, you do not remember it. ▷ **forgetting, forgot, forgotten** ▷ *noun* **forgetfulness** ▷ *adjective* **forgetful**

forget-me-not *noun* A plant with clusters of small, blue flowers, often used as a symbol of friendship.

for·give (fur-giv) *verb* To pardon someone, or to stop blaming the person for something. ▷ **forgiving, forgave, forgiven** ▷ *noun* **forgiveness** ▷ *adjective* **forgiving**

fork (fork)
1. *noun* An instrument with prongs used for eating or for lifting hay.
2. *noun* A place where a road, river, tree, etc., branches into two or more directions. ▷ *verb* **fork** ▷ *adjective* **forked**
3. *verb* If you **fork out** for something, you pay for it reluctantly. ▷ **forking, forked**

fork·lift (fork-*lift*) *noun* A vehicle with two prongs or forks at the front, used for lifting and carrying loads. *When the driver operates the controls on this forklift, the cylinder rises and chains pull up the cage and the forks, which hold the load.*

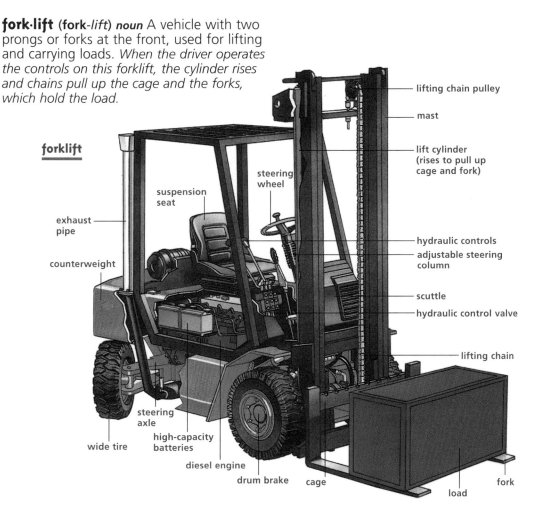

forklift

lifting chain pulley
mast
lift cylinder (rises to pull up cage and fork)
steering wheel
suspension seat
exhaust pipe
counterweight
hydraulic controls
adjustable steering column
scuttle
hydraulic control valve
lifting chain
steering axle
high-capacity batteries
wide tire
diesel engine
drum brake
cage
load
fork

F

for·lorn (for-**lorn**) *adjective* Sad or lonely. ▷ *adverb* **forlornly**

form (form)
1. *noun* Type or kind. *Which form of travel do you prefer?*
2. *noun* Shape. *The monster took on a human form.* ▷ *adjective* **formless**
3. *verb* To make up or create something. *The lines formed a rectangle.*
4. *noun* A piece of paper with questions to be filled in.
5. *verb* To make or to organize. *We formed a club.*
6. *noun* In grammar, one of the ways a word appears, depending on how it is used. *The word* children *is the plural form of the word* child.
▷ *verb* **forming, formed**

for·mal (for-muhl) *adjective*
1. Proper and not casual, as in *formal clothes.* ▷ *noun* **formal**
2. Official. *We're waiting for formal permission before we make any plans.*
▷ *adverb* **formally**

for·mat (for-mat)
1. *noun* The shape or style of something. *The new magazine has a bolder, larger format than the old one.*
2. *verb* To prepare a computer disk to be used.
▷ **formatting, formatted**

for·ma·tion (for-may-shuhn) *noun*
1. The process of making something. *We are studying the formation of crystals.*
2. A pattern or a shape. *Look at that wonderful cloud formation!*
3. The way in which the members of a group are arranged. *The tanks rolled in battle formation.*

for·mer (for-mur)
1. *noun* The first of two things that you have been talking about. *I am fond of kittens and puppies, but I really prefer the former.*
2. *adjective* Previous or earlier, as in *my former wife.*

for·mer·ly (for-mur-lee) *adverb* In the past, or at an earlier time.

for·mi·da·ble (for-muh-duh-buhl) *adjective* Frightening, as in *a formidable opponent.* ▷ *adverb* **formidably**

for·mu·la (for-myuh-luh) *noun*
1. A rule in science or math that is written with numbers and symbols.
2. A suggested set of actions. *What's your formula for success?*
3. A liquid substitute for mother's milk. *Heat the baby's formula.*
▷ *noun, plural* **formulas** *or* **formulae** (for-myuh-lee *or* for-myuh-lye)

for·mu·late (for-myuh-late) *verb* If you **formulate** a theory, you work out an idea and then state it clearly. ▷ **formulating, formulated**

for·sake (for-sayk) *verb* To give up, leave, or abandon. *Don't forsake your old friends when you move.* ▷ **forsaking, forsook** (for-suk), **forsaken**

for·sak·en (for-say-kuhn) *adjective* Abandoned or left, as in *a forsaken building.*

for·syth·i·a (for-sith-ee-uh) *noun* A bush with brilliant yellow flowers that bloom in the spring.

fort (fort) *noun*
1. A building that is strongly built to survive attacks.
2. If you **hold the fort,** you look after things for someone else while the person is away.

forte
1. (fort *or* for-tay) *noun* Your **forte** is your strong point.
2. (for-tay) *adverb* **Forte** is the Italian word for loud. It is used in music.

forth (forth) *adverb*
1. Forward, or onward. *The parade marched forth.*
2. Out from hiding. *She burst forth from behind a tree.*
3. Away, or abroad. *Their journey forth was a long time overdue.*

forth·com·ing (forth-*kum*-ing) *adjective*
1. Coming soon. *I am eager to vote in the forthcoming election.*
2. If someone is not very **forthcoming,** he or she does not tell the entire truth.

for·ti·fy (for-tuh-fye) *verb*
1. To make a place stronger against attack. *The soldiers fortified the town's defenses.* ▷ *noun* **fortification**
2. If you **fortify** yourself, you make yourself feel better and stronger. *The climbers fortified themselves against the cold with hot soup.*
3. To improve or to enrich. *The bakery fortified the bread with vitamins.*
▷ *verb* **fortifies, fortifying, fortified**

fort·night (fort-*nite*) *noun* A period of two weeks. ▷ *adjective* **fortnightly** ▷ *adverb* **fortnightly**

for·tress (for-triss) *noun* A place that is strengthened against attack. ▷ *noun, plural* **fortresses**

for·tu·nate (for-chuh-nit) *adjective* Lucky.
▷ *adverb* **fortunately**

for·tune (for-chuhn) *noun*
1. Fate or destiny. *The psychic told my fortune by looking into her crystal ball.*
2. Chance or good luck. *I had the good fortune to find a summer job.*
3. A large amount of money.

> ### ▶ Word History
> **Fortune** comes from the Latin word *fortūna*, meaning "fate" or "luck." The same Latin word in its plural form, *fortūnae*, means "possessions" or "goods," and hence fortune, today, also means riches.

fo·rum (for-uhm) *noun*
1. The town square of an ancient Roman city.
2. A public discussion of an issue. *We attended a forum on city planning.*

for·ward (for-wurd)
1. *adverb* Toward the front, or ahead. *We crept forward cautiously.* ▷ *adjective* **forward** ▷ *adverb* **forwards**
2. *adjective* Toward the future. *I am looking forward to the holidays.*
3. *noun* A player in basketball, hockey, or soccer who plays in an attacking position and tries to score goals.
4. *adjective* Bold or rude. *I don't think you should have been so forward, speaking out in class today.*

fos·sil (foss-uhl) *noun* The remains or traces of an animal or a plant from millions of years ago, preserved as rock. *Examples of different types of fossils are shown in this picture.*
▷ *verb* **fossilize**
▷ *adjective* **fossilized**

fossils

gastropod

echinoderm

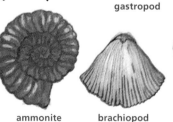
ammonite   brachiopod   trilobite

fossil fuel *noun* Coal, oil, or natural gas, formed from the remains of prehistoric plants and animals.

fos·ter (fawss-tur *or* foss-tur) *verb*
1. To look after a child who is not your own, without becoming the legal parent. ▷ *adjective* **foster**

2. To help the growth and development of. *The new club fostered a sense of community.*
▷ *verb* **fostering, fostered**

foul (foul)
1. *adjective* Very dirty or disgusting. *The sewer had a foul smell.* ▷ *noun* **foulness** ▷ *adverb* **foully**
2. *verb* To make something dirty or unpleasant. *Chemical waste fouled the water system.*
▷ **fouling, fouled**
3. *adjective* Cloudy, rainy, or stormy, as in *foul weather.*
4. *noun* An action in sports that is against the rules. ▷ *verb* **foul**
Foul sounds like **fowl.**
▷ *adjective* **fouler, foulest**

foul line *noun*
1. In baseball, either of the two lines drawn from home plate to first and third bases. A ball hit outside of the foul lines is a *foul ball.*
2. In basketball, the line on either side of the court from which a player shoots a penalty shot.

found (found) *verb* To set up or start something, such as a school. ▷ **founding, founded** ▷ *noun* **founder**

foun·da·tion (foun-day-shuhn) *noun*
1. A solid structure on which a building is built. *See* **building.**
2. The base or basis of something. *That rumor has no foundation in fact.*
3. An organization that gives money to worthwhile causes.

found·ry (foun-dree) *noun* A factory for melting and shaping metal.

foun·tain (foun-tuhn) *noun*
1. A stream or jet of water used for drinking or for decoration.
2. A rich or abundant source. *My teacher is a fountain of knowledge.*

fountain pen *noun* A pen with a point that is supplied with ink from a container inside the pen.

four (for) *noun* The whole number, written 4, that comes after three and before five. ▷ *adjective* **four**

Four-H Club *noun* A rural club for young people that teaches community values through farming and other useful skills. The four Hs stand for head, heart, hands, and health.

fourth (forth)
1. *adjective* That which comes after third and before fifth.
2. *noun* One part of something that has been divided into four equal parts, written $\frac{1}{4}$.

Fourth of July *noun* A U.S. holiday that celebrates the signing of the Declaration of Independence on July 4, 1776.

fowl (foul) *noun* A bird, such as a chicken, turkey, duck, etc., often raised for its eggs or its meat. **Fowl** sounds like **foul.** ▷ *noun, plural* **fowl** *or* **fowls**

fox (foks) *noun* A wild animal related to the dog, with thick fur, a pointed nose and ears, and a bushy tail. ▷ *noun, plural* **foxes**

fox

fox·hound (foks-hound) *noun* A breed of dog of medium size trained to hunt foxes.

foy·er (foi-ur *or* foi-ay) *noun* An entrance hall, especially of a theater, an apartment building, or a hotel.

frac·tal (frak-tuhl) *noun* A shape, often drawn on a computer, that repeats itself in a pattern over and over again.

frac·tion (frak-shuhn) *noun*
1. A part of a whole number. For example, $\frac{1}{2}$, $\frac{3}{4}$, and $\frac{7}{8}$ are all fractions.
2. A part of a whole.
3. A small amount. *Polly bought the painting for a fraction of its real value.* ▷ *adjective* **fractional** ▷ *adverb* **fractionally**

frac·ture (frak-chur) *verb* To break or crack something, especially a bone. ▷ **fracturing, fractured** ▷ *noun* **fracture**

frag·ile (fraj-il) *adjective* Delicate, or easily broken.

frag·ment (frag-muhnt) *noun* A small piece or a part that is broken off. ▷ *verb* **fragment** (frag-ment)

fra·grant (fray-gruhnt) *adjective* Having a sweet smell. ▷ *noun* **fragrance**

frail (frayl) *adjective* Weak. ▷ **frailer, frailest** ▷ *noun* **frailty**

frame (fraym)
1. *noun* A basic structure over which something is built. *Our house has a wood frame.*
2. *noun* A border that surrounds and holds something, as in *a picture frame.* ▷ *verb* **frame**
3. *noun* The way in which a person's body is built. *That football player has a large frame.*
4. *verb* (*informal*) If someone **frames** an innocent person, he or she makes the person seem guilty by giving false information or evidence.

frame·work (fraym-*wurk*) *noun* A structure that gives shape or support to something.

franc (frangk) *noun* The main unit of money in France, Belgium, Switzerland, and many African countries. **Franc** sounds like **frank.**

fran·chise (fran-chize)
1. *noun* The right to vote.
2. *noun* Permission given by a company to sell its services or distribute its products in a certain area.
3. *verb* To give the right to someone to sell a product or service in a certain area.
▷ **franchising, franchised**
▷ *noun* **franchiser**

frank (frangk) *adjective* Open and honest. **Frank** sounds like **franc.** ▷ **franker, frankest** ▷ *noun* **frankness** ▷ *adverb* **frankly**

frank·fur·ter (frangk-fur-tur) *noun* A hot dog or small smoked sausage made of beef, pork, chicken, etc.

fran·tic (fran-tik) *adjective* Wildly excited by worry or fear. ▷ *adverb* **frantically**

fraud (frawd) *noun*
1. If you practice **fraud,** you cheat or trick people. ▷ *adjective* **fraudulent** (fraw-juh-luhnt) ▷ *adverb* **fraudulently**
2. If someone is a **fraud,** the person pretends to be something he or she is not.

fray (fray)
1. *verb* To unravel. *Stan sewed elbow patches on his jacket where the fabric had frayed.* ▷ **fraying, frayed**
2. *noun* A noisy quarrel or battle.

freak (freek)
1. *noun* A person, an animal, or a plant that has not developed normally.
2. *adjective* Very odd or unusual, as in *freak weather conditions.*
3. *noun* (informal) Someone who is very enthusiastic about something, as in *an exercise freak.*
▷ *adjective* **freakish**

freck·le (frek-uhl) *noun* A small, light brown spot on your skin. ▷ *adjective* **freckled,** *adjective* **freckly**

free (free)
1. *adjective* If something is **free,** it does not cost anything.
2. *adjective* If a person or an animal is **free,** it can do what it likes. ▷ *adverb* **freely**
3. *verb* If you **free** a person or an animal, you let it go from a prison or cage. ▷ **freeing, freed**
4. *adjective* Not held back, as in *a free discussion.*
5. *adjective* Not affected by something, as in *free of disease.*
▷ *adjective* **freer, freest**

free·dom (free-duhm) *noun* The right to do and say what you like.

free·lance (free-lanss) *adjective* If you are a **freelance** worker, you do not earn a salary but are paid for each job that you do. ▷ *noun* **freelancer**

free-range *adjective* **Free-range** animals are allowed to feed and wander freely outside cages or pens.

free·way (free-*way*) *noun* A wide highway that you can travel on without paying tolls.

freeze (freez) *verb*
1. To become solid or icy at a very low temperature. *Water freezes at 0 degrees Celsius.* ▷ *adjective* **freezing**
2. To make or become very cold. *The spectators froze.*
3. To stop still because you are frightened.
4. To be damaged or killed from the cold. *The orange crop froze last winter.*
5. To keep from rising. *The government plans to freeze food prices.*
Freeze sounds like **frieze.**
▷ *verb* **freezing, froze** (frohz), **frozen**

freez·er (free-zur) *noun* A refrigerator or part of a refrigerator that freezes food quickly and keeps it from spoiling.

freight (frayt) *noun* Goods or cargo carried by trains, ships, planes, trucks, etc.

freight·er (fray-tur) *noun* A ship that carries cargo.

French fries *noun, plural* Strips of potato that are fried in deep fat or oil.

French horn *noun* A brass instrument made of a coiled tube that flares into a bell at the end. *See* **brass.**

fren·zy (fren-zee) *noun* If you are in a **frenzy,** you are wildly excited about something. ▷ *noun, plural* **frenzies** ▷ *adjective* **frenzied**

fre·quen·cy (free-kwuhn-see) *noun*
1. If something happens with **frequency,** it happens again and again.
2. The number of times that something happens. *The frequency of road accidents has increased.*
3. The number of cycles per second of a radio wave.
4. The number of vibrations per second in a light wave.
▷ *noun, plural* **frequencies**

fre·quent
1. (free-kwent) *adjective* Common, or happening often. ▷ *adverb* **frequently**
2. (free-kwent) *verb* To visit somewhere often or regularly. *Mark frequents the local park.*
▷ **frequenting, frequented**

F

fres·co (fress-koh) *noun* A painting made on a wall or ceiling while the plaster is still wet. *This ancient fresco shows a man leaping over a bull.*
▷ *noun, plural* **frescoes** *or* **frescos**

fresco

fresh (fresh) *adjective*
1. Clean or new, as in *a fresh piece of paper.*
▷ *adverb* **freshly**
2. Not frozen or canned, as in *fresh fruit.*
3. Cool or refreshing, as in *a fresh sea breeze.*
4. Not salty, as in *fresh water.*
5. Rude. *No one appreciated her fresh remarks.*
▷ *adjective* **fresher, freshest**

fresh·man (fresh-muhn) *noun* Someone in the first year of high school or college.

fresh·wa·ter (fresh-*wa*-tur) *adjective* To do with or living in water that does not contain salt, as in *freshwater fish.* ▷ *noun* **freshwater**

fret (fret)
1. *verb* To worry or get upset about something.
▷ **fretting, fretted** ▷ *noun* **fretfulness** ▷ *adjective* **fretful** ▷ *adverb* **fretfully**
2. *noun* One of the bars or ridges on the neck of a stringed musical instrument, such as a guitar. *See* **guitar.**

fric·tion (frik-shuhn) *noun*
1. Rubbing. *Friction causes heat.*
2. The force that slows down objects when they rub against each other.
3. Disagreement or anger. *There was much friction between the two teams.*

Fri·day (frye-*day or* frye-dee) *noun* The sixth day of the week, after Thursday and before Saturday.

> **Word History**
> ●
> Long ago, the pagan English named the sixth day of the week after Frigga, queen of the gods. "Frigga's day" became **Friday.**

fridge (frij) *Short for* **refrigerator.**
friend (frend) *noun*
1. Someone whom you enjoy being with and know well. ▷ *noun* **friendship**
2. Someone who supports a group or cause.

friend·ly (frend-lee) *adjective*
1. Kind and helpful.
2. Not angry or hostile, as in *friendly relations between nations.*
▷ *adjective* **friendlier, friendliest** ▷ *noun* **friendliness**

frieze (freez) *noun* A decorated or painted strip, usually along the top of a wall. **Frieze** sounds like **freeze.**

fright (frite) *noun* A sudden feeling of fear. *I had a fright when you jumped out in front of me.*

fright·en (frite-uhn) *verb*
1. To scare someone. *Eva hoped to frighten her friends with her scary Halloween costume.*
▷ *adjective* **frightening**
2. To drive away by scaring. *The cat frightened away the birds.*
▷ *verb* **frightening, frightened**

fright·ful (frite-fuhl) *adjective* Terrible or shocking. *The children created a frightful mess in the kitchen when they tried to bake a cake on their own.* ▷ *adverb* **frightfully**

frig·id (frij-id) *adjective*
1. Extremely cold. *My mom says we're in for a frigid winter this year.*
2. Unfriendly. *I got a frigid reception after I insulted my aunt.*

frill (fril) *noun* A ruffled strip of material or paper used as decoration. ▷ *adjective* **frilly**

fringe (frinj)
1. *noun* A border of cords or threads attached to something.
2. *noun* Any border or edge.
3. *verb* To form an edge or a border. *Tulips fringed the path.* ▷ **fringing, fringed**

Fris·bee (friz-bee) *noun* A trademark for a plastic disk tossed from person to person in any of various games.

frisk (frisk) *verb*
1. *(informal)* To search someone for weapons, drugs, etc.
2. To play in a lively way. *It's fun to watch the kittens frisk about the house.*
▷ *verb* **frisking, frisked**

frisk·y (friss-kee) *adjective* Playful and full of energy. ▷ *adverb* **friskily**

frit·ta·ta (free-tah-tuh) *noun* A flat omelet filled with chopped vegetables, cheese, meat, etc.

frit·ter (frit-ur)
1. *verb* To use up in a careless, wasteful way. *They frittered away their whole day.* ▷ **frittering, frittered**
2. *noun* A small fried cake containing corn, clams, fruit, or other ingredients.

friv·o·lous (friv-uh-luhss) *adjective*
1. Silly. ▷ *adverb* **frivolously**
2. Not important.

F

frog (frog *or* frawg) *noun* A small, green or brown animal with webbed feet and long back legs that it uses for jumping. Frogs are amphibians and live in or near water. *The pictures show the life cycle of the common frog. See also* **rain forest.**

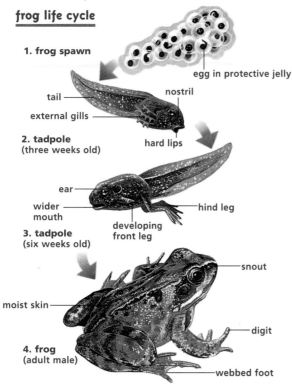

frog life cycle

1. frog spawn

egg in protective jelly

tail

nostril

external gills

2. tadpole (three weeks old)

hard lips

ear

wider mouth

hind leg

developing front leg

3. tadpole (six weeks old)

snout

moist skin

digit

4. frog (adult male)

webbed foot

frog·man (frog-muhn) *noun* An investigator or military person who swims underwater using diving equipment. ▷ *noun, plural* **frogmen**

frol·ic (frol-ik) *verb* To play happily. *The children frolicked in the sun.* ▷ **frolicking, frolicked** ▷ *noun* **frolic**

from (fruhm) *preposition*
1. Starting at. *The train headed north from Washington to New York.*
2. In relative distance to. *The garage is not far from the house.*
3. The source. *The hurricane came from the south.*
4. As opposed to. *I can't tell him from his twin brother.*
5. Out of. *The first little pig's house was made from straw.*
6. Because of. *I became sick from food poisoning.*
7. At. *I got this sundae from the ice-cream shop.*

frond (frond) *noun* A large, divided leaf on a plant such as a fern or palm. *See* **fern.**

front (fruhnt) *noun*
1. The part of something that comes first, as in *the front of a book.*

2. The part of something that faces forward.
3. The place where armies are fighting.
4. The edge of a mass of cold or warm air.
5. If you **put up a front,** you pretend to feel or think something.
▷ *adjective* **front**

fron·tier (fruhn-tihr *or* fruhn-tihr) *noun*
1. The far edge of a country, where few people live.
2. The border between two countries.
3. A subject or an area of study that is just beginning to be understood, as in *the frontiers of medicine.*

frost (frawst)
1. *noun* Powdery ice that forms on things in freezing weather.
2. *verb* If something **frosts up,** it becomes covered with frost. *The windshield frosted up overnight.*
3. *noun* Weather with a temperature below the freezing point.
4. *verb* To put frosting on, as in *to frost a cake.*
▷ *verb* **frosting, frosted**

frost·bite (frawst-*bite*) *noun* If someone suffers from **frostbite,** parts of the body, such as fingers, toes, or ears, are damaged by extreme cold. ▷ *adjective* **frostbitten**

frost·ing (frawst-ing) *noun* A sweet sugar coating used to decorate cakes and pastries.

frost·y (fraw-stee) *adjective*
1. Covered with powdery ice.
2. Very cold, as in *frosty weather.*
3. If someone is **frosty,** he or she is unfriendly.
▷ *adjective* **frostier, frostiest** ▷ *noun* **frostiness**
▷ *adverb* **frostily**

froth (frawth) *noun* Lots of small bubbles in or on top of a liquid. ▷ *verb* **froth** ▷ *adjective* **frothy**

frown (froun) *verb*
1. To move your eyebrows together and wrinkle your forehead, usually as a sign that you are annoyed or unhappy. ▷ *noun* **frown**
2. To disapprove or to be against. *The teacher frowns on rudeness.*
▷ *verb* **frowning, frowned**

fro·zen (froh-zuhn) *adjective*
1. If water is **frozen,** it has been made so cold that it has turned into ice.
2. Extremely cold. *My hands are frozen.*
3. Chilled until hard, then stored in a freezer, as in *frozen food.*
4. Plugged up with ice, as in *frozen pipes.*
5. Too frightened to move, as in *frozen with terror.*

fru·gal (froo-guhl) *adjective* If you are **frugal,** you are very careful not to waste things. ▷ *noun* **frugality** ▷ *adverb* **frugally**

fruit (froot) *noun*
1. The fleshy, juicy product of a plant that contains one or more seeds and is usually edible. *Melons and grapes are fruits.* ▷ *adjective* **fruity**
2. The part of a flowering plant that contains seeds, such as a nut or a pod.
3. The result of something. *This project is the fruit of the whole group's efforts.*
▷ *noun plural* **fruit** or **fruits**

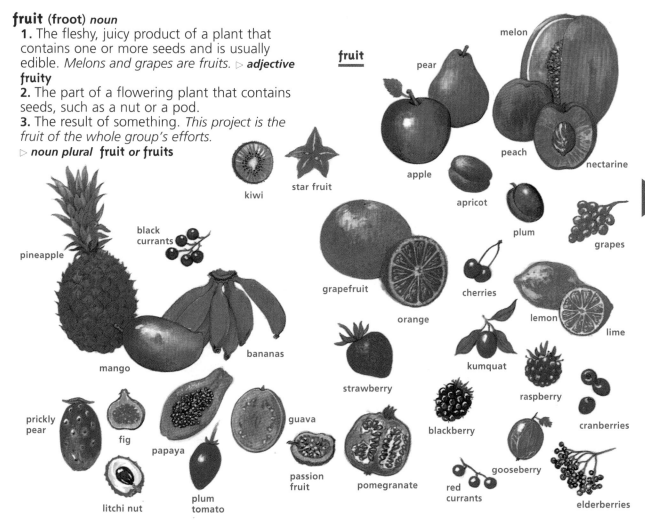

fruit

melon
pear
peach
nectarine
apple
apricot
plum
grapes
star fruit
kiwi
black currants
pineapple
grapefruit
orange
cherries
lemon
lime
bananas
kumquat
mango
strawberry
raspberry
prickly pear
fig
papaya
guava
blackberry
cranberries
passion fruit
pomegranate
gooseberry
red currants
elderberries
litchi nut
plum tomato

F

fruit·ful (froot-fuhl) *adjective* Successful or useful, as in *a fruitful discussion.* ▷ *noun* **fruitfulness** ▷ *adverb* **fruitfully**
fruit·less (froot-liss) *adjective* Unsuccessful or useless. ▷ *adverb* **fruitlessly**
frus·trate (fruhss-trate) *verb*
1. If something **frustrates** you, it prevents you from doing something. ▷ *noun* **frustration**
2. To make someone feel helpless or discouraged.
▷ *verb* **frustrating, frustrated** ▷ *adjective* **frustrated,** *adjective* **frustrating**
fry (frye) *verb* To cook food in hot fat or oil. ▷ **fries, frying, fried** ▷ *adjective* **fried**
fudge (fuhj) *noun* A sweet, rich candy made with butter, sugar, milk, and usually chocolate.
fu·el (fyoo-uhl) *noun* Something that is used as a source of heat or energy, such as coal, wood, gasoline, natural gas, etc. ▷ *verb* **fuel**
fu·gi·tive (fyoo-juh-tiv) *noun* Someone who is running away, especially from the police.
▷ *adjective* **fugitive**

> **Suffix**
> •
> The suffix **-ful** adds one of the following meanings to a root word:
> 1. Full of, as in *careful* (full of care) and *shameful* (full of shame).
> 2. Able to, as in *harmful* (able to harm).
> 3. As much as will fill, as in *cupful* (as much as will fill a cup).

ful·crum (ful-kruhm) *noun* The point on which a lever rests or turns. The support on which a seesaw balances acts as a fulcrum. ▷ *noun, plural* **fulcrums** or **fulcra** (ful-kruh)
ful·fill (ful-fil) *verb*
1. To perform or to do what is needed. *Toni fulfilled her duty and did the dishes.*
2. If you **fulfill** a need, a wish, or an ambition, you satisfy it. *The club fulfills a need for after-school activities.*
▷ *verb* **fulfilling, fulfilled** ▷ *noun* **fulfillment**

full (ful) *adjective*
1. If something is **full,** there is no room left inside it.
2. Whole or complete. *I want a full explanation.*
▷ *adverb* **fully**
3. Having a large number. *Our house was full of guests.*
▷ *adjective* **fuller, fullest**

fum·ble (fuhm-buhl) *verb*
1. To look for something in a clumsy way. *I fumbled around for my keys.*
2. To drop something or to handle it clumsily.
▷ *noun* **fumble**
▷ *verb* **fumbling, fumbled**

fume (fyoom)
1. **fumes** *noun, plural* Unpleasant or harmful gas, smoke, or vapor given off by something burning or by chemicals.
2. *verb* To be very angry. *Hector was fuming at Muriel's rudeness.* ▷ **fuming, fumed**

fun (fuhn) *noun* A good time, or something that provides enjoyment.

> ### ▶ Word History
> Years ago, some people couldn't have any **fun.** It was a fairly new word in the 18th century and not considered a word to be used by educated people. Fun may have come from the word *fon,* which meant "to make a fool of" or "to be foolish."

func·tion (fuhngk-shuhn)
1. *verb* If something **functions,** it works.
▷ **functioning, functioned**
2. *noun* A purpose, role, or job.
3. *noun* A formal social gathering, such as a wedding.

func·tion·al (fuhngk-shuh-nuhl) *adjective* If something is **functional,** it works well or is designed to work well.

fund (fuhnd)
1. *noun* Money kept for a special purpose, as in *a college fund.*
2. *noun* A supply. *This book has a fund of information on Olympic athletes.*
3. **funds** *noun, plural* Money that is ready to use. *The school lacks the funds to buy new books.*
4. *verb* If someone **funds** something, the person gives money to support it. ▷ **funding, funded**

fun·da·men·tal (fuhn-duh-men-tuhl) *adjective* Basic and necessary. *My father taught me the fundamental principles of arithmetic.* ▷ *noun, plural* **fundamentals** ▷ *adverb* **fundamentally**

fu·ner·al (fyoo-nuh-ruhl) *noun* The ceremony held after someone has died, after which the body is buried or cremated.

fun·gus (fuhn-guhss) *noun* A type of plant that has no leaves, flowers, or roots. Mushrooms and molds are both fungi. *Many fungi are extremely poisonous.* ▷ *noun, plural* **fungi** (fuhn-jye)

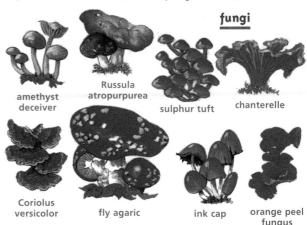

fungi

amethyst deceiver

Russula atropurpurea

sulphur tuft

chanterelle

Coriolus versicolor

fly agaric

ink cap

orange peel fungus

fun·nel (fuhn-uhl)
1. *noun* An open cone that narrows to a tube, used for pouring something into a container with a narrow neck. *See* **apparatus.**
2. *noun* A smokestack on a ship or locomotive.
3. *verb* To pour something through a funnel.
▷ **funneling, funneled**

fun·ny (fuh-nee) *adjective*
1. Amusing or humorous, as in *a funny joke.*
2. Strange. *There's a funny smell in the kitchen.*
▷ *adjective* **funnier, funniest** ▷ *adverb* **funnily**

> ### ▶ Synonyms: funny
> **Funny** describes something that causes you or other people to laugh. People, things, ideas, or situations can be funny: *Doug is a funny guy. A funny thing happened on my way to class.*
>
> **Hilarious** describes a situation so funny that people laugh almost out of control: *I thought that the movie was hilarious.*
>
> **Comical** refers to a funny person or situation: *The circus clowns offered us one comical treat after another.*
>
> **Witty** can refer to something funny or amusing through the clever use of words: *The speaker's witty remarks kept the audience listening and laughing.*
>
> **Silly** describes something foolish or lacking sense: *It was silly to eat a piece of pizza just 20 minutes before dinner.*
>
> **Laughable** describes something that turns out to be funny or causes laughter, though it was meant to be serious: *Her attempts to give the cat a bath in the tub were laughable.*

fur (fur) *noun* The soft, thick, hairy coat of an animal. **Fur** sounds like **fir**. ▷ *adjective* **furry**

fu·ri·ous (fyu-ree-uhss) *adjective*
1. Extremely angry. *I was furious when my brother yelled at my best friend.*
2. Fierce or violent, as in *a furious storm.*
▷ *adverb* **furiously**

fur·long (fur-long) *noun* A distance of 220 yards.

fur·lough (fur-loh) *noun* Time off from duty for military people.

fur·nace (fur-niss) *noun* A large enclosed metal chamber in which fuel is burned to produce heat. Furnaces are used to heat buildings or melt metals. *The picture shows how pure iron is created from iron ore in a furnace. Blasts of hot air raise the temperature of the iron mixture to the melting point, when it separates into pure iron and waste products, or slag.*

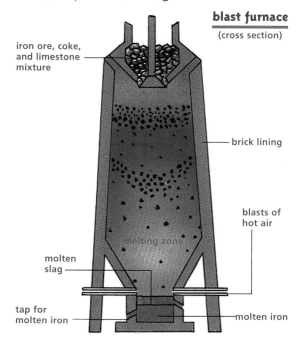

blast furnace
(cross section)

iron ore, coke, and limestone mixture

brick lining

blasts of hot air

melting zone

molten slag

tap for molten iron

molten iron

fur·nish (fur-nish) *verb*
1. To equip a room or a house with furniture.
▷ *noun, plural* **furnishings**
2. To supply something. *Can you furnish any proof of your age?*
▷ *verb* **furnishes, furnishing, furnished**

fur·ni·ture (fur-nuh-chur) *noun* The movable things such as chairs, tables, and beds that are needed in a home or an office.

fur·row (fur-oh) *noun* The groove cut by a plow when it turns over the soil.

fur·ther (fur-THur)
1. *adjective or adverb* A comparative of **far.**
2. *adverb* To a greater degree or extent. *We read no further.*

3. *adjective* Additional, as in *further information.*
4. *adverb* At a greater distance; farther.
5. *adjective* More distant or remote, as in *the further shore.*
6. *verb* To help advance or go forward. *Hard work will further your career.*

fur·ther·more (fur-THur-*mor*) *adverb* In addition, or as well.

fur·tive (fur-tiv) *adjective* Sly or sneaky, as in *a furtive glance.* ▷ *noun* **furtiveness** ▷ *adverb* **furtively**

fu·ry (fyoo-ree) *noun* Violent anger or rage.
▷ *noun, plural* **furies**

fuse (fyooz)
1. *noun* A safety device in electrical equipment that cuts off the power if something goes wrong.
2. *verb* To join two pieces of metal, plastic, etc., by heating them. ▷ **fusing, fused**
3. *noun* A cord or wick leading from a bomb that is lit to make the bomb explode.

fu·se·lage (fyoo-suh-lahzh *or* fyoo-suh-lij) *noun* The main body of an aircraft where the passengers, crew, and cargo are carried.

fu·sion (fyoo-zhuhn) *noun* The joining together of two pieces of metal, plastic, etc., caused by heating.

fuss (fuhss)
1. *verb* To be unnecessarily worried or excited about something. ▷ **fusses, fussing, fussed**
2. *noun* More talk or activity than is necessary. *Carla always makes a fuss about having visitors.*
▷ *noun, plural* **fusses**

fuss·y (fuhss-ee) *adjective*
1. Overly concerned with small details.
2. If you are a **fussy** eater, you are very particular about what you eat.
▷ *adjective* **fussier, fussiest**

fu·tile (fyoo-tuhl *or* fyoo-tile) *adjective* If an action is **futile,** it is useless and a waste of time.
▷ *noun* **futility**

fu·ton (foo-ton) *noun* A small mattress that is filled with cotton or similar material and is used on the floor or in a bed frame.

fu·ture (fyoo-chur) *noun*
1. The time to come.
2. The **future tense.**
▷ *adjective* **future**

future tense *noun* A form of a verb using "will," "be going to," or "shall" to indicate future time, as in *I will go home tomorrow.*

fuzz (fuhz) *noun* Short, soft hair or fiber.
▷ *adjective* **fuzzy**

fuzz·y (fuhz-ee) *adjective*
1. Like fuzz, or covered with fuzz.
2. Not clear or distinct, as in *a fuzzy idea.*
▷ *adjective* **fuzzier, fuzziest**

Gg

Spelling Hint: Some words that are spelled with the letter *g* are pronounced with a *g* sound as in *gate* or *go*. Some are pronounced with a *j* sound as in *gene* or *gentle*.

gab (gab) *verb* *(slang)* To chat or to gossip.

gad·get (gaj-it) *noun* A small tool that does a particular job. *We have a gadget for slicing hard-boiled eggs.*

gag (gag)
1. *verb* To tie a piece of cloth around someone's mouth in order to stop the person from talking or crying out.
2. *noun* Something put over the mouth to stop someone from making a noise.
3. *verb* If you **gag,** you feel as though you are about to choke or throw up.
4. *noun* *(informal)* A joke.
▷ *verb* **gagging, gagged**

gain (gayn)
1. *verb* To get or win something.
2. *noun* A profit, or an increase.
3. *verb* If you **gain on** someone, you start to catch up with the person.
▷ *verb* **gaining, gained**

gait (gate) *noun* A way of walking. *His gait changed from a slow walk to a trot.* **Gait** sounds like **gate.**

ga·la (gay-luh *or* gal-uh) *noun* A special event.
▷ *adjective* **gala**

gal·ax·y (gal-uhk-see)
noun A very large group of stars and planets. *This photograph of our galazy, the Milky Way, was taken from the Hubble Space Telescope.*
▷ *noun, plural* **galaxies**
▷ *adjective* **galactic**

Milky Way galaxy

gale (gale) *noun*
1. A very strong wind.
2. A noisy outburst, as in *gales of laughter.*

gal·lant (gal-uhnt) *adjective*
1. Brave and fearless.
2. Courteous and attentive.
▷ *adverb* **gallantly**

gall·blad·der (gawl-*blad*-ur) *noun* The organ in your body that stores a liquid called bile, or gall, that helps you digest food. *See* **chicken, digestion.**

gal·le·on (gal-ee-uhn) *noun* A sailing ship with three masts used in the 15th to early 18th centuries for trading and warfare.

gal·ler·y (gal-uh-ree) *noun*
1. A place where paintings, sculpture, photographs, etc., are exhibited and sometimes sold.
2. An upstairs seating area or balcony, especially in large halls and theaters.
▷ *noun, plural* **galleries**

gal·ley (gal-ee) *noun*
1. The kitchen on a boat or an airplane. *During our flight, meals were prepared in the galley. See* **aircraft, boat.**
2. A long boat with oars, used in ancient times.

gal·lon (gal-uhn) *noun* A liquid measure equal to four quarts. *If you run a shower for one minute, you use about five gallons of water.*

gal·lop (gal-uhp) *verb* When a horse **gallops,** it runs as fast as it can with all four feet leaving the ground at once. ▷ **galloping, galloped**
▷ *noun* **gallop**

gal·lows (gal-ohz) *noun* A wooden frame used in the past for hanging criminals.

ga·loot (guh-loot) *noun* *(slang)* An awkward or silly person.

gal·ore (guh-lor) *adjective* In large numbers. *There were rides galore at the fair.*

ga·losh·es (guh-losh-iz) *noun, plural* Waterproof shoes that fit over your ordinary shoes and protect them from rain and snow.

gal·va·nize (gal-vuh-nize) *verb*
1. To coat steel or iron with zinc to keep it from rusting.
2. If you **galvanize** someone into action, you shock the person into doing something.
▷ *verb* **galvanizing, galvanized**

gam·ble (gam-buhl) *verb*
1. To bet money on the outcome of a race, a game, or something that might happen.
2. To take a risk. *We gambled on the weather staying sunny all day.*
▷ *verb* **gambling, gambled** ▷ *noun* **gambler**

game (game)
1. *noun* An activity with rules that can be played by one or more people, as in *a game of tennis* or *a computer game.*
2. *noun* Wild animals, including birds, that are hunted for sport and food. *Pheasants and rabbits are two types of game.*
3. *adjective* If you are **game** to do something, you are willing to go ahead with it.
4. *adjective* Spirited and determined. ▷ *adverb* **gamely**

gan·der (gan-dur) *noun* A male goose.

gang (gang)
1. *noun* A group of people with similar interests or goals. A gang usually has a leader.
2. *noun* An organized group of criminals.
3. *verb* If several people **gang up** on you, they all turn against you. ▷ **ganging, ganged**

gang·plank (gang-*plangk*) *noun* A short bridge or piece of wood used for walking onto and off of a ship.

gan·grene (gang-**green** *or* gang-green) *noun* If someone has **gangrene,** his or her flesh decays, usually because the blood supply has been cut off to that part of the body.

gang·ster (gang-stur) *noun* A member of a criminal gang.

gang·way (gang-*way*) *noun*
1. A passageway on a ship or between buildings.
2. A gangplank.

gap (gap) *noun* A space between things.

gape (gape)
1. *verb* To open your mouth wide, usually with surprise. *The children gaped at all the presents.*
2. *verb* To open widely. *When the meteor landed, it caused a huge hole to gape in the ground.*
3. *noun* A large opening.
4. *noun* The part of a beak that opens. *See* **dolphin.**
  ▷ *verb* **gaping, gaped** ▷ *noun* **gape**

ga·rage (guh-**rahzh** *or* guh-**rahj**) *noun*
1. A building used for storing vehicles.
2. A place where cars and other vehicles are fixed. *Pam's car was towed to the garage after it broke down.*

gar·bage (gar-bij) *noun* Food or things thrown away.

gar·bled (gar-buhld) *adjective* A **garbled** message is mixed up and does not make sense.

gar·den (gard-uhn) *noun* A place where flowers, vegetables, and shrubs are grown. ▷ *noun* **gardener, noun gardening** ▷ *verb* **garden**

gar·de·nia (gar-deen-yuh) *noun* A tropical evergreen tree or bush with fragrant flowers.

gar·gle (gar-guhl) *verb* To move a liquid around your mouth without swallowing it. ▷ **gargling, gargled** ▷ *noun* **gargle**

gargoyle

gar·goyle (gar-goil) *noun* A grotesque stone head or figure carved below the roof of old buildings such as churches. Gargoyles were often used as spouts to drain water from roofs.

gar·ish (ga-rish) *adjective* Too brightly colored and overly decorated. ▷ *adverb* **garishly**

gar·land (gar-luhnd) *noun* A ring of flowers, often worn on the head.

gar·lic (gar-lik) *noun*
1. A strong-smelling plant related to an onion.
2. The strong-tasting bulb of the garlic plant, used in cooking to add flavor.

gar·ment (gar-muhnt) *noun* A piece of clothing.

gar·net (gar-nit) *noun* A dark red stone worn as jewelry or used as an abrasive.

gar·nish (gar-nish) *verb* To decorate food with small amounts of other food or spices. *The chef garnished the fish with lemon wedges.*
  ▷ **garnishes, garnishing, garnished** ▷ *noun* **garnish**

gar·ri·son (ga-ruh-suhn) *noun* A group of soldiers based in a town and ready to defend it. ▷ *verb* **garrison**

gar·ter (gar-tur) *noun* A piece of elastic worn around the top of a sock or stocking to keep it from slipping down.

garter snake *noun* A small, brown or green snake with yellow stripes on its back. A garter snake is not poisonous.

gas (gass) *noun*
1. A substance, such as air, that will spread to fill any space that contains it. *See* **molecule.**
  ▷ *adjective* **gaseous** (gass-ee-uhss *or* gash-uhss)
2. A substance that is used as a source of energy. Gas can be made from coal and can also be found underground.
3. A liquid fuel used in many vehicles. **Gas** is short for **gasoline.**
  ▷ *noun, plural* **gases**

gash (gash) *noun* A long, deep cut. *I've got a nasty gash on my knee.* ▷ *noun, plural* **gashes**
  ▷ *verb* **gash**

gas mask *noun* A mask that fits over the whole face to keep a person from breathing poisonous gas.

gas·o·hol (gass-uh-*hawl*) *noun* A motor-vehicle fuel made of about 90 percent gasoline and ten percent grain alcohol.

gas·o·line (gass-uh-**leen**) *noun* A liquid fuel made from oil, which is used in many vehicles. Also called gas.

gasp (gasp) *verb*
1. To take in breath suddenly because you are surprised, in pain, or have exercised heavily.
  ▷ *noun* **gasp**
2. To speak while out of breath. *"Help!" the boy gasped as he waved to the firefighter.*
  ▷ *verb* **gasping, gasped**

gas station *noun* A place that sells gasoline, oil, and other things needed to keep motor vehicles running. Most gas stations also have mechanics who do repairs.

G

gas·tric (gass-trik) *adjective* To do with the stomach, as in *gastric juices.*

gate (gate) *noun*
1. A frame or barrier that can be opened and closed.
2. The number of people paying to see a game, a sporting event, or a performance, such as a concert.
Gate sounds like **gait.**

gate-crash·er (krash-ur) *noun* Someone who goes to a party he or she was not invited to or to a performance without paying for a ticket.
▷ *verb* **gate-crash**

gate·way (gate-*way*) *noun*
1. An opening through which you can enter by a gate.
2. A way to get something you want. *Learning is a gateway to fulfillment and happiness.*
3. A place where people enter a country. *Miami has become a gateway to the United States for many Latin American people.*

gath·er (gaTH-ur) *verb*
1. To collect or pick things. *We gathered blackberries from the bushes beside the road.*
2. To come together in a group. *A large crowd gathered.*
3. To discover or learn something. *I gather we're not welcome here.*
4. To gain little by little. *The tornado gathered force as it approached.*
▷ *verb* **gathering, gathered**

gaud·y (gaw-dee) *adjective* If someone's clothing is **gaudy,** it is too brightly colored, and if someone's jewelry is **gaudy,** it is too showy.
▷ **gaudier, gaudiest**

gauge (gayj)
1. *verb* To judge something or make a guess about it. *We tried to gauge people's reaction to the plan.* ▷ **gauging, gauged**
2. *noun* An instrument for measuring something, as in *a pressure gauge.* ▷ *verb* **gauge**
3. *noun* A set measurement, such as the distance between two rails of a railroad track.

gaunt (gawnt) *adjective* Very thin and bony. *Mr. López has lost so much that he looks gaunt.*

gaunt·let (gawnt-lit) *noun*
A long, protective glove. In the past, gauntlets were worn by soldiers to prevent injury from weapons. *This pair of leather gauntlets was worn by a soldier in the 17th century.*

gauntlets

gauze (gawz) *noun* A very thin woven cloth used as a bandage.

gav·el (gav-uhl) *noun* A small, wooden mallet used to signal the beginning of a meeting or to call for quiet. A gavel is used by an auctioneer or a judge.

gay (gay) *adjective*
1. Happy and lively.
2. Decorated with bright colors.
▷ *adjective* **gayer, gayest** ▷ *adverb* **gaily**

gaze (gayz) *verb* To look at something steadily. *We gazed in wonder as the sun rose.* ▷ **gazing, gazed** ▷ *noun* **gaze**

ga·zelle (guh-zel) *noun* A graceful antelope found in Africa and Asia. The gazelle can run very fast.

ga·zet·teer (gaz-uh-tihr) *noun* A dictionary that lists names of places, rivers, oceans, and mountains alphabetically; a geographical dictionary.

gear (gihr)
1. **gears** *noun, plural* A set of wheels with teeth that fit together and pass on or change the movement of a machine. *The diagram below shows how gears work. The arrows show the direction of movement.*
2. *noun* Equipment or clothing, as in *hiking gear.*
3. *verb* To make suitable. *The lecture was geared to eight-year-olds.* ▷ **gearing, geared**

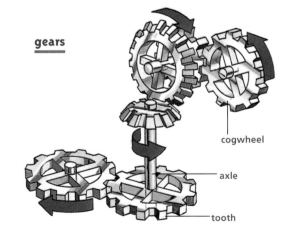

gears

cogwheel

axle

tooth

gear·shift (gihr-*shift*) *noun* A handle used to change gears in the transmission of a vehicle.

Gei·ger counter (gye-gur) *noun* An instrument that finds and measures radioactivity.

gel (jel) *noun* A thick, jellylike substance, as in *hair gel.* **Gel** sounds like **jell.**

gel·a·tin *or* **gel·a·tine** (jel-uh-tuhn) *noun* A clear substance used in making jelly, desserts, and glue that is obtained from bones and other animal tissues.

ge·la·to (juh-**lah**-toh) *noun* A soft, rich, creamy Italian ice cream. ▷ *noun, plural* **gelati** (juh-**lah**-tee)

gem (jem) *noun* A precious stone, such as a diamond, a ruby, or an emerald.

gen·der (**jen**-dur) *noun*
1. The sex of a person or creature.
2. A **gender** is a category of nouns. In English we show the gender of a noun mainly by the kind of pronoun that can refer to it. Feminine nouns such as *girl* use *she,* masculine nouns such as *boy* use *he,* neuter nouns such as *table* use *it,* and common nouns such as *children* use *they.*

gene (jeen) *noun* One of the parts of the cells of all living things. Genes are passed from parents to children and determine how you look and the way you grow. ▷ *adjective* **genetic**

ge·ne·al·o·gy (*jee*-nee-al-uh-jee or *jee*-nee-**ol**-uh-jee) *noun*
1. The study of family history. ▷ *noun* **genealogist**
2. The history of a family. *The genealogy of our family is recorded in a family tree.*
▷ *noun, plural* **genealogies**

gen·e·ral (**jen**-ur-uhl)
1. *adjective* To do with everybody or everything. *I've noticed a general improvement in the class's work.*
2. *adjective* Not detailed or specialized. *The professor gave a general overview of the course.*
3. *noun* A very high-ranking officer in the army, air force, or marines. *My dad is a four-star general.*
▷ *adverb* **generally**

gen·er·al·ize (**jen**-ur-uh-lize) *verb*
1. To create a general rule from a small number of specific examples. *After grading half of the test papers, the teacher generalized that most students understood the material.*
2. To discuss something in a vague or general way.
▷ *verb* **generalizing, generalized** ▷ *noun* **generalization**

gen·er·ate (**jen**-uh-rate) *verb* To produce something. *Dan generated a lot of comments when he grew a beard.* ▷ **generating, generated**

gen·er·a·tion (*jen*-uh-ray-shuhn) *noun*
1. All the people born around the same time, as in *the younger generation.*
2. The average amount of time between the birth of parents and that of their children. A generation is said to be about 30 years.
3. The descendants from a shared ancestor.
4. The process of bringing something into being, as in *the generation of heat by the sun.*

gen·er·a·tor (**jen**-uh-*ray*-tur) *noun* A machine that produces electricity by turning a magnet inside a coil of wire.

gen·er·ic (juh-**ner**-ik) *adjective*
1. To do with a whole group or class of

something. *Folktale is a generic term that applies to myths, legends, and fairy tales.*
2. To do with a product not sold under a trademark or copyright, as in *a generic drug.*

gen·er·ous (**jen**-ur-uhss) *adjective* People who are **generous** are happy to use their time and money to help others. ▷ *noun* **generosity** (*jen*-u-**ross**-i-tee) ▷ *adverb* **generously**

gene therapy *noun* The treatment of genetic disorders by inserting healthy genes inside the cells, replacing defective genes.

ge·net·ics (juh-**net**-iks) *noun* The study of the ways that personal characteristics are passed from one generation to another through genes. *Experts in genetics may uncover the origin of some diseases.* ▷ *adjective* **genetic** ▷ *adverb* **genetically**

ge·nial (**jeen**-yuhl or **jeen**-ee-uhl) *adjective* Friendly and welcoming, as in *a genial conversation.* ▷ *noun* **geniality** ▷ *adverb* **genially**

ge·nie (**jee**-nee) *noun* In tales from the Middle East, a **genie** is a spirit who obeys the person who summons it and grants the person's wishes.

gen·ius (**jee**-nee-uhss or **jeen**-yuhss) *noun* An unusually intelligent or talented person. ▷ *noun, plural* **geniuses**

▶ **Word History**
....
Today a **genius** is a gifted person with an unusual intelligence or talent. The word genius in Latin originally referred to a protecting spirit. The ancient Romans believed that when a person was born, a spirit (genius) was born, too, to stay with and guard that person always.

gen·teel (jen-**teel**) *adjective* Extremely polite and careful in your behavior. ▷ *noun* **gentility**

gen·tile or **Gen·tile** (**jen**-tile) *noun*
1. A person who is not Jewish.
2. In the Mormon church, a person who is not Mormon.

gen·tle (**jen**-tuhl) *adjective*
1. Not rough.
2. Kind and sensitive.
3. Not extreme, as in *a gentle slope.*
▷ *adjective* **gentler, gentlest** ▷ *noun* **gentleness** ▷ *adverb* **gently**

gen·tle·man (**jen**-tuhl-muhn) *noun*
1. A polite term for a man. *"Ladies and gentlemen,"* the announcer began.
2. A man with good manners. *Alexander is quite a gentleman.*
3. A man who belongs to a high social class.
▷ *noun, plural* **gentlemen**

gen·tle·wom·an (jen-tuhl-*wu*-muhn) *noun*
1. A woman with good manners.
2. A woman who belongs to a high social class.
▷ *noun, plural* **gentlewomen**

gen·tri·fi·ca·tion (jen-truh-fuh-**kay**-shuhn) *noun*
The rebuilding of decaying neighborhoods to attract wealthier residents.

gen·u·ine (**jen**-yoo-uhn) *adjective*
1. Real and not fake, as in *a genuine diamond.*
2. Honest or true, as in *genuine love.*
▷ *adverb* **genuinely**

ge·nus (**jee**-nuhss) *noun* A group of related plants or animals. A genus usually consists of many species. ▷ *noun, plural* **genera** (**jen**-ur-uh) or **genuses**

ge·o·de·sic (*jee*-uh-**dess**-ik) *adjective* To do with the geometry of curved surfaces, as in *a geodesic dome.*

ge·og·ra·phy (jee-**og**-ruh-fee) *noun* The study of the earth, including its people, resources, climate, and physical features. ▷ *noun* **geographer** ▷ *adjective* **geographical**

ge·ol·o·gy (jee-**ol**-uh-jee) *noun* The study of the earth's layers of soil and rock. ▷ *noun* **geologist** ▷ *adjective* **geological**

ge·o·met·ric (jee-uh-**met**-rik) *adjective*
1. To do with geometry.
2. A **geometric** shape is the outside edge or surface of a figure, such as a circle, a triangle, a rectangle, a square, or a sphere.

ge·om·e·try (jee-**om**-uh-tree) *noun* The branch of mathematics that deals with lines, angles, shapes, etc. *The picture shows some instruments used in geometry.*

ge·o·ther·mal (jee-oh-**thur**-muhl) *adjective* To do with the intense heat of the internal part of the earth and its commercial use, as in *geothermal steam* or *geothermal electricity.*

ge·ra·ni·um (juh-**ray**-nee-uhm) *noun* A garden plant with thick stems and red, pink, white, or purple clusters of flowers.

ger·bil (**jur**-buhl)
noun A small, furry rodent with long feet and a long, tufted tail. Gerbils are often kept as pets.

ger·i·at·ric (jer-ee-**at**-rik) *adjective* To do with very old people, as in *a geriatric hospital.*

germ (jurm) *noun*
1. A very small living organism that can cause disease.
2. The very beginning of something, as in *the germ of an idea.*

Ger·man·ic (jer-**man**-ik) *noun* A language that scholars suppose was the parent of modern English, German, Dutch, and other related languages. ▷ *adjective* **Germanic**

German measles *noun* A contagious illness that gives you a rash and a slight fever.

German shepherd *noun* A breed of large dog with pointed ears, a narrow nose, and black, brown, or gray fur.

ger·mi·nate (**jur**-muh-nate) *verb* When seeds or beans **germinate,** they start to grow shoots and roots. ▷ **germinating, germinated**

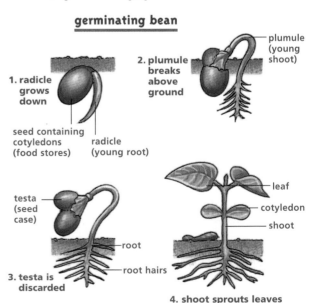

gerbil with babies

geometry instruments

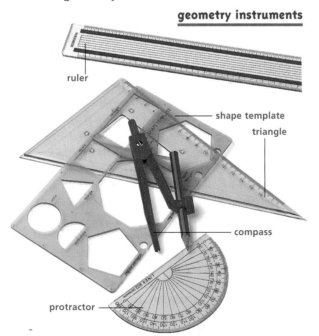

ruler
shape template
triangle
compass
protractor

germinating bean

1. radicle grows down
seed containing cotyledons (food stores)
radicle (young root)
2. plumule breaks above ground
plumule (young shoot)
testa (seed case)
root
3. testa is discarded
root hairs
leaf
cotyledon
shoot
4. shoot sprouts leaves

ges·tic·u·late (jess-tik-yuh-late) *verb* To indicate something by waving your hands about in an excited or angry way. *The two drivers gesticulated wildly as they argued over who caused the accident.* ▷ **gesticulating, gesticulated** ▷ *noun* **gesticulation**

ges·ture (jess-chur)
1. *verb* To move your head or hands in order to communicate a feeling or an idea. *The teacher gestured to Nikki that she should sit down.*
▷ **gesturing, gestured** ▷ *noun* **gesture**
2. *noun* An action that shows a feeling. *I sent Maria flowers as a gesture of friendship.*

get (get) *verb*
1. To obtain something. *Please get me a newspaper on your way home.*
2. To capture. *The police got the intruder as he was running from the scene of the crime.*
3. To become. *The puddle got bigger the more it rained.*
4. To arrive somewhere. *We got home a little after midnight.*
5. get by To manage with very little money. *Somehow we'll get by.*
6. To become sick with. *I could tell that Andy was getting the flu by how much he was sniffling.*
▷ *verb* **getting, got** (got) or **gotten** (got-in)

> ### ▶Synonyms: get
> ●
>
> **Get** is the general word that means to come to have something: *For my birthday, I hope to get a new bike. If you don't take care of yourself, you'll get a cold.*
>
> **Obtain** means to get something, usually after some effort: *The concert was sold out, but we were finally able to obtain tickets.*
>
> **Acquire** also is used when there is effort involved in getting something: *Tracy plans to acquire as many souvenirs of her vacation as she can.*
>
> **Receive** is used when you get something from someone else: *I think I will receive at least three CDs for my birthday.*
>
> **Gain** means to get something, usually as the result of cleverness or hard work: *My uncle has gained a fortune by investing carefully in real estate.*
>
> **Win** means to get something in spite of obstacles or competition: *The politician needs 1,000 more votes to win the election.*

get·a·way (get-uh-*way*) *noun* A fast escape from a situation, especially a crime. *Their getaway was quick and clean.*

gey·ser (gye-zur) *noun* A hole in the ground through which hot water and steam shoot up in bursts. *Geysers are found in volcanic areas where water is heated to the boiling point underground and then forced upward.*

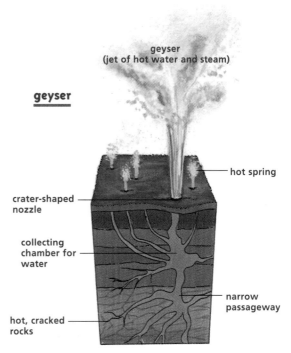

geyser

geyser
(jet of hot water and steam)

hot spring

crater-shaped nozzle

collecting chamber for water

narrow passageway

hot, cracked rocks

ghast·ly (gast-lee) *adjective*
1. Horrible, as in *a ghastly crime.*
2. *(informal)* Very bad or unpleasant, as in *a ghastly party.*
3. If you feel or look **ghastly,** you feel or look very ill.
▷ *adjective* **ghastlier, ghastliest**

ghet·to (get-oh) *noun* A usually poor neighborhood in a city where people of the same race, religion, or ethnic background live.
▷ *noun, plural* **ghettos** or **ghettoes**

ghost (gohst) *noun* A spirit of a dead person believed to haunt people or places.

ghost·ly (gohst-lee) *adjective* To do with ghosts, as in *a ghostly figure.*

ghost town *noun* A deserted town. There were many ghost towns in the American West after nearby gold and silver mines closed down.

GI (gee eye) *noun* An American soldier. GI is short for *Government Issue.*

gi·ant (jye-uhnt)
1. *noun* In folktales and fairy tales, a **giant** is a very large and strong creature.
2. *adjective* Very large, as in *giant size.*

gib·ber·ish (jib-ur-ish) *noun* Uncontrolled speech that does not make sense.

gib·bon (gib-uhn) *noun* A small ape with long, slender arms and no tail. Gibbons live mainly in southeast Asia.

gid·dy (gid-ee) *adjective* If you feel **giddy,** you feel dizzy and unsteady, either because you are ill or because you are excited. ▷ **giddier, giddiest** ▷ *noun* **giddiness** ▷ *adverb* **giddily**

gift (gift) *noun*
1. A present.
2. A special talent. *Vincent has a gift for painting.* ▷ *adjective* **gifted**

gig (gig) *noun* (informal) A booking for a musician or a band to play rock, jazz, etc., in public; a job.

gi·gan·tic (jye-gan-tik) *adjective* Huge, or enormous. ▷ *adverb* **gigantically**

gig·gle (gig-uhl) *verb* To laugh in a nervous or silly way. ▷ **giggling, giggled** ▷ *noun* **giggle** ▷ *adjective* **giggly**

gild (gild) *verb* To coat something with a thin layer of gold or gold paint. *She gilded the mirror frame.* ▷ **gilding, gilded**

gill (gil) *noun* The organ on a fish's side through which it breathes. *The gill filaments are filled with blood. As water flows over them, oxygen from the water passes into the blood, and carbon dioxide from the blood passes into the water. See also* **fish.**

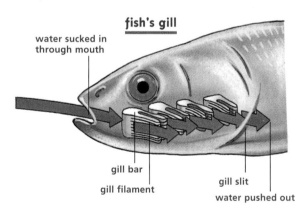

fish's gill

water sucked in through mouth

gill bar
gill filament
gill slit
water pushed out

gilt (gilt) *adjective* A **gilt** object is decorated with a thin coating of gold or gold paint. **Gilt** sounds like **guilt.**

gim·mick (gim-ik) *noun* A clever gadget, trick, or idea used to get people's attention.

gin (jin) *noun* A strong alcoholic drink made from grain and juniper berries.

gin·ger (jin-jur) *noun*
1. A plant root used to give a hot, spicy flavor to food and drink.
2. A reddish brown color. ▷ *adjective* **ginger,** *adjective* **gingery**

gin·ger·bread (jin-jur-*bred*) *noun* A cake or cookie flavored with ginger and other spices.

gin·ger·ly (jin-jur-lee) *adverb* Cautiously and carefully. *The new mother picked up her baby and placed him gingerly in his crib.*

ging·ham (ging-uhm) *noun* Checked cotton cloth.

gi·raffe (juh-raf) *noun* An African mammal with a very long neck and legs and dark spots on its coat. The giraffe is the tallest animal in the world.

giraffes

gird·er (gur-dur) *noun* A large, heavy beam made of steel or concrete, used in construction. *See* **oil rig.**

girl (gurl) *noun* A female child or young woman.

girl·friend (gurl-*frend*) *noun*
1. The girl or woman with whom someone is having a romantic relationship.
2. A female friend.

girth (gurth) *noun* The measurement around something. *The girth of that tree is huge.*

gist (jist) *noun* The main part of something. *What was the gist of her speech?*

give (giv) *verb*
1. To hand something to another person.
2. To pay. *What will you give me for this beautiful vase?*
3. To supply. *The new lamp gave us more light.*
4. To offer. *We gave thanks that the rain finally stopped.*
5. To cause to happen. *The blizzard gave the students an unexpected vacation.*
▷ *verb* **giving, gave** (gayv), **given** (giv-in)

gla·cier (glay-shur) *noun* A huge sheet of ice found in mountain valleys or polar regions. A glacier is formed when snow falls and does not melt because the temperature remains below freezing.

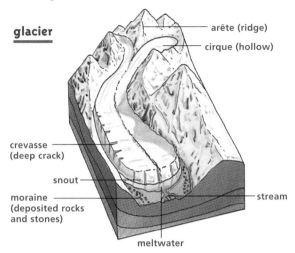

glacier

arête (ridge)

cirque (hollow)

crevasse (deep crack)

snout

moraine (deposited rocks and stones)

stream

meltwater

glad (glad) *adjective* Pleased or happy. ▷ **gladder, gladdest** ▷ *noun* **gladness** ▷ *verb* **gladden** ▷ *adverb* **gladly**

glade (glade) *noun* An open, grassy space in the middle of a wood or forest.

glad·i·a·tor (glad-ee-ay-tur) *noun* A warrior of ancient Rome who fought against other warriors or fierce animals in order to entertain the public. *The picture shows a fight between two types of gladiators.* See **amphitheater.**

gladiators

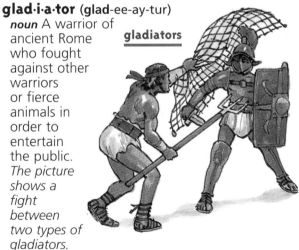

glad·i·o·lus (glad-ee-oh-luhss) *noun* A plant with a long, leafy stalk and white or brightly colored flowers. ▷ *noun, plural* **gladioli** (glad-ee-oh-lye)

glam·or·ous (glam-ur-uhss) *adjective* Attractive and exciting. *Many people consider modeling to be a very glamorous profession.*

glam·our *or* **glam·or** (glam-ur) *noun* Fashion, charm, or appeal.

glance (glanss) *verb*
1. To look at something very briefly. *Connie glanced at her watch before hurrying off to her next class.* ▷ *noun* **glance**
2. To hit something and slide off at an angle. *The ball Josh threw glanced off the backboard into the net.*
▷ *verb* **glancing, glanced** ▷ *adjective* **glancing**

gland (gland) *noun* An organ in the body that either produces natural chemicals or allows substances to leave the body, such as sweat glands. ▷ *adjective* **glandular** (glan-juh-lur)

glare (glair)
1. *noun* Very bright light that dazzles. ▷ *verb* **glare**
2. *verb* To look at someone in a very angry way. *All Sue has to do is glare at her little brother, and he starts to cry.* ▷ **glaring, glared** ▷ *noun* **glare**

glar·ing (glair-ing) *adjective*
1. Very bright and gaudy, as in *glaring colors.*
2. Very obvious, as in *a glaring error.*
▷ *adverb* **glaringly**

glass (glass) *noun*
1. A transparent material made from melted sand, used in windows, bottles, and lenses. *The picture shows two 16th-century craftsmen blowing glass.*
2. A container for drinking, made from glass or plastic. ▷ *noun, plural* **glasses**

glass-blowing

glass·es (glass-iz) *noun, plural* Lenses set in frames, worn to improve a person's eyesight.

glaze (glayz)
1. *noun* A thin coat of liquid painted on pottery before it is fired to give it a shiny finish.
2. *verb* To put glass into a window.
3. *verb* If your eyes **glaze over,** they look fixed and vacant because you are tired or bored.
▷ *verb* **glazing, glazed** ▷ *adjective* **glazed**

gla·zier (glay-zhur) *noun* A person who puts glass into windows.

gleam (gleem)
1. *verb* To shine. *Her face gleamed with happiness.* ▷ **gleaming, gleamed** ▷ *noun* **gleam**
2. *noun* A beam of light.

glee (glee) *noun* Enjoyment and delight. *The children laughed with glee at the clown's silly pranks.* ▷ *adjective* **gleeful** ▷ *adverb* **gleefully**

glen (glen) *noun* A narrow valley.

glide (glide) *verb* To move smoothly and easily. *The swan glided down the stream.* ▷ **gliding, glided** ▷ *noun* **glide**

glid·er (glye-dur) *noun* A very light aircraft that flies by floating and rising on air currents instead of by engine power.

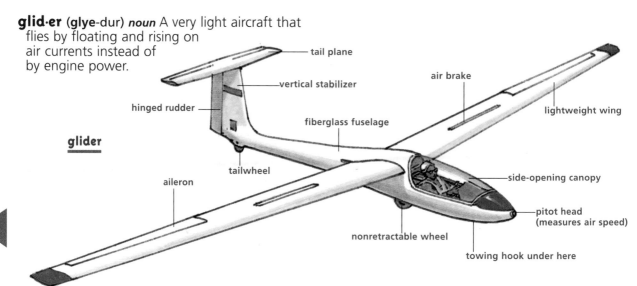

glider

tail plane

vertical stabilizer

hinged rudder

air brake

lightweight wing

fiberglass fuselage

aileron

tailwheel

side-opening canopy

pitot head (measures air speed)

nonretractable wheel

towing hook under here

glim·mer (glim-ur)
1. *verb* To shine faintly. *Stars glimmered in the sky.* ▷ **glimmering, glimmered** ▷ *noun* **glimmer**
2. *noun* A trace, as in *a glimmer of hope.*

glimpse (glimps) *verb* To see something very briefly. ▷ **glimpsing, glimpsed** ▷ *noun* **glimpse**

glint (glint)
1. *verb* To sparkle, or to flash. ▷ **glinting, glinted**
2. *noun* If you have a **glint in your eye,** you are secretly amused or excited about something.

glis·ten (gliss-uhn) *verb* To shine in a sparkling way. ▷ **glistening, glistened**

glitch (glich) *noun (informal)* Any sudden thing that goes wrong or causes a problem, usually with machinery, as in *a computer glitch.*

glit·ter (glit-ur) *verb* To sparkle with many tiny lights or reflections. ▷ **glittering, glittered**

gloat (gloht) *verb* To delight in your own good luck or someone else's bad luck. ▷ **gloating, gloated**

global warming *noun* An apparent gradual rise in the temperature of the earth's atmosphere, caused by the greenhouse effect. *See* **greenhouse effect.**

globe (glohb) *noun*
1. The world. ▷ *adjective* **global**
2. A round model of the world.
3. Anything shaped like a round ball. ▷ *adjective* **globular** (glob-yuh-lur)

glock·en·spiel (glok-uhn-speel) *noun* A musical instrument with metal plates of different sizes on a frame, which are struck to give different notes.

gloom (gloom) *noun*
1. A sense of hopelessness.
2. A dark and depressing atmosphere.

gloom·y (gloo-mee) *adjective*
1. Dull and dark, as in *a gloomy dungeon.*

2. If you are **gloomy,** you feel sad and pessimistic. ▷ *adjective* **gloomier, gloomiest**

glo·ri·fy (glor-uh-fye) *verb*
1. To praise or treat as very important or splendid. *She glorified her past with many untrue stories.*
2. To honor or promote the glory of. *This hymn glorifies God.*
▷ *verb* **glorifies, glorifying, glorified**

glo·ry (glor-ee) *noun*
1. Great fame or honor, as in *the glory of victory.*
2. Something that brings great fame or honor. *My child is my glory.*
3. Splendor or magnificence, as in *the glory of sunrise.*
▷ *noun, plural* **glories** ▷ *adjective* **glorious**

gloss (gloss *or* glawss) *noun* A shine on a surface. ▷ *noun, plural* **glosses** ▷ *adjective* **glossy**

glos·sa·ry (gloss-uh-ree) *noun* A **glossary** explains the meaning of technical or specialized words and phrases used in a book. ▷ *noun, plural* **glossaries**

glove (gluhv) *noun*
1. A warm or protective hand covering that has separate parts for the thumb and fingers.
2. A leather covering for the hand worn by players of sports such as boxing and baseball.

glow (gloh)
1. *verb* If something **glows,** it gives off a steady, low light, often because it is hot.
2. *noun* A light from something that glows.
3. *verb* To show a color suggesting brightness, warmth, or health.
4. *noun* A bright, warm, or healthy color. *There was a glow on her cheeks.*
5. *verb* To show a warm feeling. *He glowed with contentment.*
▷ *verb* **glowing, glowed** ▷ *adjective* **glowing**

G

glow·er (glou-ur) *verb* To stare angrily at someone. ▷ **glowering, glowered** ▷ *noun* **glower**

glow·worm (gloh-*wurm*) *noun* The larva of a firefly, or an adult firefly that does not have wings.

glu·cose (gloo-kose) *noun* A natural sugar found in plants that gives energy to living things.

glue (gloo) *noun* A substance used to make one surface stick to another. ▷ *verb* **glue**

glum (gluhm) *adjective* Gloomy and miserable. ▷ **glummer, glummest** ▷ *adverb* **glumly**

glut (gluht) *noun* If there is a **glut** of something, there is too much of it.

glut·ton (gluht-uhn) *noun* A person who is greedy, especially for food. ▷ *noun* **gluttony** ▷ *adjective* **gluttonous**

gnarled (narld) *adjective* Twisted and lumpy with age, as in *a gnarled oak tree.*

gnash (nash) *verb* If you **gnash** your teeth, you grind them together in anger or grief. ▷ **gnashes, gnashing, gnashed**

gnat (nat) *noun* A small insect with two wings that bites.

gnaw (naw) *verb* To keep biting on something. *The dog gnawed the bone.* ▷ **gnawing, gnawed**

gnome (nome) *noun* In folktales and fairy tales, **gnomes** are dwarflike old men.

gnu (noo) *noun* A kind of antelope that has a large head like an ox, curved horns, and a long tail. The gnu lives in Africa. **Gnu** sounds like **new**. ▷ *noun, plural* **gnus** *or* **gnu**

go (goh)
1. *verb* To move away from or toward a place. *After school I will go straight home.*
2. *verb* To work properly. *This machine won't go.*
3. *verb* To pass. *Spring has gone.*
4. *verb* To have a certain place. *That picture goes on the kitchen wall.*
5. *verb* If you are **going to** do something, you will do it in the future.
6. *verb* To be suitable. *Pie and ice cream go well together.*
7. *verb* To turn out. *How did the exam go?*
8. *adjective* Ready to happen. *All systems are go.*
▷ *verb* **goes, going, went** (went), **gone** (gon)

goad (gohd) *verb* To tease or urge someone into doing something. ▷ **goading, goaded**

goal (gohl) *noun*
1. A frame with a net into which you aim a ball in sports such as soccer and hockey.
2. When you score a **goal** in a game, you send a ball or puck into or through a goal.
3. Something that you aim for. *Shelly's goal is to go to medical school.*

goal·ie (goh-lee) *noun* Someone who guards the goal in soccer or hockey to keep the other team

from scoring. *See* **ice hockey, soccer.**

goal·keep·er (gohl-*keep*-ur) *noun* A goalie.

goat (goht) *noun* An animal with horns and a beard. Some goats are raised on farms for their milk.

goa·tee (goh-tee) *noun* A beard grown around the mouth and chin.

gob·ble (gob-uhl) *verb*
1. To eat food quickly and greedily.
2. To make the sound a turkey makes.
▷ *verb* **gobbling, gobbled**

gob·let (gob-lit) *noun* A tall drinking container with a stem and a base.

gob·lin (gob-luhn) *noun* In fairy tales, **goblins** are small, unpleasant, ugly creatures.

go-cart *noun* A very low, small, open vehicle built for racing.

God (god) *noun*
1. In Christianity, Islam, and Judaism, **God** is the creator and ruler of the universe.
2. **god** A supernatural being who is worshiped.

god·dess (god-iss) *noun* A female supernatural being who is worshiped. *The picture shows some ancient Egyptian gods and goddesses.*

Egyptian gods and goddesses

Ma'at

Re

Horus

Anubis

Osiris

Hathor

Amun

Isis

god·par·ent (god-*pair*-uhnt) *noun* Someone who promises his or her support for a child when the child is baptized into the Christian religion.

gog·gles (gog-uhlz) *noun, plural* Special glasses that fit tightly around your eyes to protect them.

gold (gohld) *noun*
1. A precious metal used in jewelry and sometimes for money. *See* **mineral.**
2. A warm, yellow color.
▷ *adjective* **gold,** *adjective* **golden**

gold·en·rod (gohld-uhn-*rod*) *noun* A tall, wild plant with many small, yellow flowers. Goldenrods bloom in late summer and in the fall.

gold·finch (gohld-*finch*) *noun* A small bird that looks very much like a canary. The male goldfinch is yellow with black markings. ▷ *noun, plural* **goldfinches**

gold·fish (gohld-*fish*) *noun* An orange-colored fish often kept in ponds and aquariums. ▷ *noun, plural* **goldfish** *or* **goldfishes**

golf (golf) *noun* A game in which players use clubs to hit a small white ball around a special course and into a hole. A golf course has either 9 or 18 holes. *The picture shows four types of clubs used for playing golf: a wood for hitting the ball long distances; an iron for medium- to short-range shots; a wedge for lifting the ball high in the air; and a putter for tapping the ball into the hole.* ▷ *noun* **golfer,** *noun* **golfing** ▷ *verb* **golf**

<u>golf equipment</u>

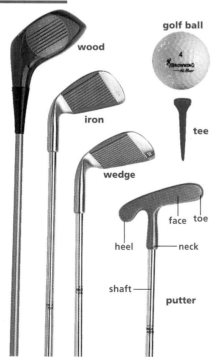

golf ball

wood

iron

tee

wedge

face   toe

heel   neck

shaft

putter

gon·do·la (gon-duh-luh) *noun*
1. A light boat with high, pointed ends, used on the canals of Venice, Italy. Gondolas are moved through the water using a single oar.
2. A railroad freight car with low sides and no roof.
3. A compartment under a hot-air balloon or a blimp.

Venetian gondola

gong (gong) *noun* A disk of metal that makes a hollow, echoing sound when it is hit with a hammer.

good (gud) *adjective*
1. Well-behaved. *Cynthia is such a good girl.*
2. Fit and well. *I'm feeling good today.*
3. Of high quality, as in *a good piece of furniture.*
4. Useful. *This pencil is good for drawing.*
5. Clever or skillful, as in *a good hitter.*
6. Kind or helpful, as in *good to animals.*
7. If you **make good** at something, you are doing well at it.
▷ *adjective* **better, best** ▷ *noun* **good**

▶ **Synonyms: good**

Good is the opposite of *bad* in most of its meanings. Sometimes good is just the right word: *The man did a good deed when he returned the lost dog to its owner. She is a good friend.* Other times you can find more colorful words to describe things that are "good."

Enjoyable can describe something good that is extremely pleasant: *We had an enjoyable time when we visited our cousins.*

Excellent describes something of very good quality, with no faults or mistakes: *That was an excellent meal.*

Capable can describe a person who is good at doing something: *He's a capable chess player.*

Well-behaved describes a person who has good manners: *Ms. Stuart's well-behaved students were rewarded with a trip to the museum.*

Tasty means full of good flavor: *For Mother's Day, Brian and Emma served their mom a tasty breakfast of pancakes and fruit.*

good-bye or **good-by** *interjection* A word said to someone who is leaving.

Good Friday *noun* A date commemorated by Christian religions as the day Jesus died on the cross; the Friday before Easter.

good-na·tured (nay-churd) *adjective* Pleasant and generally warm and kind.

good·ness (gud-niss) *noun* Generosity or kindness.

goods (gudz) *noun, plural* Things that are sold, or things that someone owns, as in *leather goods* or *household goods.*

good·will (gud-wil) *noun*
1. Kindness or cheerfulness.
2. The value a business has because of a good relationship with its customers.

goo·ey (goo-ee) *adjective* (informal) Sticky. ▷ **gooier, gooiest** ▷ *noun* **gooeyness**

goose (gooss) *noun* A large bird with a long neck and webbed feet. ▷ *noun, plural* **geese** (geess)

Canada goose

goose bumps *noun, plural* Tiny bumps on your skin that appear when you are cold or frightened.

go·pher (goh-fur) *noun* A small, furry animal related to the squirrel that lives underground. The gopher can be found throughout North America.

gore (gor)
1. *noun* Clotted blood.
2. *verb* If someone is **gored** by a bull, the person is pierced by its horns. ▷ **goring, gored**

gorge (gorj)
1. *noun* A deep valley with steep, rocky sides. *See* **river.**
2. *verb* If you **gorge** yourself, you stuff yourself with food. ▷ **gorging, gorged**

gor·geous (gor-juhss) *adjective* Really beautiful or attractive.

go·ril·la (guh-ril-uh) *noun* A very large, strong ape with dark fur found in Africa. **Gorilla** sounds like **guerrilla.**

gor·y (gor-ee) *adjective* If something is **gory,** it involves a lot of blood. ▷ **gorier, goriest**

gos·pel (goss-puhl) *noun*
1. The teachings of Jesus.

2. **Gospel** One of the first four books in the New Testament of the Bible. The gospels describe the life and teachings of Jesus.
3. If you **take something as gospel,** you believe it to be completely true.

gos·sa·mer (goss-uh-mur) *noun* A very delicate film of spiders' webs.

gos·sip (goss-ip) *noun*
1. A person who likes to talk about other people's personal business.
2. Idle talk about other people's personal business.
▷ *verb* **gossip**

> ### Word History
>
> A **gossip** was not always a nosy person. In Old English the word was *godsibb* and it referred to a godparent (from *god* "god" and *sibb* "relative"). It later came to refer to a friend or companion. We all know that friends like to talk, and gossip has come to mean someone who talks about others, or the idle talk of such people.

Goth·ic (goth-ik) *adjective* In the style of art or architecture used in western Europe between the 12th and 16th centuries. Gothic buildings have pointed arches and windows. *See* **arch.**

gouge (gouj)
1. *noun* A tool used to make deep impressions in wood or other hard materials.
2. *noun* A deep cut caused by such a tool or other object.
3. *verb* To cut something deeply with a tool that has a sharp edge.
4. *verb* To cheat or steal from someone.
▷ *verb* **gouging, gouged**

gourd (gord) *noun* A fruit with a rounded shape similar to that of a squash or pumpkin. Gourds are sometimes used for decoration and to make bowls or jugs.

gour·met (gor-may) *noun* An expert on food and wine. ▷ *adjective* **gourmet**

gov·ern (guhv-urn) *verb* To control a country, organization, etc., using laws. ▷ **governing, governed** ▷ *noun* **governor**

gov·ern·ment (guhv-urn-muhnt) *noun*
1. The control and administration of a country, state, or organization.
2. The people who rule or govern a country or state.
▷ *adjective* **governmental**

gown (goun) *noun*
1. A woman's dress, as in *a wedding gown.*
2. A loose robe worn by judges and surgeons and by students at their graduation ceremonies.

G

GP (jee pee) *noun* A family doctor who treats common illnesses and refers patients to specialists if necessary. GP is short for *general practitioner.*

grab (grab) *verb* To take hold of something suddenly and roughly. *I grabbed the handrail as I tripped on the stairs.* ▷ **grabbing, grabbed**

grace (grayss) *noun*
1. An elegant way of moving. *Anna moves with a dancer's grace.* ▷ *adjective* **graceful** ▷ *adverb* **gracefully**
2. Pleasant behavior. *Edward accepted my apology with grace.* ▷ *adjective* **gracious (gray-shuhss)** ▷ *adverb* **graciously**
3. A short prayer of thanks that is said before a meal.

grack·le (grak-uhl) *noun* A bird with a long tail and shiny black feathers; a type of blackbird. *The common grackle, shown here, can often be seen in city parks.*

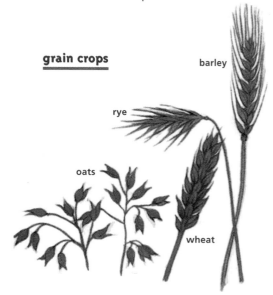
grackle

grade (grayd)
1. *noun* A mark given for work done in school. *I got a good grade in spelling last week.* ▷ *verb* **grade**
2. *noun* Quality. *The dress material was a silk of the highest grade.*
3. *noun* A class or year in a school.
4. *verb* To make more level, as in *to grade a side street.* ▷ **grading, graded**
5. *noun* The amount of slope on a road, as in *a steep grade.*

grade school *noun* An elementary school or a grammar school.

gra·di·ent (gray-dee-uhnt) *noun* A slope, or the steepness of a slope; a sloping surface.

grad·u·al (graj-yoo-uhl) *adjective* If an event is **gradual,** it takes place slowly but steadily. ▷ *adverb* **gradually**

grad·u·ate
1. **(graj-oo-it)** *noun* Someone who has completed the last year in a school and has received a diploma.
2. **(graj-oo-ate)** *verb* To finish a course of study in a school and receive a diploma.
3. **(graj-oo-ate)** *verb* To mark something such as a cup or a stick with lines so that you can measure with it.
▷ *verb* **graduating, graduated** ▷ *noun* **graduation**

graf·fi·ti (gruh-fee-tee) *noun, plural* Pictures drawn or words written on the walls of buildings, on subway cars, or on other surfaces.

graft (graft)
1. *noun* The taking of money dishonestly as a member of a government.
2. *noun* Money taken dishonestly.
3. *verb* To take the skin from one part of the body to help repair an injury to another part. *Surgeons grafted skin from Dean's leg to his burned face.*
4. *verb* To plant a shoot from one plant into a slit in another so that they grow as one.
▷ *noun* **graft** ▷ *verb* **grafting, grafted**

grain (grayn) *noun*
1. A very small particle, as in *a grain of salt.*
2. Cereal plants.
3. The seed of a cereal plant.

grain crops

barley

rye

oats

wheat

gram (grahm) *noun* A unit of measurement equal to one thousandth of a kilogram. A nickle weighs about five grams.

gram·mar (gram-ur) *noun* The rules of speaking or writing a language. ▷ *adjective* **grammatical**

grammar school *noun* A school that children attend from kindergarten through fifth or sixth grade.

gra·na·ry (gray-nuh-ree *or* **gran-uh-ree)** *noun* A building for storing grain. ▷ *noun, plural* **granaries**

grand (grand) *adjective*
1. Large and impressive, as in *the grand ballroom.*
2. Very worthy or dignified, as in *the grand lady.*
3. *(informal)* Wonderful. *We had a grand time.*
4. Complete. *The book fair took in a grand total of $1,000.*
▷ *adjective* **grander, grandest** ▷ *adverb* **grandly**

grand·child (grand-*childe*) *noun* You are the grandchild of your parents' parents. ▷ *noun, plural* **grandchildren**

grand·fa·ther (grand-*fah*-THur) *noun* The father of your mother or father.

grandfather clock *noun* A clock built into the top of a tall, narrow, usually wooden cabinet.

grand jury *noun* A group of people that meet to decide if there is enough evidence to try someone for a crime. ▷ *noun, plural* **grand juries**

grand·moth·er (grand-*muh*-THur) *noun* The mother of your mother or father.

grand·pa·rent (grand-*pa*-ruhnt) *noun* The parent of one of your parents.

grand·stand (grand-*stand*) *noun* The main area at a ballpark or stadium with seats for spectators.

gran·ite (gran-it) *noun* A hard, gray rock used in the construction of buildings.

gra·no·la (gruh-noh-luh) *noun* A food made with grains, nuts, and dried fruit and often eaten as a breakfast cereal.

grant (grant)
1. *verb* To give something, or to allow something. *We were granted permission to leave.*
2. *noun* A sum of money given by the government or another organization for a special purpose, as in *a study grant.*
3. *verb* To accept something for the sake of argument. *I'll grant you he's a great pitcher.*
4. If you **take** something **for granted,** you do not appreciate it, or you assume that you will get it. ▷ *verb* **granting, granted**

gran·u·la·ted sugar (gran-yuh-lay-tid) *noun* Sugar that is in the form of grains or tiny particles.

grape (grayp) *noun* A small fruit that grows on a vine that can be eaten fresh, dried to make currants or raisins, or crushed to make wine. *See* **fruit.**

grape·fruit (grayp-*froot*) *noun* A large, yellow citrus fruit. *See* **fruit.**

grape·vine (grayp-*vine*) *noun*
1. A climbing plant on which grapes grow.
2. If you hear information **through the grapevine,** you hear it unofficially or as a rumor.

> ## Suffix
> •
> The suffix **-graph** adds one of these meanings to a root word:
> **1.** Something that can transmit writing or an image, as in *telegraph* and *seismograph.*
> **2.** Something that is the result of having been recorded, as in *photograph.*

graph (graf) *noun* A diagram that shows the relationship between numbers or amounts. Common graphs use bars, lines, or parts of a circle to display data.

graph·ic (graf-ik) *adjective*
1. Very realistic. *Sonia told the story in graphic detail.*
2. To do with art and design.
3. To do with handwriting, as in *graphic symbols.*

graph·ics (graf-iks) *noun, plural* Images such as drawings, maps, or graphs.

graph·ite (graf-ite) *noun* A common black or gray mineral used as lead in pencils.

grap·ple (grap-uhl) *verb*
1. To wrestle with someone.
2. If you **grapple** with a problem, you think hard about all the ways it can be solved.
▷ *verb* **grappling, grappled**

grasp (grasp) *verb*
1. To seize something and hold it tightly.
2. To understand something completely. *Have you grasped what I'm telling you?*
▷ *verb* **grasping, grasped** ▷ *noun* **grasp**

grass (grass) *noun*
1. A green plant with long, thin, erect leaves that grows wild and is used for lawns.
2. Any of several other plants, such as grains, bamboo, and sugarcane.
▷ *noun, plural* **grasses** ▷ *adjective* **grassy**

grass·hop·per (grass-*hop*-ur) *noun* An insect that eats plants and has long back legs adapted for leaping. *A grasshopper sings to other grasshoppers by rubbing the hard veins on its front wings over the tiny teeth inside its back legs.*

grasshopper

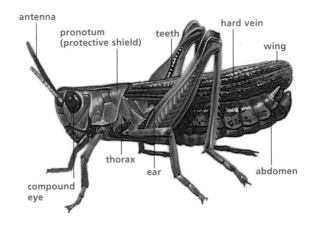

antenna
pronotum (protective shield)
teeth
hard vein
wing
thorax
ear
abdomen
compound eye

grass·land (grass-*land*) *noun* A large, open area of grass, often used as pasture for animals.

G

G

grate (grayt)
1. *verb* To shred food, such as cheese, into small, thin pieces.
2. *verb* If something **grates** on you, it annoys you.
3. *noun* A grid of metal bars in the base of a furnace or fireplace.
Grate sounds like **great**.
▷ *verb* **grating, grated**

grate·ful (grayt-fuhl) *adjective* If you are **grateful** for something that you are given, you appreciate it and are thankful for it. ▷ *adverb* **gratefully**

grat·i·fy (grat-i-fye) *verb* To give pleasure to someone by fulfilling his or her needs or desires. *The students gratified their teacher by working hard.* ▷ **gratifies, gratifying, gratified** ▷ *noun* **gratification**

grat·i·tude (grat-uh-tood) *noun* A feeling of being grateful and thankful.

grave (grayv)
1. *noun* A place where a dead person is buried.
2. *adjective* Very serious, as in *grave danger*.
▷ **graver, gravest** ▷ *adverb* **gravely**

grav·el (grav-uhl) *noun* Small, loose stones used for paths and roads.

grave·stone (grayv-stohn) *noun* A piece of carved stone that marks someone's grave.

grave·yard (grayv-yard) *noun* A piece of land, often near a church, where dead people are buried; a cemetery.

grav·i·ty (grav-uh-tee) *noun*
1. The force that pulls things down toward the surface of the earth and keeps them from floating away into space.
2. Seriousness. *The doctors told us of the gravity of Lynn's condition.*
▷ *noun, plural* **gravities**

gra·vy (gray-vee) *noun* A flavored sauce served with meat and usually made from the juices of cooked meat. ▷ *noun, plural* **gravies**

gray (gray) *noun* The color between black and white, such as the color of the sky on a rainy day. ▷ *adjective* **gray**

graze (grayz) *verb*
1. When animals **graze,** they eat grass that is growing in a field.
2. To scrape the surface off your skin. *The bullet grazed the officer's leg.* ▷ *noun* **graze**
3. To touch just barely. *The pitch grazed the batter's shirt.*
▷ *verb* **grazing, grazed**

grease (greess) *noun*
1. A thick, oily substance used on machines to help the parts move easily.
2. An oily substance found in animal fat and in hair and skin.
▷ *verb* **grease** ▷ *adjective* **greasy**

great (grayt) *adjective*
1. Very big or large. ▷ *adverb* **greatly**
2. Very important and famous. ▷ *noun* **greatness**
3. Very good, or wonderful. *We had a great time.*
Great sounds like **grate**.
▷ *adjective* **greater, greatest**

Great Dane (dayn) *noun* A very large, powerful dog with a short coat and long legs.

Great Dane

great-grandchild *noun* The son or daughter of your grandchild.

great-grandparent *noun* The father or mother of one of your grandparents.

greed (greed) *noun* Extreme selfishness; wanting everything for oneself.

greed·y (gree-dee) *adjective* If you are **greedy,** you want more of something than you need.
▷ **greedier, greediest** ▷ *adverb* **greedily**

green (green)
1. *noun* The color of grass or leaves. ▷ *adjective* **green**
2. *adjective* Not ripe, as in *green apples*.
3. *noun* An area of grass in a public place, as in *the village green*.
4. *noun* An area of ground used for an activity or sport, as in *a putting green*.
5. greens *noun, plural* Green leaves or stems used as food, as in *salad greens*.
6. *adjective* Having little experience. *The new campers were green compared with the older ones.*
▷ *adjective* **greener, greenest**

green card *noun* A permit or identification card that allows someone who is not a citizen to live and work in the United States.

green·horn (green-horn) *noun* (informal) Someone who is new to and unfamiliar with an organization, activity, or area.

green·house (green-houss) *noun* An enclosed structure used for the growth and protection of tender plants. Temperature and light are controlled in a greenhouse so that all plants can grow out of season.

greenhouse effect *noun* The warming of the atmosphere around the earth caused by gases such as carbon dioxide that collect in the atmosphere and prevent the sun's heat from escaping.

greenhouse effect

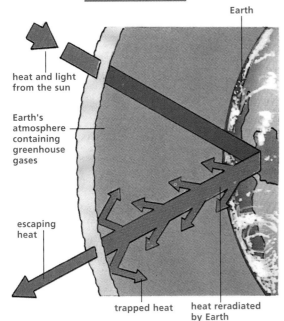

- heat and light from the sun
- Earth's atmosphere containing greenhouse gases
- escaping heat
- trapped heat
- heat reradiated by Earth
- Earth

greenhouse gases *noun, plural* Gases such as carbon dioxide and methane that are found in the earth's atmosphere and help hold heat in.

green thumb *noun* A talent for making plants grow.

greet (greet) *verb*
1. To say something friendly or welcoming to someone when you meet him or her. ▷ *noun* **greeting, noun greeter**
2. To react to something in a particular way. *Harriet greeted the news with a shout of joy.*
▷ *verb* **greeting, greeted**

gre·nade (gruh-nade) *noun* A small bomb that is thrown by hand or fired from a rifle.

grey (gray) *noun* Another spelling of **gray**.
▷ *adjective* **grey**

grey·hound (gray-hound) *noun* A thin dog with a smooth coat. A greyhound can run very fast. *See* **dog**.

grid (grid) *noun* A set of straight lines that cross each other at right angles to form a regular pattern of squares.

grid·dle (grid-uhl) *noun* A large, flat pan with a handle, used for frying food.

grid·i·ron (grid-eye-urn) *noun*
1. A griddle.
2. A playing field marked out for football.

grid·lock (grid-lok) *noun* A severe traffic jam that results in blocking all intersections in a grid of streets so that vehicles cannot move in any direction.

grief (greef) *noun* A feeling of great sadness.

griev·ance (gree-vuhnss) *noun* If you have a **grievance,** you have a real or imagined reason to feel angry or annoyed about something.

grieve (greev) *verb* To feel very sad, usually because someone whom you love has died.
▷ **grieving, grieved**

grill (gril)
1. *noun* A cooking utensil or device used outdoors that heats or cooks food.
2. *verb* To cook food on a grill.
3. *verb* (*informal*) To ask someone a lot of detailed questions in order to find out information. *The defense lawyer grilled the witness about the time of the robbery.*
▷ *verb* **grilling, grilled**

grim (grim) *adjective* Gloomy, stern, and unpleasant, as in *a grim expression.* ▷ **grimmer, grimmest** ▷ *adverb* **grimly**

gri·mace (grim-iss) *noun* A facial expression usually indicating a negative reaction to something. *A grimace spread across Calvin's face when the bully entered the cafeteria.* ▷ *verb* **grimace**

grime (grime) *noun* Dirt or soot that accumulates on a surface. ▷ *adjective* **grimy**

grin (grin) *verb* To give a large, cheerful smile.
▷ **grinning, grinned** ▷ *noun* **grin**

grind (grinde)
1. *verb* To crush something into a powder.
2. *verb* To sharpen a blade on a rough, hard surface.
3. *noun* A period of very hard work or study. *It was a grind studying for the final exam.*
▷ *verb* **grinding, ground** (ground)

grind·stone (grinde-stone) *noun*
1. A rotating stone used to sharpen or shape something.
2. If you **keep your nose to the grindstone,** you do not let anything distract you from your work.

grip (grip) *verb*
1. To hold something very tightly. ▷ *noun* **grip**
2. If something **grips** you, it holds your attention completely because it is so exciting. ▷ *adjective* **gripping**
▷ *verb* **gripping, gripped**

gris·tle (griss-uhl) *noun* A tough substance sometimes found in meat. Gristle is cartilage tissue.

G

231

grit (grit)
1. *noun* A sandy or grainy material on an otherwise smooth surface. ▷ *adjective* **gritty**
2. *noun* The ability to keep on doing something even though it is very difficult.
3. *verb* To grind your teeth together. *She gritted her teeth every time she took a cold shower.*
▷ **gritting, gritted**

grits (grits) *noun, plural* Coarsely ground grain, especially white corn, boiled and eaten as a cereal or side dish.

griz·zly bear (griz-lee) *noun* A large, brown or gray bear of western North America.

groan (grohn) *verb* To make a long, low sound showing that you are in pain or are unhappy.
▷ **groaning, groaned** ▷ *noun* **groan**

gro·cer (groh-sur) *noun* Someone who owns or runs a store selling food and household goods.
▷ *noun* **grocery**

grog·gy (grog-ee) *adjective* Sleepy or dizzy. *That cold medicine made me feel groggy.* ▷ **groggier, groggiest**

groin (groin) *noun* The hollow that marks the meeting of the inner part of your thigh and your stomach.

groom (groom)
1. *noun* A man who is about to get married or has just gotten married.
2. *verb* To take care of your appearance and your clothing. *He groomed himself well each morning.*
3. *noun* Someone who takes care of horses.
4. *verb* To brush and clean an animal such as a horse. ▷ *noun* **grooming**
▷ *verb* **grooming, groomed**

grooming kit for horses

- hoof oil
- sponge
- dander brush
- body brush
- sweat scraper
- curry comb
- mane comb
- hoof pick
- water brush
- wool dust cloth

groove (groov) *noun*
1. A long cut in the surface of something.
2. A habitual or routine way of doing something.

grope (grohp) *verb*
1. To feel about with your hands for something that you cannot see.
2. To look for or think about in an uncertain way. *The speaker had to grope for an answer to the question.*
▷ *verb* **groping, groped**

gross (grohss)
1. *adjective* Very large, as in *a gross error*.
2. *adjective* Very rude and improper, as in *gross behavior*.
3. *adjective* Unpleasantly big and ugly.
4. *noun* A group of 12 dozen, or 144, things, as in *a gross of pens*.
5. *adjective* The **gross** amount is the total amount, with nothing taken away.
▷ *adjective* **grosser, grossest** ▷ *adverb* **grossly**

gro·tesque (groh-tesk) *adjective* Very strange or ugly. *The monster had a grotesque smile.* ▷ *adverb* **grotesquely**

grouch (grouch) *noun* Someone who is in a bad mood. *What a grouch!* ▷ *noun, plural* **grouches**

grouch·y (grou-chee) *adjective* Mean, nasty, or cross. *Scrooge was a grouchy old man.*

ground (ground)
1. *noun* The surface of the earth.
2. *noun* Land used for a certain activity, as in *a parade ground*.
3. *verb* In baseball, to hit a ball that bounces along the ground. *The game ended after Julie grounded out to first base.* ▷ **grounding, grounded**
4. ground ball *noun* In baseball, a ball hit along the ground by a batter.
5. grounds *noun, plural* Reason or cause. *What grounds do you have for accusing me?*
6. grounds *noun, plural* The land surrounding a large building or group of buildings.

ground·ed (groun-did) *adjective*
1. If an aircraft is **grounded,** it cannot fly.
2. *(informal)* If you are **grounded,** you are not allowed to go out.
3. If an electrical appliance is **grounded,** it is connected directly to the earth and is safe to use.

ground·hog (ground-hog) *noun* A small, furry, burrowing animal with large front teeth. Also called a **woodchuck.**

Groundhog Day *noun* A day, February 2, said to forecast the coming of spring. If the groundhog sees its shadow, the forecast is for six more weeks of winter, but if the groundhog does not see its shadow, the forecast is for an early spring.

group (groop)
1. *noun* A number of things that go together or are similar in some way.
2. *verb* To put things into groups, or to make a group. ▷ **grouping, grouped**
3. *noun* A number of people who gather together or share a common purpose, as in *a musical group.*

grouse (grouss)
1. *noun* A small, plump game bird.
2. *verb* To complain loudly about something. ▷ **grousing, groused**

grouse

grove (grohv) *noun* A group of trees growing or planted near one another, as in *an olive grove.*

grov·el (gruhv-uhl *or* grov-uhl) *verb* To be unnaturally humble and polite to someone because you are afraid of the person or because you think he or she is very important. ▷ **groveling, groveled**

grow (groh) *verb*
1. To increase in size, length, or amount.
2. To plant something and look after it so that it lives and gets bigger.
3. To become. *Simon continues to grow lazier and lazier.*
4. If something **grows on** you, you gradually start to like it.
▷ *verb* **growing, grew** (groo)**, grown** (grohn)

growl (groul) *verb* When an animal **growls,** it makes a low, deep noise, usually because it is angry. ▷ **growling, growled** ▷ *noun* **growl**

grown-up *noun* An adult. ▷ *adjective* **grown-up**

growth (grohth) *noun*
1. The process of growing. *Here's a chart to measure your growth.*
2. A lump of body tissue either on or inside someone's body.

grub (gruhb) *noun*
1. The young form of some insects that looks like a short, white worm.
2. (*slang*) Food.

grub·by (gruhb-ee) *adjective* Dirty or sloppy. ▷ **grubbier, grubbiest** ▷ *noun* **grubbiness**

grudge (gruhj) *noun* A feeling of resentment toward someone who has hurt or insulted you in the past. *Jon bore a grudge against Daniel for months.* ▷ *verb* **grudge**

gru·el·ing (groo-uh-ling) *adjective* Very demanding and tiring, as in *a grueling job.*

grue·some (groo-suhm) *adjective* Something that is **gruesome** is disgusting and horrible.

gruff (gruhf) *adjective* Rough or rude. ▷ **gruffer, gruffest** ▷ *adverb* **gruffly**

grum·ble (gruhm-buhl) *verb* To complain about something in a grouchy way. ▷ **grumbling, grumbled**

grump·y (gruhm-pee) *adjective* Grouchy or cross. ▷ **grumpier, grumpiest** ▷ *adverb* **grumpily**

grunge (gruhnj) *noun* A type of rock music influenced by heavy metal and punk. ▷ *adjective* **grunge**

grunt (gruhnt) *verb* To make a deep, gruff sound like a pig. ▷ **grunting, grunted** ▷ *noun* **grunt**

gua·ca·mo·le (gwah-kuh-moh-lee) *noun* A dip made of avocado, tomatoes, onions, and seasonings.

guar·an·tee (ga-ruhn-tee) *noun*
1. A promise made by manufacturers that if their product breaks within a certain time or is defective, they will repair or replace it.
2. A promise that something will definitely happen.
▷ *verb* **guarantee**

guard (gard)
1. *verb* To protect a person or place from attack.
2. *verb* To watch a person carefully to prevent him or her from escaping.
3. *noun* Someone who protects or keeps watch over a person or place.
4. *noun* A football player whose job is often to protect the quarterback or tackle the opposition's quarterback.
5. *noun* A basketball player whose job is often to initiate plays.
6. *noun* An object placed near another object to provide protection, as in *a shin guard.*
7. *verb* If you **guard against** something, you try to keep it from happening.
▷ *verb* **guarding, guarded**

guard·i·an (gar-dee-uhn) *noun*
1. Someone who is not the parent of a child but who has the legal responsibility to look after him or her.
2. Someone who guards or protects something.
▷ *adjective* **guardian**

G

gua·va (gwah-vuh) *noun* A tropical tree bearing a large yellow fruit often made into jams or jellies. *See* **fruit.**

guer·ril·la (guh-ril-uh) *noun* A member of a small group of fighters or soldiers that often launches surprise attacks against an official army. **Guerrilla** sounds like **gorilla.** ▷ *adjective* **guerrilla**

guess (gess) *verb*
1. To give an answer that may be right but that you cannot be sure of. *I guess there are about 100 people here.* ▷ *noun* **guess**
2. To suppose or believe something. *I guess I can do it.*
▷ *verb* **guesses, guessing, guessed**

guest (gest) *noun*
1. Someone who has been invited to visit or to stay in another's home.
2. Someone staying in a hotel, a motel, or an inn.

gui·dance (gye-duhnss) *noun*
1. Advice or counsel, especially about a student's future plans, as in *career guidance.*
2. Direction or supervision. *We learned to draw under the guidance of an expert teacher.*

guide (gide) *verb* To help someone, usually by showing the person around a place or by leading the person across difficult country.
▷ **guiding, guided** ▷ *noun* **guide**

guide·book (gide-buk) *noun* A book containing maps and information about a place.

guided missile *noun* A missile that can be aimed directly at its target and guided during flight.

guide dog *noun* A dog trained to lead a visually impaired person.

guild (gild) *noun* A group or organization of people who do the same kind of work or have the same interests. *The Newspaper Guild is a labor union made up of reporters and editors.*

guile (gile) *noun* Cunning or artful deception.

guil·lo·tine (gil-uh-teen *or* gee-uh-teen) *noun* A large machine with a sharp blade used in the past to sever the heads of criminals.

guilt (gilt) *noun*
1. The fact of having committed a crime or done something wrong.
2. A feeling of shame or remorse for having done something wrong or having failed to do something.
Guilt sounds like **gilt.**

guilt·y (gil-tee) *adjective*
1. If you are **guilty,** you have committed a crime or done something wrong.
2. If you feel **guilty,** you feel bad because you have done something wrong or have failed to do something.
▷ *adjective* **guiltier, guiltiest** ▷ *adverb* **guiltily**

guin·ea pig (gin-ee) *noun*
1. A small mammal with smooth fur, short ears, and a very short tail, often kept as a pet.
2. A person who is used in an experiment.

guinea pig

gui·tar (guh-tar) *noun* A musical instrument with strings that you pluck or strum. *The vibrations of the strings on this electric guitar are transformed by the pickups into electrical impulses that are then amplified through a speaker. See also* **acoustic guitar.**

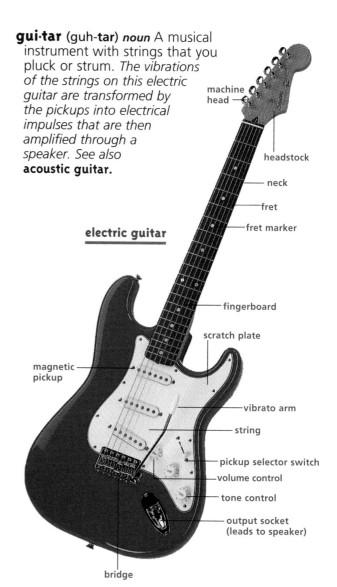

machine head

headstock

neck

fret

fret marker

electric guitar

fingerboard

scratch plate

magnetic pickup

vibrato arm

string

pickup selector switch

volume control

tone control

output socket (leads to speaker)

bridge

gulch (guhlch) *noun* A deep ravine or valley that fills with water when it rains. ▷ *noun, plural* **gulches**

gulf (guhlf) *noun*
1. A large area of sea that is partly surrounded by land, as in *the Gulf of Mexico.*
2. A difference or gap between people.

gull (guhl) *noun* Short for **seagull.**

gul·li·ble (guhl-uh-buhl) *adjective* If you are **gullible,** you believe anything you are told and you are easily tricked. ▷ *noun* **gullibility**

gul·ly (guhl-ee) *noun* A long, narrow ravine or ditch. ▷ *noun, plural* **gullies**

gulp (guhlp)
1. *verb* To swallow something quickly and noisily. ▷ **gulping, gulped**
2. *noun* A mouthful of something that is swallowed. *He took a large gulp of milk.*

gum (guhm) *noun*
1. Your **gums** are the areas of firm, pink flesh around the base of your teeth.
2. A thick liquid from any of various plants.
3. A sticky substance made from such a liquid and used as glue.
4. A sweet substance used for chewing. Also called **chewing gum.**

gum·drop (guhm-drop) *noun* A small, chewy candy covered with sugar.

gun (guhn)
1. *noun* A weapon that fires bullets through a long metal tube.
2. **gun down** *verb* To shoot someone with a gun.
3. *verb* To speed something up quickly, as in *to gun an engine.*
▷ *verb* **gunning, gunned**

> ### ▶ Word History
> The word **gun** comes from the term *Lady Gunilda,* a huge crossbow that shot large ammunition in the 14th century. Later, the word gun was used for cannons as well as hand-carried firearms.

gun·fire (guhn-fire) *noun* The firing of guns.

gun·pow·der (guhn-pou-dur) *noun* A powder that explodes easily. Gunpowder is used in large naval guns, in fireworks, and in blasting.

gun·smith (guhn-smith) *noun* Someone who makes and repairs guns.

gup·py (guhp-ee) *noun* A tiny freshwater fish popular in home aquariums. ▷ *noun, plural* **guppies**

gur·gle (gur-guhl) *verb*
1. When water **gurgles,** it makes a low, bubbling sound.
2. To make a low, bubbling sound like gurgling water. *The baby gurgled happily.*
▷ *verb* **gurgling, gurgled** ▷ *noun* **gurgle**

gush (guhsh) *verb*
1. When liquid **gushes,** it flows quickly in large amounts. ▷ *noun* **gush**
2. When a person **gushes,** he or she is embarrassingly sentimental or emotional.
▷ *verb* **gushes, gushing, gushed** ▷ *adjective* **gushing**

gust (guhst) *noun* A sudden, strong blast of wind. ▷ *adjective* **gusty**

gus·to (guhss-toh) *noun* If you do something with **gusto,** you do it with energy and enthusiasm.

gut (guht)
1. *noun* The alimentary canal in your body.
2. **guts** *noun, plural* Intestines.
3. *verb* To destroy the inside of a building.
▷ **gutting, gutted**
4. **guts** *noun, plural* (informal) Courage.

gut·ter (guht-ur) *noun* A channel or length of tubing through which rain is drained away from a road or from the roof of a building. *See* **building.**

guy (gye) *noun* (informal) A man or a boy.

guz·zle (guh-zuhl) *verb* To eat or drink something quickly and noisily. ▷ **guzzling, guzzled**

gym (jim) *noun*
1. A large room or building with special equipment for doing exercises and physical training. Gym is short for *gymnasium.*
2. A class or course in physical education.

gym·na·si·um (jim-nay-zee-uhm) *noun* A gym.

gym·nast (jim-nast) *noun* Someone who practices gymnastics.

gym·nas·tics (jim-nass-tiks) *noun* Physical exercises, often performed on apparatus, that involve difficult and carefully controlled body movements. ▷ *adjective* **gymnastic**

Gyp·sy (jip-see) *noun* A member of a group of people who originally came from India and now live mainly in Europe and North America.
▷ *noun, plural* **Gypsies**

gy·rate (jye-rate) *verb* To move around and around in a circle.
▷ **gyrating, gyrated**

gy·ro·scope (jye-ruh-skope) *noun* A wheel that spins inside a frame and causes the frame to balance in any position. Gyroscopes are used to help keep ships and aircraft steady.

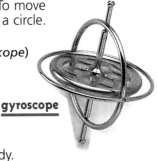
gyroscope

235

Hh

About H

Spelling Hint: Some words that begin with an *h* sound are spelled *wh*. Examples: who, wholesale, wholesome.

H

ha (hah) *interjection*
1. A word used to express joy, surprise, or triumph.
2. A word used to express laughter.

hab·it (hab-it) *noun*
1. Something that you do regularly, often without thinking about it. *Making my bed has become a habit.*
2. A piece of clothing that looks like a long, loose dress, worn by monks and nuns.
3. Clothing worn for a particular activity, as in *a riding habit.*

hab·it·a·ble (hab-uh-tuh-buhl) *adjective* If a building is **habitable,** it is safe, comfortable, and clean enough to live in.

hab·i·tat (hab-uh-*tat*) *noun* The place and natural conditions in which a plant or an animal lives. *The tiger's habitat is the forest.*

ha·bit·u·al (huh-**bich**-oo-uhl) *adjective*
1. Behaving from habit, as in *a habitual smoker.*
2. Done over and over again. *His habitual lies are upsetting his friends.*
3. Regular or usual. *Kelly's father took his habitual seat at the head of the table.*

ha·bit·u·al·ly (huh-**bich**-oo-uh-lee) *adverb* Usually or normally. *Rob is habitually optimistic.*

ha·ci·en·da (hah-see-en-duh) *noun* A large ranch or estate found in the southwestern part of the United States or in Mexico or other Spanish-speaking countries.

hack (hak)
1. *verb* To chop or cut something roughly. ▷ **hacking, hacked**
2. *noun* A short, dry cough. ▷ *verb* **hack**
3. *noun* (informal) A taxi.

hack·er (hak-ur) *noun* Someone who is expert at getting into a computer system illegally.

had·n't (had-uhnt) *contraction* A short form of *had not.*

hag·gard (hag-urd) *adjective* Someone who is **haggard** looks thin, tired, and worried.

hag·gle (hag-uhl) *verb* To argue, usually about the price of something. *We haggled with the merchant over the price of the rug and ended up buying it for less money.* ▷ **haggling, haggled**

hai·ku (hye-*koo*) *noun* A short Japanese poem in 3 lines containing a total of 17 syllables.

hail (hayl) *verb*
1. When it **hails,** small balls of ice fall from the sky. ▷ *noun* **hail**
2. To attract someone's attention. *Terry hailed a taxi.* ▷ *verb* **hailing, hailed**

hair (hair) *noun* The mass of fine, soft strands that grow on your head or body or on the body of an animal. **Hair** sounds like **hare.**

hair·cut (hair-*kuht*) *noun* When you get a **haircut,** someone cuts and styles your hair.

hair·do (hair-*doo*) *noun* The way hair is styled or arranged.

hair·dress·er (hair-*dress*-ur) *noun* Someone who cuts and styles people's hair.

hair·pin (hair-*pin*)
1. *noun* A piece of bent wire with sides that press together to hold hair in place.
2. *adjective* Shaped like a hairpin, as in *a hairpin turn. The hairpin turns in this road in Bolivia lead to the world's highest ski area.*

hairpin turns

hair-rais·ing (hair-*ray*-zing) *adjective* Extremely frightening. *The roller coaster ride was a hair-raising experience.*

hair·y (hair-ee) *adjective*
1. Covered with hair.
2. (slang) Dangerous and frightening.
▷ *adjective* **hairier, hairiest**

half (haf)
1. *noun* One of two equal parts of something. ▷ *adjective* **half**
2. *adverb* Partly or not completely. *The meal was only half cooked.*
3. *noun* One of two equal lengths of time played in games. *Jerry scored late in the first half.*
▷ *noun, plural* **halves** (havz)

half brother *noun* A brother who shares only one parent with someone else.

half·heart·ed (haf-har-tid) *adjective* Without much enthusiasm or interest. *Chris made a halfhearted attempt to read all the material before the test.* ▷ *adverb* **halfheartedly**

half-mast *noun* The position halfway between the top and bottom of a flagpole or mast. Flags are flown at this position as a sign of respect for someone who has just died.

half sister *noun* A sister who shares only one parent with someone else.

half·time (haf-*time*) *noun* A short break in the middle of a game such as football, basketball, or hockey.

half·way (haf-way)
1. *adjective* Half the distance from one point to another. *The runners reached the halfway mark in the race.*
2. *adjective* Not thorough or complete. *Halfway measures won't solve the problem.*
3. *adverb* To or at half the distance. *We ran halfway down the street.*

hal·i·but (hal-uh-buht) *noun* A type of fish found in both the Atlantic and Pacific oceans and used as food. ▷ *noun, plural* **halibut** *or* **halibuts**

hall (hawl) *noun*
1. An area of a house just inside the front door.
2. A large room used for meetings or other public events.
3. A corridor or a passageway. *There are three bedrooms off the hall.*
Hall sounds like **haul.**

hal·le·lu·jah (hal-uh-loo-yuh) *interjection* A word used to express joy and thanks.

hal·lowed (hal-ohd *or* hal-oh-id) *adjective* Sacred or holy. ▷ *verb* **hallow**

Hal·low·een *or* **Hallowe'en** (*hal*-oh-een) *noun* The evening of October 31, believed in the past to be the night when witches and ghosts were active. On Halloween, children dress up in costumes and go out to trick-or-treat.

hal·lu·ci·nate (huh-loo-suh-*nate*) *verb* To see something in your mind that is not really there. ▷ **hallucinating, hallucinated** ▷ *noun* **hallucination**

ha·lo (hay-loh) *noun*
1. A ring of light around an object. *The moon sometimes has a halo around it.*
2. A circle of light shown in pictures around the heads of angels and sacred people.

halt (hawlt) *verb* To stop. ▷ **halting, halted** ▷ *noun* **halt**

hal·ter (hawl-tur) *noun*
1. A rope or strap used to lead or tie an animal such as a horse. A halter fits over the animal's nose and behind its ears.
2. A woman's top with a band that ties behind the neck, leaving the back and shoulders bare.

halve (hav) *verb*
1. To cut or divide something into two equal parts. *Ron halved the banana so he and I could share it.*
2. To reduce something so that there is only half as much as there was. *We have halved expenses for our planned trip.*
Halve sounds like **have.**
▷ *verb* **halving, halved**

ham (ham) *noun* The meat from the upper part of a pig's hind leg that has been salted and sometimes smoked.

ham·burg·er (ham-*bur*-gur) *noun*
1. A round, flat piece of cooked beef, usually served on a bun.
2. Ground beef.

ham·let (ham-lit) *noun* A very small village.

ham·mer (ham-ur)
1. *noun* A tool with a metal head on a handle, used for hitting things such as nails. ▷ *verb* **hammer**
2. *verb* To hit something hard. *Elsa hammered at the door.* ▷ **hammering, hammered**

ham·mock (ham-uhk) *noun* A piece of strong cloth or net that is hung up by each end and used as a bed or as a place to relax.

ham·per (ham-pur)
1. *noun* A large box or basket used for carrying food or for storing dirty clothing, as in *a picnic hamper* or *a laundry hamper.*
2. *verb* To make it difficult for someone to do something. *Nina's tight shoes hampered her running.* ▷ **hampering, hampered**

ham·ster (ham-stur) *noun*
A small animal like a mouse with no tail, often kept as a pet. *Hamsters have pouches in their cheeks for storing food.*

hamster

hand (hand)
1. *noun* The part of your body on the end of your arm. The hand includes your wrist, palm, fingers, and thumb.
2. *verb* To pass or give something to someone. *Hand me a sheet of paper, please.* ▷ **handing, handed**
3. *noun* A set of cards that you hold during a game of cards.
4. *noun* One of the pointers on a clock, as in *the minute hand.*
5. If you **give** or **lend a hand** to someone, you help the person.
6. *noun* One of a ship's crew. *All hands on deck!*
7. *noun* A laborer, as in *a hired hand.*
8. If something is **at hand,** it is nearby and handy to use, or its time has come.
9. If you **have your hands full** with something, you are very busy with it.
10. If things are **out of hand,** they are not under control.
11. If you **wash your hands of** something, you refuse to have anything more to do with it.
12. If you are **in good hands,** you are well taken care of.

hand·bag (hand-*bag*) *noun* A bag in which a woman carries her wallet and other small things.

hand·ball (hand-*bawl*) *noun*
1. A game played in a large room or outdoors in which two or four players take turns hitting a small, hard rubber ball against a wall with their hands.
2. The rubber ball used for playing handball.

hand·book (hand-*buk*) *noun* A book that gives you information or advice.

hand·cuffs (hand-*kuhfs*) *noun, plural* Metal rings joined by a chain that are locked around a prisoner's wrists to prevent escape. ▷ *verb* **handcuff**

hand·ful (hand-ful) *noun*
1. The amount of something that you can hold in your hand. *Nao ate a handful of gumdrops.*
2. A small number of people or things. *We collected only a handful of old toys.*
3. *(informal)* If someone is a **handful,** he or she is difficult to cope with.

hand·i·cap (han-dee-*kap*)
1. *noun* If someone has a **handicap,** the person has a physical disability. ▷ *adjective* **handicapped**
2. *noun* A disadvantage that makes it difficult for you to do something. *Laurie's sore throat was a handicap in choir practice.*
3. *noun* A disadvantage given to skilled competitors in a sport in order to make the competition more equal, as in *a golf handicap.*
4. *verb* To state the chances that each horse in a race has of winning the race. ▷ **handicapping, handicapped** ▷ *noun* **handicapper**

hand·i·craft (han-dee-*kraft*) *noun* A skill, such as pottery or sewing, that involves making things with your hands.

hand·ker·chief (hang-kur-chif) *noun* A small square of cloth that you use for wiping off your face or hands or blowing your nose.

han·dle (han-duhl)
1. *noun* The part of an object that you use to carry, move, or hold that object, as in *a door handle.*
2. *verb* To pick something up and hold it in your hands in order to look at it carefully. *The sign in the store said, "Please handle the china with care."*
3. *verb* To deal with someone or something. *Katy is very good at handling tricky situations.* ▷ *verb* **handling, handled**

han·dle·bars (han-duhl-*barz*) *noun, plural* The bar at the front of a bicycle or motorcycle that you use for steering. *See* **bicycle.**

hand·made (hand-made) *adjective* Made by hand, not by machine.

hand-me-down *noun* An article of clothing or another item passed along for someone else's use. ▷ *noun, plural* **hand-me-downs**

hand·out (hand-*out*) *noun*
1. Money, food, or clothing that is given to a needy person.
2. A pamphlet or leaflet that is given out for free.

hand·rail (hand-*rail*) *noun* A narrow rail that can be held by the hand for support, usually used on stairways.

hand·shake (hand-*shayk*) *noun* A way of greeting or saying good-bye to someone by taking the person's hand and shaking it.

hand·some (han-suhm) *adjective*
1. Attractive in appearance. *My friends think our teacher is a handsome man.*
2. Generous, as in *a handsome contribution.*

hand·spring (hand-*spring*) *noun* A gymnastic movement in which you spring forward or backward onto both hands, then flip all the way over to land back on your feet.

hand·stand (hand-*stand*) *noun* When you do a **handstand,** you balance on your hands with your feet in the air.

hand·writ·ing (hand-*rye*-ting) *noun*
1. The style you use for forming letters and words when you write.
2. Writing done by a person, not a machine. ▷ *adjective* **handwritten**

hand·y (han-dee) *adjective*
1. Useful and easy to use. *A small iron is a handy thing to take on vacation.*
2. Skillful. *Suzie is handy with a power drill.*
3. Close by. *Is there a phone handy?* ▷ *adjective* **handier, handiest**

hang (hang) *verb*
1. To fasten something somewhere by attaching the top of it and leaving the bottom free. *Hang your coat on this hook.*
2. To kill someone by putting a rope around the person's neck and then taking the support from under the feet. The past tense and past participle of this sense of the verb is *hanged. The convicted murderer was hanged at midnight.*
3. **hang up** To end a telephone conversation by putting down the receiver.
4. **hang out** *(informal)* To spend a lot of time in a place. *The teens hang out at the mall.* ▷ *noun* **hangout**
▷ *verb* **hanging, hung** (huhng) *or* **hanged**

han·gar (hang-ur) *noun* A large building where aircraft are kept. **Hangar** sounds like **hanger.**

hang·er (hang-ur) *noun* A piece of specially shaped wood, metal, or plastic used for hanging clothes. **Hanger** sounds like **hangar.**

H

hang glider *noun* An aircraft like a giant kite with a harness for a pilot hanging below it. *The pilot controls the hang glider by moving his or her body.*
▷ *noun* **hang gliding**

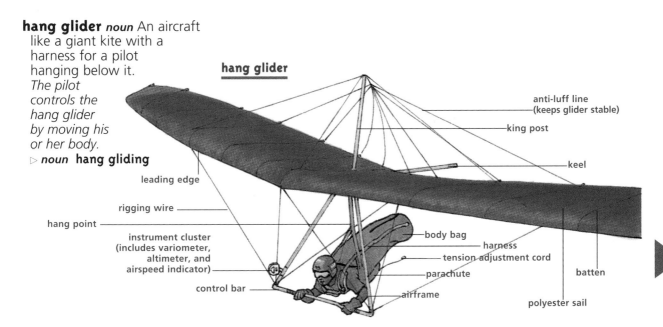

hang glider

anti-luff line
(keeps glider stable)

king post

keel

leading edge

rigging wire

hang point

instrument cluster
(includes variometer, altimeter, and airspeed indicator)

control bar

body bag

harness

tension adjustment cord

parachute

airframe

batten

polyester sail

H

hang·over (hang-*oh*-vur) *noun* A headache and a sick feeling that someone gets after drinking too much alcohol.

hang-up *noun* (informal) If you have a **hang-up** about something, it bothers you. *Ellis has a hang-up about being short.*

han·ker (hang-kur) *verb* To wish or long for something. *Denise hankers for a hamburger.*
▷ **hankering, hankered** ▷ *noun* **hankering**

Ha·nuk·kah *or* **Chanukah**
(hah-nuh-kuh) *noun* An eight-day Jewish festival that usually falls in December. Also called the Feast or Festival of Lights. *At Hanukkah, Jews light candles on a menorah, or special holder.*

Hanukkah menorah

hap·haz·ard (hap-haz-urd) *adjective* Disorganized. *The papers were scattered in a haphazard manner.* ▷ *adverb* **haphazardly**

hap·less (hap-luhss) *adjective* Unlucky or unfortunate. *The hapless boy always seemed to forget the answer when his teacher called on him.* ▷ *adverb* **haplessly** ▷ *noun* **haplessness**

hap·pen (hap-uhn) *verb*
1. To take place or to occur. *A lot has happened since you left.*
2. If you **happen** to do something, you have the chance or luck to do it.

▷ *verb* **happening, happened**

hap·py (hap-ee) *adjective*
1. Pleased and contented. ▷ *noun* **happiness**
2. Lucky or fortunate. *Meeting Bob in town was a happy coincidence.*
▷ *adjective* **happier, happiest** ▷ *adverb* **happily**

▶ **Synonyms: happy**
. . . .

Happy describes a general feeling of well-being. If you are happy, you may feel good about something you have done or seen or something that happened to you: *When I woke up, the sun was shining, and I felt happy.*

Glad describes your good feelings about something specific, such as an occasion or event: *I'm glad you can make it to my party.*

Pleased means that you have good feelings about the way something has turned out: *I was pleased that Mr. Tanaka liked my idea for having a talent show.*

Delighted describes extreme pleasure about something: *We all were delighted to hear that Ginny will play the lead in the school play.*

Joyful describes something that shows or causes joy: *The room was filled with the joyful sounds of children playing.*

Joyous is very close in meaning to joyful, but it usually refers to the event that causes joy: *It was a joyous occasion for the whole family when my cousin graduated from college.*

H

happy-go-lucky *adjective* Without any worries or troubles.

ha·rangue (huh-rang) *verb* To talk loudly or angrily at someone. *Our neighbor harangued us about cutting across his lawn.* ▷ **haranguing, harangued** ▷ *noun* **harangue**

har·ass (huh-rass *or* ha-ruhss) *verb* To pester or annoy someone. ▷ **harasses, harassing, harassed** ▷ *noun* **harassment**

har·bor (har-bur)
1. *noun* A place where ships shelter or unload their cargo.
2. *verb* To take care of someone or something, as in *to harbor a wounded bird.*
3. *verb* To hide someone, as in *to harbor a fugitive.*
▷ *verb* **harboring, harbored**

hard (hard)
1. *adjective* Firm and solid, as in *a hard bed.*
2. *adjective* Difficult, as in *a hard exam.*
3. *adjective* Strong and powerful enough to cause addiction, as in *hard drugs.*
4. *adjective* Energetic, as in *a hard worker.*
5. *adverb* Energetically, as in *to work hard.*
6. *adjective* Not gentle; severe, as in *a hard winter.*
▷ *noun* **hardness** ▷ *adjective* **harder, hardest**

▶ Synonyms: hard

Hard is the opposite of easy and describes something that requires work or effort: *The homework was so hard that Ellen spent all evening on it.*

Difficult means that extra effort and perhaps some skills are needed to do something because there are obstacles in the way: *It was difficult to communicate with the visitors because they understood only a few words of English.*

Arduous refers to something that requires continued extra effort: *The arduous journey through the ice and snow took the travelers more than a week.*

Oppressive describes something that is very difficult to bear because of harsh or extreme conditions: *The heat in the factory was so oppressive that some people became ill.*

Exhausting refers to something that requires hard work and makes you tired: *Johnny found an hour of baby-sitting more exhausting than three hours of playing basketball.*

hard-boiled *adjective*
1. Cooked by boiling until firm, as in *a hard-boiled egg.*
2. Tough and not sympathetic, as in *a hard-boiled detective.*

hard copy *noun* A printed version of a document created by a computer.

hard disk *noun* A disk inside a computer used for storing large amounts of data. *See* **computer.**

hard·en (hard-uhn) *verb*
1. To become harder, or to make something harder.
2. To make or become tough and indifferent. *The king hardened himself against the complaints of his subjects.*
▷ *verb* **hardening, hardened** ▷ *adjective* **hardened**

hard·ly (hard-lee) *adverb*
1. Scarcely or only just. *I could hardly wait to open my gifts.*
2. Surely not. *We can hardly have a picnic in the rain.*

hard·ship (hard-ship) *noun* Difficulty or suffering.

hard·ware (hard-wair) *noun*
1. Tools and other household equipment.
2. Computer equipment, such as a printer, a monitor, or a keyboard.

hard·wood (hard-wud) *noun* Strong, hard wood from various trees, such as oak, beech, or ash.

har·dy (har-dee) *adjective* If a person, an animal, or a plant is **hardy,** it is tough and can survive under very difficult conditions. ▷ **hardier, hardiest**

hare (hair) *noun* A mammal like a large rabbit with long, strong, back legs. **Hare** sounds like **hair.**

harm (harm) *verb* To injure or hurt someone or something. ▷ **harming, harmed** ▷ *noun* **harm** ▷ *adjective* **harmful**

harm·less (harm-liss) *adjective* Not able to cause injury or damage, as in *a harmless joke.* ▷ *noun* **harmlessness** ▷ *adverb* **harmlessly**

har·mon·i·ca (har-mon-uh-kuh) *noun* A small musical instrument played by blowing out and drawing in your breath through the mouthpiece. *Harmonicas contain two sets of reeds fixed to reed plates above and below the mouthpiece. The reeds are left free at one end so that they can vibrate and produce notes when air passes over them.*

harmonica

cover plate
metal reed (fixed below plate)
metal reed (fixed above plate)
slide (changes notes)
box
hole
lower reed plate inside here
mouthpiece
upper reed plate

har·mo·nize (har-muh-nize) *verb*
1. To sing or play music using harmony. *My sister and I always try to harmonize when we sing.*

2. To go together in a pleasing or agreeable way. *The colors of the couch and chairs harmonize nicely.*
▷ *verb* **harmonizing, harmonized**

har·mo·ny (har-muh-nee) *noun*
1. Agreement. *The team worked in harmony.*
2. A set of musical notes played at the same time that are part of a chord.
▷ *noun, plural* **harmonies** ▷ *adjective* **harmonious**

har·ness (har-niss)
1. *noun* A set of leather straps and metal pieces that connect a horse or another animal to a plow, cart, or wagon.
2. *noun* An arrangement of straps used to keep someone safe, as in *a parachute harness.*
3. *verb* To control and use something. *We can harness the sun to create electricity.* ▷ **harnesses, harnessing, harnessed**
▷ *noun, plural* **harnesses**

harp (harp)
1. *noun* A large, triangular musical instrument with strings that you play by plucking. ▷ *noun* **harpist**
2. *verb* If you **harp on** something, you keep talking about it.
▷ **harping, harped**

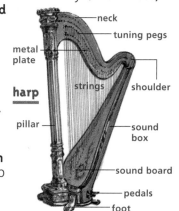

harp

- neck
- tuning pegs
- metal plate
- strings
- shoulder
- pillar
- sound box
- sound board
- pedals
- foot

har·poon (har-poon)
1. *noun* A long spear with an attached rope that can be thrown or shot out of a special gun. It is usually used for hunting large fish or whales.
2. *verb* To hit or kill with a harpoon. ▷ **harpooning, harpooned**

harp·si·chord (harp-suh-*kord*) *noun* A keyboard instrument that looks like a small piano. A harpsichord has wire strings that are plucked rather than being struck like the strings in a piano.

harsh (harsh) *adjective*
1. Cruel or rough, as in *a harsh punishment.*
2. Unpleasant or hard on the body or senses, as in *a harsh light* or *a harsh voice.*
▷ *adjective* **harsher, harshest** ▷ *adverb* **harshly**

har·vest (har-vist)
1. *noun* The gathering in of crops that are ripe, or the crops gathered in.
2. *verb* To collect or gather up crops.
▷ **harvesting, harvested**

har·vest·er (har-vi-stur) *noun* A machine used to harvest crops. *The picture shows the main parts of a combine harvester, which is used to harvest crops such as wheat, barley, and peas. Wheat is gathered and cut by the header and carried to the threshing cylinder and beater to separate the grain from the straw. The straw then travels along straw walkers, where more grain is collected and the waste is unloaded. The grain is cleaned in the cleaning shoe and stored in the grain tank, ready for unloading.*

H

combine harvester

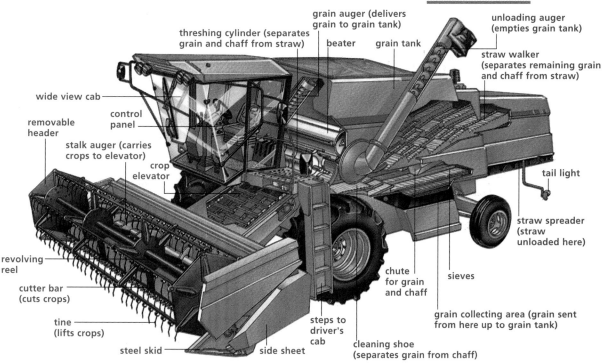

- grain auger (delivers grain to grain tank)
- threshing cylinder (separates grain and chaff from straw)
- beater
- grain tank
- unloading auger (empties grain tank)
- straw walker (separates remaining grain and chaff from straw)
- wide view cab
- control panel
- removable header
- stalk auger (carries crops to elevator)
- crop elevator
- tail light
- revolving reel
- cutter bar (cuts crops)
- tine (lifts crops)
- steel skid
- side sheet
- steps to driver's cab
- cleaning shoe (separates grain from chaff)
- chute for grain and chaff
- sieves
- grain collecting area (grain sent from here up to grain tank)
- straw spreader (straw unloaded here)

hash (hash) *noun*
1. Small pieces of meat and vegetables cooked together.
2. A mess. *Barney made a hash of his exams.*
▷ *noun, plural* **hashes**

has·n't (haz-uhnt) *contraction* A short form of *has not.*

has·sle (hass-uhl)
1. *verb (informal)* If someone **hassles** you, the person annoys you persistently about something. ▷ **hassling, hassled**
2. *noun (informal)* A troublesome nuisance. *The traffic jam made it a real hassle to drive to school.*

haste (hayst) *noun* Speed or quickness in moving or acting. *We ate breakfast in great haste so we could get to school on time.*

has·ten (hayss-uhn) *verb*
1. To move quickly.
2. To make someone or something move or happen faster. *Lots of tender, loving care hastened my grandfather's return to good health.*
▷ *verb* **hastening, hastened**

has·ty (hay-stee) *adjective* Too quick or hurried, as in *a hasty decision.* ▷ **hastier, hastiest** ▷ *adverb* **hastily**

hat (hat) *noun*
1. An item of clothing that you wear on your head.
2. hat trick Three successes in a row, such as three goals in a single game by a hockey player.

hatch (hach)
1. *verb* When an egg **hatches**, a baby bird or reptile breaks out of it.
2. *noun* A group of young birds or reptiles that have hatched.

turtles hatching

3. *verb* To devise a plot. *The mystery writer hatched another incredible story.*
4. *noun* A covered hole in a floor, deck, door, wall, or ceiling. *The sailor opened the hatch to the lower deck of the ship.*
▷ *noun, plural* **hatches** ▷ *verb* **hatches, hatching, hatched**

hatch·back (hach-*bak*) *noun* A car with a rear window that opens upward.

hatch·er·y (hach-er-ee) *noun* A place where eggs, especially chicken or fish eggs, are hatched. ▷ *noun, plural* **hatcheries**

hatch·et (hach-it) *noun* A small ax.

hatch·ling (hach-ling) *noun* A recently hatched animal.

hate (hate) *verb* To dislike or detest someone or something. ▷ **hating, hated** ▷ *noun* **hate,** *noun* **hatred**

hate·ful (hate-fuhl) *adjective* Horrible. *Denzel is hateful to his younger brother.* ▷ *adverb* **hatefully**

haugh·ty (haw-tee) *adjective* If you are **haughty,** you are very proud and look down on other people. ▷ **haughtier, haughtiest** ▷ *noun* **haughtiness** ▷ *adverb* **haughtily**

haul (hawl)
1. *verb* To pull something with difficulty. *Terri hauled the sack of potatoes into the shed.*
2. *verb* To transport with a vehicle, as in *to haul grain to the mill.*
3. *noun* A quantity of something that is caught, as in *a big haul of fish.*
4. *noun* A distance to be traveled. *The flight between Seattle and Buenos Aires is a long haul.*
Haul sounds like **hall.**
▷ *verb* **hauling, hauled**

haunch (hawnch) *noun* The hip, buttock, and upper thigh of an animal or a person. ▷ *noun, plural* **haunches**

haunt (hawnt)
1. *verb* If a ghost **haunts** a place, it visits it often. ▷ *adjective* **haunted**
2. *verb* If something **haunts** you, it stays on your mind. *Laura was haunted by the memory of the child's face.* ▷ *adjective* **haunting**
3. *noun* A place you visit often. *The community swimming pool is one of my favorite haunts in the summer.*
▷ *verb* **haunting, haunted**

have (hav) *verb*
1. To own or possess something. *I have a new bicycle.*
2. To experience or enjoy something. *Let's have some fun!*
3. To receive or get something. *Did you have lunch?*
4. To contain or consist of. *The cookies have chocolate chips in them.*
5. To be the parent or parents of. *Mom and Dad have two children.*
6. To arrange for. *Let's have the painters come at the end of the week.*
Have sounds like **halve.**
▷ *verb* **has (haz), having, had (had)**

ha·ven (hay-vuhn) *noun*
1. A harbor. *The captain of the damaged ship looked for a close haven.*
2. A safe place. *The wildlife refuge is a haven for many animals.*

have·n't (hav-uhnt) *contraction* A short form of *have not.*

hav·oc (hav-uhk) *noun* Great damage and chaos. *The floods have caused havoc.*

hawk (hawk)
1. *noun* A bird of prey with a hooked beak and sharp claws that eats other birds and small animals.
2. *verb* To offer goods for sale by shouting in the street. ▷ **hawking, hawked**

haw·thorn (haw-*thorn*) *noun* A shrub or tree of the rose family that has thorns, white or pink blossoms, and small, colorful fruits.

hay (hay) *noun* Grass that is dried and fed to farm animals. **Hay** sounds like **hey.**

hay fever *noun* An allergy to pollen or grass that makes you sneeze, makes your eyes water, and can make you wheeze.

hay·loft (hay-*loft*) *noun* A platform high above the floor of a barn where hay is stored.

hay·stack (hay-*stak*) *noun* A large pile of hay.

haz·ard (haz-urd)
1. *noun* A danger or a risk. *Keeping lots of newspapers around is a fire hazard.*
2. *verb* To risk or take a chance on something, as in *hazard a guess.* ▷ **hazarding, hazarded**

haz·ard·ous (haz-ur-duhss) *adjective* Dangerous or risky. *Smoking cigarettes is hazardous to your health.*

hazardous waste *noun* Dangerous materials that should not be thrown away without some sort of protective covering.

haze (hayz) *noun* Smoke, dust, or moisture in the air that prevents you from seeing very far.

ha·zel (hay-zuhl) *noun*
1. A small tree or shrub that produces nuts.
2. A green-brown color. ▷ *adjective* **hazel**

haz·y (hay-zee) *adjective*
1. Misty, as in *a hazy morning.*
2. If you have a **hazy** memory of something, it is vague and unclear in your mind.
▷ *adjective* **hazier, haziest** ▷ *adverb* **hazily**

H-bomb (aych) *See* **hydrogen bomb.**

he (hee) *pronoun*
1. The male person or animal mentioned before.
2. That person. *He who hesitates is lost.*

head (hed)
1. *noun* The top part of your body where your brain, eyes, nose, and mouth are.
2. *noun* The person in charge. ▷ *adjective* **head**
3. *noun* The top or front of something, as in *the head of the line* or *the head of a pin.*
4. *verb* To lead. *Admiral Peary headed an expedition to the North Pole.*
5. *verb* To move toward something. *We headed toward the exit.*
6. *noun* A single person or animal, as in *a head of cattle.*
7. *noun* A cluster of leaves or flowers, as in *a head of lettuce.*
8. If something **goes to your head,** it makes you dizzy.
9. If a compliment **goes to your head,** it makes you conceited.
10. If you **keep a cool head** in an emergency, you remain calm and relaxed.
▷ *verb* **heading, headed**

head·ache (hed-*ayk*) *noun* A pain in your head.

head·band (hed-*band*) *noun* A strip of cloth worn around the head to soak up sweat or keep hair out of the face.

head·dress (hed-*dress*) *noun* A covering, often decorative, for the head. *Below is an American Indian-type headdress, often worn as a sign of bravery or power.* ▷ *noun, plural* **headdresses**

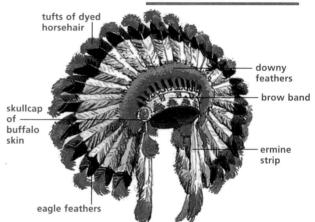

American Indian headdress

tufts of dyed horsehair
downy feathers
brow band
skullcap of buffalo skin
ermine strip
eagle feathers

head·first (hed-furst) *adverb* With the head first, or leading with the head. *She dove into the pool headfirst.*

head·ing (hed-ing) *noun* Words written as a title at the top of a page or over a section of writing in a magazine, newspaper, or book.

head·light (hed-*lite*) *noun* A bright light on the front of a vehicle that allows the driver or pilot to see ahead in the dark. *See* **car, motorcycle.**

head·line (hed-*line*) *noun* The title of a newspaper article, printed in large, usually bold type. ▷ *verb* **headline**

head·long (hed-*lawng*) *adverb*
1. With the head first. *She plunged headlong into the water.*
2. Rashly, or with little thought. *Cynthia rushed headlong into the street after the rubber ball.*

head·mas·ter (hed-*mass*-tuhr) *noun* A man who is in charge of a private day or boarding school.

head·mis·tress (hed-*miss*-triss) *noun* A woman who is in charge of a private day or boarding school. ▷ *noun, plural* **headmistresses**

H

head-on (hed-on) *adjective* With the head or front end first. *Our car was in a head-on collision with a truck.* ▷ *adverb* **head-on**

head·phones (hed-fohnz) *noun, plural* Small speakers that you wear in or over your ears.

head·quar·ters (hed-*kwor*-turz) *noun* The place from which an organization is run. ▷ *noun, plural* **headquarters**

head start *noun* An advantage, usually in a race when one runner is allowed to start first.

head·strong (hed-*strong*) *adjective* Determined to have one's own way. *Jen was headstrong; she would not listen to her parents' advice or suggestions.*

head·way (hed-*way*) *noun* Progress or forward movement. *We can't make much headway in this blizzard.*

heal (heel) *verb*
1. To cure someone or make the person healthy. ▷ *noun* **healer,** *noun* **healing**
2. To get better. *Jake's cut finger healed quickly.* **Heal** sounds like **heel.**
▷ *verb* **healing, healed**

health (helth) *noun*
1. Strength and fitness.
2. The state or condition of your body. *Aunt Agnes is in poor health.*

health food *noun* Food that is grown organically, using natural fertilizers, and prepared without preservatives.

health·y (hel-thee) *adjective*
1. If you are **healthy,** you are fit and well.
2. Something that is **healthy** makes you fit, as in *a healthy diet.*
▷ *adjective* **healthier, healthiest** ▷ *adverb* **healthily**

heap (heep)
1. *noun* A pile.
2. *verb* To pile up. ▷ **heaping, heaped**
3. *noun* (informal) A great deal of something. *There's a heap of junk in the basement.*

hear (hihr) *verb*
1. To sense sounds through your ears. ▷ *noun* **hearing**
2. To get news. *Jan heard from his friend in Norway.*
3. To listen to. *Please hear my side of the story.* **Hear** sounds like **here.**
▷ *verb* **hearing, heard** (hurd)

hearing aid *noun* A small piece of electronic equipment that people wear in or behind one or both ears to help them hear better.

hear·say (hihr-*say*) *noun* Things that you are told but have not actually seen or experienced; rumor. *I never listen to hearsay.*

hearse (hurss) *noun* A car that carries a coffin to a funeral and burial.

heart (hart) *noun*
1. The organ in your chest that pumps blood all through your body.
2. Courage or enthusiasm. *Don't lose heart when things go wrong.*
3. Love and affection. *You have won my heart.*
4. The center of something, as in *the heart of the city.*
5. If you learn something **by heart,** you memorize it.
6. hearts *noun, plural* One of the four suits in a deck of cards. Hearts have a red symbol shaped like a heart.
7. If you **take something to heart,** you think about it seriously.

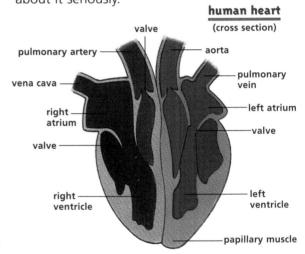

human heart
(cross section)

valve
pulmonary artery
aorta
vena cava
pulmonary vein
right atrium
left atrium
valve
valve
right ventricle
left ventricle
papillary muscle

heart attack *noun* If someone has a **heart attack,** the person's heart is not pumping blood properly to the rest of the body. The result can be extreme chest pain, collapse, or, in very severe cases, death.

heart·beat (hart-*beet*) *noun* One complete pumping movement of the heart.

heart·bro·ken (hart-*broh*-kuhn) *adjective* If you are **heartbroken,** you are sad or filled with grief.

hearth (harth) *noun* The area in front of a fireplace.

heart·less (hart-liss) *adjective* Cruel and unkind. ▷ *noun* **heartlessness** ▷ *adverb* **heartlessly**

heart·y (har-tee) *adjective*
1. Enthusiastic or sincere. *The team received a hearty welcome home after winning the state championship.* ▷ *adverb* **heartily**
2. A **hearty** meal is large and filling.
▷ *adjective* **heartier, heartiest** ▷ *noun* **heartiness**

heat (heet)
1. *noun* Great warmth.
2. *verb* To warm or cook something. ▷ **heating, heated**

H

3. noun A trial run in a race. *Linda won the first heat in the 100-meter dash.*

4. noun Passion. *In the heat of the argument, I lost my self-control.* ▷ *adjective* **heated** ▷ *adverb* **heatedly**

5. noun In physics, energy that comes from the motion of molecules passing from one substance to another, which increases temperature.

6. heat wave noun Unusually hot weather that lasts for several days.

heat·er (hee-tur) *noun* A device that produces heat, such as a radiator or a furnace.

heath (heeth) *noun* A large, wild area of grasses, ferns, and heather.

hea·then (hee-THuhn) *noun*
1. Someone who does not believe in the God of Christianity, Judaism, or Islam.
2. *(informal)* Someone who is uncivilized.

heath·er (heTH-ur) *noun* A small bush with pink, purple, or white flowers.

heave (heev)
1. verb To lift, pull, push, or throw something with great effort.
2. verb To go up and down. *Clark's chest heaved with emotion.*
3. noun The act of lifting or pulling.
▷ *verb* **heaving, heaved**

heav·en (hev-uhn) *noun*
1. In Christianity and some other religions, a glorious place where God is believed to live and where good people are believed to go after they die.
2. A wonderful place, thing, or state. *It was heaven to be on vacation.*
3. the heavens noun, plural The sky.

heav·en·ly (hev-uhn-lee) *adjective*
1. To do with heaven; divine.
2. To do with the sky or outer space, as in *heavenly bodies.*
3. Delightful or wonderful.

heav·y (hev-ee) *adjective*
1. Weighing a lot.
2. Great in amount or force, as in *heavy fighting* or *heavy rain.*
3. Slow or difficult, as in *heavy work.*
4. Difficult to digest, as in *heavy, greasy food.*
5. *(slang)* Serious and hard to cope with, as in *a heavy film.*
▷ *adjective* **heavier, heaviest** ▷ *noun* **heaviness**
▷ *adverb* **heavily**

heavy metal *noun* A type of rock-and-roll music with a strong beat and loud electric guitars.

He·brew (hee-broo)
1. noun A member of or descendant from one of the Jewish tribes of ancient times.

2. noun The language of the ancient Hebrews, used today as a language of prayer and by the people who live in Israel.
3. adjective To do with the Hebrews or their language.

heck·le (hek-uhl) *verb* To interrupt a speaker by making rude comments. ▷ **heckling, heckled** ▷ *noun* **heckler**

hect·are (hek-tair) *noun* A unit of area in the metric system. One hectare is equal to 10,000 square meters. It takes about 15 school soccer fields to make one hectare. A hectare is about $2\frac{1}{2}$ acres.

hec·tic (hek-tik) *adjective* Very busy. *Bill's been on a hectic schedule lately.* ▷ *adverb* **hectically**

hedge (hej)
1. noun A border of bushes.
2. verb To avoid giving a direct answer. *Quit hedging and answer the question.* ▷ **hedging, hedged**

heed (heed) *verb* To pay close attention to someone or something. *I will heed your good advice.* ▷ **heeding, heeded** ▷ *noun* **heed**

heel (heel) *noun*
1. The back part of your foot.
2. Something that supports or is worn on the back part of your foot.
3. If you **kick up your heels,** you are having a very good time.
Heel sounds like **heal.**

hef·ty (hef-tee) *adjective* *(informal)* Large or powerful. *Neal used to be slim, but now he's really hefty.* ▷ **heftier, heftiest** ▷ *noun* **heftiness** ▷ *adverb* **heftily**

heif·er (hef-ur) *noun* A young cow that has not had a calf.

height (hite) *noun*
1. A measurement of how high something is.
2. The most important or greatest point of something. *My new hat is the height of fashion.*

height·en (hite-uhn) *verb* To make something higher or stronger, as in *to heighten suspense.*

Heim·lich maneuver (hime-lik) *noun* An emergency action done to dislodge food from the windpipe, performed by squeezing the person from behind, below the ribs.

heir (air) *noun* Someone who has been, or will be, left money, property, or a title, as in *the heir to a fortune.* **Heir** sounds like **air.**

heir·ess (air-uhss) *noun* A girl or woman who has been, or will be, left money, property, or a title. ▷ *noun, plural* **heiresses**

heir·loom (air-*loom*) *noun* Something precious that is owned by a family member and handed down from one generation to the next.

H

hel·i·cop·ter
(hel-uh-*kop*-tur)
noun An aircraft with large rotating blades on top that can take off and land in a small space. *The picture shows a Schweizer 300C helicopter.*

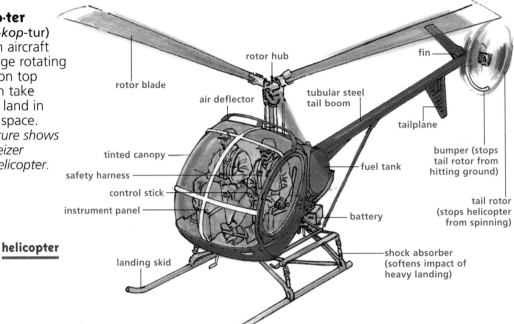

rotor hub
fin
rotor blade
air deflector
tubular steel tail boom
tailplane
tinted canopy
bumper (stops tail rotor from hitting ground)
safety harness
fuel tank
control stick
tail rotor (stops helicopter from spinning)
instrument panel
battery
shock absorber (softens impact of heavy landing)
landing skid

helicopter

Word History

The French word *hélicoptère* was borrowed into English as **helicopter**. The French word comes from the Greek *heliko*, which is a form of *helix*, which means "spiral," and *pteron*, which means "wing."

he·li·um (hee-lee-uhm) *noun* A light, colorless gas that does not burn. It is used in airships and balloons.

hell (hel) *noun*
1. In Christianity and some other religions, a place of suffering and misery where evil people are believed to go when they die.
2. A very unpleasant place, thing, or state. *It was hell having to work such long hours.*
▷ *adjective* **hellish**

hel·lo (hel-oh *or* huh-loh) *interjection* A word said in greeting when you meet a person or speak on the telephone.

helm (helm) *noun*
1. The wheel or handle used to steer a boat.
2. If someone is **at the helm** of something, such as a company, the person is in charge of it.

hel·met (hel-mit) *noun* A hard hat that protects your head during sports or dangerous activities.

help (help)
1. *verb* To assist. ▷ *noun* **helper**
2. *noun* Assistance.
3. *verb* To make feel better. *The medicine helped his cough.*

4. *verb* To avoid. *I couldn't help laughing.*
▷ *verb* **helping, helped**

help·ful (help-fuhl) *adjective* Friendly and willing to help. ▷ *noun* **helpfulness** ▷ *adverb* **helpfully**

help·ing (help-ing) *noun* A portion of food.

helping verb *noun* A verb, such as *may* or a form of *be*, that is used together with another verb to complete the meaning of that verb, as in "may marry" or "is married." A helping verb is also called an **auxiliary** *verb*.

help·less (help-liss) *adjective* If you are **helpless,** you cannot look after yourself. ▷ *noun* **helplessness** ▷ *adverb* **helplessly**

hem (hem) *verb*
1. To fold over an edge of material and sew it down. ▷ *noun* **hem**
2. If you are **hemmed in,** you are surrounded and cannot get out.
▷ *verb* **hemming, hemmed**

hem·i·sphere (hem-uhss-fihr) *noun* One half of a sphere, especially of the earth. *Canada is in the earth's northern hemisphere.*

hem·lock (hem-lok) *noun*
1. An evergreen tree similar to the pine. It has flat needles, small cones, and reddish bark.
2. A poisonous plant of the carrot family.

he·mo·glo·bin (hee-muh-*gloh*-buhn) *noun* A substance in your red blood cells that carries oxygen to all parts of your body.

he·mo·phil·i·a (hee-muh-fil-ee-uh) *noun* If people suffer from **hemophilia,** their blood does not clot properly, so they bleed severely if cut or bruised.

hem·or·rhage (hem-ur-ij) *noun* Severe bleeding from a torn or cut blood vessel.

H

hemp (hemp) *noun* A plant whose fibers are used to make rope and sacks.

hen (hen) *noun*
1. Any of various female birds.
2. A female bird raised for its eggs and its meat. *See* **chicken**.

hep·tath·lon (hep-tath-luhn) *noun* A competition made up of seven athletic events.

her (hur)
1. *pronoun* The form of **she** used as a grammatical object. *I saw her yesterday.*
2. *adjective* Belonging to or to do with her. *Her smile is nice.*

her·ald·ry (her-uhl-dree) *noun* The study of coats of arms and family histories. *The picture shows some patterns and symbols used in heraldry.*

heraldry

cross   chevron   bend

fleur-de-lis   lion rampant   lion passant

herb (urb) *noun* A plant used in cooking or medicine. ▷ *noun* **herbalist** ▷ *adjective* **herbal**

herbs

rosemary

bay

dill

sage

mint

basil

thyme

parsley

her·bi·vore (hur-buh-*vor*) *noun* An animal that eats plants rather than other animals. *Cows and rabbits are examples of herbivores.* ▷ *adjective* **herbivorous** (hur-biv-uh-ruhss)

herd (hurd)
1. *noun* A large group of animals, as in *a herd of cattle.*
2. *verb* To make people or animals move together as a group. *We were all herded into a tiny room to hear the news.* ▷ **herding, herded** ▷ *noun* **herder**
Herd sounds like **heard**.

here (hihr)
1. *adverb* At or in this place. *Put the bag here.*
2. *adverb* At this point or time. *Here the music becomes softer.*
3. *interjection* A word used to answer a roll call. *Here!*
4. *noun* This place. *The boundary is from here to that tree.*
Here sounds like **hear**.

here·af·ter (*hihr*-af-tur) *adverb* From now on.

here·by (hihr-*bye* or hihr-bye) *adverb* By means of this. *Lindsay's memo said, "I hereby resign."*

he·red·i·tar·y (huh-**red**-uh-*ter*-ee) *adjective* If something is **hereditary,** it is passed from parent to child, as in *a hereditary disease.*

he·red·i·ty (huh-**red**-uh-tee) *noun*
1. The passing on of traits from parents to children through the genes. *The speakers argued about whether a person's intelligence is a result of heredity or environment.*
2. All of the traits that are passed on in this way. *Bridget's blue eyes and red hair are part of her heredity.*

her·e·tic (her-uh-tik) *noun* Someone whose views are different from those of a particular religion or unacceptable to people in authority. ▷ *noun* **heresy** ▷ *adjective* **heretical**

her·i·tage (her-uh-tij) *noun* Valuable or important traditions handed down from generation to generation. *We value our heritage of freedom.*

her·mit (hur-mit) *noun* Someone who lives totally alone and isolated from other people.

he·ro (hihr-oh) *noun*
1. A brave or good person. ▷ *noun* **heroism**
2. The main character in a book, play, movie, or any kind of story.
▷ *noun, plural* **heroes**

he·ro·ic (hi-roh-ik) *adjective*
1. Very brave or daring. *The police officer made a heroic leap to save the child.*
2. To do with the deeds and actions of heroes. *The book is full of heroic stories from World War II.*
▷ *adverb* **heroically**

H

H

her·o·in (her-oh-uhn) *noun* A powerful, illegal, addictive drug. **Heroin** sounds like **heroine.**

her·o·ine (her-oh-uhn) *noun*
1. A brave girl or woman.
2. The main female character in a book, play, movie, or any kind of story. **Heroine** sounds like **heroin.**

her·on (her-uhn) *noun* A bird with a long, thin beak and long legs that lives near water.

her·pes (hur-peez) *noun* Any of several diseases that cause painful blisters at various places on the body. Herpes is caused by any one of several related viruses.

her·ring (her-ing) *noun* A bony fish that swims in the northern Atlantic and Pacific oceans and is used for food.

hers (hurz) *pronoun* The one or ones belonging to or to do with her. *That pen is hers.*

her·self (hur-self) *pronoun* Her and no one else. *Emily hurt herself when she tried to move the dresser without help.*

hertz (hurts) *noun* A unit for measuring the frequency of vibrations and waves, equal to one cycle per second. The abbreviation for *hertz* is *Hz.* ▷ *noun, plural* **hertz**

hes·i·tate (hez-uh-tate) *verb* To pause before you do something. *Zoe hesitated before diving into the freezing-cold water.* ▷ **hesitating, hesitated** ▷ *noun* **hesitation** ▷ *adjective* **hesitant**

hex·a·gon (hek-suh-*gon*) *noun* A shape with six straight sides. *See* **shape.** ▷ *adjective* **hexagonal**

hey (hay) *interjection* A word used to get someone's attention or to express surprise or joy. **Hey** sounds like **hay.**

hey·day (hay-*day*) *noun* Your **heyday** is the best or most successful period in your life.

hi (hye) *interjection* A word used as a greeting; hello. **Hi** sounds like **high.**

hi·ber·nate (hye-bur-nate) *verb* When animals **hibernate,** they spend the winter in a deep sleep. Animals hibernate to survive low temperatures and a lack of food. ▷ **hibernating, hibernated** ▷ *noun* **hibernation**

▶ Word History
• •
The English word **hibernate** comes from the Latin word *hibernus,* meaning "wintry." Winter is the time when certain kinds of animals hibernate.

hic·cup (hik-uhp) *noun*
1. A sudden sound in your throat caused by a spasm in your chest.
2. **hiccups** *noun, plural* The condition of having these spasms for a period of time. Sometimes called *the hiccups.*

hick·o·ry (hik-ur-ee) *noun* A tall tree of North America with hard wood and an edible nut. ▷ *noun, plural* **hickories** ▷ *adjective* **hickory**

hide (hide)
1. *verb* To go where you cannot be seen.
2. *verb* To keep something secret or concealed. *Julia managed to hide her disappointment when she wasn't selected for the team.*
3. *noun* An animal's skin used to make leather.
4. If something stays **in hiding,** it remains out of sight. ▷ *verb* **hiding, hid** (hid), **hidden** (hid-in)

hide-and-seek *noun* A game in which people hide while one person, who is "it," looks for—or seeks—them.

hid·e·ous (hid-ee-uhss) *adjective* Ugly or horrible. ▷ *noun* **hideousness** ▷ *adverb* **hideously**

hide·out (hide-*out*) *noun* A place where someone can hide, especially a criminal trying to escape from the police.

hi·er·o·glyph·ics (hye-ur-uh-glif-iks) *noun, plural* Writing used by ancient Egyptians, made up of pictures and symbols. *The hieroglyphics shown here were used as symbols for both objects and letters or sounds.*

hieroglyphics

D
hand

T
loaf

W
quail chick

F
viper

B
foot

Y
flowering reed

N
water

H
room

M
owl

K
basket

high (hye) *adjective*
1. Something that is **high** is a great distance from the ground, as in *a high mountain.* ▷ *adverb* **high**
2. Measuring from top to bottom. *The tree was 75 feet high.*

3. More than the normal level or amount, as in *high prices.* ▷ *noun* **high** ▷ *adverb* **highly** **High** sounds like **hi.**
▷ *adjective* **higher, highest**

higher education *noun* Education at a college or university.

high jump *noun* An event in a track-and-field competition in which the athlete must jump over a bar without knocking it down. ▷ *noun* **high jumper**

high·land (hye-luhnd) *noun* An area with mountains or hills. ▷ *adjective* **highland**

high·light (hye-*lite*)
1. *verb* To draw attention to something.
2. *noun* The best or most interesting part of something, as in *the highlight of our trip.*
3. *verb* To mark important words using a pen with brightly colored ink. *Highlight the verb in each sentence.*
4. highlights *noun, plural* Streaks of a light color in hair. *Denise decided to put highlights in her hair.*
▷ *verb* **highlighting, highlighted**

high-rise *noun* A very tall building. ▷ *adjective* **high-rise**

high seas *noun, plural* The open waters of an ocean or a sea that are beyond the boundaries or control of any country.

high-strung *adjective* Very nervous or excitable.

high tech (tek) *noun* The latest technology based on advanced electronics, computers, etc.

high tide *noun* The time at which the water level in an ocean, a gulf, or a bay is at its highest point.

high·way (hye-*way*) *noun* A main public road.

hi·jack (hye-*jak*) *verb* If someone **hijacks** a plane or other vehicle, the person takes illegal control of it and forces its pilot or driver to go somewhere. ▷ **hijacking, hijacked** ▷ *noun* **hijacker,** *noun* **hijacking**

hike (hike) *noun* A long walk, especially in the country. ▷ *noun* **hiker,** *noun* **hiking** ▷ *verb* **hike**

hi·lar·i·ous (huh-**lair**-ee-uhss *or* hi-**lair**-ee-uhss) *adjective* Very funny. ▷ *noun* **hilarity**

hill (hil) *noun* A raised area of land that is smaller than a mountain. ▷ *adjective* **hilly**

hill·side (hil-*side*) *noun* The sloping side of a hill. *Each spring the hillside is covered with flowers.*

hill·top (hil-*top*) *noun* The highest part of a hill. *We live in a house on a hilltop.*

hilt (hilt) *noun*
1. The handle of a sword or dagger. *See* **rapier.**
2. to the hilt To the limit; completely. *Kyle used his charm to the hilt during his meeting with the principal.*

him (him) *pronoun* The form of **he** used as a grammatical object. **Him** sounds like **hymn.**

him·self (him-**self**) *pronoun* Him and no one else. *Justin often talks to himself.*

hind (hinde) *adjective* At the back or rear. *The horse kicked up its hind legs.*

hin·der (hin-dur) *verb* If someone or something **hinders** you, it makes things difficult for you. ▷ **hindering, hindered**

Hin·du·ism (hin-doo-*iz*-uhm) *noun* A religion and philosophy practiced mainly in India. Hindus believe that they must act in harmony with universal laws and that various gods are different forms of the Supreme Deity. *This bronze statue represents Shiva, one of the main gods in Hinduism.* ▷ *noun* **Hindu** ▷ *adjective* **Hindu**

Shiva

hinge (hinj)
1. *noun* A movable metal joint on a window or a door. ▷ *adjective* **hinged**
2. *verb* To depend on something. *My future hinges on your decision.* ▷ **hinging, hinged**

hint (hint) *noun*
1. A clue or helpful tip. ▷ *verb* **hint**
2. A tiny amount; a trace. *There's a hint of salt in this soup.*

hip (hip) *noun* The part of your body below your waist that sticks out on either side, covering the joint where the thigh joins the pelvis.

hip-hop *noun* A style of dancing, art, music, and dress that originated in urban areas and became popular through break dancing, graffiti, and rap music.

hip·pie (hip-ee) *noun* A member of a cultural movement that began in the United States during the 1960s. Hippies opposed the war in Vietnam and rebelled against society by developing their own style of dress and behavior. ▷ *noun, plural* **hippies**

hip·po·pot·a·mus (*hip*-uh-**pot**-uh-muhss) *noun* A large African mammal with short legs and thick skin that lives in or near water. ▷ *noun, plural* **hippopotamuses** *or* **hippopotami** (*hip*-uh-**pot**-uh-*mye or hip*-uh-**pot**-uh-*mee*)

hippopotamus

H

249

hire (hire) *verb* To employ someone. *Is the factory hiring?* ▷ **hiring, hired**

his (hiz)
1. *adjective* Belonging to or to do with him.
2. *pronoun* The one or ones belonging to or to do with him.

His·pan·ic (hiss-pan-ik) *adjective* Coming from or to do with countries where Spanish is spoken. ▷ *noun* **Hispanic**

hiss (hiss) *verb* To make a "ssss" noise like a snake, especially to show that you do not like something or someone. *We hissed at the villains in the play.* ▷ **hisses, hissing, hissed** ▷ *noun* **hiss**

his·tor·ic (hiss-tor-ik) *adjective* If an event is **historic,** it was important in the past or will be seen as important in the future, as in *the historic first landing on the moon.*

his·tor·ic·al (hi-stor-uh-kuhl) *adjective* To do with people or events of the past, as in *an historical novel.* ▷ *adverb* **historically**

his·to·ry (hiss-tuh-ree) *noun*
1. The study of past events. ▷ *noun* **historian**
2. A description of past events. *I'm reading a history of medicine.*
▷ *noun, plural* **histories**

hit (hit)
1. *verb* To smack or strike something with your hand or with an object such as a bat or a hammer. ▷ *noun* **hit,** *noun* **hitter**
2. *verb* To knock or bump into something. *The stone hit the window.*
3. *verb* To have a bad effect on someone or something. *The factory was hit by the recession.*
4. *noun* A successful song, play, or any type of presentation. *My lasagna was a big hit with the family.*
5. *verb* (informal) If you **hit it off** with someone, you get along well with the person.
▷ *verb* **hitting, hit**

hitch (hich)
1. *verb* To fasten with a rope, etc., as in *to hitch a horse to a post.*
2. *noun* A problem. *There's been a hitch in our plans, so we can't come.*
3. *verb* To join something to a vehicle. *They hitched the trailer to the van.*
4. (slang) If you **get hitched,** you marry someone.
▷ *noun, plural* **hitches** ▷ *verb* **hitches, hitching, hitched**

hitch·hike (hich-*hike*) *verb* To travel by getting rides in other people's vehicles. *It can be very dangerous to hitchhike.* ▷ **hitchhiking, hitchhiked** ▷ *noun* **hitchhiker**

hith·er (hiTH-ur) *adverb* To or toward this place. *Come hither!*

HIV (aych eye vee) *noun*
1. A virus that can lead to AIDS. HIV stands for *Human Immunodeficiency Virus.*
2. If someone is **HIV positive,** the person has the HIV virus and his or her immune system is weak. People who are HIV positive can develop AIDS.

hive (hive) *noun*
1. A natural structure in which bees build a honeycomb. *See* **honeycomb.**
2. A box for keeping bees so that their honey can be collected. *The queen bee lays her eggs in the brood box and honey is stored in the supers. The honey-filled supers are collected from the hive.*
3. **hives** *noun, plural* A rash that appears on the skin, usually from an allergic reaction.

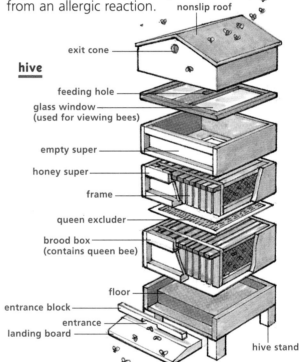

hive

nonslip roof
exit cone
feeding hole
glass window (used for viewing bees)
empty super
honey super
frame
queen excluder
brood box (contains queen bee)
floor
entrance block
entrance
landing board
hive stand

hoard (hord) *verb*
1. To collect and store things. *Squirrels hoard nuts for the winter.*
2. To buy up a lot of supplies because you think there will be a shortage.
Hoard sounds like **horde.**
▷ *verb* **hoarding, hoarded** ▷ *noun* **hoard,** *noun* **hoarder**

hoarse (horss) *adjective* A **hoarse** voice is rough and sore. **Hoarse** sounds like **horse.**

hoax (hohks) *noun* A trick or a practical joke.
▷ *noun, plural* **hoaxes**

hob·ble (hob-uhl) *verb* To walk with difficulty because you are in pain or are injured.
▷ **hobbling, hobbled**

H

hob·by (hob-ee) *noun* Something that you enjoy doing in your spare time. ▷ *noun, plural* **hobbies**

> ▶ **Word History**
> ·
> The word **hobby** comes from the word *hobbyhorse*, which used to mean a small horse. Later, a hobbyhorse referred to a play horse for children. No one is quite sure how hobby came to mean a pastime, except that both hobbies and hobbyhorses are fun.

hock·ey (hok-ee) *See* **ice hockey, field hockey.**

Hodg·kin's disease (hoj-kinz) *noun* A disease in which the lymph glands, spleen, and liver become increasingly enlarged.

hoe (hoh) *noun* A gardening tool with a long handle and a thin blade, used for weeding and loosening earth. ▷ *verb* **hoe**

hog (hog)
1. *noun* A fully grown pig.
2. *noun* (informal) A selfish person who takes more than his or her fair share, as in *a road hog.*
3. *verb* (informal) To take more than one's fair share. ▷ **hogging, hogged**

ho·gan (hoh-guhn) *noun* A Navajo house made with logs and branches and covered with earth.

hoist (hoist)
1. *verb* To lift something heavy, usually with a piece of equipment. *The crane hoisted the cars off the ship.* ▷ **hoisting, hoisted**
2. *noun* A piece of equipment used for lifting heavy objects.

hold (hohld)
1. *verb* To carry, support, or keep something. *Hold the cup carefully.* ▷ *noun* **holder**
2. *verb* To contain something or be able to contain it. *This bottle holds less than a quart.*
3. *verb* To have. *We held a secret meeting of our club.*
4. *noun* The part of a ship where the cargo is stored.
5. If you **hold out** in a difficult situation, you continue with what you are doing.
6. If someone is **held up,** the person is robbed by someone with a weapon.
▷ *verb* **holding, held** (held)

hold·up (hohld-uhp) *noun*
1. A robbery by someone who has a weapon.
2. A delay in activity. *The three-car accident caused a holdup on the freeway.*

hole (hohl) *noun*
1. A hollow place, or a gap.
2. An animal's den.
3. (informal) An unpleasant or dirty place.

hol·i·day (hol-uh-day) *noun*
1. A day on which work, school, or any regular activities are officially suspended. Labor Day and Memorial Day are holidays.
2. A religious festival or holy time, such as Passover, Christmas, or the month of Ramadan.

ho·lis·tic (hoh-liss-tik) *adjective* To do with the whole of anything rather than with its individual parts. Holistic medicine deals with the whole patient, the mind and the body, not just an isolated physical pain or symptom.

hol·low (hol-oh)
1. *adjective* If something is **hollow,** it has an empty space inside it. ▷ *noun* **hollow**
2. hollow out *verb* If you **hollow** something **out,** you take its insides out. ▷ **hollowing, hollowed**

hol·ly (hol-ee) *noun* An evergreen tree or bush with prickly leaves and red berries.

hol·ly·hock (hol-ee-hok) A tall garden plant grown for its showy spikes of large, brightly colored flowers.

ho·lo·caust (hol-uh-kost) *noun*
1. Total destruction and great loss of life, especially by fire, as in *a nuclear holocaust.*
2. the Holocaust The killing of millions of European Jews and others by the Nazis during World War II.

ho·lo·gram (hol-uh-gram) *noun* An image made by laser beams that looks three-dimensional. ▷ *noun* **holography** (huh-log-ruh-fee)

hol·ster (hohl-stur) *noun* A holder for a gun worn on a belt.

ho·ly (hoh-lee) *adjective* To do with or belonging to God or a higher being. ▷ **holier, holiest**

Holy Communion *noun* A Christian service in which people eat bread and drink wine or grape juice to symbolize the death and resurrection of Jesus.

home (home) *noun*
1. Your **home** is where you live or belong. ▷ *adverb* **home**
2. A place where you are likely to find something. *Africa is the home of many exotic animals.*
3. A place where the ill, the aged, or the homeless can receive proper care, as in *a nursing home.*
4. If you **feel at home** with someone, you feel comfortable with the person.

home·less (home-liss)
1. *adjective* Without a permanent home or place to sleep. *We volunteer at a shelter for homeless people.*
2. the homeless *noun, plural* People who have no permanent home or place to sleep. *Our spaghetti dinner raised $400 to feed the homeless.*

H

home·ly (home-lee) *adjective*
1. Not attractive in appearance; plain.
2. Not fancy or pretentious; simple, as in *a homely manner.*
▷ *adjective* **homelier, homeliest**

home·made (home-made) *adjective* Made at home or by hand, as in *homemade soup.*

home·mak·er (home-*may*-kur) *noun* Someone who takes care of a house and family. ▷ *noun* **homemaking** ▷ *adjective* **homemaking**

ho·me·op·a·thy (*hoh*-mee-*op*-uh-thee) *noun* A way of treating illness by giving people very small amounts of substances that produce the same symptoms as the illness. ▷ *noun* **homeopath** (hoh-mee-uh-*path*) ▷ *adjective* **homeopathic**

home plate *noun* In baseball, the base next to which a batter stands to hit the ball. The batter must run to all the bases and cross home plate to score a run. *See* **baseball.**

home·room (home-*room* or **home**-*rum*) *noun* A classroom in which students meet with their teacher before studying begins.

home run *noun* In baseball, a hit that allows the batter to run all the way around the bases and score a run.

home·sick (hohm-*sik*) *adjective* If you are **homesick,** you miss your home and family.

home·spun (hohm-*spuhn*) *adjective*
1. Spun or made at home, especially fabric.
2. Plain and simple, as in *homespun humor.*

home·stead (home-sted) *noun*
1. A house, especially a farmhouse, with its buildings and land.
2. In the American West, a piece of land measuring 160 acres (65 hectares) given to a settler by the U.S. government.
▷ *noun* **homesteader** ▷ *verb* **homestead**

home·work (home-*wurk*) *noun* Work assigned in school that is to be done at home.

ho·mi·cide (hom-uh-*side* or **hoh**-muh-*side*) *noun* Murder. ▷ *adjective* **homicidal**

ho·mog·e·nize (huh-**moj**-uh-nize) *verb* To mix the cream in milk so that it is spread evenly through the liquid and does not rise to the top.
▷ **homogenizing, homogenized** ▷ *noun* **homogenization**

hom·o·graph (hom-uh-*graf*) *noun* One of two or more words that have the same spelling but different meanings and possibly different pronunciations. A *bowl,* meaning a kind of dish, and to *bowl,* meaning to play a game of bowling, are homographs, as are *wind,* a current of air, and to *wind,* or coil something.

hom·o·nym (hom-uh-nim) *noun* One of two or more words that have the same pronunciation and often the same spelling but different

meanings. *Lock* meaning "a tuft of hair" and *lock* meaning "a part of a door that you open and shut with a key" are homonyms.

hom·o·phone (home-uh-*fone*) *noun* One of two or more words that have the same pronunciation but different spellings and different meanings. *To, too,* and *two* are homophones.

hon·est (on-ist) *adjective* An **honest** person is truthful and will not lie or steal or cheat anyone. ▷ *noun* **honesty** ▷ *adverb* **honestly**

hon·ey (huhn-ee) *noun* A sweet, sticky, golden-brown substance made by bees. *See* **hive, honeycomb.**

hon·ey·bee (huhn-ee-bee) *noun* A bee that collects pollen and uses it to make honey in a hive. *See* **hive, honeycomb.**

hon·ey·comb (huhn-ee-*kohm*) *noun* A wax structure made by bees and used by them to store honey, pollen, and eggs. A honeycomb consists of many rows of cells with six sides. *The picture shows the different functions of the cells in a honeycomb. For the first six days, the brood cells are unsealed so the worker bees can feed the growing larvae. Then the bees seal the cells and the larvae change into pupae, which develop into bees. See also* **hive.**

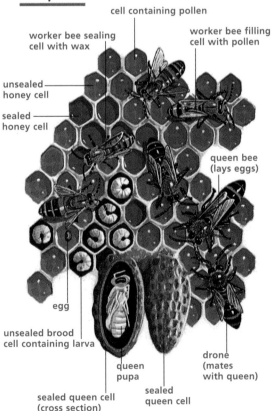

honeycomb

cell containing pollen
worker bee sealing cell with wax
worker bee filling cell with pollen
unsealed honey cell
sealed honey cell
queen bee (lays eggs)
egg
unsealed brood cell containing larva
queen pupa
sealed queen cell (cross section)
sealed queen cell
drone (mates with queen)

hon·ey·moon (huhn-ee-*moon*) *noun* A trip that a bride and groom take together after their wedding.

hon·ey·suck·le (huhn-ee-*suhk*-uhl) *noun* A climbing vine or shrub with fragrant white, red, or yellow flowers shaped like small tubes.

honk (hongk)
1. *noun* The sound a goose makes.
2. *noun* The sound a car horn makes.
3. *verb* To make the sound of a goose or a car horn. ▷ **honking, honked**

hon·or (on-ur)
1. *noun* Someone's **honor** is his or her good reputation and the respect that other people have for the person.
2. *verb* To give praise or an award. *The mayor honored Kim for her bravery.* ▷ *noun* **honor**
3. *verb* To keep an agreement. *Both parties must honor the contract.*
4. *noun* A special privilege. *"It's an honor to be here today," the speaker began at our graduation.*
▷ *verb* **honoring, honored**

hon·or·a·ble (on-ur-uh-buhl) *adjective*
1. An **honorable** action is good and deserves praise.
2. If someone is **honorable,** the person keeps his or her promises.

hon·or·ar·y (on-uh-rer-ee) *adjective* Given as an honor without the usual requirements or duties. *The university gave the governor an honorary degree.*

hood (hud) *noun*
1. The part of a jacket or coat that goes over your head. ▷ *adjective* **hooded**
2. The cover for a car's engine.

hood·lum (hood-luhm) *noun*
1. A gangster or a thug.
2. A young person who is rough, mean, or violent.

hoof (huf *or* hoof) *noun*
1. The hard covering over the foot of a horse, deer, etc. *See* **horse.**
2. The entire foot of a horse, deer, etc.
▷ *noun, plural* **hoofs** *or* **hooves** ▷ *adjective* **hoofed** *or* **hooved**

hook (huk) *noun*
1. A curved piece of metal or plastic used to fasten or hold something.
2. A curved piece of metal with a barb at one end, used to catch fish.
3. A punch in boxing made with the elbow bent, as in *a right hook.*
▷ *verb* **hook**

hooked (hukt) *adjective*
1. Curved, as in *a hooked nose.*
2. If you are **hooked** on something, you like it a lot or are addicted to it.

hoo·li·gan (hoo-luh-guhn) *noun* A noisy, violent person who makes trouble. ▷ *noun* **hooliganism**

hoop (hoop *or* hup) *noun*
1. A large ring, as in *the hoops of a barrel.*
▷ *adjective* **hooped**
2. A ring with a net attached, used as a goal in basketball.
3. **hoops** *noun, plural* (informal) Basketball. *Let's play some hoops!*

hoo·ray *See* **hurray.**

hoot (hoot) *verb*
1. To make a sound like an owl.
2. To show dislike or disapproval by making a loud shout.
▷ *verb* **hooting, hooted** ▷ *noun* **hoot**

hop (hop)
1. *verb* To move with short jumps or leaps. *Birds hop around.*
2. *verb* To jump on one foot.
3. *verb* To jump over, as in *to hop a fence.*
4. **hops** *noun, plural* The dried seed cases of hop plants, which are used to make beer.
▷ *verb* **hopping, hopped** ▷ *noun* **hop**

hope (hope)
1. *verb* To wish for or expect something.
▷ **hoping, hoped**
2. *noun* A feeling of expectation or confidence. *I have plenty of hope for the future.*
▷ *noun* **hopefulness** ▷ *adjective* **hopeful** ▷ *adverb* **hopefully**

hope·less (hope-liss) *adjective*
1. Without hope.
2. Bad, or lacking in skill. *You're hopeless at reading a map!*
▷ *noun* **hopelessness** ▷ *adverb* **hopelessly**

Ho·pi (hoh-pee) *noun* One of a group of American Indians that lives primarily in northeastern Arizona. ▷ *noun, plural* **Hopi** *or* **Hopis**

hop·scotch (hop-*skoch*) *noun* A game in which players throw a stone or other object into a pattern of numbered shapes drawn on the ground. The players hop into the shapes in a certain order and try to pick up the stone.

playing hopscotch

horde (hord) *noun* A large, noisy, moving crowd of people or animals. **Horde** sounds like **hoard.**

ho·ri·zon (huh-**rye**-zuhn) *noun*
1. The line where the sky and the earth or sea seem to meet.
2. The limit of your experience or opportunities. *Travel broadens your horizons.*

hor·i·zon·tal (hor-uh-**zon**-tuhl) *adjective* Flat and parallel to the ground, as in *a horizontal line.*
▷ *adverb* **horizontally**

hor·mone (hor-mohn) *noun* Your **hormones** are chemicals made by certain glands in your body that affect the way you grow and develop.
▷ *adjective* **hormonal**

horn (horn) *noun*
1. A hard, bony, permanent growth on the heads of some animals. ▷ *adjective* **horned**
2. The hard, bony substance that horns and hoofs are made from. ▷ *adjective* **horny**
3. A brass musical instrument that you blow, as in *a French horn. See* **brass, orchestra.**
4. A machine that gives a signal by making a loud sound, as in *a car horn.*

hor·net (hor-nit) *noun* A large, stinging wasp that lives in colonies and builds a large nest.

hor·o·scope (hor-uh-*skope*) *noun* A diagram of the stars and planets on the day when you were born, used by astrologers to try to tell your character and predict events in your life.

hor·ri·ble (hor-uh-buhl) *adjective*
1. Causing horror or fear, as in *a horrible crime.*
2. Very bad, as in *a horrible cold.*
▷ *adverb* **horribly**

hor·rid (hor-id) *adjective* Nasty or horrible.

hor·rif·ic (hor-if-ik) *adjective* Shocking.

hor·ri·fy (hor-uh-fye) *verb* If something **horrifies** you, it shocks and disgusts you. ▷ **horrifies, horrifying, horrified** ▷ *adjective* **horrifying**

hor·ror (hor-ur)
1. *noun* Great fear, terror, or shock.
2. *noun* Something that brings on such a feeling. *The family was touched by the horror of war.*
3. *adjective* Intended to cause great fear or terror, as in *a horror story.*

horse (horss)
1. *noun* A large, strong animal with hoofs that people ride or use to pull coaches, carriages, plows, etc. *The picture shows an Arabian horse.*
2. *noun* A piece of gymnastics apparatus that you jump over.
3. *verb* If you **horse around,** you get into mischief. ▷ **horsing, horsed**
Horse sounds like **hoarse.**
See also **mustang.**

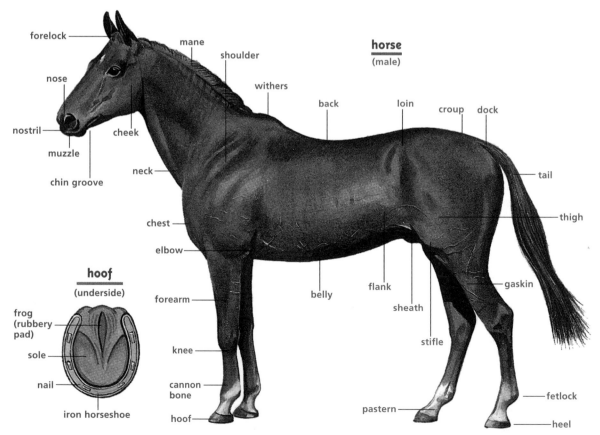

horse
(male)

forelock — mane — shoulder — withers — back — loin — croup — dock — nose — nostril — cheek — muzzle — neck — chin groove — chest — elbow — belly — flank — sheath — stifle — gaskin — thigh — tail — forearm — knee — cannon bone — hoof — pastern — fetlock — heel

hoof
(underside)

frog (rubbery pad) — sole — nail — iron horseshoe

H

horse·back (horss-*bak*)
1. *noun* The back of a horse.
2. *adverb* On the back of a horse. *They rode horseback into the mountains.*

horse·fly (horss-*flye*) *noun* A large fly. The female bites and sucks the blood of humans, horses, cattle, and other animals. ▷ *noun, plural* **horseflies**

horse·play (horss-*play*) *noun* Rough and noisy play or fun.

horse·pow·er (horss-*pou*-ur) *noun* A unit for measuring the power of an engine.

horse·shoe (horss-*shoo*) *noun*
1. A piece of metal shaped like a U and nailed to the bottom of a horse's hoof to protect it. *See* **horse.**
2. horseshoes *noun, plural* A game in which horseshoes are thrown around a metal stake.
▷ *verb* **horseshoe**

hor·ti·cul·ture (hor-tuh-*kuhl*-chur) *noun* The growing of fruits, vegetables, and flowers.
▷ *adjective* **horticultural**

hose (hohz)
1. *noun* A long, rubber or plastic tube through which liquids or gases travel.
2. *noun* Stockings or socks.
3. *verb* To wash or water something with a hose. *Will you hose the soap off the car?*
▷ **hosing, hosed**

ho·sier·y (hoh-zhur-ee) *noun* Stockings and socks.

hos·pice (hoss-piss) *noun* A place that provides care for people who are dying and comfort for their families.

hos·pi·tal (hoss-pi-tuhl) *noun* A place where you receive medical treatment and are looked after when you are sick or injured.

hos·pi·tal·i·ty (*hoss*-puh-tal-uh-tee) *noun* A generous and friendly way of treating people, especially guests, so that they feel comfortable and at home. ▷ *noun, plural* **hospitalities**
▷ *adjective* **hospitable** (hoss-pi-tuh-buhl *or* hoss-pit-uh-buhl)

host (hohst) *noun*
1. A person who entertains guests.
2. A large number. *The audience asked a host of questions.*
3. A person who is in charge of a TV show that offers conversation, music, etc., with celebrities and other guests.
4. An animal or plant from which a parasite or another organism gets nutrition.
▷ *verb* **host**

hos·tage (hoss-tij) *noun* Someone taken and held prisoner as a way of demanding money or other conditions.

hos·tel (hoss-tuhl) *noun* A building that provides inexpensive lodging or shelter for travelers, especially young people who are hiking or biking. **Hostel** sounds like **hostile.**

host·ess (hoh-stuhss) *noun*
1. A woman who entertains guests.
2. A woman who greets people in a restaurant or serves food on an airplane.
▷ *noun, plural* **hostesses**

hos·tile (hoss-tuhl) *adjective* Unfriendly or angry, as in *a hostile crowd.* **Hostile** sounds like **hostel.**

hos·til·i·ty (hoss-til-uh-tee)
1. *noun* A strong hatred or dislike.
2. hostilities *noun, plural* Acts of war.

hot (hot) *adjective*
1. Having a high temperature.
2. Very spicy and strong in taste.
3. Fiery. *Gene has a hot temper.*
4. Eager. *We were hot to get started on our trip.*
5. Recent or exciting, as in *hot news.*
▷ *adjective* **hotter, hottest**

hot-air balloon *See* **balloon.**

hot dog *noun* A long sausage usually eaten in a bun.

ho·tel (hoh-tel) *noun* A place where you pay to stay overnight. Many hotels serve meals.

hot spring *noun* A natural source of water heated by the earth's interior.

hot-water bottle *noun* A rubber container for hot water, used to warm a bed or soothe an ache.

hound (hound)
1. *noun* Any of various kinds of dog that have been bred to hunt by sight or scent.
2. *verb* To chase or pester somebody. *Reporters hounded the movie star.* ▷ **hounding, hounded**

hour (our) *noun* A unit of time equal to 60 minutes; $\frac{1}{24}$ of the time it takes the earth to make one turn on its axis. **Hour** sounds like **our.**
▷ *adverb* **hourly**

hour·glass (our-*glass*) *noun* An instrument for measuring time. It is made of two glass bulbs joined in the middle by a thin glass tube. A quantity of sand falls from the upper bulb into the lower one in exactly one hour.

house (houss)
1. *noun* A building where people live.
2. *noun* People who live in a house. *The alarm woke up the whole house.*
3. If something in a restaurant is **on the house,** it is free.
4. *verb* (houz) If you **house** someone, you provide the person with a place to stay or live.
▷ **housing, housed**

house·boat (houss-*boht*) *noun* A boat that people live on, with cooking and sleeping areas.

house·fly (houss-*flye*) *noun* A common fly found in most parts of the world. It feeds on food and garbage and spreads diseases among humans. *See* **insect.**

house·hold (houss-*hohld*)
1. *noun* All the people who live together in a house.
2. *adjective* Belonging to or to do with a house or a family. *We all share the household chores.*

House of Representatives *noun* One of the two houses of the U.S. Congress that makes laws. In this body, members are elected for two-year terms, and the number of members from each state is based on population.

house-sit *verb* To live in or take care of a home while the owners or regular residents are away. ▷ **house-sitting, house-sat** ▷ *noun* **house sitter**

house·work (houss-*wurk*) *noun* Work done to keep a house clean and tidy.

hous·ing (hou-*zing*) *noun*
1. Buildings or other shelters where people live, as in *student housing.*
2. A frame or cover that protects a machine's moving parts. *The jeweler took the watch out of its housing so he could repair it.*

hov·el (huhv-uhl *or* hov-uhl) *noun* A small, dirty house or hut. *The man lived in a hovel near the railroad tracks.*

hov·er (huhv-ur) *verb*
1. To remain in one place in the air. *Hummingbirds hover.*
2. To stay attentively nearby. *She hovered over the sick child.*
3. To linger, or to be uncertain. *Joe hovered in the doorway.*
▷ *verb* **hovering, hovered**

hov·er·craft (huhv-ur-*kraft*) *noun* A vehicle that can travel over land and water, supported by a cushion of air. *We took a ride in a hovercraft.*

how (hou) *adverb*
1. In what way, or by what means. *How do you carve a turkey?*
2. In what condition. *How are you?*
3. To what extent, amount, or degree. *How long is this play?*
4. For what reason, or why. *How did you happen to walk by at just the right time?*

how·ev·er (hou-ev-ur)
1. *conjunction* In spite of that. *It's very cold; however, we still plan to go.*
2. *adverb* In whatever way, or to whatever extent. *You have to go, however much you hate it.*

howl (houl) *verb*
1. To cry out in pain like a dog or a wolf. *I howled when I stepped on the nail.*
2. To yell out with laughter. *We howled at the great joke.*
3. To make a loud, sad noise. *The icy wind howled.*
▷ *verb* **howling, howled** ▷ *noun* **howl**

hub (huhb) *noun*
1. The center of a wheel. *See* **bicycle.**
2. The center of an organization or activity. *Wall Street in New York City is the hub of the financial world.*

huck·le·ber·ry (huhk-uhl-*ber*-ee) *noun* A shiny, dark blue or black berry similar to a blueberry that grows on a low shrub. Huckleberry can mean both the berry and the bush it grows on. ▷ *noun, plural* **huckleberries**

hud·dle (huhd-uhl)
1. *verb* To crowd together in a tight group. *We huddled together against the cold.* ▷ **huddling, huddled** ▷ *noun* **huddle**
2. *noun* A grouping of the offensive team in football to prepare for the next play. *The team formed a huddle.* ▷ *verb* **huddle**

hue (hyoo) *noun* A color, or a variety of a color.

huff (huhf) *noun* If you are **in a huff,** you are upset or very annoyed.

hug (huhg) *verb* To hold someone or something tightly in a loving or caring way. ▷ **hugging, hugged** ▷ *noun* **hug**

huge (hyooj) *adjective* Enormous or gigantic, as in *a huge amount of money.* ▷ **huger, hugest**

hulk (huhlk) *noun*
1. The remains of a wrecked ship.
2. A large, heavy person. ▷ *adjective* **hulking**

hull (huhl)
1. *noun* The frame or body of a boat or ship. *See* **hydrofoil, rescue helicopter, ship.**
2. *noun* The outer covering of certain fruits, seeds, or nuts.

almond hulls

3. *verb* To remove the outer skin of a seed or nut. ▷ **hulling, hulled**
4. *noun* The small leaves around the stem of a strawberry and some other fruits. ▷ *verb* **hull**

hum (huhm) *verb*
1. To sing a melody with your mouth closed.
2. To make a steady, buzzing noise.
▷ *verb* **humming, hummed** ▷ *noun* **hum**

hu·man (hyoo-muhn)
1. human *or* **human being** *noun* A person.
▷ *adjective* **human**
2. *adjective* Natural and understandable. *It was only human for Amy to admire her sister.*
3. human rights *noun, plural* Everyone's right to justice, fair treatment, and free speech.

hu·mane (hyoo-mayn) *adjective* Someone who is **humane** is kind and charitable. ▷ *adverb* **humanely**

hu·man·i·tar·i·an (hyoo-*man*-uh-**ter**-ee-uhn) *adjective* To do with helping people and relieving suffering. *A humanitarian medical unit has been sent into the war zone.*

hu·man·i·ty (hyoo-man-uh-tee) *noun*
1. All human beings.
2. Kindness and sympathy.
3. the humanities *noun, plural* Subjects outside the sciences, such as literature, history, and art.

hum·ble (huhm-buhl) *adjective* Modest and not proud. ▷ **humbler, humblest** ▷ *adverb* **humbly**

hum·drum (huhm-*druhm*) *adjective* A **humdrum** life is dull and filled with routine events.

hu·mid (hyoo-mid) *adjective* Damp and moist. ▷ *noun* **humidity**

hu·mil·i·ate (hyoo-mil-ee-ate) *verb* To make someone look or feel foolish or embarrassed. ▷ **humiliating, humiliated** ▷ *noun* **humiliation**

hu·mil·i·ty (hyoo-mil-uh-tee) *noun* If you show **humility,** you are not too proud, and you recognize your own faults.

hum·ming·bird (huhm-ing-*burd*) *noun* A very small, brightly colored bird that makes a humming sound when it flaps its wings rapidly. *This hummingbird is sticking its long beak into a flower so that it can suck up nectar through its hollow tongue.*

hummingbird

hum·mus (huhm-uhss) *noun* A dip or sandwich spread made of chickpeas and sesame paste.

hu·mor (hyoo-mur)
1. *noun* The funny or amusing aspect of something. *There was no humor in the story.*
2. *noun* If you have a **sense of humor,** you are quick to appreciate the funny side of life.
3. *noun* Mood or state of mind, as in *a good humor.*

4. *verb* If you **humor** someone, you keep the person happy by agreeing with him or her or doing what he or she wants. ▷ **humoring, humored**

> ### Word History
> The word **humor** started out in the Middle Ages meaning any of the four liquids believed to determine the state of a person's body and health. Humor today refers to a person's mood or state of mind. You can be in a good humor or a bad humor, but we no longer attribute these moods to the four liquids in our body.

hu·mor·ous (hyoo-mur-uhss) *adjective* Amusing.

hump (huhmp) *noun* A large lump that sticks out or up from something. *Camels have either one or two humps.* ▷ *adjective* **humped**

hump·back (huhmp-*bak*) *noun*
1. A humped or severely crooked back. Another term for a humpback is a **hunchback.**
2. A type of large whale that is black with a white underside.

hu·mus (hyoo-muhss) *noun* Rich, dark earth made from rotting vegetable and animal matter.

hunch (huhnch)
1. *verb* To lower your head into your shoulders and lean forward. *Hassan hunched over his homework.* ▷ **hunches, hunching, hunched**
2. *noun* An idea that is not backed by proof but comes from intuition. *I had a hunch that I would hear some good news.* ▷ *noun, plural* **hunches**

hunch·back (huhnch-bak) *noun*
1. A humpback.
2. A person having a humpback.

hun·dred (huhn-druhd) *noun* The whole number, written 100, that is equal to 10 × 10. ▷ *adjective* **hundred**

hun·dredth (huhn-dredth)
1. *noun* One part of something that has been divided into 100 equal parts, written $\frac{1}{100}$.
2. *noun* In decimal notation, the position of the second number to the right of the decimal point, known as *the hundredths place.* In the number 4.0129, the digit 1 is in the hundredths place.

hun·gry (huhng-gree) *adjective* Wanting food. ▷ **hungrier, hungriest** ▷ *noun* **hunger** ▷ *adverb* **hungrily**

hunk (huhngk) *noun* A large piece of something, such as bread, cheese, or meat.

H

hunt (huhnt) *verb*
1. To search for something. *Lisa hunted for her watch.*
2. To chase and kill deer, geese, or other wild animals for food or sport.
▷ *verb* **hunting, hunted** ▷ *noun* **hunt,** *noun* **hunting**

hunt·er (huhnt-ur) *noun*
1. Someone who hunts.
2. A horse or a dog that you use to help during hunting.

hur·dle (hur-duhl)
1. *noun* A small fence that you jump over in a running event. *The sequence of pictures shows a hurdler clearing a hurdle.* ▷ *noun* **hurdler**
2. *verb* To jump over something. ▷ **hurdling, hurdled**
3. *noun* An obstacle.

hurdler

hurl (hurl) *verb* To throw something with great effort. ▷ **hurling, hurled**

hur·ray *or* **hooray** (huh-ray) *or* **hurrah** (huh-rah) *interjection* A word used when people cheer.

hur·ri·cane (hur-uh-*kane*) *noun* A violent storm with high winds that starts in the regions of the Atlantic Ocean or the Caribbean Sea near the equator and then travels north, northeast, or northwest.

hur·ry (hur-ee)
1. *verb* To do things as fast as possible. ▷ **hurries, hurrying, hurried**
2. When you are **in a hurry,** you do everything very quickly and often impatiently.
▷ *adjective* **hurried**

hurt (hurt) *verb*
1. To cause physical or emotional pain. *She hurt him with her insulting remarks.* ▷ *adjective* **hurtful**
2. To be in pain. *My head hurts.*
▷ *verb* **hurting, hurt**

hur·tle (hur-tuhl) *verb* To move at great speed.
▷ **hurtling, hurtled**

hus·band (huhz-buhnd) *noun* The male partner in a marriage.

hush (huhsh)
1. *noun* A sudden period of quietness. *A hush fell over the audience as the curtain went up.*
▷ *verb* **hush** ▷ *noun, plural* **hushes**
2. *interjection* Be quiet! *Hush!*
3. hush up *verb* To keep something secret. *The government hushed up news about the scandal.*
▷ **hushes, hushing, hushed**
4. hush-hush *adjective* (*informal*) Very secret and confidential. *Lizi's news was very hush-hush.*

husk (huhsk) *noun* The outer casing of seeds or grains. *Corn is covered with a husk.*

husk·y (huhss-kee)
1. *adjective* A **husky** voice sounds low and hoarse.
2. *adjective* Large and powerful.
3. *noun* A strong dog with a thick coat, bred to pull sleds in the far North. ▷ *noun, plural* **huskies**
▷ *adjective* **huskier, huskiest** ▷ *noun* **huskiness**

hus·tle (huhss-uhl) *verb*
1. To push someone roughly in order to make the person move. *The guard hustled the prisoners out of the room.*
2. To work rapidly and energetically. *Andy hustled to finish the job by noon.* ▷ *noun* **hustler**
▷ *verb* **hustling, hustled**

hut (huht) *noun*
1. A small, primitive house.
2. A wooden shed.

hutch (huhch) *noun*
1. A pen or coop for rabbits or other small pets.
2. A wooden cupboard having open shelves on top to hold dishes.
▷ *noun, plural* **hutches**

hy·a·cinth (hye-uh-sinth) *noun* A plant related to the lily that grows from a bulb. It has a thick stem with small flowers that grow in long clusters.

hy·brid (hye-brid) *noun* A plant or an animal that has been bred from two different species or varieties. *Mules are hybrids.* ▷ *adjective* **hybrid**

hy·drant (hye-druhnt) *noun* A large outdoor pipe connected to a water supply for use against fires and in other emergencies.

hy·drau·lic (hye-draw-lik) *adjective* **Hydraulic** machines work on power created by liquid being forced under pressure through pipes.
▷ *noun* **hydraulics**

hy·dro·e·lec·tric (hye-droh-i-**lek**-trik) *adjective* To do with the production of electricity by water power that is used to turn a generator. Hydroelectric power plants are often built at dams.

hy·dro·e·lec·tric·i·ty (hye-droh-i-lek-**triss**-uh-tee) *noun* Electricity made from energy produced by running water.

hy·dro·foil (hye-druh-*foil*) *noun*
A boat with skilike attachments at the front and back used to lift the hull out of the water once the boat is traveling fast.

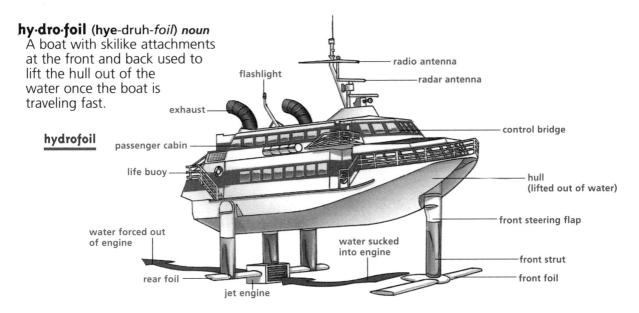

hydrofoil

Labels: flashlight · radio antenna · radar antenna · exhaust · control bridge · passenger cabin · life buoy · hull (lifted out of water) · front steering flap · water forced out of engine · water sucked into engine · front strut · rear foil · front foil · jet engine

H

hy·dro·gen (hye-druh-juhn) *noun* A colorless gas that is lighter than air and catches fire easily. *Hydrogen combines with oxygen to make water.*

hydrogen bomb *noun* An extremely powerful bomb, more powerful than the atomic bomb. Its tremendous force comes from the energy that is released when hydrogen atoms combine to form helium atoms. Also called **H-bomb.**

hy·drom·e·ter (hye-drom-uh-tur) *noun* An instrument used to measure the density of a liquid.

hy·dro·pon·ics (hye-druh-**pon**-iks) *noun* The science of growing plants in a solution of water and chemicals rather than in soil. ▷ *adjective* **hydroponic**

hy·e·na (hye-ee-nuh) *noun* A wild animal that looks somewhat like a dog. It eats meat and has a shrieking howl.

hy·giene (hye-jeen) *noun* Actions taken by people to stay healthy and keep clean. *Brushing your teeth after every meal is an example of good hygiene.* ▷ *adjective* **hygienic** (hye-gee-*en*-ik *or* hye-jen-ik) ▷ *adverb* **hygienically**

hy·gien·ist (hye-jee-nist) *noun* Someone trained to know how to keep people healthy and clean. *The dental hygienist cleaned Frank's teeth.*

hymn (him) *noun* A song of praise to God. **Hymn** sounds like **him.**

hym·nal (him-nuhl) *noun* A book of religious songs used in religious services.

hype (hipe) *noun* Exaggerated claims made about something in order to promote it. Hype is short for *hyperbole. There was a lot of hype surrounding the new film.* ▷ *verb* **hype**

hy·per·ac·tive (*hye*-pur-ak-tiv) *adjective* If someone is **hyperactive,** the person is unusually restless and has difficulty sitting quietly. ▷ *noun* **hyperactivity**

hy·phen (hye-fuhn) *noun* The punctuation mark (-) used in a word made of two or more parts or words. Words such as *half-mast, middle-aged,* and *ice-skate* use hyphens. ▷ *noun* **hyphenation** ▷ *verb* **hyphenate**

hyp·no·tize (hip-nuh-tize) *verb* To put someone into a trance. ▷ **hypnotizing, hypnotized** ▷ *noun* **hypnotism,** *noun* **hypnotist**

hy·po·chon·dri·ac (*hye*-puh-kon-dree-ak) *noun* Someone who continually thinks that he or she is ill or will become ill. ▷ *noun* **hypochondria**

hyp·o·crite (hip-uh-krit) *noun* Someone who pretends to be loyal, honest, or good. ▷ *noun* **hypocrisy** (hi-pok-ri-see) ▷ *adjective* **hypocritical** ▷ *adverb* **hypocritically**

hy·po·der·mic (*hye*-puh-**dur**-mik) *noun* A hollow needle used for giving injections.

hy·pot·e·nuse (hye-pot-uhn-*ooss*) *noun* The side opposite the right angle in a right triangle.

hy·po·ther·mi·a (*hye*-puh-**thur**-mee-uh) *noun* If someone is suffering from **hypothermia,** the person's body temperature has become dangerously low.

hy·poth·e·sis (hye-poth-uh-siss) *noun* A temporary prediction that can be tested about how a scientific investigation or experiment will turn out. ▷ *noun, plural* **hypotheses**

hys·ter·i·cal (hi-ster-uh-kuhl) *adjective* If someone is **hysterical,** the person laughs or cries a lot because he or she is very excited, frightened, or angry. ▷ *noun* **hysteria** ▷ *adverb* **hysterically**

Ii

The letter **i** is said to be based on something close at hand—the shape of the human finger. Before the 11th century, people didn't dot their *i*'s. The dot was added to help make words that had two *i*'s in a row easier to read. Without dots, *radii*, the plural of *radius*, looked like *radu* when some people wrote it.

I (eye) *pronoun* The person who is speaking or writing. *I will be home before dark.*

▶ Suffix

The suffix **-ic** or **-ical** turns a root word into an adjective by adding one of the following meanings:

1. Of or having to do with, as in *historic, historical* (having to do with history).

2. Like, as in *metallic* (like metal).

3. Made of or with, as in *alcoholic* (made with alcohol).

ice (eyess)
1. *noun* Frozen water.
2. *verb* To turn into ice.
3. *verb* To cool with ice. *We iced the fish so it wouldn't spoil.*
4. *noun* A frozen dessert made from fruit juice and sweetened water.
5. *verb* If someone **ices** a cake, the person covers it with icing. ▷ **icing, iced**

Ice Age or **ice age** *noun* A period of time in history when a large part of the earth was covered with ice.

ice·berg (eyess-berg) *noun* A huge mass of ice floating in the sea. Icebergs break off from glaciers. *The ship hit an iceberg and sank.*

▶ Word History

The word **iceberg** comes from the Danish or Norwegian *isberg* or the Dutch *ijsberg*, both of which mean "mountain of ice." It was first used in English to describe a glacier that could be seen from the ocean as a hill of ice. Eventually, though, it became the word for a floating body of ice broken off from a glacier.

ice·box (eyess-boks) *noun*
1. A box or chest kept cool with blocks of ice.
2. A refrigerator.
▷ *noun, plural* **iceboxes**

ice·break·er (eyess-*bray*-kur) *noun*
1. A ship designed to clear away ice in frozen waters so that other ships can pass through.
2. An event or comment that relieves the tension at a social gathering. *Tina's joke was a real icebreaker.*

ice·cap (eyess-*kap*) *noun* A mound of ice that covers an area of land and gets bigger as snow falls, melts, and freezes.

ice cream *noun* A sweet, frozen dessert made from milk products, various flavors, and sweeteners.

ice hockey *noun* A team game played on ice with sticks and a flat disk called a puck that skaters try to hit into their opponents' net.

ice hockey goalie
helmet — face mask — arm and chest protector with built-in shoulder pads — blocking pad — goalie's stick — puck — team jersey — catch glove — strap-on goalie's pads — skate

ice-skate *verb* To move around on ice wearing high, laced boots with blades on the bottom. ▷ **ice-skating, ice-skated** ▷ *noun* **ice-skater**

ice-skating movements
stag jump — bunny jump — revolutions in the air — death spiral

ice skate *noun* A shoe or boot with a blade on the bottom that makes it easy for the wearer to glide on ice. ▷ *noun* **ice-skating**

i·ci·cle (eye-si-kuhl) *noun* A long, thin stem of ice formed from dripping water that has frozen.

ic·ing (eye-sing) *noun* A sugar coating used to decorate cakes.

i·con (eye-kon) *noun*
1. One of several small pictures on a computer screen representing available programs or functions. *This icon shows that the computer user has mail.*
2. A picture of a holy figure that is present in some churches.

computer icon

i·cy (eye-see) *adjective*
1. Very cold, or covered with ice.
2. Unfriendly, as in *an icy stare.*
▷ *adjective* **icier, iciest**

I'd (eyed) *contraction* A short form of *I had, I would,* or *I should.*

I.D. (eye dee) Short for **identification.**

i·de·a (eye-dee-uh) *noun* A thought, a plan, or an opinion.

i·de·al (eye-dee-uhl)
1. *adjective* Very suitable or perfect. *Hamsters make ideal pets.*
2. *noun* Someone or something considered perfect. *My ideal is world peace.*
3. *noun* A standard of excellence. *We must never forget our ideals.*
▷ *adjective* **idealistic**

i·den·ti·cal (eye-den-ti-kuhl) *adjective* Exactly alike, as in *identical twins.* ▷ *adverb* **identically**

i·den·ti·fi·ca·tion (eye-den-tuh-fuh-kay-shuhn) *noun* Something that proves who you are.

i·den·ti·fy (eye-den-tuh-fye) *verb* To recognize or tell what something is or who someone is.
▷ **identifies, identifying, identified**

i·den·ti·ty (eye-den-ti-tee) *noun* Your **identity** is who you are. ▷ *noun, plural* **identities**

id·i·om (id-ee-uhm) *noun* A commonly used expression or phrase that means something different from what it appears to mean. For example, if a homework assignment is "a piece of cake," it means that it is easy. ▷ *adjective* **idiomatic**

id·i·ot (id-ee-uht) *noun* A stupid or foolish person. ▷ *adjective* **idiotic** (id-ee-ot-ik) ▷ *adverb* **idiotically**

i·dle (eye-duhl)
1. *adjective* Not busy, or not working. *The students enjoyed some idle time when their teacher stepped out of the room.* ▷ *verb* **idle** ▷ *adverb* **idly**
2. *adjective* Not active, or not in use. *The factory stood idle during the strike.*
3. *verb* To run slowly without being connected to the transmission. *The engine was idling as we waited.*

Idle sounds like **idol.**
▷ *verb* **idling, idled** ▷ *noun* **idleness,** *noun* **idler**
▷ *adjective* **idler, idlest**

i·dol (eye-duhl) *noun*
1. An image or statue worshipped as a god.
2. Someone whom people love and admire, as in *a pop idol.*
Idol sounds like **idle.**

i.e. (eye ee) An abbreviation of the Latin phrase *id est,* which means "that is" and is used to explain something further. *The winning dog at the dog show, i.e., the poodle, appeared last.*

if (if) *conjunction* A word used to show that something will happen on condition that another thing happens first. *I will pay you if you work hard.*

ig·loo (ig-loo) *noun* The traditional house of the Eskimo, or Inuit people, made in the shape of a dome out of sod, wood, stone, blocks of ice, or hard snow.

ig·ne·ous (ig-nee-uhss) *adjective* Produced by great heat or by a volcano, as in *igneous rock.*

ig·nite (ig-nite) *verb* To set fire to something, or to catch fire. ▷ **igniting, ignited**

ig·ni·tion (ig-nish-uhn) *noun*
1. The electrical system of a vehicle that uses power from the battery to start the engine.
2. The firing or blasting off of a rocket.

ig·no·rant (ig-nur-uhnt) *adjective*
1. Not aware of something. *I was completely ignorant of Ben's intentions.*
2. Not educated, or not knowing about many things.
▷ *noun* **ignorance** ▷ *adverb* **ignorantly**

ig·nore (ig-nor) *verb* To take no notice of something. *Jessica ignored their rude comments.*
▷ **ignoring, ignored**

i·gua·na (i-gwan-uh) *noun* A large tropical American lizard. An iguana has a ridge down its back and can grow to more than five feet in length. *See* **lizard.**

ill (il) *adjective*
1. Sick. *Carla was ill for a week.* ▷ *noun* **illness**
2. Bad. *Did you suffer any ill effects after your accident?* ▷ *adverb* **ill**

I'll (eye-uhl) *contraction* A short form of *I will* or *I shall.* **I'll** sounds like **aisle** and **isle.**

il·le·gal (i-lee-guhl) *adjective* Against the law. *False advertising is illegal.* ▷ *adverb* **illegally**

il·leg·i·ble (i-lej-uh-buhl) *adjective* If your handwriting is **illegible,** it is difficult to read.

il·lit·er·ate (i-lit-ur-it) *adjective* Not able to read or write. ▷ *noun* **illiteracy**

il·log·i·cal (i-loj-uh-kuhl) *adjective* Something **illogical** does not make sense. ▷ *adverb* **illogically**

il·lu·mi·nate (i-loo-muh-nate) *verb*
1. To light up something, such as a building.
2. To make something clearer and easier to understand. ▷ *adjective* **illuminating**
3. In the Middle Ages, manuscripts were **illuminated** by adding pictures and decoration to the text. *The letter L, shown here, comes from a manuscript that was illuminated by monks.*
▷ *verb* **illuminating, illuminated** ▷ *noun* **illumination** ▷ *adjective* **illuminated**

the letter "L"

il·lu·sion (i-loo-zhuhn) *noun* Something that appears to exist but does not. ▷ *adjective* **illusory** (i-loo-suh-ree)

il·lus·trate (il-uh-strate) *verb*
1. To draw pictures, by hand or by computer, for a book, magazine, or other publication.
▷ *adjective* **illustrated**
2. To make clear or explain by using examples or comparisons. *The teacher illustrated how the heart works by comparing it with a pump.*
▷ *verb* **illustrating, illustrated** ▷ *noun* **illustrator**

il·lus·tra·tion (il-uh-stray-shuhn) *noun*
1. A picture in a book, magazine, etc.
2. An example. *Lee gave lots of illustrations of her brother's talent.* ▷ *adjective* **illustrative** (i-luhss-truh-tiv)

ill will *noun* Unfriendly feeling or hatred. *We've had our disagreements, but I hope you feel no ill will toward me.*

Prefix

The prefix **im-** or **in-** changes a root word by adding one of these meanings:

1. Not, as in *immature* (not mature), *imperfect* (not perfect), or *incapable* (not capable).

2. A lack of, as in *inefficiency* (a lack of efficiency).

3. In or into, as in *imperil* (to place in peril) or *inborn* (born in).

I'm (eyem) *contraction* A short form of *I am.*

im·age (im-ij) *noun*
1. A picture you have in your mind. *I have an image of my ideal house.*
2. A representation, such as a picture or a statue.
3. Your **image** is the way that you appear to other people.
4. A picture formed in a lens or mirror.

im·age·ry (im-ij-ree) *noun* Descriptive language used by writers in poems, stories, etc. *Similes and metaphors are both types of imagery.*

i·mag·i·nar·y (i-maj-uh-ner-ee) *adjective* Existing in the imagination and not the real world. *Some children have imaginary friends.*

i·mag·i·na·tion (i-maj-uh-nay-shuhn) *noun*
1. The ability to form pictures in your mind of things that are not present or real.
2. The ability to create new images or ideas of things you have never experienced. *It took great imagination to write that science-fiction story.*

i·mag·i·na·tive (i-maj-uh-nuh-tiv) *adjective*
1. Creative or having great imagination, as in *an imaginative child.*
2. Showing imagination. *Ike told an imaginative story about a boy who grew to be 10 feet tall.*
▷ *adverb* **imaginatively**

im·ag·ine (i-maj-uhn) *verb* To picture something in your mind. ▷ **imagining, imagined**

im·be·cile (im-buh-suhl) *noun* A stupid person.

im·i·tate (im-uh-tate) *verb* To copy or mimic someone or something. ▷ **imitating, imitated** ▷ *noun* **imitation**

im·mac·u·late (i-mak-yuh-lit) *adjective* Very clean or neat. *My grandmother's house is always immaculate.* ▷ *adverb* **immaculately**

im·ma·ture (im-uh-chur *or* im-uh-tur) *adjective*
1. Young and not fully developed.
2. If someone is **immature,** he or she behaves in a silly, childish way.
▷ *noun* **immaturity** ▷ *adverb* **immaturely**

im·mea·sur·a·ble (im-ezh-ur-uh-buhl) *adjective* Too great or vast to be measured. *Billy's generosity is immeasurable.* ▷ *adverb* **immeasurably**

im·me·di·ate (i-mee-dee-it) *adjective*
1. Happening or done at once, as in *an immediate reply.*
2. Close or near. *Our immediate neighbors are very friendly.*

im·me·di·ate·ly (i-mee-dee-it-lee) *adverb*
1. Now or at once. *Come here immediately!*
2. Closely, or next. *She was immediately behind me in line.*

im·mense (i-menss) *adjective* Huge, or enormous. ▷ *noun* **immensity** ▷ *adverb* **immensely**

im·merse (i-murss) *verb*
1. To cover something completely in a liquid.
2. In some religions, to baptize someone by completely placing the person under water for a moment.
3. If you **immerse** yourself in something, you involve yourself in it completely.
▷ *verb* **immersing, immersed** ▷ *noun* **immersion** (i-mur-zhuhn)

im·mi·grant (im-uh-gruhnt) *noun* Someone who comes from abroad to live permanently in a country. ▷ *noun* **immigration** ▷ *verb* **immigrate**

im·mi·nent (im-uh-nuhnt) *adjective* About to happen, as in *imminent danger.* ▷ *adverb* **imminently**

im·mo·bi·lize (i-moh-buh-lize) *verb* To make it impossible for something or someone to move. *The accident immobilized Ellen for weeks.*
▷ **immobilizing, immobilized**

im·mor·al (i-mor-uhl) *adjective* Unfair, or without a sense of right and wrong. ▷ *noun* **immorality**
▷ *adverb* **immorally**

im·mor·tal (i-mor-tuhl)
1. *adjective* Living or lasting forever.
2. *adjective* Famous or remembered forever. *One of Shakespeare's immortal works is* Romeo and Juliet.
3. *noun* Someone or something that lives or is famous forever.
▷ *noun* **immortality**

im·mune (i-myoon) *adjective*
1. Protected against a disease.
2. Protected from physical or emotional harm. *If you are not immune to criticism, be careful what you say to others.*
▷ *noun* **immunity**

immune system *noun* The system that protects your body against disease and infection. It includes white blood cells and antibodies.

im·mu·nize (im-yuh-*nize*) *verb* To make someone immune to a disease. ▷ **immunizing, immunized**
▷ *noun* **immunization**

im·pact (im-pakt) *noun*
1. The striking of one thing against another.
2. The effect that something has on a person or a thing. *His speech had a great impact on me.*

im·pair (im-pair) *verb* To damage something or make it less effective. *The constant loud music impaired the boy's hearing.* ▷ **impairing, impaired**
▷ *noun* **impairment**

im·pal·a (im-pal-uh) *noun* A small African antelope that has curved horns and a reddish brown coat. The impala can leap great distances. ▷ *noun, plural* **impala** or **impalas**

im·par·tial (im-par-shuhl) *adjective* Fair and not favoring one person or point of view over another. ▷ *noun* **impartiality** ▷ *adverb* **impartially**

im·pa·tient (im-pay-shuhnt) *adjective*
1. In a hurry and unable to wait.
2. Easily annoyed. *Dad gets impatient when we argue.*
▷ *noun* **impatience** ▷ *adverb* **impatiently**

im·peach (im-peech) *verb* To bring formal charges against a public official who may have committed a crime or done something wrong while in office. ▷ **impeaches, impeaching, impeached** ▷ *noun* **impeachment**

im·per·a·tive (im-per-uh-tiv) *adjective*
1. Extremely important. *It is imperative that you stay off your sprained ankle for a week.*
2. Expressing a command, an order, or a request, as in *an imperative sentence.*
▷ *noun* **imperative**

im·per·fect (im-pur-fikt) *adjective* Faulty or not perfect. ▷ *noun* **imperfection** ▷ *adverb* **imperfectly**

im·pe·ri·al (im-pihr-ee-uhl) *adjective*
1. To do with an empire.
2. To do with an emperor or empress, as in *the imperial palace.*

im·per·son·al (im-pur-suh-nuhl) *adjective*
1. Lacking in warmth and feeling. *The captain had a cold, impersonal manner.*
2. To do with people generally rather than with one particular person.
▷ *adverb* **impersonally**

im·per·son·ate (im-pur-suh-nate) *verb* To pretend to be someone else, either seriously or for fun.
▷ **impersonating, impersonated** ▷ *noun* **impersonation**, *noun* **impersonator**

im·per·ti·nent (im-pur-tuh-nuhnt) *adjective* Rude and impudent, as in *impertinent behavior.* ▷ *noun* **impertinence** ▷ *adverb* **impertinently**

im·pet·u·ous (im-pech-oo-uhss) *adjective* Someone who is **impetuous** does things suddenly, without thinking first. ▷ *adverb* **impetuously**

im·plant (im-plant) *verb*
1. To establish or instill firmly and deeply. *He has implanted his own love of music in all his children.*
2. To put an organ or a device into the body by surgery. *The doctors implanted a new liver into the patient.*
▷ *verb* **implanting, implanted** ▷ *noun* **implant** (im-plant)

im·ple·ment
1. (im-pluh-muhnt) *noun* A tool or a utensil.
2. (im-pluh-ment) *verb* To put something such as a plan or an idea into action. *The government implemented the emergency relief plan by sending food and water to the area hit by the hurricane.*
▷ **implementing, implemented** ▷ *noun* **implementation**

im·pli·ca·tion (im-pluh-kay-shuhn) *noun*
1. The meaning or significance of something. *We had no way of knowing the implications of our decision to move to the city.*
2. Something suggested but not actually said. *When Harry asked what time it was, the implication was that he wanted to go.*

im·ply (im-plye) *verb* To suggest or mean something without actually saying it. *The look on Von's face implied that he was sorry.*
▷ **implies, implying, implied**

263

im·po·lite (im-puh-**lite**) *adjective* If someone is **impolite,** he or she behaves in a rude manner. ▷ *adverb* **impolitely**

im·port (im-**port** *or* im-port) *verb* To bring into a place or country from elsewhere. *Russia imports a lot of grain.* ▷ **importing, imported** ▷ *noun* **import** (im-port), *noun* **importer**

im·por·tant (im-**port**-uhnt) *adjective*
1. Something **important** is worth taking seriously and can have a great impact, as in *an important discovery.* ▷ *adverb* **importantly**
2. An **important** person is powerful and holds a high position.
▷ *noun* **importance**

im·pose (im-**poze**) *verb*
1. To force to accept by legal means, as in *to impose taxes* or *to impose a prison sentence.*
2. To take advantage of someone or make unfair demands. *I won't impose on you by staying for dinner.*
▷ *verb* **imposing, imposed** ▷ *noun* **imposition**

im·pos·si·ble (im-**poss**-uh-buhl) *adjective* If something is **impossible,** it cannot be done or cannot be true. ▷ *noun* **impossibility** ▷ *adverb* **impossibly**

im·pos·tor (im-**poss**-tur) *noun* Someone who pretends to be something that he or she is not. *The man who says he is Elvis is an impostor.*

im·prac·ti·cal (im-**prak**-tuh-kuhl) *adjective* Not sensible, or not useful, as in *an impractical plan.*

im·press (im-**press**) *verb*
1. To make people think highly of you. *Charlie's work impressed his teacher.*
2. To have an effect on someone's mind. *The Statue of Liberty impressed the group.*
▷ *verb* **impresses, impressing, impressed**
▷ *adjective* **impressive**

im·pres·sion (im-**presh**-uhn) *noun*
1. An idea or a feeling. *I had the impression that Sid didn't like me.*
2. An imitation of someone. *Tom did his impression of the principal.*
3. If something **makes an impression** on you, it has a strong effect on you.

im·pres·sion·a·ble (im-**presh**-uh-nuh-buhl) *adjective* If someone is **impressionable,** the person is easily influenced.

im·print
1. (im-print) *noun* A mark made by pressing or stamping something on a surface. *His sneakers made imprints in the sand.* ▷ *verb* **imprint** (im-**print**)
2. (im-print) *noun* A strong influence. *Immigrants from many countries have made a strong imprint on the American way of life.*
3. (im-**print**) *verb* To fix firmly in the mind or memory. ▷ **imprinting, imprinted**

im·pris·on (im-**priz**-uhn) *verb* To put someone in prison, or to lock the person up. ▷ **imprisoning, imprisoned** ▷ *noun* **imprisonment**

im·prop·er (im-**prop**-ur) *adjective*
1. Incorrect, as in *an improper response.*
2. Showing bad manners or bad taste. *It is improper to burp at the table.*
3. An **improper fraction** is a fraction whose numerator is greater than its denominator, as in $\frac{5}{4}$ or $\frac{11}{8}$.
▷ *adverb* **improperly**

im·prove (im-**proov**) *verb* To get better, or to make something better. ▷ **improving, improved** ▷ *noun* **improvement** ▷ *adjective* **improved**

im·pro·vise (im-**pruh**-vize) *verb*
1. To do the best you can with what is available. *We improvised a shelter from some old blankets.*
2. When actors or musicians **improvise,** they make up material on the spot. ▷ *noun* **improvisation** (im-*prov*-uh-**zay**-shuhn)
▷ *verb* **improvising, improvised** ▷ *noun* **improviser**

im·pu·dent (im-**pyuh**-duhnt) *adjective* Rude, bold, and outspoken, as in *an impudent remark.*
▷ *noun* **impudence** ▷ *adverb* **impudently**

im·pulse (im-**puhlss**) *noun*
1. A sudden desire to do something.
2. A sudden push or thrust.
3. A pulse of energy, as in *an electrical impulse.*

im·pul·sive (im-**puhl**-siv) *adjective* Acting on impulse, or done on impulse, as in *an impulsive person.* ▷ *adverb* **impulsively**

im·pure (im-**pyoor**) *adjective*
1. Unclean or contaminated, as in *impure water.*
2. Mixed with foreign substances, as in *an impure metal.*
▷ *adverb* **impurely**

in (in)
1. *preposition* Inside. *Your socks are in the top drawer.*
2. *preposition* Into. *Get in the house.*
3. *preposition* During, as in *in the autumn.*
4. *adverb* In or into some condition, relation, or place, as in *to join in* or *to fall in.*
5. *adverb* Inside a certain place. *The rain is keeping us in today.*
In sounds like **inn.**

in·a·bil·i·ty (in-uh-**bil**-uh-tee) *noun* Lack of power or ability to do something.

in·ac·cu·rate (in-**ak**-yuh-rit) *adjective*
1. Not very precise or correct.
2. Off the mark; not on target.
▷ *noun* **inaccuracy** ▷ *adverb* **inaccurately**

in·ad·e·quate (in-**ad**-uh-kwit) *adjective* Not enough or not good enough. ▷ *adverb* **inadequately**

in·ap·pro·pri·ate (in-uh-**proh**-pree-it) *adjective* Unsuitable for the time, place, etc. *Sara's shoes are inappropriate for hiking.* ▷ *adverb* **inappropriately**

in·ar·tic·u·late (in-ar-**tik**-yuh-lit) *adjective* Not able to express oneself very clearly in words.

in·au·di·ble (in-**aw**-duh-buhl) *adjective* Not loud enough to be heard. ▷ *noun* **inaudibility** ▷ *adverb* **inaudibly**

in·au·gu·rate (in-**aw**-gyuh-*rate*) *verb*
1. To swear a public official into office with a formal ceremony, as in *to inaugurate the president of the United States.*
2. To formally open, or to begin to use publicly, as in *to inaugurate a new plan.*
▷ *verb* **inaugurating, inaugurated**

in·au·gu·ra·tion (in-aw-gyuh-**ray**-shuhn) *noun* The ceremony of swearing in a public official.

in·born (in-*born*) *adjective* If you have an **inborn** skill or quality, you have it from birth and it is natural to you. *Jan has an inborn sense of style.*

in·can·des·cent (in-kan-**dess**-uhnt) *adjective*
1. Glowing with intense light and heat, as in *an incandescent bulb.*
2. Radiant or brightly shining, as in *an incandescent smile.*

incandescent bulb

in·ca·pa·ble (in-**kay**-puh-buhl) *adjective* If someone is **incapable** of doing something, he or she is unable to do it.

in·cense
1. (**in**-senss) *noun* A substance that is burned to give off a sweet smell.
2. (in-**senss**) *verb* To make very angry. *The governor's speech about budget cuts incensed the state employees.* ▷ **incensing, incensed**

in·cen·tive (in-**sen**-tiv) *noun* Something that encourages you to make an effort. *The chance of winning a prize was an incentive to work hard.*

in·ces·sant (in-**sess**-uhnt) *adjective* Nonstop or continuous, as in *incessant noise.* ▷ *adverb* **incessantly**

inch (inch)
1. *noun* A unit of length equal to $\frac{1}{12}$ of a foot. The diameter of a quarter measures about an inch.
2. *noun* A very small amount or distance. *We couldn't budge the boulder an inch.*
3. *verb* To move very slowly. *Miriam inched her way through the crowd.* ▷ **inches, inching, inched** ▷ *noun, plural* **inches**

inch·worm (**inch**-wurm) *noun* A caterpillar that moves by arching and stretching its body.

in·ci·dent (**in**-suh-duhnt) *noun* Something that happens; an event.

in·ci·den·tal·ly (in-suh-**dent**-uh-lee) *adverb* By the way. *We're leaving tomorrow, and, incidentally, I can't find my toothbrush.*

in·cin·er·a·tor (in-**sin**-uh-ray-tur) *noun* A furnace for burning garbage and other waste materials.

in·ci·sion (in-**sizh**-uhn) *noun* A clean cut made by a knife or blade. *The surgeon made an incision in order to take out my appendix.*

in·cite (in-**site**) *verb* If you **incite** someone to do something, you provoke the person or urge him or her to do it. ▷ **inciting, incited**

in·cline (in-**kline**) *verb* To lean, or to slope. ▷ **inclining, inclined** ▷ *noun* **incline** (**in**-kline)

in·clined (in-**klinde**) *adjective*
1. Leaning, or sloping.
2. If you are **inclined to** do something, you like to do it or tend to do it. ▷ *noun* **inclination** (in-kluh-**nay**-shuhn)

in·clude (in-**klood**) *verb* To contain something or someone as part of something else. *The cost of the meal includes dessert.* ▷ **including, included**

in·clu·sive (in-**kloo**-siv) *adjective* Including and covering everything. *The work week is Monday to Friday inclusive.*

in·co·her·ent (*in*-koh-**hihr**-uhnt) *adjective* Not clear, or not logical. *There was an incoherent message on my answering machine.* ▷ *adverb* **incoherently**

in·come (**in**-kuhm) *noun* The money that someone earns or receives regularly.

income tax *noun* A payment made to the government based on the amount of money a person makes. ▷ *noun, plural* **income taxes**

in·com·pat·i·ble (*in*-kuhm-**pat**-uh-buhl) *adjective* If people are **incompatible,** they cannot get along, and if objects are **incompatible,** they cannot be used together. ▷ *noun* **incompatibility**

in·com·pe·tent (in-**kom**-puh-tuhnt) *adjective* If someone is **incompetent** at something, she or he cannot do it well or effectively. ▷ *noun* **incompetence** ▷ *adverb* **incompetently**

in·com·plete (*in*-kuhm-**pleet**) *adjective* Not finished or not complete. ▷ *adverb* **incompletely**

in·com·pre·hen·si·ble (*in*-kom-pri-**hen**-suh-buhl) *adjective* Impossible to understand. *This portion of the novel is incomprehensible.*

in·con·ceiv·a·ble (*in*-kuhn-**see**-vuh-buhl) *adjective* Impossible to believe or imagine. *It is inconceivable that your dog ate your homework again.* ▷ *adverb* **inconceivably**

in·con·clu·sive (*in*-kuhn-**kloo**-siv) *adjective* Not clear, or not certain, as in *inconclusive results.* ▷ *adverb* **inconclusively**

in·con·sid·er·ate (*in*-kuhn-**sid**-ur-it) *adjective* Someone who is **inconsiderate** does not think about other people's needs or feelings. ▷ *adverb* **inconsiderately**

in·con·spic·u·ous (*in*-kuhn-**spik**-yoo-uhss) *adjective* Something that is **inconspicuous** cannot be seen easily or does not attract attention. ▷ *adverb* **inconspicuously**

in·con·ven·ience (*in*-kuhn-**vee**-nyuhnss) *noun*
1. Trouble or difficulty.
2. Something that causes trouble or difficulty. *Walking far to school is a real inconvenience.* ▷ *verb* **inconvenience**

in·con·ven·ient (*in*-kuhn-**vee**-nyuhnt) *adjective* If something is **inconvenient,** it causes trouble or difficulty. ▷ *adverb* **inconveniently**

in·cor·po·rate (*in*-**kor**-puh-*rate*) *verb*
1. When you **incorporate** something into another thing, you make it a part of that thing. *We've incorporated a new song into our show.*
2. To make or become a corporation. ▷ *verb* **incorporating, incorporated** ▷ *noun* **incorporation** ▷ *adjective* **incorporated**

in·cor·rect (*in*-kuh-**rekt**) *adjective* Wrong. ▷ *adverb* **incorrectly**

in·crease (*in*-**kreess**) *verb* To grow in size or number. ▷ **increasing, increased** ▷ *noun* **increase** (*in*-kreess) ▷ *adverb* **increasingly**

in·cred·i·ble (*in*-**kred**-uh-buhl) *adjective* Unbelievable or amazing. *Jack's beanstalk grew to an incredible size.* ▷ *adverb* **incredibly**

in·cred·u·lous (*in*-**krej**-uh-luhss) *adjective* Not able to believe something or accept that something is true. *When our favorite teacher told us she was retiring, we were incredulous.* ▷ *adverb* **incredulously**

in·crim·i·nate (*in*-**krim**-uh-*nate*) *verb* To show that someone is guilty of a crime or another wrong action. *The man incriminated his friend in the robbery.* ▷ **incriminating, incriminated** ▷ *noun* **incrimination**

in·cu·bate (*ing*-**kyuh**-bate) *verb*
1. To keep eggs warm before they hatch.
2. To keep a premature or sick baby safe and warm in a specially heated apparatus.
3. To nurture, or to allow to develop, as in *to incubate an idea.* ▷ *verb* **incubating, incubated** ▷ *noun* **incubation**

in·cu·ba·tor (*ing*-kyuh-*bay*-tur) *noun*
1. A heated apparatus in which premature or sick babies are kept safe and warm.
2. A container in which eggs are kept warm until they hatch.

incubator

in·cur·a·ble (*in*-**kyur**-uh-buhl) *adjective* If someone has an **incurable** disease, the person cannot be made well.

in·debt·ed (*in*-**det**-id) *adjective*
1. Owing thanks or gratitude to someone for a favor. *I am indebted to Pablo for his help.*
2. Owing money; in debt. ▷ *noun* **indebtedness**

in·de·cent (*in*-**dee**-suhnt) *adjective* Unpleasant, rude, or shocking, as in *indecent language.* ▷ *noun* **indecency** ▷ *adverb* **indecently**

in·deed (*in*-**deed**) *adverb* Certainly. *We are indeed lucky to be in good health.*

in·def·i·nite (*in*-**def**-uh-nit)
1. *adjective* Not clear, or not certain, as in *an indefinite amount of time.* ▷ *adverb* **indefinitely**
2. **indefinite article** *noun* The grammatical term for *a* or *an,* used before a noun when it refers to something general or not specific, as in *a baseball* or *an orange.*

in·dent (*in*-**dent**) *verb* To start a line of writing or typing a few spaces in from the margin. ▷ **indenting, indented** ▷ *noun* **indent** (*in*-dent) *noun* **indentation**

in·de·pen·dence (*in*-di-**pen**-duhnss) *noun* Freedom; the condition of being independent.

Independence Day *noun* A U.S. holiday, celebrated on July 4th, to commemorate the signing of the Declaration of Independence in 1776. Also known as *the Fourth of July.*

in·de·pend·ent (*in*-di-**pen**-duhnt)
1. *adjective* Free from the control of other people or things. *The colonists wanted to be independent of England.*

2. *adjective* If someone is **independent,** the person does not want or need much help from other people.
3. independent clause *noun* A sentence that can stand alone and be grammatical, as the sentence *"He likes to swim."* See **dependent clause.**
▷ *adverb* **independently**

in·de·struc·ti·ble (in-di-struhk-tuh-buhl) *adjective* If something is **indestructible,** it cannot be destroyed. ▷ *adverb* **indestructibly**

in·dex (in-deks)
1. *noun* An alphabetical list that shows you where to find things in a book. *In this book, the index is found at the back.* ▷ *noun, plural* **indexes** or **indices** (in-di-*seez*)
2. *verb* To supply with an index. *It helps readers if a book has been indexed.* ▷ **indexes, indexing, indexed** ▷ *noun* **indexer**

index finger *noun* The finger next to the thumb, used for pointing.

In·di·an (in-dee-uhn)
1. *noun* Someone who is from India.
2. *adjective* To do with India, its people, or its culture.
3. *noun* A Native American. See **American Indian.**
4. *adjective* To do with American Indians.

in·di·cate (in-duh-kate) *verb*
1. To show or prove something. *The report indicates that the company is losing money quickly.* ▷ *adjective* **indicative** (in-dik-uh-tiv)
2. To point something out clearly. *A road sign indicates the route to the beach.*
▷ *verb* **indicating, indicated** ▷ *noun* **indicator**

in·di·ca·tion (in-di-kay-shuhn) *noun* Something that indicates or points out. *A fever is an indication of infection.*

in·dict (in-dite) *verb* To officially charge someone with a crime. *The man was indicted for murder.*
▷ **indicting, indicted** ▷ *noun* **indictment**

in·dif·fer·ent (in-dif-uhr-uhnt) *adjective*
1. If someone is **indifferent** to something, the person is not interested in it. ▷ *noun* **indifference** ▷ *adverb* **indifferently**
2. Poor in quality. *Toby produced an indifferent piece of work.*

in·di·ges·tion (in-duh-jess-chuhn) *noun* If you have **indigestion,** your stomach is uncomfortable and you are having difficulty digesting food.

in·dig·nant (in-dig-nuhnt) *adjective* If you are **indignant,** you are upset and annoyed because you feel that something is not fair. *Adam was indignant when he was accused of cheating.*
▷ *noun* **indignation** ▷ *adverb* **indignantly**

in·di·go (in-duh-goh) *noun*
1. A plant with dark purple berries from which a dark blue dye can be made.
2. A dark violet-blue color or dye. See **spectrum.**

in·di·rect (in-dye-rekt *or* in-duh-**rekt**) *adjective*
1. Not in a straight line, as in *an indirect route.*
2. Not directly connected. *Making new friends is an indirect benefit of joining the drama club.*
3. Not to the point. *Steve answered my question in an indirect way.*
▷ *adverb* **indirectly**

in·dis·pen·sa·ble (in-diss-pen-suh-buhl) *adjective* If someone or something is **indispensable** to an organization, the person or thing is absolutely necessary to its smooth running. ▷ *adverb* **indispensably**

in·dis·tin·guish·a·ble (in-diss-ting-gwi-shuh-buhl) *adjective* When two people or things are **indistinguishable,** you cannot tell the difference between them. *The twins are virtually indistinguishable.* ▷ *adverb* **indistinguishably**

in·di·vid·u·al (in-duh-vij-oo-uhl)
1. *adjective* Single and separate. *Slowly, I got to know the individual members of the group.*
2. *noun* A person, as in *a strange individual.*
3. *adjective* Unusual or different. *Ricky has a very individual hairstyle.*
▷ *adverb* **individually**

in·di·vid·u·al·i·ty (in-duh-*vij*-oo-al-uh-tee) *noun* The qualities that set a person apart from all others.

in·di·vis·i·ble (in-duh-viz-uh-buhl) *adjective* Not able to be divided or broken into pieces.
▷ *adverb* **indivisibly**

in·door (in-dor) *adjective* Used, done, or built inside. *An indoor mall is a nice place to shop on a rainy day.*

in·doors (in-dorz) *adverb* Inside a building.

in·dulge (in-duhlj) *verb*
1. To let someone have his or her own way. *Nathan's grandparents indulge him by buying him anything he wants.* ▷ *adjective* **indulgent**
2. If you **indulge in** something, you allow yourself to enjoy it.
▷ *verb* **indulging, indulged** ▷ *noun* **indulgence**

in·dus·tri·al (in-duhss-tree-uhl) *adjective* To do with businesses and factories. *The industrial area of the city is busy during the day and quiet at night.* ▷ *adverb* **industrially**

in·dus·tri·al·ize (in-duhss-tree-uh-*lize*) *verb* To set up businesses and factories in an area.
▷ **industrializing, industrialized** ▷ *noun* **industrialization**

in·dus·try (in-duh-stree) *noun*
1. Manufacturing companies and other businesses, taken together. *Our town needs more industry.*
2. A single branch of business or trade, as in *the tourist industry.*
3. Hard work or effort.
▷ *noun, plural* **industries**

inefficient ▶ inflammation

in·ef·fi·cient (in-uh-**fish**-uhnt) *adjective* If someone or something is **inefficient,** the person or thing does not work very well and wastes time and energy. ▷ *noun* **inefficiency** ▷ *adverb* **inefficiently**

in·e·qual·i·ty (*in*-i-**kwol**-uh-tee) *noun* The treatment of people or things in an unequal and unfair way. ▷ *noun, plural* **inequalities**

in·ert (in-**urt**) *adjective*
1. Lifeless or not moving.
2. An **inert** gas is characterized by great stability and extremely low reaction rates.

in·er·tia (in-**ur**-shuh) *noun*
1. A lazy, tired feeling.
2. The **inertia** of an object is its resistance to any change in motion. *Inertia makes it hard to get something moving when it is still and hard to make something stop when it is moving.*

in·ev·i·ta·ble (in-**ev**-uh-tuh-buhl) *adjective* If something is **inevitable,** it is sure to happen. ▷ *noun* **inevitability** ▷ *adverb* **inevitably**

in·ex·pen·sive (in-ik-**spen**-siv) *adjective* Not costing a lot of money. ▷ *adverb* **inexpensively**

in·ex·pe·ri·enced (*in*-ik-**spihr**-ee-uhnst) *adjective* An **inexperienced** person has had little practice in doing something.

in·ex·pli·ca·ble (in-ik-**splik**-uh-buhl *or* in-ek-**spluh**-kuh-buhl) *adjective* If something is **inexplicable,** it cannot be explained. *It is inexplicable how that huge crater was formed.* ▷ *adverb* **inexplicably**

in·fa·mous (**in**-fuh-muhss) *adjective* If someone or something is **infamous,** the person or thing has a very bad reputation. *Jesse James was an infamous outlaw.*

in·fant (**in**-fuhnt) *noun* A newborn child. Babies are considered infants until the time they can walk. ▷ *noun* **infancy** ▷ *adjective* **infant**

in·fan·try (**in**-fuhn-tree) *noun* The part of an army that fights on foot.

in·fat·u·at·ed (in-**fach**-yoo-ay-tid) *adjective* If you are **infatuated** with someone or something, you like the person or thing so much that you stop thinking clearly and sensibly. *Pat is infatuated with the movie star.* ▷ *noun* **infatuation**

in·fect (in-**fekt**) *verb* To cause disease or contaminate by introducing germs or viruses. *Mosquitoes can infect people with diseases.* ▷ **infecting, infected** ▷ *adjective* **infected**

in·fec·tion (in-**fek**-shuhn) *noun* An illness caused by germs or viruses. *The infection was treated with an antibiotic.*

in·fec·tious (in-**fek**-shuhss) *adjective*
1. An **infectious** disease can spread from one person to another by germs or viruses in the air or on objects.

2. If a mood is **infectious,** it spreads easily, as in *infectious laughter.*

in·fer (in-**fur**) *verb* To draw a conclusion after considering all the facts. *We inferred from Tim's absence that he wanted to leave our club.* ▷ **inferring, inferred** ▷ *noun* **inference**

in·fe·ri·or (in-**fihr**-ee-ur) *adjective* If something is **inferior** to something else, it is not as good. ▷ *noun* **inferiority**

in·fer·tile (in-**fur**-tuhl) *adjective*
1. Land that is **infertile** is useless for growing crops and plants.
2. Unable to reproduce or have offspring. ▷ *noun* **infertility**

in·fes·ted (in-**fess**-tid) *adjective* If an object or a place is **infested,** it is full of animal or insect pests. ▷ *noun* **infestation** ▷ *verb* **infest**

in·fil·trate (in-**fil**-*trate*) *verb* To join an enemy's side secretly in order to spy or cause some sort of damage. ▷ **infiltrating, infiltrated** ▷ *noun* **infiltration**

in·fi·nite (**in**-fuh-nit) *adjective* Endless. *Life is filled with infinite possibilities.* ▷ *noun* **infinity** ▷ *adverb* **infinitely**

in·fin·i·tive (in-**fin**-uh-tiv) *noun* The basic form of a verb, often preceded by *to;* for example, *to run, to be, to write.*

in·firm (in-**furm**) *adjective* Weak or ill. *The elderly woman was blind and infirm.* ▷ *noun* **infirmity**

in·fir·ma·ry (in-**fur**-mur-ee) *noun* A place where sick people are cared for. *The camp has an infirmary.*

in·flame (in-**flame**) *verb*
1. To make hot, red, or swollen, usually as the result of an infection or injury.
2. To stir up or excite the emotions of a person or group. *The speaker inflamed the crowd's hatred.* ▷ *verb* **inflaming, inflamed**

in·flam·ma·ble (in-**flam**-uh-buhl) *adjective* An **inflammable** substance can catch fire easily.

Word History

There is much confusion over the meaning of the word **inflammable**. It comes from the Latin *in,* meaning "in," and *flamma,* meaning "flames." Unfortunately, another meaning of *in* is "not," which would make the word incorrectly mean "not capable of burning." For safety and clarity, people in the 20th century started using the word *flammable* to describe something that is able to burn.

in·flam·ma·tion (in-fluh-**may**-shuhn) *noun* Redness, swelling, heat, and pain, usually caused by an infection or injury.

in·flat·a·ble (in-flay-tuh-buhl) *adjective* An **inflatable** object can be filled with air and expanded. *The picture shows an inflatable life raft with its safety equipment.* ▷ *noun* **inflatable**

inflatable life raft and safety equipment

- battery-operated light
- pressure relief valve
- tie tapes
- pullover canopy
- canopy arch
- outer lifeline
- outer envelope
- handheld flares
- floating anchor (rolled up)
- pump and hose
- extending boarding ladder
- stabilizing pocket
- twin buoyancy tubes
- inflation canister
- instruction manual
- bailer
- first-aid kit
- leak stoppers
- throw ring and line
- raft repair kit (glue and patches)
- waterproof flashlight
- spare batteries
- chemical light sticks
- paddles with handles

in·flate (in-flate) *verb* To make something expand by blowing or pumping air into it. ▷ **inflating, inflated**

in·fla·tion (in-flay-shuhn) *noun*
1. A general increase in prices. ▷ *adjective* **inflationary**
2. The act of making something expand by blowing air into it.

in·flex·i·ble (in-flek-suh-buhl) *adjective* Not able to bend or change; rigid. ▷ *noun* **inflexibility** ▷ *adverb* **inflexibly**

in·flict (in-flikt) *verb* To cause suffering to someone or something, as in *to inflict damage.* ▷ **inflicting, inflicted** ▷ *noun* **infliction**

in·flu·ence (in-floo-uhnss) *verb* To have an effect on someone or something. ▷ **influencing, influenced** ▷ *noun* **influence**

in·flu·en·tial (in-floo-en-shuhl) *adjective* Having the power to change or affect someone or something, as in *an influential senator.*

in·flu·en·za (in-floo-en-zuh) See **flu.**

in·fo·mer·cial (in-foh-mur-shuhl) *noun* A program-length television commercial with demonstrations, interviews, and detailed information about a service or product.

in·form (in-form) *verb*
1. To tell someone something. *Lee informed me that he was leaving.*
2. If you **inform on** a criminal, you give the police information about the person.
▷ *verb* **informing, informed** ▷ *noun* **informer,** *noun* **informant**

in·for·mal (in-for-muhl) *adjective*
1. Relaxed and casual, as in *an informal party.* ▷ *noun* **informality**
2. **Informal** language is used in everyday speech but not usually in formal speaking or in writing. *Saying that Ivy has "classy clothes" is an informal way of saying that she has "elegant clothes."* ▷ *adverb* **informally**

in·for·ma·tion (in-fur-may-shuhn) *noun* Facts and knowledge.

information su·per·high·way (soo-pur-hye-way) *noun* A vast network of information available to a computer user with a modem.

information technology *noun* The use of computers and other electronic equipment to find, create, store, or communicate information.

in·for·ma·tive (in-for-muh-tiv) *adjective* If something or someone is **informative,** the thing or person provides useful information.

in·fre·quent (in-free-kwuhnt) *adjective* Not happening very often. ▷ *adverb* **infrequently**

in·fu·ri·ate (in-fyur-ee-ate) *verb* If someone or something **infuriates** you, the person or thing makes you extremely angry. ▷ **infuriating, infuriated** ▷ *adjective* **infuriating** ▷ *adverb* **infuriatingly**

ingenious ▶ insane

in·gen·ious (in-jee-nee-uhss) *adjective* Inventive and original, as in *an ingenious plan.* ▷ *noun* ingenuity (in-ji-noo-i-tee) ▷ *adverb* ingeniously

in·got (ing-uht) *noun* A mass of metal that has been shaped into a block or bar.

in·gre·di·ent (in-gree-dee-uhnt) *noun* One of the items that something is made from, such as an item of food in a recipe.

in·hab·it (in-hab-it) *verb* If you **inhabit** a place, you live there. ▷ **inhabiting, inhabited** ▷ *noun* **inhabitant**

in·hale (in-hayl) *verb* To breathe in. *It feels great to inhale that clean, fresh air.* ▷ **inhaling, inhaled** ▷ *noun* **inhalation** (in-huh-lay-shuhn)

in·hal·er (in-hay-lur) *noun* A small device from which you may inhale medicine through your mouth. *Sean uses an inhaler for his asthma.*

in·her·it (in-her-it) *verb*
1. To receive money, property, or a title from someone who has died. ▷ *noun* **inheritance**
2. If you **inherit** a particular characteristic, it is passed down to you from your parents.
▷ *verb* **inheriting, inherited**

in·hu·man (in-hyoo-muhn) *adjective* Cruel and brutal, as in *inhuman treatment.* ▷ *noun* **inhumanity** ▷ *adverb* **inhumanly**

in·i·tial (i-nish-uhl)
1. *noun* The first letter of a name or word.
2. *adjective* First, or at the beginning. *My initial reaction to the intruder was to scream.* ▷ *adverb* **initially**
3. *verb* To write your initials on. *Dr. Morris initialed the prescription.* ▷ **initialing, initialed**

i·ni·ti·ate (i-nish-ee-ate) *verb*
1. To introduce or start something new. *I initiated a discussion on today's topic.*
2. To bring someone into a club or group, often with a ceremony.
▷ *verb* **initiating, initiated** ▷ *noun* **initiation**

in·i·tia·tive (i-nish-ee-uh-tiv) *noun* If you take the **initiative,** you do what is necessary without other people telling you to do it.

in·ject (in-jekt) *verb* To use a needle and syringe to put medicine or nourishment into someone's body. ▷ **injecting, injected** ▷ *noun* **injection**

in·jure (in-jur) *verb* To hurt or harm yourself or someone else. *Bev injured herself when she fell off her bicycle.* ▷ **injuring, injured**

in·ju·ry (in-juh-ree) *noun* Damage or harm. ▷ *noun, plural* **injuries** ▷ *adjective* **injurious** (in-jur-ee-uhss)

in·jus·tice (in-juhss-tiss) *noun*
1. Unfairness or lack of justice.
2. An unfair situation or action. *You did me an injustice when you penalized me for no reason.*

ink (ingk) *noun* A colored liquid used for writing and printing. ▷ *adjective* **inky**

in·land (in-luhnd) *adjective* Away from the sea. *The inland states are very warm in summer.* ▷ *adverb* **inland**

in·let (in-let) *noun* A narrow body of water that leads inland from a larger body of water, such as an ocean.

in·mate (in-mayt) *noun* Someone who has been sentenced to live in a prison or other institution where one is under supervision.

inn (in) *noun* A small hotel that often includes a restaurant. **Inn** sounds like **in.**

in·ner (in-ur) *adjective*
1. Inside, or near the center. *The inner part of the earth's core is extremely hot.*
2. Private. *Nobody can know your inner thoughts.*

in·ning (in-ing) *noun* A part of a baseball game in which each team gets a turn at bat.

in·no·cent (in-uh-suhnt) *adjective*
1. Not guilty.
2. Not knowing about something. *Tanya was innocent of her aunt's plans.*
▷ *noun* **innocence** ▷ *adverb* **innocently**

in·no·va·tion (in-uh-vay-shuhn) *noun* A new idea or invention. ▷ *verb* **innovate** ▷ *adjective* **innovative**

in·nu·mer·ate (in-noo-mur-uht) *adjective* Unable to do basic math problems or understand the concepts behind them. ▷ *noun* **innumeracy**

in·oc·u·late (in-ok-yuh-late) *verb* To inject a weakened form of a disease into someone's body so that the person becomes protected against it. *The child was inoculated against mumps.*
▷ **inoculating, inoculated** ▷ *noun* **inoculation**

in·pa·tient (in-pay-shuhnt) *noun* Someone who stays in the hospital while being treated.

in·put (in-put) *noun*
1. Advice. *Our team benefited from Karen's input.*
2. Information fed into a computer. ▷ *verb* **input**
3. Something that is put in, as energy to be used by a machine.

in·quest (in-kwest) *noun* An official investigation or inquiry. *The coroner held an inquest after the accident.*

in·quire (in-kwire) *verb* To ask about someone or something. *Monica inquired about the time of the next commuter train.* ▷ **inquiring, inquired** ▷ *adjective* **inquiring** ▷ *adverb* **inquiringly**

in·quir·y (in-kwye-ree *or* in-kwuh-ree) *noun* A study or an investigation, especially an official or scientific one. ▷ *noun, plural* **inquiries**

in·quis·i·tive (in-kwiz-uh-tiv) *adjective* Questioning or curious. *What an inquisitive mind you have!* ▷ *noun* **inquisitiveness** ▷ *adverb* **inquisitively**

in·sane (in-sayn) *adjective*
1. Mentally ill.
2. Very foolish. *What an insane idea!*
▷ *noun* **insanity** (in-san-i-tee) ▷ *adverb* **insanely**

in·san·i·tar·y (in-san-uh-*ter*-ee) *adjective* Dirty and unhealthy.

in·scribe (in-skribe) *verb*
1. To carve or engrave letters on a surface.
2. To write a special message or dedication in a book.
▷ *verb* **inscribing, inscribed** ▷ *adjective* **inscribed**

in·scrip·tion (in-skrip-shuhn) *noun* A carved, engraved, or specially written message. *There are inscriptions under most statues.*

in·sect (in-sekt) *noun* A small creature with three pairs of legs, one or two pairs of wings, three main sections to its body, an exoskeleton, and no backbone. *The picture shows a variety of insects.*

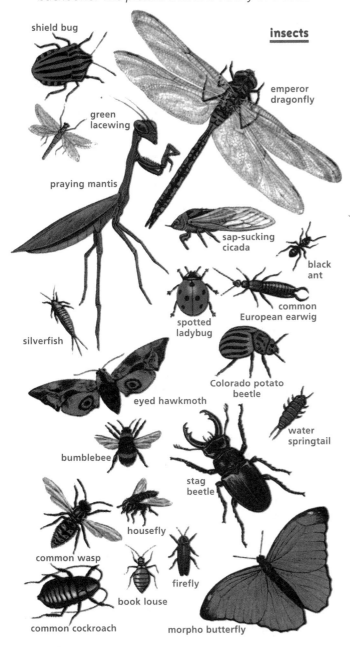

insects

shield bug
green lacewing
emperor dragonfly
praying mantis
sap-sucking cicada
black ant
silverfish
spotted ladybug
common European earwig
eyed hawkmoth
Colorado potato beetle
water springtail
bumblebee
stag beetle
housefly
common wasp
firefly
book louse
common cockroach
morpho butterfly

in·sec·ti·cide (in-sek-tuh-*side*) *noun* A chemical used to kill insects. *The farmer sprayed the fields with insecticides.*

in·se·cure (*in*-si-kyoor) *adjective*
1. Unsafe, or not fastened tightly. *The lock on the front door is very insecure.*
2. Anxious and not confident. *Paula felt very insecure on her first day at her new school.*
▷ *noun* **insecurity** ▷ *adverb* **insecurely**

in·sen·si·tive (in-sen-suh-tiv) *adjective* Thoughtless and unsympathetic to other people's feelings. *Matt made an insensitive comment about Jim's weight.* ▷ *noun* **insensitivity** ▷ *adverb* **insensitively**

in·sert
1. *verb* (in-surt) To put something inside something else. *Insert a coin in the slot.*
▷ **inserting, inserted** ▷ *noun* **insertion**
2. *noun* (in-surt) Something that is put inside something else. *This magazine has an insert on mountain bikes.*

in·side (*in*-side *or* in-*side*)
1. *noun* The interior or inner part of something.
▷ *adjective* **inside** (in-side)
2. *preposition* In less than. *We were back home inside an hour.*
3. *preposition* Within. *Put it inside the bag.*
4. *adverb* (*in*-side) Into. *He went inside.*

in·sid·i·ous (in-sid-ee-uhss) *adjective*
1. Quietly harmful or deceitful, as in *an insidious enemy.*
2. Working in a hidden but harmful way, as in *an insidious disease.*

in·sight (in-site) *noun* If you have **insight** into something or someone, you understand something about that matter or person that is not obvious. *The therapist had a lot of insight into her patient's problems.*

in·sig·ni·a (in-sig-nee-uh) *noun* A badge, emblem, or design that shows someone's rank or membership in an organization. *Justin wore the Marine Corps insignia.*

in·sig·nif·i·cant (in-sig-**nif**-uh-kuhnt) *adjective* Unimportant. ▷ *noun* **insignificance** ▷ *adverb* **insignificantly**

in·sin·cere (*in*-sin-sihr) *adjective* Someone who is **insincere** is not genuine or honest. ▷ *noun* **insincerity** ▷ *adverb* **insincerely**

in·sip·id (in-sip-id) *adjective* Dull or tasteless, as in *an insipid television program.*

in·sist (in-sist) *verb* If you **insist** on something, you demand it very firmly. *Sally insisted on wearing her jeans.* ▷ **insisting, insisted** ▷ *noun* **insistence** ▷ *adjective* **insistent**

in·so·lent (in-suh-luhnt) *adjective* Insulting and outspoken. *Sometimes teenagers are insolent to adults.* ▷ *noun* **insolence** ▷ *adverb* **insolently**

in·sol·u·ble (in-sol-yuh-buhl) *adjective*
1. A substance that is **insoluble** will not dissolve in water or other liquid.
2. A problem that is **insoluble** cannot be solved.

in·som·ni·a (in-som-nee-uh) *noun* If you have **insomnia,** you often find it very hard to fall asleep or stay asleep. ▷ *noun* **insomniac** (in-som-nee-ak)

in·spect (in-spekt) *verb* To look at something very carefully. *The crew inspected the plane before takeoff.* ▷ **inspecting, inspected** ▷ *noun* **inspection**

in·spec·tor (in-spek-tur) *noun*
1. Someone who checks or examines things. *The inspector checked the elevators every three months.*
2. A senior police officer. *Dave's mom is an inspector in the local police department.*

in·spire (in-spire) *verb*
1. To fill someone with an emotion, an idea, or an attitude. *Maggie's attitude inspired confidence in her fellow workers.*
2. To influence and encourage someone to do something. *The rock concert inspired me to take guitar lessons.*
▷ *verb* **inspiring, inspired** ▷ *noun* **inspiration** (*in*-spihr-ay-shuhn) ▷ *adjective* **inspiring,** *adjective* **inspirational** (*in*-spihr-ay-shuhn-uhl)

in·stall (in-stawl) *verb* To put something in place, ready to be used. *We have had a new computer installed in our classroom.* ▷ **installing, installed** ▷ *noun* **installation** (*in*-stuhl-lay-shuhn)

in·stall·ment (in-stawl-muhnt) *noun*
1. If you pay for something in **installments,** you pay for it in regular, small amounts over a period of time.
2. One part of a story printed or shown in separate parts. *The movie will be shown on television in two installments.*

in·stance (in-stuhnss) *noun*
1. An example. *Nancy gave me several instances of when I had interrupted her.*
2. for instance As an example. *Her interests include, for instance, the science club and hiking.*

in·stant (in-stuhnt)
1. *adjective* Happening right away, as in *instant results.* ▷ *adverb* **instantly**
2. *noun* A moment. *It was over in an instant.*
▷ *adjective* **instantaneous** (*in*-stuhn-tay-nee-uhss) ▷ *adverb* **instantaneously**
3. *adjective* Already mixed and prepared, needing only to be heated with added liquid, as in *instant pudding.*

in·stead (in-sted) *adverb* In place of another. *Bill really wanted ice cream but ordered sherbet instead.*

in·step (in-*step*) *noun* The top part of your foot, between your toes and your ankle.

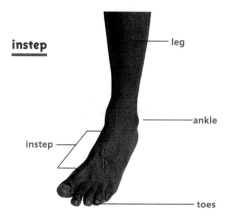

in·still (in-stil) *verb* To put into a person's mind slowly, over a period of time. *The teacher instilled a sense of pride in his students.*
▷ **instilling, instilled**

in·stinct (in-stingkt) *noun*
1. Behavior that is natural rather than learned. *Ducks swim by instinct.* ▷ *adjective* **instinctual** (in-stingk-choo-uhl)
2. If you have an **instinct** about something, you know or feel something without being told about it. *I had an instinct that she was not telling the truth.*
▷ *adjective* **instinctive** ▷ *adverb* **instinctively**

in·sti·tute (in-stuh-toot)
1. *noun* An organization set up to promote or represent the interests of a particular cause or group of people. *The new institute will study the American family.*
2. *verb* To begin, to set up, or to found. *A special committee instituted an inquiry into the missing money.* ▷ **instituting, instituted**

in·sti·tu·tion (in-stuh-too-shuhn) *noun*
1. A large organization where people live or work together, such as a hospital or a college.
▷ *adjective* **institutional**
2. A well-established custom or tradition. *Sunday dinner is an institution in our house.*

in·struct (in-struhkt) *verb*
1. To teach a subject or a skill. *Ginger instructed me in tap dancing.* ▷ *noun* **instructor**
2. To give an order. *The captain instructed her crew to set sail.*
▷ *verb* **instructing, instructed**

in·struc·tion (in-struhk-shuhn) *noun*
1. The act of teaching or giving lessons. *We learned to sing in harmony without instruction.*
2. instructions *noun, plural* Directions on how to do something, or orders on what to do, as in *to follow instructions.*

I

in·stru·ment (in-struh-muhnt) *noun*
1. An object that you use to make music. *The picture shows a range of musical instruments from around the world.* ▷ *noun* **instrumentalist** ▷ *adjective* **instrumental**
2. A tool or apparatus for delicate or scientific work, as in *surgical instruments.*

musical instruments

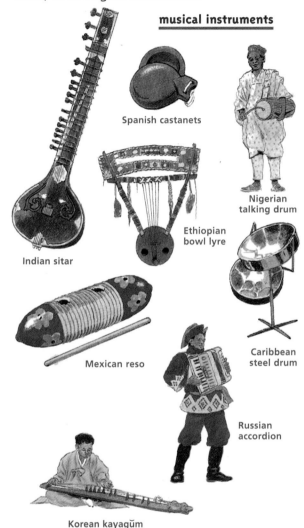

Spanish castanets

Nigerian talking drum

Ethiopian bowl lyre

Indian sitar

Mexican reso

Caribbean steel drum

Russian accordion

Korean kayagŭm

in·suf·fi·cient (in-suh-fish-uhnt) *adjective* Not enough or inadequate. *I had insufficient funds in my bank account to pay my bills.* ▷ *adverb* **insufficiently**

in·su·late (in-suh-late) *verb* To cover something with material in order to stop heat or electricity from escaping. *We insulated our attic before the winter.* ▷ **insulating, insulated** ▷ *noun* **insulation,** *noun* **insulator** ▷ *adjective* **insulating**

in·su·lin (in-suh-luhn) *noun* A hormone produced in the pancreas that regulates the amount of sugar that you have in your body. People who have diabetes need to be given insulin.

in·sult (in-suhlt) *verb* To say or do something rude and upsetting to somebody. *Jeremy insulted his friend by calling him a liar.* ▷ **insulting, insulted** ▷ *noun* **insult** (in-suhlt) ▷ *adjective* **insulting**

in·sur·ance (in-shu-ruhnss) *noun* When you take out **insurance,** you pay money to a company that agrees to pay you in the event of sickness, fire, accident, or other loss.

in·sure (in-shur) *verb* To take out insurance on something. *Dad insures both our family cars.* ▷ **insuring, insured** ▷ *adjective* **insured**

in·tact (in-takt) *adjective* Not broken or harmed; complete. *Our books survived the flood intact.*

in·take (in-take) *noun*
1. The amount of something taken in. *Runners often increase their intake of carbohydrates before a race.*
2. The act of taking something in, as in *a sharp intake of breath.*

in·te·ger (in-tuh-jur) *noun* The whole numbers and their opposites. Examples of integers include ⁻3, ⁻2, ⁻1, 0, 1, 2, and 3.

in·te·grate (in-tuh-grate) *verb*
1. To combine several things or people into one whole. *Mr. Platt integrated all of the students' ideas into the story.*
2. To include people of all races.
▷ *verb* **integrating, integrated** ▷ *adjective* **integrated**

in·te·gra·tion (in-tuh-gray-shuhn) *noun* The act or practice of making facilities open to people of all races.

in·teg·ri·ty (in-teg-ruh-tee) *noun* If someone has **integrity,** the person is honest and sticks to his or her principles.

in·tel·lect (in-tuhl-ekt) *noun* The power of the mind to think, reason, understand, and learn. *Albert Einstein was a genius who was known for his great intellect.*

in·tel·lec·tu·al (in-tuh-lek-choo-uhl)
1. *adjective* Involving thought and reason. *Brenda enjoys intellectual puzzles.*
2. *noun* Someone who spends most of his or her time thinking and studying.
▷ *adverb* **intellectually**

in·tel·li·gent (in-tel-uh-juhnt) *adjective* Someone who is **intelligent** is quick to understand, think, and learn. ▷ *noun* **intelligence** ▷ *adverb* **intelligently**

in·tel·li·gi·ble (in-tel-uh-juh-buhl) *adjective* If something is **intelligible,** it can be understood. ▷ *adverb* **intelligibly**

in·tend (in-tend) *verb*
1. If you **intend** to do something, you mean to do it. ▷ **intending, intended**
2. If something is **intended** for you, it is meant to be yours.

in·tense (in-tenss) *adjective*
1. Very strong, as in *intense heat* or *intense happiness*.
2. Showing strong feelings about something. *When Jill concentrates, she gets an intense look on her face.*
▷ *noun* **intensity** ▷ *adverb* **intensely**

in·ten·si·fy (in-ten-suh-*fye*) *verb* To make something more powerful or concentrated. *The police intensified their search.* ▷ **intensifies, intensifying, intensified**

in·tent (in-tent)
1. *adjective* If you are **intent on** doing something, you are determined to do it. *Bryan is intent on going to college.*
2. *noun* An aim or a purpose.
▷ *adverb* **intently**

in·ten·tion (in-ten-shuhn) *noun* A thing that you mean to do. *It's my intention to win this race.*
▷ *adjective* **intentional**

in·ter·ac·tive (in-tur-ak-tiv) *adjective*
1. Describing action between people, groups, or things.
2. An **interactive** computer program allows users to make choices in order to control and change it in some ways. *The virtual reality system shown below uses a type of interactive computer program.*
▷ *verb* **interact**

interactive computer program

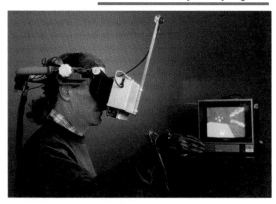

in·ter·cept (*in*-tur-sept) *verb* To stop the movement of someone or something. *Our star player intercepted the pass.* ▷ **intercepting, intercepted** ▷ *noun* **interception**

in·ter·change·a·ble (*in*-tur-chaynj-uh-buhl) *adjective* Easily switched with someone or something else. *Socks are interchangeable because each one can go on either foot.* ▷ *adverb* **interchangeably**

in·ter·com (in-tur-*kom*) *noun* A microphone-and-speaker system that allows you to listen and talk to someone in another room or building. **Intercom** is short for *intercommunication system*.

in·ter·est (in-tur-ist *or* in-trist)
1. *verb* If something **interests** you, you want to know more about it. ▷ **interesting, interested**
2. *noun* A feeling of curiosity or concern, as in *an interest in sports*.
3. *noun* The power to cause such curiosity or concern. *Music is of no interest to me.*
4. *noun* A legal share, as in a business.
5. *noun* A fee paid for borrowing money.
6. If it is **in your interest** to do something, it will help you.
▷ *adjective* **interested**, *adjective* **interesting**

in·ter·face (in-tur-*fayss*) *noun* The point at which two different things meet. *A keyboard is one type of interface between a computer and its user.* ▷ *verb* **interface**

in·ter·fere (*in*-tur-fihr) *verb*
1. To involve yourself in a situation that has nothing to do with you.
2. To hinder. *The noise interfered with my work.*
▷ *verb* **interfering, interfered** ▷ *adjective* **interfering**

in·ter·fer·ence (*in*-tur-fihr-uhnss) *noun*
1. An unwelcome involvement in the affairs of others. *I can't stand any more interference from our neighbors.*
2. When you get **interference** on your television or radio, something interrupts the signal so that you cannot see or hear the program properly.
3. In sports, the illegal obstruction of an opponent. *A penalty was called for pass interference.*

in·ter·ga·lac·tic (*in*-tur-guh-lak-tik) *adjective* Between galaxies, as in *intergalactic space travel*.

in·te·ri·or (in-tihr-ee-ur) *noun* The inside of something, especially a building. ▷ *adjective* **interior**

in·ter·jec·tion (in-tur-jek-shuhn) *noun* A word spoken suddenly and used to express surprise, pain, or delight. *"Oh!" and "Hello!" are interjections.*

in·ter·me·di·ate (*in*-tur-mee-dee-*it*) *adjective* In between two things, or in the middle. *I am in the intermediate swimming class.*

in·ter·mis·sion (*in*-tur-mish-uhn) *noun* A short break in a play or concert. *We bought candy during the play's intermission.*

in·ter·mit·tent (*in*-tur-mit-uhnt) *adjective* Stopping and starting, as in *intermittent rain*. ▷ *adverb* **intermittently**

in·tern (in-turn) *noun*
1. Someone who is learning a skill or job by working with an expert in that field.
2. A newly graduated doctor of medicine who is working at a hospital to get practical experience.
▷ *noun* **internship** ▷ *verb* **intern**

in·ter·nal (in-tur-nuhl) *adjective*
1. Happening or existing inside someone or something, as in *internal bleeding.* ▷ *adverb* **internally**
2. To do with matters inside a country, as in *internal affairs.*

in·ter·na·tion·al (in-tur-nash-uh-nuhl) *adjective* Involving different countries, as in *international trade.* ▷ *adverb* **internationally**

in·ter·plan·e·tar·y (*in*-tur-plan-uh-ter-ee) *adjective* Between planets. *Science fiction is filled with stories about interplanetary travel.*

in·ter·pret (in-tur-prit) *verb*
1. If someone **interprets** for people speaking different languages, the person translates for them. ▷ *noun* **interpreter**
2. To decide what something means. *I interpreted his hug as a sign of friendship.*
▷ *verb* **interpreting, interpreted** ▷ *noun* **interpretation**

in·ter·ro·gate (in-ter-uh-*gate*) *verb* To question someone in detail. *The police interrogated the suspect for hours.* ▷ **interrogating, interrogated** ▷ *noun* **interrogation**

in·ter·rupt (*in*-tuh-ruhpt) *verb*
1. To stop or hinder for a short time. *The TV program was interrupted by a news flash.*
2. To start talking before someone else has finished talking. *Don't interrupt me!*
▷ *verb* **interrupting, interrupted** ▷ *noun* **interruption** ▷ *adjective* **interruptive**

in·ter·sect (in-tur-sekt) *verb* To meet or cross something. *Route 44 intersects Route 2 at Davidsonville.* ▷ **intersecting, intersected**

in·ter·sec·tion (*in*-tur-sek-shuhn or in-tur-*sek*-shuhn) *noun* The point at which two things meet and cross each other.

in·ter·state (*in*-tur-state) *adjective* Connecting, between, or having to do with two or more states, as in *an interstate highway.*

interstate highway sign

in·ter·val (in-tur-vuhl) *noun* A time between two events, or a space between two objects.

in·ter·vene (*in*-tur-veen) *verb*
1. If you **intervene** in a situation, you get involved in it in order to change what is happening. *Bobby intervened to prevent his brothers from fighting.* ▷ *noun* **intervention** (*in*-tur-**ven**-shuhn)
2. If a period of time **intervenes** between events, it comes between them.
▷ *verb* **intervening, intervened**

in·ter·view (in-tur-*vyoo*) *noun* A meeting at which someone is asked questions, as in *a job interview* or *a radio interview.* ▷ *verb* **interview**

in·tes·tine (in-tess-tin) *noun* A long tube extending below the stomach that digests food and absorbs liquids and salts. It consists of the **small intestine** and the **large intestine.**

in·ti·mate (in-tuh-mit) *adjective* Friends who are **intimate** are very close and share their feelings with one another. ▷ *noun* **intimacy** (in-tuh-muh-see) ▷ *adverb* **intimately**

in·tim·i·date (in-tim-uh-*date*) *verb* To frighten. *The bully tried to intimidate us.* ▷ **intimidating, intimidated** ▷ *noun* **intimidation** ▷ *adjective* **intimidating**

in·to (in-too *or* in-tuh) *preposition*
1. To the inside of. *She went into the tent.*
2. To the occupation of. *I think I'll go into astronomy.*
3. To the condition or form of. *The cat got into trouble.*
4. Against. *Her car bumped into ours.*
5. Toward. *The kite flew into the wind.*

in·tol·er·a·ble (in-tol-ur-uh-buhl) *adjective* If something is **intolerable,** it is difficult to endure. ▷ *adverb* **intolerably**

in·tol·er·ant (in-tol-ur-uhnt) *adjective* People who are **intolerant** get unreasonably angry when others think or behave differently from them. ▷ *noun* **intolerance** ▷ *adverb* **intolerantly**

in·tox·i·cate (in-tok-suh-*kate*) *verb*
1. To make drunk, especially with alcohol.
2. To excite or to make enthusiastic, as in *an intoxicating aroma.*
▷ *verb* **intoxicating, intoxicated** ▷ *noun* **intoxication**

in·tran·si·tive (in-tran-suh-tiv) *adjective* **Intransitive** verbs stand on their own and do not need an object. *The verbs "to laugh," and "to sneeze" are intransitive. See* **transitive.**

in·trep·id (in-trep-id) *adjective* An **intrepid** person is courageous and bold.

in·tri·cate (in-truh-kit) *adjective* Detailed and complicated, as in *an intricate pattern.* ▷ *noun* **intricacy** ▷ *adverb* **intricately**

in·trigue

1. (in-**treeg**) *verb* To fascinate or interest someone very much. *Kit's story intrigued me.* ▷ **intriguing, intrigued** ▷ *adjective* **intriguing**

2. (**in**-treeg *or* in-**treeg**) *noun* A secret plot or scheme. ▷ *verb* **intrigue** (in-**treeg**)

in·tro·duce (in-truh-**dooss**) *verb*

1. To bring in something new. *The company is introducing a new product next month.*

2. To cause to be known by name. *We introduced ourselves to our new neighbors.*

3. To start. *She introduced the report with a series of statistics.*

▷ *verb* **introducing, introduced**

in·tro·duc·tion (in-truh-**duhk**-shuhn) *noun*

1. Your **introduction** to something is your first experience of it. *I can still remember my introduction to rock climbing.*

2. The act of introducing one person to another.

3. The opening words of a book, speech, etc.

▷ *adjective* **introductory**

in·tro·vert (in-truh-**vurt**) *noun* A shy person who keeps his or her thoughts and feelings to himself or herself. ▷ *adjective* **introverted**

in·trude (in-**trood**) *verb* To force your way into a place or situation where you are not wanted or invited. ▷ **intruding, intruded** ▷ *noun* **intruder,** *noun* **intrusion** ▷ *adjective* **intrusive**

in·tu·i·tion (*in*-too-**ish**-uhn) *noun* A feeling about something that cannot be explained logically. *My intuition tells me that you will win this race.*

▷ *verb* **intuit** ▷ *adjective* **intuitive**

In·u·it (in-**oo**-it *or* in-**yoo**-it)

noun A person, or a group of people, from the Arctic north of Canada, Alaska, and Greenland. Inuits are also known as **Eskimos**. *This Inuit is fishing through a hole in the ice.*

▷ *adjective* **Inuit**

Inuit

in·un·date

(in-uhn-*date*) *verb*

1. To flood. *The village was inundated by water.*

2. To overwhelm someone with a large quantity of something. *We were inundated with presents.*

▷ *verb* **inundating, inundated** ▷ *noun* **inundation**

in·vade (in-**vade**) *verb* To send armed forces into another country in order to take it over. *The soldiers invaded the island.* ▷ **invading, invaded** ▷ *noun* **invader,** *noun* **invasion**

in·va·lid

1. (**in**-vuh-lid) *noun* Someone who is bedridden or must limit his or her activity because he or she is seriously ill.

2. (in-**val**-id) *adjective* If a ticket, library card, etc., is **invalid,** it cannot be used for some reason.

in·val·u·a·ble (in-**val**-yuh-buhl) *adjective* Very useful or precious. ▷ *adverb* **invaluably**

in·vent (in-**vent**) *verb*

1. To think up and create something new.

▷ *noun* **inventor**

2. To make something up. *Leon invented a story to explain why he was soaking wet.*

▷ *verb* **inventing, invented** ▷ *noun* **invention**

in·ven·tive (in-**ven**-tiv) *adjective* Good at thinking up new ideas or ways of doing things; creative.

in·ven·to·ry (in-**vuhn**-*tor*-ee)

1. *noun* A complete list of items someone owns.

2. *noun* All the items on hand for sale in a store.

▷ *noun, plural* **inventories**

3. *verb* To count and list the items available for sale in a store. ▷ **inventories, inventorying, inventoried**

in·vert (in-**vurt**) *verb*

1. To turn something upside down. *If you invert a 6, it looks like a 9.*

2. To reverse the order of something. *If you invert the letters of the word "stop" you get "pots."*

▷ *verb* **inverting, inverted**

in·ver·te·brate (in-**vur**-tuh-brit) *noun* A creature without a backbone. *Octopuses, earthworms, and snails are examples of invertebrates.*

▷ *adjective* **invertebrate**

snails

in·vest (in-**vest**) *verb*

1. To give or lend money to something, such as a company, in the belief that you will get more money back in the future. *We invested in a new ice-cream franchise.* ▷ *noun* **investment,** *noun* **investor**

2. To give time or effort to something. *I've invested a lot of time in practicing the trumpet.* ▷ *verb* **investing, invested**

in·ves·ti·gate (in-**vess**-tuh-gate) *verb* If you **investigate** something, such as a crime, you find out as much as possible about it. ▷ **investigating, investigated** ▷ *noun* **investigation,** *noun* **investigator** ▷ *adjective* **investigative**

in·vin·ci·ble (in-**vin**-suh-buhl) *adjective* If someone is **invincible,** that person cannot be beaten or defeated. ▷ *adverb* **invincibly**

in·vis·i·ble (in-**viz**-uh-buhl) *adjective* Something that is **invisible** cannot be seen. ▷ *noun* **invisibility** ▷ *adverb* **invisibly**

in·vite (in-**vite**) *verb* To ask someone to do something or to go somewhere. ▷ **inviting, invited** ▷ *noun* **invitation** (in-vi-**tay**-shuhn)

in·voice (in-**voiss**) *noun* An itemized bill for goods shipped to a customer or for work done or to be done for a customer. ▷ *verb* **invoice**

in·vol·un·tar·y (in-**vol**-uhn-ter-ee) *adjective*
1. Not done willingly or by choice. *The suspect claimed that his confession was involuntary.*
2. Done without a person's control. *Breathing is an involuntary act.*

in·volve (in-**volv**) *verb* To include something as a necessary part. *The project involves library research.* ▷ **involving, involved** ▷ *noun* **involvement**

in·volved (in-**volvd**) *adjective*
1. If you are **involved** in or with something, you take a part in it or are mixed up in it. *I am involved in planning the picnic.*
2. Complicated, as in *an involved story.*

in·ward (in-**wurd**) *adverb* Toward the inside. *The door opens inward.* ▷ *adjective* **inward**

i·o·dine (**eye**-uh-*dine*) *noun*
1. A chemical element found in seaweed and salt water that is used in medicine and photography.
2. A brown medicine containing iodine and alcohol that is used to kill germs on wounds.

i·on (**eye**-uhn *or* **eye**-on) *noun* An electrically charged atomic particle. Ions are either positive or negative.

IQ (**eye kyoo**) *noun* A measure of a person's intelligence. IQ stands for *Intelligence Quotient.*

i·rate (**eye**-rate *or* eye-**rate**) *adjective* Extremely angry or annoyed. *Dad was irate when I damaged the car.* ▷ *adverb* **irately**

i·ris (**eye**-riss) *noun*
1. The round, colored part of the eye around the pupil. *See* **eye.**
2. A plant with long, thin leaves and large purple, white, or yellow flowers.

I·rish set·ter (**eye**-rish **set**-ur) *noun* A large hunting dog with a silky, red coat. These dogs originally were bred in Ireland.

i·ron (**eye**-urn)
1. *noun* A strong, hard metal used to make such things as gates and railings. It is also found in some foods as well as in your body's red blood cells. ▷ *adjective* **iron**
2. *noun* A piece of electrical equipment with a handle and a heated surface, used to smooth creases out of clothing. *This picture shows the main parts inside a steam iron.* ▷ *verb* **iron**
3. *verb* If you **iron out** a problem, you solve it. ▷ **ironing, ironed**

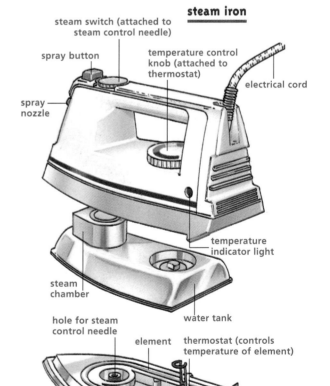

steam iron

Suffix

The suffix **-ion** turns a root word into a noun by adding one of these meanings:
1. The act of, as in *participation* (the act of participating).
2. A state of being, as in *confusion* (the state of being confused).

Iron Age *noun* A period of history when iron was commonly used to make tools and weapons. Different parts of the world experienced an Iron Age at different times. *During the Iron Age in western Europe, starting about 1,000 B.C., most people were farmers living in small settlements like the one reconstructed in this picture.*

Iron Age settlement

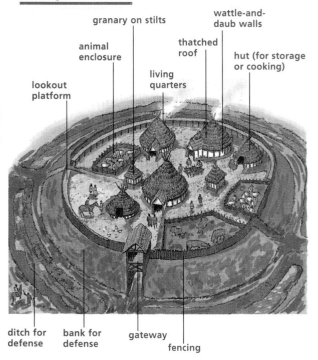

granary on stilts
wattle-and-daub walls
animal enclosure
thatched roof
living quarters
hut (for storage or cooking)
lookout platform
ditch for defense
bank for defense
gateway
fencing

i·ron·ic (eye-ron-ik) *adjective*
1. If a situation is **ironic,** the actual result differs from the expected result. *It was ironic that the clumsiest boy in the class became a famous dancer.*
2. Mildly sarcastic. *"What a great job you did on that!" said Rosa, with an ironic smile.* ▷ *adverb* **ironically**

i·ro·ny (eye-ruh-nee) *noun* A way of speaking or writing that means the opposite of what the words say. Saying *"Beautiful weather, isn't it?"* when it is raining is an example of irony.

I·ro·quois (ihr-uh-kwoi) *noun* A member of a confederation of American Indian tribes originally of New York. ▷ *noun, plural* **Iroquois**

ir·ra·tio·nal (i-rash-uh-nuhl) *adjective* Not sensible, or not logical. *A phobia is an irrational fear of something.* ▷ *adverb* **irrationally**

ir·reg·u·lar (i-reg-yuh-luhr) *adjective*
1. Not standard in shape, timing, size, etc., as in *irregular bus service.*
2. Not following the normal pattern. *It's most*

irregular to come to school in slippers. ▷ *noun* **irregularity**
3. An **irregular** verb is one whose main parts are not formed according to a regular pattern. *Sink is irregular because its past tense is* sank *rather than* sinked.
▷ *adverb* **irregularly**

ir·rel·e·vant (i-rel-uh-vuhnt) *adjective* If something is **irrelevant,** it has nothing to do with a particular subject. *The story contained many irrelevant details.* ▷ *noun* **irrelevance** ▷ *adverb* **irrelevantly**

ir·re·sist·i·ble (ihr-i-ziss-tuh-buhl) *adjective* Too tempting to resist. *The fudge was irresistible.* ▷ *adverb* **irresistibly**

ir·re·spon·si·ble (ihr-i-spon-suh-buhl) *adjective* Reckless and lacking a sense of responsibility. *It was irresponsible to leave the children alone in the house.* ▷ *noun* **irresponsibility** ▷ *adverb* **irresponsibly**

ir·re·vers·i·ble (ihr-uh-**ver**-suh-buhl) *adjective* Unable to be changed or undone. *The president's decision to go to war was irreversible.*

ir·ri·gate (ihr-uh-*gate*) *verb* To supply water to crops by artificial means, such as channels and pipes. *The farmer irrigated his fields.* ▷ **irrigating, irrigated** ▷ *noun* **irrigation**

ir·ri·ta·ble (ihr-uh-tuh-buhl) *adjective* Someone who is **irritable** is cross and grumpy. ▷ *adverb* **irritably**

ir·ri·tate (ihr-uh-tate) *verb*
1. If something **irritates** you, it annoys you.
2. To make sore or sensitive. *Dylan screamed so loudly, he irritated his throat.*
▷ *verb* **irritating, irritated** ▷ *noun* **irritation**
▷ *adjective* **irritating** ▷ *adverb* **irritatingly**

> ### ▶ Suffix
> The suffix **-ish** turns a root word into an adjective by adding one of the following meanings:
> 1. Having characteristics of or like something, as in *childish* (like a child).
> 2. Somewhat, as in *reddish* (somewhat red).

Is·lam (iss-luhm *or* i-slahm) *noun* The religion based on the teachings of Muhammad. Muslims believe that Allah is God and that Muhammad is Allah's prophet. The religion is based on prayer, fasting, charity, and pilgrimage, as taught through the Koran.
▷ *adjective* **Islamic**

is·land (eye-luhnd) *noun* A piece of land surrounded by water.

isle (eye-uhl) *noun* A small island. **Isle** sounds like aisle and **I'll**.

is·n't (iz-uhnt) *contraction* A short form of *is not*. *Maria isn't going to be in school today.*

i·so·late (eye-suh-*late*) *verb*
1. To keep something or someone separate. *Polly was isolated because she had a highly infectious illness.* ▷ *noun* **isolation**
2. To discover and identify something. *We've isolated the fault in your computer program.*
▷ *verb* **isolating, isolated**

i·so·met·rics (eye-suh-met-riks) *noun* A system of physical exercises that strengthens muscles by using pressure against an unmoving object such as a wall or your own hand. Two hands pushing against each other create an isometric exercise.
▷ *adjective* **isometric**

i·sos·ce·les (eye-soss-uh-leez) *adjective* An isosceles triangle has two equal sides. *See* **shape.**

is·sue (ish-oo)
1. *noun* The main topic for debate or decision. *What issues will be covered at the meeting?*
2. *noun* An edition of a newspaper or magazine.
3. *verb* To send out, or to give out. *The school issued us the necessary equipment.*
4. *verb* To come out of. *Muffled cries issued from the locked closet.*
▷ *verb* **issuing, issued**

isth·mus (iss-muhss) *noun* A narrow strip of land that lies between two bodies of water and connects two larger land masses. *Panama is an isthmus connecting North and South America.*

it (it)
1. *pronoun* A thing, part, person, or situation mentioned earlier or later. *You can't see it, but there's a squirrel on the other side of that tree.*
2. *pronoun* The subject of some verbs that shows an action or condition. *It is snowing. It is hot today.*
3. *noun* The player in a game who has to perform the main action, such as trying to find others in hide-and-seek.

i·tal·ic (i-tal-ik *or* eye-tal-ik) *noun* A sloping form of print used to emphasize certain words or to make them stand out. *The sentence you are reading is printed in italic.* ▷ *verb* **italicize**
▷ *adjective* **italic**

itch (ich) *verb* If your skin **itches**, it is uncomfortable and you want to scratch it.
▷ **itches, itching, itched** ▷ *noun* **itch** ▷ *adjective* **itchy**

i·tem (eye-tuhm) *noun* One of a number of things, as in *an item of clothing.*

i·tem·ize (eye-tuh-*mize*) *verb* To list the individual units or parts of something. *The archaeologist itemized the artifacts that she found at the dig site.* ▷ **itemizing, itemized** ▷ *adjective* **itemized**

i·tin·er·ant (eye-tin-uh-ruhnt) *adjective* Traveling from place to place, usually to find or do work. *Many small towns in the West used to depend on itinerant judges who went from town to town trying cases.*

i·tin·er·ar·y (eye-tin-uh-rer-ee) *noun* A detailed plan of a journey. *Before signing up for the tour, I requested an itinerary to get an idea of whether or not I would enjoy it.* ▷ *noun, plural* **itineraries**

its (its) *adjective* Related to or belonging to something. *The puppy chased its tail.*

it's (its) *contraction* A short form of *it is* or *it has*. *It's time for us to go home.*

it·self (it-self) *pronoun* It and nothing else. *This machine works by itself.*

▶ Suffix
• •
The suffix **-ity** turns a root word into a noun by adding the following meaning to the root word: The state or quality of being, as in *civility* (the quality of being civil) and *joviality* (the state of being jovial).

▶ Suffix
• •
The suffix **-ive** turns a root word into an adjective by adding the following meaning to the root word: Tending to do something, as in *active* (tending to act), *possessive* (tending to possess), *corrective* (tending to correct).

I've (eyev) *contraction* A short form of *I have*. *I've got the perfect book to help you with your report.*

i·vo·ry (eye-vur-ee) *noun*
1. The natural substance from which the tusks of elephants and some other animals are made.
2. A creamy-white color.
▷ *adjective* **ivory**

i·vy (eye-vee) *noun* An evergreen climbing or trailing plant that has pointed leaves.

ivy

jab (jab)
1. *verb* To poke somebody with something sharp. *Katy jabbed her elbow into my ribs.*
▷ **jabbing, jabbed**
2. *noun* A short, quick punch. *The boxer hit his opponent with a jab from the left.*

jab·ber (jab-ur) *verb* To talk in a fast, confused, or foolish way that is hard to understand. *Stan's jabbering distracted Julie from the video game she was playing.* ▷ **jabbering, jabbered** ▷ *noun* **jabber**

jack (jak) *noun*
1. A tool used to raise a vehicle off the ground for repair. ▷ *verb* **jack**
2. A picture playing card with a value between that of a ten and a queen.
3. A small, metal piece with six points used in the game of jacks.
4. jacks A game played with jacks and a rubber ball. *Jacks is my favorite game.*

jack·al (jak-uhl) *noun* A kind of wild dog of Africa and Asia that feeds off dead animals.

jack·et (jak-it) *noun*
1. A short coat.
2. An outer covering for a book or record.

jack·ham·mer (jak-*ham*-ur) *noun* A machine that is operated by air that is compressed. It is used to drill rock, concrete, and similar hard materials.

jack·knife (jak-*nife*)
1. *noun* A large knife with a blade that folds into a handle.
2. *noun* A type of dive in which a diver bends the body double in the air, then straightens out before striking the water headfirst.
3. *verb* To fold in like a jackknife. **jackknifing, jackknifed**
▷ *noun, plural* **jackknives**

jack-o'-lan·tern (jak-uh-*lan*-turn) *noun* A pumpkin with a face carved into it and a candle inside, used at Halloween.

jack·pot (jak-*pot*) *noun* The top prize in a game or contest. *Donna's parents won the jackpot in the state lottery.*

jack·rab·bit (jak-*rab*-it) *noun* A large hare, common in the western part of the United States. The jackrabbit has very long ears and strong back legs for leaping.

Ja·cuz·zi (ja-koo-zee) *noun* Trademark for a large bath with underwater jets of water that massage your skin.

jade (jayd) *noun*
1. A hard, green stone used for making ornaments and jewelry.
2. A green color.
▷ *adjective* **jade**

jag·ged (jag-id) *adjective* Uneven and sharp, as in *a jagged edge.*

jag·uar (jag-wahr) *noun* A large wildcat, similar to a leopard, found in the southwestern United States, Mexico, and South and Central America.

jaguar

jail (jayl)
1. *noun* A building for keeping people who are awaiting trial or who have been found guilty of minor crimes. ▷ *noun* **jailer**
2. *verb* To put someone in jail. ▷ **jailing, jailed**

jail·bird (jayl-burd) *noun* (informal) A prisoner or a convict.

jam (jam)
1. *noun* A sweet, thick food made from boiled fruit and sugar.
2. *noun* A situation in which things or people cannot move, as in *a traffic jam.*
3. *verb* To squeeze or wedge something into a tight space. *Alvin jammed his bag into the locker.*
4. *noun* (informal) A difficult situation. *Jeff was in a terrible jam—he'd gone to take his test without a pencil.*
5. *verb* To become stuck and not work. *The key jammed in the lock.*
6. *verb* To bruise or crush by squeezing. *I jammed my finger in the door.*
7. (informal) When musicians have a **jam** or **jam session,** they play together without any planning. ▷ *verb* **jam**
▷ *verb* **jamming, jammed**

jan·gle (jang-guhl) *verb* To make a loud, unpleasant, ringing sound. *Alice's bracelet jangled on her wrist.* ▷ **jangling, jangled**

jan·i·tor (jan-uh-tur) *noun* Someone whose job is to look after and clean a school or some other building.

Jan·u·ar·y (jan-yoo-er-ee) *noun* The first month on the calendar. January is followed by February and has 31 days.

> ▶ **Word History**
> ●●●●●●●●●●●●●●●●●●●●●●●●●●●●●●●●●
>
> Is there such a thing as a "month with two faces"? The Roman god Janus was often shown with two faces since he was the protector of gates and doors. His month, **January**, "looks two ways," back to the last year and ahead to the new one.

Jap·a·nese beetle (*jap*-uh-**neez**) *noun* An insect that eats leaves and can destroy plants, brought to the United States from Japan.

jar (jar)
1. *noun* A container with a wide mouth.
2. *verb* To jolt or shake something or someone. *The fall jarred my knee.*
3. *verb* If something **jars** you, it makes you feel uncomfortable or annoyed.
4. *verb* If something **jars** with the facts, it conflicts with them.
▷ *verb* **jarring, jarred**

jar·gon (jar-guhn) *noun* Words used by people in a particular business or activity that others cannot easily understand, as in *computer jargon.*

jaun·dice (jawn-diss) *noun* A disease, usually of the liver, that turns the skin yellow.

jaunt (jawnt) *noun* A short pleasure trip or outing.

jaun·ty (jawn-tee) *adjective* Giving a carefree and self-confident impression. *Sophie wore her cap at a jaunty angle.* ▷ **jauntier, jauntiest** ▷ *adverb* **jauntily**

jave·lin (jav-uh-luhn) *noun* A light, metal spear that is thrown for distance in a track-and-field event.

jaw (jaw)
1. *noun* Either of two bones between your nose and your chin that hold your teeth. *See* **skeleton.**
2. *noun* The lower part of your face.
3. **jaws** *noun, plural* The parts of a tool that close to grip an object, as in *the jaws of a clamp.*
4. *verb* (slang) To talk for a long time in a boring way. ▷ **jawing, jawed**

jay·walk (jay-*wawk*) *verb* To cross a street carelessly, taking no notice of traffic or signals. ▷ **jaywalking, jaywalked** ▷ *noun* **jaywalker**

jazz (jaz) *noun* A lively, rhythmical type of music in which players often improvise, or make up their own tunes and add new notes in unexpected places. Jazz was started by African Americans between 1900 and 1905 in New Orleans, Louisiana. ▷ *adjective* **jazzy**

jeal·ous (jel-uhss) *adjective*
1. If you are **jealous** of someone, you want what he or she has.
2. Afraid that a person you love cares more for someone else than for you.
▷ *noun* **jealousy** ▷ *adverb* **jealously**

jeans (jeenz) *noun, plural* Pants for casual wear made of denim or similar strong cloth.

> ▶ **Word History**
> ●●●●●●●●●●●●●●●●●●●●●●●●●●●●●●●●●●
>
> **Jeans** are a common garment today. The word probably comes from the name of the fabric used to make them, *gene fustion. Gene* is the Middle English form of Genoa, a city in Italy where such fabric was made, and *fustion* referred to a cotton cloth. Jeans shifted its meaning to the garment made from this cloth.

Jeep (jeep) *noun* Trademark for a small, powerful vehicle used for driving over rough country.

jeer (jihr) *verb* To scorn someone in a loud, unpleasant way. *The audience jeered at the singer when he showed up an hour late.*
▷ **jeering, jeered** ▷ *noun* **jeer** ▷ *adverb* **jeeringly**

Je·ho·vah (ji-hoh-vuh) *noun* A name for God in the Old Testament.

Jell-O (jel-oh) *noun* Trademark for a dessert made with gelatin and a flavoring, which is boiled and then allowed to set.

jel·ly (jel-ee) *noun* A sweet, thick food made from boiled fruit and sugar. ▷ *noun, plural* **jellies**

jel·ly·fish (jel-ee-*fish*) *noun* A sea creature with a body that is soft and quivering like jelly and has trailing tentacles. *The picture shows how a jellyfish has its mouth in the center, with feelers or arms stretching out from it.* ▷ *noun, plural* **jellyfish** *or* **jellyfishes**

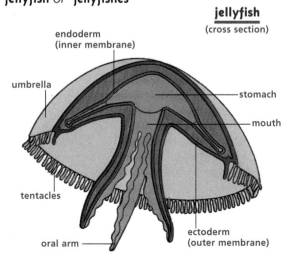

jellyfish
(cross section)

endoderm
(inner membrane)

umbrella

stomach

mouth

tentacles

oral arm

ectoderm
(outer membrane)

J

jeop·ard·y (jep-ur-dee) *noun* If someone's job or life is **in jeopardy,** it is in danger or is threatened in some way. ▷ *verb* **jeopardize**

jerk (jurk)
1. *verb* To move or pull something very suddenly and sharply. ▷ **jerking, jerked**
2. *noun* A sudden movement as something starts up. *The old car moved forward with a jerk.*
3. *noun* An annoyingly stupid or foolish person. ▷ *adjective* **jerky** ▷ *adverb* **jerkily**

jest (jest) *noun* A joke or something said in fun. ▷ *verb* **jest**

jest·er (jes-tur) *noun* An entertainer at a court in the Middle Ages.

Je·sus (jee-zuhss) *noun* The founder of Christianity. Also called *Jesus Christ. See* **Christ.**

jet (jet) *noun*
1. A stream of liquid or gas forced through a small opening with great pressure.
2. An aircraft powered by jet engines. ▷ *verb* **jet**

jet engine *noun* An engine that is powered by a stream of gases made by burning a mixture of fuel and air inside the engine itself. *The picture shows a turbofan jet engine that is used on many airplanes. Air is sucked in by the fan, squeezed by the compressors, then mixed with fuel and burned in the combustion chamber. The gases produced in the chamber are forced out through a series of turbines that drive the compressors and the fan. See also* **hydrofoil.**

jet turbofan engine

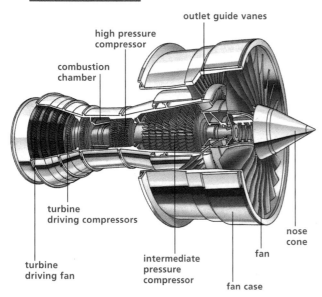

outlet guide vanes
high pressure compressor
combustion chamber
turbine driving compressors
turbine driving fan
intermediate pressure compressor
fan case
fan
nose cone

jet lag *noun* A feeling of tiredness or confusion after a long plane flight from a different time zone.

jet propulsion *noun* A way of moving an aircraft in one direction by using a stream of hot gas propelled in the opposite direction.

jet·sam (jet-suhm) *noun* Part of a ship's cargo that is thrown or lost overboard.

jet stream *noun* A very strong current of wind, usually found between seven and nine miles above the earth's surface. Jet streams usually move west to east at speeds reaching over 200 miles per hour.

jet·ti·son (jet-uh-suhn) *verb* To throw overboard, or to throw out something that you no longer need. *I'm going to clean out my room and jettison all those old toys.* ▷ **jettisoning, jettisoned**

jet·ty (jet-ee) *noun* A wall built out into the sea to give an area shelter from the waves. Boats moor and unload beside jetties. ▷ *noun, plural* **jetties**

Jew (joo) *noun*
1. Someone who is descended from the ancient Hebrew tribes of Israel.
2. Someone who practices the religion of Judaism.

jew·el (joo-uhl) *noun*
1. A precious stone, such as a diamond, a ruby, or an emerald.
2. A person or thing that is greatly admired or valued.

jew·el·er (joo-uh-lur) *noun* A person who designs, makes, repairs, or sells jewelry.

jew·el·ry (joo-uhl-ree) *noun* Ornaments that you wear, such as rings, bracelets, and necklaces, often made of jewels, gold, etc.

Jew·ish (joo-ish) *adjective* To do with Jews, their religion, or their culture.

jib (jib) *noun* A triangular sail that is set in front of the mast and attached to the bow of a ship. *See* **sail, ship.**

jif·fy (jif-ee) *noun* A very short time; a moment. *I'll be with you in a jiffy.* ▷ *noun, plural* **jiffies**

jig (jig) *noun*
1. A fast, lively dance, or the music played during this dance. ▷ *verb* **jig**
2. *(informal)* If **the jig is up,** the trick you are playing or the secret you are keeping is over because someone has caught on to you.

jig·saw puzzle (jig-*saw*) *noun* A wooden or cardboard puzzle made up of pieces of a picture that have to be put together.

jin·gle (jing-guhl) *noun*
1. A tinkling or ringing sound made by the movement of small bells, keys, etc. ▷ *verb* **jingle**
2. A simple, upbeat song used to advertise a product.

J

jinx (jingks) *noun* A person or thing that is supposed to bring bad luck. ▷ *noun, plural* **jinxes** ▷ *verb* **jinx**

job (job) *noun*
1. A task or a chore.
2. The work that someone does for a living.

jock·ey (jok-ee)
1. *noun* Someone who rides horses in races. ▷ *verb* **jockey**
2. *verb* If you **jockey for position** with someone, you try to beat him or her at something, often by unfair actions. ▷ **jockeying, jockeyed**

jockey

joc·u·lar (jok-yuh-lur) *adjective* Joking, or liking to make jokes.

jodh·purs (jod-purz) *noun, plural* Pants worn for horseback riding. Jodhpurs are loose around the top part of the leg and fit tightly below the knee.

jog (jog) *verb*
1. To run at a slow, steady pace. ▷ *noun* **jogger**
2. To shake or to push. *Someone jogged my elbow.*
3. If something **jogs your memory**, it reminds you of something.
▷ *verb* **jogging, jogged** ▷ *noun* **jogging**

join (join) *verb*
1. To fasten two things together. ▷ *noun* **join**
2. To come together with something or someone. *Please join us for supper.*
3. To become a member of a club or group.
4. **join up** To become a member of the armed forces.
▷ *verb* **joining, joined**

join·er (joi-nur) *noun*
1. Someone who makes wooden furniture and house fittings such as door frames. ▷ *noun* **joinery**
2. A person who enjoys joining a lot of clubs or groups.

joint (joint)
1. *noun* A place where two bones meet; for example, your knee or elbow. There are four main types of joints in your body: fixed, sliding, hinge, and ball-and-socket. *This diagram of a human hip joint shows how the ball at the top of the femur fits into the socket of the pelvis.*
2. *noun* A place where two or more things meet or come together. ▷ *adjective* **jointed**
3. *adjective* Done or shared by two or more people, as in *a joint effort.* ▷ *adverb* **jointly**
4. *noun (informal)* A cheap, unattractive place to eat, drink, or spend the night.

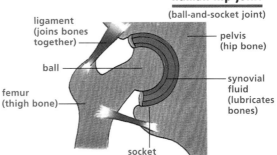

human hip joint
(ball-and-socket joint)

ligament (joins bones together)

pelvis (hip bone)

ball

synovial fluid (lubricates bones)

femur (thigh bone)

socket

jo·jo·ba (hoh-hoh-buh) *noun* A large evergreen shrub or small tree that grows in the southwestern part of the United States and Mexico. Jojoba oil is used in products such as shampoos and lotions.

joke (joke) *verb* To say funny things or play tricks on people in order to make them laugh.
▷ **joking, joked** ▷ *noun* **joke**

jol·ly (jol-ee) *adjective* Happy and cheerful.
▷ **jollier, jolliest**

jolt (johlt)
1. *verb* To move with sudden, rough jerks. *The cart jolted along the track.* ▷ **jolting, jolted**
▷ *noun* **jolt**
2. *noun* A sudden surprise or shock. *The news of his death gave me quite a jolt.*

jon·quil (jon-kwil) *noun* A plant that grows from bulbs and has long, narrow leaves and fragrant, white or yellow flowers. The jonquil is a kind of daffodil.

jos·tle (joss-uhl) *verb* To bump or push roughly. *I always get jostled by the crowds in stores before Christmas.* ▷ **jostling, jostled**

jot (jot) *verb* To write something down quickly. *I've jotted down some ideas.* ▷ **jotting, jotted**

joule (jool) *noun* A unit for measuring energy or work done. Joule is a term used by physicists.

jour·nal (jur-nuhl) *noun*
1. A diary in which you regularly write down your thoughts and experiences.
2. A magazine or newspaper.

jour·na·lism (jur-nuhl-iz-uhm) *noun* The work of gathering and reporting news for newspapers, magazines, and other media.

jour·nal·ist (jur-nuhl-ist) *noun* Someone who collects information and writes articles for newspapers, magazines, television, or radio. ▷ *adjective* **journalistic**

jour·ney (jur-nee) *noun* A long trip. ▷ *verb* **journey**

joust (joust *or* juhst) *noun* A battle between two knights riding horses and armed with lances. *The picture shows a medieval joust.* ▷ *verb* **joust**

jousting knights triple-pronged lance | helmet | caparison (saddle cloth) | chanfron | shield with heraldic crest

jo·vi·al (joh-vee-uhl) *adjective* Someone who is **jovial** is cheerful and enjoys talking and laughing with other people. ▷ *noun* **joviality** ▷ *adverb* **jovially**

jowl (joul) *noun* A layer of loose flesh that hangs down around the throat or lower jaw.

joy (joi) *noun*
1. A feeling of great happiness.
2. A person or thing that brings great happiness to someone. *The walk through the woods was a real joy.* ▷ *adjective* **joyous**

joy·ful (joi-fuhl) *adjective* Very happy. ▷ *noun* **joyfulness** ▷ *adverb* **joyfully**

joy·stick (joi-*stik*) *noun* A lever used to control movement in a computer game or in an aircraft.

ju·bi·lant (joo-buh-luhnt) *adjective* Very happy and delighted. *Josh was jubilant about winning the race.* ▷ *noun* **jubilation** ▷ *adverb* **jubilantly**

ju·bi·lee (joo-buh-lee) *noun* A big celebration to mark the anniversary of a special event.

Ju·da·ism (joo-dee-iz-uhm) *noun* The religion of the Jewish people, based chiefly on a belief in one God and the teachings of the Torah, the first five books of the Old Testament. *The picture shows a symbol of Judaism, the Star of David.*

Star of David

judge (juhj)
1. *noun* A person who listens to cases before a court and decides how a guilty person should be punished. ▷ *verb* **judge**

2. *verb* To decide who is the winner of a competition. ▷ *noun* **judge**
3. *verb* To form an opinion about something or someone. *After meeting Nat, I judged him to be honest.*
▷ *verb* **judging, judged**

judg·ment *or* **judge·ment** (juhj-muhnt) *noun*
1. An opinion of something or someone. *I think your judgment of the situation is right.*
2. A decision made by a judge.
3. The ability to decide or form opinions wisely. *They showed good judgment in deciding not to drink and drive.*

ju·di·cial (joo-dish-uhl) *adjective* To do with a court of law or a judge. ▷ *adverb* **judicially**

ju·di·cious (joo-dish-uhss) *adjective* Sensible and wise, as in *a judicious decision.* ▷ *adverb* **judiciously**

ju·do (joo-doh) *noun* A sport in which two people fight each other using quick, controlled movements, each trying to throw the other to the ground. *This sequence shows a basic forward throw in judo called Harai goshi.*

judo
(forward throw)

jug (juhg) *noun* A container with a narrow neck and a small handle.

jug·ger·naut (juhg-ur-*nawt*) *noun* A very powerful force that can destroy anything in its path.

jug·gle (juhg-uhl) *verb* To keep a set of balls, clubs, or other objects moving through the air by repeatedly throwing them up and catching them again, one after another. ▷ **juggling, juggled** ▷ *noun* **juggler**

juggling equipment | balls | clubs or tenpins

juice (joos) *noun* Liquid that comes out of fruit, vegetables, or meat. ▷ *adjective* **juicy**

juke·box (jook-*boks*) *noun* A machine that plays music or records when you put coins into it.
▷ *noun, plural* **jukeboxes**

Ju·ly (juh-**lye** *or* joo-**lye**) *noun* The seventh month on the calendar, after June and before August. July has 31 days.

> ### Word History
> The ancient Romans named most of their months for gods. **July**, however, was kept for the great general and statesman of Rome, Julius Caesar, whose birthday falls in July. The English spelling was at first *Julie* and then July.

jum·ble (**juhm**-buhl) *verb* To mix things up so that they are messy and not well organized.
▷ **jumbling, jumbled** ▷ *noun* **jumble**

jum·bo (**juhm**-boh)
1. *adjective* Very large, as in *jumbo shrimp*.
2. jumbo jet *noun* (*informal*) A very large jet airplane that can carry hundreds of passengers. *See* **aircraft.**

jump (juhmp)
1. *verb* To push off with your legs and feet and move through or into the air.
2. *noun* The distance covered by a jump, as in *a long jump*.
3. *verb* To move or get up suddenly, as in *to jump in surprise*.
4. *noun* A sudden rise or increase, as in *a jump in prices*.
5. *verb* If you **jump at** something, you accept it eagerly.
▷ *verb* **jumping, jumped**

> ### Synonyms: jump
> **Jump** means to propel yourself into or through the air, using the power of your feet and legs. You can jump down from a height, or straight up, or in any direction: *In the movie, the sheriff jumped onto the stagecoach as it passed under the bridge.*
>
> **Leap** means to jump quickly or in a dramatic way: *Lucia leaped into the air when Valerie's pet hamster crawled up her leg.*
>
> **Spring** means to jump up suddenly as if there were springs underneath you: *My puppy springs up and runs into the kitchen whenever he hears me pour food in his bowl.*
>
> **Vault** means to jump up and over something, using your hands or a pole: *Shelly vaulted over the fence to get to her neighbor's yard.*
>
> **Hurdle** means to jump up and over something, especially while running: *The horse and rider hurdled the last brick wall and finished the race in record time.*

jum·per (**juhm**-pur) *noun* A sleeveless dress, usually worn over a shirt or sweater. *Abby wears a jumper when it's cold outside.*

jumper cables *noun, plural* Thick wires that are used to connect the batteries of two cars so that one can be started using the other's battery.

jump rope *noun*
1. A rope used for exercise and children's games. The jump rope is swung over the head and under the feet as the player jumps up to let it pass.
2. A game in which this rope is used.

junc·tion (**juhngk**-shuhn) *noun* A place where roads or railroad lines meet or join. *Ride one mile to the junction of Bay Street and Alden Avenue, and turn right.*

June (joon) *noun* The sixth month on the calendar, after May and before July. June has 30 days.

> ### Word History
> There are two theories as to the origin of the word **June**. Many scholars point to the Latin *Junius,* the name of a powerful Roman family. Other scholars, however, believe that the ancient Romans named this month for Juno, the goddess who protected women.

jun·gle (**juhng**-guhl) *noun* Land in warm, tropical areas near the equator that is thickly covered with trees, vines, and bushes.

> ### Word History
> **Jungle** goes back to the ancient Indian word *jangala,* which meant a dry land without plants. Later, the word came to mean any kind of uncultivated land. When the English occupied India, the word passed into English, where it came to mean land overgrown with vegetation or the vegetation itself.

jun·ior (**joo**-nyur)
1. *adjective* **Junior** is used after the name of a son who has the same name as his father. It means "the younger of two," as in *John Smith, Jr.*
2. *adjective* Not very important in rank or position, as in *a junior manager*.
3. *adjective* For young children, as in *a junior encyclopedia.*
4. *noun* A third-year high school or college student.

junior high school *noun* A school between elementary school and high school. It usually includes the seventh and eighth grades and sometimes includes the ninth grade.

ju·ni·per (joo-nuh-pur) *noun* An evergreen bush or tree similar to a pine. It bears purple fruit that look like berries.

juniper tree

junk (juhngk) *noun*
1. Old metal, wood, rags, or other items that are thrown away.
2. Things that are worthless or useless. *My room is full of junk!*
3. A Chinese sailing boat with square sails and a flat bottom. *Junks have been used for trading for hundreds of years.*

Chinese junk

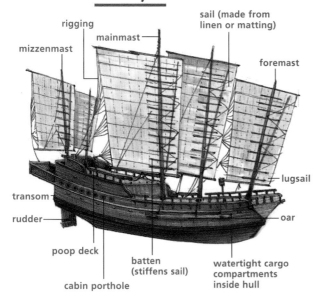

rigging
mizzenmast
mainmast
sail (made from linen or matting)
foremast
transom
lugsail
rudder
oar
poop deck
batten (stiffens sail)
watertight cargo compartments inside hull
cabin porthole

junk food *noun* Food that is not good for you because it contains a lot of calories, fat, sugar, salt, and/or chemical additives. Potato chips, candy, and cookies are all considered junk food.

junk mail *noun* Advertisements, catalogs, and other mail that you receive without having asked for them.

junk·yard (juhnk-*yard*) *noun* An area used to collect, store, and sometimes sell discarded materials, such as old or wrecked cars.

Ju·pi·ter (joo-puh-tur) *noun* The fifth planet from the sun. Jupiter is the largest planet in our solar system.

ju·ror (jur-ur) *noun* A member of a jury.

ju·ry (ju-ree) *noun* A group of people at a trial that listens to the facts and decides whether the person accused of a crime is innocent or guilty. ▷ *noun, plural* **juries**

just (juhst)
1. *adjective* Fair and right, as in *a just decision.* ▷ *adverb* **justly**
2. *adverb* Exactly. *That cantaloupe weighs just two pounds.*
3. *adverb* A very little while ago. *I'm afraid that Henry has just left.*
4. *adverb* Barely. *We just made the train.*
5. *adverb* Nothing more than. *It's just a small scratch.*

jus·tice (juhss-tiss) *noun*
1. Fair and impartial behavior or treatment.
2. The system of laws and judgment in a country.
3. A judge.
4. **justice of the peace** Someone who hears cases in local courts of law and marries couples.

jus·ti·fy (juhss-tuh-fye) *verb* If you **justify** an action, you give a reason or explanation to show that it is fair or reasonable. *How can you justify spending so much money on clothes?* ▷ **justifies, justifying, justified** ▷ *noun* **justification**

jut (juht) *verb* To stick out. *The cliff jutted into the sea.* ▷ **jutting, jutted**

jute (joot) *noun* A strong fiber that is woven to make rope and a coarse material called burlap. Jute comes from a plant that grows in tropical Asia.

ju·ve·nile (joo-vuh-nuhl *or* joo-vuh-*nile*)
1. *noun* A young person who is not yet an adult according to the law.
2. *adjective* Of or for young people, as in *juvenile books.*
3. *adjective* Childish or immature, as in *juvenile behavior.*
4. **juvenile delinquent** *noun* A young person who breaks the law. ▷ *noun* **juvenile delinquency**

jux·ta·pose (juhk-stuh-*poze*) *verb* To place things side by side, especially to compare or contrast them. *When you juxtapose the two pictures, you see how much bigger our new house is than our old one.* ▷ **juxtaposing, juxtaposed** ▷ *noun* **juxtaposition** (juhk-stuh-puh-zi-shuhn)

J

Kk

About K ◀

Spelling Hint: Words that begin with a *k* sound are spelled with a *k* or a *c*. Examples: kabob, keen, capital, clever, coin.

ka·bob *or* **ke·bob** (kuh-bob) *noun* Small pieces of meat or vegetables cooked on a skewer.

Ka·bu·ki (kuh-boo-kee) *noun* A type of Japanese drama traditionally performed by men in elaborate costumes.

ka·lei·do·scope (kuh-lye-duh-*skope*) *noun* A tube that you twist or turn as you look into it to see changing patterns made by mirrors and pieces of colored glass. ▷ *adjective* **kaleidoscopic**

kan·ga·roo (*kang*-guh-**roo**) *noun* An animal of Australia with short front legs and long, powerful back legs that are used for leaping. The female carries her young in a pouch for about six months after birth.

kar·a·o·ke (kah-ree-oh-kee) *noun* A form of entertainment originated in Japan in which people sing the words of popular songs while a machine plays the background music.

ka·ra·te
(kah-**rah**-tee) *noun* A form of self-defense in which people fight each other using controlled kicks and punches. *The man in the picture is landing after a front jump kick.*

karate

▶ Word History

Karate is a Japanese word meaning "empty hands," because in that martial art, no weapons are required to defeat an opponent.

ka·ty·did (kay-tee-did) *noun* A large, green insect that is related to the grasshopper. The male rubs its front wings together to make a shrill noise that sounds like its name.

kay·ak (kye-ak) *noun* A covered, narrow boat in which you sit and move through water by paddling. Kayaks were first used by the Eskimo.

kayak

curved paddle blade
safety helmet
shaft
life preserver
deck
spray skirt (keeps water out)

keel (keel)
1. *noun* A long beam along the bottom of a boat or ship that holds it together. *See* **ship.**
2. keel over *verb* (informal) To fall over in one smooth, steady movement. ▷ **keeling, keeled**

keen (keen) *adjective*
1. Very sharp, as in *a keen blade.*
2. Able to notice things easily, as in *a keen sense of smell.*
3. Quick or alert, as in *a keen mind.*
4. Eager or enthusiastic. *I am keen on sports.*
▷ *adjective* **keener, keenest**

keep (keep) *verb*
1. To have something and not get rid of it. *Let's keep these books.*
2. To stay the same. *We ran around to keep warm.*
3. To continue doing something. *Dottie kept laughing at me.*
4. To store. *We'll keep the new car in the garage.*
5. To hold back or to stop. *The blizzard kept us from going outside.*
6. To carry out or to fulfill, as in *to keep a promise.*
▷ *verb* **keeping, kept** (kept)

keep·er (kee-pur) *noun* Someone who looks after or guards something.

keg (keg) *noun* A small barrel.

kelp (kelp) *noun* A large, edible, brown seaweed. When kelp is burned, the ashes can be used to produce iodine, fertilizer, and other products.
▷ *noun, plural* **kelp**

ken·nel (ken-uhl) *noun*
1. A shelter where dogs and cats are kept.
2. A place where dogs and cats are raised and trained or looked after while their owners are away.

ker·chief (kur-chif) *noun* A piece of cloth, usually square, worn around the head or neck.

ker·nel (kur-nuhl) *noun*
1. A grain or seed of corn, wheat, or other cereal plant.
2. The soft part inside the shell of a nut that is good to eat.
3. The central or most important part of something, as in *a kernel of truth.*

ker·o·sene (ker-uh-*seen*) *noun* A thin, colorless fuel that is made from petroleum.

K

ketch·up (kech-uhp) *noun* A thick, red sauce that is made with tomatoes, onions, salt, sugar, and spices.

> ### ▶ Word History
> •
>
> Some people write **ketchup** and others write **catsup**. Both these words come from the Chinese term *ke-tsiap* or "fish sauce." The original ketchup did not include tomatoes as an ingredient. American sailors were the first to add them to an early type of ketchup the British made from mushrooms.

ket·tle (ket-uhl) *noun* A metal pot used for boiling liquids or cooking foods.

ket·tle·drum (ket-uhl-*druhm*) *noun* A large drum with a metal body shaped like a bowl and a deep, booming sound.

key (kee)
1. *noun* A piece of metal shaped to fit into a lock to open it or to start an engine.
2. *noun* Something that provides a solution or an explanation, as in *the key to the mystery*.
3. *noun* One of the buttons on a computer or typewriter.
4. *noun* One of the black or white bars that you press on a piano.
5. *adjective* Very important, as in *a key decision*.
6. *noun* A list or chart that explains the symbols on a map.
7. *noun* A group of musical notes based around one particular note, as in *a song in the key of F*. **Key** sounds like **quay**.

key·board (kee-*bord*) *noun*
1. The set of keys on a computer, typewriter, piano, etc.
2. An **electronic keyboard** has keys like a piano and buttons that produce other sounds. It is worked by electricity.

key·hole (kee-*hole*) *noun* The hole in a lock where a key fits.

key·pad (kee-*pad*) *noun* A small panel of keys or buttons used for operating an electronic machine such as a calculator.

kha·ki (kak-ee *or* kah-kee) *noun*
1. A yellow-brown color.
2. A strong cotton cloth of this color, often used for soldiers' uniforms.
▷ *adjective* **khaki**

kib·butz (ki-buts) *noun* A small community in Israel in which all the people live and work together. ▷ *noun, plural* **kibbutzim** (ki-but-seem)

kick (kik)
1. *verb* To hit something with your foot.
▷ **kicking, kicked** ▷ *noun* **kick**

2. *noun* (informal) A feeling of excitement or pleasure. *Dan gets a kick out of baby-sitting for his nephew.*

kick·off (kik-*of*) *noun* A kick of the ball that begins the action in a game of football or soccer.

kid (kid)
1. *noun* (informal) A child.
2. *noun* A young goat. *The kid in the picture is standing in some old metal storage drums.*
3. *verb* To make fun of or tease someone. *Are you kidding me?* ▷ **kidding, kidded**

kid

kid·nap (kid-*nap*) *verb* The illegal activity of capturing someone and keeping the person as a prisoner, usually until certain demands are met.
▷ **kidnapping, kidnapped** ▷ *noun* **kidnapper**

kid·ney (kid-nee) *noun* One of a pair of organs in your body that remove waste matter from your blood and turn it into urine. *See* **organ**.

kill (kil) *verb*
1. To end the life of a person, an animal, or a plant. ▷ *noun* **killer**
2. To end or to destroy. *Failing the test killed my chances of getting an A in English.*
3. To hurt very much. *My back is killing me.*
▷ *verb* **killing, killed**

kiln (kil *or* kiln) *noun* A very hot oven used to bake objects made of clay until they are hard and dry.

ki·lo·gram (kil-uh-*gram*) *noun* A unit of mass or weight in the metric system equal to 1,000 grams or 2.2 pounds. This dictionary weighs about one kilogram.

ki·lo·hertz (kil-uh-*hurts*) *noun* A unit for measuring the frequency of radio waves. One kilohertz is equal to 1,000 vibrations per second. ▷ *noun, plural* **kilohertz**

ki·lo·joule (kil-uh-*jool*) *noun* A unit for measuring energy or work done. One kilojoule is equal to 1,000 joules.

ki·lo·me·ter (kuh-lom-uh-tur *or* kil-uh-*mee*-tur) *noun* A unit of length in the metric system equal to 1,000 meters, or about 0.6 miles. The Golden Gate Bridge in San Francisco, California, is about one kilometer long.

ki·lo·watt (kil-uh-*waht*) *noun* A unit for measuring electrical power. One kilowatt equals 1,000 watts.

kilt (kilt) *noun* A pleated, plaid skirt worn by Scottish men as part of a traditional costume.

ki·mo·no (kuh-**moh**-nuh) *noun* A long, loose robe with wide sleeves and a sash, worn in Japan.

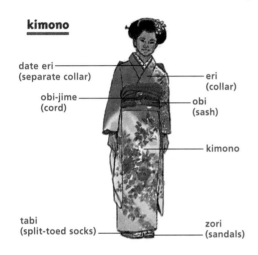

kimono

date eri (separate collar)
eri (collar)
obi-jime (cord)
obi (sash)
kimono
tabi (split-toed socks)
zori (sandals)

kin (kin) *noun* A person or people related to you.

kind (kinde)
1. *adjective* Friendly, helpful, and generous. ▷ **kinder, kindest** ▷ *noun* **kindness** ▷ *adverb* **kindly**
2. *noun* A group of the same or similar things; a category. *The beagle is one kind of dog.*
3. *noun* A type or sort. *That's the kind of book that makes us laugh.*

kin·der·gar·ten (kin-dur-*gart*-uhn) *noun* A class for children ages four to six.

▶ Word History

Kindergarten is the German word for "children's garden." The first kindergarten was opened in Germany in 1837 by Friedrich Wilhelm August Froebel. Froebel, who had an unhappy childhood, spent his life opening schools where children could play and explore the world.

kin·dle (kin-duhl) *verb*
1. To make something start to burn. *The campers quickly kindled a fire.*
2. To stir up or to excite. *Our visit to the castle kindled my interest in history.*
▷ *verb* **kindling, kindled**

kin·dling (kind-ling) *noun* Small, thin pieces of wood used for starting fires.

ki·net·ic (ki-net-ik) *adjective* To do with movement, or caused by movement, as in *kinetic energy.* ▷ *adverb* **kinetically**

king (king) *noun*
1. A man from a royal family who is the ruler of his country.
2. A chess piece that can move one square in any direction. *See* **chess.**
3. A playing card with a picture of a king on it.

king·dom (king-duhm) *noun*
1. A country that has a king or queen as its ruler.
2. One of the main groups into which all living things are divided, such as the animal kingdom and the plant kingdom.

king·fish·er (king-*fish*-ur) *noun* A small bird with bright feathers and a long bill that lives near water and catches fish for food.

kingfisher

kink (kingk) *noun*
1. A tight curl or twist in a rope, wire, hose, chain, or hair. ▷ *adjective* **kinky**
2. A painful or stiff feeling in a neck or back muscle.
3. An imperfection that is likely to cause problems. *The kink in the computer program caused a delay in our results.*

kin·ship (kin-ship) *noun*
1. A family relationship.
2. Any close connection. *Juan immediately felt a kinship with Meg because they were both new at the school.*

ki·osk (kee-osk) *noun* A small structure with one or more open sides, often used as a stand for selling newspapers.

kiss (kiss) *verb* To touch someone with your lips to greet the person or to show that you like or love him or her. ▷ **kisses, kissing, kissed** ▷ *noun* **kiss**

kit (kit) *noun*
1. A set of parts that you put together to make something, as in *a model airplane kit.*
2. A set of tools and materials for a certain purpose, as in *a sewing kit* or *a first-aid kit.*

kitch·en (kich-uhn) *noun* A room in which food is prepared and cooked.

kite (kite) *noun* A frame covered with paper or material that is attached to a long piece of string and flown in the wind.

The picture shows a stunt kite, which can be made to perform turns, dips, and loops.

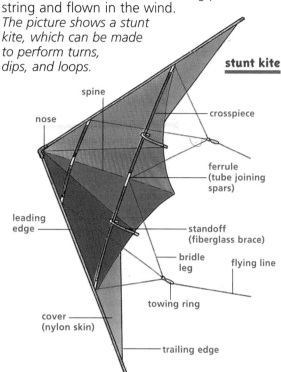

stunt kite

- spine
- nose
- crosspiece
- ferrule (tube joining spars)
- leading edge
- standoff (fiberglass brace)
- bridle leg
- flying line
- towing ring
- cover (nylon skin)
- trailing edge

kit·ten (kit-uhn) *noun* A young cat.

kit·ty (kit-ee) *noun*
1. A kitten. *Here, kitty, kitty.*
2. An amount of money contributed by everyone in a group and then used to buy something.
▷ *noun, plural* **kitties**

ki·wi (kee-wee) *noun*
1. A bird from New Zealand that cannot fly.
2. A small, round fruit with brown, fuzzy skin and green flesh. Kiwis are grown in New Zealand. Also called **kiwifruit**. *See* **fruit**.

klutz (kluhts) *noun* (slang) A clumsy person.

knack (nak) *noun* An ability to do something difficult or tricky. *Greg has a knack for diplomacy.*

knap·sack (nap-sak) *noun* A canvas or leather bag used to carry books or supplies on your back.

knave (nayv) *noun* (old-fashioned) A dishonest man or boy.

knead (need) *verb* When you **knead** dough, you press, fold, and stretch it to make it smooth. **Knead** sounds like **need**. ▷ **kneading, kneaded**

knee (nee) *noun* The joint between your upper and lower leg that you bend when you walk.

kneel (neel) *verb* To bend your legs and put your knees on the ground. *Arthur knelt down to scrub the floor.* ▷ **kneeling, knelt** (nelt)

knick·ers (nik-urz) *noun, plural* Loose, short pants that end just below the knee.

knick·knack (nik-nak) *noun* A small object used as a decoration.

knife (nife)
1. *noun* A tool with a sharp blade used for cutting things. ▷ *noun, plural* **knives**
2. *verb* To stab someone with a knife. ▷ **knifing, knifed**

knight (nite) *noun*
1. In medieval times, a **knight** was a warrior who fought on horseback. A king or noble would give a knight land, and in return the knight would fight for him. *See also* **joust**.
▷ *adjective* **knightly**
2. In Great Britain, a man who has been given the title "Sir" as a reward for service to his country. ▷ *noun* **knighthood** ▷ *verb* **knight**
3. A chess piece with a horse's head that always has to move three squares at a time. *See* **chess**. **Knight** sounds like **night**.

mounted knight

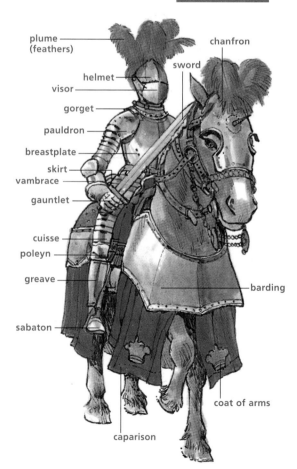

- plume (feathers)
- chanfron
- sword
- helmet
- visor
- gorget
- pauldron
- breastplate
- skirt
- vambrace
- gauntlet
- cuisse
- poleyn
- greave
- barding
- sabaton
- coat of arms
- caparison

knit (nit) *verb*
1. To make cloth or clothing by looping yarn together either by hand with long, pointed needles or by machine. ▷ *noun* **knitting**
2. When a bone **knits,** it heals after it has been broken.
▷ *verb* **knitting, knitted** *or* **knit**

knob (nob) *noun*
1. A small, round handle on a drawer or door.
2. A control button on a radio, television, or other device.
3. A roundish lump. *The trunk of the tree was covered with knobs.*

knock (nok) *verb*
1. To bang or hit something or someone. *Knock the nails into the wall with a hammer.* ▷ *noun* **knock**
2. To hit and cause to fall. *The skidding car knocked over a telephone pole.*
3. To criticize harshly. *Critics knocked the new movie.*
4. knock out To make someone unconscious.
▷ *verb* **knocking, knocked**

knock·er (nok-ur) *noun* A piece of metal attached to a door that you use to knock on the door.

knoll (nohl) *noun* A small hill.

knot (not)
1. *noun* A fastening made by looping and twisting one or more pieces of string or rope.
2. *verb* To make a knot in. ▷ **knotting, knotted**
3. *noun* A small, hard spot in a piece of wood where a branch once joined the main trunk.
4. *noun* A unit for measuring the speed of a ship or an aircraft, equal to 6,076 feet per hour.
Knot sounds like **not.**

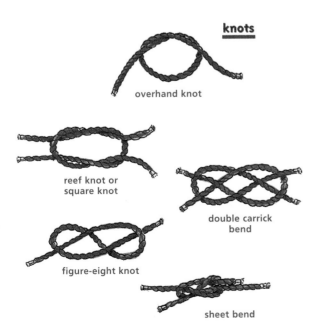
knots
overhand knot
reef knot or square knot
double carrick bend
figure-eight knot
sheet bend

knot·ty (not-ee) *adjective*
1. Having many knots, as in *knotty pine.*
2. Difficult to understand or solve, as in *a knotty problem.*
▷ *adjective* **knottier, knottiest**

know (noh) *verb* To be familiar with a person, place, or piece of information. **Know** sounds like **no.** ▷ **knowing, knew** (noo), **known** (nohn)

know-how *noun* The knowledge and skill needed to complete a task or job correctly.

know·ledge (nol-ij) *noun*
1. The things that someone knows; information. *The quiz tested our knowledge.*
2. Awareness or a clear idea. *The knowledge that he would be punished stopped the boy from misbehaving.*

knowl·edge·a·ble (nol-ij-uh-buhl) *adjective* If you are **knowledgeable,** you know a lot. *Chico is very knowledgeable about music.*

knuck·le (nuhk-uhl) *noun* One of the joints in a finger.

ko·a·la (koh-ah-luh) *noun* An Australian animal that looks like a small bear and lives in eucalyptus trees. *See* **eucalyptus.**

kook (kook) *noun* (slang) Someone who acts in a silly or strange way or who has crazy ideas.
▷ *adjective* **kooky**

kook·a·bur·ra (kuk-uh-*bur*-uh) *noun* An Australian bird that makes a loud, cackling sound like the sound of someone laughing.

kookaburra

Ko·ran *or* **Qur'an** (kor-ahn *or* kor-an) *noun* The holy book of the Muslim religion.

ko·sher (koh-shur) *adjective* **Kosher** food is food that has been prepared according to the laws of the Jewish religion.

kung fu (kuhng foo) *noun* One of the Chinese martial arts in which a person uses punches, kicks, and blocks for self-defense. Kung fu is similiar to karate.

Kwan·za *or* **Kwan·zaa** (kwahn-zuh) *noun* An African-American holiday based on a traditional African harvest festival. Kwanza is celebrated for seven days beginning on December 26 and ending on New Year's Day, January 1. Each day is devoted to a different principle, such as faith, creativity, unity, and purpose.

K

Ll

About L

Spelling Hint: Words that begin with the *lye* sound are usually spelled *li* or *ly*. Examples: line, liar, Lyme (disease), lyre.

lab (lab) Short for **laboratory**.

la·bel (lay-buhl)
1. *noun* A piece of paper, cloth, or plastic that is attached to something and gives information about it.
2. *noun* A word or phrase that describes something. *Philadelphia has the label "City of Brotherly Love."*
3. *verb* To attach a label to something or to give something a label. ▷ **labeling, labeled**

la·bor (lay-bur)
1. *verb* To work hard. *Nick labored all weekend at his term paper.* ▷ **laboring, labored** ▷ *noun* **labor,** *noun* **laborer**
2. *noun* The work of giving birth to a baby.
3. *noun* People employed to do work, especially physical work. *Labor and management agreed on a new contract.*

lab·o·ra·tor·y (lab-ruh-*tor*-ee) *noun* A room, building, or institute containing special equipment for people to use in scientific experiments. ▷ *noun, plural* **laboratories**

Labor Day *noun* A legal holiday in the United States to honor people who work. It is celebrated on the first Monday in September.

labor union *noun* An organized group of workers set up to help improve working conditions and pay.

lace (layss)
1. *noun* Thin material made from cotton or silk with a pattern of small holes and delicate stitches. ▷ *adjective* **lacy**
2. *noun* A long piece of thin string, cord, or leather used to tie shoes.
3. *verb* To tie something together with a lace. *Lace up your shoes.* ▷ **lacing, laced**

lack (lak)
1. *verb* To be without something that you need. *The refugees lack food.* ▷ **lacking, lacked**
2. *noun* If there is a **lack** of something, there is not enough of it, as in *a lack of rain.*
3. *noun* Something that is needed or is missing. *The most serious lack in his diet is protein.*

lac·quer (lak-ur)
1. *noun* A liquid coating that is put on wood or metal to give it a shiny finish and protect it.
2. *verb* To coat with this liquid. ▷ **lacquering, lacquered**

la·crosse (luh-krawss) *noun* A ball game for two teams in which each player has a long stick with a small net on the end. The players use the net to run with the ball, pass it or throw it to one another, and aim to score goals.

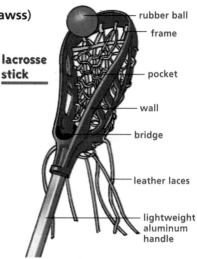

lacrosse stick

rubber ball
frame
pocket
wall
bridge
leather laces
lightweight aluminum handle

lad (lad) *noun* A boy or a young man.

lad·der (lad-ur) *noun* A metal, wooden, or rope structure that is used to climb up and down. Ladders are made from two long, upright pieces linked by a series of horizontal pieces called rungs.

lad·en (layd-uhn) *adjective* Carrying a lot of things. *Matt arrived laden with presents.*

la·dle (lay-duhl) *noun* A large, deep spoon with a long handle, used for serving soup, casseroles, etc. ▷ *verb* **ladle**

la·dy (lay-dee) *noun*
1. A woman.
2. A girl or woman who has good manners.
3. Lady In Great Britain, a title used by a woman who has either earned the title herself as a reward for service to her country or who is married to a lord or a man with the title "Sir." ▷ *noun, plural* **ladies**

la·dy·bug (lay-dee-*buhg*) *noun* A small, round beetle that usually has red or orange wings and black spots. Ladybugs eat insects, such as aphids, that are harmful to plants.

▶ Word History

Not all **ladybugs** are female. This insect did not get its name because of gender but because of religion. The ladybug honors Mary, the mother of Jesus, who is referred to as "Our Lady" in Christianity. Because these colorful beetles helped farmers by feeding on other, harmful insects, the name was seen as a tribute.

lag (lag)
1. *verb* To move so slowly that you fall behind the others. *The slower joggers lagged behind and soon were out of sight.*

2. *noun* A delay. *After we turned on the old TV set, there was a slight lag before a picture appeared on the screen.*
3. *verb* To drop, or to lessen. *Our interest in the dull game lagged.* ▷ *noun* **lag**
▷ *verb* **lagging, lagged**

la·goon (luh-**goon**) *noun* A shallow pool of seawater separated from the sea by a narrow strip of land.

laid-back *adjective* *(informal)* Very relaxed and calm.

lair (lair) *noun* A place where a wild animal rests and sleeps.

lake (lake) *noun* A large body of fresh water surrounded by land.

lamb (lam) *noun*
1. A young sheep.
2. Meat from a young sheep.

lame (laym) *adjective*
1. Someone who is **lame** has an injured leg and so is unable to walk freely. ▷ *noun* **lameness**
2. Weak or unconvincing, as in *a lame excuse.*
▷ *adverb* **lamely**

la·ment (luh-**ment**)
1. *verb* To feel or show great sadness. *Ramón lamented the death of his grandmother.*
▷ **lamenting, lamented**
2. *noun* A sad song, especially one about someone's death.

lamp (lamp) *noun* A light that uses gas, oil, or electricity.

LAN (lan) *noun* A system of computers in a small area that are linked by cables so that users can share information and equipment. LAN stands for *Local Area Network.*

lance (lanss)
1. *noun* A long spear used in the past by soldiers riding horses. *See* **joust.**
2. *verb* To cut open with a sharp knife. *The doctor lanced the boil.* ▷ **lancing, lanced**

land (land)
1. *noun* The part of the earth's surface that is not covered by water.
2. *noun* Earth or soil. *The pioneers looked for good land to farm.*
3. *verb* To come down from the air to the land or water. *The plane landed safely.*
4. *noun* A country. *Canada is a vast land.*
5. *verb* To succeed in getting something. *I've landed a place on the team.*
6. *verb* To cause you to end up somewhere. *His rude behavior landed him in trouble.*
▷ *verb* **landing, landed**

land·fill (land-*fil*) *noun*
1. Garbage that is stacked and covered with earth.

2. landfill site A large area where garbage is buried.

land·ing (land-ing) *noun*
1. The act of coming to land or coming ashore after a flight or voyage, as in *a rough landing.*
2. The place on a dock or pier where boats load and unload.
3. A level area of floor at the top of a staircase.
4. landing strip A level area of ground that aircraft use for taking off and landing.

land·la·dy (land-*lay*-dee) *noun* A woman who owns and rents out an apartment, a room, a house, or other property. ▷ *noun, plural* **landladies**

land·lord (land-*lord*) *noun* A man who owns and rents out an apartment, a room, a house, or other property.

land·mark (land-*mark*) *noun*
1. An object in a landscape that can be seen from far away. *The statue of the mayor is a familiar landmark in our city.*
2. An important event. *The invention of the telephone is a landmark in the history of communication.*
3. A building or place selected and pointed out as important, as in *a historical landmark.*

land·scape (land-*skape*) *noun*
1. A large area of land that you can view from one place.
2. A painting, drawing, or photograph that shows such a stretch of land.
3. landscape gardening The designing, shaping, and planting of a garden in an attractive way.

land·slide (land-*slide*) *noun*
1. A sudden slide of earth and rocks down the side of a mountain or a hill.
2. An election victory in which the winner gets many more votes than anyone else.

lane (layn) *noun*
1. A narrow road or street.
2. One of the strips marked on a main road that is wide enough for a single line of vehicles.
3. One of the strips, each wide enough for one person, into which a track or swimming pool is divided.
4. A narrow wooden path on which bowling balls are rolled.

lan·guage (lang-gwij) *noun*
1. The words and grammar that people use to talk and write to each other.
2. Speech used by one country or group of people, as in *the Spanish language.*
3. A set of signs, symbols, or movements used to express meaning, as in *sign language.*

lank·y (lang-kee) *adjective* Someone who is **lanky** is very tall and thin. ▷ **lankier, lankiest**

lan·tern
(lan-turn)
noun A light with a protective frame around it. *Lanterns can be made from paper, such as the ones shown here, or from glass and metal.*

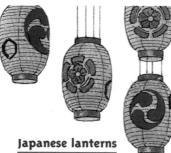

Japanese lanterns

> ### Word History
>
> The word **lantern** comes from the Greek word *lampein,* meaning "to shine." Lantern is an example of an ancient word for a thing that is still used but has changed in some way. In olden times, lanterns held candles or burning oil. Today, most lanterns are powered by electricity.

lan·yard (lan-yurd) *noun* A cord worn around the neck to which you can attach a knife or a whistle.

lap (lap)
1. *noun* The flat area formed by the top part of your legs when you are sitting down.
2. *noun* One time over or around something. *Sol ran four laps around the track.*
3. *verb* To lie partly over something else. *The insect's wings lap over each other.*
4. *verb* When water **laps** against something, it moves gently against it.
5. *verb* When an animal **laps up** a drink, it flicks the liquid up into its mouth with its tongue.
▷ *verb* **lapping, lapped**

la·pel (luh-pel) *noun* The part of the collar of a coat or jacket that folds back over itself.

lapse (laps)
1. *noun* A small mistake or failure, as in *a lapse of memory.* ▷ *verb* **lapse**
2. *noun* The passing of time. *After a lapse of two years, Jo-Jo returned.*
3. *verb* To drop or fall off little by little. *The story was so boring that our interest soon lapsed.*
4. *verb* To come to an end. *Our magazine subscription lapsed last month.*
▷ *verb* **lapsing, lapsed**

lap·top (lap-top) *noun* A portable computer that is so small and light that you can use it on your lap.

larch (larch) *noun* A tall tree with small cones and needles that drop off in the fall. The larch is related to the pine.

lard (lard) *noun* A solid, white grease made from the melted-down fat of pigs and hogs. Lard is used in cooking.

lar·der (lar-dur) *noun* A small room or pantry in which food is stored.

large (larj)
1. *adjective* Great in size or amount. ▷ **larger, largest** ▷ *noun* **largeness**
2. If a person or an animal is **at large,** it is free. *There's a tiger at large in the town.*

large intestine *noun* The thick, lower end of the digestive system, containing the appendix, colon, and rectum. *See* **digestion, organ.**

large·ly (larj-lee) *adverb* Mostly. *Rosie's story is largely untrue.*

la·ri·at (la-ree-uht) *noun* A lasso.

lark (lark) *noun*
1. A small, brown bird that flies very high in the sky and has a beautiful song.
2. Something silly that you do for fun or as a joke. *As a lark, we played on the beach during the snowstorm.*

lark·spur (lark-spur) *noun* A tall plant that has long stalks of blue, purple, or white flowers.

lar·va (lar-vuh) *noun* An insect at the stage of development between an egg and a pupa when it looks like a worm. A caterpillar is the larva of a moth or a butterfly. *See* **caterpillar.** ▷ *noun, plural* **larvae** (lar-vee)

lar·yn·gi·tis (la-rin-jye-tiss) *noun* A swelling of the throat caused by an infection. It causes hoarseness.

lar·ynx (la-ringks) *noun* The upper part of the windpipe. The larynx holds your vocal cords.

la·sa·gna *or* **la·sa·gne** (luh-zah-nyuh) *noun* An Italian dish made with layers of wide noodles, chopped meat or vegetables, tomato sauce, and cheese.

la·ser (lay-zur) *noun*
1. A device that makes a very narrow, powerful beam of light that can be used for light shows, for cutting things, or for medical operations. Laser stands for *Light Amplification by Stimulated Emission of Radiation.*
2. laser beam A concentrated beam of light made by a laser. Laser beams are used to read compact disks. *See* **compact disk.**

laser printer *noun* A computer printer that reproduces high-quality images using a laser.

lash (lash)
1. *noun* One of the small hairs that grow around your eyelid.
2. *noun* A stroke with a whip. ▷ *verb* **lash**
3. *verb* To tie things together very firmly using rope or cord.
4. *verb* To whip back and forth. *The caged lion lashed its tail as the trainer approached.*

L

5. lash out *verb* To hit or to speak out against someone suddenly and angrily.
▷ *verb* **lashes, lashing, lashed** ▷ *noun, plural* **lashes**

lass (lass) *noun* A girl or a young woman. ▷ *noun, plural* **lasses**

las·so (lass-oh *or* lass-oo) *noun* A length of rope with a large loop at one end that can be thrown over an animal to catch it. Also called a lariat. ▷ *noun, plural* **lassos** *or* **lassoes** ▷ *verb* **lasso**

last (last)
1. adjective Coming at the end or after everything else. *Jane was the last one to leave.*
▷ *adverb* **lastly**
2. adjective Being the only one left. *He ate the last piece of meat.*
3. adjective Most recent. *I saw Dominic last week.*
4. noun The last person or thing.
5. verb To go on for a particular length of time. *The movie will last for 90 minutes.*
6. verb To stay in good condition. *My sneakers lasted one year.*
▷ *verb* **lasting, lasted**

last·ing (last-ing) *adjective* Something that is **lasting** keeps going for a long time.

latch (lach)
1. noun A lock or fastening for a door. ▷ *noun, plural* **latches** ▷ *verb* **latch**
2. verb If you **latch on to** someone or something, you become very attached to and dependent on it. ▷ **latches, latching, latched**

latch·key (lach-kee) *noun*
1. A key that opens a door with a latch.
2. Latchkey children have to let themselves in when they return from school because there is nobody else at home yet.

late (late) *adjective*
1. When someone or something is **late,** it comes after the expected time. ▷ *noun* **lateness**
▷ *adverb* **late**
2. Near the end of a period of time, as in *the late 20th century.*
3. No longer alive, as in *the late Elvis Presley.*
▷ *adjective* **later, latest**

late·com·er (late-kuhm-ur) *noun* Someone who arrives late.

late·ly (late-lee) *adverb* Recently.

la·tent (late-uhnt) *adjective* Present but not very obvious or strong, as in *latent fingerprints* or *a latent talent.*

lat·er·al (lat-ur-uhl) *adjective* On, from, or to the side. *The quarterback threw a lateral pass.*

la·tex (lay-teks) *noun*
1. A milky liquid that comes from certain plants. This natural liquid is used to make rubber. *See* **rubber.**
2. A similar liquid that is produced artificially and is used to make rubber, paints, and chewing gum.
▷ *noun, plural* **latexes**

lathe (layTH) *noun* A machine that holds a piece of wood or metal while turning it against a cutting tool that shapes it.

lath·er (laTH-ur) *noun* A thick, creamy foam formed when soap is mixed with water. ▷ *verb* **lather**

Lat·in (lat-uhn) *noun* The language of the ancient Romans.

La·ti·na (lah-tee-nuh *or* luh-tee-nuh) *noun*
1. A woman or girl who was born in or lives in Latin America.
2. A woman or girl born in Latin America who lives in the United States.
▷ *adjective* **Latina**

Latin America *noun* All of the Americas found south of the United States where the languages spoken are based on Latin. Latin America includes Mexico as well as the countries of Central America and South America.

Latin-American *adjective* To do with the people, cultures, and countries of Mexico, Central America, and South America. ▷ *noun* **Latin American**

La·ti·no (lah-tee-noh *or* luh-tee-noh) *noun*
1. A person who was born in or lives in Latin America.
2. A person born in Latin America who lives in the United States.
▷ *adjective* **Latino**

lat·i·tude (lat-uh-tood) *noun* The position of a place, measured in degrees north or south of the equator. ▷ *adjective* **latitudinal**

lat·ter (lat-ur)
1. noun The second of two things just mentioned. *I like apples and pears, but I prefer the latter.*
2. adjective Later. *It snowed during the latter part of our vacation.*

lat·tice (lat-iss) *noun* A structure made from strips of wood, metal, etc., that cross each other, often diagonally, forming a pattern of diamond shapes. ▷ *adjective* **latticed**

laugh (laf) *verb* When you **laugh,** you make a sound to show that you think that something is funny. ▷ **laughing, laughed** ▷ *noun* **laugh,** *noun* **laughter**

laugh·a·ble (laf-uh-buhl) *adjective* If something is **laughable,** it is ridiculous and cannot be taken seriously.

laugh track *noun* Previously recorded laughter of a studio audience that is added to the sound track of a television program.

L

launch (lawnch)
1. *verb* To put a boat or ship into the water.
2. *verb* To send a rocket up into space.
3. *verb* To start or introduce something new. *The charity launched a campaign to help the homeless.*
4. *noun* A type of boat that is often used for sightseeing. ▷ *noun, plural* **launches**
5. **launching pad** *or* **launch pad** *noun* A place where rockets leave the ground to go into space. ▷ *verb* **launches, launching, launched** ▷ *noun* **launch**

laun·der (lawn-dur) *verb* To wash and iron clothes. *I have to launder my shirt before I can wear it to the party.* ▷ **laundering, laundered**

Laun·dro·mat (lawn-druh-*mat*) *noun* Trademark for a place where you pay to use washing machines and clothes dryers.

laun·dry (lawn-dree) *noun*
1. Clothes, towels, sheets, and other such items that are being washed or are about to be washed.
2. A place where washing is done.
▷ *noun, plural* **laundries**

lau·rel (lor-uhl) *noun*
1. An evergreen bush or tree with smooth, shiny leaves.
2. A wreath made from laurel leaves, given to heroes and poets in ancient Rome.
3. If you **rest on your laurels,** you rely on your past achievements and do not try anymore.

la·va (lah-vuh *or* la-vuh) *noun*
1. The hot, liquid rock that pours out of a volcano when it erupts.
2. The rock formed when this liquid has cooled and hardened.
See **volcano.**

> ▶ **Word History**
> ••
> **Lava** comes from the Latin and French word *lavare,* meaning "to fall" or "to slide." Lava slides or falls down the side of a volcano after an eruption.

lav·a·to·ry (lav-uh-*tor*-ee) *noun* A bathroom.
▷ *noun, plural* **lavatories**

lav·en·der (lav-uhn-dur) *noun*
1. A plant with pale purple flowers that have a pleasant smell.
2. A pale purple color, the color of lavender flowers. ▷ *adjective* **lavender**

lav·ish (lav-ish)
1. *adjective* Generous or extravagant, as in *lavish gifts.* ▷ *adverb* **lavishly**
2. *verb* If you **lavish** attention, money, care, etc., on someone, you give the person a lot of it.
▷ **lavishes, lavishing, lavished**

law (law) *noun*
1. A rule made by the government that must be obeyed.
2. A statement in science or math about what always happens whenever certain events take place, as in *the law of gravity.*
3. The profession and work of a lawyer, as in *a career in law.*

law·a·bid·ing (uh-bye-ding) *adjective* If you are **law-abiding,** you obey the laws of a government.

law·ful (law-fuhl) *adjective* Permitted by the law, as in *a lawful agreement.* ▷ *noun* **lawfulness** ▷ *adverb* **lawfully**

lawn (lawn) *noun* An area covered with grass, usually next to a house.

lawn mow·er (moh-ur) *noun* A machine that people use to cut grass.

law·suit (law-*soot*) *noun* A legal action or case brought against a person or a group in a court of law.

law·yer (law-yur *or* loi-ur) *noun* A person who is trained to advise people about the law and who acts and speaks for them in court.

lax (laks) *adjective* Relaxed or not strict, as in *lax discipline.* ▷ *noun* **laxity,** *noun* **laxness** ▷ *adverb* **laxly**

lay (lay) *verb*
1. To put or to place. *Lay the clothes on the bed.*
2. To produce an egg or eggs.
3. If a person has been **laid off,** he or she has been dismissed from a job, often for a short period of time.
4. If you are **laid up,** you are in bed with an injury or illness.
Lay sounds like **lei.** ▷ *verb* **laying, laid** (layd)

lay·er (lay-ur) *noun* A thickness or coating of something, as in *a layer of dust.* ▷ *verb* **layer** ▷ *adjective* **layered**

lay·off (lay-*of*) *noun* A period in which people are temporarily dismissed from work because there is not enough for them to do.

lay·out (lay-*out*) *noun* The pattern or design of something, as in *the layout of a book.*

la·zy (lay-zee) *adjective* If you are **lazy,** you do not want to work or be active. ▷ **lazier, laziest** ▷ *noun* **laziness** ▷ *verb* **laze** ▷ *adverb* **lazily**

lead
1. (leed) *verb* To show someone the way, usually by going in front of the person. *Gary led his friends to the treasure chest he had found.*
2. (leed) *verb* To be in charge, as in *to lead a discussion.* ▷ *noun* **leadership**
3. (leed) *noun* A person's position at the front. *Olga took the lead in the race.*
4. (leed) *noun* A piece of helpful advice or information. *I got several good leads on how to research job opportunities.*

5. (leed) *noun* The main actor or role in a play, movie, etc.
6. (led) *noun* A soft, gray metal.
7. (led) *noun* The black or gray material used in pencils; graphite.
8. (leed) *noun* A leash.
▷ *verb* **leading, led** (led) ▷ *noun* **leader**

leaf (leef)
1. *noun* A flat and usually green part of a plant or tree that grows out from a stem, twig, branch, etc. Leaves make food by the process of photosynthesis, giving off oxygen as a by-product. *The pictures show the main external and internal parts of a leaf. Photosynthesis happens mainly in the palisade cells, while respiration takes place around the spongy mesophyll cells.*
▷ *adjective* **leafy**
2. *noun* A page of a book.
3. *verb* To turn pages and glance at them quickly. *Waiting in the dentist's office, Rose leafed through a magazine.* ▷ **leafing, leafed**
4. *noun* A flat, removable part of a table. *Before the dinner party we added two extra leaves to the table.*
▷ *noun, plural* **leaves**

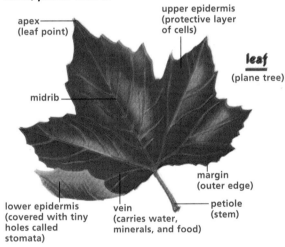

leaf
(plane tree)

apex (leaf point)
upper epidermis (protective layer of cells)
midrib
margin (outer edge)
lower epidermis (covered with tiny holes called stomata)
vein (carries water, minerals, and food)
petiole (stem)

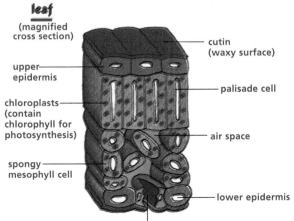

leaf
(magnified cross section)

cutin (waxy surface)
upper epidermis
palisade cell
chloroplasts (contain chlorophyll for photosynthesis)
air space
spongy mesophyll cell
lower epidermis
stoma (opens to allow gases in and out)

leaf·let (leef-lit) *noun*
1. A single sheet of paper giving information or advertising something.
2. A small or young leaf.

league (leeg) *noun*
1. A group of people with a common interest or activity, such as a group of sports teams or a political organization.
2. A measure of distance equal to about three miles.

leak (leek) *verb*
1. If a container **leaks,** water, gas, or another fluid escapes from it. ▷ *adjective* **leaky**
2. If a liquid or gas **leaks,** it escapes through a hole or crack in a container.
3. If someone **leaks** a story or information, the person tells it to someone else who is not meant to know it.
Leak sounds like **leek.**
▷ *verb* **leaking, leaked** ▷ *noun* **leak**

lean (leen)
1. *verb* To bend toward or over something. *The mother leaned over her baby.*
2. *verb* To rest your body against something for support. *Floyd leaned against the railing.*
3. *verb* To rely on for help. *I lean on my dad whenever I have a problem.*
4. *adjective* Slim and muscular.
5. *adjective* If meat is **lean,** it has very little or no fat. ▷ *noun* **lean**
▷ *verb* **leaning, leaned** ▷ *adjective* **leaner, leanest**

leaning *noun* If you have a **leaning** toward something, you are interested in it or tend to like it.

leap (leep) *verb* To jump or jump over something.
▷ **leaping, leaped** or **leapt** (leept or lept) ▷ *noun* **leap**

leap·frog (leep-frog) *noun* A game in which one player bends over and another jumps over his or her back, using the hands for support.
▷ *verb* **leapfrog**

leap year *noun* A year that has 366 days, caused by adding an extra day in February. A leap year comes every fourth year. *The years 1988 and 1992 were leap years.*

learn (lurn) *verb*
1. To gain knowledge or a skill.
2. To memorize. *I had to learn a poem by heart.*
3. To discover some news. *I learned that Abdul was going away.*
▷ *verb* **learning, learned** or **learnt**

learn·ed (lur-nid) *adjective* Having much knowledge or education, as in *a learned scholar.*

learning disabled *adjective* Having difficulty in learning a basic skill, such as reading, because of a physical condition, such as dyslexia. Abbreviated *LD.* ▷ *noun* **learning disability**

L

lease (leess) *noun* An agreement that a landlord and tenant sign when renting an apartment, a house, or other property. ▷ *verb* **lease**

leash (leesh) *noun* A strap, cord, or chain that you use to hold and control an animal. ▷ *noun, plural* **leashes**

least (leest)
1. *noun* The smallest amount. *Of all the children, Sue eats the least.* ▷ *adjective* **least**
2. *adverb* Less than anything else. *Turnips are my least favorite vegetable.*
3. at least Not less or fewer than. *We need at least another week's vacation.*

leath·er (leTH-ur) *noun* Animal skin that is treated with chemicals and used to make shoes, bags, and other goods. ▷ *adjective* **leathery**

leave (leev)
1. *verb* To go away, as in *to leave for a vacation.*
2. *verb* To let something stay or remain. *Leave the dishes; I'll do them later.*
3. *verb* To give property to someone through a will, after death. *Grandmother left Dad her house in the country.*
4. *verb* To quit. *Joanne will leave her job when she finds a better one.*
5. *noun* Time away from work, as in *maternity leave.*
6. *verb* To have remaining. *Subtracting 2 from 7 leaves 5.*
7. leave behind *verb* If you **leave** something **behind,** you forget to bring it.
8. leave out *verb* If you **leave** something **out,** you do not include it.
▷ *verb* **leaving, left** (left)

lec·ture (lek-chur) *noun*
1. A talk given to a class or an audience in order to teach something. ▷ *noun* **lecturer**
2. A scolding that lasts a long time.
▷ *verb* **lecture**

ledge (lej) *noun*
1. A narrow shelf that sticks out from a wall, as in *a window ledge.*
2. A narrow, flat shelf on the side of a mountain or cliff.

lee (lee) *noun* The side of something such as a ship or mountain that is away from the wind; shelter. *The goats stood in the lee of the hill to wait out the storm.* ▷ *adjective* **lee**

leech (leech) *noun*
1. A worm that lives in water or wet earth and survives by sucking blood from animals. In the past, doctors often used leeches to take blood from patients. Leeches are still used for that purpose in some parts of the world. *See* **parasite.**
2. A person who clings to others, hoping to get something from them.
▷ *noun, plural* **leeches**

leek (leek) *noun* A long, white vegetable with green leaves at one end. It tastes like a mild onion. **Leek** sounds like **leak.** *See* **vegetable.**

leer (lihr) *noun* A sly or evil grin. ▷ *verb* **leer**

left (left) *noun*
1. The side you begin to read from in a line of English writing. *Turn left at the corner.* ▷ *adjective* **left** ▷ *adverb* **left**
2. In politics, people **on the left** have liberal or radical views.

left-hand·ed (han-did) *adjective* If you are **left-handed,** you use your left hand more easily than your right hand. ▷ *noun* **left-hander**

left·o·vers (left-oh-vurz) *noun, plural* The part of a meal that has not been eaten and can be used for another meal.

leg (leg) *noun*
1. The part of your body between your hip and your foot.
2. The part of a pair of pants that covers a leg.
3. A part of a chair, table, etc., on which it stands.
4. A **leg** of a journey is one part or stage of it.
5. Either of two sides of a triangle besides the base.
6. *(informal)* If you **pull** someone's **leg,** you make fun of the person by telling him or her something untrue.
7. If something is **on its last legs,** it is about to collapse or die.

leg·a·cy (leg-uh-see) *noun*
1. Money or property that has been left to someone in a will.
2. Something handed down from one generation to another.
▷ *noun, plural* **legacies**

le·gal (lee-guhl) *adjective*
1. To do with the law, as in *legal documents.*
2. Lawful, or allowed by law. ▷ *verb* **legalize** ▷ *adverb* **legally**

leg·end (lej-uhnd) *noun*
1. A story handed down from earlier times. Legends are often based on fact, but they are not entirely true. ▷ *adjective* **legendary**
2. The words written beneath or beside a map or chart to explain it.

leg·gings (leg-ingz) *noun, plural* A covering for the legs that fits like tights.

leg·i·ble (lej-uh-buhl) *adjective* If handwriting or print is **legible,** it can be read fairly easily. ▷ *noun* **legibility** ▷ *adverb* **legibly**

le·gion (lee-juhn)
1. *noun* A unit in the Roman army.
2. *noun* A large body of soldiers or former soldiers.
3. *adjective* Very many, or numerous. *Melissa's faults are legion.*

leg·is·la·tion (lej-uh-**slay**-shuhn) *noun* Laws that have been proposed or made. *The government has introduced new legislation to deal with drug offenders.* ▷ *noun* **legislator** ▷ *verb* **legislate**

leg·is·la·ture (lej-iss-*lay*-chur) *noun* A group of people who have the power to make or change laws for a country or state.

le·git·i·mate (luh-**jit**-uh-mit) *adjective*
1. Lawful or rightful.
2. Reasonable, as in *a legitimate complaint.*
▷ *adverb* **legitimately**

le·gume (**leg**-yoom) *noun* A plant with seeds that grow in pods. Peas, beans, lentils, and peanuts are legumes.

leg warmer *noun* A knitted leg covering usually worn from the ankle to the thigh.

lei (lay) *noun*
A necklace of leaves or flowers, often given as a gift of welcome in Hawaii. *As you can see from this photo, leis come in many different colors.* **Lei** sounds like **lay.**

Hawaiian leis

lei·sure (lee-zhur *or* **lezh**-ur) *noun* Free time, when you do not have to work or study. ▷ *adjective* **leisure**

lei·sure·ly (**lee**-zhur-lee *or* **lezh**-ur-lee) *adjective* Not hurried or not rushed. *We enjoyed a long, leisurely breakfast.*

lem·on (**lem**-uhn) *noun* A yellow citrus fruit with a thick skin and a sour taste. *See* **fruit.**

lem·on·ade (lem-uh-**nade**) *noun* A drink made from lemon juice, water, and sugar.

lend (lend) *verb* To let someone have something that you expect to get back. *Felicia looked so cold sitting in the movie theater that I decided to lend her my jacket.* ▷ **lending, lent** (lent)

length (lengkth) *noun*
1. The distance from one end of something to the other.
2. The amount or extent from beginning to end, as in *the length of a vacation* or *the length of a book.* ▷ *adjective* **lengthy**
3. A piece of something, as in *a length of rope.*

length·en (**lengk**-thuhn) *verb* To make something longer. ▷ **lengthening, lengthened**

length·wise (**lengkth**-*wize*) *adverb* In the direction of the longest side. *Fold the paper lengthwise.* ▷ *adjective* **lengthwise**

le·ni·ent (**lee**-nyuhnt *or* **lee**-nee-uhnt) *adjective* Gentle and not strict. ▷ *adverb* **leniently**

lens (lenz) *noun*
1. A piece of curved glass or plastic in a pair of glasses or in a camera, telescope, etc. Lenses bend light rays so that you can focus a camera or see things magnified through a telescope or microscope. *The diagram shows how concave and convex lenses make light rays bend in different ways. See also* **telescope.**
2. The clear part of your eye that focuses light on the retina. *See* **eye.**
▷ *noun, plural* **lenses**

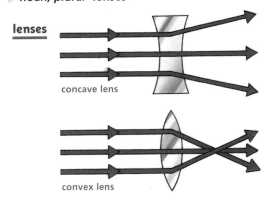

lenses

concave lens

convex lens

L

Lent (lent) *noun* The 40 days before Easter, not including Sundays, in the Christian church's year. *Some people give up certain foods for Lent.*

len·til (**len**-tuhl) *noun* The flat, round seed of a plant related to beans and peas. Lentils are often cooked in soups.

leop·ard (**lep**-urd) *noun* A large, wildcat with a spotted coat found in Africa, India, and eastern Asia.

leopard

le·o·tard (**lee**-uh-*tard*) *noun* A tight, one-piece garment worn for dancing or exercise.

lep·ro·sy (**lep**-ruh-see) *noun* A disease caused by a bacterium that attacks the skin, nerves, and muscles. Leprosy can cause a person to lose feeling or become paralyzed in the areas that are affected.

> ## Suffix
>
> The suffix **-less** adds one of these meanings to a root word:
>
> 1. Without, as in *doubtless* (without doubt) or *effortless* (without effort).
>
> 2. Unable to be, as in *countless* (unable to be counted).

less (less)
1. *adjective* Smaller, or in smaller quantities. *There is much less fat in milk than in butter.*
▷ *adverb* **less**
2. *adjective* Made up of a smaller number than wanted, needed, or expected. *I have less paper in my notebook than I should have.*
3. *preposition* Minus. *We bought it for the sale price, less a 10 percent discount.*

les·sen (less-uhn) *verb* To get smaller in size, strength, importance, etc. *The noise lessened as the teacher approached the classroom.* **Lessen** sounds like **lesson.** ▷ **lessening, lessened**

les·son (less-uhn) *noun*
1. Some information or skill that you need to learn or study. *Do your math lesson.*
2. A set period in school when pupils are taught, or a session when a skill is taught.
3. An experience that teaches you something. *My attempt to juggle school with a part-time job taught me a lesson.*
Lesson sounds like **lessen.**

let (let) *verb*
1. To allow or permit something. *My mother let me go over to my friend's house after dinner.*
2. To allow to pass or go. *Let the cat out.*
3. To rent out a house or an apartment.
4. If you are **let down** by someone, you are disappointed by the person because the person did not do something that he or she promised.
▷ *verb* **letting, let**

le·thal (lee-thuhl) *adjective* If something is **lethal,** it can kill, as in *a lethal poison.* ▷ *adverb* **lethally**

let's (lets) *contraction* A short form of *let us. Let's go to the movies tonight.*

let·ter (let-ur) *noun*
1. A mark that is part of an alphabet. A letter stands for a sound or sounds and is used in writing, as in *the letter A.* ▷ *verb* **letter**
2. A message that you write to someone or that someone writes to you.

letter car·ri·er (kar-ee-ur) *See* **mail carrier.**

let·ter·ing (let-ur-ing) *noun* Letters that have been drawn, painted, or printed on something, such as a sign or a greeting card.

let·tuce (let-iss) *noun* A green, leafy salad vegetable. *See* **vegetable.**

leu·ke·mi·a (loo-kee-mee-uh) *noun* A serious disease in which the blood makes too many white cells.

lev·ee (lev-ee) *noun*
1. A bank built up near a river to prevent flooding.
2. A place for boats or ships to land.
Levee sounds like **levy.**

lev·el (lev-uhl)
1. *adjective* Flat and smooth, as in *a level surface.*
2. *adjective* At the same height. *My window is level with one in the next house.*
3. *noun* A floor or story of a structure. *Our car is parked on the upper level.*
4. *noun* A height, as in *sea level.*
5. *noun* A position or rank in a series. *My mom has risen to the level of company vice president.*
6. *verb* To flatten. *The tornado leveled every building on the street.*
7. *verb* If something **levels off,** it stops rising or falling and stays the same.
8. *noun* A tool used to show if a surface is flat.
▷ *verb* **leveling, leveled**

lev·er (lev-ur *or* lee-vur) *noun*
1. A bar that you use to lift an object by placing one end under the object and pushing down on the other end. ▷ *verb* **lever**
2. A bar or a handle that you use to work or control a machine.

lev·i·tate (lev-i-tate) *verb*
1. To rise in the air and float, in seeming defiance of gravity.
2. To cause to rise in the air and float.
▷ *noun* **levitation**

lev·y (lev-ee)
1. *verb* To impose or collect by lawful actions or by force. *The government levied a tax on gasoline.* ▷ **levies, levying, levied**
2. *noun* A tax. ▷ *noun, plural* **levies**
Levy sounds like **levee.**

li·a·ble (lye-uh-buhl) *adjective*
1. Likely. *Judy is liable to get angry when she hears the news.*
2. If you are **liable** for something you have done, you are responsible for it by law.
▷ *noun* **liability**

li·ar (lye-ur) *noun* Someone who tells lies. *Once you know that someone is a liar, it becomes difficult to believe anything that he or she says.*

lib·er·al (lib-ur-uhl) *adjective*
1. Generous, as in *a liberal donation.*
2. More than enough, as in *a liberal helping of food.*
3. Broad-minded and tolerant, especially of other people's ideas.
4. In favor of political change and reform.
▷ *noun* **liberal,** *noun* **liberalism**

lib·er·ate (lib-uh-*rate*) *verb* To set someone free. ▷ **liberating, liberated** ▷ *noun* **liberation,** *noun* **liberator**

lib·er·at·ed (lib-uh-*ray*-tid) *adjective* Someone who is **liberated** has been set free or feels free.

lib·er·ty (lib-ur-tee) *noun* Freedom. ▷ *noun, plural* **liberties**

li·brar·y (lye-brer-ee) *noun* A place where books, magazines, newspapers, records, and videos are kept for reading or borrowing. ▷ *noun, plural* **libraries,** ▷ *noun* **librarian**

lice (lisse) *noun, plural* Small insects without wings that live on animals or people. *Lice* is the plural form of **louse.**

li·cense (lye-suhnss)
1. *noun* A document giving permission for you to do something or own something, as in *a driver's license.*
2. *verb* If someone is **licensed** to do something, such as practice medicine, he or she has official permission to do it. ▷ **licensing, licensed**

li·chen (lye-ken)
noun A flat, mosslike growth on rocks, trees, etc. Lichen is made up of a kind of algae and a fungus that grow together.

Himalayan lichen

lick (lik) *verb*
1. To pass your tongue over something. ▷ *noun* **lick**
2. To touch something lightly. *Small waves licked the shore.*
3. To defeat. *We licked their team last week.*
▷ *noun* **licking**
▷ *verb* **licking, licked**

lic·o·rice (lik-ur-ish *or* lik-ur-iss) *noun*
1. A plant with a sweet, edible root that is used to flavor medicine and candy.
2. A candy flavored with licorice.

lid (lid) *noun*
1. A top or a cover, as in *a lid on a jar.*
2. An eyelid.

lie (lye)
1. *verb* To get into or be in a flat, horizontal position.
2. *verb* To be or be placed somewhere. *The cottage lies in a deep valley.*
3. *verb* To stay in a certain place or condition, as in *to lie hidden.*
4. *noun* A statement that is not true.
5. *verb* To say something that is not true. The past tense of this sense of the verb is *lied.*
Lie sounds like **lye.**
▷ *verb* **lying, lay** (lay), **lain** (layn) *or* **lying, lied**

lieu·ten·ant (loo-ten-uhnt) *noun* An officer of low rank in the armed forces.

life (life) *noun*
1. The quality that separates people, animals, and plants from things such as rocks and machines that are not alive. Life is the quality that makes it possible for things to grow and reproduce.
2. Your **life** is the time from your birth until your death.
3. A living person. *No lives were lost in the crash.*
4. Living things. *There was little plant life out in the desert.*
5. Energy, or a feeling of being alive. *I am full of life today!*
▷ *noun, plural* **lives** (livez)

life·boat (life-*boht*) *noun* A strong boat usually carried on a larger ship that is used to save lives during shipwrecks or other emergencies.

life cycle *noun* The series of changes each living thing goes through from birth to death.

life·guard (life-*gard*) *noun* Someone who is trained to save swimmers in danger.

life jacket *noun* A jacket that will keep you afloat if you fall into the water.

L

life jacket

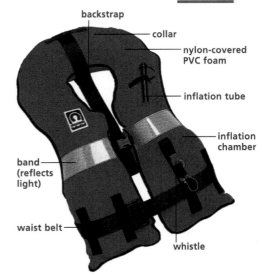

backstrap
collar
nylon-covered PVC foam
inflation tube
inflation chamber
band (reflects light)
waist belt
whistle

life·less (life-liss) *adjective*
1. Dead or without life, as in *a lifeless body* or *a lifeless planet.*
2. Boring or dull, as in *a lifeless party.*
▷ *noun* **lifelessness** ▷ *adverb* **lifelessly**

life·like (life-*like*) *adjective* Looking alive or real, as in *a lifelike drawing.*

life·long (life-*long*) *adjective* Lasting for a lifetime, as in *lifelong friends.*

life preserver ▶ lighthouse

life pre·serv·er (pri-**zurv**-er) *noun* A belt, vest, or ring that can be filled with air and used to keep a person afloat in water.

life span *noun* The period of time a person, an animal, a plant, or an object is expected to live or last. ▷ *noun, plural* **life spans**

life·style (life-*stile*) *noun* A way of living. *Ralph has a very glamorous lifestyle.*

life·time (life-*time*) *noun* The period of time that a person lives or an object lasts.

lift (lift)
1. *verb* To raise something or someone.
2. *verb* To rise into the air. *The kite slowly lifted as the wind picked up.* ▷ *noun* **lift**
3. *verb* To rise and disappear. *The fog lifted.*
4. *noun* A ride, especially in a car.
5. *noun* A happy feeling. *Her compliment gave me a lift.*
▷ *verb* **lifting, lifted**

lift·off (lift-*of*) *noun* The movement of a rocket or spacecraft as it rises from its launching pad.

lig·a·ment (lig-uh-muhnt) *noun* A tough band of tissue that connects bones and holds some organs in place. *See* **joint.**

light (lite)
1. *verb* To start something burning. ▷ *noun* **light**
2. *verb* To make something bright and visible. *Gabe turned on the lamp to light the room.*
3. *noun* Brightness; for example, from the sun or a lamp.
4. *adjective* Pale in color, as in *light blue.*
5. *noun* An object that gives out light, such as a flashlight or lamp.
6. *adjective* Gentle, as in *a light rain.*
7. *adjective* Weighing little. ▷ *noun* **lightness**
8. *adjective* Moving easily or gracefully. *The dancer was light on his feet.*
9. *adjective* Not serious, as in *a light novel.*
10. *adjective* Low in calories or fat, as in *a diet of light foods.*
11. If you **shed light** or **throw light on** something, you make it clear.
12. If you **see the light,** you understand something for the first time.
▷ *verb* **lighting, lighted** *or* **lit** (lit) ▷ *adjective* **lighter, lightest**

light·en (lite-uhn) *verb*
1. To make brighter or lighter. *The new lamp really lightens the room.*
2. To make or become lighter in color. *Spending the summer in the sun lightened Alan's hair.*
3. To make or become lighter in weight or quantity. *Karen's help lightened her mother's load of work.*
4. To make or become more cheerful. *A visit from my Aunt Martha always lightens my mood.*
▷ *verb* **lightening, lightened**

light·house (lite-*houss*) *noun* A tower set in or near the sea. A lighthouse has a flashing light at the top that guides ships or warns them of danger.

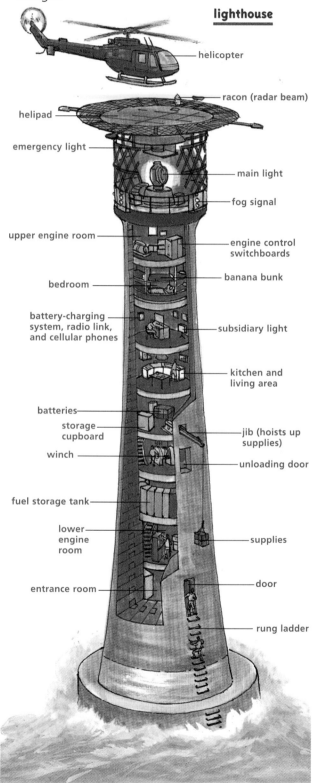

lighthouse

helicopter
racon (radar beam)
helipad
emergency light
main light
fog signal
upper engine room
engine control switchboards
bedroom
banana bunk
battery-charging system, radio link, and cellular phones
subsidiary light
kitchen and living area
batteries
storage cupboard
jib (hoists up supplies)
winch
unloading door
fuel storage tank
lower engine room
supplies
entrance room
door
rung ladder

L

302

light·ning (lite-ning) *noun* A flash of light in the sky when electricity moves between clouds or between a cloud and the ground.

lightning bug See **firefly.**

light pen *noun* A penlike device used to draw or to change or move information or images on a computer screen.

light·weight (lite-*wayt*) *adjective*
1. Not heavy, as in *a lightweight coat.*
2. Not important or not serious.

light-year *noun* A unit for measuring distance in space. A light-year is the distance that light travels in one year.

lik·a·ble (lye-kuh-buhl) *adjective* Easy to like, as in *a likable person.*

> ### Suffix
> ●
> The suffix **-like** adds the following meaning to a root word:
> Similar to or resembling, as in *lifelike* (similar to life) or *childlike* (resembling a child).

like (like)
1. *verb* To enjoy or be pleased by something or someone. *I really like ice cream.* ▷ *noun* **liking**
2. *verb* To wish for or want something. *I'd like a glass of juice, please.*
3. *preposition* Similar to. *I want a hat like yours.*
4. *preposition* Typical of. *It's just like Daisy to be late.*
5. *preposition* Such as. *I do well in subjects like reading and language arts.*
6. *adjective* Similar or equal, as in *a like amount.*
7. *conjunction* (informal) As if. *He looked like he might be sick.*
▷ *verb* **liking, liked**

like·ly (like-lee) *adjective* Probable. ▷ **likelier, likeliest** ▷ *noun* **likelihood**

like·wise (like-*wize*) *adverb* Also, or in the same way. *I'll dance, and you do likewise.*

li·lac (lye-luhk *or* lye-lak) *noun*
1. A shrub or tree with large clusters of fragrant purple, pink, or white flowers.
2. A pale purple color.

lilac

lil·y (lil-ee) *noun* Any of several plants that grow from bulbs and have flowers that are shaped like trumpets. See **pistil.** ▷ *noun, plural* **lilies**

lily of the valley *noun* A plant of the lily family with broad leaves and a stem covered with small, white flowers shaped like bells. ▷ *noun, plural* **lilies of the valley**

limb (lim) *noun*
1. A part of a body used in moving or grasping. Arms, legs, wings, and flippers are limbs. *That monkey is using its tail as a fifth limb.*
2. A branch of a tree.

lim·ber (lim-bur)
1. *adjective* Bending or moving easily. *Gymnasts must be limber.*
2. *verb* When you **limber up,** you stretch your muscles before exercising. ▷ **limbering, limbered**

lime (lime) *noun*
1. A small, green citrus fruit shaped like a lemon. See **fruit.**
2. A white substance or powder that is made up of calcium and oxygen. Lime is used to make cement and as a fertilizer.

lime·light (lime-*lite*) *noun* If you are **in the limelight,** you are the center of attention.

lim·er·ick (lim-ur-ik) *noun* A funny poem made up of five lines that rhyme in a particular pattern.

lime·stone (lime-*stohn*) *noun* A hard rock used in building and in making lime and cement. Limestone is formed from the remains of shells or coral.

lim·it (lim-it)
1. *noun* A point beyond which someone or something cannot or should not go, as in *the speed limit.* ▷ *adjective* **limitless** ▷ *adverb* **limitlessly**
2. *verb* To keep within a certain area or amount. *I've limited myself to three cups of tea a day.* ▷ **limiting, limited** ▷ *noun* **limitation**
3. limits *noun, plural* Boundaries. *Don't go beyond the park limits.*

lim·it·ed (lim-uh-tid) *adjective* Small and unable to increase, as in *limited shelf space.*

limp (limp)
1. *verb* To walk in an uneven way, usually because of an injury. ▷ **limping, limped** ▷ *noun* **limp**
2. *adjective* Floppy and not firm, as in *a limp handshake.* ▷ **limper, limpest** ▷ *adverb* **limply**

Lin·coln's Birthday (ling-kinz) *noun* A holiday on February 12 when some states celebrate the birth of Abraham Lincoln (1809–1865), 16th President of the United States. The holiday is observed in some states on Presidents' Day, the third Monday in February.

303

L

line (line)
1. *noun* A long, thin mark made by a pen, pencil, or other tool.
2. *noun* A row of people or words.
3. *noun* A long, thin rope, string, or cord, as in *a fishing line.*
4. *noun* A boundary, as in *the state line.*
5. *noun* A short letter. *Drop us a line when you get there.*
6. *noun* A wire or set of wires that connect points in a telephone or telegraph system.
7. *noun* A transportation system that runs on a specific route. *We need a new bus line in our neighborhood.*
8. lines *noun, plural* Words that you speak in a play. *Don't forget your lines.*
9. *noun* In mathematics, a set of points extending in a straight path without end in either direction.
10. *verb* To make a lining for something.
11. *noun* An attitude or approach to something. *My dad takes a firm line on discipline.*
12. *verb* To form a straight line. *Cars lined up at the gas station.*
▷ *verb* **lining, lined**

lin·e·ar (lin-ee-ur) *adjective*
1. Using or having to do with lines, as in *a linear drawing.*
2. To do with length. Feet, miles, centimeters, and kilometers are linear measures.

lin·en (lin-uhn) *noun*
1. Cloth made from the flax plant.
2. Household items, such as tablecloths and sheets, that were once made of linen.

lines·per·son (linez-per-suhn) *noun* An official who decides whether the ball has gone over the boundary line in games such as football, soccer, hockey, and tennis. *See* **soccer.**

lin·ger (ling-gur) *verb* To stay or wait around. *The fans lingered outside the stadium.* ▷ **lingering, lingered** ▷ *adjective* **lingering**

lin·gui·ne (ling-gwee-nee) *noun* Pasta cut into long, thin strips.

lin·guist (ling-gwist) *noun* Someone who studies languages or speaks them well.

lin·ing (lye-ning) *noun* The layer or coating that covers the inside of something, as in *the stomach lining* or *the lining of a coat.*

link (lingk)
1. *noun* One of the separate rings that make up a chain.
2. *noun* A connection between things or people.
3. *verb* To join objects, ideas, or people together.
▷ **linking, linked**

li·no·le·um (luh-noh-lee-uhm) *noun* A material with a strong, shiny surface and a canvas or cloth back. Linoleum is used as a floor covering, most commonly in kitchens.

lin·seed oil (lin-seed) *noun* Oil from the seed of certain flax plants used to make paints, varnishes, printing inks, patent leather, and linoleum. *See* **artist.**

lint (lint) *noun* Very small bits of thread or fluff from cloth.

li·on (lye-uhn) *noun* A large, light brown wildcat found in Africa and southern Asia. Male lions have manes.

li·on·ess (lye-uh-ness) *noun* A female lion.

lip (lip) *noun*
1. Your **lips** are the fleshy edges of your mouth.
2. The edge or rim of a container or hole.
3. If you **keep a stiff upper lip** when something bad or frightening happens, you remain calm and not afraid.

lip-read *verb* When deaf or hearing impaired people **lip-read,** they watch someone's lips while the person is talking in order to understand what the person is saying. ▷ **lip-reading, lip-read** ▷ *noun* **lip reading**

lip·stick (lip-stik) *noun* A small, crayonlike stick used to color the lips.

liq·ue·fy (lik-wuh-fye) *verb* To make something solid into a liquid. ▷ **liquefies, liquefying, liquefied**

liq·uid (lik-wid) *noun* A wet substance that you can pour. ▷ *adjective* **liquid**

liquid crystal display *noun* A way of showing numbers and letters on clocks, calculators, etc. Different parts of a grid of liquid crystals reflect light as electronic signals are sent to them. Abbreviated LCD. *See* **calculator.**

liq·uor (lik-ur) *noun* A strong alcoholic drink, such as whiskey, gin, or vodka.

li·ra (lihr-uh) *noun* The main unit of money in Italy and Turkey. ▷ *noun, plural* **lire** (lihr-uh)

lisp (lisp) *noun* A way of talking in which you say "th" instead of "s." ▷ *verb* **lisp**

list (list)
1. *noun* A series of items, names, numbers, etc., often written in a particular order.
2. *verb* To put into a list. *Tim listed all of his chores for the day before leaving the house.*
3. *verb* When a ship **lists,** it leans to one side.
▷ *verb* **listing, listed**

lis·ten (liss-uhn) *verb* To pay attention so that you can hear something. ▷ **listening, listened** ▷ *noun* **listener**

li·ter (lee-tur) *noun* A unit of measurement in the metric system. A liter is the amount held by a rectangular container 10 centimeters by 10 centimeters by 10 centimeters. A liter is about 1.1 quarts.

lit·er·a·cy (lit-ur-uh-see) *noun* The ability to read and write.

lit·er·al·ly (lit-ur-uh-lee) *adverb*
1. Word for word. *We translated the Spanish story literally.*
2. Actually. *The flood moved boats from the harbor to literally miles inland.*
3. If you **take** someone **literally,** you believe the person's exact words.

lit·er·ate (lit-ur-it) *adjective*
1. Able to read and write.
2. Highly educated.

lit·er·a·ture (lit-ur-uh-chur) *noun* Written works that have lasting value or interest. Literature includes novels, plays, short stories, essays, and poems. ▷ *adjective* **literary**

lit·mus paper (lit-muhss) *noun* Paper soaked in a dye that changes from red to blue in a base solution and from blue to red in an acid solution.

lit·ter (lit-ur) *noun*
1. Bits or scraps of paper or other garbage scattered around carelessly. ▷ *verb* **litter**
2. A group of kittens, puppies, baby pigs, etc., born at the same time to one mother.
3. A stretcher for carrying a sick or wounded person.

lit·tle (lit-uhl)
1. *adjective* Small in size or amount.
2. *noun* A small amount of something. *I'll have just a little.*
3. *adjective* Not much. *We have little time.*
▷ *adjective* **littler** or **less, littlest** or **least**

> ▶ **Synonyms: little**
> •
>
> ▶ **Little** is the opposite of *big* and has to do with size more than importance: *It's hard to imagine your parents as little children.*
>
> ▶ **Small** also means little, but it refers to something's number, capacity, or value, as in *a small audience, a small pitcher,* or *a small raise in pay.*
>
> ▶ **Minute** describes something that is extremely small: *Even a minute amount of poison can be fatal.*
>
> ▶ **Miniature** refers to something that has been scaled down to a very small size: *Every detail of the model airplane is authentic, right down to the miniature pilot sitting in the cockpit.*
>
> ▶ **Diminutive** describes something that is unusually or abnormally small: *We were surprised that such a large woman would have such diminutive hands.*
>
> ▶ **Tiny** is an informal way of saying "extremely small," or "minute": *The spot of ink on the sweater is so tiny that you can hardly see it.*

live
1. (liv) *verb* To be alive. *Some cats live for 20 years.*
2. (live) *adjective* Alive or living. *You can buy live lobsters at the fish store.*
3. (liv) *verb* To have your home somewhere. *Josie lives in Chicago.*
4. (liv) *verb* To support oneself. *He lives on a small salary.*
5. (live) *adjective* Broadcast or televised as it is happening.
6. (live) *adjective* Burning, as in *live coals.*
7. (live) *adjective* If an electrical wire is **live,** it is carrying electricity that can give you a shock.
8. (live) *adjective* Unexploded, as in *a live bomb.*
9. If you **live and let live,** you are tolerant and able to accept or respect the behavior, customs, beliefs, or opinions of others.
10. If you can **live with** a difficult situation, you can put up with it or bear it.
▷ *verb* **living, lived**

live·li·hood (live-lee-*hud*) *noun* The way that you make money to support yourself.

live·ly (live-lee) *adjective*
1. Active and full of life, as in *a lively dance step.*
2. Bright. *Red is a lively color.*
3. Exciting, as in *a lively debate.*
4. Creative, as in *a lively imagination.*
▷ *adjective* **livelier, liveliest** ▷ *noun* **liveliness**

liv·er (liv-ur) *noun*
1. The organ in a human or animal body that cleans the blood. The liver also produces bile, which helps digest food. *See* **digestion, organ.**
2. A food prepared from the liver of a calf, pig, or other animal.

liv·er·y (liv-ur-ee) *noun*
1. A uniform worn by servants or members of a profession.
2. A stable where horses are taken care of for a fee.

lives·tock (live-stok) *noun* Animals raised on a farm or ranch, such as horses, sheep, and cows.

liv·id (liv-id) *adjective*
1. Having a pale, usually white or somewhat blue color. *His face was livid with rage.*
2. Very angry. *I am livid that you yelled at me.*
3. Purple or dark in color because of a bruise.

liv·ing (liv-ing)
1. *adjective* Alive now; not dead.
2. *noun* Money to live on. *Joe earns his living by painting.*
3. *adjective* Still active or in use. *Spanish is a living language.*

living room *noun* A lounge or sitting room in a house.

L

liz·ard (liz-urd) *noun* A reptile with a scaly body, four legs, and a long tail. *The picture shows parts of a lizard and some of the different types.*

lizard

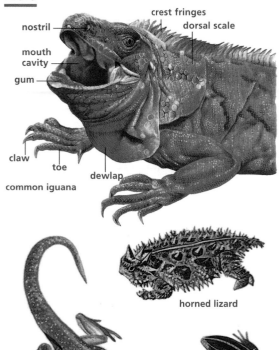

nostril
mouth cavity
gum
crest fringes
dorsal scale
claw
toe
dewlap
common iguana

horned lizard

collared lizard

skink

frilled lizard

lla·ma (lah-muh) *noun* A large South American mammal raised for its wool and used to carry loads. The llama is related to the camel.

load (lohd)
1. *noun* Something that is carried, especially something heavy.
2. *noun* The amount carried at one time. *We need four loads of dirt for the yard.*
3. *verb* To put things onto or into something. *Bobby loaded the car with camping equipment.*

4. *verb* To put a bullet into a gun, film into a camera, or a program into a computer.
5. *noun, plural* (informal) If you have **loads** of something, you have lots of it.
▷ *verb* **loading, loaded**

loaf (lohf)
1. *noun* Bread baked in one piece.
2. *noun* Food in the shape of a loaf of bread, as in *meat loaf.*
3. *verb* To spend time doing little or nothing.
▷ **loafing, loafed**
▷ *noun, plural* **loaves** (lohvz)

loaf·er (loh-fur) *noun*
1. Someone who is lazy and does not do much.
2. Loafer A trademark for a flat, casual shoe.

loam (lohm) *noun* Loose, rich soil made of sand, clay, and decayed leaves and plants. ▷ *adjective* **loamy**

loan (lohn)
1. *noun* The act of lending something to someone.
2. *noun* Something borrowed, especially money.
3. *verb* To lend something to someone.
▷ **loaning, loaned**
Loan sounds like **lone.**

loathe (lohTH) *verb* To hate or dislike someone or something. ▷ **loathing, loathed** ▷ *noun* **loathing**

loath·some (lohTH-suhm) *adjective* Very unpleasant or disgusting, as in *a loathsome disease.*

lob (lob) *verb* To throw or hit a ball high into the air. ▷ **lobbing, lobbed** ▷ *noun* **lob**

lob·by (lob-ee) *noun*
1. A hall or room at the entrance to a building.
2. A group of people who try to persuade politicians to act or vote in a certain way. ▷ *verb* **lobby**
▷ *noun, plural* **lobbies**

lob·ster (lob-stur) *noun* A sea creature with a hard shell and five pairs of legs. The front pair are large, heavy claws. Lobsters can be eaten and turn red when they are cooked.

lobster

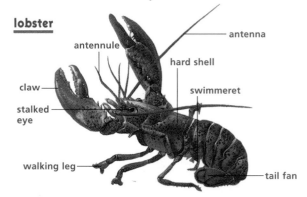

antennule
antenna
hard shell
claw
swimmeret
stalked eye
walking leg
tail fan

lo·cal (loh-kuhl)
1. *adjective* Near your house, or to do with the area where you live, as in *a local newspaper.*
▷ *adverb* **locally**
2. *noun* A train, subway, or bus that makes all the stops on a route. ▷ *adjective* **local**
3. *adjective* Affecting only a part of the body, as in *a local anesthetic.*

lo·cal·i·ty (loh-**kal**-uh-tee) *noun* An area or a neighborhood. ▷ *noun, plural* **localities**

lo·cate (loh-kate) *verb*
1. To find out where something is.
2. To put or place somewhere. *The company located its fifth store in a popular mall.*
3. To settle in a particular place. *My family has located in Texas.*
▷ *verb* **locating, located**

lo·ca·tion (loh-**kay**-shuhn) *noun*
1. The place or position where someone or something is.
2. If a movie or television program is made **on location,** it is filmed out of the studio.

lock (lok)
1. *verb* To fasten something with a key.
2. *noun* A part of a door, box, etc., that you can open and shut with a key.
3. *verb* To join or link together. *We locked arms and formed a circle.*
4. *noun* A part of a canal with gates at each end where boats are raised or lowered to different water levels.
5. *noun* A tuft of hair. *The child's head was covered with curly locks.*
▷ *verb* **locking, locked**

lock·er (lok-ur) *noun* A small chest or closet that can be locked and where you can leave your belongings.

lock·et (lok-it) *noun* A piece of jewelry that women wear on a chain around their necks and that often contains a photograph, lock of hair, or other memento.

lock·jaw (lok-*jaw*) *See* **tetanus.**

lock·smith (lok-*smith*) *noun* Someone who makes and repairs locks and keys.

lo·co·mo·tion (*loh*-kuh-**moh**-shuhn) *noun* The act of moving from one place to another, or the ability to do so.

lo·co·mo·tive (*loh*-kuh-**moh**-tiv) *noun* An engine used to push or pull railroad cars.
See **steam locomotive.**

lo·cust (loh-kuhst) *noun*
A type of grasshopper that eats and destroys crops. Locusts fly in large swarms of up to two billion.

locust

lode·stone (lohd-*stohn*) *noun* A stone with iron in it that acts as a magnet.

lodge (loj)
1. *noun* A small house, cottage, or cabin, often used for a short stay, as in *a ski lodge.*
2. *verb* If you **lodge** with someone, you stay in the person's house and usually pay him or her money.
3. *verb* If something **lodges** somewhere, it gets stuck there.
4. *noun* A beaver's home. *See* **beaver.**
5. *verb* To bring to someone in authority, as in *to lodge a complaint.*
▷ *verb* **lodging, lodged**

lodg·er (loj-ur) *noun* Somebody who pays to live in a room in someone else's house. ▷ *noun* **lodgings**

loft (loft) *noun*
1. A room or space under the roof of a building.
2. An upper story in a business building used for living or as an artist's studio.

loft·y (lof-tee) *adjective*
1. Very tall and imposing, as in *a lofty skyscraper.*
2. Thinking of oneself as better than other people, as in *a lofty manner.*
▷ *adjective* **loftier, loftiest**

log (log)
1. *noun* A part of a tree that has been chopped down or has fallen down.
2. *verb* To cut down trees. ▷ *noun* **logger**
3. *noun* A written record kept by the captain of a ship.
4. *noun* A written record of something. *Liza kept a log of her progress.* ▷ *verb* **log**
5. *verb* When you **log on** or **log in** to a computer, you begin to use it; for example, by entering a name or a password.
6. *verb* When you have finished using a computer, you **log off** or **log out.**
▷ *verb* **logging, logged**

lo·gan·ber·ry (loh-guhn-*ber*-ee) *noun* A large, dark red berry that grows on a prickly shrub. The loganberry is a cross between the blackberry and the raspberry.

log·ic (loj-ik) *noun*
1. Careful and correct reasoning or thinking.
2. The study of the rules for forming careful reasoning.
3. A particular way of thinking.
▷ *adjective* **logical** ▷ *adverb* **logically**

lo·go (loh-goh) *noun* A symbol that represents a particular company or organization.

loin (loin) *noun*
1. In people or animals, the part of the sides and back of the body between the ribs and the hip. *See* **horse.**
2. A cut of meat from this part of an animal.

L

loi·ter (loi-ter) *verb* To stand around, usually because you have nothing to do. ▷ **loitering, loitered** ▷ *noun* **loiterer**

loll (lol) *verb*
1. To sit or stand in a lazy or relaxed way. *Wayne lolled on the sofa.*
2. To hang loosely. *The wolf's tongue lolled out of its mouth.*
▷ *verb* **lolling, lolled**

lol·li·pop (lol-ee-*pop*) *noun* A piece of hard candy on a stick.

lone (lohn) *adjective*
1. Alone or solitary. *The lone hawk sat on a high branch.*
2. Only or single, as in *the lone survivor of a plane crash.*
Lone sounds like **loan.**

lone·ly (lone-lee) *adjective*
1. If you are **lonely,** you are sad because you are by yourself. ▷ *noun* **loneliness**
2. Far from other people or things, as in *a lonely cabin.*
▷ *adjective* **lonelier, loneliest**

lone·some (lohn-suhm) *adjective*
1. If you are **lonesome,** you are sad because you feel alone. *With her best friend away, Allie was lonesome even when she was at school.*
2. Not often visited or used by people, as in *a lonesome road.*

long (lawng)
1. *adjective* More than the average length, distance, time, etc., as in *a long walk.*
2. *adjective* From one end to the other. *The path was about two miles long.*
3. *adjective* Taking a lot of time. *Is the movie very long?*
4. *adverb* For a long time. *The plane is long overdue.*
5. *adverb* Throughout the length or duration of, as in *all week long.*
6. *noun* A long time. *He was not gone for long.*
7. *verb* If you **long for** something, you want it very much. ▷ **longing, longed** ▷ *noun* **longing**
▷ *adjective* **longer, longest**

long-distance *adjective*
1. Covering or able to cover a long distance, as in *a long-distance runner.*
2. Connecting distant places, as in *a long-distance telephone call.*
▷ *adverb* **long-distance**

long·hand (lawng-*hand*) *noun* Ordinary writing in which you use a pencil or pen to write the words out in full, without abbreviations.

lon·gi·tude (lon-juh-*tood*) *noun* The position of a place, measured in degrees east or west of a line that runs through the Greenwich Observatory in London, England. On a map or globe, lines of longitude are drawn from the North Pole to the South Pole. ▷ *adjective* **longitudinal**

long-range *adjective*
1. To do with the future, as in *long-range plans.*
2. Designed to travel a long way, as in *long-range missiles.*

long·ship (long-*ship*) *noun* A long, narrow ship with many oars and a sail, used especially by the Vikings. *The Vikings used longships to carry warriors to new lands.*

Viking longship

deck (made from loose planks with storage room beneath)

coarse woolen sail

sea chest (containing sailors' belongings)

yard

mast

mast rest

sail rest

rigging

stern head

shield

wooden oar

storage sacks

steerboard (oar for steering)

overlapping oak planks (sealed with sheep's wool and tar)

long-term *adjective* To do with a long period of time, as in *long-term plans.*

long-wind·ed (win-did) *adjective* Unnecessarily long and boring, as in *a long-winded speech.*

loo·fah (loo-fuh) *noun* A rough sponge that you use to wash yourself with in the bath.

look (luk)
1. *verb* To use your eyes to see things.
2. *verb* To turn your eyes or attention. *Look at the camera.*

3. *noun* A glance or expression on someone's face, as in *an angry look.*

4. *verb* To seem or to appear. *It looks as if the weather will be rainy all week.*

5. *noun* Appearance. *Dylan has a new look about him since he had his hair styled last week.*

6. *verb* To face in a certain direction. *The hotel looks onto the beach.*

7. *verb* If you **look after** someone or something, you take care of him, her, or it.

8. *verb* If you **look down on** someone, you think that you are better than the person.

9. *verb* If you **look forward to** something, you wait for it eagerly.

10. *verb* If you **look** something **up,** you try to find out about it in a book or other reference.

11. *verb* If you **look up to** a person, you respect him or her.
▷ *verb* **looking, looked**

looking glass *noun* A mirror.

look·out (luk-*out*) *noun* Someone who keeps watch over something. *The soldiers posted a lookout outside the fort.*

loom (loom)

1. *verb* To appear in a sudden or frightening way. *Suddenly, a tall figure loomed out of the shadows.*
▷ **looming, loomed**
2. *noun* A machine used for weaving cloth. *The picture shows a woman working on a traditional Bangladeshi backstrap loom.*

loom

loon (loon) *noun* A large diving bird with webbed feet, short legs, and a speckled back. The cry of the loon sounds like wild laughter.

loop (loop) *noun* A curve or circle in a piece of string, rope, etc. ▷ *verb* **loop**

loose (looss) *adjective*

1. Not fastened or attached firmly. *The car wouldn't start because of a loose wire.*

2. Free. *The dog was loose in the street.*

3. Not fitting tightly, as in *loose pants.*

4. Not contained or bound together, as in *loose papers.*

5. Not placed or packed tightly together, as in *loose gravel* or *a loose weave.*
▷ *adjective* **looser, loosest** ▷ *adverb* **loosely**

loose-leaf *adjective* Holding or made to hold pages that have holes and are easily removed, as in *a loose-leaf notebook.*

loos·en (loo-suhn) *verb*

1. To make something less tight.

2. To set free. *We loosened the dog from the leash.*

3. If you **loosen up,** you become more relaxed and often less shy.
▷ *verb* **loosening, loosened**

loot (loot)

1. *verb* To steal from stores or houses in a riot or a war. ▷ **looting, looted** ▷ *noun* **looter**

2. *noun* Stolen money or valuables.
Loot sounds like **lute.**

lop·sid·ed (lop-sye-did) *adjective* Unbalanced, with one side heavier, larger, or higher than the other.

lord (lord) *noun*

1. A person who has great power or authority over others. In the Middle Ages, a lord lived in a castle and had many people under his rule.
▷ *adjective* **lordly**

2. Lord A name for God.

3. Lord In Great Britain, a title for a man of noble birth. Some British men earn this title as a reward for service to their country.

lose (looz) *verb*

1. If you **lose** something, you do not have it anymore.

2. To fail to keep or hold onto something. *Don't lose your temper.*

3. To be beaten or defeated in a game, argument, etc. ▷ *noun* **loser**

4. To waste. *The hikers will lose time if they stop to pick flowers.*
▷ *verb* **losing, lost (lost)**

loss (loss) *noun*

1. The losing of something, as in *the loss of a race* or *a memory loss.*

2. Something that is lost. *We all suffered great losses when a flood hit our town.*
▷ *noun, plural* **losses**

lot (lot)

1. *noun* A large number or amount. *A lot of apples rolled off the pile.*

2. *noun* A piece of land, as in *a vacant lot.*

3. a lot or **lots** *adverb* Much. *He feels a lot worse today.*

4. *noun* A group of objects or people. *This kitten is the cutest of the lot.*

5. If you and other people **draw lots,** everyone in the group picks objects, such as straws, to decide who will do or get something.

lo·tion (loh-shuhn) *noun* A thin cream that is used to clean, soften, or heal the skin.

lot·ter·y (lot-ur-ee) *noun* A way of raising money in which people buy tickets with the aim of winning a prize. ▷ *noun, plural* **lotteries**

L

lo·tus (loh-tuhss) *noun* A water plant with pink, yellow, or white flowers. ▷ *noun, plural* **lotuses**

lotus

loud (loud) *adjective*
1. Noisy, or producing a lot of sound. ▷ *adverb* **loud,** *adverb* **loudly**
2. Very bright and colorful, as in *a loud tie.* ▷ *adjective* **louder, loudest**

loud·speak·er (loud-*spee*-kur) *noun* A machine that turns electrical signals into sounds that are loud enough to be heard in a large room or area. *See* **speaker.**

lounge (lounj)
1. *verb* To stand, sit, or lie in a lazy or relaxed way. ▷ **lounging, lounged**
2. *noun* A comfortable room where people can sit and relax.

louse (louss) *noun*
1. A small, wingless insect that often lives on people or animals and sucks their blood. Lice can spread some diseases. ▷ *noun, plural* **lice**
2. (*slang*) Someone who is mean. ▷ *noun, plural* **louses**

lov·a·ble (luhv-uh-buhl) *adjective* Easy to love, as in *a lovable kitten.* ▷ *adverb* **lovably**

love (luhv)
1. *verb* To like someone or something very much. ▷ **loving, loved**
2. *noun* A strong liking for something, as in *a love of music.*
3. If you are **in love** with someone, you are passionately fond of him or her.
4. *noun* In tennis, a score of zero.

love·ly (luhv-lee) *adjective*
1. If someone is **lovely,** the person is beautiful to look at or has a very attractive personality. ▷ *noun* **loveliness**
2. Enjoyable. *We had a lovely day.* ▷ *adjective* **lovelier, loveliest**

low (loh) *adjective*
1. Not high or not tall, as in *a low branch.*
2. Below the usual level. *The reservoir was low during the drought.*
3. Below average, as in *a low grade.*
4. A **low** sound is quiet and soft or deep in pitch.

5. Not having enough. *We were low on gas.*
6. If someone feels **low,** the person is sad or depressed.
▷ *adjective* **lower, lowest**

lower
1. *verb* To move or bring something down, as in *to lower a flag.*
2. *adjective* Not as high as something else.
3. *verb* To make or become less. *The store lowered its prices.*
4. *verb* To make less loud. *Lower your voices.*
▷ *verb* **lowering, lowered**

low·er·case (*loh*-er-kasse) *adjective* Using letters that are not capitals. *Except for the first "e," this entire sentence is in lowercase letters.* ▷ *noun* **lowercase** ▷ *verb* **lowercase**

loy·al (*loi*-uhl) *adjective* Firm in supporting or faithful to one's country, family, friends, or beliefs. ▷ *noun* **loyalty** ▷ *adverb* **loyally**

LSD (el ess dee) *noun* A strong drug that causes people to see frightening, dreamlike things. LSD is illegal in the United States and in many other countries.

lu·bri·cate (loo-bruh-*kate*) *verb* To add a substance such as oil or grease to the parts of a machine so that it runs more smoothly.
▷ **lubricating, lubricated** ▷ *noun* **lubricant,** *noun* **lubrication**

luck (luhk) *noun*
1. Something that happens to someone by chance. *This game is just a matter of luck.*
2. Good fortune or success. *Wish me luck!*

luck·y (luhk-ee) *adjective*
1. Someone who is **lucky** is fortunate, and good things seem to happen to him or her.
2. Something that is **lucky** happens by chance and is fortunate, as in *a lucky guess.* ▷ *adverb* **luckily**
3. A **lucky** number, charm, etc., is one that you think will bring you good luck.
▷ *adjective* **luckier, luckiest**

lu·di·crous (loo-duh-kruhss) *adjective* Ridiculous or foolish. ▷ *adverb* **ludicrously**

lug (luhg) *verb* To carry something with great difficulty or effort. ▷ **lugging, lugged**

lug·gage (luhg-ij) *noun* Suitcases and bags that you take with you when you travel.

luke·warm (luke-*worm*) *adjective*
1. Slightly warm.
2. Not enthusiastic, as in *a lukewarm response.*

lull (luhl)
1. *verb* To make someone feel peaceful, safe, or sleepy. *The sound of the waves on the shore lulled Fay to sleep.* ▷ **lulling, lulled**
2. *noun* A short pause or break during a period of fighting or activity.

L

lul·la·by (luhl-uh-*bye*) *noun* A gentle song sung to send a baby to sleep. ▷ *noun, plural* **lullabies**

lum·ber (luhm-bur)
1. *noun* Wood or timber that has been sawed.
2. *verb* To move along heavily and clumsily. *Several hippopotamuses lumbered into view.*
▷ **lumbering, lumbered**

lum·ber·jack (luhm-bur-*jak*) *noun* Someone whose job is to cut down trees and get the logs to a sawmill.

lu·mi·nous (loo-muh-nuhss) *adjective* Shining or glowing, as in a *luminous campfire.* ▷ *adverb* **luminously**

lump (luhmp)
1. *noun* A shapeless piece of something, as in *a lump of clay.*
2. *noun* A swelling or a bump. *Look at this lump on my head!*
3. *verb* To put or bring together. *We lumped our savings to buy the radio.*
4. *adjective* Whole, as in *a lump sum.*
5. *verb* To form lumps.
▷ *verb* **lumping, lumped**

lu·nar (loo-nur) *adjective* To do with the moon, as in *a lunar eclipse.*

lunch (luhnch) *noun* The meal that you eat in the middle of the day. ▷ *noun, plural* **lunches** ▷ *verb* **lunch**

lung (luhng) *noun* One of a pair of baglike organs inside your chest that you use to breathe. The lungs supply the blood with oxygen and rid the blood of carbon dioxide. *See* **organ, respiration.**

lunge (luhnj) *verb* To move forward quickly and suddenly. *I lunged to catch the dish before it fell.* ▷ **lunging, lunged** ▷ *noun* **lunge**

lu·pus (loo-puhss) *noun* A disease marked by severe skin sores, body aches, shortness of breath, and heart or kidney problems.

lurch (lurch)
1. *verb* To move in an unsteady, jerky way. *The train lurched to a halt.* ▷ **lurches, lurching, lurched** ▷ *noun* **lurch**
2. If someone **leaves you in the lurch,** you are left in a difficult situation, without any help.

lure (loor)
1. *verb* To attract and perhaps lead someone or some creature into a trap. ▷ **luring, lured**
2. *noun* An attraction. *I can never resist he lure of the sea.*

lurk (lurk) *verb* To lie hidden, especially for an evil purpose. *The thief lurked in the darkness.* ▷ **lurking, lurked**

lus·cious (luhsh-uhss) *adjective* Delicious. *Our wonderful meal was topped off by a luscious dessert.* ▷ *adverb* **lusciously**

lush (luhsh) *adjective* Growing thickly and healthily, as in *lush vegetation.* ▷ **lusher, lushest**

lust (luhst) *verb* If you **lust after** something, you want or desire it very strongly. *Jimmy has always lusted after power.* ▷ **lusting, lusted** ▷ *noun* **lust** ▷ *adjective* **lustful**

lus·ter (luhss-tur) *noun* A bright shine or glow of soft reflected light. *Washing and waxing the car gave it a nice luster.*

lute (loot) *noun* A stringed instrument with a body shaped like a pear, played by plucking the strings. **Lute** sounds like **loot.**

lux·u·ry (luhk-shuh-ree *or* luhg-zhuh-ree) *noun*
1. Something that you do not really need but that is enjoyable to have. ▷ *adjective* **luxury**
2. If you live **in luxury,** you are surrounded by expensive and beautiful things that make your life very comfortable and pleasant. ▷ *adjective* **luxurious**

lye (lye) *noun* A strong substance used in making soap and detergents. Lye is made by soaking wood ashes in water. **Lye** sounds like **lie.**

Lyme disease (lime) *noun* A bacterial disease transmitted by the bite of a tick. Symptoms include a round, red sore where the tick was attached, fever, chills, and weakness. If it is not treated early, it can lead to joint pain, arthritis, and heart and nerve problems.

lymph (limf) *noun* A clear liquid that carries nourishment and oxygen to body cells and carries away waste products.

lynx (lingks)
noun A wildcat with long legs, a short tail, light brown or orange fur, and tufts of hair on its ears. ▷ *noun, plural* **lynx** or **lynxes**

lynx

lyre (lire) *noun* A small, stringed, harplike instrument played mostly in ancient Egypt, Israel, and Greece. *See* **instrument.**

lyr·ic (lihr-ik)
1. lyrics *noun, plural* The words of a song.
2. *noun* A short poem that expresses strong feelings, especially love.

lyr·i·cal (lihr-uh-kuhl) *adjective*
1. Expressing a strong, personal emotion. *In a lyrical voice, Peggy read her poem to the class.*
2. Like a song, or fit for singing, as in *the lyrical sounds of a nightingale.*

L

Mm

Spelling Hint: Words
that begin with a *mye-*
sound are usually spelled *mi* or *my*.
Examples: minor, mine, mynah, myself.

ma'am (mam) *noun (informal)* Short for **madam**.

ma·ca·bre (muh-**kahb** *or* muh-**kah**-bruh) *adjective*
Gruesome and frightening. *Edgar Allan Poe
wrote macabre tales of murder and mystery.*

mac·a·ro·ni (mak-uh-**roh**-nee) *noun* A food made
from dough, usually in the shape of short,
hollow tubes. *See* **pasta.**

Mach (mahk) *noun* A unit for measuring an
aircraft's speed. Mach 1 is the speed of sound,
762 miles per hour at sea level.

ma·chet·e (muh-**shet**-ee) *noun* A long, heavy
knife with a broad blade, used as a tool and
weapon. *Sugarcane is cut with a machete.*

ma·chine (muh-**sheen**)

noun
1. A piece
of equipment
made up
of moving
parts
that
is used
to do
a job.
*The vise in
the picture
is a machine.*

vise

2. A simple device that makes it easier to move
something. Levers, screws, and pulleys are
simple machines.
3. **machine gun** A gun that can fire bullets very
quickly without needing to be reloaded.

ma·chin·er·y (muh-**shee**-nuh-ree) *noun* A group
of machines, or the parts of a machine.

ma·chin·ist (muh-**shee**-nist) *noun* A person who
is skilled in running machines that make tools
and parts.

mack·er·el (mak-uh-ruhl) *noun* A shiny, dark blue
saltwater fish that can be eaten. ▷ *noun, plural*
mackerel *or* **mackerels**

mad (mad) *adjective*
1. Insane. ▷ *noun* **madness**
2. Very angry. *Don't be mad at me.*
3. Very foolish, as in *a mad romance.*
4. Having the disease rabies, as in *a mad dog.*
5. *(informal)* If you are **mad about** someone, you
like the person very much.
▷ *adjective* **madder, maddest** ▷ *adverb* **madly**

▷ Synonyms: mad

Mad usually means foolish or crazy, but it also is
used to describe someone who is very angry
about something: *Bobby was mad that we didn't
wait for him after school.* The adjectives that
follow are similar to mad, but they describe
feelings or actions of different origins or degrees.

Angry, like mad, can be used to describe
someone who feels upset about something and
shows it: *I was so angry at Camila for breaking my
bike that I yelled at her.*

Indignant describes a person who is angry
because he or she feels that something is unfair:
*The people were indignant that the mayor named
his friend to an important government post.*

Irate often refers to someone who does
something about his or her anger: *The irate
customer demanded her money back because the
television set did not work.*

Enraged describes someone who is filled with
rage, usually as a result of being annoyed or
provoked: *The louder our neighbors play their
music, the more enraged my mother becomes.*

Furious describes someone who is full of intense
anger, or fury, to the point of losing control: *Mr.
Thompkins was so furious when his car was
broken into that he made himself sick.*

mad·am (mad-uhm) *noun* A formal title for a
woman, used in speaking and writing. *Can I
help you, madam?*

mag·a·zine (mag-uh-zeen) *noun*
1. A publication that contains news, articles,
photographs, advertisements, etc. Most
magazines are issued on a regular basis, such as
weekly or monthly, throughout the year.
2. A room or building for storing ammunition or
weapons. *See* **ship.**
3. The part of a gun that holds the bullets.

▷ Word History

The word **magazine** comes from the Arabic word
makhzan, meaning "storehouse." A magazine could
be thought of as a storehouse of information.

mag·got (mag-uht) *noun* The larva of certain flies.
Maggots are found in decaying animal matter.

Ma·gi (may-jye) *noun, plural* In the New
Testament, the three wise kings who visited the
baby Jesus, bringing gifts.

mag·ic (maj-ik) *noun*
1. The power that some people believe exists to make impossible things happen by using charms or spells. ▷ *adjective* **magical** ▷ *adverb* **magically**
2. Clever tricks done to entertain people.
▷ *adjective* **magic** ▷ *noun* **magician** (muh-jish-uhn)

mag·is·trate (maj-uh-strate) *noun*
1. A government official who has the power to enforce the law.
2. A judge who has limited power, such as a justice of the peace.

mag·lev (mag-lev) *noun* A short form of *magnetic levitation,* a system of high-speed train transportation in which the train uses powerful magnets to float above its track.

mag·ma (mag-muh) *noun* Melted rock found beneath the earth's surface. Magma flows as lava out of volcanoes and becomes igneous rock when it cools. *See* **volcano.**

mag·ne·si·um (mag-nee-zee-uhm) *noun* A light, silver-white metal that burns with a dazzling white light. It is often used in making fireworks and is also combined with other metals to make alloys.

mag·net (mag-nit) *noun* A piece of metal that attracts iron or steel. Magnets have two ends or poles, a north pole and a south pole. *The diagram illustrates a law of magnetism: the like poles of two magnets repel each other, while the unlike poles attract each other.* ▷ *noun* **magnetism** ▷ *adjective* **magnetic**

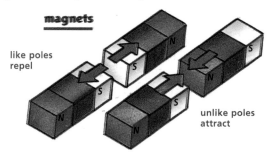

magnets

like poles repel

unlike poles attract

magnetic field *noun* The area around a magnet or electric coil that has the power to attract other metals, usually iron or steel.

magnetic pole *noun*
1. Either of the two points of a magnet where its magnetic force seems to be strongest.
2. Either of the two points of the earth's surface where the earth's magnetic pull is strongest. One of these points is near the North Pole; the other is near the South Pole.

magnetic tape *noun* A thin ribbon of plastic coated with a magnetic material on which sound, television images, and other information can be stored.

mag·net·ize (mag-nuh-tize) *verb* To make a piece of material magnetic, either by exposing it to an electric coil or by attaching a magnet to it.
▷ **magnetizing, magnetized** ▷ *noun* **magnetization**

mag·nif·i·cent (mag-nif-i-sent) *adjective* Very impressive or beautiful. *The king lived in a magnificent palace.* ▷ *adverb* **magnificently**

mag·ni·fy (mag-nuh-fye)
1. *verb* To make something appear larger so that it can be seen more easily. ▷ *noun* **magnification** ▷ *adjective* **magnified**
2. *verb* To make something seem greater or more important than it really is. *Sophie always magnifies her problems.*
3. magnifying glass *noun* A glass lens that makes things look bigger.
▷ *verb* **magnifies, magnifying, magnified**

mag·ni·tude (mag-nuh-tood) *noun* The size or importance of something. *Once she had seen the mess, Jo realized the magnitude of her task.*

mag·no·li·a (mag-nohl-yuh) *noun* A tree or tall shrub that has large, fragrant, white, pink, purple, or yellow flowers.

▶ **Word History**
• •
The **magnolia** was named for a French professor, Pierre Magnol (1638–1715), who published a book classifying plants. The magnolia is found in southeast Asia and the southeastern United States. Mississippi is known as the Magnolia State.

mag·pie (mag-*pye*) *noun* A noisy, black and white bird with a large beak and long tail feathers. Magpies often collect shiny objects. They are related to crows.

ma·hog·a·ny (muh-hog-uh-nee) *noun*
1. A tropical tree with hard, dark, reddish-brown wood that is used for making furniture.
2. The wood from this tree.
3. A dark, reddish brown color.

maid (mayd) *noun*
1. A female servant who is paid to do housework.
2. A young, unmarried woman.
3. maid of honor An unmarried bridesmaid who is given special honor at a wedding.

maid·en (mayd-uhn)
1. *noun* A young, unmarried woman.
2. *adjective* A **maiden** voyage or flight is the first one made by a particular ship or plane.

maiden name *noun* The surname that a married woman used before she was married. Some women continue to use their maiden names after they marry, and some use their husbands' names instead.

mail (mayl) *noun*
1. Letters, cards, and packages sent through a post office. ▷ *verb* **mail**
2. Armor made by joining together small metal rings. *See* **centurion.**
3. If you buy something by **mail order,** you order it and pay for it and then the item is sent to you. **Mail** sounds like **male.**

▶ **Word History**
• •
▶ Today we think of **mail** as being the letters and
▶ packages delivered to us, but originally the word
▶ referred to the bag the mail was delivered in. The
▶ word comes from the old French word *male,* which
▶ referred to a leather sack.

---

mail·box (mayl-*boks*) *noun*
1. A box in which letters are put so that they can be picked up by a mail carrier.
2. A private box for letters and packages delivered to a home or business.

mail car·ri·er (ka-ree-ur) *noun* A person who delivers the mail to a house or office or picks it up from mailboxes. Also called a **letter carrier.**

mail·man (mayl-*man*) *noun* A mail carrier. ▷ *noun, plural* **mailmen**

maim (maym) *verb* To injure someone so badly that part of the person's body is damaged for life. ▷ **maiming, maimed**

main (mayn)
1. *adjective* Largest, or most important, as in *the main reason.*
2. *noun* A large pipe or wire that supplies water, gas, or electricity to a building.
Main sounds like **mane.**

main·frame (mayn-*fraym*) *noun* A large and very powerful computer.

main·land (mayn-luhnd) *noun* The chief or largest land mass of a country, territory, or continent, as opposed to its islands or peninsulas.

main·ly (mayn-lee) *adverb* For the most part. *Our town is mainly on the south side of the river.*

main·stay (mayn-*stay*) *noun*
1. A heavy rope or cable that supports or steadies the mast of a sailing ship.
2. Something or someone who acts as the chief support of something. *Carlos is the mainstay of the soccer team.*

main·stream (mayn-*streem*)
1. *noun* The most common direction or trend of a movement. *The candidate's political beliefs are well within the mainstream of U.S. politics.*
2. *verb* To place a child with disabilities in a regular classroom. ▷ **mainstreaming, mainstreamed**

main·tain (mayn-tayn) *verb*
1. To keep a machine or building in good condition.
2. To continue to say that something is so. *The suspect maintains that he is innocent.*
3. To continue something and not let it come to an end. *We have always maintained a close friendship.*
4. To give money to support somebody, as in *to maintain a family.*
▷ *verb* **maintaining, maintained** ▷ *noun* **maintenance** (mayn-tuh-nuhnss)

maize (mayz) *noun* Corn. **Maize** sounds like **maze.**

ma·jes·tic (muh-jess-tik) *adjective*
1. Having great dignity; royal.
2. Having great power and beauty. *The ocean is majestic when it storms.*
▷ *adverb* **majestically**

maj·es·ty (maj-uh-stee) *noun*
1. Greatness and dignity. *The queen walks with majesty.*
2. The highest power or authority, as in *the majesty of the law.*
3. The formal title for a king or a queen is *His Majesty* or *Her Majesty.*

ma·jor (may-jur)
1. *adjective* Larger, greater, or more important.
2. *noun* An officer in the army and other branches of the armed forces who ranks above a captain.
3. *adjective* A **major** scale in music has a semitone between the third and fourth and the seventh and eighth notes.
4. *noun* The main subject studied at a college or university.

ma·jor·ette (may-jur-et) *noun* A girl or woman who leads a band or twirls a baton in a parade.

ma·jor·i·ty (muh-jor-uh-tee) *noun*
1. More than half of a group of people or things. *The majority of students came by bike.*
2. The number of votes by which someone wins an election.
3. When someone reaches his or her **majority,** the person becomes an adult by law.
▷ *noun, plural* **majorities**

make (make)
1. *verb* To build or produce something. *We helped Dad make dinner.*
2. *verb* To do something. *Wally made two phone calls.*
3. *verb* To cause something to happen. *Pepper makes me sneeze.*
4. *verb* To add up to. *Six and 5 make 11.*
5. *verb* To earn. *My sister makes money by delivering newspapers.*
6. *noun* A particular brand or type of product. *What make is your bicycle?*

M

7. verb To turn out to be. *Amy will make a good teacher.*

8. verb To cause to become. *Your letters always make me happy.*

9. verb To win a place or spot on a team. *Ed has a good chance to make the soccer team.*

10. verb To **make believe** is to pretend or imagine.

11. verb If you can **make** something **out,** you can see it, but just barely.

12. verb If you **make up** with someone, you go back to being friends after a quarrel.

13. verb If you **make up** a test, you take it later because you could not take it on time.
▷ *verb* **making, made (made)**

make-believe

1. noun Playful pretense or imagination. *That fairy tale is only make-believe.*

2. adjective Imaginary, or not real. *We built a make-believe fort.*

make·shift (make-*shift*) **adjective** A **makeshift** object is made from whatever is available and is only meant to be used for a short time.

make·up (make-*uhp*)
noun

Kabuki makeup

1. Lipstick, powder, eyeshadow, and other cosmetics. *The picture shows some of the dramatic makeup used in Japanese Kabuki theater.*

2. The way something is put together. *The makeup of the class is half girls and half boys.*

3. Personality. *It's not in Lee's makeup to be rude.*

ma·lar·i·a (muh-**lair**-ee-uh) **noun** A serious tropical disease that people get from mosquito bites. Symptoms include chills, fever, and sweating.

male (male) **noun** A person or animal of the sex that can father young. **Male** sounds like **mail.**
▷ *adjective* **male**

mal·ice (mal-iss) **noun** A desire or intent to hurt someone; spite.

ma·li·cious (muh-**lish**-uhss) **adjective** Showing or done from malice, as in *malicious gossip.*
▷ *adverb* **maliciously**

ma·lign (muh-**line**) **verb** To say mean, untrue things about someone. ▷ **maligning, maligned**

ma·lig·nan·cy (muh-**lig**-nuhn-see) **noun** A malignant tumor. ▷ *noun, plural* **malignancies**

ma·lig·nant (muh-**lig**-nuhnt) **adjective**

1. A **malignant** growth or disease is dangerous because it tends to spread and eventually causes death. *Cancer is a malignant disease.*

2. Nasty and evil. *The villain gave a malignant grin.* ▷ *adverb* **malignantly**

mall (mawl) **noun**

1. A large, enclosed shopping center.

2. A shaded, public walk.
Mall sounds like **maul.**

mal·lard (mal-urd) **noun** A common wild duck of North America, Europe, and northern Asia. The male has a green head, a white band around the neck, and a dark body.

mal·le·a·ble (mal-ee-uh-buhl) **adjective** If a substance is **malleable,** it is easily molded into a different shape.

mal·let (mal-it) **noun**

1. A hammer with a short handle and a heavy wooden head.

2. A wooden club with a long handle, used to hit the ball in croquet or polo.

mal·nu·tri·tion (*mal*-noo-**trish**-uhn) **noun** A harmful condition caused by not having enough food or by eating the wrong kinds of food.

malt (mawlt) **noun** Grain, usually barley, that has been soaked in warm water, allowed to sprout, and then dried. ▷ *adjective* **malted**

malted milk **noun** A sweetened drink of milk, malted flavoring, and sometimes ice cream.

mal·treat (mal-**treet**) **verb** To treat a person or an animal cruelly. ▷ **maltreating, maltreated** ▷ *noun* **maltreatment**

mam·mal (mam-uhl) **noun** A warm-blooded animal with a backbone. Female mammals produce milk to feed their young. *Human beings, cows, and dolphins are all mammals.*

mam·moth (mam-uhth)

1. noun
An extinct animal like a large elephant, with long, curved tusks and shaggy hair. Mammoths lived during the Ice Age.

woolly mammoth

2. adjective Huge. *Building a skyscraper is a mammoth task.*

man (man)

1. noun An adult male human being. ▷ *noun* **manhood,** *noun* **manliness** ▷ *adjective* **manly**

2. noun The human race.

3. noun A piece used in games such as chess and checkers.

4. verb To be in charge of a piece of equipment. *We need some people to man the phones.*
▷ **manning, manned**
▷ *noun, plural* **men (men)**

man·age (man-ij) *verb*
1. To be in charge of a store, business, etc. *Terry manages a small electrical company.* ▷ *noun* **management**
2. To be able to do something that is difficult or awkward. *Can you manage to carry all those bags?* ▷ *verb* **managing, managed**

man·a·ger (man-uh-jur) *noun* Someone in charge of a store, business, etc., or in charge of a group of people at work. ▷ *adjective* **managerial** (man-uh-jeer-ee-uhl)

man·a·tee (man-uh-tee) *noun* A large mammal with flippers and a flat tail that lives in warm waters and eats plants.

manatee

man·da·rin (man-dur-in) *noun*
1. A high official in ancient China.
2. Mandarin The official language of the People's Republic of China.
3. A small, sweet orange with a thin rind that is easy to peel. It is also called a **mandarin orange.**

man·date (man-date) *noun*
1. Instructions or support given by voters to their government representatives through the votes cast in an election. *The president received a clear mandate to balance the budget.*
2. An order given by an authority, as in *the king's mandate.*
▷ *verb* **mandate**

man·do·lin (man-duh-lin *or* man-duh-**lin**) *noun* A small, guitarlike instrument with metal strings and a body that is shaped like a pear.

mane (mayn) *noun* The long, thick hair on the head and neck of a male lion or a horse. **Mane** sounds like **main.** See **horse.**

ma·neu·ver (muh-noo-ver)
1. *noun* A difficult movement that needs planning and skill. *The pilots performed a series of exciting maneuvers.*
2. *verb* To move something carefully into a particular position. ▷ **maneuvering, maneuvered**
3. When an army is **on maneuvers,** a large number of soldiers, tanks, etc., are moved around an area in order to train for battle.

man·ger (mayn-jur) *noun* A large, open box that holds food for cattle and horses.

man·gle (mang-guhl) *verb* To spoil or destroy something by cutting, tearing, or crushing it. *The car was completely mangled in the crash.*
▷ **mangling, mangled** ▷ *adjective* **mangled**

man·go (mang-goh) *noun* A yellow-red tropical fruit with a sweet taste. ▷ *noun, plural* **mangoes** or **mangos**

man·hole (man-hohl) *noun* A covered hole in the street that leads to sewers or underground pipes or wires.

man·hood (man-hud) *noun*
1. The time or state of being an adult man. *Jake felt he had entered manhood once he found an apartment and got a job.*
2. Men as a group. *The editorial about lazy husbands seemed an insult to all manhood.*

ma·ni·ac (may-nee-ak) *noun*
1. Someone who is insane or acts in a wild or violent manner. ▷ *adjective* **maniacal** (muh-nye-uh-kuhl)
2. A person who is very enthusiastic about something, as in *a sports maniac.*

man·i·cure (man-uh-kyur) *noun* The cleaning, shaping, and polishing of the fingernails. ▷ *verb* **manicure**

ma·nip·u·late (muh-nip-yuh-late) *verb*
1. To influence people in a clever way so that they do what you want them to do. ▷ *adjective* **manipulative**
2. To use your hands in a skillful way. *Karen manipulated the plane's controls expertly.*
▷ *verb* **manipulating, manipulated** ▷ *noun* **manipulation**

man·kind (man-kinde) *noun* The human race, or human beings as a group.

man-made *adjective* Something that is **man-made** is made by people and not produced naturally. *Nylon is a man-made fiber.*

man·ner (man-ur) *noun*
1. The way in which you do something. *Look at the manner in which Garth plays the drums.*
2. The way that someone behaves. *Kate has a very gentle manner.*
3. Kind. *We saw all manner of birds at the zoo.*
4. manners *noun, plural* Polite behavior.
Manner sounds like **manor.**

man·or (man-ur) *noun*
1. A lord's estate in the Middle Ages.
2. A mansion.
Manor sounds like **manner.**

man·sion (man-shuhn) *noun* A very large and grand house.

man·slaught·er (man-slaw-tur) *noun* The crime of killing someone without intending to do so.

man·tel (man-tuhl) *noun* A wooden or stone shelf above a fireplace. **Mantel** sounds like **mantle.**

man·tle (man-tuhl) *noun*
1. A loose cloak without sleeves.
2. Something that covers or hides like a mantle. *Our footprints were covered by a mantle of snow.*
3. The part of the earth between the crust and the core. The mantle is about 1,800 miles thick. *See* **earth.**
Mantle sounds like **mantel.**

man·u·al (man-yoo-uhl)
1. *adjective* Operated or done by hand rather than automatically, as in *a manual typewriter.*
▷ *adverb* **manually**
2. *noun* A book of instructions that tells you how to do something.
3. *adjective* If you do **manual** labor, you work hard physically.

man·u·fac·ture (man-yuh-fak-chur) *verb*
1. To make something, often with machines.
▷ *noun* **manufacturing,** *noun* **manufacturer**
2. To invent something or to make something up. *Eric manufactured an excuse for his lateness.*
▷ *verb* **manufacturing, manufactured**

ma·nure (muh-noo-ur) *noun* Animal waste put on land to improve the quality of the soil and to make crops grow better.

man·u·script (man-yuh-skript) *noun*
1. The original handwritten or typed pages of a book, poem, piece of music, etc., before it is printed.
2. A handwritten document, as in *a medieval manuscript.*

man·y (men-ee)
1. *adjective* Numerous. *A clock has many parts.*
▷ **more, most**
2. *pronoun* A large number of people or things. *Many were late for the party because of a snowstorm.*
3. *noun* A large number. *Many of the animals had diseases.*
▷ *noun* **more,** *noun* **most**

map (map)
1. *noun* A detailed plan of an area, showing features such as towns, roads, rivers, mountains, etc.
2. *verb* To make a map of a place.
3. *verb* If you **map** something **out,** you plan it.
▷ *verb* **mapping, mapped**

ma·ple (may-puhl) *noun* A tree with large leaves having five points. Maples are grown for their hard wood and their sap, which is used to make syrup and sugar.

mar·a·thon (mar-uh-thon) *noun*
1. A race for runners over a distance of 26 miles and 385 yards.

2. Any long race or competition that tests the participants' ability to hold up under pain, stress, and fatigue.

> ### Word History
> When the Greeks defeated the Persians in the city of Marathon in 490 B.C., a messenger was sent to Athens with the news. Legend has it that he covered the 24 miles so quickly that he dropped dead after delivering the message. His run was commemorated in 1896, when a **marathon** was included in the first modern Olympic games, in London, England. The distance was lengthened to 26 miles, 385 yards so that the runners would finish the race right in front of the box where Britain's king and queen were seated.

mar·ble (mar-buhl) *noun*
1. A hard stone with colored patterns in it, used for buildings and sculptures.
2. A small, hard glass ball used in a children's game.
3. **marbles** A children's game in which these balls are rolled along the ground.

march (march)
1. *verb* When soldiers **march,** they walk together with uniform steps. ▷ *noun* **march**
2. *noun* A piece of music with a strong beat to which you can march.
3. *verb* To walk somewhere quickly and in a determined way. *Mom marched down to the building superintendent's office to complain about the lack of heat.*
4. *noun* A large group of people walking together in order to protest or express their opinion about something. ▷ *verb* **march**
▷ *noun, plural* **marches** ▷ *verb* **marches, marching, marched**

March *noun* The third month on the calendar, after February and before April. March has 31 days.

> ### Word History
> The Roman new year at one time began with the month of **March.** The beginning of the year, the Romans felt, was a good time to wage war, so they named this first month after Mars, the god of war. Later, March became the third month, as it is today.

mare (mair) *noun* The female of certain animals, such as the horse, donkey, and zebra.

mar·ga·rine (mar-juh-ruhn) *noun* A yellow spread similar to butter that is usually made from vegetable oil.

mar·gin (mar-juhn) *noun*
1. The long, blank space that runs down the edge of a page.
2. An amount, especially of time, in addition to what is needed. *When traffic is heavy, allow a margin of 30 minutes for driving to school.*
3. A difference between two amounts, especially a small one. *Mr. Edwards won the election by a very narrow margin.*
▷ *adjective* **marginal**

mar·i·gold (ma-ruh-*gohld*) *noun* A garden plant that has orange, yellow, or red flowers.

mar·i·juan·a (ma-ruh-*wah*-nuh) *noun* A drug made from the dried leaves and flowering tops of the hemp plant. Marijuana is illegal in the United States and many other countries.

ma·ri·na (muh-*ree*-nuh) *noun* A small harbor where boats, yachts, etc., are kept.

mar·i·na·ra (*mair*-uh-*nair*-uh) *adjective* Made with tomatoes, as in *marinara sauce.* Marinara comes from an Italian word that means "in sailor style." ▷ *noun* **marinara**

ma·rine (muh-*reen*)
1. *adjective* To do with the sea, as in *marine life.*
2. *adjective* To do with ships or navigation.
3. *noun* A soldier trained to fight on land and water.
4. Marine *noun* A member of the U.S. Marine Corps.

Marine Corps *noun* One of the armed forces of the United States. Marines are trained to fight on both land and water.

mar·i·o·nette (ma-ree-uh-*net*) *noun* A puppet that is moved by pulling strings or wires attached to various parts of its body. A marionette is usually made of wood.

mar·i·time (ma-ruh-*time*) *adjective*
1. To do with the sea, ships, or navigation.
2. Of, relating to, or near the sea.

mark (mark)
1. *noun* A small scratch or stain on something.
2. *noun* A written sign or symbol, as in *a question mark.*
3. *noun* A line or an object that shows position. *Put your foot on the mark before the race begins.*
4. *noun* A number or letter put on a piece of work to show how good it is.
5. *verb* To show something clearly. *The road sign marked the way to the beach.* ▷ **marking, marked**
6. *noun* Something that shows clearly. *A mark of good manners is saying "please."*
7. *noun* A unit of money in Germany.
8. If you **make your mark,** you become successful.
▷ *verb* **mark**

mar·ket (mar-kit) *noun*
1. A place where people buy and sell food or goods. ▷ *verb* **market**
2. A store where specific kinds of goods are sold, as in *a fish market.*
3. A demand for something. *There is a very large market for video games in the United States.*
4. If a product is **on the market,** it is available and can be bought.

market research *noun* When people or companies do **market research,** they collect information about the products that customers buy and what customers want and need.

marks·man (marks-muhn) *noun* Someone who is expert at shooting a gun. ▷ *noun, plural* **marksmen**

mar·ma·lade (mar-muh-lade) *noun* A jam made from oranges or other citrus fruit.

ma·roon (muh-*roon*)
1. *noun* A dark reddish brown color. ▷ *adjective* **maroon**
2. *verb* If someone is **marooned** on a desert island, the person is stuck there and cannot leave. ▷ **marooning, marooned**

mar·quee (mar-*kee*) *noun* A large awning or rooflike structure over a theater entrance. It displays the name of the current play or movie.

mar·riage (ma-rij) *noun*
1. The state of being married, or the relationship between husband and wife.
2. The wedding ceremony.

mar·ried (ma-reed) *adjective* Someone who is **married** has a spouse.

mar·row (ma-roh) *noun* The soft substance inside bones that is used to make blood cells: *See* **bone.**

mar·ry (ma-ree) *verb*
1. When people **marry,** they go through a ceremony in which they promise to spend their lives together.
2. To perform a marriage ceremony.
▷ *verb* **marries, marrying, married**

Mars (marz) *noun* The fourth planet in distance from the sun. Mars is the seventh-largest planet in our solar system. It has two moons. *See* **planet.**

marsh (marsh) *noun* An area of wet, low land.
▷ *adjective* **marshy**

marshal (mar-shuhl)
1. *noun* An officer of a federal court who has duties similar to those of a sheriff.
2. *noun* An official who investigates suspicious fires.
3. *noun* A person who helps organize a public event such as a parade.
4. *verb* To gather together a group of people or things and arrange them in a sensible order. *The general marshaled his troops.* ▷ **marshaling, marshaled**
Marshal sounds like **martial.**

marsh·mal·low (marsh-*mal*-loh) *noun* A soft, spongy kind of white candy.

mar·su·pi·al (mar-soo-pee-uhl) *noun* The name for a large group of animals that includes the kangaroo, the koala, and the opossum. Female marsupials carry their young in pouches at their abdomens.

mar·tial (mar-shuhl)
1. *adjective* To do with war or soldiers.
2. **martial art** *noun* A style of fighting or self-defense that comes mostly from the Far East; for example, judo or karate.
3. **martial law** *noun* Rule by the army in time of war or disaster.
Martial sounds like **marshal**.

mar·tin (mart-uhn) *noun* A swallow with a forked tail and long wings.

Martin Lu·ther King Day (looth-ur) *noun* A national holiday celebrated on the third Monday of January to honor the birth of Dr. Martin Luther King, Jr., the African-American civil rights leader who was assassinated in 1968.

Martin Luther King, Jr.

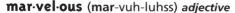

mar·tyr (mar-tur) *noun* Someone who is killed or made to suffer because of his or her beliefs. ▷ *noun* **martyrdom**

mar·vel (mar-vuhl) *verb* If you **marvel** at something, you are filled with surprise and wonder. ▷ **marveling, marveled** ▷ *noun* **marvel**

mar·vel·ous (mar-vuh-luhss) *adjective*
1. Causing surprise, wonder, or amazement.
2. Very good or outstanding. *What a marvelous dinner you cooked me last night.* ▷ *adverb* **marvelously**

mas·car·a (mass-ka-ruh) *noun* A substance put on eyelashes to color them and make them look thicker.

mas·cot (mass-kot) *noun* Something that is supposed to bring good luck, especially an animal kept by a sports team.

mas·cu·line (mass-kyuh-lin) *adjective*
1. To do with men.
2. Someone who is **masculine** has qualities that are supposed to be typical of men. ▷ *noun* **masculinity**

mash (mash)
1. *verb* To crush food into a soft mixture. ▷ **mashes, mashing, mashed** ▷ *noun* **mash**
2. *noun* A mixture of crushed grain and water that is fed to livestock and poultry. ▷ *noun, plural* **mashes**

mask (mask)
1. *noun* A covering worn over the face to hide, protect, or disguise it. *This mask, made in New Guinea, would have been worn by a boy at a special ceremony to celebrate his adulthood.* ▷ *adjective* **masked**
2. *verb* To cover up or disguise something. *A smile masked his actual disgust.* ▷ **masking, masked** ▷ *noun* **mask**

mask

ma·son (may-suhn) *noun* Someone who builds or works with stone, cement, or bricks.

ma·son·ry (may-suhn-ree) *noun* Something that is made of stone, cement, or bricks.

mas·quer·ade (mass-kuh-rade)
1. *noun* A party or event at which all the people dress up in costumes.
2. *verb* To dress up in order to disguise yourself at a party or other event. *I'm going to masquerade as a clown.*
3. *verb* To pretend to be something you are not. *She masqueraded as my friend until I finally figured her out.* ▷ *noun* **masquerade** ▷ *verb* **masquerading, masqueraded**

mass (mass) *noun*
1. A lump or pile of matter that has no particular shape, as in *a mass of snow*.
2. A large number of people or things together. ▷ *verb* **mass** ▷ *adjective* **mass**
3. In physics, the **mass** of an object is the amount of physical matter that it contains. *Mass is measured in grams or ounces.*
4. **the masses** *noun, plural* The ordinary people. *This show is designed to appeal to the masses.*

Mass *noun* The main religious service in the Roman Catholic Church and certain other churches.

mas·sa·cre (mass-uh-kur) *noun* The brutal killing of a very large number of people, often in battle. ▷ *verb* **massacre**

mas·sage (muh-sahzh) *verb* To rub someone's body with the fingers and hands in order to loosen the muscles or to help the person relax. ▷ **massaging, massaged** ▷ *noun* **massage**

mas·sive (mass-iv) *adjective* Large, heavy, and solid. *Thirty people sat at the massive mahogany table.* ▷ *adverb* **massively**

mass media *noun, plural* Different forms of communication that reach a large number of people. Television, radio, and newspapers are all mass media.

mass production *noun* The method of making identical things in a factory. Items that are mass-produced are usually made in large quantities by people or machines on an assembly line.
▷ *verb* **mass-produce**

mass transit *noun* A system of subways, buses, and trains that carry people in large numbers into and around major cities.

mast (mast) *noun* A tall pole that stands on the deck of a boat or ship and supports its sails. *See* **dinghy, ship.**

mas·ter (mass-tur)
1. *noun* A person with power, rule, or authority over another. *The dog came when its master whistled.*
2. *noun* An expert. *O. Henry was a master of the short story.*
3. *verb* If you **master** a subject or skill, you become very good at it.
4. *verb* If you **master** a fear, you overcome it.
5. *noun* A male teacher, especially in a private school.
6. *adjective* Most important or largest, as in *the master bedroom.*
▷ *verb* **mastering, mastered**

mas·ter·mind (mass-tur-*minde*) *verb* If you **mastermind** a course of action, you plan it and control the way that it is carried out.
▷ **masterminding, masterminded**

mas·ter·piece (mass-tur-*peess*) *noun*
1. An outstanding piece of work, especially in the areas of art, literature, music, etc.
2. A person's finest achievement.

mat (mat) *noun*
1. A thick pad of material used for covering a floor, wiping your feet, protecting a table, etc.
2. A large, thick floor pad used to protect wrestlers, gymnasts, and other athletes.
3. A thick, tangled mass, especially of hair.
▷ *verb* **mat**
Mat sounds like **matte.**

mat·a·dor (mat-uh-dor) *noun* A bullfighter.

match (mach)
1. *noun* A small, thin piece of wood or cardboard with a chemical tip that is struck to produce a flame.
2. *noun* Someone or something that is similar to or goes well with another. *These pants are a good match for your jacket.*
3. *verb* To go well with. *Joe's expensive taste in clothes didn't match his budget.*
4. *noun* Someone or something that is equal to another. *You are no match for our lead runner in speed.*
5. *verb* To equal. *She matched our donation.*

6. *noun* A game or a sporting competition, as in *a tennis match.*
7. *verb* To put into competition. *The football game matched two powerful college teams.*
▷ *noun, plural* **matches** ▷ *verb* **matches, matching, matched**

mate (mate)
1. *noun* One of a pair. *Can you find the mate to this glove?*
2. *noun* A husband or a wife.
3. *noun* The male or female partner of a pair of animals.
4. *verb* To join together for breeding. ▷ **mating, mated** ▷ *noun* **mating**
5. *noun* A ship's officer.
6. *noun* A friend.

ma·te·ri·al (muh-*tihr*-ee-uhl)
1. *noun* Cloth or fabric.
2. *noun* The substances from which something is made. *What materials do you need to build a house?*
3. *adjective* Made from or having to do with matter, as in *the material world.*
4. *adjective* To do with the well-being of the body. *Good food and warm clothes are material needs.*

ma·te·ri·al·is·tic (muh-*tihr*-ee-uh-liss-tik) *adjective* People who are **materialistic** are overly concerned with money and possessions. ▷ *noun* **materialism**

ma·te·ri·al·ize (muh-*tihr*-ee-uh-*lize*) *verb* To appear, or to become real. ▷ **materializing, materialized**

ma·ter·nal (muh-*tur*-nuhl) *adjective* To do with being a mother, as in *maternal feelings.*

ma·ter·ni·ty (muh-tur-nuh-tee) *noun*
1. Motherhood.
2. maternity leave Time that a woman is allowed away from her job to have a baby.
3. maternity ward The part of a hospital for women who have just had or are about to have a baby.

math (math) *noun* Short for **mathematics.**

math·e·ma·ti·cian (*math*-uh-muh-tish-uhn) *noun* A person who is very good at or specializes in mathematics.

math·e·mat·ics (math-uh-mat-iks) *noun* The study of numbers, quantities, shapes, and measurements and how they relate to each other. ▷ *adjective* **mathematical**

mat·i·nee (mat-uhn-ay) *noun* An afternoon performance of a play or showing of a movie.

mat·ri·mo·ny (mat-ruh-*moh*-nee) *noun* Marriage.
▷ *adjective* **matrimonial**

ma·trix (may-triks) *noun* In math, a **matrix** is an arrangement of numbers or other items in columns and rows. A chart showing the standings of major league baseball teams is a type of matrix. ▷ *noun, plural* **matrices** (may-tri-*seez*)

ma·tron (may-truhn) *noun*
1. An older woman who is married or widowed.
2. A woman who has some authority in an institution.
3. **matron of honor** A married bridesmaid who is given special honor at a wedding.

matte (mat) *adjective* Not shiny, as in *a matte finish.* **Matte** sounds like **mat.**

mat·ter (mat-ur)
1. *noun* Anything that has weight and takes up space, as a solid, liquid, or gas.
2. *noun* Content, or material, as in *undigested matter.*
3. *noun* A subject of discussion, interest, or concern, as in *a legal matter* or *a business matter.*
4. *noun* Something that needs to be dealt with. *Let's sort this matter out now.*
5. *noun* Written or printed material, as in *reading matter.*
6. *verb* If something **matters,** it is important. ▷ **mattering, mattered**

mat·tress (mat-riss) *noun* A thick pad made of strong cloth filled with soft material and often coiled springs. A mattress is used on or as a bed. ▷ *noun, plural* **mattresses**

ma·ture (muh-chur *or* muh-tyur) *adjective*
1. Adult or fully grown.
2. Ripe, as in *mature fruit.*
3. Behaving in a sensible, adult way. *Edmund is very mature for his age.* ▷ *adverb* **maturely** ▷ *noun* **maturity** ▷ *verb* **mature**

maul (mawl) *verb* To handle someone or something in a rough and possibly damaging way. **Maul** sounds like **mall.** ▷ **mauling, mauled**

mau·so·le·um (maw-suh-lee-uhm *or* maw-zuh-lee-uhm) *noun* A large building that houses a tomb or tombs.

mauve (mohv) *noun* A light purple color. ▷ *adjective* **mauve**

max·i·mum (mak-suh-muhm) *noun* The greatest possible amount, or the upper limit. *Two hours is the maximum allowed for the test.* ▷ *adjective* **maximum**

may (may) *verb* A helping verb that is used in the following ways:
1. To say that something is possible or likely. *I may have to leave in five minutes.*
2. To ask or give permission. *May I drive your car? Yes, you may.*
3. To express hope or a wish. *May you live long and prosper!*

May (may) *noun* The fifth month on the calendar, after April and before June. May has 31 days.

Word History
Planting a garden in **May** seems especially appropriate because the ancient Romans named the month in honor of the earth goddess, Maia.

Ma·ya (mye-uh) *noun* A member of a group of American Indian tribes that live in southern Mexico and Central America. The Maya had a highly structured civilization that flourished until about A.D. 1000. They were conquered by the Spanish during the 16th century. ▷ *noun, plural* **Maya** *or* **Mayas** ▷ *adjective* **Mayan**

may·be (may-bee) *adverb* Perhaps. *Maybe I spoke too soon when I said this party was boring.*

May·day (may-day) *noun* **Mayday** is a word used all over the world to ask for help or rescue.

may·hem (may-hem) *noun*
1. The crime of deliberately injuring someone seriously.
2. A situation of confusion or violent destruction.

may·on·naise (may-uh-naze *or* may-uh-naze) *noun* A salad dressing or creamy sauce made from egg yolks, oil, and vinegar or lemon juice.

may·or (may-ur) *noun* The leader of a town or city government.

maze (mayz) *noun* A complicated network of paths or lines, made as a puzzle to find your way through. *The picture shows a maze made of hedges located in Colonial Williamsburg, Virginia. It is based on a 17th-century maze at Hampton Court, England.* **Maze** sounds like **maize.**

maze
(aerial view)

me (mee) *pronoun* The form of **I** used as a grammatical object. *Give the paper to me.*

mead·ow (med-oh) *noun* A field of grass, often used for animals to graze in.

mead·ow·lark (med-oh-*lark*) *noun* A North American songbird with a pointed bill and a yellow chest with a black crescent across it.

mea·ger (mee-gur) *adjective* Very little, or barely enough, as in *a meager meal of broth and toast.*

meal (meel) *noun*
1. Food that is served and eaten, usually at a particular time of day. Breakfast, lunch, and dinner are meals.
2. Grain that has been ground.

mean (meen)
1. *verb* To try to express. *What does this painting mean?*
2. *verb* To intend to do something. *I mean to go skating tomorrow.*
3. *verb* To be defined as. *The word* thin *means "skinny."*
4. *verb* To matter. *Your friendship means a lot to me.*
5. *adjective* Not kind, or not nice. ▷ *noun* **meanness**
6. *noun* In mathematics, an average. *The mean of 3, 5, and 10 is 6, found by adding the three numbers and dividing by three.*
7. *adjective* (slang) Good and skillful. *Alice plays a mean game of baseball.*
▷ *verb* **meaning, meant** ▷ *adjective* **meaner, meanest**

me·an·der (mee-an-dur) *verb* When a river **meanders,** it winds or turns, usually through a flat part of a valley. ▷ **meandering, meandered**

mean·ing (mee-ning) *noun*
1. The idea behind something spoken or written.
2. The importance or significance of something. *What is the meaning of life?*

mean·time (meen-*time*) *noun* The time in between. *We leave early tomorrow morning. In the meantime, let's get some sleep!*

mean·while (meen-*wile*) *adverb*
1. In or during the time between. *I had the car washed; meanwhile I did my shopping.*
2. At the same time. *George went to explore. Meanwhile, Harry cleaned up the campsite.*

mea·sles (mee-zuhlz) *noun, plural* An infectious disease causing fever and a rash. Measles is caused by a virus. The word measles can be used with a singular or a plural verb.

mea·sly (mee-zlee) *adjective* (informal) Inadequate, or not very generous, as in *a measly amount of soup.* ▷ **measlier, measliest**

meas·ure (mezh-ur)
1. *verb* To find out the size, capacity, weight, etc., of something. *Would you please measure the height of that cabinet for me?* ▷ *noun* **measurement**
2. *verb* To have as a measurement. *The photograph measures 8 by 10 inches.*
3. *noun* A unit of measurement. *Feet and yards are measures of length.*

4. *noun* An action intended to achieve a result. *What measures can we take to fight crime?*
5. *noun* An amount or an extent, as in *a measure of truthfulness.*
6. *noun* A bar of music.
▷ *verb* **measuring, measured**

meat (meet) *noun*
1. The flesh of an animal that can be eaten.
2. The edible part of a fruit or nut.
3. The most important part of something, as in *the meat of a book.*
Meat sounds like **meet.**
▷ *adjective* **meaty**

me·chan·ic (muh-kan-ik) *noun* Someone who is skilled at operating or repairing machinery.

me·chan·i·cal (muh-kan-uh-kuhl) *adjective*
1. To do with machines or tools, as in *mechanical skill.*
2. Operated by machinery, as in *a mechanical toy.*
3. Acting or done as if by a machine, without thought or feeling, as in *a mechanical task.*
▷ *adverb* **mechanically**

me·chan·ics (muh-kan-iks) *noun* A part of physics that deals with the way forces affect still or moving objects.

mech·a·nism (mek-uh-*niz*-uhm) *noun* A system of moving parts inside a machine.

med·al (med-uhl) *noun* A piece of metal shaped like a coin, star, or cross that is given to someone for being brave or for service to his or her country or as a prize for some sporting achievement. **Medal** sounds like **meddle.**

med·dle (med-uhl) *verb* To interfere in someone else's business. **Meddle** sounds like **medal.**
▷ **meddling, meddled** ▷ *noun* **meddler**

med·dle·some (med-uhl-suhm) *adjective* A **meddlesome** person interferes in other people's business.

me·di·a (mee-dee-uh) *noun, plural* A plural of **medium.**

me·di·an (mee-dee-uhn) *noun*
1. The middle number in a set of numbers listed in order from smallest to largest. If there is no middle number, the median is the average of the two middle numbers. *In the set 5, 10, 15, the median is 10. In the set 2, 4, 6, 8, the median is the average of 4 + 6, or 5.*
2. A strip of land dividing two or more lanes of traffic going in opposite directions.
▷ *adjective* **median**

med·ic (med-ik) *noun* Someone trained to give medical help in an emergency or during a battle.

Med·i·caid (med-uh-*kade*) *noun* A system for providing medical aid for those unable to afford it. Medicaid is paid for by state and federal governments.

med·i·cal (med-uh-kuhl) *adjective* To do with doctors or medicine, as in *medical school.*
▷ *adverb* **medically**

Med·i·care (med-uh-*kair*) *noun* A system for providing medical care to citizens over the age of 65 under the federal Social Security program.

med·i·cine (med-uh-suhn) *noun*
1. A drug or other substance used in treating illness. ▷ *adjective* **medicinal**
2. The study of diseases and how to discover, treat, and prevent them. *You must study medicine in order to become a doctor.*

me·di·e·val (mee-dee-vuhl *or* med-ee-ee-vuhl) *adjective* To do with the Middle Ages, the period of history between approximately A.D. 500 and 1450. *The picture shows a medieval tapestry.*

medieval tapestry

me·di·o·cre (me-dee-oh-kur) *adjective* Of average or less than average quality. ▷ *noun* **mediocrity** (*mee-dee-ok-ri-tee*)

med·i·tate (med-i-tayt) *verb*
1. To think very deeply about something.
2. To relax the mind and body by a regular program of mental exercise.
▷ *verb* **meditating, meditated** ▷ *noun* **meditation**

me·di·um (mee-dee-uhm)
1. *adjective* Average or middle. *Kevin is of medium height.*
2. *noun* The substance or surroundings in which something lives. *Water is the medium for whales and fish.*
3. *noun* A means for communicating information to large numbers of people. *Television is probably the most popular medium in the United States.*
4. *noun* A substance or means through which something acts or is carried. *The air is a medium for sound waves.*
5. *noun* Someone who claims to make contact with spirits of the dead. ▷ *noun, plural* **mediums** ▷ *noun, plural* **media** (mee-dee-uh) *or* **mediums**

med·ley (med-lee) *noun*
1. A musical piece that consists of bits and pieces of different songs. *The group performed a medley of old rock 'n' roll songs.*
2. A mixture or assortment of things. *As we walked, we listened to a medley of city noises, with people shouting, car horns honking, and trucks rumbling by.*

meek (meek) *adjective* Quiet, humble, and obedient, as in *a meek servant.* ▷ **meeker, meekest** ▷ *adverb* **meekly**

meet (meet)
1. *verb* To come face to face with someone or something.
2. *verb* To come together. *The two paths meet at the summit of the mountain.*
3. *verb* To be introduced to. *I'd like you to meet my parents.*
4. *verb* To keep an appointment with. *I'll meet you at the library at four o'clock.*
5. *verb* To come together. *The town council will meet on Friday.*
6. *verb* To satisfy, or to be equal to. *He did not meet the requirements for the job.*
7. *noun* A sports contest, as in *a track meet.* **Meet** sounds like **meat.**
▷ *verb* **meeting, met** (met)

meet·ing (mee-ting) *noun* An arranged event in which people come together, often to discuss something.

meg·a·byte (meg-uh-*bite*) *noun* A unit used to measure the capacity of a computer's memory. A megabyte is 1 million bytes.

meg·a·phone (meg-uh-*fone*) *noun* A device shaped like a cone that is used to make the voice sound louder. *The cheerleaders used megaphones when they shouted to the crowd.*

mel·an·cho·ly (mel-uhn-*kol*-ee) *adjective* Very sad. ▷ *noun* **melancholy** ▷ *adjective* **melancholic**

mel·low (mel-oh)
1. *adjective* Soft, full, and soothing, as in *mellow music* or *a mellow color.*
2. *verb* If someone **mellows,** she or he becomes gentler and more relaxed. ▷ **mellowing, mellowed**
3. *adjective* Soft, sweet, and fully ripe, as in *a mellow peach.*
▷ *adjective* **mellower, mellowest**

me·lo·di·ous (muh-loh-dee-uhss) *adjective* Pleasant to hear. *Our doorbell has a melodious tone.* ▷ *noun* **melodiousness** ▷ *adverb* **melodiously**

mel·o·dra·mat·ic (*mel*-uh-druh-**mat**-ik) *adjective* Overly dramatic, sentimental, or emotional, as in *a melodramatic play.* ▷ *noun* **melodrama**

mel·o·dy (mel-uh-dee) *noun* A tune. ▷ *noun, plural* **melodies** ▷ *adjective* **melodic** (muh-lod-ik)

mel·on (mel-uhn) *noun* A large, round, juicy fruit. Melons grow on vines. *See* **fruit.**

melt (melt) *verb*
1. When a substance **melts,** it changes from a solid to a liquid because of heat.
2. To dissolve. *Sugar melts in water.*
3. To disappear or fade slowly. *The dark clouds melted away.*
4. To soften and become more gentle and more understanding. *The child's sobs melted our hearts.*
▷ *verb* **melting, melted**

melt·down (melt-*doun*) *noun* The melting of the heated core of a nuclear reactor, resulting in the release of radiation into the atmosphere.

mem·ber (mem-bur) *noun*
1. A person, animal, or thing that belongs to a group. ▷ *noun* **membership**
2. A part of a human or animal body, especially an arm or a leg.

mem·brane (mem-brayn) *noun* A very thin layer of tissue or skin that lines or covers certain organs or cells. *See* **cell, egg.**

me·men·to (muh-men-toh) *noun* A small item kept to remember a place, an experience, or a person.

mem·o (mem-oh) *noun* Short for **memorandum.**

mem·o·ra·ble (mem-ur-uh-buhl) *adjective* Easily remembered or worth remembering. *What a memorable day we had!* ▷ *adverb* **memorably**

mem·o·ran·dum (*mem*-uh-ran-duhm) *noun*
1. A brief written reminder.
2. A short letter written to people who work in the same office or organization.
▷ *noun, plural* **memorandums** *or* **memoranda** (*mem*-uh-ran-duh)

me·mo·ri·al (muh-mor-ee-uhl)
1. *noun* Something that is built or done to help people continue to remember a person or an event. Monuments, statues, and plaques often are used as memorials.
2. *adjective* Meant to help people remember someone or something, as in *a memorial service.*

Memorial Day *noun* A holiday celebrated in the United States on the last Monday of May to honor Americans who have died in wars.

mem·o·rize (mem-uh-rize) *verb* To learn something by heart. *Miguel has to memorize the speech by Saturday.* ▷ **memorizing, memorized**

mem·o·ry (mem-uh-ree) *noun*
1. The power to remember things.
2. Something that you remember from the past.
3. Honor and respect for someone or something in the past. *The statue was built in memory of*

the soldiers who died in the war.
4. The part of a computer in which information is stored.
▷ *noun, plural* **memories**

men·ace (men-iss) *noun* A threat or a danger. *Drunk drivers are a menace to everyone else on the road.* ▷ *adjective* **menacing**

mend (mend) *verb*
1. To fix or repair something, as in *to mend a sock.*
2. To heal or to improve. *My broken arm is mending slowly.*
▷ *verb* **mending, mended**

me·no·rah (muh-nor-uh) *noun* A special holder for seven or nine candles, used in the Jewish religion. Menorahs for nine candles are used during Hanukkah, the Jewish "Festival of Lights." *See* **Hanukkah.**

men·tal (men-tuhl) *adjective* To do with or done by the mind, as in *mental health* or *mental calculations.* ▷ *adverb* **mentally**

men·tion (men-shuhn) *verb* To speak or write about something briefly. *Polly mentioned that she would be away on Tuesday.* ▷ **mentioning, mentioned** ▷ *noun* **mention**

men·u (men-yoo) *noun*
1. A list of foods served in a restaurant.
2. A list of choices shown on a computer screen.

me·ow (mee-ou) *verb* To make a noise like a cat.
▷ **meowing, meowed** ▷ *noun* **meow**

mer·ce·nar·y (mur-suh-ner-ee)
1. *noun* A soldier who is paid to fight for a foreign army. ▷ *noun, plural* **mercenaries**
2. *adjective* If someone is **mercenary,** the person is mainly interested in making money.

mer·chan·dise (mur-chuhn-dize *or* mur-chuhn-disse) *noun* Goods that are bought or sold.

mer·chant (mur-chuhnt) *noun*
1. Someone who sells goods for profit.
2. Someone who owns or manages a store.
3. A country's **merchant marine** is made up of ships and crews that carry goods for trade.

mer·cu·ry (mur-kyuh-ree) *noun* A poisonous, silvery, liquid metal. Mercury is used in thermometers and barometers.

Mer·cu·ry (mur-kyuh-ree) *noun* The second-smallest planet in our solar system and the closest planet to the sun. *See* **planet.**

mer·cy (mur-see) *noun*
1. If you show **mercy** to someone, you do not treat or punish the person as severely as he or she may deserve.
2. Something to be thankful for. *Your help was a real mercy.*
▷ *noun, plural* **mercies** ▷ *adjective* **merciful**
▷ *adverb* **mercifully**

mere (mihr) *adjective* Nothing more than. *He was a mere child when he wrote his first book.*
▷ *adjective* **merest**

mere·ly (mihr-lee) *adverb* Only or simply. *Don't blame me; I'm merely the messenger.*

merge (murj) *verb* When two things **merge,** they join together to form a whole. *The two roads run alongside each other before they merge.*
▷ **merging, merged**

merg·er (mur-jur) *noun* The act of making two businesses, teams, etc., into one.

me·rid·i·an (muh-rid-ee-uhn) *noun* An imaginary circle on the earth's surface, passing through the North and South poles.

mer·it (mer-it)
1. *noun* If something has **merit,** it is very good or valuable.
2. *noun* A good point or quality in a person or thing. *What are the merits of your invention?*
3. *verb* To deserve or to be worthy of.
▷ **meriting, merited**
4. merits *noun, plural* The actual facts of a matter. *The judge will decide the case on its merits.*

mer·maid (mur-mayd) *noun* An imaginary sea creature with the upper body of a woman and the tail of a fish.

mer·ry (mer-ee) *adjective* Cheerful or joyful, as in *a merry song.* ▷ **merrier, merriest**

me·sa (may-suh) *noun* A hill or mountain with steep sides and a flat top.

> **Word History**
> •
> Spanish explorers encountered many **mesas** in the American Southwest. The explorers named these geographical features with the Spanish word for "table."

mesh (mesh)
1. *noun* A net made of threads, wires, or lines woven together with open spaces between them. *The strainer is made of fine mesh.* ▷ *noun, plural* **meshes**
2. *verb* To fit together. *Our ideas finally meshed.*
▷ **meshes, meshing, meshed**

mess (mess)
1. *noun* A dirty or untidy state or thing. *My room is a mess!* ▷ *adjective* **messy** ▷ *adverb* **messily**
2. *noun* An unpleasant, difficult, or confusing state or thing. *My life is a mess!*
3. *verb* If you **mess** something **up,** you make it dirty or untidy or you make it go wrong.
▷ **messes, messing, messed**
4. *noun* A meal served to a group of soldiers, sailors, or campers.

5. *noun* A group of soldiers, sailors, or campers who eat together.
▷ *noun, plural* **messes**

mes·sage (mess-ij) *noun*
1. Information sent to someone.
2. The meaning of something. *The message of the movie was that truth wins out.*

mes·sen·ger (mess-uhn-jur) *noun* Someone who carries messages or does errands.

me·tab·o·lism (muh-**tab**-uh-*liz*-uhm) *noun* The process by which our bodies change the fuel we eat into the energy we need to breathe, digest, and carry on all other important life functions.

met·al (met-uhl) *noun* A chemical substance, such as iron, copper, or silver, that is usually hard and shiny, is a good conductor of heat and electricity, and can be melted and formed into shapes. ▷ *adjective* **metallic** (muh-**tal**-ik)

met·a·mor·phic (*met*-uh-**mor**-fik) *adjective* Resulting from or having to do with metamorphosis.

met·a·mor·pho·sis (met-uh-mor-fuh-siss) *noun*
1. The series of changes certain animals go through as they develop from eggs to adults. *A caterpillar goes through a metamorphosis to become a butterfly.*
2. Any complete or great change in appearance, form, or character. *Between losing weight and getting a new hairdo, Josie has gone through quite a metamorphosis.*
▷ *noun, plural* **metamorphoses** (*met*-uh-**mor**-fuh-seez)

met·a·phor (met-uh-*for* or met-uh-*fur*) *noun* A way of describing something by calling it something else; for example, "The princess is a shining jewel, and her father is a raging bull."

me·te·or (mee-tee-ur) *noun* A piece of rock or metal from space that enters the earth's atmosphere at high speed, burns, and forms a streak of light as it falls to the earth.

> **Word History**
> •
> The word **meteor** comes from the Greek word *meteoron,* meaning "something high in the air," because meteors are seen as streaks of light high in the air.

me·te·or·ite (mee-tee-ur-*rite*) *noun* A remaining part of a meteor that falls to earth before it has burned up.

me·te·o·rol·o·gist (*mee*-tee-ur-**ol**-oh-jist) *noun* Someone who specializes in meteorology.

M

me·te·or·ol·o·gy (mee-tee-uh-**rol**-uh-jee) *noun*
The study of the earth's atmosphere and, in particular, its climate and weather. ▷ *adjective* **meteorological**

me·ter (**mee**-tur) *noun*
1. The basic unit of length in the metric system. A meter is equal to 39.37 inches, or about $3\frac{1}{4}$ feet. A meter is about the length of a baseball bat.
2. An instrument for measuring the quantity of something, especially the amount of something that has been used, as in *a gas meter* or *a parking meter.* ▷ *verb* **meter**
3. The pattern of rhythm in a line of poetry formed by stressing some syllables and not stressing others.

meth·ane (**meth**-ane) *noun* A colorless, odorless gas that burns easily and is used for fuel.

meth·od (**meth**-uhd) *noun* A way of doing something.

me·thod·i·cal (muh-**thod**-uh-kuhl) *adjective* Careful, logical, and following an orderly system. *The police made a methodical search of the suspect's house.* ▷ *adverb* **methodically**

me·tic·u·lous (muh-**tik**-yuh-luhss) *adjective* Very careful and precise. ▷ *adverb* **meticulously**

met·ric (**met**-rik) *adjective* To do with a measuring system based on units of 10. Meters, liters, kilograms, and degrees Celsius are basic metric measurements.

metric system *noun* A system of measurement based on counting by 10s. In the metric system, the meter is the basic unit of length, the kilogram is the basic unit of mass or weight, and the liter is the basic unit of liquid volume.

met·ro·nome (**met**-ruh-*nome*) *noun* A device that produces a regular beat that helps musicians keep time as they play.

met·ro·pol·i·tan (*met*-ruh-**pol**-uh-tuhn) *adjective*
1. To do with a large city, as in *a metropolitan police force.*
2. To do with a large city and its surrounding communities, as in *the Los Angeles metropolitan area.*

mi·crobe (**mye**-krobe) *noun* A germ or other living thing that is too small to be seen without a microscope; a microorganism.

mi·cro·chip (**mye**-kroh-*chip*) *noun* A very thin piece of silicon with electronic circuits printed on it, used in computers and other electronic equipment. *See* **chip.**

mi·cro·com·pu·ter (**mye**-kroh-kuhm-*pyoo*-tur) *noun* A computer that sits on a desk or can be carried in a case.

mi·cro·or·gan·ism (*mye*-kroh-**or**-guh-niz-uhm) *noun* A living thing that is too small to be seen without a microscope. *Bacteria and viruses are microorganisms.*

mi·cro·phone (**mye**-kruh-*fone*) *noun* An instrument that changes sound into an electric current to make the sound louder, record it, or transmit it to radio or television stations. *When sound waves enter the diaphragm inside a moving coil microphone, they make it vibrate. These vibrations are transferred to a wire coil that moves inside a magnet, producing a constantly changing electric current. The current is sent down wires to an amplifier or to recording or transmitting equipment.*

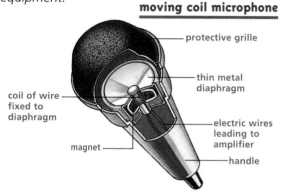

moving coil microphone

protective grille
thin metal diaphragm
coil of wire fixed to diaphragm
electric wires leading to amplifier
magnet
handle

mi·cro·scope (**mye**-kruh-*skope*) *noun* An instrument with powerful lenses. A microscope magnifies very small things so that they look large enough to be seen and studied.

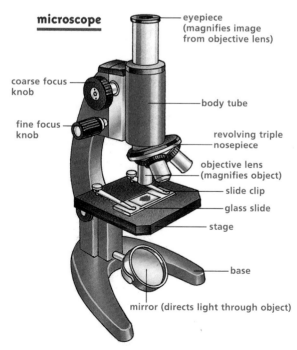

microscope

eyepiece (magnifies image from objective lens)
coarse focus knob
body tube
fine focus knob
revolving triple nosepiece
objective lens (magnifies object)
slide clip
glass slide
stage
base
mirror (directs light through object)

mi·cro·scop·ic (mye-kruh-**skop**-ik) *adjective* Too small to be seen without a microscope. ▷ *adverb* **microscopically**

M

mi·cro·wave (mye-kroh-*wave*) *noun*
1. An electromagnetic wave that can pass through solid objects. Microwaves are used in radar. They are also used to send messages over long distances and to cook food in microwave ovens.
2. **microwave oven** An oven that cooks food very quickly by beaming microwaves into it. The microwaves make the moisture in the food vibrate and become hot, and this heat is passed through the food so that it cooks from the inside.

mid·day (mid-day) *noun* Noon, or 12 o'clock in the middle of the day. ▷ *adjective* **midday**

mid·dle (mid-uhl)
1. *adjective* Half of the way between two things, sides, or outer points. ▷ *noun* **middle**
2. If you are **in the middle** of doing something, you are involved in doing it. *I'm in the middle of watching this program.*

middle-aged *adjective* Someone who is **middle-aged** is between 40 and 60 years old.

Middle Ages *noun* The period of European history between approximately A.D. 500 and 1450.

middle class *noun* The group of people whose income level places them between the upper class (wealthy) and the lower class (poor). ▷ *adjective* **middle-class**

Middle East *noun* A region made up of Egypt, Iran, Iraq, Israel, Saudi Arabia, Syria, Turkey, and other countries. The Middle East overlaps parts of two continents, Asia and Africa. ▷ *adjective* **Middle Eastern**

Middle English *noun* The English language that was spoken from around A.D. 1150 to 1475.

mid·get (mij-it) *noun* A very small thing or person.

mid·night (mid-*nite*) *noun* Twelve o'clock in the middle of the night. ▷ *adjective* **midnight**

mid·way
1. (mid-way) *adverb and adjective* Half of the way. *The car broke down midway between our house and the mall.*
2. (mid-*way*) *noun* The area of a circus, carnival, or fair in which games, rides, and other amusements are located.

Mid·west (mid-west) *noun* The north-central region of the United States bordered by the Appalachian Mountains on the east; the Rocky Mountains on the west; Canada on the north; and Missouri, Oklahoma, and the Ohio River on the south.

mid·wife (mid-*wife*) *noun* A person who assists women in childbirth. ▷ *noun, plural* **midwives** ▷ *noun* **midwifery** (mid-wif-uh-ree)

might (mite)
1. *noun* Strength or force. ▷ *adjective* **mighty** ▷ *adverb* **mightily**
2. *verb* The past tense of **may.**
Might sounds like **mite.**

mi·graine (mye-grayn) *noun* A very bad headache that can cause nausea and vomiting. Migraines usually cause pain on only one side of the head.

mi·grant (mye-gruhnt)
1. *noun* Someone or something that migrates.
2. *adjective* To do with someone who moves around doing seasonal work, as in *a migrant laborer.*

mi·grate (mye-grate) *verb*
1. To move from one country or region to another.
2. When birds **migrate,** they fly away at a particular time of year to live in another region or climate.
▷ *verb* **migrating, migrated** ▷ *noun* **migration** ▷ *adjective* **migratory**

mild (milde) *adjective*
1. Moderate and not too harsh, as in *mild weather.*
2. Someone who is **mild** is gentle and not aggressive.
▷ *adjective* **milder, mildest** ▷ *noun* **mildness** ▷ *adverb* **mildly**

mil·dew (mil-doo) *noun* A thin coating of white, powdery fungus that can grow on damp cloth, paper, etc. ▷ *verb* **mildew** ▷ *adjective* **mildewed,** *adjective* **mildewy**

mile (mile) *noun* A unit of length equal to 5,280 feet. It takes about 20 minutes to walk one mile.

mile·stone (mile-*stone*) *noun*
1. A stone marker found at the side of a road that tells the distance in miles to a certain point or points.
2. An important event or development. *Arriving in the United States was a milestone in my grandmother's life.*

mil·i·tant (mil-uh-tuhnt) *adjective* Someone who is **militant** is prepared to fight or to be very aggressive in support of a cause in which he or she believes. ▷ *noun* **militancy** ▷ *adverb* **militantly**

mil·i·tar·y (mil-uh-*ter*-ee)
1. *adjective* To do with soldiers, the armed forces, or war, as in *a military career* or *a military hospital.*
2. *noun* The armed forces of a country.

mi·li·tia (muh-lish-uh) *noun* A group of citizens who are trained to fight but who only serve in time of emergency, as in the National Guard.

milk (milk)
1. *noun* The white liquid produced by female mammals to feed their young. People drink milk from cows and sometimes goats or other animals. ▷ *adjective* **milky**
2. *verb* To take milk from a cow or other animal. ▷ **milking, milked**
3. *noun* A white liquid that is made in plants, as in *coconut milk.*
4. milk teeth *noun, plural* Your first set of teeth, which fall out and are replaced by your permanent teeth.

Milky Way *noun* The galaxy that includes the earth and our solar system. The Milky Way is made up of more than 100 billion stars and can be seen as a hazy white streak across the night sky.

mill (mil) *noun*
1. A building containing machinery for grinding grain into flour or meal. *See* **windmill.**
2. A large factory with machinery for processing textiles, wood, paper, steel, etc.
3. A small machine used for grinding something into powder, as in *a pepper mill.*
▷ *verb* **mill**

mil·len·ni·um (muh-len-ee-uhm) *noun* A period of a thousand years. ▷ *noun, plural* **millenniums** *or* **millennia** (muh-len-ee-uh) ▷ *adjective* **millennial**

mil·let (mil-it) *noun* A grass like wheat that is raised for its small, edible seeds.

mil·li·gram (mil-i-*gram*) *noun* In the metric system, a measure equal to $\frac{1}{1000}$ gram.

mil·li·me·ter (mil-i-*mee*-tur) *noun* In the metric system, a measure equal to $\frac{1}{1000}$ meter.

mil·lion (mil-yuhn) *noun*
1. A thousand thousands (1,000,000).
2. A very large number. *I've told you a million times not to do that!*

mil·lion·aire (*mil*-yuhn-air) *noun* Someone whose money and property are worth at least a million dollars.

mime (mime) *noun*
1. A form of acting in which actions are used instead of words.
2. A performer who expresses himself or herself without words.
▷ *verb* **mime**

mim·ic (mim-ik) *verb* To imitate someone else's speech or actions, especially to make fun of the person. ▷ **mimicking, mimicked** ▷ *noun* **mimic**

min·a·ret (*min*-uh-ret *or* min-uh-ret) *noun* The tall, thin tower of a mosque, from which Muslims are called to prayer.

mince (minss) *verb* To cut or chop into very small pieces. ▷ **mincing, minced**

mince·meat (minss-*meet*) *noun* A sweet mixture of finely chopped dried fruit, spices, etc., used in pies.

mind (minde)
1. *noun* The part of you that thinks, feels, understands, reasons, and remembers.
2. *verb* To look after something or someone.
3. *verb* To care or to be bothered about something. *Would you mind driving me to the store?*
4. *noun* An opinion or a point of view. *Andrew spoke his mind about the school's dress code.*
5. *noun* Attention. *I can't keep my mind focused.*
6. *noun* Memory. *The appointment slipped my mind.*
7. *verb* To watch out for something. *Mind the step!*
▷ *verb* **minding, minded**

mine (mine)
1. *pronoun* The one or ones belonging to or having to do with me. *This bike is mine.*
2. *verb* To dig up minerals that are underground. ▷ **mining, mined** ▷ *noun* **mine,** *noun* **miner**
3. *noun* A bomb placed underground or underwater.
4. *noun* A rich supply. *The dictionary is a mine of information.*

min·er·al (min-ur-uhl) *noun* A substance found in nature that is not an animal or a plant. Gold, salt, and copper are all minerals. ▷ *adjective* **mineral**

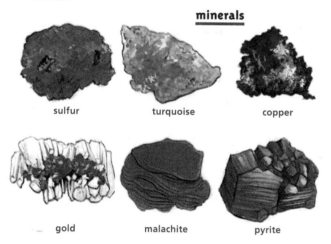

minerals

sulfur   turquoise   copper

gold   malachite   pyrite

min·gle (ming-guhl) *verb* To mix together. *The guests mingled easily at the party.* ▷ **mingling, mingled**

min·i·a·ture (min-ee-uh-chur) *adjective* Smaller than the usual size, as in *a miniature golf course.* ▷ *noun* **miniature**

min·i·mize (min-uh-mize) *verb*
1. To make something as small as possible. *Charlotte minimized the risk of getting lost by taking a map along on her hike.*

2. To make something seem as unimportant or insignificant as possible. *When we told our parents about our adventure, we minimized the danger.*
▷ *verb* **minimizing, minimized**

min·i·mum (min-uh-muhm) *noun* The smallest possible amount, or the lowest limit. *We need a minimum of six people to play this game.*
▷ *adjective* **minimum**

min·i·ser·ies (min-ee-*sihr*-eez) *noun* A television production of a story presented as a series of daily or weekly programs.

min·i·skirt (min-ee-*skurt*) *noun* A very short skirt.

min·is·ter (min-uh-stur)
1. *noun* A person who is authorized to lead religious ceremonies in a church, especially a Protestant church.
2. *noun* Someone sent by a government to represent it overseas.
3. *verb* To help or serve someone. ▷ **ministering, ministered**
▷ *noun* **ministry** ▷ *adjective* **ministerial**

mink (mingk) *noun*
1. A small animal with dark brown, luxurious fur, often raised for its pelt.
2. A coat made from this animal's fur.
▷ *noun, plural* **mink** or **minks**

min·now (min-oh) *noun* A tiny freshwater fish.

mi·nor (mye-nur)
1. *adjective* Less important or less serious. *We will deal with minor matters after the main issues have been discussed.*
2. *noun* Someone under adult age.
3. *adjective* A **minor** scale in music has a semitone between the second and third notes.

mi·nor·i·ty (muh-**nor**-uh-tee *or* mye-**nor**-uh-tee) *noun*
1. A small number or part within a bigger group. *Only a minority were against the proposal.*
2. A group of people of a particular race, ethnic group, or religion living among a larger group of a different race, ethnic group, or religion.
▷ *noun, plural* **minorities**

min·strel (min-struhl) *noun* A medieval musician and poet.

mint (mint) *noun*
1. A plant whose leaves have a strong scent and are used for flavoring. *See* **herb.**
2. A candy flavored with mint.
3. A place where coins are manufactured. ▷ *verb* **mint**
4. *(informal)* A very large amount of money. *That limousine must have cost a mint.*

min·u·end (min-yoo-*end*) *noun* The number from which another number is subtracted. In the problem 75 – 32, 75 is the minuend and 32 is the subtrahend.

mi·nus (mye-nuhss)
1. *adjective* In math, a **minus** sign (–) is used in a subtraction problem. *6 minus 4 equals 2, or 6 – 4 = 2.* ▷ *noun* **minus**
2. *preposition* Without. *I went to school minus my sandwiches.*
3. *adjective* Less than zero. *The temperature was minus six degrees Fahrenheit last night.*
4. *adjective* Slightly less or lower than. *I got a B minus on my last test.*

min·ute
1. (min-it) *noun* A unit of time equal to 60 seconds.
2. (min-it) *noun* A short period of time. *Can I see you for a minute?*
3. (mye-**noot**) *adjective* Very small.
4. (mye-**noot**) *adjective* Careful and complete. *The detective made a minute check of the carpet to see if it contained any clues.*
5. minutes (min-its) *noun, plural* The written record of what is said at a meeting.
▷ *adjective* **minuter, minutest** ▷ *adverb* **minutely**

min·ute·man (min-it-*man*) *noun* A volunteer soldier in the American Revolutionary War who was ready to fight at a minute's notice. ▷ *noun, plural* **minutemen**

mir·a·cle (mihr-uh-kuhl) *noun*
1. An amazing event that cannot be explained by the laws of nature.
2. A remarkable and unexpected event. *It was a miracle that no one died in the fire.*
▷ *adjective* **miraculous** (mi-**rak**-yuh-luhss) ▷ *adverb* **miraculously**

mi·rage (muh-**razh**) *noun* Something that you think you see in the distance, such as water, that is not really there. Mirages are caused by the bending of light rays by layers of air at different temperatures.

mir·ror (mihr-ur) *noun*
1. A metal or glass surface that reflects the image of whatever is in front of it.
2. Something that gives a true picture. *This book is a mirror of life during the Civil War.*
▷ *verb* **mirror**

> **Prefix**
> •
> The prefix **mis-** adds the following meanings to a root word: Bad, wrongly, or badly, as in *misconduct* (bad conduct), *mispronounce* (to pronounce wrongly), or *misbehave* (to behave badly).

mis·be·have (*miss*-bee-**hayv**) *verb* To behave badly. ▷ **misbehaving, misbehaved** ▷ *noun* **misbehavior**

mis·cal·cu·late (miss-kal-kyuh-late) *verb* To figure something out incorrectly, or to judge a situation wrongly. ▷ **miscalculating, miscalculated** ▷ *noun* **miscalculation**

mis·car·riage (miss-ka-rij *or* miss-ka-rij) *noun*
1. When a pregnant woman has a **miscarriage**, she gives birth to a fetus that is not sufficiently formed to live. ▷ *verb* **miscarry**
2. A **miscarriage of justice** occurs when the legal system fails to come to the right decision or verdict.

mis·cel·la·ne·ous (miss-uh-lay-nee-uhss) *adjective* Assorted or of different types. *The drawer was full of miscellaneous socks, but I couldn't find a pair.* ▷ *noun* **miscellany**

mis·chief (miss-chif) *noun* Playful behavior that may cause annoyance or harm to others. *My brother is always up to some sort of mischief.* ▷ *adjective* **mischievous** (miss-chuh-vuhss *or* miss-chee-vee-uhss) ▷ *adverb* **mischievously**

mis·con·duct (miss-kon-duhkt) *noun* Dishonest, irresponsible, or immoral action, especially by someone in a position of responsibility.

mi·ser (mye-zur) *noun* A very stingy person who spends as little as possible in order to hoard money. ▷ *noun* **miserliness** ▷ *adjective* **miserly**

mis·er·a·ble (miz-ur-uh-buhl) *adjective*
1. Sad, unhappy, or dejected.
2. Causing great discomfort or unhappiness, as in *a miserable cold* or *miserable weather.* ▷ *noun* **misery** ▷ *adverb* **miserably**

mis·fit (miss-fit) *noun* Someone or something not suited to the people or situation around it.

mis·for·tune (miss-for-chuhn) *noun*
1. An unlucky event. *The closing of the park is a great misfortune for the neighborhood.*
2. Bad luck. *It was my misfortune to miss the plane.*

mis·giv·ing (miss-giv-ing) *noun* A feeling of worry or doubt. *We had misgivings about our plan to play a trick on my sister.*

mis·guid·ed (miss-gye-did) *adjective* If you are **misguided**, you have the wrong idea about something. ▷ *adverb* **misguidedly**

mis·hap (miss-hap) *noun* An unfortunate accident.

mis·lay (miss-lay) *verb* To lose something for a short while because you have put it in a place where you cannot find it. *Juanita mislaid one of her shoes.* ▷ **mislaying, mislaid**

mis·lead (miss-leed) *verb* To give someone the wrong idea about something. ▷ **misleading, misled** ▷ *adjective* **misleading** ▷ *adverb* **misleadingly**

mis·place (miss-playss) *verb* To put something down somewhere and then forget where it is. ▷ **misplacing, misplaced** ▷ *noun* **misplacement**

mis·print (miss-print) *noun* A mistake in a book, newspaper, etc., where the letters have been printed incorrectly. ▷ *verb* **misprint** (miss-print)

mis·pro·nounce (miss-proh-nounss) *verb* To say a word incorrectly. ▷ **mispronouncing, mispronounced**

miss (miss)
1. *verb* To fail to hit or reach something. *The batter missed the ball.* ▷ *noun* **miss**
2. *verb* To fail to catch, see, meet, or do something. *Guillermo missed the train by seconds.*
3. *verb* To fail to attend or be present for. *I missed my doctor's appointment.*
4. *verb* To be unhappy because something or someone is not with you. *I miss my brother.*
5. *verb* To avoid or to escape. *I just missed being hit by the avalanche.*
6. *noun* A title given to a girl or an unmarried woman. It is written **Miss** before a name, as in *Miss Smith.* ▷ *noun, plural* **misses** *or* **Misses** ▷ *verb* **misses, missing, missed**

mis·sile (miss-uhl) *noun* A weapon that is thrown or shot at a target, as in *an atomic missile.*

missing (miss-ing) *adjective*
1. Lacking, as in *missing information.*
2. Lost, as in *a missing child.*

mis·sion (mish-uhn) *noun*
1. A special job or task. *Our mission is to collect clothing for the flood victims.*
2. A group of people who are sent to do a special job. *My mom and dad are part of the rescue mission.*
3. A church or other place where missionaries live and work. *Sister Mary Paul taught English classes at the mission.*

mis·sion·ar·y (mish-uh-ner-ee) *noun* Someone who is sent by a church or religious group to teach that group's faith and do good works, especially in a foreign country. ▷ *noun, plural* **missionaries**

mis·spell (miss-spel) *verb* To spell something incorrectly. ▷ **misspelling, misspelled** ▷ *noun* **misspelling**

mist (mist) *noun* A cloud of tiny water droplets in the air. ▷ *verb* **mist** ▷ *adjective* **misty**

mis·take (muh-stake)
1. *noun* An error or a misunderstanding.
2. *verb* To believe that someone or something is another. *I always mistake Tracy for her older sister.*
▷ **mistaking, mistook, mistaken** ▷ *adjective* **mistaken** ▷ *adverb* **mistakenly**

mis·ter (miss-tur) *noun* A title for a man. It is written **Mister** or **Mr.** before a name.

mis·tle·toe (miss-uhl-*toh*) *noun* An evergreen plant that grows as a parasite on trees. Mistletoe has white berries and is often used as a Christmas decoration.

mistletoe

mis·treat (miss-treet) *verb* To treat roughly, cruelly, or badly. ▷ **mistreating, mistreated** ▷ *noun* **mistreatment**

mis·tress (miss-triss) *noun* A woman with power, responsibility, or control over something. *My mother is the mistress of this house.* ▷ *noun, plural* **mistresses**

mis·trust (miss-truhst) *verb* To be suspicious of someone. ▷ **mistrusting, mistrusted** ▷ *noun* **mistrust**

mis·un·der·stand (*miss*-uhn-dur-**stand**) *verb* To understand incorrectly. *I misunderstood the directions.* ▷ **misunderstanding, misunderstood**

misunderstanding *noun*
1. A failure to understand.
2. A disagreement between people.

mis·use (miss-yooz) *verb* To use something in the wrong way. ▷ **misusing, misused** ▷ *noun* **misuse** (miss-**yooss**)

mite (mite) *noun*
1. A tiny animal with eight legs that is related to the spider. A mite lives off plants, animals, or stored food.
2. A small person or thing. *The kitten was just a mite.*
3. A small amount of anything.
Mite sounds like **might.**

mitt (mit) *noun* A padded leather glove that protects a person's hand when he or she catches a baseball or softball.

mit·ten (mit-uhn) *noun* A warm covering for the hand with one part for the thumb and another for the rest of the fingers.

mix (miks) *verb*
1. To combine or blend different things. *Mix all the ingredients together.*
2. If something **mixes** you **up,** it confuses you.
▷ *adjective* **mixed-up**
▷ *verb* **mixes, mixing, mixed** ▷ *noun* **mix**

mixed number *noun* A number made up of a whole number and a fraction, such as $6\frac{1}{2}$.

mix·ture (miks-chur) *noun* Something consisting of different things mixed together.

mix-up *noun* A confused situation. *We were late for dinner because there was a mix-up over when we would eat.* ▷ *noun, plural* **mix-ups**

moan (mohn) *verb*
1. To make a low, sad sound, usually because you are in pain or are unhappy.
2. To complain in a sad way. *"I don't want to go,"* Isabelle moaned.
▷ *verb* **moaning, moaned** ▷ *noun* **moan**

moat (moht) *noun* A deep, wide ditch dug all around a castle, fort, or town and filled with water to prevent attacks. Moats were used in the Middle Ages. *See* **castle.**

mob (mob)
1. *noun* A large and dangerous crowd of people, as in *an angry mob.*
2. *noun* Any large crowd.
3. *verb* To crowd around excitedly. *Fans mobbed the movie star.* ▷ **mobbing, mobbed**

mo·bile
1. (moh-buhl *or* moh-beel *or* moh-bile) *adjective* Able to move, as in *a mobile home.* ▷ *noun* **mobility**
2. (moh-beel) *noun* A sculpture made of several items balanced at different heights and hanging from a central wire or thread.

mobile home *noun* A large trailer people can live in.

mobile phone *noun* A telephone that you can carry around with you.

moc·ca·sin (mok-uh-suhn) *noun* A soft leather shoe or slipper without a heel. Moccasins originally were worn by American Indians.

mock (mok)
1. *verb* To make fun of someone in an unpleasant way. ▷ **mocking, mocked** ▷ *noun* **mockery**
2. *adjective* False or imitation, as in *a mock battle.*

mock·ing·bird (mok-ing-*burd*) *noun* A gray and white songbird of North and South America that can imitate the calls of other birds.

mode (mohd) *noun*
1. A way of doing something. *Buses are a popular mode of transportation in many cities.*
2. In mathematics, the most frequent number in a set of numbers. *In the set 3, 3, 3, 4, 4, 5, 6, 7, the mode is 3 because it appears most often.*

mod·el (mod-uhl)
1. *adjective* Small or miniature, as in *a model railroad.* ▷ *noun* **model**
2. *adjective* Perfect or ideal, as in *a model child.*
3. *noun* Someone who poses for an artist or a photographer or who wears clothing in order to show how the clothing looks. ▷ *noun* **modeling**
▷ *verb* **model**
4. *noun* A thing or person who is a good example. *Ted is a model of good behavior.*
5. *noun* A particular type or design of product. *This car is the very latest model.*
▷ *adjective* **model**

mo·dem (moh-duhm) *noun* A piece of electronic equipment used to send information between computers by telephone lines.

M

mod·er·ate

1. (mod-ur-it) *adjective* Not extreme, as in *moderate speed.* ▷ *adverb* **moderately**
2. (mod-uh-*rate*) *verb* To make or become less extreme. ▷ *noun* **moderation**
3. (mod-ur-it) *noun* A person with moderate opinions.
4. (mod-uh-*rate*) *verb* To lead or preside over a meeting. ▷ *noun* **moderator**
▷ *verb* **moderating, moderated**

mod·ern (mod-urn) *adjective*

1. To do with the present or the recent past, as in *modern art.*
2. Up-to-date or new in style, as in *modern appliances.*

mod·ern·ize (mod-ur-nize) *verb* To make something more modern or up-to-date.
▷ **modernizing, modernized** ▷ *noun* **modernization**

mod·est (mod-ist) *adjective*

1. People who are **modest** are not boastful about their abilities, possessions, or achievements. ▷ *noun* **modesty**
2. Not large or extreme, as in *a modest salary.*
▷ *adverb* **modestly**

mod·i·fy (mod-uh-fye) *verb*

1. To change something slightly. ▷ *noun* **modification**
2. To limit the meaning of a word or phrase. *Adjectives modify nouns and pronouns.* ▷ *noun* **modifier**
▷ *verb* **modifies, modifying, modified**

mod·ule (moj-ool) *noun* A separate, independent section that can be linked to other parts to make something larger, as in *a space module.*

Mohammed See **Muhammad.**

Mo·hawk (moh-hawk) *noun* A member of a group of American Indians that lives primarily in eastern New York, in the Mohawk River valley. The Mohawk are part of the Iroquois Confederation.

Mo·he·gan (moh-hee-guhn) or **Mo·hi·can** (moh-hee-kuhn) *noun* A member of a group of American Indians that originally lived in southeastern Connecticut. ▷ *noun, plural* **Mohegan, Mohegans** or **Mohican, Mohicans**

moist (moist) *adjective* Slightly wet. ▷ **moister, moistest** ▷ *noun* **moisture** ▷ *verb* **moisten**

mo·lar (moh-lur) *noun* A broad, flat tooth at the back of the mouth used for grinding food. See **teeth, tooth.**

mo·las·ses (muh-lass-iz) *noun* A thick, sweet syrup made when sugarcane is processed into sugar.

mold (mohld)

1. *noun* A furry fungus that grows on old food or damp surfaces. ▷ *noun* **moldiness** ▷ *adjective* **moldy**

2. *verb* To model or shape something. *Mold the clay into the shape of a cat.* ▷ **molding, molded**
3. *noun* A hollow container that you can pour liquid into so that it sets in that shape, as in *a gelatin mold.*

mole (mohl) *noun*

1. A small, furry mammal that digs tunnels and lives underground.
2. A small growth on the skin.

mole

mol·e·cule (mol-uh-kyool) *noun* The smallest part of a substance that contains all the chemical properties of that substance. *The diagrams show how molecules are tightly packed in solids, loosely linked in liquids, and widely spaced in gases. This means that solids usually keep their shape, liquids can flow, and gases can spread out easily.* ▷ *adjective* **molecular** (muh-lek-yuh-lur)

molecules

molecules in a solid

molecules in a liquid

molecules in a gas

mol·lusk (mol-uhsk) *noun* An animal with a soft body and no spine. A mollusk is usually protected by a hard shell. *Snails and oysters are mollusks.*

mol·ly·cod·dle (mol-ee-*kod*-uhl) *verb* To look after someone too carefully. *Ms. Avery mollycoddled Vincent; she never let him go to the park to play with his friends.* ▷ **mollycoddling, mollycoddled** ▷ *noun* **mollycoddler**

molt (mohlt) *verb* When a bird or an animal **molts,** its outer covering of fur, feathers, or skin comes off so that a new covering can grow.
▷ **molting, molted**

mol·ten (mohlt-uhn) *adjective* Melted by heat. *Lava is molten rock.*

mom (mom) *noun* (informal) Mother.

mo·ment (moh-muhnt) *noun*

1. A very brief period of time. *I saw the rocket for only a moment.* ▷ *adjective* **momentary**
▷ *adverb* **momentarily**

2. If something is happening **at this moment,** it is happening now.

mo·men·tum (moh-**men**-tuhm) *noun* The force or speed that an object has when it is moving. *Our car gained momentum as we drove down the mountain.*

mon·arch (**mon**-urk) *noun*
1. A ruler, such as a king or queen, who often inherits his or her position. ▷ *noun* **monarchy**
2. A large, orange and black butterfly.

mon·as·ter·y (**mon**-uh-*ster*-ee) *noun* A group of buildings where monks live and work. ▷ *noun, plural* **monasteries** ▷ *adjective* **monastic** (muh-**nass**-tik)

Mon·day (**muhn**-day *or* **muhn**-dee) *noun* The second day of the week, after Sunday and before Tuesday.

> ### ▶ Word History
> ●
> The Romans were honoring the moon when they named **Monday**. In mythology, the moon was the wife of the sun. Since the sun has his day of the week, Sunday, the moon deserved her own day, too. "Moon day" was *luna dia* in Latin. In Old English the translation became "moon's day," and that gradually became Monday in modern English.

mon·ey (**muhn**-ee) *noun* The coins and bills that people use to buy things. ▷ *noun, plural* **moneys** *or* **monies** ▷ *adjective* **monetary** (**mon**-i-*ter*-ee)

mon·goose (**mon**-*gooss*) *noun* An animal that resembles a ferret, having a slender body, a long tail, and brown or black fur. Mongooses are known for their ability to kill poisonous snakes. ▷ *noun, plural* **mongooses** *or* **mongeese**

mon·grel (**muhng**-gruhl *or* **mong**-gruhl) *noun* An animal, especially a dog, that is a mixture of different breeds.

mon·i·tor (**mon**-uh-tur)
1. *noun* A student who is given a special job to do in the classroom, as in *a chalkboard monitor.*
2. *verb* To keep a check on something over a period of time. ▷ **monitoring, monitored**
3. *noun* A person or a device that keeps track of or monitors people, machines, or a situation.
4. *noun* The visual display unit of a computer. *See* **computer.**
5. *noun* A television screen used in a studio to show what is being recorded or transmitted.

monk (muhngk) *noun* A man who lives in a religious community and has promised to devote his life to God.

mon·key (**muhng**-kee)
1. *noun* An animal like a small ape, usually with a tail. Monkeys have hands and feet that are adapted for climbing and for grasping objects.
2. *verb* To play in a silly or mischievous way. *Stop monkeying around.* ▷ **monkeying, monkeyed**

monkey wrench *noun* A tool with a grip that adjusts to fit different sizes of nuts and bolts.

mon·o·cle (**mon**-uh-kuhl) *noun* A glass lens worn to improve the eyesight of one eye.

mon·o·gram (**mon**-uh-*gram*) *noun* A design made from two or more letters, usually someone's initials. ▷ *verb* **monogram** ▷ *adjective* **monogrammed**

mon·o·lin·gual (*mon*-uh-**ling**-gwuhl) *adjective* Able to speak only one language.

mon·o·logue (**mon**-uh-*log*) *noun* A long speech by one person.

mon·o·nu·cle·o·sis (*mon*-oh-noo-klee-**oh**-siss) *noun* An infectious illness that gives you a sore throat, swollen glands, and a high temperature.

mo·nop·o·lize (muh-**nop**-uh-lize) *verb* To keep something all to yourself. *Rafael monopolized the conversation.* ▷ **monopolizing, monopolized**

mo·nop·o·ly (muh-**nop**-uh-lee) *noun*
1. The complete control of something, especially a service or the supply of a product. ▷ *adjective* **monopolistic** (muh-*nop*-uh-**liss**-tik)
2. A group or company that has such control. ▷ *noun, plural* **monopolies**

mon·o·rail (**mon**-uh-*rayl*) *noun*
1. A railroad that runs on one rail, usually high off the ground.
2. A railroad track that has only one rail.

mo·not·o·nous (muh-**not**-uh-nuhss) *adjective* If something is **monotonous,** it goes on and on in a dull and boring way, as in *a monotonous job.* ▷ *noun* **monotony** ▷ *adverb* **monotonously**

mon·soon (mon-soon) *noun*
1. A very strong wind that blows across the Indian Ocean and southern Asia. In the summer it blows from the ocean toward the land and brings very heavy rains. In the winter it blows from the land toward the ocean, bringing hot, dry weather.
2. The rainy summer season brought on by the monsoon.

mon·ster (**mon**-stur)
1. *noun* A large, fierce, or horrible creature.
2. *noun* A very evil or cruel person.
3. *adjective* Huge, as in *a monster whale.* ▷ *noun* **monster**

mon·strous (**mon**-struhss) *adjective*
1. Horrible or frightening, as in *a monstrous creature.*
2. Huge.
3. Evil and shocking, as in *a monstrous crime.* ▷ *noun* **monstrosity** (mon-**stross**-i-tee) ▷ *adverb* **monstrously**

month (muhnth) *noun* One of the 12 parts that make up a year. ▷ *adjective* **monthly** ▷ *adverb* **monthly**

mon·u·ment (mon-yuh-muhnt) *noun*
1. A statue, building, etc., that is meant to remind people of an event or a person, as in *a war monument.*
2. An important work or achievement. *The discovery of penicillin was a monument in medical research.*

mon·u·men·tal (mon-yuh-**men**-tuhl) *adjective* Very large or very important, as in *a monumental mistake* or *a monumental decision.*
▷ *adverb* **monumentally**

mood (mood) *noun* Your **mood** is the way that you are feeling.

mood·y (moo-dee) *adjective*
1. Gloomy or unhappy. ▷ *adverb* **moodily**
2. A **moody** person has frequent changes of mood or feelings.
▷ *adjective* **moodier, moodiest** ▷ *noun* **moodiness**

moon (moon) *noun*
1. The satellite that moves around the earth once each month and reflects light from the sun. *The first diagram shows how the moon moves around Earth, while the second identifies the different phases of the moon as they are seen from Earth during the course of a month.*
2. A satellite of a planet. *Mars has two moons.*

the moon's motion

Earth

sun's rays

moon

phases of the moon

| new moon (invisible) | crescent moon (waxing) | half-moon (first quarter) | gibbous moon (waxing) |

| full moon | gibbous moon (waning) | half-moon (last quarter) | crescent moon (waning) |

moon·light (moon-*lite*)
1. *noun* The light of the moon that you can see at night. ▷ *adjective* **moonlit**
2. *verb* (informal) Someone who **moonlights** holds two jobs, one during the day and one at night.
▷ **moonlighting, moonlighted**

moor (mor)
1. *verb* If you **moor** a boat, you tie it up or anchor it. ▷ **mooring, moored** ▷ *noun, plural* **moorings**
2. *noun* An open, grassy area, often covered with heather and marshes.

moose (mooss) *noun* A large, heavy animal of the deer family that lives in the cold forests of North America, Europe, and Asia. The male has very large, broad antlers. **Moose** sounds like **mousse.** ▷ *noun, plural* **moose**

▶ Word History
• •
The **moose** got its name from the American Indians. In one Indian language of the eastern United States, the word *mus* means "he strips off the bark," because a moose strips off and eats the bark of trees. Many English words for plants and animals have come from American Indian languages, and the meanings are very descriptive.

mop (mop)
1. *noun* A long stick with a sponge or bundle of cloth or string at one end, used to clean floors.
2. *verb* To clean a floor or soak up liquid with a mop, cloth, or sponge. ▷ **mopping, mopped**
3. *noun* A thick, tangled mass, as in *a mop of hair.*

mope (mope) *verb* To be gloomy and depressed.
▷ **moping, moped**

mo·ped (moh-ped) *noun* A heavy bicycle with a small engine.

mor·al (mor-uhl)
1. *adjective* To do with right and wrong. *Carl faced the moral dilemma of saying nothing or telling the truth.*
2. *adjective* Good and honest. *A moral person would never lie or cheat.*
3. *noun, plural* Your **morals** are your beliefs about what is right and wrong.
4. *noun* The lesson taught by a story.
▷ *noun* **morality** ▷ *adverb* **morally**

mo·rale (muh-ral) *noun* The state of mind or spirit of a person or group. *The team's morale was low after it lost its third game in a row.*

mor·bid (mor-bid) *adjective* Someone who is **morbid** is very interested in death and gruesome things. ▷ *adverb* **morbidly**

more (mor)
1. *adjective* Greater in number, size, extent, or degree. *César did more work than anyone else.*
2. *adjective* Additional or further. *I added more flour to the dough.*
3. *adverb* To a greater extent or degree. *Please be more careful.*

M

4. *adverb* In addition or again. *He woke up, then fell asleep once more.*

5. *noun* An extra amount. *I want more to eat.*

6. *pronoun* A greater number. *More will be rich than will starve.*

7. more or less Roughly or nearly.

more·o·ver (mor-oh-vur) *adverb* Beyond what has already been said. *"I'm sorry I was rude," Joyce apologized. "Moreover, I promise that it won't happen again."*

Mor·mon (mor-muhn) *noun* A member of the Church of Jesus Christ of Latter-day Saints, a religion founded in 1830 by Joseph Smith at Fayette, New York.

morn·ing (mor-ning) *noun* The time of day between midnight and noon or sunrise and noon. **Morning** sounds like **mourning.**

morning glory *noun* A climbing vine with flowers of different colors. The flowers open early in the morning and close in the afternoon. ▷ *noun, plural* **morning glories**

mo·rose (muh-rohss) *adjective* Gloomy or depressed. *Ever since his grandfather died, Jack has been morose.* ▷ *adverb* **morosely**

morph (morf) *verb* To change in shape, especially as done by computer animation. *The cartoon tiger morphed into a young man.* ▷ **morphing, morphed**

Morse code (morss) *noun* A way of signaling that uses light or sound in a pattern of dots and dashes to represent letters. *This picture shows the word "Morse" in Morse code.*

mor·sel (mor-suhl) *noun* A small piece of food, as in *a morsel of bread.*

mor·tal (mor-tuhl)

1. *adjective* Unable to live forever. *All humans are mortal.* ▷ *noun* **mortality**

2. *adjective* Causing death, as in *a mortal wound.* ▷ *adverb* **mortally**

3. *adjective* Very hostile, as in *mortal enemies.*

4. *adjective* Very great or intense. *He has a mortal fear of snakes.*

5. *noun* A human being.

mor·tar (mor-tur) *noun*

1. A mixture of lime, sand, water, and cement that is used for building. *Bricks are laid with mortar.*

2. A deep bowl used with a pestle for crushing things.

3. A very short cannon that fires shells or rockets high in the air.

mort·gage (mor-gij) *noun* A loan from a bank to buy a house. ▷ *verb* **mortgage**

mor·tu·ar·y (mor-choo-er-ee) *noun* A room or building where dead bodies are kept until burial. ▷ *noun, plural* **mortuaries**

mo·sa·ic (moh-zay-ik) *noun* A pattern or picture made up of small pieces of colored stone, tile, or glass. *This ancient Roman mosaic represents a Byzantine empress.*

mosaic

Mo·ses (moh-ziss *or* moh-ziz) *noun* In the Old Testament, a Hebrew prophet and giver of laws who led the ancient Jews out of Egypt.

mo·sey (moh-zee) *verb* (informal) To walk slowly or aimlessly. ▷ **moseying, moseyed**

mosh·ing (mosh-ing) *noun* At rock music concerts, the activity of swaying, dancing, and flinging yourself around while banging into other people.

Moslem (moz-luhm) See **Muslim.**

mosque (mosk) *noun* A building used by Muslims for worship. See **architecture.**

mos·qui·to (muh-skee-toh) *noun* A small insect, the female of which bites and sucks blood from animals and humans. Mosquitoes can spread diseases such as malaria and yellow fever. ▷ *noun, plural* **mosquitoes** *or* **mosquitos**

mosquito

sucking tube

moss (mawss *or* moss) *noun* A small, furry, green plant that grows on damp soil, rocks, and tree trunks. Mosses do not have roots, flowers, or fruit but reproduce from spores. See **spore.** ▷ *noun, plural* **mosses** ▷ *adjective* **mossy**

most (mohst)

1. *adjective* Greatest in number, amount, or degree. *My little brother always gets the most attention.*

2. *adjective* The majority of. *Most athletes avoid junk foods.*

3. *noun* The greatest number, amount, or degree. *One hour is the most I can spare.*

4. *adverb* Very. *She is a most unusual person.*

5. *adverb* To the greatest degree or extent. *That is the most disgusting thing I have ever seen.*

M

most·ly (mohst-lee) *adverb* Mainly or usually.

mo·tel (moh-tel) *noun* A roadside hotel that provides parking spaces adjacent to the rooms.

moth (mawth) *noun* An insect similar to a butterfly but having a thicker body, a duller color, and antennae shaped like feathers. Unlike butterflies, moths usually fly at night. *The emperor moth is found in Europe and in Asia.*

emperor moth
(male)

moth·er (muhTH-ur)
1. *noun* A female parent. ▷ *noun* **motherhood** ▷ *verb* **mother** ▷ *adjective* **motherly**
2. *noun* The source or origin of something. *Necessity is the mother of invention.*
3. *adjective* Native, as in *mother country*.

mother-in-law *noun* Someone's **mother-in-law** is the mother of his or her spouse. ▷ *noun, plural* **mothers-in-law**

Mother's Day *noun* A day set aside for honoring mothers, observed every year on the second Sunday in May.

mo·tion (moh-shuhn)
1. *noun* Movement. *The motion of the boat made me feel sick.*
2. *verb* To tell someone something through a movement. *The teacher motioned Deirdre to sit down.* ▷ **motioning, motioned**

3. *noun* A formal suggestion made at a meeting or in a court of law. ▷ *verb* **motion**

mo·tion·less (moh-shun-liss) *adjective* Not moving. *The cat stayed motionless, waiting for the bird to come closer.* ▷ *adverb* **motionlessly**

motion picture *noun* A series of still pictures on a strip of film. When the film is run at high speed through a projector, the individual pictures blend into one another so that the people and things in the pictures appear to move.

mo·ti·vate (moh-tuh-*vate*) *verb* To encourage someone to do something. *The coach tried to motivate her team to win.* ▷ **motivating, motivated** ▷ *noun* **motivation** ▷ *adjective* **motivated**

mo·tive (moh-tiv) *noun* A reason for doing something. *Pat's motive for getting good grades was his desire to go to college.*

mo·to·cross (moh-tuh-*kross*) *noun* A cross-country motorcycle race.

mo·tor (moh-tur)
1. *noun* A machine that provides the power to make something run or work. See **engine.**
2. *adjective* To do with a motor or something run by a motor, as in *motor vehicles* or *motor oil.*
3. *verb* To drive. ▷ **motoring, motored** ▷ *noun* **motoring**

mo·tor·bike (moh-tur-*bike*) *noun*
1. A bicycle powered by a small motor.
2. A small or light motorcycle.

mo·tor·cy·cle (moh-tur-*sye*-kuhl) *noun* A heavy vehicle with two wheels and an engine.

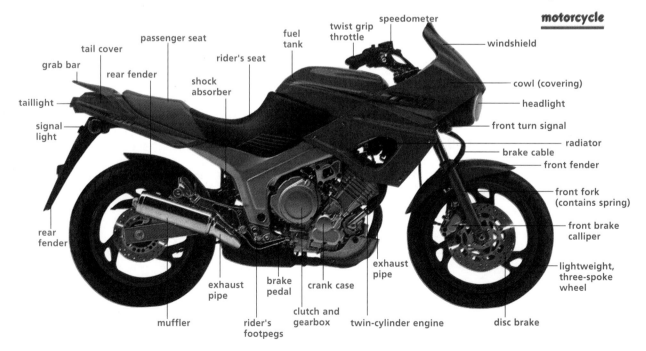

motorcycle

- speedometer
- twist grip throttle
- fuel tank
- windshield
- passenger seat
- rider's seat
- tail cover
- grab bar
- rear fender
- shock absorber
- cowl (covering)
- taillight
- headlight
- signal light
- front turn signal
- radiator
- brake cable
- front fender
- front fork (contains spring)
- front brake calliper
- rear fender
- exhaust pipe
- lightweight, three-spoke wheel
- muffler
- exhaust pipe
- brake pedal
- crank case
- clutch and gearbox
- rider's footpegs
- twin-cylinder engine
- disc brake

mo·tor·ist (moh-tur-ist) *noun* Someone who travels by car.

mot·tled (mot-uhld) *adjective* If something is **mottled,** it is covered with patches of different colors.

mot·to (mot-oh) *noun* A short sentence that is meant to guide behavior or state what someone believes or stands for. *My motto is "Be prepared."* ▷ *noun, plural* **mottoes** or **mottos**

mound (mound) *noun*
1. A hill or a pile, as in *a mound of garbage.* ▷ *verb* **mound**
2. A slightly raised area for the pitcher in the center of a baseball diamond.

mount (mount)
1. *verb* To get on or to climb up. *Sheila mounted her horse. We mounted the stairs.*
2. *verb* To rise or to increase. *Excitement mounted as the great day drew near.*
3. *verb* To set in place for display. *I mounted my new stamps in an album.*
4. *noun* A horse or other animal used for riding.
5. *noun* Mountain. This word is usually used as part of a name, as in *Mount Everest.*
▷ *verb* **mounting, mounted**

moun·tain (moun-tuhn) *noun*
1. A very high piece of land.
2. A large amount of something, as in *a mountain of work.*

mountain bike *noun* A strong bicycle with many gears and heavy tire treads that can be ridden on rough or hilly ground. *See* **bicycle.**

moun·tain·eer (moun-tuh-**nihr**) *noun* Someone who climbs mountains for sport. ▷ *noun* **mountaineering**

mountain lion *noun* A large, powerful wildcat, found in the mountains of North, Central, and South America. The mountain lion is also known as a **cougar, puma,** or **panther.**

mourn (morn) *verb* To be very sad and grieve for someone who has died. ▷ **mourning, mourned** ▷ *noun* **mourner,** *noun* **mourning**

mourn·ful (morn-fuhl) *adjective* Feeling, showing, or filled with grief, as in *a mournful song.* ▷ *adverb* **mournfully**

mouse (mouss) *noun*
1. A small, furry animal with a pointed nose, small ears, and a long tail.
2. A small control box that you use to move the cursor on your computer screen.
See **computer.**
▷ *noun, plural* **mice** (misse)

harvest mouse

mousse (mooss) *noun*
1. A cold dessert containing beaten egg whites or whipped cream and gelatin. Mousse is like a light and fluffy pudding.
2. A substance that you use to style your hair. **Mousse** sounds like **moose.**

moustache *See* **mustache.**

mous·y (mou-see) *adjective*
1. **Mousy** hair is light brown.
2. Quiet and shy. ▷ *noun* **mousiness** ▷ *adverb* **mousily**

mouth
1. (mouth) *noun* The opening in the body through which people and animals take in foods.
2. (mouth) *noun* An opening that looks like a mouth, as in *the mouth of a jar* or *the mouth of a cave.*
3. (mouth) *noun* The part of a river where it empties into another body of water.
4. (mouTH) *verb* If you **mouth** words, you say them, sometimes insincerely, and sometimes by only moving your lips. ▷ **mouthing, mouthed**

mouth organ *noun* A harmonica. *See* **harmonica.**

mouth·piece (mouth-*peess*) *noun*
1. The part of a telephone that you talk into.
2. The part of a musical instrument that you blow over or into. *See* **bagpipes, recorder, saxophone.**
3. (*informal*) Someone who acts as a spokesperson for an individual or a group.

move (moov)
1. *verb* To change place or position. *Akiko moved to the front row.*
2. *verb* To change where you live or work. *We moved to Denver.*
3. *noun* A step or a movement. *The runner made a quick move to third base.*
4. *verb* If you are **moved** by something such as a movie or a piece of music, it makes you feel emotional.
5. *verb* To put or keep in motion. *Wind moves a windmill.*
6. *verb* To cause someone to do something. *What moved you to buy such an expensive gift?*
7. *noun* An action planned to bring about a result. *In a move to get elected, the candidate promised that she would lower taxes.*
8. *noun* A person's turn to change the position of a playing piece in games such as chess or checkers.
▷ *noun* **move** ▷ *verb* **moving, moved** ▷ *adjective* **moving,** *adjective* **movable** or **moveable**

move·ment (moov-muhnt) *noun*
1. The act of moving from one place to another. *The boxer's movements were lightning quick.*
2. A group of people who have joined together to support a cause, as in *the civil rights movement.*
3. One of the main parts of a long piece of classical music.

337

movie ▶multiply

mov·ie (moo-vee) *noun* A motion picture.

mow (moh) *verb* To cut grass, grain, hay, etc.
▷ **mowing, mowed, mown** (mohn) ▷ *noun* **mower**

mph or **m.p.h.** (em-pee-aych) An abbreviation for *miles per hour. This car's top speed is 130 mph.*

Mr. (miss-ter) *noun* A title put in front of a man's name, as in *Mr. James Brown.*

Mrs. (miss-iz) *noun* A title put in front of a married woman's name, as in *Mrs. Clare White.*

Ms. (miz) *noun* A title put in front of a woman's name that does not indicate whether she is married or unmarried, as in *Ms. Anna Black.*

much (muhch)
1. *adjective* Great in amount or degree. *I don't have much money left. It's too much trouble.*
2. *adverb* Very. *I was much disturbed by her odd behavior.*
3. *noun* A large amount of something. *I don't eat much.*

mu·ci·lage (myoo-suh-lij) *noun* A kind of glue.

muck (muhk) *noun*
1. Anything that is dirty, wet, sticky, or slimy, such as mud or manure.
2. *(informal)* Anything that is messy or disgusting.

mu·cus (myoo-kuhss) *noun* A slimy fluid that coats and protects the inside of your mouth, nose, throat, and other breathing passages.
▷ *adjective* **mucous** (myoo-kuhss)

mud (muhd) *noun* Earth that is wet, soft, and sticky.

mud·dle (muh-duhl)
1. *verb* To mix things up or confuse them. *Because she was nervous, she muddled the facts in her speech.* ▷ **muddling, muddled**
2. *noun* A mess or confusion. *Because he did not keep good records, his checking account was in a muddle.*
▷ *adjective* **muddled**

mud·dy (muhd-ee)
1. *adjective* If something is **muddy,** it is covered with wet, sticky earth. ▷ **muddier, muddiest**
2. *verb* To make something muddy or unclear.
▷ **muddies, muddying, muddied**

mud·guard (muhd-gard) *noun* A guard placed over the wheel of a bicycle to keep the rider from getting splashed. *See* **motorcycle.**

muf·fin (muhf-uhn) *noun* A small cake or bread shaped like a cupcake.

muf·fle (muhf-uhl) *verb* To make a sound quieter or duller. *Hannah put a handkerchief over her mouth to muffle her laughter.* ▷ **muffling, muffled**

muf·fler (muhf-lur) *noun*
1. A device that reduces the noise made by an engine. *See* **car.**
2. A warm scarf.

mug (muhg)
1. *noun* A large, heavy cup with a handle.
2. *verb (informal)* To attack someone and try to steal the person's money. ▷ **mugging, mugged**
▷ *noun* **mugger**

mug·gy (muh-gee) *adjective* If the weather is **muggy,** it is warm and damp. ▷ **muggier, muggiest** ▷ *noun* **mugginess**

Mu·ham·mad (moo-ham-id) or **Mo·ham·mad** (moh-ham-id) *noun* The founder of the Islamic religion. Muslims believe that Muhammad is God's main prophet.

mul·ber·ry (muhl-ber-ee) *noun* A tree with edible, dark purple berries. Mulberry leaves are sometimes used as food for silkworms.

mule (myool) *noun*
1. An animal produced by mating a female horse with a male donkey.
2. A stubborn person.

mul·ti·cul·tur·al (muhl-ti-kuhl-chuh-ruhl) *adjective* Involving or made up of people from different races or religions, as in *a multicultural community.* ▷ *adverb* **multiculturally**

mul·ti·lin·gual (muhl-ti-ling-gwuhl) *adjective* Using or able to use several different languages. *Some translators are multilingual.*

mul·ti·me·di·a (muhl-ti-mee-dee-uh) *adjective* Using or combining different kinds of communication technologies, such as video and printed text. ▷ *noun* **multimedia**

mul·ti·na·tion·al (muhl-tee-nash-uhn-uhl) *noun* A company that has factories or offices in more than one country. ▷ *adjective* **multinational**

mul·ti·ple (muhl-tuh-puhl)
1. *adjective* Involving many parts or many things. *Theresa suffered multiple injuries.*
2. *noun* A number into which a smaller number can go an exact number of times. *The multiples of 5 are 0, 5, 10, 15, 20, etc.*
3. *adjective* A **multiple-choice** test gives you a number of answers for each question, from which you have to choose one.

multiple scle·ro·sis (skluh-roh-suhss) *noun* A serious disease in which small areas of the brain and spinal cord are destroyed. It causes paralysis and muscle tremors.

mul·ti·pli·cand (muhl-tuh-pluh-kand) *noun* A number that is to be multiplied by another number. In the problem 2 × 8, 2 is the multiplicand.

mul·ti·pli·er (mul-tuh-plye-ur) *noun* The number by which you multiply another. In the problem 2 × 8, 8 is the multiplier.

mul·ti·ply (muhl-tuh-plye) *verb*
1. To add the same number to itself several times. *If you multiply 3 times 4, you get 12.*

M

2. To grow in number or amount. *The weeds keep multiplying.*
▷ *verb* **multiplies, multiplying, multiplied** ▷ *noun* **multiplication**

mul·ti·ra·cial (*muhl*-tee-ray-shuhl) *adjective* Involving people of different races, as in *a multiracial community.* ▷ *adverb* **multiracially**

mul·ti·tude (*muhl*-ti-tood) *noun*
1. A crowd of people.
2. A large number of things. *The new club offers a multitude of activities.*
▷ *adjective* **multitudinous**

mum·ble (*muhm*-buhl) *verb* To speak quietly and unclearly, with the mouth closed. ▷ **mumbling, mumbled**

mum·my (*muh*-mee) *noun* A dead body that has been preserved with special salts and resins and wrapped in cloth to make it last for a very long time. The ancient Egyptians placed the mummies of their rulers in elaborate coffins. *The illustration shows Tutankhamun's mummy and the three coffins that held it. The large picture shows the second coffin in more detail.*
▷ *noun, plural* **mummies** ▷ *verb* **mummify**
▷ *adjective* **mummified**

mumps (muhmps) *noun, plural* An infectious illness caused by a virus that makes the glands at the sides of your face swell up and become sore. The word mumps can be used with a singular or a plural verb.

munch (muhnch) *verb* To chew with a crunching sound. *We munched on carrots.* ▷ **munches, munching, munched**

mun·dane (muhn-dayn) *adjective* Boring and ordinary. *His mundane life seemed to consist of nothing but working, eating, and sleeping.*

mu·nic·i·pal (myoo-niss-uh-puhl) *adjective* To do with a city or town and its services. *The mayor promised that all municipal workers would receive a raise in pay.*

mu·ral (myu-ruhl) *noun* A painting on a wall.

mur·der (mur-dur) *verb* To kill someone deliberately. ▷ **murdering, murdered** ▷ *noun* **murder,** *noun* **murderer**

murk·y (mur-kee) *adjective* Dark, cloudy, or gloomy. *The murky waters of the river hid the sunken boat from our view.* ▷ **murkier, murkiest**

M

mummy and coffins of Tutankhamun

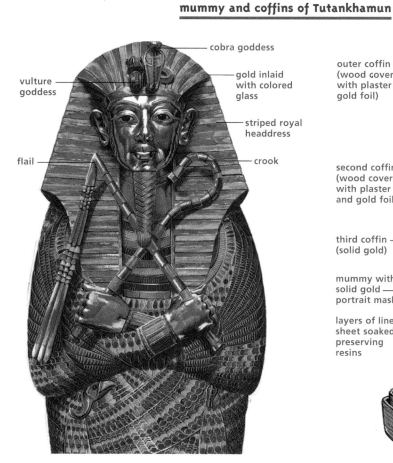

vulture goddess
cobra goddess
gold inlaid with colored glass
striped royal headdress
flail
crook

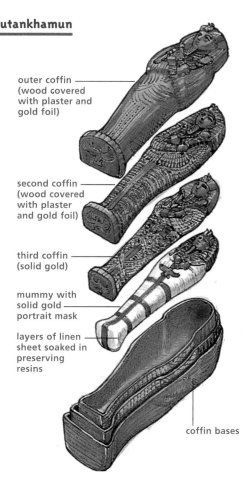

outer coffin (wood covered with plaster and gold foil)

second coffin (wood covered with plaster and gold foil)

third coffin (solid gold)

mummy with solid gold portrait mask

layers of linen sheet soaked in preserving resins

coffin bases

mur·mur (mur-mur) *verb*
1. To talk very quietly.
2. To make a quiet, low, continuous sound. *The wind murmured in the trees.*
▷ *verb* **murmuring, murmured** ▷ *noun* **murmur**

mus·cle (muhss-uhl) *noun*
1. One of the parts of your body that produces movement. Your muscles are attached to your skeleton and pull on your bones to make them move. *The diagram shows the muscles that move your arm.*
2. Strength or power. *This job requires muscle.* **Muscle** sounds like **mussel.**

upper arm muscles

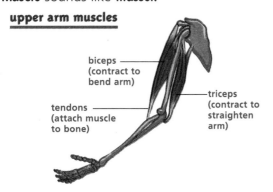

biceps (contract to bend arm)

tendons (attach muscle to bone)

triceps (contract to straighten arm)

muse (myooz) *verb* To think deeply or to reflect. *Before going to sleep, I like to muse on the events of the day.* ▷ **musing, mused** ▷ *noun* **musing**

mu·se·um (myoo-zee-uhm) *noun* A place where interesting objects of art, history, or science are displayed.

mush (muhsh) *noun*
1. A thick cereal made with cornmeal boiled in water or milk.
2. A thick, soft mass. *The snow soon turned to mush.*

mush·room (muhsh-room *or* muhsh-rum)
1. *noun* A small fungus that is usually shaped like an umbrella. Many mushrooms can be eaten, but some are poisonous.
2. *verb* To grow or spread quickly. *New housing developments have mushroomed around the town.* ▷ **mushrooming, mushroomed**

mu·sic (myoo-zik) *noun*
1. A pleasant arrangement of sounds, such as in a song.
2. The art of combining sounds in a pleasing way.
3. Printed or written signs or notes that represent musical sounds. *Can you read music?* See **notation.**

mu·si·cal (myoo-zuh-kuhl)
1. *adjective* If you are **musical,** you are very interested in music or you can play an instrument well. ▷ *adverb* **musically**

2. *adjective* To do with music, as in *musical instruments.*
3. *noun* A play or movie that includes singing and dancing.
4. *adjective* Pleasing to the ear. *We heard the musical sounds of children's laughter.*

musical instrument *noun* An instrument on which you can play music. *See* **brass, percussion, strings, woodwind.**

mu·si·cian (myoo-zish uhn) *noun* Someone who plays, sings, or composes music.

musk (muhsk) *noun* A substance with a strong odor, produced by some male deer, that is used in perfume, medicine, and soap.

mus·ket (muhss-kit) *noun* A gun with a long barrel that was used before the rifle was invented.

mus·ket·eer (*muhss*-kuh-**tihr**) *noun* A soldier who carried a musket.

musk·rat (muhsk-*rat*) *noun* A small, North American rodent with webbed hind feet, a flat tail, and thick, brown fur. Muskrats live in and around water. ▷ *noun, plural* **muskrat** *or* **muskrats**

Mus·lim (muhz-luhm) *or* **Mos·lem** (moz-luhm) *noun* Someone who follows the religion of Islam. ▷ *adjective* **Muslim** *or* **Moslem**

mus·lin (muhz-luhn) *noun* A cotton fabric used to make sheets, curtains, and clothing.

mus·sel (muhss-uhl) *noun* A type of shellfish that you can eat. **Mussel** sounds like **muscle.**

mussel

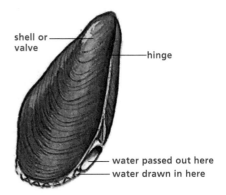

shell or valve

hinge

water passed out here

water drawn in here

must (muhst)
1. *verb* To have to do something. *I must go before the rain starts.*
2. *verb* To be forced or required to do something. *People must eat to survive.*
3. *verb* To be definitely doing something. *He must be lying.*
4. *noun* Something that you need. *This book is a must.*

mus·tache *or* **mous·tache** (muh-**stash** *or* muhss-*tash*) *noun* The hair that grows on a person's upper lip.

mus·tang (muhss-tang) *noun* A wild horse found mostly on the western plains of the United States. Mustangs are descended from horses brought to America by the Spaniards.

mustang

mus·tard (muhss-turd) *noun* A spicy paste or powder made from the pungent seeds of the mustard plant.

mus·ter (muhss-tur) *verb*
1. To assemble in a group. *The soldiers mustered in the field.*
2. To gather something together. *Jackie mustered all her strength for the final lap.*
▷ *verb* **mustering, mustered**

must·n't (muhss-uhnt) *contraction* A short form of *must not. We mustn't forget to bring Grandpa his birthday present.*

must·y (muhss-tee) *adjective* If something or someplace is **musty,** it smells of dampness, decay, or mold. ▷ **mustier, mustiest** ▷ *noun* **mustiness**

mu·tant (myoot-uhnt) *noun* A living thing that has developed different characteristics because of a change in its parents' genes. ▷ *noun* **mutation** ▷ *verb* **mutate**

mute (myoot)
1. *adjective* Silent, or unable to speak. ▷ *adverb* **mutely**
2. *noun* Someone who cannot speak.
3. *noun* Something that can be fitted to a musical instrument to make it play more softly. ▷ *verb* **mute**

mu·ti·late (myoo-tuh-*late*) *verb* To injure or damage something or someone seriously. *The storm mutilated the store's awning.*
▷ **mutilating, mutilated** ▷ *noun* **mutilation**

mu·ti·ny (myoot-uh-nee) *noun* A revolt against someone in charge, especially in the navy.
▷ *noun, plural* **mutinies** ▷ *noun* **mutineer**
▷ *verb* **mutiny** ▷ *adjective* **mutinous**

mutt (muht) *noun* A dog of mixed breed.

mut·ter (muht-ur) *verb* To speak in a low, unclear way with the mouth nearly closed. *Wayne angrily muttered his complaints.* ▷ **muttering, muttered** ▷ *noun* **mutter**

mut·ton (muht-uhn) *noun* Meat from a sheep.

mu·tu·al (myoo-choo-uhl) *adjective* Shared or joint, as in *a mutual friend.* ▷ *adverb* **mutually**

muz·zle (muhz-uhl) *noun*
1. An animal's nose, mouth, and jaws. See **dog, reindeer.**
2. A cover for an animal's mouth to keep it from biting. ▷ *verb* **muzzle**
3. The open end of a gun barrel.

my (mye) *adjective* Belonging to or having to do with me. *My work is done.*

my·nah or **my·na** (mye-nuh) *noun* A dark brown bird originally found in Asia that is known for its ability to imitate the human voice.

my·ri·ad (mihr-ee-uhd) *noun* A large number. *As we entered the hall, we were dazzled by a myriad of lights.* ▷ *adjective* **myriad**

my·self (*mye*-self) *pronoun* Me and no one else. *I have hurt myself.*

mys·te·ri·ous (miss-tihr-ee-uhss) *adjective* Very hard to explain or understand, as in *a mysterious stranger.* ▷ *adverb* **mysteriously**

mys·ter·y (miss-tur-ee) *noun*
1. Something that is hard to explain or understand. *It is a mystery to me how you can be so cruel.*
2. A story containing a puzzling crime that has to be solved, as in *a murder mystery.*
▷ *noun, plural* **mysteries**

mys·ti·fy (miss-tuh-fye) *verb* To puzzle or confuse someone. *The magician mystified his audience.* ▷ **mystifies, mystifying, mystified**
▷ *noun* **mystification**

myth (mith) *noun*
1. A story that expresses the beliefs of a group of people, tells about gods or goddesses, or gives reasons for something that happens in nature, such as thunder.
2. A false idea that many people believe. *It is a myth that porcupines shoot their quills.*

myth·i·cal (mith-i-kuhl) *adjective*
1. To do with myths. *The unicorn is a mythical creature.*
2. Imaginary or not real, as in *a mythical community of aliens.*

my·thol·o·gy (mi-thol-uh-jee) *noun* A collection of myths. ▷ *noun, plural* **mythologies** ▷ *adjective* **mythological**

About N

Spelling Hint: Some words that begin with an n- sound are spelled *gn, kn,* or *pn.* Examples: gnat, gnash, knead, knight, pneumatic, pneumonia.

nag (nag)
1. *verb* To annoy by scolding, complaining, or criticizing all the time. *My parents sometimes nag me about my messy room.* ▷ **nagging, nagged**
2. *noun* A horse, especially one that is old or worn-out.

nail (nayl) *noun*
1. A small, pointed piece of metal that you hammer into something. ▷ *verb* **nail**
2. The hard covering at the ends of your fingers and toes.

na·ive or **na·ïve** (nah-eev) *adjective* If you are **naive,** you are not very experienced and may believe or trust people too much. ▷ **naiver, naivest** ▷ *noun* **naiveté** or **naïveté** (nah-eev-tay) ▷ *adverb* **naively**

na·ked (nay-kid) *adjective*
1. Wearing no clothing. ▷ *noun* **nakedness** ▷ *adverb* **nakedly**
2. Bare or without the usual covering, as in *a naked branch.*
3. Without anything added, as in *the naked truth.*
4. Without the aid of a telescope or other optical instrument. *You can't see the planet Pluto with the naked eye.*

name (naym)
1. *noun* What a person, an animal, a place, or a thing is called. *What is your name?* ▷ *verb* **name**
2. *noun* A bad or insulting word or phrase used to describe a person or thing. *I ignored the class bully when he called me names.*
3. *noun* Reputation. *The bully's constant fighting has given him a bad name.*
4. *verb* To speak of or to mention. *Name your favorite color.*
5. *verb* To choose or to appoint. *The mayor named a new police commissioner.*
▷ *verb* **naming, named**

nan·ny (nan-ee) *noun*
1. Someone trained to look after young children in the children's home.
2. A female goat.
3. *(informal)* Grandmother.
▷ *noun, plural* **nannies**

nap (nap)
1. *verb* To sleep for a short time. ▷ **napping, napped** ▷ *noun* **nap**
2. *noun* The soft, fuzzy surface on certain kinds of cloth.

nape (nape) *noun* The back of your neck.

nap·kin (nap-kin) *noun* A square piece of paper or cloth used to protect clothes while eating and to wipe hands and lips.

nar·cis·sist (nar-si-sist) *noun* Someone who is overly interested in his or her own looks or body. *Jim spends all his time looking at himself in the mirror; he's such a narcissist.* ▷ *noun* **narcissism** ▷ *adjective* **narcissistic**

nar·cis·sus (nar-siss-uhss) *noun* A plant that grows from a bulb and has yellow or white flowers and long, thin leaves. The daffodil is a kind of narcissus. ▷ *noun, plural* **narcissuses** or **narcissus**

nar·cot·ic (nar-kot-ik) *noun* An often addictive drug that can be prescribed by a doctor to relieve pain. ▷ *adjective* **narcotic**

nar·rate (na-rate or na-rate) *verb* To tell a story. ▷ **narrating, narrated** ▷ *noun* **narration,** *noun* **narrator**

nar·ra·tive (na-ruh-tiv)
1. *noun* A story, or an account of something that has happened.
2. *adjective* Telling a story, as in *a narrative poem.*

nar·row (na-roh) *adjective*
1. Not broad or wide, as in *a narrow street.* ▷ *verb* **narrow**
2. Limited, or small. *She has a narrow circle of friends.*
3. If you have a **narrow** escape, you only just get away.
4. If you are **narrow-minded,** you stick to your own ideas and do not want to listen to new ones.
▷ *adjective* **narrower, narrowest** ▷ *noun* **narrowness** ▷ *adverb* **narrowly**

na·sal (nay-zuhl) *adjective*
1. To do with your nose, as in *nasal congestion.*
2. Spoken through the nose rather than the mouth. *M, n,* and *ng* are nasal sounds.

nas·tur·tium (nuh-stur-shuhm) *noun* A plant with yellow, red, or orange flowers that are sometimes eaten in salads.

nas·ty (nass-tee) *adjective*
1. Cruel or unkind. ▷ *adverb* **nastily**
2. Very unpleasant, as in *cold, nasty weather.*
3. Harmful or severe, as in *a nasty fall.*
▷ *noun* **nastiness** ▷ *adjective* **nastier, nastiest**

na·tion (nay-shuhn) *noun* A large group of people who live in the same part of the world and often share the same language, customs, and government.

na·tion·al (nash-uh-nuhl) *adjective* To do with, belonging to, or characteristic of a nation as a whole, as in *a national library* or *a national costume.* ▷ *adverb* **nationally**

National Guard *noun* A volunteer military organization with units in each state of the United States. Each National Guard unit is under the control of the governor of the state. However, the president can take command of the National Guard during a state of war or emergency.

na·tion·al·ist (nash-uh-nuh-list) *noun* Someone who is proud of his or her country or who fights for its independence. ▷ *noun* **nationalism** ▷ *adjective* **nationalistic**

na·tion·al·i·ty (nash-uh-nal-uh-tee) *noun*
1. Your **nationality** is the status you have in a country by having been born there or by becoming a citizen.
2. A group of people who share a common language, culture, and history. *America is a land of many nationalities.*
▷ *noun, plural* **nationalities**

na·tion·al·ize (nash-uh-nuh-*lize*) *verb* If an industry is **nationalized,** its ownership is transferred from a private company to the government. ▷ **nationalizing, nationalized** ▷ *noun* **nationalization**

national park *noun* A large section of land set aside by the government for public use. *The picture shows Grand Canyon National Park in Arizona.*

Grand Canyon National Park

na·tive (nay-tiv)
1. *noun* Someone born in a particular place. *Warren is a native of New Hampshire.*
2. *noun* A person, an animal, or a plant that originally lived or grew in a certain place. *The kangaroo is a native of Australia.*
3. *adjective* Belonging to a person because of where he or she was born. *Japanese is my grandmother's native language.*
4. Your **native country** is the country where you were born.
▷ *adjective* **native**

Native American *noun* One of the original inhabitants of North, Central, or South America or a descendant of these. Native Americans are sometimes called **American Indians**. ▷ *adjective* **Native American**

> ### ▶ Language Note
>
> Many people now use **Native American** instead of *Indian* or *American Indian* because Native American corrects a mistake originally made by Christopher Columbus in naming the peoples he found living in the New World. Native American also sets apart the peoples originally living in North, Central, and South America from those in India. In addition, many writers use Native American when they want to emphasize ethnic pride.
>
> The terms *Indian* and *American Indian* are neither old-fashioned nor offensive to Native Americans. For a very long time, *Indian* has been an important part of expressions such as *Indian summer* (the warm weather in late fall) and *Indian pony* (a small, very sturdy horse). *Indian* is also used in terms such as *Indian paintbrush* (a wildflower with brightly colored flowers) and *Indian pudding* (pudding made from cornmeal, molasses, and milk). *American Indian* is part of expressions such as *American Indian art.*

Na·tiv·i·ty (nuh-**tiv**-uh-tee *or* nay-**tiv**-uh-tee) *noun* The birth of Jesus, or a display or scene commemorating it.

NATO (nay-toh) *noun* A group of countries, including the United States and Britain, that help each other defend themselves. NATO stands for *North Atlantic Treaty Organization.*

nat·u·ral (nach-ur-uhl)
1. *adjective* Found in or produced by nature rather than being artificial or made by people, as in *natural rock formations.*
2. *adjective* Normal or usual. *It's only natural to need a rest after a long run.*
3. *adjective* Present from birth rather than being learned. *She is a natural athlete.*
4. *adjective* Lifelike or closely following nature. *The flowers in the painting look very natural.*
5. *adjective* Not faked or not forced. *She spoke in a sincere and natural manner.*
6. *noun* A person who is good at something because of a special talent or ability. *Martina is a natural at tennis.*
7. *adjective* In music, a **natural** note is one that is not sharp or flat.
8. *adjective* In a musical score, a **natural** sign shows that the next note is natural. *See* **notation.**
▷ *noun* **natural** ▷ *adverb* **naturally**

N

natural gas *noun* A gas that is found beneath the earth's surface. It consists mainly of methane and is used for heating and cooling.

natural history *noun* The study of animals and plants.

na·tu·ral·ist (nach-ur-uh-list) *noun* Someone who studies animals and plants.

nat·u·ral·ize (nach-ur-uh-*lize*) *verb* To give citizenship to someone who was born in another country. ▷ **naturalizing, naturalized**

natural resource *noun* A material found in nature that is necessary or useful to people. Forests, water, and minerals are some natural resources.

na·ture (nay-chur) *noun*
1. Everything in the world that is not made by people, such as plants, animals, the weather, etc.
2. The character of someone or something. *Trevor has a very generous nature. Stories of a scary nature don't interest me.*

naught (nawt) *noun*
1. Nothing. *All our plans came to naught.*
2. Zero. *Four minus naught equals four.*

naught·y (naw-tee) *adjective* Badly behaved, or disobedient. ▷ **naughtier, naughtiest** ▷ *noun* **naughtiness** ▷ *adverb* **naughtily**

nau·se·a (naw-zee-uh *or* naw-zhuh) *noun* A feeling of being sick to your stomach. ▷ *adjective* **nauseous** (naw-shuhss), *adjective* **nauseated**

nau·ti·cal (naw-tuh-kuhl)
1. *adjective* To do with ships, sailing, or navigation.
2. **nautical mile** *noun* A unit for measuring distance at sea or in the air. One nautical mile equals 6,076 feet.

Na·va·jo *or* **Na·va·ho** (nav-uh-hoh) *noun* One of a group of American Indians that lives primarily in New Mexico, Arizona, and Utah. ▷ *noun, plural* **Navajo, Navajos** *or* **Navaho, Navahos**

na·val (nay-vuhl) *adjective* To do with a navy or warships. **Naval** sounds like **navel.**

na·vel (nay-vuhl) *noun* The small, round hollow in your stomach where your umbilical cord was attached when you were born. **Navel** sounds like **naval.**

nav·i·gate (nav-uh-gate) *verb*
1. To travel in a ship, an aircraft, or other vehicle using maps, compasses, the stars, etc., to guide you. *Sextants like the one above were used to navigate at sea in the 18th and 19th centuries. They helped the navigator work out the ship's position on a map by measuring the angle between the sun and the horizon or the angle between stars.*

2. To sail on or across. *We navigated the river on a rubber raft.*
▷ *verb* **navigating, navigated** ▷ *noun* **navigation,** *noun* **navigator**

sextant
mirror, index sunshade, telescope, index arm (movable arm), viewing window, horizon- and sun-viewing glass, handle, magnifying glass, arc

na·vy (nay-vee) *noun* The entire military sea force of a country, including ships, aircraft, weapons, land bases, and people. ▷ *noun, plural* **navies**

navy blue *noun* A very dark blue color. ▷ *adjective* **navy blue**

Na·zi (not-see *or* nat-see) *noun*
1. A member of the group, led by Adolf Hitler, that ruled Germany from 1933 to 1945. Nazis attempted to rid the human race of people they considered "impure" by killing millions of Jews, Gypsies, and other peoples from eastern Europe. They fought World War II to try to spread their beliefs around the world.
2. **nazi** *or* **Nazi** A person with beliefs similar to those of the Nazis, especially a cruel, violently racist person.
▷ *adjective* **Nazi** *or* **nazi**

near (nihr)
1. *preposition* Close to. *Alex lives near me.*
2. *adverb* Close. *Don't come near.* ▷ *adjective* **near**
3. *verb* To come closer to something. *The train neared the station.* ▷ **nearing, neared**
4. *adjective* Narrow or close. *We had a near escape from the fire.*
5. *adjective* Closely related or associated. *My aunt is my nearest relative.*
▷ *noun* **nearness** ▷ *adjective and adverb* **nearer, nearest**

near·by (nihr-bye) *adjective* Not far away. *My cousins live in a nearby town.* ▷ *adverb* **nearby**

near·ly (nihr-lee) *adverb* Almost or not quite. *We are nearly home.*

near·sight·ed (nihr-sye-tid) *adjective* Able to see nearby objects more clearly than faraway ones.

N

neat (neet) *adjective*
1. Orderly and clean. ▷ *noun* **neatness**
2. Done in a clever or skillful way. *Hector did a neat job of solving the mystery.*
▷ *adjective* **neater, neatest** ▷ *adverb* **neatly**

neb·u·la (neb-yuh-luh) *noun* A bright, cloudlike mass that can be seen in the night sky. Nebulae are made up of stars or gases and dust. ▷ *noun, plural* **nebulae** (neb-yuh-*lee* or neb-yuh-*lye*) or **nebulas**

nec·es·sar·y (ness-uh-ser-ee) *adjective* If something is **necessary,** you have to do it or have it. ▷ *adverb* **necessarily**

ne·ces·si·ty (nuh-sess-uh-tee) *noun*
1. A very strong need or requirement. *Necessity made us ask for help.*
2. Necessities are the things you cannot live without, such as food and shelter.

neck (nek) *noun*
1. The part of your body that joins your head to your shoulders.
2. The narrow part of a garment that fits around your neck.
3. A narrow part of something, as in *the neck of a bottle.*

neck·er·chief (nek-ur-*cheef* or nek-ur-chif) *noun* A scarf or square of cloth worn around the neck.

neck·lace (nek-liss) *noun* A piece of jewelry worn around the neck.

neck·tie (nek-*tye*) *noun* A long, narrow strip of cloth that is tied around the neck and knotted. A necktie is worn under a shirt collar, usually with suits or jackets.

nec·tar (nek-tur) *noun* A sweet liquid that bees collect from flowers and turn into honey.

nec·tar·ine (*nek*-tuh-**reen**) *noun* A fruit similar to a peach but with a smooth skin.

need (need)
1. *verb* To want or require something urgently. *The refugees need food and shelter.*
2. *noun* Something that you have to have. *Food, clothing, and shelter are basic needs.*
3. *verb* To have to do something. *I need to practice for the concert tomorrow.*
4. *noun* A necessity or an obligation. *There is no need for you to shout.*
5. *noun* Poverty or hardship. *The beggar lived in need.*
Need sounds like **knead.**
▷ *verb* **needing, needed**

nee·dle (nee-duhl)
1. *noun* A thin, pointed piece of metal with a hole for thread at one end, used for sewing. *See* **pin.**
2. *noun* A long, thin, pointed rod used for knitting.
3. *noun* A thin, hollow tube with a sharp point

that doctors use for injections or taking blood.
4. *noun* A pointer on an instrument such as a compass. *See* **compass.**
5. *noun* A very thin, pointed leaf on a fir tree or pine tree.
6. *verb* (*informal*) If someone **needles** you, the person annoys you. ▷ **needling, needled**

need·less (need-liss) *adjective* If something is **needless,** it is not necessary. *Buying a new stereo would be a needless expense.* ▷ *adverb* **needlessly**

nee·dle·work (need-uhl-*wurk*) *noun* Work that is done with a needle, such as embroidery or lace.

needlework

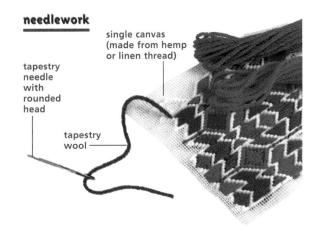

single canvas (made from hemp or linen thread)

tapestry needle with rounded head

tapestry wool

need·n't (need-uhnt) *contraction* A short form of *need not. We needn't worry about the storm because the weather forecast has changed.*

need·y (nee-dee) *adjective* Very poor or in need.
▷ **needier, neediest**

neg·a·tive (neg-uh-tiv)
1. *adjective* Giving the answer "no." *I asked Bill if he wanted to eat, but his reply was negative.*
2. *adjective* If someone has a **negative** attitude, that person is not optimistic or helpful. ▷ *adverb* **negatively**
3. *noun* A photographic film used to make prints. A negative shows light areas as dark and dark areas as light.
4. *adjective* A **negative** number is less than zero.
5. *adjective* Having one of two opposite kinds of electrical charge.
6. *adjective* Showing that a disease or condition is not present. *The allergy tests were negative.*
▷ *noun* **negative**

neg·lect (ni-glekt)
1. *verb* To fail to take care of someone or something. ▷ *adjective* **neglectful**
2. *verb* To fail to do something, especially from carelessness. *She neglected to turn off the iron.*
3. *noun* If a person, building, etc., is suffering from **neglect,** it has not been looked after properly.
▷ *verb* **neglecting, neglected**

neg·li·gent (neg-luh-juhnt) *adjective* Careless or not attentive to one's duties. *The negligent driver did not stop at the light.* ▷ *noun* **negligence**

ne·go·ti·ate (ni-**goh**-shee-ate *or* ni-**goh**-see-ate) *verb* To bargain or discuss something so that you can come to an agreement. *The baseball players and owners negotiated an end to the strike.* ▷ **negotiating, negotiated** ▷ *noun* **negotiation,** *noun* **negotiator**

Ne·gro (**nee**-groh) *noun* A member of a race of people with dark skin, hair, and eyes, thought to have come originally from central and southern Africa. *See* **African American.** ▷ *noun, plural* **Negroes**

neigh (nay) *noun* The sound that a horse makes. ▷ *verb* **neigh**

neigh·bor (**nay**-bur) *noun*
1. Someone who lives next door to you or near to you.
2. A person, place, or thing that is next to or near another. *Canada and the United States are neighbors.*
3. Another human being. *Love thy neighbor.*

neigh·bor·hood (**nay**-bur-*hud*) *noun*
1. Your **neighborhood** is the local area around your house.
2. In a city or town, a small area or section where people live. *I grew up in an Italian-American neighborhood.*

nei·ther (**nee**-THur *or* **nye**-THur)
1. *adjective* Not either. *Neither one of my brothers likes spinach.*
2. *pronoun* Not either one. *Bob and Alice cheated; neither played fairly.*
3. *conjunction* Nor. *My brother doesn't like spinach, and neither do I.*
4. *conjunction* Used with **nor** to show two negative choices or possibilities. *Neither Mark nor David is home.*

ne·on (**nee**-on) *noun* A colorless, odorless gas that glows when an electric current is passed through it. Neon is used in lights and signs.

neph·ew (**nef**-yoo) *noun* Someone's **nephew** is the son of his or her brother, sister, brother-in-law, or sister-in-law.

Nep·tune (**nep**-toon) *noun* The eighth planet in distance from the sun. Neptune is the fourth-largest planet in our solar system. *See* **planet.**

nerd (nurd) *noun (slang)* A person who is considered unattractive or clumsy but who also has the reputation of being very smart or expert at something, as in *a computer nerd.* ▷ *adjective* **nerdy**

nerve (nurv) *noun*
1. A **nerve** is one of the thin fibers that send messages between your brain or spinal cord and other parts of your body so that you can move and feel.
2. Courage. *You need lots of nerve to be a lion tamer.*
3. *(informal)* Boldness or rudeness. *Harry's got a lot of nerve, answering back like that!*
4. *noun, plural (informal)* If someone suffers from **nerves,** he or she is worried or frightened.

nerv·ous (**nur**-vuhss)
1. *adjective* Easily upset or tense. *Thunder and lightning make me nervous.*
2. *adjective* Fearful or timid. *I am nervous about my doctor's appointment.*
3. *adjective* To do with the nerves, as in *nervous energy.*
4. *noun* If someone has a **nervous breakdown,** the person becomes very depressed and feels unable to cope with his or her problems.
▷ *noun* **nervousness** ▷ *adverb* **nervously**

nervous system *noun* A system in the body that includes the brain, spinal cord, and nerves. In vertebrates, the nervous system controls all the actions of the body.

> ### Suffix
> •
> The suffix **-ness** adds the following meaning to a root word: Quality or state, as in *goodness* (the quality of being good) and *happiness* (the state of being happy).

nest (nest)
1. *noun* A place built by birds and many other animals to lay their eggs and/or bring up their young. *Wasps' nests are built by a queen wasp from wood that has been chewed up and mixed with saliva. The queen lays her eggs in the cells, and the eggs develop into worker wasps that enlarge and strengthen the nest.*
2. *verb* To make or settle in a nest or home. ▷ **nesting, nested**
3. *noun* A cozy place or shelter.

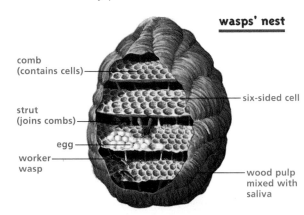

wasps' nest

comb (contains cells)
strut (joins combs)
egg
worker wasp
six-sided cell
wood pulp mixed with saliva

nes·tle (ness-uhl) *verb* To settle into a comfortable position. *The baby nestled against her mother's shoulder.* ▷ **nestling, nestled**

net (net)
1. *noun* Material made from fine threads or ropes that are knotted together with holes in between them.
2. *noun* A bag made from such material that is attached to a pole and used to catch fish, butterflies, etc.
3. *verb* To catch with or as if with a net. *We netted five trout on our fishing trip.*
4. *noun* A **net amount** of money is the amount left after everything necessary, such as taxes and expenses, has been taken away.
5. *noun* The **net weight** of something is its weight without packaging.

net·tle (net-uhl) *noun* A weed with sharp hairs that sting you if you touch them.

net·work (net-*wurk*)
1. *noun* A large number of lines forming a crisscross pattern, as in *a network of railroad tracks.*
2. *noun* A system of things that are connected to each other, as in *a television network.*
3. *verb* To connect computers so that they can work together. ▷ **networking, networked** ▷ *noun* **network**
4. *noun* A group of people who exchange professional or social information with each other. ▷ *verb* **network** ▷ *noun* **networking**

neu·rot·ic (nu-rot-ik) *adjective* If someone is **neurotic,** the person is very scared or worried, usually about something imaginary. ▷ *adverb* **neurotically**

neu·ter (noo-tur)
1. *adjective* Neither masculine nor feminine.
2. *adjective* In some languages, nouns that are neither masculine nor feminine in gender are **neuter.** In English, the pronoun *it* refers to neuter nouns, such as *table.*

neu·tral (noo-truhl)
1. *adjective* If a country or a person is **neutral** in a war or an argument, it does not support either side. *Switzerland usually stays neutral when its neighbors are at war.* ▷ *noun* **neutrality** ▷ *adverb* **neutrally**
2. *noun* When a car is in **neutral,** the gears are arranged so that they cannot pass on power to the wheels.
3. *adjective* **Neutral** colors are pale and not colorful. *Laura wears neutral colors, such as beige and gray.*
4. *adjective* In chemistry, a **neutral** substance is neither an acid nor a base.

neu·tral·ize (noo-truh-*lize*) *verb* To stop something from working or from having an effect. *The medicine quickly neutralized the poison.* ▷ **neutralizing, neutralized**

neu·tron (noo-tron) *noun* One of the extremely small parts in the nucleus of an atom. The neutron has no electrical charge. See **atom.**

nev·er (nev-ur) *adverb* At no time or not ever. *I have never been to the North Pole.*

nev·er·the·less (nev-ur-THuh-less) *adverb* In spite of that; yet. *Eduardo was cold and hungry; nevertheless, he kept on walking.*

new (noo) *adjective*
1. Just made or begun.
2. Seen, known, or thought of for the first time. *The astronomer discovered a new star.*
3. Unfamiliar or strange. *The teacher saw many new faces in his class.*
4. Not yet used to or experienced at. *Marva is new to driving.*
5. Recently arrived or established in a place, position, relationship, or role. *The new student felt lonely and out of place.*
6. Not yet worn or used. *I bought a new pair of sneakers.*
7. Repeating or beginning again, as in *a new year.*
8. Taking the place of one that came before. *Our new librarian is stricter than our old one.*
New sounds like **gnu** and **knew.**
▷ *adjective* **newer, newest**

new·born (noo-*born*) *adjective*
1. Recently born, as in *a newborn baby.* ▷ *noun* **newborn**
2. Fresh or renewed. *After taking a walk, I attacked my math assignment with newborn determination.*

new·com·er (noo-*kuhm*-ur) *noun* Someone who has just come to a place. *Eric was a newcomer to our school last year, but now he's running for class president.*

New Eng·land (ing-gluhnd) *noun* A region of the northeastern United States made up of six states: Maine, New Hampshire, Vermont, Massachusetts, Rhode Island, and Connecticut.

news (nooz) *noun* Fresh or recent information or facts. *The news about the elections was exciting.*

news·cast (nooz-kast) *noun* A television or radio program that presents the news. ▷ *noun* **newscaster**

news·pa·per (nooz-*pay*-pur) *noun* A publication made up of several pages of paper containing news reports, articles, letters, etc. Newspapers are usually published daily.

news·stand (nooz-stand) *noun* A place where newspapers and magazines and sometimes books and snacks are sold.

N

newt (noot) *noun*
A small salamander with short legs and a long tail that lives on land but lays its eggs in water.

marbled newt

New Testament *noun* A collection of writings that makes up the second section of the Christian Bible. It deals with the life and teachings of Jesus Christ and his disciples.

new·ton (noot-uhn) *noun* A unit used by physicists for measuring force.

New Year's Day *noun* January 1, a holiday celebrating the first day of the new year.

next (nekst)
1. *adjective* Immediately following. *We'll catch the next train.*
2. *adjective* Nearest or closest. *I live in the next house.*
3. *adverb* Immediately after. *They dropped us off next.*

next door *adverb* In or at the nearest house, building, etc. *We live next door.* ▷ *adjective* **next-door**

Nez Percé (nez purss) *noun* One of a group of American Indians that lives primarily in Washington, Oregon, and Idaho. French explorers called them Nez Percé, or "pierced nose," because they wore nose pendants.
▷ *noun, plural* **Nez Percé** or **Nez Percés**

nib·ble (nib-uhl) *verb* To bite something gently, or to take small bites of something. ▷ **nibbling, nibbled** ▷ *noun* **nibble**

nice (nisse) *adjective*
1. Pleasant. *I hope we have nice weather for the picnic.*
2. Kind. *It was nice of you to help.*
3. Polite. *It isn't nice to talk with your mouth full of food.*
▷ *adjective* **nicer, nicest** ▷ *adverb* **nicely**

Synonyms: nice

Nice is a word used to describe someone you like or something that makes you feel good: *We had a nice time at the party.* Nice is often used when a more specific word would be better. Here are some synonyms to help you say exactly what you mean:

Pleasing and **pleasant** both mean that something is agreeable and gives pleasure to someone: *The new wallpaper in our house has a pleasing effect. In this pleasant weather, we love to be outdoors.*

Delightful means that something or someone is highly pleasing: *Our visitor from England has a delightful sense of humor.*

Wonderful means that something or someone is terrific or nice to an unusual degree: *Johnny is the most wonderful friend a person could have.*

Fantastic also describes something that is much better than just nice: *Between going to the ball game and the beach, I had a fantastic day.*

niche (nich) *noun*
1. A hollow place in a wall that is often used to hold or display a statue.
2. A place, position, or situation for which someone is especially suited. *Richard can't seem to find his niche in school.*

nick (nik)
1. *noun* A small cut or chip on a surface or an edge. ▷ *verb* **nick**
2. If something happens **in the nick of time,** it happens at the last moment or just in time.

nick·el (nik-uhl) *noun*
1. A hard, silver-gray metal that is added to alloys to make them strong.
2. A coin of the United States equal to five cents.

nick·name (nik-name) *noun*
1. A descriptive name used with or instead of a person's real name. *Many left-handed pitchers have the nickname "Lefty."*
2. A familiar or shortened form of a name. *"Marty" is a nickname for "Martin."*
▷ *verb* **nickname**

Word History

The word **nickname** owes its current form to sloppy pronunciation. Nickname comes from the Old English word *ekename,* meaning "an extra name." After people said "an ekename" enough, it evolved into "a nekename" and then "a nickname."

nic·o·tine (nik-uh-teen) *noun* A poisonous and addictive substance found in tobacco.

niece (neess) *noun* Someone's **niece** is the daughter of his or her brother, sister, brother-in-law, or sister-in-law.

night (nite) *noun* The time between sunset and sunrise, when it is dark.

night·fall (nite-*fawl*) *noun* The period of time at dusk when the light of day is ending and night begins.

night·gown (nite-*goun*) *noun* A loose dress that girls or women wear in bed.

night·in·gale (nite-uhn-*gale*) *noun* A small, brown and white bird that lives in Europe and Asia. The male is known for its beautiful song.

night·ly (nite-lee) *adverb* Done or happening every night. *The doctor visits nightly.* ▷ *adjective* **nightly**

night·mare (nite-*mair*) *noun* A frightening or unpleasant dream or experience.

nim·ble (nim-buhl) *adjective* If you are **nimble**, you move quickly and lightly. ▷ **nimbler, nimblest** ▷ *adverb* **nimbly**

nine (nine) *noun* The whole number, written 9, that comes after 8 and before 10. ▷ *adjective* **nine**

nin·ja (nin-juh) *noun* A person who is highly trained in ancient Japanese martial arts, especially one hired as a spy or an assassin.

nip (nip) *verb*
1. To bite or pinch sharply but not hard. *The puppy nipped my fingers.*
2. To cut off by pinching. *I nipped the dead leaves off the plant.*
3. To sting, or to chill. *The freezing air nipped my ears.* ▷ *adjective* **nippy**
▷ *verb* **nipping, nipped** ▷ *noun* **nip**

nip·ple (nip-uhl) *noun*
1. The small, raised part at the center of a breast or an udder.
2. A small rubber cap with a hole, attached to the top of a baby's bottle.

ni·tro·gen (nye-truh-juhn) *noun* A colorless, odorless gas that makes up about four-fifths of the earth's air.

nits (nits) *noun, plural* Eggs laid by lice.

no (noh)
1. *adverb* Not so; a negative response to a question.
2. *adverb* Not at all. *The newborn kitten was no larger than a child's hand.*
3. *interjection* A word used to show surprise, wonder, or disbelief. *No! That can't be true!*
4. *adjective* Not any. *There was no hope.*
5. *adjective* Not a. *That guy is no friend of mine.*

6. *noun* A word used to show refusal or denial. *I thought I had a good idea, but it was met with a chorus of noes.*
7. *noun* A negative vote or voter.
No sounds like **know.**
▷ *noun, plural* **noes**

no. The abbreviation for **number.**

no·ble (noh-buhl) *adjective*
1. If someone is **noble,** the person acts in a way that is idealistic and considerate. ▷ *adverb* **nobly**
2. A **noble** family is aristocratic and of high rank.
▷ *noun* **noble,** *noun* **nobleman,** *noun* **noblewoman**
3. Impressive or magnificent in appearance, as in *a noble redwood tree.*
▷ *adjective* **nobler, noblest** ▷ *noun* **nobility** (noh-**bil**-i-tee)

no·bod·y (noh-*bod*-ee or noh-*buh*-dee)
1. *pronoun* Not a single person. *There was nobody there.*
2. *noun* If someone is a **nobody,** he or she is not considered to be important. ▷ *noun, plural* **nobodies**

noc·tur·nal (nok-tur-nuhl) *adjective*
1. To do with the night, or happening at night, as in *a nocturnal journey.* ▷ *adverb* **nocturnally**
2. A **nocturnal** animal is active at night. *The flying fox is a nocturnal animal.*

nocturnal flying fox

nod (nod) *verb*
1. To move your head up and down, especially to say yes.
2. To let the head fall forward with a quick motion, especially when you are sleepy.
3. To show or say something by nodding. *My father nodded his approval.*
4. To bend or to sway. *The flowers nodded in the breeze.*
▷ *verb* **nodding, nodded** ▷ *noun* **nod**

noise (noiz) *noun* A sound, especially a loud or unpleasant one. ▷ *noun* **noisiness**

nois·y (noi-zee) *adjective* Loud. ▷ **noisier, noisiest**
▷ *adverb* **noisily**

N

no·mad (noh-mad) *noun*
1. A member of a tribe that wanders around instead of living in one place. *The picture shows the camp of some Bedouin nomads.*
2. A person who wanders from place to place.
▷ *adjective* **nomadic**

nomads

nom·i·nate (nom-uh-nate) *verb* To suggest that someone would be the right person to do a job or to receive an honor. *I nominate George to be our team leader.* ▷ **nominating, nominated** ▷ *noun* **nomination**

nom·i·nee (nom-uh-nee) *noun* Someone who is chosen to run in an election, to fill a position, or to be considered for an award or an honor.

▶ Prefix

The prefix **non-** adds one of the following meanings to a root word:

1. Not, as in *nontoxic* (not toxic) and *nonfiction* (not fiction).

2. Lacking or without, as in *nonsense* (lacking sense) and *nonfat* (without fat).

If the root word is a proper noun, *non-* is added with a hyphen, as in *non-Catholic* (not Catholic) and *non-British* (not British).

none (nuhn)
1. *pronoun* No one or not one. *Many people accepted my invitation, but none came to my party.*
2. *pronoun* Not any or no part. *None of the birthday cake was left.*
3. *adverb* Not at all. *The rescue team arrived none too soon.*
None sounds like **nun.**

none·the·less (nuhn-THuh-less) *adverb* In spite of that. *Harriet fell off her horse three times; nonetheless, she completed the course.*

non·fic·tion (non-fik-shuhn) *noun* Writing that is not fiction, especially information about real things, people, and events. *Biographies are nonfiction.*

non·sense (non-senss) *noun*
1. If something is **nonsense,** it is silly or has no meaning.
2. Talk, writing, or behavior that is silly or annoying.
▷ *adjective* **nonsensical**

non·stop (non-stop) *adjective* Without any stops or breaks, as in *a nonstop flight from New York to Los Angeles.* ▷ *adverb* **nonstop**

noo·dle (noo-duhl) *noun* A flat strip of dried dough, usually made from flour, water, and eggs.

noon (noon) *noun* Twelve o'clock in the middle of the day.

no one *pronoun* Not a single person. *There was no one in the park.*

noose (nooss) *noun* A large loop at the end of a piece of rope that closes up as the rope is pulled.

nor (nor) *conjunction* And not. Nor is often used with **neither.** *Neither Judy nor I was able to go to school this week because we both had colds.*

nor·mal (nor-muhl)
1. *adjective* Usual or regular. *The normal time for my piano lesson is 5:00 P.M.*
2. *adjective* Healthy. *He has a normal heartbeat.*
3. *noun* The usual condition. *My appointment at the dentist took longer than normal.*
▷ *noun* **normality,** *noun* **normalcy** ▷ *adverb* **normally**

north (north)
1. *noun* One of the four main points of the compass. North is to your right when you face the direction where the sun sets. ▷ *adverb* **north**
2. North *noun* Any area or region lying in this direction.
3. the North *noun* In the United States, the region that is north of Maryland, the Ohio River, and Missouri, especially the states that fought against the Confederacy in the Civil War.
4. *adjective* To do with or existing in the north, as in *the north shore of the lake.* ▷ *adjective* **northern**

North A·mer·ic·a (uh-mer-i-kuh) *noun* The continent in the Western Hemisphere that includes the United States, Canada, Mexico, and Central America. ▷ *noun* **North American** ▷ *adjective* **North American**

North·east (north-eest) *noun* The area of the United States to the north and east, including New England, New York, and sometimes New Jersey and Pennsylvania.

Northern Hemisphere *noun* The half of the earth that is north of the equator.

northern lights *noun, plural* Colorful streams of light that appear at night in the far northern sky. Northern lights are also called the **aurora borealis.**

North Pole *noun* The most northern point on earth, located at the upper tip of the earth's axis. The North Pole is in the Arctic.

North Star *noun* A bright star in the northern sky located directly over the North Pole.

North·west (north-west) *noun* The area of the United States to the north and west that includes Washington, Oregon, and Idaho.

N

nose (nohz)
1. *noun* The part of your face that you use when you smell and breathe.
2. *noun* The pointed part at the front of some aircraft. *See* **aircraft.**
3. *verb* To move forward slowly and carefully. *The ship nosed toward the pier.* ▷ **nosing, nosed**

nose cone *noun* The front section of a missile, rocket, or jet engine that is shaped like a cone to reduce friction with the air. *See* **aircraft, jet engine.**

nosh (nosh)
1. *noun* A snack or a light meal. ▷ *noun, plural* **noshes**
2. *verb* To eat a snack. *We noshed on cheese and crackers until our cousins arrived.* ▷ **noshes, noshing, noshed** ▷ *noun* **nosher**

nos·tal·gic (noss-tal-jik) *adjective* People who are **nostalgic** like to think about the past and are sad because things have changed since then. ▷ *noun* **nostalgia** (noss-tal-juh) ▷ *adverb* **nostalgically**

nos·tril (noss-truhl) *noun* Your **nostrils** are the two openings in your nose through which you breathe and smell.

nos·y (noh-zee) *adjective* Someone who is **nosy** is too interested in things that do not concern him or her. ▷ **nosier, nosiest** ▷ *adverb* **nosily**

not (not) *adverb* At no time or in no way. *Not* is used to make a statement negative. *You may not go. It did not snow.* **Not** sounds like **knot.**

no·ta·ble (noh-tuh-buhl)
1. *adjective* Important, remarkable, or worthy of notice. *The director's first movie was a notable success.* ▷ *adverb* **notably**
2. *noun* An important or well-known person. *The mayor expected many notables at the annual town banquet.*

no·ta·tion (noh-tay-shuhn) *noun*
1. A series of signs or symbols used to represent elements in a system such as music or math. *An example of musical notation is shown here.*
2. A short note. *The book had notations in the margins.*

notch (noch) *noun*
1. A cut or nick shaped like a *V*. ▷ *verb* **notch**
2. A narrow opening between mountains.

note (noht)
1. *noun* A short letter or message. *Write me a note when you arrive.*
2. *noun* A word, phrase, or short sentence written down to remind you of something. *I took notes during the lecture.*
3. *noun* A piece of paper money.
4. *noun* A musical sound, or the symbol that represents it. *See* **notation.**
5. *verb* To notice a fact and pay attention to it. *Please note the price increase.*
6. *verb* To write something down. *I've noted your name in my book.*
▷ *verb* **noting, noted**

note·book (noht-*buk*) *noun*
1. A small pad or book of paper used for writing notes.
2. A very small portable computer.

noth·ing (nuhth-ing)
1. *pronoun* Not anything at all. *There was nothing in the cupboard.*
2. *pronoun* Not anything important. *I did nothing all weekend.*
3. *noun* Zero. *The final score was three to nothing.*

no·tice (noh-tiss)
1. *verb* To see something, or to become aware of it. *Did you notice the smell?* ▷ **noticing, noticed** ▷ *adjective* **noticeable** ▷ *adverb* **noticeably**
2. *noun* Attention or observation. *They escaped notice by hiding behind a tree.*
3. *noun* A written message put in a public place to tell people about something.
4. *noun* A warning or an announcement. *The enemy planes attacked without notice.*
5. If someone **gives notice,** the person notifies his or her employer that he or she will be leaving that job shortly.

N

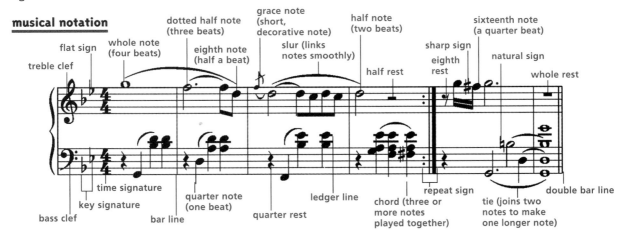

musical notation

treble clef · flat sign · whole note (four beats) · dotted half note (three beats) · eighth note (half a beat) · grace note (short, decorative note) · slur (links notes smoothly) · half note (two beats) · half rest · sharp sign · eighth rest · sixteenth note (a quarter beat) · natural sign · whole rest

bass clef · key signature · time signature · bar line · quarter note (one beat) · quarter rest · ledger line · chord (three or more notes played together) · repeat sign · tie (joins two notes to make one longer note) · double bar line

no·ti·fy (noh-tuh-fye) *verb* To tell someone about something officially or formally. *The hospital notified us about the test results.* ▷ **notifies, notifying, notified** ▷ *noun* **notification**

no·tion (noh-shun) *noun*
1. An idea. *I haven't the slightest notion why he said that.*
2. A desire or a whim. *I had a sudden notion to go on a picnic.*
3. notions *noun, plural* Small, useful items such as needles, pins, buttons, thread, and ribbons.

no·to·ri·ous (noh-tor-ee-uhss) *adjective* If someone is **notorious,** the person is well known for something bad. *The people across the hall are notorious for their loud parties.*

noun (noun) *noun* A word that names a person, place, or thing. *The words* dog, France, *and* happiness *are all nouns.*

nour·ish (nur-ish) *verb* To give a person or an animal enough food to keep him or her strong and healthy. ▷ **nourishes, nourishing, nourished** ▷ *noun* **nourishment** ▷ *adjective* **nourishing**

nov·el (nov-uhl)
1. *noun* A book that tells a long story about made-up people and events. ▷ *noun* **novelist**
2. *adjective* New and unusual, as in *a novel idea.*

nov·el·ty (nov-uhl-tee) *noun* Something new, interesting, and unusual. *Television was a novelty in the 1940s.* ▷ *noun, plural* **novelties** ▷ *adjective* **novelty**

No·vem·ber (noh-vem-bur) *noun* The eleventh month on the calendar, after October and before December. November has 30 days.

▶ Word History

November got its name from the Latin word *novem,* meaning "nine." November might seem like an odd name for the 11th month of the year. November started out as the 9th month, but then the Romans changed their ancient calendar. They decided to keep some of the old names, even though their positions on the calendar changed.

nov·ice (nov-iss) *noun*
1. A beginner or someone who is not very experienced. *Even though Gloria was a novice, she won the race.*
2. Someone who joins a religious order for a trial period before taking vows.

now (nou)
1. *adverb* At present. *Let's not discuss this now.*
2. *adverb* At once. *Come over here now.*
3. *adverb* In the recent past. *He left just now.*

4. *noun* The present time. *The time to make a decision is now.*
5. *conjunction* Since. *Now that you're gone, things aren't the same.*

no·where (no-wair)
1. *adverb* Not any place. *There was nowhere to hide.*
2. *noun* An unknown or unimportant place or state of being. *The boxer rose from nowhere to become an Olympic champion.*

noz·zle (noz-uhl) *noun* A spout that directs the flow of liquid from the end of a hose or tube. *See* **aerosol, fire extinguisher.**

nu·cle·ar (noo-klee-ur)
1. *adjective* To do with a nucleus.
2. *adjective* To do with the energy created by splitting atoms.
3. nuclear power *noun* Power created by splitting atoms.
4. nuclear weapon *noun* A weapon that uses the power created by splitting atoms.
5. nuclear reactor *noun* A large machine that produces nuclear power in a power station.

nu·cle·us (noo-klee-uhss) *noun*
1. A central or core part around which other parts are grouped. *The nucleus of the city was the busy business district.*
2. The central part of an atom, made up of neutrons and protons. *See* **atom.**
3. The central part of a cell, containing the chromosomes. *See* **cell.**
▷ *noun, plural* **nuclei** (noo-klee-eye)

nude (nood)
1. *adjective* Naked. ▷ *noun* **nudist,** *noun* **nudity**
2. *noun* A naked human figure, especially one in a painting or sculpture.

nudge (nuhj) *verb* To give someone or something a small push, often with the elbow. ▷ **nudging, nudged** ▷ *noun* **nudge**

nug·get (nuhg-it) *noun*
1. A small lump or chunk of something, especially precious metal, as in *a nugget of gold.*
2. A tiny bit or a tidbit, as in *a nugget of wisdom.*

nui·sance (noo-suhnss) *noun* Someone or something that annoys you and causes problems for you. *Dogs that run wild in the street can be a nuisance.*

nuke (nook)
1. *verb* (slang) To attack with nuclear weapons.
2. *verb* (slang) To cook in a microwave. *Dinner will be ready as soon as I nuke the potatoes.*
3. *noun* (slang) A nuclear weapon.
▷ *verb* **nuking, nuked**

numb (nuhm) *adjective*
1. Unable to feel anything, or unable to move. *My hands were numb with cold.*

2. Stunned. *When Jennifer heard that she had lost the school election by only a few votes, she was too numb to speak.*
▷ *noun* **numbness** ▷ *verb* **numb**

num·ber (nuhm-bur)
1. *noun* A word or symbol used for counting and for adding and subtracting.
2. *verb* To give a number to something. *Kenny numbered the cards from 1 to 10.*
3. *verb* To amount to a number. *The crowd numbered at least 300.*
4. *noun* A number that identifies someone or something, as in *a license number* or *a telephone number.*
5. *noun* A large quantity or group. *A number of fans gathered around the rock star.*
6. If **your days are numbered,** they are limited.
▷ *verb* **numbering, numbered**

nu·mer·al (noo-mur-uhl) *noun* A written symbol that represents a number, such as 8 or VIII.

nu·mer·a·tor (noo-muh-*ray*-tur) *noun* In fractions, the **numerator** is the number above the line. The numerator shows how many parts of the denominator are taken. *In the fraction $\frac{2}{3}$, the numerator is 2.*

nu·mer·i·cal (noo-mer-uh-kuhl) *adjective* To do with numbers, as in *numerical order.* ▷ *adverb* **numerically**

nu·mer·ous (noo-mur-uhss) *adjective* Many, or made up of a large number. *Tracy has made numerous friends at school.*

nun (nuhn) *noun* A woman who lives in a religious community and has promised to devote her life to God. **Nun** sounds like **none.**

nurse (nurss)
1. *noun* Someone who looks after people who are ill, usually in a hospital.
2. *verb* To look after someone who is ill. *My grandmother nursed me back to health.*
3. *noun* A woman hired to take care of children.
4. *verb* To feed offspring milk from a breast.
5. *verb* To treat with care. *I nursed my cold until it got better.*
▷ *verb* **nursing, nursed**

nurs·er·y (nur-sur-ee) *noun*
1. A baby's bedroom.
2. A place where babies and very young children are looked after while their parents are at work.
3. A place where you can buy trees and plants.
4. nursery rhyme A short poem for very young children.
5. nursery school A school for children aged three to five years old, before they go to kindergarten.
▷ *noun, plural* **nurseries**

nur·ture (nur-chur) *verb* To tend to the needs of someone, especially a child. ▷ **nurturing, nurtured** ▷ *noun* **nurturer**

nut (nuht) *noun*
1. A fruit or seed with a hard shell called a hull and one or more softer kernels inside that can usually be eaten. *See* **hull.**
2. The edible kernel of a nut.
3. A small metal piece with a hole in the middle that screws on to a bolt and holds it in place.
4. A strange or silly person.
▷ *adjective* **nutty**

nut·meg (nuht-meg) *noun* An aromatic spice made by grinding up the seeds of an evergreen tree that grows in Indonesia and elsewhere in the tropics. *See* **spice.**

nu·tri·ent (noo-tree-uhnt) *noun* Something that is needed by people, animals, and plants to stay strong and healthy. Proteins, minerals, and vitamins are all nutrients.

nu·tri·tious (noo-trish-uhss) *adjective* Food that is **nutritious** contains substances that your body can use to help you stay healthy and strong.
▷ *noun* **nutrition** ▷ *adverb* **nutritiously**

nuz·zle (nuhz-uhl) *verb*
1. To rub or touch with the nose as an animal does.
2. To cuddle or lie close to someone or something. *The puppy nuzzled against the boy.*
▷ *verb* **nuzzling, nuzzled**

ny·lon (nye-lon) *noun*
1. A strong synthetic fiber used to make clothing, carpets, fishing lines, etc.
2. nylons *noun, plural* Women's stockings made from nylon.

N

Word History

Nylon is a synthetic material that was first produced in large quantities in the early 1940s. One of its most popular early uses was in women's stockings, the forerunners to pantyhose. Before World War II, stockings often were made of silk, but during the war, silk was in short supply. Nylon stockings, or nylons, became the widely used substitute.

nymph (nimf) *noun*
1. In ancient Greek and Roman stories, a beautiful female spirit or goddess who lived in a forest, a meadow, a mountain, or a stream.
2. A young form of an insect, such as a grasshopper, that changes into an adult by repeatedly shedding its skin.

Oo

oak (ohk) *noun* A large hardwood tree that produces acorns. *The picture shows a 1,000-year-old oak tree in Goose Island, Texas.*

oak

oar (or) *noun* A wooden pole with a flat blade at one end, used for rowing a boat. **Oar** sounds like **or** and **ore.**

oar·lock (or-*lok*) *noun* A curved piece of metal on the side of a rowboat, used for holding the oar in place while you row.

o·a·sis (oh-ay-siss) *noun* A place in a desert where there is water and plants and trees grow.
▷ *noun, plural* **oases** (oh-ay-seez)

oat (oht) *noun* The grain of a kind of grass plant used as food for humans and feed for animals. *See* **grain.**

oath (ohth) *noun*
1. A serious, formal promise. *The witness took an oath to tell the truth in court.*
2. A swear word.

oat·meal (oht-*meel*) *noun*
1. Meal made from oats that have been ground or pressed flat by a roller.
2. A cereal made from this meal.

o·be·di·ent (oh-bee-dee-uhnt) *adjective* If you are **obedient,** you do what you are told to do.
▷ *noun* **obedience** ▷ *adverb* **obediently**

o·bese (oh-beess) *adjective* Very fat. ▷ *noun* **obesity**

o·bey (oh-bay) *verb*
1. To do what someone tells you to do. *Karen always obeys her mother.*
2. To carry out, or to follow, as in *to obey the law* or *to obey orders.*
▷ *verb* **obeying, obeyed**

o·bi (oh-bee) *noun* A Japanese sash worn with a kimono. *See* **kimono.**

ob·ject
1. (ob-jikt) *noun* Something that you can see and touch but is not alive. *Several objects were placed on the table.*
2. (ob-jikt) *noun* A person or thing toward which attention, discussion, feeling, thought, or action is directed. *His wild ideas were the object of much criticism.*
3. (ob-jikt) *noun* The thing that you are trying to achieve. *The object of this game is to get the ball into the net.*
4. (ob-jikt) *noun* The **object** or **direct object** of a verb is the noun that receives the action of the verb. In *"Heather liked Hannah,"* Hannah is the object of the verb *liked.* Prepositions are also followed by objects, as *him* after the preposition *to* in *"Give the book to him."* The **indirect object** of a verb is the noun to which something is given or for which something is done. In *"We gave her a watch,"* her is the indirect object.
5. (uhb-jekt) *verb* If you **object** to something, you dislike it or disagree with it. ▷ **objecting, objected** ▷ *noun* **objection,** *noun* **objector**

ob·jec·tion·a·ble (uhb-jek-shuh-nuh-buhl) *adjective* Unpleasant and likely to offend people, as in *objectionable behavior.*

ob·jec·tive (uhb-jek-tiv)
1. *noun* An aim that you are working toward. *Our objective is to produce a car that does not pollute.*
2. *adjective* Influenced by or based on facts, not feelings; fair. *News reporters must try to be objective.* ▷ *noun* **objectivity** ▷ *adverb* **objectively**

ob·li·gate (ob-li-gate) *verb* To make someone do something because of a law, promise, contract, or sense of duty. *The contract obligates the singer to perform five shows over the next two weeks.* ▷ **obligating, obligated**

ob·li·ga·tion (ob-luh-gay-shuhn) *noun* Something that it is your duty to do. *All citizens have the obligation to vote.* ▷ *adjective* **obligatory** (uh-**blig**-uh-*tor*-ee)

o·blige (uh-blije) *verb*
1. If you are **obliged** to do something, you have to do it. *I felt obliged to pay for the lamp that I broke.*
2. To do someone a favor. *Our car wasn't working, so our friends obliged us by driving us into town.* ▷ *adjective* **obliging** ▷ *adverb* **obligingly** ▷ *verb* **obliging, obliged**

o·blit·er·ate (uh-blit-uh-rate) *verb* To destroy something completely. *In A.D. 79, a volcano obliterated the ancient city of Pompeii, Italy.* ▷ **obliterating, obliterated**

ob·long (ob-*lawng*)
1. *adjective* Greater in length than in width. *The roses were delivered in an oblong box.*
2. *noun* A shape with four straight sides and four right angles. An oblong is longer than it is wide.

ob·nox·ious (uhb-**nok**-shuhss) *adjective* Very unpleasant, annoying, or offensive. *That show-off is really obnoxious.* ▷ *adverb* **obnoxiously**

o·boe (oh-boh) *noun* A woodwind instrument with a thin body and a double-reed mouthpiece. An oboe makes a high sound. *See* **orchestra, woodwind.** ▷ *noun* **oboist**

ob·scene (uhb-**seen**) *adjective* Indecent and shocking, as in *obscene language.* ▷ **obscener, obscenest** ▷ *noun* **obscenity** (uhb-**sen**-i-tee) ▷ *adverb* **obscenely**

ob·scure (uhb-**skyoor**)
1. *adjective* Not well known. *Even the librarian had never heard of the obscure author.* ▷ *noun* **obscurity**
2. *adjective* Not easy to understand. *The scientist's explanation was much too complicated and obscure for the class to grasp.*
3. *verb* To make it difficult to see something. *The column obscured our view of the stage.*
▷ **obscuring, obscured**
▷ *adjective* **obscurer, obscurest**

ob·serv·ant (uhb-**zur**-vuhnt) *adjective* If you are **observant,** you are good at noticing things.
▷ *adverb* **observantly**

ob·ser·va·tion (ob-zur-**vay**-shuhn) *noun*
1. The careful watching of someone or something. *The patient is under close observation.*
2. Something that you have noticed by watching carefully. *We made several observations during our experiment.*
3. A remark. *Mr. Jones made the observation that the ground was very wet.*

ob·serv·a·to·ry (uhb-**zur**-vuh-tor-ee) *noun* A building containing telescopes and other scientific instruments for studying the sky and the stars. *Scientists photographed the eclipse from the observatory.* ▷ *noun, plural* **observatories**

ob·serve (uhb-**zurv**) *verb*
1. To watch someone or something carefully. *The police have been observing the house.*
2. To notice something by looking or watching. *I observed that Henry had torn his pants.*
3. To make a remark. *Christine observed that the train was late again.*
4. To follow or to obey. *Drivers must observe the speed limit.*
5. To celebrate. *In the United States, people observe Independence Day on July 4th.*
▷ *verb* **observing, observed** ▷ *noun* **observer,** *noun* **observance**

ob·sess (uhb-**sess**) *verb* If something **obsesses** you, you think about it all the time. ▷ **obsesses, obsessing, obsessed** ▷ *noun* **obsession** ▷ *adjective* **obsessive**

ob·so·lete (ob-suh-*leet* or ob-suh-**leet**) *adjective* Out-of-date and no longer used. *Some computers are now obsolete.*

ob·sta·cle (ob-stuh-kuhl) *noun* Something that gets in your way or prevents you from doing something. *Bad grades are an obstacle to making the team.*

ob·sti·nate (ob-stuh-nit) *adjective* If someone is **obstinate,** the person is stubborn and unwilling to change his or her mind. ▷ *noun* **obstinacy** ▷ *adverb* **obstinately**

ob·struct (uhb-**struhkt**) *verb*
1. To block a road or path. *Fallen trees obstructed the road.*
2. To stand or be in the way of. *I told the people who were standing that they were obstructing my view of the baseball game.*
3. To prevent something from happening, or to make something difficult. *Ray obstructed all of our attempts to make him clean his room.*
▷ *verb* **obstructing, obstructed** ▷ *noun* **obstruction** ▷ *adjective* **obstructive**

obtain (uhb-**tayn**) *verb* To get or be given something. *Hector obtained the information he needed by checking an encyclopedia.*
▷ **obtaining, obtained**

ob·tuse (uhb-**tooss**) *adjective*
1. If someone is **obtuse,** he or she is slow to understand things.
2. An **obtuse** angle is an angle of between 90 and 180 degrees.

ob·vi·ous (ob-vee-uhss) *adjective* If something is **obvious,** it is easy to see or understand. *His frown was an obvious sign that he was unhappy.* ▷ *adverb* **obviously**

oc·ca·sion (uh-**kay**-zhuhn) *noun*
1. A time when something happens. *Ramón had been to Los Angeles on several occasions.*
2. A special or important event. *Graduation is a happy occasion.*

oc·ca·sion·al (uh-**kay**-zhuh-nuhl) *adjective* Happening from time to time. *Except for an occasional thunderstorm, we had wonderful weather last summer.* ▷ *adverb* **occasionally**

oc·cu·pa·tion (ok-yuh-**pay**-shuhn) *noun*
1. A job. ▷ *adjective* **occupational**
2. The taking over and controlling of a country or an area by an army. *The enemy force's occupation of the town lasted several months.*

355

oc·cu·py (ok-yuh-pye) *verb*
1. To live in a building, room, etc. *Who occupies this house?* ▷ *noun* **occupant,** *noun* **occupier**
2. To take up or to fill. *Gardening occupies much of my grandfather's free time.*
3. If an army **occupies** a country or an area, it captures it and takes control of it.
4. To keep someone busy and happy. *The children were occupied for hours on their computer.*
▷ *verb* **occupies, occupying, occupied**

oc·cur (uh-kur) *verb*
1. To happen. *When did the accident occur?* ▷ *noun* **occurrence**
2. If something **occurs to you,** you suddenly think of it.
▷ *verb* **occurring, occurred**

o·cean (oh-shuhn) *noun*
1. The entire body of salt water that covers about 71 percent of the earth's surface.
2. One of the four main parts of this vast body of water. *This map shows the four main oceans of the world.*

oceans

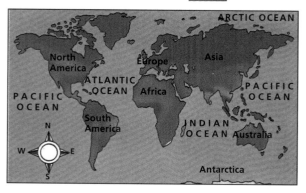

o·cean·og·ra·phy (oh-shuh-**nog**-ruh-fee) *noun* The science that deals with the oceans and the plants and animals that live in them. ▷ *noun* **oceanographer**

oce·lot (oss-uh-lot) *noun* A wildcat of medium size with spotted fur. The ocelot lives mostly in the southwestern United States, Central America, and parts of South America.

o'clock (uh-klok) *adverb* A word used when saying what the time is. *O'clock* is short for "of the clock." *It's three o'clock.*

oc·ta·gon (ok-tuh-gon *or* ok-tuh-guhn) *noun* A shape with eight sides and eight angles. *See* **shape.** ▷ *adjective* **octagonal** (ok-tag-uh-nuhl)

oc·ta·he·dron (ok-tuh-**hee**-druhn) *noun* A solid shape with eight faces that are usually triangular. *See* **shape.**

oc·tave (ok-tiv *or* ok-tave) *noun* The eight-note gap in a musical scale between a note and the next note of the same name above or below it.

Oc·to·ber (ok-toh-bur) *noun* The 10th month on the calendar, after September and before November. October has 31 days.

> ## Word History
> **October** is another month whose name is misleading. October was the eighth month on the ancient Roman calendar, getting its name from *octo,* which is Latin for "*eight.*" When the Romans adopted a new calendar, October became the tenth month.

oc·to·pus (ok-tuh-puhss) *noun* A sea animal with a soft body and eight long tentacles that it uses to catch its prey. The tentacles have suckers that help the octopus move along the ocean bottom and grasp prey. ▷ *noun, plural* **octopuses** *or* **octopi** (ok-tuh-pye)

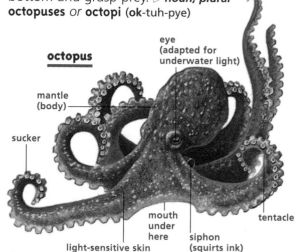

octopus

eye (adapted for underwater light)
mantle (body)
sucker
mouth under here
light-sensitive skin (changes color for camouflage)
siphon (squirts ink)
tentacle

> ## Word History
> When the Greeks gave the **octopus** its name, they called it "the creature with eight feet," *oktopous.* They might more properly have called it "the creature with eight arms," *oktobrach.*

odd (od) *adjective*
1. Strange, or difficult to explain and understand. *When my car started making an odd noise, I took it to my mechanic. It is odd that he hasn't called me yet.* ▷ *adjective* **odder, oddest** ▷ *adverb* **oddly**
2. An **odd** number cannot be divided exactly by two; it does not have two as a factor. *1, 13, 47, and 895 are all odd numbers.*
3. Not matching, as in *odd socks.*
4. Occasional. *I earn extra money by doing odd jobs on Saturdays.*

odd·i·ty (od-uh-tee) *noun* Someone or something that seems unusual or strange. *Having red hair is an oddity in our family.*

odds (odz) *noun, plural* The probability of something happening. *The odds are that last year's champion will win the tournament again this year.*

ode (ohd) *noun* A long poem, usually rhymed and often written to praise some person or thing.

o·di·ous (oh-dee-uhss) *adjective* Hateful or disgusting, as in *an odious crime.*

o·dor (oh-dur) *noun* A smell.

of (uhv *or* ov) *preposition*
1. Belonging to. *You are a friend of mine.*
2. Made with, as in *a ring of gold.*
3. Named or called. *The city of Baltimore is known for its aquarium.*
4. Containing or holding. *I carried a glass of orange juice to the table.*
5. Before or until. *It is 20 minutes of five.*
6. About or concerning. *I thought of you last night.*

off (of *or* awf)
1. *preposition* Away from. *Please take those books off the table.*
2. *adverb* Away from a place. *They went off for the day.*
3. *adverb* Not turned on or not working. *Frank has turned the computer off.*
4. *adverb* In the future. *The carnival is just four days off.*
5. *adjective* Not at work. *Uncle Mike is off all week.*
6. *adjective* Not as good as usual. *His handball game is off.*
7. *adjective* Wrong. *His estimate for the cost of the job was off by several hundred dollars.*

of·fend (uh-fend) *verb* To make someone feel hurt or angry. *His rude remarks offended me.*
▷ **offending, offended**

of·fend·er (uh-fen-dur) *noun* Someone who commits a crime or causes offense.

of·fense
1. (uh-fenss) *noun* A crime.
2. (uh-fenss) If you **cause offense,** you upset someone.
3. (uh-fenss) If you **take offense,** you feel upset by something that someone has done or said.
4. (aw-fenss) *noun* In sports, the team that is attacking or trying to score.

of·fen·sive (uh-fen-siv)
1. *adjective* Causing anger or hurt feelings, as in *an offensive remark.*
2. *adjective* Unpleasant, as in *an offensive odor.*
3. *noun* An attack, usually a military one.
4. *adjective* Attacking. *The army took offensive action.*

of·fer (of-ur) *verb*
1. To ask someone if he or she would like something. *Can I offer you some cake?*
2. To say that you are willing to do something for someone. *I offered to take the message.*
3. To put forward or suggest something. *They offered no new ideas.*
▷ *verb* **offering, offered** ▷ *noun* **offer**

of·fer·ing (of-ur-ing) *noun* A contribution. *The family gave an offering at church.*

off·hand (of-hand) *adjective* Done, made, or said without much thought or preparation, as in *offhand remarks.* ▷ *adverb* **offhand**

of·fice (of-iss) *noun*
1. A room or building in which people work, usually sitting at desks.
2. An important and usually powerful position. *She is running for the office of governor.*
3. The people who work in an office. *Most of the office came to work early today.*

of·fi·cer (of-uh-sur) *noun*
1. Someone who is in charge of other people, especially in the armed forces or the police.
2. Someone who has a responsible position in a club or similar group.

of·fi·cial (uh-fish-uhl)
1. *adjective* If something is **official,** it has been approved by someone in authority. *There will be an official inquiry into the accident.* ▷ *adverb* **officially**
2. *noun* Someone who holds an important position in an organization, as in *a government official.*
3. *noun* In sports, the person who enforces the rules of the game. *The official called a penalty on one of our players.*

off·peak *adjective* Happening when there is less activity or demand, as in *off-peak travel.*

off·putting *adjective* Discouraging or disturbing, as in *an off-putting announcement.*

off·set (of-set) *verb* To balance, or to make up for. *Jason's strengths offset his weaknesses.*
▷ **offsetting, offset**

off·shoot (of-shoot) *noun*
1. A stem that grows from the main stalk of a plant.
2. Something that develops or grows from something else. *David's report was an offshoot of the class project.*

off·side (of-side) *adjective* If a player is **offside** in football or hockey, he or she has broken the rules of the game by moving forward, ahead of the ball or puck.

off·spring (of-spring) *noun* An animal's or a human's young. ▷ *noun, plural* **offspring**

off-the-wall *adjective* (informal) Very odd or unusual. *Jane has an off-the-wall sense of humor, but she has a serious side, too.*

O

of·ten (of-uhn) *adverb* Many times. *We often go for walks in the woods.*

o·gre (oh-gur) *noun*
1. A fierce, cruel giant or monster in fairy tales and folktales.
2. Any person who is cruel or frightening.

oh (oh) *interjection* A word used to express happiness, surprise, disappointment, or pain. **Oh** sounds like **owe**.

ohm (ohm) *noun* A unit for measuring how much resistance a substance gives to the flow of electricity running through it.

oil (oil)
1. *noun* A thick, greasy liquid that burns easily and does not mix with water. Different types of oil are used for heating buildings, for cooking, and for making machines run smoothly. ▷ *adjective* **oily**
2. *verb* To cover or fill something with oil. *You should oil your bicycle chain regularly.* ▷ **oiling, oiled**
3. *noun* A paint that is used by an artist and contains oil. *See* **artist**.

oil rig *noun* A large platform used as a base for drilling for oil under the sea or under the ground. *The picture shows the Kittiwake oil rig in the North Sea.*

oil well *noun* A deep hole that is dug or drilled in the ground to get crude oil.

oint·ment (oint-muhnt) *noun* A thick, often greasy substance put on the skin to heal or protect it.

O·jib·wa (oh-jib-way) *noun* A member of a group of American Indians that lives primarily near Lake Superior in the United States and Canada. The Ojibwa are also called **Chippewa**. ▷ *noun, plural* **Ojibwa** *or* **Ojibwas**

o·kay *or* **OK** (oh-kay)
1. *adjective* All right.
2. *verb* If you **okay** something, you agree to it or approve it. ▷ **okaying, okayed**
3. *noun* Agreement or approval. *Dad gave his okay to our plans.*

ok·ra (oh-kruh) *noun* The sticky, green pods of a tall plant. Okra is used in soups and stews and eaten as a vegetable. *See* **vegetable**.

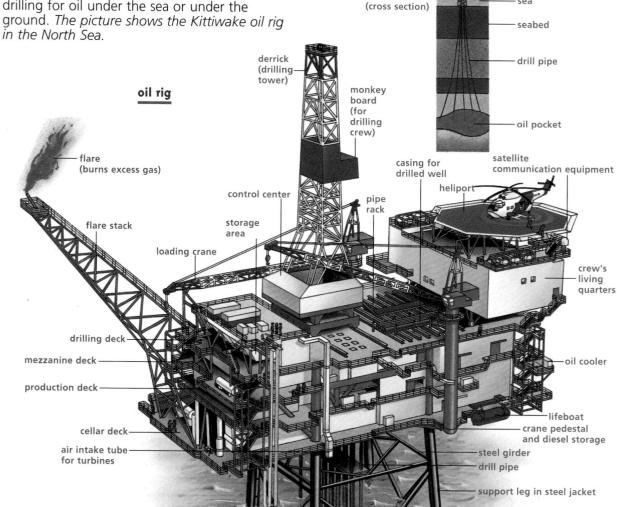

seabed
(cross section)

- rig
- sea
- seabed
- drill pipe
- oil pocket

oil rig

- derrick (drilling tower)
- monkey board (for drilling crew)
- flare (burns excess gas)
- control center
- flare stack
- storage area
- loading crane
- pipe rack
- casing for drilled well
- satellite communication equipment
- heliport
- crew's living quarters
- drilling deck
- mezzanine deck
- production deck
- oil cooler
- cellar deck
- lifeboat
- crane pedestal and diesel storage
- air intake tube for turbines
- steel girder
- drill pipe
- support leg in steel jacket

old (ohld) *adjective*
1. Someone who is **old** has lived for a long time.
2. Something that is **old** has existed or been used for a long time.
3. Of a certain age. *He is nine years old.*
4. Worn out by a lot of use, as in *old clothing.*
5. Former, or from an earlier time. *I still miss my old neighborhood.*
▷ *adjective* **older, oldest**

Synonyms: old

Old means not young or new and can refer to people, animals, things, or ideas: *The old car lurched down the street.*

Elderly refers to people who are old: *My great-grandfather, at age 90, is an elderly man.*

Antique refers to objects that are old and usually have retained or increased their value over time: *My grandparents have several antique rocking chairs in their living room.*

Ancient describes something that occurred in or survived from the distant past: *We learned about the cave dwellers in our unit on ancient history.*

Obsolete describes an object or a practice that is out-of-date and has been replaced by something more modern: *My mom bought a computer four years ago, but it's already obsolete.*

---

old age *noun* The time when a person is old.

old·en (ohl-din) *adjective* Very old or ancient. *In olden days, people rode in buggies pulled by horses.*

Old English *noun* The English language that was spoken before A.D. 1150.

old-fash·ioned (fash-uhnd) *adjective*
1. No longer fashionable or popular. *We found some old-fashioned clothes in my grandmother's trunk.*
2. Attached to or keeping the ways, ideas, or customs of an earlier time, as in *an old-fashioned wedding.*

Old Testament *noun* A collection of writings that makes up the Jewish Bible and the first part of the Christian Bible. It is the story of Jewish history and religion.

ol·ive (ol-iv) *noun* A small, black or green fruit that is eaten whole or crushed for its oil. ▷ *noun* **olive oil**

O·lym·pic games (oh-lim-pik) *noun, plural* A competition in summer and winter sports held every four years for athletes from all over the world. After 1992, the schedules of the summer and winter competitions were staggered. The Summer Games take place every four years, starting from 1992. The Winter Games take place every four years, starting from 1994. Also known as the *Olympics. See* **flag**.

om·buds·man (om-budz-muhn or om-buhdz-muhn) *noun* A person whose job is to investigate and settle the complaints of people who feel they have been wronged. An ombudsman can work for a government or for a private organization. ▷ *noun, plural* **ombudsmen**

om·e·let *or* **om·e·lette** (om-lit) *noun* Eggs that have been beaten, cooked in a pan without stirring, and folded over. Omelets can be filled with vegetables, meat, or cheese.

o·men (oh-muhn) *noun* A sign or warning about something that will happen in the future.

om·i·nous (om-uh-nuhss) *adjective* If something is **ominous,** it makes you feel that something bad is going to happen, as in *an ominous black cloud* or *an ominous silence.* ▷ *adverb* **ominously**

omit (oh-mit) *verb* To leave something out. *Hans omitted a line from the song.* ▷ **omitting, omitted** ▷ *noun* **omission**

om·ni·bus (om-nuh-buhss) *noun* A collection of stories or television programs that were previously published or shown separately.

om·ni·vore (om-nuh-vor) *noun* An animal that eats both plants and meat. Bears are omnivores. ▷ *adjective* **omnivorous** (om-niv-ur-uhss)

once (wuhnss)
1. *adverb* One time. *I've only been to London once.*
2. *adverb* In the past. *Parts of this country were once covered by ice.*
3. *conjunction* After something has happened. *I'll tell you all about it once we get home.*
4. at once *adverb* Immediately. *Take those muddy shoes off at once!*

on·com·ing (on-*kuhm*-ing) *adjective* Coming nearer or approaching. *We swerved to avoid hitting the oncoming car.*

one (wuhn)
1. *noun* The whole number, written 1, that comes after 0 and before 2.
2. *noun* A singular thing. *One is enough.*
3. *adjective* Single or alone. *Let's just get one pizza.*
4. *adjective* Some. *One day I'll beat my brother at tennis.*
5. *pronoun* A certain person or thing. *One of my shoes is lost.*
6. *pronoun* Any person. *One can see the fine craftsmanship in this table.*
One sounds like **won**.

O

one-sid·ed (sye-did) *adjective*
   1. Favoring one group, or showing one side. *Doug's account of the argument is one-sided.*
   2. Not equal or even. *The soccer match was very one-sided, with our team losing 9 to 1.*

one-way *adjective*
   1. A **one-way** street allows traffic to travel in only one direction.
   2. A **one-way** ticket allows you to travel to a place but not back again.

on·go·ing (on-*goh*-ing) *adjective* If something is **ongoing,** it continues to happen or develop, as in *an ongoing argument.*

on·ion (*uhn*-yuhn) *noun* A round vegetable with a strong smell and taste. Onions are the edible bulbs of a plant. *See* **vegetable.**

Word History

The word **onion** comes from the Latin word *unio,* which means "oneness" or "union." If you cut an onion in half, you'll find out why. This vegetable is a "union" of many different layers. Throughout history, the onion has been a symbol of strength. Civil War general Ulysses S. Grant once refused to move his troops until he received a shipment of onions to keep his soldiers strong.

---

on-line *adjective* Connected to, or available from a central computer or a system of computers and modems, as in *on-line information.* ▷ *adverb* **on-line**

on·ly (*ohn*-lee)
   1. *adverb* Not more than; just. *There were only three people in the store.*
   2. *adjective* With nothing or no one else. *Maria was the only person there.*
   3. *conjunction* But. *We would have gotten here earlier, only the car broke down.*
   4. *noun* An **only child** has no brothers or sisters.

on·o·mat·o·poe·ia (on-uh-*mat*-uh-*pee*-uh) *noun* The use of a word that sounds like the thing it stands for. *"Buzz" and "sizzle" are examples of onomatopoeia.* ▷ *adjective* **onomatopoeic** (on-uh-*mat*-uh-**pee**-ik) *or* **onomatopoetic** (on-uh-*mat*-uh-**poh**-et-ik)

on·set (on-*set*) *noun*
   1. The beginning. *The squirrels prepared for the onset of winter by storing up acorns.*
   2. An attack or an assault. *The army's onset devastated the little town.*

on·to (on-*too or* on-tuh) *preposition* To a position on or upon. *It fell onto my lap.*

on·ward (on-wurd) *or* **on·wards** (on-wurdz) *adverb* Forward, as in *from 1987 onward.* ▷ *adjective* **onward**

ooze (ooz)
   1. *verb* To flow out slowly. *Mud oozed from my shoes.* ▷ **oozing, oozed**
   2. *noun* Very soft mud, usually found underwater in a pond or stream.

o·pal (oh-puhl) *noun* A mineral used as a gem that shows different colors, depending on how it is held to the light.

o·paque (oh-pake) *adjective* Not letting light through, or not transparent. *The water in the stream was muddy and opaque.*

o·pen (oh-puhn)
   1. *adjective* Not shut, closed, or sealed. *The door is open. There is an open container of milk in the refrigerator.* ▷ *verb* **open**
   2. *adjective* Not covered or enclosed, as in *open land* or *open air.*
   3. *adjective* If you are **open** about something, you are honest about it. ▷ *noun* **openness** ▷ *adverb* **openly**
   4. *adjective* Not limited or restricted, as in *an open discussion.*
   5. *verb* To start or begin something. *The story opens in a dark forest.*
   6. *noun* If you have an **open mind,** you are able to accept new ideas.
   7. *verb* To begin working hours. *The bank opens at nine o'clock.* ▷ *adjective* **open** ▷ *verb* **opening, opened**

o·pen·ing (oh-puh-ning)
   1. *noun* A hole or space in something. *We crept through a small opening in the hedge.*
   2. *adjective* Coming at the beginning, as in *the opening lines of a play.* ▷ *noun* **opening**
   3. *noun* A chance or opportunity, as in *a job opening.*
   4. *noun* The first time a play is performed.

op·er·a (op-ur-uh) *noun* A play in which all or most of the words are sung and the singers are accompanied by an orchestra. ▷ *adjective* **operatic** (op-uh-rat-ik)

op·er·ate (op-uh-rate) *verb*
   1. To work or to run. *The engine operates well.*
   2. To make something work. *Can you operate a computer?*
   3. To cut open someone's body to repair a damaged part or remove a diseased part. ▷ *verb* **operating, operated**

op·er·a·tion (op-uh-ray-shuhn) *noun*
   1. The cutting open of someone's body to repair a damaged part or remove a diseased part.
   2. An event that has been carefully planned and involves a lot of people, as in *a massive security operation.*
   3. If something is **in operation,** it is working. ▷ *adjective* **operational**

op·er·a·tor (op-uh-*ray*-tur) *noun*
1. Someone who helps people make telephone calls.
2. Someone who works a machine or device, as in *an elevator operator.*

op·er·et·ta (*op*-uh-ret-uh) *noun* A short opera in which some of the lines are spoken.

oph·thal·mol·o·gist (*of*-thuhl-mol-uh-jist or *op*-thuhl-mol-uh-jist) *noun* A medical doctor who specializes in the structure, function, and diseases of the eye. ▷ *noun* **ophthalmology**

o·pin·ion (uh-pin-yuhn) *noun*
1. The ideas and beliefs that you have about something. *What's your opinion of our new teacher?*
2. An expert's judgment, as in *a doctor's opinion.*
3. **opinion poll** A way of finding out what people think about something by questioning a selection of people.

o·pos·sum (uh-poss-uhm) *noun* A gray, furry animal that lives mostly in trees and carries its young in a pouch. When threatened, the opossum lies very still and seems to be dead. It is also called a *possum.*

op·po·nent (uh-poh-nuhnt) *noun* Someone who is against you in a fight, contest, debate, or election.

op·por·tu·ni·ty (op-ur-too-nuh-tee) *noun* A chance to do something. *Carla's job gives her the opportunity to travel.* ▷ *noun, plural* **opportunities**

op·pose (uh-poze) *verb* To be against something and try to prevent it from happening. *Katie opposed the city's plan to raise bus and subway fares.* ▷ **opposing, opposed**

op·po·site (op-uh-zit)
1. *preposition* If something is **opposite** you, it is facing you.
2. *adjective* Located or facing directly across. *We stared at the opposite side of the river.*
3. *adjective* Facing or moving the other way. *Sue ran in the opposite direction when she saw me.*
4. *adjective* Completely different. *I thought I had written a great book report, but my teacher came to the opposite conclusion.*
5. *noun* A person, thing, or idea that is completely different from another. *The words* short *and* tall *are opposites.*

op·po·si·tion (op-uh-zish-uhn) *noun*
1. When there is **opposition** to something, people are against it. *There was a lot of opposition to the plans for a new supermarket.*
2. The person or team that you play against in a match or competition.

op·press (uh-press) *verb*
1. To treat people in a cruel, unjust, and hard

way. *The dictator oppressed his people.* ▷ *noun* **oppression,** *noun* **oppressor**
2. If something **oppresses** you, it makes you feel worried or weighed down.
▷ *verb* **oppresses, oppressing, oppressed**
▷ *adjective* **oppressive**

opt (opt) *verb*
1. To choose to have or do something. *Lydia opted to learn German.*
2. **opt out** To choose not to take part in something. *Brian opted out of the contest.*
▷ *verb* **opting, opted**

op·ti·cal (op-tuh-kuhl)
1. *adjective* To do with eyes or eyesight.
2. *adjective* Designed to aid sight. *Microscopes and telescopes are optical instruments.*
3. **optical illusion** *noun* Something that you think you see that is not really there.

op·ti·cian (op-tish-uhn) *noun* Someone who makes or sells glasses and contact lenses.

op·ti·mis·tic (op-tuh-miss-tik) *adjective* People who are **optimistic** always believe that things will turn out successfully or for the best. ▷ *noun* **optimism,** *noun* **optimist**

op·tion (op-shuhn) *noun* Something that you can choose to do. *You have the option of staying home.*

op·tion·al (op-shuh-nuhl) *adjective* If something is **optional,** you can choose whether or not to have it or do it. ▷ *adverb* **optionally**

op·tom·e·trist (op-tom-i-*trist*) *noun* A person who is licensed to test your vision and prescribe glasses or contact lenses.

> **Suffix**
> •
> The suffix **-or** adds the following meaning when added to a root word: One who, as in *actor* (one who acts) and *conductor* (one who conducts).

or (or) *conjunction*
1. A word used to introduce choices or alternatives. *You may stay or leave.*
2. A word used to indicate that words or phrases have the same meaning. *The word "teenager" refers to a young person or an adolescent.*
3. A word used with *either* or *whether* to show choices. *You can either eat the cake now or save it.*
Or sounds like **oar** and **ore.**

o·ral (or-uhl) *adjective*
1. Spoken, not written, as in *an oral report.*
2. To do with your mouth, as in *oral hygiene.*
▷ *adverb* **orally**

or·ange (or-inj) *noun*
1. The color of carrots, or a mixture of red and yellow. ▷ *adjective* **orange**
2. A round citrus fruit with a thick, orange skin and sweet, juicy flesh.

o·rang·u·tan (uh-**rang**-uh-*tan*) *noun* A large ape with long, reddish brown hair and very long, strong arms. Orangutans live in Borneo and Sumatra.

orangutans

or·bit (**or**-bit)
1. *noun* The invisible path followed by an object circling a planet, the sun, etc. ▷ *adjective* **orbital**
2. *verb* To travel around a planet, the sun, etc. ▷ **orbiting, orbited**

or·chard (**or**-churd) *noun* A field or farm where fruit trees are grown.

or·ches·tra (**or**-kuh-struh) *noun* A large group of musicians who play their instruments together. *The diagram shows the positions of the main instruments in a symphony orchestra, which usually plays classical music.* ▷ *adjective* **orchestral** (or-**kess**-truhl)

or·chid (**or**-kid) *noun* A plant with colorful and often unusually shaped flowers. *The Vanda tricolor orchid shown here grows in southeast Asia.*

orchid

or·dain (or-**dane**) *verb*
1. To bring someone into the priesthood or ministry. ▷ *noun* **ordination**
2. To order by law. *The king ordained that all young people must attend school.*
▷ *verb* **ordaining, ordained**

or·deal (or-**deel**) *noun* A very difficult or painful experience. *Being lost in the woods was quite an ordeal.*

or·der (**or**-dur)
1. *verb* To tell someone that he or she has to do something. *Ken's mom ordered him to clean his room.*
2. *verb* To ask for something in a restaurant.
3. *verb* To ask a manufacturer or store to send you something. *I've ordered a new television.*
4. *noun* Arrangement, as in *alphabetical order* or *numerical order.*
5. *noun* Neatness. *Leave the house in good order when you go out.*
6. *noun* Good behavior. *Can we have some order in this classroom?*
7. *noun* A written request to pay money to someone, as in *a postal money order.*
8. *noun* A community of people living under the same religious rules, as in *an order of monks.*
9. If you put things **in order,** you arrange them so that each thing is in the right place.
10. If an object is **out of order,** it is broken and does not work.
11. If a person is **out of order,** he or she is behaving badly.
▷ *verb* **ordering, ordered** ▷ *noun* **order**

symphony orchestra

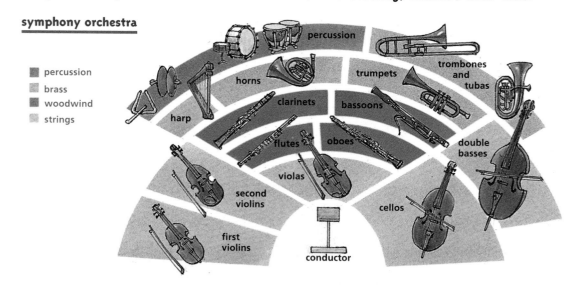

- percussion
- brass
- woodwind
- strings

percussion
trombones and tubas
horns
trumpets
clarinets
bassoons
harp
flutes
oboes
double basses
violas
second violins
cellos
first violins
conductor

or·der·ly (or-dur-lee)
1. *adjective* Neat, with everything in its place. *You keep such an orderly desk.*
2. *adjective* Well behaved, as in *an orderly crowd.*
3. *noun* A hospital attendant who cleans and does other jobs.
▷ *noun* **orderliness**

or·di·nal number (ord-uhn-uhl) *noun* A number that shows the position of something in a series, such as first, second, third, fourth, etc.

or·di·nar·y (ord-uh-*ner*-ee) *adjective*
1. Commonly used or usual. *She finally stopped yelling and returned to her ordinary tone of voice.* ▷ *adverb* **ordinarily**
2. Average, or not distinguished in any way. *My brother loved the book, but I thought it was very ordinary.*

ore (or) *noun* A rock that contains metal, as in *iron ore.* **Ore** sounds like **oar** and **or.**

or·gan (or-guhn) *noun*
1. A large musical instrument with one or more keyboards and pipes of different lengths. ▷ *noun* **organist**
2. A part of the body that does a particular job. *The diagram shows the main human organs used for breathing and for digesting and excreting food. The kidneys are shown separately because they are positioned behind the intestines. See also* **circulation, digestion, respiration.**

human organs

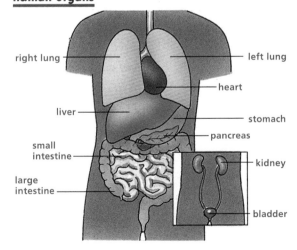

right lung — left lung — heart — liver — stomach — pancreas — small intestine — kidney — large intestine — bladder

or·gan·ic (or-gan-ik) *adjective*
1. Using only natural products and no chemicals, pesticides, etc., as in *organic farming.* ▷ *adverb* **organically**
2. To do with or coming from living things. *Decaying leaves, manure, and other organic matter can be used to enrich the soil.*

or·gan·ism (or-guh-*niz*-uhm) *noun* A living plant or animal. *Bacteria are organisms.*

or·gan·i·za·tion (or-guh-nuh-**zay**-shuhn) *noun*
1. A number of people joined together for a particular purpose. *I belong to an organization that finds homes for stray cats and dogs.*
2. The task of planning and running something. *We left the organization of the party to Jeffrey.*
3. The way something is planned or arranged. *The Constitution set out the rules for the organization of the U.S. government.*

or·gan·ize (or-guh-nize) *verb*
1. To plan and run an event. ▷ *noun* **organizer**
2. To arrange things neatly and in order. *Look how well Celia has organized the books on her shelves.*
▷ *verb* **organizing, organized**

O·ri·ent (or-ee-uhnt) *noun* The countries of the Far East, especially Japan and China. ▷ *adjective* **Oriental**

o·ri·en·teer·ing (or-ee-uhn-tihr-ing) *noun* A sport in which people have to find their way across rough country as fast as they can, using a map and compass.

origami bird

o·ri·ga·mi (or-uh-**gah**-mee) *noun* The Japanese art of paper folding. *This picture shows an example of origami.*

or·i·gin (or-uh-jin) *noun*
1. The cause or source of something, or the point where something began. *What was the origin of this argument?*
2. Ancestry, or birth. *Ida Wong's parents are of Chinese origin.*

o·rig·i·nal (uh-rij-uh-nuhl)
1. *adjective* First, or earliest. *The original cameras were made without lenses.* ▷ *adverb* **originally**
2. *adjective* New, or unusual. *What an original idea!* ▷ *noun* **originality**
3. *noun* A work of art that is not a copy.
▷ *adjective* **original**

o·rig·i·nate (uh-rij-uh-nate) *verb* To begin from somewhere or something. *This drawing originated from a doodle.* ▷ **originating, originated** ▷ *noun* **origination**

o·ri·ole (or-ee-*ohl*) *noun* A songbird that is found all over the world. The male is usually bright orange or yellow with black markings.

or·na·ment (or-nuh-muhnt) *noun* A small, attractive object used as a decoration, as in *a Christmas tree ornament.* ▷ *adjective* **ornamental**

or·nate (or-nayt) *adjective* Richly decorated. *The ornate wedding gown was covered with rows of pearls, sequins, and beads.* ▷ *adverb* **ornately**

or·ner·y (or-nur-ee) *adjective* Stubborn and mean.

or·ni·thol·o·gy (or-nuh-**thol**-uh-jee) *noun* The study of birds. ▷ *noun* **ornithologist**

363

or·phan (or-fuhn) *noun* A child whose parents are dead. ▷ *adjective* **orphaned**

or·phan·age (or-fuh-nij) *noun* A place where orphans live and are looked after.

or·tho·don·tist (or-thuh-don-tist) *noun* A dentist who straightens uneven teeth.

or·tho·dox (or-thuh-doks) *adjective*
1. Members of a religion are described as **orthodox** if they believe in its older, more traditional teachings.
2. **Orthodox** views and beliefs are ones that are accepted by most people.
▷ *noun* **orthodoxy**

or·tho·pe·dic (or-thuh-pee-dik) *adjective* To do with the branch of medicine that deals with bones and joints. ▷ *noun* **orthopedics**

os·mo·sis (oz-moh-siss *or* oss-moh-siss) *noun* The process by which a fluid passes through a membrane from a less concentrated solution to a more concentrated solution until the solutions reach the same level of concentration.

os·trich (oss-trich) *noun* A large African bird that can run very fast but cannot fly. The ostrich is the largest of all living birds and often weighs as much as 300 pounds (140 kilograms). *See* **bird**. ▷ *noun, plural* **ostriches**

oth·er (uhTH-ur)
1. *adjective* Different; not the same as mentioned. *I found one shoe, but I can't find the other one.* ▷ *pronoun* **other**
2. *adjective* Remaining. *My other friends are homesick.*
3. *adjective* More or extra. *There are other gloves in the closet.*
4. *adjective* In the recent past. *It rained the other day.*
5. **others** *pronoun* The rest. *Where are the others?*

oth·er·wise (uhTH-ur-wize)
1. *conjunction* Or else. *Catch the express bus; otherwise you will be late.*
2. *adverb* In a different way. *We didn't have very good seats, but otherwise the concert was excellent.*

ot·ter (ot-ur) *noun* A furry mammal with webbed feet that lives in or near water and eats fish. Otters are related to weasels and minks.

otter

ouch (ouch) *interjection* A cry of pain. *Ouch! That hurt.*

ought (awt) *verb* A helping verb used in the following ways:

1. To show an obligation or a duty. *You ought to obey the speed limit.*
2. To show what is expected or likely. *These sneakers are my size, so they ought to fit.*
3. To offer advice. *You ought to get some sleep.*

ounce (ounss) *noun*
1. A unit of weight equal to $\frac{1}{16}$ of a pound. A mouse weighs a little less than one ounce, and a tennis ball weighs two ounces.
2. A **fluid ounce** is a unit used in liquid measurement. There are 16 fluid ounces in a pint and 32 fluid ounces in a quart.
3. A small amount. *Ginny doesn't have an ounce of common sense.*

our (our *or* ar) *pronoun* Belonging to or to do with us. *That is our problem.*

ours (ourz *or* arz) *pronoun* The one or ones belonging to or to do with us. *That car is ours.*

our·selves (our-selvz *or* ar-selvz) *pronoun* Us and no one else. *We're proud of ourselves.*

> ### ▶ Word History
> •
> The suffix **-ous** adds the following meaning when added to a root word: Full of, as in *joyous* (full of joy) and *dangerous* (full of danger).

oust (oust) *verb* To force someone out of a position or job. *Glenn has been ousted as captain of the team.* ▷ **ousting, ousted**

out (out)
1. *adverb* Away from the inside or center. *I went out to play. The rescuers spread out and looked for the missing children.*
2. *adverb* Away from home or work. *Let's go out for dinner.*
3. *adverb* Into the open, or into public view. *The roses are out. Is his new book out yet?*
4. *adverb* No longer burning or lit. *The fire went out.*
5. *adverb* No longer taking part in a game. *You're out if you get a question wrong.*
6. *adverb* Aloud. *Izzy called out for help.*
7. *adjective* In baseball, no longer a batter or base runner. ▷ *noun* **out**

out·board motor (out-bord) *noun* A motor with a propeller that can be attached to the rear of a small boat.

out·break (out-brake) *noun* A sudden start of something such as disease or war.

out·burst (out-burst) *noun* A sudden pouring out of strong emotion, as in *an outburst of anger.*

out·cast (out-kast) *noun* Someone who is not accepted by other people. *When he first came to this country, the foreign student felt like an outcast.*

out·come (out-*kuhm*) *noun* The result of something. *The outcome of the election surprised everyone.*

out·cry (out-*krye*) *noun* If there is an **outcry** about something, a lot of people complain loudly about it. *There was an outcry over the rise in crime.* ▷ *noun, plural* **outcries**

out·dat·ed (out-*day*-tid) *adjective* Old-fashioned or out-of-date. *Typewriters are becoming outdated.*

out·do (*out*-doo) *verb* If you **outdo** someone, you do something better than he or she does. ▷ **outdoes, outdoing, outdid, outdone**

out·doors (*out*-dorz) *adverb* Outside in the open air. ▷ *noun* **outdoors** ▷ *adjective* **outdoor**

out·er (ou-tur) *adjective* On the outside or furthest from the middle, as in *the outer edge.*

outer space *noun* Space beyond the earth's atmosphere.

out·fit (out-fit)
1. *noun* A set of clothes.
2. *noun* A group of people who work together or form a unit, as in *a commercial outfit* or *a military outfit.*
3. *verb* To furnish someone with all the equipment he or she needs to do something. *We outfitted ourselves with our hiking equipment.* ▷ **outfitting, outfitted**

out·go·ing (out-goh-ing) *adjective* Someone who is **outgoing** is very sociable and friendly.

out·grow (*out*-groh) *verb* To grow too big or too old for something. *I outgrew my clothing. He outgrew his fear of the dark.* ▷ **outgrowing, outgrew, outgrown**

out·ing (out-ing) *noun* A short trip taken for pleasure. *We enjoyed our outing to the beach.*

out·law (out-*law*)
1. *noun* A criminal, especially one who is running away from the law.
2. *verb* To forbid something by law. *The town outlawed keeping wild animals as pets.* ▷ **outlawing, outlawed**

out·lay (out-*lay*) *noun* Money spent on something.

out·let (out-let) *noun*
1. A pipe or hole that lets out liquid or gas.
2. A place where appliances can be plugged in and connected to a supply of electrical current.
3. A store where a company's products can be bought at a discount.
4. An activity that lets you express your feelings. *Exercise is a good outlet for energy.*

out·line (out-*line*) *noun*
1. A line that shows the edge of something. *We saw an outline of the building against the night sky.*
2. The basic points or ideas about something. *Give me an outline of the movie's plot.*
▷ *verb* **outline**

out·look (out-*luk*) *noun*
1. Your general attitude toward things. *Yoshi has a very positive outlook.*
2. A situation that seems likely to happen. *The outlook for tomorrow's weather is quite good.*

out·num·ber (out-*nuhm*-bur) *verb* To be larger in number than another group. *In this class girls outnumber boys.* ▷ **outnumbering, outnumbered**

out-of-date *adjective* Old-fashioned or obsolete. *Ms. Kimball's impressions of teenagers are hopelessly out-of-date.*

out·pa·tient (out-*pay*-shuhnt) *noun* Someone who goes to a hospital for treatment but does not stay there overnight.

out·post (out-*pohst*) *noun*
1. A military camp set up away from the main group of soldiers to guard against a surprise attack.
2. A remote settlement.

out·put (out-*put*) *noun*
1. The amount produced by a person, machine, or business. *The factory increased its output by hiring more workers.*
2. Information produced by a computer. ▷ *verb* **output**

out·rage (out-*raje*) *noun*
1. An act of violence or cruelty. *The people have suffered enough from the outrages of terrorism.*
2. Extreme anger. *The reporter was full of outrage when she returned from the war.*
▷ *verb* **outrage**

out·ra·geous (*out*-ray-juhss) *adjective* Very shocking or offensive. *We stopped shopping at that store because it charges outrageous prices.*
▷ *adverb* **outrageously**

out·right (out-*rite*)
1. *adjective* Total or complete, as in *an outright lie.*
2. *adverb* Instantly. *He was killed outright.*

out·set (out-*set*) *noun* The start or the beginning. *I knew from the outset that the show would be a success.*

out·side
1. (*out*-side) *adverb* Out of a building, or in the open air. *The children played outside until it started to rain.*
2. (*out*-side) *noun* The outer surface, side, or part. *The outside of the box was painted pink.*
▷ *adjective* **outside**
3. (*out*-side) *preposition* Beyond the limits or boundaries of. *My friends live just outside Denver.*
4. **outside chance** (*out*-side) A very small chance.

out·skirts (out-*skurts*) *noun, plural* The outer edges of an area, as in *the outskirts of town.*

out·smart (*out*-smart) *verb* To be more clever than someone else. *Sonia outsmarted her brother by borrowing the car before he got home.* ▷ **outsmarting, outsmarted**

O

out·spo·ken (out-spoh-kuhn) *adjective* If you are **outspoken,** you express your views strongly and clearly, especially when you are criticizing someone.

out·stand·ing (*out*-stand-ing) *adjective*
1. Extremely good, as in *an outstanding performance.*
2. Not yet paid or dealt with, as in *an outstanding bill.*

out·ward (out-wurd) *or* **out·wards** (out-wurdz)
1. *adjective* Appearing on the surface. *Philip's outward appearance was calm, but really he was very nervous.* ▷ *adverb* **outwardly**
2. *adverb* Toward the outside. *The front door opens outward.* ▷ *adjective* **outward**

out·wit (*out*-wit) *verb* To fool or get the better of someone by being more clever than the person. ▷ **outwitting, outwitted**

o·val (oh-vuhl) *noun* A shape like an egg.
▷ *adjective* **oval**

o·va·ry (oh-vur-ee) *noun*
1. The part of a flowering plant in which seeds are formed.
2. The female organ that produces eggs.
▷ *noun, plural* **ovaries**

o·va·tion (oh-vay-shuhn) *noun* A response with loud applause and cheering. *The performers received a standing ovation.*

ov·en (uhv-uhn) *noun* An enclosed space, as in a stove, where food is baked or roasted.

o·ver (oh-vur)
1. *preposition* Above or on top of something. *We hung the painting over the couch.*
2. *preposition* More than. *My sandwich cost over seven dollars.*
3. *adjective* Finished. *The match was over in two hours.*
4. *preposition* Across. *Don't step over the line.*
5. *adverb* Remaining or surplus. *After we divided up the oranges, there were two left over.*
6. *adverb* Again. *I helped Juan do his paper over.*
7. *adverb* Leaning or falling downward. *The lamp fell over when Doug ran into it.*
8. If you **get over** an illness or experience, you recover from it and are no longer ill or upset.

o·ver·all (oh-vur-awl) *adverb* Generally, or considering everything. *Overall, I think the party was a success.* ▷ *adjective* **overall** (oh-vur-*awl*)

o·ver·alls (oh-vur-*awlz*) *noun, plural* Loose pants with shoulder straps and a panel covering the chest.

o·ver·bear·ing (*oh*-vur-**bair**-ing) *adjective* Very domineering or bossy.

o·ver·board (oh-vur-*bord*) *adverb*
1. Over the side of a boat. *The sailor fell overboard during the battle.*

2. If you **go overboard** about something, you are overly enthusiastic about it.

o·ver·cast (oh-vur-*kast*) *adjective* An **overcast** sky is covered with clouds.

o·ver·coat (oh-vur-*kote*) *noun* A heavy coat worn in cold weather.

o·ver·come (oh-vur-kuhm) *verb*
1. To defeat or deal with something such as a feeling or a problem. *I must overcome my fear of spiders.*
2. If someone is **overcome** by smoke, emotion, guilt, etc., the person is so strongly affected by it that he or she is made unconscious or helpless.
▷ *verb* **overcoming, overcame, overcome**

o·ver·do (oh-vur-doo) *verb* To do too much. *If you overdo the exercise, you'll be sore in the morning.* ▷ **overdoes, overdoing, overdid, overdone** ▷ *adjective* **overdone**

o·ver·dose (oh-vur-*dohss*) *noun* A quantity of a drug so large that it can kill you or make you seriously ill. ▷ *verb* **overdose** (oh-vur-*dohss*)

o·ver·draft (oh-vur-*draft*) *noun* An amount of money taken out of the bank when there is not enough money in the account. ▷ *adjective* **overdrawn**

o·ver·dress (oh-vur-*dress*) *verb* To wear clothes that are too warm or too formal for an occasion. *As usual, my uncle overdressed and wore a three-piece suit to the picnic.*
▷ **overdresses, overdressing, overdressed**

o·ver·due (oh-vur-doo) *adjective* Late. *My library books are overdue.*

o·ver·eat (*oh*-vur-*eet*) *verb* To eat too much food.
▷ **overeating, overate**

o·ver·flow (oh-vur-*floh*) *verb*
1. To flow over the edges of something. *The bath water overflowed the tub.*
2. To flood. *Heavy rains caused the river to overflow its bank.*
▷ *verb* **overflowing, overflowed**

o·ver·grown (oh-vur-grohn) *adjective* An **overgrown** garden is covered with weeds because it has not been looked after.

o·ver·hand (oh-vur-*hand*) *adjective* Done with your arm raised above your shoulder, as in *an overhand pitch.*

o·ver·haul (oh-vur-*hawl*) *verb* To examine carefully all the parts of a piece of equipment and make any repairs that are neeeded. *The mechanic overhauled our car's engine.*
▷ **overhauling, overhauled** ▷ *noun* **overhaul** (oh-vur-*hawl*)

o·ver·head
1. (*oh*-vur-**hed**) *adverb* Above your head. *The airplane flew overhead.* ▷ *adjective* **overhead** (oh-vur-hed)

2. (oh-vur-*hed*) *noun* Regular business expenses such as wages, rent, telephone, heating, and lighting.

o·ver·hear (oh-vur-hihr) *verb* To hear what someone else is saying when the person does not know that you are listening. ▷ **overhearing, overheard**

o·ver·joyed (oh-vur-joid) *adjective* If you are **overjoyed,** you are extremely happy.

o·ver·lap (oh-vur-lap) *verb* To cover part of something. *The feathers of a bird overlap.* ▷ **overlapping, overlapped** ▷ *noun* **overlap** (oh-vur-*lap*)

o·ver·load (oh-vur-lode) *verb*
1. To give something or someone too much to carry or too much work to do. *The teacher overloaded the students with homework.*
2. To send too much electricity through a circuit or device so that it burns out. *Don't overload the circuit.*
▷ *verb* **overloading, overloaded** ▷ *noun* **overload** (oh-vur-*lode*)

o·ver·look (oh-vur-luk) *verb*
1. To be able to look down on something from a window or room. *Our room overlooked the beach.*
2. To fail to notice something. *Daisy overlooked the extra costs.*
3. To choose to ignore something wrong that someone has done. *I overlooked Dylan's rude remarks.*
▷ *verb* **overlooking, overlooked**

o·ver·ly (oh-vur-lee) *adverb* Very or excessively. *Oliver is always overly cautious.*

o·ver·night
1. (oh-vur-nite) *adverb* During or through the night. *We had a storm overnight.*
2. (oh-vur-nite) *adverb* Suddenly. *Tony's luck changed overnight.*
3. (oh-vur-nite) *adjective* For one night. *I took an overnight trip.*
4. (oh-vur-nite) *adjective* Used for short trips. *It didn't take me long to pack my overnight bag.*

o·ver·pass (oh-vur-*pass*) *noun* A road or bridge that crosses over another road or a railroad.
▷ *noun, plural* **overpasses**

o·ver·pop·u·la·tion (oh-vur-*pop*-yuh-**lay**-shuhn) *noun* The condition in which the large population of humans or other animals is too great to be sustained by the natural resources available in the area.

o·ver·pow·er (oh-vur-pou-ur) *verb*
1. To defeat someone because you are stronger than he or she is. *The wrestler overpowered his opponent and won the match.*

2. If something **overpowers** you, it affects you very strongly. *I was overpowered by the disgusting smell.*
▷ *verb* **overpowering, overpowered**

o·ver·rat·ed (oh-vur-ray-tid) *adjective* If you think that something is **overrated,** you do not think that it is as good as many other people think it is.

o·ver·rule (oh-vur-rool) *verb* If someone in authority **overrules** a decision, the person says that the decision was wrong and has to be changed. ▷ **overruling, overruled**

o·ver·run (oh-vur-ruhn) *verb*
1. To spread all over a place in large numbers. *The town was overrun with rats.*
2. To flood beyond. *The river overran its banks.*
3. To go beyond. *The runner overran third base and was tagged out.*
▷ *verb* **overrunning, overran, overrun**

o·ver·seas (oh-vur-seez)
1. *adverb* Abroad or across the seas. *We traveled overseas to Italy.*
2. *adjective* To do with foreign countries or countries across the sea, as in *overseas trade.*

o·ver·sight (oh-vur-*site*) *noun* A careless mistake. *It was an oversight not to invite you.*

o·ver·sleep (oh-vur-sleep) *verb* To sleep for longer than intended. ▷ **oversleeping, overslept**

o·ver·take (oh-vur-take) *verb*
1. To catch up to someone. *With a fast sprint, I overtook the other joggers.*
2. To come upon suddenly or by surprise. *A blizzard overtook the mountain climbers.*
▷ *verb* **overtaking, overtook, overtaken**

o·ver·throw (oh-vur-throh) *verb*
1. To defeat a leader or ruler and remove the person from power by force.
2. To throw a ball too far, past where it should go. *The player overthrew the plate, allowing a runner to score.*
▷ *verb* **overthrowing, overthrew, overthrown**
▷ *noun* **overthrow**

o·ver·time (oh-vur-*time*) *noun* Time spent working beyond normal working hours.
▷ *adjective* **overtime** ▷ *adverb* **overtime**

o·ver·ture (oh-vur-chur) *noun* A piece of music played at the start of a musical, an opera, or a ballet.

o·ver·turn (oh-vur-turn) *verb*
1. To turn something over so that it is upside down or on its side.
2. To reverse a decision that someone else has made. *The judge overturned the verdict.*
▷ *verb* **overturning, overturned**

o·ver·weight (oh-vur-*wate*) *adjective* Weighing more than is normal, desirable, or allowed.

o·ver·whelm (oh-vur-**welm**) *verb*
1. To defeat or overcome completely. *Our forces overwhelmed the enemy soldiers.*
2. To have a very strong effect. *I was overwhelmed by the applause.*
▷ *verb* **overwhelming, overwhelmed** ▷ *adjective* **overwhelming**

o·ver·work (oh-vur-**wurk**) *verb* To work too hard.
▷ **overworking, overworked**

owe (oh) *verb*
1. To have to pay money to someone, especially money that you have borrowed.
2. To have a duty to do something for someone in return for something the person has done for you. *I owe you a favor.*
3. To be grateful to someone for giving you something. *My sister owes her life to the brave firefighters.*
Owe sounds like **oh.**
▷ *verb* **owing, owed**

owl (oul) *noun* A bird that has a round head, large eyes, and a hooked bill. Owls hunt at night and live mainly on mice and other small animals. *The tawny owl, shown here, is found in Europe.*

tawny owl

flexible neck

forward-facing eyes

hooked beak

talon

own (ohn)
1. *adjective* Belonging to oneself or itself. *I'm using my own pen. The camera comes equipped with its own flash.*
2. *verb* To possess or have something. *I own a collection of baseball cards.* ▷ *noun* **owner**
3. *verb* If you **own up** to something, you confess that you have done something wrong.
4. on your own Alone or by yourself.
▷ *verb* **owning, owned**

ox (oks) *noun*
1. The adult male of domestic cattle, used as a work animal or for beef.
2. Any of several animals that are related to cattle, such as the buffalo, bison, or yak.
▷ *noun, plural* **oxen** (oks-in)

ox·ford (oks-furd) *noun*
1. A low shoe with laces over the top of the foot.
2. A cotton cloth used to make lightweight clothing.

ox·i·dize (ok-suh-*dize*) *verb* To combine with oxygen. When something oxidizes, it burns or rusts. ▷ **oxidizing, oxidized** ▷ *noun* **oxidizer,** *noun* **oxidation**

ox·y·gen (ok-suh-juhn) *noun* A colorless gas found in the air. Humans and animals need oxygen to breathe, and fires need it to burn. Oxygen makes up 21 percent of the earth's atmosphere.

ox·y·mo·ron (ok-si-mor-on) *noun* A short phrase in which the words seem to contradict each other; for example, "a wise fool."

> ### Word History
> •
> The word **oxymoron** comes from two Greek words meaning "sharply foolish." *Deafening silence* is an oxymoron.

oy·ster (oi-stur) *noun* A flat, edible shellfish that lives in shallow coastal waters and has a shell made up of two hinged parts. *See* **pearl.**

o·zone (oh-zone) *noun*
1. A form of oxygen that has a pale blue color and a strong smell. This gas is formed when an electrical discharge passes through the air. It can be poisonous in large quantities.
2. ozone layer A layer of ozone high above the earth's surface that blocks out some of the sun's harmful rays. *Recently, scientists have discovered a hole in the ozone layer above Antarctica, probably caused by the use of chemicals such as chlorofluorocarbons. In this satellite picture, the hole in the ozone layer is light orange. See also* **atmosphere.**

hole in the ozone layer

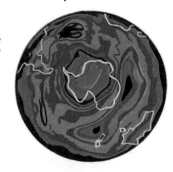

About P ◀

Spelling Hint: Words
that begin with a *pye*-
sound are spelled *pi* or *py*.
Examples: pie, pipe, pylon, python. ◀

pace (payss)
1. *noun* A step or a stride. *The treasure was buried 10 paces from the tree.*
2. *noun* The average length of a step when you are walking, about $2\frac{1}{2}$ feet for an adult.
3. *verb* To measure distance in paces. *Pace off the length of the driveway.*
4. *noun* A rate of speed. *We had to walk at a rapid pace in order to catch the bus.*
5. *verb* To walk back and forth. *Archie paced the hall.*
▷ *verb* **pacing, paced**

pace·mak·er (payss-*may*-kur) *noun* An electronic device put into someone's body to help the heart beat more regularly.

pac·i·fist (pass-uh-fist) *noun* Someone who strongly believes that war and violence are wrong and who refuses to fight. ▷ *noun* **pacifism**

pac·i·fy (pass-uh-fye) *verb* If you **pacify** someone, you make the person feel calmer. ▷ **pacifies, pacifying, pacified**

pack (pak)
1. *verb* To put objects into a box, case, bag, etc. *She packed three trunks with clothes for college. We packed our books in boxes before we moved.* ▷ *noun* **packing**
2. *verb* To fill a space tightly. *A huge crowd packed the stadium.*
3. *noun* A group of something such as animals, people, or things, as in *a pack of wolves* or *a pack of cards.*
4. *noun* A bundle of things tied or wrapped together for carrying.
5. *noun* A sturdy bag for carrying things on the back.
6. *noun* A large quantity or amount, as in *a pack of lies.*
▷ *verb* **packing, packed**

pack·age (pak-ij) *noun*
1. A parcel, or a bundle of something that is packed, wrapped, or put into a box. *I received a package in the mail.*
2. A carton, box, or case that can be packed with something. *The ingredients were listed on the package.*
▷ *verb* **package**

pack·ag·ing (pak-uh-jing) *noun* The wrapping on something, especially something that you buy.

pack animal *noun* An animal, usually a horse or mule, that can carry heavy supplies.

pack·et (pak-it) *noun* A small container or package, as in *a packet of seeds.*

pact (pakt) *noun* An agreement, often between two countries, as in *a peace pact.*

pad (pad)
1. *verb* To walk around softly. *She padded down the corridor in her bedroom slippers.*
2. *noun* A wad or cushion of soft material, usually used to absorb liquid, give comfort, or provide protection. ▷ *verb* **pad**
3. *noun* Sheets of paper fastened together, as in *a memo pad.*
4. *noun* The soft part on the bottom of the feet of dogs and many other animals.
5. *noun* A platform from which a rocket is fired, as in *a launching pad.*
6. *verb* To add words to a speech or piece of writing just to make it longer.
7. *verb* If you **pad a bill,** you charge someone for more work than you really did.
▷ *verb* **padding, padded**

padding *noun* Cotton, foam rubber, or any other material used to make or stuff a pad.

pad·dle (pad-uhl)
1. *noun* A short, wide oar used to move and steer some boats. See **inflatable, kayak.** ▷ *verb* **paddle**
2. *noun* A small board with a short handle used to strike a ball in table tennis and other games.
3. *noun* A flat, wooden tool used for stirring, mixing, or beating.
4. *verb* To spank with a paddle or the hand.
▷ **paddling, paddled**

paddle wheel *noun* A large wheel with paddles arranged around it. *Paddle wheels propel some steamboats through water.*

paddle wheel

pad·dock (pad-uhk) *noun* An enclosed field or area where horses can graze or exercise.

P

pad·dy (pad-ee)
noun A wet field where rice is grown. ▷ *noun, plural* **paddies**

paddy

pad·lock (pad-*lok*) *noun* A lock with a metal bar shaped like a U that can be put through an opening or link and snapped shut.

pa·gan (pay-guhn) *noun* Someone who is not a member of the Christian, Jewish, or Muslim religion. A pagan may worship many gods or have no religion at all. ▷ *adjective* **pagan**

page (payj)
1. *noun* One side of a sheet of paper in a book, newspaper, or magazine.
2. *noun* In the past, a **page** was a boy servant. Today, a page assists someone, such as a senator, by running errands or by being a messenger. A page can also be a boy attendant at a wedding.
3. *verb* To find someone by calling out or announcing the person's name or by using a pager. *Ann had her mother paged when they got separated in the department store.* ▷ **paging, paged**

pag·eant (paj-uhnt) *noun* A public show where people walk in processions or act out historical scenes, as in *a beauty pageant* or *a Thanksgiving pageant.* ▷ *noun* **pageantry**

pag·er (pay-jur) *noun* A small, electronic beeping device that people such as doctors wear so that they can be reached in emergencies.

pa·go·da (puh-goh-duh) *noun* A shrine or temple in eastern religions. A pagoda is shaped like a tower with many roofs that curve upward. *See* **architecture.**

pail (payl) *noun* A bucket. **Pail** sounds like **pale.**

pain (payn) *noun*
1. A feeling of physical hurt or great unhappiness. ▷ *verb* **pain**
2. pains *noun, plural* Efforts or trouble. *David took great pains over his essay.*
Pain sounds like **pane.**

pain·ful (payn-fuhl) *adjective* If something is **painful,** it hurts you physically or makes you very unhappy. ▷ *adverb* **painfully**

pain·kill·er (payn-*kil*-ur) *noun* A pill or other medicine taken to stop pain.

pain·less (payn-liss) *adjective* Free from pain. *Don's medical examination was relatively painless.* ▷ *adverb* **painlessly**

pains·tak·ing (paynz-*tay*-king) *adjective* Careful and thorough, as in *a painstaking worker* or *painstaking research.* ▷ *adverb* **painstakingly**

paint (paynt)
1. *noun* A liquid that you use to color surfaces such as walls or to make pictures.
2. *verb* To use paint to make a picture or cover a surface. ▷ **painting, painted** ▷ *noun* **painter,** *noun* **painting**

paint·brush (paynt-*bruhsh*) *noun* A brush for spreading paint. *See* **artist.** ▷ *noun, plural* **paintbrushes**

pair (pair)
1. *noun* Two things that match or go together, as in *a pair of socks.* ▷ *verb* **pair**
2. *noun* One thing that is made up of two parts, as in *a pair of scissors* or *a pair of glasses.*
3. *noun* Two persons or animals that are alike or that work together, as in *a pair of dancers* or *a pair of horses.*
4. pair off *verb* To form a pair or into pairs. *The teacher had her students pair off for their dance lesson.*
Pair sounds like **pare** and **pear.**

pa·ja·mas (puh-jam-uhz *or* puh-jahm-uhz) *noun, plural* A set of clothes to sleep in consisting of a loose shirt and pants or shorts.

▶ Word History

Pajamas is a combination of two Persian words: *pae* or *pay,* which means "leg," and *jama,* the word for "clothing." The word pajamas was brought to India and passed into English during the United Kingdom's long rule over India. Originally referring to loose, lightweight trousers, pajamas came to be applied to any two-piece set of clothes for sleeping.

pal (pal) *noun* A good friend or a buddy.

pal·ace (pal-iss) *noun* A large, grand residence for a king, queen, or other ruler.

▶ Word History

The word **palace** can trace its origins to one of the seven great hills of Rome, the Palatine Hill. In ancient times Rome's emperors and leading citizens built their big and beautiful houses on it. The Latin *palatium* became the French *palais,* and the English palace.

pal·ate (pal-it) *noun*
1. The roof of your mouth.
2. A person's sense of taste. *Sweet-and-sour pork is a dish designed to delight the palate with its range of flavors.*
Palate sounds like **palette.**

P

pale (payl)
1. *adjective* Having a light skin color, often because of an illness. *His face looked thin and pale.* ▷ *noun* **pallor** (pal-ur)
2. *adjective* Not bright in color. *Naomi's dress was pale green.*
3. *verb* To become pale. *Vincent's face paled with fright.* ▷ **paling, paled**
Pale sounds like **pail.**
▷ *noun* **paleness** ▷ *adjective* **paler, palest**

pa·le·on·tol·o·gy (*pale*-ee-uhn-tol-uh-jee) *noun* The science that deals with fossils and other ancient life forms. Someone who studies paleontology is called a *paleontologist.*

Pa·le·o·zo·ic (*pay*-lee-uh-**zoh**-ik) *noun* An era in the earth's history that began about 600 million years ago and ended about 200 million years ago. During this time, land plants, fish, amphibians, and reptiles began to appear.
▷ *adjective* **Paleozoic**

pal·ette (pal-it) *noun* A flat board with a hole for the thumb. A palette is used to mix paints on.
Palette sounds like **palate.** *See* **artist.**

pal·in·drome (pal-in-*drohm*) *noun* A word, sentence, or number that reads the same backward as forward. *Hannah, Bob, Otto, and the number 96769 are all palindromes.*

pal·i·sade (*pal*-uh-**sayd**) *noun* A line of steep cliffs, often bordering a river.

pal·lid (pal-id) *adjective* If you are **pallid,** your skin looks pale.

palm (pahm)
1. *noun* The flat surface on the inside of your hand.
2. *noun* A tall, tropical tree with large leaves shaped like feathers or fans at the top.
3. *verb* To hide something in your palm. *The magician palmed a quarter and made us think it had disappeared.* ▷ **palming, palmed**

pal·met·to (pal-met-oh) *noun* A kind of palm tree with leaves shaped like fans. Palmettos grow in the southern United States. ▷ *noun, plural* **palmettos** *or* **palmettoes**

palm·ist·ry (pah-muh-stree) *noun* The practice of telling people's fortunes by looking at the lines in the palms of their hands. ▷ *noun* **palmist**

pal·o·mi·no (*pal*-uh-**mee**-noh) *noun* A golden-tan or cream horse with a white mane and tail.
▷ *noun, plural* **palominos**

pam·pas (pam-puhz) *noun, plural* Large, treeless plains in South America. The pampas are mainly in central Argentina and Uruguay.

pam·per (pam-pur) *verb* To take very good care of yourself or someone else with food, kindness, or anything special. ▷ **pampering, pampered**

pam·phlet (pam-flit) *noun* A small, thin booklet that usually contains an essay or information on one particular topic.

pan (pan)
1. *noun* A wide, shallow metal container that is used for cooking.
2. *verb* To look for gold by washing earth in a pan or sieve. *Many people panned for gold in California during the late 1840s.*
3. *verb* To move a movie or television camera over a wide area in order to follow an action. *The camera panned on the speeding car.*
4. *verb* (informal) To criticize someone or something harshly. *The drama critic panned the play and the playwright.*
▷ *verb* **panning, panned**

pan·cake (pan-*kake*) *noun* A thin, flat cake made from batter and cooked in a pan or on a griddle.

pan·cre·as (pan-kree-uhss) *noun* A gland near your stomach that makes a fluid that helps you digest food. The pancreas also makes insulin, a hormone that helps your body use glucose. *See* **digestion.**

pan·da (pan-duh) *noun*
1. An animal found in China that looks like a bear and has thick, black and white fur. It is also called a *giant panda. The picture shows a giant panda eating a bamboo shoot.*

giant panda

2. A small, reddish brown animal that is found in Asia. It looks like a raccoon and has short legs; a long, bushy tail with rings; and a white face. It is also called a *lesser panda.*

pan·de·mo·ni·um (*pan*-duh-moh-nee-uhm) *noun* Chaos or confusion.

pane (payn) *noun* A sheet of glass or plastic in a window or door. **Pane** sounds like **pain.**

pan·el (pan-uhl) *noun*
1. A flat piece of wood or other material made to form part of a surface such as a wall. ▷ *noun* **paneling** ▷ *verb* **panel**
2. A board with controls or instruments on it.
3. A group of people chosen to do something such as judge a competition, discuss a topic, or serve on a jury. ▷ *noun* **panelist**

pang (pang) *noun* A sudden, brief pain or emotion, as in *hunger pangs* or *a pang of regret*.

pan·ic (pan-ik)
1. *noun* A sudden feeling of great terror or fright, often affecting many people at once. *When the ship hit an iceberg, panic spread among the passengers.* ▷ *verb* **panic** ▷ *adjective* **panicky**
2. **panic-stricken** *adjective* Struck with a sudden fear. *The panic-stricken children fled to safety at the first signs of a storm.*

pan·o·ram·a (*pan*-uh-ram-uh) *noun* A wide or complete view of an area. *You can see a panorama of New York City from the top of the Empire State Building.* ▷ *adjective* **panoramic**

pan·sy (pan-zee) *noun* A small garden flower with five rounded petals that are often purple, yellow, or white. ▷ *noun, plural* **pansies**

pansy

pant (pant) *verb* To breathe quickly and loudly because you are exhausted. *Josephine was panting by the time she caught up with us.* ▷ **panting, panted**

pan·ther (pan-thur) *noun*
1. A large leopard with a black coat.
2. Another name for a **cougar, mountain lion,** and **puma.**

pan·to·mime (pan-tuh-mime) *noun*
1. The telling of a story with gestures, body movements, and facial expressions rather than words. ▷ *verb* **pantomime**
2. A play or scene acted out with gestures instead of words.

pan·try (pan-tree) *noun* A small room or a closet in or near a kitchen where food, plates, pans, and other kitchen supplies are kept. ▷ *noun, plural* **pantries**

pants (pants) *noun, plural* A piece of clothing with two legs that covers the lower part of your body.

pan·ty hose (pan-tee) *noun, plural* An undergarment, similar to tights, that covers the hips, legs, and feet and is often made of nylon.

pa·pa·ya (puh-pah-yuh) *noun* The yellow or orange sweet fruit that grows on a tropical American tree. It looks like a melon.

pa·per (pay-pur)
1. *noun* A thin piece or sheet of material made from wood pulp and rags. Paper is used for writing, printing, drawing, wrapping, and covering walls.
2. *noun* A single sheet of paper.
3. *noun* A document, or a sheet of paper with something printed or written on it. *Mr. Hernández keeps all of his important papers in a safe at his office.*
4. *noun* A written report or essay for school. *Our English teacher requires us to write a paper every week.*
5. *noun* A newspaper. *I always read the morning paper.*
6. *verb* To put wallpaper up, or to cover something with paper. ▷ **papering, papered**

pa·per·back (pay-pur-*bak*) *noun* A book with a paper cover.

paper clip *noun* A bent piece of thin wire that is used to hold sheets of paper together.

pa·per·weight (pay-pur-*wate*) *noun* A heavy, often decorative object used to hold down papers on a desk or other flat surface.

pa·per·work (pay-pur-*wurk*) *noun* Work that includes writing reports and keeping records.

pa·pier-mâ·ché (pay-pur muh-**shay**) *noun* Paper that has been soaked in glue. Before hardening, this material can be molded into dolls, toys, furniture, etc. ▷ *adjective* **papier-mâché**

pa·poose (pa-**pooss**) *noun* An American Indian baby or young child.

pap·ri·ka (pa-**preek**-uh *or* pap-ruh-kuh) *noun* A reddish orange spice made from powdered sweet red peppers. *See* **spice.**

pa·py·rus (puh-**pye**-ruhss) *noun*
1. A tall water plant that grows in northern Africa and southern Europe.
2. Paper made from the stems of this plant. The ancient Egyptians wrote on papyrus. ▷ *noun, plural* **papyri** (puh-**pye**-ree) *or* **papyruses**

par (par) *noun*
1. An equal level. *Her singing is on a par with yours.*
2. An accepted or normal level. *I must get my grades up to par so that I can stay on the football team.*
3. In golf, the number of strokes it should take a player to get the ball into the hole or finish a particular course.

par·a·ble (pa-ruh-buhl) *noun* A fable or story that has a moral or religious lesson.

par·a·chute (pa-ruh-*shoot*) *noun* A large piece of strong but lightweight fabric attached to thin ropes. A parachute is used to drop people or loads safely from airplanes. ▷ *noun* **parachutist** ▷ *verb* **parachute**

parachute

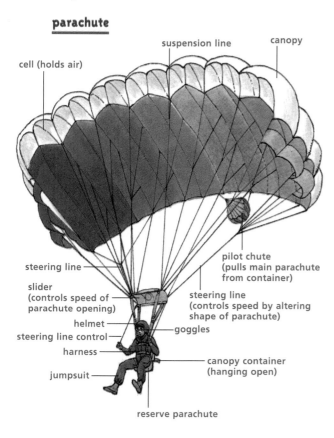

cell (holds air)
suspension line
canopy
steering line
slider (controls speed of parachute opening)
helmet
steering line control
harness
jumpsuit
pilot chute (pulls main parachute from container)
steering line (controls speed by altering shape of parachute)
goggles
canopy container (hanging open)
reserve parachute

> ### ▶ Word History
>
> The French word **parachute** can be broken down into *para*, which means "to protect or ward off," and *chute*, which means "fall." The word came into English in the late 1700s, long before the invention of the airplane. Parachutes were first used in connection with balloon travel.

pa·rade (puh-rade)
1. *noun* A procession of people and vehicles as part of a ceremony or festivity. ▷ *verb* **parade**
2. *verb* If you **parade** something, you show it off. ▷ **parading, paraded**

par·a·dise (pa-ruh-*dise*) *noun*
1. A place that is considered extremely beautiful and that makes people feel happy and contented, as in *a vacation paradise.*
2. In some religions, **paradise** is another word for heaven.

par·a·dox (pa-ruh-*doks*) *noun*
1. A statement that seems to contradict itself but in fact may be true. *The phrase "a well-known secret agent" is an example of a paradox.*
2. A person or thing that seems to contradict itself. *My brother is a real paradox. Some days he's the nicest guy in the world; other times he's just plain mean to me.*
▷ *noun, plural* **paradoxes** ▷ *adjective* **paradoxical**

par·af·fin (pa-ruh-fin) *noun* A white, waxy substance used in making candles and for sealing jars.

par·a·graph (pa-ruh-*graf*) *noun* A short passage in a piece of writing that begins on a new line and usually is indented. A paragraph is made up of one or more sentences about a single subject or idea.

par·a·keet (pa-ruh-*keet*) *noun* A small parrot with brightly colored feathers and a long, pointed tail. Parakeets often are kept as pets.

par·a·le·gal (*pa*-ruh-lee-guhl) *noun* Someone who is trained and paid to assist a lawyer.
▷ *adjective* **paralegal**

par·al·lel (pa-ruh-*lel*)
1. *adjective* If two straight lines are **parallel,** they stay the same distance from each other, and they never cross or meet.
2. *noun* If a situation has a **parallel,** there is another situation very similar to it. ▷ *verb* **parallel**
3. *noun* Any of the imaginary lines that circle the earth parallel to the equator. On a map, parallels represent degrees of latitude.
4. If electrical parts are connected **in parallel,** each one can receive power even when the others are not being used.

par·al·lel·o·gram (*pa*-ruh-**lel**-uh-*gram*) *noun* A quadrilateral with opposite sides that are equal in length and parallel. *See* **shape.**

pa·ral·y·sis (puh-**ral**-uh-siss) *noun* A loss of the power to move or feel a part of the body.

par·a·lyze (pa-ruh-lize) *verb*
1. To cause paralysis in.
2. To make someone or something helpless or unable to function. *A blizzard paralyzed the airport.*
▷ *verb* **paralyzing, paralyzed**

par·a·me·ci·um (*pa*-ruh-**mee**-see-uhm *or* *pa*-ruh-**mee**-shee-uhm) *noun* A microscopic organism with only one cell that lives in fresh water. It is shaped like a slipper. ▷ *noun, plural* **paramecia** (*pa*-ruh-**mee**-see-uh *or* *pa*-ruh-**mee**-shee-uh)

par·a·mount (pa-ruh-mount) *adjective* Above all others in rank, power, or importance. *A good education is of paramount importance in today's world.*

P

par·a·pher·na·lia (*pa*-ruh-fur-**nay**-lyuh) *noun*
Numerous pieces of equipment, belongings, and other personal items. *Before the school year ended, I had to clean out all the paraphernalia from my desk.*

par·a·phrase (**pa**-ruh-*fraze*) *verb* If you **paraphrase** speech or writing, you say or write it again in a different way. ▷ **paraphrasing, paraphrased** ▷ *noun* **paraphrase**

par·a·ple·gic (pa-ruh-**plee**-jik) *noun* Someone who has no feeling or movement in the lower part of his or her body, usually because of an injury or a disease of the spinal cord. ▷ *adjective* **paraplegic**

par·a·site (**pa**-ruh-*site*) *noun*
1. An animal or plant that gets its food by living on or inside another animal or plant. *Leeches are parasites that use suckers to attach themselves to people or other animals and feed on their blood.*
2. A person who gets money, food, and shelter from another without doing anything in return.
▷ *adjective* **parasitic** (pa-ruh-**sit**-ik)

leech

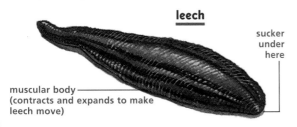

sucker under here

muscular body
(contracts and expands to make leech move)

P

par·a·sol (**pa**-ruh-sol) *noun* A small, light umbrella that shades you from the sun.

par·a·troops (**pa**-ruh-*troops*) *noun, plural* Soldiers who are trained to jump by parachute into battle. ▷ *noun* **paratrooper**

par·cel (**par**-suhl)
1. *noun* A package, or something that is packed, wrapped, or put into a box.
2. *noun* A section or plot of land.
3. *verb* To divide into parts and give out. *The art teacher began the class by parceling out supplies.*
▷ **parceling, parceled**

parch (parch) *verb*
1. To make very dry. *The hot sun parched the soil.*
2. To make very thirsty.
▷ *verb* **parches, parching, parched** ▷ *adjective* **parched**

parch·ment (**parch**-muhnt) *noun* Heavy, paperlike material made from the skin of sheep or goats and used for writing on.

par·don (**pard**-uhn)
1. *verb* To forgive or excuse someone, or to release the person from punishment. *The governor pardoned the prisoner.* ▷ **pardoning, pardoned** ▷ *noun* **pardon**

2. *interjection* You say **I beg your pardon** as a polite way of asking someone to repeat what he or she has said or asking someone for forgiveness.

pare (pair) *verb*
1. To cut off the outer layer. *She pared the apple with a knife.*
2. To reduce or make less step by step, as if by cutting. *He pared down his book report until it was only one page long.*
Pare sounds like **pair** and **pear**.
▷ *verb* **paring, pared**

par·ent (**pa**-ruhnt *or* **pair**-uhnt) *noun*
1. A mother or a father.
2. A plant or an animal that produces offspring.
▷ *noun* **parenthood** ▷ *verb* **parent** ▷ *adjective* **parental**

pa·ren·the·sis (puh-**ren**-thuh-siss) *noun* One of the curved lines ( ) used to enclose a word or phrase in a sentence or to enclose symbols or numbers in a mathematical expression. ▷ *noun, plural* **parentheses** (puh-**ren**-thuh-seez)

par·ish (**pa**-rish) *noun*
1. An area that has its own church and minister or priest.
2. The people who live in a parish.
3. In Louisiana, a county.

pa·rish·ion·er (puh-**rish**-uh-nur) *noun* Someone who lives in the parish of a church.

park (park)
1. *noun* An area of land with trees, benches, and sometimes playgrounds, used by the public for recreation.
2. *noun* An area of land set aside by the government so that it can be kept in its natural state.
3. *verb* To leave a car or other vehicle in a space in a garage or lot or at the curb of a street. *My mother parked the car near the library because she had a lot of heavy books to return.* ▷ **parking, parked**

par·ka (**par**-kuh) *noun* A large, heavy jacket suitable for winter weather. It has a hood and is usually made of fur or filled with down.

parking meter *noun* A machine that you put money into in order to pay for parking. The meter allows you a certain amount of time for each coin you put into it.

park·way (**park**-*way*) *noun* A wide highway or road that has grass, bushes, trees, and flowers planted down the middle or along the sides.

par·lia·ment (**par**-luh-muhnt) *noun* The group of people who have been elected to make the laws in some countries, such as Canada, the United Kingdom, and Israel. ▷ *adjective* **parliamentary**

par·lor (par-lur) *noun*
1. A formal living room, especially in an old house, that is used for receiving guests.
2. A room or rooms used for a business, as in *an ice-cream parlor*.

pa·ro·chi·al (puh-roh-kee-uhl) *adjective*
1. To do with a church parish, as in *a parochial school*.
2. Having a narrow, short-sighted point of view.

par·o·dy (pa-ruh-dee) *noun* An imitation of a serious piece of writing or song that makes fun of the original work. ▷ *noun, plural* **parodies** ▷ *verb* **parody**

pa·role (puh-role) *noun* The early release of a prisoner, usually for good behavior, on the condition that the person behave according to the law. ▷ *verb* **parole**

par·ox·ysm (pa-ruhk-*siz*-uhm) *noun* A sudden outburst or fit, as in *a paroxysm of laughter*.

par·rot (pa-ruht)
noun
scarlet macaw
1. A tropical bird with a curved beak and brightly colored feathers. Some parrots can learn to repeat things that are said to them. *The scarlet macaw shown here is one of the largest members of the parrot family.*
2. Someone who repeats or imitates words without understanding what they mean. ▷ *verb* **parrot**

parse (parss) *verb* When you **parse** a sentence, you identify its subject and object and the parts of speech of its words. ▷ **parsing, parsed**

pars·ley (par-slee) *noun* A leafy, green herb with small leaves, used as food decoration or as seasoning. *See* **herb.**

pars·nip (par-snip) *noun* A plant with a pale yellow root eaten as a vegetable. Parsnips resemble carrots. *See* **vegetable.**

par·son (par-suhn) *noun* A minister, especially a Protestant minister.

part (part)
1. *noun* A portion or division of a whole. *I fell asleep during the last part of the movie.*
2. *noun* A piece in a machine or device. *Our television has a broken part.*
3. *noun* An expected share of responsibility or work. *If you all do your part, the school carnival will be a success.*

4. *noun* A character or role in a play or film. *He played the part of Hamlet.*
5. *noun* A line in your hair where the hair is combed in two directions. ▷ *verb* **part**
6. *verb* To separate or to divide. *We parted at the crossroads.*
7. *adjective* Not completely or entirely. *My grandfather is part Cherokee.*
8. *verb* If you **part with** something, you give it away or give it up.
9. If you **take part,** you participate or join with others in an activity.
▷ *verb* **parting, parted**

Synonyms: part

A **part** is anything less than all of something. A part may be very small or very large, just as long as it is not the whole thing: *Part of the story takes place in Indiana. Part of Jaime's tooth broke off when he bit into the apple.*

A **piece** is a fragment of something that is separated from the whole: *We found the last piece of the jigsaw puzzle under the couch.*

A **portion** is a share of something, usually one that is assigned or given to someone: *When Tony finished his portion of roast beef, he asked if he could have some more.*

A **section** is a part that is often separate or distinct in some way: *Julia ate a section of grapefruit. My dad loves to read the sports section of the newspaper.*

A **component** is a part that is important in helping to complete the whole: *Math is one component of a good education.*

A **division** is one of the parts into which something large has been organized: *Sharon's mom works for the magazine division at the publishing company.*

par·tial (par-shuhl) *adjective*
1. Not complete. *Our vacation was only a partial success.* ▷ *adverb* **partially**
2. Someone who is **partial** favors one person or side more than another.
3. If you are **partial to** a particular food or drink, you are especially fond of it.
▷ *noun* **partiality** (*par*-shee-al-uh-tee)

par·tic·i·pate (par-tiss-uh-*pate*) *verb* To join with others in an activity or event. *To participate in the study, all I had to do was answer a few questions.* ▷ **participating, participated** ▷ *noun* **participant,** *noun* **participation**

P

par·ti·ci·ple (par-tuh-*sip*-uhl) *noun* A form of a verb that is used with a helping verb or that can be used as an adjective. English has two participles: the **present participle,** ending in -ing, as in "walking" or "singing" and a **past participle,** ending in -ed or sometimes -en, as in "finished" or "swollen."

par·ti·cle (par-tuh-kuhl) *noun* An extremely small piece or amount of something.

particle physics *noun* The study of the behavior of the minute parts of atoms.

par·tic·u·lar (pur-tik-yuh-lur)
1. *adjective* Individual or special. *I want this particular painting.*
2. *adjective* Very careful about details. *My teacher is particular about neat homework.*
3. *adjective* Special or unusual. *Pay particular attention to his instructions.*
4. *noun* A fact or a detail. *Please send me some particulars about the course.*
5. in particular Especially. *All the rides are fun, but there's one in particular that you must try.*
▷ *adverb* **particularly**

part·ing (part-ing)
1. *noun* A departure or a separation, as in *an emotional parting.*
2. *adjective* To do with a departure or separation, as in *a parting handshake.*

par·ti·tion (par-tish-uhn)
1. *noun* A movable wall or panel used to divide an area or a room. *See* **building.**
2. *verb* To section something off or to separate something. *We partitioned the dining room from the living room with a screen.*
3. *verb* To divide into sections or parts. *The town partitioned the land into lots for houses.*
▷ *verb* **partitioning, partitioned**

part·ly (part-lee) *adverb* In part or to some extent. *He was partly to blame for the accident.*

part·ner (part-nur) *noun*
1. One of two or more people who do something together, as in *business partners* or *dancing partners.* ▷ *noun* **partnership**
2. Someone on your side in a game, as in *a tennis partner.*

part of speech *noun* A grammatical class into which a word can be placed according to the way it is used in a phrase or sentence, such as **noun, verb, adjective,** etc. ▷ *noun, plural* **parts of speech**

par·tridge (par-trij) *noun* A plump game bird that has gray, brown, and white feathers.

part-time *adjective* If you have a **part-time** job, you work at it for a few hours or a few days each week. ▷ *noun* **part-timer** ▷ *adverb* **part time**

par·ty (par-tee) *noun*
1. An organized occasion when people enjoy themselves in a group. ▷ *verb* **party**
2. A group of people working together. *The search party found the stranded hikers.*
3. An organized group of people with similar political beliefs who try to win elections. *The Democratic and Republican parties are the two largest political parties in the United States.*
▷ *noun, plural* **parties** ▷ *adjective* **party**

pass (pass)
1. *verb* To go by someone or something. *I always pass the library on my way to school.*
2. *verb* To give something to somebody. *Pass the salt, please.*
3. *verb* To kick, throw, or hit a ball to someone on your team in a sport or game. ▷ *noun* **pass, noun** **passer**
4. *verb* To succeed in a test or course. *My mom passed all her exams, and now she can practice law.* ▷ *noun* **pass**
5. *verb* To move on or to go by. *The days passed quickly.*
6. *verb* To approve or to make into law. *The Senate passed the gun control bill.*
7. *noun* A narrow passage in a mountain range.
8. *noun* Written permission. *Do you have a hall pass?*
9. *noun* A free ticket. *I won two passes to the ball game.*
10. pass away *verb* To die.
11. pass out *verb* To faint.
12. *verb* If you **pass** something **up,** you give up the opportunity to have or do it.
▷ *noun, plural* **passes** ▷ *verb* **passes, passing, passed**

pas·sage (pass-ij) *noun*
1. A hall or a corridor.
2. A short section in a book or piece of music.
3. A journey by ship or airplane.
4. Approval of a bill into law by a legislature. *At this time, passage of the bill is uncertain.*

pas·sage·way (pass-ij-*way*) *noun* An alley, a hallway, a tunnel, or anything that allows you to pass from one place to another. *The old mansion has many secret passageways.*

pas·sen·ger (pass-uhn-jur) *noun* Someone besides the driver who travels in a car or other vehicle.

pass·er·by (pass-ur-*bye*) *noun* Someone who happens to be passing. ▷ *noun, plural* **passersby**

pas·sion (pash-uhn) *noun*
1. A very strong feeling, such as anger, love, or hatred.
2. Great love or enthusiasm. *He has a passion for football.*

pas·sion·ate (pash-uh-nit) *adjective* Having or showing very strong feelings, as in *a passionate speech.* ▷ *adverb* **passionately**

pas·sive (pass-iv) *adjective*
1. If you are **passive,** you let things happen to you and do not fight back or resist. ▷ *adverb* **passively**
2. A **passive** verb's subject has something done to it rather than doing the action itself. In the sentence "The ball was kicked by the football player," the verb is passive, but in the sentence "The football player kicked the ball," the verb is active.

passive smoking *noun* The breathing in of smoke from other people's cigarettes, cigars, or pipes.

Pass·o·ver (pass-oh-vur) *noun* An important Jewish holiday celebrated in the spring. It celebrates the Jews' escape from slavery in Egypt.

pass·port (pass-port) *noun* An official booklet that proves that you are a citizen of a certain country and allows you to travel abroad.

pass·word (pass-wurd) *noun* A secret word, code, or phrase that you need to know to get into a guarded area or a computer system.

past (past)
1. *noun* The period of time before the present. *In the past, people traveled by stagecoach.* ▷ *adjective* **past**
2. *adjective* Just finished or ended. *The past month was rainy.*
3. *preposition* By, after, or beyond. *We went past the exit.* ▷ *adverb* **past**
4. *adjective* Former. *The past president of the club has moved away.*
5. *noun* The **past tense.**

pas·ta (pah-stuh) *noun* A food made from flour and water. Pasta is made into shapes and dried. *The picture shows a selection of different types of pasta.*

pasta

farfalle
(bows)

tagliatelle
(ribbons)

spaghetti

rigatoni
(tubes)

fusilli
(twists)

macaroni

conchiglie
(shells)

paste (payst)
1. *noun* A soft, sticky mixture used to stick things together.
2. *noun* Any soft, creamy mixture, as in *tomato paste.*
3. *verb* To stick with paste. *He will paste the newspaper article into his scrapbook.*
4. *verb* On a computer, to insert at the cursor text or graphics copied or cut from another location.
▷ *verb* **pasting, pasted**

pas·tel (pa-stel *or* pass-tel) *noun*
1. A chalky crayon that is used in drawing.
2. A picture made with pastels.
3. A light, soft shade of a color.
▷ *adjective* **pastel**

pas·teur·ize (pass-chuh-rize *or* pass-tuh-rize) *verb* To heat milk or another liquid to a temperature that is high enough to kill harmful bacteria.
▷ *noun* **pasteurization** ▷ *adjective* **pasteurized**

▶ **Word History**
• •
The first person to **pasteurize** milk was the French doctor, scientist, and inventor Louis Pasteur (1822–1895). The process was named after him.

pas·time (pass-time) *noun* A hobby, a sports activity, or an entertainment that makes the time pass in an enjoyable way. *Watching basketball is my favorite pastime.*

pas·tor (pass-tur) *noun* A minister or priest in charge of a church or parish.

pas·tor·al (pass-tur-uhl) *adjective*
1. To do with the countryside.
2. To do with or from a pastor, as in *pastoral guidance.*

past participle *noun* A form of a verb that ends in -ed or -en and can be used with a helping verb to show that an action or a condition is completed. In the sentence "I have wrapped his gift," the word "wrapped" is a past participle. A past participle is also used to help form a passive verb, such as "kicked" in the sentence "The ball was kicked." Past participles may also be used as adjectives, such as "swollen" in "a swollen ankle."

pas·try (pay-stree) *noun*
1. A dough that is rolled out and used for pie crusts.
2. Pies, tarts, and other baked goods made with pastry. ▷ *noun, plural* **pastries**

past tense *noun* A form of a verb that is used to indicate past time, as "went" in "She went to school late yesterday."

P

377

pas·ture (pass-chur) *noun* Grazing land for animals.

pas·ty (pay-stee) *adjective* If you look **pasty,** you have a pale and sickly complexion. ▷ **pastier, pastiest**

pat (pat)
1. *verb* To tap or stroke something gently with your hand. *Erika patted the frightened kitten to calm it down.* ▷ **patting, patted** ▷ *noun* **pat**
2. *noun* A small, flat piece, as in *a pat of butter.*
3. *noun* If you give someone a **pat on the back,** you praise the person and say that he or she has done well.

patch (pach)
1. *verb* To put a small piece of material on a hole, rip, or worn place in order to mend it. ▷ *noun* **patch**
2. *noun* A small part or area of something. *The black dog had a patch of white fur on his back.*
3. *noun* A small piece of ground. *We planted tomatoes in our vegetable patch.*
4. patch up *verb* To settle or to smooth over. *We patched up our quarrel.*
▷ *noun, plural* **patches** ▷ *verb* **patches, patching, patched**

patch·work (pach-*wurk*) *noun* Fabric with a pattern made by sewing small patches of different material together. Some quilts are patchwork.

patch·y (pach-ee) *adjective* Uneven; made up of or similar to patches, as in *patchy fog.*
▷ **patchier, patchiest**

pâ·té (pah-tay) *noun* A spread made of meat, fish, or vegetables that is usually eaten on toast or crackers.

pat·ent (pat-uhnt)
1. *noun* A legal document giving the inventor of some item sole rights to manufacture or sell the item.
2. *verb* To obtain a patent for. ▷ **patenting, patented**
3. *adjective* Obvious or open. *Leo told a patent lie.* ▷ *adverb* **patently**
4. patent leather *noun* Very shiny leather used for shoes, belts, handbags, and other accessories.

pat·er·nal (puh-tur-nuhl) *adjective*
1. To do with or like a father. *He has paternal concern for the young couple who live next door.*
2. Related through your father. *My paternal grandparents come from Cuba.*
▷ *adverb* **paternally**

path (path) *noun*
1. A trail or track for walking.
2. The line or route along which a person or thing moves. *Scientists tracked the path of the hurricane.*

pa·thet·ic (puh-thet-ik) *adjective*
1. Causing pity, sorrow, or sympathy. *The cold, hungry kitten was a pathetic sight.*
2. Feeble or useless, as in *a pathetic attempt.*
▷ *adverb* **pathetically**

pa·tience (pay-shuhnss) *noun* If you have **patience,** you can put up with problems and delays without getting angry or upset.

pa·tient (pay-shuhnt)
1. *adjective* If you are **patient,** you are good at putting up with problems and delays and don't get angry or upset. ▷ *adverb* **patiently**
2. *noun* Someone who is receiving treatment from a doctor or other health-care provider.

pa·ti·o (pat-ee-oh) *noun* A paved area next to a house, used for relaxing or eating outdoors.
▷ *noun, plural* **patios**

pa·tri·arch (pay-tree-ark) *noun*
1. The male head of a family or tribe. *Grandpa is the patriarch of our family.*
2. An older man in a group, tribe, or village who is respected and who holds a place of honor.

pa·tri·ot (pay-tree-uht) *noun* Someone who loves his or her country and is prepared to fight for it.
▷ *noun* **patriotism** ▷ *adjective* **patriotic**

pa·trol (puh-trohl)
1. *verb* To walk or travel around an area to protect it or to keep watch on people. *Police patrol the area regularly.* ▷ **patrolling, patrolled**
2. *noun* A group of people who protect and watch an area, as in *a highway patrol.*
3. *noun* A group of soldiers, sometimes aboard ships or airplanes, sent out to find or learn about the enemy.

pa·tron (pay-truhn) *noun*
1. A regular customer, as in *a restaurant patron.*
2. Someone who gives money to or helps another person, an activity, or a cause, as in *a patron of the arts.* ▷ *noun* **patronage**

pa·tron·ize (pay-truh-*nize* or pat-ruh-*nize*) *verb*
1. To talk or act as though you are better than another person or persons.
2. If you **patronize** a store, restaurant, or other business, you go there regularly.
▷ *verb* **patronizing, patronized**

patron saint *noun* A saint who is believed to look after a particular country or group of people.

pat·ter (pat-ur)
1. *verb* To make light, quick sounds. *I love to hear the rain patter on my umbrella.* ▷ **pattering, pattered** ▷ *noun* **patter**
2. *noun* Fast talk. *The magician kept up a steady patter while he performed his tricks.*

P

pat·tern (pat-urn) *noun*
1. A repeating arrangement of colors, shapes, and figures. *The material has a pattern of flowers.* ▷ *adjective* **patterned**
2. A sample or model that you can copy from. *I made my dress from a pattern.*
3. A repeated set of actions or characteristics. *There was a pattern to the crimes.*
▷ *verb* **pattern**

pat·ty (pat-ee) *noun*
1. A round, flat piece of chopped or ground food, as in *a hamburger patty.*
2. A round, flat piece of candy, as in *a mint patty.*
▷ *noun, plural* **patties**

pau·per (paw-pur) *noun* A very poor person who receives most of his or her money through charity or welfare.

pause (pawz) *verb* To stop for a short time. *Gretchen paused in the middle of her walk to enjoy the scenery.* ▷ **pausing, paused** ▷ *noun* **pause**

pave (payv) *verb*
1. To cover a road or other surface with a hard material such as concrete or asphalt.
2. pave the way To lead the way, or to make progress easier. *His experiments paved the way for future research.*
▷ *verb* **paving, paved**

pave·ment (payv-muhnt) *noun*
1. A hard material, such as concrete or asphalt, that is used to cover roads or sidewalks.
2. A paved road, or a sidewalk.

pa·vil·ion (puh-vil-yuhn) *noun*
1. An open building that is used for shelter or recreation or for a show or an exhibit, as in a park or at a fair.
2. One of a group of buildings, especially a building that is part of a hospital.

paw (paw) *noun* The foot of an animal having four feet and claws.

pawn (pawn)
1. *verb* To leave a valuable item at a pawnbroker's in return for a loan. The item is returned to you if you repay your debt or may be sold if you fail to do so. ▷ **pawning, pawned**
2. *noun* The smallest piece in the game of chess having the lowest value. *See* **chess.**
3. *noun* A person or thing that is used to get something or gain an advantage.

pawn·brok·er (pawn-broh-kur) *noun* A person whose business is to make loans to people who leave valuable objects as security for the loans.

pay (pay)
1. *verb* To give money for something. ▷ *noun* **payment**
2. *verb* To be worthwhile or advantageous. *It pays to be polite.*
3. *verb* To give or offer something. *Celeste paid me a compliment.*
4. *verb* To suffer. *Ed paid for his mistake.*
5. *noun* Wages or salary.
▷ *verb* **pays, paying, paid**

pay-per-view *noun* A service for cable television viewers in which customers order and view a single movie or televised event for a fee.

pay·roll (pay-rohl) *noun*
1. A list of workers who are paid by a company, along with the amount each is to be paid.
2. The total of all money paid to workers. *The guard picked up the payroll from the bank.*

PC (pee see)
1. *noun* Short for **personal computer.**
2. *adjective* (informal) Someone who is **PC** makes a great effort to be sensitive to the needs and wishes of all groups, including minorities, women, and the disabled, for example. PC stands for *Politically Correct.*

PE (pee ee) *noun* A period in school during which you play sports or do any kind of physical exercise. PE stands for *Physical Education.*

pea (pee) *noun* A small, round, green vegetable that grows as a seed in a pod. *See* **vegetable.**

peace (peess) *noun*
1. A period without war or fighting. ▷ *noun* **peacetime**
2. Calmness of mind or environment. *I'd like some peace and quiet.*
3. Public security, or law and order. *In frontier times, a sheriff's job was to keep the peace.*
Peace sounds like **piece.**
▷ *adjective* **peaceful** ▷ *adverb* **peacefully**

peach (peech) *noun*
1. A soft, round, sweet fruit with a fuzzy, reddish yellow skin and a pit at the center. *See* **fruit.** ▷ *noun, plural* **peaches**
2. A pink-yellow color. ▷ *adjective* **peach**

pea·cock (pee-kok) *noun* A large bird that is related to the pheasant. The male peacock has brilliant blue and green feathers that spread out in a fan shape when the peacock raises its tail.

peacock

379

peak (peek) *noun*
1. The pointed top of a high mountain.
2. A mountain with a pointed top.
3. The highest or best point. *Carl reached the peak of his athletic career when he won the Olympic gold medal.* ▷ *verb* **peak**
4. The brim, or the curved front part of a cap. **Peak** sounds like **peek.**

peal (peel)
1. *verb* When bells **peal,** they ring out loudly. ▷ **pealing, pealed**
2. *noun* A loud sound or series of sounds, as in *a peal of bells* or *peals of laughter.* **Peal** sounds like **peel.**

pea·nut (pee-nuht) *noun* A nutlike seed that grows in underground pods. Peanuts are eaten roasted or made into peanut butter and cooking oil.

peanut butter *noun* A thick, light brown spread made from ground, roasted peanuts.

pear (pair) *noun* A juicy, sweet, yellow, green, red, or brown fruit with a smooth skin. **Pear** sounds like **pair** and **pare.** *See* **fruit.**

pearl (purl)
noun
1. A small, round object that grows inside oysters and is used to make valuable jewelry.
2. A valuable person, thing, or idea, as in *pearls of wisdom.*

oyster

oyster shell

mother-of-pearl lining pearl

peas·ant (pez-uhnt) *noun* Someone who owns a small farm or works on a farm, especially in Europe and some Asian nations.

peat (peet) *noun* Dark brown, partly decayed plant matter that is found in bogs and swamps. Peat can be used as fuel or compost.

peb·ble (peb-uhl) *noun* A small, round stone. ▷ *adjective* **pebbly**

pe·can (pee-kan *or* pi-kahn) *noun* A sweet nut with a thin, smooth shell. Pecans grow on large trees.

peck (pek)
1. *verb* When a bird **pecks** at something, it strikes it or picks it up with its beak. ▷ **pecking, pecked** ▷ *noun* **peck**
2. *noun* (*informal*) A quick kiss. *Aunt Doris gave me a peck on the cheek.* ▷ *verb* **peck**
3. *noun* A unit of measure for dry things, such as fruit, vegetables, and grain. A peck is equal to eight quarts or $\frac{1}{4}$ of a bushel.

pe·cu·liar (pi-kyoo-lyur) *adjective*
1. Strange or odd.
2. **peculiar to** Belonging to or having to do with a certain person, group, place, or thing. *Kangaroos are peculiar to Australia.*
▷ *noun* **peculiarity** ▷ *adverb* **peculiarly**

ped·al (ped-uhl)
1. *noun* A lever on a bicycle, car, piano, etc., that you push with your foot.
2. *verb* To make something work or move by using a pedal or pedals. ▷ **pedaling, pedaled**
Pedal sounds like **peddle.**

ped·dle (ped-uhl) *verb* To travel around selling things. *When my grandfather was a boy, he used a horse and wagon to peddle fruits and vegetables.* **Peddle** sounds like **pedal.** ▷ **peddling, peddled** ▷ *noun* **peddler**

ped·es·tal (ped-i-stuhl) *noun*
1. A base for a statue.
2. Any base or support, as for a large vase.
3. If you put someone **on a pedestal,** you admire and respect the person excessively.

pe·des·tri·an (puh-dess-tree-uhn) *noun* Someone who travels on foot.

pe·di·a·tric·ian (pee-dee-uh-tri-shuhn) *noun* A doctor who specializes in the care and treatment of babies and children. ▷ *noun* **pediatrics**

ped·i·gree (ped-uh-gree) *noun* A line or list of ancestors, especially of an animal. *My dog's pedigree includes many champion show dogs.*

peek (peek) *verb* To look at something secretly or quickly. *It was difficult not to peek at the present that arrived a few days before my birthday.* **Peek** sounds like **peak.** ▷ **peeking, peeked** ▷ *noun* **peek**

peel (peel)
1. *noun* The tough outer skin of a fruit.
2. *verb* To remove the skin of a vegetable or a fruit. *Please peel the potatoes.*
3. *verb* To remove or to pull off. *Before you paint this wall, you must peel off the wallpaper.*
4. *verb* To come off in pieces or strips. *I got so sunburned that the skin on my back peeled.*
Peel sounds like **peal.**
▷ *verb* **peeling, peeled**

peep (peep)
1. *verb* To peek or look secretly at something. ▷ **peeping, peeped** ▷ *noun* **peep**
2. *noun* The sharp sound that a young bird or chicken makes. ▷ *verb* **peep**

peer (pihr)
1. *verb* To look hard at something that is difficult to see. *He peered at the note but could not read it in the dim light.* ▷ **peering, peered**

P

2. *noun* An equal, or a person of the same age, rank, or standing as another, as in *a jury of one's peers.*

3. *noun* A member of the British nobility, such as a duke or an earl. ▷ *noun* **peerage**

Peer sounds like **pier.**

peg (peg) *noun* A thin piece of wood, metal, or plastic, used to hold things down or hang things up. ▷ *verb* **peg**

Pe·king·ese (*peek*-uhn-eez) *noun* A breed of small dog originally from China. A Pekingese has a long, silky coat and a flat face. ▷ *noun, plural* **Pekingese**

pel·i·can (pel-uh-kuhn)

noun A large water bird with a pouch below its beak where it holds the fish that it catches.

pelican

pel·let (pel-it) *noun* A small, hard ball of something, such as food or ice.

pell-mell (pel-mel) *adverb* In a confused or disorderly way. *The frightened child rushed pell-mell into the crowd.*

pelt (pelt)

1. *verb* To strike or beat again and again. *Hail pelted the windshield.* ▷ **pelting, pelted**

2. *noun* An animal's skin with the hair or fur still on it.

pen (pen)

1. *noun* An instrument used for writing or drawing with ink. ▷ *verb* **pen**

2. *noun* A small, enclosed area for sheep, cattle, pigs, or other animals.

3. *verb* To keep or shut up in a pen. ▷ **penning, penned**

▶ **Word History**
. . . .
The English word **pen** comes from the Latin word *penna,* which means "feather." People once wrote with quill pens crafted from bird feathers.

pe·nal·ize (pee-nuh-*lize* or pen-uh-*lize*) *verb* To make someone suffer a penalty or punishment for something the person has done wrong. *The referee penalized the basketball player for shoving.* ▷ **penalizing, penalized**

pen·al·ty (pen-uhl-tee) *noun*

1. A punishment. *In my town, the penalty for littering is a $100.00 fine.*

2. In sports, a disadvantage or punishment that a team or player suffers for breaking the rules. *The referee called a penalty of 10 yards against the football team.*

pen·cil (pen-suhl) *noun* An instrument used for drawing and writing. A pencil is made from a stick of graphite in a covering usually made of wood. ▷ *verb* **pencil**

pen·dant (pen-duhnt) *noun* A hanging ornament, especially one worn on a necklace.

pen·du·lum (pen-juh-luhm *or* pen-dyuh-luhm) *noun* A weight in a large clock that moves from side to side and helps keep the clock ticking regularly.

pen·e·trate (pen-uh-trate) *verb*

1. To go inside or through something. *The nail penetrated Nick's shoe.*

2. To understand or to solve, as in *to penetrate a mystery.*

▷ *verb* **penetrating, penetrated** ▷ *noun* **penetration**

pen·guin (pen-gwin *or* peng-gwin) *noun* A water bird of the Antarctic region that cannot fly. The penguin uses its wings as flippers for underwater swimming. *See* **polar.**

pen·i·cil·lin (pen-uh-sil-uhn) *noun* A drug made from a mold called *penicillium* that kills bacteria and helps fight some diseases. Penicillin was the first antibiotic. It was discovered in 1928 by Sir Alexander Fleming, a British scientist.

pen·in·su·la (puh-nin-suh-luh)

noun A piece of land that sticks out from a larger land mass and is almost completely surrounded by water. *The map shows Florida, which is a peninsula.*

▷ *adjective* **peninsular**

peninsula

Florida

▶ **Word History**
. . . .
Peninsula comes from the Latin words *paene,* which means "almost," and *insula,* which means "island." A peninsula is indeed almost an island. All but one side is surrounded by water.

pe·nis (pee-niss) *noun* The male organ for urinating. ▷ *noun, plural* **penises** *or* **penes** (pee-neez)

pen·i·tent (pen-uh-tuhnt) *adjective* If you are **penitent,** you are extremely sorry for what you have done wrong. ▷ *noun* **penitent,** *noun* **penitence**

pen·i·ten·tia·ry (pen-uh-**ten**-chur-ee) *noun* A state or federal prison for people found guilty of serious crimes. ▷ *noun, plural* **penitentiaries**

pen·knife (pen-*nife*) *noun* A small knife with blades that fold into a case. *The penknife shown here is a Swiss Army knife.* ▷ *noun, plural* **penknives**

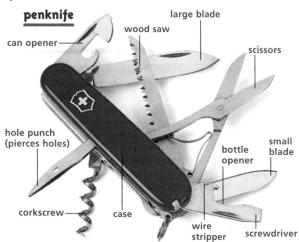

penknife

can opener
wood saw
large blade
scissors
hole punch (pierces holes)
bottle opener
small blade
corkscrew
case
wire stripper
screwdriver

pen name *noun* A made-up name used by an author instead of his or her real name. *Mark Twain is the pen name of Samuel Langhorne Clemens.*

pen·nant (pen-uhnt) *noun*
1. A long, triangular flag, often with the name of a school or team on it.
2. A triangular flag that symbolizes a championship, especially in professional baseball. *My favorite team won the pennant last year.*

pen·ni·less (pen-ee-liss) *adjective* If you are **penniless,** you have absolutely no money.

pen·ny (pen-ee) *noun* The coin that is the smallest unit of money in the United States and Canada. A penny equals one cent. One hundred pennies equal one dollar. ▷ *noun, plural* **pennies**

pen pal *noun* Someone, often from another country, who exchanges letters with you.

pen·sion (pen-shuhn) *noun* An amount of money paid regularly to someone who has retired from work. ▷ *noun* **pensioner**

pen·ta·gon (pen-tuh-gon) *noun*
1. A flat shape with five sides. *See* **shape.**
▷ *adjective* **pentagonal** (pen-**tag**-uh-nuhl)
2. the Pentagon A building with five sides in Arlington, Virginia, that is the headquarters of the U.S. Department of Defense.

pent·house (pent-houss) *noun* An apartment located on the top floor of a tall building.

pen·ul·ti·mate (pi-**nuhl**-tuh-mit) *adjective* Next to last. *Y is the penultimate letter in the alphabet.*

pe·o·ny (pee-uh-nee) *noun* A garden plant with large flowers that may be red, pink, or white. ▷ *noun, plural* **peonies**

peo·ple (pee-puhl) *noun*
1. Persons or human beings.
2. A collection of human beings who make up a nation, race, tribe, or group, as in *the American people.* ▷ *noun, plural* **peoples**
3. Family or relatives. *His people come from Korea.*

pep (pep)
1. *noun* Great energy and high spirits. *She was full of pep.* ▷ *adjective* **pep**
2. *verb* If something **peps** you **up,** it fills you with energy. ▷ **pepping, pepped**

pep·per (pep-ur) *noun*
1. A spicy powder made from the dried berries of a tropical climbing plant. ▷ *verb* **pepper**
▷ *adjective* **peppery**
2. A hollow vegetable that is usually red, green, or yellow. *See* **vegetable.**

pep·per·mint (pep-ur-*mint*) *noun*
1. A kind of mint plant. The oil from peppermint leaves is used as a flavoring, especially in candy and toothpaste.
2. A candy flavored with peppermint oil.
▷ *adjective* **peppermint**

per (pur) *preposition* In each or for each. *His job pays $7.00 per hour.* **Per** sounds like **purr.**

per·ceive (pur-seev) *verb*
1. To become aware of through the senses, especially through sight or hearing. *I perceived a small, dark figure in the distance.*
2. To understand. *She perceived that I was angry.*
▷ *verb* **perceiving, perceived** ▷ *noun* **perception**

per·cent (pur-sent) *noun* A part that is one one-hundredth. A quarter is 25 percent of one dollar. Percent is also written using the percent symbol %.

per·cent·age (pur-sen-tij) *noun*
1. A fraction or proportion of something expressed as a number out of a hundred.
2. A part considered in relation to the whole; a proportion. *What percentage of the class is out?*

per·cep·ti·ble (pur-sep-tuh-buhl) *adjective* Noticeable and clear. *There was a perceptible difference in Kareem's height after the summer.*
▷ *adverb* **perceptibly**

per·cep·tive (pur-sep-tiv) *adjective* If you are **perceptive,** you are quick to notice things or to understand situations.

perch (purch)
1. *noun* A bar or branch on which a bird can rest. ▷ *verb* **perch**
2. *noun* Any raised place where a person can sit or stand.

P

3. *verb* To sit or stand on the edge of something, often high up. ▷ **perches, perching, perched**

4. *noun* An edible freshwater fish. *See* **fish.**
▷ *noun, plural* **perches** *or* **perch** *(fish only)*

per·chance (pur-chanss) *adverb* Perhaps or possibly.

per·cus·sion instrument (pur-kuhsh-uhn) *noun* A musical instrument, such as a drum, that is played by being hit or shaken. *The picture shows a variety of small percussion instruments.* ▷ *noun* **percussionist**

percussion instruments

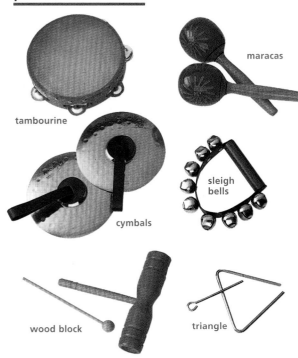

tambourine

maracas

cymbals

sleigh bells

wood block

triangle

per·en·ni·al (puh-ren-ee-uhl)
1. *noun* A plant that lives and flowers for more than two years. *Roses are perennials.*
2. *adjective* Lasting for a long time, or never ending. *If you seem to have a perennial cold, your problem might be allergies.* ▷ *adverb* **perennially**

per·e·stroi·ka (per-uh-stroi-kuh) *noun* The policy of economic and governmental reform begun in the former Soviet Union during the mid-1980s.

per·fect
1. (pur-fikt) *adjective* Without any flaws or mistakes, as in *a perfect apple* or *a perfect copy.* ▷ *noun* **perfection** ▷ *adverb* **perfectly**
2. (pur-fekt) *verb* To succeed with effort in making something work well. *After much practice, Bill perfected his juggling skills.*
▷ **perfecting, perfected**

per·fo·rate (pur-fuh-rayt) *verb*
1. To make a hole in.

2. To make a row of small holes through. *The printer perforated the edge of the subscription form so that it would be easier to tear out of the magazine.*
▷ *verb* **perforating, perforated** ▷ *noun* **perforation**
▷ *adjective* **perforated**

per·form (pur-form) *verb*
1. To do something or carry something out. *He performed many useful tasks around the house.*
2. To give a show in public. *Our class will perform a play during the Spring Festival.*
▷ *verb* **performing, performed**

per·form·ance (pur-for-muhnss) *noun*
1. The public presentation of a play, movie, or piece of music.
2. The way something works. *Engineers tested the car's performance on slippery roads.*

per·form·er (pur-for-mur) *noun* Someone who entertains an audience in public.

per·fume (pur-fyoom *or* pur-fyoom) *noun*
1. A liquid you put on your skin to make yourself smell pleasant.
2. Any pleasing smell or odor.
▷ *verb* **perfume** ▷ *adjective* **perfumed**

per·haps (pur-haps) *adverb* Maybe or possibly.

per·il (per-uhl) *noun*
1. Danger. *A police officer's life is often in peril.*
2. Something dangerous.
▷ *adjective* **perilous** ▷ *adverb* **perilously**

pe·rim·e·ter (puh-rim-uh-tur) *noun*
1. The outside edge of an area.
2. The distance around the edge of a shape or an area.

pe·ri·od (pihr-ee-uhd) *noun*
1. A length of time. *Rocky left the room for a short period.*
2. A part of a school day. *After lunch we have a free period.*
3. The punctuation mark (.) used to show that a sentence has ended or that a word has been abbreviated.

pe·ri·od·ic (*pihr*-ee-od-ik) *adjective* Happening or repeating at regular intervals. *Once a year we take the cat to the vet for her periodic shots.*
▷ *adverb* **periodically**

pe·ri·od·i·cal (*pihr*-ee-od-uh-kuhl) *noun* A journal or magazine that is published at regular intervals, most often once a week or once a month.

pe·riph·er·al (puh-rif-ur-uhl)
1. *noun* An external device, such as a printer or modem, that is connected to and controlled by a computer.
2. *adjective* To do with the outer part or edge of something, as in *peripheral vision.* ▷ *adverb* **peripherally**

P

pe·riph·er·y (puh-rif-ur-ee) *noun* The outside edge of something. ▷ *noun, plural* **peripheries**

per·i·scope (per-uh-*skope*) *noun* A vertical tube with prisms or mirrors at each end that allows you to see something from a position a long way below it. Periscopes are often used in submarines. *The diagram shows how a periscope works.*

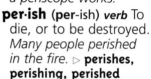
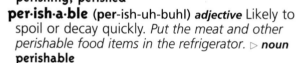

periscope

prism (tilts up or down)

light from image

lens (enlarges and sharpens image)

line of sight

eyepiece — prism

per·ish (per-ish) *verb* To die, or to be destroyed. *Many people perished in the fire.* ▷ **perishes, perishing, perished**

per·ish·a·ble (per-ish-uh-buhl) *adjective* Likely to spoil or decay quickly. *Put the meat and other perishable food items in the refrigerator.* ▷ *noun* **perishable**

per·ju·ry (pur-jur-ee) *noun* The act of lying in a court of law while under oath to tell the truth. *Perjury is a crime.* ▷ *noun, plural* **perjuries** ▷ *verb* **perjure**

perk (purk)
1. *verb* To lift up briskly or alertly. *The dogs perked up their ears when they heard the car in the driveway.*
2. *verb* If you **perk up,** you become more cheerful. ▷ *adjective* **perky**
3. *noun* (informal) An extra advantage that comes from doing a particular job. *One of the perks of working in this restaurant is the free food.*
▷ *verb* **perking, perked**

perm (purm) *noun* (informal) A process in which hair is treated with chemicals to give it curls or waves that last for several months. Perm is short for *permanent wave.*

per·ma·nent (pur-muh-nuhnt) *adjective* Lasting or meant to last for a long time, as in *a permanent job.* ▷ *noun* **permanence** ▷ *adverb* **permanently**

per·me·ate (pur-mee-*ate*) *verb* To spread or pass through something. *A delicious smell permeated the house.* ▷ **permeating, permeated**

per·mis·si·ble (pur-miss-uh-buhl) *adjective* If something is **permissible,** it is allowed.

per·mis·sion (pur-mish-uhn) *noun* If you give **permission** for something, you say that you will allow it to happen.

per·mis·sive (pur-miss-iv) *adjective* Someone who is **permissive** is not strict and allows freedom where others would not. ▷ *noun* **permissiveness**

per·mit
1. (pur-mit) *verb* To allow something. ▷ **permitting, permitted**
2. (pur-mit) *noun* A written statement giving permission for something, as in *a hunting permit.*

per·mu·ta·tion (pur-myuh-**tay**-shuhn) *noun* One of the ways in which a series of things can be arranged or put in order. *There are six permutations of the numbers 1, 2, and 3: 123, 132, 213, 231, 312, and 321.*

per·pen·dic·u·lar (pur-puhn-dik-yuh-lur)
1. *noun* A line that is at right angles to another line or to a surface. ▷ *adjective* **perpendicular**
2. *adjective* Straight up and down or extremely steep, as in *the perpendicular face of a mountain.*

per·pet·u·al (pur-pech-oo-uhl) *adjective* Without ending or changing, as in *perpetual motion.* ▷ *adverb* **perpetually**

per·pet·u·ate (pur-pech-oo-ate) *verb* To make something last or continue for a very long time. *The war memorial perpetuates the memory of the soldiers who died in combat.* ▷ **perpetuating, perpetuated** ▷ *noun* **perpetuation**

per·plex (pur-pleks) *verb* To make someone puzzled or unsure. *Her sudden change in attitude perplexed us.* ▷ **perplexes, perplexing, perplexed** ▷ *noun* **perplexity** ▷ *adjective* **perplexed**

per·se·cute (pur-suh-kyoot) *verb* To continually treat someone cruelly and unfairly, especially because of that person's ideas or political beliefs. ▷ **persecuting, persecuted** ▷ *noun* **persecution**

per·se·vere (pur-suh-**veer**) *verb* If you **persevere** at something, you keep on trying and do not give up, even if you are faced with obstacles or difficulties. ▷ **persevering, persevered** ▷ *noun* **perseverance**

per·sim·mon (pur-sim-uhn) *noun* An orange-red fruit that is shaped like a plum and is sweet and soft when ripe.

per·sist (pur-sist *or* pur-zist) *verb*
1. To last or to continue steadily. *Her cold persisted all week.*
2. To keep on doing something in spite of obstacles or warnings. *If you persist in teasing your brother, you will be sent to your room.*
▷ *verb* **persisting, persisted** ▷ *noun* **persistence** ▷ *adjective* **persistent** ▷ *adverb* **persistently**

per·son (pur-suhn) *noun*
1. An individual human being.
2. In grammar, the *first person* refers to "I" or "we"; the *second person* refers to "you"; the *third person* refers to "he," "she," "it," or "they."
3. in person Physically present. *The actor looked shorter in person than on TV.*

per·son·al (pur-suh-nuhl) *adjective*
1. Private, or to do with one person only, as in *personal property.*
2. Done or made in person, as in *a personal appearance.*

personal computer *noun* A small desktop or portable computer that can be used by an individual at home, at school, or in an office.

per·son·al·i·ty (*pur*-suh-**nal**-uh-tee) *noun*
1. All of the qualities or traits that make one person different from others. *Sally has a very outgoing personality.*
2. A famous person, as in *a show business personality.*
▷ *noun, plural* **personalities**

per·son·al·ly (pur-suhn-uh-lee) *adverb*
1. Without assistance; directly. *I invited them personally.*
2. For oneself. *Don't take the remark personally.*
3. As an individual. *I don't like my boss personally, but I think he's good at his job.*

per·son·nel (purss-uh-nel) *noun* The group of people who work for a company or an organization. ▷ *noun, plural* **personnel** ▷ *adjective* **personnel**

per·spec·tive (pur-**spek**-tiv) *noun*
1. A particular way of looking at a situation. *From my perspective, she's the best person for the job.*
2. The way things or events relate to each other in size or importance. *If you put your problems into proper perspective, you'll see that most of them are very minor.*
3. If a picture is **in perspective,** distant objects are drawn smaller than nearer ones so that the view looks as someone would see it.

per·spire (pur-spire) *verb* To sweat. ▷ **perspiring, perspired** ▷ *noun* **perspiration**

per·suade (pur-swade) *verb* To succeed in making someone do or believe something by giving the person good reasons. ▷ **persuading, persuaded** ▷ *noun* **persuasion** ▷ *adjective* **persuasive**

per·tain (pur-tane) *verb* To be connected or related. *The president's speech pertained to the state of the U.S. economy.* ▷ **pertaining, pertained**

per·ti·nent (purt-uh-nuhnt) *adjective* To do with what is being discussed or considered. *Your remarks are pertinent to the subject at hand.*

per·turb (pur-turb) *verb* To make someone uncomfortable or anxious. *Harry's questions perturbed me.* ▷ **perturbing, perturbed**

per·verse (pur-vurss) *adjective* Deliberately unreasonable and stubborn. ▷ *noun* **perversity**

pe·se·ta (puh-**say**-tuh) *noun* The main unit of money in Spain.

pe·so (pay-soh) *noun* The main unit of money in Mexico, the Philippines, and several South and Central American countries. ▷ *noun, plural* **pesos**

pes·si·mis·tic (pess-uh-**miss**-tik) *adjective* People who are **pessimistic** are gloomy and always think that the worst will happen. ▷ *noun* **pessimism,** *noun* **pessimist** ▷ *adverb* **pessimistically**

pest (pest) *noun*
1. An insect that destroys or damages flowers, fruits, or vegetables.
2. Any creature that causes serious interference with human activity.
3. A persistently annoying person.

pes·ter (pess-tur) *verb* To keep annoying other people, often by asking or telling them something over and over again. ▷ **pestering, pestered**

pes·ti·cide (pess-tuh-*side*) *noun* A chemical used to kill pests, such as insects.

pes·tle (pess-uhl *or* pess-tuhl) *noun* A short stick with a thick, rounded end used to crush things such as herbs and medicine in a bowl called a mortar.

pet (pet)
1. *noun* A tame animal kept for company or pleasure.
2. *noun* Somebody's favorite person or thing, as in *teacher's pet.*
3. *verb* To stroke or pat an animal in a gentle, loving way. ▷ **petting, petted**
▷ *adjective* **pet**

pet·al (pet-uhl) *noun* One of the colored outer parts of a flower. *See* **flower.**

pe·ti·tion (puh-**tish**-uhn) *noun* A letter signed by many people asking those in power to change their policy or actions or telling them how the signers feel about a certain issue or situation. *We signed a petition asking for the computer room to be opened an hour earlier.* ▷ *verb* **petition**

pet·ri·fied (pet-ruh-fide) *adjective*
1. If you are **petrified,** you are unable to move because you are so frightened.
2. Petrified wood is dead wood that has turned into stone because minerals have seeped into its cells.
▷ *verb* **petrify**

pe·tro·le·um (puh-**troh**-lee-uhm) *noun* A thick, oily liquid found below the earth's surface. It is used to make gasoline, kerosene, heating oil, and many other products.

pet·ti·coat (pet-ee-*kote*) *noun* A thin garment worn underneath a skirt or dress.

pet·ty (pet-ee) *adjective*
1. Trivial and unimportant, as in *petty complaints.*
2. Mean or spiteful, as in *petty gossip.*
▷ *adjective* **pettier, pettiest**

pe·tu·nia (puh-**too**-nyuh) *noun* A garden plant with colorful flowers shaped like trumpets.

pew (pyoo) *noun* A long, wooden bench with a high back that people sit on in church.

pew·ter (**pyoo**-tur) *noun*
1. A metal made of tin mixed with lead or copper. Pewter is used to make plates, pitchers, and other utensils.
2. Utensils made of pewter. *Grandma has a collection of pewter.*
▷ *adjective* **pewter**

pH (pee aych) *noun* A measure of how acidic or alkaline a substance is. The initials pH stand for *Potential of Hydrogen. Acids have pH values under 7, and alkalis have pH values over 7. If a substance has a pH value of 7, it is neutral.*

phan·tom (**fan**-tuhm) *noun* A ghost.

phar·aoh (**fair**-oh) *noun* The title of kings of ancient Egypt.

phar·ma·cist (**far**-muh-sist) *noun* A trained person who prepares and sells drugs and medicines.

phar·ma·cy (**far**-muh-see) *noun* A drugstore.
▷ *noun, plural* **pharmacies**

phase (faze)
1. *noun* A stage in something or someone's growth or development. *My two-year-old sister is going through a crying phase.*
2. *noun* A stage of the moon's change in shape as it appears from earth. *See* **moon.**
3. *noun* One part or side of something. *Let's go over every phase of the problem.*
4. phase in *verb* To start something gradually.
5. phase out *verb* To stop something gradually.
▷ *verb* **phasing, phased**

pheas·ant (**fez**-uhnt) *noun* A large, brightly colored bird with a long tail that is hunted for sport and for food. Peacocks, partridges, grouse, and quail are types of pheasant.

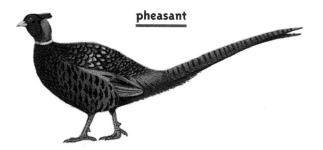

pheasant

phe·nom·e·nal (fuh-**nom**-uh-nuhl) *adjective* Amazing or astonishing. *The rock group's first album was a phenomenal success.* ▷ *adverb* **phenomenally**

phe·nom·e·non (fe-**nom**-uh-non) *noun*
1. An event or a fact that can be seen or felt. *An earthquake is a natural phenomenon.*
2. Something very unusual and remarkable.
▷ *noun, plural* **phenomena** *or* **phenomenons**

phil·an·thro·pist (fuh-**lan**-thruh-pist) *noun* A person who helps others by giving time or money to causes and charities.

phil·o·den·dron (fil-uh-**den**-druhn) *noun* A tropical American climbing vine with leaves that are shaped like hearts. The philodendron is a popular indoor plant.

phil·o·soph·i·cal (fil-uh-**sof**-uh-kuhl) *adjective*
1. To do with philosophy.
2. If you are **philosophical,** you accept difficulties and problems calmly.
▷ *adverb* **philosophically**

phi·los·o·phy (fuh-**loss**-uh-fee) *noun*
1. The study of truth, wisdom, the nature of reality, and knowledge.
2. The systematic study of the basic ideas in any field, as in *the philosophy of science.*
3. A person's **philosophy** is his or her basic ideas and beliefs on how life should be lived.
▷ *noun* **philosopher**

phlegm (flem) *noun* The thick substance that you cough up when you have a cold.

pho·bi·a (**foh**-bee-uh) *noun* An extremely strong fear. *John has a phobia of spiders.* ▷ *adjective* **phobic**

phone (fohn) *noun* Short for **telephone.** ▷ *verb* **phone**

pho·net·i·cal·ly (fuh-**net**-ik-lee) *adverb* If something is spelled **phonetically,** it is spelled as it is pronounced, sometimes by using special symbols to represent sounds. The words in this dictionary are spelled phonetically in parentheses.

pho·net·ics (fuh-**net**-iks) *noun* The study of the sounds that are used in speaking.

pho·no·graph (**foh**-nuh-*graf*) *noun* A machine that picks up and reproduces the sounds that have been recorded in the grooves cut into a record. *CD players are replacing phonographs.*

phos·pho·res·cence (*foss*-fuh-**ress**-uhnss) *noun*
1. Light that is given off from a substance after the source of energy has been removed.
2. The light that is given off by a living thing, such as a fish or an insect.
▷ *adjective* **phosphorescent**

phos·pho·rus (**foss**-fur-uhss) *noun* A chemical element that glows in the dark. It is used in making matches, fertilizers, glass, and steel.

pho·to (foh-toh) *noun* Short for **photograph.**

pho·to·cop·i·er (foh-toh-*kop*-ee-ur) *noun* A machine that copies documents using a special lens and ink called *toner.*

pho·to·cop·y (foh-toh-*kop*-ee) *noun* A copy of a document made by a photocopier. ▷ *verb* **photocopy**

photo finish *noun* A very close end to a race, where a photograph has to be studied to decide which racer has won. ▷ *noun, plural* **photo finishes**

pho·to·gen·ic (foh-tuh-**jen**-ik) *adjective* If someone is **photogenic,** he or she looks very good in photographs. *Bill was so photogenic that his friends all encouraged him to become a model.*

pho·to·graph (foh-tuh-*graf*) *noun* A picture taken by a camera on film and then developed on paper. ▷ *verb* **photograph**

pho·to·gra·phy (fuh-**tog**-ruh-fee) *noun* The creation of pictures by exposing film inside a camera to light. *The single-lens reflex camera shown here is used in professional and amateur photography. The reflex mirror sends light from the lens through the prism to the viewfinder, so you see the same image that falls on the film. When you press the shutter-release button, the mirror swings up, the shutter opens, and light hits the film.* ▷ *noun* **photographer** ▷ *adjective* **photographic**

pho·to·jour·nal·ist (*foh*-toh-**jurn**-uh-list) *noun* A photographer who takes photographs of news events and tells the story of what has happened through the photos. ▷ *noun* **photojournalism**

pho·to·syn·the·sis (foh-toh-**sin**-thuh-siss) *noun* A chemical process by which green plants make their food. Plants use energy from the sun to turn water and carbon dioxide into food, and they give off oxygen as a by-product.

phrase (fraze)
1. *noun* A group of words that have a meaning but do not form a sentence. *In the dark* is a phrase.
2. *verb* To put into words in a particular way. ▷ **phrasing, phrased**

phys·i·cal (fiz-uh-kuhl) *adjective*
1. To do with the body, as in *physical education.*
2. To do with matter and energy. *Chemistry is a physical science.*
3. To do with nature or natural objects. *I need a map that shows the mountains, rivers, and other physical features of the United States.*

physical fitness *noun* The state of being in good health as a result of exercising and eating nutritious foods.

physical therapy *noun* The treatment of diseased or injured muscles and joints by physical and mechanical means, such as exercise, massage, and heat. ▷ *noun* **physical therapist**

single-lens reflex camera

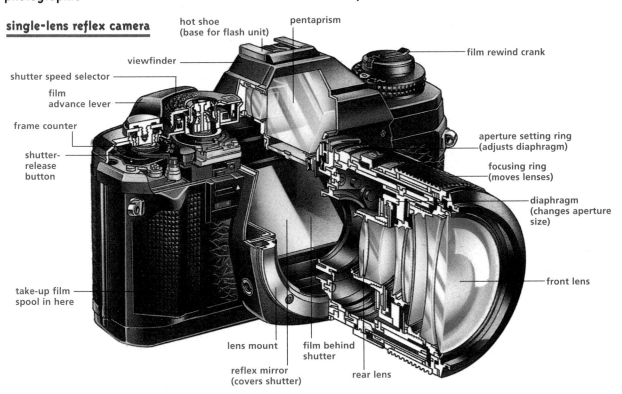

hot shoe (base for flash unit), pentaprism, viewfinder, film rewind crank, shutter speed selector, film advance lever, frame counter, shutter-release button, aperture setting ring (adjusts diaphragm), focusing ring (moves lenses), diaphragm (changes aperture size), take-up film spool in here, front lens, lens mount, film behind shutter, reflex mirror (covers shutter), rear lens

phy·si·cian (fuh-**zish**-uhn) *noun* Someone with a medical degree who has been trained and licensed to treat injured and sick people; a doctor. Physicians are also authorized to write prescriptions for medicine.

phys·ics (**fiz**-iks) *noun* The science that deals with matter and energy. It includes the study of light, heat, sound, electricity, motion, and force. ▷ *noun* **physicist**

pi (pye) *noun* In math, a symbol (π) for the ratio of the circumference of a circle to its diameter. Pi equals about 3.1416. **Pi** sounds like **pie**.

pi·an·o (pee-**an**-oh *or* **pyan**-oh)
1. *noun* A large keyboard instrument that produces musical sounds when padded hammers inside the piano strike tuned metal strings. ▷ *noun* **pianist** ▷ *noun, plural* **pianos**
2. *adverb* Softly. This word is used in music.

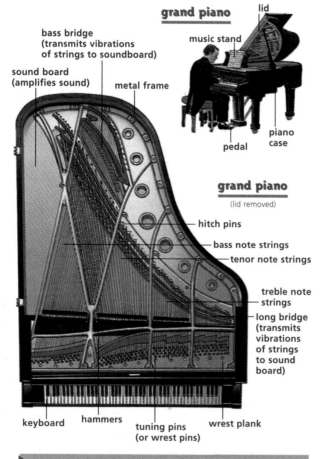

grand piano

bass bridge (transmits vibrations of strings to soundboard)

sound board (amplifies sound)

metal frame

lid

music stand

piano case

pedal

grand piano
(lid removed)

hitch pins

bass note strings

tenor note strings

treble note strings

long bridge (transmits vibrations of strings to sound board)

keyboard

hammers

tuning pins (or wrest pins)

wrest plank

Word History

In Italian, **piano** means "soft." The name for the instrument comes from the phrase *piano e forte,* or "soft and loud." This refers to the fact that a piano's tones can vary from soft to loud.

pic·co·lo (**pik**-uh-loh) *noun* An instrument that looks like a flute but is smaller and has a higher pitch. See **woodwind**. ▷ *noun, plural* **piccolos**

pick (pik)
1. *verb* To choose or to select. *During the card trick, I had to pick a number.* ▷ *noun* **pick**
2. *verb* To collect or to gather. *Have you picked all the strawberries?*
▷ *noun* **picker**
3. *noun* A tool with pointed metal ends, used for breaking up soil or rocks.
4. *noun* A small piece of plastic or metal used to strum or pluck banjo or guitar strings.
▷ *verb* **pick**
5. *verb* To cause on purpose. *He's trying to pick a fight.*
6. *verb* If you **pick on** someone, you tease the person or treat him or her in a mean way.
7. *verb* If you **pick at** something, you take bits off it. *I wasn't hungry, so I just picked at my food.*
▷ *verb* **picking, picked**

picks

Synonyms: pick

Pick means to decide on something from among a number of possibilities. You can pick something at random or because you've made a specific decision: *I picked a comedy at the video store because I needed a good laugh.*

Choose means to decide on something after giving the matter some thought: *Ms. Chang will choose the best paper after she reads them all.*

Select means to pick something after carefully considering the choices: *After much thought, I think I selected the perfect gift for my mother's birthday.*

Prefer means that you have chosen something because you like it better or best: *Cindy prefers books to magazines, football to baseball, and movies to TV.*

Elect means to choose someone for office by voting: *The town will elect a new mayor on June 8.*

pick·ax *or* **pick·axe** (**pik**-aks) *noun* A tool with a long handle and a metal head. One end of the head is a sharp blade, and the other is a pick. A pickax can be used to cut through roots, loosen soil, and break up rocks. ▷ *noun, plural* **pickaxes**

pick·er·el (pik-ur-uhl) *noun* A freshwater fish found in the waters of North America. The pickerel has a long, pointed head and is used for food. ▷ *noun, plural* **pickerel** *or* **pickerels**

pick·et (pik-it)
1. *verb* To stand outside a place to make a protest and sometimes to try to prevent people from entering. ▷ **picketing, picketed** ▷ *noun* **picket,** *noun* **picketer**
2. *noun* A pointed stake that is driven into the ground to hold something in place or to build a fence.

pick·le (pik-uhl)
1. *verb* To preserve food in vinegar or salt water. ▷ **pickling, pickled**
2. *noun* Any food, such as a cucumber, that has been pickled.
3. *noun* (informal) A difficult situation. *Peter hadn't done his homework, and he was in a pickle because there was a surprise quiz.*

pick·pock·et (pik-*pok*-it) *noun* Someone who steals from people's pockets or handbags.

pick·up (pik-*uhp*) *noun*
1. An increase in speed. *Our car has good pickup.*
2. A small truck with a driver's cab and an open back.

pick·y (pik-ee) *adjective* (informal) Fussy or choosy. *My brother is a picky eater.* ▷ **pickier, pickiest**

pic·nic (pik-nik) *noun* A party or trip that includes a meal eaten out of doors. ▷ *noun* **picnicker** ▷ *verb* **picnic**

pic·to·graph (pik-toh-*graf*) *noun*
1. A picture used as a symbol in ancient writing systems.
2. Another name for **picture graph.**

pic·to·ri·al (pik-**tor**-ee-uhl) *adjective* Using pictures. *My book about birds is a pictorial guide.* ▷ *adverb* **pictorially**

pic·ture (pik-chur)
1. *noun* An image of something, such as a painting, photograph, or drawing. ▷ *verb* **picture**
2. *noun* An image on a television screen. *The TV picture keeps jumping up and down.*
3. *noun* A movie or a motion picture.
4. *verb* To imagine something. *Before I met him, I pictured Jim as tall.*
5. *verb* To describe something in words. *The writer pictured the horrors of the Civil War.*
▷ *noun* **picture**
▷ *verb* **picturing, pictured**

picture graph *noun* A graph that shows information by means of picture symbols instead of lines or bars. Another name for picture graph is **pictograph.**

pic·tur·esque (pik-chuh-**resk**) *adjective* If a place or view is **picturesque,** it is beautiful to look at.

pie (pye) *noun* Pastry filled with fruit, custard, meat, or vegetables and baked in an oven. **Pie** sounds like **pi.**

piece (peess) *noun*
1. A bit or section of something larger. *The novelist read a piece from her new book.*
2. A part that has been broken, torn, or cut from a whole, as in *a piece of broken glass* or *a piece of pie.*
3. Something written or made, as in *a musical piece* or *a piece of pottery.*
4. A coin. *I put a 25-cent piece into the pay phone to make my call.*
5. A small object used in playing checkers, chess, and other board games.
Piece sounds like **peace.**

piece·work (peess-*wurk*) *noun* Work completed and paid for by the piece, not by the time it takes to do it.

pier (pihr) *noun*
1. A platform of metal, stone, concrete, or wood that extends over a body of water. A pier can be used as a landing place for ships and boats.
2. A pillar supporting a bridge.
Pier sounds like **peer.**

pierce (pihrss) *verb*
1. To make a hole in something. *Joanie had her ears pierced.*
2. To pass into or through, as if with a sharp instrument. *The coyote's cries pierced the stillness.*
▷ *verb* **piercing, pierced**

pierc·ing (pihr-sing) *adjective* Very loud and shrill. *A piercing scream shattered the silence.*

pig (pig) *noun*
1. A farm animal with a blunt snout that is raised for its meat.
2. (informal) A greedy, messy, or disgusting person.

pi·geon (pij-uhn) *noun* A plump bird sometimes used for racing or for carrying messages. Pigeons are often found in cities. They are related to doves.

pigeon

389

pig·gy·back (pig-ee-*bak*) *adverb* If someone carries you **piggyback,** the person carries you on his or her shoulders or back.

pig·gy bank (pig-ee) *noun* A small bank, often in the shape of a pig, used mainly by children for saving coins.

pig·ment (pig-muhnt) *noun* A substance that gives color to something. There is pigment in paints and in your skin.

pig·pen (pig-*pen*) *noun* An enclosed area where pigs are kept. It is also called a **sty** or a **pigsty.**

pig·sty (pig-*stye*) *noun*
1. A pigpen.
2. (informal) A very messy and often dirty place. *His room is a pigsty.*
▷ *noun, plural* **pigsties**

pig·tail (pig-*tayl*) *noun* A length of hair that has been divided into three sections and braided.

pike (pike) *noun*
1. A large, thin freshwater fish with a flat snout and very sharp teeth.
2. A type of dive in which the diver bends at the waist to touch the toes while in midair, then enters the water with the body fully extended.

pile (pile) *noun*
1. A heap or mound of something, as in *a pile of old newspapers.* ▷ *verb* **pile**
2. A very great amount of something. *I have a pile of homework to do.*
3. A heavy wood or steel beam that is driven into the ground to support a bridge or pier.
4. The raised loops or pieces of yarn that form the surface of a carpet.

pil·fer (pil-fur) *verb* To steal small amounts of something or small things. ▷ **pilfering, pilfered** ▷ *noun* **pilferer,** *noun* **pilferage**

pil·grim (pil-gruhm) *noun*
1. Someone who goes on a journey to worship at a holy place. ▷ *noun* **pilgrimage**
2. **the Pilgrims** *noun, plural* The group of people who left England because of religious persecution, came to America, and founded Plymouth Colony in 1620.

pill (pil) *noun* A small, solid tablet of medicine, such as aspirin.

pil·lar (pil-ur) *noun* A column that supports part of a building or that stands alone as a monument. *See* **temple.**

pil·low (pil-oh) *noun* A large, soft cushion on which you put your head when you are sleeping. Some pillows are used to support the back or to sit on.

pil·low·case (pil-oh-*kayss*) *noun* A cloth cover that you put over a pillow on a bed to keep it clean.

pi·lot (pye-luht)
1. *noun* Someone who flies an aircraft.

2. *noun* Someone who steers a ship in and out of port.
3. *verb* To control or guide something. *I was asked to pilot a class project.* ▷ **piloting, piloted**
4. *adjective* Done as an experiment, as in *a pilot television program.* ▷ *noun* **pilot**

pim·ple (pim-puhl) *noun* A small, raised spot on the skin that is sometimes painful and filled with pus. ▷ *adjective* **pimply**

pin (pin)
1. *noun* A thin, pointed piece of metal, usually used to fasten material together. *Pins are often used in sewing, as shown below.*
2. *noun* A piece of jewelry or a badge fastened to clothing with a pin or clasp. *I wore my favorite pin on the lapel of my blazer.*
3. *verb* To fasten things together with a pin.
4. *verb* To hold something or someone firmly in position. *I pinned a notice on the board.*
5. *noun* One of 10 pieces of wood shaped like bottles that are knocked over in bowling.
6. *noun* In golf, the flag that indicates where the hole is on the green. *My mom's putt was inches from the pin.*
▷ *verb* **pinning, pinned**

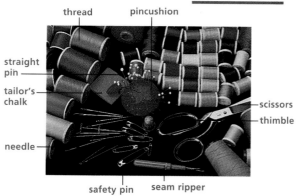

sewing supplies

thread · pincushion · straight pin · tailor's chalk · needle · scissors · thimble · safety pin · seam ripper

pi·ña·ta (peen-yah-tuh) *noun* A decorated container filled with candies and gifts. It is hung from the ceiling to be broken with sticks by blindfolded children. Piñatas are popular at Latin American parties and celebrations.

pin·ball (pin-*bawl*) *noun* A game in which you shoot small balls around a number of obstacles and targets on a slanted table.

pin·cer (pin-sur)
1. *noun* The pinching claw of a crustacean such as a crab. *See* **crab.**
2. **pincers** *noun, plural* A tool with jaws for gripping and pulling things.

pinch (pinch)
1. *verb* To squeeze someone's skin painfully between the thumb and index finger. ▷ *noun* **pinch**

2. *noun* A small amount of something, as in *a pinch of salt.*

3. *verb* To make thin or wrinkled. *His lips were pinched with rage.*

4. *noun* An emergency or time of need. *If you're in a pinch, I can lend you some money.*
▷ *verb* **pinches, pinching, pinched** ▷ *noun, plural* **pinches**

pin·cush·ion (pin-*kush*-uhn) *noun* A small cushion used to stick pins in when they are not being used. *See* **pin.**

pine (pine)
1. *noun* A tall evergreen tree that produces cones and leaves that look like needles.
2. *verb* If you **pine for** someone, you feel very sad because the person has gone away and you miss him or her. ▷ **pining, pined**

pine·ap·ple (pine-*ap*-uhl) *noun* A large, tropical fruit with yellow flesh and a tough, prickly skin. Pineapples grow on plants with long, stiff leaves. *See* **fruit.**

Ping-Pong (ping-*pong*) *noun* Another word for table tennis. Ping-Pong is a trademark. *See* **table tennis.**

pink (pingk) *noun* A pale red color made by mixing red and white. ▷ *adjective* **pink,** *adjective* **pinkish**

pink·eye (pingk-*eye*) *noun* A highly contagious disease that causes the surface of the eyeball and the inside of the eyelid to become red, sore, and itchy.

pin·point (pin-*point*)
1. *adjective* Very exact or precise. *The expert gunner fired with pinpoint accuracy.*
2. *verb* If you **pinpoint** something, you locate it exactly. *The sailors used sonar to pinpoint the enemy submarine.* ▷ **pinpointing, pinpointed**

pins and needles *noun, plural*
1. A prickly, tingling feeling that you get when some of the blood supply to part of your body has been cut off.
2. If you are **on pins and needles,** you are very nervous about something that is going to happen soon.

pin·stripe (pin-*stripe*) *noun* A fabric with a very narrow stripe woven into it. *Bert's new suit is black with blue pinstripes.*

pint (pinte) *noun* A unit of measure equal to half a quart or 16 fluid ounces.

pin·to (pin-toh) *noun*
1. A horse or pony that has spots or patches of two or more colors.
2. A type of kidney bean that is spotted. It is grown mainly in the southwestern part of the United States and is used for food.
▷ *noun, plural* **pintos**

pin·wheel (pin-*weel*) *noun* A toy wheel that spins in the wind. It is made of colored paper or plastic that is pinned to a stick.

pi·o·neer (pye-uh-*neer*) *noun*
1. One of the first people to work in a new and unknown area. *The Wright brothers were pioneers of flight.*
2. Someone who explores unknown territory and settles there. *The pioneers who settled the American West were brave and determined.*
▷ *verb* **pioneer**

pi·ous (pye-uhss) *adjective* Someone who is **pious** practices his or her religion faithfully and seriously. ▷ *adverb* **piously**

pipe (pipe)
1. *noun* A tube, usually used to carry a liquid or gas.
2. *verb* To send something along pipes, tubes, or wires.
▷ **piping, piped**
3. *noun* A tube with a bowl on the end of it, used for smoking tobacco. Pipes are usually made of wood.
4. *noun* A tube with holes in it, used as a musical instrument or as part of an instrument. *This set of pipes, called panpipes, is from Peru.*
5. **piped music** *noun* Music that can be heard through speakers all over a building.

panpipes

pipe·line (pipe-*line*) *noun*
1. A line of large pipes that carry water, gas, or oil over long distances.
2. A direct route for sending information or supplies. *The senator has a direct pipeline to the president's office.*

pip·ing (pye-ping)
1. *noun* A system of pipes.
2. *noun* A shrill sound or call, as in *the piping of tiny frogs.*
3. *noun* A thin, pipelike line of decoration on a cake, piece of clothing, or furniture.
4. *adjective* If food is **piping hot,** it is very, very hot.

pi·rate (pye-rit)
1. *noun* Someone who attacks and steals from ships at sea. ▷ *noun* **piracy**
2. *verb* If someone **pirates** a tape, computer game, or anything that has been created by someone else, the person makes copies from the original and sells them illegally. ▷ **pirating, pirated**
▷ *adjective* **pirated**

P

pis·ta·chi·o (pi-stash-ee-oh) *noun*
 1. A small, green nut with a hard shell that is sometimes dyed red.
 2. A light green color.
 ▷ *noun, plural* **pistachios**

pis·til (piss-tuhl) *noun* The female part of a flower that is shaped like a stalk. It is the place where the seeds are produced. The pistil includes the ovule, the style, and the stigma of a flower. *See* **flower**. **Pistil** sounds like **pistol**.

lily

pistil —

pis·tol (piss-tuhl) *noun* A small gun designed to be held in the hand. **Pistol** sounds like **pistil**.

pis·ton (piss-tuhn) *noun* A disk or cylinder that moves back and forth in a large cylinder. Automobile engines have pistons. Their back-and-forth movement is converted to rotational motion. *See* **engine, steam locomotive**.

pit (pit)
 1. *noun* A hole in the ground.
 2. *noun* The large, hard seed in the middle of some fruits, such as peaches and plums.
 3. *verb* If two people are **pitted against** each other, they are made to compete with each other. ▷ **pitting, pitted**
 4. *noun* When a race car makes a **pit stop**, it pulls to the side of the racecourse for fuel and repairs.
 5. *(informal)* If something is **the pits**, it is the worst.

pi·ta (pee-tuh) *noun* A thin, flat bread that can be separated into two layers to form a pocket for meat, vegetables, or another filling.

pitch (pich)
 1. *verb* To throw or toss something, such as a baseball or horseshoe. ▷ *noun* **pitch**
 2. *verb* To fall or plunge forward. *The ship pitched in the heavy seas. I tripped on my shoelace and pitched down the stairs.*
 3. *verb* When you **pitch** a tent, you put it up.
 4. *noun* A dark, sticky substance that is made from tar or petroleum. Pitch is used to waterproof roofs and pave streets.

5. *noun* A high point or degree, as in *a high pitch of excitement.*
 6. *noun* The highness or lowness of a musical sound.
 7. *noun* *(informal)* A talk meant to persuade you to do or buy something, as in *a sales pitch.*
 ▷ *noun, plural* **pitches** ▷ *verb* **pitches, pitching, pitched**

pitc·her (pich-ur) *noun*
 1. A container with an open top for liquids. Pitchers usually have a handle and a lip or spout.
 2. A baseball player who throws the ball to the batter.

pitch·fork (pich-fork) *noun* A large fork with a long handle and two or three prongs, used for lifting and throwing hay.

pit·fall (pit-fawl) *noun* A hidden danger or difficulty.

pit·i·ful (pit-i-fuhl) *adjective*
 1. Causing or deserving pity. *The lost mountain climbers were in a pitiful state when they were found.*
 2. Useless or worthless. *This essay is a pitiful effort.*
 ▷ *adverb* **pitifully**

pit·i·less (pit-ee-liss) *adjective* If someone is **pitiless,** he or she shows no pity or sympathy for anyone. ▷ *adverb* **pitilessly**

pit·y (pit-ee)
 1. *verb* If you **pity** someone, you feel sorry for the person. ▷ **pities, pitying, pitied** ▷ *adverb* **pityingly**
 2. *noun* A feeling of sorrow or sympathy for the suffering of another. ▷ *noun, plural* **pities**

piv·ot (piv-uht)
 1. *noun* A central point on which something turns or balances.
 2. *verb* To turn suddenly as if on a pivot.
 ▷ **pivoting, pivoted** ▷ *adjective* **pivotal**

pix·el (piks-uhl) *noun* One of the tiny dots on a video screen or computer monitor that make up the visual image.

pix·ie *or* **pix·y** (pik-see) *noun* A small elf or fairy in legends and fairy tales. ▷ *noun, plural* **pixies**

piz·za (peet-suh) *noun* A flat pie that is baked with toppings of tomato sauce, cheese, etc.

plac·ard (plak-ard) *noun* A poster, sign, or notice that is put up in a public place. *The concert was announced on placards around the city.*

pla·cate (play-kate) *verb* To make someone calm or less angry, often by giving the person something that he or she wants. *The company tried to placate the angry strikers by agreeing to sit down and talk.* ▷ **placating, placated**

P

place (playss)
1. *noun* A particular area or location. *We visited many interesting places on our trip.*
2. *noun* A particular position or rank. *My cake won first place in the baking contest.*
3. *noun* A space for a person or thing. *Please save me a place at the table.*
4. *verb* To put something somewhere deliberately and carefully. *Kim placed the goldfish bowl out of the cat's reach.*
5. *verb* To identify by putting in context. *I know I've met you somewhere, but I can't place you.*
6. If something is **in place,** it is in its proper spot or location.
▷ *verb* **placing, placed**

plac·id (plass-id) *adjective* Calm or peaceful, as in *a placid disposition* or *a placid lake.* ▷ *adverb* **placidly**

pla·gia·rize (play-juh-*rize*) *verb* To steal and pass off the ideas or words of another as one's own.
▷ **plagiarizing, plagiarized** ▷ *noun* **plagiarism,** *noun* **plagiarist**

plague (playg)
1. *noun* A very serious disease that spreads quickly to many people and often causes death.
2. *verb* If something **plagues** you, it troubles and annoys you. *The explorers were plagued by flies.*
▷ **plaguing, plagued**

plaid (plad) *noun* A pattern of squares in cloth formed by weaving stripes of different widths and colors that cross each other.

plain (plane)
1. *adjective* Easy to see or hear. *She was in plain view.*
2. *adjective* Easy to understand. *The meaning of his actions is perfectly plain.*
3. *adjective* Simple or not fancy, as in *plain food* or *plain dress.*

4. *adjective* Simple and straightforward. *Just give me the plain facts.*
5. *adjective* Not beautiful or handsome, as in a *plain face.*
6. *noun* A large, flat area of land.
Plain sounds like **plane.**
▷ *adjective* **plainer, plainest**

plain·tive (playn-tiv) *adjective* Sad and mournful. *The kitten let out a plaintive cry.* ▷ *adverb* **plaintively**

plait (playt *or* plat) *noun* A length of hair that has been divided into three sections and braided. ▷ *verb* **plait** ▷ *adjective* **plaited**

plan (plan)
1. *verb* To work out ahead of time how you will do something.
2. *noun* An idea about how you intend to do something, as in *plans for the future.*
3. *verb* If you **plan** to do something, you intend to do it. *I plan to go shopping today.*
4. *noun* A diagram or drawing that shows how the parts of something are arranged or put together, as in *plans for a new building.*
▷ *verb* **planning, planned**

plane (plane) *noun*
1. A machine with wings that flies through the air. Plane is short for **airplane.** *See* **aircraft.**
2. A hand tool with a sharp blade used for smoothing wood. *See* **woodwork.** ▷ *verb* **plane**
3. A level of difficulty or achievement. *The lecture was on such a high plane that few people could understand it.*
4. In geometry, a flat surface. *A cube has six planes.*
Plane sounds like **plain.**

plan·et (plan-it) *noun* One of the nine large heavenly bodies circling the sun. *This picture shows the planets of our solar system in their correct order but not drawn to scale.* ▷ *adjective* **planetary**

P

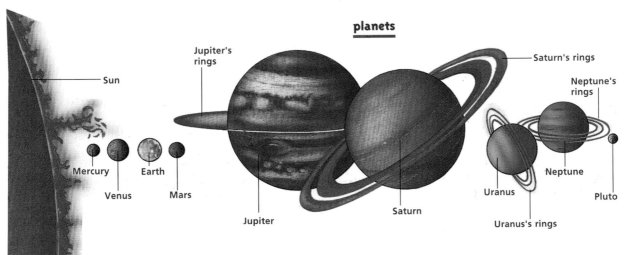

planets

plan·e·tar·i·um (*plan*-uh-**tair**-ee-uhm) *noun* A building with equipment for reproducing the positions and movements of the sun, moon, planets, and stars by projecting their images onto a curved ceiling.

plank (plangk) *noun* A long, flat piece of wood used, for example, for flooring in a house.

plank·ton (**plangk**-tuhn) *noun* Animals and plants, usually tiny, that drift or float in oceans and lakes.

plant (plant)
1. *noun* A living organism with a green pigment called chlorophyll that allows the organism to make food from the energy of the sun. Many land plants have stems, roots, and leaves. *See also* **flower.**
2. *verb* To put a plant or seed in the ground so that it can grow.
3. *verb* To put something firmly in place. *My teacher planted in my mind the idea of becoming a doctor.*
4. *noun* The buildings and equipment used to make a product, such as cars, chemicals, or electricity; a factory.
▷ *verb* **planting, planted**

buttercup
petal
flower bud
flower
internode (area between two nodes)
axillary bud
leaf node
leaf
leaf stalk or petiole
stem
root
root hairs

plan·tain (**plan**-tuhn) *noun* A tropical fruit that looks like a banana but is eaten cooked.

plan·ta·tion (plan-**tay**-shuhn) *noun* A large farm found in warm climates where crops such as coffee, tea, rubber, and cotton are grown.

plaque (plak) *noun*
1. A plate with words inscribed on it, usually placed on a wall in a public place.
2. The coating made from food, bacteria, and saliva that forms on your teeth and can cause tooth decay.

plas·ma (**plaz**-muh) *noun* The clear, yellow, liquid part of the blood. Red and white blood cells float in the watery plasma. *See* **blood.**

plas·ter (**plass**-tur)
1. *noun* A substance made of lime, sand, and water, used by builders to put a smooth finish on walls and ceilings. ▷ *noun* **plasterer** ▷ *verb* **plaster**
2. *verb* To cover or coat something as if you were using plaster. *The little boy plastered his bedroom walls with animal posters.* ▷ **plastering, plastered**
3. plaster cast *noun* A hard, white case that holds broken bones together so that they can heal properly.

plas·tic (**plass**-tik) *noun* A synthetic substance that is light and strong and can be molded into different shapes and thicknesses. Cellophane and vinyl are plastics.

plastic surgery *noun* Operations on skin and body tissue. Plastic surgery can be used to repair damage or to improve someone's appearance.

plate (playt) *noun*
1. A flat dish used for food.
2. A flat sheet of metal, as in *a license plate* or *plates of armor.*
3. A color illustration in a book.
4. Home base in baseball. *In this photograph, baseball legend Reggie Jackson manages to touch the plate and score a run as he slides to avoid the catcher's tag.*
5. One of the sheets of rock that make up the earth's outer crust.

home plate

pla·teau (pla-**toh**) *noun* An area of high, flat land.

▶ **Word History**
• •
From an old French word meaning "flat," **plateau** names a hill with a flat top. The same French word became the modern English *plate.* *Platform* comes from the same root.

plate·let (plate-lit) *noun* A tiny, flat body in the blood that helps the blood clot. *See* **blood.**

plat·form (plat-*form*) *noun*
1. A flat, raised structure where people can stand, as in *a train platform* or *a speaker's platform.*
2. A statement of beliefs of a group. *The political party's platform stressed tax cuts.*

plat·ing (play-ting) *noun* A thin coating or layer of metal, usually gold or silver.

plat·i·num (plat-uhn-uhm) *noun* A very valuable silvery-white metal that is often used in jewelry.

pla·toon (pluh-toon) *noun* A group of soldiers made up of two or more squads. A platoon is usually commanded by a lieutenant.

plat·ter (plat-ur) *noun* A large, shallow plate used to serve food. *Dad served the turkey on a platter.*

plat·y·pus (plat-uh-puhss *or* plat-uh-puss) *noun* An Australian mammal with webbed feet and a broad bill. The platypus is one of the few mammals that lay eggs. ▷ *noun, plural* **platypuses**

platypus

plau·si·ble (plaw-zuh-buhl) *adjective* Believable. *Gus gave a plausible reason for being so late.* ▷ *adverb* **plausibly**

play (play)
1. *verb* To take part in a game or other enjoyable activity.
2. *noun* Fun or recreation. *The children spent hours at play.*
3. *noun* A story that is acted, usually on a stage or in a theater.
4. *noun* A move, a turn, or an action in a game. *The goalie made a great play. It's your play next.*
5. *verb* To make music on. *Branford plays the saxophone.*
6. *verb* To take part in a sport or game. *Our team plays the Suns tomorrow.*
7. *verb* To act a part in a play. *I played the role of a knight.*
8. *verb* To act or to behave. *She is not playing fair.*
▷ *noun* **player** ▷ *verb* **playing, played**

play·ful (play-fuhl) *adjective*
1. Frisky and willing to play. *My new puppy is very playful.*
2. Humorous, or meant to amuse or tease. *Tina's playful remark reminded me that I was taking the whole situation much too seriously.*

play·ground (play-*ground*) *noun* An outdoor area, often with swings, slides, seesaws, and other equipment where children can play.

playing card *noun* A card used in a game. The most common group of playing cards has 52 cards divided into four suits called spades, clubs, hearts, and diamonds.

play·mate (play-*mate*) *noun* A child who plays with another child or children.

play·pen (play-*pen*) *noun* A usually square folding structure that is a safe place for a baby to play in.

play·room (play-*room*) *noun* A room in which children can play.

play·wright (play-*rite*) *noun* Someone who writes plays.

pla·za (plaz-uh *or* plah-zuh) *noun*
1. A public square.
2. An open area near large city buildings that often has walkways, trees, shrubs, and places to sit down.

plea (plee) *noun*
1. An extremely emotional request, as in *a plea for mercy.*
2. A defendant's answer to a charge in a court of law. *The courtroom grew very noisy after the man entered a plea of not guilty.*

plead (pleed) *verb*
1. If you **plead** with someone, you beg the person to do something.
2. To say whether you are guilty or not guilty in a court of law. *He pleaded guilty to robbery.*
▷ *verb* **pleading, pleaded** *or* **pled** (pled)

pleas·ant (plez-uhnt) *adjective*
1. Enjoyable or giving pleasure. *We spent a pleasant afternoon in the park.*
2. Likeable or friendly, as in *a pleasant personality.*
▷ *adverb* **pleasantly**

please (pleez)
1. *verb* To satisfy or to give pleasure. *Your present pleased me greatly.* ▷ *adjective* **pleased,** *adjective* **pleasing**
2. *adverb* A polite word used when you ask for something. It means "be so kind as to." *Please be quiet.*
3. *verb* To choose or to prefer. *They think they can do whatever they please.*
▷ *verb* **pleases, pleasing, pleased**

P

pleas·ure (plezh-ur) *noun*
1. A feeling of enjoyment or satisfaction. *They smiled with pleasure.*
2. Something that gives you a feeling of enjoyment or satisfaction. *Reading is one of my greatest pleasures.* ▷ *adjective* **pleasurable**

pleat (pleet) *noun* One of a series of parallel folds in a piece of clothing such as a skirt. ▷ *adjective* **pleated**

pledge (plej) *verb* To make a sincere promise. *I pledge never to betray your trust.* ▷ **pledging, pledged** ▷ *noun* **pledge**

plen·ti·ful (plen-ti-fuhl) *adjective* Existing in large amounts. *Food was plentiful at the feast.* ▷ *adverb* **plentifully**

plen·ty (plen-tee) *noun* A great number or amount that is more than enough. *There's plenty of space for us to work here.*

pli·a·ble (plye-uh-buhl) *adjective*
1. If an object or material is **pliable,** it can be easily bent or shaped.
2. If a person is **pliable,** he or she can be influenced easily.

pli·ers (plye-urz) *noun, plural* A tool with two handles and jaws that can grip and bend objects or cut wire. *See* **tool.**

plight (plite) *noun* A situation of great danger or hardship. *Everyone is saddened by the terrible plight of the earthquake victims.*

plod (plod) *verb*
1. To walk in a slow and heavy way. *We plodded through the snow.*
2. To work in a dull, slow way. *We plodded through the long homework assignment.* ▷ *verb* **plodding, plodded** ▷ *noun* **plodder**

plot (plot)
1. *verb* To make a secret plan, usually to do something wrong or illegal. ▷ *noun* **plot**
2. *noun* A small area of land, as in *a vegetable plot.*
3. *noun* The main story of a novel, movie, play, or any work of fiction.
4. *verb* To mark out something, such as a graph or a route on a map.
▷ *verb* **plotting, plotted**

plo·ver
(pluhv-ur *or* ploh-vur) *noun* A bird with long, pointed wings and a short bill that runs along the shore to find food.

black-bellied plover

plow (plou)
1. *noun* A piece of farm equipment pulled by an animal or a tractor and used to turn over soil before seeds are planted. *The picture shows a wooden model of an ancient Egyptian plow.*

Egyptian plow

plow   ox   yoke

2. *noun* A device used to remove or push aside matter, such as snow from roads and sidewalks.
3. *verb* To turn over soil using a plow.
4. *verb* If you **plow through** something, you work hard to get through it.
▷ *verb* **plowing, plowed**

pluck (pluhk)
1. *verb* To pull feathers out of a bird. *We have to pluck the chicken before we can cook it.*
2. *verb* To play notes on a stringed instrument by pulling on the strings with your fingers or by using a pick.
3. *noun* Courage and bravery. *It took pluck to stand in front of the audience and give the speech.* ▷ *adjective* **plucky** ▷ *adverb* **pluckily**
4. *verb* To pick fruit or flowers.
▷ *verb* **plucking, plucked** ▷ *adjective* **plucked**

plug (pluhg)
1. *noun* An object pushed into a hole to block it. ▷ *verb* **plug**
2. *noun* A device at the end of a wire that is put into an electrical outlet to make a connection with a source of electricity. Plugs have metal prongs.
3. *noun* Short for **spark plug.**
4. *verb* (informal) To gain publicity for something by talking about it, usually on radio or television. *The singer plugged her new CD on the talk show.*
5. *verb* To work in a steady way. *Mark plugged away at his term paper until he was finally done.*
▷ *verb* **plugging, plugged**

plum (pluhm) *noun* A fruit that is soft when ripe and has a purple or yellow skin. *See* **fruit.**

plum·age (ploo-mij) *noun* A bird's feathers. *The peacock's plumage is truly beautiful.*

plumb·er (pluhm-ur) *noun* Someone who puts in and repairs water and sewage systems, from pipes to sinks to toilets.

plumb·ing (pluhm-ing) *noun* The system of water pipes in a building.

plume (ploom) *noun*
1. A long, fluffy feather often used as an ornament on clothing.

2. Something that looks like a feathery plume. *A plume of smoke rose from the chimney.* ▷ *verb* **plume**

plump (pluhmp) *adjective* Somewhat fat or round in shape, as in *a plump baby* or *a plump cushion.* ▷ **plumper, plumpest**

plun·der (pluhn-dur) *verb* To steal things by force, often during a battle. ▷ **plundering, plundered** ▷ *noun* **plunder**

plunge (pluhnj) *verb*
1. To dive into water. *Tom plunged into the pool.*
2. To put or push something in suddenly or with force. *The sergeant showed the new recruits how to plunge their bayonets into the training dummy.*
3. To fall steeply or sharply. *The cliffs plunged to the sea. The temperature plunged.*
4. To do something suddenly, or to make something happen suddenly. *We plunged into action.*
▷ *verb* **plunging, plunged** ▷ *noun* **plunge**

plu·ral (ploor-uhl) *noun* The form of a word used for two or more of something. The plural of *child* is *children.* ▷ *adjective* **plural**

plus (pluhss)
1. *noun* In math, a sign (+) used in addition. Also called a *plus sign.* ▷ *noun, plural* **pluses**
2. *preposition* Added to. *Three plus three equals six.*
3. *preposition* In addition to. *The dining room set consists of a table plus six chairs.*
4. *adjective* Slightly higher than, as in *a grade of B plus.*

Plu·to (ploo-toh) *noun* The ninth and smallest planet in our solar system. Pluto is the farthest planet from the sun and can be seen only through a telescope. *See* **planet.**

plu·to·ni·um (ploo-toh-nee-uhm) *noun* A radioactive metallic element that is made artificially from uranium. Plutonium is used as a fuel in nuclear reactors. It is also used to make atomic bombs.

ply·wood (plye-wud) *noun* Board made from several thin sheets of wood that have been glued together. Plywood is used for building and carpentry.

P.M. (pee em) The initials of the Latin phrase *post meridiem,* which means "after midday." It is used to indicate the time between noon and 11:59 in the evening. *School ends at 3 P.M.*

pneu·mat·ic (noo-mat-ik) *adjective*
1. Filled with air. *My bike has pneumatic tires.*
2. Operated by compressed air. *The workers used a pneumatic drill to break up the sidewalk.*

pneu·mo·nia (noo-moh-nyuh) *noun* A serious disease that causes the lungs to become inflamed and filled with a thick fluid that makes breathing difficult.

poach (pohch) *verb*
1. To catch fish or animals illegally on someone else's land.
2. To cook food, such as eggs or fish, by heating it in gently boiling liquid.
▷ *verb* **poaches, poaching, poached**

poach·er (pohch-ur) *noun*
1. A person who hunts or fishes illegally on someone else's land.
2. A pot designed to poach eggs or fish.

pock·et (pok-it)
1. *noun* A small cloth pouch that is sewn into clothing and used for carrying small items.
2. *verb* To take something secretly. *The thief pocketed the money and ran.* ▷ **pocketing, pocketed**
3. *noun* A small area or an isolated group. *The army met pockets of resistance along the way.*
4. *adjective* Small enough to be carried in your pocket, as in *a pocket calculator.*

pock·et·book (pok-it-buk) *noun* A woman's purse or handbag that is used to carry personal items such as a wallet and keys.

pock·et·knife (pok-it-nife) *noun* A small knife with a blade or blades that fold into the handle. A small pocketknife is called a **penknife.** *See* **penknife.** ▷ *noun, plural* **pocketknives**

pocket money *noun* Money for minor expenses, such as bus fare or snacks.

pod (pod) *noun* A long case that holds the seeds of certain plants, as in *a pea pod.*

po·em (poh-uhm) *noun* A piece of writing set out in short lines, often with a noticeable rhythm and some words that rhyme. Many poems are written to help the reader or listener share an experience or feel a strong emotion. In a poem, words are often chosen for their sounds as well as their meanings.

po·et (poh-uht) *noun* Someone who writes poetry.

po·et·ry (poh-i-tree) *noun*
1. Literary work in the form of poems. *Do you write poetry?*
2. Anything that has the effect of a poem. *The dancer's graceful movements were poetry in motion.*
▷ *adjective* **poetic**

poin·set·ti·a (poin-set-uh *or* poin-set-ee-uh) *noun* A decorative plant with large red, white, or pink leaves that look like flower petals.

poinsettias

397

point (point)
1. *verb* To show where something is by using your index finger.
2. *noun* The sharp end of something, as in *a pencil point.* ▷ *adjective* **pointed**
3. *noun* A dot in writing, as in *a decimal point.*
4. *noun* The main purpose behind something that is said or done. *The point of the presentation was to get people thinking.*
5. *noun* A specific place or stage. *Don't go beyond this point.*
6. *noun* A unit for scoring in a game. *The score was two points to one.*
7. *noun* In geometry, a location in space with no dimension.
8. *noun* A particular time or moment. *At that point, a quiet hush settled over the audience.*
9. *noun* A quality or a trait. *Her sense of humor is one of her best points.*
10. *verb* To aim at someone or something. *Don't point that gun at me!*
▷ *verb* **pointing, pointed**

point-blank *adjective*
1. Very close. *He fired the gun at point-blank range.*
2. Plain and blunt, as in *point-blank questions.*

point·less (point-liss) *adjective* If something is **pointless**, it is useless. *It's pointless to take your ice skates to the beach.* ▷ *adverb* **pointlessly**

point of view *noun* An attitude, a viewpoint, or a way of looking at or thinking about something. *From my point of view, it is better to make gifts than to buy them.*

poise (poiz)
1. *verb* To balance. *The glass was poised on the edge of the table.* ▷ **poising, poised**
2. *noun* Composure or self-confidence.

poised (poizd) *adjective* If you are **poised,** you are self-confident and do not lose your composure.

poi·son (poi-zuhn) *noun* A substance that can kill or harm someone if it is swallowed, inhaled, or sometimes even touched. ▷ *verb* **poison** ▷ *adjective* **poisonous**

poison ivy *noun* A shrub or climbing vine with clusters of three shiny, green leaves. Poison ivy causes an itchy rash on most people who touch it.

poison sumac *noun* A variety of sumac that can cause a rash similar to that from poison ivy.

poke (pohk) *verb*
1. To jab sharply with a finger or pointed object. ▷ *noun* **poke**
2. To stick out or thrust quickly. *The groundhog poked its head out of the hole.*
3. To move slowly. *My little brother poked along behind me.* ▷ *adjective* **poky** or **pokey**
▷ *verb* **poking, poked**

pok·er (poh-kur) *noun*
1. A long, metal tool used for stirring up a fire.
2. A card game in which a player bets that the value of his or her cards is greater than that of the cards held by the other players.

po·lar (poh-lur) *adjective* To do with or near the icy regions around the North or South Pole.

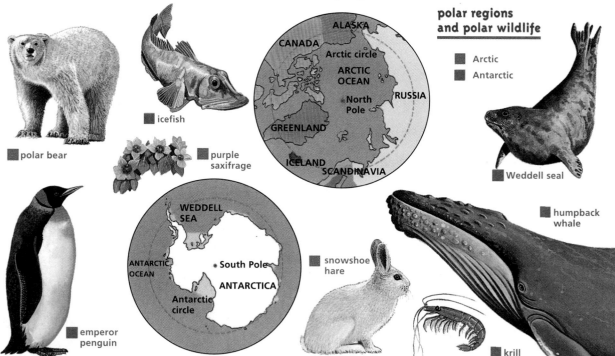

polar regions and polar wildlife

- polar bear
- icefish
- purple saxifrage
- ■ Arctic
- ■ Antarctic
- ALASKA
- CANADA
- Arctic circle
- ARCTIC OCEAN
- North Pole
- RUSSIA
- GREENLAND
- ICELAND
- SCANDINAVIA
- Weddell seal
- WEDDELL SEA
- ANTARCTIC OCEAN
- South Pole
- ANTARCTICA
- Antarctic circle
- snowshoe hare
- humpback whale
- emperor penguin
- krill

polar bear *noun* A large bear with thick, white fur that lives in Arctic regions. *See* **polar.**

pole (pohl) *noun*
1. A long, smooth piece of wood, metal, or plastic, as in *a telephone pole.*
2. One of the two geographical points that are farthest away from the equator, the North Pole or the South Pole. *See* **polar.**
3. One of the two opposite ends of a magnet. *See* **magnet.**
4. If two people or things are **poles apart,** they are very different or have very different ideas. **Pole** sounds like **poll.**

pole·cat (pohl-*kat*) *noun*
1. A European animal of the weasel family that has brown or black fur. A polecat gives off a strong, unpleasant odor when attacked or frightened.
2. Any of a group of North American skunks.

pole vault *noun* A jump over a high bar using a flexible pole. *The picture sequence shows an athlete performing a pole vault.* ▷ *noun* **pole-vaulter** ▷ *verb* **pole-vault**

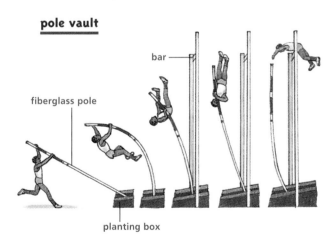

pole vault

bar
fiberglass pole
planting box

po·lice (puh-leess)
1. *noun, plural* The people whose job is to keep order, make sure that the law is obeyed, and stop any crimes that are being committed. ▷ *noun* **policeman,** *noun* **policewoman**
2. *verb* To guard or patrol an area and keep order. *Government agents policed the airport until the president's plane took off.* ▷ **policing, policed**

police officer *noun* A member of a police department. A police officer can be a man or a woman.

pol·i·cy (pol-uh-see) *noun*
1. A general plan or principle that people use to help them make decisions or take action. *What is the government's policy on giving aid to starving nations?*

2. An insurance contract.
▷ *noun, plural* **policies**

po·li·o (poh-lee-oh) *noun* An infectious viral disease that attacks the brain and spinal chord. Polio occurs mainly in children. In serious cases, it can cause paralysis. This disease is now easily prevented with a vaccine. Polio is short for *poliomyelitis.*

pol·ish (pol-ish)
1. *verb* To rub something to make it shine. *One of my chores is to polish the furniture.* ▷ **polishes, polishing, polished** ▷ *noun* **polish**
2. *noun* A cleaning substance used to make things shine, as in *shoe polish.* ▷ *noun, plural* **polishes**

pol·ished (pol-isht) *adjective*
1. Smooth and shiny.
2. If you give a **polished** performance, you are well rehearsed and perform confidently.

po·lite (puh-lite) *adjective* Having good manners; being well behaved and courteous to others. ▷ **politer, politest** ▷ *noun* **politeness** ▷ *adverb* **politely**

pol·i·ti·cian (pol-uh-**tish**-uhn) *noun* Someone who runs for or holds a government office, such as a senator.

pol·i·tics (pol-uh-tiks) *noun*
1. The debate and activity involved in governing a country.
2. *noun, plural* The activities of politicians and political parties.
3. *noun, plural* An individual's beliefs about how the government should be run. *Her politics are conservative.*
▷ *adjective* **political** ▷ *adverb* **politically**

pol·ka (pole-kuh *or* poke-uh) *noun* A fast dance in which couples swirl around the floor in a circular pattern. The polka came from central Europe.

polka dot *noun* One of many round dots that are repeated to form a regular pattern on fabric or other materials.

poll (pohl) *noun*
1. A survey of people's opinions or beliefs.
▷ *verb* **poll**
2. **polls** *noun, plural* The place where votes are cast and recorded during an election. *When do the polls close?*
Poll sounds like **pole.**

pol·len (pol-uhn) *noun*
1. Tiny yellow grains produced in the anthers of flowers. Pollen grains are the male cells of flowering plants.
2. **pollen count** A measurement of the level of pollen in the air, which indicates how badly people with pollen allergies will be affected.

P

399

pol·li·nate (pol-uh-nate) *verb* To carry or transfer pollen from the stamen to the pistil of the same flower or another flower where female cells can be fertilized to produce seed. *Insects, birds, the wind, and some animals can help pollinate plants.* ▷ **pollinating, pollinated** ▷ *noun* **pollination**

pol·lut·ant (puh-loot-uhnt) *noun* Anything that pollutes or contaminates is a **pollutant.**

pol·lute (puh-loot) *verb* To contaminate or make dirty or impure, especially with industrial waste or other products produced by humans. *Oil from the damaged tanker polluted the ocean.* ▷ **polluting, polluted**

pol·lu·tion (puh-loo-shuhn) *noun*
1. Harmful materials that damage or contaminate the air, water, and soil, such as chemicals, gasoline exhaust, and industrial waste.
2. The act of polluting or the state of being polluted.

po·lo (poh-loh) *noun* A game played on horseback by two teams of four players. The players try to hit a small ball using long, wooden mallets.

pol·y·es·ter (*pol*-ee-ess-tur) *noun* A synthetic substance used to make plastic products and fabric.

pol·y·gon (pol-ee-gon) *noun* A flat, closed figure with three or more straight sides. Triangles, squares, pentagons, and hexagons are all polygons.

> ### Word History
> A **polygon** has at least three straight sides and therefore at least three angles. This word comes from two Greek words meaning "many" and "angle." You can see the combining form *poly-* in other English words, such as *polyester* and *polystyrene.*

pol·y·mer (pol-uh-mur) *noun* A natural or synthetic compound made up of small, simple molecules linked together in long chains of repeating units.

pol·yp (pol-ip) *noun*
1. A small sea animal with a tubular body and a round mouth surrounded by tentacles. Coral is an example of a polyp.
2. A tumor or mass on the lining of the nose, mouth, or other body passage open to the outside.

pol·y·sty·rene (*pol*-ee-stye-reen) *noun* A light, stiff plastic often used to make disposable cups, foams, and packing materials. Styrofoam is one form of polystyrene.

pol·y·un·sat·u·rates (*pol*-ee-uhn-sach-uh-ruhts) *noun, plural* Vegetable fats and oils thought to be healthier for you than other fats. ▷ *adjective* **polyunsaturated**

pome·gran·ate (pom-uh-*gran*-it) *noun* A round, reddish yellow fruit that has a tough skin, red flesh, and many seeds. Pomegranates have a tart flavor.

pomp (pomp) *noun* An elaborate and stately ceremony or display. *The prince and princess were married with great pomp.*

pomp·ous (pom-puhss) *adjective* Conceited and haughty or arrogant. A pompous person thinks that he or she is better than others. ▷ *adverb* **pompously**

pon·cho (pon-choh) *noun*
1. A cloak that looks like a blanket with a hole in the center for the head. Ponchos were originally worn in South America.
2. A similar waterproof garment with a hood.
▷ *noun, plural* **ponchos**

pond (pond) *noun* An enclosed body of fresh water that is smaller than a lake.

pon·der (pon-dur) *verb* To think about things carefully. *Philosophers ponder the meaning of life.* ▷ **pondering, pondered**

pon·der·ous (pon-dur-uhss) *adjective*
1. Heavy and slow or clumsy. *Elephants are ponderous animals.*
2. Hard to understand and dull. *The politician gave a ponderous speech.*
▷ *adverb* **ponderously**

po·ny (poh-nee) *noun*
1. A breed of horse that stays small when fully grown.
2. Any horse, especially a small one.
▷ *noun, plural* **ponies**

Pony Express *noun* A mail service in which a series of riders carried the mail on horseback from Missouri to California. Pony Express service started in April 1860 and ended in October 1861. *This picture of a Pony Express rider was drawn by British artist George Henry Andrews.*

Pony Express

P

po·ny·tail (poh-nee-*tayl*) *noun* A hairdo that looks like a pony's tail, in which the hair is tied with a band and hangs behind the head.

poo·dle (poo-duhl) *noun* A breed of dog with thick, curly hair that is usually cut in a fancy style. Poodles range in size from the fairly large standard poodle to the very small toy poodle.

▶ Word History

While we think of **poodles** as French, the breed's name actually comes from the German word *Pudlehund*, which means "splashing hound" or "dog that splashes in the water." These intelligent dogs are excellent at retrieving, even if it means getting a little wet.

pool (pool)
1. *noun* A small area of still water.
2. *noun* A swimming pool.
3. *noun* A game in which players use a stick called a cue to hit colored balls into pockets on a table.
4. *noun* A group of people who share something, as in *a typing pool* or *a car pool.*
5. *verb* If people **pool** their money or ideas, they put them together to be shared. ▷ **pooling, pooled**

poor (poor *or* por) *adjective*
1. If someone is **poor,** he or she does not have much money.
2. Low in quality or standard, as in *poor eyesight* or *a poor crop.*
3. Unfortunate and deserving sympathy or pity. *Poor Alex had to walk home in the pouring rain.*
▷ *adjective* **poorer, poorest**

poor·ly (poor-lee) *adverb* Badly. *The room was poorly lit.*

pop (pop)
1. *verb* To explode with a small bang or bursting sound. *The balloon popped.* ▷ *noun* **pop**
2. *noun* A sweet, carbonated soft drink. Also called *soda pop.*
3. *verb* To move or appear quickly or unexpectedly. *Laura popped a mint into her mouth. My aunt popped in for a brief visit.*
4. *noun* (informal) Father.
5. *verb* If you **pop out** in baseball, you hit a fly ball that is caught by a player on the other team.
▷ *verb* **popping, popped**

pop·corn (pop-*korn*) *noun* Kernels of corn that are heated until they swell up and burst open with a popping sound. The kernels become fluffy and can be eaten as a snack.

pope *or* **Pope** (pohp) *noun* The head of the Roman Catholic church.

pop·lar (pop-lur) *noun* A tall tree with wide leaves. The aspen and the cottonwood are both poplar trees.

pop music *noun* (informal) Modern popular music with a strong, and usually fast, beat. ▷ *noun* **pop**

pop·py (pop-ee) *noun* A garden plant with large, usually red, showy flowers. Poppies produce cases through which its seeds may escape when shaken by the wind. ▷ *noun, plural* **poppies**

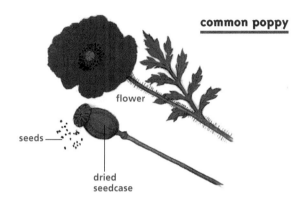

common poppy

flower

seeds

dried seedcase

pop·u·lar (pop-yuh-lur) *adjective*
1. Liked or enjoyed by many people. *The park is a popular spot for picnics in the summer.* ▷ *noun* **popularity** ▷ *adverb* **popularly**
2. Having many friends, or liked by many people. *Jana is the most popular girl in our class.*
3. Of or for the people. *In the United States, local officials are elected by popular vote.*

pop·u·lat·ed (pop-yuh-*lay*-tid) *adjective* If a place is **populated,** it has people living there. *The summer resort is heavily populated in July and August.*

pop·u·la·tion (*pop*-yuh-**lay**-shuhn) *noun*
1. The total number of people who live in a place. *The populations of our town is 15,025.*
2. All of the people living in a certain place. *The entire population of the town was evacuated after the flood.*

por·ce·lain (por-suh-lin) *noun* Very fine china, often used to make ornaments or cups and saucers. *This 18th-century porcelain figure was made in Germany.*

porcelain figure

P

porch (porch) *noun* A structure with a roof that is attached to the outside of a house, usually near a door. ▷ *noun, plural* **porches**

por·cu·pine (por-kyuh-*pine*) *noun* A large rodent covered with long, sharp quills that are used for protection.

Malaysian porcupine

▶ **Word History**
· ·
Because it looks like a tiny pig covered with spikes, the **porcupine** was given its name from the Latin words *porcus*, meaning "pig," and *spina*, meaning "thorn." *Pork*, or meat from a pig, comes from the same root.

pore (por)
1. *noun* One of the tiny holes in your skin through which you sweat. *See* **skin**.
2. *verb* To read or study something carefully. *After poring over the directions, I was sure I could put together my new model airplane.* ▷ **poring, pored**
Pore sounds like **pour**.

pork (pork) *noun* The meat from a pig.

po·rous (por-uhss) *adjective* Something that is **porous** is full of tiny holes and lets liquid or gas through it.

por·poise (por-puhss) *noun* An ocean mammal with a rounded head and a short, blunt snout. The porpoise is related to but is usually smaller than the dolphin and the whale.

▶ **Word History**
· ·
The **porpoise**'s name comes from a French word that in turn comes from the Latin words *porcus*, meaning "pig," and *piscis*, meaning "fish." The porpoise's nose is rounded like that of a pig.

por·ridge (por-ij *or* par-ij) *noun* A breakfast food made by boiling oats or other grains in milk or water until the mixture is thick.

port (port) *noun*
1. A harbor or place where boats and ships can dock or anchor safely.

2. A town or city with a harbor where ships can dock and load and unload cargo. *San Francisco, New Orleans, and New York are some important U.S. ports.*
3. The left side of a ship or an aircraft as one faces forward. ▷ *adjective* **port**
4. A strong, sweet red wine.

port·a·ble (por-tuh-buhl) *adjective* Able to be carried or moved easily, as in *a portable radio.*

port·cul·lis (port-kuhl-iss) *noun* A heavy grating in the entrance to a castle that was used as an extra defense. *This view of a castle gatehouse shows how the portcullis and drawbridge were raised and lowered.* ▷ *noun, plural* **portcullises**

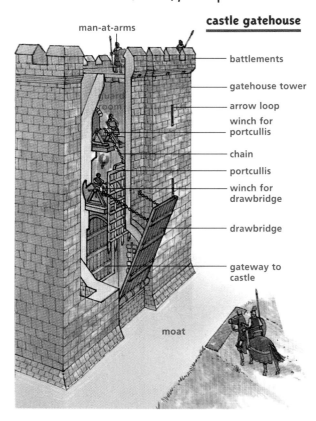

castle gatehouse

man-at-arms

battlements
gatehouse tower
arrow loop
winch for portcullis
chain
portcullis
winch for drawbridge
drawbridge
gateway to castle

moat

por·ter (por-tur) *noun*
1. Someone who carries luggage for people at a railroad station or hotel.
2. A person who waits on train passengers.

port·hole (port-*hohl*) *noun* A small, round window in the side of a ship or boat. *See* **boat, junk, underwater.**

por·ti·co (por-tuh-koh) *noun* A porch or walkway with a roof that is supported by columns. *We visited an old plantation that had a portico at the entrance.* ▷ *noun, plural* **porticos** *or* **porticoes**

por·tion (por-shuhn) *noun*
1. A part or piece of something. *He spent a large portion of the evening doing his homework.*

2. An amount of food that is served to someone. *I'd like another portion of mashed potatoes.*
▷ *verb* **portion**

port·ly (port-lee) *adjective* Heavy or stout. *His white beard and portly appearance make him look like Santa Claus.* ▷ *noun* **portliness**

por·trait (por-trit *or* por-trayt) *noun*
1. A drawing, painting, or photograph of a person.
2. A written description. *The author painted a glowing portrait of life in the city.*

por·tray (por-tray) *verb*
1. To describe in words. *In the book, the villain is portrayed as a greedy ogre.*
2. To make a picture of something or someone.
3. To act a part in a play or movie. *In the movie I just saw, my favorite actress portrays a tough lawyer.*
▷ *verb* **portraying, portrayed** ▷ *noun* **portrayal**

pose (pohz) *verb*
1. To keep your body in a particular position so that you can be photographed, painted, or drawn. ▷ *noun* **pose**
2. To pretend to be someone else in order to deceive people. *The thieves posed as police officers.*
3. If you **pose a question,** you ask it.
▷ *verb* **posing, posed**

posh (posh) *adjective* (informal) Very stylish or expensive. *After they won the lottery, they ate only at posh restaurants.* ▷ **posher, poshest**

po·si·tion (puh-zish-uhn)
1. *noun* The place where someone or something is. *We changed the position of our chairs so we could see better.*
2. *verb* To put something in a particular place. *Position the pictures carefully.* ▷ **positioning, positioned**
3. *noun* A person's opinion or point of view on a particular issue or subject. *What is your position on the governor's plan to lower taxes?*
4. *noun* The way in which someone is standing, sitting, or lying, as in *an upright position.*
5. *noun* The right place to be. *We got in position for the class picture.*
6. *noun* A particular job. *I'm applying for the position of baby-sitter.*

pos·i·tive (poz-uh-tiv) *adjective*
1. Sure or certain. *I'm positive that I left my pencil here.*
2. Helpful or constructive. *He gave me some positive comments about ways I could improve my short story.*
3. Showing approval or acceptance. *I received many positive replies to my invitation.*
4. A **positive** number is more than zero.

5. Having one of two opposite kinds of electrical charge. *A magnet has a positive pole and a negative pole.*
6. If a medical test is **positive,** it shows that a particular disease or organism is present.
▷ *adverb* **positively**

pos·se (poss-ee) *noun* A group of people gathered together by a sheriff to help capture a criminal.

pos·ses·sion (puh-zesh-uhn) *noun*
1. Something that you own. ▷ *verb* **possess**
2. If something is **in your possession,** you own it or have it.

pos·ses·sive (puh-zess-iv)
1. *adjective* If someone is **possessive,** the person wants to keep someone or something for him- or herself and does not want to share it.
2. *noun* The form of a noun or pronoun that shows that something belongs to the one referred to. *In "This ball is mine" and "Tom's hat," "mine" and "Tom's" are possessives.* ▷ *adjective* **possessive**

pos·si·ble (poss-uh-buhl) *adjective* If something is **possible,** it might happen or it might be true.
▷ *noun* **possibility** ▷ *adverb* **possibly**

pos·sum (poss-uhm) *noun*
1. An opossum.
2. When a person or an animal **plays possum,** he, she, or it pretends to be asleep or dead.

post (pohst)
1. *noun* A long, thick piece of wood, concrete, or metal that is fixed in the ground to support or mark something, as in *a fence post.*
2. *verb* To put up a notice or an announcement of information. *The winners' names were posted on the bulletin board.*
3. *noun* A place where someone on duty is supposed to be. *The guard never left his post.*
4. *noun* A military base where soldiers are stationed or trained, as in *an army post.*
5. *noun* A particular job that someone has. *Mr. Jarvis holds the post of ambassador.*
6. *verb* To assign someone to a post.
7. *verb* To mail a letter or package. ▷ *noun* **post**
8. keep posted *verb* (informal) To give someone information or the latest news. *Please keep me posted on how she's recovering from her illness.*
▷ *verb* **posting, posted**

> ### Prefix
> •
> The prefix **post-** adds one of the following meanings to a root word:
> 1. After, as in *postwar* (after the war).
> 2. Later, as in *postpone* (put off till later).

post·age (poh-stij) *noun* The cost of sending a letter or package by mail.

postage stamp *noun* A small printed piece of paper issued by a government and attached to mail to show that postage has been paid. *See* **stamp.**

Post·al Service (pohst-uhl) *noun* The agency that is in charge of selling stamps and delivering the mail. Though the Postal Service is run by the U.S. government, it is an independent agency.

post·card (pohst-kard) *noun* A card, sometimes with a picture on one side, that you send by mail. A postcard does not require an envelope to be mailed.

post·er (poh-stur) *noun* A large, printed sign that often has a picture. A poster can be put up as an advertisement, a notice, or a decoration.

post·hu·mous (pohst-chuh-muhss) *adjective* Coming or happening after death. *The soldier who was killed in action received a posthumous medal.* ▷ *adverb* **posthumously**

post·man (pohst-muhn) *noun* A mail carrier. ▷ *noun, plural* **postmen**

post·mark (pohst-mark) *noun* An official stamp on a piece of mail that cancels the postage stamp and shows the place and date of mailing.

post·mast·er (pohst-mass-tur) *noun* The head of a post office, if the person is a man.

post·mis·tress (pohst-miss-triss) *noun* The head of a post office, if the person is a woman.

post office *noun* The place where people go to buy stamps and to send letters and packages.

post·pone (pohst-pone) *verb* To put something off until later or another time. *The outdoor concert was postponed because of the rain.* ▷ **postponing, postponed** ▷ *noun* **postponement**

post·script (pohst-skript) *noun* A short message beginning "P.S." that is added to the end of a letter, after the writer's signature.

pos·ture (poss-chur) *noun* The position of your body when you stand, sit, or walk.

post·war (pohst-war) *adjective* After or later in time than a war, as in *the postwar period.*

pot (pot) *noun*
1. A deep, round container used for cooking or storing food.
2. A container made of clay or plastic that is used for growing plants.
▷ *verb* **pot**

po·tas·si·um (puh-tass-ee-uhm) *noun* A silvery-white, metallic chemical element. It is used in making fertilizers, explosives, and soap, and is found in foods such as bananas and potatoes. Potassium is necessary for good nutrition.

po·ta·to (puh-tay-toh) *noun* The thick underground tuber of a leafy plant. This vegetable was originally grown in South America. *See* **vegetable.** ▷ *noun, plural* **potatoes**

po·tent (poht-uhnt) *adjective* Powerful or strong, as in *a potent drug.* ▷ *noun* **potency** ▷ *adverb* **potently**

po·ten·tial (puh-ten-shuhl)
1. *noun* Your **potential** is what you are capable of achieving in the future.
2. *noun* If an idea or a place has **potential,** you think that it has promise and that you can develop it into something better.
3. *adjective* Possible but not yet actual or real, as in *a potential danger* or *a potential customer.*
▷ *adverb* **potentially**

pot·hole (pot-hohl) *noun* A hole in the surface of a road.

pot·ter (pot-ur) *noun* Someone who makes objects out of clay, such as bowls, plates, or vases.

pot·ter·y (pot-ur-ee) *noun*
1. Objects made of baked clay, such as bowls, plates, or vases. Pottery can be used for decorative or practical purposes.
2. A place where clay objects are made. ▷ *noun, plural* **potteries**

pouch (pouch) *noun*
1. A leather or fabric bag.
2. A flap of skin in which kangaroos and other marsupials carry their young.
▷ *noun, plural* **pouches**

poul·try (pohl-tree) *noun* Farm birds raised for their eggs and meat. Chickens, turkeys, ducks, and geese are poultry.

pounce (pounss) *verb* To jump on something suddenly and grab hold of it. *The lion pounced on its prey.* ▷ **pouncing, pounced**

pound (pound)
1. *noun* A unit of weight equal to 16 ounces. A soccer ball weighs about one pound.
2. *noun* A unit of money used in England, Ireland, and several other countries.
3. *verb* To keep hitting something noisily and with force. *The rain pounded on the roof.*
4. *verb* To beat quickly or heavily. *Scary stories make my heart pound.*
5. *noun* A place where stray dogs and other animals are kept.
▷ *verb* **pounding, pounded**

pour (por) *verb*
1. To make something flow in a steady stream. *I'll pour the tea.*
2. To rain heavily. *It poured all night.*
3. To move somewhere quickly and in large numbers. *People poured out of the stadium onto the street.*
Pour sounds like **pore.**
▷ *verb* **pouring, poured**

P

pout (pout) *verb* To push out your lips when you are angry or disappointed about something.
▷ **pouting, pouted** ▷ *noun* **pout**

pov·er·ty (pov-ur-tee) *noun* The state of being poor. *Homeless people live in extreme poverty.*

pow·der (pou-dur)
1. *noun* Tiny particles made by grinding, crushing, or pounding a solid substance.
▷ *adjective* **powdery,** *adjective* **powdered**
2. *noun* A cosmetic or other preparation made from powder.
3. *verb* To make or turn something into powder.
4. *verb* To cover something with powder. *Gloria powdered her nose.*
▷ *verb* **powdering, powdered**

pow·er (pou-ur) *noun*
1. The strength or ability to do something. *It took all my power to move the heavy couch.*
2. The authority or right to command, control, or make decisions. *The president has the power to veto a bill.*
3. A person, group, or nation that has great strength, influence, or control over others. *The United States is a major world power.*
4. Electricity or other forms of energy.
5. In mathematics, the number of times you use a number as a factor in multiplication. Three to the fifth power means 3 as a factor 5 times and equals $3 \times 3 \times 3 \times 3 \times 3$, or 243.

pow·er·ful (pou-ur-fuhl) *adjective* Having great power, strength, or authority, as in *a powerful punch* or *a powerful king.*

pow·er·less (pou-ur-liss) *adjective* Having no power, strength, or authority. *We were powerless to help them.*

prac·ti·cal (prak-tuh-kuhl) *adjective*
1. To do with experience or practice rather than theory and ideas. *Do you have any practical experience in teaching?*
2. Useful. *White is not a practical color for a carpet because it shows dirt.*
3. Sensible, or showing good judgment. *A practical person would never think of doing this huge job alone.*

practical joke *noun* A mischievous trick often done to make someone look or feel foolish.

prac·ti·cal·ly (prak-tik-lee) *adverb*
1. Almost or nearly. *It's practically impossible to get there by bus.*
2. In a sensible way. *Henry tackled the job very practically.*

prac·tice (prak-tiss)
1. *noun* The repetition of an action regularly in order to improve a skill. *After school I have piano practice.*

2. *noun* A custom or a habit. *How old is the practice of sending birthday cards?*
3. *noun* The business of a doctor, lawyer, or other professional. *After he received his degree, Daniel opened his medical practice.*
4. *verb* If someone **practices** a religion, he or she follows its teachings and attends its services or ceremonies.
5. *verb* To put something into action. *Practice what you preach.*
6. in practice *adverb* What really happens rather than what is meant to happen. *The idea sounded good in theory but failed in practice.*
▷ *verb* **practicing, practiced**

prai·rie (prair-ee) *noun* A large area of flat or rolling grassland with few or no trees.

prairie dog *noun* A small burrowing mammal that is related to the squirrel. Prairie dogs live mainly in the plains of west-central North America. They dig elaborate underground burrows and live in large colonies. Their call sounds like a dog's bark.

black-tailed prairie dog

prairie schooner *noun* A large covered wagon used by pioneers to journey westward to the Pacific coast over the flat, grassy prairies of central North America.

praise (praze)
1. *noun* Words of approval or admiration.
2. *verb* To express praise to someone. *The teacher praised the class for its cooperation.*
3. *verb* To worship and express thanks to. *The preacher praised God.*
▷ *verb* **praising, praised**

prance (pranss) *verb*
1. To walk or move in a lively or proud way.
2. When a horse **prances,** it springs forward on its hind legs.
▷ *verb* **prancing, pranced**

prank (prangk) *noun* A playful or mischievous trick.

pray (pray) *verb*
1. To talk to God to give thanks or ask for help.
2. To hope very much that something happens. *We're praying that it will be sunny tomorrow.*
Pray sounds like **prey**.
▷ *verb* **praying, prayed**

pray·er (pray-ur) *noun*
1. The act of praying.
2. An expression of appeal or thanks to God.
3. A set of words used in praying.
4. Something requested or prayed for.

praying man·tis (man-tiss) *noun* An insect that is related to the grasshopper. When it rests, the praying mantis folds its front legs, which then look like hands folded in prayer. *See also* **camouflage, insect.** ▷ *noun, plural* **praying mantises** *or* **praying mantes** (man-teez)

praying mantis

Prefix

The prefix **pre-** adds the following meaning to a root word: Before, as in *precede* (to go before), *prewar* (before the war), or *prepare* (be ready before something happens).

preach (preech) *verb*
1. To give a religious talk to people, especially during a church service. ▷ *noun* **preacher**
2. To tell other people what you think they should do, often in a boring or annoying way. *He is always preaching to me about not wasting my money on foolish things.*
▷ *verb* **preaches, preaching, preached**

pre·car·i·ous (pri-kair-ee-uhss) *adjective* Unsafe and risky. *The glass was perched in a precarious position on the edge of the table.* ▷ *adverb* **precariously**

pre·cau·tion (pri-kaw-shuhn) *noun* Something you do in order to prevent something dangerous or unpleasant from happening. *Let's take along a first-aid kit as a precaution.*
▷ *adjective* **precautionary**

pre·cede (pree-seed) *verb* If one thing **precedes** something else, it comes before it. *A short cartoon preceded the main feature.* ▷ **preceding, preceded** ▷ *adjective* **preceding**

pre·ce·dent (press-uh-duhnt) *noun* Something done, said, or written that becomes an example to be followed in the future. *My parents' decision not to let my older sister drive the family car set a precedent for me and my brother.*

pre·cinct (pree-singkt) *noun*
1. An area or a district in a city or town, as in *a police precinct* or *an election precinct*.
2. A police station in such a district.

pre·cious (presh-uhss) *adjective*
1. Rare and valuable, as in *a precious gem*.
2. Very special or dear, as in *precious memories*.

prec·i·pice (press-uh-piss) *noun* A steep cliff.

pre·cip·i·tate (pri-sip-i-tate) *verb*
1. To rain, sleet, hail, or snow.
2. To make something happen suddenly or sooner than expected. *The bombing of Pearl Harbor precipitated the United States' involvement in World War II.*
▷ *verb* **precipitating, precipitated**

pre·cip·i·ta·tion (*pri*-sip-i-tay-shuhn) *noun* The falling of water from the sky in the form of rain, sleet, hail, or snow.

pre·cise (pri-sisse) *adjective* Very accurate or exact. *The precise time is 9:04 P.M.* ▷ *noun* **precision** ▷ *adverb* **precisely**

pre·co·cious (pri-koh-shuhss) *adjective* If a child is **precocious,** he or she is very advanced in intelligence for his or her age.

pred·a·tor (pred-uh-tur) *noun* An animal that lives by hunting other animals for food. Lions, sharks, and hawks are predators. ▷ *adjective* **predatory**

pred·e·ces·sor (pred-uh-sess-ur) *noun* Someone who held an office or a job before another person.

pre·dic·a·ment (pri-dik-uh-muhnt) *noun* An awkward or difficult situation.

pred·i·cate (pred-i-kit) *noun* The part of a sentence or clause that tells what the subject does or what is done to the subject. In the sentence "The kitten purred softly," the predicate is "purred softly."

pre·dict (pri-dikt) *verb* To say what you think will happen in the future. *Can you predict tomorrow's weather?* ▷ **predicting, predicted** ▷ *noun* **prediction**

pre·dom·i·nate (pri-**dom**-uh-*nate*) *verb* To be greater in power or number than others. *A cold weather system is predominating in the Midwest. Girls predominate in our class.* ▷ **predominating, predominated** ▷ *noun* **predominance** ▷ *adjective* **predominant**

preen (preen) *verb* When birds **preen** themselves, they clean and arrange their feathers with their beaks. ▷ **preening, preened**

pref·ace (**pref**-iss) *noun* An introduction to a book or speech.

pre·fer (pri-**fur**) *verb* To like one thing better than another. *I prefer oranges to apples.* ▷ **preferring, preferred** ▷ *noun* **preference**

pre·fix (**pree**-fiks) *noun* A word part added to the beginning of a word or root to change the meaning. *Sub-, un-, and re-* are all prefixes. *The prefix* pre-, *which means "before," is used in the words* prehistoric *and* premature. ▷ *noun, plural* **prefixes**

preg·nant (**preg**-nuhnt) *adjective* A woman who is **pregnant** has an embryo or a fetus growing in her uterus. ▷ *noun* **pregnancy**

pre·his·tor·ic (*pree*-hi-**stor**-ik) *adjective* Belonging to a time before history was recorded in written form. *Dinosaurs are prehistoric animals.* ▷ *noun* **prehistory**

prej·u·dice (**prej**-uh-diss) *noun*
1. An opinion or a judgment formed unfairly or without knowing all the facts.
2. A fixed, unreasonable, or unfair opinion about someone based on the person's race, religion, or other characteristic.
3. Hatred or unfair treatment that results from having fixed opinions about some group of people.
▷ *verb* **prejudice** ▷ *adjective* **prejudiced,** *adjective* **prejudicial**

pre·lim·i·nar·y (pri-**lim**-uh-ner-ee) *adjective* Preparing the way for something important that comes later. *We were given a preliminary talk before the course started.* ▷ *noun* **preliminary**

pre·ma·ture (*pree*-muh-**choor** *or* *pree*-muh-**toor**) *adjective* Happening, appearing, or done too soon, as in *a premature baby* or *a premature decision.* ▷ *adverb* **prematurely**

pre·med·i·tat·ed (pree-**med**-uh-*tay*-tid) *adjective* Planned in advance, as in *a premeditated attack.* ▷ *verb* **premeditate**

pre·mier (pri-**mihr**)
1. *adjective* Leading or top, as in *America's premier rock group.*
2. *noun* A prime minister.

pre·miere (pri-**mihr** *or* pruh-**myair**) *noun* The first public performance of a film, play, or work of music or dance.

prem·ise (**prem**-iss) *noun*
1. A statement or principle that is accepted as true or taken for granted. *The author started his novel with the premise that human beings could survive a nuclear war.*
2. premises *noun, plural* Land and the buildings on it. *A burglar was seen entering the premises.*

pre·mi·um (**pree**-mee-uhm) *noun*
1. Something that is free or less expensive than usual when you buy something else.
2. Money that is paid to take out and maintain an insurance policy.
3. If something is **at a premium,** it is rare and valued very highly.

pre·mo·ni·tion (*pree*-muh-**nish**-uhn *or* prem-uh-**nish**-uhn) *noun* A feeling that something is going to happen, especially something bad or harmful.

pre·oc·cu·pied (pree-**ok**-yuh-pide) *adjective* If you are **preoccupied,** your thoughts are completely taken up with something, and you can't keep your attention on anything else. ▷ *noun* **preoccupation**

pre·pare (pri-**pair**) *verb*
1. To make or to get ready. *I'm preparing for the test by studying every night. I have to prepare for the party.*
2. To put together various parts or ingredients. *Have you prepared lunch?*
▷ *verb* **preparing, prepared** ▷ *noun* **preparation**

prep·o·si·tion (prep-uh-**zish**-uhn) *noun* A word such as "with" or "on" that shows the relation of a noun or pronoun to other items in a sentence, as in the sentence "The book with a red cover is on the table."

pre·pos·ter·ous (pri-**poss**-tur-uhss) *adjective* Ridiculous and absurd, as in *a preposterous idea.* ▷ *adverb* **preposterously**

prep school (prep) *noun* A private school that prepares students for college. Prep school is short for *preparatory school.*

pre·school (**pree**-skool)
1. *adjective* To do with children who are younger than elementary-school age.
2. *noun* A school for children who are too young for elementary school, such as a child care center or a nursery school.

pre·scribe (pri-**skribe**) *verb*
1. To say what should be done. *The football coach prescribed some tough rules for training.*
2. When doctors **prescribe** medicine for a patient, they write a prescription.
▷ *verb* **prescribing, prescribed**

pre·scrip·tion (pri-**skrip**-shuhn) *noun* An order for drugs or medicine written by a doctor to a pharmacist. A prescription specifies what type and quantity of medicine to give.

pres·ence (prez-uhnss) *noun*
1. Being in a place at a certain time. *We would appreciate your presence at our party.*
2. The area immediately near a person or thing. *I'm shy in the presence of strangers.*

pre·sent
1. (pri-**zent**) *verb* To give someone a gift or a prize in a formal way. *I would like to present you with this medal.*
2. (**prez**-uhnt) *noun* Something that you give to somebody, as in *a birthday present*.
3. (**prez**-uhnt) *noun* The time that is happening now.
4. (**prez**-uhnt) *noun* The **present tense**.
5. (**prez**-uhnt) *adjective* If someone is **present** in a place, he or she is there.
6. (pri-**zent**) *verb* To introduce something, such as a television program.
▷ *verb* **presenting, presented** ▷ *noun* **presenter**

pres·en·ta·tion (*prez*-uhn-**tay**-shuhn *or* *pree*-zen-**tay**-shuhn) *noun*
1. The act of giving a prize or present, as in *the presentation of awards*.
2. The way that something is produced and the way it looks. *Your work is good, but your presentation needs improvement.*

pres·ent·ly (**prez**-uhnt-lee) *adverb*
1. Soon or shortly. *"I will be down presently," she called.*
2. Now or at the present time. *We are presently studying the Middle Ages.*

present participle *noun* A form of a verb that ends in "ing" and can be used with a helping verb to form certain tenses and to show that an action or condition is not completed. In the sentence "I am working," the word "working" is a present participle. Present participles may also be used as adjectives, as "thinking" in "A thinking man."

present tense *noun* A form of the verb that is used to indicate present time, as "likes" in "He likes cereal for breakfast."

pre·serv·a·tive (pri-**zur**-vuh-tiv) *noun* Something used to preserve an item, especially a chemical used to keep food from spoiling. ▷ *adjective* **preservative**

pre·serve (pri-**zurv**)
1. *verb* To protect something so that it stays in its original state. ▷ *noun* **preserve,** *noun* **preservation** (*prez*-ur-**va**-shuhn)
2. *verb* To treat food so that it does not become spoiled.
3. **preserves** *noun, plural* Jam. *I love to put apricot preserves on my toast.*
▷ *verb* **preserving, preserved**

pre·side (pri-**zide**) *verb* To be in charge of something. *Gina presided over the meeting.*
▷ **presiding, presided**

pres·i·dent *or* **President** (**prez**-uh-duhnt) *noun*
1. The elected leader or chief executive of a republic. *These portraits of U.S. presidents are carved out of rock at Mount Rushmore in South Dakota.*
2. The head of a company, society, college, club, or organization.
▷ *noun* **presidency** ▷ *adjective* **presidential**

Mount Rushmore

Washington   Jefferson   T. Roosevelt   Lincoln

president-elect *noun* The person who has won the election for president but has not yet been sworn into office.

Presidents' Day *noun* A holiday observed in most of the United States on the third Monday in February, celebrating the birthdays of George Washington and Abraham Lincoln.

press (press)
1. *verb* To push firmly. *Press the button to ring the doorbell.*
2. *verb* To persuade strongly. *Eddie was pressed into taking a role in the play.*
3. *verb* To smooth out the creases in clothes with an iron. ▷ *noun* **presser**
4. *noun* A machine for printing.
5. **the press** *noun* The news media and the people who produce them.
▷ *noun, plural* **presses** ▷ *verb* **presses, pressing, pressed**

pressing *adjective* Urgent and needing immediate attention. *I must run because I have a pressing appointment.*

pres·sure (**presh**-ur) *noun*
1. The force produced by pressing on something, as in *blood pressure* or *water pressure*.
2. Strong influence, force, or persuasion. *Kathy is under a lot of pressure to finish her work this week.* ▷ *verb* **pressure**
3. A burden or a strain. *He could not handle the pressure of making life-and-death decisions.*

pres·sur·ize (**presh**-uh-*rize*) *verb* To seal off an aircraft cabin, a spacecraft, or a diving chamber so that the air pressure inside is the same as the pressure at the earth's surface. ▷ **pressurizing, pressurized** ▷ *adjective* **pressurized**

pres·tige (pre-steezh *or* pre-steej) *noun* The great respect and high status that come from being successful, powerful, rich, or famous. ▷ *adjective* **prestigious**

pre·sum·a·bly (pri-zoo-muh-blee) *adverb* Probably. *If you have graduated from high school, you presumably know how to read and write.*

pre·sume (pri-zoom) *verb*
1. To think that something is true without being certain or having all the facts. *I presume that you like ice cream, so I bought you a cone.*
2. To dare. *Don't presume to tell me what to do!* ▷ *verb* **presuming, presumed** ▷ *noun* **presumption**

pre·tend (pri-tend) *verb*
1. To make believe. *The little girl pretended she was an astronaut.*
2. To claim falsely. *I do not pretend to be a computer expert.*
3. To give a false show in order to trick or deceive. *He pretended illness, but his mother said he had to go to school and take his test.* ▷ *verb* **pretending, pretended** ▷ *noun* **pretense**

pre·text (pree-tekst) *noun* A false reason or excuse given to hide a real reason. *Joe left the boring party on the pretext that he had to get up early the next morning.*

pret·ty (prit-ee)
1. *adjective* Attractive and pleasing to look at. ▷ *noun* **prettiness** ▷ *adverb* **prettily**
2. *adverb* Quite, as in *a pretty bad movie.*

pret·zel (pret-suhl) *noun* Dough that has been shaped into a stick or a knot and baked until it is crisp. Pretzels are usually salted on the outside.

pre·vail (pri-vayl) *verb*
1. To succeed in spite of difficulties. *Justice prevailed when the innocent woman was acquitted.*
2. To be common or usual. *Poverty and crime prevail in many cities.* ▷ *adjective* **prevalent** ▷ *verb* **prevailing, prevailed**

pre·vent (pri-vent) *verb*
1. To stop something from happening. *Brushing your teeth prevents tooth decay.*
2. To keep someone from doing something. *Our neighbor's loud party prevented us from sleeping.* ▷ *verb* **preventing, prevented** ▷ *noun* **prevention**

pre·ven·tive (pri-ven-tiv)
1. *adjective* Meant to prevent or stop something, as in *preventive medicine.*
2. *noun* Something that prevents, especially something that prevents a disease. *The vaccine is a preventive against polio.*

pre·view (pree-vyoo) *noun* A showing of a play or a screening of a movie before it is released to the general public. ▷ *verb* **preview**

pre·vi·ous (pree-vee-uhss) *adjective* Former, or happening before. *I like this school more than my previous one.* ▷ *adverb* **previously**

prey (pray)
1. *noun* An animal that is hunted by another animal for food.
2. *verb* When an animal **preys on** another animal, it hunts it and then eats it. *Owls prey on mice.*
3. *verb* To rob, attack, or take advantage of someone who is helpless or unable to fight back. *The robber preyed on frail senior citizens.*
4. *noun* The victim of an attack or robbery. **Prey** sounds like **pray.** ▷ *verb* **preying, preyed**

price (prisse)
1. *noun* The amount that you have to pay for something.
2. *verb* To give something a price. ▷ **pricing, priced**
3. *noun* The cost at which something is gained. *The battle was won at the price of hundreds of lives.*

price·less (prisse-liss) *adjective* If something is **priceless,** it is too precious for anyone to put a value on it.

prick (prik) *verb*
1. To make a small hole in something with a sharp point. ▷ *noun* **prick**
2. To raise up. *The dog pricked up his ears when he heard the whistle.* ▷ *verb* **pricking, pricked**

prick·le (prik-uhl) *noun* A small, sharp point, such as a thorn. ▷ *adjective* **prickly**

prickly pear *noun* A cactus with yellow flowers and fruit shaped like a pear. See **fruit.**

pride (pride) *noun*
1. Self-respect, or a sense of your own importance or worth.
2. A feeling of satisfaction in something that you or someone else has achieved. *Sarah takes pride in her work.* ▷ *verb* **pride**
3. A too-high opinion of your own importance and cleverness.

priest (preest) *noun* In certain Christian and other religions, a member of the clergy who can lead services and perform rites. ▷ *noun* **priesthood** ▷ *adjective* **priestly**

prim (prim) *adjective* Someone who is **prim** is stiffly formal and proper. ▷ **primmer, primmest**

pri·ma don·na (pree-muh don-uh) *noun*
1. A female opera or concert star.
2. *(informal)* Someone who is demanding, mean, or conceited. ▷ *noun, plural* **prima donnas**

P

pri·mar·i·ly (prye-**mair**-uh-lee) *adverb* Chiefly or mainly. *Kenny was primarily interested in dinosaurs.*

pri·mar·y (prye-mair-ee *or* prye-muh-ree)
1. *adjective* Most important, chief, or main, as in *a primary concern.*
2. *adjective* First or earliest, as in *primary education.*
3. *noun* An election to choose a party candidate who will run in the general election.

primary colors *noun, plural* In painting, the **primary colors** are red, yellow, and blue, which can be mixed to make all the other colors.

primary school *noun* A school that includes the first three or four grades and sometimes kindergarten.

pri·mate (prye-mate) *noun* Any member of the group of intelligent mammals that includes humans, apes, and monkeys.

prime (prime)
1. *adjective* Of first importance or quality, as in *prime beef.*
2. *verb* To prepare a surface to be painted.
3. *verb* To pour water into a dry pump in order to start it working properly.
▷ *verb* **priming, primed**

prime minister *noun* The person in charge of a government in some countries. Both Great Britain and Canada have prime ministers.

prime number *noun* A number that has exactly two factors. *The numbers 2, 3, 5, 7, 11, 13, 17, and 19 are the first eight prime numbers.*

pri·me·val (prye-mee-vuhl) *adjective* Belonging to the earliest period of the earth, as in *primeval oceans.*

prim·i·tive (prim-uh-tiv) *adjective*
1. Very simple or crude. *Cave dwellers used primitive tools and weapons.*
2. Uncivilized, basic, and crude. *Conditions at the campsite were very primitive.*
3. To do with an early stage of development. *The mammoth was a primitive form of elephant.*

prim·rose (prim-*rohz*) *noun* A small garden plant with clusters of brightly colored flowers.

prince (prinss) *noun*
1. The son of a king or queen.
2. The husband of a queen.
3. A nobleman of high rank.

prin·cess (prin-suhss *or* prin-sess) *noun*
1. The daughter of a king or queen.
2. The wife of a prince.
3. A noblewoman of high rank.
▷ *noun, plural* **princesses**

prin·ci·pal (prin-suh-puhl)
1. *adjective* Most important, chief, or main. *She is a principal dancer with the ballet company. My principal reason for moving was the offer of a better job.* ▷ *adverb* **principally**

2. *noun* The head of a public school.
Principal sounds like **principle.**

prin·ci·ple (prin-suh-puhl)
1. *noun* A basic truth, law, or belief. *Our government is based on the principle that all people are created equal.*
2. *noun* A basic rule that governs a person's behavior. *It's against Stephanie's principles to lie.*
3. If you agree to someone's plan **in principle,** you are happy with the general idea but not necessarily with the details.
Principle sounds like **principal.**

print (print)
1. *verb* To produce words or pictures on a page with a machine that uses ink. *Color pictures are usually printed by combining four colors of ink on white paper. This is called four-color printing. The picture below has been magnified so that you can see how it is made up of millions of overlapping dots of black, yellow, cyan (blue), and magenta (red).* ▷ *noun* **printer**
2. *verb* To write using letters that are separate.
3. *noun* A photograph or a printed copy of a painting or drawing.
4. *verb* To publish. *The newspaper printed my letter to the editor.*
▷ *verb* **printing, printed** ▷ *adjective* **printed**

printed picture

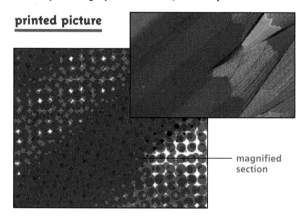

magnified section

printing press *noun* A large machine that prints words and designs by pressing sheets of paper against a surface, such as a metal plate, that has ink on it.

print·out (print-*out*) *noun* A printed copy of information stored in a computer.

pri·or (prye-ur) *adjective* Earlier. *Peter can't come to the meeting because of a prior appointment.*

pri·or·i·ty (prye-or-uh-tee) *noun* Something that is more important or more urgent than other things.

prism (priz-uhm) *noun* A clear glass or plastic shape that bends light or breaks it up into the colors of the spectrum. Prisms usually have a triangular base. *See* **periscope, shape, spectrum.**

P

pris·on (priz-uhn) *noun* A building where people are made to live as punishment for a crime.

pris·on·er (priz-uhn-ur) *noun*
1. Someone who is in prison.
2. Any person who has been captured or is held by force, as in *a prisoner of war.*

pri·vate (prye-vit)
1. *adjective* If something is **private,** it belongs to or concerns one person or group and no one else. *My diary is one of my private possessions.* ▷ *noun* **privacy**
2. *adjective* Not meant to be shared, as in *a private conversation* or *a private telephone number.* ▷ *adverb* **privately**
3. *adjective* Not holding a public office, as in *a private citizen.*
4. *noun* A soldier of the lowest rank.

private school *noun* A school where parents pay for their children's education, as opposed to a public school, which is supported by tax dollars.

priv·i·lege (priv-uh-lij) *noun* A special right or advantage given to a person or a group of people. ▷ *adjective* **privileged**

prize (prize)
1. *noun* A reward for winning a game or competition.
2. *verb* To value something very much. *I prize my freedom.* ▷ **prizing, prized** ▷ *adjective* **prized**

pro (proh)
1. *preposition* If you are **pro** something, you are in favor of it.
2. *noun* A shortened form of **professional,** often used in sports, as in *a golf pro.*
3. **pros and cons** (konz) Advantages and disadvantages. *We debated the pros and cons of the proposed law.*

prob·a·ble (prob-uh-buhl) *adjective* Likely to happen or be true. *It's probable that André will win the tennis match.* ▷ *noun* **probability** ▷ *adverb* **probably**

pro·ba·tion (proh-bay-shuhn) *noun*
1. A period of time for testing a person's behavior or job qualifications.
2. If someone who has committed a crime is put on **probation,** he or she is not sent to prison but is allowed to go free under the close supervision of a probation officer.

probe (prohb) *noun*
1. A thorough examination or investigation.
2. A tool or device used to explore or examine something, as in *a space probe.* ▷ *verb* **probe**

prob·lem (prob-luhm) *noun*
1. A difficult situation that needs to be figured out or overcome.

2. A puzzle or question to be solved, as in *a math problem.*

pro·ce·dure (pruh-see-jur) *noun* A way of doing something, especially by a series of steps. *Follow the usual procedure for leaving the building.*

pro·ceed
1. (pruh-seed) *verb* To move forward or continue. ▷ **proceeding, proceeded**
2. **proceeds** (proh-seedz) *noun, plural* The **proceeds** of an event are the sum of money that it raises. *The proceeds from the book fair went to buy a new encyclopedia.*

proc·ess (pross-ess *or* proh-sess)
1. *noun* An organized series of actions that produce a result. *We studied the process of making rubber.* ▷ *noun, plural* **processes**
2. *verb* To prepare or change by a series of steps. *The newspaper was processed so it could be used again.* ▷ **processes, processing, processed** ▷ *noun* **processing,** *noun* **processor** ▷ *adjective* **processed**

pro·ces·sion (pruh-sesh-uhn) *noun* A number of people walking or driving along a route as part of a public festival, a religious service, or a parade.

pro·claim (pruh-klaym) *verb* If someone **proclaims** something, the person announces it publicly. ▷ **proclaiming, proclaimed** ▷ *noun* **proclamation**

pro·cras·ti·nate (proh-krass-tuh-*nate*) *verb* To put off doing something that you have to do simply because you don't want to do it. ▷ **procrastinating, procrastinated** ▷ *noun* **procrastination,** *noun* **procrastinator**

prod (prod) *verb*
1. To poke or jab something or someone. *I prodded Mitch to wake him up.*
2. To push or urge someone into action. *My parents had to prod me to study for my test.* ▷ *verb* **prodding, prodded** ▷ *noun* **prod**

prod·i·gy (prod-uh-jee) *noun* A **prodigy** is an extremely smart or talented child or young person. ▷ *noun, plural* **prodigies**

pro·duce
1. (pruh-dooss) *verb* To make something. *This factory produces cars.*
2. (prod-ooss *or* proh-dooss) *noun* Things that are produced or grown for eating, especially fruits and vegetables.
3. (pruh-dooss) *verb* To bring something out for people to see. *Nick produced a mouse from his pocket.*
4. (pruh-dooss) *verb* To be in charge of putting on a play or making a movie or TV program. ▷ *noun* **producer** ▷ *verb* **producing, produced**

prod·uct (prod-uhkt) *noun*
   1. Something that is manufactured or made by a natural process, as in *a dairy product.*
   2. The result you get when you multiply two numbers. *The product of 3 times 5 is 15.*

pro·duc·tion (pruh-duhk-shuhn) *noun*
   1. The process of manufacturing or growing something.
   2. The total amount produced. *Production is down this year.*
   3. A play, an opera, a show, or any form of entertainment that is presented to others.
   4. production line A system of manufacturing in which the product moves along slowly while different things are added or done to it.

pro·duc·tive (pruh-duhk-tiv) *adjective* Making a lot of products or producing good results. *We had a productive meeting.* ▷ *noun* **productivity**

pro·fess (pruh-fess) *verb*
   1. To state openly or to make known. *I will profess my feelings for her at the Valentine's Day dance.*
   2. To say something insincerely, or to pretend that something is true. *He professed to be a great player, but he couldn't even make the junior high basketball team.*
   ▷ *verb* **professes, professing, professed**

pro·fes·sion (pruh-fesh-uhn) *noun*
   1. An occupation for which you need special training or study. *Medicine, teaching, and law are all professions.*
   2. The whole group of people in a profession, as in *the medical profession.*
   3. Something that you state openly. *He made a sudden profession of love.*

pro·fes·sion·al (pruh-fesh-uh-nuhl)
   1. *noun* A member of a profession, such as a doctor, teacher, nurse, or lawyer. ▷ *adjective* **professional**
   2. *adjective* Making money for doing something others do for fun, as in *a professional athlete.*
   ▷ *noun* **professional**

pro·fes·sor (pruh-fess-ur) *noun* A teacher of the highest teaching rank at a college or university.

pro·fi·cient (pruh-fish-uhnt) *adjective* If you are **proficient** at doing something, you are able to do it properly and skillfully. ▷ *noun* **proficiency** ▷ *adverb* **proficiently**

pro·file (proh-file) *noun*
   1. A side view or drawing of someone's head.
   2. A brief account of someone's life.
   ▷ *verb* **profile**

prof·it (prof-it)
   1. *noun* The amount of money left after all the costs of running a business have been subtracted from all the money earned. *We had a profit of $5,000.*

   2. *noun* A gain or a benefit. *Hard work always yields a profit.*
   3. *verb* To gain or benefit in some way. *You will profit by doing well in school.* ▷ **profiting, profited**
   Profit sounds like **prophet.**

prof·it·a·ble (prof-i-tuh-buhl) *adjective* Producing a profit. *They have a profitable business.*

pro·found (pruh-found) *adjective* Very deeply felt or thought, as in *profound sadness.* ▷ *adverb* **profoundly**

pro·fuse (pruh-fyooss) *adjective* Plentiful or more than enough. *I offered my mother my profuse apologies for breaking the vase.* ▷ *noun* **profusion** (pruh-fyoo-zhuhn), *noun* **profuseness**

pro·gram (proh-gram *or* proh-gruhm)
   1. *noun* A television or radio show.
   2. *noun* A theater or concert **program** is a booklet that gives you information about the performance.
   3. *noun* A schedule or plan for doing something. *The citizens' group proposed a new program to help the homeless in our city.*
   4. *noun* A series of instructions, written in a computer language, that control the way a computer works.
   5. *verb* To give a computer or other machine instructions to make it work in a certain way.
   ▷ **programming, programmed**
   ▷ *noun* **programming**

pro·gram·mer (proh-gram-ur) *noun* Someone whose job is to program a computer.

prog·ress
   1. (pruh-gress) *verb* To move forward or to improve. *How are you progressing with your fitness program?* ▷ **progresses, progressing, progressed**
   2. (prog-ruhss) *noun* A forward movement or improvement. *The teacher saw some progress in the student's work.*
   3. (prog-ruhss) If something is **in progress,** it is happening. *Road construction will be in progress all this week.*

pro·gress·ive (pruh-gress-iv)
   1. *adjective* Moving forward or happening steadily. *Lou's work in math showed progressive improvement.*
   2. *adjective* In favor of improvement, progress, or reform, especially in political or social matters. *The liberal candidate had many progressive ideas for protecting the environment.*
   3. *noun* Someone who favors improvement or reform, especially in political, social, or educational matters.

pro·hib·it (proh-hib-it) *verb* To stop or ban something officially. *The law now prohibits smoking in this restaurant.* ▷ **prohibiting, prohibited** ▷ *noun* **prohibition**

proj·ect

1. (proj-ekt) *noun* A plan or a proposal. *The Senate approved the highway project.*
2. (proj-ekt) *noun* A school assignment worked on over a period of time. *We are starting a project on the Romans.*
3. (pruh-jekt) *verb* To stick out. *The branch projected into the road.* ▷ *adjective* **projecting**
4. (pruh-jekt) *verb* To show an image on a screen.
5. (pruh-jekt) *verb* To look ahead or to forecast. *The company has projected a loss for next year.*
6. (pruh-jekt) *verb* If you **project** your voice, you make it carry very far.
7. (proj-ekt) *noun* A group of apartment buildings planned and built as a unit.
▷ *verb* **projecting, projected**

pro·jec·tile (pruh-jek-tuhl) *noun* An object, such as a bullet or missile, that is thrown or shot through the air. *The arrow in the picture is a projectile heading toward a target.*

projectile

pro·jec·tion (pruh-jek-shuhn) *noun*
1. Something that sticks out, as in *a rock projection.*
2. A forecast or a prediction.
3. A **map projection** is a way of representing the globe on a flat page.

pro·jec·tor (pruh-jek-tur) *noun* A machine that shows slides or movies on a screen.

pro·li·fic (pruh-lif-ik) *adjective* Very productive or producing a large quantity. *The prolific author had written more than 40 books.*

pro·logue (proh-lawg) *noun* A short speech or piece of writing that introduces a play, story, or poem.

pro·long (pruh-lawng) *verb* To make something last longer. *Debbie prolonged the suspense by not giving Pete his birthday present until after dinner.*
▷ **prolonging, prolonged**

prom·e·nade (prom-uh-nade or prom-uh-nahd)
1. *noun* A walk taken for pleasure.
2. *verb* To walk for pleasure. *We love to promenade along the upper deck of the ocean liner.* ▷ **promenading, promenaded**
3. *noun* A place for taking a leisurely walk.

prom·i·nent (prom-uh-nuhnt) *adjective*
1. Very easily seen, as in *a prominent landmark.*
2. Famous or important. *He is a prominent politician.*
▷ *noun* **prominence**

prom·ise (prom-iss)
1. *verb* If you **promise** to do something, you give your word that you will do it. ▷ **promising, promised**
2. *noun* A pledge given by someone that he or she will do something.
3. *noun* Someone who shows **promise** seems likely to do well in the future. ▷ *adjective* **promising**

prom·on·tor·y (prom-uhn-tor-ee) *noun* A high point of land or rock that sticks out into a body of water. *This promontory is part of the cliffs of Mohr in Ireland.*

promontory

pro·mote (pruh-mote) *verb*
1. To move someone to a more important job or to a higher grade in school.
2. To help with the growth or development of something. *Sugary foods promote tooth decay.*
3. To make the public aware of something or someone. *Rob is busy promoting his latest book.*
▷ *verb* **promoting, promoted**

pro·mo·tion (pruh-moh-shuhn) *noun*
1. Advancement to a more important job or a higher grade in school.
2. Encouragement.

prompt (prompt)
1. *adjective* Very quick and without delay. *I received a prompt answer to my question.*
2. *adjective* On time. *Please be prompt for dinner.*
3. *verb* To move someone to action. *The anger in her voice prompted me to drop the discussion.*
4. *verb* To remind actors of their lines when they have forgotten them during a play. ▷ *noun* **prompter**
▷ *verb* **prompting, prompted** ▷ *adjective* **prompter, promptest** ▷ *adverb* **promptly**

prone (prohn) *adjective*
1. Likely to act, feel, or be a certain way. *She is prone to mischief.*
2. Lying flat or face down, as in *a prone position.*

prong (prong) *noun* One of the sharp points of a fork or other tool.

P

pro·noun (proh-*noun*) *noun* A word that is used in place of a noun. "I," "me," "he," and "it" are all pronouns.

pro·nounce (pruh-nounss) *verb*
1. To say words in a particular way. *You pronounce* present *two different ways, depending on the meaning you are using.*
2. To make a formal announcement. *The mayor pronounced the fair open.* ▷ *noun* **pronouncement**
▷ *verb* **pronouncing, pronounced**

pro·nun·ci·a·tion (pruh-*nuhn*-see-ay-shuhn) *noun* The way in which a word is pronounced.

proof (proof) *noun* Facts or evidence that something is true. *The lawyer claimed to have proof that his client was innocent. Do you have proof of your age?*

proof·read (proof-*reed*) *verb* If you **proofread** something, you read it carefully and correct any mistakes in spelling, punctuation, and grammar that you find. ▷ **proofreading, proofread** ▷ *noun* **proofreader**

prop (prop)
1. *verb* To support something that would otherwise fall down. *Bob propped the ladder against the wall.* ▷ **propping, propped**
2. *noun* Something used as a support.
3. *noun* In the theater, movies, or television a **prop** is any item that an actor needs to carry or use. Prop is short for **property.**

prop·a·gan·da (prop-uh-gan-duh) *noun* Information that is spread to influence the way people think, gain supporters, or damage an opposing group. Propaganda is often incomplete or biased information.

pro·pel (pruh-pel) *verb* To drive or push something forward. *The aircraft was propelled by twin jet engines.* ▷ **propelling, propelled** ▷ *noun* **propulsion**

pro·pel·lant (pruh-pel-uhnt) *noun*
1. A chemical or fuel that when burned propels something.
2. A compressed gas or a liquid that releases the contents of an aerosol can. *See* **aerosol.**

pro·pel·ler (pruh-pel-ur) *noun* A set of rotating blades that provide force to move a vehicle through water or air.

prop·er (prop-ur) *adjective*
1. Right or suitable for a given purpose or occasion. *Do you have the proper tools for the job? The restaurant requires proper attire; no bathing suits are allowed.*
2. Stiffly formal. *Claudia is very prim and proper.*

prop·er·ly (prop-ur-lee) *adverb*
1. In a correct, appropriate, or suitable way. *Can he do the job properly? Are you properly equipped for your camping trip?*
2. In an exact or strict sense. *Properly speaking, whales are not fish; they are mammals.*

proper noun *noun* A **proper noun** is the name of a particular person, place, or thing, such as *Jane, New York,* and *Washington Monument.* A proper noun starts with a capital letter.

prop·er·ty (prop-ur-tee) *noun*
1. Anything that is owned by an individual. *Whose property is this pen?*
2. Buildings and land belonging to someone. *Two fierce dogs guarded the property.*
3. A special quality or characteristic of something, as in *the properties of a liquid.*
▷ *noun, plural* **properties**

proph·e·cy (prof-uh-see) *noun* A prediction.
▷ *noun, plural* **prophecies** ▷ *verb* **prophecy**
(prof-uh-sye)

proph·et (prof-it) *noun*
1. A person who speaks or claims to speak for God.
2. Someone who predicts what will happen in the future.
Prophet sounds like **profit.**

pro·por·tion (pruh-por-shuhn) *noun*
1. A part of something. *A large proportion of the class supported me.*
2. The size, number, or amount of something in relation to another thing. *The proportion of girls to boys in the school is two to one.*
3. In mathematics, a statement that two ratios are equal.
4. If something is **in proportion** to something else, it is the correct size in relation to it. *Gus has large eyes, but they are in proportion to the rest of his features.*
5. proportions *noun, plural* The **proportions** of something are its measurements or size.
▷ *adjective* **proportional** ▷ *adverb* **proportionally**

pro·pose (pruh-poze) *verb*
1. To suggest a plan or an idea. *Carla proposed that we all go swimming.*
2. To ask someone to marry you.
▷ *verb* **proposing, proposed** ▷ *noun* **proposal**

pro·po·si·tion (*prop*-uh-zi-shuhn) *noun*
1. An offer, or a suggestion. *The neighbors considered my proposition to mow their lawn for a reasonable fee.*
2. Anything brought up for discussion. *The proposition before the class is whether or not to put on a class play.*

pro·pul·sion (pruh-puhl-shuhn) *noun* The force by which a plane, rocket, etc., is pushed along, as in *jet propulsion.*

prose (proze) *noun* Ordinary written or spoken language, as opposed to verse or poetry. Short stories and essays are examples of prose.

P

pros·e·cute (pross-uh-kyoot) *verb* To begin and carry out a legal action in a court of law against a person accused of a crime. ▷ *noun* **prosecution**

pros·e·cu·tor (pross-uh-*kyoo*-tur) *noun* A lawyer who represents the government in criminal trials.

pros·pect (pross-pekt)
1. *noun* Something that is looked forward to or expected. *I was excited by the prospect of owning my own dog.*
2. *noun* A view or a scene.
3. *verb* To explore or search for something, especially gold or silver. ▷ **prospecting, prospected** ▷ *noun* **prospector**
4. *noun* A possible customer or winner in a political or athletic contest.

pro·spec·tive (pruh-spek-tiv) *adjective*
1. Possible or likely. *I've calculated my prospective earnings for my weekend baby-sitting job.*
2. Future or likely to become, as in *a prospective buyer* or *a prospective bride.*

pro·spec·tus (pruh-spek-tuhss) *noun* A brochure giving information about a company or any organization. ▷ *noun, plural* **prospectuses**

pros·per (pross-pur) *verb* To be successful or to thrive. ▷ **prospering, prospered** ▷ *noun* **prosperity** ▷ *adjective* **prosperous**

pros·the·sis (pross-thee-siss) *noun* An artificial device that replaces a missing part of a body. *The accident victim's prosthesis looked and worked a lot like a real leg.* ▷ *noun, plural* **prostheses** (pross-thee-seez)

pro·tect (pruh-tekt) *verb* To guard or keep something safe from harm, attack, or injury. *Skaters wear helmets to protect their heads.* ▷ **protecting, protected** ▷ *noun* **protection,** *noun* **protector** ▷ *adjective* **protective**

pro·tein (proh-teen) *noun* A substance found in all living plant and animal cells. Foods such as meat, cheese, eggs, beans, and fish are sources of dietary protein.

pro·test
1. (pruh-**test**) *verb* To object to something strongly and publicly. *The students protested against the increase in college tuition.* ▷ **protesting, protested**
2. (proh-**test**) *noun* A demonstration or statement against something, as in *a protest against war.*

Prot·es·tant (prot-uh-stuhnt) *noun* A Christian who does not belong to the Roman Catholic or the Orthodox church. ▷ *adjective* **Protestant**

pro·tist (proh-tist) *noun* Any organism from the kingdom *Protista.* Protists include amoebas, paramecia, and some algae.

pro·ton (proh-ton) *noun* One of the very small parts in the nucleus of an atom. A proton carries a positive electrical charge. *See* **atom.**

pro·to·plasm (proh-tuh-*plaz*-uhm) *noun* A jellylike substance that makes up the living matter of all cells.

pro·to·type (proh-tuh-*tipe*) *noun* The first version of an invention that tests an idea to see if it will work.

prototype car

pro·to·zo·an (proh-tuh-**zoh**-uhn) *noun* A microscopic animal with one cell that reproduces by dividing. Paramecia and amoebas are protozoans. ▷ *noun, plural* **protozoans** *or* **protozoa** (proh-tuh-**zoh**-uh)

pro·trac·tor (proh-**trak**-tur) *noun* A semicircular instrument used for measuring and drawing angles. Protractors are marked off in degrees. They are usually made of transparent plastic. *See* **geometry.**

pro·trude (proh-**trood**) *verb* To stick or jut out. *The rocks protruded into the sea.* ▷ **protruding, protruded** ▷ *noun* **protrusion**

proud (proud) *adjective*
1. If you are **proud,** you are pleased and satisfied with what you or someone else has achieved.
2. If you are **proud,** you have self-respect and a sense of your own importance.
3. If you are **proud,** you think too highly of your own value or abilities.
▷ *adjective* **prouder, proudest**

prove (proov) *verb* To show that something is true. *The experiment proved our hypothesis. The lawyer tried to prove that her client was innocent.* ▷ **proving, proved**

prov·erb (prov-urb) *noun* A wise old saying that tells a common truth. *"A stitch in time saves nine" is a proverb.*

pro·vide (pruh-vide)
1. *verb* To supply the things that someone needs. ▷ *noun* **provider,** *noun* **provision**
2. *verb* To set down as a rule or condition. *The Constitution provides that all adult citizens have the right to vote.*
3. provided *conjunction* On condition that or as long as. *I will go swimming provided that you come, too.*
▷ *verb* **providing, provided**

P

prov·ince (prov-uhnss) *noun* A district or a region of some countries. Canada is made up of provinces.

pro·vin·cial (pruh-vin-shuhl) *adjective*
1. To do with a province, as in *a provincial government.*
2. Narrow-minded or having a limited or prejudiced point of view. *Her grandparents have very provincial attitudes; they think girls should never wear pants.*

pro·vi·sion (pruh-vizh-uhn) *noun*
1. The act of providing something. *We made provisions for a photographer to be at the wedding.*
2. Something that is named as a condition in an agreement, a law, or a document. *A provision of the treaty bans the production of new nuclear weapons.*
3. **provisions** *noun, plural* A supply of groceries or food.

pro·vi·sion·al (pruh-vizh-uh-nuhl) *adjective* If something is **provisional,** it is temporary or not yet final, as in *a provisional government* or *provisional plans.* ▷ *adverb* **provisionally**

pro·voke (pruh-voke) *verb*
1. To annoy someone and make the person angry.
2. To bring on or to arouse. *The editorial provoked a heated debate.*
▷ *verb* **provoking, provoked** ▷ *noun* **provocation** ▷ *adjective* **provocative**

prow (prou) *noun* The bow or front part of a boat or ship.

prow·ess (prou-iss) *noun* Skill or bravery. *Cathy's prowess on the ski slopes is well known.*

prowl (proul) *verb* To move around quietly and secretly, like an animal looking for prey.
▷ **prowling, prowled** ▷ *noun* **prowler**

prox·im·i·ty (prok-sim-uh-tee) *noun* Nearness.

pru·dent (prood-uhnt) *adjective* If you are **prudent,** you are cautious and think carefully before you do something. ▷ *noun* **prudence** ▷ *adverb* **prudently**

prune (proon)
1. *noun* A dried plum.
2. *verb* To cut off branches from a tree or bush in order to make it grow more strongly.
▷ **pruning, pruned**

pry (prye) *verb*
1. If you **pry,** you ask someone personal or nosy questions about things he or she does not want to discuss.
2. To remove, raise, or pull apart with force, as with a lever. *I pried the lid off the crate.*
3. To get with difficulty or much effort. *The police tried to pry a confession out of the suspect.*
▷ *verb* **pries, prying, pried**

P.S. (pee ess) Short for **postscript** or **public school.**

psalm (sahm) *noun* A sacred song or poem, especially one from the Book of Psalms in the Bible.

pseu·do·nym (sood-uh-nim) *noun* A false name, especially one used by an author instead of his or her real name.

psy·chi·a·trist (sye-kye-uh-trist) *noun* A medical doctor who is trained to treat emotional and mental illness. ▷ *noun* **psychiatry** ▷ *adjective* **psychiatric** (sye-kee-at-rik)

psy·chic (sye-kik) *adjective* Someone who is **psychic** claims to be able to tell what people are thinking or to predict the future. ▷ *noun* **psychic**

psy·cho·log·i·cal (sye-kuh-loj-uh-kuhl) *adjective*
1. To do with psychology.
2. To do with or arising from the mind. *Her problem is psychological, not physical.*

psy·chol·o·gist (sye-kol-uh-jist) *noun* Someone who studies people's minds and emotions and the ways that people behave.

psy·chol·o·gy (sye-koh-luh-jee) *noun* The study of the mind, the emotions, and human behavior.

psy·cho·path (sye-kuh-*path*) *noun* Someone who is mentally unbalanced, especially a person who is violent or dangerous. ▷ *adjective* **psychopathic**

pter·o·dac·tyl (ter-uh-dak-til) *noun* A prehistoric flying reptile with wide wings supported by very large fourth fingers.

pub (puhb) *noun* A bar where adults can go to drink alcohol.

pu·ber·ty (pyoo-bur-tee) *noun* The time when a person's body changes from a child's to an adult's.

pub·lic (puhb-lik)
1. *adjective* To do with the people or the community, as in *public safety* or *public opinion.*
2. *adjective* If something is **public,** it belongs to or can be used by everybody, as in *public transportation* or *a public beach.*
3. *adjective* Working for the government of a town, city, or country, as in *a public official* or *a public servant.*
4. **the public** *noun* People in general.
▷ *adjective* **publicly**

pub·li·ca·tion (puhb-luh-kay-shuhn) *noun*
1. A book, magazine, or newspaper.
2. The production and distribution of a book, magazine, or newspaper.

pub·lic·i·ty (puh-bliss-uh-tee) *noun* Information about a person or an event that is given out to get the public's attention or approval. *The movie received a lot of publicity in the newspapers.*

pub·li·cize (puhb-luh-*size*) *verb* If you **publicize** an event, you make it known to as many people as possible. ▷ **publicizing, publicized**

P

public opinion *noun* The views or beliefs of most of the people in a town, city, or country, usually found out through a public opinion poll.

public relations *noun, plural* The methods or activities an organization or a business uses to promote goodwill or a good image with the public.

public school *noun* A school that provides free education. Public schools are supported by taxes.

pub·lish (puhb-lish) *verb* To produce and distribute a book, magazine, newspaper, or any other printed material so that people can buy it.
▷ **publishes, publishing, published** ▷ *noun* **publisher,** *noun* **publishing**

puck (puhk) *noun* A hard, round, flat piece of rubber used in ice hockey. See **ice hockey.**

puck·er (puhk-ur) *verb* To wrinkle or to fold. *Eating a lemon always makes me pucker my lips.*
▷ **puckering, puckered** ▷ *noun* **pucker**

pud·ding (pud-ing) *noun* A sweet, soft dessert, as in *rice pudding* or *chocolate pudding.*

pud·dle (puhd-uhl) *noun* A small pool of water or other liquid, as in *a puddle of spilled milk.*

pueb·lo (pweb-loh) *noun*
1. A village consisting of stone and adobe buildings built next to and on top of each other. Pueblos were built by American Indian tribes in the southwestern United States. *The picture shows a pueblo in Taos, New Mexico.* ▷ *noun, plural* **pueblos**
2. Pueblo A member of an American Indian tribe of New Mexico and Arizona. ▷ *noun, plural* **Pueblo** *or* **Pueblos**

pueblo

puff (puhf)
1. *noun* A short, sudden burst of air, breath, or smoke.
2. *noun* Anything that looks soft, light, and fluffy, as in *puffs of clouds.*
3. *verb* To blow or come out in puffs. *Smoke puffed from the chimney.*
4. *verb* If something **puffs up,** it swells. *The mosquito bite puffed up.*
▷ *verb* **puffing, puffed** ▷ *adjective* **puffy**

puf·fin (puf-uhn) *noun* A seabird of northern regions that has black and white feathers, a short neck, and a colorful beak.

puffin

pug (puhg) *noun* A dog with short hair, a flat nose, a wrinkled face, and a curled tail.

pug·na·cious (puhg-**nay**-shuhss) *adjective* If someone is **pugnacious,** he or she often picks fights.
▷ *adverb* **pugnaciously**

pull (pul)
1. *verb* To move something forward or toward you. *An ox pulled the cart. He pulled the door open.*
2. *verb* To tug or pluck something, as in *to pull weeds.*
3. *noun* The act of pulling something, or the effort required to pull something, as in *a big pull.*
4. *noun* Attraction or influence, as in *the pull of a magnet.*
5. *verb* To stretch or strain a part of the body. *I pulled a muscle in my leg.*
6. *verb* If you **pull** something **off,** you do it with great success.
7. *verb* If you **pull through,** you get through a hard, painful, or dangerous time.
▷ *verb* **pulling, pulled**

pul·ley (pul-ee) *noun*
1. A wheel with a grooved rim in which a rope or chain can run. A pulley is used to lift loads more easily.
2. A lifting machine made from a rope or chain and a set of pulleys linked together. *The diagram shows how a pulley is used to lift a heavy load.*

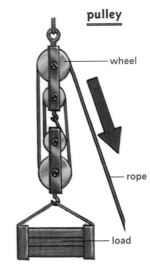
pulley
— wheel
— rope
— load

pull·o·ver (pul-oh-vur) *noun* A shirt or sweater that you can pull over your head.

P

pulp (puhlp) *noun*
1. The soft, juicy, or fleshy part of fruits and vegetables.
2. Any soft, wet mixture, as in *wood pulp*.
3. The soft inner part of a tooth.
▷ *verb* **pulp**

pul·pit (puhl-pit) *noun* A raised, enclosed platform in a church where a minister stands to speak to a congregation.

pul·sate (puhl-sate) *verb* To beat or vibrate regularly. *Rock music pulsated through the house. The heart pulsates.* ▷ **pulsating, pulsated**

pulse (puhlss) *noun* A steady beat or throb, especially the feeling of the heart moving blood through your body. ▷ *verb* **pulse**

pu·ma (pyoo-muh *or* poo-muh) *noun* Another name for a **cougar, mountain lion,** and **panther.**

pum·ice (puhm-iss) *noun* A light, grayish volcanic rock that is used for cleaning, smoothing, or polishing.

pum·mel (puhm-uhl) *verb* To punch someone or something repeatedly. ▷ **pummeling, pummeled**

pump (puhmp)
1. *noun* A machine that forces liquids or gases from one place or container into another, as in *a bicycle pump* or *a water pump*.
2. *verb* To empty or fill using a pump. *We pumped out the water that had leaked into our basement. I pumped air into the flat tire.*
3. **pumps** *noun, plural* Formal women's shoes with a medium to high heel.
4. *verb* If you **pump** someone for information, you keep asking the person questions.
▷ *verb* **pumping, pumped**

pump·kin (puhmp-kin) *noun* A big, round, orange fruit that grows on a vine along the ground. People often carve faces in pumpkins at Halloween.

pumpkins

pun (puhn) *noun* A joke based on one word that has two meanings or two words that sound the same but have different meanings. Here is an example of a pun: *People work as bakers because they knead (need) the dough.* ▷ *verb* **pun**

punch (puhnch)
1. *verb* To hit something or someone with your fist. ▷ *noun* **punch,** *noun* **puncher**
2. *noun* A drink made by mixing fruit juices, often with soda and spices.
3. *noun* A metal tool used for making holes.
4. *verb* To make a hole in something. *Ted punched a hole in his report so he could fasten the pages together.*
5. **punch line** *noun* The last line of a joke or story that makes it funny or surprising.
▷ *verb* **punches, punching, punched**

punc·tu·al (puhngk-choo-uhl) *adjective* If you are **punctual,** you arrive right on time. ▷ *noun* **punctuality** ▷ *adverb* **punctually**

punc·tu·a·tion (puhngk-choo-ay-shuhn) *noun*
1. The use of periods, commas, and other marks to make the meaning of written material clear. ▷ *verb* **punctuate**
2. One or more punctuation marks.

punctuation mark *noun* A written mark, such as a comma, period, colon, semicolon, question mark, or exclamation point, used in punctuating.

punc·ture (puhngk-chur) *noun* A hole made by a sharp object. ▷ *verb* **puncture**

pun·gent (puhn-juhnt) *adjective* If something is **pungent,** it tastes or smells strong or sharp, as in *a pungent odor*.

pun·ish (puhn-ish) *verb* If you **punish** someone, you make the person suffer for committing a crime or for behaving badly. ▷ **punishes, punishing, punished** ▷ *noun* **punishment**

punk (puhngk) *noun*
1. *(slang)* A young person who is inexperienced or always getting into trouble.
2. A style of music and dress that became popular in the late 1970s. People who dressed in this style wore black clothes, used safety pins for decoration, and had brightly colored hair.
3. **punk rock** Loud, hard rock music that became popular in the late 1970s.

punt (puhnt)
1. *noun* A boat with a flat bottom that you push along with a long pole. ▷ *verb* **punt**
2. *verb* To kick a football or soccer ball dropped from the hands before it strikes the ground.
▷ **punting, punted** ▷ *noun* **punt,** *noun* **punter**

pu·ny (pyoo-nee) *adjective* Small and weak, or unimportant. ▷ **punier, puniest** ▷ *noun* **puniness** ▷ *adverb* **punily**

pu·pa (pyoo-puh) *noun* An insect at the stage of development between a larva and an adult. *See* **caterpillar.** ▷ *noun, plural* **pupas** *or* **pupae** (pyoo-pee)

pu·pil (pyoo-puhl) *noun*
1. Someone who is being taught, especially in school.
2. The round, black part of your eye that lets light travel through it. *See* **eye.**

> **Word History**
> ●
> Have you ever looked into the **pupil** of someone's eye? If so, you probably saw a tiny reflection of whatever the person was looking at. This tiny image gave the pupil its name. It is based on the Latin word *pūpilla,* or "tiny doll."

pup·pet (puhp-it) *noun* A toy in the shape of a person or an animal that you control by pulling strings that are attached to it or by moving your hand inside it.

pup·py (puhp-ee) *noun* A young dog. ▷ *noun, plural* **puppies**

pur·chase (pur-chuhss)
1. *verb* To buy something. *My parents purchased a new sofa for the living room.* ▷ **purchasing, purchased** ▷ *noun* **purchaser**
2. *noun* Something that has been bought. *We carried our purchases into the house.*
3. *noun* The act of purchasing. *We saved our money for the purchase of a new stereo.*

pure (pyoor) *adjective*
1. Not mixed with anything else, as in *pure gold.*
2. Not dirty or not polluted, as in *pure water.*
3. Innocent or free from evil or guilt, as in *a pure heart* or *a pure mind.*
4. Complete or nothing but, as in *pure luck* or *pure nonsense.*
▷ *adjective* **purer, purest** ▷ *noun* **purity**

pure·bred (pyoor-bred) *adjective* Having ancestors of the same breed or kind of animal. *One of my dogs is a purebred poodle; the other is a mutt.*

pu·ree *or* **pu·rée** (pyoo-ray) *noun* A thick paste made from food that has been put through a sieve or blender, as in *tomato puree.* ▷ *verb* **puree** *or* **purée**

purge (purj) *verb* To clean something out by getting rid of unwanted things. *We purged the house of all our old clothes.* ▷ **purging, purged** ▷ *noun* **purge**

pu·ri·fy (pyoor-uh-fye) *verb* To make something pure or clean. *We need a filter to purify our water.* ▷ **purifies, purifying, purified** ▷ *noun* **purification**

Pur·i·tan (pyoor-uh-tuhn) *noun* One of a group of Protestants in 16th- and 17th-century England who sought simple church services and a strict moral code. Many Puritans fled England and settled in America.

pur·ple (pur-puhl) *noun* The color that is made by mixing red and blue. ▷ *adjective* **purple**

pur·pose (pur-puhss) *noun*
1. A goal or an aim. *My purpose in getting a part-time job is to save money for college.*
2. The reason why something is made or done, or an object's function. *What's the purpose of this TV dial?*
3. **on purpose** Deliberately rather than by accident.
▷ *adjective* **purposeful** ▷ *adverb* **purposely**

purr (pur) *verb*
1. When a cat **purrs,** it makes a low, soft sound in its throat.
2. To make a low sound like a cat. *The new car purred up the driveway.*
Purr sounds like **per.**
▷ *verb* **purring, purred** ▷ *noun* **purr**

purse (purss)
1. *noun* A handbag or a pocketbook.
2. *noun* A small container in which people keep their money.
3. *noun* A sum of money given as a prize in an athletic contest.
4. *verb* If you **purse** your lips, you press them together into wrinkles. ▷ **pursing, pursed**

pur·sue (pur-soo) *verb*
1. To follow or chase someone in order to catch him or her. *The police pursued the robber.* ▷ *noun* **pursuer**
2. To continue something. *We'll pursue this argument later.*
▷ *verb* **pursuing, pursued**

pur·suit (pur-soot) *noun*
1. If you are in **pursuit** of someone, you are trying to catch the person.
2. An activity, hobby, or interest. *Collecting baseball cards is one of my favorite pursuits.*

pus (puhss) *noun* A thick, yellow liquid that comes out of an infected wound or sore.

push (push)
1. *verb* To make something move by pressing on or against it. *I pushed my bike up the hill.*
2. *verb* To shove or press roughly. *He pushed me off the sidewalk.*
3. *verb* To press yourself forward. *We pushed through the crowd.*
4. *noun* An act of pushing or shoving.
5. *verb* To try very hard to sell or do something. *The new cars are due in next week, so the dealer is pushing last year's models.*
6. *noun* A great effort or drive, as in *a final push to victory.*
▷ *noun, plural* **pushes** ▷ *noun* **pusher** ▷ *verb* **pushes, pushing, pushed**

P

419

push-up *noun* An exercise in which you raise your body off the floor from a lying position by pushing with your arms.

pus·sy willow (puss-ee) *noun* A shrub with soft, gray, furry flowers on long, thin branches.

put (put) *verb*

1. To place, lay, or move something. *I put the book on the desk.*

2. To express in words. *How can I put this so that you'll understand?*

3. To cause someone to undergo or experience something. *Allie put me to a great deal of trouble.*

4. If you **put** something **off,** you delay doing it.

5. If you **put** someone **up,** you let the person sleep overnight at your house.

6. If you **put up with** something, you allow it to continue.

▷ *verb* **putting, put**

pu·trid (pyoo-trid) *adjective* Decaying or rotten.

putt (puht) *verb* To hit a golf ball lightly into the hole on a green. ▷ **putting, putted** ▷ *noun* **putt,** *noun* **putter**

put·ter (puht-ur) *verb* To work aimlessly without getting much done. *Cassie puttered around the house all day.* ▷ **puttering, puttered**

put·ty (puht-ee) *noun* A kind of soft cement made of powdered chalk and linseed oil. It dries hard and is used to fasten windows into frames and to fill holes in wood.

puz·zle (puhz-uhl)

1. *noun* A game or an activity in which you have to think hard in order to solve problems, as in *a crossword puzzle.*

2. *noun* Someone or something that is hard to understand.

3. *verb* If something **puzzles** you, it makes you confused or unsure. ▷ **puzzling, puzzled** ▷ *adjective* **puzzled,** *adjective* **puzzling**

py·lon (pye-lon) *noun*

1. A tall, metal tower that supports electrical cables.

2. A small rubber cone sometimes found on a road or highway, for example, where construction is being done.

pyr·a·mid (pihr-uh-mid) *noun*

1. A solid shape with a polygon as a base and triangular sides that meet at a point on top. Most pyramids have a square base and four triangular sides. *See* **shape.**

2. An ancient Egyptian stone monument where pharaohs and their treasures were buried. *The picture shows a reconstruction of how a pyramid was built and a view of the Great Pyramid at Giza in Egypt.*

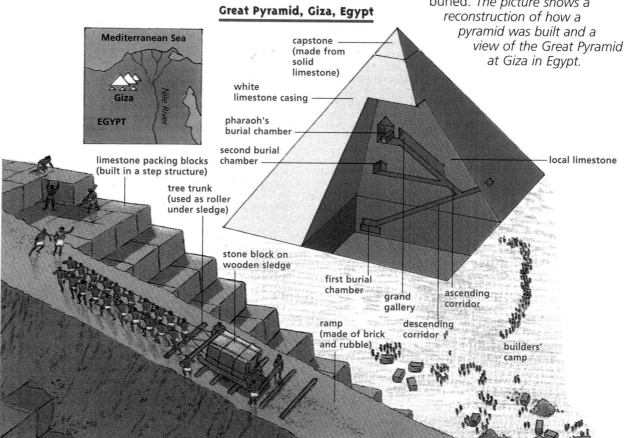

Great Pyramid, Giza, Egypt

Mediterranean Sea

Giza

EGYPT

Nile River

capstone (made from solid limestone)

white limestone casing

pharaoh's burial chamber

second burial chamber

local limestone

limestone packing blocks (built in a step structure)

tree trunk (used as roller under sledge)

stone block on wooden sledge

first burial chamber

grand gallery

ascending corridor

descending corridor

ramp (made of brick and rubble)

builders' camp

P

Qq

About Q ◀

The letter **Q** is usually followed by a *u*. Q rarely appears at the end of an English word. Words that have been adopted into English from other languages are the main exceptions. Examples: Iraq, Iraqi.

quack (kwak)
1. *verb* When ducks **quack,** they make a sharp, loud sound. ▷ **quacking, quacked** ▷ *noun* **quack**
2. *noun* A dishonest person who pretends to be a doctor or an expert. ▷ *adjective* **quack**

quad (kwahd) *noun* An rectangular yard with buildings around it, especially at a college. Quad is short for **quadrangle.**

quad·ran·gle (kwahd-*rang*-guhl) *noun*
1. A closed shape with four sides and four angles; a quadrilateral.
2. A quad, as at a college.

quad·rant (kwahd-ruhnt) *noun* A quarter of a circle, or a quarter of the circumference of a circle.

quad·ri·lat·er·al (*kwahd*-ruh-lat**-ur-uhl)** *noun* A closed shape with four sides and four angles. Squares and rectangles are quadrilaterals.
▷ *adjective* **quadrilateral**

quad·ru·ped (kwahd-ruh-ped) *noun* An animal with four feet. Horses are quadrupeds.

qua·dru·ple (kwah-droo-puhl *or* kwahd-ruh-puhl)
1. *verb* To multiply something by four.
▷ **quadrupling, quadrupled**
2. *adjective* Four times as big, or four times as many.

qua·dru·plet (kwah-droo-plit) *noun* One of four babies born at the same time to one mother.

quag·mire (kwag-mire *or* kwahg-mire) *noun* A soggy area of ground.

qua·hog (kwaw-*hawg* *or* kwaw-*hog*) *noun* A round, edible clam with a thick, heavy shell found on the eastern coast of North America. Quahog is an American Indian word.

quail (kwayl) *noun*
A small, plump bird with gray or brown feathers that are often speckled with white. *This Gambel's quail is found in the southwestern United States and northwestern Mexico.*

quail

quaint (kwaynt) *adjective* Charming and old-fashioned, as in *a quaint little fishing village.*
▷ **quainter, quaintest** ▷ *noun* **quaintness** ▷ *adverb* **quaintly**

quake (kwake)
1. *verb* To shake and to tremble with fear. *I quaked when the monster appeared on the screen.*
2. *verb* To shake or to tremble. *The earth quaked.*
3. *noun* An earthquake, or a trembling of the ground. *This picture shows a house in the Marina District of San Francisco, California, after an October 1989 quake.*
4. *noun* Any trembling or shaking.
▷ *verb* **quaking, quaked**

quake

Quak·er (kway-kur) *noun* A member of the Society of Friends, a Christian group founded in 1650 that prefers simple religious services and opposes war.

qual·i·fi·ca·tion (*kwahl*-uh-fuh-kay**-shuhn)** *noun* A skill or an ability that makes you able to do a job or a task or carry out an office. *Teaching experience is a qualification for a job as school principal.*

qual·i·fy (kwahl-uh-fye) *verb*
1. To reach a level or standard that allows you to do something. *Winning the match qualified us to play in the final.* ▷ *adjective* **qualified**
2. To limit or restrict something. *Victoria qualified the statement "I don't like boys." by adding the word "some" to her sentence.*
3. To limit or modify the meaning of a word or phrase. *Adjectives qualify nouns.*
▷ *verb* **qualifies, qualifying, qualified**

qual·i·ty (kwahl-uh-tee) *noun*
1. Grade or degree of fineness. *You can tell it is a cheap video by its poor quality.*
2. A special characteristic of someone or something. *Heather has all the right qualities to be a doctor.*
▷ *noun, plural* **qualities**

qualm (kwahm *or* kwahlm) *noun* A feeling of worry or uneasiness. *I had serious qualms about getting home so late.*

quan·da·ry (kwahn-duh-ree) *noun* If you are **in a quandary** about something, you are confused and do not know what to do about it. ▷ *noun, plural* **quandaries**

quan·ti·ty (kwahn-tuh-tee) *noun*
1. An amount or a number. *The package contains a small quantity of jelly beans.*
2. A large number or amount. *Restaurants buy food in quantity.*
▷ *noun, plural* **quantities**

quar·an·tine (kwor-uhn-teen) *noun* When a person, animal, plant, etc., is put in **quarantine,** it is kept away from others to stop a disease from spreading. ▷ *verb* **quarantine**

> ### Word History
> Quarantine comes from the Italian word *quaranta,* meaning "forty." The first quarantines date back to the Middle Ages, when sailors and other travelers were suspected of carrying diseases from one country to another. People on ships arriving from countries with widespread disease had to wait 40 days before they were allowed on shore.

quark (kwork) *noun* In physics, any of several particles that are believed to come in pairs. A quark is smaller than an atom.

quar·rel (kwor-uhl)
1. *verb* To argue or to disagree.
2. *noun* An argument.
3. *verb* To find fault. *I can't quarrel with your decision.*
▷ *verb* **quarreling, quarreled**

quar·rel·some (kwor-uhl-suhm) *adjective* A person who is **quarrelsome** argues with others a lot.

quar·ry (kwor-ee) *noun*
1. A place where stone, slate, etc., is dug from the ground. *The photographer looked down into a marble quarry to take this picture.*
▷ *verb* **quarry**
2. A person or an animal that is being chased or hunted.
▷ *noun, plural* **quarries**

marble quarry

quart (kwort) *noun* A unit of liquid measure equal to 32 ounces, or two pints. Milk is commonly sold in quarts.

quar·ter (kwor-tur)
1. *noun* One of four equal parts. ▷ *verb* **quarter**
2. *noun* A coin of the United States and Canada equal to 25 cents, or $\frac{1}{4}$ of a dollar.
3. *noun* One of four periods, usually 15 minutes each, that make up a game of football, basketball, soccer, etc.
4. *noun* A part of a town. *The French Quarter in New Orleans is a great place to hear jazz.*
5. quarters *noun, plural* Lodgings, or rooms where people live.
6. *verb* To provide people, usually soldiers, with food and lodging. ▷ **quartering, quartered**

quar·ter·back (kwor-tur-*bak*) *noun* In football, the player who leads the offense by passing the ball or handing it off to a runner.

quart·er·ly (kwor-tur-lee)
1. *adjective* Happening once every three months. *Carlos receives quarterly interest on his savings account.*
2. *adverb* Once every three months. *Some magazines are published quarterly.*

quar·tet (kwor-tet) *noun*
1. A piece of music that is played or sung by four people.
2. Four people who play music or sing together.

quartz (kworts) *noun* A hard mineral that comes in many different forms and colors. Quartz is used to make very accurate clocks, watches, and electronic equipment.

quartz crystal

qua·sar (kway-zar *or* kway-sar) *noun* A heavenly body that is larger than a star but smaller than a galaxy. Quasars give off powerful radio waves and huge amounts of light and radioactivity.

quash (kwahsh) *verb*
1. To crush or to stop by force, as in *to quash a rebellion.*
2. To reject an idea or a decision. *The court of appeals quashed the conviction.*
▷ *verb* **quashes, quashing, quashed**

qua·ver (kway-vur)
1. *verb* To shake or to tremble. *Charlie's voice quavered because he was so nervous.*
▷ **quavering, quavered** ▷ *noun* **quaver**
2. *noun* A musical note representing half of one beat.

quay (kee) *noun* A place where boats can stop to load or unload. *The picture shows a ship being unloaded at a quay.* **Quay** sounds like **key.**

quay

quea·sy (kwee-zee) *adjective*
1. Sick to your stomach, or nauseated.
2. Uneasy or troubled. *I had a queasy feeling that I was lost.*
▷ *adjective* **queasier, queasiest** ▷ *noun* **queasiness**

queen (kween) *noun*
1. A woman from a royal family who is the ruler of her country.
2. The wife of a king.
3. A playing card that has a picture of a queen on it.
4. The most powerful chess piece. It can move in any direction. *See* **chess.**
5. A female bee, wasp, or ant that can lay eggs. *See* **honeycomb.**

queer (kwihr) *adjective* Odd or strange. ▷ **queerer, queerest** ▷ *adverb* **queerly**

quell (kwel) *verb* To stop or crush by force, as in *to quell a disturbance.* ▷ **quelling, quelled**

quench (kwench) *verb*
1. If you **quench** a fire, you put it out.
2. If you **quench** your thirst, you drink until you are no longer thirsty.
▷ *verb* **quenches, quenching, quenched**

que·ry (kwihr-ee)
1. *noun* A question or doubt about something. *The editor had several queries for the author.*
▷ *noun, plural* **queries**
2. *verb* To ask a question to. *Let's query your mother about her plans for the afternoon.*
3. *verb* To express doubt about something. *I queried whether we'd have time to go to the store before lunch.*
▷ *verb* **queries, querying, queried**

quest (kwest) *noun*
1. A long search. *Many pioneers traveled to California in a quest for gold.* ▷ *verb* **quest**
2. In the Middle Ages, a journey taken by a knight to perform a feat or to find something.

ques·tion (kwess-chuhn)
1. *noun* A sentence that asks something. *Bernado has a question about the homework assignment.*
2. *noun* A problem, or something that needs to be asked about. *We need to tackle the question of the price of school lunches.*
3. *verb* To ask questions. *The police officer will question the suspect.*
4. *verb* To be doubtful about something. *I question the truth of that statement.*
5. *noun* Doubt. *Without question, Toby is the best person for the job.*
▷ *verb* **questioning, questioned**

question mark *noun* The punctuation mark (?) used in writing to show that a sentence is a question.

ques·tion·naire (*kwess*-chuh-**nair**) *noun* A list of questions used to get information or to find out about people's opinions.

quet·zal (ket-sal) *noun* A bird of Mexico and Central America with crimson and green feathers. The male has long, flowing tail feathers.

queue (kyoo)
1. *noun* A line of people waiting for something.
2. *verb* To wait in a line of people. ▷ **queuing, queued**
Queue sounds like **cue.**

quib·ble (kwib-uhl) *verb* To argue about unimportant things. *During their divorce, my parents quibbled about everything.* ▷ **quibbling, quibbled** ▷ *noun* **quibble**

quiche (keesh) *noun* A food made up of a pastry crust and a filling of eggs, cream or milk, cheese, vegetables, etc.

quick (kwik) *adjective*
1. Fast, as in *a quick lunch.* ▷ *verb* **quicken**
▷ *adverb* **quick,** *adverb* **quickly**
2. Clever and lively, as in *a quick sense of humor* or *a quick mind.*
▷ *adjective* **quicker, quickest**

quick·sand (kwik-*sand*) *noun* Loose, wet sand that you can sink into.

qui·et (kwye-uht)
1. *adjective* Not loud. *We all spoke in quiet voices.*
2. *adjective* Peaceful and calm. *We spent a quiet afternoon by the river.*
3. *noun* The state of being quiet. *The teacher asked for quiet.*
▷ *noun* **quietness** ▷ *verb* **quiet** ▷ *adjective* **quieter, quietest** ▷ *adverb* **quietly**

quill (kwil) *noun*
1. The long, hollow central part of a bird's feather.
2. One of the long, pointed spines on a porcupine. *See* **porcupine.**
3. **quill pen** A pen made from a bird's feather, with its quill carved to form a point.

quilt (kwilt) *noun*
A warm, usually padded, covering for a bed. ▷ *verb* **quilt**

quilt·ed (kwil-tid) *adjective* If material is **quilted,** it is padded and sewn in lines or patterns.

quin·tet (kwin-tet) *noun*
1. A piece of music that is played or sung by five people.
2. Five people who play music or sing together.

quin·tup·let (kwin-**tuhp**-lit) *noun* One of five babies born at the same time to one mother. *This picture shows a set of quintuplets at age 10. The photographs on the table show the same boys and girls when they were six months old.*

quill pen

— nib

quintuplets

quip (kwip) *noun* A witty or clever remark.

quirk (kwerk) *noun*
1. A peculiar trait or a strange way of acting. *Bill has the annoying quirk of cracking his knuckles when he is nervous.* ▷ *noun* **quirkiness** ▷ *adjective* **quirky**
2. A sudden twist or turn. *It was a quirk of fate that we each came around the corner and met when we did.*

quit (kwit) *verb*
1. To stop doing something. *Dad has promised to quit smoking.*

2. To leave something. *Betsy decided to quit her job.*
▷ *verb* **quitting, quit** *or* **quitted** ▷ *noun* **quitter**

quite (kwite) *adverb*
1. Completely. *I haven't quite finished.*
2. Actually or really. *Winning the marathon was quite an achievement.*
3. Rather or very. *The concert was quite good.*

quiv·er (kwiv-ur)
1. *verb* To tremble or to vibrate. *Nancy's voice quivered as she gave her oral report.*
▷ **quivering, quivered** ▷ *noun* **quiver**
2. *noun* A case for arrows.

quix·ot·ic (kwik-**sot**-ik) *adjective* If a person is **quixotic,** he or she is caught up in doing noble deeds or in trying to achieve goals that are impractical. *Alonso's attempts to make right all the wrongs in the world are quixotic.*

▶ **Word History**
• •
The word **quixotic** comes from the novel *Don Quixote,* written by Miguel de Cervantes in two parts from 1605 to 1615. Don Quixote is an idealistic old man who wanders the world looking for adventures in which he can fight evil and injustice.

quiz (kwiz)
1. *noun* A short test. ▷ *noun, plural* **quizzes**
2. *verb* To question someone closely. *The attorney quizzed the witness carefully.* ▷ **quizzes, quizzing, quizzed**

quo·ta (kwoh-tuh) *noun* A fixed amount or share of something. *Immigration laws often set quotas that limit the number of immigrants from different countries.*

quo·ta·tion (kwoh-tay-shuhn) *noun*
1. A sentence or short passage from a book, play, speech, etc., that is repeated by someone else.
2. The act of repeating another person's words.

quotation mark *noun* The punctuation mark (" or ') used in writing to show where speech begins and ends.

quote (kwote)
1. *verb* To repeat words that were spoken or written by someone else. *Rebecca quoted Martin Luther King, Jr., in her speech.* ▷ **quoting, quoted**
2. *noun* A quotation.

quo·tient (kwoh-shuhnt) *noun* The number that you get when you divide one number by another. In the problem 12 divided by 4, the quotient is 3.

Rr

About R ◀

Spelling Hint: Some words that begin with an *r* sound are spelled *rh* or *wr*. Examples: rhinoceros, rhubarb, rhythm, wrench, wristwatch, wrong.

rab·bi (rab-eye) *noun* A Jewish religious leader and teacher.

rab·bit (rab-it) *noun* A small, furry mammal with long ears that lives in a hole that it digs in the ground. *See* **angora.**

rab·ble (rab-uhl) *noun* A noisy crowd of people.

ra·bies (ray-beez) *noun* An often fatal disease that can affect humans, dogs, bats, and other warm-blooded animals. Rabies is caused by a virus that attacks the brain and spinal cord and is spread by the bite of an infected animal.
▷ *adjective* **rabid** (rab-id)

rac·coon (ra-koon) *noun* A mammal with rings on its tail and black and white face markings that look like a mask.

race (rayss)
1. *noun* A test of speed. ▷ *verb* **race**
2. *noun* One of the major groups into which human beings can be divided. People of the same race share the same physical characteristics, such as skin color, which are passed on from generation to generation.
3. *verb* To run or move very fast. *Angela raced down the hall to get to her next class.*
▷ **racing, raced**

race car *noun* A car designed to race at very high speeds. *The picture shows a Ford Formula 1 race car.*

race relations *noun, plural* The way that people of different races get along with each other when they live in the same community.

race·track (rayss-trak) *noun* A round or oval course that is used for racing.

ra·cial (ray-shuhl) *adjective*
1. To do with a person's race, as in *racial characteristics.*
2. Between races, as in *racial prejudice* or *racial harmony.*

rac·ist (ray-sist) *adjective* Someone who is **racist** thinks that a particular race is better than others or treats people unfairly or cruelly because of their race. ▷ *noun* **racism,** *noun* **racist**

rack (rak)
1. *noun* A framework for holding or hanging things, as in *a clothes rack.*
2. *noun* An instrument of torture used in the past to stretch the body of a victim.
3. *verb* If you **rack your brains,** you think very hard. *I racked my brains to remember his name.*
▷ **racking, racked**

rack·et (rak-it) *noun*
1. **racket** or **racquet** A stringed frame with a handle that you use in games such as tennis, squash, and badminton. *See* **badminton.**
2. A very loud noise.
3. A dishonest activity. *The police exposed a gambling racket.*

rac·quet (rak-it) *See* **racket.**

rac·quet·ball (rak-it-bawl) *noun* A game played by two or four players who use short rackets to hit a small rubber ball against the walls, floor, and ceiling of an enclosed court.

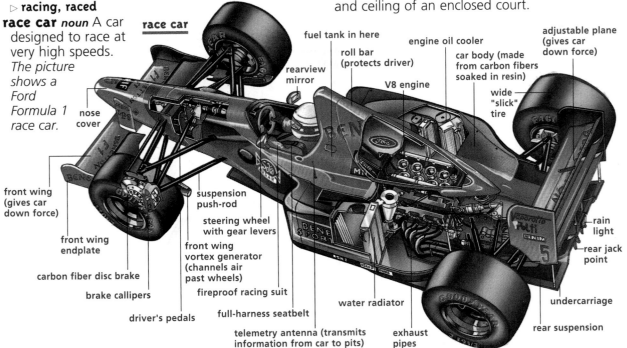

race car

fuel tank in here
engine oil cooler
adjustable plane (gives car down force)
roll bar (protects driver)
car body (made from carbon fibers soaked in resin)
rearview mirror
V8 engine
wide "slick" tire
nose cover
front wing (gives car down force)
suspension push-rod
steering wheel with gear levers
front wing endplate
front wing vortex generator (channels air past wheels)
carbon fiber disc brake
fireproof racing suit
rain light
rear jack point
brake callipers
driver's pedals
full-harness seatbelt
water radiator
undercarriage
telemetry antenna (transmits information from car to pits)
exhaust pipes
rear suspension

R

ra·dar (ray-dar) *noun*
1. Planes and ships use **radar** to find solid objects by reflecting radio waves off them and by receiving the reflected waves. Radar stands for *RAdio Detecting And Ranging*.
2. radar trap A system using radar equipment that is set up by the police to catch speeding drivers.

ra·di·al (ray-dee-uhl) *adjective*
1. Spreading out from the center or arranged like rays.
2. To do with a kind of automobile or truck tire whose design makes it grip the road better than traditional tires. ▷ *noun* **radial**

ra·di·ant (ray-dee-uhnt) *adjective*
1. Bright and shining.
2. Someone who is **radiant** looks very healthy and happy.
▷ *noun* **radiance**

ra·di·ate (ray-dee-*ate*) *verb*
1. To give off rays of light or heat.
2. To spread out from the center.
3. To send out something strongly. *Mario radiates confidence.*
▷ *verb* **radiating, radiated**

ra·di·a·tion (*ray*-dee-ay-shuhn) *noun*
1. The sending out of rays of light, heat, etc.
2. Particles that are sent out from a radioactive substance.

ra·di·a·tor (ray-dee-*ay*-tur) *noun*
1. A metal container through which hot liquid or steam circulates, sending heat into a room.
2. A metal device through which a liquid, usually water, circulates to cool a vehicle's engine. *See* **car, race car.**

rad·i·cal (rad-i-kuhl) *adjective*
1. If a change is **radical,** it is thorough and has a wide range of important effects. ▷ *adverb* **radically**
2. Someone who is **radical** believes in extreme political change. ▷ *noun* **radical**

ra·di·o (ray-dee-oh)
1. *noun* A way of communicating using electromagnetic waves broadcast from a central antenna.
2. *noun* A device that sends or receives these broadcasts and converts them into sound.
3. *verb* To send a message using a radio.
▷ **radios, radioing, radioed**
▷ *noun, plural* **radios** ▷ *adjective* **radio**

ra·di·o·ac·tive (*ray*-dee-oh-ak-tiv) *adjective*
Radioactive materials are made up of atoms whose nuclei break down, giving off harmful radiation. ▷ *noun* **radioactivity**

ra·di·og·ra·phy (*ray*-dee-og-ruh-fee) *noun* The process of taking X-ray photographs of people's bones, organs, etc. ▷ *noun* **radiographer**

rad·ish (rad-ish) *noun* A small, red and white root vegetable that you eat in salads. *See* **vegetable.**
▷ *noun, plural* **radishes**

ra·di·um (ray-dee-uhm) *noun* A radioactive element sometimes used to treat cancer.

ra·di·us (ray-dee-uhss) *noun*
1. A straight line segment drawn from the center of a circle to its outer edge. *See* **circle.**
2. The outer bone in your lower arm. *See* **skeleton.**
3. A circular area around a thing or a place. *Most of my friends live within a radius of one mile from my house.*
▷ *noun, plural* **radii** (ray-dee-eye)

ra·don (ray-don) *noun* An odorless, colorless, radioactive gas that can seep up from the earth and rocks. Radon is a chemical element produced by radium.

raf·fle (raf-uhl) *noun* A way of raising money by selling tickets and then giving prizes to people with winning tickets. ▷ *verb* **raffle**

raft (raft)
1. *noun* A floating platform often made from logs tied together.
2. *verb* To travel by raft. ▷ **rafting, rafted** ▷ *noun* **rafting**
3. *noun* An inflatable rubber craft with a flat bottom. *The picture shows an inflatable raft traveling through fast-moving water.*

inflatable raft

rag (rag)
1. *noun* A piece of old cloth.
2. rags *noun, plural* Very old, worn-out clothing.

rage (rayj)
1. *noun* Violent anger.
2. *verb* To be violent or noisy. *The wind raged around the house.* ▷ **raging, raged**

rag·ged (rag-id) *adjective* Old, torn, and worn-out. ▷ *adjective* **raggedy** ▷ *adverb* **raggedly**

rag·time (rag-*time*) *noun* An early style of jazz having a strong, syncopated rhythm.

rag·weed (rag-*weed*) *noun* A weed whose pollen is a cause of hay fever in the fall.

raid (rayd) *noun*
1. A sudden, surprise attack on a place. ▷ *noun* **raider**
2. A sudden visit by the police to search for criminals, drugs, etc.
▷ *verb* **raid**

rail (rayl) *noun*
1. A fixed bar supported by posts.
2. Railroad. *Thomas loves traveling by rail.*
▷ *adjective* **rail**

rail·ing (ray-ling) *noun* A wooden or metal bar that is a part of a fence or a staircase.

rail·road (rayl-*rohd*) *noun*
1. A track of double rails for a train.
2. A system of transport using trains.

rail·way (rayl-*way*) *noun* A railroad, or the tracks of a railroad.

rain (rayn)
1. *noun* Water that falls in drops from clouds.
2. *noun* A falling of rain.
3. *verb* To fall in rain. *It's raining today.*
4. *verb* To fall or pour like rain. *Tears rained down their faces.*
Rain sounds like **reign** and **rein.**
▷ *verb* **raining, rained** ▷ *adjective* **rainy**

rain·bow (rayn-*boh*) *noun* An arc of different colors caused by the bending of sunlight as it shines through water vapor. *See* **spectrum.**

rain·coat (rayn-*koht*) *noun* A waterproof coat that keeps you dry when it is raining.

rain·drop (rayn-*drop*) *noun* A drop of rain.

rain·fall (rayn-*fawl*) *noun* The amount of rain that falls in one place in a certain time.

rain forest *noun* A dense, tropical forest where a lot of rain falls. *Shown here are a map with the main rain forests of the world and several examples of rain forest wildlife.*

raise (rayz)
1. *verb* To lift something up. *Raise your hand if you know the answer.*
2. *verb* If you **raise** money, you collect it for a particular cause or charity.
3. *verb* To look after children or young animals until they are grown. *Martha has raised five sons.*
4. *noun* An increase in salary. ▷ *verb* **raise**
5. *verb* To ask or to bring up, as in *to raise an objection.*
▷ *verb* **raising, raised**

rai·sin (ray-zuhn) *noun* A dried grape.

rake (rayk)
1. *noun* A garden tool with metal teeth used to level soil or to collect leaves, grass cuttings, etc.
2. *verb* To use a rake. *Bernard is raking the leaves.*
3. *verb* (informal) If you **rake it in,** you make a lot of money.
▷ *verb* **raking, raked**

hyacinth macaw
(South America)

orchid

carpenter bee
(Southeast Asia)

poison arrow frog
(South America)

R

**rain forests and
rain forest wildlife**

ruffed lemur
(Madagascar)

golden cock-of-the-rock
(South America)

rain forest

NORTH AMERICA

EUROPE

ASIA

Central America

The Amazon

SOUTH AMERICA

India

Borneo

Papua New Guinea

AUSTRALIA

Madagascar

Zaire

Sumatra

palm weevil
(Africa)

pangolin
(Africa)

ral·ly (ral-ee)
1. *verb* To bring together again. *The officer rallied his troops.*
2. *verb* To join together to help or support a person or thing. *My friends rallied to my defense.*
3. *verb* To regain strength, energy, or health. *The patient rallied overnight.*
4. *noun* A large meeting, as in *a political rally.*
5. *noun* In racket games such as tennis, a **rally** is a long exchange of shots.
▷ ***noun, plural*** **rallies** ▷ ***verb*** **rallies, rallying, rallied**

ram (ram)
1. *noun* A male sheep.
2. *verb* To crash into something with great force. *The car rammed into the pole.*
3. *verb* To push something into a space. *Kitty rammed her clothes into the bag.*
▷ ***verb*** **ramming, rammed**

RAM (ram) *noun* The part of a computer's memory that is lost when you turn the computer off. RAM stands for *Random Access Memory.*

Ram·a·dan (rahm-i-*dahn*) *noun* The ninth month of the Muslim year, when Muslims fast each day from sunrise to sunset.

ram·ble (ram-buhl) *verb*
1. To wander about without direction or purpose.
2. To go on a long walk for pleasure.
3. To speak or write extensively without sticking to the point.
▷ ***verb*** **rambling, rambled** ▷ ***noun*** **ramble, *noun*** **rambler**

ram·bling (ram-bling) *adjective* Going or growing in many directions, as in *a rambling speech* or *a rambling rose.*

ramp (ramp) *noun* A sloping passageway or roadway linking one level with another.

ram·page (ram-payj) *noun* If someone goes **on a rampage,** the person rushes around in a noisy and destructive way. ▷ ***verb*** **rampage**

ram·pant (ram-puhnt) *adjective* Wild and without restraint, as in *a rampant growth of weeds.*

ram·part (ram-part) *noun* The surrounding wall or embankment of a fort or castle built to protect against attack.

ram·shack·le (ram-*shak*-uhl) *adjective* Rickety or likely to fall apart, as in *a ramshackle cottage.*

ranch (ranch) *noun* A large farm for cattle, sheep, or horses. ▷ ***noun, plural*** **ranches** ▷ ***noun*** **rancher** ▷ ***verb*** **ranch**

ran·cid (ran-sid) *adjective* **Rancid** food is food that has spoiled.

ran·dom (ran-duhm) *adjective*
1. Without any order or purpose. *Beth took random courses in college before deciding to study history.* ▷ ***adverb*** **randomly**

2. If you make a **random** selection from a group of items, each item in the group has the same chance of being chosen.
3. If you do something **at random,** you do it without any plan or method.

range (raynj)
1. *verb* To vary between one extreme and the other. *The dogs ranged in size from tiny terriers to enormous Great Danes.* ▷ ***noun*** **range**
2. *noun* The distance that a bullet or rocket can travel or a person can see.
3. *noun* A place for shooting at targets or testing rockets.
4. *noun* An area of open land used for a special purpose, as in *a cattle range.*
5. *noun* A long chain of mountains.
6. *verb* To wander over a large area. *Cattle ranged over the plains.*
7. *noun* A cooking stove.
▷ ***verb*** **ranging, ranged**

rang·er (rayn-jur) *noun* Someone in charge of a park or forest.

rank (rangk)
1. *noun* An official position or job level. *Stephen rose to the rank of colonel.*
2. *verb* To assign a position to. *Our team is ranked first.* ▷ **ranking, ranked** ▷ ***noun*** **rank**
3. *noun* Social class. *People of all ranks supported the cause.*
4. *adjective* Having a strong and unpleasant odor or taste.
5. *adjective* Complete or absolute, as in *a rank amateur.*
▷ ***adjective*** **ranker, rankest**

ran·sack (ran-sak) *verb* To search a place wildly, usually looking for things to steal. *The intruder ransacked the house.* ▷ **ransacking, ransacked**

ran·som (ran-suhm) *noun* Money that is demanded before someone who is being held captive can be set free. ▷ ***verb*** **ransom**

rant (rant) *verb* To talk or shout in a loud and angry manner. *Steve ranted about how he had been cheated.* ▷ **ranting, ranted**

rap (rap)
1. *verb* To hit something sharply and quickly. *Bettina rapped on the window.* ▷ ***noun*** **rap**
2. *noun* A type of song in which the words are spoken in a rhythmical way to a musical background. ▷ ***noun*** **rapper** ▷ ***verb*** **rap**
3. *verb* (slang) To talk.
Rap sounds like **wrap.**
▷ ***verb*** **rapping, rapped**

rap·id (rap-id) *adjective* Very fast or quick, as in *a rapid heartbeat.* ▷ ***noun*** **rapidity** ▷ ***adverb*** **rapidly**

rap·ids (rap-idz) *noun, plural* A place in a river where the water flows very fast.

ra·pi·er (ray-pee-ur) *noun* A long sword with two edges, often used in duels in the 16th and 17th centuries. *This rapier was made in Italy in the 16th century.*

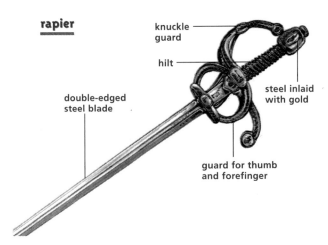

rapier

knuckle guard

hilt

steel inlaid with gold

double-edged steel blade

guard for thumb and forefinger

rap·ture (rap-chur) *noun* Great happiness, joy, or delight. *My brother stared in rapture at his new bicycle.*

rare (rair) *adjective*
1. Not often seen, found, or happening. *The musician made a rare appearance.* ▷ *noun* **rarity** ▷ *adverb* **rarely**
2. Rare meat is very lightly cooked.
3. Unusually good or excellent, as in *a rare beauty* or *a rare gift.*
▷ *adjective* **rarer, rarest**

ras·cal (rass-kuhl) *noun*
1. Someone who is very mischievous.
2. A dishonest person.

rash (rash)
1. *noun* An occurrence of spots or red patches on the skin caused by an allergy or illness. ▷ *noun, plural* **rashes**
2. *adjective* If you are **rash,** you act quickly, without thinking first. ▷ **rasher, rashest** ▷ *adverb* **rashly**

rasp (rasp)
1. *verb* To speak in a harsh voice. *The drill sergeant rasped an order to the troops.* ▷ **rasping, rasped**
2. *noun* A harsh, grating sound. *The rusty gate closed with a rasp.*
3. *noun* A coarse file used for smoothing metal or wood.

rasp·ber·ry (raz-ber-ee) *noun*
1. A small, sweet, black or red berry with very small seeds. Raspberries grow on prickly bushes. *See* **fruit.**
2. A dark purple-red color.
▷ *noun, plural* **raspberries**

rat (rat) *noun*
1. A rodent that looks like a large mouse and has a long tail. Rats sometimes spread disease.
2. *(informal)* A disloyal or treacherous person.
3. rat race A very stressful routine or competition at work.

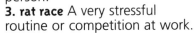

rat

rate (rayt)
1. *noun* A degree of speed. *Rhonda spends money at an alarming rate.*
2. *noun* A charge or a fee. *Mitch charges very high rates for his work.*
3. *noun* A standard amount used to calculate a total. *The rate of the telephone call was 15 cents for each minute.*
4. *verb* To judge the quality or worth of a person or thing. *The critic rated the restaurant as very good.*
5. *verb* To place in a particular position or rank. *Gwen rated the brands of ice cream according to price.*
▷ *noun* **rating** ▷ *verb* **rating, rated**

rath·er (ra-THur) *adverb*
1. Fairly or quite. *It's rather a long way to walk.*
2. More willingly. *I would rather be at the beach than at school.*
3. More correctly. *That man is my father, or rather my stepfather.*

rat·i·fy (rat-uh-fye) *verb* To agree to or approve officially. *Members of Congress ratified the bill.*
▷ **ratifies, ratifying, ratified** ▷ *noun* **ratification**

ra·ti·o (ray-shee-oh *or* ray-shoh) *noun* A comparison of two quantities or numbers using division. Ratios are usually expressed as fractions, or using the word "to." *The ratio of the number of a human being's fingers to eyes is $\frac{10}{2}$ or 10 to 2; the ratio is also $\frac{5}{1}$ or 5 to 1, five times as many fingers as eyes.*

ra·tion (rash-uhn *or* ray-shuhn)
1. *noun* A limited amount or share, especially of food. ▷ *noun* **rationing**
2. *verb* To give out in limited amounts. *During World War II, the government rationed gasoline.*
▷ **rationing, rationed**

ra·tion·al (ra-shuh-nuhl) *adjective*
1. Sensible and logical. *We made a rational decision to turn the two small stores into one.*
2. Calm, reasonable, and sane, as in *rational behavior.*
▷ *adverb* **rationally**

R

rat·tle (rat-uhl)
  1. *verb* To make a rapid series of short, sharp noises. *The windows rattled.* ▷ ***noun* rattle**
  2. *verb* To talk or say quickly. *The teacher rattled off the answers.*
  3. *verb* To upset or embarrass. *Speaking in front of the group rattled Jim.*
  4. *noun* A baby's toy that makes a rattling sound.
  5. *noun* The end part of a rattlesnake's tail that produces a rattling sound.
  ▷ ***verb* rattling, rattled**

rat·tle·snake (rat-uhl-*snayk*) ***noun*** A poisonous snake of North and South America with a tail that rattles as it shakes.

rattlesnake

rattle

rau·cous (raw-kuhss) ***adjective***
  1. Harsh or loud, as in *a raucous voice.*
  2. Loud and rowdy, as in *a raucous party.*
  ▷ ***adverb* raucously**

rave (rayv) ***verb***
  1. To speak in a wild, uncontrolled way. *He raved like a lunatic.*
  2. *(informal)* To praise something enthusiastically. *We raved about the movie.*
  ▷ ***verb* raving, raved**

ra·vel (rav-uhl) ***verb*** To fray, or separate into single loose threads; to unravel. *My sweater raveled at the sleeve when I caught a thread on a nail.* ▷ **raveling, raveled**

ra·ven (ray-vuhn)
  noun A large, black bird of the crow family.

raven

rav·en·ous (rav-uh-nuhss) ***adjective*** Very hungry.

ra·vine (ruh-veen) ***noun*** A deep, narrow valley with steep sides.

rav·i·o·li (rav-ee-oh-lee) ***noun*** Square pockets of pasta that can be filled with meat, vegetables, or cheese.

raw (raw) ***adjective***
  1. Food that is **raw** has not been cooked.
  2. Not treated, processed, or refined. *Milk is raw before it is pasteurized.*
  3. Not trained or inexperienced, as in *a raw recruit.*
  4. Having the skin rubbed off, as in *a raw wound.*
  5. Unpleasantly damp and chilly, as in *raw weather.*
  ▷ ***adjective* rawer, rawest**

raw·hide (raw-*hide*) ***noun*** The skin of cattle or other animals before it has been soaked in a special solution and made into leather.

raw material ***noun*** A substance that is treated or processed and made into a useful finished product. *Crude oil is the raw material from which we get gasoline.*

ray (ray) ***noun***
  1. A narrow beam of light or other radiation, as in *the rays of the sun.*
  2. A type of fish with a flat body; large, winglike fins; and a small, whiplike tail.
  3. A tiny amount, as in *a ray of hope.*
  4. Part of a line that extends on and on in one direction from a single point.

giant devil ray

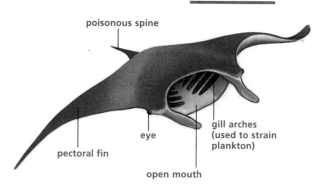

poisonous spine

gill arches (used to strain plankton)

eye

pectoral fin

open mouth

ray·on (ray-on) ***noun*** A synthetic fabric made from cellulose that has the look and feel of silk.

ra·zor (ray-zur) ***noun*** An instrument with a sharp blade used to shave hair from the skin.

> ## Prefix
> •
> The prefix **re-** adds one of the following meanings to a root word:
>
> 1. Again, as in *reelect* (to elect again) or *rerun* (to run again).
>
> 2. Back or backward, as in *return* (to turn back) or *revoke* (to take back).

reach (reech)
1. *verb* To stretch out to something with your hand. *Can you reach the top shelf?*
2. *verb* To extend, or to go as far as. *Our garden reaches right to the river.*
3. *noun* The distance a person or thing can reach.
4. *noun* An expanse, as in *vast reaches of the sea.*
5. *verb* To arrive somewhere. *We eventually reached the summit.*
6. *verb* To contact. *Alison reached her mother by phone.*
7. *noun* The act of reaching.
▷ *verb* **reaches, reaching, reached** ▷ *noun, plural* **reaches**

re·act (ree-akt) *verb*
1. To respond to something that happens. *The firefighters reacted quickly to the alarm.*
2. If a substance **reacts** with another, a chemical change takes place in one or both of the substances as they are mixed together.
▷ *verb* **reacting, reacted**

re·act·ion (ree-ak-shuhn) *noun* An action in response to something; a response.

re·ac·tion·ar·y (ree-ak-shuh-ner-ee) *adjective* If someone is **reactionary,** the person is against change and wants to return things to the way they were in the past. ▷ *noun* **reactionary**

re·ac·tor (ree-ak-tur) *noun* A large machine in which nuclear energy is produced by splitting atoms under controlled conditions.

read (reed) *verb*
1. To look at written or printed words and understand what they mean.
2. To say aloud something that is written. *I read the book to Rachel.*
3. To learn by reading. *We're reading about life in the Middle Ages.*
4. To understand some form of communication. *Hilary can read my mind.*
5. To show or to register. *The speedometer reads 55 miles per hour.*
▷ *verb* **reading, read** (red)

read·i·ly (red-uhl-ee) *adverb* Easily or willingly. *Michael readily listened to his parents.*

read·y (red-ee) *adjective*
1. Prepared. *When I finish studying, I'll be ready for the test.*
2. Willing. *She is ready to work hard.*
3. Likely or about to do something. *I was ready to scream.*
4. Quick, as in *a ready answer.*
▷ *adjective* **readier, readiest**

real (ree-uhl *or* reel) *adjective*
1. True and not imaginary. *The real story isn't quite so dramatic.*
2. Genuine and not artificial. *I prefer real flowers to plastic ones.*

real estate *noun* Land and the buildings that are on it.

re·al·is·tic (ree-uh-liss-tik) *adjective*
1. Very much like the real thing, as in *a realistic painting.*
2. If you are **realistic,** you view things as they really are. *Jolene is realistic about her chances of winning.*
▷ *noun* **realism** ▷ *adverb* **realistically**

re·al·i·ty (ree-al-uh-tee) *noun*
1. Truth, or the actual situation. *Being a model looks glamorous, but the reality is that it is hard work.*
2. The facts of life that must be faced. *After vacation, we must return to reality.*
▷ *noun, plural* **realities**

re·al·ize (ree-uh-lize) *verb*
1. To become aware that something is true. *John realized that he hadn't been working hard enough.*
2. To make real or to achieve. *After years of study, Juan finally realized his dream of becoming a professional musician.*
▷ *verb* **realizing, realized** ▷ *noun* **realization**

re·al·ly (ree-uh-lee *or* ree-lee) *adverb*
1. Actually, or in reality. *Are the rumors really true?*
2. Very. *I'm really happy right now.*

realm (relm) *noun*
1. An area or field of knowledge or interest, as in *the realm of science.*
2. A kingdom. *He was king of the whole realm.*

reap (reep) *verb*
1. To cut grain or to gather a crop by hand or machine.
2. To get as a reward. *The actor reaped high praise for his fine performance.*
▷ *verb* **reaping, reaped**

re·ap·pear (ree-uh-pihr) *verb* To come into sight again. *The moon reappeared from behind the cloud.* ▷ **reappearing, reappeared** ▷ *noun* **reappearance**

rear (rihr)
1. *verb* To breed and bring up young animals. *The tiger reared her cubs.*
2. *verb* To care for and raise. *My aunt reared seven children.*
3. *noun* The back of something. ▷ *adjective* **rear**
4. *verb* If a horse **rears,** it rises up on its back legs.
5. *verb* To lift up. *The lion reared its head and roared.*
▷ *verb* **rearing, reared**

re·ar·range (ree-uh-raynj) *verb* To arrange things differently. *I rearranged the furniture in my room.*
▷ **rearranging, rearranged**

R

rea·son (ree-zuhn)
1. *noun* The cause of something, or the motive behind someone's action. *There was no reason to doubt his honesty.*
2. *noun* An explanation or an excuse. *Here is my reason for being late.*
3. *verb* To think in a logical way. *Aaron reasoned that it would be quicker to walk.* ▷ *noun* **reason**
4. *verb* If you **reason** with someone, you try to persuade the person that what you suggest is sensible.
▷ *verb* **reasoning, reasoned**

rea·son·a·ble (ree-zuhn-uh-buhl) *adjective*
1. Fair. *Your offer seems reasonable to me.*
2. Sensible. *Hal won't make a fuss; he's always very reasonable.*
3. Costing a fair price. *The chair was reasonable.*
▷ *adverb* **reasonably**

rea·son·ing (ree-zuhn-ing) *noun*
1. The process of thinking in an orderly fashion, drawing conclusions from facts. *Scientific thought is based on reasoning.*
2. The reasons used in this process. *I don't agree with your reasoning.*

re·as·sure (ree-uh-shur) *verb* To calm someone and give the person confidence or courage. *The doctor reassured the woman before the operation.* ▷ **reassuring, reassured** ▷ *noun* **reassurance** ▷ *adjective* **reassuring**

re·bel (reb-uhl) *noun* Someone who fights against a government or against the people in charge of something. ▷ *verb* **rebel** (ri-bel)
▷ *adjective* **rebellious** (ri-bel-yuhss)

re·bel·lion (ri-bel-yuhn) *noun*
1. Armed fight against a government.
2. Any struggle against the people in charge of something.

re·boot (ree-boot) *verb* To start a computer again. *Jim rebooted the computer after installing the new software.* ▷ **rebooting, rebooted**

re·buke (ri-byook) *verb* To scold someone because he or she has done something wrong.
▷ **rebuking, rebuked** ▷ *noun* **rebuke**

re·call (ri-kawl) *verb*
1. To remember something. *I definitely recall your saying that you would help me.*
2. To order someone to return. *The witness was recalled to the stand.*
3. To call back a purchased product that has a defect. *The company recalled thousands of infant car seats that had defective buckles.*
▷ *verb* **recalling, recalled** ▷ *noun* **recall** (ri-kawl *or* ree-kawl)

re·cap (ree-kap) *verb* (informal) To repeat the main points of what has been said. *Recap is short for recapitulate. The announcer recaps the news every hour.* ▷ **recapping, recapped** ▷ *noun* **recap**

re·cede (ri-seed) *verb*
1. To move back. *After the flood, the water slowly receded.*
2. To fade gradually. *Hopes of rescue receded as night fell.*
▷ *verb* **receding, receded** ▷ *adjective* **receding**

re·ceipt (ri-seet) *noun* A piece of paper showing that money, goods, mail, or a service has been received.

re·ceive (ri-seev) *verb*
1. To get or accept something. *I received a letter from my pen pal.*
2. To experience. *I received a shock when I heard the bad news.*
3. To greet or to welcome. *The hostess received her guests at the door.*
▷ *verb* **receiving, received**

re·ceiv·er (ri-see-vur) *noun*
1. The part of a telephone that you hold in your hand.
2. A piece of equipment that receives radio or television signals and changes them into sounds or pictures.
3. A person who receives something.

re·cent (ree-suhnt) *adjective* Happening, made, or done a short time ago. *The city is still recovering from a recent storm. Have you seen the most recent issue of that magazine?* ▷ *adverb* **recently**

re·cep·ta·cle (ri-cep-ti-kuhl) *noun* A container. *Throw that wrapper in the trash receptacle.*

re·cep·tion (ri-sep-shuhn) *noun*
1. The way in which someone or something is received. *We gave our visitors a warm reception. The reception on our television is very bad.*
2. A formal party.

re·cep·tion·ist (ri-sep-shuh-nist) *noun* A person whose job is to greet people in an office, clinic, etc., or when they call on the telephone.

re·cess (ree-sess *or* ri-sess) *noun*
1. A break from work for rest or relaxation.
▷ *verb* **recess**
2. A part of a room set back from the main area.
▷ *noun, plural* **recesses** ▷ *adjective* **recessed**

re·ces·sion (ri-sesh-uhn) *noun* A time when business slows down and more workers than usual are unemployed.

rec·i·pe (ress-i-pee) *noun* Instructions for preparing and cooking food.

> ## Word History
>
> Originally, **recipe** came from the Latin word *recipere,* meaning "to receive." It was first used by doctors, who wrote it at the top of instructions for making medicines. The word later also came to apply to instructions for making food.

re·cip·i·ent (ri-**sip**-ee-uhnt) *noun* A person who receives something. *The recipient of first prize wins a vacation in Hawaii.*

re·cit·al (ri-**sye**-tuhl) *noun*
1. A musical performance by a single performer or by a small group of musicians or dancers.
2. A detailed account or report. *The speaker gave a long recital of the events that led to the Civil War.*

re·cite (ri-**site**) *verb*
1. To say aloud something that you have learned by heart. *Joelle recited the poem.*
2. To tell about in detail. *He slowly recited the story of his life.*
▷ *verb* **reciting, recited** ▷ *noun* **recitation** (*ress*-i-**tay**-shuhn)

reck·less (**rek**-liss) *adjective* If you are **reckless,** you are careless about your own or other people's safety. ▷ *adverb* **recklessly**

reck·on (**rek**-uhn) *verb*
1. To calculate or to count up. *I reckon that I owe you $10.00.* ▷ *noun* **reckoning**
2. To think or to have an opinion. *I reckon that our team will win.*
▷ *verb* **reckoning, reckoned**

re·claim (ri-**klaym**) *verb*
1. To get back something that is yours. *Stacy reclaimed her bag from the safe.*
2. To make land suitable for farming, etc., by clearing it or draining it. ▷ *noun* **reclamation** (*rek*-luh-**may**-shuhn)
▷ *verb* **reclaiming, reclaimed**

re·cline (ri-**kline**) *verb* To lean or lie back. *I reclined on the couch.* ▷ **reclining, reclined**

rec·og·nize (**rek**-uhg-*nize*) *verb*
1. To see someone and know who the person is. *Even from far away, Margaret recognized Camila.*
▷ *adjective* **recognizable** ▷ *adverb* **recognizably**
2. To understand a situation and accept it as true or right. *They recognized their duty to vote in the presidential election.*
▷ *verb* **recognizing, recognized** ▷ *noun* **recognition** (*rek*-uhg-**ni**-shuhn)

rec·ol·lect (rek-uh-**lekt**) *verb* To remember or to recall. *Do you recollect the day we first met?*
▷ **recollecting, recollected** ▷ *noun* **recollection**

rec·om·mend (rek-uh-**mend**) *verb*
1. To suggest as being good or worthy. *My dentist recommended this toothpaste.*
2. To advise. *I recommend that you forget your differences and make up.*
▷ *verb* **recommending, recommended** ▷ *noun* **recommendation**

rec·on·cile (rek-uhn-*sile*) *verb*
1. To make or become friendly again after an argument or a fight. *The couple reconciled after a short separation.* ▷ *noun* **reconciliation**

2. If you **reconcile yourself** to something, you decide to put up with it. *I reconciled myself to working over the holidays.*
▷ *verb* **reconciling, reconciled**

re·con·sid·er (*ree*-kuhn-**sid**-ur) *verb* To think again about a previous decision, especially with the idea of making a change. *The mayor reconsidered his opposition to raising taxes.*
▷ **reconsidering, reconsidered**

re·con·struct (*ree*-kuhn-**struhkt**) *verb*
1. To rebuild something that has been destroyed.
2. To carefully piece together past events. *The police reconstructed the events leading to the robbery.*
▷ *verb* **reconstructed, reconstructing** ▷ *noun* **reconstruction**

rec·ord
1. (ri-**kord**) *verb* To write down information so that it can be kept. *Record your thoughts in this diary.* ▷ *noun* **record** (**rek**-urd)
2. (**rek**-urd) *noun* The facts about what a person or group has done. *Because the prisoner had a good record, she was granted parole.*
3. (**rek**-urd) *noun* A disk with grooves on which sound, especially music, is recorded to be played by a phonograph. Also called *a phonograph record.*
4. (ri-**kord**) *verb* To put music or other sounds onto a tape, compact disk, or record.
5. (**rek**-urd) *noun* If you set a **record** in something such as a sport, you do it better than anyone has ever done it before.
▷ *verb* **recording, recorded**

re·cord·er (ri-**kor**-dur) *noun*
1. A machine for recording sounds on magnetic tape.
2. A woodwind musical instrument that is a form of flute. You play the recorder by blowing into the mouthpiece and covering holes with your fingers to make different notes.

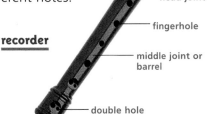

mouthpiece
lip
window
head joint
fingerhole
middle joint or barrel
double hole
foot joint

recorder

R

re·cord·ing (ri-**kor**-ding) *noun*
  1. A tape, compact disk, or record.
  2. The sounds on a tape, compact disk, or record.

re·cov·er (ri-**kuhv**-ur) *verb*
  1. To get better after an illness or a difficulty. *They recovered from the accident.*
  2. To get back something that has been lost or stolen. *The police recovered a lot of stolen goods.*
  3. To make up for. *In order to recover the time we had lost, we skipped lunch.*
  ▷ *verb* **recovering, recovered** ▷ *noun* **recovery**

rec·re·a·tion (rek-ree-**ay**-shuhn) *noun* The games, sports, hobbies, etc., that people enjoy in their spare time. ▷ *adjective* **recreational**

re·cruit (ri-**kroot**)
  1. *noun* Someone who has recently joined the armed forces or any group or organization.
  2. *verb* To get a person to join. *The coach is recruiting new players for the basketball team.*
  ▷ **recruiting, recruited** ▷ *noun* **recruitment**

rec·tan·gle (rek-*tang*-guhl) *noun* A shape with four sides and four right angles. *See* **shape.**
  ▷ *adjective* **rectangular**

rec·ti·fy (rek-tuh-*fye*) *verb* To make right or correct, as in *to rectify a mistake.* ▷ **rectifies, rectifying, rectified**

rec·tum (rek-tuhm) *noun* The lowest portion of the large intestine, ending at the anus. *See* **digestion.** ▷ *adjective* **rectal**

re·cu·per·ate (ri-**koo**-puh-*rate*) *verb* To recover slowly from an illness or injury. ▷ **recuperating, recuperated** ▷ *noun* **recuperation**

re·cur (ri-**kur**) *verb* To appear or happen again. *The same problem recurs every time I use the computer.* ▷ **recurring, recurred** ▷ *noun* **recurrence** ▷ *adjective* **recurrent**

re·cy·cle (ree-**sye**-kuhl) *verb* To process old items such as glass, plastic, newspapers, and aluminum cans so that they can be used to make new products. ▷ **recycling, recycled** ▷ *adjective* **recyclable**

recycling aluminum cans

red (red) *noun* One of the three primary colors, along with blue and yellow. Red is the color of beets and blood. ▷ *adjective* **red,** *adjective* **reddish**

red blood cell *noun* A cell in your blood that carries oxygen from your lungs to all the tissues and cells of your body.

red·coat (red-*koht*) *noun* A British soldier during the time of the Revolutionary War and later wars. These soldiers' uniforms included bright red coats.

Red Cross *noun* An international organization that helps victims of disasters of all kinds, from floods and earthquakes to war and famine.

re·deem (ri-**deem**) *verb*
  1. To exchange something for money or merchandise. *Caroline redeemed the coupon for a set of free drinking glasses.*
  2. To save, or to make up for. *Glen redeemed his reputation by scoring three goals.*
  ▷ *verb* **redeeming, redeemed** ▷ *noun* **redemption** (ri-**demp**-shuhn)

red-hand·ed (han-did) *adjective* If you catch someone **red-handed,** you catch the person in the act of doing something wrong. *The police caught the thief red-handed.*

red herring *noun* Something that distracts a person's attention from the real issue. *In the story, the discovery of a bloody knife was a red herring.*

red tape *noun* Rules, regulations, and paperwork that make it difficult to get things done.

re·duce (ri-**dooss** *or* ri-**dyooss**) *verb*
  1. To make something smaller or less. *The store will reduce its prices during the sale.* ▷ *noun* **reduction** (ri-**duhk**-shuhn)
  2. To lose body weight by dieting.
  ▷ *verb* **reducing, reduced**

re·dun·dant (ri-**duhn**-duhnt) *adjective* Using too many words for what you mean to say or write. *Saying "three triplets" is redundant.* ▷ *noun* **redundancy**

red·wood (red-*wood*) *noun* An evergreen tree found along the western coast of the United States, especially in northern California. The world's tallest redwood, found in Humboldt County, California, is 362 feet (110 meters) tall.

reed (reed) *noun*
  1. A tall grass with long, thin, hollow stems that grows in or near water.
  2. A piece of thin wood, metal, or plastic in the mouthpieces of some musical instruments, such as the clarinet, oboe, and saxophone. When you blow over the reed, it vibrates and makes a sound. *See* **woodwind.**

reef (reef) *noun*
  1. A strip of rock, sand, or coral close to the surface of the ocean or another body of water.
  2. reef knot A square knot. *See* **knot.**

R

reek (reek) *verb* To smell strongly of something unpleasant. *The room reeked of tobacco smoke.* **Reek** sounds like **wreak.** ▷ **reeking, reeked**

reel (reel)
1. *verb* To stagger around unsteadily. *The drunk man reeled down the street.*
2. *noun* A spool on which thread, film, etc., is wound. *See* **angling.** ▷ *verb* **reel**
3. *noun* A type of folk dance that is lively and spirited.
4. *verb* If you **reel** something **off,** you say it very fast.
▷ *verb* **reeling, reeled**

re·e·lect (ree-ee-lekt) *verb* To elect for another term, as in *to reelect the president.* ▷ **reelecting, reelected** ▷ *noun* **reelection**

re·en·try (ree-en-tree) *noun* The return of a spacecraft or missile to the earth's atmosphere. ▷ *noun, plural* **reentries** ▷ *verb* **reenter**

ref (ref) Short for **referee.**

re·fer (ri-fur) *verb*
1. If you **refer** to a book, you look in it for information.
2. If you **refer** to something while talking or writing, you mention it.
3. To send someone for additional or more detailed information, advice, etc. *My doctor has referred me to a specialist.* ▷ *noun* **referral**
▷ *verb* **referring, referred**

ref·er·ee (ref-uh-ree) *noun* Someone who supervises a sports match or a game and makes sure that the players obey the rules. ▷ *verb* **referee**

ref·er·ence (ref-uh-renss) *noun*
1. A mention of someone or something. *There was a reference to you in the speech.*
2. A written statement about someone's character and abilities. *You will need references for this job.*
3. A book, magazine, etc., that you use in order to produce a piece of work. *Please list your references at the end of your essay.*

reference book *noun* A book that you use to find information quickly and easily. *Encyclopedias, dictionaries, atlases, and almanacs are reference books.*

ref·er·en·dum (ref-uh-ren-duhm) *noun* A vote by the people on a public measure. *The ballot included a referendum on building a new school.* ▷ *noun, plural* **referendums** *or* **referenda**

re·fill (ree-fil) *verb* To fill something again. *The waitress refilled Meg's coffee cup.* ▷ **refilling, refilled** ▷ *noun* **refill** (ree-fil)

re·fine (ri-fine) *verb* To purify, or to remove unwanted matter from a substance such as oil or sugar. ▷ **refining, refined**

re·fined (ri-fined) *adjective*
1. A **refined** person is very polite and has elegant manners and tastes.
2. Purified or processed, as in *refined sugar.*

re·fin·er·y (ri-fye-nuh-ree) *noun* A factory where raw materials are purified and made into finished products. *Oil refineries turn crude oil into gasoline, jet fuel, and other products.* ▷ *noun, plural* **refineries**

re·fit (ree-fit) *verb* To repair something, or to supply it with new parts or equipment. *The old ship was refitted with a new mast.* ▷ **refitting, refitted**

re·flect (ri-flekt) *verb*
1. To show an image of something on a shiny surface such as a mirror. *The lake reflected my face.*
2. When rays of light or heat are **reflected,** they bounce off an object. *The diagram shows how a light beam is reflected when it hits a mirror.*
3. To think carefully. *Bernardo reflected on the meaning of life.*
4. To bring blame or discredit. *His bad behavior reflects on his parents.*
5. To show or to express. *Amanda's clothes reflect her good taste.*
▷ *verb* **reflecting, reflected** ▷ *noun* **reflection**

reflection

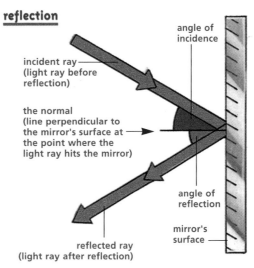

angle of incidence

incident ray (light ray before reflection)

the normal (line perpendicular to the mirror's surface at the point where the light ray hits the mirror)

angle of reflection

mirror's surface

reflected ray (light ray after reflection)

re·flec·tive (ri-flek-tiv) *adjective*
1. Acting like a mirror.
2. Serious and thoughtful. ▷ *adverb* **reflectively**

re·flec·tor (ri-flek-tur) *noun* A shiny surface or device that bounces back light or heat.

re·flex (ree-fleks) *noun* An automatic action that happens without a person's control or effort. *Blinking and sneezing are reflexes.* ▷ *noun, plural* **reflexes** ▷ *adjective* **reflex**

reflex angle *noun* An angle between 180 degrees and 360 degrees.

re·for·est (ree-for-est) *verb* To replant trees where all the original trees were cut down or destroyed by fire or disaster. ▷ **reforesting, reforested** ▷ *noun* **reforestation**

re·form (ri-form)
1. *verb* To improve something that is unsatisfactory, or to correct something that is wrong. *The candidate believes that tax laws need to be reformed.*
2. *verb* To change for the better. *The thief promised to reform and live an honest life.*
3. *noun* An improvement, or the correcting of something unsatisfactory, as in *health care reform.* ▷ *verb* **reforming, reformed**

re·for·ma·to·ry (ri-for-muh-*tor*-ee) *noun* A special school or institution for young people who have broken the law. ▷ *noun, plural* **reformatories**

re·fract (ri-frakt) *verb* When a light ray or a sound wave is **refracted,** it changes direction because it has traveled from one medium into another. *The diagram shows how a light ray is refracted as it moves from the air into glass and then back into the air.* ▷ **refracting, refracted** ▷ *noun* **refraction**

refraction

angle of incidence

incident ray
(light ray before refraction)

the normal
(line perpendicular to the glass block's surface at the point where the light ray enters the glass)

angle of refraction

angle equal to angle of incidence

glass block

refracted ray
(light ray after refraction)

re·frain (ri-frayn)
1. *verb* To stop yourself from doing something. *Please refrain from standing on the seats.* ▷ **refraining, refrained**
2. *noun* A regularly repeated part of a song or poem.

re·fresh (ri-fresh) *verb* If something **refreshes** you, it makes you feel fresh and strong again. ▷ **refreshes, refreshing, refreshed** ▷ *adjective* **refreshing**

re·fresh·ments (ri-fresh-muhnts) *noun, plural* Drink and food.

re·frig·er·a·tor (ri-frij-uh-*ray*-tur) *noun* A cabinet with a very cold interior, used for storing food and drink. *Refrigerators are kept cool inside by a substance called refrigerant that circulates constantly. The diagram shows how refrigerant evaporates inside the refrigerator, drawing heat away from the food, and condenses outside the refrigerator, sending out the heat that it has gained.* ▷ *noun* **refrigeration** ▷ *verb* **refrigerate**

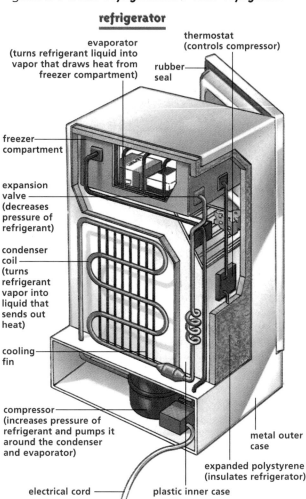

refrigerator

thermostat
(controls compressor)

evaporator
(turns refrigerant liquid into vapor that draws heat from freezer compartment)

rubber seal

freezer compartment

expansion valve
(decreases pressure of refrigerant)

condenser coil
(turns refrigerant vapor into liquid that sends out heat)

cooling fin

compressor
(increases pressure of refrigerant and pumps it around the condenser and evaporator)

metal outer case

expanded polystyrene
(insulates refrigerator)

electrical cord

plastic inner case

re·fu·el (ree-fyoo-uhl) *verb* To take on more fuel. *The plane to Antarctica had to refuel in Brazil.* ▷ **refueling, refueled**

ref·uge (ref-yooj) *noun*
1. Protection or shelter from danger or trouble. *The frightened kitten took refuge under the couch.*
2. A place that provides protection or shelter, as in *a wildlife refuge.*

ref·u·gee (*ref*-yuh-jee *or* ref-yuh-jee) *noun* A person who is forced to leave his or her home because of war, persecution, or a natural disaster.

R

re·fund (ri-fuhnd) *verb* To give money back to the person who paid it. *The store owner refunded my money because the bread that I bought from him was stale.* ▷ **refunding, refunded** ▷ *noun* **refund** (ree-fuhnd)

re·fuse
1. (ri-fyooz) *verb* To say you will not do something or accept something. *Alec refused to go on the amusement park ride by himself.* ▷ **refusing, refused** ▷ *noun* **refusal**
2. (ref-yooss) *noun* Rubbish or trash.

re·gal (ree-guhl) *adjective* To do with or fit for a king or queen, as in *a regal manner.* ▷ *adverb* **regally**

re·gale (ri-gale) *verb*
1. To give great pleasure, delight, or entertainment. *The old man regaled his grandchildren with tales of his adventures at sea.*
2. To entertain lavishly with a lot of food and drink. *The king regaled his guests with a feast.*
▷ *verb* **regaling, regaled**

re·gard (ri-gard)
1. *verb* To have an opinion about something. *Douglas regards racists with contempt.*
2. *noun* A good opinion; esteem. *I have a high regard for volunteer workers.*
3. *verb* To look at closely. *The cats regarded each other with suspicion.*
4. *verb* To respect or to consider. *Melissa regards her sister's privacy.*
5. *noun* Respect or consideration, as in *no regard for danger.*
6. regards *noun, plural* If someone sends you his or her **regards,** the person sends you best wishes.
▷ *verb* **regarding, regarded**

re·gard·ing (ri-gar-ding) *preposition* About or concerning. *The teacher wrote a note regarding Maureen's lateness.*

re·gard·less (ri-gard-liss)
1. *adjective* Without considering anything or anyone else. *Nina drove at high speed, regardless of the other drivers.*
2. *adverb* In spite of everything. *I know the truth might hurt, but I'm going to tell it regardless.*

re·gat·ta (ri-gat-uh) *noun* A boat race, or a series of boat races.

reg·gae (reg-ay) *noun* A type of rhythmic popular music that comes from the West Indies.

re·gime (ri-zheem) *noun* A government that rules a people during a specific period of time. *The new regime plans to focus on fighting crime and improving education.*

reg·i·ment (rej-uh-muhnt) *noun* A military unit made up of two or more battalions.

re·gion (ree-juhn) *noun* An area or a district. *In which region of the country do you live?*
▷ *adjective* **regional** ▷ *adverb* **regionally**

reg·is·ter (rej-uh-stur)
1. *noun* A book in which names or official records are kept, as in *a class register.*
2. *verb* To enter something on an official list. *All cars must be registered.*
3. *noun* The range of notes produced by a musical instrument or a voice.
4. *verb* To show an emotion. *Alicia's face registered dismay.*
5. *noun* A machine that automatically records and counts, as in *a cash register.*
6. *verb* To show on a scale or other device. *His temperature registered 98.6 degrees Fahrenheit on the thermometer.*
▷ *verb* **registering, registered** ▷ *noun* **registration**

registered nurse *noun* A nurse who has completed certain training and is licensed by the state in which he or she practices.

re·gret (ri-gret) *verb* To be sad or sorry about something. *I regretted losing my temper.*
▷ **regretting, regretted** ▷ *noun* **regret** ▷ *adjective* **regretful**

re·gret·ta·ble (ri-gret-uh-buhl) *adjective* If something is **regrettable,** it is unfortunate and you wish that it had not happened. ▷ *adverb* **regrettably**

reg·u·lar (reg-yuh-lur) *adjective*
1. Usual or normal. *This is my regular route home.*
2. According to habit or usual behavior, as in *a regular customer.*
3. Always happening or occurring at the same time, as in *regular meals.*
4. Even or steady, as in *a regular heartbeat.*
5. A **regular** verb is one whose main parts are formed according to a regular pattern. *Love is a regular verb because its past tense is loved.*
▷ *noun* **regularity** (reg-yuh-la-ri-tee) ▷ *adverb* **regularly**

reg·u·late (reg-yuh-late) *verb*
1. To control or to manage. *Laws are passed to regulate behavior.*
2. To adjust or to keep at some standard. *A thermostat can be used to regulate the temperature in a room.*
▷ *verb* **regulating, regulated**

reg·u·la·tion (reg-yuh-lay-shuhn) *noun*
1. An official rule or order, as in *the regulations of a sport.*
2. The act of controlling or adjusting something, as in *government regulation of the banking industry.*

re·gur·gi·tate (ree-gur-juh-tate) *verb* To bring food from the stomach back into the mouth. *Many birds regurgitate food and feed it to their young.* ▷ **regurgitating, regurgitated**

re·hearse (ri-hurss) *verb*
1. To practice for a public performance. *The cast rehearsed the play.*
2. To review or recount something in order. *He rehearsed his plans for the trip.*
▷ *verb* **rehearsing, rehearsed** ▷ *noun* **rehearsal**

reign (rayn) *verb*
1. To rule as a king or queen. *The queen reigned for 50 years.* ▷ *noun* **reign**
2. To be widespread. *Peace and harmony reigned throughout the country.*
Reign sounds like **rain** and **rein**.
▷ *verb* **reigning, reigned**

re·im·burse (ree-im-burss) *verb* To pay someone back the money the person has had to spend on your behalf. *The company will reimburse you for your expenses.* ▷ **reimbursing, reimbursed** ▷ *noun* **reimbursement**

rein (rayn) *noun*
1. reins *noun, plural* Straps attached to a bridle to control or guide a horse. *See* **tack.**
2. Any method or device for controlling.
Rein sounds like **rain** and **reign**.

rein·deer (rayn-*dihr*)
noun A deer that lives in the earth's far north regions. Both male and female reindeer have large, branching antlers.
▷ *noun, plural* **reindeer**

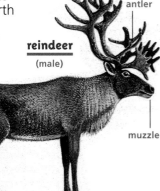

reindeer (male)
antler
muzzle

re·in·force (*ree*-in-**forss**) *verb* To strengthen something. *Concrete bridges are reinforced by metal rods.* ▷ **reinforcing, reinforced**

re·in·force·ment (*ree*-in-**forss**-muhnt) *noun*
1. Something that strengthens.
2. reinforcements *noun, plural* Extra troops sent to strengthen a fighting force.

re·ject
1. (ri-**jekt**) *verb* To refuse to accept something. *Julio rejected all offers of help.* ▷ **rejecting, rejected** ▷ *noun* **rejection**
2. (ree-jekt) *noun* Something that has been discarded. *Put the torn clothing over there with the other rejects.*

re·joice (ri-**joiss**) *verb* To be very happy about something. *We rejoiced at the wonderful news.*
▷ **rejoicing, rejoiced**

re·lapse (ri-laps *or* ree-laps) *noun* The act of falling back to a former condition, especially the return of an illness after you were feeling better. *Pat recovered from the flu, but now she's had a relapse.* ▷ *verb* **relapse** (ri-laps)

re·late (ri-late) *verb*
1. To narrate, or to tell the story of. *The lawyer related how the crime occurred.*
2. If things **relate** to each other, there is a connection between them. *All the questions at the meeting related to the new schedule.*
3. If people **relate** to each other, they get along well together or understand each other. *The Millers really relate well to their kids.*
▷ *verb* **relating, related**

re·lat·ed (ri-lay-tid) *adjective*
1. If you are **related** to someone, you are both part of the same family.
2. Having some connection, as in *related events.*

re·la·tion (ri-lay-shuhn) *noun*
1. A connection between two or more things. *There is a relation between exercise and health.*
2. A member of your family.

re·la·tion·ship (ri-lay-shuhn-ship) *noun*
1. The way in which people get along together. *Although they sometimes argue, my parents basically have a good relationship.*
2. The way in which things are connected. *There is a relationship between how much you study and how well you do on a test.*

rel·a·tive (rel-uh-tiv)
1. *noun* A member of your family.
2. *adjective* Compared with others. *They live in relative luxury compared with their neighbors.*

rel·a·tive·ly (rel-uh-tiv-lee) *adverb* Compared with others. *I am relatively old compared with you.*

re·lax (ri-laks) *verb*
1. To rest and take things easy. *We relaxed on vacation.*
2. To become less tense and anxious. *Try to relax before taking the test.*
3. To make less strict. *The new principal has relaxed the rules at our school.*
▷ *verb* **relaxes, relaxing, relaxed** ▷ *noun* **relaxation** (ree-lak-say-shuhn)

re·lay (ree-lay)
1. *noun* A team race in which members of the team take turns running and passing a baton from one runner to the next.
2. *verb* To pass a message on to someone else. *Yoko relayed the news to the others.* ▷ **relaying, relayed**

re·lease (ri-leess) *verb*
1. To free something or someone. *The boy*

released the trapped squirrel.
2. If a CD, film, etc., is **released,** it is made available to the public for the first time.
▷ *verb* **releasing, released** ▷ *noun* **release**

rel·e·gate (rel-uh-gate) *verb*
1. To send to a place or position of less importance. *The old clothes were relegated to the garbage heap.*
2. To turn over or assign a task to another person. *I relegated the job of writing the story to the newest reporter on the school paper.*
▷ *verb* **relegating, relegated**

re·lent (ri-lent) *verb* To become less strict or more merciful. *My mom was going to punish me, but at the last minute she relented.* ▷ **relenting, relented**

re·lent·less (ri-lent-liss) *adjective* Endless and determined. *Sheila practices the trumpet with relentless enthusiasm.* ▷ *adverb* **relentlessly**

rel·e·vant (rel-uh-vuhnt) *adjective* If something is **relevant,** it is directly concerned with what is being discussed or dealt with. ▷ *noun* **relevance**

re·li·a·ble (ri-lye-uh-buhl) *adjective* Trustworthy or dependable. ▷ *noun* **reliability** ▷ *adverb* **reliably**

rel·ic (rel-ik) *noun*
1. Something that has survived from the past.
2. Some object belonging to a saint or other holy person.

re·lief (ri-leef) *noun*
1. A feeling of freedom from pain or worry. *It's such a relief to know that you're safe.*
2. Aid given to people in special need, as in *flood relief.*
3. Freedom from a job or duty, especially when one person takes over for another.
4. Figures or details that are raised from a surface. *The top of the building included tigers carved in relief.*
5. relief map A map that uses shading or a model that uses relief to show areas of high and low ground.

re·lieve (ri-leev) *verb*
1. To ease someone's trouble or pain. *The medicine relieved my cough.*
2. If you **relieve** someone, you take over a duty from the person.
▷ *verb* **relieving, relieved**

re·lig·ion (ri-lij-uhn) *noun*
1. Belief in God or gods.
2. A specific system of belief, faith, and worship. Some world religions are Buddhism, Christianity, Hinduism, Islam, and Judaism.
3. The practice of your belief through worship, obedience, and prayer.
▷ *adjective* **religious**

rel·ish (rel-ish)
1. *verb* To enjoy something greatly. *Wesley relishes sleeping late on weekends.* ▷ **relishes,**

relishing, relished ▷ *noun* **relish**
2. *noun* A mixture of spices and chopped vegetables, such as olives or pickles, used to flavor food. ▷ *noun, plural* **relishes**

re·luc·tant (ri-luhk-tuhnt) *adjective* If you are **reluctant,** you do not want to do something. *I was reluctant to lend him money because I knew he would never pay me back.* ▷ *noun* **reluctance** ▷ *adverb* **reluctantly**

re·ly (ri-lye) *verb* If you **rely on** something or someone, you need and trust the thing or person. *I relied on my friends to help me.* ▷ **relies, relying, relied** ▷ *noun* **reliance** ▷ *adjective* **reliant**

re·main (ri-mayn) *verb*
1. To stay in the same place. *While we rode our bikes, my sister remained at home.*
2. To be left behind or left over. *Only three bananas remained in the fruit bowl.*
3. To continue being. *We remained loyal fans.*
▷ *verb* **remaining, remained**

re·main·der (ri-mayn-dur) *noun*
1. The amount left over. *I'll put the remainder of my allowance in the bank.*
2. The number found when one number is subtracted from another. *If you subtract 5 from 20, the remainder is 15.*
3. The number left over when one number cannot be divided evenly by another. *If you divide 7 by 2, the quotient is 3 with a remainder of 1.*

re·mains (ri-maynz) *noun, plural*
1. Things left over. *What shall I do with the remains of my lunch?*
2. Parts of something that was once alive.
3. A dead body.

re·mark (ri-mark) *verb*
1. To make a comment about something. *My mother remarked that I looked nice.*
2. To notice or to observe.
▷ *verb* **remarking, remarked** ▷ *noun* **remark**

re·mark·a·ble (ri-mar-kuh-buhl) *adjective* Worth noticing; extraordinary. *The computer is a remarkable invention.* ▷ *adverb* **remarkably**

re·me·di·al (ri-mee-dee-uhl) *adjective* Intended to help or correct something, as in *a remedial reading program.*

rem·e·dy (rem-uh-dee) *noun* Something that relieves pain, cures a disease, or corrects a disorder. *Will there ever be a remedy for the common cold?* ▷ *noun, plural* **remedies** ▷ *verb* **remedy**

re·mem·ber (ri-mem-bur) *verb*
1. To recall or to bring back to mind. *I'll always remember Marco. Try to remember the answer.*
2. To keep in mind carefully. *Please remember that you have a test tomorrow.*

re·mind (ri-minde) *verb* To make someone remember something. *Please remind me to lock the door.* ▷ **reminding, reminded**

re·mind·er (ri-minde-ur) *noun* Something that helps a person remember.

rem·i·nisce (*rem*-uh-**niss**) *verb* To think or talk about the past and things that you remember. *The couple reminisced about their first date.* ▷ **reminiscing, reminisced** ▷ *noun* **reminiscence**

re·mis·sion (ri-mish-uhn) *noun* If a person with a disease starts to have less pain or the symptoms of the disease start to disappear, the disease is in **remission.** *After he underwent chemotherapy treatments, his leukemia went into remission.*

rem·nant (**rem**-nuhnt) *noun* A piece or part of something that is left over, as in *a remnant of material.*

re·mod·el (ree-mod-uhl) *verb* To make a major change to the structure or design of something. *The owners remodeled their restaurant so that it would seat more people.* ▷ **remodeling, remodeled**

re·morse (ri-morss) *noun* A strong feeling of guilt and regret about something wrong that you have done. *The criminal felt no remorse for his horrible crime.* ▷ *adjective* **remorseful** ▷ *adverb* **remorsefully**

re·mote (ri-moht) *adjective*
1. Far away, isolated, or distant, as in *a remote island.*
2. Extremely small or slight, as in *a remote possibility.*
▷ *adjective* **remoter, remotest** ▷ *noun* **remoteness**
▷ *adverb* **remotely**

remote control *noun* A system for operating machines from a distance, usually by radio signals or by a light beam. ▷ *adjective* **remote-controlled**

re·move (ri-moov) *verb*
1. To take something away. *They removed the boxes from the garage.*
2. To take off or away. *Please remove your shoes before you enter the restaurant.*
▷ *verb* **removing, removed** ▷ *noun* **removal**

Re·nais·sance (ren-uh-sahnss)
noun The revival of art and learning in Europe between the 14th and 16th centuries. The Renaissance was inspired by an interest in the ancient Greeks and Romans. *This picture is based on "Study for the Head of Leda," a pen-and-ink drawing by Leonardo da Vinci, one of the leading artists of the Italian Renaissance.*

Italian Renaissance drawing

ren·der (ren-dur) *verb*
1. To make or cause to become. *She was rendered helpless by an injury to her spinal cord.*
2. To give or to deliver. *The jury rendered a guilty verdict.*
▷ *verb* **rendering, rendered**

ren·dez·vous (ron-duh-*voo* or ron-day-voo) *noun*
1. An appointment to meet at a certain time or place.
2. The place chosen for a meeting. *The restaurant is a famous rendezvous for young couples.*
▷ *verb* **rendezvous**

re·new (ri-noo or ri-nyoo) *verb*
1. To replace something old with something new. *I renewed the finish on the table.*
2. To start something again after a break. *We renewed our efforts to complete the puzzle after dinner.*
3. To extend the period of a library loan, club membership, magazine subscription, etc.
▷ *verb* **renewing, renewed** ▷ *noun* **renewal**
▷ *adjective* **renewable,** *adjective* **renewed**

renewable energy *noun* Power from sources that can never be used up, such as wind, waves, and the sun.

ren·o·vate (ren-uh-*vate*) *verb* To restore something to good condition, or to make it more modern. *They renovated their old house.*
▷ **renovating, renovated** ▷ *noun* **renovation**

re·nowned (ri-nound) *adjective* Famous or well-known. *Edgar Allan Poe is renowned for his scary stories.* ▷ *noun* **renown**

rent (rent)
1. *noun* Money paid by a tenant to the owner of a property in return for living in it or using it.
2. *verb* To get or give the right to use something in return for payment. *Jack rented a car on his trip.* ▷ **renting, rented**

rent·al (ren-tuhl) *noun*
1. The amount paid to rent something.
2. Something that is hired or rented, such as a car or property. *My parents don't want to buy a house; they're looking for a rental.*
▷ *adjective* **rental**

re·pair (ri-pair) *verb* To make something work again, or to put back together something that is broken. *The man repaired the watch.* ▷ **repairing, repaired** ▷ *noun* **repair**

re·pa·tri·a·tion (ree-*pay*-tree-ay-shuhn) *noun* The return of someone to the country where he or she was born or where he or she is a citizen, as in *the repatriation of the prisoners of war.* ▷ *verb* **repatriate**

re·pay (ri-pay) *verb*
1. To pay or give something back. *Please repay the money you owe.*

2. To give or do something in return. *How can I repay you for your kindness?*
▷ *verb* **repaying, repaid** ▷ *noun* **repayment**

re·peal (ri-**peel**) *verb* To do away with something officially, such as a law. ▷ **repealing, repealed** ▷ *noun* **repeal**

re·peat (ri-**peet**) *verb* To say or do something again. *Jane repeated the message. I'll never repeat that mistake.* ▷ **repeating, repeated** ▷ *noun* **repeat** (ri-**peet** *or* ree-**peet**)

re·pel (ri-**pel**) *verb*
1. To drive away. *The army repelled the enemy forces.*
2. To disgust someone. *His violence repelled me.*
▷ *verb* **repelling, repelled**

re·pel·lent (ri-**pel**-uhnt)
1. *noun* A chemical that keeps insects and other pests away, as in *a mosquito repellent*.
2. *adjective* Disgusting, as in *a repellent smell*.

re·pent (ri-**pent**) *verb* To be deeply sorry for the bad things that you have done. *She repented her terrible behavior.* ▷ **repenting, repented** ▷ *noun* **repentance** ▷ *adjective* **repentant**

rep·er·toire (**rep**-ur-*twar*) *noun* The collection of songs, jokes, stories, etc., that an entertainer is prepared to perform in public.

rep·e·ti·tion (rep-uh-**tish**-uhn) *noun* The repeating of words or actions. *Young children learn the alphabet by repetition.* ▷ *adjective* **repetitious,** *adjective* **repetitive** (ri-**pet**-i-tiv)

re·place (ri-**playss**) *verb*
1. To put one thing or person in place of another. *Computers have replaced typewriters.*
2. To put something back where it was. *I replaced the playing card in the deck.*
3. To provide substitutes for. *We replaced the old tires.*
▷ *verb* **replacing, replaced** ▷ *noun* **replacement**

re·play
1. (ri-**play**) *verb* To play back a tape in order to see or hear something again. ▷ **replaying, replayed** ▷ *noun* **replay** (ree-play)
2. (ree-play) *noun* A second contest between two teams or players when the first contest has ended in a tie. ▷ *verb* **replay** (ri-**play**)

rep·li·ca (**rep**-luh-kuh) *noun* An exact copy of something, especially a copy made on a smaller scale than the original. *Inside the bottle was a replica of an old sailing ship.* ▷ *verb* **replicate**

re·ply (ri-**plye**) *verb* To give an answer or a response. *Brad replied to the letter he had received.* ▷ **replies, replying, replied** ▷ *noun* **reply**

re·port (ri-**port**)
1. *noun* A written or spoken account of something that has happened.
2. *verb* To give a report. *Cynthia reported the fire to the fire department.*
3. *verb* If you **report** someone, you make an official complaint about the person.
4. *verb* To appear for duty. *Please report for work on Monday morning.*
5. *verb* If you **report to** someone, you work for him or her.
▷ *verb* **reporting, reported**

report card *noun* A listing of a student's grades that is compiled and sent home several times a year. A report card can also include comments from a teacher about a student's behavior.

re·port·er (ri-**por**-tur) *noun* Someone who gathers and reports the news for radio, television, or a newspaper or magazine. *Television, radio, and newspaper reporters question lawyers (bottom, right) after a day in court.*

reporters

rep·re·sent (rep-ri-**zent**) *verb*
1. To speak or act for someone else. *My lawyer represented me.*
2. To stand for something. *On a map, water is usually represented by the color blue.*
▷ *verb* **representing, represented** ▷ *noun* **representation**

rep·re·sen·ta·tive (rep-ri-**zen**-tuh-tiv) *noun*
1. Someone who is chosen to speak or act for others. *I wrote to my representative in Congress.*
2. A person or thing that is typical of a group. *This church is a good representative of Gothic architecture.* ▷ *adjective* **representative**

re·press (ri-**press**) *verb*
1. If you **repress** an emotion, such as anger, you keep it under control and do not show it.
2. To keep people under very strict control. *The dictator repressed the citizens of his country.*
▷ *verb* **represses, repressing, repressed** ▷ *noun* **repression** ▷ *adjective* **repressed**

re·prieve (ri-**preev**) *verb* To postpone a punishment, especially a death sentence. ▷ **reprieving, reprieved** ▷ *noun* **reprieve**

rep·ri·mand (**rep**-ruh-*mand*) *verb* To criticize someone sharply or formally. *The teacher reprimanded the student.* ▷ **reprimanding, reprimanded** ▷ *noun* **reprimand**

re·pri·sal (ri-**prye**-zuhl) *noun* An act of revenge.

R

re·proach (ri-prohch) *verb* To blame someone, or to show that you disapprove of something the person has done or said. *Annie reproached me for forgetting her birthday.* ▷ **reproaches, reproaching, reproached** ▷ *noun* **reproach**

re·pro·duce (ree-pruh-**dooss**) *verb*
1. To make a copy of something. *This machine reproduces color photographs.*
2. When animals **reproduce,** they breed and produce offspring.
▷ *verb* **reproducing, reproduced** ▷ *noun* **reproduction** (ree-pruh-**duhk**-shuhn)

rep·tile (**rep**-tile *or* **rep**-tuhl) *noun* A cold-blooded animal that crawls across the ground or creeps on short legs. Reptiles have backbones and reproduce by laying eggs. *The picture shows a range of reptiles from around the world.*
▷ *adjective* **reptilian** (rep-**til**-ee-uhn *or* rep-**til**-yuhn)

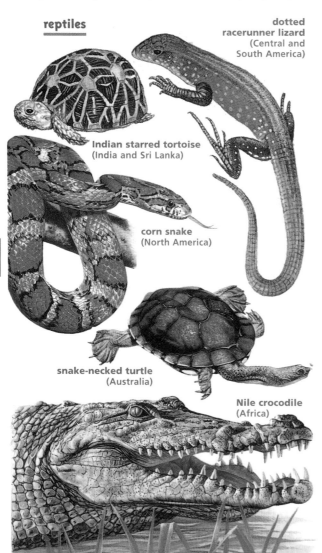

reptiles

dotted racerunner lizard
(Central and South America)

Indian starred tortoise
(India and Sri Lanka)

corn snake
(North America)

snake-necked turtle
(Australia)

Nile crocodile
(Africa)

re·pub·lic (ri-**puhb**-lik) *noun*
1. A form of government in which the people have the power to elect representatives who manage the government. Republics often have presidents.
2. A country that has such a form of government. The United States is a republic.

re·pub·li·can (ri-**puhb**-li-kuhn) *adjective* To do with a republic or in favor of a republic, as in *a republican government.*

Republican Party
noun One of the main political parties in the United States. *In the 19th century, artist Thomas Nast chose the elephant as the symbol of the Republican Party.*

symbol of the Republican Party

re·pug·nant (ri-**puhg**-nuhnt) *adjective* Very unpleasant and disgusting. *Melissa found the job of cleaning out the stables totally repugnant.*

re·pulse (ri-**puhlss**) *verb*
1. To drive or force back. *Our army repulsed the enemy's attack.*
2. To reject something, as in *to repulse an offer.*
▷ *verb* **repulsing, repulsed**

re·pul·sive (ri-**puhl**-siv) *adjective* Very distasteful or disgusting. *This medicine smells repulsive.*
▷ *noun* **repulsion** ▷ *adverb* **repulsively**

rep·u·ta·ble (rep-yuh-tuh-buhl) *adjective* Reliable and trustworthy. *Always buy electrical equipment from a reputable dealer.* ▷ *adverb* **reputably**

rep·u·ta·tion (rep-yuh-**tay**-shuhn) *noun* Your worth or character, as judged by other people. *Mark has a reputation for working hard.*

re·pute (ri-**pyoot**) *noun* Fame; reputation.

re·put·ed (ri-**pyoo**-tid) *adjective* Supposed to be or thought to be. *The reputed murderer was brought before the judge.* ▷ *adverb* **reputedly**

re·quest (ri-**kwest**)
1. *verb* To ask for something politely. *Visitors are requested to be seated.* ▷ **requesting, requested**
2. *noun* Something that you ask for. *The band played our request.*

re·qui·em (**rek**-wee-uhm) *noun*
1. A church service in which prayers are said for someone who has died.

2. A piece of music composed in memory of a dead person, often a musical setting of the requiem service.

re·quire (ri-kwire) *verb*

1. To need something. *All animals require food to survive.*

2. If you are **required** to do something, you must do it.

▷ *verb* **requiring, required**

re·quire·ment (ri-kwire-muhnt) *noun* Something that you need to do or have. *The ability to swim 100 yards is a requirement of this sailing course.*

re·read (ree-reed) *verb* To read something again. *Kerry reread the train schedule anxiously.*

▷ **rereading, reread** (ree-red)

re·run

1. (ree-ruhn) *verb* To run again. *After a tie was declared, we had to rerun the race.* ▷ **rerunning, reran**

2. (ree-*ruhn*) *noun* A television program that has been shown before.

res·cue (ress-kyoo)

1. *verb* To save someone who is in danger or is trapped somewhere. *The lifeguard rescued the drowning swimmer.* ▷ **rescuing, rescued** ▷ *noun* **rescue,** *noun* **rescuer**

2. rescue helicopter *noun* A specially equipped helicopter used to search for and rescue people on land and at sea. *The picture shows a Sea King rescue helicopter.*

re·search (ri-surch *or* ree-surch)

1. *verb* To study and find out about a subject, usually by reading a lot of books about it or by doing experiments. *Ariel researched the Civil War for her project.* ▷ **researches, researching, researched**

2. *noun* A study or an investigation in a particular field, usually to learn new facts or solve a problem, as in *medical research.* ▷ *noun* **researcher**

re·sem·ble (ri-zem-buhl) *verb* To be or look like something or someone. *Lucy resembles her Aunt Matilda.* ▷ **resembling, resembled** ▷ *noun* **resemblance**

re·sent (ri-zent) *verb* To feel hurt or angry about something that has been done or said to you. *I resent that you always interfere in my private affairs.* ▷ **resenting, resented** ▷ *noun* **resentment** ▷ *adjective* **resentful**

res·er·va·tion (*rez*-ur-vay-shuhn)

1. *noun* An arrangement to save space or a seat for someone. *Do you have a reservation for this flight?*

2. *noun* An area of land set aside by the government for a special purpose, as in *a tribal reservation.*

3. *noun, plural* If you have **reservations** about something, you feel doubtful about it.

rescue helicopter

tail rotor

hydraulic rescue winch

radar scanner

winch operator

cabin door

rotor blade

horizontal stabilizer

rotor hub

engine under here

engine air intake duct

window

tail wheel

waterproof floor

footstep

crash-resistant fuel system

steel lifeline

winchman

stretcher

immersion suit

sponson

flotation bag (used for water landing)

exhaust

undercarriage

boat-shaped hull

dual pilot cockpit

landing lights

R

re·serve (ri-zurv)
1. *verb* To arrange for something to be kept for later use. *Harvey reserved a seat on the train.*
2. *verb* To save for a special purpose or later use. *Let's reserve our strength for the trip home.*
3. *verb* To keep for oneself. *The defendant reserves the right to remain silent.*
4. *noun* A protected place where animals can live and breed safely, as in *a nature reserve.*
5. reserves *noun, plural* The part of the armed forces that is kept ready to serve in an emergency.
▷ *verb* **reserving, reserved**

re·served (ri-zurvd) *adjective*
1. If a seat, table, or room is **reserved,** it is kept for someone to use later.
2. A **reserved** person behaves in a quiet, shy way and does not show his or her feelings much.

res·er·voir (rez-ur-*vwar* or rez-ur-*vor*) *noun* A natural or artificial holding area for storing a large amount of water.

res·i·dence (rez-uh-duhnss) *noun* The place where somebody lives.

res·i·dent (rez-uh-duhnt) *noun* Someone who lives in a particular place, as in *the residents of a community.*

res·i·den·tial (rez-i-den-shuhl) *adjective* To do with a neighborhood or an area where people live, as in *a residential section of the city.*

res·i·due (rez-uh-doo or rez-uh-dyoo) *noun*
1. What is left after something burns up or evaporates.
2. Anything that remains after the main part has been taken away.
▷ *adjective* **residual** (re-zid-yoo-uhl)

re·sign (ri-zine) *verb*
1. To give up a job, a position, or an office voluntarily. *The coach resigned so that he could spend more time with his family.*
2. If you **resign yourself** to something, you accept it without complaining or worrying about it. ▷ *adjective* **resigned**
▷ *verb* **resigning, resigned** ▷ *noun* **resignation** (rez-ig-**nay**-shuhn)

res·in (rez-in) *noun* A yellow or brown, sticky substance that oozes from pine, balsam, and other trees and plants. Resin is used to make varnishes, lacquers, plastics, glue, and rubber. *See* **mummy.**

re·sist (ri-zist) *verb*
1. To refuse to accept; to oppose. *Jessie resisted her mother's attempts to make her clean her room.*
2. To fight back. *The villagers resisted the advancing army.*
3. To stop yourself from doing something that you would like to do, as in *to resist temptation.*
▷ *verb* **resisting, resisted**

re·sis·tance (ri-ziss-tuhnss) *noun*
1. Fighting back. *Resistance is useless; you must surrender.*
2. The ability to fight off or overcome something. *He developed a sore throat because his resistance was low.*
3. A force that opposes the motion of an object. *We must consider air resistance in determining our speed.*
4. The ability of a substance or an electrical circuit to oppose an electrical current passing through it because the electricity is turned into heat.

res·o·lute (rez-uh-*loot*) *adjective* Someone who is **resolute** is strongly determined to do something.
▷ *adverb* **resolutely**

res·o·lu·tion (rez-uh-loo-shuhn) *noun*
1. A promise to yourself that you will try hard to do something, as in *New Year's resolutions.*
2. The state of being very determined. *She approached the difficult task with great resolution.*

re·solve (ri-zolv) *verb*
1. To decide that you will try hard to do something. *Shane resolved to find a part-time job.*
▷ *noun* **resolve**
2. To deal with a problem or difficulty successfully. *We resolved the problem.*
▷ *verb* **resolving, resolved**

res·o·nant (rez-uh-nuhnt) *adjective*
1. Having a full, deep sound. *The opera singer's voice is rich and resonant.*
2. Able to amplify sounds or make them last longer. *Guitars are made of resonant wood.*
▷ *noun* **resonance** ▷ *verb* **resonate**

re·sort (ri-zort)
1. *noun* A place where people go for rest and relaxation, as in *a ski resort.*
2. *verb* If you **resort to** something, you turn to it because you do not have any other choices. *When the child's pleas didn't work, he resorted to tears.* ▷ **resorting, resorted**
3. *noun* If you do something as **a last resort,** you do it because everything else has failed.

re·sound (ri-zound) *verb*
1. To be filled with sound. *The theater resounded with cheers when the actors took their bows.*
2. To make a long, loud, echoing sound. *The chorus of voices resounded through the auditorium.*
▷ *verb* **resounding, resounded**

re·source (ri-sorss or ree-sorss) *noun*
1. Something valuable or useful to a place or a person. *Fresh water is one of our great natural resources.*
2. Something that you can go to for help or support. *The library is a good resource for anyone doing a research report.*

re·source·ful (ri-**sorss**-fuhl or ri-**zorss**-fuhl)
adjective If you are **resourceful,** you are good at knowing what to do or where to get help in any situation.

re·spect (ri-**spekt**)
1. *verb* To admire and have a high opinion of someone. *In our family, children are taught to respect their elders.* ▷ **respecting, respected**
2. *noun* A feeling of admiration or consideration for someone that makes you take the person seriously.
3. *noun* A detail or particular part of something. *In many respects, Guy's plan is a good one.*
4. respects *noun, plural* Regards or greetings. *Please give my respects to your parents.*

re·spect·a·ble (ri-**spek**-tuh-buhl) *adjective*
1. If someone is **respectable,** he or she behaves honestly and decently.
2. Reasonably good. *Brian got a respectable grade.*
▷ *adverb* **respectably**

re·spect·ful (ri-**spekt**-fuhl) *adjective* Showing proper respect, consideration, or courtesy. *I am respectful of my elders.* ▷ *adverb* **respectfully**

re·spec·tive (ri-**spek**-tiv) *adjective* Belonging to or having to do with each one. *After getting off the school bus, they went to their respective homes.*
▷ *adverb* **respectively**

res·pi·ra·tion (*ress*-puh-**ray**-shuhn) *noun* The process of taking in oxygen and sending out carbon dioxide, beginning with breathing in and ending with breathing out. *The diagram shows the main organs used in respiration. Air is drawn into the lungs and travels to the alveoli, where oxygen from the air passes into the blood. Carbon dioxide from the blood passes into the alveoli and is breathed out.*
▷ *adjective* **respiratory** (*ress*-pi-ruh-*taw*-ree)

human respiration system

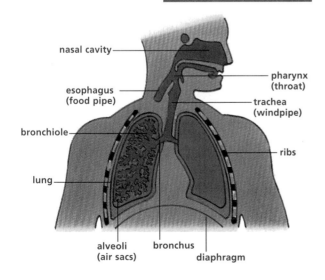

nasal cavity

esophagus
(food pipe)

bronchiole

lung

pharynx
(throat)

trachea
(windpipe)

ribs

alveoli
(air sacs)

bronchus

diaphragm

re·spond (ri-**spond**) *verb*
1. To reply or to give an answer. *Please respond to the invitation in writing.*
2. To react to something. *Nancy did not respond to her brother's taunts.*
▷ *verb* **responding, responded** ▷ *noun* **response**

re·spon·si·bil·i·ty (ri-*spon*-suh-**bil**-uh-tee) *noun*
1. A duty or a job. *It's my responsibility to provide food at the picnic.*
2. If you **take responsibility** for something bad that has happened, you agree that you are to blame for it.
▷ *noun, plural* **responsibilities**

re·spon·si·ble (ri-**spon**-suh-buhl) *adjective*
1. If someone is **responsible** for something, he or she has to do it, and it is the person's fault if it goes wrong.
2. If a person is **responsible,** he or she is sensible and can be trusted.
3. Being the cause. *Drunk driving is responsible for many accidents.*
4. Having or involving important duties, as in *a responsible job.*
▷ *adverb* **responsibly**

rest (rest)
1. *verb* To relax, or to sleep. *We rested after lunch.*
2. *noun* A stopping of work or some activity.
3. *noun* Sleep. *I need eight hours of rest at night.*
4. *noun* The others, or the remaining part of something. *I came in first and beat all the rest.*
5. *verb* To lean on something. *Rest your bicycles against the wall.*
6. *verb* To stop and stay in one place. *The spotlight rested on his face.*
7. *noun* The state or fact of not moving. *We came to a rest.*
8. *noun* A period of silence in a piece of music. *See* **notation.**
9. *verb* To finish presenting evidence in a court of law. *The prosecution rests.*
Rest sounds like **wrest.**
▷ *verb* **resting, rested**

res·tau·rant (**ress**-tuh-ruhnt or **ress**-tuh-*rahnt*) *noun* A place where people pay to eat meals.

rest·less (**rest**-liss) *adjective* If someone is **restless,** the person finds it hard to keep still or to concentrate on anything. ▷ *adverb* **restlessly**

re·store (ri-**stor**) *verb*
1. To bring back or to establish again. *The judge tried to restore order in the court after the spectators cheered the verdict.*
2. To bring back to an original condition. *Catherine restored the old table.* ▷ *noun* **restorer**
3. To give or bring something back. *Please restore the pen to its owner.*
▷ *verb* **restoring, restored** ▷ *noun* **restoration**

R

re·strain (ri-strayn) *verb*
1. To prevent someone from doing something. *We managed to restrain Jon from eating too much.*
2. To hold back. *Please restrain your temper.*
▷ *verb* **restraining, restrained** ▷ *noun* **restraint**

re·strained (ri-straynd) *adjective* If someone is **restrained,** the person is very quiet and controlled.

re·strict (ri-strikt) *verb* To confine or keep within limits. *Please restrict yourselves to one cookie each.* ▷ **restricting, restricted** ▷ *noun* **restriction** ▷ *adjective* **restricted**

rest room *noun* A bathroom, especially in a public building.

re·sult (ri-zuhlt)
1. *noun* Something that happens because of something else.
2. *verb* If one thing **results in** something else, it causes it. *His carelessness resulted in an accident.* ▷ **resulting, resulted**

re·sume (ri-zoom) *verb* To start doing something again after a break. *We will resume our discussion after lunch.* ▷ **resuming, resumed**

re·su·mé (re-zuh-may) *noun* A brief list of all the jobs, education, and awards a person has had.

re·sus·ci·tate (ri-suhss-uh-tate) *verb* To make conscious again, or to bring back from a near-death condition. *The doctor resuscitated the accident victim.* ▷ **resuscitating, resuscitated** ▷ *noun* **resuscitation**

re·tail (ree-tayl)
1. *adjective* To do with the sale of goods directly to customers, as in *a retail store.* ▷ *noun* **retail** ▷ *verb* **retail**
2. *noun* The **retail price** of goods is the price at which they are sold in stores.

re·tail·er (ree-tay-lur) *noun* Someone who sells goods to the public, usually in a store. *The retailer in this 1937 photograph by Berenice Abbott can be seen through the bakery window.*

retailers

re·tain (ri-tayn) *verb*
1. To keep something. *Please retain your receipt.*
2. To hold in or to contain. *Sponges retain water.* ▷ *noun* **retention**
3. If you **retain** a lawyer, you pay him or her a fee to represent you. ▷ *verb* **retaining, retained**

re·tal·i·ate (ri-tal-ee-ate) *verb* To do something unpleasant to someone because the person has done something unpleasant to you. *Gerald retaliated when Les punched him.* ▷ **retaliating, retaliated** ▷ *noun* **retaliation** ▷ *adjective* **retaliatory**

re·tard (ri-tard) *verb* To slow down. *The children's poor diet retarded their growth.* ▷ **retarding, retarded**

retarded *adjective* Slow in mental abilities. ▷ *noun* **retardation**

retch (rech) *verb* When you **retch,** you feel your throat and stomach move as if you are going to vomit. ▷ **retches, retching, retched** ▷ *noun* **retch**

ret·i·cent (ret-uh-suhnt) *adjective* If someone is **reticent,** he or she is unwilling to tell people what he or she knows, thinks, or feels. ▷ *noun* **reticence**

ret·i·na (ret-uhn-uh) *noun* The lining at the back of the eyeball. The retina is sensitive to light and sends images of the things you see to the brain. *See* **eye.**

re·tire (ri-tire) *verb*
1. To give up work, usually because of your age. *My grandfather retired when he was 67.* ▷ *noun* **retirement** ▷ *adjective* **retired**
2. To go to bed. *We retired at 10 P.M.*
3. To go to a private place. *The jury has retired to consider its verdict.*
4. To put out in baseball. *The pitcher retired the batter, and the game was over.* ▷ *verb* **retiring, retired**

retiring *adjective* Shy and reserved. *Chris has a retiring personality, but that doesn't keep him from making friends.*

re·tort
1. (ri-tort) *verb* To answer someone quickly or sharply. *When the children teased Dylan, he retorted by sticking out his tongue.* ▷ **retorting, retorted** ▷ *noun* **retort**
2. (ri-tort *or* ree-tort) *noun* A glass container with a round body and a long neck. Retorts are used in laboratories.

re·trace (ri-trayss) *verb* To go back over something. *I retraced my steps to look for the lost button.* ▷ **retracing, retraced**

re·treat (ri-treet)
1. *verb* To move back or withdraw from a difficult situation. *The enemy retreated into the woods.* ▷ **retreating, retreated** ▷ *noun* **retreat**
2. *noun* A quiet place where you can go to relax, to think, or to be alone.

R

re·trieve (ri-treev) *verb*
1. To get or bring something back. *Felicia retrieved her umbrella from the closet.*
2. To locate information in storage, especially by using a computer.
▷ *verb* **retrieving, retrieved** ▷ *noun* **retrieval**

re·triev·er (ri-**tree**-vur) *noun* Any of several popular breeds of large dogs. Retrievers can be trained to find and bring back game shot by hunters.

re·tro·rock·et (**ret**-roh-*rok*-it) *noun* A small rocket that fires out of the front of a spacecraft to slow it down or turn it.

ret·ro·vi·rus (**ret**-roh-*vye*-ruhss) *noun* Any of a group of viruses that contain RNA instead of the usual DNA. When retroviruses enter the cells of their hosts, they make copies of themselves and attach themselves permanently to the chromosomes of the cells that they attack.
▷ *noun, plural* **retroviruses**

re·turn (ri-**turn**)
1. *verb* To go back. *It's time to return home.*
2. *verb* To take or send something back. *Please return my book.*
3. *verb* To appear or happen again. *Autumn returns each year.*
4. *verb* To give back in the same way, as in *to return a compliment.*
5. *noun* The act of returning.
6. *noun* Money made as a profit. *The returns from the book fair were excellent.*
7. *noun* An official form, as in *a tax return.*
8. **in return** In exchange for something, or as a payment for something.
9. **return ticket** *noun* A ticket that allows you to travel to a place and back again.
▷ *verb* **returning, returned**

re·un·ion (ree-**yoon**-yuhn) *noun* A meeting between people who have not seen each other for a long time.

re·us·a·ble (ree-**yoo**-zuh-buhl) *adjective* If something is **reusable,** it can be used again rather than thrown away.

rev (rev)
1. *verb* (informal) To make an engine run quickly and noisily. *Mimi revved up the car's engine.*
▷ **revving, revved**
2. *noun* (informal) A revolution of an engine that is running. *Rev is short for revolutions per minute.*

re·veal (ri-**veel**) *verb*
1. To make known. *Carmen would not reveal the location of her secret hiding place.*
2. To show or bring into view. *The clouds parted to reveal a beautiful blue sky.*
▷ *verb* **revealing, revealed** ▷ *adjective* **revealing**

rev·el (**rev**-uhl) *verb* If you **revel in** something, you enjoy it very much. *Peter reveled in his work.*
▷ **reveling, reveled**

rev·e·la·tion (rev-uh-**lay**-shuhn) *noun* A very surprising fact that is made known. *It was a revelation to Janet that ducks can fly.*

re·venge (ri-**venj**) *noun* Action that you take to pay someone back for harm that the person has done to you or to someone you care about. *The widow swore to get revenge on her husband's killer.* ▷ *verb* **revenge**

rev·e·nue (**rev**-uh-*noo* or **rev**-uh-*nyoo*) *noun*
1. The money that a government gets from taxes and other sources.
2. The money that is made from property or other investments.

re·ver·ber·ate (ri-**vur**-buh-*rate*) *verb* To echo loudly and repeatedly. *The scream reverberated around the cave.* ▷ **reverberating, reverberated** ▷ *noun* **reverberation**

rev·er·ence (**rev**-ur-uhnss) *noun* Great respect and love. *Everyone expressed reverence for the retiring teacher.* ▷ *verb* **revere** (ri-**veer**) ▷ *adjective* **reverent** ▷ *adverb* **reverently**

re·verse (ri-**vurss**)
1. *verb* To turn something around, upside down, or inside out. *You can reverse this jacket.*
▷ *adjective* **reversible**
2. *noun* The opposite. *You may think this is fun, but it's quite the reverse.*
3. *adjective* Opposite in position, order, or direction. *The answers are on the reverse side of the page.*
4. *noun* The back or rear side of something, as in *the reverse of a record album.*
5. *verb* To transfer telephone fees to someone receiving the call. *Liz reversed the charges.*
6. *verb* To change to the opposite position. *The verdict was reversed by a higher court.*
7. *noun* A position of gears that allows a motor vehicle to move backward. *Stuart put the car in reverse and backed it into the garage.*
▷ *verb* **reversing, reversed** ▷ *adjective* **reversal**

re·vert (ri-**vurt**) *verb* To go back to the way things were. *Despite her resolutions, Gina soon reverted to her old habits.* ▷ **reverting, reverted** ▷ *noun* **reversion** (ri-**vur**-zhuhn)

re·view (ri-**vyoo**)
1. *noun* A piece of writing that gives an opinion about a new book, play, movie, etc. ▷ *noun* **reviewer** ▷ *verb* **review**
2. *verb* To study something carefully in order to see whether changes are necessary. *The budget will be reviewed each year.*
3. *verb* To study or go over again. *Yong reviewed her notes before the quiz.*
4. *verb* To make a formal inspection of. *The general reviewed the troops.*
▷ *verb* **reviewing, reviewed** ▷ *noun* **review**

447

re·vise (ri-vize) *verb*
1. To change and correct something, often to bring it up-to-date. *The new city guide has been thoroughly revised.*
2. To change or to make different. *I'm sure he'll revise his opinion when he hears the facts.*
▷ *verb* **revising, revised** ▷ *noun* **revision** (ri-**vi**-zhuhn)

re·vive (ri-vive) *verb*
1. To bring someone back to consciousness after he or she has been unconscious. *The doctor revived the patient.*
2. To bring something back into use. *We've revived a play from the 1950s.*
3. To give new strength or freshness to. *A good night's sleep revived the weary traveler.*
▷ *verb* **reviving, revived** ▷ *noun* **revival**

re·voke (ri-voke) *verb* To take away or to cancel. *His driver's license was revoked.* ▷ **revoking, revoked** ▷ *noun* **revocation** (re-vuh-**kay**-shuhn)

re·volt (ri-vohlt)
1. *verb* To fight against authority. *The people revolted against the dictator.*
2. *noun* A rebellion against a government or an authority.
3. *verb* If something **revolts** you, you find it horrible and disgusting.
▷ *verb* **revolting, revolted**

revolting *adjective* Disgusting, as in *a revolting smell.*

rev·o·lu·tion (rev-uh-**loo**-shuhn) *noun*
1. A violent uprising by the people of a country that changes its system of government.
2. A very large, important change. *The invention of the airplane caused a revolution in travel.*
3. Movement of one object around another. *It takes the earth about 365 days to make one revolution around the sun.*
▷ *adjective* **revolutionary**

Revolutionary War *noun* The war in which the 13 American colonies won their independence from Great Britain. The war lasted from 1775 to 1783 and is also known as the *American Revolution. This painting by John Trumbull shows the Battle of Bunker Hill, the first large battle of the war.*

Battle of Bunker Hill

rev·o·lu·tion·ize (rev-uh-**loo**-shuh-*nize*) *verb* To change something totally. *The introduction of the printing press revolutionized communication.*
▷ **revolutionizing, revolutionized**

re·volve (ri-volv) *verb*
1. To keep turning in a circle or orbit around a central point or object. *The moon revolves around the earth.*
2. To spin around or to rotate. *The car's wheels revolved slowly.*
3. revolve around To center or focus on. *Jack's life revolves around his family.*
▷ *verb* **revolving, revolved**

re·volv·er (ri-**vol**-vur) *noun* A small firearm that stores bullets in a cylinder and can fire several shots before it needs to be loaded again.

re·ward (ri-word) *noun* Something that you receive for doing something good or useful.
▷ *verb* **reward**

re·ward·ing (ri-**wor**-ding) *adjective* If something is **rewarding,** it gives you pleasure and satisfaction, as in *a rewarding job.*

re·word (ree-wurd) *verb* To say or write something using different words. *Erin reworded the sentence.* ▷ **rewording, reworded**

Reye's syndrome (rize *or* raze) *noun* A rare children's disease with symptoms of high fever, vomiting, and swelling of the liver and brain.

rheumatic fever *noun* A serious disease, especially in children, that causes fever, joint pain, and possible heart damage.

rheu·ma·tism (roo-muh-*tiz*-uhm) *noun* A disease that causes the joints and muscles to become swollen, stiff, and painful. ▷ *adjective* **rheumatic** (roo-ma-tik)

rhi·noc·er·os (rye-**noss**-ur-uhss) *noun* A large mammal from Africa and Asia and has thick skin and one or two large horns on its nose.

rhinoceros

▶ Word History
• •
Rhinoceros comes from a Greek word meaning "animal with a horn on its nose." It is based on *rhin,* "nose," and *keros,* "having a horn."

rho·do·den·dron (roh-duh-**den**-druhn) *noun* A large evergreen shrub with showy clusters of flowers that have a shape like a bell.

> ▶ **Word History**
> ●
> **Rhododendron** comes from two Greek words: *rhodon,* meaning "rose," and *dendron,* meaning "tree." The flowers of the rhododendron resemble roses.

rhom·bus (rom-buhss) *noun* A shape that has four straight sides of equal length but usually does not have right angles. *See* **shape.** ▷ *noun, plural* **rhombuses** *or* **rhombi** (rom-*bye*)

rhu·barb (roo-barb) *noun* A plant with long, red or green stems that can be cooked and eaten and leaves that are poisonous.

rhyme (rime)
1. *verb* If words **rhyme,** they end with the same sounds. The word *seat* rhymes with *beet* and *feet.* ▷ **rhyming, rhymed** ▷ *noun* **rhyme**
2. *noun* A short poem.

rhythm (riTH-uhm) *noun* A regular beat in music, poetry, or dance.

rhyth·mic (riTH-mik) *adjective* To do with or having a rhythm. *I love to sit on the beach and listen to the rhythmic sound of the waves.*
▷ *adjective* **rhythmical** ▷ *adverb* **rhythmically**

rib (rib) *noun*
1. One of the curved bones that enclose your chest and protect your heart and lungs. *See* **skeleton.**
2. Something that looks or functions like a rib, as in *the ribs of an umbrella.*

rib·bon (rib-uhn) *noun*
1. A long, thin band of material used for tying up hair or for decorating a present.
2. A long, thin band of material used for something other than decoration, as in *a typewriter ribbon.*

rice (risse) *noun*
The seeds of a tall grass that is grown in flooded fields. Rice is cooked and eaten. *The photograph shows people threshing rice in Bali, Indonesia. See also* **paddy.**

threshing rice

rich (rich) *adjective*
1. Someone who is **rich** has a lot of money and possessions.
2. If something is **rich** in a particular thing, it contains a lot of it. *Milk is rich in calcium.*
3. Food that is **rich** contains a lot of fat or sugar and makes you feel full very quickly.
4. Fertile, as in *rich soil.*
5. riches *noun, plural* Great wealth.
▷ *adjective* **richer, richest** ▷ *adverb* **richly**

rick·et·y (rik-uh-tee) *adjective* Old, weak, and likely to break. *The rickety gate was hanging on one hinge.*

rick·sha *or* **rick·shaw** (rik-*shaw*) *noun* A small carriage with two wheels and a cover that usually is pulled by one person. Rickshas originally were used in Asia.

ric·o·chet (rik-uh-*shay*) *verb* If a stone or bullet **ricochets,** it hits a wall or another hard surface and bounces off in a different direction.
▷ **ricocheting, ricocheted**

rid (rid)
1. *verb* To remove something that is unwanted. *I must rid my house of mice.* ▷ **ridding, rid**
2. If you **get rid of** something, you throw it away or otherwise remove it.
3. If you **get rid of** a cold, you overcome it.

rid·dle (rid-uhl) *noun* A question that seems to make no sense but that has a clever answer. For example: *What has four wheels and flies?* Answer: *A garbage truck.*

ride (ride)
1. *verb* To travel on an animal or in a vehicle.
▷ *noun* **rider**
2. *noun* A journey on an animal or in a vehicle.
3. *noun* A device or machine such as a merry-go-round that people ride for fun.
4. *verb* To be supported or carried along. *The surfers rode the waves.*
▷ *verb* **riding, rode** (rohd), **ridden** (rid-in)

ridge (rij) *noun*
1. A narrow raised strip on something. *Corduroy has ridges.*
2. A long, narrow chain of mountains or hills.
▷ *adjective* **ridged**

rid·i·cule (rid-uh-kyool) *verb* To make fun of someone or something. *Many people ridiculed the inventor's seemingly crazy new idea.*
▷ **ridiculing, ridiculed** ▷ *noun* **ridicule**

ri·dic·u·lous (ri-dik-yuh-luhss) *adjective* Extremely silly or foolish, as in *a ridiculous hat* or *a ridiculous idea.* ▷ *adverb* **ridiculously**

ri·fle (rye-fuhl)
1. *noun* A gun with a long barrel that is fired from the shoulder.
2. *verb* To search through and rob. *The burglar rifled the safe.* ▷ **rifling, rifled**

R

rig (rig)
1. verb To provide or to equip. *The car is rigged with an alarm.*
2. verb To equip a ship with the necessary masts, sails, ropes, etc.
3. noun The arrangement of masts, sails, ropes, etc., on a boat or ship.
4. noun A large structure on land or in the sea, used to drill for oil or gas under the ground. *See* **oil rig.**
5. noun A carriage led by a horse or horses that is used for moving people or goods.
6. noun A truck that has a small cab for the driver and a larger trailer in back, used for hauling commercial goods.
7. noun Equipment or gear used for a special purpose.
8. verb To control something dishonestly. *Natalie rigged the competition so that she came in first.*
9. verb If you **rig up** something, you make it quickly from whatever you can find.
▷ **verb** **rigging, rigged**

rigging **noun** The ropes and wires on a boat or ship that support and control the sails. *See* **junk.**

right (rite)
1. adjective On the side opposite the left. ▷ **noun** **right** ▷ **adverb** **right**
2. adjective Correct. *I got the right answers.*
3. adverb Correctly. *I did it right.*
4. adjective Good, fair, and acceptable. *It's not right to be cruel to animals.*
5. adjective Suitable. *He's just right for the job.*
6. adverb Exactly. *We managed to park right outside the movie theater.*
7. adverb Immediately. *We have to leave right now.*
8. adverb Toward the right. *Turn right at the light.*
9. adverb In a straight line. *Brenda walked right to the front of the line.*
10. noun Something that the law says you can have or do, as in *the right to vote.*
11. In politics, people **on the right** have conservative views.
Right sounds like **write.**
▷ **adverb** **rightly**

right angle **noun** An angle of 90 degrees, such as one of the angles of a square.

righ·teous (rye-chuhss) **adjective**
1. Someone who is **righteous** does not do anything that is bad or against the law. ▷ **noun** **righteousness** ▷ **adverb** **righteously**
2. With good reason. *When I saw the mess they had made, I was filled with righteous anger.*

right-hand·ed (hand-id) **adjective** If you are **right-handed,** you use your right hand more easily than your left hand. ▷ **noun** **right-hander**

right triangle **noun** A triangle that includes one right angle. *See* **shape.**

rig·id (rij-id) **adjective**
1. Stiff and difficult to bend. *The soldiers stood at rigid attention.*
2. Very strict and difficult to change, as in *a rigid rule.*
▷ **noun** **rigidity** ▷ **adverb** **rigidly**

rile (rile) **verb** To annoy or to irritate. *We really riled Mom when we knocked the lamp off the table.* ▷ **riling, riled** ▷ **adjective** **riled**

rim (rim) **noun** The outside or top edge of something. *The white bowl has a blue rim.*

rind (rinde) **noun** The tough outer layer on melons, citrus fruits, and some cheeses.

cantaloupe rind

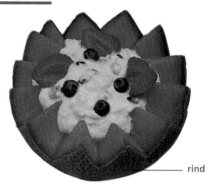

rind

ring (ring)
1. noun A circle. *Dance in a ring.*
2. verb To make or form a ring around. *Houses ringed the lake.*
3. noun A thin band worn on your finger as a piece of jewelry.
4. verb To make or cause to make a clear, musical sound. *The phone rang. I'll ring the doorbell.* ▷ **noun** **ring**
5. noun A telephone call. *Give me a ring soon.*
6. noun The area in which a boxing or wrestling match takes place.
7. noun A group of people working together for some unlawful purpose, as in *a smuggling ring.*
Ring sounds like **wring.**
▷ **verb** **ringing, rang** (rang), **rung** (ruhng)

ring·lead·er (ring-lee-dur) **noun** The leader of a group of people who commit crimes or do things that are wrong.

ring·let (ring-lit) **noun** A long, spiral curl of hair.

rink (ringk) **noun** An area with a specially prepared surface that is used for ice-skating, roller-skating, or hockey.

rinse (rinss)
1. verb To wash something in clean water without using any soap. *Rinse out your bathing suit.* ▷ **noun** **rinse**

R

2. verb To wash lightly. *Rinse the plates before you put them in the dishwasher.*
3. noun A special liquid that you can put on hair to color it slightly.
▷ *verb* **rinsing, rinsed**

ri·ot (rye-uht)
1. verb If people **riot,** they behave in a noisy, violent, and usually uncontrollable way.
▷ **rioting, rioted** ▷ *noun* **riot, noun rioter, noun rioting** ▷ *adjective* **riotous**
2. noun (informal) A person or thing that is extremely funny.

rip (rip) *verb*
1. To tear something. *Jeremy ripped his jacket on a nail.* ▷ *noun* **rip**
2. (slang) If someone **rips** you **off,** the person sells you a faulty product or charges you an unfair amount of money for something. ▷ *noun* **rip-off**
▷ *verb* **ripping, ripped**

ripe (ripe) *adjective* Ready to be harvested, picked, or eaten, as in *ripe fruit.* ▷ **riper, ripest**
▷ *noun* **ripeness** ▷ *verb* **ripen**

rip·ple (rip-uhl) *noun*
1. A very small wave on the surface of a lake, pond, etc.
2. Anything that looks like a ripple. *The ripples in the pavement came from years of heavy traffic.*
3. A small wave of sound, as in *a ripple of laughter.*
▷ *verb* **ripple**

rise (rize)
1. verb To go or move upward. *The balloon rose slowly into the air.*
2. verb To stand up. *The audience rose to its feet.*
3. verb To get out of bed. *Ruben rises at 7:00 every morning.*
4. verb To increase. *Prices have risen dramatically this year.* ▷ *noun* **rise**
5. verb To move up in position, rank, or importance. *She rose to the position of company president.*
6. verb To rebel. *The people rose up against the cruel tyrant.*
7. noun An upward slope, as in *the rise of a hill.*
8. noun The beginning of something. *The 18th century saw the rise of democracy in America.*
▷ *verb* **rising, rose (rohz), risen (riz-in)**

risk (risk)
1. noun The possibility of loss or harm; danger.
▷ *adjective* **risky**
2. verb To expose to risk. *Joel risked his life to save the kitten.*
3. verb To take the risk or chance of. *Don't risk being late.*
▷ *verb* **risking, risked**

rit·u·al (rich-oo-uhl) *noun*
1. A set of actions that is always performed in the same way as part of a religious ceremony or social custom. *A bar mitzvah is a Jewish ritual.*

2. An action or set of actions that you repeat often. *Eating a good breakfast is part of my morning ritual.*
▷ *adjective* **ritual** ▷ *adverb* **ritually**

ri·val (rye-vuhl)
1. noun Someone whom you are competing against. ▷ *noun* **rivalry** ▷ *adjective* **rival**
2. verb To be as good as something or someone else. *No team can rival us at ice hockey.*
▷ **rivaling, rivaled**

riv·er (riv-ur) *noun* A large natural stream of fresh water that flows into a lake or an ocean. *The picture shows how a river develops and changes as it flows from its source to its mouth.*

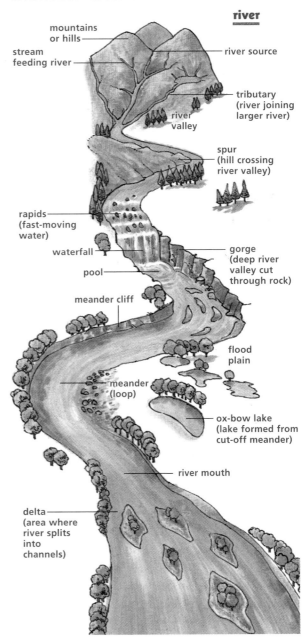

river

mountains or hills
stream feeding river
river source
tributary (river joining larger river)
river valley
spur (hill crossing river valley)
rapids (fast-moving water)
waterfall
pool
gorge (deep river valley cut through rock)
meander cliff
flood plain
meander (loop)
ox-bow lake (lake formed from cut-off meander)
river mouth
delta (area where river splits into channels)

R

riv·et (riv-it)

1. *noun* A strong metal bolt that is used to fasten pieces of metal together. ▷ *noun* **riveter** ▷ *verb* **rivet**

2. *verb* If you are **riveted** by something, you find it so interesting that you cannot stop watching it or listening to it. ▷ **riveting, riveted** ▷ *adjective* **riveting**

RNA (ar en ay) *noun* The complex molecule produced by living cells and viruses that is responsible for manufacturing the protein in a cell. RNA stands for *RiboNucleic Acid*.

road (rohd) *noun*

1. A wide path with a smooth surface on which vehicles and people travel.

2. The route or path a person takes to achieve a goal, as in *the road to success*.

Road sounds like **rode**.

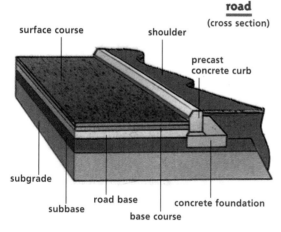

road
(cross section)

surface course
shoulder
precast concrete curb
subgrade
road base
subbase
base course
concrete foundation

road map *noun* A map for motorists that shows the streets and highways of an area.

road·run·ner (rohd-*ruhn*-ur) *noun* A small bird with brown-black feathers and a long tail found mainly in the southwestern United States. It gets around by running very fast instead of flying.

road·side (rohd-*side*) *noun* The area beside a road. ▷ *adjective* **roadside**

roam (rohm) *verb* To wander around without any particular purpose. *I roamed the streets until dark.* ▷ **roaming, roamed**

roar (ror) *verb*

1. To make a loud, deep noise. *The lion roared. The crowd roared.*

2. To laugh very loudly. *We roared at the joke.* ▷ *verb* **roaring, roared** ▷ *noun* **roar**

roast (rohst)

1. *verb* To cook meat or vegetables in a hot oven. *Jamal roasted a chicken.*

2. *noun* A piece of meat that has been cooked in a hot oven, as in *a rib roast*.

3. *adjective* Roasted. *Do you like roast beef?*

4. *verb* To be very hot. *We roasted in the sun.* ▷ *adjective* **roasting** ▷ *verb* **roasting, roasted** ▷ *adjective* **roasted**

rob (rob) *verb* To steal something from somebody. *The police caught the men who robbed the store.* ▷ **robbing, robbed** ▷ *noun* **robber**

rob·ber·y (rob-uh-ree) *noun* The act or crime of stealing money or goods. ▷ *noun, plural* **robberies**

robe (rohb) *noun*

1. A piece of clothing like a long, loose coat. *The judge wore a long, black robe.*

2. A bathrobe.

rob·in (rob-in) *noun* A songbird that has a reddish orange chest. *The American robin is almost twice as large as the European robin.*

European robin

American robin

ro·bot (roh-bot *or* roh-buht) *noun* A machine that is programmed to do jobs that are usually performed by a person. ▷ *adjective* **robotic**

> ### Word History
> The word **robot** comes from the Czech word *robota*, which means "forced labor" or "drudgery." Karel Capek coined the new meaning in his 1921 play called *R.U.R.* or *Rossum's Universal Robots*.

robotic arm

noun A mechanical arm that works like a human arm to control tools or to operate machines. *The arrows on this picture of a robotic arm show the six directions in which it can move. See also* **space shuttle, underwater.**

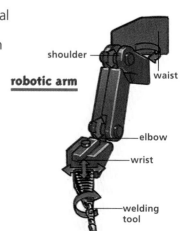

robotic arm

shoulder
waist
elbow
wrist
welding tool

ro·bot·ics (roh-**bot**-iks) *noun* The study of making and using robots.

ro·bust (roh-**buhst**) *adjective*
1. Strong and healthy, as in *a robust child*.
2. Powerfully built, as in *a robust athlete*.
3. Rich; strong in flavor, as in *robust coffee*.
▷ *adverb* **robustly**

rock (rok)
1. *noun* A large stone.
2. *noun* The very hard mineral matter that forms an important part of the earth's crust.
3. *verb* To move gently backward and forward or from side to side. *The mother rocked the baby's cradle.*
4. *verb* To shake or move violently. *The bomb blast rocked the building.*
5. *noun* Popular music with a very strong beat and a simple tune; rock 'n' roll. Also called *rock music.*
▷ *verb* **rocking, rocked**

rock climbing *noun* The sport of climbing steep rock faces, usually with the help of ropes and other equipment. *The picture shows a climber with various pieces of equipment that are used in rock climbing.*

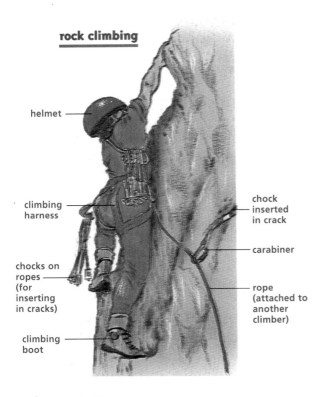

rock climbing

- helmet
- climbing harness
- chocks on ropes (for inserting in cracks)
- climbing boot
- chock inserted in crack
- carabiner
- rope (attached to another climber)

rock·et (rok-it)
1. *noun* A vehicle shaped like a long tube with a pointed end that can travel very fast. Rockets are used for space travel and for carrying missiles. See **space shuttle**.

2. *verb* To go up very quickly. *Housing prices rocketed last spring.* ▷ **rocketing, rocketed**

rocking chair *noun* A chair mounted on curved runners that allow the sitter to rock back and forth.

rocking horse *noun* A toy horse mounted on curved runners so that it can rock back and forth.

rock 'n' roll (rok-uhn-**rohl**) *noun* A kind of popular music with a strong beat and a simple tune. ▷ *adjective* **rock 'n' roll**

rod (rod) *noun*
1. A long, thin pole or stick.
2. A unit of length equal to $5\frac{1}{2}$ yards or $16\frac{1}{2}$ feet.

ro·dent (rohd-uhnt) *noun* A mammal with large, sharp front teeth that it uses for gnawing things. *Rats, beavers, and squirrels are all rodents.*

ro·de·o (roh-**dee**-oh *or* roh-**day**-oh) *noun* A contest in which cowboys and cowgirls compete at riding wild horses and bulls and catching cattle with lassos.

rodeo rider

Word History

Rodeo was first used to mean rounding up and counting cattle. It comes from the Spanish word *rodear*, which means "to surround." Only recently has rodeo come to mean an exhibition of roping and riding skills.

roe (roh) *noun* The eggs of a fish.

rogue (rohg) *noun*
1. A dishonest person.
2. A vicious and dangerous animal, especially an elephant, that lives apart from the herd.

role (rohl) *noun*
1. The part that a person acts in a play. *Julian played the role of Hamlet.*
2. The job or purpose of a person or thing. *Marcia's role is to supervise the workers.*
Role sounds like **roll**.

R

roll (rohl)
  1. *verb* To move along by turning over and over. *The ball rolled down the hill.*
  2. *verb* To make something into the shape of a ball or tube. *Charlie rolled the clay into balls.*
  3. *noun* Something that is in the shape of a tube, as in *a roll of film.*
  4. *verb* To flatten something by pushing a rounded object over it. *Roll out the pie dough.*
  5. *noun* A small, round piece of baked bread dough.
  6. *noun* A list of names. *Check the class roll.*
  7. *verb* To move in a side-to-side or up-and-down way. *The boat rolled in the waves.*
  8. *verb* To make a deep, loud sound. *The drums rolled.*
  9. *verb* (informal) To start. *Let's get rolling.*
  Roll sounds like **role.**
  ▷ *verb* **rolling, rolled** ▷ *noun* **roll**

roll·er (roh-lur) *noun*
  1. A cylinder or rod that has something rolled around it, such as a window shade.
  2. A cylinder that is used to spread, squeeze, smooth, or crush something, as in *a paint roller.*

roller coast·er (kohss-tur) *noun* An amusement park ride consisting of a train of cars that travels fast over a track that rises, falls, and curves.

roller-skating *noun* The sport of moving about on shoes or boots with wheels attached to them. ▷ *noun* **roller skate** ▷ *verb* **roller-skate**

rolling pin *noun* A cylinder, often made of wood, that is used to flatten out dough.

ROM (rom) *noun* Permanent computer memory that can be read but not changed. The initials ROM stand for *Read-Only Memory.*

Ro·man (roh-muhn)
  1. *noun* A person who lived in ancient Rome.
  2. *noun* A person who was born or is living in modern Rome, Italy.
  3. *adjective* To do with the people or culture of ancient or modern Rome.
  4. **roman** *noun* A style of type with upright letters. This sentence is printed in roman.

Roman Catholic
  1. *noun* A member of the Roman Catholic church.
  2. *adjective* To do with the Roman Catholic church and its beliefs, as in *a Roman Catholic service.*

Roman Catholic church *noun* A Christian church that has the pope as its leader.

ro·mance (roh-manss *or* roh-manss) *noun*
  1. An affectionate relationship between people who are in love.
  2. A poem or story about the loves and adventures of heroes and heroines.
  3. A quality of mystery, excitement, and adventure. *The faraway setting added to the novel's romance.*

Romance language *noun* One of a group of languages that developed from Latin. The Romance languages include Spanish, Italian, French, Portuguese, and Romanian.

Roman numerals *noun, plural* Letters used by the ancient Romans to represent numbers. Roman numerals are sometimes used today; for example, on some clocks.

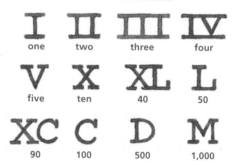

Roman numerals

I	II	III	IV
one	two	three	four
V	X	XL	L
five	ten	40	50
XC	C	D	M
90	100	500	1,000

ro·man·tic (roh-man-tik) *adjective*
  1. To do with love. *How romantic of Jeremy to send you roses!*
  2. Imaginative but not practical, as in *romantic ideas.*

romp (romp) *verb* To play in a noisy, carefree, and energetic way. *The boys love romping in the ocean.* ▷ **romping, romped** ▷ *noun* **romp**

roof (roof *or* ruf) *noun*
  1. The covering on the top of a house, building, or vehicle.
  2. The top part of something, as in *the roof of your mouth.*

roof rack *noun* A frame for carrying luggage, placed on top of a car.

rook (ruk)
  1. *noun* A chess piece, also known as a castle, that can move in straight lines but not diagonally across the board. *See* **chess.**
  2. *verb* (informal) To cheat someone. *The gambler rooked the others in a card game.* ▷ **rooking, rooked**

rook·ie (ruk-ee) *noun*
  1. Someone who has just joined a group and lacks experience and training, especially an inexperienced police officer.
  2. An athlete who is in his or her first season with a professional sports team.

room (room *or* rum)
  1. *noun* One of the separate parts of a house or building with its own doorway and walls.
  2. *noun* Enough space for something. *Is there room for us all to go in your car?*

3. *noun* An opportunity or a chance. *There's plenty of room for improvement in her work.*
4. *verb* To share a room or living space with one or more people. ▷ **rooming, roomed**

room·mate (room-*mate*) *noun* Someone who shares a room or living space with one or more people.

room·y (roo-mee) *adjective* Large, or having a lot of space. *The house looked small but it was quite roomy inside.* ▷ **roomier, roomiest**

roost (roost)
1. *noun* A place where birds rest or build nests.
2. *verb* When birds **roost,** they settle somewhere for the night. ▷ **roosting, roosted**

roost·er (roo-stur) *noun* A fully grown male chicken.

root (root *or* rut)
1. *noun* The part of a plant or tree that grows under the ground. *Water and dissolved foods are absorbed from the soil through root hairs and travel up the roots to the plant's stem through xylem and phloem vessels.*
2. *verb* To form roots. *I tried to plant a tree but it didn't root.*
3. *noun* A part that functions like a root or resembles one, as in *the root of a tooth.*
4. *noun* The source, origin, or cause of something. *Let's get to the root of the problem.*
5. *noun* A word to which a prefix or suffix is added to make another word. *Hungry* is the root of *hungriest.*
6. *verb* To cheer. *I rooted for my sister's team.*
7. *noun, plural* Your **roots** are where your family comes from or where you grew up. Many Americans have their roots in Europe, Africa, or Asia.
▷ *verb* **rooting, rooted**

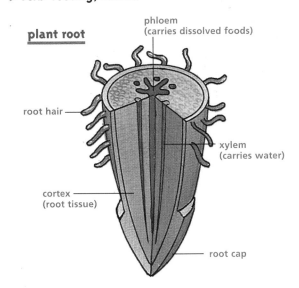

plant root

phloem (carries dissolved foods)

root hair

xylem (carries water)

cortex (root tissue)

root cap

root canal *noun*
1. A groove in a tooth's root through which the nerve passes.
2. A dental procedure to replace the pulp in a tooth's root with another substance in order to save the tooth.

rope (rohp)
1. *noun* A strong, thick cord made from twisted or woven fibers.
2. *verb* To fasten with a cord. *Heather roped the cartons together.*
3. *verb* To catch with a lasso or rope. *The cowhand roped the steer.*
4. *verb* To separate an area or object with ropes. *The police roped off the scene of the crime before they started their investigation.*
▷ *verb* **roping, roped**

rose (roze) *noun*
1. A garden flower that usually has a sweet smell and grows on a bush with thorns. Roses may be red, pink, yellow, or white.
2. A light pink color. ▷ *adjective* **rose**

rose·bud (roze-*buhd*) *noun* The bud from which the rose flower blooms.

Rosh Ha·sha·na (rohsh huh-shah-nuh) *noun* The Jewish New Year, occurring in September or October.

ros·y (roh-zee) *adjective*
1. Pink, as in *rosy cheeks.*
2. Hopeful, as in *a rosy future.*
▷ *adjective* **rosier, rosiest**

rot (rot) *verb* To make or become rotten; to decay. *Damp air rotted the magazines in the basement. Fruit rots if it is not refrigerated.*
▷ **rotting, rotted** ▷ *noun* **rot**

ro·ta·ry (roh-tuh-ree) *adjective* Having a part or parts that turn around and around or rotate, as in *a rotary telephone dial* or *a rotary engine.*

ro·tate (roh-tate) *verb*
1. To turn around and around like a wheel. *The earth rotates on its axis once a day.*
2. To take turns doing or using things in a fixed order that is repeated. *The teacher rotates the classroom jobs. Farmers rotate their crops.*
▷ *verb* **rotating, rotated** ▷ *noun* **rotation**
▷ *adjective* **rotational**

ro·ta·tor cuff (roh-tay-tur *or* roh-**tay**-tur) *noun* The muscles and tendons that attach the upper arm to the shoulder and allow the arm to rotate in the socket.

ro·tor (roh-tur) *noun*
1. The part of an engine or other machine that turns or rotates.
2. The blades of a helicopter that turn and lift the helicopter into the air. *See* **helicopter.**

rot·ten (rot-uhn) *adjective*
1. Food that is **rotten** has gone bad or started to decay from the action of bacteria or fungi.
2. Wood that is **rotten** is weak and likely to crack, break, or give way.
3. *(informal)* Very bad or unpleasant, as in *a rotten trick* or *rotten weather*.

Rott·wei·ler (rot-wye-lur) *noun* One of a breed of powerful black and brown dogs with short hair and a short tail, often used as guard dogs.

rouge (roozh) *noun* Red or pink makeup put on the cheeks to make them look less pale.

rough (ruhf)
1. *adjective* A **rough** surface is not smooth but has dents or bumps in it.
2. *adjective* Someone who is **rough** is not gentle or polite and may fight with people or use violence.
3. *adjective (informal)* Difficult and unpleasant. *Martha had a rough time at her last job.*
4. *adjective* Vague or not exact. *I've got a rough idea of where Ray lives.*
5. *adjective* **Rough** work is work that you do as preparation for the final piece, as in *a rough sketch.*
6. *verb (informal)* If you **rough it,** you manage without the usual comforts of home. ▷ **roughing, roughed**
Rough sounds like **ruff.**
▷ *adjective* **rougher, roughest** ▷ *adverb* **roughly**

rough·age (ruhf-ij) *noun* The fiber found in cereals, vegetables, and other foods, which passes through the body but is not digested. Roughage helps food move through the intestines.

round (round)
1. *adjective* Shaped like a circle or a ball.
2. *adjective* Having a curved surface or outline. *The table had round corners.*
3. *noun* Something round in shape. *We cut the carrot into rounds.*
4. rounds *noun, plural* A regular route or course of action followed by a mail carrier, doctor, guard, etc.
5. *noun* A long burst, as in *a round of applause.*
6. *noun* A series of repeated actions or events, as in *the latest round of talks.*
7. *noun* A period of play in a sport or contest. *The boxer was knocked out in the third round.*
8. *noun* A complete game, as in *a round of golf.*
9. *noun* A simple song in which people start singing one after another so that they are singing different parts of the song at the same time.
10. *noun* One shot fired by a weapon or by each person in a military unit.
11. *verb* To make or become round. *I used sandpaper to round the corners of the table.*
12. *verb* To go around. *The bus rounded the corner.*
13. *preposition* Around. *The hikers gathered round the campfire.*
14. *adverb* Around. *The ballerina spun round and round.*
15. round off *verb* To make into a round number. *I rounded off 33.7 to 34.*
16. round up *verb* To gather together. *I rounded up the children for lunch.*
▷ *verb* **rounding, rounded** ▷ *adjective* **rounder, roundest,** *adjective* **rounded**

round·a·bout (round-uh-*bout*) *adjective* Indirect in travel, thought, or conversation. *He told me the truth in a roundabout way.*

round·house (round-*houss*) *noun* A circular building with a large turntable in the center, used for storing, repairing, and switching locomotive engines.

round number *noun* A number rounded off to the nearest whole number or to the nearest ten, hundred, thousand, etc. Rounding off 158 to the nearest ten gives you a round number of 160. Rounding off 158 to the nearest hundred gives you a round number of 200.

round trip *noun* A trip to a place and back again. *The round trip from my house to your house and back to my house again takes an hour.*

round·up (round-*uhp*) *noun*
1. The gathering together of cattle for branding or shipping to market.
2. A gathering together of people, things, or facts, as in *a news roundup.*

cattle roundup

rouse (rouz) *verb*
1. To wake someone up. *The alarm roused Bill.*
2. To make someone feel interested or excited. *His fiery speech roused the crowd.* ▷ *adjective* **rousing**
▷ *verb* **rousing, roused**

R

rout (rout)
1. *noun* A complete or overwhelming defeat.
2. *verb* To defeat or beat totally. *Our team routed their team by a score of 20–2.*
3. *verb* To drive or force out. *The fighting routed the civilians from their homes.*
▷ *verb* **routing, routed**

route (root *or* rout) *noun*
1. The road or course that you follow to get from one place to another.
2. A series of places or customers visited regularly by a person who delivers or sells something, as in *a newspaper route.*

rou·tine (roo-teen)
1. *noun* A regular way or pattern of doing things. *Taking out the garbage is part of my daily routine.*
2. *adjective* Something that is **routine** is normal and not at all difficult or unusual, as in *routine chores* or *a routine checkup.*

row
1. (roh) *noun* A line of people or things side by side, as in *a row of chairs.*
2. (roh) *verb* To use oars in order to move a boat through water. ▷ **rowing, rowed** ▷ *noun* **rower**
3. (roh) *noun* A trip made by rowboat.
4. (rou) *noun* A noisy fight or quarrel.

row·boat (roh-*boht*) *noun* A small boat that is moved through the water by using oars.

row·dy (rou-dee) *adjective* Wild and noisy. *Don't play such rowdy games.* ▷ **rowdier, rowdiest** ▷ *noun* **rowdiness** ▷ *adverb* **rowdily**

roy·al (roi-uhl) *adjective*
1. To do with or belonging to a king or queen or a member of his or her family. *The royal jewels are priceless.* ▷ *noun* **royalty**
2. Magnificent or fit for a king or queen, as in *a royal welcome.*

RSVP (ar ess vee pee) The initials of the French phrase *Répondez S'il Vous Plaît,* which means "please reply." RSVP is often written at the bottom of an invitation.

rub (ruhb) *verb*
1. To press one thing against another and move one or both backward and forward. *Josefina rubbed her hands in delight.*
2. To put or spread on by using pressure. *Rub some sunscreen on your arms and legs.*
3. To clean, polish, or make smooth by pressing something against a surface and moving it back and forth. *I rubbed the table with a damp sponge.* ▷ *noun* **rub**
4. *(informal)* If you **rub it in,** you keep telling someone about his or her mistakes. ▷ *verb* **rubbing, rubbed**

rub·ber (ruhb-ur)
noun
1. A substance made from the milky sap of a rubber tree or produced artificially. Rubber is strong, elastic, and waterproof and is used for making tires, balls, boots, etc. *The picture shows liquid rubber, or latex, being collected.*
2. rubbers *noun, plural* Low boots that protect shoes from water.

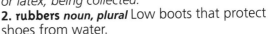
rubber tapping
area of removed bark
diagonal cut
trunk of rubber tree
funnel
latex (rubber particles in liquid)
cup

rubber band *noun* A loop of thin rubber that can be stretched and used to hold things together.

rubber stamp
1. *noun* A stamp with a rubber end. Raised letters or a design in the rubber can be inked to print something over and over.
2. rubber-stamp *verb* *(informal)* To approve or vote for without question.

rub·bish (ruhb-ish) *noun*
1. Things that you throw away because they are not useful or valuable.
2. Nonsense. *Don't talk rubbish.*

rub·ble (ruhb-uhl) *noun* Broken bricks and stones. *All that was left of their house was a pile of rubble.*

ru·ble (roo-buhl) *noun* The main unit of money in Russia and some of the other countries formed from the Soviet Union in 1989.

ru·by (roo-bee) *noun*
1. A dark red precious stone. ▷ *noun, plural* **rubies**
2. A dark red color.
▷ *adjective* **ruby**

rud·der (ruhd-ur) *noun* A hinged wood or metal plate attached to the back of a boat, ship, or airplane. A rudder is used for steering. *See* **aircraft, dinghy, ship.**

rude (rood) *adjective*
1. Not polite, as in *rude behavior* or *a rude answer.* ▷ *noun* **rudeness**
2. Roughly or crudely made. *In some countries, farmers still use rude wooden plows.*
▷ *adjective* **ruder, rudest** ▷ *adverb* **rudely**

ruff (ruhf) *noun*
1. A tall, pleated collar formerly worn by men and women.
2. A collar of feathers or hair on certain birds or animals.
Ruff sounds like **rough.**

ruf·fi·an (ruhf-ee-uhn) *noun* A rough or violent person.

457

ruf·fle (ruhf-uhl)
1. *verb* To disturb something that was smooth so that it becomes uneven or messy. *The breeze ruffled the water. She ruffled his hair.*
2. *verb* To make someone feel annoyed, worried, or unsettled. *That last question really ruffled the speaker.*
3. *noun* A strip of gathered material such as lace or ribbon used as a decoration or trimming.
▷ *verb* **ruffling, ruffled**

rug (ruhg) *noun* A thick mat made from wool or other fibers that is used to cover part of a floor.

rug·by (ruhg-bee) *noun* A form of football played by two teams that kick, pass, or carry an oval ball.

rug·ged (ruhg-id) *adjective*
1. Rough and uneven, or having a jagged outline, as in *rugged mountain peaks.*
2. Tough and strong. *You need a rugged vehicle to make it over those mountains.*
3. Harsh or difficult. *Settlers of the frontier led a very rugged life.*

ru·in (roo-in)
1. *verb* To spoil or destroy something completely. *The storm ruined our picnic.*
2. *noun* The destruction of something.
3. *verb* To make someone lose all of his or her money. *Jeff was almost ruined by the legal costs of the case.*
4. *noun* Loss of wealth or social position.
5. **ruins** *noun, plural* The remains of something that has collapsed or been destroyed. *The picture shows the ruins of a Roman theater in Alexandria, Egypt.*
▷ *verb* **ruining, ruined**

ruins

rule (rool)
1. *noun* An official instruction that tells you what you must or must not do.
2. *verb* To govern or have power and authority over something, usually a country.
3. *noun* Control, or government. *The people were unhappy under the rule of the dictator.*
4. *verb* To make an official decision or judgment. *The judge ruled that the father should be allowed to see his children.* ▷ *noun* **ruling**
5. *noun* Something that is usually done. *Jeans and sneakers are the rule among the kids in my town.*

6. *verb* If you do something **as a rule,** you usually do it.
7. *verb* If you **rule** something **out,** you decide that it is not possible or not wanted.
▷ *verb* **ruling, ruled**

rul·er (roo-lur) *noun*
1. A long, flat piece of wood, plastic, or metal that you use for measuring and drawing straight lines.
2. Someone who rules a country.

rum (ruhm) *noun* A strong alcoholic drink made from sugarcane.

rum·ble (ruhm-buhl) *verb* To make a low, rolling noise like the sound of thunder. ▷ **rumbling, rumbled** ▷ *noun* **rumble**

rum·mage (ruhm-ij) *verb* To look for something by moving things around in an untidy or careless way. *Ned rummaged in his backpack for candy.*
▷ **rummaging, rummaged**

ru·mor (roo-mur) *noun* Something said by many people although it may not be true. ▷ *verb* **rumor** ▷ *adjective* **rumored**

rump (ruhmp) *noun* The back part of an animal, above its hind legs.

rum·ple (ruhm-puhl) *verb* To wrinkle or to crease.
▷ **rumpling, rumpled** ▷ *adjective* **rumpled**

run (ruhn)
1. *verb* To move along quickly using your legs.
2. *noun* The act of running, as in *to take a run.*
3. *noun* A pace of running. *We broke into a run.*
4. *verb* To function or to work. *Most heavy trucks run on diesel fuel.*
5. *verb* To be in charge of something. *Olivia runs a small business.*
6. *verb* To travel a regular route. *A bus runs to the city every morning.*
7. *verb* To take part in an election. *Alonzo is running for class president.*
8. *verb* To continue. *The fair runs for one week.*
9. *verb* To flow in a steady stream. *Melted wax ran down the candle.*
10. *verb* To do something as if by running. *I have to run some errands.*
11. *verb* To operate a computer program. *Can you run that program again?*
12. *noun* A small enclosure for animals, as in *a dog run.*
13. *noun* Freedom to move about or use something. *Our dog has the run of the yard.*
14. *noun* A series of actions that continue to happen. *The team had a run of eight losses.*
15. *noun* A length of torn stitches. *I have a run in my stocking.* ▷ *verb* **run**
16. *noun* In baseball, a score made by touching home plate after touching all three bases.
17. *verb* If you **run away,** you escape from a place or leave it secretly.
18. *verb* If you have **run out of** something, you have used it all and have none left.

19. *verb* If you **run into** or **run across** someone or something, you meet the person or find the thing by chance.
▷ *verb* **running, ran (ran), run**

> **Synonyms: run**
>
> **Run** means to move along steadily with springing steps at a speed faster than a walk: *Rob can walk a mile in 20 minutes, but he can run a mile in 8 minutes.*
>
> **Jog** means to run at a slow but steady pace: *My dog loves to prance around me as I jog.*
>
> **Trot** means to go at a pace between a walk and a run. It is used mainly to describe the gait of horses: *The winning horse trotted around the track for a victory lap.*
>
> **Dash** means to move with sudden speed: *When the rain began, we dashed into the nearest store.*
>
> **Race** means to run with great speed: *The nurse raced over to help the man who had collapsed.*
>
> **Sprint** means to run at top speed for a short distance: *Toward the end of the one-mile race, the runners put on a burst of speed and sprinted across the finish line.*

run·a·way (ruhn-uh-*way*)
  1. *noun* A child who has run away from home.
  2. *adjective* Out of control, as in *a runaway train.*
  3. *adjective* Very easy, as in *a runaway victory.*
run-down *adjective*
  1. Old and in need of repair. *The run-down house was not a safe place for anyone to live.*
  2. Tired or weak. *Whenever I feel run-down, I catch a cold.*
rung (ruhng) *noun* One of the horizontal bars on a ladder. **Rung** sounds like **wrung.**
run·ner (ruhn-ur) *noun*
  1. Someone who runs in a race.
  2. The long, narrow part of an object that enables it to move or slide, as the blade on an ice skate or a sled.
  3. A long, narrow carpet, often used on stairs.
runner-up *noun* The person or team that comes in second in a race or competition. ▷ *noun, plural* **runners-up**
running mate *noun* A person who runs for public office on another candidate's ticket. *The person running for vice president is the presidential candidate's running mate.*
run·ny (ruhn-ee) *adjective*
  1. If something is **runny,** it flows or moves like a liquid, as in *runny custard.*

2. If you have a **runny** nose, it tends to drip mucus. ▷ *adjective* **runnier, runniest**
run·way (ruhn-*way*) *noun* A strip of level land that aircraft use for taking off and landing.
rup·ture (ruhp-chur) *verb* To break open or to burst. *His appendix ruptured. The steam pipe ruptured.* ▷ **rupturing, ruptured** ▷ *noun* **rupture**
ru·ral (rur-uhl) *adjective* To do with the countryside or farming, as in *a rural area* or *a rural economy.*
ruse (rooz) *noun* A clever trick meant to confuse or mislead someone. *The magician's story was just a ruse to keep everyone's attention away from what he was really doing.*
rush (ruhsh)
  1. *verb* To go somewhere quickly, or to do something quickly. ▷ **rushes, rushing, rushed**
  2. *noun* The act of rushing.
  3. *noun* A sudden burst of speed or activity. *We were in a rush to get home.*
  4. *adjective* Requiring or done with speed or urgency. *I placed a rush order for a present for my parents' anniversary.*
  5. rushes *noun, plural* Tall plants with hollow stems that grow in damp places. ▷ *noun, plural* **rushes**
rust (ruhst)
  1. *noun* The reddish brown substance that can form on iron and steel when they are exposed to moisture and air. ▷ *adjective* **rusty**
  2. *noun* A reddish brown color.
  3. *verb* To become covered with rust. *The door hinges have rusted.* ▷ **rusting, rusted**
  4. *noun* Red or brown disease spots on plants, caused by a fungus.
rus·tic (ruhss-tik) *adjective* To do with the country. *He built a rustic cabin in the woods.*
rus·tle (ruhss-uhl) *verb*
  1. When leaves, papers, etc., **rustle,** they make a soft, crackling sound as they move together gently. ▷ *noun* **rustle**
  2. To steal horses or cattle. ▷ *noun* **rustler,** *noun* **rustling**
  3. *(informal)* If you **rustle up** something, you make or provide it quickly. *José rustled up some food.* ▷ *verb* **rustling, rustled**
rut (ruht) *noun*
  1. A deep, narrow track made in the ground by wheels or by continuous use.
  2. If someone is **in a rut,** he or she keeps doing things in the same dull, boring way.
ruth·less (rooth-liss) *adjective* Someone who is **ruthless** is cruel and has no pity. ▷ *noun* **ruthlessness** ▷ *adverb* **ruthlessly**
rye (rye) *noun*
  1. A cereal grass grown and used to make flour and whiskey.
  2. A dark brown bread made from rye flour.

R

Ss

Spelling Hint: Some words that begin with a *sye* sound are spelled *ci, cy, psy,* or *sci.* Examples: cider, cite, cyberspace, cyclone, psychic, psychology, science, scientist.

Sab·bath (sab-uhth) *noun* The day of rest and worship in some religions. The Jewish Sabbath is from sundown Friday to sundown Saturday, while for most Christians the Sabbath is Sunday.

sa·ber (say-bur) *noun* A heavy sword with a curved blade and one cutting edge.

saber-toothed tiger (tootht) A prehistoric animal related to the lion and tiger that had long, curved teeth in its upper jaw.

saber-toothed tiger

sa·ble (say-buhl) *noun*
1. A small animal that looks like a weasel. Sable are found in northern Europe and northern Asia. Their soft, brown fur is very valuable. ▷ *noun, plural* **sable** or **sables**
2. The color of a sable, either black or dark brown. ▷ *adjective* **sable**

sab·o·tage (sab-uh-*tahzh*) *noun* The deliberate damage or destruction of property, or an act that interferes with work or another activity. *Enemy agents use sabotage to stop or slow down a nation's war efforts.* ▷ *verb* **sabotage**

sab·o·teur (*sab*-uh-tur) *noun* A person who deliberately damages or destroys property in order to hinder the enemy's war efforts.

sac (sak) *noun* An animal or plant part that is shaped like a bag or pouch. It often contains a liquid. **Sac** sounds like **sack.**

sac·cha·rin (sak-uh-rin *or* sak-rin) *noun* A very sweet artificial compound with no calories that is used instead of sugar to sweeten food.

sac·cha·rine (sak-uh-rin) *adjective*
1. Overly or sickeningly sweet. *My mother doesn't enjoy watching those sorts of saccharine movies.*
2. To do with or related to sugar.

sack (sak)
1. *noun* A large bag that is made of strong material and is used for storing or carrying potatoes, flour, etc.
2. *verb* If an employer **sacks** someone, the employer fires the person from a job.
3. *verb* To steal things from a place that has been captured in a war or battle. Sack is another word for **loot** or **plunder.**
Sack sounds like **sac.**
▷ *verb* **sacking, sacked**

sa·cred (say-krid) *adjective*
1. Holy, or to do with religion, as in *sacred music* or *sacred ground.*
2. Very important and deserving great respect, as in *a sacred promise.*

sac·ri·fice (sak-ruh-fisse)
1. *verb* To give up something important or enjoyable for a good reason. *I sacrificed my free time to help my brother with his homework.*
▷ **sacrificing, sacrificed** ▷ *noun* **sacrifice**
2. *noun* The offering of something to God or a god. ▷ *adjective* **sacrificial**
3. *noun* In baseball, a **sacrifice hit** is a bunt that advances a base runner but results in the batter being put out.
4. *noun* In baseball, a **sacrifice fly** is a fly ball to the outfield that is caught but still allows a base runner to advance.
▷ *verb* **sacrifice**

sac·ri·lege (sak-ruh-lij) *noun* An action that shows disrespect for something holy or very important.
▷ *adjective* **sacrilegious** (*sak*-ruh-lij-uhss) ▷ *adverb* **sacreligiously**

sad (sad) *adjective*
1. Unhappy or sorrowful. ▷ *noun* **sadness** ▷ *verb* **sadden** ▷ *adverb* **sadly**
2. Something that is **sad** makes you feel unhappy, as in *sad news* or *a sad sight.*
▷ *adjective* **sadder, saddest**

sad·dle (sad-uhl)
1. *noun* A leather seat for a rider on the back of a horse. See **tack.** ▷ *verb* **saddle**
2. *noun* A seat on a bicycle or motorcycle.
3. *verb* If someone **saddles** you with an unpleasant job or responsibility, the person leaves you to deal with it. ▷ **saddling, saddled**

sa·fa·ri (suh-fah-ree) *noun* A trip taken, especially in Africa, to see or hunt large wild animals.

> ### Word History
> **Safari** comes from the Arabic word *safara*, meaning "travel." Although safaris at one time were hunting expeditions into the African jungle, today they are often sightseeing trips, as the original word implies.

safe (sayf)
1. *adjective* If something is **safe**, it is not in danger of being harmed or stolen. ▷ *noun* **safety** ▷ *adverb* **safely**
2. *adjective* Not dangerous or not risky. *Is this ladder safe?*
3. *adjective* Careful. *My dad is a safe driver.*
4. *adjective* In baseball, a hitter is **safe** if he or she reaches a base without being tagged by an opposing player or called out by the umpire.
5. *noun* A strong box in which you can lock away money or valuables.
▷ *adjective* **safer, safest**

safe·guard (sayf-*gard*)
1. *verb* To protect someone or something. *A vaccination will safeguard you against smallpox.*
▷ **safeguarding, safeguarded**
2. *noun* Something that protects. *Following a healthy diet is a safeguard against disease.*

safety belt *noun*
1. A belt or harness that fastens a person who works at great heights to a fixed object. Safety belts prevent falls. *People who build skyscrapers wear safety belts.*
2. Another word for **seat belt**.

safety pin *noun* A pin that is bent into the shape of a clasp. It has a guard at one end that covers and holds the point. *See* **pin.**

sag (sag) *verb*
1. To hang or sink downward. *The bed sagged in the middle.*
2. To lose strength. *His spirits sagged after he failed the test.*
▷ *verb* **sagging, sagged**

sage (sayj)
1. *noun* An herb with leaves that are often used in cooking. *See* **herb.**
2. *adjective* Wise, as in *sage advice.*
3. *noun* A very wise person.

sage·brush (sayj-bruhsh) *noun* A shrub that grows on the dry plains of the western United States. Sagebrush has silver-green leaves and large clusters of yellow or white flowers.

sail (sayl)
1. *noun* A large sheet of strong cloth such as canvas that makes a boat or ship move when it catches the wind. *The picture shows the main parts of the sails on a sailing dinghy. See also* **ship.**
2. *verb* To travel in a boat or ship. ▷ *noun* **sailing**
3. *verb* When a boat or ship **sails**, it starts out on a voyage.
4. *verb* To glide or move smoothly. *The kite sailed across the sky.*
5. *noun* An arm of a windmill. *See* **windmill.**
Sail sounds like **sale.**
▷ *verb* **sailing, sailed**

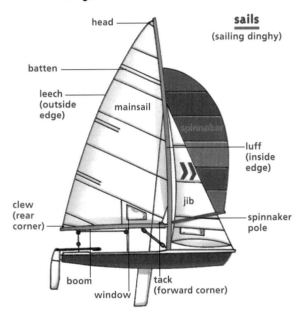

sails
(sailing dinghy)

head
batten
leech (outside edge)
mainsail
spinnaker
luff (inside edge)
jib
clew (rear corner)
spinnaker pole
boom
window
tack (forward corner)

sail·board (sayl-*bord*) *noun* A flat board with a mast and sail fixed to it, used for windsurfing. *See* **windsurfing.**

sail·boat (sayl-*boht*) *noun* A boat that is moved through the water by the wind blowing against its sail or sails.

sail·or (say-lur) *noun*
1. Someone who works on a ship as a member of the crew.
2. A member of a country's navy.

saint (saynt) *noun*
1. A man or woman honored by the Christian church because of his or her very holy life. The short form of *Saint* is *St.* The picture shows a painting of Saint Peter from a 13th-century manuscript.
2. A very kind and patient person. ▷ *adjective* **saintly,** *adjective* **sainted**

Saint Peter

Saint Ber·nard (bur-**nard**) *noun* A large, powerful dog with a big head and fur that is white and reddish brown. The Saint Bernard was originally used to locate lost travelers in the snowy mountains of Switzerland.

sake (sayk) *noun*
1. A benefit or an advantage. *The family moved to a new house for the sake of the children.*
2. A reason or a purpose. *I added many details to the story for the sake of being realistic.*

sal·ad (**sal**-uhd) *noun*
1. A mixture of raw vegetables usually served with a dressing.
2. A mixture of cold foods, as in *a fruit salad.*

sal·a·man·der (**sal**-uh-*man*-dur) *noun* An animal that looks like a small lizard. Salamanders are amphibians. They live in or near fresh water and have smooth, moist skin.

salamander

sal·a·ry (**sal**-uh-ree) *noun* The fixed amount of money someone is paid for his or her work.
▷ *noun, plural* **salaries** ▷ *adjective* **salaried**

sale (sayl) *noun*
1. The act of selling something. *The salesperson lowered the price to make the sale.*
2. A period of time when items are sold at lower-than-usual prices.
3. sales *noun, plural* The number or amount of things sold. *Sales were high in June.*
4. for sale Available for people to buy.
5. on sale For sale at reduced prices.
Sale sounds like **sail.**

sales·man (**saylz**-muhn) *noun* A man who sells goods or services. ▷ *noun, plural* **salesmen**

sales·per·son (**saylz**-*pur*-suhn) *noun* A man or woman who sells goods or services. ▷ *noun, plural* **salespeople**

sales·wom·an (**saylz**-*wum*-uhn) *noun* A woman who sells goods or services. ▷ *noun, plural* **saleswomen**

sa·lin·i·ty (suh-**lin**-uh-tee) *noun* Saltiness, or the amount of salt in something. *We measured the salinity of the water to see if it was safe to drink.*
▷ *adjective* **saline** (**say**-leen *or* **say**-line)

sa·li·va (suh-**lye**-vuh) *noun* The clear liquid in your mouth that keeps it moist and helps you swallow and begin to digest food.

salm·on (**sam**-uhn) *noun*
1. A large fish with a silvery skin and pink flesh. Most salmon live in salt water but swim to fresh water to lay their eggs. ▷ *noun, plural* **salmon**
2. A yellow-pink color.

Atlantic salmon

sal·mo·nel·la (*sal*-muh-**nel**-uh) *noun* Any of a group of bacteria that are shaped like rods and that can cause food poisoning, stomach inflammation, and typhoid fever in humans and other warm-blooded animals. ▷ *noun, plural* **salmonellas** *or* **salmonellae** (*sal*-muh-**nel**-ee)

sa·loon (suh-**loon**) *noun* A bar where people can buy and drink alcoholic beverages.

sal·sa (**sahl**-suh) *noun*
1. A hot, spicy tomato sauce that can be flavored with onions and hot peppers.
2. A popular style of music that originated in Puerto Rico. It has been influenced by jazz and rock.

salt (sawlt) *noun*
1. A common white substance found in sea water and under the ground. Salt is used to season and preserve food. ▷ *noun* **saltiness** ▷ *verb* **salt** ▷ *adjective* **salt,** *adjective* **salty**
2. In chemistry, a compound formed from an acid and a base.
3. If you take something with **a grain of salt,** you do not believe that it is absolutely true.

> ## Language Note
> •
> In olden times **salt** was the main way of keeping meat and some other foods from spoiling. In fact, it was so important that Roman soldiers were paid in salt. This "salt money" was called a *salary,* from the Latin root of salt, *sal.* This same root is in the Latin word *salsa,* meaning "salted," and gives us English *salsa* and *sauce.*

salt·wa·ter (**sawlt**-*wah*-tur) *adjective* To do with water that is very salty, such as that found in the oceans and in certain inland bodies of water. *Most sharks are saltwater fish.*

S

sa·lute (suh-loot) *verb*
1. When soldiers **salute,** they raise their right hands to their foreheads as a sign of respect.
2. To praise or honor someone for something that the person has done. *The school saluted Jill for her bravery.*
▷ *verb* **saluting, saluted** ▷ *noun* **salute**

sal·vage (sal-vij) *verb* To rescue property from a shipwreck, fire, or any disaster. ▷ **salvaging, salvaged** ▷ *noun* **salvage,** *noun* **salvager**

sal·va·tion (sal-vay-shuhn) *noun*
1. The state of being saved from sin, evil, harm, or destruction.
2. Someone or something that saves or rescues.

salve (sav) *noun* An ointment or a cream that relieves pain and helps heal wounds, burns, or sores.

same (saym)
1. *adjective* Exactly alike, or identical in every way. *Two girls wore the same dress to the party.*
2. *adjective* Being the very one and not another. *This is the same seat I had yesterday.*
3. *adjective* Not changed or different. *She's the same thoughtful person she's always been.*
4. *pronoun* The identical person or thing. *Malcolm ordered a hamburger, and I asked for the same.*
5. the same In an identical manner. *He treats all his students the same.*

sam·ple (sam-puhl)
1. *noun* A small amount of something that shows what the whole of it is like. *The doctor took a blood sample.*
2. *verb* To try a small amount of something to see if you like it. *Gerald sampled the cheese before buying it.* ▷ **sampling, sampled**

sam·u·rai (sam-oo-*rye*)
noun A Japanese warrior who lived in medieval times. *This samurai is defending himself from attack with his naginata, a long rod with a curved blade at the end.*
▷ *noun, plural* **samurai**
▷ *adjective* **samurai**

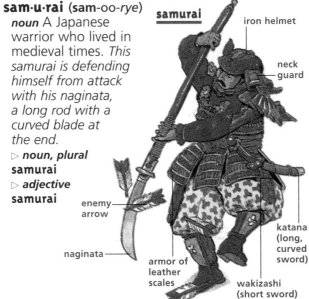

samurai
iron helmet
neck guard
enemy arrow
naginata
armor of leather scales
katana (long, curved sword)
wakizashi (short sword)

sanc·tion (sangk-shuhn)
1. *verb* To permit or to give approval.
▷ **sanctioning, sanctioned**
2. *noun* Permission or approval.
3. sanctions *noun, plural* Punishment for breaking the law or for unacceptable behavior. *One country sometimes imposes sanctions against another country by refusing to trade with it.*

sanc·tu·ar·y (sangk-choo-er-ee) *noun*
1. Safety or protection. *The outlaws found sanctuary in the deep, dark woods.*
2. A natural area where birds or animals are protected from hunters.
3. A holy or sacred place, such as a church, temple, or mosque.
▷ *noun, plural* **sanctuaries**

sand (sand)
1. *noun* The tiny grains of rock that make up beaches and deserts. ▷ *adjective* **sandy**
2. *verb* To sprinkle or cover with sand. *People sand icy roads in winter.*
3. *verb* To smooth or polish a surface with sandpaper or a sanding machine.
▷ *verb* **sanding, sanded**

san·dal (san-duhl) *noun* A light, open shoe with straps that go over the foot.

sand·bag (sand-*bag*) *noun* A sturdy bag filled with sand and used as a protection against floods, bullets, or explosives. ▷ *verb* **sandbag**

sand·bar (sand-*bar*) *noun* A ridge of sand in a river or bay or along an ocean's shore. Sandbars are built up by the action of waves or currents.

sand·box (sand-*boks*) *noun* A large, wooden box with low sides that is filled with sand and used by children to play in.

sand·pa·per (sand-*pay*-pur) *noun* Paper coated with grains of sand and used for rubbing against surfaces to make them smooth. ▷ *verb* **sandpaper**

sand·pip·er (sand-*pye*-pur) *noun* A small bird with a long bill; long, slender legs; and brown or gray feathers. Sandpipers feed in flocks along the seashore.

sand·stone (sand-*stohn*) *noun* A kind of rock made up mostly of sandlike grains of quartz cemented together by lime or other materials.

sand·wich (sand-wich) *noun* Two or more pieces of bread around a filling of cheese, meat, or some other food. ▷ *noun, plural* **sandwiches**

sane (sayn) *adjective*
1. Someone who is **sane** has a healthy mind.
2. Sensible, or showing good judgment. *Janet has a very sane approach to Josie's problems.*
▷ *adjective* **saner, sanest** ▷ *noun* **sanity** ▷ *adverb* **sanely**

S

san·i·tar·y (san-uh-*ter*-ee) *adjective* Clean and free from germs.

san·i·ta·tion (san-uh-tay-shuhn) *noun* Systems for cleaning the water supply and disposing of sewage. Sanitation protects people from dirt and disease.

sap (sap)
1. *noun* The liquid that flows through a plant, carrying water and food from one part of the plant to another.
2. *verb* To gradually weaken something. *Hunger had sapped Ali's strength.* ▷ **sapping, sapped**

sap·ling (sap-ling) *noun* A young tree.

sap·phire (sa-fire) *noun* A clear, deep-blue precious stone.

sar·cas·tic (sar-kass-tik) *adjective* If you are **sarcastic,** you use bitter or mocking words that are meant to hurt or make fun of someone or something. ▷ *noun* **sarcasm** ▷ *adverb* **sarcastically**

sar·dine (sar-deen) *noun* A small saltwater fish, often sold in cans as food.

sa·ri (sah-ree) *noun* A long piece of light material worn wrapped around the body and over one shoulder. Saris are worn mainly by Indian and Pakistani women and girls. *The picture shows an Indian woman wearing a sari.*

sari

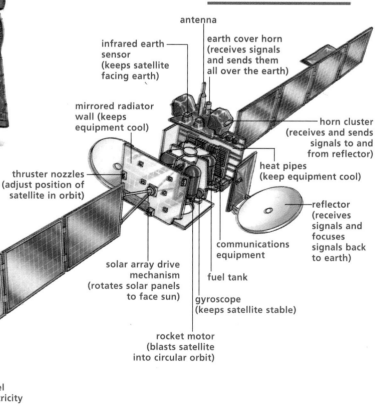

sa·rong (suh-rong) *noun* A piece of cloth wrapped around the body like a skirt or dress. Sarongs were originally worn by Malaysian men and women.

sash (sash) *noun*
1. A wide strip of material worn around the waist or over one shoulder as an ornament or as part of a uniform.
2. A frame that holds the glass in a window or door.
▷ *noun, plural* **sashes**

sa·shi·mi (sah-**shee**-mee or sah-**shuh**-mee) *noun* A Japanese dish made up of thinly sliced raw fish served with a sauce for dipping.

Sa·tan (say-tuhn) *noun* The Devil in the Old Testament. Satan is described as an evil spirit that has permanently been sent away from the presence of God and confined to hell.

satch·el (sach-uhl) *noun* A bag or small suitcase sometimes carried over the shoulder.

sat·el·lite (sat-uh-*lite*) *noun*
1. A spacecraft that is sent into orbit around the earth, the moon, or another heavenly body. *The picture shows the main parts of a communications satellite that sends television and telephone signals to earth.*
2. A moon or other heavenly body that travels in an orbit around a larger heavenly body. *See* **moon.**

communications satellite

antenna

infrared earth sensor (keeps satellite facing earth)

earth cover horn (receives signals and sends them all over the earth)

mirrored radiator wall (keeps equipment cool)

horn cluster (receives and sends signals to and from reflector)

heat pipes (keep equipment cool)

thruster nozzles (adjust position of satellite in orbit)

reflector (receives signals and focuses signals back to earth)

communications equipment

thermal blanket cover (layers of protective foil)

solar array drive mechanism (rotates solar panels to face sun)

fuel tank

gyroscope (keeps satellite stable)

rocket motor (blasts satellite into circular orbit)

solar sailing flap (helps control satellite's position)

solar array panel (generates electricity from sun)

S

satellite dish *noun* A receiver for radio or television signals sent by satellite. Satellite dishes are shaped like a dish and are often attached to walls outside a home or building. ▷ *noun, plural* **satellite dishes**

sat·in (sat-uhn) *noun* A very smooth fabric that is shiny on one side and dull on the other. Satin is made of silk or a synthetic material.

sat·ire (sat-ire) *noun* A type of clever, mocking humor that points out the faults in certain people or ideas. ▷ *noun* **satirist** ▷ *adjective* **satirical** (suh-tihr-i-kuhl)

sat·is·fac·tion (sat-iss-fak-shuhn) *noun* A feeling of being content because you have accomplished something that you wanted to do or have done something well.

sat·is·fac·to·ry (sat-iss-fak-tuh-ree) *adjective* Good enough but not outstanding. ▷ *adverb* **satisfactorily**

sat·is·fy (sat-iss-*fye*) *verb*
1. To please someone by doing enough or giving the person enough. *The pizzas soon satisfied the hungry children.*
2. To convince or to free from doubt. *Jackson's alibi satisfied the police.*
▷ *verb* **satisfies, satisfying, satisfied** ▷ *adjective* **satisfied**

sat·u·rate (sach-uh-rate) *verb* To soak thoroughly or to fill completely. *The rain saturated my shoes.*
▷ **saturating, saturated** ▷ *noun* **saturation**
▷ *adjective* **saturated**

saturation point *noun* The level at which an object is filled to its greatest capacity. *When the cloud reached its saturation point, it started to rain.*

Sat·ur·day (sat-ur-dee *or* sat-ur-*day*) *noun* The seventh day of the week, after Friday and before Sunday.

> ▶ **Word History**
> •
> **Saturday**, the seventh day of the week, and the planet **Saturn** share a common history. Both were named for Saturn, the Roman god of farming.

Sat·urn (sat-urn) *noun* The sixth planet in distance from the sun. Saturn is the second-largest planet in our solar system. It has 10 moons and is surrounded by rings that are thought to be made of ice, rock, and frozen gases. *See* **planet.**

sauce (sawss) *noun*
1. A thick liquid served with food to make it taste better.

2. Stewed fruit eaten as dessert or as a side dish, as in *cranberry sauce.*

sauce·pan (sawss-*pan*) *noun* A metal or glass cooking pot with a handle and sometimes a lid.

sau·cer (saw-sur) *noun* A small, shallow plate that is placed under a cup.

sau·na (saw-nuh *or* sou-nuh) *noun*
1. A bath using dry heat, or a steam bath in which the steam is made by throwing water on hot stones. Saunas originated in Finland.
2. A room for such a bath.

saun·ter (sawn-tur) *verb* To walk in a slow, leisurely, or casual way. ▷ **sauntering, sauntered**

sau·sage (saw-sij) *noun* Chopped and seasoned meat stuffed into a thin case shaped like a tube.

sav·age (sav-ij)
1. *adjective* Not tamed, or not under human control, as in *a savage beast.*
2. *adjective* Fierce, dangerous, or violent, as in *a savage battle.* ▷ *adverb* **savagely**
3. *adjective* Not civilized, as in *a savage society.*
4. *noun* A person who lives in a way that is not civilized.
5. *noun* A fierce or violent person.

sa·van·na *or* **sa·van·nah** (suh-van-uh) *noun* A flat, grassy plain with few or no trees. Savannas are found in tropical areas.

save (sayv) *verb*
1. To rescue someone or something from danger.
2. If you **save** time, space, energy, etc., you make the best use of it and do not waste it.
3. To keep money to use in the future rather than spend it now.
4. To stop a ball or puck from going into a goal in soccer or hockey. ▷ *noun* **save**
5. To copy a file from a computer's RAM (random access memory) onto a disk or other storage device in order to keep it or protect it from being erased.
▷ *verb* **saving, saved** ▷ *noun* **saver**

sav·ings (say-vingz) *noun, plural* Money that you have saved.

sa·vor·y (say-vuh-ree) *adjective* Pleasing to the taste or smell, as in *savory cooking odors.*

saw (saw)
1. *noun* A tool used for cutting wood with sharp teeth on its blade.
2. *verb* To cut something with a saw. ▷ **sawing, sawed, sawn** (sawn)
3. *verb* Past tense of **see.**

saw·dust (saw-*duhst*) *noun* Tiny particles of wood that fall off when you saw wood.

saw·mill (saw-*mil*) *noun* A place where people use machines to saw logs into lumber.

S

sax·o·phone

(sak-suh-*fone*) *noun* A wind instrument made of brass, with a mouthpiece, keys for the fingers, and a body that is usually curved.
▷ *noun* **saxophonist**

say (say)

1. *verb* To speak. *What did you say?*
2. *verb* To state, or to express in words. *The sign says this is a one-way street.*
3. *verb* To repeat or to recite, as in *to say one's prayers.*
4. *noun* The chance to speak. *When it's your turn, you'll have your say.*
▷ *verb* **saying, said** (sed)

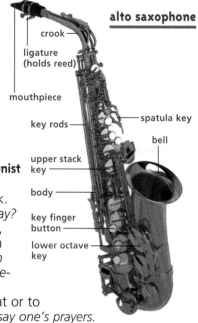

alto saxophone

crook
ligature (holds reed)
mouthpiece
key rods
spatula key
bell
upper stack key
body
key finger button
lower octave key

Synonyms: say

Say means to express something out loud using words. *Said*, the past tense of say, is often used in writing about conversations. For example: *"My mom says that it's too late to go to the store now," said Tony. "Okay," said Eloise. "How about tomorrow?"* Here are some other words that can sometimes take the place of say.

State means to announce or declare something in very straightforward terms: *The lawyer asked the witness to state his name, address, and occupation.*

Report means to give a detailed account of something that has happened: *My mom reported every word of her conversation with my teacher.*

Remark means to point out or offer a comment or an opinion on something: *After reading the article, Jed remarked that he thought the author didn't know what he was talking about.*

Exclaim means to cry out or say something with sudden emotion, such as surprise or anger: *"I can't believe you ate that entire cake!" exclaimed Simon.*

Declare means to say something formally or officially: *The mayor declared that next week will be Be Kind to Animals Week in our town.*

say·ing (say-ing) *noun* A well-known phrase or proverb that gives advice. "Don't cry over spilt milk" is a saying.

sa·yo·na·ra (*sah*-yoh-**nar**-uh) *interjection* A Japanese word meaning "good-bye."

scab (skab) *noun*
1. The hard covering that forms over a wound when it is healing.
2. *(informal)* Someone who takes the job of a union worker who is on strike.

scab·bard (skab-urd) *noun* A case that holds a sword, dagger, or bayonet when it is not in use.

scaf·fold (skaf-uhld) *noun* The structure made of wooden planks and ropes or metal poles that workers stand on when they are working above the ground on a building.

scald (skawld) *verb* To burn with very hot liquid or steam. ▷ **scalding, scalded** ▷ *noun* **scald** ▷ *adjective* **scalding**

scale (skale)

1. *noun* One of the small pieces of hard skin that cover the body of a fish, snake, or other reptile. ▷ *adjective* **scaly**
2. *verb* To remove all the scales from.
3. *noun* A series of musical notes going up or down in order.
4. *noun* A series of numbers, units, etc., that is used to measure something, as in *a scale for measuring the strength of earthquakes.*
5. *noun* The ratio between the measurements on a map or model and the actual measurements, as in *a scale of one inch represents 100 miles.*
6. *noun* An instrument used for weighing things.
7. *verb* To climb up something. *Joel scaled the mountain.*
8. *noun* A series of stages or steps. *The pay scale ranged from $7.00 per hour to $15.00 per hour.*
▷ *verb* **scaling, scaled**

sca·lene triangle (skay-leen) *noun* In geometry, a triangle whose three sides each have different lengths.

scalene triangle

scal·lion (skal-yuhn) *noun* An onion with long, grasslike leaves and a small bulb.

scal·lop (skol-uhp *or* skal-uhp) *noun*
1. A shellfish with two hinged shells or valves. Scallops move around by opening and closing their valves rapidly.
2. One of a series of curves in a border that looks like the edge of a scallop shell.
▷ *verb* **scallop** ▷ *adjective* **scalloped**

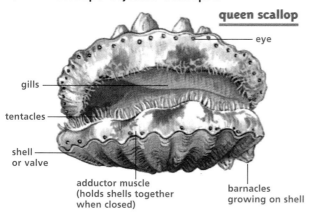

queen scallop

eye
gills
tentacles
shell or valve
adductor muscle (holds shells together when closed)
barnacles growing on shell

scalp (skalp) *noun* The skin covering the top of your head where your hair grows. *See* **brain.**

scal·pel (skal-puhl) *noun* A small, sharp knife used by surgeons.

scam·per (skam-pur) *verb* To run lightly and quickly. *The rabbit scampered away.*
▷ **scampering, scampered**

scan (skan) *verb*
1. To read quickly, without looking for details. *I didn't have time to read the whole newspaper, so I just scanned the headlines.*
2. To look at closely and carefully, or to examine. *We scanned the horizon for ships.*
3. If a machine **scans** something, it moves a beam of light over the object in order to examine it or search for something. ▷ *noun* **scanner**
▷ *verb* **scanning, scanned** ▷ *noun* **scan**

scan·dal (skan-duhl) *noun*
1. A dishonest or immoral act that shocks people and disgraces those involved.
2. Harmful gossip.
▷ *adjective* **scandalous**

Scan·di·na·vi·an (skan-duh-nay-vee-uhn) *noun*
1. Someone who was born in or is a citizen of Norway, Denmark, or Sweden. Iceland and Finland also are sometimes considered Scandinavian countries.
2. The languages spoken by people in these countries.
▷ *adjective* **Scandinavian**

scant (skant) *adjective*
1. Barely enough, or not enough. *The hiker brought only scant supplies for the trip so that his load would not be too heavy.*

2. Not quite the full amount, as in *a scant teaspoonful of salt.*

scant·y (skan-tee) *adjective* Not enough, or not big enough. *We had only scanty information.*
▷ **scantier, scantiest**

scape·goat (skape-goht) *noun* Someone who is unfairly made to take all the blame for something.

scar (skar) *noun* A mark left on your skin by a cut or wound that has healed. ▷ *verb* **scar**

scarce (skairss) *adjective* Something that is **scarce** is hard to find because there is so little of it. *Fresh water is scarce on the island.* ▷ *noun* **scarcity**

scarce·ly (skairss-lee) *adverb*
1. Hardly. *I've scarcely seen my cousin all year.*
2. Certainly not. *After the way they treated us, I would scarcely forgive them.*

scare (skair)
1. *verb* To frighten a person or an animal.
▷ **scaring, scared**
2. *noun* Widespread fear or panic, as in *a bomb scare.*
▷ *adjective* **scared,** *adjective* **scary**

scare·crow (skair-kroh) *noun* A figure made of straw that is shaped and dressed to look like a person and put in a field to frighten birds away from crops.

scarf (skarf) *noun* A strip of material worn around the neck or head for decoration or warmth. ▷ *noun, plural* **scarfs** *or* **scarves** (skarvz)

scar·let (skar-lit) *noun* A bright red color.
▷ *adjective* **scarlet**

scarlet fever *noun* A highly contagious disease that occurs mostly in children. It causes a bright red rash, a sore throat, and high fever.

scat·ter (skat-ur) *verb*
1. To throw things over a wide area. *We scattered the seed over the lawn.*
2. To hurry away in different directions. *The insects scattered when I turned over the log.*
▷ *verb* **scattering, scattered**

scat·ter·brained (skat-ur-braynd) *adjective* If you are **scatterbrained,** you are unable to concentrate and are always losing or forgetting things.

scav·enge (skav-uhnj) *verb* To search among garbage for food or something useful.
▷ **scavenging, scavenged** ▷ *noun* **scavenger**

sce·nar·i·o (suh-nair-ee-oh *or* suh-nah-ree-oh) *noun*
1. An outline of a movie, a play, or an opera that summarizes the story.
2. An outline of a series of events that might happen in a particular situation.
▷ *noun, plural* **scenarios**

S

scene (seen) *noun*
1. A view or a picture. *Sheila paints country scenes.*
2. A part of a story, play, movie, etc., that shows what is happening in one particular place and time.
3. The place where something happens. *The ambulance rushed across town to the scene of the accident.*
4. If you **make a scene,** you get very angry with someone or behave badly in public.

scen·er·y (see-nur-ee) *noun*
1. The natural countryside of an area, such as trees, hills, mountains, and lakes.
2. The painted boards and screens that are used on stage as the background to a play, an opera, or a ballet.

sce·nic (see-nik) *adjective* A **scenic** place has beautiful natural surroundings.

scent (sent)
1. *noun* A pleasant smell, as in *the scent of roses.* ▷ *adjective* **scented**
2. *noun* A liquid that you put on your skin to make you smell pleasant.
3. *noun* The odor or trail of a hunted animal or person. *The dogs picked up the scent of a fox.*
4. *noun* The sense of smell.
5. *verb* If you **scent** danger or victory, you start to feel that it is near. ▷ **scenting, scented**
Scent sounds like **cent** and **sent.**

scep·ter (sep-tur) *noun* A rod or staff carried by a king or queen as a symbol of authority.

sched·ule (skej-ool *or* skej-ul)
1. *noun* A plan, program, or timetable.
2. *verb* If you **schedule** an event, you plan it for a particular time. ▷ **scheduling, scheduled**

scheme (skeem)
1. *noun* A plan or plot for doing something.
2. *verb* To plan or plot something, especially something secret or dishonest. ▷ **scheming, schemed** ▷ *noun* **schemer** ▷ *adjective* **scheming**

schol·ar (skol-ur) *noun*
1. A person who has a great deal of knowledge.
2. A serious student. ▷ *adjective* **scholarly**

schol·ar·ship (skol-ur-ship) *noun*
1. A grant or prize that pays for you to go to college or to follow a course of study.
2. Knowledge achieved from studying hard.

school (skool) *noun*
1. A place where people go to be taught.
2. Learning that takes place in school. *Jeremy likes school.* ▷ *noun* **schooling** ▷ *verb* **school**
3. All the people in a school. *The whole school went on a field trip.*
4. A part of a university, as in *a medical school.*
5. A group of fish or other sea creatures, as in *a school of porpoises.*

schoon·er (skoo-nur) *noun* A fast ship with two masts, a narrow hull, and sails that run lengthwise.

sci·ence (sye-uhnss) *noun*
1. The study of nature and the physical world by testing, experimenting, and measuring.
2. Any of the branches or fields of such study, as biology, physics, or geology.
▷ *noun* **scientist** ▷ *adjective* **scientific** ▷ *adverb* **scientifically**

▶ **Word History**
• •
The word **science** comes from the Latin word *scientia*, which means "knowledge." Although *science* was used in English as early as 1340, the word *scientist* was not coined until 500 years later, by author William Whelwell.

science fiction *noun* Stories about life in the future or life on other planets.

scis·sors (siz-urz) *noun, plural* A sharp tool with two blades used for cutting paper, fabric, etc. See **pin.**

scoff (skof *or* skawf) *verb* To be scornful and mocking about someone or something. *Nat scoffed at my idea of painting my room purple.* ▷ **scoffing, scoffed**

scold (skohld) *verb* To tell someone in an angry way that he or she has done something wrong or done a bad job. ▷ **scolding, scolded**

sco·li·o·sis (*skoh-lee-oh-siss*) *noun* An abnormal curving of the spine to the side. Scoliosis usually occurs during adolescence.

scone (skohn) *noun* A round biscuit often eaten with butter.

scoop (skoop)
1. *verb* To lift or pick up something. *Jan scooped up a handful of snow.* ▷ **scooping, scooped**
2. *noun* A utensil shaped like a spoon with a short handle and a deep hollow to pick things up with, as in *an ice-cream scoop.*
3. *noun* A story reported in a newspaper before other papers have a chance to report it.
▷ *verb* **scoop**

scoot·er (skoo-tur) *noun*
1. A child's vehicle with a handle, two wheels, and a board that you stand on with one foot while pushing against the ground with the other.
2. A small motorcycle.

scope (skohp) *noun*
1. A range of opportunity. *Flower gardening gives Aunt Martha scope for her creativity in design.*
2. The area or range of operation. *What is the scope of this investigation?*

S

scorch (skorch)
1. *verb* To burn something slightly, usually with an iron. ▷ *noun* **scorch**
2. *verb* To dry up something. *The front lawn has been scorched by the sun.*
3. *adjective* If the weather is **scorching,** it is extremely hot.
▷ *verb* **scorches, scorching, scorched**

score (skor)
1. *verb* To make a point or points in a game, contest, or test. ▷ *noun* **scorer**
2. *noun* The number of points made by each person or team in a game, contest, or test.
3. *noun* A written piece of music.
4. *verb* To arrange a piece of music so that it can be played by different instruments.
5. *verb* To cut a line or lines in a surface. *I scored the loaf of bread before baking it.*
6. *noun* Twenty. *The skyscraper was built four score years ago, so it is 80 years old.*
7. **scores** *noun, plural* A large number. *I've received scores of letters.*
8. *(informal)* If you **know the score,** you are well informed about the situation.
▷ *verb* **scoring, scored**

scorn (skorn)
1. *noun* A feeling of hatred or contempt for someone or something thought of as bad, worthless, or low. *Gerry is full of scorn for any new ideas.*
2. *verb* To treat with scorn. *Don't scorn the man's attempt to make a better life for himself.*
3. *verb* If you **scorn** an offer, you refuse it because you think it is not worth your while.
▷ *verb* **scorning, scorned** ▷ *adjective* **scornful**

scor·pi·on (skor-pee-uhn) *noun* An animal related to the spider that has a poisonous sting in its tail.

Sahara scorpion

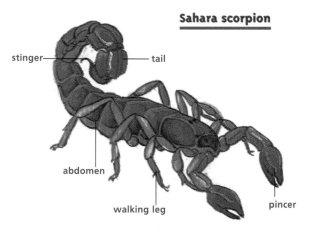

stinger — tail
abdomen
walking leg — pincer

scoun·drel (skoun-druhl) *noun* A wicked person, especially someone who cheats and lies.

scour (skour) *verb*
1. To clean or polish something by rubbing it hard. *Neil scoured the bathtub.* ▷ *noun* **scourer**
2. To search an area thoroughly. *Police scoured the building for clues.*
▷ *verb* **scouring, scoured**

scourge (skurj) *noun* A cause of great harm and suffering.

scout (skout)
1. *noun* Someone sent to find out and bring back information.
2. *verb* To look or search for something. *We scouted around for firewood.* ▷ **scouting, scouted**

scowl (skoul) *verb* To make an angry frown.
▷ **scowling, scowled** ▷ *noun* **scowl**

scrag·gy (skrag-ee) *adjective* Thin and bony. *Anthony is tall and scraggy.* ▷ **scraggier, scraggiest** ▷ *noun* **scragginess**

scram·ble (skram-buhl) *verb*
1. To climb over rocks or hills.
2. To rush or struggle to get somewhere or something. *Jessica scrambled to get to the front row.*
3. To mix up or mix together. *Scramble the letters in the game.*
4. To alter an electronic signal so that it requires a special receiver to decode the message. *The cable television company scrambled its signal so that only subscribers could receive it.* ▷ *noun* **scrambler**
5. **scrambled eggs** Egg yolks and whites mixed together and cooked in a pan.
▷ *verb* **scrambling, scrambled** ▷ *noun* **scramble** ▷ *adjective* **scrambled**

scrap (skrap)
1. *noun* A small piece of paper, food, etc.
2. *noun* Metal salvaged from old cars or machines.
3. *verb* To get rid of something. *We had to scrap our plans because of the weather.*
4. *verb (informal)* To fight or to quarrel. ▷ *noun* **scrap**, *noun* **scrapper**
▷ *verb* **scrapping, scrapped**

scrap·book (skrap-buk) *noun* A book with blank pages on which you mount pictures, newspaper clippings, and other items you wish to keep.

scrape (skrape)
1. *verb* To clean, peel, or scratch something with a sharp object. ▷ *noun* **scrape,** *noun* **scraper**
2. *noun (informal)* An awkward situation. *Mindy's always getting into scrapes.*
3. **scrape together** *verb* To gather or collect with great difficulty. *He managed to scrape together a few dollars.*
4. **scrape by** *verb* To manage or make your way with difficulty. *The man scraped by on his small salary.*
▷ *verb* **scraping, scraped**

S

scratch (skrach) *verb*
 1. To scrape lightly a part of you that itches.
 2. To make a mark or cut.
 3. To scrape with the fingernails or claws. *The dog scratched at the door until we let him in.*
 4. *(informal)* To erase or cancel something. *Please scratch my answer.*
 5. *(informal)* If you do something **from scratch,** you start from the beginning.
 6. *(informal)* If something is not **up to scratch,** it is not good enough.
 ▷ *verb* **scratches, scratching, scratched** ▷ *noun* **scratch**

scratch·y (skrach-ee) *adjective*
 1. Causing an itch, as in *a scratchy fabric.*
 2. Rough and itchy, as in *a scratchy throat.*
 ▷ *adjective* **scratchier, scratchiest**

scrawl (skrawl)
 1. *verb* To write in a quick, sloppy way.
 ▷ **scrawling, scrawled**
 2. *noun* A sloppy handwriting that is difficult to read.

scream (skreem)
 1. *verb* To make a loud, shrill, piercing cry or sound. ▷ **screaming, screamed** ▷ *noun* **scream**
 2. *noun* *(informal)* A very funny thing or person. *Angie is such a scream.*

screech (skreech) *verb* To make a high, unpleasant sound. *The car screeched to a halt.*
 ▷ **screeches, screeching, screeched** ▷ *noun* **screech**

screen (skreen)
 1. *noun* Wire or plastic netting in a frame. *Screens keep insects out.*
 2. *noun* A light, movable partition used to hide or divide a room. ▷ *verb* **screen**
 3. *noun* The front of a television set or computer monitor.
 4. *noun* The white surface that movies or slides are projected onto.
 5. *verb* To show on a screen. *The movie was screened in the auditorium.*
 6. *verb* To examine carefully in order to make a selection, or to separate into groups. *During the meeting, Ms. Thomas asked her assistant to screen her telephone calls and put only the most important ones through.*
 ▷ *verb* **screening, screened**

screen saver *noun* A computer program that prolongs the life of a monitor by providing a changing or fading image when the machine is on but not is use.

screw (skroo)
 1. *noun* A metal fastener like a nail with a groove in its head and a spiral thread.
 2. *verb* To fasten something with screws.
 3. *verb* If you **screw on** a lid, you turn or twist it.

4. *verb* To twist into an unnatural position. *The baby screwed up his face.*
 5. *verb* *(informal)* If you **screw up,** you make a really bad mistake.
 ▷ *verb* **screwing, screwed**

screw·driv·er (skroo-*drye*-vur) *noun* A tool with a tip that fits into the groove in the head of a screw so that you can turn it. *See* **tool.**

scrib·ble (skrib-uhl) *verb*
 1. To write or draw carelessly or quickly. *Dorothy scribbled the directions as I talked.*
 2. To make meaningless marks with a pencil, pen, or crayon. *I scribbled in the margins of my notebook.*
 ▷ *verb* **scribbling, scribbled** ▷ *noun* **scribble**

scribe (skribe) *noun* A person who copies books, letters, contracts, and other documents by hand.

scrim·mage (skrim-ij) *noun*
 1. In football, the rough contact that occurs as soon as the ball is picked up off the ground and snapped to another player.
 2. A game played for practice in football and other sports.
 ▷ *verb* **scrimmage**

script (skript) *noun*
 1. The written text of a play, a movie, or a television or radio show. ▷ *verb* **script**
 2. Writing in which the letters are joined together.

scrip·ture (skrip-chur) *noun*
 1. A sacred book.
 2. Scripture The Bible.

scroll

scroll (skrohl)
 1. *noun* A piece of paper or parchment with writing on it that is rolled up into the shape of a tube. *The picture shows a Torah scroll made of parchment.*
 2. *verb* To move the text on a computer screen up and down so that you can see more of it. ▷ **scrolling, scrolled**

scrounge (skrounj) *verb*
 1. To get things from people without paying. *Can I scrounge a sandwich from you?*
 2. To get or collect things with difficulty. *He scrounged up enough money to pay for lunch.*
 ▷ *verb* **scrounging, scrounged** ▷ *noun* **scrounger**

scrub (skruhb)
 1. *verb* To clean something by rubbing it hard.
 ▷ **scrubbing, scrubbed** ▷ *noun* **scrub**
 2. *noun* Low bushes or short trees that cover a piece of ground.

scruff·y (skruhf-ee) *adjective* Shabby and messy.
▷ **scruffier, scruffiest** ▷ *adverb* **scruffily**

scru·ple (skroo-puhl) *noun* A strong feeling about what is right that keeps you from doing something wrong. *Alonzo wouldn't cheat on the test because he has scruples.*

scru·pu·lous (skroo-pyuh-luhss) *adjective*
1. Having strict beliefs about what is right and proper.
2. Careful and exact. *Glenn is scrupulous about money.*
▷ *adverb* **scrupulously**

scru·ti·nize (skroot-uh-*nize*) *verb* To examine or study something closely. *The doctor scrutinized the X ray.* ▷ **scrutinizing, scrutinized** ▷ *noun* **scrutiny**

scu·ba diving (skoo-buh) *noun* Underwater swimming with an air tank on your back that is connected to your mouth by a hose. Scuba stands for *Self-Contained Underwater Breathing Apparatus.* ▷ *noun* **scuba diver**

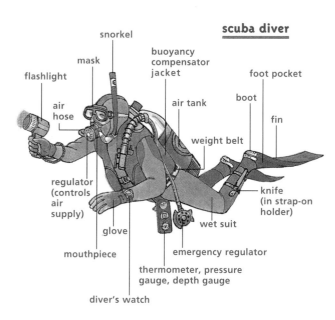

scuba diver

snorkel
mask
flashlight
buoyancy compensator jacket
foot pocket
boot
air hose
air tank
fin
weight belt
regulator (controls air supply)
knife (in strap-on holder)
glove
wet suit
mouthpiece
emergency regulator
thermometer, pressure gauge, depth gauge
diver's watch

scuff (skuhf) *verb* To scratch or scrape something and leave a mark. *He scuffed his new shoes on the sidewalk.* ▷ **scuffing, scuffed**

scuf·fle (skuhf-uhl) *noun* A confused and disorderly struggle or fight. ▷ *verb* **scuffle**

scull (skuhl) *noun*
1. One of a pair of lightweight oars used to propel a boat through water.
2. A small, light boat that is propelled by oars, often used for racing.
Scull sounds like **skull.**
▷ *verb* **scull**

sculp·ture (skuhlp-chur) *noun*
1. Something carved or shaped out of stone, wood, metal, marble, or clay or cast in bronze or another metal.
2. The art or work of making sculpture.
▷ *noun* **sculptor** ▷ *verb* **sculpt**

scum (skuhm) *noun* A filmy layer that forms on the surface of a liquid or body of water, especially stagnant water.

scur·ry (skur-ee) *verb* To hurry, or to run with short, quick steps. ▷ **scurries, scurrying, scurried**

scur·vy (skur-vee) *noun* A disease characterized by bleeding gums and great weakness. Scurvy is caused by a lack of *vitamin C* in the diet. Vitamin C is found in citrus fruits and other fruits and vegetables.

scuz·zy (skuhz-ee) *adjective (slang)* Dirty, grimy, or disgusting in some way. ▷ **scuzzier, scuzziest**

scythe (siTHe)
noun A tool with a large, curved blade used for cutting grass or crops by hand.

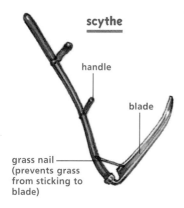

scythe

handle
blade
grass nail (prevents grass from sticking to blade)

sea (see) *noun*
1. The body of salt water that covers nearly three-fourths of the earth's surface; the ocean.
2. A body of salt water that is a part of an ocean yet is partly enclosed by land, such as the Caribbean Sea.
3. An overwhelming amount or number, as in *a sea of troubles.*
Sea sounds like **see.**

sea anemone *noun* A sea animal with a body shaped like a tube and a mouth opening that is surrounded by brightly colored tentacles.

sea·board (see-bord) *noun* The land along or near the ocean shore. *The eastern seaboard is one of the most crowded areas of our country.*

sea·far·er (see-*fair*-ur) *noun* A sailor or someone who travels by sea.

sea·far·ing (see-*fair*-ing) *adjective*
1. Earning one's living by working at sea, as in *a seafaring merchant.*
2. To do with sailors or the sea, as in *a seafaring vessel* or *seafaring tales.*

sea·food (see-*food*) *noun* Edible fish and shellfish.

sea·gull (see-*guhl*) *noun* A gray and white bird that is commonly found near the sea.

S

sea horse *noun* A small ocean fish with a head shaped like that of a horse and a long, curling tail.

sea horse

seal (seel)
1. *noun* A sea mammal that lives in coastal waters and has thick fur and flippers. *See* **polar.**
2. *verb* To close something up. *We've sealed off the old well.* ▷ **sealing, sealed** ▷ *noun* **seal,** *noun* **sealant**
3. *noun* A design pressed into wax and made into a stamp. A seal is used to make a document official or to close up a letter or an envelope. ▷ *verb* **seal**

sea level *noun* The average level of the surface of the ocean, used as a starting point from which to measure the height or depth of any place. *The mountain is 2,000 feet above sea level.*

sea lion *noun* A large seal found mostly in the Pacific Ocean. It has ears that stick out and large flippers.

sea lion

flipper

seam (seem) *noun*
1. A line of sewing that joins two pieces of material.
2. A band of mineral or metal in the earth, as in *a seam of coal.*
Seam sounds like **seem.**

seam·stress (seem-struhss) *noun* A woman who sews for a living. ▷ *noun, plural* **seamstresses**

sea·plane (see-*plane*) *noun* An airplane that can take off from and land on water. A seaplane has floats attached to its underside.

sea·port (see-*port*) *noun*
1. A port or harbor for seafaring ships.
2. A city or town with such a port or harbor.

search (surch)
1. *verb* To explore or examine something carefully and thoroughly. ▷ **searches, searching, searched** ▷ *noun* **search,** *noun* **searcher**
2. **search warrant** *noun* An order from a court that allows the police to go into a building to look for certain items or people.

search·ing (sur-ching) *adjective* Deep and thorough; probing. *He asked me a lot of searching questions.*

search·light (surch-*lite*) *noun* A large, powerful lamp that can be turned to focus in a particular direction.

sea·shell (see-*shel*) *noun* The shell of a sea animal such as an oyster or a clam. *See* **shell.**

sea·shore (see-*shor*) *noun* The sandy or rocky land next to the sea.

sea·sick (see-*sik*) *adjective* If you are **seasick,** you feel nauseous and dizzy because of the rolling or tossing movement of a boat or ship.

sea·son (see-zuhn)
1. *noun* One of the four natural parts of the year. The four seasons are spring, summer, autumn or fall, and winter. ▷ *adjective* **seasonal** ▷ *adverb* **seasonally**
2. *noun* A part of the year when a certain activity or event takes place, as in *the rainy season* or *the football season.*
3. *verb* To add flavor to food with herbs, salt, or spices. ▷ **seasoning, seasoned**
4. If a food is **in season,** it is fresh and easily available.
5. **season ticket** *noun* A ticket for a series of events in a season, such as to all the home games of a sports team or performances of a ballet or an opera company.

sea·son·ing (see-zuhn-ing) *noun* An herb or spice that is added to food to give it more flavor.

seat (seet)
1. *noun* Something such as a chair or bench that you can sit on.
2. *noun* Anyplace where you can sit.
3. *verb* To cause to sit. *Jack seated himself on the arm of the sofa.*
4. *noun* The part of the body you sit on, or the fabric that covers it. *Hank tore the seat of his jeans.*
5. *noun* The central location of something. *Ottawa is the seat of the national government in Canada.*
6. *verb* To have room for people to sit down. *This table seats six.*
▷ *verb* **seating, seated**

seat belt *noun* A strap or harness that holds a person securely in the seat of a car, a truck, or an airplane for protection in case of an accident. *See* **car.**

S

sea ur·chin (ur-chin) *noun* A sea creature with a hard, spiny shell. The spines are used for protection and also help the sea urchin move around.

sea·weed (see-*weed*) *noun* Any of various types of algae that grow in the sea and need sunlight to make their own food. *The picture shows examples of brown, green, and red seaweed growing underwater.* ▷ *noun, plural* **seaweed**

seaweed

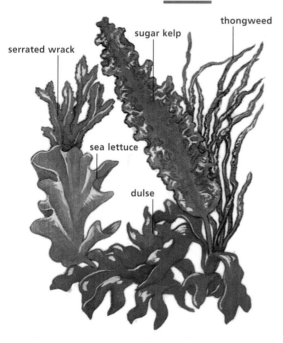

serrated wrack

sugar kelp

thongweed

sea lettuce

dulse

se·cede (si-seed) *verb* To formally withdraw from a group or an organization, often to form another organization. *By 1861, 11 southern states had seceded from the Union to form the Confederate States of America.* ▷ **seceding, seceded** ▷ *noun* **secession**

se·clud·ed (si-kloo-did) *adjective* Quiet and private. *The cabin is in a secluded valley.* ▷ *noun* **seclusion**

sec·ond (sek-uhnd)
1. *noun* A unit of time equal to $\frac{1}{60}$ of a minute.
2. *noun* Any very short period of time.
3. *adjective* Next after the first. ▷ *noun* **second** ▷ *adverb* **second,** *adverb* **secondly**
4. seconds *noun, plural* Another, or a second, helping of food. *Ethan always asks for seconds.*
5. *verb* If you **second** a motion at a meeting, you formally support it. ▷ **seconding, seconded** ▷ *noun* **seconder**

sec·on·dar·y (sek-uhn-der-ee) *adjective*
1. Less important, as in *a secondary problem* or *a secondary cause.* ▷ *adverb* **secondarily**
2. Based on something that is not original. *He used secondary sources to do his research.*
3. To do with the second stage of something, as in *secondary education.*

secondary school *noun* A school between elementary school and college.

sec·ond·hand (sek-uhnd-*hand*) *adjective*
1. If something is **secondhand,** it belonged to another person first.
2. Selling used goods, as in *a secondhand furniture store.*

second-rate *adjective* Not very good, as in *second-rate merchandise.*

se·cret (see-krit)
1. *noun* Something that is kept hidden or that only a few people know. *The location of the treasure is a secret.*
2. *adjective* Not known by many people. *My secret wish is to be an actress.*
3. in secret Privately.
▷ *noun* **secrecy** ▷ *adverb* **secretly**

secret agent *noun* A spy or someone who obtains secret information, usually from another government.

sec·re·tar·y (sek-ruh-ter-ee) *noun*
1. Someone whose job is to prepare letters, answer the telephone, keep records, make appointments, and do other office work for an employer. ▷ *adjective* **secretarial**
2. A person in charge of a cabinet department in a government, as in *the secretary of defense.*
▷ *noun, plural* **secretaries**

se·crete (si-kreet) *verb*
1. To produce a liquid. *Some snakes secrete poison.* ▷ *noun* **secretion**
2. To hide. *The pirate secreted his loot in a cave.*
▷ *verb* **secreting, secreted**

se·cre·tive (see-kri-tiv *or* si-kree-tiv) *adjective* Tending to be silent about some matter, as in *a secretive man.*

sect (sekt) *noun* A group whose members share the same beliefs and practices or follow the same leader. A sect is often a religious group that has broken away from a larger church.

sec·tion (sek-shuhn) *noun*
1. A part or division of something, as in *the tail section of an airplane.*
2. A part of an area. *I like to see the old section of any city I visit.*
3. A **cross section.**

sec·tor (sek-tur) *noun*
1. A part of a circle made by drawing two straight lines from the center to different places on the circumference. See **circle.**
2. A part or division of a city or group of people, as in *the public and private sectors.*

S

se·cure (si-kyoor)
1. *adjective* If you feel **secure,** you feel safe and sure of yourself.
2. *adjective* Safe, firmly closed, or well protected. *The money is secure in the safe.*
3. *verb* If you **secure** something, you make it safe, especially by closing it tightly. *The guards secured the president's home.*
4. *adjective* Firm and steady, or strong, as in *a secure ladder* or *a secure lock.*
5. *adjective* Certain or guaranteed, as in *a secure job.*
6. *verb* To get. *Zena secured four tickets to the concert.*
▷ *noun* **security** ▷ *verb* **securing, secured** ▷ *adverb* **securely**

se·dan (si-dan) *noun* An enclosed car for four or more people.

se·date (si-date)
1. *adjective* Calm and not hurried. *We strolled along at a sedate pace.*
2. *adjective* Serious or dignified, as in *a sedate judge.*
3. *verb* To make someone calm or sleepy, especially by giving the person medicine. *The nurse sedated the patient.* ▷ **sedating, sedated**
▷ *noun* **sedation**
▷ *adverb* **sedately**

sed·a·tive (sed-uh-tiv) *noun* A drug that makes you quiet and calm.

sed·i·ment (sed-uh-muhnt) *noun*
1. Solid pieces of matter that settle at the bottom of a liquid. ▷ *noun* **sedimentation**
2. Rocks, sand, or dirt that has been carried to a place by water, wind, or a glacier.

sed·i·men·tar·y (*sed-uh-men-tuh-ree*) *adjective* **Sedimentary** rock is formed by layers of sediment in the ground being pressed together. *The bands of color in sedimentary rock, seen here in the Grand Canyon, indicate changes in the types of sediment involved.*

Grand Canyon

see (see) *verb*
1. To use your eyes, to look at, or to notice something or someone.
2. To understand or to recognize. *I see what you mean.*
3. To find out or to discover. *I need to see what our friends want.*
4. To visit and spend some time with someone. *Ivy is going over to see Phyllis this afternoon.*
5. To date someone regularly. *Are you seeing anyone?*
6. If you **see about** something, you deal with it.
7. If you **see through** someone or something, you are not deceived or tricked by the person or thing.
8. If you **see** a job **through,** you continue doing it right to the end.
See sounds like **sea.**
▷ *verb* **seeing, saw, seen** (seen)

seed (seed) *noun*
1. *noun* The part of a flowering plant from which a new plant can grow, especially a grain, nut, or kernel. *See* **germinate.**
2. *noun* The source or beginning of something, as in *the seeds of hope.*
3. *verb* To plant land with seeds.
4. *verb* To remove seeds from. *I seeded the watermelon before eating it.*
▷ *verb* **seeding, seeded**

seed·ling (seed-ling) *noun* A young plant that has been grown from a seed.

seek (seek) *verb*
1. To look or search for something. ▷ *noun* **seeker**
2. To try. *Joseph will seek to win the election.*
3. To ask for. *The survivors sought help.*
▷ *verb* **seeking, sought** (sawt)

seem (seem) *verb*
1. To appear to be, or to give the impression of being. *They seem happy.*
2. To appear to oneself. *I seem to have forgotten my keys.*
Seem sounds like **seam.**
▷ *verb* **seeming, seemed**

seep (seep) *verb* To flow or trickle slowly. *Some water has seeped through the ceiling.* ▷ **seeping, seeped** ▷ *noun* **seepage**

see·saw (see-*saw*)
1. *noun* A long board balanced on a support in the middle. When people sit on opposite sides, one end goes up as the other goes down.
2. *verb* To ride on a seesaw.
3. *verb* To move up and down or back and forth. *The price of gasoline has seesawed.*
▷ *verb* **seesawing, seesawed**

seethe (seeTH) *verb*
1. To be very angry or excited. *She was seething with rage.*
2. If a liquid **seethes,** it bubbles or boils.
▷ *verb* **seething, seethed** ▷ *adjective* **seething**

S

see-through *adjective* Able to be seen through; transparent, as in *a see-through material.*

seg·ment (seg-muhnt) *noun*
1. A part or section of something. *Lucy divided the orange into segments.*
2. In geometry, the straight path that connects two points.
▷ *verb* **segment** ▷ *adjective* **segmental**

seg·re·gate (seg-ruh-gate) *verb* To separate or keep people or things apart from the main group. *The warden segregated the violent prisoners.*
▷ **segregating, segregated** ▷ *adjective* **segregated**

seg·re·ga·tion (seg-ruh-gay-shuhn) *noun* The act or practice of keeping people or groups apart. Segregation of schools and public facilities along racial lines is illegal in the United States.

seis·mo·graph (size-muh-*graf*) *noun* An instrument that detects earthquakes and measures their power. ▷ *noun* **seismography** (size-mo-gruh-fee)

seize (seez) *verb*
1. To grab or take hold of something suddenly. *I seized the rail to keep myself from falling down the steps.*
2. To arrest or capture someone or something. *Police seized the burglars as they came out of the building. The enemy seized the ship.*
▷ *verb* **seizing, seized**

sei·zure (see-zhur) *noun*
1. A **seizure** is a sudden attack of illness, or a spasm.
2. The act of seizing something or someone.

sel·dom (sel-duhm) *adverb* Rarely. *We seldom see our neighbors because they leave for work early and get home late.*

se·lect (si-lekt)
1. *verb* To pick out or to choose. ▷ **selecting, selected** ▷ *noun* **selector**
2. *adjective* Carefully chosen as the best. *The scholarship winners were part of a select group.*

se·lec·tion (suh-lek-shuhn) *noun*
1. The act of picking or choosing something. *Because there were so many beautiful cats at the pet shop, I had a hard time making a selection.*
2. A person or thing that has been chosen.

se·lec·tive (si-lek-tiv) *adjective* If you are **selective,** you choose carefully.

self (self) *noun* One's individual nature or personality. *He was upset this morning and not like his usual self.* ▷ *noun, plural* **selves**

self-centered *adjective* Thinking only about yourself; selfish.

self-confident *adjective* If you are **self-confident,** you are sure of your own abilities or worth.
▷ *noun* **self-confidence** ▷ *adverb* **self-confidently**

self-conscious *adjective* If you are **self-conscious,** you think that people are looking at you, and you worry about what they are thinking.
▷ *adverb* **self-consciously**

self-control *noun* Control of your feelings and behavior. ▷ *adjective* **self-controlled**

self-defense *noun* The act of protecting yourself against attacks or threats.

self-de·struct (di-struhkt) *verb* To destroy itself or oneself. *I once read a story about a computer that self-destructed when it realized that it could never love anyone.* ▷ **self-destructing, self-destructed** ▷ *noun* **self-destruction** ▷ *adjective* **self-destructive**

self-employed *adjective* If you are **self-employed,** you work for yourself, not an employer. You are your own boss.

self-esteem *noun* A feeling of personal pride and of respect for yourself.

self-explanatory *adjective* If something is **self-explanatory,** it does not need any further explanation. *These instructions are self-explanatory.*

self·ish (sel-fish) *adjective* Someone who is **selfish** puts his or her own feelings and needs first and does not think of others. ▷ *noun* **selfishness** ▷ *adverb* **selfishly**

self-respect *noun* Pride in yourself and your abilities. ▷ *adjective* **self-respecting**

self-rising flour *noun* Flour containing baking powder, which makes cakes or breads rise.

self-service *adjective* If a store or gas station is **self-service,** you help yourself to what you want and then pay a cashier.

self-start·er (star-tur) *noun* Someone who has the ability or willingness to take a first step in doing or learning something.

self-sufficient *adjective* Able to take care of one's own needs without help from others.
▷ *noun* **self-sufficiency**

sell (sel) *verb*
1. To give something in exchange for money. *Julie sold me her tickets to the baseball game.*
▷ *noun* **seller**
2. To offer for sale. *This store sells sports equipment.*
3. To be sold or to be on sale. *A rare baseball card can sell for $1,000.*
4. To help the sale of something. *TV commercials are used to sell new products.*
5. *(informal)* To make someone believe or want something. *The travel agent tried to sell us the idea of a Caribbean vacation.*
Sell sounds like **cell.**
▷ *verb* **selling, sold** (sohld)

S

sem·a·phore (sem-uh-*for*) *noun* A system of making signals by means of flags or your arms. *The picture shows the message SOS in semaphore.* ▷ *verb* semaphore

semaphore

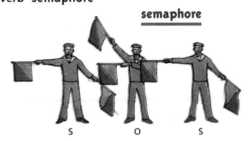

S   O   S

se·mes·ter (suh-**mess**-tur) *noun* One of two terms that make up a school year. *Our fall semester begins the day after Labor Day.*

sem·i·cir·cle (sem-i-*sur*-kuhl) *noun* A half of a circle. ▷ *adjective* semicircular

sem·i·co·lon (sem-i-*koh*-luhn) *noun* The punctuation mark (;) used to separate parts of a sentence. A semicolon shows a greater separation of thoughts or ideas than a comma does.

sem·i·con·duc·tor (*sem*-ee-kuhn-**duhk**-tur) *noun* A substance, such as silicon, whose ability to conduct electricity is not as good as a conductor, such as copper, but is better than an insulator, such as plastic. Semiconductors are used in electronic devices, including personal computers.

sem·i·fi·nal (sem-ee-*fye*-nuhl or sem-eye-*fye*-nuhl) *noun* A match or game to decide who will play in the final. ▷ *noun* semifinalist ▷ *adjective* semifinal

sem·i·nar·y (sem-uh-*ner*-ee) *noun* A school that trains students to become priests, ministers, or rabbis. ▷ *noun, plural* seminaries

Sem·i·nole (sem-uh-nole) *noun* A member of a tribe of American Indians that originally lived in Florida. After the United States acquired Florida in 1819, the government attempted to force the Seminoles to move to the Indian Territory in Oklahoma. They resisted, but after fighting three wars, many were sent west. Today, the Seminoles largely live in Oklahoma, but some still live in Florida. ▷ *noun, plural* Seminoles or Seminole

sen·ate (sen-it) *noun*
1. A body of officials elected to make laws.
2. Senate One of the two houses of the U.S. Congress that make laws. Each state has two senators. Senators are elected every six years. Most states have similar legislative bodies. ▷ *noun* senator or Senator

send (send) *verb*
1. To make someone or something go somewhere, as in *to send a letter,* or *to send someone on an errand.* ▷ *noun* sender
2. To write to ask for something. *We sent away for the free offer.*

3. If you **send for** something or someone, you make it come to you. *Let's send for pizza. Should we send for the police?* ▷ *verb* sending, sent

send-off *noun* (informal) If you are given a **send-off,** people gather to wish you well for a journey, new job, etc.

se·nile (see-nile or sen-ile) *adjective* Weak in mind and body because of old age. ▷ *noun* senility (si-nil-i-tee)

sen·ior (see-nyur)
1. *adjective* When a father and son have identical names, **senior** is placed after the surname to indicate the father, as in *John Doe, Senior.*
2. *adjective* Someone who is **senior** to you is older or has a higher rank. ▷ *noun* seniority
3. *noun* A student in the fourth year of high school or college. ▷ *adjective* senior

senior citizen *noun* An elderly person, especially someone who is older than 65 and has retired.

sen·sa·tion (sen-say-shuhn) *noun*
1. The ability to feel or be aware of something through one of the senses, as in *the sensation of touch.*
2. A feeling or an awareness. *The mountain climber had no sensation in her toes because she had severe frostbite. When I heard a noise behind me, I had a strong sensation that I was being followed.*
3. Something that causes a lot of excitement and interest. *The telephone caused a big sensation when it was first invented.* ▷ *adjective* sensational ▷ *adverb* sensationally

sense (senss)
1. *noun* One of the powers a living being uses to learn about its surroundings. Sight, hearing, touch, taste, and smell are the five senses.
2. *noun* A feeling, as in *a sense of pride* or *a sense of failure.*
3. *noun* An understanding or an appreciation, as in *a good sense of humor.*
4. *noun* Good judgment. *Have the sense to eat a healthy breakfast.*
5. *noun* Meaning. *Frances is persistent, in the best sense of the word.*
6. *verb* To feel or be aware of something. *I sensed that Gene was angry.* ▷ sensing, sensed
7. If something **makes sense,** it is understandable or logical.

sense·less (senss-liss) *adjective*
1. Pointless or without meaning. *What a senseless waste of money!* ▷ *adverb* senselessly
2. Unconscious. *The batter was knocked senseless by a wild pitch.*

sense organ *noun* An organ in the body that receives information, or stimuli, from its surroundings. The human sense organs include the eyes, ears, nose, taste buds, and skin.

S

sen·si·ble (sen-suh-buhl) *adjective* If you are **sensible,** you think carefully and do not do stupid or dangerous things. ▷ *adverb* **sensibly**

sen·si·tive (sen-suh-tiv) *adjective*
1. Easily offended or hurt. *Max is sensitive to criticism.*
2. Painful. *The infected tooth was very sensitive.*
3. Aware of other people's feelings. *The counselor was sensitive to Joelle's problems.*
4. Able to react to the slightest change, as in *a sensitive measuring device.*
▷ *noun* **sensitivity** ▷ *adverb* **sensitively**

sen·sor (sen-sur) *noun* An instrument that can detect changes in heat, sound, pressure, etc., and send the information to a controlling device.

sen·tence (sen-tuhnss) *noun*
1. A group of words that expresses a complete thought, having a subject and a verb. A written sentence begins with a capital letter and ends with a period, a question mark, or an exclamation point.
2. A punishment given to a guilty person in court. *The murderer was given a life sentence.*
▷ *verb* **sentence**

sen·ti·ment (sen-tuh-muhnt) *noun*
1. An opinion about a specific matter. *Popular sentiment is against lowering the voting age.*
2. A thought or an attitude that is based on feeling or emotion instead of reason. *Watching the Americans receive their Olympic gold medals stirred Alan's patriotic sentiment.*
3. Tender or sensitive feeling. *I tried to find a Valentine's Day card that would express my sentiment.*

sen·ti·ment·al (sen-tuh-**men**-tuhl) *adjective* To do with emotion, romance, or feelings. *This ring has sentimental value because it was my mother's.*
▷ *noun* **sentimentality** ▷ *adverb* **sentimentally**

sen·try (sen-tree) *noun* A person who stands guard and warns others of danger. ▷ *noun, plural* **sentries**

se·pal (see-puhl) *noun* The green outer covering of a flower bud. The sepal opens to allow the flower to bloom and remains to protect the petals.

sep·a·rate
1. (sep-uh-rate) *verb* To part or divide something or some people. *Separate the orange into sections. Separate those fighting boys.*
2. (sep-ur-it) *adjective* Different, individual, or not together. *The three children have separate bedrooms.* ▷ *adverb* **separately**
3. (sep-uh-rate) *verb* If a husband and wife **separate,** they stop living together.
4. separates (sep-ur-its) *noun, plural* Clothes, such as a skirt and blouse, that you can wear together or with other clothes.
▷ *verb* **separating, separated** ▷ *noun* **separation**

Sep·tem·ber (sep-tem-bur) *noun* The ninth month on the calendar, after August and before October. September has 30 days.

> ### Word History
> In ancient Rome, the year began in March, making **September** the seventh month. That's why our ninth month, September, takes its name from the Latin word *septem,* which means "seven."

se·quel (see-kwuhl) *noun* A book or movie that continues the story of an earlier work.

se·quence (see-kwuhnss) *noun*
1. The following of one thing after another in a regular or fixed order. *The letters of the alphabet follow each other in sequence.*
2. A series or collection of things that follow in order. *This sequence of four photographs shows our house during the different seasons of the year.* ▷ *adjective* **sequential** (see-kwen-shuhl)

se·quoi·a (suh-**kwoi**-uh) *noun* A giant evergreen tree that can reach a height of over 300 feet (90 meters). Sequoias have thick, reddish brown bark and grow mostly in California. Redwoods are a type of sequoia. *The photograph shows one such tree at California's Sequoia National Park.*

sequoia

> ### Word History
> The **sequoia,** among the largest and tallest of trees, was named in honor of the Cherokee Indian scholar Sequoyah, who was born around 1770. Sequoyah spent 12 years developing a written alphabet for the spoken Cherokee language. The giant tree was named for him shortly after his death in 1847.

S

ser·en·dip·i·ty (ser-uhn-dip-uh-tee) *noun* A fortunate accident in which you find something valuable or pleasing when you were not looking for it. *It was serendipity when the box fell off the shelf and I discovered my dad's forgotten collection of baseball cards.* ▷ *adjective* **serendipitous**

se·rene (suh-reen) *adjective* Calm and peaceful, as in *a serene setting.* ▷ *noun* **serenity** (suh-ren-i-tee) ▷ *adverb* **serenely**

serf (surf) *noun* In medieval times, a farm worker who was owned by a lord and treated as a slave. **Serf** sounds like **surf.** See **feudalism.** ▷ *noun* **serfdom**

ser·geant (sar-juhnt) *noun* An officer in the army or Marine Corps who is appointed from among the enlisted personnel. A sergeant ranks above a corporal and is in charge of enlisted troops.

se·ri·al (sihr-ee-uhl) *noun* A story that is told in several parts. The parts are presented one at a time on television or radio or in a magazine. **Serial** sounds like **cereal.** ▷ *noun* **serialization** ▷ *verb* **serialize**

serial number *noun* A number that identifies a member of the armed forces or a vehicle, an appliance, or another product.

se·ries (sihr-eez) *noun*
1. A group of related things that follow in order. *I took a series of swimming lessons.*
2. A number of television or radio programs that are linked in some way. *On Sunday nights I watch a detective series.*
3. Electrical parts that are connected **in series** allow electricity to pass through them one after the other.
▷ *noun, plural* **series**

se·ri·ous (sihr-ee-uhss) *adjective*
1. Solemn and thoughtful. *As the priest began his sermon, his voice took on a serious tone.*
2. Sincere or not joking. *Are you serious about leaving school?*
3. Very bad, or dangerous. *She has a serious illness.*
4. Important and requiring a lot of thought. *My brother is making serious plans for college.*
▷ *noun* **seriousness** ▷ *adverb* **seriously**

ser·mon (sur-muhn) *noun*
1. A speech given during a religious service.
2. Any serious talk, especially one that deals with morals or correct behavior. *My parents gave me a sermon about the importance of studying.*
▷ *verb* **sermonize**

ser·o·pos·i·tive (sihr-oh-poz-uh-tiv) *adjective* If a blood test is **seropositive,** it means that the antibody the doctor was looking for is present in the blood. ▷ *noun* **seropositivity** (sihr-oh-*po*-zuh-**tiv**-uh-tee)

ser·pent (sur-puhnt) *noun* A snake. *This Aztec jewelry is made in the shape of a serpent with two heads.*

serpent pendant

ser·rat·ed (ser-ay-tid) *adjective* A **serrated** knife has teeth like a saw.

se·rum (sihr-uhm) *noun*
1. The clear, thin, liquid part of the blood. It separates from blood when a clot forms.
2. A liquid used to prevent or cure a disease. Serum is taken from the blood of an animal that has had the disease and is already immune to it.
▷ *noun, plural* **serums** or **sera** (sihr-uh)

serv·ant (sur-vuhnt) *noun* Someone who works in another person's house doing housework, cooking, or other chores.

serve (surv) *verb*
1. To work for someone as a servant. *The housekeeper served our family for years.*
2. To give someone food, or to help someone find items in a store. *The waiter served us our food quickly.*
3. To do your duty in some form of service. *I would like to serve on a jury.*
4. To supply. *The recipe serves four people, but I plan to double it for my party.*
5. To spend. *The criminal served his full sentence in jail.*
6. In games such as tennis and volleyball, to begin play by hitting the ball. ▷ *noun* **serve**
▷ *verb* **serving, served** ▷ *noun* **server**

serv·ice (sur-viss) *noun*
1. The **service** in a store, restaurant, etc., is the way that the staff helps and takes care of you.
2. Work that helps others. *He spends much of his time in service to the homeless. He needs the services of a doctor.*
3. Employment as a servant.
4. A system or way of providing something useful or necessary. *Mail service is slow in our town.*
5. A branch of the armed forces. *After high school, my father spent four years in the service.*
6. A religious ceremony or meeting.
7. A branch of the government, as in *the postal service* or *the foreign service.*
8. The repairing of a car or an appliance. *We brought the television in for service.*

S

9. A complete set of matched dishes, as in *a dinner service.*
10. A serve in tennis, volleyball, or any game in which a ball is hit over a net.
▷ *verb* **service**

service station *noun* Another term for **gas station.**

ses·a·me (sess-uh-mee) *noun* A small oval seed, or the tropical plant from which this seed comes. Sesame seeds and their oil are used in cooking and baking.

ses·sion (sesh-uhn) *noun*
1. A formal meeting, as in *a session of the Supreme Court.*
2. A series of meetings of a court or legislature. *This session of Congress ends next week.*
3. A period of time used for an activity. *Our training session on our new computers will run all morning.*

set (set)
1. *noun* A group of things that go together, as in *a chess set.*
2. *noun* The stage or scenery for a play or movie.
3. *adjective* Ready. *Are we all set to leave?*
4. *adjective* Fixed. *The meeting begins at a set time every week.*
5. *verb* To put or to place. *He set the book back on its shelf.*
6. *verb* To lay out, arrange, or put in order. *Set the table for four people.*
7. *verb* To begin or to start. *I set to work on my project.*
8. *verb* To decide on. *Have they set a date for their wedding?*
9. *verb* To model for other people to follow. *My teacher sets a good example.*
10. *verb* If a liquid **sets,** it becomes hard or solid.
11. *verb* When the sun **sets,** it goes below the horizon.
12. *noun* A device for sending out or receiving electronic signals, as in *a television set.*
13. *noun* In math, a collection of items that are grouped together or have something in common.
14. If you **set** something **up,** you get it ready for use or arrange it. *Carl set up enough chairs for all of his guests.*
15. If you **set aside** something, you save it for another time.
16. If you **set out** for a place, you begin your trip.
17. If you are **set on** something, you want it very much and are determined to get or achieve it.
▷ *verb* **setting, set**

set·back (set-*bak*) *noun* Something that delays you or keeps you from making progress. *The builders promised that the house would be built by September, despite setbacks caused by the weather.*

set·tee (se-tee) *noun* A small sofa.

settee

set·tle (set-uhl) *verb*
1. To decide or agree on something. *We settled the argument by tossing a coin.*
2. To make yourself comfortable. *Jessie settled down with a good book.*
3. To make a home or to live in a new place. *Pioneers settled the West.* ▷ *noun* **settler**
4. To sink. *Our sidewalk has settled and cracked.*
5. To calm. *The medicine settled my stomach.*
6. If you **settle in,** you get used to your new house, school, etc.
7. If you **settle up,** you pay a bill or an account.
▷ *verb* **settling, settled**

set·tle·ment (set-uhl-muhnt) *noun*
1. An agreement or a decision about something that was in doubt. *The strike dragged on because the two sides could not reach a settlement.*
2. A small village or group of houses.
3. A colony or group of people who have left one place to make a home in another.

set·up (set-*uhp*) *noun* The way that something is organized or arranged. *The teacher changed the setup of our classroom while we were on vacation.*

sev·en (sev-uhn) *noun* The whole number, written 7, that comes after six and before eight.
▷ *adjective* **seven**

sev·enth (sev-uhnth)
1. *adjective* That which comes after sixth and before eighth.
2. *noun* One part of something that has been divided into seven equal parts, written $\frac{1}{7}$.

sev·er (sev-ur) *verb*
1. To cut off or apart, as in *to sever a limb.*
2. To end or to break off. *The two countries have severed all ties.*
▷ *verb* **severing, severed**

sev·er·al (sev-ur-uhl)
1. *adjective* More than two, but not many. *Several days passed before Tim returned our call.*
2. *noun* More than two, or a few, people or things. *Several of the guests were late.*

S

se·vere (suh-veer) *adjective*
1. Strict, harsh, or demanding, as in *severe punishment* or *severe criticism*.
2. Painful or dangerous, as in *a severe burn* or *a severe illness*.
3. Violent, or causing great discomfort or difficulty, as in *a severe storm*.
▷ *adjective* **severer, severest** ▷ *noun* **severity** (suh-ver-i-tee) ▷ *adverb* **severely**

sew (soh) *verb* To make, repair, or fasten something with stitches made by a needle and thread. **Sew** sounds like **so.** ▷ **sewing, sewed, sewn** (sohn) ▷ *noun* **sewing**

sew·age (soo-ij) *noun* Liquid and solid waste that is carried away in sewers and drains.

sewage plant *noun* A place where sewage is treated to make it safe and not poisonous.

sew·er (soo-ur) *noun* An underground pipe that carries away liquid and solid waste.

sewing machine *noun* A machine for sewing very fast or making special stitches.

sex (seks) *noun*
1. One of the two classes of most living things, male or female, into which people and many other living things are divided. *The symbols used for the male and female sexes are shown here.*
2. The fact or condition of being male or female. *The sex of the candidate should not be important in our decision.*
▷ *noun, plural* **sexes**

male

female

sex·ist (sek-sist) *adjective* Someone who is **sexist** discriminates against members of one or the other sex. *It is sexist to assume that girls can't play football or that boys can't sew.* ▷ *noun* **sexism,** *noun* **sexist**

shab·by (shab-ee) *adjective*
1. Worn, neglected, or in need of repair. *I changed into shabby clothes before going out to work in the garden.* ▷ *noun* **shabbiness**
2. Unfair or mean. *That was a shabby trick Ken played on you.*
▷ *adjective* **shabbier, shabbiest** ▷ *adverb* **shabbily**

shack (shak) *noun* A small, roughly built hut or house.

shack·les (shak-uhlz) *noun, plural* A pair of metal rings locked around the wrists or ankles of a prisoner or a slave.

shad (shad) *noun* A food fish related to the herring. Shad live along the coasts of Europe and North America and swim up freshwater rivers to lay their eggs, or roe. ▷ *noun, plural* **shad**

shade (shayd)
1. *verb* To shelter something from the light. *A large hat shaded her face.*
2. *noun* A device that provides shelter from light, as in *a lamp shade* or *a window shade.*
3. *noun* An area that is sheltered from the light. *Come and sit in the shade and have a cold drink.*
▷ *adjective* **shady**
4. *noun* The degree of darkness of a color. *The artist used several shades of green to paint his jungle scene.*
5. *verb* To make part of a drawing darker than the rest. *Shade in that area with your piece of charcoal.*
6. *noun* A small amount or difference. *Randall is a shade shorter than his father. The word* bad *has many shades of meaning.*
7. shades *noun, plural* (slang) Sunglasses.
▷ *noun* **shading** ▷ *verb* **shading, shaded**

shad·ow (shad-oh)
1. *noun* A dark shape made by something blocking out light. ▷ *adjective* **shadowy**
2. *noun* A faint trace or suggestion, as in *a shadow of a doubt.*
3. *verb* To follow someone closely and watch the person carefully and usually secretly. *Detectives shadowed the thieves all the way back to their hideout.* ▷ **shadowing, shadowed**

shaft (shaft) *noun*
1. The long, narrow rod of a spear, an arrow, or a paddle. *See* **kayak.**
2. A rotating rod that transmits power to wheels or propellers.
3. A thin beam of light.
4. A long, narrow passage that goes straight down, as in *a mine shaft* or *an elevator shaft.*
5. The central stem of a feather. *See* **feather.**

shag·gy (shag-ee) *adjective* Having long, rough hair or wool, as in *a shaggy dog* or *a shaggy carpet.* ▷ **shaggier, shaggiest**

shake (shayk) *verb*
1. To move quickly up and down or back and forth. *Shake the bottle before you open it. The trees shook in the wind.*
2. To remove or scatter something by making short, quick movements. *I shook the rain from my umbrella.*
3. To tremble, or to cause to tremble. *I shook with cold. The earthquake shook our house.*
4. To upset. *The news we received from our cousins shook my family.*
5. To clasp someone's hand as a way of greeting or agreeing with the person.
▷ *verb* **shaking, shook** (shuk)**, shaken** (shay-kin)
▷ *noun* **shake**

S

shak·y (shay-kee) *adjective*
1. Unsteady and wobbly. *The calf stood up on shaky legs.*
2. Trembling or shaking. *The nervous student gave her report in a shaky voice.*
▷ *adjective* **shakier, shakiest**

shale (shayl) *noun* A rock that is formed from hardened clay or mud. It has many thin layers that separate easily.

shall (shal) *verb* A helping verb that is used in the following ways:
1. To show an action that will take place in the future. *I shall arrive tomorrow.*
2. To show that an action is required. *You shall clean up your room before going out.*
3. To ask a question, or to offer a suggestion. *Shall we dance?*

shal·low (shal-oh) *adjective*
1. Not deep. *I like to wade in the shallow water.*
2. Lacking depth of thought, feeling, or knowledge, as in *a shallow mind.*
▷ *adjective* **shallower, shallowest**

sham (sham) *noun* Something that is false and not what it seems to be. ▷ *adjective* **sham**

sham·bles (sham-buhlz) *noun* If something is a **shambles,** it is very badly organized and chaotic. *The basketball game turned into a shambles after the fans surged onto the court.*

shame (shame) *noun*
1. A feeling of guilt and sadness about something wrong or foolish that you have done.
2. Dishonor or disgrace. *His arrest brought shame to his entire family.* ▷ *verb* **shame**
3. A pity, or a sad thing to have happened. *It's a shame that Alexandra can't come with us for dinner tonight.*

sham·poo (sham-poo) *noun* A soapy liquid used for washing hair, carpets, or upholstery. ▷ *verb* **shampoo**

▶ Word History
• •
Shampoo, one of the very few English words that end in -oo, comes from India. It developed from the Hindi word *champo,* meaning "massage" or "knead," which describes the action of working soap into your hair.

sham·rock (sham-rok) *noun* A small, green plant with three leaves. The shamrock is the national emblem of Ireland.

shan·ty (shan-tee) *noun*
1. A roughly built hut or cabin. A shanty is usually made of wood.

2. A **sea shanty** is a song sung by sailors in rhythm with their work.
▷ *noun, plural* **shanties**

shape (shayp)
1. *noun* The form or outline of an object or a figure. *The picture shows a range of flat and solid shapes.*
2. *verb* To mold something into a shape.
3. *noun* Good or fit condition. *Exercise helps keep you in shape.*
4. shape up *verb* (informal) To develop. *The new team is shaping up well.*
▷ *verb* **shaping, shaped**

flat shapes

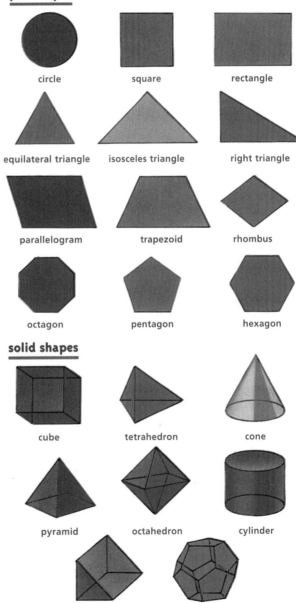

circle   square   rectangle

equilateral triangle   isosceles triangle   right triangle

parallelogram   trapezoid   rhombus

octagon   pentagon   hexagon

solid shapes

cube   tetrahedron   cone

pyramid   octahedron   cylinder

prism   dodecahedron (12 faces)

S

481

shape·less (shape-liss) *adjective* Having no clearly defined shape, or having an unattractive shape. *I was amazed at the beautiful sculpture that you made from a shapeless mass of clay.*

share (shair)
1. *verb* To divide something between two or more people. *Elaine shared her sandwich.*
2. *noun* The portion of something that someone receives or that is assigned to someone. *I hope you do your share of the work.*
3. *verb* To use together. *My cousins share a house.*
4. *verb* To take part. *Jeff shared in the fun.*
5. *noun* One of many equal parts into which the ownership of a business is divided. *I own 10 shares of stock in a computer company.*
▷ *verb* **sharing, shared**

share·ware (shair-wair) *noun* Computer software that has a copyright but is provided free on a trial basis. If a person decides to continue using the software, he or she is expected to pay a fee to the author. ▷ *noun, plural* **shareware**

shark (shark) *noun*
1. A large and often fierce fish that feeds on meat and has very sharp teeth.
2. Someone who cheats people.

tiger shark

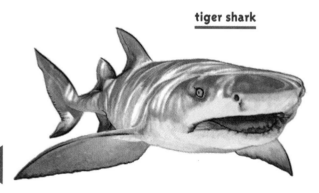

sharp (sharp) *adjective*
1. Having an edge or a point that cuts or pierces easily, as in *a sharp knife* or *a sharp needle.*
2. Pointed, as in *a sharp mountain peak.*
3. Able to think or notice things quickly, as in *a sharp mind* or *sharp eyes.*
4. Sudden and dramatic. *There is a sharp turn in the road.*
5. Strong, biting, or harsh, as in *a sharp cheese, sharp words,* or *a sharp wind.*
6. Clearly outlined, as in *a sharp picture.*
7. Exactly. *Be here at three o'clock sharp.*
8. In music, a **sharp** note is one that is higher in pitch than the usual note. *C sharp is a semitone higher than C.* ▷ *noun* **sharp**
9. (slang) Very attractive. *That's a sharp outfit!*
▷ *adjective* **sharper, sharpest**

shat·ter (shat-ur) *verb*
1. To break into tiny pieces. *The mirror shattered when I dropped it.*
2. To destroy completely or to ruin. *His life was shattered by a tragic car accident.*
▷ *verb* **shattering, shattered**

shave (shayv)
1. *verb* To remove hair with a razor or an electric shaver. ▷ *noun* **shave**
2. *verb* To cut off or slice in thin layers.
3. (informal) If you have **a close shave,** you only just manage to escape from something.
▷ *verb* **shaving, shaved**

shawl (shawl) *noun* A piece of soft material that is worn over the shoulders or around the head.

Shaw·nee (shaw-nee) *noun* A member of an American Indian tribe that once lived in the central Ohio valley. The Shawnee now live mainly in Oklahoma. ▷ *noun, plural* **Shawnee** or **Shawnees**

she (shee) *pronoun* The female person or animal mentioned before. *I like Sheila; she is my friend.*

sheaf (sheef) *noun* A bundle, as in *a sheaf of papers.* ▷ *noun, plural* **sheaves**

shear (shihr) *verb*
1. To clip or cut with scissors or shears. *The gardener sheared the hedge.*
2. To cut the fleece off a sheep. *The picture shows a farmer shearing a sheep with electric clippers.* **Shear** sounds like **sheer.**
▷ *verb* **shearing, sheared** *or* **shorn (shorn)**

sheepshearing

shears (shihrz) *noun, plural* A large cutting tool with two blades. Shears are used for cutting hedges, trimming grass, etc.

sheath (sheeth) *noun* A holder for a knife, sword, or dagger. *See* **dagger.**

shed (shed)
1. *noun* A small building used for storing things.
2. *verb* To let something fall or drop off. *Some reptiles shed their skin. Some trees shed their leaves. People shed tears.*
3. *verb* To give off or to supply. *The lecture shed little light on the subject.*
▷ *verb* **shedding, shed**

she'd (sheed) *contraction* A short form of *she had* or *she would. She'd never been to a big city before. She'd help you if she could.*

sheen (sheen) *noun* A shine on a surface.

sheep (sheep) *noun* A farm animal raised for its wool and meat. *See* **flock.** ▷ *noun, plural* **sheep**

sheep·dog (sheep-dog) *noun* A working farm dog that guards and rounds up sheep.

sheep·ish (sheep-ish) *adjective* If someone looks **sheepish,** the person looks embarrassed or ashamed, often because he or she has done something foolish. ▷ *adverb* **sheepishly**

sheer (shihr) *adjective*
1. Extremely thin and transparent, as in *sheer stockings.*
2. Total and complete, as in *sheer nonsense* or *sheer exhaustion.*
3. Extremely steep. *There was a sheer drop to the rocks below.*
Sheer sounds like **shear.**
▷ *adjective* **sheerer, sheerest**

sheet (sheet) *noun*
1. A large, thin, rectangular piece of cloth used to cover a bed.
2. A thin, flat piece of paper, glass, metal, or other material.

sheik (sheek *or* shake) *noun* The head of an Arab tribe, village, or family.

shelf (shelf) *noun*
1. A horizontal board on a wall or in a cupboard, used for holding or storing things.
2. Something flat that looks like a shelf, such as a ledge of rock.
▷ *noun, plural* **shelves** (shelvz)

shell (shel)
1. *noun* A hard outer covering or case. Nuts, tortoises, shellfish, and eggs all have shells.
2. *noun* A type of small bomb that is fired from a cannon.
3. *noun* A metal or paper case that holds a bullet and its explosive. It is fired from a gun.
4. *verb* To remove something from its shell.
5. *verb* To bombard, or attack with shells.
▷ *verb* **shelling, shelled**

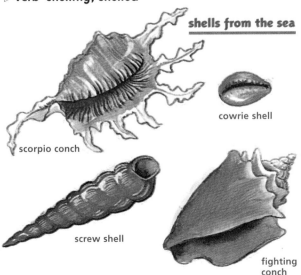

shells from the sea

scorpio conch

cowrie shell

screw shell

fighting conch

she'll (sheel) *contraction* A short form of *she will* or *she shall. She'll arrive next week. She'll water my plants while I'm away.*

shel·lac (shuh-lak) *noun* A hard varnish used on wooden floors and furniture to protect them and give them a shiny finish.

shell·fish (shel-fish) *noun* A sea creature with a shell, such as a shrimp, crab, lobster, or mussel. Many shellfish are edible. ▷ *noun, plural* **shellfish** *or* **shellfishes**

shel·ter (shel-tur) *noun*
1. A place where you can keep covered in bad weather or stay safe and protected from danger, as in *a bus shelter* or *a bomb shelter.*
2. Protection. *During the tornado, they took shelter in their basement.*
3. A place where a homeless person, a victim of a disaster, or an animal that is not wanted can stay.
▷ *verb* **shelter**

shelve (shelv) *verb*
1. To put something off for a while. *The project was shelved because of lack of funds.*
2. To put something on a shelf or shelves. *The librarian shelved the books.*
▷ *verb* **shelving, shelved**

shep·herd (shep-urd)
1. *noun* Someone whose job is to look after sheep.
2. *verb* To watch over or to guide. *The ski patrol shepherded us out of the area hit by an avalanche.*
▷ **shepherding, shepherded**

sher·bet (shur-buht) *or* **sher·bert** (shur-burt) *noun* A frozen dessert made of fruit juices, water, sugar, and milk, egg white, or gelatin.

sher·iff (sher-if) *noun* The chief person in charge of enforcing the law in a county.

sher·ry (sher-ee) *noun* A strong, sweet wine.
▷ *noun, plural* **sherries**

she's (sheez) *contraction* A short form of *she is* or *she has. She's almost ready. She's been at the computer for hours.*

Shet·land pony (shet-luhnd) *noun* A small horse with a long mane and tail and a rough coat, originally bred in Scotland's Shetland Islands.

shield (sheeld)
1. *noun* A piece of armor carried to protect the body from attack.
2. *noun* A protective barrier, as in *a heat shield.*
3. *verb* To protect something or someone. *The parasol shielded us from the sun.* ▷ **shielding, shielded**
4. *noun* A police officer's badge.

S

shift (shift)
  1. *verb* To change or move something. *I used to respect the mayor, but my opinion of her has shifted. Abby shifted her books to her other arm.*
  2. *noun* A movement or a change. *I detect a shift in your attitude.*
  3. *noun* A set period of several hours' continuous work, as in *the night shift.*
  4. *verb* To change the gears in a motor vehicle that does not have an automatic transmission. *Shift into second gear.* ▷ ***noun*** **shift**
  ▷ ***verb*** **shifting, shifted**

shii·ta·ke (shee-tah-kee) ***noun*** A dark brown, edible Asian mushroom.

shil·ling (shil-ing) ***noun***
  1. A coin that was used in Great Britain until 1971. Twenty shillings equaled one pound.
  2. A coin that is used in several African countries, including Kenya, Somalia, Tanzania, and Uganda. One shilling equals 100 cents.

shim·mer (shim-ur) ***verb*** To shine with a faint, unsteady light. ▷ **shimmering, shimmered**

shin (shin)
  1. *noun* The front part of your leg between your knee and your ankle.
  2. *verb* To climb by using your hands and legs to pull you up, as in *to shin up a tree.* ▷ **shinning, shinned**

shine (shine) ***verb***
  1. To give off a bright light.
  2. To be bright; to make bright or polish. *His face is shining with joy. Please shine those shoes.*
  3. If someone **shines** at something, the person is very good at it.
  ▷ ***verb*** **shining, shone** (shohn) *or* **shined** ▷ ***noun*** **shine**

shin·gle (shing-guhl) ***noun*** A thin, flat piece of wood or other material used to cover roofs or outside walls. Shingles are put on in overlapping rows so that water runs off them. ▷ ***verb*** **shingle**

Shin·to (shin-toh) ***noun*** The main religion of Japan, which involves the worship of ancestors and the spirits of nature.

> **Suffix**
> •
> The suffix **-ship** adds one of the following meanings to a root word:
>
> 1. The state or quality of being, as in *friendship* (the state of being a friend) and *leadership* (the quality of being a leader).
>
> 2. The art or skill of, as in *scholarship* (the skill of a scholar).

ship (ship)
  1. *noun* A large boat that can travel across deep water. *The two pictures show HMS (His Majesty's Ship)* Victory, *a British warship from 1805. The cross section shows a reconstruction of life on board the* Victory.
  2. *noun* An airplane, an airship, or a spacecraft.
  3. *verb* To send on a ship, a truck, a train, or an airplane. *I will ship my clothes to camp in a trunk.*
  4. *verb* To go on a ship, usually to work. *The sailor shipped as a crew member.*
  ▷ ***verb*** **shipping, shipped**

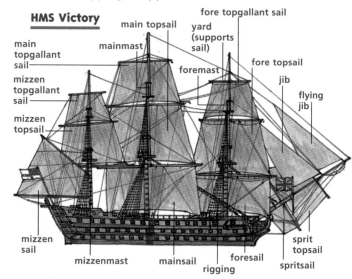

HMS Victory

fore topgallant sail · main topsail · yard (supports sail) · main topgallant sail · mainmast · foremast · fore topsail · mizzen topgallant sail · jib · flying jib · mizzen topsail · mizzen sail · mizzenmast · mainsail · foresail · rigging · spritsail · sprit topsail

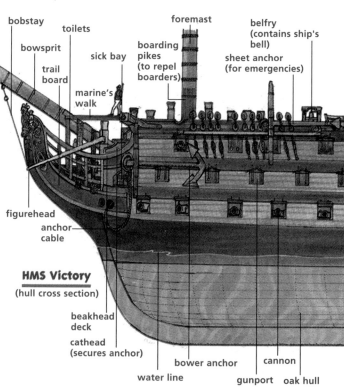

bobstay · toilets · foremast · belfry (contains ship's bell) · bowsprit · sick bay · boarding pikes (to repel boarders) · sheet anchor (for emergencies) · trail board · marine's walk · figurehead · anchor cable · beakhead deck · cathead (secures anchor) · water line · bower anchor · cannon · gunport · oak hull

HMS Victory
(hull cross section)

S

ship·ment (ship-muhnt) *noun*
1. A package or a group of packages that is sent from one place to another. *Our shipment of clothes finally arrived yesterday.*
2. The act of shipping. *The library bundled the books for shipment overseas.*

ship·shape (ship-shayp) *adjective* Clean, neat, and in good order. *I cleaned my room until it was shipshape.*

ship·wreck (ship-rek) *noun*
1. The wrecking or destruction of a ship at sea. ▷ *verb* **shipwreck**
2. The remains of a wrecked ship. ▷ *adjective* **shipwrecked**

ship·yard (ship-yard) *noun* A place where ships are built or repaired.

shirk (shurk) *verb* To avoid doing something that should be done. *Robert shirked his responsibilities at home.* ▷ **shirking, shirked** ▷ *noun* **shirker**

shirt (shurt) *noun* A piece of clothing that you wear on the top half of your body. Shirts usually have a collar and sleeves.

shish ka·bob *or* **shish ke·bob** (shish kuh-bob) *noun* Small pieces of meat and vegetables cooked on a skewer.

shiv·er (shiv-ur) *verb* To shake with cold or fear. ▷ **shivering, shivered** ▷ *noun* **shiver** ▷ *adjective* **shivery**

shoal (shole) *noun*
1. A stretch of shallow water.
2. A large group of fish swimming together.

shock (shok)
1. *noun* A sudden, violent event, such as an accident or a death, that upsets or disturbs you greatly.
2. *noun* The mental or emotional upset caused by such an event.
3. *noun* If a person goes into **shock,** he or she suffers a serious lowering of blood pressure and may lose consciousness. Shock may be caused by severe injury or great emotional upset.
4. *verb* To surprise, horrify, or disgust someone. *The news of the murders shocked us all.* ▷ **shocking, shocked** ▷ *adjective* **shocking**
5. *noun* A sudden, violent impact.
6. *noun* The violent effect of an electric current passing through someone's body. ▷ *verb* **shock**
7. *noun* A thick, bushy mass. *Jason has a shock of golden curls.*

shod·dy (shod-ee) *adjective* Carelessly produced and of poor quality, as in *shoddy goods.* ▷ **shoddier, shoddiest** ▷ *noun* **shoddiness**

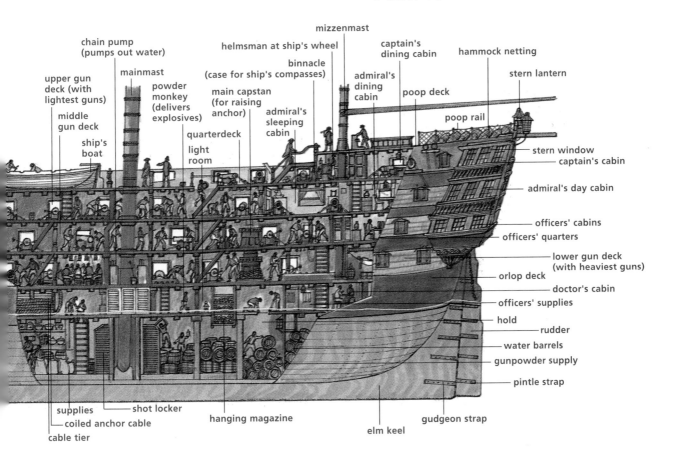

chain pump (pumps out water)
helmsman at ship's wheel
mizzenmast
captain's dining cabin
hammock netting
binnacle (case for ship's compasses)
admiral's dining cabin
poop deck
stern lantern
upper gun deck (with lightest guns)
mainmast
powder monkey (delivers explosives)
main capstan (for raising anchor)
admiral's sleeping cabin
poop rail
middle gun deck
admiral's sleeping cabin
quarterdeck
stern window
captain's cabin
ship's boat
light room
admiral's day cabin
officers' cabins
officers' quarters
lower gun deck (with heaviest guns)
orlop deck
doctor's cabin
officers' supplies
hold
rudder
water barrels
gunpowder supply
pintle strap
supplies
shot locker
hanging magazine
coiled anchor cable
cable tier
elm keel
gudgeon strap

S

485

shoe (shoo)
1. *noun* An outer covering for the foot. Shoes are usually made of leather or vinyl.
2. *noun* A horseshoe.
3. *noun* The part of a brake that presses against a wheel to slow or stop it.
4. *verb* To fit a shoe or shoes on a horse.
▷ **shoeing, shod** (shod) *or* **shoed**

shoe·horn (shoo-*horn*) *noun* A narrow piece of plastic or metal that you use to help your heel slip easily into a shoe.

shoe·lace (shoo-*layss*) *noun* A cord or string used for fastening a shoe.

shoot (shoot)
1. *verb* To wound or kill a person or an animal with a bullet or an arrow.
2. *verb* To fire a gun.
3. *verb* To make a movie or video. *The movie was shot in Italy.*
4. *verb* To move very fast. *The race car shot past.*
5. *noun* A young plant that has just appeared above the soil, or a new part of a plant that is just beginning to grow. *See* **germinate.**
6. *verb* To aim and drive a ball, puck, etc., toward a goal or net.
7. *verb* To strive for. *I'm shooting for an A on my paper.*
▷ *verb* **shooting, shot**

shooting star *noun* A meteor, or piece of rock from space that burns up as it enters the earth's atmosphere.

shop (shop)
1. *noun* A place where goods are displayed and sold, as in *a hat shop* or *a pet shop.*
2. *noun* A place where a particular kind of work is done, as in *a flower shop* or *a repair shop.*
3. *verb* To go to stores in order to buy goods.
▷ **shopping, shopped** ▷ *noun* **shopper,** *noun* **shopping**

shop·keep·er (shop-*kee*-pur) *noun* Someone who owns or runs a small shop or store.

shop·lift·er (shop-*lif*-tur) *noun* Someone who takes something from a store without paying for it. ▷ *noun* **shoplifting** ▷ *verb* **shoplift**

shopping center *noun* A group of stores with one central parking lot.

shore (shor) *noun* The land along the edge of an ocean, a river, or a lake.

short (short)
1. *adjective* Less than the average length, height, distance, time, etc., as in *a short book, a short girl, a short walk, a short wait.* ▷ *noun* **shortness** ▷ *adverb* **short**
2. *adjective* If you are **short of** something, you have less of it than you need. *Henry is very short of money at the moment.*
3. *adjective* Brief in a rude or unfriendly way; curt. *Her short manner made everybody tense.*
4. *adverb* Suddenly. *The car stopped short at the red light.*
5. *noun* A **short circuit.**
6. shorts *noun, plural* Pants that reach to or above the knees.
7. shorts *noun, plural* A man's or boy's underwear.
8. short for *adjective* Shortened from something longer. *The word* dorm *is short for* dormitory.
▷ *adjective and adverb* **shorter, shortest**

short·age (shor-*tij*) *noun* When there is a **shortage** of something, there is not enough of it. *There is a water shortage because it hasn't rained in weeks.*

short·bread (short-*bred*) *noun* A rich cookie made with flour, sugar, and shortening.

short circuit *noun* An electric circuit that bypasses a device that was designed to be included in the circuit. Sometimes a short circuit can cause a fire or blow a fuse. ▷ *verb* **short-circuit**

short·com·ing (short-*kuhm*-ing) *noun* A failing or weak point in something or someone. *One of Tim's shortcomings is that he is always late.*

short·en (short-uhn) *verb* To make short or shorter. *Dad shortened the cuffs on his pants.*
▷ **shortening, shortened**

short·en·ing (short-uhn-ing) *noun* Butter, lard, or other fat used in baking.

short·hand (short-*hand*) *noun* A system of writing symbols instead of words. Shorthand is used for taking notes quickly.

short-hand·ed (han-did) *adjective* If you are **short-handed,** you do not have enough people to do a job.

short·ly (short-lee) *adverb* Soon or presently. *The train will be arriving shortly.*

short-range *adjective* Not reaching far in time or distance. *A short-range weather forecast tells us what tomorrow's weather will be like.*

short·sight·ed (short-sye-tid) *adjective*
1. Not aware of future consequences. *He made a shortsighted decision.*
2. Nearsighted.
▷ *noun* **shortsightedness**

short·stop (short-*stop*) *noun* In baseball or softball, the player whose position is between second and third base.

short-tem·pered (tem-purd) *adjective* Someone who is **short-tempered** becomes angry very quickly and easily.

shot (shot)
1. *verb* The past tense and past participle of **shoot.**
2. *noun* The firing of a gun. *I think I heard a shot.*
3. *noun* A person who shoots. *She is a good shot.*

4. noun A single bullet fired from a gun.
5. noun A single metal ball or pellet fired from a gun or cannon. ▷ **noun, plural shots** or **shot**
6. noun A throw or thrust of a ball or puck toward a net or other goal in sports such as basketball, hockey, soccer, and golf.
7. noun The distance or range over which something such as a missile or bullet can travel. *The cannon fired a very long shot.*
8. noun A photograph.
9. noun (informal) An injection. *I got a flu shot before the winter.*
10. noun A heavy metal ball thrown at a track-and-field event.
11. noun (informal) An attempt. *Tonya had a shot at beating the record.*

shot·gun (shot-*guhn*) **noun** A gun with a long barrel that fires cartridges filled with pellets.

shot put

shot-putter

noun A track-and-field event in which a heavy metal ball is thrown as far as possible. *The photograph shows an athlete about to* put, *or* push, *the* shot, *or ball, into the air.*
▷ **noun shot-putter, noun shot-putting**

should (shud) **verb** A helping verb that is used in the following ways:
1. To show a duty or an obligation. *You should be doing your homework right now.*
2. To show that something is likely or expected. *We should arrive at the station soon.*
3. To show that something might happen. *If we should see a gas station, let's stop and ask directions.*

shoul·der (shohl-dur)
1. noun The part of your body between your neck and your upper arm.
2. noun A similar part on an animal's body.
3. noun The sloping side or edge of a road or highway.
4. verb To push with your shoulder or shoulders. *I shouldered my way through the crowd.*
5. verb To take on a burden, as in *to shoulder the blame* or *to shoulder a responsibility.*
▷ **verb shouldering, shouldered**

shoulder blade noun One of two large, flat bones in the upper back, just below the shoulder.

should·n't (shud-uhnt) **contraction** A short form of *should not. We shouldn't stay up so late.*

shout (shout) **verb** To call out loudly. ▷ **shouting, shouted** ▷ **noun shout**

shove (shuhv) **verb** To push hard or roughly. ▷ **shoving, shoved** ▷ **noun shove**

shov·el (shuhv-uhl)
1. noun A tool with a long handle and a flattened scoop, used for moving material.
2. verb To move things with a shovel. *Maria shoveled the snow off the path.* ▷ **shoveling, shoveled**

show (shoh)
1. verb To let see or be seen. *Show me the picture. Show the book to them.*
2. verb To explain or demonstrate to someone. *Show me how to do it.*
3. verb To make known or clear. *He showed his happiness by whistling on the way home from school.*
4. verb To guide or lead someone. *Let me show you to your seat.*
5. verb To be visible. *That stain won't show.*
6. noun A public performance or exhibition.
7. verb If someone **shows up,** the person comes to a place.
▷ **verb showing, showed, shown (shohn)**

> **Synonyms: show**

Show means to let someone see or examine something: *Brian showed his mother his art project before taking it to school.*

Display means to show something in a careful way so others can see it: *The store displays all the new books on a table near the front.*

Exhibit means to display something in public so that it is easy for people to see: *After the judges choose the winners, we will exhibit all of the students' paintings in the library.*

Present can mean to offer something for view: *My class is going to present a play about the experiences of immigrant children.*

Reveal means to uncover or show something that previously had been hidden: *Moving the picture revealed a secret hiding place in the wall.*

Parade suggests that someone is showing off something: *The little girl paraded past her friends in her brand-new clothes.*

S

show business *noun* The world of the theater, movies, television, and other forms of entertainment.

show·er (shou-er)
1. *noun* A piece of equipment that produces a fine spray of water for washing your body.
2. *verb* To wash yourself under a shower.
3. *noun* A brief rainfall. ▷ *adjective* **showery**
4. *verb* To fall in large numbers. *Leaves showered from the tree.* ▷ *noun* **shower**
5. *verb* To give someone lots of things. *Rosie showered me with presents.*
6. *noun* A party at which a woman who is about to marry or give birth is honored and receives presents.
▷ *verb* **showering, showered**

show-off *noun* Someone who behaves in a bragging way about his or her possessions or abilities. ▷ *verb* **show off**

show·room (shoh-*room*) *noun* A room used to display goods for sale, as in *a car showroom.*

show·y (shoh-ee) *adjective*
1. Striking, or attracting attention because of color or size, as in *showy flowers.*
2. Flashy, or too bright and colorful, as in *a showy dress.*

shrap·nel (shrap-nuhl) *noun* Small pieces of metal scattered by an exploding shell or bomb.

shred (shred) *noun*
1. A long, thin strip of cloth or paper that has been torn off something. ▷ *verb* **shred**
2. A small amount; a bit, as in *a shred of truth* or *a shred of evidence.*

shred·der (shred-ur) *noun* A machine for cutting documents into tiny pieces so that no one can read them.

shrew (shroo) *noun*
1. A small mammal with a long nose and small eyes. Shrews eat insects. *The picture shows a white-toothed shrew with her young.*
2. A nagging, scolding woman.

shrew with young

shrewd (shrood) *adjective* Clever, experienced, and sharp in dealing with practical situations, as in *a shrewd businessman* or *a shrewd shopper.*
▷ **shrewder, shrewdest** ▷ *adverb* **shrewdly**

shriek (shreek) *verb* To cry out or scream in a shrill, piercing way. ▷ **shrieking, shrieked** ▷ *noun* **shriek**

shrill (shril) *adjective* Having a high, sharp sound. *The shrill blast of the whistle signaled the beginning of the race.* ▷ **shriller, shrillest**

shrimp (shrimp) *noun* A small, edible shellfish with a pair of claws and a long tail.

shrine (shrine) *noun*
1. A holy building that often contains sacred objects. *The photograph shows the Marble Temple, a Buddhist shrine in Bangkok, Thailand.*
2. A place that is honored for its history or because it is connected to something important. *That cemetery is a national shrine.*

shrine

shrink (shringk)
1. *verb* If something **shrinks,** it becomes smaller, often after being wet. *Our savings shrank. That blouse will shrink if you wash it in hot water.*
2. *verb* To draw back because you are frightened or disgusted. *The beautiful princess shrank from the hideous beast.*
3. *noun* (slang) A psychiatrist or a psychologist.
▷ *verb* **shrinking, shrank** (shrangk) *or* **shrunk** (shruhngk), **shrunk** *or* **shrunken**

shriv·el (shriv-uhl) *verb* If something **shrivels,** it shrinks and becomes wrinkled, often after drying in heat or sunlight. ▷ **shriveling, shriveled** ▷ *adjective* **shriveled**

shroud (shroud)
1. *noun* A cloth used to wrap a dead body for burial.
2. *noun* Something that covers or hides. *A shroud of mist settled over the harbor.*
3. *verb* To cover or hide with a thin veil or haze. *Fog shrouded the highway.* ▷ **shrouding, shrouded**

shrub (shruhb) *noun* A plant or bush with woody stems that branch out at or near the ground.

shrub·ber·y (shruhb-ur-ee) *noun* A number of shrubs planted together.

shrug (shruhg) *verb* To raise your shoulders in order to show doubt or lack of interest.
▷ **shrugging, shrugged** ▷ *noun* **shrug**

shrunk·en (shruhngk-uhn)
1. *verb* A past participle of **shrink.**

S

2. *adjective* Made smaller. *I couldn't believe that the shrunken sweater I took out of the washing machine had ever fit me.*

shud·der (shuhd-ur) *verb* To shake violently from cold or fear. ▷ **shuddering, shuddered** ▷ *noun* **shudder**

shuf·fle (shuhf-uhl) *verb*
1. To walk slowly, hardly raising your feet from the floor or ground.
2. To mix playing cards so that they are in a different order.
3. To move something from one place to another, as in *to shuffle papers.*
▷ *verb* **shuffling, shuffled** ▷ *noun* **shuffle**

shun (shuhn) *verb* To avoid someone or something on purpose. *Keith shunned any contact with the outside world.* ▷ **shunning, shunned**

shunt (shuhnt) *verb* To move something off to one side. *The engine shunted the boxcars onto a siding.* ▷ **shunting, shunted** ▷ *noun* **shunt**

shut (shuht) *verb*
1. To block an opening or close something with a door, lid, cover, etc. *Shut the door behind you, please.* ▷ *adjective* **shut**
2. To confine or to enclose. *The animal was shut inside a cage.*
3. shut down To stop operating or to close down. *The local factory has shut down.*
4. shut out To stop the opposing team from scoring any points.
5. shut up To stop talking or to make someone stop talking.
▷ *verb* **shutting, shut**

shut·ter (shuht-ur) *noun*
1. A movable cover that protects the outside of a window and keeps out the light.
2. The part of a camera that opens to expose the film to light when a picture is taken. *See* **photography.**

shut·tle (shuht-uhl) *noun*
1. The part of a loom that carries the thread from side to side.
2. A bus, a subway, a train, or an aircraft that travels frequently between two places. ▷ *verb* **shuttle**
3. *See* **space shuttle.**

shy (shye)
1. *adjective* If someone is **shy,** he or she is bashful and does not feel comfortable around people or with strangers. ▷ *noun* **shyness** ▷ *adverb* **shyly**
2. *adjective* Easily frightened or startled; timid. *Most wild deer are too shy to get close to people.*
3. *adjective* Lacking, or short. *I am $5.00 shy of the amount I need to buy a new basketball.*
4. *verb* If a horse **shies,** it moves backward or

sideways suddenly because it is frightened or startled. ▷ **shying, shied**
▷ *adjective* **shier, shiest**

Si·a·mese cat (sye-uh-meez) *noun* A slender breed of cat that has blue eyes, short hair, and a pale brown or gray coat. Its ears, paws, and tail are often dark.

sib·ling (sib-ling) *noun* A brother or a sister.

sick (sik) *adjective*
1. Suffering from a disease; ill. ▷ *noun* **sickness**
2. Nauseated, or feeling as though you are going to vomit.
3. Tired or disgusted. *I'm sick of your silly excuses.*
4. Upset or very unhappy. *Yolanda is sick about having to move away from her friends.*
▷ *adjective* **sicker, sickest**

sick·en (sik-uhn) *verb* If something **sickens** you, it makes you feel nauseated or disgusted.
▷ **sickening, sickened** ▷ *adjective* **sickening**
▷ *adverb* **sickeningly**

sick·le (sik-uhl) *noun* A tool with a short handle and a curved blade that is used for cutting grain, grass, or weeds.

sickle-cell anemia *noun* A form of anemia in which many normal red blood cells take on a sickle shape and cannot carry oxygen. Sickle-cell anemia is an inherited disease occurring mainly in people of African ancestry.

sick·ly (sik-lee) *adjective*
1. Weak and often ill. *My grandfather is sickly and usually rests in bed.*
2. Caused by or showing sickness, as in *a sickly complexion.*
▷ *adjective* **sicklier, sickliest**

side (side)
1. *noun* A line segment in a figure, or a surface of a shape or an object. *A square has four equal sides. Write on both sides of the paper.*
2. *noun* An outer part of something that is not the front or the back. *We need to paint the west side of the house.*
3. *noun* The right or left part of the body. *I fell and scraped my right side.*
4. *noun* One of two opposing individuals, groups, teams, or positions. *Our side won the game. I took Randall's side during the argument.*
5. *noun* The area next to someone. *When Emma heard the bad news, her parents were at her side.*
6. *noun* A line of ancestors. *She is my aunt on my mother's side.*
7. *verb* If you **side** with someone, you support the person in an argument. ▷ **siding, sided**
8. *adjective* At or near one side, as in *a side door.*

side·board (side-bord) *noun* A piece of dining room furniture with a large, flat surface and drawers or cabinets below.

S

side·burns (side-*burnz*) *noun, plural* The hair that grows down the sides of a man's face.

side effect *noun* A usually negative effect of taking a medicine besides the intended effect.

side·line (side-*line*) *noun*
1. A line that marks the side boundary of the playing area in sports such as football, basketball, and soccer.
2. An activity or work done in addition to a regular job. *My mother's sideline is coaching the girls' soccer team.*

side·show (side-*shoh*) *noun* A small show in addition to the main attraction at a fair or circus.

side·step (side-*step*) *verb*
1. To step to one side. *He was running right at me, so I sidestepped to avoid being hit.*
2. To avoid a problem or decision. *The politician sidestepped the reporter's question about the budget and talked about his trip to China instead.*
▷ *verb* **sidestepping, sidestepped**

side·track (side-*trak*) *verb* To distract someone from what he or she is doing or saying.
▷ **sidetracking, sidetracked**

side·walk (side-*wawk*) *noun* A paved path beside a street.

side·ways (side-*wayz*)
1. *adjective* To or from one side. *Take three sideways steps.*
2. *adverb* With one side forward. *To get through this narrow tunnel, you'll have to walk sideways.*
3. *adjective* Moving or directed toward one side, as in *a sideways glance.*

sid·ing (sye-ding) *noun*
1. A section of railroad track used for storing or shunting cars.
2. Material that covers the outside of a house.

siege (seej) *noun* The surrounding of a place such as a castle or city to cut off supplies and then wait for those inside to surrender.

si·er·ra (see-er-uh) *noun* A chain of hills or mountains with peaks that look like sharp, jagged teeth.

> ### Word History
> •
> The word **sierra** was borrowed from a Spanish word that means "saw." From a distance, a sierra looks like the jagged teeth of a saw.

si·es·ta (see-ess-tuh) *noun* An afternoon nap or rest, usually taken after a midday meal.

sieve (siv) *noun* A container with lots of small holes in it, used for separating large pieces from small pieces or liquids from solids. ▷ *verb* **sieve**

sift (sift) *verb*
1. To put a substance through a sieve to get rid of lumps or large chunks.
2. To examine something carefully. *Police sifted through the evidence for clues.*
▷ *verb* **sifting, sifted**

sigh (sye) *verb* To breathe out deeply, often to express sadness or relief. ▷ **sighing, sighed**
▷ *noun* **sigh**

sight (site)
1. *noun* The ability to see. *She lost her sight in an accident.*
2. *noun* The act of seeing. *It was love at first sight.*
3. *noun* The range or distance a person can see. *Don't let your little brother out of your sight.*
4. *noun* A view or a scene. *The New York skyline is a marvelous sight.*
5. *verb* To see or to spot. *The sailors were happy to sight land.* ▷ **sighting, sighted**
6. *noun* A small metal device on a rifle that helps in aiming. ▷ *verb* **sight**
7. *noun* Something funny or odd to look at. *Carl was a sight in his costume.*
Sight sounds like **cite** and **site**.

sight·se·er (site-see-ur) *noun* Someone who travels for pleasure to see interesting places.
▷ *noun* **sightseeing** ▷ *verb* **sightsee**

sign (sine)
1. *noun* A symbol that stands for something, as in *a dollar sign* or *a minus sign.*
2. *noun* A public notice giving information, as in *a road sign.*
3. *verb* To write your name in your own way.
▷ **signing, signed**
4. *noun* A trace, or evidence left by someone. *There was no sign of breaking and entering.*
5. *noun* Something that points out what is to come. *Blooming flowers are a sign of spring. Some people believe that finding a four-leaf clover is a sign of good luck.*

sig·nal (sig-nuhl) *noun*
1. Anything agreed upon to send a message or warning, as in *a traffic signal.* ▷ *verb* **signal**
2. One of many electrical pulses transmitted for radio, television, or telephone communications.

sig·na·ture (sig-nuh-chur) *noun* The individual way that you write your name, usually in script. *This is how John Hancock's signature looks on the Declaration of Independence.*

John Hancock's signature

sig·nif·i·cant (sig-**nif**-uh-kuhnt) *adjective*
Important, or meaning a great deal, as in *a significant event.* ▷ *noun* **significance** ▷ *adverb* **significantly**

sign language *noun* A language in which hand gestures, in combination with facial expressions and larger body movements, are used instead of speech. Sign language often is used by people with hearing impairments. *The woman in the picture is using sign language for the word* good. *See Appendix.*

sign language

sign·post (**sine**-pohst) *noun* A post with signs on it to direct travelers.

Sikh (seek) *noun* A member of a religious sect of India that believes in a single god. ▷ *noun* **Sikhism**

si·lage (**sye**-lij) *noun* Cut grass or hay that is stored in a silo and used as animal feed.

si·lenc·er (**sye**-luhn-sur) *noun* An attachment that reduces noise from a gun.

si·lent (**sye**-luhnt) *adjective* Absolutely quiet.
▷ *noun* **silence** ▷ *adverb* **silently**

sil·hou·ette (sil-oo-**et**) *noun*
1. A drawing made by filling in the outline of a figure with a solid color, usually black.
2. A dark outline seen against a light background. ▷ *verb* **silhouette**

sil·i·con (**sil**-uh-kuhn) *noun* A chemical element found in sand and rocks and used to make glass, microchips, and transistors.

silk (silk) *noun* A soft, shiny fabric made from fibers produced by a silkworm.

silk·worm (**silk**-wurm) *noun* A caterpillar that spins a cocoon of silk threads.

life cycle of a silkworm

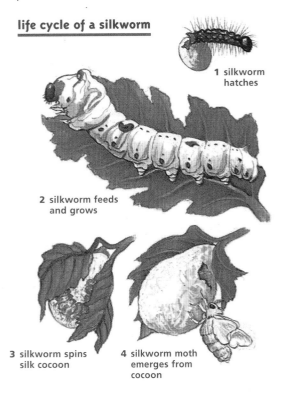

1 silkworm hatches

2 silkworm feeds and grows

3 silkworm spins silk cocoon

4 silkworm moth emerges from cocoon

silk·y (**sil**-kee) *adjective* Made of silk or like silk in texture; smooth, as in *silky hair.*

sill (sil) *noun* A piece of wood or stone that runs across the bottom of a door or window.

sil·ly (**sil**-ee) *adjective*
1. Stupid or not sensible, as in *a silly mistake.*
2. Ridiculous or laughable, as in *a silly idea.*
▷ *adjective* **sillier, silliest** ▷ *noun* **silliness**

si·lo (**sye**-loh) *noun*
1. A tall, round tower used to store food for farm animals.
2. An underground shelter for a guided missile.
▷ *noun, plural* **silos**

silt (silt) *noun* The fine particles of soil that are carried along by flowing water and eventually settle to the bottom of a river or lake.

sil·ver (**sil**-vur) *noun*
1. A soft, shiny, white metal that is used to make jewelry, coins, bowls, and utensils.
2. Coins made from silver or metal with a silver color.
3. Forks, spoons, and other items made of or coated with silver; silverware.
4. The color of silver.
▷ *adjective* **silver,** *adjective* **silvery**

S

491

sil·ver·smith (sil-vur-*smith*) *noun* Someone who makes or repairs silver objects.

sil·ver·ware (sil-vur-*wair*) *noun* Objects made of or coated with silver, especially forks, spoons, and knives. *The photograph shows silverware from the Hanover pattern, designed in 1730.*

silverware

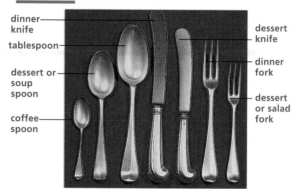

dinner knife
tablespoon
dessert or soup spoon
coffee spoon
dessert knife
dinner fork
dessert or salad fork

sim·i·lar (sim-uh-lur) *adjective* Alike, or of the same type. ▷ *noun* **similarity** (sim-uh-**lair**-i-tee) ▷ *adverb* **similarly**

sim·i·le (sim-uh-lee) *noun* A way of describing something by comparing it with something else. A simile uses the word *like* or *as*. For example: *Her eyes are like stars. His smile is as warm as the sun.*

sim·mer (sim-ur) *verb*
1. To boil very gently. ▷ *noun* **simmer**
2. simmer down (informal) To calm down.
▷ *verb* **simmering, simmered**

sim·ple (sim-puhl) *adjective*
1. Easy, or not hard to understand or do, as in *a simple test* or *a simple task.*
2. With nothing added, as in *the simple truth.*
3. Plain, or not fancy, as in *a simple meal.*
▷ *adjective* **simpler, simplest** ▷ *noun* **simplicity** (sim-**pliss**-i-tee)

sim·pli·fy (sim-pluh-fye) *verb* To make something easier or less complicated. *The cook simplified the recipe.* ▷ **simplifies, simplifying, simplified** ▷ *noun* **simplification**

sim·ply (sim-plee) *adverb*
1. In a simple way, or plainly. *Jan dressed simply.*
2. Merely, or just. *If you need help, simply ask me.*
3. Very. *You look simply marvelous.*

sim·u·la·tion (sim-yuh-lay-shuhn) *noun*
1. The act of pretending. *Before the moon walk, the astronauts went through a simulation under water.*
2. A copy or an imitation.
▷ *verb* **simulate**

sim·u·la·tor (sim-yuh-*lay*-tur) *noun* A machine that allows you to experience what it is like to fly a plane, drive a car, etc., by using computer technology, film, and mechanical movement.

si·mul·ta·ne·ous (sye-muhl-tay-nee-uhss) *adjective* Happening at the same time. ▷ *adverb* **simultaneously**

sin (sin) *noun* Bad or evil behavior that goes against moral and religious laws. ▷ *noun* **sinner** ▷ *verb* **sin** ▷ *adjective* **sinful** ▷ *adverb* **sinfully**

since (sinss)
1. *conjunction* From the time that. *I've lived here since I was three.*
2. *conjunction* As, or because. *Since you've been so helpful, we'll give you a treat.*
3. *adverb* Ago; before now. *I have long since forgotten our argument.*
4. *adverb* From the past until now. *Tony left the party in a huff and hasn't been seen since.*
5. *preposition* From or during the time after. *I've been here since July.*

sin·cere (sin-sihr) *adjective* If you are **sincere**, you are honest and truthful in what you say and do. ▷ **sincerer, sincerest** ▷ *noun* **sincerity** (sin-**ser**-i-tee) ▷ *adverb* **sincerely**

sin·ew (sin-yoo) *noun* A strong fiber or band of tissue that connects a muscle to a bone; a tendon.

sing (sing) *verb*
1. To produce words and musical sounds with your voice.
2. To perform by singing, as in *to sing a song.*
3. To produce musical sounds. *Not all birds sing.*
▷ *verb* **singing, sang** (sang), **sung** (suhng) ▷ *noun* **singer**

singe (sinj) *verb* To burn something slightly.
▷ **singeing, singed**

sin·gle (sing-guhl)
1. *adjective* One and no more than one. *A single rose remained on the bush.*
2. *adjective* Intended for one person or family, as in *a single room.*
3. *adjective* Not married.
4. single out *verb* To choose. *The firefighter was singled out for a medal.* ▷ **singling, singled**
5. *noun* A recording with one song on each side.
6. *noun* A hit in baseball that allows the runner to get to first base. ▷ *verb* **single**

single-hand·ed (han-did) *adjective* Done alone or without help from others, as in *a single-handed rescue.* ▷ *adverb* **single-handedly**

single-mind·ed (mine-did) *adjective* If you are **single-minded,** you concentrate on achieving one aim.

sin·gu·lar (sing-gyuh-lur) *noun* The form of a word used for one thing or one person. *Chair* and *singer* are singulars. ▷ *adjective* **singular**

sin·is·ter (sin-uh-stur) *adjective* Seeming evil and threatening. *I get chills whenever I hear his sinister laugh.*

S

sink (singk)
1. *noun* A basin used for washing. A sink has faucets for hot and cold water and a drain.
2. *verb* To go down slowly. *The ship sank.*
3. *verb* To make go under the surface. *A violent hurricane can sink a ship.* ▷ *noun* **sinking**
4. *verb* To fall or drop into a certain state. *I sank into a deep sleep.*
5. *verb* To become lower in amount. *Our food supply sank to an all-time low.*
6. *verb* To fall in pitch or volume. *Their voices sank to a whisper.*
7. *verb* To penetrate or go through or into deeply. *The water sank into the earth.*
▷ *verb* **sinking, sank** (sangk), **sunk** (suhngk)

si·nus (sye-nuhss) *noun* One of the eight hollow spaces above the eyes and on either side of the nose that lead to the nose. *See* **brain.** ▷ *noun,* **plural sinuses**

Sioux (soo) *noun* A member of a tribe of American Indians of Minnesota, North and South Dakota, and Wyoming.

sip (sip) *verb* To drink slowly, taking in small amounts. ▷ **sipping, sipped** ▷ *noun* **sip**

si·phon (sye-fuhn) *noun* A bent tube through which liquid can drain upward and then down to a lower level. Air pressure causes this to happen. ▷ *verb* **siphon**

sir (sur) *noun*
1. A formal term for a man used in speaking and writing, as in *Dear Sir* and *Can I help you, sir?*
2. Sir The title of someone who has been made a knight, as in *Sir Lancelot.*

si·ren (sye-ruhn) *noun* A device that makes a loud, shrill sound. A siren is often used as a signal or warning, as in *a police car siren.*

sis·ter (siss-tur) *noun*
1. A girl or woman who has the same parents as another person. ▷ *adjective* **sisterly**
2. A nun.
3. A woman who shares an interest or cause with another.

sis·ter·hood (siss-tur-hud) *noun*
1. The warm, close feeling between sisters or any women.
2. A group of women who share a common interest, aim, or cause.

sister-in-law *noun* Someone's **sister-in-law** is the sister of his or her spouse or the wife of his or her brother. ▷ *noun, plural* **sisters-in-law**

sit (sit) *verb*
1. To rest on your buttocks.
2. To be in a place or on a surface. *Books sit on shelves.*
3. To pose. *I had to sit for our family portrait.*

4. To take a place as an official member of a club or legislature. *My uncle sits in Congress.*
5. To hold a session or meeting. *The Supreme Court will sit next month.*
6. To baby-sit. *I sit for the neighbors' children.*
7. If you **sit in** for someone, you take the person's place temporarily.
▷ *verb* **sitting, sat** (sat)

sit·com (sit-*kom*) *noun* (*informal*) A humorous television program that features the same group of characters each week. Sitcom is short for *situation comedy.*

site (site) *noun* The place where something is or happens, as in *the site of the battle.* **Site** sounds like **cite** and **sight.**

sitting room *noun* A room in a home or hotel in which people can sit and relax or talk with others.

sit·u·ate (sich-oo-ate) *verb* To place something in a particular spot or location. *The baseball stadium is situated near several bus stops.*
▷ **situating, situated**

sit·u·a·tion (sich-oo-ay-shuhn) *noun* The circumstances that exist at a particular time. *The flood has produced a desperate situation.*

sit-up *noun* An exercise for stomach muscles that is done by lying and moving to a sitting position without lifting the feet or legs.

six (siks) *noun* The whole number, written 6, that comes after five and before seven. ▷ *adjective* **six**

sixth (siksth)
1. *adjective* That which comes after fifth and before seventh.
2. *noun* One part of something that has been divided into six equal parts, written $\frac{1}{6}$.

siz·a·ble *or* **size·a·ble** (size-uh-buhl) *adjective* Fairly large. *My parents made a sizable donation to their favorite charity.*

size (size) *noun*
1. The measurement of how large or small something is.
2. One in a series of standard measurements for clothing, shoes, etc. *What size is that dress?*

siz·zle (siz-uhl) *verb* To make a hissing noise, especially when frying. *I heard the bacon sizzling in the pan.* ▷ **sizzling, sizzled**

skate (skayt)
1. *noun* A boot with a blade on the bottom. Skates are used for gliding over ice.
2. *noun* A roller skate.
3. *verb* To glide or move along on skates.
▷ **skating, skated**
4. *noun* A large, flat, saltwater fish with a long, narrow tail and two wide side fins that are shaped like wings. Skates are related to sharks and rays.

skate·board (skate-*bord*) *noun* A small board with wheels that you stand on and ride.

ske·dad·dle (ski-dad-uhl) *verb* (*informal*) To move along quickly or to run away from something that scares you. ▷ **skedaddling, skedaddled**

skel·e·ton (skel-uh-tuhn) *noun* The framework of bones that supports and protects the body of an animal with a backbone.

skep·ti·cal (skep-tuh-kuhl) *adjective* If you are **skeptical** about something, you doubt that it is really true. ▷ *noun* **skeptic**, *noun* **skepticism** ▷ *adverb* **skeptically**

sketch (skech) *noun*
1. A quick, rough drawing of something. ▷ *verb* **sketch**
2. A short essay, especially one that describes a person.
3. A short play that is usually humorous.
▷ *noun, plural* **sketches**

sketch·y (skech-ee) *adjective*
1. Roughly drawn or done without detail.
2. Incomplete and not very clear. *The dazed woman could only give a sketchy description of the man who stole her purse.*
▷ *adjective* **sketchier, sketchiest**

skew·er (skyoo-ur) *noun* A long, metal pin for holding pieces of meat or vegetables while they are cooking. ▷ *verb* **skewer**

ski (skee) *noun*
1. One of a pair of long, narrow runners that you fasten to boots and use for gliding over snow.
2. A water ski.
▷ *noun* **skiing** ▷ *verb* **ski**

human skeleton

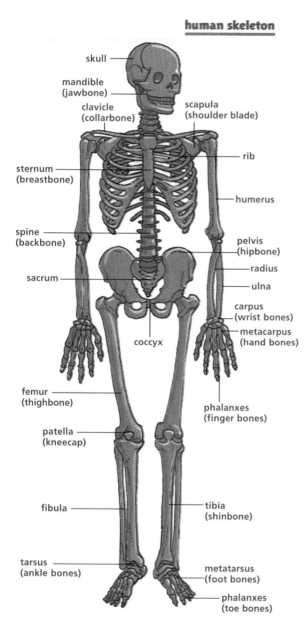

- skull
- mandible (jawbone)
- clavicle (collarbone)
- scapula (shoulder blade)
- rib
- sternum (breastbone)
- humerus
- spine (backbone)
- pelvis (hipbone)
- radius
- sacrum
- ulna
- carpus (wrist bones)
- metacarpus (hand bones)
- coccyx
- femur (thighbone)
- phalanxes (finger bones)
- patella (kneecap)
- fibula
- tibia (shinbone)
- tarsus (ankle bones)
- metatarsus (foot bones)
- phalanxes (toe bones)

ski

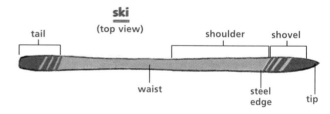

ski (top view)

- tail
- shoulder
- shovel
- waist
- steel edge
- tip

ski boot and ski

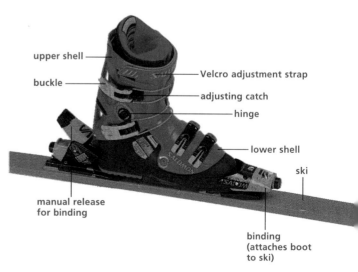

- upper shell
- buckle
- Velcro adjustment strap
- adjusting catch
- hinge
- lower shell
- ski
- manual release for binding
- binding (attaches boot to ski)

▶ Word History

Skeleton comes from the Greek expression *soma skeleton*, or "dried-up body." The Greeks observed that buried bodies eventually became dry bones.

S

skid (skid)
1. *verb* To slide out of control on a slippery surface. *The car skidded on the ice.* ▷ **skidding, skidded** ▷ *noun* **skid**
2. *noun* A runner on the bottom of a helicopter. *See* **helicopter.**

skiff (skif) *noun* A boat small enough to be sailed or rowed by one person.

skill (skil) *noun* The ability to do something well. ▷ *adjective* **skillful,** *adjective* **skilled**

skil·let (skil-it) *noun* A frying pan.

skim (skim) *verb*
1. To take something off the top of a liquid. *My grandmother skimmed the fat from the soup.* ▷ *adjective* **skimmed**
2. To read through something quickly, just to get the main ideas.
3. To glide across a surface. ▷ *verb* **skimming, skimmed**

skim milk *noun* Milk from which the cream has been removed. It is also called *skimmed milk.*

skin (skin)
1. *noun* The outer covering of tissue on the bodies of humans and animals.
2. *noun* The outer layer of a fruit or vegetable, as in *a banana skin.*
3. *verb* To scrape your skin. *I skinned both knees when I fell off my bike.*
4. *verb* To remove the skin from a killed animal. ▷ *verb* **skinning, skinned**

human skin
(magnified cross section)

- hair shaft
- dermis
- epidermis (protective layer)
- pore
- muscle
- sebaceous gland (oil gland)
- sweat duct
- hair follicle
- sweat gland
- blood vessel
- nerve fiber

skin·ny (skin-ee) *adjective* Very thin. ▷ **skinnier, skinniest**

skip (skip) *verb*
1. To move along in a bouncy way, hopping on each foot in turn. ▷ *noun* **skip**
2. To jump over, as in *to skip rope.*
3. To leave something out or to pass over. *I skipped the gory scenes in my book.*
4. *(informal)* To leave a place quickly or secretly. *The robbery suspect skipped town.*
5. To go past one grade in school by going to the next one. *She skipped ninth grade.* ▷ *verb* **skipping, skipped**

skipping

skirt (skurt)
1. *noun* A piece of clothing worn by women and girls that hangs from the waist.
2. *verb* To pass around a place or to lie around its border or edge. *A walking path skirts the lake.*
3. *verb* To avoid a question, a discussion, or an issue because it is difficult or because you are afraid that others might disagree with you. ▷ *verb* **skirting, skirted**

skit (skit) *noun* A short, usually funny play.

skit·tish (skit-ish) *adjective* Easily frightened or excited, as in *a skittish horse.*

skull (skuhl) *noun* The bony framework of the head that protects the brain. **Skull** sounds like **scull.** *See* **skeleton.**

S

skunk (skuhngk) *noun*
1. A black and white mammal with a bushy tail. Skunks spray liquid with a foul smell when they are threatened.
2. *(informal)* A really mean person.

sky (skye) *noun* The upper atmosphere, or the area of space that seems to arch over the earth.
▷ *noun, plural* **skies**

sky·box (skye-*boks*) *noun* An elevated, enclosed room at a sports stadium where spectators can watch the action in privacy and luxury.

sky·div·ing (skye-*div*-ing) *noun* The sport of jumping from an airplane and falling as far as safely possible before opening a parachute. Skydiving often involves stunts or formation work. *The picture shows a skydiving formation called the star.* ▷ *noun* **skydiver** ▷ *verb* **skydive**

skydiving

sky·lark (skye-*lark*) *noun* A brown and white European bird that sings while flying.

sky·light (skye-*lite*) *noun* A window in a roof or ceiling.

sky·line (skye-*line*) *noun*
1. The outline of buildings, mountains, or other objects seen against the sky from a distance.
2. The horizon, or the line at which the earth and sky seem to meet.

sky·rock·et (skye-*rok*-it)
1. *noun* A type of firework that shoots into the air and explodes in a shower of sparks of many colors.
2. *verb* To rise suddenly and quickly. *Sales of the book skyrocketed after the author appeared on television.* ▷ **skyrocketing, skyrocketed**

sky·scrap·er (skye-*skray*-pur) *noun* A very tall building.

slab (slab) *noun* A broad, flat, thick piece of something, as in *a slab of concrete* or *a slab of bread*.

slack (slak) *adjective*
1. Not tight or not firm; loose. *When the breeze died down, the kite string went slack.*
2. Not busy. *In a recession, business is slack for many stores.*
3. If you are **slack** in your work, you do not try very hard at it.
▷ *adjective* **slacker, slackest** ▷ *verb* **slacken**

slacks (slaks) *noun, plural* Pants for casual wear. *I wore a sweater and slacks to the party.*

sla·lom (slah-luhm
or slal-uhm)
noun An athletic
event in which
competitors ski
down a hill,
zigzagging
between
gates.

slalom skier

slam (slam) *verb*
1. To close something heavily and loudly. *Jessica slammed the book shut.*
2. To strike something with great force. *The truck slammed into a car. The batter slammed the ball into center field.*
▷ *verb* **slamming, slammed** ▷ *noun* **slam**

slan·der (slan-dur) *noun* An untrue spoken statement that damages someone's reputation.
▷ *verb* **slander** ▷ *adjective* **slanderous**

slang (slang) *noun* Colorful or lively words and phrases used in ordinary conversation but not in formal speech or writing. Slang often gives new and different meanings to old words.

slant (slant)
1. *verb* To slope, or to be at an angle. *My handwriting slants to the right.* ▷ **slanting, slanted**
▷ *noun* **slant**
2. *noun* A point of view. *These new facts give a very different slant to the story.* ▷ *verb* **slant**

slap (slap) *verb*
1. To hit someone or something with the palm of your hand. ▷ *noun* **slap**
2. To throw down or put on with great force. *The officer slapped the handcuffs on the criminal.*
▷ *verb* **slapping, slapped**

slap·dash (slap-*dash*) *adjective* Slapdash work is done carelessly and in a hurry.

S

slap·stick (slap-*stik*) *noun* Comedy that stresses loud, rough action or horseplay, such as a clown slipping on a banana peel.

slash (slash) *verb*
1. To use a knife or blade to make a sharp, sweeping cut in something. ▷ *noun* **slash**
2. To reduce something dramatically. *The store has slashed all its prices.*
▷ *verb* **slashes, slashing, slashed**

slat (slat) *noun* A long, narrow strip of wood or metal. *The fence was made of redwood slats.*

slate (slayt) *noun*
1. A blue-gray rock that can be split into thin layers. Slate is sometimes used to make roofs.
2. A tile for roofs or floors made from slate.
3. A dark blue-gray color.
4. A complete list of candidates who are running for office.

slaugh·ter (slaw-tur)
1. *verb* To kill animals for their meat.
▷ **slaughtering, slaughtered** ▷ *noun* **slaughter**
2. *noun* The brutal killing of large numbers of people. ▷ *verb* **slaughter**

slave (slayv)
1. *noun* Someone who is owned by another person and thought of as property. ▷ *noun* **slavery**
2. *noun* A person who is controlled by a habit or by influence. *When I grow up, I don't want to be a slave to cigarettes.*
3. *verb* To work very hard. *I've slaved all day over my homework.* ▷ **slaving, slaved**
4. *noun* A person who works as hard as a slave.

slay (slay) *verb* To kill in a violent way. *The knight went off to slay the dragon.* **Slay** sounds like **sleigh.** ▷ **slaying, slayed, slew** (sloo), **slain** (slayn)

sled (sled)
noun A vehicle with wooden or metal runners used for traveling over snow and ice.
▷ *verb* **sled**

sledge·ham·mer (slej-*ham*-ur) *noun* A heavy hammer with a long handle. A sledgehammer is usually held with both hands.

a boy and his sled

sleek (sleek) *adjective* Smooth and shiny.
▷ **sleeker, sleekest**

sleep (sleep) *verb* To rest in an unconscious state.
▷ **sleeping, slept** (slept) ▷ *noun* **sleep**

sleeping bag *noun* A padded bag in which you sleep, especially when you are camping.

sleep·walk·er (sleep-*wawk*-ur) *noun* Someone who walks in his or her sleep. ▷ *verb* **sleepwalk**

sleep·y (slee-pee) *adjective* Drowsy, or ready for sleep. ▷ **sleepier, sleepiest** ▷ *noun* **sleepiness**

sleet (sleet) *noun* Partly frozen rain. ▷ *verb* **sleet**

sleeve (sleev) *noun* The part of a shirt, coat, or other garment that covers your arm.

sleigh (slay) *noun* A sled, usually pulled by horses or other animals. **Sleigh** sounds like **slay.**

slen·der (slen-dur) *adjective*
1. Slim or thin.
2. Small and inadequate in amount. *We just get by on my dad's slender income.*
▷ *adjective* **slenderer, slenderest**

sleuth (slooth) *noun* A detective, or anyone good at finding out facts. ▷ *verb* **sleuth**

slice (slisse) *noun* A thin, flat piece cut from something larger, as in *a slice of bread.* ▷ *verb* **slice**

slick (slik)
1. *adjective* Very smooth or slippery. *The roads were slick after the rain.* ▷ *verb* **slick**
2. *noun* A pool of oil covering an area of water or road.
3. *adjective* Very fast, efficient, and professional, as in *a slick performance.*
▷ *adjective* **slicker, slickest**

slide (slide)
1. *verb* To move smoothly over a surface. *Amy is sliding down the banister.*
2. *noun* A smooth surface on which people can slide. *There was a slide in the yard.*
3. *verb* To move or fall suddenly. *The car hit an icy patch and slid off the road.*
4. *noun* A transparency inside a frame that you view by projecting the image onto a screen.
5. *noun* A small piece of glass on which you place a specimen in order to view it under a microscope. *See* **microscope.**
6. *noun* A large mass of snow, earth, or rock that slides down suddenly from a great height.
▷ *verb* **sliding, slid** (slid) ▷ *noun* **slide**

slight (slite)
1. *adjective* Small or not very important, as in *a slight delay.* ▷ *adverb* **slightly**
2. *adjective* Slender. *The jockey has a slight build.*
3. *verb* To treat something as unimportant or to do something carelessly. *Don't slight your work.*
4. *verb* To insult someone or to treat a person coldly. ▷ *noun* **slight**
▷ *verb* **slighting, slighted** ▷ *adjective* **slighter, slightest**

S

slim (slim)
  1. *adjective* Thin and graceful.
  2. *adjective* Very small. *We have a slim chance of winning.*
  3. *verb* To try to reduce your weight. *Slim down with a diet.* ▷ **slimming, slimmed**
  ▷ *adjective* **slimmer, slimmest**

slime (slime) *noun* A soft, slippery substance, such as mud. ▷ *adjective* **slimy**

sling (sling)
  1. *noun* A loop of cloth used to support a broken arm.
  2. *noun* A loop of leather used for throwing stones.
  3. *noun* A strong loop of cable, chain, or rope used to raise heavy objects. *Cargo was placed aboard the freighter with heavy slings.*
  4. *verb* To hang or throw something loosely or in a rough way. *Sling your bag on the top bunk.*
  ▷ **slinging, slung** (sluhng)

sling·shot (sling-shot) *noun* A piece of metal or wood shaped like a Y with an elastic band attached. Slingshots are used for shooting small stones.

slip (slip)
  1. *verb* To lose your balance on a slippery surface. ▷ *noun* **slip**
  2. *verb* To move quickly and quietly. *She slipped away into the night.*
  3. *verb* To put on or take off quickly and easily. *He sat down and slipped off his shoes.*
  4. *verb* To escape. *The task slipped my mind.*
  5. *verb* To move or slide from a place. *The stool slipped out from under me.*
  6. *noun* A small mistake. ▷ *verb* **slip**
  7. *noun* A light garment worn under a skirt or dress.
  8. *noun* A small piece, as in *a slip of paper.*
  9. *noun* A small shoot or twig cut from a plant for grafting or planting.
  ▷ *verb* **slipping, slipped**

slip·per (slip-ur) *noun* A soft, light shoe that you wear indoors, as in *bedroom slippers.*

slip·per·y (slip-ur-ee) *adjective* Smooth, oily, or wet and very hard to grip onto.

slip·shod (slip-shod) *adjective* Careless and untidy. *You did a slipshod job of cleaning your room.*

slit (slit) *verb* To make a long, narrow cut in something. ▷ **slitting, slit** ▷ *noun* **slit**

slith·er (sliTH-ur) *verb* To slip and slide along like a snake. ▷ **slithering, slithered**

sliv·er (sliv-ur) *noun* A very thin and sometimes pointed piece of something, as in *a sliver of cake* or *a sliver of wood.*

slo·gan (sloh-guhn) *noun* A phrase or motto used by a business, a group, or an individual to express a goal or belief.

sloop (sloop) *noun* A sailboat with one mast and sails that are set from front to back.

slop (slop) *verb* To splash or spill liquid. *Water slopped from the pail.* ▷ **slopping, slopped**

slope (slohp) *verb* To be at an angle. *The wall slopes to the left.* ▷ **sloping, sloped** ▷ *noun* **slope** ▷ *adjective* **sloping**

slop·py (slop-ee) *adjective*
  1. Messy, as in *sloppy clothes.*
  2. Carelessly done. *My teacher said my work was sloppy.*
  3. Wet or slushy, as in *sloppy weather.*
  ▷ *adjective* **sloppier, sloppiest** ▷ *noun* **sloppiness** ▷ *adverb* **sloppily**

slot (slot) *noun* A small, narrow opening or groove.

sloth (slawth *or* sloth) *noun*
  1. A mammal with long arms and legs, curved claws, and a shaggy coat. Sloths move very slowly and hang upside down in trees. They live in Central and South America.
  2. Laziness. ▷ *adjective* **slothful**

three-toed sloth with baby

slouch (slouch)
  1. *verb* To sit, stand, or walk in a lazy way, with your shoulders and head drooping. *Don't slouch when you walk.* ▷ **slouches, slouching, slouched** ▷ *noun* **slouch**
  2. *noun* An awkward, lazy, or incompetent person. *Dan's no slouch at football.* ▷ *noun, plural* **slouches**

slov·en·ly (sluhv-uhn-lee) *adjective* Careless, untidy, and dirty, as in *a slovenly appearance.* ▷ *noun* **slovenliness**

slow (sloh)
  1. *adjective* Not fast. ▷ *noun* **slowness** ▷ *adverb* **slowly**
  2. *adjective* Behind the right time. *My watch is five minutes slow.*

3. *verb* To cut down your speed. *Slow down in a school zone.* ▷ **slowing, slowed**
4. *adjective* Not busy. *Business was slow all week.*
5. *adjective* Not able to learn or understand quickly. *He is slow in math.*
6. *adverb* In a slow way. *Go slow.*
▷ *adjective and adverb* **slower, slowest**

sludge (sluhj) *noun* Soft, thick mud.

slug (sluhg)
1. *noun* A soft, slimy creature that is similar to a snail but has no shell. *A slug moves in a series of waves in which it lifts up part of its foot and then puts it down further forward. The foot is covered with mucus for protection and to help it cling to surfaces.*
2. *noun* A bullet.
3. *noun* A metal disk that is used in place of a coin, often illegally.
4. *verb* To hit with force. *The batter slugged the ball.* ▷ **slugging, slugged** ▷ *noun* **slug**

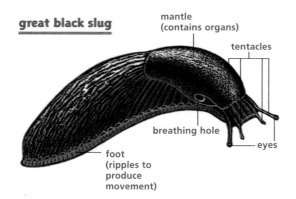

great black slug
mantle (contains organs)
tentacles
breathing hole
eyes
foot (ripples to produce movement)

slug·gish (sluhg-ish) *adjective* Moving slowly and lacking in energy. ▷ *noun* **sluggishness**

slum (sluhm) *noun* An overcrowded, poor, and neglected area of housing in a town or city.

slum·ber (sluhm-bur)
1. *verb* To sleep. *We slumbered until dawn.*
▷ **slumbering, slumbered**
2. *noun* Sleep. *The noise disturbed our slumber.*

slump (sluhmp)
1. *verb* To sink down heavily and suddenly. *Pat fainted and slumped to the ground.* ▷ **slumping, slumped**
2. *noun* A sudden drop or decline, as in *a slump in sales* or *a batting slump.* ▷ *verb* **slump**

slur (slur)
1. *verb* To pronounce words unclearly by running sounds into one another. ▷ **slurring, slurred**
2. *noun* If something is a **slur** on your character, it is insulting or damaging.

slurp (slurp) *verb* To drink or eat something noisily. ▷ **slurping, slurped**

slush (sluhsh) *noun* Snow or ice that has partly melted. ▷ *adjective* **slushy**

sly (slye) *adjective* Crafty, cunning, and secretive. ▷ **slier, sliest** ▷ *adverb* **slyly**

smack (smak)
1. *verb* To hit someone or something with the palm of your hand.
2. *verb* To strike or hit something noisily and with force. *The car smacked into a tree.*
3. *verb* To close and open the lips quickly, making a sharp sound.
4. *noun* A loud kiss.
▷ *verb* **smacking, smacked** ▷ *noun* **smack**

small (smawl)
1. *adjective* Little.
2. *adjective* Not important. *It is a small problem.*
3. *adjective* Low, soft, or weak, as in *a small voice.*
4. **small talk** *noun* Conversation about unimportant things.
▷ *adjective* **smaller, smallest**

small intestine *noun* The long, coiled part of the digestive system between the stomach and the large intestine, where most nutrients are removed from food and passed into the bloodstream. *See* **organ.**

small·pox (smawl-*poks*) *noun* A very contagious disease that causes chills, high fever, and pimples that can leave permanent scars.

smart (smart)
1. *adjective* Clever and quick in thinking; bright.
2. *verb* To sting or to hurt. *This burn smarts.*
▷ **smarting, smarted**
3. *adjective* Nicely dressed, tidy, and clean.
4. *adjective* Fashionable or stylish.
▷ *noun* **smartness** ▷ *adjective* **smarter, smartest**
▷ *adverb* **smartly**

smash (smash)
1. *verb* To break something into a lot of pieces by hitting or dropping it.
2. *verb* To collide violently with something. *The runaway truck smashed into the telephone pole.*
3. *verb* To destroy or defeat completely.
4. **smash hit** *noun* (informal) A recording, movie, or show that is very successful.
▷ *verb* **smashes, smashing, smashed**

smear (smihr) *verb*
1. To rub something sticky or greasy over a surface.
2. To become messy or blurred. *The paint smeared on the canvas.*
3. To try to damage someone's reputation by telling untrue stories about the person.
▷ *verb* **smearing, smeared** ▷ *noun* **smear**

smell (smel)

1. *verb* To sense an odor with your nose. *I can smell dinner cooking.*

2. *noun* An odor or a scent. *A lovely smell wafted up from the kitchen.*

3. *verb* To give off a smell or odor. *Perfume smells nice.*

4. *verb* To give off an unpleasant odor. *Garbage smells!* ▷ *adjective* **smelly**

5. *verb* To sniff. *I love to smell the roses.*

6. *noun* The ability to notice smells. *Dogs have an excellent sense of smell.*

▷ *verb* **smelling, smelled** or **smelt**

smelt (smelt)

1. *verb* To melt ore so that the metal can be removed. ▷ **smelting, smelted**

2. *noun* A thin, silvery food fish that lives in cold ocean waters and swims up rivers to lay its eggs.

smile (smile) *verb* To widen your mouth and turn it up at the corners to show that you are happy or amused. ▷ **smiling, smiled** ▷ *noun* **smile**

smirk (smurk) *verb* To smile in a smug, knowing, or annoying way. ▷ **smirking, smirked** ▷ *noun* **smirk**

smock (smok) *noun* A garment that looks like a long, loose shirt. Smocks are worn over other clothes to keep them from getting dirty.

smog (smog) *noun* A mixture of fog and smoke that sometimes hangs in the air over cities and industrial areas. *The photograph shows smog in Los Angeles, California.*

smog

smoke (smohk)

1. *noun* The mixture of gas and tiny carbon particles that is given off when something burns. ▷ *adjective* **smoky**

2. *verb* To give off smoke. *Our campfire was still smoking this morning.*

3. *verb* To hold a cigarette or cigar in your mouth and inhale its smoke. ▷ *noun* **smoker,** *noun* **smoking**

4. *verb* To preserve food by hanging it in smoke. *This salmon has been smoked.* ▷ *adjective* **smoked** ▷ *verb* **smoking, smoked**

smoke alarm *noun* Another name for a **smoke detector.**

smoke detector *noun* A device that warns people of smoke or fire by letting out a loud, piercing sound.

smoke·stack (smoke-*stak*) *noun* A chimney that allows smoke or gases to escape from a factory, a ship, or a locomotive.

smol·der (smohl-dur) *verb*

1. To burn and smoke slowly with no flames. *After the fire was put out, the ashes smoldered for hours.*

2. To show hidden anger, hate, or jealousy. *His eyes smoldered with hate.*

3. To exist or continue in a hidden state. *Rage smoldered in the mind of the victim.*

▷ *verb* **smoldering, smoldered**

smooth (smooTH)

1. *adjective* A **smooth** surface is even and flat, not rough or bumpy, as in *a smooth road.*

2. *adjective* Happening easily, with no problems or difficulties, as in *a smooth landing.* ▷ *adverb* **smoothly**

3. *verb* To make things more even and flat. ▷ **smoothing, smoothed**

4. *adjective* Able or skillful, as in *a smooth dancer.* ▷ *noun* **smoothness** ▷ *adjective* **smoother, smoothest**

smoth·er (smuTH-ur) *verb*

1. To cover someone's nose and mouth so that the person cannot breathe.

2. To cover something thickly. *Karen smothered the french fries with ketchup.*

3. To hide or to hold back, as in *to smother a yawn.* ▷ *verb* **smothering, smothered**

smudge (smuhj) *verb* To make a messy mark by rubbing something. ▷ **smudging, smudged** ▷ *noun* **smudge** ▷ *adjective* **smudged**

smug (smuhg) *adjective* If you are **smug,** you are so pleased with yourself that you annoy other people. ▷ **smugger, smuggest** ▷ *noun* **smugness** ▷ *adverb* **smugly**

smug·gle (smuhg-uhl) *verb*

1. To bring goods into a country illegally. ▷ *noun* **smuggler**

2. To take something into or out of a place secretly. *We smuggled Jim's present into the house.* ▷ *verb* **smuggling, smuggled**

snack (snak) *noun* A small, light meal. ▷ *verb* **snack**

snag (snag)

1. *noun* A small, unexpected problem or difficulty.

2. *verb* To catch on something. *I snagged my sleeve on a nail.* ▷ **snagging, snagged** ▷ *noun* **snag**

S

snail (snayl) *noun*
 1. A small animal with no legs; a soft, slimy body; and a shell on its back. *See* **invertebrate.**
 2. A person who moves slowly.

snake (snayk) *noun* A long, thin reptile that has no legs and slithers along the ground. In the United States, only rattlesnakes, copperheads, water moccasins, and coral snakes have poisonous bites. *The diagram shows the internal organs of a snake. See also* **adder, venom.**

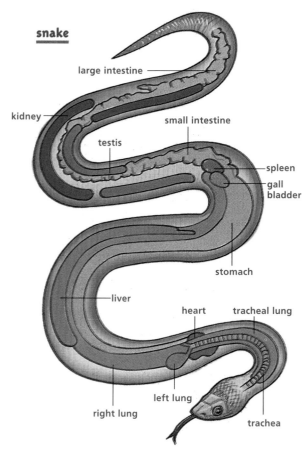

snake

- large intestine
- kidney
- testis
- small intestine
- spleen
- gall bladder
- stomach
- liver
- heart
- tracheal lung
- right lung
- left lung
- trachea

snap (snap)
 1. *verb* To break with a sudden loud, cracking sound. *The twigs snapped beneath our feet.*
 2. *noun* A sudden cracking sound. *The alligator's mouth closed with a snap.*
 3. *verb* To bite or grab suddenly with the mouth or teeth. *The dog snapped at me.*
 4. *verb* To speak sharply and angrily. *Don't snap at me.*
 5. *verb* To open or close with a click or snapping sound. *The lock snapped shut.*
 6. cold snap *noun* A brief period of cold weather.
 7. *noun* (*informal*) A snapshot.
 8. *verb* In football, to pick the ball up off the ground and pass it to another player.

9. *noun* A **snap decision** is a decision that is made very quickly.
 ▷ *noun* **snap** ▷ *verb* **snapping, snapped**
 ▷ *adjective* **snappy**

snap·drag·on (snap-*dra*-guhn) *noun* A garden plant with brightly colored flowers that grow on spikes. Each flower has two petals that look like lips. The petals open and close when pressed.

snap·shot (snap-*shot*) *noun* A photograph taken with a simple camera.

snare (snair)
 1. *noun* A trap for catching birds or animals.
 2. *verb* To catch a bird or an animal in a snare.
 ▷ **snaring, snared**

snare drum *noun* A small drum with strings or wires stretched across its base that produce a rattling sound when hit. *See* **drum.**

snarl (snarl) *verb*
 1. If an animal **snarls,** it shows its teeth and makes a growling sound.
 2. To say something angrily.
 ▷ *verb* **snarling, snarled** ▷ *noun* **snarl**

snatch (snach)
 1. *verb* To take or grab something quickly.
 ▷ **snatches, snatching, snatched** ▷ *noun* **snatch**
 2. *noun* A small part. *I overheard snatches of their conversation.* ▷ *noun, plural* **snatches**

sneak (sneek)
 1. *verb* To move quietly and secretly. *Melissa sneaked up on me from behind.* ▷ *adjective* **sneaky** ▷ *adverb* **sneakily**
 2. *verb* To bring someone or something in where it is not supposed to be. *Jerry sneaked the turtle into the house without anyone noticing.*
 3. *adjective* Done secretly or with no warning, as in *a sneak attack.*
 4. *noun* Someone who is tricky and dishonest.
 ▷ *verb* **sneaking, sneaked** *or* **snuck** (snuhk)

sneak·ers (snee-kurz) *noun, plural* Athletic shoes with rubber soles.

sneer (snihr) *verb* To smile in a hateful, mocking way. *The boxer sneered at his opponent.*
 ▷ **sneering, sneered** ▷ *noun* **sneer**

sneeze (sneez) *verb* To push air out through your nose and mouth suddenly, often because you have a cold. ▷ **sneezing, sneezed** ▷ *noun* **sneeze**

▶ **Word History**

Sneeze was originally spelled and pronounced *fnese* in Old English, but the *f* was mistaken for an *s* because the two letters looked very similar then. *Fnese* is related to the Greek word *pneuma,* meaning "breath." You see that root in *pneumatic* and *pneumonia.*

S

snick·er (snik-ur)
1. *noun* A mean or disrespectful little laugh.
2. *verb* To laugh in such a way. *The children snickered at her terrible joke.* ▷ **snickering, snickered**

sniff (snif) *verb*
1. To breathe in strongly through your nose.
2. To smell something.
▷ *verb* **sniffing, sniffed** ▷ *noun* **sniff**

snif·fle (snif-uhl) *verb* To breathe noisily through your nose, usually because you have a cold.
▷ **sniffling, sniffled** ▷ *noun* **sniffle**

snip (snip) *verb* To cut something using small, quick cuts of shears or scissors. ▷ **snipping, snipped** ▷ *noun* **snip**

snipe (snipe)
1. *verb* To shoot at a person or persons from a hidden place. ▷ **sniping, sniped** ▷ *noun* **sniper**
2. *noun* A marsh bird with a long bill and brown feathers spotted with black and white.

sniv·el (sniv-uhl) *verb* To cry or complain in a noisy, whining way. *The children sniveled when they were sent to their room.* ▷ **sniveling, sniveled**

snob (snob) *noun*
1. Someone who looks down on people who are not rich, successful, or intelligent.
2. A person who thinks that he or she is better than or superior to others.
▷ *noun* **snobbery**

snoop (snoop)
1. *verb* (informal) To pry or look around in a sly or sneaky way. ▷ **snooping, snooped**
2. *noun* A nosy person who pries into other people's business. ▷ *adjective* **snoopy**

snoot·y (snoo-tee) *adjective* (informal) A **snooty** person acts like a snob. ▷ **snootier, snootiest**

snooze (snooz) *verb* (informal) To sleep lightly for a short time, usually during the day. ▷ **snoozing, snoozed** ▷ *noun* **snooze**

snore (snor) *verb* To breathe noisily through your mouth while you are asleep. ▷ **snoring, snored** ▷ *noun* **snore**

snor·kel (snor-kuhl) *noun* A tube that you use to breathe through when you are swimming underwater. *See* **scuba diving.** ▷ *noun* **snorkeling**

snort (snort) *verb*
1. To breathe out noisily through your nose.
2. To show scorn, anger, or disbelief by snorting.
▷ *verb* **snorting, snorted** ▷ *noun* **snort**

snout (snout) *noun* The long front part of an animal's head. It includes the nose, mouth, and jaws.

snow (snoh)
1. *noun* White crystals of ice that form when water vapor freezes in the air.
2. *verb* When it **snows**, snow falls from the sky.
▷ **snowing, snowed** ▷ *adjective* **snowy**

snow·ball (snoh-*bawl*)
1. *noun* Snow pressed into a ball.
2. *verb* If something **snowballs,** it grows rapidly. *Once we started inviting friends, the party snowballed.* ▷ **snowballing, snowballed**

snow·flake
(snoh-*flake*)
noun A single flake or crystal of snow.

snowflake
(magnified)

snow·man
(snoh-*man*) *noun*
A figure built to resemble a person by stacking large balls of snow.
▷ *noun, plural* **snowmen**

snow·mo·bile (snoh-moh-*beel*) *noun* A vehicle with an engine and skis or runners, used to travel over snow.

snow·plow (snoh-*plou*)
1. *noun* A device or vehicle used to push snow off a road, sidewalk, or other surface.
2. *verb* When you **snowplow** in skiing, you go down the slope slowly with the tips of your skis pointing inward and the ends pointing out.
▷ **snowplowing, snowplowed** ▷ *noun* **snowplow**

snow·shoe (snoh-*shoo*) *noun* A webbed frame that is shaped like a racket and attached to a boot to keep the foot from sinking into the snow.

snow·storm (snoh-*storm*) *noun* A storm with strong winds and heavy snow.

snub (snuhb) *verb* To treat someone coldly or with disrespect; to ignore a person. *Our new neighbors snubbed us by pretending they didn't see us wave.* ▷ **snubbing, snubbed** ▷ *noun* **snub**

snuff (snuhf)
1. *noun* Powdered tobacco used for sniffing. Snuff was very popular in the 18th century.
2. snuff out *verb* To extinguish, as in *to snuff out a candle.* ▷ **snuffing, snuffed**

snuf·fle (snuhf-uhl) *verb* To breathe noisily and with difficulty, as when you have a cold.
▷ **snuffling, snuffled**

snug (snuhg) *adjective*
1. Cozy and comfortable. *The cabin was warm and snug.*
2. Fitting closely or tightly. *The jacket was a little snug, so I gave it to my younger sister.*
▷ *adjective* **snugger, snuggest** ▷ *adverb* **snugly**

snug·gle (snuhg-uhl) *verb* To lie close to someone, or to hold something close for warmth or protection or to show affection. *The little boy fell asleep snuggling his teddy bear.*
▷ **snuggling, snuggled** ▷ *adjective* **snuggly**

S

so (soh)
1. adverb In this or that way. *If you want to throw a sinking pitch, hold the baseball so.*
2. adverb To that extent. *I'm so hungry I could eat a horse.*
3. adverb Very. *The puppy is so cute.*
4. adverb Very much. *I miss her so.*
5. conjunction Therefore. *I was bored, so I left the party early.*
6. adverb Too or also. *I dance, and so does he.*
7. adjective True. *Say it isn't so.*
8. conjunction In order that. *Open the window so we can get some air.*
9. pronoun More or less. *Use a teaspoon or so.*
10. pronoun That way, or the same. *Our parents are strict and have always been so.*
11. interjection A word that shows surprise, shock, or annoyance. *So! This is where you've been hiding.*
So sounds like **sew.**

soak (sohk) *verb*
1. To make something completely wet. *The rain soaked my clothes.*
2. To put something in water and leave it there. *My mother soaked the dirty tablecloth overnight.*
3. When something **soaks up** liquid, it absorbs it or takes it in.
▷ *verb* **soaking, soaked**

soak·ing (soh-king) *adjective* Very wet.

soap (sohp) *noun* A substance used for washing and cleaning. Soap is usually made from fat and lye. ▷ *verb* **soap** ▷ *adjective* **soapy**

soap opera *noun* A television series about the tangled loves and lives of a group of people. Soap operas stress suspense and exaggerated emotions.

▷ Word History
· ·
The term **soap opera** dates back to 1939, when *Newsweek* magazine used it to describe the melodramatic 15-minute plays then featured on the radio. *Newsweek* used the word *opera* because the plays were similar to short operas. *Soap* referred to soap manufacturers, the sponsors of many of these programs.

soar (sor) *verb*
1. To fly very high in the air.
2. To rise or increase very quickly. *Gas prices are expected to soar this summer.*
Soar sounds like **sore.**
▷ *verb* **soaring, soared**

sob (sob) *verb* To breathe in short bursts or gasps because you have been crying a lot. ▷ **sobbing, sobbed** ▷ *noun* **sob**

so·ber (soh-bur)
1. adjective Not drunk.
2. adjective Serious or solemn. *He gave me a sober warning.*
3. verb To make someone more serious, solemn, or sober. *The injury to our teammate sobered us quickly.* ▷ **sobering, sobered**
4. adjective Sober colors are dark and dull.
▷ *adjective* **soberer, soberest** ▷ *adverb* **soberly**

sob story *noun* A sad tale intended to evoke sympathy. ▷ *noun, plural* **sob stories**

soc·cer (sok-ur) *noun* A game played by two teams of 11 players who try to score by kicking a ball into goals at each end of a field. *The picture shows players on half a soccer field.*

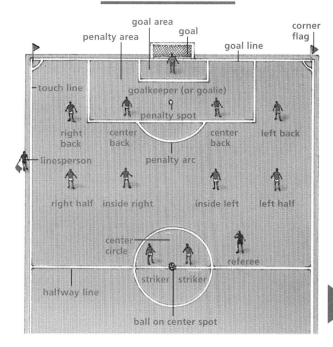

soccer field and players

goal area
penalty area
goal
goal line
corner flag
touch line
goalkeeper (or goalie)
penalty spot
right back
center back
center back
left back
linesperson
penalty arc
right half
inside right
inside left
left half
center circle
referee
striker   striker
halfway line
ball on center spot

so·cia·ble (soh-shuh-buhl) *adjective* A **sociable** person is friendly and enjoys talking to people and spending time with them. ▷ *noun* **sociability** ▷ *adverb* **sociably**

so·cial (soh-shuhl)
1. adjective To do with the way that people live together as a society, as in *social problems.*
2. adjective To do with people getting together in a friendly way or for companionship, as in *a social visit* or *a social club.*
3. adjective Friendly or sociable. *I'm a very social person.*
4. adjective Social animals live in groups rather than on their own.
5. noun A party or a gathering of people.
▷ *adverb* **socially**

so·cial·ism (soh-shuh-*liz*-uhm) *noun* An economic system in which the production of goods by factories, businesses, and farms is controlled to a high degree by a government instead of by the owners of the factories, businesses, and farms. ▷ *noun* **socialist** ▷ *adjective* **socialist**

Social Security *noun* A U.S. government program that pays money to people who are elderly, retired, unemployed, or disabled. Workers and employers also contribute funding. Also spelled **social security.**

social studies *noun* A subject in school that includes geography, history, and government.

so·ci·e·ty (suh-**sye**-uh-tee) *noun*
1. All people, or people as a group. *Laws are made to protect society.*
2. All the people who live in the same country or area and share the same laws and customs. *Americans live in a democratic society.*
3. An organization for people who share the same interests. *Noah is a member of the local music society.*
4. The wealthiest part of society that often sets or follows current fashions and style.
▷ *noun, plural* **societies**

so·ci·ol·o·gy (*soh*-see-**ol**-uh-jee) *noun* The study of the ways in which people live together in different societies. ▷ *noun* **sociologist** ▷ *adjective* **sociological**

sock (sok)
1. *noun* A piece of clothing that you wear on your foot.
2. *verb* (informal) To hit someone very hard.
▷ **socking, socked**

sock·et (sok-it) *noun* A hole or hollow place where something fits in, as in *an electric socket* or *an eye socket.*

sod (sod)
1. *noun* The top layer of soil and the grass attached to it.
2. *noun* A piece of sod that is held together by matted roots and cut in a square or strip.
3. *verb* To cover with pieces of sod.
▷ **sodding, sodded**

sod

so·da (soh-duh) *noun*
1. A soft drink made with soda water.
2. A drink made with soda water, flavoring, and ice cream.
3. Soda water.
4. Baking soda.

soda fountain *noun* A counter where ice cream, soft drinks, and light meals are served.

soda water *noun* A drink with bubbles, made by mixing water with carbon dioxide gas.

sod·den (sod-uhn) *adjective* Soaking wet.

so·di·um (soh-dee-uhm) *noun* A chemical found in salt.

sodium bi·car·bon·ate (bye-kar-buh-nit) *noun* A white substance used in baking powder, fire extinguishers, and medicines. Also called **baking soda.**

so·fa (soh-fuh) *noun* A long, soft seat with arms and a back and room for two or more people; a couch.

soft (sawft) *adjective*
1. Something that is **soft** is not stiff or hard and is easily pressed or bent into a different shape, as in *a soft pillow.* ▷ *noun* **softness**
2. Smooth and gentle to touch. *Babies have very soft skin.*
3. Pleasantly quiet and gentle, as in *soft music* or *a soft breeze.* ▷ *adverb* **softly**
4. Kind, as in *a soft heart.*
▷ *adjective* **softer, softest** ▷ *verb* **soften**

soft·ball (sawft-bawl) *noun* A sport, similar to baseball, that is played on a smaller field with a larger, softer ball that is pitched underhand.

soft drink *noun* A beverage, made with soda water, that contains no alcohol.

soft·heart·ed (sawft-har-tid) *adjective* If someone is **softhearted,** he or she is very kind, sympathetic, and generous to others.

soft·ware (sawft-wair) *noun* Computer programs that control the workings of the equipment, or hardware, and direct it to do specific tasks.

sog·gy (sog-ee) *adjective* Very wet; soaked, as in *soggy ground.* ▷ **soggier, soggiest**

soil (soyl)
1. *noun* Dirt or earth in which plants grow.
2. *noun* A land or a country. *During World War II, American soldiers fought on foreign soil.*
3. *verb* If you **soil** something, you make it dirty or stain it. ▷ **soiling, soiled**

so·lace (sol-iss)
1. *noun* Comfort, or relief from sorrow or grief. *The widow found solace in new friends.*
2. *noun* Something that gives such comfort. *Her children were a solace to her.*
3. *verb* To comfort or console someone who is sad or grieving. *I solaced myself with a hot cup of soup.* ▷ **solacing, solaced**

S

so·lar (soh-lur) *adjective*
 1. To do with the sun, as in *a solar eclipse.*
 2. Powered by energy from the sun.
solar energy *noun* Energy from the sun that can be used for heating and generating electricity. *Solar panels such as the one shown are fixed to roofs and use solar energy to produce hot water.*

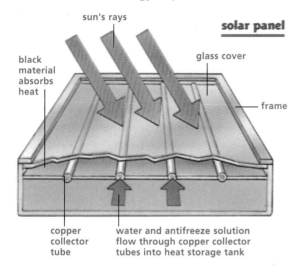

sun's rays

solar panel

glass cover

black material absorbs heat

frame

copper collector tube

water and antifreeze solution flow through copper collector tubes into heat storage tank

solar heating *noun* Heating powered by energy from the sun.
solar system *noun* The sun and the bodies that move in orbit around it. In our solar system there are nine planets, many moons, and also asteroids and comets. *See* **planet.**
sol·der (sod-ur) *verb* To join pieces of metal by putting a small amount of hot, liquid metal between them. The liquid metal hardens as it cools. *He soldered the wires together.*
 ▷ **soldering, soldered** ▷ *noun* **solder**
sol·dier (sole-jur) *noun* Someone who is in the army.

sole (sole)
 1. *noun* The bottom part of the foot.
 2. *noun* The bottom part of a shoe, boot, or sock. ▷ *verb* **sole**
 3. *noun* A kind of edible ocean flatfish.
 4. *adjective* Only. *I was the sole survivor.* ▷ *adverb* **solely**
Sole sounds like **soul.**
sol·emn (sol-uhm) *adjective* Grave or very serious, as in *a solemn occasion* or *a solemn promise.*
 ▷ *noun* **solemnness,** *noun* **solemnity** (suh-**lem**-ni-tee) ▷ *adverb* **solemnly**
sol·id (sol-id)
 1. *adjective* Hard and firm; not a liquid or gas. *The water had frozen solid.* ▷ *noun* **solidity**
 2. *adjective* Not mixed with anything else, as in *solid gold.*
 3. *adjective* Not hollow, as in *a solid block of ice.*
 4. *adjective* Dependable, as in *solid citizens.*
 5. *adjective* Not interrupted. *I jogged for a solid hour.*
 6. *noun* A three-dimensional geometric figure that encloses a part of space. *Cubes and pyramids are solids.* ▷ *adjective* **solid**
sol·i·dar·i·ty (*sol*-uh-da-ruh-tee) *noun* Unity; agreement among a group of people that they will work or fight together to achieve their goal.
so·lid·i·fy (suh-**lid**-uh-fye) *verb* To become hard and firm. ▷ **solidifies, solidifying, solidified**
sol·id·ly (sol-id-lee) *adverb*
 1. Firmly and strongly. *This house is very solidly built.*
 2. Without stopping. *Alma worked solidly for two hours.*
sol·i·tar·y (sol-uh-*ter*-ee) *adjective*
 1. If someone is **solitary,** the person spends a lot of time alone.
 2. Single. *There was not one solitary person on the beach.*

S

soldiers

| Roman legionnaire | 11th-century European knight | 15th-century European knight | 17th-century British cavalryman | 18th-century Prussian musketeer | 19th-century US private |

sol·i·tary con·fine·ment (kuhn-fine-muhnt) *noun* A punishment in which a prisoner is put in a cell alone and is not allowed to see or talk to anybody.

so·lo (soh-loh)
1. *noun* A piece of music that is played or sung by one person, with or without accompaniment. ▷ *noun, plural* **solos** ▷ *noun* **soloist**
2. *adjective* Done by one person. *After playing a duet with Jill, I played a solo piece.* ▷ *adverb* **solo**
3. *verb* To fly a plane alone, especially for the first time. ▷ **soloing, soloed**

sol·u·ble (sol-yuh-buhl) *adjective* A substance that is **soluble** can be dissolved in liquid.

so·lu·tion (suh-loo-shuhn) *noun*
1. The answer to a problem; an explanation.
2. A mixture made up of a substance that has been dissolved in a liquid.

solve (solv) *verb* To find the answer to a problem. ▷ **solving, solved** ▷ *noun* **solver**

sol·vent (sol-vuhnt)
1. *noun* A liquid that makes other substances dissolve.
2. *adjective* Having enough money to pay one's debts.

som·ber (som-bur) *adjective*
1. Dark and gloomy, as in *a rainy, chilly, somber day.*
2. Very sad or depressed. *Many disappointments put Carl in a somber mood.*

som·bre·ro (som-brer-oh) *noun* A tall straw or felt hat with a wide brim that is worn in Mexico and the southwestern United States. ▷ *noun, plural* **sombreros**

> ### Word History
> . . . .
> **Sombrero** is taken from a Spanish word that was formed from two Latin word parts meaning "under" and "shade." The wide brim of a sombrero casts a lot of shade.

some (suhm)
1. *adjective* A number of things, or an amount of something that is not named or known. *There were some children in the park.*
2. *pronoun* A certain number of people or things. *Some of us are going to the park.*
3. *adjective* (informal) Remarkable. *That was some soccer match!*
Some sounds like **sum.**

some·bod·y (suhm-bod-ee *or* suhm-buh-dee)
1. *pronoun* A person who is not specified or known.
2. *noun* An important or famous person. *When I grow up, I'm going to be somebody.*

some·day (suhm-day) *adverb* At some future time. *Someday I'm going to be a famous author.*

some·how (suhm-hou) *adverb* In some way. *Somehow the rabbit managed to get away.*

some·one (suhm-wuhn) *pronoun* Somebody; some person. *Someone has taken my pen!*

som·er·sault (suhm-ur-sawlt) *noun* When you do a **somersault,** you tuck your head into your chest and roll in a complete circle forward or backward. ▷ *verb* **somersault**

some·thing (suhm-thing)
1. *pronoun* A thing that is not specified or known. *You'd better take something for that cough. There's something moving in the bushes.*
2. *adverb* A little bit. *My sister looks something like our cousin.*

some·time (suhm-time) *adverb* At a time that is not specified or known. *I'll do my homework sometime tomorrow.*

some·times (suhm-timez) *adverb* Now and then; at some times but not at others. *Rachel sometimes takes a nap in the afternoon.*

some·what (suhm-waht)
1. *adverb* Rather. *My idea is somewhat like yours.*
2. *pronoun* Something. *The news was somewhat of a surprise.*

some·where (suhm-wair) *adverb*
1. To, in, or at a place that is not specified or known. *My aunt lives somewhere in Ohio.* ▷ *noun* **somewhere**
2. At some time, or in some amount. *We plan to arrive somewhere between seven and eight. I'm looking for a gift that costs somewhere around $25.*

son (suhn) *noun* Someone's **son** is his or her male child. **Son** sounds like **sun.**

so·nar (soh-nar) *noun* An instrument that is used to calculate how deep the water is or where underwater objects are. It works by sending sound waves through the water and listening for when they bounce back off something. Sonar stands for *SOund Navigation And Ranging.*

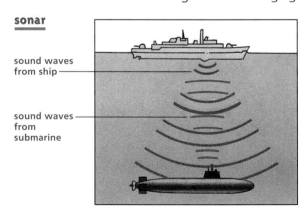

sonar

sound waves from ship

sound waves from submarine

so·na·ta (suh-nah-tuh) *noun* A piece of music for one or two instruments that is in three or four movements, or sections.

S

song (sawng *or* song) *noun*
1. A piece of music with words for singing.
2. The musical sounds made by a whale, a bird, or an insect.
3. If you buy something **for a song,** you get it at a very cheap price.

song·bird (sawng-*burd*) *noun* A bird that has a musical call or song. Larks, finches, and orioles are songbirds.

son·ic (son-ik) *adjective*
1. To do with sound waves.
2. To do with the speed of sound in air, or about 741 miles per hour at sea level.

sonic boom *noun* The loud noise produced by a vehicle when it travels faster than the speed of sound and breaks through the sound barrier.

son-in-law *noun* Someone's **son-in-law** is the husband of his or her daughter. ▷ *noun, plural* **sons-in-law**

son·net (son-it) *noun* A poem with 14 lines and a fixed pattern of rhymes.

soon (soon) *adverb*
1. In a short time. *I'll visit you soon.*
2. Too early. *The alarm rang too soon this morning.*
3. Quickly; without delay. *Come back soon.*
4. **sooner** If you would **sooner** do something, you would prefer to do that thing.
▷ *adverb* **sooner, soonest**

soot (sut) *noun* Black powder that is produced when a fuel such as coal, wood, or oil is burned. Soot often collects in chimneys. *After cleaning out a chimney, this chimney sweep has a face that is covered with soot.* ▷ *adjective* **sooty**

chimney sweep

soothe (sooTH) *verb*
1. To calm someone who is angry or upset. *Fran tried to soothe the screaming baby.*
2. To relieve something that is painful. *This cream should soothe your rash.*
▷ *verb* **soothing, soothed** ▷ *adjective* **soothing**

so·phis·ti·ca·ted (suh-fiss-tuh-*kay*-tid) *adjective*
1. People who are **sophisticated** have a lot of knowledge about the world.
2. A **sophisticated** machine is cleverly designed and able to do difficult or complicated things.
▷ *noun* **sophistication**

soph·o·more (sof-*mor* or sof-uh-*mor*) *noun* A student in the second year of high school or college.

sop·ping (sop-ing) *adjective* Extremely wet. *My clothes were sopping after the rainstorm.*

so·pran·o (suh-*pran*-oh) *noun*
1. The highest singing voice. ▷ *adjective* **soprano**
2. Someone who sings in a soprano voice.
▷ *noun, plural* **sopranos**

sor·bet (sor-bay *or* sor-buht) *noun* A frozen dessert made with fruit juice.

sor·cer·er (sor-sur-er) *noun* Someone who performs magic by controlling evil spirits; a wizard. ▷ *noun* **sorcery**

sor·did (sor-did) *adjective*
1. Dirty or filthy, as in *a sordid slum.*
2. Evil and disgusting, as in *a sordid murder.*
▷ *noun* **sordidness** ▷ *adverb* **sordidly**

sore (sor)
1. *adjective* Painful, as in *sore muscles.* ▷ *noun* **soreness**
2. *noun* An area of painful skin on your body. *That sore on your arm looks infected.*
3. *adjective* Angry. *Eric was sore at his friends.*
▷ *adjective* **sorer, sorest**
Sore sounds like **soar.**

sor·rel (sor-uhl *or* so-ruhl) *noun*
1. A reddish brown color.
2. A horse of this color with a mane and tail of a lighter color.
3. A plant with long clusters of small flowers and edible leaves that are shaped like hearts.

sor·row (so-roh) *noun* Great sadness or grief.
▷ *adjective* **sorrowful** ▷ *adverb* **sorrowfully**

sor·ry (so-ree) *adjective*
1. Feeling sadness, sympathy, or regret because you have done something wrong or because someone is suffering. *I'm sorry I hurt your feelings. I'm sorry you are ill.*
2. If someone or something is **in a sorry state,** it is in very bad condition.
▷ *adjective* **sorrier, sorriest**

sort (sort)
1. *noun* A type or a kind. *What sort of dog is that?*
2. *verb* To arrange or separate things into groups. *I will sort my socks into pairs.* ▷ **sorting, sorted**

SOS (ess oh ess) *noun* A signal sent out by a ship or plane to say that it is in need of urgent help. The initials SOS stand for *Save Our Ship.*

S

soul (sole)
1. *noun* The spiritual part of a person that is often thought to control the ability to think, feel, and act.
2. *noun* A person. *You mustn't tell another soul.*
3. *adjective* To do with African Americans or black culture, as in *soul music* and *soul food.* **Soul** sounds like **sole.**

sound (sound)
1. *noun* Something that you hear.
2. *noun* One of the noises that make up human speech. *Write begins with an r sound.*
3. *verb* If a horn or bell **sounds,** it makes a noise.
4. *verb* To give an impression. *That sounds like a good idea.*
5. *verb* To be said or pronounced. The word *sore* sounds like *soar.*
6. *adjective* Healthy, as in *a sound mind.*
7. *adjective* Sensible, as in *sound advice.*
8. *adjective* Deep. *After being up all night, I fell into a sound sleep.*
9. *noun* A long, narrow arm of water between two bodies of water or between the mainland and an island.
▷ *verb* **sounding, sounded**

sound barrier *noun* When a vehicle goes through the **sound barrier,** the sound waves produced by that vehicle are moving more slowly than the vehicle itself. As a result, all of the sound waves that people on the ground usually hear as a roar get bunched together into a single boom. *In this photo Chuck Yeager poses in front of the X–1, the plane he was flying in 1947 when he became the first human ever to break the sound barrier.*

Chuck Yeager

sound bite *noun* A statement or a small portion of a political speech that is recorded and played on a newscast or other program.

sound effects *noun, plural* Noises that are used to make a play, a movie, or a radio or television program seem more realistic.

sound·proof (sound-*proof*) *adjective* A **soundproof** room does not let any sound in or out of it. ▷ *verb* **soundproof**

sound track *noun*
1. A recording of music from a movie or play.
2. The narrow strip on a motion-picture film or videotape that carries the sound recording.

sound wave *noun* A wave or series of vibrations in the air, in a solid, or in a liquid that can be heard.

soup (soop)
1. *noun* A liquid food made with vegetables, meat, or fish. ▷ *adjective* **soupy**
2. *verb* (slang) If you **soup up** an engine or motor vehicle, you increase its power. ▷ **souping, souped**

sour (sour)
1. *adjective* Something that is **sour** has a sharp, acid taste, such as a lemon.
2. *adjective* Disagreeable. *Ralph has a very sour expression.*
3. *verb* To make or become acid through spoiling. *We left the milk out and it soured.*
▷ **souring, soured**
▷ *noun* **sourness**

source (sorss) *noun*
1. The place, person, or thing from which something comes, as in *the source of the problem.*
2. The place where a stream or river starts.
3. Someone or something that provides information. *An encyclopedia is a useful reference source.*

sour·dough (sour-*doh*) *noun* A fermented dough used in making breads and rolls.

south (south)
1. *noun* One of the four main points of the compass. South is to your left when you face the direction where the sun sets. ▷ *adjective* **south** ▷ *adverb* **south**
2. South *noun* Any area or region that is lying in this direction.
3. *adjective* To do with or existing in the south, as in *the south side of the city.*
4. the South *noun* In the United States, the states lying south of Pennsylvania and the Ohio River and east of the Mississippi River. The South includes those states that fought for the Confederacy against the Union (or North) in the Civil War.

South·east (south-*eest*) *noun* The area of the United States to the south and east that stretches from Virginia to Florida and Louisiana.

south·ern (suhTH-urn) *adjective*
1. In or toward the south.
2. Coming from the south, as in *a southern wind.*
3. Southern To do with the part of the United States that is in the South.

Southern Hemisphere *noun* The half of the earth that is south of the equator.

South Pole *noun* The most southern part of the earth, located at the bottom tip of the earth's axis. The South Pole is at Antarctica. *See* **polar.**

South·west (*south-west*) *noun* The area of the United States that includes the states west of the Mississippi River and south of Missouri and Kansas.

south·west·er (*south-wess-tur*) *noun*
1. A waterproof hat with a wide brim at the back to keep your neck dry.
2. A long, waterproof coat worn especially by sailors during stormy weather.

sou·ve·nir (*soo-vuh-nihr* or *soo-vuh-nihr*) *noun* An object that you keep to remind you of a place, a person, or an event.

sov·er·eign (*sov-ruhn*)
1. *noun* A king or queen.
2. *adjective* Having the highest power, as in *a sovereign ruler.*
3. *adjective* Independent, as in *a sovereign nation.*

So·vi·et Union (*soh-vee-et*) *noun* A former federation of 15 republics that included Russia, Ukraine, and other nations of eastern Europe and northern Asia. Also called *Union of Soviet Socialist Republics.*

sow
1. (*soh*) *verb* To scatter seeds over the ground so that they will grow; to plant. ▷ **sowing, sowed, sown** (*sohn*) *or* **sowed**
2. (*sou*) *noun* An adult female pig.

soy·bean (*soi-been*) *noun* A seed that grows in pods on bushy plants. Soybeans are a good source of protein and oil.

soy sauce (*soi*) *noun* A dark liquid that is made from soaked and fermented soybeans. It is used as a sauce to flavor food.

space (*spayss*)
1. *verb* To leave an empty area between things. *Space your lines evenly as you write.* ▷ **spacing, spaced**
2. *noun* The universe beyond the earth's atmosphere. Also called **outer space.**
3. *noun* An empty or available area. *There's space for a few more things in this suitcase. We found a parking space at the shopping center.*
4. *noun* A period of time. *All of the guests arrived within a space of 15 minutes.*
5. *noun* The open area in which all objects are located. Space has height, width, and depth.

space bar *noun* A bar at the bottom of a computer or typewriter keyboard that adds a space to the right of a character when pressed.

space·craft (*spayss-kraft*) *noun* A vehicle that travels or is used in space.

space·ship (*spayss-ship*) *noun* A spacecraft designed and built to break free of earth's atmosphere and travel into space.

space shuttle *noun* A spacecraft designed to carry astronauts into space and back to earth. A space shuttle is made up of four parts (the orbiter, the external fuel tank, and two booster rockets) that separate after the launch. The orbiter returns to earth. *This picture shows a space shuttle and how the parts separate.*

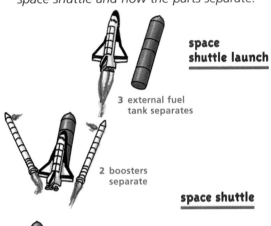

space shuttle launch

3 external fuel tank separates

2 boosters separate

space shuttle

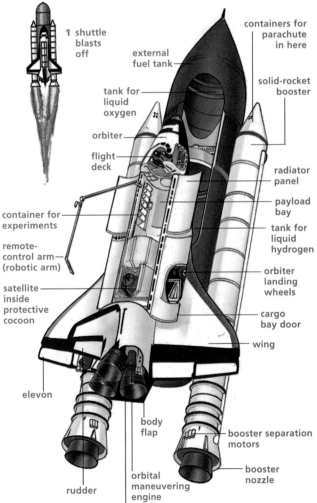

1 shuttle blasts off

external fuel tank

tank for liquid oxygen

orbiter

flight deck

container for experiments

remote-control arm (robotic arm)

satellite inside protective cocoon

elevon

containers for parachute in here

solid-rocket booster

radiator panel

payload bay

tank for liquid hydrogen

orbiter landing wheels

cargo bay door

wing

booster separation motors

booster nozzle

body flap

orbital maneuvering engine

rudder

main engine

S

space station *noun* A spacecraft large enough to house a crew for long periods of time. Space stations are placed in orbit and are used for scientific observation and as a launching site for other spacecraft.

space·suit (spayss-*soot*) *noun* The protective clothing that an astronaut wears in space. *See* **astronaut.**

space·walk (spayss-*wawk*) *noun* A period of time during which an astronaut leaves his or her spacecraft and moves around in space. ▷ *noun* **spacewalker** ▷ *verb* **spacewalk**

spa·cious (spay-shuhss) *adjective* If something is **spacious,** it is very large and roomy. *We moved from our small apartment to a spacious house.*

spade (spayd) *noun*
1. A tool with a flat blade and a long handle. Spades are used for digging. ▷ *verb* **spade**
2. spades *noun, plural* One of the four suits in a deck of cards. Spades have a black symbol that looks like a heart with a stalk.

spa·ghet·ti (spuh-get-ee) *noun* Long, thin strands of pasta made of flour and water and cooked by boiling. *See* **pasta.**

span (span)
1. *noun* The distance between two points. The span of a bridge is its length from one end to the other.
2. *noun* The full reach or length of something, as in *the wing span of an airplane* or *a person's life span.*
3. *noun* A length of time.
4. *verb* To reach over or stretch across something. *A bridge spans this river.* ▷ **spanning, spanned**

spank (spangk) *verb* To hit someone with an open hand or a flat object, especially on the buttocks, as a punishment. ▷ **spanking, spanked**

spare (spair)
1. *adjective* Kept for use when needed, as in *a spare tire.* ▷ *noun* **spare**
2. *adjective* Not taken up by work; free, as in *spare time.*
3. *adjective* Lean and thin. *Abraham Lincoln was tall and spare.*
4. *verb* To give or make something available. *Can you spare a few minutes?*
5. *verb* To show mercy, or to not hurt someone, as in *to spare a life* or *to spare someone's feelings.*
6. *verb* To free from the need to do something. *She spared us from having to wash the dishes.*
7. *noun* The knocking down of all 10 pins in bowling with two rolls of the ball.
▷ *verb* **sparing, spared**

spark (spark)
1. *noun* A small bit of burning material thrown off by a fire.

2. *noun* A quick flash of light, as in *an electrical spark.*
3. *noun* A small bit or trace, as in *a spark of enthusiasm.*
4. *verb* To make something happen. *The concert sparked my interest in music.* ▷ **sparking, sparked** ▷ *verb* **spark**

spar·kle (spar-kuhl) *verb*
1. To shine with many flashing points of light; to glitter. *Her eyes sparkled with excitement.*
2. To bubble. *Soda water sparkles.*
3. To accomplish something in a brilliant or lively way. *The pianist sparkled at last night's concert.*
▷ *verb* **sparkling, sparkled** ▷ *noun* **sparkle**

spark plug *noun* One of the parts of a gasoline engine that supplies an electrical spark to ignite the fuel-and-air mixture in a cylinder. Spark plugs are screwed into the cylinders and connected to the distributor, which supplies the current to create the spark. *See also* **engine.**

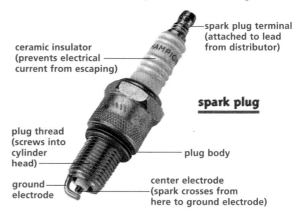

ceramic insulator (prevents electrical current from escaping)

spark plug terminal (attached to lead from distributor)

spark plug

plug thread (screws into cylinder head)

plug body

ground electrode

center electrode (spark crosses from here to ground electrode)

spar·row (spa-roh) *noun* A small, common songbird with brown, white, and gray feathers and a short bill.

sparse (sparss) *adjective* Thinly spread; not crowded or dense, as in *sparse vegetation.*
▷ *adverb* **sparsely**

spasm (spaz-uhm) *noun*
1. A sudden tightening of a muscle that cannot be controlled.
2. A short, sudden burst of energy, activity, or emotion, as in *a spasm of laughter.*

spat (spat) *noun* A short, unimportant argument or quarrel.

spat·ter (spat-ur) *verb* To scatter or splash in drops or small bits. *She spattered paint all over her clothes.* ▷ **spattering, spattered**

spat·u·la (spach-uh-luh) *noun*
1. A tool with a broad, flat blade that bends easily. It is used to mix, spread, or lift food or to mix paint.
2. An instrument with a flat blade used by doctors and scientists. *See* **apparatus.**

spawn (spawn)
1. *noun* The eggs produced by fish and amphibians. *See* **frog.**
2. *verb* To produce a large number of eggs. *Most salmon live in salt water but swim to fresh water to spawn.* ▷ **spawning, spawned**

speak (speek) *verb*
1. To talk, or to say words out loud.
2. To tell or make known your ideas, opinions, or feelings. *Can I speak to you about a problem I'm having?*
3. To deliver a speech.
4. To talk in a certain language. *At home we speak English and Spanish.*
5. If you **speak out** or **speak up,** you speak loudly or you speak openly and honestly about what you really believe.
▷ *verb* **speaking, spoke** (spohk), **spoken** (spoh-kin)

speak·er (spee-kur) *noun*
1. The one who is speaking.
2. Somebody who gives a speech in public.
3. A loudspeaker, especially one attached to a sound system. *The diagram shows a speaker. Electrical signals from a sound system flow into the coil of wire, creating a magnetic force that makes the coil move backward and forward, toward and away from the magnet. The moving coil makes the cone vibrate and produce sounds.*

speaker

cabinet

grille

tweeter
(high-range
speaker)

magnet

coil of
wire

woofer
(low-range
speaker)

speaker cone
(made from paper or plastic)

spear (spihr)
1. *noun* A weapon with a long handle and a pointed head.
2. *noun* A long blade, shoot, or stalk of a plant, as in *asparagus spears.*
3. *verb* To pick up with something sharp. *I speared the piece of cheese with a toothpick.*
▷ **spearing, speared**

spear·mint (speer-*mint*) *noun* A mint plant with leaves that are shaped like spears and are used to flavor candy and food.

spe·cial (spesh-uhl)
1. *adjective* Different or unusual, as in *a special occasion* or *a special request.* ▷ *adverb* **specially**
2. *adjective* Particular. *You need a special pass to get backstage.*
3. *noun* A television program intended as a single show rather than as one in a series.

spe·cial·ist (spesh-uh-list) *noun* An expert at one particular job or area. *Her doctor is a specialist in heart disease.*

spe·cial·ize (spesh-uh-*lize*) *verb* To focus on one area of work, or to learn a lot about one subject. *Alice specializes in comic book art.* ▷ **specializing, specialized** ▷ *noun* **specialization**

spe·cial·ty (spesh-uhl-tee) *noun*
1. The thing that you are particularly good at. *Sam's specialty is playing the guitar.*
2. A particular product or service. *That store's specialty is greeting cards.*
▷ *noun, plural* **specialties**

spe·cies (spee-sheez *or* spee-seez) *noun* One of the groups into which animals and plants of the same genus are divided according to their shared characteristics. Members of the same species can mate and have offspring. *The lion and cheetah are two different species of cat.*
▷ *noun, plural* **species**

spe·cif·ic (spi-sif-ik) *adjective* Particular, definite, or individually named. *Corinne insists on a specific brand of cereal for breakfast.* ▷ *adverb* **specifically**

spec·i·fi·ca·tions (spess-uh-fuh-**kay**-shuhnz) *noun, plural* Detailed information and instructions about something that is to be built or made. *The architect drew up specifications for the house.*

spec·i·fy (spess-uh-*fye*) *verb* To mention something in an exact way. *Please specify your sweater size on the catalog order form.*
▷ **specifies, specifying, specified**

spec·i·men (spess-uh-muhn) *noun* A sample, or an example used to stand for a whole group, as in *a butterfly specimen* or *a blood specimen.*
▷ *adjective* **specimen**

speck (spek) *noun*
1. A small spot or mark. *Some specks of paint got on my shoes.*
2. A tiny particle or bit, as in *a speck of dust.*

speck·led (spek-uhld) *adjective* Covered with small, irregular spots or marks, as in *a speckled egg.*

spec·ta·cle (spek-tuh-kuhl) *noun* A remarkable and dramatic sight. *The fireworks were quite a spectacle.*

S

spec·ta·cles (spek-tuh-kuhlz) *noun, plural*
Eyeglasses.

spec·tac·u·lar (spek-tak-yuh-lur) *adjective*
Remarkable or dramatic, as in *a spectacular sunset.* ▷ *adverb* **spectacularly**

spec·ta·tor (spek-tay-tur) *noun* Someone who watches an event and does not participate in it.
▷ *adjective* **spectator**

spec·ter (spek-tur) *noun* A ghost. ▷ *adjective* **spectral**

spec·trum (spek-truhm) *noun*
1. The range of colors that is revealed when light shines through a prism or through drops of water, as in a rainbow. *When white light travels through a prism, it is refracted, or bent. Since each of the colors in light travels at a slightly different speed, each bends at a different angle and the range of colors spreads out in a spectrum.*
2. A wide range of things or ideas.
▷ *noun, plural* **spectrums** *or* **spectra** (spek-truh)

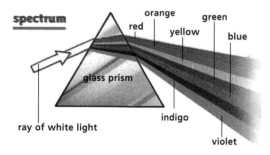

spec·u·late (spek-yuh-late) *verb*
1. To wonder or guess about something without knowing all the facts.
2. To invest in something that is risky, such as a business or a stock.
▷ *verb* **speculating, speculated** ▷ *noun* **speculation,** *noun* **speculator**

speech (speech) *noun*
1. The ability to speak.
2. A talk given to a group of people. ▷ *noun, plural* **speeches**
3. The way in which someone speaks. *I can tell by your speech that you're from the South.*

speech·less (speech-liss) *adjective* Unable to speak. *He was speechless with rage.*

speed (speed)
1. *noun* The rate at which something moves.
2. *noun* The rate of any action. *I'm taking a class to improve my reading speed.*
3. *verb* To travel very fast or faster than is allowed. ▷ **speeding, sped** (sped) *or* **speeded**
4. *noun* Quickness of movement.

speed bump *noun* A ridge of asphalt or hard rubber that has been laid across a road or parking lot to make drivers slow down.

speed·om·e·ter (spi-dom-uh-tur) *noun* An instrument in a vehicle that shows how fast you are traveling. *See* **motorcycle.**

spell (spel)
1. *verb* To write or say the letters of a word in their correct order.
2. *verb* To mean. *The captain's injury spelled trouble for the team.*
3. *verb* To take someone's place for a time. *During our cross-country car trip, my parents spelled each other at the wheel.*
4. *noun* A period of time, usually a short one, as in *a spell of rainy weather.*
5. *noun* A word or words supposed to have magical powers.
6. *verb* If you **spell out** an idea or a plan, you explain it clearly and in detail.
▷ *verb* **spelling, spelled**

spell checker *noun* A computer program that searches for misspelled words by comparing each word in a document to correctly spelled words.

spe·lunk·ing (spi-luhng-king) *noun* If you go **spelunking,** you explore caves. ▷ *noun* **spelunker**

spend (spend) *verb*
1. To use money to buy things.
2. To pass time. *We will spend our vacation at the beach.*
3. If you **spend** time or energy, you use it.
▷ *verb* **spending, spent** (spent)

sperm (spurm) *noun* One of the reproductive cells from a male that is capable of fertilizing eggs in a female.

sphere (sfihr) *noun*
1. A solid shape like a basketball or globe, with all points of the shape the same distance from the center of the shape. ▷ *adjective* **spherical** (sfihr-uh-kuhl *or* sfer-uh-kuhl)
2. An area of activity, interest, or knowledge. *Poetry is in my sphere of interest.*

sphinx (sfingks) *noun*
1. In Egyptian mythology, a creature with the body of a lion and the head of a man, ram, or hawk.
2. **the Sphinx** A large statue of this creature in Giza, Egypt.
▷ *noun, plural* **sphinxes**

the Sphinx

spice (spisse) *noun*
1. A substance with a distinctive smell or taste used to flavor foods. *The picture shows a range of spices.*
2. Anything that adds excitement or interest. *Variety is the spice of life.* ▷ *verb* **spice**

spices

cloves

powdered turmeric

paprika

nutmeg

caraway seeds

cinnamon sticks

allspice

cumin seeds

spi·cy (spye-see) *adjective* Containing lots of spices; having a pungent taste. *My father makes very spicy chili.* ▷ **spicier, spiciest**

spi·der (spye-dur) *noun* A small animal with eight legs, a body divided into two parts, and no wings. Spiders spin webs to trap insects for food. *The picture shows a selection of spiders from around the world.*

spiders

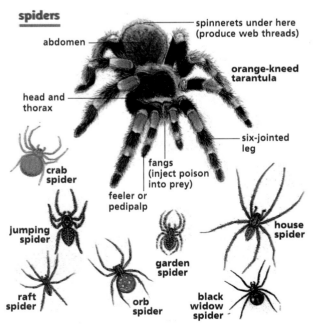

abdomen

spinnerets under here (produce web threads)

orange-kneed tarantula

head and thorax

six-jointed leg

crab spider

fangs (inject poison into prey)

feeler or pedipalp

jumping spider

garden spider

house spider

raft spider

orb spider

black widow spider

spike (spike)
1. *noun* A large, heavy nail often used to fasten rails to railroad ties. ▷ *verb* **spike**
2. *noun* A pointed piece of metal attached to the sole of a shoe to help athletes get and keep firm footing.
3. *noun* An ear of wheat or grain, such as corn.
4. *noun* A long cluster of flowers on one stem.
5. *verb* To hit a volleyball down and over the net with force so that it is difficult to return.
▷ **spiking, spiked**
▷ *noun* **spike** ▷ *adjective* **spiked**

spill (spil)
1. *verb* If you **spill** something, you let the contents of a container fall out, often accidentally.
2. *verb* To run out or flow over. *Tears spilled from her eyes.*
3. *noun* A serious fall. *Mike took a bad spill off his motorcycle.*
▷ *verb* **spilling, spilled** *or* **spilt** (spilt)

spin (spin)
1. *verb* To make thread by twisting fine fibers together. *The picture shows a spinning jenny, a machine invented in the 18th century that could spin up to eight threads at once.*

spinning jenny

2. *verb* To make a web or cocoon by giving off a liquid that hardens into thread. *Spiders spin webs.*
3. *verb* To rotate or to whirl around. *The earth spins.*
4. *verb* To tell or to relate. *The old sea captain spins a good tale.*
5. *verb* To feel dizzy, or as if your head is whirling around. *The roller coaster made my head spin.*
6. *noun* A short ride. *We took the new car out for a spin around the block.*
7. *noun* A special interpretation or point of view. *The senator put a positive spin on the poll results.*
▷ *verb* **spinning, spun** (spuhn)

spin·ach (spin-ich) *noun* A dark green, leafy vegetable. *See* **vegetable.**

spinal column *noun* A series of connected bones in your back that support and protect the spinal cord. Spinal column is another term for **backbone.**

spinal cord *noun* A thick cord of nerve tissue that starts at the brain and runs through the center of the spinal column. The spinal cord carries impulses to and from the brain and links the brain to the rest of the nerves in the body.

S

513

spin·dle (spin-duhl) *noun* The round stick or rod on a spinning wheel that holds and winds thread.

spin·dly (spind-lee) *adjective* Long, thin, and rather weak. *The newborn colt stood on spindly legs.* ▷ **spindlier, spindliest**

spine (spine) *noun*
1. The backbone. *See* **skeleton.** ▷ *adjective* **spinal**
2. A hard, sharp, pointed growth, such as a thorn or quill, on some plants and animals.
▷ *adjective* **spiny**
3. The central, vertical piece of a book's cover. *See* **book.**

spinning wheel *noun* A device worked by hand consisting of a large wheel and a spindle. A spinning wheel is used to spin fibers into thread or yarn.

spin-off *noun*
1. An object or product that was first used in a different or unrelated way. *The coating Teflon is a spin-off from the space program.*
2. A television show starring a character who had a popular but less important role on an earlier program. ▷ *verb* **spin off**

spin·ster (spin-stur) *noun* A woman who has never been married.

spi·ral (spye-ruhl)
adjective A **spiral** pattern winds around in circles like a spring. *The chambers inside a nautilus shell are arranged in a spiral pattern.*
▷ *noun* **spiral**
▷ *verb* **spiral**

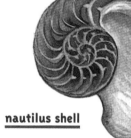

nautilus shell

spire (spire) *noun* A structure that comes to a point at the top. Spires are often built on top of church steeples. *See* **cathedral.**

spir·it (spihr-it)
1. *noun* The part of a person that is believed to control thoughts and feelings; the soul.
2. *noun* Enthusiasm and determination in a person or group of people. *We shared a spirit of hope.* ▷ *adjective* **spirited**
3. *noun* A ghost.
4. *noun, plural* **spirits** A person's mood or state of mind. *The patient is recovering nicely and is in good spirits.*
5. *noun* The real meaning or intent, as in *the spirit of the law.*
6. *verb* To carry off mysteriously or secretly.
▷ **spiriting, spirited**

spir·i·tu·al (spihr-uh-choo-uhl)
1. *adjective* To do with the soul and not with physical things. ▷ *adverb* **spiritually**
2. *adjective* To do with religion.
3. *noun* A type of religious folk song that was originated by African Americans in the South.

spit (spit)
1. *verb* To force saliva out of your mouth.
2. *noun* Saliva.
3. *verb* To make an angry, hissing sound. *The cat spat at the puppy.*
4. *noun* A long, pointed rod that holds meat over a fire for cooking.
5. *noun* A narrow point of land that sticks out into water.
▷ *verb* **spitting, spat** (spat) *or* **spit**

spite (spite)
1. *noun* Deliberate nastiness. ▷ *adjective* **spiteful**
▷ *adverb* **spitefully**
2. *verb* To be mean or nasty to. *Grace played that trick on Alan just to spite him* ▷ **spiting, spited**
3. in spite of Without being hindered by; regardless, or in defiance of. *Dan ran the marathon in spite of his cold.*

splash (splash) *verb*
1. To throw a liquid. *Jim splashed water on his face.*
2. To make wet by splashing.
▷ *verb* **splashes, splashing, splashed** ▷ *noun* **splash**

splash·down (splash-*doun*) *noun* The landing of a spacecraft in the ocean.

splen·did (splen-did) *adjective*
1. Very beautiful or impressive; brilliant, as in *a splendid performance.*
2. Very good; excellent, as in *a splendid idea.*
▷ *adverb* **splendidly**

splen·dor (splen-dur) *noun* Great or magnificent beauty. *We stood speechless as we gazed out at the ocean's splendor.*

splint (splint) *noun* A piece of wood, plastic, or metal used to support an injured limb.

splin·ter (splin-tur)
1. *noun* A thin, sharp piece of wood, glass, metal, etc.
2. *verb* To break into thin, sharp pieces.
▷ **splintering, splintered**

split (split)
1. *verb* To break along the grain, as in *to split logs.*
2. *verb* To divide. *The partners split the profits.*
3. *verb* To burst or break apart by force. *The seam split. Scientists can split atoms.*
4. *noun* A crack or a break.
5. *noun* An acrobatic or dance move in which you slide to the floor with your legs spread in opposite directions.
▷ *verb* **splitting, split**

spoil (spoil)
1. *verb* To ruin or wreck something.
2. *verb* To become rotten or unfit for eating.
3. *adjective* If children are **spoiled,** their parents have pampered them and allowed them to have their own way too often.
▷ *verb* **spoiling, spoiled** *or* **spoilt**

spoke (spoke)
1. *verb* The past tense of **speak.**
2. *noun* One of the thin rods that connect the rim of a wheel to the hub. *See* **bicycle.**

sponge (spuhnj) *noun*
1. A sea animal that has a rubbery skeleton with many holes that absorb water. The dried skeletons of sponges are often used for washing and cleaning.
2. A cleaning pad made of plastic or another artificial material that absorbs water.
▷ *verb* **sponge** ▷ *adjective* **spongy**

spon·sor (spon-sur)
1. *verb* To give money and support to people who are doing something worthwhile, often for charity. ▷ *noun* **sponsorship**
2. *verb* To pay the costs of a radio or television broadcast in return for having your products advertised. ▷ *noun* **sponsor**
3. *noun* A person who is responsible for someone or something. *The senator is the sponsor of the new law.*
▷ *verb* **sponsoring, sponsored**

spon·ta·ne·ous (spon-tay-nee-uhss) *adjective*
1. Without previous thought or planning, as in *spontaneous applause.*
2. Happening by itself, without any apparent outside cause, as in *a spontaneous explosion.*
▷ *noun* **spontaneity** (spon-tuh-**nee**-uh-tee *or* spon-tuh-**nay**-uh-tee) ▷ *adverb* **spontaneously**

spool (spool) *noun* A reel on which film, tape, thread, etc., is wound.

spoon (spoon) *noun* A utensil with a handle on one end and a surface shaped like a shallow bowl on the other. Spoons are used for eating, stirring, and measuring. *See* **silverware.** ▷ *verb* **spoon**

spore (spor) *noun*
A plant cell that develops into a new plant. Spores are produced by plants that do not flower, such as fungi, mosses, and ferns. *The picture shows some moss spore cases. When the cases open, the spores are spread by the wind. See also* **fern.**

moss spore cases

sport (sport) *noun*
1. A game involving physical activity. A sport can be played professionally or for pleasure.
2. A person who plays fair and accepts losing with good grace, as in *a good sport.*

sports·man·ship (sports-muhn-ship) *noun* Fair and reasonable behavior, especially in playing a sport. *The tennis player displayed great sportsmanship, even after losing her match.*

spot (spot)
1. *noun* A small mark or stain. *He had a spot of gravy on his tie.*
2. *noun* An area on the skin or fur that is different from the area around it. *A dalmatian is white with black spots.* ▷ *adjective* **spotted**
3. *noun* A place or a location. *This looks like a good spot for a picnic.*
4. *noun* A small amount of something. *Ed always has a spot of tea with his dinner.*
5. *verb* To notice something or someone. *Angelina spotted her friend in the crowd.*
▷ **spotting, spotted**
6. If something **hits the spot,** it is satisfying and is exactly the right thing to have at that moment.
7. If you are **in a tight spot,** you are in a lot of trouble and will not get out of it easily.

spot·less (spot-liss) *adjective*
1. Absolutely clean. *Bill scrubbed the kitchen sink until it was spotless.*
2. Without a flaw or weak part, as in *a spotless reputation.*
▷ *adverb* **spotlessly**

spot·light (spot-*lite*) *noun*
1. A powerful beam of light used to light up a small area.
2. A lamp that sends a strong beam of light. A spotlight is used in a reading area, on a theater stage, or in an exhibit to highlight items on display.
3. If someone is **in the spotlight,** he or she is in the news or is the focus of a lot of public attention.
▷ *verb* **spotlight**

spouse (spouss) *noun* A husband or a wife.

spout (spout)
1. *noun* A pipe, a tube, or an opening through which liquid flows or is poured. *Tea kettles have spouts.*
2. *verb* To shoot or pour out with force. *Volcanoes spout lava.* ▷ **spouting, spouted**

sprain (sprayn) *verb* To injure a joint by twisting or tearing its muscles or ligaments. *Liza sprained her ankle when she fell.* ▷ **spraining, sprained**
▷ *noun* **sprain**

S

sprawl (sprawl) *verb*
1. To sit or lie with your arms and legs spread out carelessly. *Jason sprawled on the grass.*
2. To spread out in all directions. *The city sprawled for miles.* ▷ *noun* **sprawl**
▷ *verb* **sprawling, sprawled**

spray (spray) *verb* To scatter liquid in very fine drops. ▷ **spraying, sprayed** ▷ *noun* **spray**

spread (spred)
1. *verb* To unfold or to stretch out. *Jan spread out the map on the table. The bird spread its wings.*
2. *verb* To cover a surface with something. *We spread peanut butter on the bread.* ▷ *noun* **spread**
3. *verb* To reach out or extend over an area. *The fire spread quickly.*
4. *verb* To scatter or make known. *Spread the news.*
5. *noun* (informal) An elaborate meal put on a table. *Grandma laid out a nice spread for Thanksgiving dinner.*
▷ *verb* **spreading, spread**

spread·sheet (spred-*sheet*) *noun*
1. A wide sheet of paper that is divided into rows and columns. Spreadsheets are used for organizing financial records.
2. A computer program that allows you to keep track of budgets and other financial records in a spreadsheet format.

spree (spree) *noun* A period of eating, drinking, shopping, etc., without restraint and usually to excess.

spring (spring)
1. *noun* The season between winter and summer, when the weather becomes warmer and plants and flowers begin to grow.
2. *verb* To jump suddenly. *The lion sprang at the zebra.* ▷ *noun* **spring**
3. *verb* To appear suddenly. *Flowers sprang up everywhere.*
4. *verb* To make known suddenly. *He is always springing surprises on us.*
5. *noun* A coil of metal that moves back to its original shape or position after being stretched or pushed down.
6. *noun* A place where water rises up from underground and becomes a stream.
▷ *verb* **springing, sprang** (sprang), **sprung** (spruhng)

spring·board (spring-*bord*) *noun* A flexible board used in diving or gymnastics to help a person jump high in the air.

spring-cleaning *noun* A thorough cleaning of a place, usually done once a year.

spring fever *noun* A lazy or restless feeling that often is associated with the coming of spring.

sprin·kle (spring-kuhl) *verb*
1. To scatter something in small drops or bits. *Sprinkle grated cheese on top of the dish.*

2. To rain in small amounts. *We thought it would pour, but it barely sprinkled.*
▷ *verb* **sprinkling, sprinkled** ▷ *noun* **sprinkle**

sprin·kler (springk-lur) *noun* A device that attaches to a hose and sprays water over a lawn or garden.

sprint (sprint)
1. *verb* To run fast for a short distance. *Gerry sprinted across the park so that he wouldn't be late for school.* ▷ **sprinting, sprinted**
2. *noun* A very fast race run over a short distance. ▷ *noun* **sprinter** ▷ *adjective* **sprint**

sprint start

"on your mark"   "get set"   "go"

sprock·et (sprok-it) *noun* A wheel with a rim made of toothlike points that fit into the holes of a chain. The chain then drives the wheel. *See* **bicycle.**

sprout (sprout)
1. *verb* When a plant **sprouts,** it starts to grow and produce shoots or buds.
2. *noun* A new or young plant growth, such as a bud or shoot.
3. sprouts *noun, plural* The young edible shoots of various plants that are often eaten raw.
4. *verb* To grow, appear, or develop suddenly or quickly. *Shopping malls have sprouted up all along the highway.*
▷ *verb* **sprouting, sprouted**

spruce (sprooss) *noun* An evergreen tree with short leaves shaped like needles, drooping cones, and wood that is often used in making pulp for paper.

spur (spur)
1. *noun* A spike or spiked wheel on the heel of a rider's boot. Spurs are used to make a horse go faster or obey commands.
2. *verb* If something **spurs** you **on,** it encourages or motivates you. ▷ **spurring, spurred** ▷ *noun* **spur**

spurt (spurt)
1. *verb* When liquid **spurts,** it flows or gushes suddenly in short bursts. ▷ **spurting, spurted** ▷ *noun* **spurt**
2. *noun* A sudden burst of energy, growth, or speed. ▷ *verb* **spurt**

sput·ter (spuht-ur) *verb*
1. To make popping, spitting, or coughing noises. *The old car sputtered down the street.*
2. To speak quickly and in a confused way. *Sam sputtered in excitement when he found out he had won the contest.*

3. To spit out small bits of food or saliva, especially when you are talking in an excited way. ▷ *verb* **sputtering, sputtered**

spy (spye)
1. *verb* To watch something closely from a hidden place.
2. *verb* To sight. *The sailor spied land in the distance.*
3. *noun* Someone, especially a government agent, who secretly collects information about an enemy. ▷ *noun, plural* **spies** ▷ *verb* **spy** ▷ *verb* **spies, spying, spied**

squab·ble (skwahb-uhl) *noun* A noisy argument or quarrel, usually over something unimportant. ▷ *verb* **squabble**

squad (skwahd) *noun* A small group of people involved in the same activity, such as soldiers, football players, or police officers.

squad·ron (skwahd-ruhn) *noun* A group of ships, cavalry troops, or other military units.

squal·id (skwahl-id) *adjective* Filthy and gloomy, usually because of neglect or poverty. *Conditions in the apartment were squalid.*

squall (skwawl) *noun* A sudden, violent wind that usually brings rain, snow, or sleet with it.

squa·lor (skwah-lur) *noun* The condition of being dirty, gloomy, and very poor. *After the war, the refugees lived in squalor.*

squan·der (skwahn-dur) *verb* To spend money wastefully and use it up. *Alec squandered his entire allowance.* ▷ **squandering, squandered**

square (skwair)
1. *noun* A shape with four equal sides and four right angles. *See* **shape.** ▷ *adjective* **square**
2. *verb* To multiply a number by itself. *Four squared equals 16.* ▷ **squaring, squared**
3. *noun* A number is a **square** is if it can be expressed as the product of the same two numbers. Four is the square of 2 because $2 \times 2 = 4$.
4. *noun* An open area in a town or city with streets on all four sides. Squares are often used as parks.
5. *adjective* Honest or fair, especially in business affairs. *They offered us a square deal.*
6. *adjective* Nutritious and filling, as in *a square meal.*
7. *adjective* (slang) Not cool or not hip; old-fashioned, as in *square ideas.* ▷ *noun* **square** ▷ *adjective* **squarer, squarest**

square dance *noun* A dance in which sets of four couples form the sides of a square and move to the commands called out by the leader, or caller.

square root *noun* A number that, when multiplied by itself, gives a particular number. The square root of 25 is 5, because $5 \times 5 = 25$. The symbol for a square root is $\sqrt{\ }$; $\sqrt{25} = 5$.

squash (skwahsh)
1. *verb* To crush or to flatten. ▷ **squashes, squashing, squashed**
2. *noun* A game played by two people who hit a small rubber ball against the walls of an enclosed court with rackets.
3. *noun* A fleshy fruit that grows on a vine in many shapes, sizes, and colors. Squash are related to pumpkins and gourds. They are cooked and eaten as vegetables. *See* **vegetable.** ▷ *noun, plural* **squash** *or* **squashes**

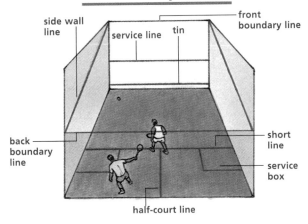

international squash court

side wall line · service line · tin · front boundary line · back boundary line · short line · service box · half-court line

squat (skwaht)
1. *verb* To crouch, or sit on your heels with your knees bent. ▷ *noun* **squat**
2. *verb* To live without permission on empty land or in an empty house that does not belong to you. ▷ *noun* **squatter**
3. *adjective* Short and broad. ▷ **squatter, squattest** ▷ *verb* **squatting, squatted**

squawk (skwawk)
1. *noun* A loud, harsh screech like the sound made by some parrots.
2. *verb* To make this sound.
3. *verb* (informal) To complain loudly. *Stop squawking and do your chores.*
4. *noun* (informal) Any loud complaint or protest. ▷ *noun* **squawker** ▷ *verb* **squawking, squawked**

squeak (skweek) *verb* To make a short, high sound like the noise of a mouse. ▷ **squeaking, squeaked** ▷ *noun* **squeak** ▷ *adjective* **squeaky**

squeal (skweel) *verb*
1. To make a shrill, high sound or cry. *The children squealed with delight. The tires squealed as the car sped around the corner.*
2. (informal) To betray a friend or secret; to turn informer. ▷ *verb* **squealing, squealed** ▷ *noun* **squeal**

squea·mish (skwee-mish) *adjective* Easily sickened or nauseated. *I am squeamish at the sight of blood.* ▷ *adverb* **squeamishly**

S

squeeze (skweez) *verb*
1. To press something firmly together from opposite sides. ▷ *noun* **squeezer**
2. To force something into or through a space. *We squeezed into the crowded elevator.*
3. To hug someone.
▷ *verb* **squeezing, squeezed** ▷ *noun* **squeeze**

squid (skwid) *noun* A sea animal with a long, soft body and 10 tentacles. Squid swim by squirting water out of their bodies with great force. ▷ *noun, plural* **squid** *or* **squids**

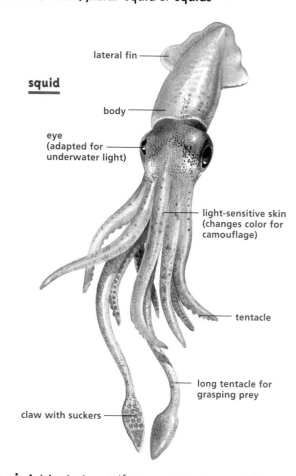

squid

lateral fin

body

eye
(adapted for underwater light)

light-sensitive skin
(changes color for camouflage)

tentacle

long tentacle for grasping prey

claw with suckers

squint (skwint) *verb* If you **squint** at something, you nearly close your eyes in order to see it more clearly. ▷ **squinting, squinted** ▷ *noun* **squint**

squire (skwire) *noun*
1. In medieval times, a **squire** was a young nobleman who accompanied and helped a knight.
2. An English country gentleman.

squirm (skwurm) *verb*
1. To wriggle about uncomfortably. *The children squirmed during the long, boring movie.*
2. To feel uncomfortable because you are embarrassed or ashamed. *The defendant squirmed in front of the judge.*
▷ *verb* **squirming, squirmed**

squir·rel (skwurl)
noun A rodent that climbs trees and has a bushy tail. *The gray squirrel shown here is found in North America and Europe.*

gray squirrel

squirt (skwurt)
verb To send out a stream of liquid. *Patty turned on the hose and squirted her brothers.*
▷ **squirting, squirted** ▷ *noun* **squirt**

squish·y (skwish-ee) *adjective* (*informal*) Soft and soggy. *The ground felt squishy after the rain.*

stab (stab)
1. *verb* To wound someone by piercing the person with a knife or other sharp instrument.
▷ *noun* **stab**
2. *verb* To stick or drive a pointed object into something. *The farmer stabbed the pitchfork into the bale of hay.*
3. *noun* A sharp, brief feeling or pang, as in *a stab of pain* or *a stab of guilt.*
4. (*informal*) If you **make a stab** at something, you make an attempt at doing it.
▷ *verb* **stabbing, stabbed**

sta·ble (stay-buhl)
1. *noun* A building or a part of a building where horses or cattle are kept. ▷ *verb* **stable**
2. *adjective* Firm and steady. *Before you climb the ladder, be sure it is stable.* ▷ *verb* **stabilize**
3. *adjective* Safe and secure. *The children had a stable home life.*
▷ *adjective* **stabler, stablest**

stac·ca·to (stuh-kah-toh) *adverb* In music, when you play notes **staccato,** you make them short, sharp, and separate from each other.

stack (stak)
1. *verb* To pile things up, one on top of another.
▷ **stacking, stacked**
2. *noun* A large, neat pile of hay, straw, or grain.
3. *noun* A neat pile of something arranged in layers, as in *a stack of books.*
4. *noun* A chimney or a smokestack.

sta·di·um (stay-dee-uhm) *noun* A large structure in which sports events and concerts are held. It usually has an open field surrounded by rows of rising seats. ▷ *noun, plural* **stadiums** *or* **stadia** (stay-dee-uh)

staff (staf)
1. *noun* A group of people who work for a company, an institution, or a person, as in *a newspaper staff.* ▷ *noun, plural* **staffs**

2. verb To provide an organization with employees. *The supervisor staffed her office with young, creative workers.* ▷ **staffing, staffed**

3. noun A stick or pole used as a support in walking or as a weapon, as in *a shepherd's staff.*

4. noun A flagpole.

5. noun The set of lines and spaces on which music is written.
▷ **noun, plural staffs** or **staves**

stag (stag)
noun An adult male deer.

red deer stag

stage (stayj)
1. noun A raised platform on which actors and other entertainers perform.

2. noun The profession of acting. *She left the stage because there were no good parts for older women.*

3. noun A level of progress. *Because you have done so well, you can move to the next stage.*

4. noun A period of development. *Ken's baby sister will enter the toddler stage when she finally learns to walk.*

5. noun A stagecoach.

6. verb To organize a public performance or event. *Our school is staging a play.* ▷ **staging, staged**

stage·coach (stayj-*kohch*) **noun** A coach pulled by a horse or horses and used in the past to carry passengers and mail over long distances.
▷ **noun, plural stagecoaches**

stagecoach

stag·ger (stag-ur) **verb**
1. To walk or stand unsteadily.

2. If you are **staggered** by something, you are astonished and overwhelmed.

3. When you **stagger** events, you time them so that they do not happen at the same time. *The guards staggered their breaks so that someone was always on duty.* ▷ **adjective staggered** ▷ **verb staggering, staggered**

stag·ger·ing (stag-ur-ing) **adjective** Amazing or astonishing. *Uncle Clarence bought the mansion for a staggering amount of money.*

stag·nant (stag-nuhnt) **adjective**
1. Not moving or not flowing; still.

2. Foul or polluted as a result of not moving.

3. Not active or not growing, as in *a stagnant economy.*

stag·nate (stag-nayt) **verb**
1. When water **stagnates,** it becomes dirty or polluted, changes color, and often gives off a foul odor.

2. If situations or persons **stagnate,** they remain the same for a long time, when they should be changing.
▷ **verb stagnating, stagnated** ▷ **noun stagnation**

staid (stayd) **adjective** If you are **staid,** you are sedate, proper, and serious. ▷ **staider, staidest** ▷ **noun staidness** ▷ **adverb staidly**

stain (stayn)
1. noun A mark or spot that is hard to remove, as in *a grass stain.*

2. verb To make a mark that is hard to remove. *The paint stained my coat.* ▷ **staining, stained**

3. noun A dye used to color wood.

stained glass **noun** Colored pieces of glass held together by lead strips, forming a picture, pattern, or design. Stained glass is often used in church windows. *The picture shows part of a window of stained glass from Chartres Cathedral in France.*
▷ **adjective stained-glass**

stained glass

stain·less steel (stayn-liss) **noun** A type of steel that does not rust or tarnish.

stair (stair) **noun**
1. One of a group of steps that allows you to walk from one level of a building to another.

2. stairs noun, plural Another word for **stairway. Stair** sounds like **stare.**

S

519

stair·way (stair-*way*) *noun* A flight of steps with a railing and a structure that supports it.

stake (stayk)
1. noun A thick, pointed post that can be driven into the ground. ▷ *verb* **stake**
2. verb To bet. *Jim staked his money on the race.* ▷ staking, staked
3. noun Something, especially money, that is bet or risked, as in *high stakes.*
4. noun If you have **a stake** in something, you are involved in it or you have put money, time, or effort into it.
5. If something is **at stake,** it is at risk.
6. If you **pull up stakes,** you leave a place.
Stake sounds like **steak.**

sta·lac·tite (stuh-**lak**-*tite*) *noun* A thin piece of rock shaped like an icicle that hangs from the roof of a cave. Stalactites are made from calcium minerals dissolved in drops of water that have slowly solidified. *The picture shows stalactites in a cave.*

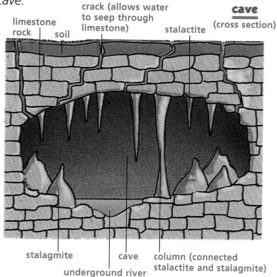

limestone rock   soil   crack (allows water to seep through limestone)   stalactite   **cave** (cross section)

stalagmite   cave   column (connected stalactite and stalagmite)   underground river

sta·lag·mite (stuh-**lag**-*mite*) *noun* A thin piece of rock shaped like an icicle that sticks up from the floor of a cave. Stalagmites are made from calcium minerals dissolved in drops of water that have slowly solidified. *The picture shows stalagmites in a cave.*

stale (stayl) *adjective*
1. No longer fresh, as in *stale bread* or *stale air.*
2. No longer new or interesting, as in *a stale joke* or *stale news.*
▷ *adjective* **staler, stalest**

stale·mate (stayl-*mayt*) *noun*
1. A situation in an argument or game of chess in which neither side can win or make any more moves.
2. Any position or situation that results in a deadlock, with no progress possible.

stalk (stawk)
1. noun The long main part or stem of a plant from which the leaves and flowers grow.
2. verb To hunt or track a person or an animal in a quiet, secret way. *The leopard stalked its prey.* ▷ *noun* **stalker**
3. verb To walk in an angry, stiff way. *Harvey stalked out of the room in a huff.*
▷ *verb* **stalking, stalked**

stall (stawl)
1. verb When a car **stalls,** its engine stops running.
2. noun A counter or booth where things are displayed for sale at a market.
3. noun A section in a stable or barn where a single animal is kept, as in *a horse stall.*
4. verb To delay doing something on purpose. *Stop stalling!* ▷ *noun* **stall**
▷ *verb* **stalling, stalled**

stal·lion (stal-yuhn) *noun* An adult male horse.

sta·men (stay-muhn) *noun* The part of a flower that produces pollen. It consists of a thin stalk, called the filament, and a tip, called the anther, that has pollen on it. *See* **flower.**

stam·i·na (stam-uh-nuh) *noun* The energy and strength to keep doing something for a long time. *You need stamina for long-distance running.*

stam·mer (stam-ur) *verb* To speak in an unsure way, stopping often and repeating certain sounds. People sometimes stammer when they are nervous or excited. ▷ **stammering, stammered** ▷ *noun* **stammer**

stamp (stamp)
1. noun A small piece of paper that you stick onto a letter or package to show that you have paid for it to be sent; a postage stamp. *The picture shows a selection of U.S. postage stamps.*
2. noun An object used to print a mark by pressing it against a pad of ink and then transferring the ink onto paper.
3. verb To bang your foot down.
▷ **stamping, stamped**
▷ *noun* **stamp**

postage stamps

stam·pede (stam-peed) *verb* When people or animals **stampede,** they make a sudden, wild rush in one direction, usually because something has frightened them. ▷ **stampeding, stampeded** ▷ *noun* **stampede**

stand (stand)

1. *verb* To be on or get on your feet with your body upright.

2. *verb* To put something in an upright position. *Stand the vase on the table.*

3. *verb* To be located. *My house stands on a hill.*

4. *verb* To be in a certain rank or order. *Maya stands first in her class.*

5. *verb* To have an opinion or to take a position. *Where do you stand on capital punishment?* ▷ *noun* **stand**

6. *verb* To continue without any change. *My offer still stands.*

7. *noun* An object on which you put things, as in *a music stand.*

8. stands *noun, plural* A covered area for spectators at a ballpark or stadium.

9. *noun* A small booth, counter, or stall where goods are sold, as in *a hot dog stand.*

10. stand for *verb* To represent. *The initials U.S. stand for United States.*

hot dog stand

11. *verb* If you cannot **stand** something, you hate it or are unable to bear it.

12. *verb* If you **stand by** someone, you support the person when he or she is in trouble.

13. *verb* If something **stands out,** it can be seen or noticed easily.

14. If you **take a stand** on an issue, you state your opinion in a clear and forceful way. ▷ *verb* **standing, stood** (stud)

stan·dard (stan-durd)

1. *noun* A rule or model that is used to judge or measure how good something is. *New cars must meet safety and pollution standards.*

2. *noun* The flag or banner of a nation or military group.

3. *adjective* Usual or average. *What is the standard fee?*

4. *adjective* Used or accepted as a standard, rule, or model. *The meter is a standard unit of length in the metric system.*

5. *adjective* Widely used or accepted as correct, as in *standard spelling* or *standard English.*

stand·by (stand-bye) *noun* Someone or something that is ready to be used if needed. *We brought a second camera on our trip as a standby in case the first one broke.*

stand-in *noun* Someone who takes the place of another person when that person cannot be there or cannot do something. ▷ *verb* **stand in**

stand·ing (stan-ding) *noun*

1. Position, rank, or reputation.

2. If you are **in good standing** with a group of people, you are respected by them and accepted within that group.

3. standings *noun, plural* The positions or rankings of all the teams within a sport during a regular season of play.

stand·still (stand-stil) *noun* If something is at a **standstill,** it has come to a complete halt.

stand-up *adjective* A **stand-up** comic or comedian performs while standing alone on a stage or in front of a camera. ▷ *noun* **stand-up**

stan·za (stan-zuh) *noun* One of the groups of lines into which a poem or song is divided; a verse.

sta·ple (stay-puhl) *noun*

1. A thin piece of wire that is shaped like a U and punched through sheets of paper to hold them together. ▷ *noun* **stapler** ▷ *verb* **staple**

2. Any food or product that is used regularly and kept in large amounts. *Flour, salt, and sugar are staples.*

3. A main product that is grown or produced in a country or region. *Timber is a staple of many economies.*

star (star)

1. *noun* A ball of burning gases in space. A star is seen from the earth as a tiny point of light in the night sky. ▷ *adjective* **starry**

2. *noun* A shape with five or more points.

3. *noun* A person who plays a leading role in a movie, television program, or play.

4. *noun* A person who is outstanding in some field, as in *a basketball star.*

5. *verb* To take the leading role in a movie, television program, or play. ▷ **starring, starred**

star·board (star-burd) *noun* The right-hand side of a ship or an aircraft. ▷ *adjective* **starboard**

starch (starch) *noun*

1. A white substance found in such foods as potatoes, bread, and rice. Starch is very filling and gives you energy.

2. A substance used for making cloth stiff. ▷ *verb* **starch**

S

stare (stair) *verb* To look directly at someone or something for a long time without moving your eyes. **Stare** sounds like **stair.** ▷ **staring, stared** ▷ *noun* **stare**

star·fish (star-*fish*) *noun* A sea animal with five or more arms. A starfish is shaped like a star. ▷ *noun, plural* **starfish**

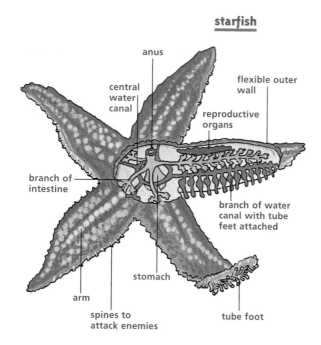

starfish

anus

central water canal

flexible outer wall

reproductive organs

branch of intestine

branch of water canal with tube feet attached

arm

stomach

spines to attack enemies

tube foot

stark (stark) *adjective*
1. Bare and grim; having little or no plant life. *The landscape was stark after the forest fire.*
2. Complete or extreme, as in *stark poverty.*
▷ *adjective* **starker, starkest**

star·ling (star-ling) *noun* A plump bird with pointed wings, a yellow bill, a short tail, and brown or green-black feathers. Starlings are found in most parts of the world.

Stars and Stripes *noun* The flag of the United States. The red and white stripes represent the 13 original colonies. The white stars represent the 50 states.

start (start)
1. *verb* To begin to move, act, or happen. *Have you started your book report? The movie starts in 10 minutes.*
2. *verb* To make something move, act, or happen. *Start the car. I didn't start the fight.*
3. *noun* The beginning of something.
4. *verb* To jump in surprise. *Jeremy started at the loud noise.* ▷ *noun* **start**
5. *noun* An advantage at the beginning of a race. *You can have a 10-yard start.*
▷ *verb* **starting, started**

star·tle (star-tuhl) *verb* To surprise or frighten someone and make the person jump. *Maria was so startled when Ken walked through the door that she dropped the spoon she was holding.*
▷ **startling, startled** ▷ *adjective* **startled,** *adjective* **startling**

starve (starv) *verb*
1. To suffer or die from lack of food. ▷ *noun* **starvation**
2. To need or want something very much. *The lost kitten was starving for love and attention.*
▷ *verb* **starving, starved**

starv·ing (starv-ing) *adjective*
1. Suffering or dying from lack of food.
2. *(informal)* Very hungry.

state (state)
1. *verb* To say something in words; to tell or explain. *Please state your name.* ▷ **stating, stated**
2. *noun* A group of people united under one government; a nation.
3. *noun* Any of the political and geographical units that make up a country such as the United States. *Alaska is the 50th state.* ▷ *noun* **statehood**
4. *noun* The way that something is, or the condition it is in. *The office was in a state of confusion.*
5. *(informal)* If someone is **in a state,** he or she is upset.

state·ly (state-lee) *adjective* Grand, dignified, or majestic, as in *a stately mansion* or *a stately manner.*

state·ment (state-muhnt) *noun*
1. Something that is said in words.
2. A list of all the amounts paid into and out of a bank account.

state-of-the-art *adjective* Very advanced and up-to-date, as in *a state-of-the-art computer system.*

stat·ic (stat-ik)
1. *adjective* Not moving, changing, or growing, as in *a static situation* or *a static population.*
2. *noun* The crackling noises that you hear when static electricity in the air interferes with a radio or television signal.

static electricity *noun* Electricity that builds up in an object and stays there. Static electricity can be produced when one object rubs against another.

sta·tion (stay-shuhn) *noun*
1. A place where tickets for trains, buses, or other vehicles are sold and where passengers are let on and off.
2. A building where a service is provided, as in *a fire station, a police station,* or *a gas station.*
3. A place with equipment to send out television or radio signals.

S

4. A place where a person or thing stands or is supposed to stand. *The guard could not leave his station.*

sta·tion·ar·y (stay-shuh-*ner*-ee) *adjective*
1. Not moving or not able to be moved. *When it's raining, I exercise indoors on a stationary bicycle.*
2. Not changing, as in *stationary prices.*
Stationary sounds like **stationery.**

sta·tion·er·y (stay-shuh-*ner*-ee) *noun*
1. Writing materials, such as paper, envelopes, pens, and notebooks.
2. Paper and envelopes used to write letters.
Stationery sounds like **stationary.**

station wagon *noun* A motor vehicle with a large, enclosed cargo area behind the rear seats, where the trunk would ordinarily be. The rear seats can be folded down for extra storage space.

sta·tis·tic (stuh-*tiss*-tik) *noun* A fact or piece of information expressed as a number or percentage. ▷ *adjective* **statistical** ▷ *adverb* **statistically**

stat·ue (stach-oo) *noun* A model of a person or an animal made from metal, stone, wood, or any solid material.

sta·tus (stay-tuhss *or* stat-uhss) *noun*
1. A person's rank or position in a group, an organization, or a society.
2. The state of affairs or condition of a situation. *Please give me a report on the status of the situation.*

stat·ute (stach-oot) *noun* A rule or a law.

stave (stayv)
1. *noun* One of the long, thin strips of wood that form the sides of a barrel.
2. *noun* The set of lines and spaces on which music is written; a staff.
3. *verb* To break or smash a hole in something. *An iceberg staved the hull of the* Titanic.
4. *verb* If you **stave** something **off**, you manage to keep it away.
▷ *verb* **staving, staved** *or* **stove** (stohv)

stay (stay)
1. *verb* To remain in one place or condition. *Stay where you are. They stayed friends for many years.*
2. *verb* To spend time somewhere. *We stayed at the party until midnight.*
3. *noun* A period of time spent somewhere as a visitor. *Have you had an enjoyable stay?*
▷ *verb* **staying, stayed**

stead·fast (sted-*fast*) *adjective* Firm and steady or not changing, as in *steadfast loyalty* or *a steadfast gaze.*

stead·y (sted-ee)
1. *adjective* Continuous and not changing much, as in *a steady rain.* ▷ *adverb* **steadily**
2. *adjective* Firm or stable; not shaky, as in *a steady hand* or *a steady chair.*
3. *verb* To stop something from moving about or shaking. *The captain steadied the ship.* ▷ **steadies, steadying, steadied**
4. *adjective* Sensible and dependable, as in *a steady worker.*
5. *adjective* Regular, as in *a steady customer.*
▷ *adjective* **steadier, steadiest**

steak (stayk) *noun* A thick slice of meat or fish. **Steak** sounds like **stake.**

steal (steel)
1. *verb* To take something that does not belong to you.
2. *verb* To do something in a secret or tricky way. *I wanted to steal a look at my birthday presents.*
3. *verb* To get to the next base in baseball without a hit or an error. *The runner stole second.* ▷ *noun* **steal**
4. *noun* Something bought at a very low price; a bargain.
Steal sounds like **steel.**
▷ *verb* **stealing, stole** (stohl), **stolen** (stohl-in)

stealth·y (stel-thee) *adjective* Secret and quiet. *We crept away with stealthy steps.* ▷ **stealthier, stealthiest** ▷ *noun* **stealth** ▷ *adverb* **stealthily**

steam (steem)
1. *noun* The vapor that is formed when water boils. ▷ *verb* **steam**
2. *verb* To cook using steam, as in *to steam vegetables.*
3. *noun* The mist formed when water vapor condenses.
4. *verb* When glass **steams up,** it becomes covered with condensation.
5. *(informal)* If you **let off steam** or **blow off steam,** you release the energy or angry feelings that you have stored up.
6. *(informal)* If you **run out of steam,** you have no more energy left.
▷ *verb* **steaming, steamed**

steam·boat (steem-*boht*) *noun* A boat powered by a steam engine.

steam engine *noun* An engine powered by steam. Coal or wood burned in a boiler heats the water in a tank. As the water in the tank boils, it creates steam. This steam is forced into cylinders where it pushes pistons to operate machinery. *See* **steam locomotive.**

steam·er (stee-mur) *noun*
1. A boat powered by steam.
2. A large, covered pot used to cook foods with steam.

S

steam locomotive

noun An engine powered by steam and used for pulling trains. Steam locomotives were used on most trains in the United States until about 1940. Today, most trains are powered by diesel engines. *The steam produced by this steam locomotive forced the pistons to move. The pistons drove the connecting rods and crank rods, which are connected to the driving wheels.*

lamp bracket
engine main frame
chimney
smoke box
steam collector dome
handrail
boiler casing
firebox
steam locomotive
safety valve
whistle
cab
tender (car for fuel and water)
smokebox door handles
outside steam pipe
brake pipe
buffer
coupling (joins the locomotive to the cars)
guard iron
leading wheel
cylinder cover
sand pipe
piston rod
front driving wheel
connecting rod
return crank rod
crank
middle driving wheel
coupling rod
back driving wheel
brake rods
axle box
trailing wheel
4472

steam·roll·er (steem-*roh*-lur) *noun* A heavy vehicle that is used to flatten road surfaces.

steam·ship (steem-*ship*) *noun* A ship powered by a steam engine.

steed (steed) *noun* A horse, especially one that is spirited.

steel (steel)
1. *noun* A hard, strong metal made chiefly from iron.
2. *verb* To prepare oneself by becoming determined and hard, like steel. *I steeled myself for my parents' questions when I came home late.*
▷ **steeling, steeled**
Steel sounds like **steal**.

steel band *noun* A group that plays music on drums made from oil barrels.

steel wool *noun* A mass of very fine threads of steel. Steel wool is used for cleaning, smoothing, and polishing things.

steep (steep)
1. *adjective* Sharply sloping up or down, as in *a steep hill*. ▷ **adverb steeply**
2. *adjective* Sharp or rapid. *There was a steep drop in attendance during the snowy months.*
3. *verb* To soak something in a liquid. *Steep the tea bag for a long time if you like strong tea.*
4. *verb* To be full of something. *Our family is steeped in tradition.*
5. *adjective* Very high, as in *steep prices*.
▷ **verb steeping, steeped** ▷ **adjective steeper, steepest**

stee·ple (stee-puhl) *noun* A high tower on a church or other building. It usually has a spire on top.

stee·ple·chase (stee-puhl-*chayss*) *noun* A long horse race with fences and water jumps.

steer (stihr)
1. *verb* To make a vehicle go in a particular direction. *She steered the boat into the harbor.*
2. *verb* To be guided. *This car steers easily.*
3. *verb* To guide or to direct. *The bodyguard steered the actor through the crowd of fans.*
4. *noun* A young male of the domestic cattle family raised especially for its beef.
▷ **verb steering, steered**

steering wheel *noun* The wheel in a vehicle used to control its direction.

steg·o·sau·rus (steg-uh-**sor**-uhss) *noun* A dinosaur that fed on plants and had bony plates along its back, a small head, and a long tail with spikes. *See* **dinosaur**.

> ## ▶ Word History
> •
> The word **stegosaurus** comes from two Greek words meaning "roof" and "lizard." This dinosaur gets this name because the scales on its back look like parts of a roof.

stem (stem)
1. *noun* The long main part of a plant from which the leaves and flowers grow. *See* **plant**.
2. stem from *verb* To originate or come from. *The quarrel stemmed from a misunderstanding.*
3. *verb* To stop something from flowing or spreading. *The rescue team tried to stem the flow of oil from the tanker.*
▷ **verb stemming, stemmed**

stench (stench) *noun* A strong, unpleasant smell, as in *the stench at the garbage dump*. ▷ **noun, plural stenches**

S

sten·cil (sten-suhl) *noun* A piece of paper, plastic, or metal with a design cut out of it. A stencil can be painted over to transfer the design onto a surface. ▷ *verb* **stencil**

step (step)
1. *noun* One of the flat surfaces on a stairway.
2. **steps** *noun, plural* A set of stairs.
3. *verb* To move your foot forward and put it down in walking, climbing, or dancing. ▷ **stepping, stepped** ▷ *noun* **step**
4. *noun* The distance covered by a step. *We live a few steps from the school.*
5. *noun* The sound of someone walking. *Can you hear steps behind you?*
6. *noun* One of the things that you need to do in order to make or achieve something. *This recipe is in six steps.*
7. *noun* If you do something **step by step,** you do it in a gradual and steady way.
8. *noun* (informal) If someone says that you should **watch your step,** the person is telling you to be careful.
Step sounds like **steppe.**

step·fam·i·ly (step-fam-lee) *noun* The family of your stepfather or stepmother.

step·fa·ther (step-faTH-ur) *noun* Someone's **stepfather** is the man who married that person's mother after the death or divorce of the person's father.

step·moth·er (step-muhTH-ur) *noun* Someone's **stepmother** is the woman who married that person's father after the death or divorce of the person's mother.

steppe (step) *noun* Any of the vast, treeless plains found in southeastern Europe and Asia. **Steppe** sounds like **step.**

ste·re·o (ster-ee-oh *or* stirh-ee-oh) *noun* A phonograph, radio, or other sound system that uses two or more channels of sound so that the listener hears sounds in a more natural way. ▷ *adjective* **stereo**

ste·re·o·type (ster-ee-oh-tipe *or* stirh-ee-oh-tipe) *noun* An overly simple picture or opinion of a person, group, or thing. *It is a stereotype to say all old people are forgetful.* ▷ *verb* **stereotype** ▷ *adjective* **stereotypical** (ster-ee-oh-tip-i-kuhl)

ster·ile (ster-uhl) *adjective* Free from germs and dirt.

ster·i·lize (ster-uh-lize) *verb* To clean something so thoroughly that you make it free from germs and dirt. *You can sterilize baby bottles by boiling them in water.* ▷ **sterilizing, sterilized** ▷ *noun* **sterilization** (ster-uh-li-zay-shuhn)

ster·ling silver (stur-ling) *noun* A metal that is made of 92.5 percent pure silver.

stern (stern)
1. *adjective* Strict or harsh, as in *a stern teacher* or *a stern lecture.* ▷ **sterner, sternest**
2. *noun* The back end of a ship or boat.

ste·roid (stihr-oid *or* ster-oid) *noun* A chemical substance found naturally in plants and animals, including humans. The use of steroids by athletes to enhance their strength and performance is banned in most sports competitions.

steth·o·scope (steth-uh-skope) *noun* A medical instrument used by doctors and nurses to listen to the sounds from a patient's heart, lungs, and other areas.

stethoscope; flexible tube; ear piece; ear tube; Y-joint; stainless steel chest piece

stew (stoo)
1. *noun* A dish made of meat or fish and vegetables cooked slowly in liquid.
2. *verb* To cook something for a long time over low heat. ▷ *adjective* **stewed**
3. *noun* If you are **in a stew** about something, you are upset and worried about it.
4. *verb* If you **stew** about something, you worry about it. ▷ **stewing, stewed**

stew·ard (stoo-urd) *noun*
1. A man who serves passengers on an airplane or a ship.
2. Someone who serves food and drink at a hotel, club, or restaurant, as in *a wine steward.*

stew·ard·ess (stoo-ur-diss) *noun* A woman who serves passengers, especially on an airplane.

stick (stik)
1. *noun* A long, thin piece of wood.
2. *noun* Something shaped like a stick, as in *a stick of gum, a stick of dynamite,* or *carrot sticks.*
3. *verb* To glue or fasten one thing to another. *I stuck the stamp on the envelope.* ▷ *adjective* **sticky**
4. *verb* To push something with a point into something else. *Fran stuck her finger with a needle.*
5. *verb* To remain attached, as if glued. *Peanut butter sticks to the roof of my mouth.*
6. *verb* If something **sticks,** it becomes fixed in a particular position. *This door keeps sticking.*
7. *verb* If something **sticks out,** it is prominent, often because it is higher or longer than other things nearby.
8. *verb* (informal) If you **stick up for** someone, you support or defend the person.
9. *verb* If you **stick to** something, you keep at it. ▷ *verb* **sticking, stuck** (stuhk)

525

stick·er (stik-ur) *noun* A paper or plastic label with glue on the back.

stiff (stif) *adjective*
1. Difficult to bend or turn. *The new leather shoes were stiff.*
2. If you feel **stiff,** your muscles hurt, often because you have overworked them.
3. Not flowing easily; thick. *Beat the egg whites until they are stiff.*
4. Difficult or severe, as in *stiff competition* or *stiff punishment.*
5. Not natural or easy in manner; formal. *After I had a fight with my friend, our conversations became stiff.*
6. Strong and steady; powerful, as in *a stiff wind.*
   ▷ *verb* **stiffen** ▷ *adjective* **stiffer, stiffest** ▷ *adverb* **stiffly**

sti·fle (stye-fuhl) *verb*
1. To hold back or to stop, as in *to stifle a yawn* or *to stifle someone's creativity.*
2. To feel smothered because of a lack of fresh or cool air. *I'm stifling in this stuffy room.*
   ▷ *verb* **stifling, stifled** ▷ *adjective* **stifling**

stig·ma (stig-ma) *noun*
1. A mark of shame or embarrassment. *Frederick feels the stigma of dropping out of school before graduation.*
2. The part of a flower that receives the pollen in pollination. *See* **flower.**
   ▷ *noun, plural* **stigmata** (stig-mat-uh) *or* **stigmas**

still (stil)
1. *adjective* Without sound; quiet; silent. *The house was dark and still.*
2. *adjective* Without motion; quiet and calm. *The water in the lake was still.* ▷ *noun* **still** ▷ *verb* **still**
3. *adverb* Without moving. *Please try to sit still.*
4. *adverb* Even now. *Are you still here?*
5. *adverb* All the same; nevertheless. *You are late, but you may still participate.*
6. *adverb* Even; yet. *After three weeks of freezing weather, it became still colder.*
   ▷ *noun* **stillness** ▷ *adjective* **stiller, stillest**

stilt (stilt) *noun*
1. One of two poles, each with a rest or strap for the foot, used to raise the wearer above the ground in walking.
2. One of the posts that holds a building, pier, or other structure above the ground or water level. *The beach house was built on stilts in case of high tides.*

stim·u·lant (stim-yuh-luhnt) *noun* A substance that stimulates activity in a part of the body. *Coffee contains a stimulant.* ▷ *adjective* **stimulant**

stim·u·late (stim-yuh-late) *verb*
1. To encourage something to grow or develop.

2. If someone or something **stimulates** you, it fills you with exciting new ideas.
   ▷ *verb* **stimulating, stimulated** ▷ *noun* **stimulation** ▷ *adjective* **stimulating**

stim·u·lus (stim-yuh-luhss) *noun*
1. Anything that excites or causes an action.
2. Something that causes or speeds up a reaction in a person, an animal, or a plant. *Your eyes, ears, and nose receive stimuli from your surroundings.*
   ▷ *noun, plural* **stimuli** (stim-yuh-lye)

sting (sting)
1. *verb* To pierce or wound with a small, sharp point. *Bees and wasps can sting you.*
2. *verb* To hurt with or as if with a sharp or throbbing pain. *My eyes are stinging. That remark really stings.*
3. *noun* A stinger. *See* **scorpion.**
   ▷ *noun* **sting** ▷ *verb* **stinging, stung** (stuhng)

sting·er (sting-ur) *noun* A sharp, pointed part of an insect or animal that can be used to sting.

sting·ray (sting-ray) *noun*
A fish with a flat body; large, winglike fins; and a long tail with poisonous spines that can cause a painful wound.

stingray

stin·gy (stin-jee) *adjective* Not willing to give or spend money; not generous. ▷ **stingier, stingiest** ▷ *adverb* **stingily**

stink (stingk) *verb*
1. To give off a strong, unpleasant smell. ▷ *noun* **stink**
2. *(slang)* To be very bad or worthless. *That idea stinks.*
   ▷ *verb* **stinking, stank** (stangk), **stunk** (stuhngk) ▷ *adjective* **stinky**

stir (stur)
1. *verb* To mix a liquid by moving a spoon or stick around and around in it.
2. *verb* To move or cause to move slightly. *The air barely stirred. The breeze stirred the leaves.*
3. *verb* To excite or cause strong feelings in. *Her fiery speech stirred the crowd.*
4. *noun* If you cause **a stir,** you make people excited about something.
   ▷ *noun* **stir** ▷ *verb* **stirring, stirred**

stir-fry *verb* To fry food quickly over high heat in a lightly oiled pan or wok while stirring continuously. ▷ **stir-fries, stir-frying, stir-fried**

S

stir·rup
(stur-uhp)
noun
1. A ring or loop that hangs down from a saddle and holds a rider's foot. *See also* **tack.**
2. One of the three small bones in the middle ear. It looks somewhat like a stirrup.

stirrup

> ### ▶ Word History
> •
> Two Old English words, *stig,* which meant "a climbing up," and *rap,* or "rope," were used to make the word **stirrup.** At one time, a stirrup was a loop of rope that hung from a saddle.

stitch (stich)
1. *noun* A complete movement of a needle with thread on it, used in sewing and embroidery and to close wounds. *See* **embroidery.**
2. *noun* A loop of yarn produced in knitting or crocheting.
3. *verb* To make stitches in sewing or knitting.
4. *verb* To close up a wound with stitches. *The doctor stitched the cut.*
5. *noun* A sudden, sharp pain in your side caused by running.
6. *(informal)* If you are **in stitches,** you cannot stop laughing.
▷ *noun, plural* **stitches** ▷ *verb* **stitches, stitching, stitched**

stock (stok)
1. *verb* If a store **stocks** a product, it keeps a supply of the product to sell.
2. *noun* All the products that a factory, warehouse, or store has to sell.
3. *noun* Cattle, sheep, pigs, and other animals raised on a ranch or farm; livestock.
4. *noun* A liquid used in cooking, made from the juices of meat or vegetables, as in *chicken stock.*
5. *noun* If you own **stock** in a company, you have invested money in it and own a part of the company.
6. *noun* Ancestors. *My family is from Irish stock.*

7. *verb* If you **stock up** on something, you buy a large supply of it.
▷ *verb* **stocking, stocked**

stock·ade (stok-ade) *noun*
1. A fence or enclosure made of strong posts set firmly in the ground to protect against attacks.
2. A jail for people in the military.

stock·bro·ker (stok-*broh*-kur) *noun* Someone whose job is buying and selling stocks and shares in companies for other people.

stock car *noun* A car for racing, made from a regular model sold to the public.

stock·hold·er (stok-*hohl*-dur) *noun* Someone who owns shares, or stock, in a company.

stock·ing (stok-ing) *noun* A tight, knitted covering for the foot and leg.

stock·pile (stok-*pile*) *verb* To build up a large supply of food or weapons that you can use in the future. *The family stockpiled canned goods before the blizzard.* ▷ **stockpiling, stockpiled**
▷ *noun* **stockpile**

stocks (stoks) *noun, plural* A heavy, wooden frame with holes in it used to hold people by their ankles and sometimes their wrists. Stocks were once used to punish people publicly for minor offenses such as drunkenness.

stock·y (stok-ee) *adjective* A **stocky** person has a short, heavy build. ▷ **stockier, stockiest** ▷ *adverb* **stockily**

stock·yard (stok-*yard*) *noun* An enclosed area where livestock are kept before being shipped or slaughtered.

stodg·y (stoj-ee) *adjective*
1. Very dull or boring, as in *a stodgy speech.*
2. Very old-fashioned and stuffy. ▷ *adjective* **stodgier, stodgiest**

sto·ic (stoh-ik) *noun* A person who is not moved or affected by pain or pleasure. ▷ *adjective* **stoic,** *adjective* **stoical** ▷ *adverb* **stoically**

stoke (stohk) *verb* To put more fuel on a fire in order to keep it burning. ▷ **stoking, stoked**

stom·ach (stuhm-uhk)
1. *noun* The muscular, pouchlike organ of your body where chewed food begins to be digested. *See* **digestion, organ.**
2. *noun* The front part of your body, between your chest and thighs, containing this organ; the belly or abdomen.
3. *verb* If you cannot **stomach** something, you cannot bear it. ▷ **stomaching, stomached**

stomp (stomp) *verb*
1. To walk heavily or loudly across a floor. *The tired skiers stomped in, covered with snow.*
2. To bang your foot down, especially in anger.
▷ *noun* **stomp**
▷ *verb* **stomping, stomped**

S

stone (stone)
 1. **noun** Naturally hardened mineral matter that is found in the earth; rock. *Granite is a kind of stone.* ▷ **adjective** **stony**
 2. **noun** A small piece of this material. *Please don't throw stones.*
 3. **verb** To hit with stones. ▷ **stoning, stoned**
 4. **noun** A valuable jewel or gem. *Diamonds and rubies are precious stones.*
 5. **noun** A hard seed found in the middle of a fruit such as a cherry or peach.
Stone Age **noun** A period in history when stone was commonly used to make tools and weapons. Different parts of the world experienced a Stone Age at different times. *Tools made from flint, like thoses shown here, were common during the Stone Age.*

Stone Age tools

stone·wall (stone-*wawl*) **verb** To ignore a question, or to stand in the way of an investigation by refusing to give information. *The coach stonewalled the press by not allowing his players to answer questions after the game.*
 ▷ **stonewalling, stonewalled**
stone·washed (stone-*washt*) **adjective** **Stonewashed** jeans are washed with stones that soften and fade the fabric.
stool (stool) **noun** A seat with no back or arms.
stoop (stoop)
 1. **verb** To bend forward and down, often with the knees bent. *Ben stooped to pick up the book he had dropped.*
 2. **verb** To walk, sit, or stand with your head and shoulders bent forward.
 3. **verb** To lower yourself to do something; to condescend or degrade yourself. *Don't stoop to his level if he starts an argument.*
 4. **noun** A small porch with steps outside a doorway.
 ▷ **verb** **stooping, stooped** ▷ **noun** **stoop**

stop (stop)
 1. **verb** When something **stops,** it comes to an end. *The music stopped. The rain finally stopped.*
 2. **verb** If you **stop** something, you put an end to it or prevent it from continuing or moving. *The teacher stopped us from running. Stop the car.*
 3. **verb** To be no longer moving or working. *My watch has stopped.*
 4. **verb** To close up or block an opening. *Hair stopped up the bathtub drain.*
 5. **noun** The act of stopping. *A sudden stop threw packages onto the floor of the car.*
 6. **noun** One of the regular places on a route where someone pauses, such as the place where a bus or train picks up and drops off passengers.
 7. **noun** A brief stay or visit. *We made a stop at the Grand Canyon.*
 ▷ **verb** **stopping, stopped**

> ### Synonyms: stop
>
> **Stop**, the opposite of **start**, means to keep something from continuing or to bring an action to an end: *I wish my brother would stop bothering me! Ms. Morales stopped the car when she saw the dog run into the street.*
>
> **Cease** means to bring something to an end, usually with the idea that it will not start again: *The rioting ceased after the mayor appealed for calm.*
>
> **Discontinue** means to give up or stop something that has been going on for a while: *The electronics company will discontinue its line of record players because most people now listen to tapes or CDs.*
>
> **Quit** means to stop or leave, often suddenly or for good: *Carolyn quit her job to go back to college.*
>
> **Halt** means to stop some kind of movement, such as marching or traveling: *The police halted traffic so the ambulance could zoom up the street.*

stop·light (stop-*lite*) **noun**
 1. Another word for **traffic light.**
 2. A light on the rear part of a motor vehicle that comes on when the driver steps on the brakes.
stop·per (stop-ur) **noun** A piece of cork or plastic that fits into the top of a container such as a test tube, jar, or bottle in order to close it.
stop·watch (stop-*wahch*) **noun** A watch that you can start and stop at any time. A stopwatch is used to measure the exact time of a race, contest, or other event.

stor·age (stor-ij) *noun* If you put something **in storage,** you put it away in a place where it can be kept until it is needed.

store (stor)
1. *noun* A place where things are sold, as in *a grocery store, a toy store,* or *a department store.*
2. *noun* A supply or stock of something kept for future use, as in *a store of wood* or *a store of weapons.*
3. *verb* To put things away until they are needed.
4. *verb* To copy data into the memory of a computer or onto a floppy disk or other storage device.
▷ *verb* **storing, stored**

store·keep·er (stor-*kee*-pur) *noun* Someone who owns or runs a store.

stork (stork) *noun* A large bird with long, thin legs; a long neck; and a long, straight bill. The stork is a wading bird that lives in marshes, swamps, and grasslands.

storm (storm)
1. *noun* Heavy rain, snow, sleet, or hail accompanied by strong winds. Some storms also can have thunder and lightning. ▷ *verb* **storm**
2. *noun* A sudden, strong outburst, as in *a storm of applause* or *a storm of protest.*
3. *verb* To attack suddenly or violently. *The army stormed the fort.*
4. *verb* If you **storm out** of a place, you rush out angrily or violently.
▷ *verb* **storming, stormed** ▷ *adjective* **stormy**

sto·ry (stor-ee) *noun*
1. A spoken or written account of something that happened, as in *a news story* or *the story of the first Thanksgiving.*
2. A tale made up to entertain people, as in *a science fiction story.*
3. A lie. *Stop telling stories about me.*
4. A floor or level of a building.
▷ *noun, plural* **stories**

stout (stout) *adjective*
1. Quite fat; large and heavily built.
2. Strong and sturdy. *You need a stout pair of boots for hiking.*
3. Brave or determined. *Her stout heart helped her survive the war.*
▷ *adjective* **stouter, stoutest**

stove (stohv) *noun* A piece of equipment used for cooking or for heating a room. A stove can be fueled by gas, electricity, wood, or oil.

stow (stoh) *verb* To put away or to store. *The sailor stowed her gear under her bunk. We stowed the trunk in the attic.* ▷ **stowing, stowed**
▷ *noun* **stowage**

stow·a·way (stoh-uh-*way*) *noun* Someone who hides in a plane, ship, or other vehicle to avoid paying a fare. ▷ *verb* **stow away**

strag·gle (strag-uhl) *verb* To follow slowly behind a group of people; to wander or stray.
▷ **straggling, straggled** ▷ *noun* **straggler**

straight (strayt)
1. *adjective* Not bent or not curved. *The shortest distance between two points is a straight line.*
2. *adjective* Not curly or not wavy, as in *straight hair.*
3. *adjective* Not crooked or not stooping, as in *straight posture.*
4. *adjective* Level or even, as in *a straight hem.*
5. *adjective* Honest, sincere, or correct. *I gave the officer a straight answer.*
6. *adverb* Immediately or directly. *Go straight home after school.*
Straight sounds like **strait.**
▷ *verb* **straighten** ▷ *adjective* **straighter, straightest** ▷ *adverb* **straight**

straight·a·way (strayt-uh-*way*) *adverb* At once.

straight·for·ward (*strayt*-for-wurd) *adjective* Honest and open, as in *a straightforward answer.*

strain (strayn)
1. *verb* To draw or pull tight; to stretch. *As the wind increased, the ship strained at the anchor.*
2. *noun* Stress or tension.
3. *verb* If you **strain** a mixture, you pour it through a sieve or colander to separate the solids from the liquid. ▷ *noun* **strainer**
4. *verb* If you **strain** a muscle in your body, you damage it by pulling it or overusing it.
5. *verb* If you **strain** to do something, you try very hard to do it.
▷ *verb* **straining, strained** ▷ *adjective* **strained**

strait (strayt) *noun*
1. A narrow strip of water that connects two larger bodies of water.
2. *noun, plural* If you are in **dire straits,** you are in a very difficult situation.
Strait sounds like **straight.**

strand (strand)
1. *noun* One of the threads or wires that are twisted together to form a rope, string, or cable.
2. *noun* Something that looks like a thread, as in *a strand of hair* or *a strand of spaghetti.*
3. *noun* Something made up of objects strung or twisted together, as in *a strand of pearls.*
4. *verb* To force onto the shore; to drive onto a beach, reef, or sandbar. *The storm stranded the injured whale on the shore.*
5. *verb* To leave in a strange or unpleasant place, especially without any money or way to depart. *When our car broke down, we were stranded in the middle of the hot desert.*
▷ *verb* **stranding, stranded**

S

strange (straynj) *adjective*
1. Different from the usual; odd or peculiar. *The costume came with a strange green wig.*
2. Not known, heard, or seen before; not familiar. *I called home and was surprised when a strange voice answered the phone.*
3. Ill at ease; not comfortable. *I felt strange at my new school.*
▷ *adjective* **stranger, strangest** ▷ *noun* **strangeness**
▷ *adverb* **strangely**

strang·er (strayn-jur) *noun*
1. Someone you do not know.
2. Someone who is in a place where he or she has not been before. *I am a stranger in this city.*

stran·gle (strang-guhl) *verb*
1. To kill someone by squeezing the person's throat so that he or she cannot breathe.
2. To be unable to breathe; to choke. *The firefighters strangled in the smoky building.*
▷ *verb* **strangling, strangled** ▷ *noun* **strangler,**
noun **strangulation**

strap (strap)
1. *noun* A strip of leather or other material used to fasten things together.
2. *verb* To fasten things or hold things in place with straps. ▷ **strapping, strapped**

strat·e·gy (strat-uh-jee) *noun* A clever plan for winning a military battle or achieving a goal.
▷ *noun, plural* **strategies** ▷ *noun* **strategist** ▷ *adjective*
strategic (struh-tee-jik) ▷ *adverb* **strategically**

strat·o·sphere (strat-uh-sfihr) *noun* The layer of the earth's atmosphere that begins about 7 miles (11 kilometers) above the earth and ends about 31 miles (50 kilometers) above the earth. Clouds rarely form here, and the air is very cold and thin.

straw (straw) *noun*
1. The dried stalks of wheat, barley, oats, or other cereal plants that are left after the grain has been removed.
2. A thin, hollow plastic or paper tube through which you can drink.

straw·ber·ry (straw-ber-ee) *noun* The red, juicy fruit of a small, low plant of the rose family. See **fruit.** ▷ *noun, plural* **strawberries**

stray (stray)
1. *verb* To wander away or to get lost.
▷ **straying, strayed** ▷ *adjective* **stray**
2. *noun* A lost cat or dog. *The stray followed me home after I fed it.*

streak (streek)
1. *noun* A long, thin mark or stripe, as in *a streak of gray in her hair* or *a streak of lightning.*
▷ *adjective* **streaky**
2. *noun* A character trait. *She has a mean streak.*
3. *noun* A small series. *Our team was on a winning streak.*

4. *verb* To move very fast. *The sprinter streaked past us.* ▷ **streaking, streaked**

stream (streem)
1. *noun* A body of flowing water, especially a brook or a small river.
2. *noun* A steady flow of anything, as in *a stream of cars* or *a stream of light.*
3. *verb* To move or flow steadily. *Fans streamed out of the stadium.*
4. *verb* To float or to wave. *The flag streamed in the breeze.*
▷ *verb* **streaming, streamed**

stream·er (stree-mur) *noun* A long, thin strip of colored paper or material used as a decoration.

stream·lined (streem-lined) *adjective*
1. If a car, plane, or boat is **streamlined,** it is designed so that it can move through air or water very quickly and easily. See **aerodynamic.**
2. If a government or system for doing something is **streamlined,** it is made simpler or more efficient.

street (street) *noun*
1. A road in a city or town, often with sidewalks, houses, or other buildings along it.
2. Everyone who lives or works on a street. *The whole street heard about the new neighbors.*

street·car (street-kar) *noun* A vehicle that holds many passengers and runs on rails through city streets. Streetcars are powered by electricity.

street·light (street-lite) *noun* A light mounted on a pole by the side of a street to help drivers and pedestrians see at night.

street·wise (street-wize) *adjective* If you are **streetwise,** you know how to survive in towns or cities without getting into trouble.

strength (strengkth *or* strenth) *noun*
1. The quality of being strong; force; power. *I'm building up my strength by lifting weights.*
2. The power to resist or hold up under strain or stress; toughness. *Test the strength of the rope before you climb it.*
3. A person's good point, or the thing that the person can do well. *Jackie's strength is her ability to solve problems.*

stren·u·ous (stren-yoo-uhss) *adjective*
1. Needing great energy or effort, as in *strenuous exercise.*
2. Very active or energetic, as in *strenuous opposition.*
▷ *adverb* **strenuously**

stress (stress)
1. *noun* Worry, strain, or pressure. *My dad is under a lot of stress at work.* ▷ *noun, plural*
stresses ▷ *adjective* **stressful**
2. *verb* To pronounce a word with more loudness or emphasis on a certain syllable.

S

3. verb If you **stress** something, you claim that it is important. *Our doctor stresses good eating habits.*
▷ **noun stress** ▷ **verb stresses, stressing, stressed**

stretch (strech)
1. verb To spread out your arms, legs, or body to full length. *I always stretch when I first wake up.*
2. verb To extend or to spread out. *The highway stretches for miles.*
3. verb To make something bigger, longer, or greater. *Rubber bands stretch. We shop carefully so we can stretch our dollars.*
4. noun *(slang)* An unbroken space of time, especially time spent in a prison. *He was in for a long stretch.*
5. noun An unbroken length or distance. *Late at night, this stretch of highway is dark and deserted.*
6. stretch out verb To lie at full length.
▷ **noun stretch** ▷ **noun, plural stretches** ▷ **verb stretches, stretching, stretched**

stretch·er (strech-ur) noun A piece of canvas attached to two poles, used for carrying an injured or sick person.

strew (stroo) verb
1. To scatter, sprinkle, or throw here and there. *We strewed grass seed on the lawn.*
2. To cover a surface with things that have been scattered or sprinkled. *The highway was strewn with litter.*
▷ **verb strewing, strewed, strewn (stroon)**

strict (strikt) adjective
1. If someone is **strict,** the person makes you obey rules exactly and behave properly.
2. If a rule is **strict,** it is enforced all the time.
3. Complete or total. *This trick needs strict concentration.*
▷ **adjective stricter, strictest** ▷ **noun strictness**
▷ **adverb strictly**

stride (stride) verb To walk with long steps.
▷ **striding, strode (strode), stridden (strid-uhn)**
▷ **noun stride**

strife (strife) noun A bitter conflict between enemies; a fight or a struggle.

strike (strike)
1. verb To hit or attack someone or something.
2. verb When a clock **strikes,** it indicates the time with a ring or another sound.
3. verb To make an impression on someone. *Sal struck me as silly.*
4. verb To find or discover suddenly. *The miner struck gold.*
5. verb If you **strike** a match, you light it.
6. verb When people **strike,** they refuse to work because of an argument or a disagreement with their employer over wages or working conditions. ▷ **noun striker**
7. noun In baseball, a ball pitched over the plate between the batter's chest and knees, or any pitch that is swung at and missed.

8. noun In bowling, the act of knocking down all 10 pins with the first ball.
▷ **noun strike** ▷ **verb striking, struck (struhk)**

strik·ing adjective Unusual or noticeable in some way. *My grandmother looks very striking in her new dress.* ▷ **adverb strikingly**

string (string)
1. noun A thin cord or rope.
2. noun A thin wire on a musical instrument such as a guitar or violin. ▷ **verb string**
▷ **adjective stringed**
3. verb To put a row of objects on a piece of string or wire. *Natasha likes to string beads to make a necklace.*
4. noun A number of things of the same or similar kind all in a row. *There was a string of thefts at school.*
5. string out verb If you **string** something **out,** you stretch or lengthen it. *We strung out the game until bedtime.*
▷ **verb stringing, strung (struhng)**

string bean noun A long, thin, green pod that is eaten as a vegetable. See **vegetable.**

strings (stringz) noun, plural Stringed instruments that are played with a bow or plucked. *The picture shows the main parts of a violin and other instruments in the strings section of an orchestra.*

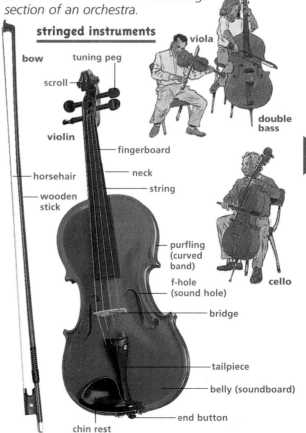

stringed instruments

bow
tuning peg
scroll
violin
horsehair
wooden stick
viola
double bass
fingerboard
neck
string
cello
purfling (curved band)
f-hole (sound hole)
bridge
tailpiece
belly (soundboard)
end button
chin rest

S

strip (strip)
1. *verb* To take off clothing; to undress.
2. *verb* To pull, tear, or take something off. *Jo stripped the wallpaper off the wall.*
3. *noun* A long, narrow piece of something, as in *a strip of paper* or *a strip of land.*
▷ *verb* **stripping, stripped**

stripe (stripe) *noun* A narrow band of color. *The flag of the United States has red and white stripes on it.* ▷ *verb* **stripe** ▷ *adjective* **striped**

strive (strive) *verb* To make a great effort to do something. *Strive to do your best.* ▷ **striving, strove** (strohv), **striven** (striv-in)

strobe (strohb) *noun* A light that flashes on and off very quickly.

stroke (strohk)
1. *verb* To pass your hand gently over something. *You may stroke the kitten.* ▷ **stroking, stroked** ▷ *noun* **stroke**
2. *noun* An unexpected action or event that has a powerful effect, as in *a stroke of lightning* or *a stroke of good luck.*
3. *noun* A hit or a blow, as in *the stroke of an ax.*
4. *noun* A line drawn by a pen, pencil, or brush.
5. *noun* When someone has a **stroke,** there is a sudden lack of oxygen in part of the brain caused by the blocking or breaking of a blood vessel.
6. *noun* A method of moving in swimming or rowing, or a method of hitting the ball in tennis.

stroll (strohl) *noun* A slow, relaxed walk. ▷ *verb* **stroll**

strong (strong) *adjective*
1. Powerful or having great force, as in *strong arms* or *a strong wind.*
2. Hard to break; firm, as in *a strong rope* or *strong beliefs.*
3. Having a sharp or bitter taste or odor, as in *a strong cheese* or *a strong smell.*
▷ *adjective* **stronger, strongest** ▷ *adverb* **strongly**

strong·hold (strong-hohld) *noun* A fortress, or a place that is well protected against attack or danger.

struc·ture (struhk-chur) *noun*
1. Something that has been built, such as a house, an office building, a bridge, or a dam.
2. The organization of something or the way that it is put together, as in *the structure of government* or *the structure of a cell.*
▷ *verb* **structure** ▷ *adjective* **structural**

strug·gle (struhg-uhl) *verb*
1. If you **struggle** with something, you try very hard, or make a great effort, to do it.
2. If you **struggle** with someone, you fight or battle the person.
▷ *verb* **struggling, struggled** ▷ *noun* **struggle**

strum (struhm) *verb* To play a musical instrument such as a guitar or harp by brushing your fingers over the strings. ▷ **strumming, strummed** ▷ *noun* **strum**

strut (struht)
1. *verb* To walk with a swagger or in an arrogant manner. *The bully strutted across the playground.* ▷ **strutting, strutted**
2. *noun* A wooden or metal supporting bar. *See* **hydrofoil.**

stub (stuhb)
1. *noun* A short part of something that remains after the rest has been used or torn off, as in *a pencil stub* or *a check stub.* ▷ *adjective* **stubby**
2. *verb* To hurt your toe or foot by banging it against something. *I stubbed my toe on the leg of the table.* ▷ **stubbing, stubbed**

stub·ble (stuhb-uhl) *noun*
1. Short, spiky stalks of grain that are left in a field after harvesting.
2. The short, rough hairs that grow on a man's face if he does not shave.
▷ *adjective* **stubbly**

stub·born (stuhb-urn) *adjective*
1. Not willing to give in or change; set on having your own way.
2. Hard to treat or deal with, as in *a stubborn cold.*
▷ *noun* **stubbornness** ▷ *adverb* **stubbornly**

stuck-up *adjective* (informal) Conceited and snobby.

stu·dent (stood-uhnt) *noun*
1. Someone who studies at a school.
2. Someone who studies or observes something on his or her own, as in *a student of human nature.*

stu·di·o (stoo-dee-oh) *noun*
1. A room or building in which an artist or a photographer works.
2. A place where movies, television and radio shows, or recordings are made.
3. A place that transmits radio or television programs.
4. A one-room apartment.
▷ *noun, plural* **studios**

stu·di·ous (stoo-dee-uhss) *adjective* If you are **studious,** you like or tend to study very hard.
▷ *noun* **studiousness** ▷ *adverb* **studiously**

stud·y (stuhd-ee)
1. *verb* To spend time learning a subject or skill by reading about it or by practicing it.
2. *noun* A room used for studying or reading.
▷ *noun, plural* **studies**
3. *verb* To examine something carefully. *Glenna studied the map until she found her street on it.*
▷ *verb* **studies, studying, studied** ▷ *noun* **study**

stuff (stuhf)
1. *noun* The material or ingredients something is made of. *What kind of stuff is in this stew?*
2. *noun* Personal belongings. *I put my stuff in my school bag.*
3. *noun* Useless or worthless things; junk. *The garage is full of old stuff.*
4. *verb* To fill something tightly. *James stuffed his pockets with candy.*
5. *verb* To put something into something else. *Don't forget to stuff the turkey.*
6. *verb* To fill yourself with too much food. *Stop stuffing yourself.*
7. If you are **stuffed up,** you have a cold or an allergy and cannot breathe through your nose.
▷ ***verb*** **stuffing, stuffed**

stuff·ing (stuhf-ing) ***noun***
1. Soft material used to fill pillows, cushions, and other articles made of or covered with cloth.
2. A mixture of chopped food that is cooked inside poultry and other food.

stuf·fy (stuhf-ee) ***adjective***
1. A **stuffy** room is hard to breathe in because it lacks fresh air.
2. A **stuffy** person is dull, old-fashioned, and easily shocked. ▷ ***adverb*** **stuffily**
▷ ***adjective*** **stuffier, stuffiest** ▷ ***noun*** **stuffiness**

stum·ble (stuhm-buhl) ***verb***
1. To trip, or to walk in an unsteady way.
2. To make mistakes when you are talking or reading aloud; to speak or act in a confused way.
3. To come upon or discover something unexpectedly. *We stumbled on a valuable baseball card while cleaning out the attic.*
▷ ***verb*** **stumbling, stumbled**

stump (stuhmp)
1. *noun* The part of a tree trunk that is left when a tree is cut down.
2. *noun* A short or broken-off piece of anything, as in *a pencil stump.*
3. *verb* *(informal)* To puzzle or to confuse. *The problem stumped me.* ▷ **stumping, stumped**

stump·y (stuhm-pee) ***adjective*** Short and thick. *My dog has a stumpy tail.* ▷ **stumpier, stumpiest**

stun (stuhn) ***verb*** If something **stuns** you, it shocks or dazes you or knocks you out.
▷ **stunning, stunned**

stun·ning (stuhn-ing) ***adjective***
1. *(informal)* Extremely beautiful.
2. Amazing or remarkable, as in *a stunning victory.*
3. Hard enough to knock you out, as in *a stunning blow.*
▷ ***adverb*** **stunningly**

stunt (stuhnt)
1. *noun* An act that shows great skill or daring. *As a stunt, the man in the photograph below jumped from one plane to the other.*
2. *noun* Something that is done to show off or attract attention.
3. *verb* To stop the proper growth of something.
▷ **stunting, stunted** ▷ ***adjective*** **stunted**
4. *noun* A **stunt person** takes the place of an actress or actor in an action scene or when a special skill or great risk is called for. Also called a *stunt double.*

stunt

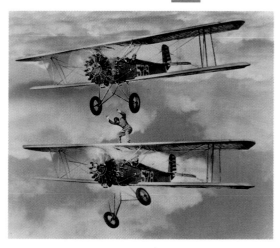

stu·pen·dous (stoo-pen-duhss) ***adjective*** Amazing or awesome. *He impressed the judges with a stupendous dive.* ▷ ***adverb*** **stupendously**

stu·pid (stoo-pid) ***adjective***
1. Slow to learn or understand; not intelligent.
2. Lacking common sense; foolish or silly. *Chasing a ball onto the street without looking for traffic is a stupid thing to do.*
▷ ***adjective*** **stupider, stupidest** ▷ ***noun*** **stupidity**
▷ ***adverb*** **stupidly**

stur·dy (stur-dee) ***adjective*** Strong and firm; solidly made or built. *I stood on a sturdy ladder to paint the ceiling. The weight lifter has a sturdy build.* ▷ **sturdier, sturdiest**

stur·geon (stur-juhn) ***noun*** A large fish covered with rows of bony, pointed scales. It is used for food and prized for its eggs, known as *caviar.*

stut·ter (stuht-ur) ***verb*** If you **stutter** when you speak, you repeat the first sound of a word before you are able to say the whole word.
▷ **stuttering, stuttered** ▷ ***noun*** **stutter,** ***noun*** **stutterer**

sty (stye) ***noun***
1. A pen in which pigs live. ▷ ***noun, plural*** **sties**
2. A red, painful swelling on the eyelid. ▷ ***noun, plural*** **sties** *or* **styes**

S

style (stile)
1. *noun* The way in which something is written, spoken, made, or done. *That writer's style is hard to follow. Our house is decorated in a modern style.*
2. *noun* The way in which people act and dress in a particular time period, especially the most recent one; fashion. *She was dressed in the latest style.*
3. *noun* If you have **style,** you have an elegant manner.
4. *verb* To arrange or design something. *The model's hair was styled before her picture was taken.* ▷ **styling, styled** ▷ *noun* **style,** *noun* **stylist**
5. *noun* The part of a flower that extends from the ovary and supports the stigma. *See* **flower.**

sty·lish (stile-ish) *adjective* To do with the latest style; fashionable. ▷ *adverb* **stylishly**

Sty·ro·foam (stye-ruh-fohm) *noun* The trademark for a very lightweight, rigid plastic that is used in many items, from building insulation to drinking cups.

sub·con·scious (suhb-kon-shuhss) *noun* The part of the mind where hidden thoughts are as well as the feelings you are not aware of. ▷ *adjective* **subconscious** ▷ *adverb* **subconsciously**

sub·con·ti·nent (suhb-kon-tuh-nuhnt) *noun* A large area of land that is part of a continent but is considered a separate geographical or political unit. *India is a subcontinent of Asia.*

sub·di·vide (*suhb*-duh-**vide** *or* **suhb**-duh-*vide*) *verb*
1. To divide into smaller, even parts something that has already been divided. *I cut the apple in half, then subdivided each half into quarters.*
2. To divide an area of land into lots for building homes.
▷ *verb* **subdividing, subdivided** ▷ *noun* **subdivision**

sub·due (suhb-doo) *verb*
1. To defeat in battle; to conquer.
2. To control. *Try to subdue your anger.*
▷ *verb* **subduing, subdued**

sub·dued (suhb-dood) *adjective*
1. Unusually quiet and controlled. *Nicole seemed subdued after her outburst.*
2. Not harsh or not strong, as in *subdued lighting.*

sub·ject
1. (suhb-jikt) *noun* The person or thing that is discussed or thought about in a book, newspaper article, conversation, etc.
2. (suhb-jikt) *noun* An area of study, such as geography or mathematics.
3. (suhb-jikt) *noun* A word or group of words in a sentence that tells whom or what the sentence is about. The subject of a sentence usually

precedes the verb. In the sentence "John likes milk," *John* is the subject.
4. (suhb-jikt) *noun* A person or thing that is studied or examined. *Scientists often use mice as subjects when they do experiments.*
5. (suhb-jikt) *noun* A person who lives in a kingdom or under the authority of a king or queen.
6. (suhb-jikt) If you are **subject to** something, you are likely to be affected by it. *Laura is subject to terrible colds.*
7. (suhb-jekt) *verb* If you **subject** someone to something, you force the person to go through it. *Our neighbors subjected us to loud music all night.* ▷ **subjecting, subjected**

sub·jec·tive (suhb-jek-tiv) *adjective* To do with your feelings or opinions rather than with actual facts. *The driver's account of the accident was purely subjective.* ▷ *adverb* **subjectively**

sub·ma·rine (suhb-muh-reen *or* suhb-muh-**reen**) *noun* A ship that can travel both on the surface and under the water.

sub·merge (suhb-murj) *verb*
1. To sink or plunge beneath the surface of a liquid, especially water. *The submarine submerged quickly.*
2. To cover with water or another liquid. *The flood submerged most of the town.*
▷ *verb* **submerging, submerged**

sub·mit (suhb-mit) *verb*
1. To hand in or to put something forward. *Did you submit your contest entry before the deadline? May I submit a plan to the committee?*
2. To agree to obey something. *I submitted to the judge's decision.*
▷ *verb* **submitting, submitted** ▷ *noun* **submission**

sub·or·di·nate (suh-bord-uhn-it)
1. *adjective* Less important; lower in rank. *Sergeants are subordinate to captains.*
2. *noun* Someone who is lower in rank or importance and can be told what to do. *The president of the company asked one of her subordinates to open the mail.*
▷ *verb* **subordinate** (suh-bord-uh-nate)

sub·scribe (suhb-skribe) *verb*
1. To pay money regularly for a product or service such as a newspaper, magazine, or cable television. ▷ *noun* **subscriber,** *noun* **subscription**
2. To agree with or go along with a belief or an idea. *I subscribe to the belief that people are basically good.*
▷ *verb* **subscribing, subscribed**

sub·se·quent (suhb-suh-kwuhnt) *adjective* Coming after, or following. *Jim lost the first match but played better in the subsequent ones.*
▷ *adverb* **subsequently**

S

sub·set (suhb-*set*) *noun* In math, a **subset** is a set of items that are all members within another set. For example, the numbers 1 through 10 are a subset of the numbers 1 through 1,000.

sub·side (suhb-side) *verb*
1. To sink to a lower or more normal level. *It took several days for the flood waters to subside.*
2. To become less intense or active. *Gradually, the noise subsided.*
▷ *verb* **subsiding, subsided**

sub·sid·i·ar·y (suhb-sid-ee-*er*-ee) *adjective* Minor, or less important, as in *a subsidiary role.* ▷ *noun* **subsidiary**

sub·si·dy (suhb-suh-dee) *noun* Money that a government or person contributes to help a worthy enterprise or in order to make goods or services cheaper. *The town received a subsidy for housing.* ▷ *noun, plural* **subsidies** ▷ *verb* **subsidize**

sub·stance (suhb-stuhnss) *noun*
1. Something that has weight and takes up space; matter. *Solid objects, powders, and liquids are substances.*
2. The material that something is made of.
3. The important part of something. *What is the substance of your argument?*

sub·stan·tial (suhb-**stan**-shuhl) *adjective*
1. Large. *I received a substantial raise in my allowance when I agreed to do more chores.*
2. Solidly built; strong or firm, as in *a substantial bridge.*
3. Not imaginary; real. *The danger of fire was quite substantial.*
▷ *adverb* **substantially**

sub·sti·tute (suhb-stuh-toot) *noun* Something or someone used in place of another, such as a teammate who plays when another player is injured. ▷ *noun* **substitution** ▷ *verb* **substitute**

sub·ti·tle (suhb-*tye*-tuhl) *noun*
1. The second, less important title of a book, a movie, an essay, a song, etc. The subtitle usually explains a bit about the title.
2. subtitles *noun, plural* The translated words that appear on the screen when a movie in another language is shown.

sub·tle (suht-uhl) *adjective*
1. Not strong; faint or delicate, as in *a subtle flavor.*
2. Clever or disguised, as in *a subtle plan.*
▷ *adjective* **subtler, subtlest** ▷ *noun* **subtlety,** *noun* **subtleness** ▷ *adverb* **subtly**

sub·tract (suhb-trakt) *verb* To take one number away from another. *If you subtract 2 from 6, you get 4.* ▷ **subtracting, subtracted** ▷ *noun* **subtraction**

sub·tra·hend (suhb-truh-*hend*) *noun* In math, a number that is subtracted from another number. In the equation $7 - 4 = 3$, 4 is the subtrahend.

sub·urb (suhb-urb) *noun* An area or a district on or close to the outer edge of a city. A suburb is made up mostly of homes, with few businesses. ▷ *noun* **suburbia** (suh-**bur**-bee-uh), *noun* **suburbanite** ▷ *adjective* **suburban**

sub·way (suhb-*way*) *noun* An electric train or a system of trains that runs underground in a city. *The photograph shows a train pulling into a subway station in San Francisco, California.*

<u>subway</u>

suc·ceed (suhk-seed) *verb*
1. To manage to do something. *Bill succeeded in fixing the car.*
2. To do well or to get what you want. *Carlotta succeeds at everything she does.*
3. To take over from someone in an important position. *Kim succeeded her mother as president of the company.*
▷ *verb* **succeeding, succeeded**

suc·cess (suhk-sess) *noun*
1. A good or favorable outcome; desired results.
2. A person or thing that has achieved success. *The experiment was a success.*
▷ *noun, plural* **successes** ▷ *adjective* **successful** ▷ *adverb* **successfully**

suc·ces·sion (suhk-sesh-uhn) *noun*
1. A number of persons or things that follow one after another in order; a series. *Our team has had a succession of losses.*
2. The coming of one person or thing after another. *The party guests arrived in quick succession.*
3. The order in which one person after another takes over a title, a throne, or an estate.

suc·ces·sive (suhk-sess-iv) *adjective* Following in a logical or sequential order. *Her flowers have won three successive blue ribbons at the fair.*
▷ *adverb* **successively**

suc·ces·sor (suhk-sess-ur) *noun* One who follows another in a position or sequence. *She is my successor as class president.*

S

suc·cu·lent (suhk-yuh-luhnt) *adjective* Juicy, as in *a succulent peach.* ▷ *noun* **succulence**

such (suhch)
1. *adjective* Of the same or that kind. *I've never seen such a magic trick before.*
2. *adjective* Like, or similar. *I like skating, skiing, and other such winter sports.*
3. *adjective* So much, or so great. *We had such fun at the carnival.*
4. *pronoun* Others of that kind. *We'll buy paint, wallpaper, and such to decorate the house.*

suck (suhk) *verb*
1. To draw something into your mouth using your tongue and lips. *George sucked the soda through the straw.*
2. To pull strongly or draw in. *The vacuum cleaner sucked up my ring.*
3. To hold in the mouth and lick. *The baby sucked his thumb.*
▷ *verb* **sucking, sucked** ▷ *noun* **suck**

suck·er (suhk-ur) *noun*
1. A body part of certain animals that is used to stick to surfaces. *See* **octopus.**
2. *(slang)* Someone who is easily cheated or fooled.
3. A piece of candy, such as a lollipop, that is held in the mouth and licked.

suc·tion (suhk-shuhn) *noun* The act of drawing air out of a space to create a vacuum. This causes the surrounding air or liquid to be sucked into the empty space. Vacuum cleaners and drinking straws work by suction.

sud·den (suhd-uhn) *adjective*
1. Happening without warning; unexpected, as in *a sudden storm.*
2. Quick, hasty, or abrupt, as in *a sudden decision* or *a sudden stop.*
▷ *noun* **suddenness** ▷ *adverb* **suddenly**

sudden infant death syndrome *noun* The death, usually during sleep, of a seemingly healthy infant for no known cause. Also known as *SIDS* or *crib death.*

suds (suhdz) *noun, plural* The bubbles that form on top of a substance such as water containing soap.

sue (soo) *verb* To start a suit or case against someone in a court of law. ▷ **suing, sued**

suede (swayd) *noun* Soft leather with a velvetlike surface.

su·et (soo-it) *noun* A hard fat from cattle and sheep that is used in cooking.

suf·fer (suhf-ur) *verb*
1. To have pain, discomfort, or sorrow. *The wounded soldier suffered. The new student suffered from loneliness.*
2. To experience or undergo something unpleasant. *The army suffered defeat.*

3. To be damaged, or to become worse. *If you don't study, your grades will suffer.*
▷ *verb* **suffering, suffered** ▷ *noun* **suffering**

suf·fi·cient (suh-fish-uhnt) *adjective* If something is **sufficient,** it is enough or adequate. *We left sufficient food for the cats when we were away.*
▷ *adverb* **sufficiently**

suf·fix (suhf-iks) *noun* A syllable or syllables added at the end of a word or root that change its meaning. For example, *-ness, -ly,* and *-ful* are all suffixes. *The suffix -ness is used in* sadness *and* happiness. ▷ *noun, plural* **suffixes**

> ### ▶ Word History
> **Suffix** comes from the Latin word parts *sub,* meaning "below," and *figere,* meaning "to fasten." A suffix, like *-ship,* is fastened or attached to the end of a word or word root to form a new word.

suf·fo·cate (suhf-uh-kate) *verb*
1. To kill by cutting off the supply of air or oxygen.
2. To die from lack of oxygen.
3. To have difficulty breathing. *I'm suffocating in this hot room.*
▷ *verb* **suffocating, suffocated** ▷ *noun* **suffocation**

suf·frage (suhf-rij) *noun* The right to vote. *Susan B. Anthony was one of the leaders in the fight for women's suffrage during the 19th century.*

sug·ar (shug-ur) *noun* A sweet substance that comes from sugar beets and sugarcane and is used in foods and drinks. ▷ *adjective* **sugary**

sugar beet *noun* A root vegetable from which sugar is produced.

sugar beet

sugar·cane (shug-ur-kayn) *noun* A tall, tropical grass that has sugar in its woody stems.

sug·gest (suhg-jest) *verb*
1. To put something forward as an idea or a possibility. *I suggested going to the mountains for our next vacation.*
2. To bring or call to mind. *Those soft, fluffy clouds suggest sheep to me.*
3. To hint or show indirectly. *This painter uses different colors to suggest his feelings.*
▷ *verb* **suggesting, suggested** ▷ *noun* **suggestion**

su·i·cide (soo-uh-*side*) *noun* If someone commits **suicide,** the person kills him- or herself on purpose. ▷ *adjective* **suicidal** ▷ *adverb* **suicidally**

suit (soot)
1. *noun* A set of matching clothes, usually a man's jacket and pants or a woman's jacket and skirt.
2. *noun* One of the four types of playing cards in a deck of cards. The four suits are clubs, diamonds, hearts, and spades.
3. *noun* A case that is brought before a court of law; a lawsuit.
4. *verb* To be acceptable and convenient. *Does Wednesday suit you?*
5. *verb* If a haircut or an outfit **suits** you, it makes you look good.
▷ *verb* **suiting, suited**

suit·a·ble (soo-tuh-buhl) *adjective* If something is **suitable,** it is right for a particular purpose.
▷ *noun* **suitability** ▷ *adverb* **suitably**

suit·case (soot-*kayss*) *noun* A flat bag used for carrying clothes and belongings when you travel.

suite *noun*
1. (sweet) A group of rooms that are connected, as in *a hotel suite.*
2. (sweet *or* soot) A set of matching items, as in *a bedroom suite.*
3. (sweet) A piece of music made up of several parts.

suit·or (soo-tur) *noun* A man who courts a woman.

sul·fur (suhl-fur) *noun* A yellow chemical element used in gunpowder, matches, and fertilizer. *See* **mineral.**

sulfur di·ox·ide (dye-ok-side) *noun* A poisonous gas found in some industrial waste. Sulfur dioxide causes air pollution.

sulk (suhlk) *verb* If you **sulk,** you are angry and silent. ▷ **sulking, sulked** ▷ *noun* **sulk** ▷ *adjective* **sulky**

sul·len (suhl-uhn) *adjective* Gloomy and silent because you feel angry, bitter, or hurt. *Deirdre was sullen when she wasn't picked to be on the team.* ▷ *adverb* **sullenly**

sul·tan (suhlt-uhn) *noun* An emperor or ruler of some Muslim countries.

sul·try (suhl-tree) *adjective* If the weather is **sultry,** it is hot and humid. ▷ **sultrier, sultriest**
▷ *noun* **sultriness**

sum (suhm)
1. *noun* An amount of money.
2. *noun* A number that you get from adding two or more numbers together.
3. *verb* If you **sum up,** you go through the main points of what has been said. ▷ **summing, summed**
4. **sum** *or* **sum total** *noun* The whole or final amount. *What is the sum total of your savings?*
Sum sounds like **some.**

su·mac (soo-mak) *noun* A bush or tree with pointed leaves and clusters of flowers or red berries.

sum·ma·ry (suhm-ur-ee) *noun* A short statement that gives the main points or ideas of something that has been said or written.
▷ *noun, plural* **summaries** ▷ *verb* **summarize**

sum·mer (suhm-ur) *noun* The season between spring and autumn, when the weather is warmest. ▷ *adjective* **summery**

sum·mit (suhm-it) *noun*
1. The highest point; the top, as in *the summit of a mountain.*
2. A meeting of important leaders from different countries.

sum·mon (suhm-uhn) *verb*
1. To call or request someone to come. *Summon the next witness, please.*
2. If you **summon up** courage, you make a great effort to be brave.
▷ *verb* **summoning, summoned**

sum·mons (suhm-uhnz) *noun* An order to appear in court. ▷ *noun, plural* **summonses** ▷ *verb* **summons**

su·mo wrestling (soo-moh) *noun* A Japanese form of wrestling. ▷ *noun* **sumo wrestler**

sun (suhn)
1. *noun* The star that the earth and other planets revolve around and that gives us light and warmth. Sometimes written **Sun.**
2. *noun* Any star that is the center of a system of planets.
3. *noun* Light and warmth from the sun. *Don't stay too long in the sun.*
4. *verb* If you **sun** yourself, you sit or lie in the sun. ▷ **sunning, sunned**
Sun sounds like **son.**

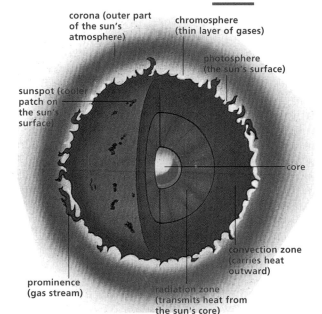

the sun

corona (outer part of the sun's atmosphere)

chromosphere (thin layer of gases)

photosphere (the sun's surface)

sunspot (cooler patch on the sun's surface)

core

convection zone (carries heat outward)

prominence (gas stream)

radiation zone (transmits heat from the sun's core)

sun·bathe (suhn-*bayTH*) *verb* To sit or lie in sunlight in order to make your body suntanned. ▷ **sunbathing, sunbathed** ▷ *noun* **sunbath**

sun·burn (suhn-burn) *noun* Sore, red skin caused by staying in sunlight too long. ▷ *adjective* **sunburned** *or* **sunburnt**

sun·dae (suhn-dee *or* suhn-*day*) *noun* Ice cream served with one or more toppings, such as syrup, whipped cream, nuts, or fruit.

Sun·day (suhn-dee *or* suhn-*day*) *noun* The first day of the week, after Saturday and before Monday.

> ### ▶ Word History
> In ancient Rome, the first day of the week was dedicated to the sun. The Romans originally called the day *dies solis,* which meant "day of the sun." The Old English language translated the Roman phrase into "sun's day," which later became **Sunday**

sun·di·al (suhn-*dye*-uhl) *noun* An instrument that shows the time by using the sun's light. A pointer casts a shadow that moves slowly around a flat, marked dial.

sundial

sun·down (suhn-*doun*) *noun* Sunset, the time of day just before nightfall, when the sun dips below the horizon.

sun·flow·er (suhn-*flou*-ur) *noun* A large flower with yellow petals and a dark center. Sunflower plants can grow as large as 12 feet high.

sun·glass·es (suhn-*glass*-iz) *noun, plural* Dark glasses that protect your eyes from the glare of sunlight.

sunk·en (suhng-kuhn) *adjective*
1. Below the surface, as in *sunken treasure.*
2. Below the other areas nearby. *Our house has a sunken living room.*
3. Very hollow, as in *sunken cheeks.*

sun·light (suhn-*lite*) *noun* The light of the sun.

sun·rise (suhn-*rize*) *noun* The time in the morning when the sun appears above the horizon.

sun·screen (suhn-*skreen*) *noun* A cream or lotion containing a chemical that protects the skin from the harmful rays of the sun.

sun·set (suhn-*set*) *noun* The time in the evening when the sun sinks below the horizon.

sun·shine (suhn-*shine*) *noun* The light from the sun.

sun·stroke (suhn-*strohk*) *noun* An illness caused by staying in hot sunlight too long. Symptoms of sunstroke include fever, dizziness, and headaches.

sun·tan (suhn-*tan*) *noun* If you have a **suntan,** your skin is brown because you have been in the rays of strong sunlight. ▷ *adjective* **suntanned**

su·per (soo-pur)
1. *adjective* Very good; excellent.
2. *noun* *(informal)* Short for **superintendent.**

su·perb (su-purb) *adjective* Excellent or outstanding, as in *a superb meal* or *a superb performance.* ▷ *adverb* **superbly**

su·per·fi·cial (soo-pur-fish-uhl) *adjective*
1. On the surface, as in *a superficial cut.*
2. Not deep, or not thorough. *My interest in music is only superficial.*
▷ *adverb* **superficially**

su·per·flu·ous (suh-pur-floo-uhss) *adjective* More than is needed or wanted; not necessary, as in *a superfluous remark.*

su·per·her·o (soo-pur-*hihr*-oh) *noun* A fictional character with superhuman powers such as extraordinary strength or the ability to fly.
▷ *noun, plural* **superheroes**

su·per·hu·man (soo-pur-**hyoo**-muhn) *adjective* Having or requiring characteristics or abilities beyond those of an ordinary human. *Taking care of three kids and working six days a week seemed like a superhuman task, but Alan's mom does it.*

su·per·in·ten·dent (soo-pur-in-ten-duhnt) *noun*
1. An official who directs or manages an organization, as in *superintendent of schools.*
2. A person in charge of a building; a janitor.

su·pe·ri·or (suh-**pihr**-ee-ur *or* soo-**pihr**-ee-ur)
1. *adjective* Higher in rank or position, as in *a superior officer.*
2. *adjective* Above average in quality or ability; excellent, as in *a superior piece of writing* or *a superior team.*
3. *noun* A person who has a higher rank or position than others.
4. *adjective* If someone acts in a **superior** way, the person behaves as if he or she were better than other people.
▷ *noun* **superiority**

su·per·la·tive (suh-pur-luh-tiv) *adjective*
1. **Superlative** adjectives and adverbs are used to describe the greatest or highest degree of things or actions. *Biggest* is the superlative form of *big,* and *most quickly* is the superlative form of *quickly.* ▷ *noun* **superlative**
2. The very best, as in *a superlative performance.*
▷ *adverb* **superlatively**

su·per·mar·ket (soo-pur-*mar*-kit) *noun* A large store that sells food and household items.

su·per·nat·u·ral (*soo*-pur-**nach**-ur-uhl) *noun* If something is **supernatural,** it involves things that natural laws cannot explain, as in *supernatural forces.* ▷ *adverb* **supernaturally**

su·per·no·va (*soo*-pur-**noh**-vuh) *noun* An extremely bright exploding star that can give off millions of times more light than the sun. ▷ *noun, plural* **supernovas** *or* **supernovae** (*soo*-pur-**noh**-vee)

su·per·son·ic (*soo*-pur-**son**-ik) *adjective* Faster than the speed of sound. *The picture shows the Concorde, a plane that flies at supersonic speeds.*

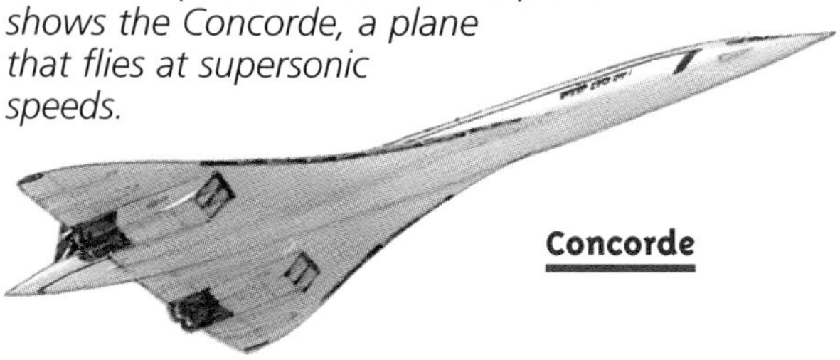

Concorde

su·per·sti·tion (*soo*-pur-**sti**-shuhn) *noun* A belief that some action not connected to a future event can influence the outcome of the event. A common superstition is that if you walk under a ladder you will have bad luck. ▷ *adjective* **superstitious**

su·per·tank·er (*soo*-pur-*tang*-kur) *noun* A very large oil tanker used to transport large amounts of crude oil to refineries.

su·per·vise (soo-pur-*vize*) *verb* To watch over or direct a group of people; to be in charge of. ▷ **supervising, supervised** ▷ *noun* **supervision**

su·per·vi·sor (soo-pur-*vye*-zur) *noun* Someone who watches over and directs the work of other people. *Ms. Jones will be your supervisor during your training period.*

sup·per (suhp-ur) *noun* An evening meal.

sup·ple (suhp-uhl) *adjective* If you are **supple,** you can move or bend your body easily. ▷ **suppler, supplest** ▷ *noun* **suppleness**

sup·ple·ment (suhp-luh-muhnt)
1. *noun* Something added to complete another thing or to make up for what is missing. *This newspaper has a color supplement that focuses on health.*
2. *verb* To add to something. *Joan supplements her diet with extra vitamins.* ▷ **supplementing, supplemented**
▷ *adjective* **supplementary**

sup·ply (suh-plye)
1. *verb* To provide something that is needed or wanted. *Forests supply trees for lumber. An encyclopedia supplies information.* ▷ **supplies, supplying, supplied** ▷ *noun* **supplier**

2. *noun* An amount of something that is available for use. *Our supply of firewood is running low.* ▷ *noun, plural* **supplies**
3. supplies *noun, plural* Materials needed to do something. *In late August, I bought all new school supplies.*

sup·port (suh-port) *verb*
1. To hold something up in order to keep it from falling.
2. To earn a living for; to provide for. *My mother supports two children.*
3. To help and encourage someone. *We all supported Carmen when she got into trouble.*
▷ *adjective* **supportive**
4. To believe in someone or favor something. *We support environmentalists.*
5. To show to be true. *My findings support your theory.*
▷ *verb* **supporting, supported** ▷ *noun* **support,** *noun* **supporter**

sup·pose (suh-poze) *verb*
1. To imagine or assume that something is true or possible. *Let's suppose that people were able to fly like birds.*
2. To believe or to guess. *I suppose she's right.*
3. To expect. *It is supposed to snow this week.*
▷ *verb* **supposing, supposed** ▷ *adjective* **supposed**

sup·press (suh-press) *verb*
1. To stop something from happening. *The dictator suppressed the revolution.*
2. To hide or control something. *Carly tried to suppress her giggles.*
▷ *verb* **suppresses, suppressing, suppressed**
▷ *noun* **suppression**

su·preme (suh-preem) *adjective* Greatest, best, or most powerful. ▷ *noun* **supremacy** ▷ *adverb* **supremely**

Supreme Court *noun* The highest and most powerful court in the United States. It has the power to overturn decisions made in lower courts and also to declare laws unconstitutional. The Supreme Court consists of nine justices.

sure (shoor)
1. *adjective* Having no doubt; certain; confident. *Are you sure he's right?*
2. *adjective* Certain to happen; impossible to avoid, as in *a sure defeat.*
3. *adjective* Firm or steady, as in *sure footing* or *a sure grip.*
4. *adverb* Without a doubt; certainly. *Sure, I'll be there.*
▷ *adjective* **surer, surest**

sure·ly (shoor-lee) *adverb* With certainty; absolutely; without a doubt. *You are surely welcome to come to the party.*

S

surf (surf)
1. *noun* Waves as they break on the shore.
2. *verb* To ride on breaking waves using a surfboard. ▷ **surfing, surfed** ▷ *noun* **surfer,** *noun* **surfing**
Surf sounds like **serf.**

surfing

sur·face (sur-fiss)
1. *noun* The outside or outermost layer of something, as in *the surface of the earth.*
2. *noun* One of the sides of something that has several sides. *Dice have six surfaces.*
3. *noun* Outward appearance. *On the surface he seemed like a nice enough guy.*
4. *verb* To come to the surface or to appear. *The submarine surfaced when it was damaged. The lost coins surfaced after several years.* ▷ **surfacing, surfaced**

surf·board (surf-bord) *noun* A narrow board that surfers stand on to ride breaking waves. *See* **surf.**

surge (surj)
1. *verb* To rush or sweep forward with force, like a wave. *The crowd surged forward as the gate was opened.* ▷ **surging, surged**
2. *noun* A sudden, strong rush.
3. *noun* A sudden increase, as in *a surge in prices* or *a surge of interest.* ▷ *verb* **surge**

sur·geon (sur-juhn) *noun* A doctor who performs operations.

sur·ger·y (sur-jer-ee) *noun*
1. Medical treatment that involves repairing, removing, or replacing injured or diseased parts of the body. Surgery is done by cutting the patient open or by using lasers. ▷ *adjective* **surgical**
2. The branch of medicine that deals with injury and disease in this way.
3. An operation performed by a surgeon.

sur·ly (sur-lee) *adjective* If someone is **surly,** he or she is mean, rude, and unfriendly. ▷ **surlier, surliest**

sur·name (sur-name) *noun* A person's last name or family name.

sur·pass (sur-pass) *verb*
1. To be better, greater, or stronger than another person or thing. *Today Patrick surpassed his previous record.*
2. To go beyond the limits or powers of. *Her beauty surpasses description.*
▷ *verb* **surpasses, surpassing, surpassed**

sur·plus (sur-pluhss) *noun* An amount greater than what is used or needed; excess, as in *a surplus of grain.* ▷ *adjective* **surplus**

sur·prise (sur-prize) *verb*
1. To amaze or astonish someone by doing or saying something unexpected. *Al's outburst surprised us all.*
2. To come upon suddenly and without warning. *He arrived home early and surprised a thief.*
▷ *verb* **surprising, surprised** ▷ *noun* **surprise**
▷ *adjective* **surprising**

sur·ren·der (suh-ren-dur) *verb* To give up, or to admit that you are beaten in a fight or battle.
▷ **surrendering, surrendered** ▷ *noun* **surrender**

sur·round (suh-round) *verb* To be on every side of something. *A fence surrounds the garden.*
▷ **surrounding, surrounded**

sur·round·ings (suh-roun-dingz) *noun, plural* The things or conditions around something or someone. *People work better in cheerful surroundings.*

sur·vey
1. (sur-vay) *noun* A report or study on what people think about something. *We are conducting a survey of reactions to the new shopping center.* ▷ *verb* **survey (sur-vay or sur-vay)**
2. (sur-vay) *verb* To look at the whole of a scene or situation. *Mom surveyed the mess with horror.*
3. (sur-vay) *verb* To measure an area in order to make a map or plan. *They surveyed the building site.* ▷ *noun* **survey (sur-vay),** *noun* **surveyor**
▷ *verb* **surveying, surveyed**

sur·vive (sur-vive) *verb*
1. To stay alive through or after some dangerous event. *Only one passenger survived the car crash.*
2. To continue to live or exist. *Humans need food and water to survive.*
▷ *verb* **surviving, survived** ▷ *noun* **survival**

sur·vi·vor (sur-vye-vur) *noun* Someone who lives through a disaster or horrible event. *The train crash left over 100 survivors.*

su·shi (soo-shee) *noun* A Japanese dish made of raw fish or seafood pressed into rice.

sus·pect
1. (suh-spekt) *verb* To think that something may be true; to guess or suppose. *The doctor suspected something more serious than flu.*
▷ *adjective* **suspect (suhss-pekt or suh-spekt)**
2. (suh-spekt) *verb* To think that someone is guilty with little or no proof.

3. (suh-**spekt**) *verb* To have doubts about; to distrust. *She said she really wants to help, but I suspect her sincerity.*

4. (**suhss**-pekt) *noun* Someone thought to be responsible for a crime.

▷ *verb* **suspecting, suspected**

sus·pend (suh-**spend**) *verb*

1. To attach something to a support so that it hangs downward. *We suspended the banner from the gym ceiling.*

2. To keep from falling as if attached from above. *The hummingbird was suspended over the flower.*

3. To stop something for a short time. *Work was suspended for the holidays.*

4. To punish someone by stopping the person from taking part in an activity for a short while. *Sophie was suspended from school for a week.*

▷ *verb* **suspending, suspended** ▷ *noun* **suspension**

sus·pend·ers (suh-**spen**-durz) *noun, plural* A pair of elastic straps worn over the shoulders and attached to pants or a skirt to hold up the garment.

sus·pense (suh-**spenss**) *noun* An anxious and uncertain feeling caused by having to wait to see what happens. *We were all in suspense as we waited to learn the winners of the contest.*

sus·pen·sion bridge (suh-**spen**-shuhn) *noun* A bridge hung from cables or chains strung from towers.

sus·pi·cion (suh-**spish**-uhn) *noun*

1. A thought, based more on feeling than on fact, that something is wrong or bad.

2. If you are **under suspicion,** people think that you may have done something wrong.

sus·pi·cious (suh-**spish**-uhss) *adjective*

1. If you feel **suspicious,** you think that something is wrong or bad, but you have little or no proof to back up your feelings.

2. If you think that someone seems or looks **suspicious,** you have a feeling that the person has done something wrong and cannot be believed or trusted.

sus·tain (suh-**stayn**) *verb*

1. To keep something going. *Jeremy sustained a conversation with his cousin for over two hours.*

2. If something **sustains** you, it gives you the energy and strength to keep going. *The hot soup sustained the walkers for miles.*

3. To suffer something. *Tracey sustained some nasty bruises.*

▷ *verb* **sustaining, sustained**

swag·ger (**swag**-ur) *verb* To walk or act in a bold, conceited way. *Billy swaggered down the hall, trying to look important.* ▷ **swaggering, swaggered** ▷ *noun* **swagger**

swal·low (**swahl**-oh)

1. *verb* To make food or drink travel down from your mouth to your stomach. ▷ *noun* **swallow**

2. *verb* To cause to disappear as if by swallowing. *The raging flood swallowed the house.*

3. *verb* To keep back. *I swallowed my pride.*

4. *noun* A migrating bird with long wings and a forked tail.

5. *verb* (*informal*) To accept or believe without question. *The story is too wild to swallow.*

▷ *verb* **swallowing, swallowed**

swallow

swamp (swahmp)

1. *noun* An area of wet, spongy ground; a marsh. ▷ *adjective* **swampy**

2. *verb* To fill with or sink in water. *The stormy seas swamped the boat.*

3. *verb* To overwhelm. *I am swamped with homework.*

▷ *verb* **swamping, swamped**

swan (swahn) *noun* A large water bird with white feathers, webbed feet, and a long, graceful neck. *The picture shows a female swan with her young.*

swan and cygnets

swank·y (**swang**-kee) *adjective* (*informal*) Very elegant or stylish, as in *a swanky restaurant.*

swap (swahp) *verb* (*informal*) To trade or exchange one thing for another. *I'll swap you my CD for a video game.* ▷ **swapping, swapped** ▷ *noun* **swap**

swarm (sworm)
  1. *noun* A group of people or insects that gather or move in large numbers.
  2. *verb* When bees **swarm,** they fly together in a thick mass.
  3. *verb* If a place **is swarming** with people or animals, it is filled with them.
  ▷ *verb* **swarming, swarmed**

a swarm of bees

swar·thy (swor-THee) *adjective* A **swarthy** person has dark skin. ▷ **swarthier, swarthiest**

swas·ti·ka (swahss-tuh-kuh) *noun* An ancient symbol consisting of a cross with the arms bent at right angles. During the 20th century, the swastika became a symbol of aggression and hatred when it was adopted as the emblem of the Nazi party in Germany.

swat (swaht) *verb* To hit with a quick, sharp blow. *James swatted the bee.* ▷ **swatting, swatted** ▷ *noun* **swat**

sway (sway) *verb*
  1. To move or swing from side to side. *The corn swayed in the wind.*
  2. To change or influence the way someone thinks or acts. *The candidate's speech swayed the voters.*
  ▷ *verb* **swaying, swayed** ▷ *noun* **sway**

swear (swair) *verb*
  1. To make a formal, solemn promise. *I swear to tell the truth.*
  2. To use rude or bad language; to curse.
  ▷ *verb* **swearing, swore** (swor), **sworn** (sworn)

sweat (swet) *verb* When you **sweat,** a salty liquid comes out through the pores in your skin because you are hot or nervous. Sweat is another word for **perspire.** *See* **skin.** ▷ **sweating, sweat** *or* **sweated** ▷ *noun* **sweat**

sweat·er (swet-ur) *noun* A knitted piece of clothing that you wear on the top half of your body.

sweat·shirt (swet-*shurt*) *noun* A heavy, collarless, casual top with long sleeves.

sweep (sweep) *verb*
  1. To clean or clear away with a brush or broom.
  2. To move or carry rapidly and forcefully. *The fire swept through the building.*
  3. To touch or brush lightly. *A wisp of hair swept her face.*
  4. To move or pass over a wide area quickly and steadily. *The telescope swept the night sky.*
  ▷ *verb* **sweeping, swept** (swept) ▷ *noun* **sweep**

sweep·ing (sweep-ing) *adjective* Something that is **sweeping** affects many things or people. *Sweeping changes in the firm meant many job losses.*

sweet (sweet)
  1. *adjective* Food that is **sweet** has a taste like that of sugar or honey, as in *a sweet peach.*
  2. *adjective* Pleasant in taste, smell, or sound, as in *the sweet smell of roses* or *sweet music.*
  3. *adjective* Gentle and kind; good-natured, as in *a sweet disposition.*
  4. *noun* A piece of candy or other food that tastes sweet.
  ▷ *adjective* **sweeter, sweetest** ▷ *adverb* **sweetly**

sweet·en (sweet-uhn) *verb* To make something sweet or sweeter, usually by adding sugar. *I like to sweeten iced tea before drinking it.*
  ▷ **sweetening, sweetened**

sweet·heart (sweet-*hart*) *noun*
  1. Either person of a loving couple. *They've been sweethearts since high school.*
  2. A lovable person. *She's a real sweetheart.*

sweet potato *noun* The thick, sweet, orange root of a vine. Sweet potatoes are eaten as vegetables. *See* **vegetable.** ▷ *noun, plural* **sweet potatoes**

swell (swel)
  1. *verb* To grow larger, greater, or stronger. *Jake's ankle swelled after he twisted it. The fans' cheers swelled to a roar.* ▷ *noun* **swelling**
  ▷ **swelling, swelled, swollen**
  2. *noun* A long, rolling wave or waves. *A boat rocked gently in the swell.*
  3. *adjective* (slang) Wonderful. *We had a swell time today.*

swel·ter·ing (swel-tur-ing) *adjective* **Sweltering** weather is very hot. ▷ *verb* **swelter**

swerve (swurv) *verb* To change direction quickly, usually to avoid something. *The car swerved to avoid the squirrel.* ▷ **swerving, swerved** ▷ *noun* **swerve**

swift (swift)
  1. *adjective* Moving or able to move very fast, as in *a swift runner.* ▷ *noun* **swiftness** ▷ *adverb* **swiftly**
  2. *adjective* Happening or done quickly, as in *a swift reply.*

3. *noun* A migrating bird with long, narrow wings. A swift is similar to a swallow. *See* **bird.**
▷ *adjective* **swifter, swiftest**

swig (swig) *verb* To drink in large gulps, usually from a bottle or other container. ▷ **swigging, swigged** ▷ *noun* **swig**

swim (swim) *verb*
1. To move through the water using the arms and legs or the fins, flippers, or tail. ▷ *noun* **swim,** *noun* **swimmer**
2. To float on or be covered by liquid. *The potatoes were swimming in gravy.*
▷ *verb* **swimming, swam** (swam)**, swum** (swuhm)

swim·suit (swim-*soot*) *noun* Clothing worn for swimming; a bathing suit.

swin·dle (swin-duhl) *verb* To cheat someone out of money, property, etc. ▷ **swindling, swindled** ▷ *noun* **swindle,** *noun* **swindler**

swine (swine) *noun*
1. A pig or a hog.
2. A hateful, vicious, or greedy person.

swing (swing)
1. *verb* To move back and forth.
2. *verb* To move on a hinge or pivot. *The door swung shut.*
3. *verb* To move or turn with a curved, sweeping motion. *The batter swung at the pitch.* ▷ *noun* **swing**
4. *noun* A piece of play equipment on which you can sit and move back and forth.
5. *noun* A style of lively jazz music originally played by large dance bands in the 1930s.
▷ *verb* **swinging, swung** (swuhng)

swipe (swipe) *verb*
1. *(informal)* To hit something or somebody with a hard, sweeping blow. ▷ *noun* **swipe**
2. *(slang)* To steal something. *Max swiped my chocolate bar.*
▷ *verb* **swiping, swiped**

swirl (swurl) *verb* To move in circles; to whirl. *The water swirled around the drain.* ▷ **swirling, swirled** ▷ *noun* **swirl**

swish (swish)
1. *verb* To move with a soft, rustling sound. *My skirt swished along the floor as I walked.*
▷ **swishes, swishing, swished**
2. *noun* A soft, rustling sound. *I love to hear the swish of the branches in the breeze.* ▷ *noun, plural* **swishes**

switch (swich)
1. *verb* To trade one thing for another. *Let's switch seats.*
2. *verb* To change from one thing to another. *My mom switched from drinking coffee to drinking tea.*
3. *noun* A change or a trade. *There was a switch in the program.*

4. *verb* To turn a piece of electrical equipment on or off. *Switch on the TV.*
5. *noun* A device that interrupts the flow of electricity in a circuit, as in *a light switch.*
6. *noun* A long, thin stick or rod used for whipping.
7. *noun* A quick, jerking motion. *The cow drove the flies away with a switch of its tail.*
8. *noun* A section of railroad track used to move a train from one track to another. ▷ *verb* **switch** ▷ *verb* **switches, switching, switched** ▷ *noun, plural* **switches**

switch·board (swich-*bord*) *noun* The control center or panel for connecting the lines of a telephone system.

swiv·el (swiv-uhl) *verb* To turn or rotate on the spot. *Sharon swiveled in her seat.* ▷ **swiveling, swiveled**

swol·len (swohl-in)
1. *verb* The past participle of **swell.**
2. *adjective* Made large by swelling, as in *a swollen gland.*

swoon (swoon) *verb* To faint, often from excitement. ▷ **swooning, swooned**

swoop (swoop) *verb* To rush down or pounce upon suddenly. *The owl swooped down on its prey.* ▷ **swooping, swooped** ▷ *noun* **swoop**

sword (sord) *noun* A weapon with a handle and a long, sharp blade.

Viking sword

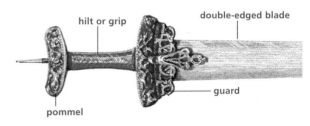

hilt or grip
double-edged blade
pommel
guard

sword·fish (sord-*fish*) *noun* A large saltwater food fish with a swordlike bone sticking out from its upper jaw. ▷ *noun, plural* **swordfish**

syc·a·more (sik-uh-*mor*) *noun* A North American tree with smooth, brown bark that peels off in layers.

syl·la·ble (sil-uh-buhl) *noun* A unit of sound in a word. A syllable contains a vowel and possibly one or more consonants. *The word* long *contains one syllable.*

syl·la·bus (sil-uh-buhss) *noun* An outline or a summary of work that must be covered for a particular course of study. ▷ *noun, plural* **syllabuses** or **syllabi** (sil-uh-bye)

sym·bol (sim-buhl) *noun* A design or an object that represents something else. *On many maps, a small, green pine tree is the symbol for a forest.* **Symbol** sounds like **cymbal.**

sym·bol·ize (sim-buh-lize) *verb* To stand for or represent something else. *The dove symbolizes peace.* ▷ **symbolizing, symbolized**

sym·met·ri·cal (si-met-ruh-kuhl) *adjective* Having matching points, parts, or shapes on both sides of a dividing line. The capital letters *M* and *X* are symmetrical because you can draw a line dividing them into two matching halves. ▷ *adverb* **symmetrically**

symmetrical shapes

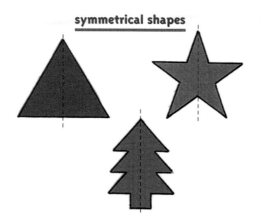

sym·me·try (sim-uh-tree) *noun* A balanced arrangement of parts on either side of a line or around a central point.

sym·pa·thize (sim-puh-thize) *verb*
1. To understand or appreciate other people's troubles.
2. To be in agreement. *We sympathize with your views on social issues.*
▷ *verb* **sympathizing, sympathized**

sym·pa·thy (sim-puh-thee) *noun*
1. The understanding and sharing of other people's troubles. *After her accident, Yoko's friends gave her lots of sympathy.*
2. If you are **in sympathy** with somebody's aims or actions, you agree with the person and support him or her.
▷ *adjective* **sympathetic** (sim-puh-thet-ik)

sym·pho·ny (sim-fuh-nee) *noun*
1. A long piece of music for an orchestra. A symphony is usually in four parts called movements.
2. A large orchestra that usually plays classical music. *See* **orchestra.**
▷ *noun, plural* **symphonies** ▷ *adjective* **symphonic** (sim-fon-ic)

symp·tom (simp-tuhm) *noun*
1. Something that shows that you have an illness. *A rash is one of the symptoms of measles.*
2. An indication of something. *Josh's failing grades were a symptom of his lack of interest in school.*

syn·a·gogue (sin-a-gog) *noun* A building used by Jewish people for worship and religious study.

syn·chro·nize (sing-kruh-nize) *verb* If two watches are **synchronized,** they are made to show the same time. ▷ **synchronizing, synchronized** ▷ *noun* **synchronization**

syn·co·pate (sing-kuh-pate) *verb* To stress beats in a piece of music that are not normally stressed. ▷ **syncopating, syncopated** ▷ *noun* **syncopation** ▷ *adjective* **syncopated**

syn·drome (sin-drohm) *noun* A group of signs and symptoms that occur together and are characteristic of a particular disease or disorder.

syn·o·nym (sin-uh-nim) *noun* A word that means the same or nearly the same as another word. *The word* rapid *is a synonym for* quick.

syn·on·y·mous (si-non-uh-muhss) *adjective*
1. Having the same or almost the same meaning. *The words* gigantic *and* huge *are synonymous.*
2. Having the same implication or reference. *To many people, the owl is synonymous with wisdom.*

syn·op·sis (si-nop-siss) *noun* A brief summary of a longer piece of writing. ▷ *noun, plural* **synopses** (si-nop-seez)

syn·tax (sin-taks) *noun* The rules of grammar that govern the way words are put together to make phrases and sentences. ▷ *adjective* **syntactic** (sin-tak-tik)

syn·the·siz·er (sin-thuh-sye-zur) *noun* An electronic keyboard instrument that can make a variety of sounds and imitate other musical instruments.

syn·thet·ic (sin-thet-ik) *adjective* Something that is **synthetic** is manufactured or artificial rather than found in nature. ▷ *noun* **synthetic** ▷ *adverb* **synthetically**

sy·phon (sye-fuhn) Another spelling of **siphon.**

sy·ringe (suh-rinj) *noun* A tube with a plunger and a hollow needle, used for giving injections.

syr·up (sihr-uhp *or* sur-uhp) *noun*
1. A sweet, thick liquid made by boiling sugar and water, usually with some flavoring, as in *chocolate syrup.*
2. A sweet, thick liquid made by boiling down the sap of a tree or plant, as in *maple syrup.*
▷ *adjective* **syrupy**

sys·tem (siss-tuhm) *noun*
1. A group of things or parts that exist or work together in an organized way, as in *the solar system* or *a computer system.*
2. A way of organizing or arranging things, as in *the educational system* or *a system of government.*
3. An orderly way of doing something; a method. *I need a better system for studying.*
▷ *adjective* **systematic** ▷ *adverb* **systematically**

S

tab (tab) *noun*
1. A small flap or loop that is attached to something. Tabs are used for labeling, pulling, or opening. *File folders and soda cans have tabs.*
2. *(informal)* If you **keep tabs on** someone, you watch the person closely to see what he or she is doing.
3. *(informal)* If you **pick up the tab,** you pay the bill in a restaurant.

tab·by (tab-ee) *noun*
1. A cat with a striped coat.
2. Any domestic cat, especially a female. *See* **cat.**

tab·er·na·cle (tab-ur-*nak*-uhl) *noun*
1. A building used for worship.
2. A case or box for holy objects.

ta·ble (tay-buhl) *noun*
1. A piece of furniture with a flat top resting on legs.
2. A chart that lists facts and figures, usually in columns.
3. Food put on a table. *Grandma set a nice table.*
4. If you **turn the tables** on someone, you reverse the situation so that things are in your favor.
5. If something is done **under the table,** it is done in secret or illegally.

ta·ble·cloth (tay-buhl-*klawth*) *noun* A piece of material used to protect or decorate a table.

table manners *noun, plural* The way you behave when you are eating.

ta·ble·spoon (tay-buhl-*spoon*) *noun* A large spoon that you use to serve food or as a measure in cooking. A tablespoon is equal to three teaspoons. ▷ *noun* **tablespoonful**

tab·let (tab-lit) *noun*
1. A pad of writing paper glued together at one end.
2. A small, solid piece of medicine that you swallow.
3. A piece of stone with writing carved on it.

table tennis *noun* A game for two or four players who use wooden paddles to hit a small, light ball over a low net on a table. Table tennis is also known as **Ping-Pong.**

tab·loid (tab-loid) *noun* A newspaper that contains brief articles and many pictures. The pictures and articles are often intended to stir up interest or excitement. ▷ *adjective* **tabloid**

ta·boo (tuh-boo *or* ta-boo) *adjective* If a subject is **taboo,** you may upset or offend people if you talk about it. *Death is a taboo subject in some societies.* ▷ *noun* **taboo**

tab·u·lar (tab-yuh-lur) *adjective* Set out in the form of a table or chart. *Please present your results in tabular form.* ▷ *verb* **tabulate**

tac·it (tass-it) *adjective* If something is **tacit,** it is understood or agreed to without being stated. *My parents have given their tacit approval to my staying up late.* ▷ *adverb* **tacitly**

tac·i·turn (tass-uh-turn) *adjective* If someone is **taciturn,** the person is quiet and shy and does not talk much. ▷ *adverb* **taciturnly**

tack (tak)
1. *noun* A small nail with a sharp point and a large, flat head.
2. *noun* A course of action. *If you have trouble solving a problem one way, try a different tack.*
3. *verb* To add or attach something extra or different. *Many senators wanted to tack an amendment onto the president's bill.*
4. *verb* If you **tack** material, you sew it loosely before doing it neatly. ▷ *noun* **tack**
5. *verb* To sail in a zigzag course against the wind.
6. *noun* Equipment that you need to ride a horse, such as a saddle and bridle. *The English-style saddle and bridle shown in detail below are worn by the horse on the left. The horse on the right is wearing western-style tack.*
▷ *verb* **tacking, tacked**

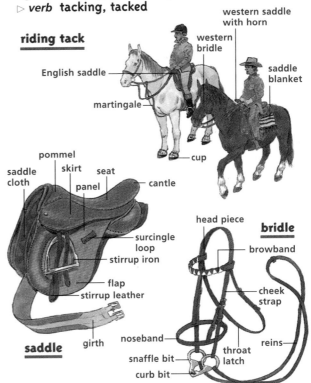

riding tack

English saddle · western bridle · western saddle with horn · saddle blanket · martingale · cup

saddle · pommel · skirt · seat · cantle · saddle cloth · panel · surcingle loop · stirrup iron · flap · stirrup leather · girth

bridle · head piece · browband · cheek strap · noseband · reins · snaffle bit · throat latch · curb bit

tack·le (tak-uhl)
1. *verb* In football, if you **tackle** someone, you knock or throw the person to the ground in order to stop forward progress. ▷ *noun* **tackle**, *noun* **tackler**
2. *verb* To deal with a problem or difficulty. *We must tackle the problem of vandalism.*
3. *noun* The equipment that you need for a particular activity, as in *fishing tackle.*
4. *noun* A system of ropes and pulleys used to raise, lower, or move heavy loads.
▷ *verb* **tackling, tackled**

ta·co (tah-koh) *noun* A Mexican food consisting of a fried tortilla that is folded around one or more fillings such as beef, chicken, or cheese.
▷ *noun, plural* **tacos**

tact (takt) *noun* If you handle a person or situation with **tact,** you are sensitive and do not upset or hurt anyone. *The woman used tact when she told my brother that he didn't get the job.* ▷ *adjective* **tactful** ▷ *adverb* **tactfully**

tac·tics (tak-tiks) *noun, plural* Plans or methods to win a game or battle or achieve a goal.
▷ *adjective* **tactical** ▷ *adverb* **tactically**

tad·pole (tad-pole) *noun* A young frog or toad that is in the larva stage of development. It lives in water, breathes through gills, and has a long tail but no legs. *See* **frog.**

> ### Word History
> ●
> The **tadpole** gets its name from its shape. *Tad* is from the Middle English word for "toad," and *pole* is from the Middle English word for "head." Since a tadpole's head takes up most of its body, the name "toad-head" seems an appropriate one.

taf·fy (taf-ee) *noun* A thick, sweet, chewy candy that is made of brown sugar or molasses and butter. The ingredients are boiled together, then stretched and folded over and over until the mixture holds its shape. ▷ *noun, plural* **taffies**

tag (tag)
1. *noun* A label, as in *a price tag* or *a name tag.*
2. *noun* A children's game in which the player called "It" has to chase the other players and touch one of them. ▷ *verb* **tag**
3. *verb* In baseball, to put a runner out by touching him or her with the ball. ▷ *noun* **tag**
4. *verb* If you **tag along** with someone, you follow the person. *Henry wasn't part of the gang; he just tagged along.*
▷ *verb* **tagging, tagged**

tail (tayl)
1. *noun* A part that sticks out at the back end of an animal's body and is often long and slender.
2. *noun* Something that is shaped like a tail, as in *the tail of a kite* or *the tail of a comet.*
3. *noun* The rear part or end of something. *We joined the tail of the procession.*
4. tails *noun* The side of a coin opposite the head, or main side.
5. *verb* (informal) If you **tail** someone, you follow the person closely. ▷ **tailing, tailed** ▷ *noun* **tail**
Tail sounds like **tale.**

tail·gate (tale-gayt)
1. *noun* A board or gate at the rear of a station wagon or truck that can be folded down or removed for loading and unloading.
2. *verb* To drive so closely behind another vehicle that you do not have room to stop in an emergency.
3. *verb* To set up a picnic on the tailgate of a vehicle, especially in the parking lot of a sports stadium.
▷ *verb* **tailgating, tailgated**

tai·lor (tay-lur)
1. *noun* Someone who makes or alters clothes.
▷ *verb* **tailor**
2. *verb* To design or alter something so that it suits someone perfectly. *The computer company will tailor its system to meet our needs.*
▷ **tailoring, tailored**

take (tayk) *verb*
1. To get, seize, or capture something with the hands. *Ken is trying to take my pen.*
2. To move, carry, or remove something. *Take your plate into the kitchen.*
3. To accept something. *Do you take credit cards?*
4. To use something. *This camera takes most types of film.*
5. To receive or to accept. *Dolores took the news well.*
6. To do or perform an action. *Ed takes a shower every night.*
7. To tolerate, or to permit. *My parents don't take disobedience.*
8. To win something. *Sandra took first place in the race.*
9. To lead. *I take my dog for a walk twice a day.*
10. To understand or believe something. *I take it that you are not hungry, because you haven't touched your food.*
11. If you **take after** someone in your family, you look or act like the person.
12. (informal) If you are **taken in** by someone, you believe the lies that the person tells you.
13. If you **take off** something, you remove it.
14. If you **take up** something, you begin it, as in *I am taking up French;* or you shorten it, as in *I will take up the hem of my skirt before the party.*

T

15. If you **take to** something or someone, you like the thing or person.
▷ *verb* **taking, took** (tuk), **taken** (tayk-in)

take·off (tayk-*awf*) *noun* The beginning of a flight, when an aircraft leaves the ground. ▷ *verb* **take off**

take·out (tayk-out) *noun*
1. A restaurant selling meals that you take and eat somewhere else. ▷ *adjective* **take-out**
2. Food that you buy from a take-out restaurant.

take·o·ver (tayk-oh-vur) *noun*
1. If there is a **takeover** of a company, one company buys enough shares of stock in another to control it.
2. If there is a **takeover** of a country, a new group or individual seizes possession or control.
▷ *verb* **take over**

talc (talk) *noun* A soft mineral that is ground up to make talcum powder, face powder, paint, and plastics.

tal·cum powder (tal-kuhm) *noun* A fine, white powder made from talc. You can use talcum powder to dry your body or to make it smell nice.

tale (tayl) *noun*
1. A story, as in *a fairy tale.*
2. A story that is not true; a lie. *Don't tell tales.*
Tale sounds like **tail.**

tal·ent (tal-uhnt) *noun*
1. A natural ability or skill.
2. A person with talent.
▷ *adjective* **talented**

talk (tawk)
1. *verb* To say words; to speak. ▷ *noun* **talker**
2. *verb* To discuss. *Can we talk business?*
3. *verb* To speak to a person or group in a persuasive way. *Lucy talked Charlie into going on the roller coaster.*
4. *noun* A conversation. *We need to have a talk about what happened this morning.*
5. *noun* A speech or a lecture. *My mom is giving a talk to my class about her work as a lawyer.*
▷ *verb* **talking, talked**

talk·a·tive (taw-kuh-tiv) *adjective* If you are **talkative,** you talk a lot.

talk show *noun* A television or radio program in which a host interviews or has discussions with guests, audience members, and callers.

tall (tawl) *adjective*
1. Higher than usual; not short or low, as in *a tall building.*
2. Having a certain height. *She is five feet tall.*
3. Hard to believe; exaggerated, as in *a tall tale.*
▷ *adjective* **taller, tallest**

tal·low (tal-oh) *noun* Fat from cattle and sheep that is used mainly to make candles and soap.

tal·ly (tal-ee)
1. *noun* An account, a record, or a score. *Keep a tally of what I owe you.*

2. *verb* To add up an account, record, or score. *The waiter tallied up our bill. These figures don't quite tally.*
3. *verb* To match, or to agree. *His account of the accident doesn't tally with mine.*
▷ *verb* **tallies, tallying, tallied**

Tal·mud (tal-muhd *or* tal-mud) *noun* The collection of Jewish civil and religious laws.

tal·on (tal-uhn) *noun* A sharp claw of a bird of prey such as an eagle, a hawk, or a falcon. *The picture shows an eagle in flight, with its talons ready to catch its prey.*

eagle
talons—

ta·ma·le (tuh-mah-lee) *noun* A Mexican dish consisting of seasoned chopped meat rolled in cornmeal dough. The mixture is wrapped in husks of corn and steamed.

tam·bou·rine (tam-bur-een) *noun* A small, round musical instrument that is similar to a drum. It has jingling metal disks around the rim and is played by shaking or striking it with the hand. *See* **percussion.**

tame (taym) *adjective*
1. Taken from a wild or natural state and trained to live with or be useful to people. *At the circus we saw a tame elephant that could perform tricks.* ▷ *verb* **tame** ▷ *noun* **tamer**
2. Gentle or not afraid; not shy. *The deer was so tame that it ate food from my hand.*
3. Not very exciting; dull.
▷ *adjective* **tamer, tamest** ▷ *adverb* **tamely**

tam·per (tam-pur) *verb* To interfere with something so that it becomes damaged or broken. ▷ **tampering, tampered**

tan (tan)
1. *noun* A light yellow-brown color. ▷ *adjective* **tan**
2. *noun* If you have a **tan,** your skin has become darker because you have been out in the sun a lot. ▷ *verb* **tan**
3. *verb* To make animal hide into leather by soaking it in a solution containing chemicals found in the bark and wood of many trees.
▷ **tanning, tanned** ▷ *noun* **tannery**

tan·dem (tan-duhm) *noun* A bicycle for two people, with one seat behind the other.

tan·door·i (tan-door-ee) *noun* An Indian method of cooking meat, bread, or any food by baking it in a clay pot.

tan·gent (tan-juhnt) *noun*
1. In geometry, a straight line that touches the edge of a curve in one place. *See* **circle.**
2. If you **go off on a tangent,** you suddenly start talking about something other than the main topic of discussion.

tan·ger·ine (*tan*-juh-**reen**) *noun* A sweet, orange citrus fruit that is smaller than an orange and easier to peel.

tan·gle (tang-guhl) *verb* To twist together in a confused mass; to snarl. ▷ **tangling, tangled** ▷ *noun* **tangle**

tan·gram (tang-gram) *noun* A Chinese puzzle made of a square cut into various shapes that you can put together to make a number of different patterns.

tang·y (tang-ee) *adjective* Having a strong, sharp flavor or odor. *I like the tangy taste of grapefruit.* ▷ **tangier, tangiest** ▷ *noun* **tang**

tank (tangk) *noun*
1. A large container for liquid or gas. *See* **aquarium.**
2. An armored combat vehicle equipped with heavy guns. Most tanks can travel over rough ground because they move on two continuous belts of metal treads.

tank·er (tang-kur) *noun* A ship, a truck, or an airplane that is equipped with tanks for carrying liquids. *The picture shows an oil tanker.*

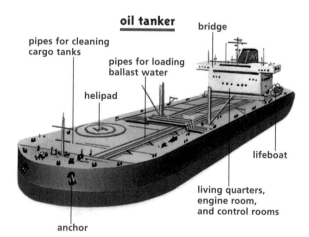

oil tanker

pipes for cleaning cargo tanks
bridge
pipes for loading ballast water
helipad
lifeboat
living quarters, engine room, and control rooms
anchor

tan·trum (tan-truhm) *noun* An outburst of anger or bad temper.

tap (tap)
1. *verb* To hit something gently or lightly. *I tapped on the window.* ▷ *noun* **tap**
2. *noun* A small metal plate attached to the soles of shoes.

3. *verb* To make or do by tapping again and again. *He tapped out a rhythm with his fingers.*
4. *verb* To make a hole in order to draw off a liquid, as in *to tap a maple tree for its sap.*
5. *verb* To listen in on a telephone conversation using a secret device. *The police tapped the suspect's phone.* ▷ *noun* **tap**
6. *noun* A device used to control the flow of a liquid in a pipe; a faucet.
▷ *verb* **tapping, tapped**

tap dancing *noun* Dancing in which shoes with taps are worn to make rhythmical clicking sounds with the feet. ▷ *noun* **tap dancer** ▷ *verb* **tap-dance**

tape (tayp)
1. *noun* A thin strip of material, paper, or plastic, as in *adhesive tape.*
2. *verb* To fasten together, wrap, or bind with tape.
3. *noun* A long piece of magnetic ribbon used for recording sound or pictures. Tape is usually contained in a plastic case, or cassette. *The picture shows an audiocassette tape, which records sound.*
4. *verb* To record sound and/or pictures on tape.
▷ *verb* **taping, taped**

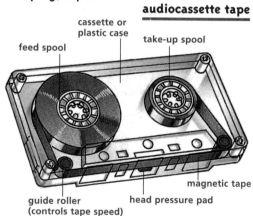

audiocassette tape

cassette or plastic case
feed spool
take-up spool
guide roller (controls tape speed)
head pressure pad
magnetic tape

tape measure *noun* A long, thin piece of ribbon or steel marked in inches or centimeters so that you can measure things easily.

ta·per (tay-pur)
1. *verb* To make or become narrower at one end. *Wendy tapered the legs of her pants.*
2. *verb* To become smaller or less; to diminish. *The storm finally tapered off.*
3. *noun* A slender candle.
Taper sounds like **tapir.**
▷ *verb* **tapering, tapered**

tape recorder *noun* A machine that you use to play back or record music and sound on magnetic tape. ▷ *noun* **tape recording** ▷ *verb* **tape-record**

tap·es·try (tap-uh-stree) *noun* A heavy piece of cloth with pictures or patterns woven into it. *See* **medieval.** ▷ *noun, plural* **tapestries**

ta·pir (tay-pur) *noun* A large animal that has hoofs and a long, flexible snout. The tapir looks like a pig. It is found in Central America, South America, and southern Asia and is distantly related to the horse and rhinoceros. **Tapir** sounds like **taper.**

taps (taps) *noun* A bugle call played at the end of the day in military camps as a signal that all lights must be put out. Taps is also played at military funerals.

tar (tar) *noun* A thick, black, sticky substance used for paving roads and patching roofs. Tar is made from coal or wood. ▷ *verb* **tar**

ta·ran·tu·la (tuh-ran-chuh-luh) *noun* A large, hairy spider found mainly in warm regions. Its bite is painful but not seriously poisonous to people. *See* **spider.**

tar·dy (tar-dee) *adjective* Not on time; late. *Several students were tardy this morning.* ▷ **tardier, tardiest** ▷ *noun* **tardiness**

tar·get (tar-git)
1. *noun* A mark, a circle, or an object that is aimed or shot at. ▷ *verb* **target**
2. *noun* Someone or something that is criticized or made fun of. *My little brother is always the target of Gwen's jokes.*
3. *noun* A goal or an aim.
4. *verb* If you **target** something, you concentrate on it. *The publicity campaign is targeted at a young audience.* ▷ **targeting, targeted**

tar·iff (ta-rif) *noun* A tax charged on goods that are imported or exported.

tar·nish (tar-nish) *verb* If something **tarnishes,** it becomes duller or less bright. ▷ **tarnishes, tarnishing, tarnished** ▷ *noun* **tarnish**

tar·pau·lin (tar-puh-lin) *noun* A heavy, waterproof covering, usually made of canvas, that is used to protect playing fields, boats, or any outdoor item from wet weather. A tarpaulin is also called a *tarp.*

tart (tart)
1. *noun* A small pie or pastry that usually contains fruit.
2. *adjective* If food is **tart,** it tastes sour or sharp.
3. *adjective* A **tart** remark is mean, sharp, or bitter in tone. ▷ *adverb* **tartly**
▷ *adjective* **tarter, tartest** ▷ *noun* **tartness**

tar·tan (tart-uhn) *noun* A type of plaid, or a woolen cloth with a plaid pattern. Tartan is used especially for Scottish kilts.

tar·tar (tar-tur) *noun*
1. A yellow substance that forms on the teeth. Tartar consists of food particles, saliva, and calcium. If not removed, it becomes hard.

2. tartar sauce A sauce made with mayonnaise and chopped pickles, often served with fish.

task (task) *noun* A piece of work to be done, especially work assigned by another person; a job or duty.

task force *noun* A group formed for a limited period of time to deal with a specific problem.

tas·sel (tass-uhl) *noun*
1. A bunch of threads tied at one end and used as a decoration on shoes, clothing, graduation caps, furniture, or rugs.
2. Something that is like a tassel, such as the tassel of silk on an ear of corn.
▷ *adjective* **tasseled**

taste (tayst)
1. *noun* Your sense of **taste** allows you to identify a food by its taste, or flavor.
2. *noun* The **taste** of a food is its flavor; for example, sweet, sour, salty, or bitter. ▷ *adjective* **tasty**
3. *noun* If you have good **taste,** you make good choices of furnishings, clothes, etc. ▷ *adjective* **tasteful**
4. *verb* To have a certain flavor. *Sugar tastes sweet.*
5. *verb* To try a bit of food or drink to see if you like it. *Would you like to taste this soup that I made?* ▷ *noun* **taste**
▷ *verb* **tasting, tasted**

taste bud *noun* One of the clusters of cells in the tongue that sense whether something is sweet, sour, salty, or bitter.

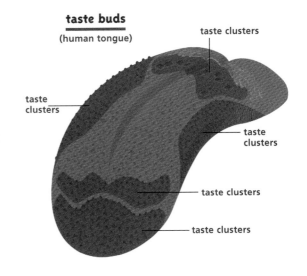

taste buds
(human tongue)

taste clusters

taste clusters

taste clusters

taste clusters

taste clusters

taste·less (tayst-liss) *adjective*
1. Having little or no flavor; bland. *This plain oatmeal is tasteless.*
2. Showing little sense of what is appropriate; lacking tact; rude, as in *a tasteless remark.*

tat·tered (tat-urd) *adjective* Old and torn, as in *a tattered jacket.*

tat·tle (tat-uhl) *verb* To tell someone in authority that someone else is doing something wrong. ▷ **tattling, tattled** ▷ *noun* **tattler**

tat·tle·tale (tat-uhl-*tale*) *noun* A **tattletale** is someone who tells other people's secrets.

tat·too (ta-too) *noun* A picture or phrase that has been printed onto somebody's skin with pigments and needles. ▷ *verb* **tattoo**

taunt (tawnt) *verb* To try to make someone angry or upset by teasing him or her. *The gang taunted George with jokes about his height.* ▷ **taunting, taunted** ▷ *noun* **taunt**

taut (tawt) *adjective* Stretched tight, as in *a taut rope.* ▷ **tauter, tautest**

tav·ern (tav-urn) *noun*
1. A place where people can sit and drink alcoholic beverages; a bar.
2. An inn.

taw·ny (taw-nee) *adjective* Having a light, sandy-brown color, as in *a tawny lion.* ▷ **tawnier, tawniest**

tax (taks)
1. *noun* Money that people and businesses must pay in order to support a government, as in *a sales tax* or *an income tax.* ▷ *noun, plural* **taxes** ▷ *noun* **taxation** ▷ *verb* **tax**
2. *verb* To make heavy demands on; to strain. *His rude behavior taxed my patience.* ▷ **taxes, taxing, taxed** ▷ *adjective* **taxing**

tax·i (tak-see)
1. *noun* A car with a driver whom you pay to take you where you want to go.
2. *verb* When planes **taxi,** they move along the ground before taking off or after landing. ▷ **taxies, taxiing, taxied**

T cell (tee) *noun* Any of a group of cells found in the lymph glands that help protect the body against disease.

tea (tee) *noun*
1. A drink made from the leaves of a shrub that is grown in China, Japan, and India.
2. This shrub or its dried leaves.
3. A similar drink made from the leaves of other plants, as in *herb tea.*
4. A light afternoon meal.
5. A late-afternoon social gathering at which tea and other refreshments are served.

teach (teech) *verb* To give a lesson, or to show someone how to do something. *Joel is going to teach me how to swim.* ▷ **teaches, teaching, taught** (tawt) ▷ *noun* **teacher**

tea·ket·tle (tee-*ket*-uhl) *noun* A kettle with a handle and a spout. A teakettle is used for boiling water.

teal (teel) *noun*
1. Any of several small ducks with short necks. Teal live in rivers and marshes. The males often have brightly colored feathers.
2. A dark color between green and blue.
▷ *adjective* **teal**
▷ *noun, plural* **teal** *or* **teals**

teal

team (teem)
1. *noun* A group of people who work together or play a sport together, as in *a team of doctors* or *a hockey team.* ▷ *noun* **teamwork**
2. *noun* Two or more horses or oxen that are harnessed together to do work.
3. *verb* If two or more people **team up,** they join together to do something. ▷ **teaming, teamed** **Team** sounds like **teem.**

team·mate (teem-*mate*) *noun* A fellow member of a team.

tear
1. (tihr) *noun* A drop of clear, salty liquid that comes from your eye. ▷ *adjective* **tearful**
2. (tair) *noun* A rip in a piece of paper or other substance.
3. (tair) *verb* To pull or be pulled apart by force. *Tear the paper into strips. This material tears easily.*
4. (tair) *verb* To make a hole in by pulling; to rip. *I tore my pants on a nail.*
5. (tair) *verb* To move very quickly. *Louise tore down the street.*
▷ *verb* **tearing, tore** (tor), **torn** (torn)

tease (teez) *verb* To mock someone by playfully saying unkind and hurtful things to the person; to kid. ▷ **teasing, teased** ▷ *noun* **tease,** *noun* **teaser**

tea·spoon (tee-*spoon*) *noun* A small spoon that you use for stirring liquids or as a measure in cooking. A teaspoon equals $\frac{1}{3}$ tablespoon. ▷ *noun* **teaspoonful**

tech·ni·cal (tek-nuh-kuhl) *adjective*
1. To do with science, engineering, or the mechanical or industrial arts. *At a technical school, you can learn how to be an electrician, an auto mechanic, or a dental assistant.*

2. Using words that only experts in a particular field or subject understand. *The conversation about computers became very technical.*
▷ *adverb* **technically**

tech·ni·cian (tek-**nish**-uhn) *noun* Someone who works with specialized equipment or does practical laboratory work, as in *a lighting technician* or *a dental technician.*

tech·nique (tek-**neek**) *noun* A method or way of doing something that requires skill, as in the arts, sports, or the sciences.

tech·nol·o·gy (tek-**nol**-uh-jee) *noun* The use of science and engineering to do practical things, such as make businesses and factories more efficient.
▷ *noun, plural* **technologies**
▷ *adjective* **technological** (tek-noh-**log**-i-kuhl)

ted·dy bear (**ted**-ee) *noun* A stuffed toy bear made from soft, furry material.

teddy bear

Word History
• •

Morris Michtom, a candy store owner from Brooklyn, New York, made the first **teddy bear** in 1902 as a tribute to President Theodore "Teddy" Roosevelt. When he heard that Roosevelt had refused to shoot a small, helpless bear cub on one of his hunting trips, Michtom decided to name his brown stuffed bears after the president.

te·di·ous (**tee**-dee-uhss *or* **tee**-juhss) *adjective* Tiring and boring. *Working on an assembly line is a tedious job.* ▷ *adverb* **tediously**

teem (teem) *verb*
1. To be very full; to swarm. *The jungle was teeming with insects.*
2. To rain very hard; to pour.
Teem sounds like **team.**

teen·ag·er (**teen**-ayj-ur) *noun* A person who is between the ages of 13 and 19. ▷ *adjective* **teenage** *or* **teenaged**

teens (teenz) *noun, plural* The years of a person's life between 13 and 19. *Tanya is in her teens.*

tee·pee (**tee**-pee) Another spelling of **tepee.**

teeth (teeth) *noun, plural* The white, bony parts of the mouth that are used for biting and chewing food. *The diagram shows a lower set of adult teeth.*

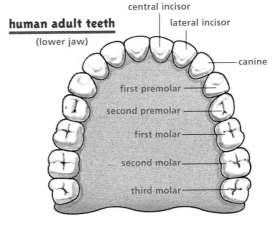

human adult teeth (lower jaw)

central incisor
lateral incisor
canine
first premolar
second premolar
first molar
second molar
third molar

teethe (teeTH) *verb* If a baby is **teething,** new teeth are coming through his or her gums.
▷ **teething, teethed**

Tef·lon (**tef**-lon) *noun* The trademark for a synthetic coating used on cooking utensils to prevent sticking.

Prefix
• •

The prefix **tele-** means "far away" in Greek. You can see this form in many words, including *telegraph* (a device that lets you send messages far away), *telephone* (a machine that lets you talk to someone far away), and *telescope* (an instrument that allows you to see images that are far away).

tel·e·cast (**tel**-uh-*kast*) *noun* A program broadcast by television. ▷ *verb* **telecast**

tel·e·com·mu·ni·ca·tion (*tel*-uh-kuh-myoo-nuh-**kay**-shuhn) *noun*
1. The science that deals with the sending of messages over long distances by telephone, satellite, radio, and other electronic means. Also called *telecommunications.*
2. Any message sent this way.
See **satellite.**

tel·e·com·mute (*tel*-uh-kuh-**myoot**) *verb* To do your work by staying at home and communicating with your office by means of a computer with a modem, a fax machine, or any other form of electronic communication.
▷ **telecommuting, telecommuted** ▷ *noun* **telecommuter**

tel·e·gram (**tel**-uh-*gram*) *noun* A message that is sent by telegraph. ▷ *verb* **telegram**

T

tel·e·graph (tel-uh-*graf*) *noun* A device or system for sending messages over long distances. It uses a code of electrical signals sent by wire or radio. The telegraph was invented by Samuel Morse in 1837. ▷ *noun* **telegrapher** (tuh-**leg**-ruh-fur) ▷ *verb* **telegraph**

tel·e·mar·ket·ing (*tel*-uh-**mar**-kuh-ting) *noun* The selling of goods and services by telephone.

te·lem·e·try (tuh-**lem**-uh-tree) *noun* The use of radio waves to transmit and record information about pressure, speed, or temperature from a measuring instrument.

tel·e·phone (tel-uh-*fone*) *noun*
1. A system for sending sounds over distances by changing them into electrical signals. The signals are sent by wires or radio waves and then changed back into sounds.
2. A device for sending and receiving sounds, especially speech, in this way. The telephone was invented by Alexander Graham Bell in 1876. ▷ *verb* **telephone**

tel·e·pho·to lens (*tel*-uh-**foh**-toh) *noun* A camera lens that makes distant objects seem larger and closer.

tel·e·scope (tel-uh-*skope*) *noun* An instrument that makes distant objects seem larger and closer. Telescopes are used especially for studying the stars and other heavenly bodies. *The picture shows a refracting telescope and a diagram of how light travels through it.* ▷ *adjective* **telescopic** (*tel*-uh-**skop**-ik)

tel·e·vise (tel-uh-*vize*) *verb* To broadcast by television. ▷ **televising, televised**

tel·e·vi·sion (tel-uh-**vizh**-uhn) *noun*
1. A piece of equipment with a screen that receives and shows moving pictures with sound.
2. The sending of sounds and moving pictures along radio waves to be picked up by a television set. *The diagram shows in simplified form how moving pictures are produced inside a television cathode-ray tube. Radio waves are changed into electrical signals that cause beams of electrons to sweep continuously across a fluorescent screen. As the beams hit the screen's phosphor stripes, they create constantly changing dots of colored light, which the viewer sees as moving images.*

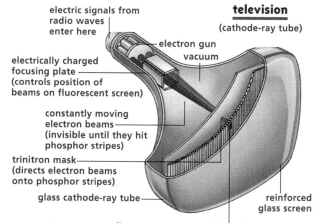

television
(cathode-ray tube)

electric signals from radio waves enter here

electron gun

vacuum

electrically charged focusing plate (controls position of beams on fluorescent screen)

constantly moving electron beams (invisible until they hit phosphor stripes)

trinitron mask (directs electron beams onto phosphor stripes)

glass cathode-ray tube

reinforced glass screen

fluorescent screen of phosphor stripes (stripes glow when hit by electron beams)

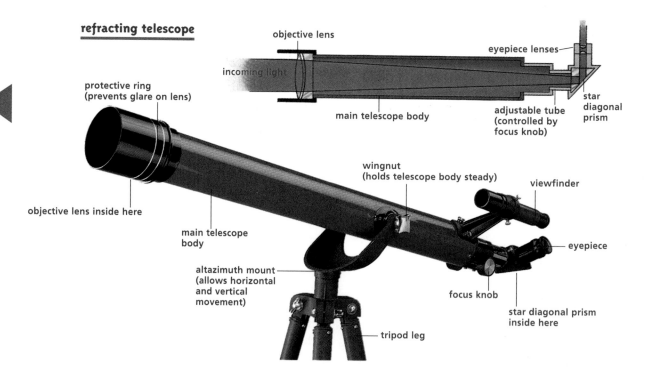

refracting telescope

objective lens

eyepiece lenses

incoming light

main telescope body

adjustable tube (controlled by focus knob)

star diagonal prism

protective ring (prevents glare on lens)

wingnut (holds telescope body steady)

viewfinder

objective lens inside here

main telescope body

eyepiece

altazimuth mount (allows horizontal and vertical movement)

focus knob

star diagonal prism inside here

tripod leg

T

tell (tel) *verb*
1. To put into words; to say. *Please tell the truth.*
2. To give the story; to report or describe. *Tell me what really happened.*
3. To show something. *The red light tells you that the engine is too hot.*
4. To order or to command. *The librarian told us to lower our voices.*
5. To recognize or to identify. *It was hard to tell who it was in the dark.*
6. If you **tell** someone **off,** you scold the person because he or she has done something wrong.
7. If you **tell on** someone, you report to someone else what that person has done.
▷ *verb* **telling, told** (tohld)

tel·ler (tel-ur) *noun*
1. Someone who tells or relates stories.
2. A bank employee who gives out and receives money.

tem·per (tem-pur)
1. *noun* A tendency to get angry. *He has quite a temper.*
2. *noun* A person's usual state of mind; disposition. *A person with an even temper rarely gets upset.*
3. *noun* A calm state of mind; self-control. *She lost her temper and started screaming at everyone.*
4. *verb* To make less harsh; to moderate. *Please temper your anger.*
5. *verb* To make hard or strong, as in *to temper steel.*
▷ *verb* **tempering, tempered**

tem·per·a·ment (tem-pur-uh-muhnt) *noun* Your nature or personality; the way you usually think, act, or respond to other people or to situations. *Laura has a calm temperament.*

tem·per·a·men·tal (tem-pur-uh-men-tuhl) *adjective* Moody, unpredictable, or too sensitive. *Since his best friend moved away, Alex has been very temperamental.* ▷ *adverb* **temperamentally**

tem·per·ate (tem-pur-it) *adjective* If an area has a **temperate** climate, it has neither very high nor very low temperatures.

tem·per·a·ture (tem-pur-uh-chur) *noun*
1. The degree of heat or cold in something, usually measured by a thermometer.
2. If you have a **temperature,** your body is hotter than normal because you are ill. Normal human body temperature is generally around 98.6 degrees Fahrenheit.

tem·pest (tem-pist) *noun*
1. A violent storm.
2. A violent or noisy commotion; an uproar.

tem·plate (tem-plate) *noun*
1. A shape or pattern that you draw or cut around to make the same shape in paper, metal, material, etc. *Josh used a template to draw a triangle. See* **geometry.**

2. In computers, a document or pattern that is used to create similar documents. For example, a magazine designer could use a template for a page that follows the same general format from issue to issue.

tem·ple (tem-puhl) *noun*
1. The flat area on either side of the forehead, above the cheek and in front of the ear.
2. A building used for worship. *This reconstruction of the Parthenon, a temple dedicated to the Greek goddess Athena, shows how it would have looked in the 5th century* B.C.

The Parthenon, Athens, Greece

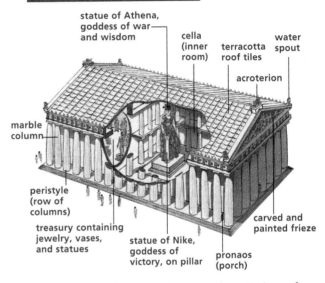

statue of Athena, goddess of war and wisdom — cella (inner room) — terracotta roof tiles — water spout — acroterion — marble column — peristyle (row of columns) — treasury containing jewelry, vases, and statues — statue of Nike, goddess of victory, on pillar — pronaos (porch) — carved and painted frieze

tem·po (tem-poh) *noun* The speed or timing of a piece of music. ▷ *noun, plural* **tempos** *or* **tempi** (tem-pee)

tem·po·rar·y (tem-puh-*rer*-ee) *adjective* If something is **temporary,** it lasts for only a short time. ▷ *adverb* **temporarily**

tempt (tempt) *verb*
1. If you **tempt** someone, you try to get the person to do or want something that is wrong or foolish. ▷ *noun* **tempter** ▷ *adjective* **tempting**
2. To appeal strongly to; to attract. *His offer tempts me.*
▷ *verb* **tempting, tempted**

temp·ta·tion (temp-tay-shuhn) *noun*
1. Something that you want to have or do, although you know it is wrong. *Ben overcame the temptation of continuing to play ball because he wanted to get home to do his homework.*
2. The act of being tempted.

ten (ten) *noun* The whole number, written 10, that comes after 9 and before 11. ▷ *adjective* **ten**

ten·ant (ten-uhnt) *noun* Someone who rents a room, a house, an apartment, an office, or land that belongs to someone else.

553

tend (tend) *verb*
1. If something **tends** to happen, it often or usually happens.
2. If you **tend** a person, an animal, or a plant, you take care of it.
▷ *verb* **tending, tended**

ten·den·cy (ten-duhn-see) *noun* If you have a **tendency** to do something, you often or usually do it. ▷ *noun, plural* **tendencies**

ten·der (ten-dur) *adjective*
1. Sore or painful. *Sal's bruises were still tender.*
2. Soft. *The steak was so tender, I was able to cut it with my fork.*
3. Gentle and kind. *She gave the new baby a tender kiss.* ▷ *adverb* **tenderly**
▷ *noun* **tenderness**

ten·don (ten-duhn) *noun* A strong, thick cord or band of tissue that joins a muscle to a bone or other body part. *See* **muscle.**

ten·e·ment (ten-uh-muhnt) *noun* A run-down apartment building, especially one that is crowded and in a poor part of a city.

ten·nis (ten-iss) *noun* A game played on a court by two or four players who use rackets to hit a ball over a net.

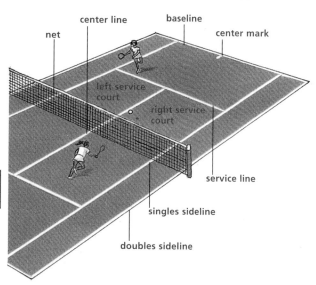

tennis court

center line
baseline
net
center mark
left service court
right service court
service line
singles sideline
doubles sideline

ten·or (ten-ur) *noun*
1. A male singing voice that is quite high.
▷ *adjective* **tenor**
2. A singer with a tenor voice.

tense (tenss)
1. *adjective* If you are **tense,** you are nervous or worried. *Miriam is always tense before an exam.*
▷ *adverb* **tensely**
2. *adjective* Stretched tight and stiff. *Your muscles will be tense if you don't warm up before a game.*

3. *noun* A form of a verb that shows whether an action happened in the past, is happening in the present, or will happen in the future. *I was, I am,* and *I will be* are examples of the past, present, and future tenses of the verb *to be.*
▷ *noun* **tenseness** ▷ *verb* **tense** ▷ *adjective* **tenser, tensest**

ten·sion (ten-shuhn) *noun*
1. A feeling of worry, nervousness, or suspense. *Tension mounted as the votes were counted.*
2. The tightness or stiffness of a rope, wire, etc. *The tension of a guitar string determines, in part, the sound that the string makes.*
3. If there is **tension** between two people, there is difficulty or strain in their relationship.

tent (tent) *noun* A portable shelter made of nylon or canvas supported by poles and ropes.

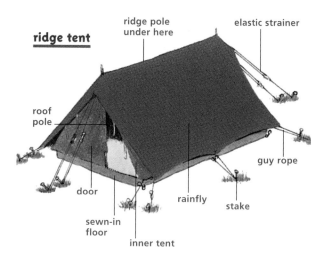

ridge tent

ridge pole under here
elastic strainer
roof pole
guy rope
door
rainfly
stake
sewn-in floor
inner tent

ten·ta·cle (ten-tuh-kuhl) *noun* One of the long, flexible limbs of some animals, such as the octopus and squid. Tentacles are used for moving, feeling, and grasping. *See* **jellyfish, octopus, slug, squid.**

ten·ta·tive (ten-tuh-tiv) *adjective* Hesitant or unsure. *Nick made a tentative attempt to join in the game.* ▷ *adverb* **tentatively**

ten·ter·hooks (ten-tur-*huks*) *noun, plural* If you are **on tenterhooks,** you are in suspense waiting for something to happen.

tenth (tenth)
1. *noun* One part of something that has been divided into 10 equal parts, written $\frac{1}{10}$.
2. *adjective* That which comes after ninth and before eleventh.
3. *noun* In decimal notation, the position to the right of the decimal point is known as **tenths place.** In the number 4.0129, the digit 0 is in tenths place.

T

ten·u·ous (ten-yoo-uhss) *adjective* Not very strong or substantial; shaky. *He had a tenuous grasp of the test material.* ▷ *adverb* **tenuously**

te·pee (tee-*pee*) *noun* A tent shaped like a cone and made from animal skins by North American Indians.

tepee

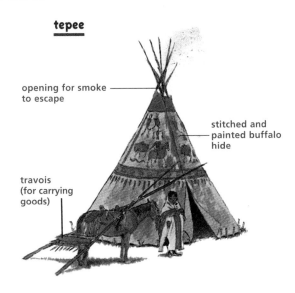

- opening for smoke to escape
- stitched and painted buffalo hide
- travois (for carrying goods)

tep·id (tep-id) *adjective* Slightly warm; lukewarm.

ter·i·ya·ki (ter-ee-yah-kee) *noun* A Japanese dish of chicken, meat, or fish that has been soaked in soy sauce and broiled or grilled.

term (turm) *noun*
1. A word with a specific meaning in some particular field, as in *musical terms* or *computer terms.*
2. A definite or limited period of time. *A president's term of office is four years.*
3. A part of the school year.
4. **terms** *noun, plural* The conditions of an agreement, a contract, a will, or a sale.
5. **terms** *noun, plural* A relationship between people. *After the argument, we were on good terms again.*

ter·mi·nal (tur-muh-nuhl)
1. *noun* A station at either end of a transportation line, as in *an airport terminal.*
2. *noun* A computer keyboard and screen linked to a network.
3. *adjective* If someone has a **terminal** illness, he or she cannot be cured and will die from it.
4. **Terminal velocity** is the maximum speed an object can reach falling through the air. ▷ *adverb* **terminally**

ter·mi·nate (tur-muh-nate) *verb* To stop or to end. *The train terminates here. We decided to terminate our agreement.* ▷ **terminating, terminated**

ter·mite (tur-mite) *noun* An antlike insect that eats wood. Termites build large mounds, where they live together in colonies. *The picture shows the inside of a termite mound.*

termite mound

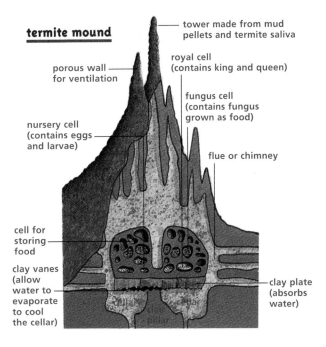

- tower made from mud pellets and termite saliva
- royal cell (contains king and queen)
- porous wall for ventilation
- fungus cell (contains fungus grown as food)
- nursery cell (contains eggs and larvae)
- flue or chimney
- cell for storing food
- clay vanes (allow water to evaporate to cool the cellar)
- clay plate (absorbs water)

ter·race (ter-iss) *noun*
1. A paved, open area next to a house; a patio.
2. A balcony of an apartment building.
3. A raised, flat platform of land with sloping sides.
▷ *adjective* **terraced**

ter·ra-cot·ta (ter-uh kot-uh) *noun* A hard, waterproof clay used in making pottery and roofs. ▷ *adjective* **terra-cotta**

ter·rain (tuh-rayn) *noun* Ground, or land. *The terrain was very rocky.*

ter·ra·pin (ter-uh-pin) *noun*
A North American turtle that lives in or near fresh water or along seashores. *The picture shows a diamondback terrapin from the East Coast of the United States. The diamondback gets its name from the shapes on its shell.*

terrapin

ter·rar·i·um (tuh-rer-ee-uhm) *noun* A glass or plastic container for growing small plants or raising small land animals. ▷ *noun, plural* **terrariums** or **terraria** (tuh-rer-ee-uh)

ter·res·tri·al (tuh-**ress**-tree-uhl) *adjective* To do with the earth, or living on the earth. *Humans are terrestrial creatures.*

ter·ri·ble (ter-uh-buhl) *adjective*
1. Causing great fear or terror, as in *a terrible flood* or *a terrible roar.*
2. Very great; extreme or severe, as in *terrible suffering* or *terrible heat.*
3. Very bad or unpleasant, as in *a terrible movie.*
▷ *adverb* **terribly**

ter·ri·er (ter-ee-ur) *noun* Any of several breeds of small, lively dogs that were originally bred for hunting small animals that live in burrows.

West Highland white terriers

> ## Word History
>
> •
>
> The **terrier** got its name from *terra,* the Latin word for "earth." Terriers are common house pets today, but originally these dogs helped hunters by digging into burrows, or holes in the earth, to drive out the animals inside.

ter·ri·fic (tuh-**rif**-ik) *adjective*
1. Very good or excellent; wonderful, as in *a terrific idea.*
2. Very great; extreme or severe. *Rod set off at a terrific speed.*
3. Causing great fear or terror. *We had a terrific windstorm last night.*
▷ *adverb* **terrifically**

ter·ri·fy (ter-uh-fye) *verb* To frighten greatly; to fill someone with terror. ▷ **terrifies, terrifying, terrified** ▷ *adjective* **terrifying** ▷ *adverb* **terrifyingly**

ter·ri·to·ry (ter-uh-tor-ee) *noun*
1. Any large area of land; a region, as in *enemy territory.*

2. The land and waters under the control of a state, nation, or ruler.
3. A part of the United States not admitted as a state.
▷ *noun, plural* **territories** ▷ *adjective* **territorial**

ter·ror (ter-ur) *noun*
1. Very great fear.
2. A person or thing that causes very great fear.

ter·ror·ist (ter-ur-ist) *noun* Someone who uses violence and threats to frighten people into obeying. ▷ *noun* **terrorism**

ter·ror·ize (ter-uh-*rize*) *verb* To frighten someone a great deal. ▷ **terrorizing, terrorized**

terse (turss) *adjective* Brief and abrupt. *When I asked Aunt Susan her age, she gave a very terse reply.* ▷ **terser, tersest**

tes·sel·late (tess-uh-late) *verb* When shapes **tessellate,** they fit together exactly on a flat surface, without leaving gaps. *The picture shows how hexagons tessellate.*
▷ **tessellating, tessellated** ▷ *noun* **tessellation** ▷ *adjective* **tessellated**

tessellating shapes

test (test)
1. *noun* A set of questions, problems, or tasks used to measure your knowledge or skill.
2. *noun* A way of studying something to find out what it is like, what it contains, or how good it is, as in *a road test, a blood test,* or *an eye test.*
3. *verb* To try something out. *Sam tested the rice to find out if it was cooked.* ▷ **testing, tested**

tes·ta·ment (tess-tuh-muhnt) *noun*
1. A written statement of what you believe.
2. **Testament** Either of the two main divisions of the Christian Bible, the New Testament or the Old Testament.

tes·ti·fy (tess-tuh-fye) *verb* To state the truth, or to give evidence in a court of law. ▷ **testifies, testifying, testified**

tes·ti·mo·ny (tess-tuh-*moh*-nee) *noun* A statement given by a witness who is under oath in a court of law. ▷ *noun, plural* **testimonies**

test pilot *noun* A pilot who flies new airplanes in order to test them for safety and strength.

test tube *noun* A narrow glass tube that is closed at one end. Test tubes are used in laboratory tests and experiments. *See* **apparatus.**

T

tet·a·nus (tet-nuhss) *noun* A serious disease caused by bacteria getting into a cut or wound. Tetanus makes your muscles, especially those in your jaw, become very stiff. It can be fatal. Another word for tetanus is **lockjaw.**

teth·er (teTH-ur) *noun*
1. A rope or chain that is used to tie up an animal so that it cannot move far. ▷ *verb* **tether**
2. If you are **at the end of your tether,** you have run out of patience or energy.

Tex-Mex (teks meks) *adjective* To do with a style of cooking or music that originated in southern Texas and combines Mexican and American culture.

text (tekst) *noun*
1. The main section of writing in a book, other than the pictures or index.
2. The original or exact words of a speaker or writer.
3. The topic or theme of a piece of writing or a speech.
4. A textbook.
5. In a computer word processing program, data in the form of words and sentences, as opposed to art, graphs, and so on.

text·book (tekst-buk) *noun* A book used to teach and study a subject.

tex·tile (tek-stuhl *or* tek-stile) *noun* A fabric or cloth that has been woven or knitted.

tex·ture (teks-chur) *noun* The look and feel of something, especially its roughness or smoothness.

than (THan) *conjunction*
1. In comparison with. *She is taller than I am.*
2. Except; besides. *Can we elect someone other than those nominated?*

thank (thangk)
1. *verb* To tell someone that you are grateful. *We thanked him for the ride.*
2. *verb* To blame or to hold responsible. *We have her to thank for this terrible mess.*
3. thanks *interjection* An expression showing that you are grateful.
4. thanks *noun, plural* Gratitude. *We expressed our thanks.*
▷ *verb* **thanking, thanked**

thank·ful (thangk-fuhl) *adjective* Glad, or grateful. *Helena was thankful for dry clothing after the flood.* ▷ *adverb* **thankfully**

thank·less (thangk-liss) *adjective*
1. Not appreciated. *Cleaning up after my dog is a thankless job.*
2. Not likely to give thanks or show gratitude, as in *a thankless child.*

Thanks·giv·ing Day (thangks-giv-ing) *noun*
1. A holiday observed in the United States on the fourth Thursday in November. It commemorates the first Pilgrims' harvest feast, which was held in 1621. This holiday is set apart for giving thanks and feasting.
2. A similar holiday observed in Canada on the second Monday in October.

that (THat)
1. *pronoun* A person or thing mentioned or indicated. *That was a delicious cake.*
2. *pronoun* A thing farther away than or contrasted with another thing. *This is a chocolate cake, and that is a carrot cake.*
3. *pronoun* Used to introduce a clause that defines a word before it. In the sentence *I took a bite of the cake that he baked,* "that he baked" defines which cake is meant.
4. *adjective* Used to indicate a person, place, or thing present or already mentioned. *He made that cake yesterday.*
5. *adjective* Used to indicate a person or thing farther away than or contrasted with another thing. *This cake is his, and that one is mine.*
6. *conjunction* Used to show reason or cause. *I'm sorry that you can't try the chocolate cake.*
7. *conjunction* Used to introduce a clause in a sentence. *She thinks that she will try every cake on the table.*
8. *conjunction* Used to indicate a result. *We ate so much cake that we couldn't even think about eating dinner.*
9. *adverb* To that extent; so. *Was the cake really that good?*
▷ *pronoun, plural* **those** ▷ *adjective, plural* **those**

thatch (thach) *noun* A roof covering made from straw or reeds. *The picture shows some features of a roof made of thatch.* ▷ *noun, plural* **thatches** ▷ *verb* **thatch** ▷ *adjective* **thatched**

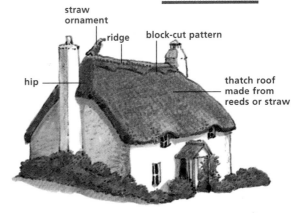

thatched cottage

straw ornament
ridge
block-cut pattern
hip
thatch roof made from reeds or straw

that's (THats) *contraction* A short form of *that is.* "*That's the best offer I've had all day,*" I said.

thaw (thaw)
  1. *verb* To melt.
  2. *verb* To become room temperature after being frozen. *Leave the turkey to thaw overnight.*
  3. *noun* A time when snow and ice melt because the weather has become warmer.
  ▷ *verb* **thawing, thawed**

the (THuh *or* THee)
  1. *definite article* Used before a noun or noun phrase that stands for a particular or previously mentioned person or thing. *The chair in the hall is an antique.*
  2. *definite article* Used to show that a thing is the only one of it there is, as in *the Colosseum* or *the Mississippi River.*
  3. *definite article* Used to show that a person or thing is thought of as the best, most important, or greatest, and therefore one of a kind. *It was the movie to see last year.*
  4. *definite article* Used to make a singular noun general. *The hippopotamus lives in central and southern Africa.*
  5. *adverb* To that degree; that much; by that much. *I'd like to see you—the sooner the better.*

the·a·ter *or* **the·a·tre** (thee-uh-tur) *noun*
  1. A building where plays or movies are shown.
  2. The work of writing, producing, or acting in plays.

the·at·ri·cal (thee-at-ruh-kuhl) *adjective*
  1. To do with the theater, as in *theatrical costumes.*
  2. If something is **theatrical,** it is done in an exaggerated way to create a dramatic effect.

thee (THee) *pronoun* An old word for **you.**

theft (theft) *noun* The act of stealing. *Keith is being punished for theft.*

their (THair) *adjective* Belonging to or to do with them. *Have the students brought their books?* **Their** sounds like **there** and **they're.**

theirs (THairz) *pronoun* The one or ones belonging to or to do with them. *That idea was theirs.*

them (THem) *pronoun* **Them** is the form of **they** that is used as the object of a verb or preposition. *Do you see them? The gift is from them.*

theme (theem) *noun*
  1. The main subject or idea of a piece of writing or a talk. *The theme of this book is that good triumphs over evil.*
  2. A short essay or piece of writing on one subject.
  3. The main melody in a piece of music.
  4. theme park A park with rides and attractions based on a subject, such as space travel.

them·selves (THuhm-selvz) *pronoun*
  1. Them and no one else; their own selves. *The children dressed themselves. They blamed themselves.*

2. Their usual or true selves. *They're not themselves today.*

then (THen)
  1. *adverb* At that time. *I didn't know Emily then.*
  2. *adverb* After that; next. *Eat first, then talk.*
  3. *adverb* In that case; therefore. *If you can't go, then give the ticket to me.*
  4. *noun* That time. *Justine's family eats dinner at 6:30 so we have to get to her house by then.*

the·ol·o·gy (thee-ol-uh-jee) *noun* The study of religion and religious beliefs. ▷ *adjective* **theological**

the·o·rem (thee-ur-uhm *or* thihr-uhm) *noun* A statement, especially in mathematics, that can be proved to be true.

the·o·ry (thee-ur-ee *or* thihr-ee) *noun*
  1. An idea or a statement that explains how or why something happens, as in *the theory of evolution.*
  2. An idea or opinion based on some facts or evidence but not proved. *The police have a theory about who robbed the bank.*
  3. The rules and principles of an art or a science, rather than its practice. *I'm taking a class on music theory.*
  4. If something should happen **in theory,** you expect it to happen but it may not.
  ▷ *adjective* **theoretical** ▷ *adverb* **theoretically**

ther·a·py (ther-uh-pee) *noun* A treatment for an illness, an injury, or a disability, as in *art therapy* or *speech therapy.* ▷ *noun, plural* **therapies** ▷ *noun* **therapist**

there (THair)
  1. *adverb* To, in, or at that place. *Let's not go there again.*
  2. *pronoun* A word used to introduce a sentence in which the verb comes before the subject. *There is a man at the door.*
  3. *noun* That place. *Let's meet at the diner and leave from there.*
  There sounds like **their** and **they're.**

there·af·ter (*THair*-af-tur) *adverb* Afterward; after that; from that time on. *It rained for 40 days, but it was sunny every day thereafter.*

there·by (THair-*bye* *or* THair-**bye**) *adverb* In that way; by that means. *We stopped watching TV, thereby giving ourselves more time to talk.*

there·fore (THair-*for*) *adverb* As a result; for that reason. *Stanley is ill; therefore Joe must take his place.*

therm (thurm) *noun* A unit for measuring heat.

ther·mal (thur-muhl)
  1. *adjective* To do with heat or holding in heat. *I wear thermal underwear when I go skiing.*
  2. *noun* A rising current of warm air.

T

ther·mom·e·ter (thur-**mom**-uh-tur) *noun* An instrument used to measure temperature. *The picture shows a clinical thermometer, which is used to measure body temperature. The bulb is usually placed under the tongue, and as the mercury heats up, it expands and rises up the tube.*

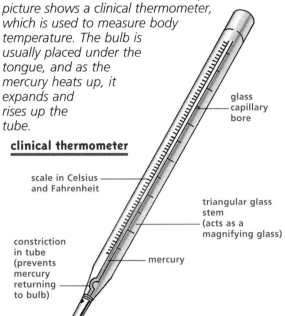

clinical thermometer

scale in Celsius and Fahrenheit

glass capillary bore

triangular glass stem (acts as a magnifying glass)

constriction in tube (prevents mercury returning to bulb)

mercury

thin-walled glass bulb

ther·mos bottle (thur-**muhss**) *noun* A container that keeps liquids hot or cold for many hours. The vacuum between its two glass walls prevents heat or cold from escaping.

thermos

(cross section)

cup
stopper
outer glass wall
vacuum
inner glass wall
liquid
body
tip protector

Word History

In 1892 Sir James Dewar, a Scottish chemist, made the first **thermos bottle** to store liquid gases at low temperatures. This container was called a Dewar Flask after its inventor until a company began to sell a version of it to the public. The bottle got its new name, thermos, from the name of the company that sold it.

ther·mo·stat (thur-muh-*stat*) *noun* A device that senses temperature changes and turns on switches that control furnaces, refrigerators, air conditioners, and other heating and cooling systems. *See* **refrigerator.**

the·sau·rus (thi-**sor**-uhss) *noun* A book containing lists of synonyms and antonyms.
▷ *noun, plural* **thesauri** (thi-**sor**-eye) *or* **thesauruses**

these (THeez) *pronoun, plural* The plural of **this.** *I'll buy these.* ▷ *adjective, plural* **these**

the·sis (**thee**-siss) *noun* An idea or argument that is to be debated or proved. ▷ *noun, plural* **theses** (**thee**-seez)

they (THay) *pronoun*
1. The people, animals, or things mentioned before. *My parents said that they couldn't come.*
2. People in general. *They say that it will snow.*

they'd (THayd) *contraction* A short form of *they had* or *they would.*

they'll (THay-uhl) *contraction* A short form of *they will* or *they shall.*

they're (THair) *contraction* A short form of *they are.* **They're** sounds like **their** and **there.**

they've (THayv) *contraction* A short form of *they have. They've got a lot to learn about teamwork.*

thick (thik) *adjective*
1. Great in width or depth; not thin, as in *a thick wall.*
2. As measured from one side or surface to the other. *This wall is one foot thick.*
3. Growing, being, or having parts that are close together; dense, as in *thick hair* or *a thick forest.*
4. Not flowing or pouring easily, as in *thick soup.*
▷ *adjective* **thicker, thickest** ▷ *noun* **thickness**
▷ *verb* **thicken** ▷ *adverb* **thick,** *adverb* **thickly**

thick·et (**thik**-it) *noun* A thick growth of plants, bushes, or small trees.

thief (theef) *noun* Someone who steals things.
▷ *noun, plural* **thieves** (theevz) ▷ *verb* **thieve** (theev) ▷ *adjective* **thieving**

thigh (thye) *noun* Your **thigh** is the top part of your leg, between your knee and your hip.

thim·ble (**thim**-buhl) *noun* A small cap made of metal, wood, plastic, or porcelain. It is worn while sewing to protect the finger that pushes the needle through the cloth. *See* **pin.**

thin (thin) *adjective*
1. Small in width or depth; not thick, as in *a thin sheet of paper.*
2. Not fat; lean; slender, as in *a thin waist.*
3. Not close together; not dense, as in *thin hair.*
4. Flowing or pouring easily, as in *thin soup.*
5. Not deep or firm; weak, as in *a thin voice.*
6. Easily seen through; flimsy, as in *a thin excuse.*
▷ *adjective* **thinner, thinnest** ▷ *noun* **thinness**
▷ *verb* **thin** ▷ *adverb* **thinly**

T

thing (thing)
1. *noun* An object, idea, or event.
2. things *noun, plural* Belongings. *Don't leave your things here.*
3. things *noun, plural* The general state of affairs. *How are things with you?*

think (thingk) *verb*
1. To use your mind; to form ideas or to make decisions. *Think before you speak.* ▷ *noun* **thinker**
2. To have an idea or opinion. *I think I'll go to bed now. I think she's a great teacher.*
3. To have as a thought; to imagine. *I think I heard a knock at the door.*
4. To remember. *Try to think about the good times you had with your grandmother.*
5. To be thoughtful or considerate. *He always thinks of other people's feelings.*
▷ *verb* **thinking, thought**

Synonyms: think

Think is a general term for the process of forming a thought or an idea in your mind: *I told my parents that I would think about what I want for my birthday.*

Imagine describes the process of picturing something as you think about it: *Our teacher asked us to imagine that we were in another city and to write about what we saw.*

Consider means to think about all the possibilities of a situation before making a decision or taking action: *Heather considered three different musical instruments before she decided to learn to play the drums.*

Reflect describes the process of recalling a memory or an event in a calm, unhurried manner: *Hector reflected on the first summer he spent with his grandfather.*

Ponder means to weigh a problem in your mind carefully and quietly, often for a long time: *Celia pondered what to say to Jeff for weeks before she got up the nerve to speak to him.*

third (thurd)
1. *adjective* That which comes after second and before fourth. *Tuesday is the third day of the week.*
2. *noun* One part of something that has been divided into three equal parts, written $\frac{1}{3}$.
▷ *adverb* **thirdly**

Third World *noun* The poorer, underdeveloped countries of the world.

thirst (thurst) *noun*
1. A dry feeling in the mouth, caused by a need to drink liquids.
2. A need or desire for liquid.
3. A longing for something. *Jesse has a great thirst for adventure.*
▷ *verb* **thirst**

thirst·y (thur-stee) *adjective* If you are **thirsty,** you need or want to drink something. ▷ **thirstier, thirstiest** ▷ *adverb* **thirstily**

this (THiss)
1. *pronoun* A person or thing present, nearby, or just mentioned. *This is my book.*
2. *pronoun* Something that is nearer or is being compared. *This is old, and that is new.*
3. *pronoun* Something about to be said. *This will make you change your mind.*
4. *adjective* Used to indicate a person or thing present, nearby, or just mentioned. *This book is the one I want.*
5. *adjective* Used to indicate a person or thing nearer than or contrasted with another thing. *This book is old, and that one is new.*
6. *adverb* To this extent; so. *Are they always this late?*
▷ *pronoun, plural* **these** ▷ *adjective, plural* **these**

this·tle
(thiss-uhl)
noun
A wild plant that has prickly leaves and purple, pink, white, blue, or yellow flowers.

spear thistle

thong (thong) *noun*
1. A narrow strip of leather used to fasten things together.
2. A sandal held to the foot with a piece of leather or plastic that goes between the first two toes.

tho·rax (thor-aks) *noun*
1. The part of your body between your neck and your abdomen.
2. The part of an insect's body between its head and its abdomen. *See* **beetle.**

thorn (thorn) *noun* A sharp point on the branch or stem of a plant such as a rose.

thorn·y (thor-nee) *adjective*
1. Covered with thorns, as in *a thorny plant.*
2. Difficult. *This is a thorny problem.*
▷ *adjective* **thornier, thorniest**

thor·ough (thur-oh) *adjective* If you are **thorough,** you do a job carefully and completely. ▷ *noun* **thoroughness** ▷ *adverb* **thoroughly**

thor·ough·fare (thur-oh-*fair*) *noun* A main road.

those (THoze) *pronoun, plural* The plural of **that.** *The purple boots are nice, but I prefer those in the window.* ▷ *adjective, plural* **those**

thou (THou) *pronoun* An old word for **you.**

though (THoh)
1. *conjunction* In spite of the fact that; although. *I'm still hungry though I've just had breakfast.*
2. *conjunction* Yet; but; however. *You wrote a good report, though you could have included more details.*
3. *adverb* However; nevertheless. *He's quite friendly; I don't like him, though.*

thought (thawt)
1. *verb* Past tense and past participle of **think.**
2. *noun* The act of thinking. *He didn't hear me because he was deep in thought.*
3. *noun* An idea or an opinion. *Do you have any thoughts on what we should do next?*
4. *noun* Close attention to something. *Give some thought to your career plans.*

thought·ful (thawt-fuhl) *adjective*
1. Serious and involving a lot of thought. *I got an "A" because my teacher said I wrote a thoughtful essay.*
2. A **thoughtful** person considers other people's feelings and needs.
▷ *adverb* **thoughtfully**

thought·less (thawt-liss) *adjective*
1. Careless. *It was thoughtless of you to forget to turn off the iron.*
2. A **thoughtless** person does not consider other people's feelings and needs.
▷ *adverb* **thoughtlessly**

thou·sand (thou-zuhnd) *noun* The whole number, written 1,000, that is equal to 10 times 100. ▷ *adjective* **thousand**

thou·sandth (thou-zuhndth)
1. *noun* One of a thousand equal parts, also written $\frac{1}{1000}$ or 0.001.
2. *adjective* Having to do with the last in a sequence of 1,000 items. *The thousandth person who comes into the store today will win a vacation in South America.*
3. *noun* In decimal notation, the position of the third number to the right of the decimal point is known as the *thousandths place.* In the number 4.0129, the digit 2 is in the thousandths place.

thrash (thrash) *verb*
1. To give someone a severe beating.
2. To move wildly or violently. *Restless, he thrashed around in bed.*

3. To beat someone thoroughly in a game. *Caroline always thrashes me at tennis.*
4. If you **thrash out** an idea or a problem, you talk about it until something is decided.
▷ *verb* **thrashes, thrashing, thrashed** ▷ *noun* **thrashing**

thread (thred)
1. *noun* A strand of cotton, silk, etc., used for sewing. *See* **pin.**
2. *verb* To pass a thread through something such as the eye of a needle or a set of beads.
3. *verb* To make one's way by following a winding or twisting course. *He threaded his way through the crowd.*
4. *noun* The theme or main idea that connects different ideas or events. *I can't follow the thread of this story.*
5. *noun* The raised, spiral ridge around a screw or nut.
▷ *verb* **threading, threaded**

thread·bare (thred-*bair*) *adjective* If your clothes are **threadbare,** they are old and worn out.

threat (thret) *noun*
1. A warning that punishment or harm will follow if a certain thing is done or not done.
2. A sign or possibility that something harmful or dangerous might happen. *The sky held a threat of snow.*
3. A person or thing regarded as a danger. *A drunk driver is a threat to everyone on the road.*

threat·en (thret-uhn) *verb* If someone or something **threatens** you, it frightens you or puts you in danger. ▷ **threatening, threatened**

three (three) *noun* The whole number, written 3, that comes after 2 and before 4. ▷ *adjective* **three**

three-dimensional or **3-D** (three dee) *adjective*
1. Having three dimensions, such as length, width, and height; solid; not flat. *Cubes and spheres are three-dimensional shapes.*
2. Having or seeming to have depth, as in a three-dimensional drawing.

thresh (thresh) *verb* To separate the grain or seed from a cereal plant such as wheat by beating. Today most farmers use combine harvesters to thresh their crops. *See* **harvest, rice.** ▷ **threshes, threshing, threshed**

thresh·old (thresh-ohld) *noun*
1. The bottom of a door frame. A threshold is usually made of a piece of wood, metal, or stone.
2. The beginning of something. *We are on the threshold of a great adventure.*

thrift·y (thrif-tee) *adjective* Someone who is **thrifty** does not waste money, food, supplies, or anything. ▷ **thriftier, thriftiest** ▷ *noun* **thrift**

thrill (thril) *noun* A strong feeling of excitement and pleasure. ▷ *verb* **thrill** ▷ *adjective* **thrilling**

thril·ler (thril-ur) *noun* An exciting story that is filled with action, mystery, or suspense.

thrive (thrive) *verb* To do well and flourish. *Roses thrive in our garden.* ▷ **thriving, thrived** ▷ *adjective* **thriving**

throat (throht) *noun*
1. The front of your neck.
2. The passage that runs from your mouth into your stomach or lungs.

throb (throb) *verb* To beat loudly or rapidly; to pound. *The loud music throbbed in my ears.* ▷ **throbbing, throbbed** ▷ *noun* **throb**

throne (throhn) *noun*
1. An elaborate chair for a king or queen.
2. The power or authority of a king or queen.

throng (throng) *noun* A large crowd of people. ▷ *verb* **throng**

throt·tle (throt-uhl)
1. *verb* If you **throttle** someone, you squeeze the person's throat so that he or she cannot breathe. ▷ **throttling, throttled** ▷ *noun* **throttle**
2. *noun* A valve in a vehicle's engine that opens to let steam, fuel, or fuel and air flow into it, thereby controlling the speed. ▷ *verb* **throttle**

through (throo)
1. *preposition* In one side and out the other. *I walked through the hall and into the kitchen.*
2. *preposition* To many places in; around. *We traveled through Europe.*
3. *preposition* By way of; because of. *Peter got the job through a friend.*
4. *preposition* As a result of. *We lost the game through inexperience.*
5. *preposition* From the beginning to the end of. *School goes through June.*
6. *preposition* In the midst of; among or between. *A hiking path winds through the trees.*
7. *preposition* Finished with. *We are through the worst part now.*
8. *adverb* From one side or end to the other. *Many people were blocking the door, but Lily managed to squeeze through.*
9. *adverb* Completely. *When he came in from the storm, Jack was soaked through.*
10. *adverb* From beginning to end. *I read the book through again.*
11. *adjective* Allowing passage from one end or side to the other. *I live on a through street.*
12. *adjective* Finished. *Are you through with your homework?*

through·out (throo-out)
1. *preposition* All the way through. *Chicken pox spread throughout the school.*
2. *adverb* In every part; everywhere. *The movie was scary throughout.*

through·way (throo-*way*) *noun* Another spelling of **thruway.**

throw (throh) *verb*
1. To send through the air; to fling, hurl, or toss. *Dean threw the ball.* ▷ *noun* **throw**
2. To make someone or something fall to the ground. *The horse reared up and threw its rider.*
3. To put on or take off quickly or carelessly. *I threw on my coat and left.*
4. To put in a certain condition or place. *The bomb scare threw everyone into a panic.*
5. *(informal)* If something **throws** you, it confuses you.
6. throw away To get rid of something.
7. throw up *(informal)* To vomit.
▷ *verb* **throwing, threw** (throo), **thrown** (throhn)

thrush (thruhsh)
noun Any of several songbirds. Robins, bluebirds, and nightingales are types of thrushes.
▷ *noun, plural* **thrushes**

song thrush

thrust (thruhst)
1. *verb* To push something suddenly and hard.
▷ **thrusting, thrust** ▷ *noun* **thrust**
2. *noun* The forward force produced by the engine of a jet or rocket.
3. *noun* The **thrust** of an argument is its main point.

thru·way (throo-*way*) *noun* A wide highway used for high-speed, long-distance travel. A thruway usually has four or more lanes.

thud (thuhd) *noun* The dull thump made when a heavy object falls to the ground. ▷ *verb* **thud**

thug (thuhg) *noun* A rough, violent person.

thumb (thuhm)
1. *noun* The short, thick finger that you have on each hand.
2. *verb* To turn over the pages of a book. *Gabriella thumbed through her photo album.*
▷ **thumbing, thumbed**
3. If someone is **all thumbs,** the person is very clumsy.

thumb·tack (thuhm-*tak*) *noun* A small pin with a flat, round head, used for fastening paper on bulletin boards, walls, and other surfaces.

thump (thuhmp)
1. *noun* A blow with a blunt, heavy object.
2. *noun* A dull, heavy sound made by such a blow. *The newspaper landed on the front porch with a thump.*

T

3. verb To beat heavily and rapidly; to pound or throb. *My heart thumped with excitement.*
▷ **thumping, thumped**

thun·der (thuhn-dur)
1. noun The loud, rumbling sound that comes after a flash of lightning. Thunder is caused by the expansion of air that has been heated by lightning.
2. verb To make a loud noise like thunder. *The trucks thundered past.* ▷ **thundering, thundered**
▷ **noun thunder**

thun·der·storm (thuhn-dur-*storm*) **noun** A rainstorm with thunder and lightning.

Thurs·day (thurz-dee *or* thurz-*day*) **noun** The fifth day of the week, after Wednesday and before Friday.

> ### ▶ Word History
> •
> There's no proof that it thunders more on **Thursday** than on any other day, but it would be appropriate if that were the case. Thursday is named for Thor, the ancient god of thunder.

thus (THuhss) **adverb**
1. In this way. *Hold the tennis racket thus.*
2. As a result. *She got terrific grades and was thus able to get into a good college.*

thwart (thwort) **verb** If you **thwart** somebody's plans, you prevent them from happening or succeeding. ▷ **thwarting, thwarted**

thy (THye) **pronoun** An old word for **your.**

thyme (time) **noun** An herb related to mint. Its aromatic leaves are used to flavor food. *See* **herb. Thyme** sounds like **time.**

ti·ar·a (tee-er-uh *or* tee-ah-ruh) **noun** A piece of jewelry like a small crown.

tick (tik)
1. noun The light clicking sound that a clock or watch makes.
2. verb To make such a sound. *The clock was ticking.*
3. verb To mark by ticking. *The clock ticked off the seconds.*
4. noun A mark that someone makes to show that an answer is correct or that something has been done.
5. verb To mark with a tick. *Hugh ticked off his answers.*
6. noun A very small insect that looks like a spider. Ticks suck blood from under the skin of animals and people.
7. verb If you **tick** someone **off,** you make the person extremely angry.
▷ **verb ticking, ticked**

tick·et (tik-it) **noun**
1. A printed piece of paper or card that proves you have paid to do something such as ride on a train or sit in a movie theater.
2. A written order to pay a fine or appear in court for breaking a traffic law.
3. A price tag or a label.
4. The list of candidates belonging to a particular political party, to be voted on in an election.
▷ **verb ticket**

tick·le (tik-uhl) **verb**
1. To keep touching or poking someone gently, often causing the person to laugh.
2. To have a tingling or scratching feeling. *The dust in the attic made my nose tickle.*
3. To please, delight, or amuse. *The children were tickled by the circus dog's tricks.*
▷ **verb tickling, tickled** ▷ **noun tickle**

tick·lish (tik-lish) **adjective**
1. Easily tickled. *The boy was very ticklish.*
2. Requiring sensitivity or delicate treatment, as in *a ticklish situation.*

tick-tack-toe *or* **tic-tac-toe** (tik tak toh) **noun** A game played on a grid of nine squares. Two players take turns putting an X or an O in an empty square. The winner is the first person to get three X's or O's in a row.

tidal wave **noun** A huge, forceful ocean wave set into motion by an underwater earthquake, a volcanic eruption, or very strong winds.

tid·bit (tid-bit) **noun** A choice or pleasing bit of food or gossip.

tid·dle·dy·winks *or* **tid·dly·winks** (tid-lee-*wingks*) **noun** A game in which each player tries to flick plastic counters into a cup.

tide (tide) **noun**
1. The constant change in sea level that is caused by the pull of the sun and the moon on the earth. ▷ **adjective tidal**
2. Something that changes like the tides of the sea. *The tide of public opinion turned against the candidate.*

> ### ▶ Word History
> •
> The words **tide** and *time* used to have the same meaning, and today tide still means "time" in some words. For example, *Yuletide* means Yule— or Christmas—time. In its more common meaning, tide refers to the regular rise and fall of the oceans' surfaces, which take place at timely, often predictable, intervals.

tid·ings (tye-dingz) **noun, plural** News or information.

T

ti·dy (tye-dee) *adjective* Neat, or in proper order. ▷ **tidier, tidiest** ▷ *noun* **tidiness** ▷ *verb* **tidy**

tie (tye)
1. *verb* To join two pieces of string or cord together with a knot or bow. ▷ **ties, tying, tied** ▷ *noun* **tie**
2. *noun* A long piece of fabric that is worn knotted around the collar of a shirt; a necktie.
3. *noun* Something that holds or bonds people together, as in *strong family ties.*
4. *noun* A situation in which two people or teams have exactly the same score in a competition. *There was a tie for second place.* ▷ *verb* **tie**

tie·break·er (tye-*bray*-kur) *noun* A special or extra game played to decide a tie game.

tier (tihr) *noun* One of several rows or layers placed one above the other. A tier can be found in a large structure such as a concert hall or stadium, or on something smaller, like a wedding cake.

ti·ger (tye-gur) *noun* A large, striped, wild cat that lives in Asia. The tiger is the largest member of the cat family.

tiger and cubs

tiger lily *noun* A type of lily that is shaped like a trumpet and has red or orange flowers and black spots.

tight (tite) *adjective*
1. Fitting closely, as in *tight shoes* or *a tight belt.*
2. Fastened or held firmly; secure, as in *a tight knot* or *a tight grip.*
3. Fully stretched; not loose, as in *a tight rope.*
4. Not letting water or air pass through, as in *a tight seal.*
5. (informal) Stingy with money.
6. Having little time to spare. *I am on a tight schedule today.*
7. Difficult. *Knowing what you've done puts me in a tight situation.*

8. Even or almost even in score; close, as in *a tight game.*
▷ *adjective* **tighter, tightest** ▷ *verb* **tighten**
▷ *adverb* **tightly**

tight·rope (tite-*rope*) *noun* A stretched high wire on which circus performers balance.

tights (titess) *noun, plural* A garment that fits closely and covers the hips, legs, and feet.

tile (tile) *noun*
A square of stone, plastic, or baked and glazed clay. Tiles are often used for covering floors or walls. *The picture shows a ceramic tile made in Delft in the Netherlands.*

Dutch ceramic tile

till (til)
1. *preposition and conjunction* Another word for **until.**
2. *noun* A drawer or box in a store, used to hold money; part of a cash register.
3. *verb* To prepare land for growing crops. *A plow is used to till the soil.* ▷ **tilling, tilled**

till·er (til-ur) *noun* A handle attached to the rudder of a boat. The tiller is used to steer the boat.

tilt (tilt) *verb* To lean, tip, or slant to one side. *The picture was tilted at a weird angle.* ▷ **tilting, tilted** ▷ *noun* **tilt**

tim·ber (tim-bur) *noun*
1. Cut wood used for building; lumber.
2. A long, heavy piece of wood; a beam.
3. Trees; forest, as in *an acre of timber.*

tim·ber·line (tim-bur-*line*) *noun* The highest point at which trees can grow on a mountain, or the farthest northern point in the arctic regions where trees can grow. The timberline on a mountain is also known as the *tree line.*

time (time)
1. *noun* The past, present, and future measured in seconds, minutes, hours, and so on. *Time seemed to pass quickly during our vacation.*
2. *noun* A particular moment shown on a clock or watch. *What is the time now?* ▷ *noun* **timer**
3. *noun* A particular period. *School was a time of great happiness.*
4. *verb* To measure how long something takes. *I'll time you while you run.*
5. *verb* To choose the moment for something. *Harry timed his entrance perfectly.* ▷ *adjective* **timely**
6. *noun* One in a series of repeated actions. *I just finished reading that book for the third time.*

T

7. *noun* The beat in a piece of music. *We kept time by clapping.*
Time sounds like **thyme.**
▷ *verb* **timing, timed**

time·less (time-liss) *adjective*
1. Not affected, changed, or weakened by time, as in *timeless beauty.*
2. Not referring to a particular time or date, as in *a timeless story of good versus evil.*
▷ *adverb* **timelessly**

time·ta·ble (time-*tay*-buhl) *noun* A printed chart of the times when buses, trains, planes, or boats arrive and depart; a schedule.

time zone *noun* A region in which the same time is used. The earth is divided into 24 time zones. Each zone is 15 degrees of longitude in width and usually observes a clock time one hour earlier than the zone immediately to its east.

tim·id (tim-id) *adjective* Shy and easily frightened. *At the beginning of the year, Rita was too timid to raise her hand in class.* ▷ *noun* **timidity** (ti-mid-i-tee) ▷ *adverb* **timidly**

tin (tin) *noun*
1. A soft, silvery metal that does not rust easily. It is used to coat steel cans and can be mixed with other metals to make pewter and bronze. Tin is a chemical element.
2. A container that is made of or coated with tin.

tin·foil (tin-*foil*) *noun* A paper-thin, flexible sheet of tin or aluminum used for wrapping food.

tinge (tinj) *noun*
1. A very small amount of added color. *Beige is white with a tinge of tan.*
2. A slight trace. *Katie's smile had a tinge of sadness to it.*
▷ *verb* **tinge**

tin·gle (ting-guhl) *verb* To sting, prick, or tickle. *Their skin tingled from the cold.* ▷ **tingling, tingled** ▷ *noun* **tingle**

tin·ker (ting-kur)
1. *verb* To make repairs in a clumsy or unskilled way. *Fred tinkered with the engine.* ▷ **tinkering, tinkered**
2. *noun* A person who travels from place to place mending pots, pans, and other metal kitchen utensils.

tin·kle (ting-kuhl) *verb* To make a light, ringing sound such as that made by a small bell.
▷ **tinkling, tinkled** ▷ *noun* **tinkle**

tint (tint)
1. *noun* A variety of a color, often one with white added.
2. *noun* A pale, delicate color.
3. *verb* To give a slight color to. *My mother tints her hair. I asked the optician to tint the lenses in my new pair of glasses.* ▷ **tinting, tinted**
▷ *adjective* **tinted**

ti·ny (tye-nee) *adjective* Very small; minute.
▷ **tinier, tiniest**

tip (tip)
1. *verb* To make something lean or fall over. *Justin tipped back his chair.* ▷ *noun* **tip**
2. *verb* To lean or to fall over. *The cans of dog food tipped over because they were piled too high.*
3. *noun* The end part or point of something, as in *the tips of the fingers* or *the tip of a spear.*
4. *noun* A useful hint, as in *a sewing tip.*
5. *noun* A sum of money given in addition to the bill to a taxi driver, waitress, etc., as thanks for his or her services. ▷ *verb* **tip**
6. *verb* To raise or touch your hat as a greeting to someone. *The gentleman tipped his hat at Mary.*
▷ *verb* **tipping, tipped**

tip·toe (tip-*toh*) *verb* To walk very quietly on or as if you were on the tips of your toes.
▷ **tiptoeing, tiptoed**

tire (tire)
1. *noun* A band of rubber that fits around the rim of a wheel and usually is filled with air.
2. *verb* To make or become weak or unable to continue because of a need for rest.
▷ *adjective* **tired**
3. *verb* To bore or to become bored. *I soon tired of Terry's chatter.*
▷ *verb* **tiring, tired** ▷ *noun* **tiredness**

changing a tire

tire·some (tire-suhm) *adjective* Tiring, boring, or annoying, as in *tiresome behavior.*

tis·sue (tish-oo) *noun*
1. Soft, thin paper used for wiping, wrapping, etc.
2. A mass of similar cells that form a particular part or organ of an animal or a plant, as in *muscle tissue.*

ti·tle (tye-tuhl) *noun*
1. The name of a book, movie, song, painting, or other work. ▷ *verb* **title**
2. A word used to show a person's status, rank, or occupation. *Ms., Dr., Lord,* and *Senator* are titles.
3. Legal ownership, or a document that shows legal ownership.
4. A championship.

Tlin·git (tling-kuht *or* kling-kuht) *noun* One of a group of American Indians that lives on the islands and coast of southern Alaska. ▷ *noun, plural* **Tlingit** *or* **Tlingits**

T

to (too) *preposition*
1. Toward; in the direction of. *The kitten started walking to me.*
2. As far as. *The astronauts went to the moon.*
3. On, against, or in contact with. *Nail the wreath to the door.*
4. In or for each. *There are four quarts to a gallon.*
5. Until. *Our booth is open from nine to eight.*
6. Compared with. *The score was nine to eight.*
7. For the attention, benefit, or purpose of. *Mom came to my rescue.*
8. Concerning or regarding. *What do you say to that?*
9. Before. *It's 10 minutes to two.*
10. Used before a verb to form an infinitive. *I'd like to go now.*
11. Used to show the receiver of an action. *We gave the trophy to her.*
12. In agreement with. *Dinner was not cooked to my liking.*
To sounds like **too** and **two.**

toad (tohd) *noun* An amphibian that looks like a frog but has a rougher, drier skin. Toads live mainly on land.

toad·stool (tohd-*stool*) *noun* A mushroom, especially one that is poisonous.

toast (tohst)
1. *noun* Bread browned by heat. ▷ *verb* **toast**
2. *verb* To warm thoroughly. *We toasted our cold feet by the fire.*
3. *verb* To drink in honor of someone. *Let's toast the bride and groom.* ▷ *noun* **toast**
▷ *verb* **toasting, toasted**

toast·er (tohss-tur) *noun* An electrical appliance that toasts bread.

to·bac·co (tuh-bak-oh) *noun* The chopped, dried leaves of the tobacco plant. Tobacco is used for smoking or chewing. ▷ *noun, plural* **tobaccos**

to·bog·gan (tuh-bog-uhn)
1. *noun* A long, flat sled with a front edge that turns up. A toboggan has no runners.
2. *verb* To travel by toboggan, especially downhill. ▷ **tobogganing, tobogganed**

toboggan

to·day (tuh-day)
1. *noun* This present day or time. *Today is my birthday.*
2. *adverb* On or during this day. *I'm going out today.*
3. *adverb* Nowadays, or at the present time. *Today many people spend more time watching sports than playing them.*

tod·dler (tod-lur) *noun* A young child who has just learned to walk.

toe (toh) *noun*
1. One of the five slender parts at the end of your foot.
2. The part of a shoe, boot, sock, or stocking that covers the toes.
Toe sounds like **tow.**

tof·fee (tof-ee) *noun* A hard, chewy candy made by boiling sugar and butter together.

to·fu (toh-foo) *noun* A soft, cheeselike food made from soybeans. Tofu is also called *bean curd.*

to·ga (toh-guh) *noun* A piece of clothing worn by men in ancient Rome. It was wrapped around the body and draped over the left shoulder.

to·geth·er (tuh-geTH-ur) *adverb*
1. With one another. *The boys arrived together.*
2. Into one group, mass, or place. *Mix the cake ingredients together.*
3. At the same time. *All of the horses started the race together.*
4. In agreement or cooperation. *We completed the class project by working together.*

toil (toil)
1. *verb* To work very hard for a long time. *They toiled in the mines.*
2. *verb* To move slowly with pain or effort. *The hikers toiled up the mountain.*
3. *noun* Hard, exhausting work.
▷ *verb* **toiling, toiled** ▷ *noun* **toiler**

toi·let (toi-lit) *noun*
1. A large bowl that can be flushed with water. A toilet is used for disposing of human wastes.
2. A room containing a toilet; a bathroom.

to·ken (toh-kuhn) *noun*
1. Something that stands for something else; a sign or symbol. *Randy gave Sue a ring as a token of his love.*
2. A piece of stamped metal that can be used in place of money. *The machines at the penny arcade require tokens instead of coins.*

tol·er·ance (tol-ur-uhnss) *noun*
1. The willingness to respect or accept the customs, beliefs, or opinions of others.
2. The ability to put up with or endure something such as pain or hardship. *Mom's tolerance was tested when all the kids started screaming at once.*
▷ *adjective* **tolerant**

tol·er·ate (tol-uh-*rate*) *verb* If you **tolerate** something, you put up with it or endure it. *It is difficult to tolerate rude people.* ▷ **tolerating, tolerated** ▷ *noun* **toleration**

toll (tohl)
1. *verb* To ring a bell slowly and regularly. ▷ **tolling, tolled** ▷ *noun* **toll**
2. *noun* A charge or tax paid for using a highway, bridge, or tunnel.
3. *noun* A charge for a service such as a long-distance telephone call.
4. If something **takes its toll,** it results in serious damage or suffering. *Famine has taken its toll in many African countries.*

tom·a·hawk (tom-uh-*hawk*)
noun A small ax once used by some North American Indians as a tool or weapon. *This decorated tomahawk was used by the Shawnee people.*

tomahawk

to·ma·to
(tuh-**may**-toh *or* tuh-**mat**-oh) *noun* A red, juicy fruit eaten as a vegetable either raw or cooked. *See* **fruit.** ▷ *noun, plural* **tomatoes**

tomb (toom)
noun A grave, room, or building for holding a dead body. *The photograph shows the Tomb of the Unknowns in Arlington National Cemetery, Arlington, Virginia.*

Tomb of the Unknowns

tom·boy (tom-*boi*) *noun* A girl who enjoys activities that were once associated with boys, such as climbing trees or playing football.

tomb·stone (toom-*stone*) *noun* A carved block of stone that marks the place where someone is buried. It usually gives the dead person's name and dates of birth and death.

tom·cat (tom-*kat*) *noun* A male cat.

to·mor·row (tuh-**mor**-oh) *noun*
1. The day after today.
2. The future, as in *the world of tomorrow.*
▷ *adverb* **tomorrow**

ton (tuhn) *noun* A unit of weight equal to 2,000 pounds in the United States and Canada and 2,240 pounds in Great Britain. A small automobile weighs about one ton.

tone (tohn) *noun*
1. A single sound, especially one that is musical, thought of in terms of its pitch, length, quality, or loudness, as in *the deep tones of an organ.*
2. A way of speaking or writing that shows a certain feeling or attitude. *Rosa's tone was soft and gentle.*
3. The general quality, feeling, or style of something. *The tone of the speech was positive.*
4. In music, a **tone** is the difference in pitch between two musical notes.
5. A tint or shade of a color.
6. The normal, healthy firmness of the muscles.

tongs (tongz *or* tawngz) *noun, plural* A tool with two connected arms used for picking up things.

tongue (tuhng) *noun*
1. The movable muscle in your mouth that is used for tasting, swallowing, and talking. *See* **taste.**
2. The tongue of an animal such as a cow, cooked and used as food.
3. A language. *The exchange student spoke to her friends in her native tongue.*
4. The ability to speak. *Have you lost your tongue?*
5. The flap of material under the laces of a shoe.
6. When you **hold your tongue,** you stop yourself from saying something.

tongue twister *noun* A sentence or verse that is very hard to say or repeat quickly, such as "red leather, yellow leather."

ton·ic (ton-ik) *noun* Something that makes you feel stronger or refreshed. *Our vacation was a real tonic.*

to·night (tuh-**nite**) *noun* This evening or night.
▷ *adverb* **tonight**

ton·sil·li·tis (*ton*-suh-**lye**-tiss) *noun* An illness that makes your tonsils infected and painful.

ton·sils (ton-suhlz) *noun, plural* Two flaps of soft tissue that lie one on each side of the throat.

too (too) *adverb*
1. As well; also; in addition. *Is Jane coming too?*
2. More than enough. *The heavy metal band was too noisy for Grandma.*
3. Very; extremely. *They were too kind.*
Too sounds like **to** and **two.**

tool ▶ topical

tool (tool) noun
1. A piece of equipment that you use to do a particular job.
2. Anything that helps you accomplish something. *A thesaurus is a useful tool for writing.*

household tools

- locking pliers
- hammer
- screwdrivers
- voltage tester
- electrician's pliers
- wrench
- adjustable wrench
- Phillips screwdriver
- files
- utility knife
- chisel
- soldering iron
- hacksaws

tool·box (tool-*boks*) *noun* A box designed for storing or carrying hand tools.

toot (toot) *verb* To sound a horn or whistle in short blasts. ▷ **tooting, tooted** ▷ *noun* **toot**

tooth (tooth) noun
1. One of the white, bony parts of your mouth that you use for biting and chewing food. *See also* **teeth.**
2. One of a row of parts that stick out on a saw, comb, or gear. *See* **gear.**
▷ *noun, plural* **teeth**

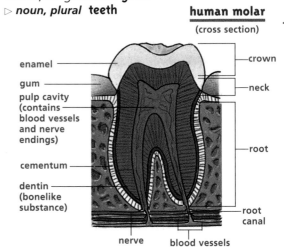

human molar (cross section)

- enamel
- gum
- pulp cavity (contains blood vessels and nerve endings)
- cementum
- dentin (bonelike substance)
- crown
- neck
- root
- root canal
- nerve
- blood vessels

tooth·ache (tooth-*ake*) *noun* A pain in or near a tooth.

tooth·brush (tooth-*bruhsh*) *noun* A small brush that is used to clean the teeth.

tooth·paste (tooth-*payst*) *noun* A paste that is put on a toothbrush and used to clean the teeth.

tooth·pick (tooth-*pik*) *noun* A small, thin piece of wood or plastic that is used to remove food from between the teeth.

top (top)
1. *noun* The highest point or part of something, as in *the top of a hill* or *the top of a page.*
2. *noun* A cover or a lid, as in *a bottle top.*
3. *noun* The highest rank or position. *My sister is at the top of her class.*
4. *noun* A piece of clothing for the upper part of your body.
5. *noun* The highest or greatest degree or pitch. *He yelled at the top of his voice.*
6. *verb* To do better than. *Bert's time in the dash tops the old record.* ▷ **topping, topped**
7. *noun* A toy that is shaped like a cone and spins on a pointed end.
▷ *verb* **top** ▷ *adjective* **top**

to·paz (toh-paz) *noun* A clear mineral that is used as a gem. It is usually a color ranging from yellow to brown.

top·ic (top-ik) *noun* The subject of a discussion, study, lesson, speech, or piece of writing.

top·i·cal (top-uh-kuhl) *adjective*
1. Of interest now; in the news at present.
2. A **topical** anesthetic is used to make a specific part of the body numb.

to·pog·ra·phy (tuh-pog-ruh-fee) *noun* The detailed description of the physical features of an area, including hills, valleys, mountains, plains, and rivers. ▷ *noun* **topographer**

top·ple (top-uhl) *verb*
1. To fall over, usually from a height.
2. To make something fall, as in *to topple a government.*
▷ *verb* **toppling, toppled**

top·soil (top-*soil*) *noun* The top or surface layer of soil. Topsoil is good for planting because it contains decaying leaves, grass, and other organic matter.

top·sy-tur·vy (top-see tur-vee) *adjective* Upside down, mixed-up, or confused. *The tornado left the house in a topsy-turvy mess.* ▷ *adverb* **topsy-turvy**

To·rah (tor-uh *or* toh-ruh) *noun* The sacred scroll kept in a Jewish synagogue on which is written in Hebrew the first five books of the Bible: Genesis, Exodus, Leviticus, Numbers, and Deuteronomy.

torch (torch)
1. *noun* A flaming light that can be carried in the hand.
2. *noun* A tool that gives off a very hot flame used to weld or cut metals; a blowtorch.
3. *verb* If you **torch** somethng, you set fire to it.
▷ **torches, torching, torched**
▷ *noun, plural* **torches**

to·re·a·dor (tor-ee-uh-*dor*) *noun* A bullfighter.

tor·ment
1. (tor-ment) *verb* To upset or annoy someone deliberately. *Jed torments his younger brother.*
▷ **tormenting, tormented** ▷ *noun* **tormentor**
2. (tor-ment) *noun* Great pain or suffering. *The years of torment showed on the woman's wrinkled face.*

tor·na·do (tor-nay-doh) *noun* A violent, whirling column of air that appears as a dark cloud shaped like a funnel. A tornado travels rapidly and usually destroys everything in its narrow path. ▷ *noun, plural* **tornadoes** or **tornados**

tor·pe·do (tor-pee-doh) *noun* An underwater missile that explodes when it hits a target, such as a ship. ▷ *noun, plural* **torpedoes** ▷ *verb* **torpedo**

tor·rent (tor-uhnt) *noun* A violent, swiftly flowing stream of water or any liquid. ▷ *adjective* **torrential**

tor·rid (tor-id) *adjective* Extremely hot; burning; scorching, as in *a torrid climate.* ▷ *noun* **torridness** ▷ *adverb* **torridly**

tor·so (tor-soh) *noun* The part of your body between your neck and your waist, not including your arms; the trunk. ▷ *noun, plural* **torsos**

tor·til·la (tor-tee-yuh) *noun* A round, flat bread made from cornmeal or flour. Tortillas are often served with a topping or filling.

tor·toise (tor-tuhss) *noun* A turtle, especially one that lives on land. *The giant tortoise in the picture is shown with finches.*

giant tortoise

tor·ture (tor-chur)
1. *verb* To cause someone extreme pain or mental suffering. *Carlos was tortured with stomach pains for a week while he had the flu.*
▷ **torturing, tortured**
2. *noun* The act of causing extreme pain as a punishment or as a way of forcing someone to do or say something against his or her will.
3. *noun* Extreme pain or mental suffering; torment.

toss (tawss) *verb*
1. To throw something with little force. *Toss me that pencil, will you?*
2. To move, fling, or rock back and forth. *The high waves tossed the boat.*
3. To mix a salad lightly.
4. To throw a coin into the air to decide something according to which side lands face up.
▷ *verb* **tosses, tossing, tossed** ▷ *noun* **toss**
▷ *adjective* **tossed**

tot (tot) *noun* A small child.

to·tal (toh-tuhl)
1. *adjective* Making up the whole amount; entire. *What is the total amount of my bill?*
2. *adjective* Complete; utter. *The party was a total surprise.* ▷ *adverb* **totally**
3. *noun* A number gotten by adding; a sum. *Add up these figures and give me the total.* ▷ *verb* **total**
4. *verb* (informal) To completely demolish. *Bill totaled his car in an accident.* ▷ **totaling, totaled**

tote (toht) *verb* To carry or haul something. *I toted that umbrella everywhere, and it never rained.* ▷ **toting, toted**

to·tem pole (**toh**-tuhm) *noun* A pole carved and painted with animals, plants, and other natural objects that represent a family or clan. Certain North American Indians placed totem poles in front of their homes. *The totem pole shown here is in Stanley Park, Vancouver, British Columbia, Canada.*

totem pole

tot·ter (**tot**-ur) *verb*
1. To walk in an unsteady way. *The baby tottered slowly across the yard.*
2. To tremble or rock as if about to fall; to sway. *Many buildings tottered during the earthquake.*
▷ *verb* **tottering, tottered**

tou·can (**too**-kan) *noun* A brightly colored tropical American bird that has a very large beak.

toucan

touch (tuhch)
1. *verb* To make contact with your hand or another area of your body. *Penny touched the hot stove.*

2. *verb* To make gentle contact with another object. *The falling leaf touched his cheek.*
3. *noun* The act of touching. *Her touch was soft.*
4. *verb* To affect emotionally. *I was touched by the tender story of the girl who found her birth mother.*
5. *noun* Your sense of **touch** is your ability to feel things with your fingers or other parts of your body.
6. *noun* A very small amount. *The cook added a touch of salt to the stew.*
7. If you **keep in touch** with someone, you contact the person regularly by telephone, letter, E-mail, etc.
▷ *noun, plural* **touches** ▷ *verb* **touches, touching, touched**

touch·down (**tuhch**-doun) *noun*
1. In football, a play in which the ball is carried over the opponent's goal line, scoring six points.
2. The moment when an aircraft or a spacecraft lands.

touch·ing (**tuhch**-ing) *adjective* Something that is **touching** makes you feel compassion, sympathy, or other tender emotions. ▷ *adverb* **touchingly**

touch·y (**tuhch**-ee) *adjective* Irritable and easily annoyed; sensitive. *Brian was feeling touchy. That's a touchy subject.* ▷ **touchier, touchiest**
▷ *noun* **touchiness**

tough (tuhf) *adjective*
1. Strong and difficult to damage, as in *tough boots.*
2. Hard to cut or chew, as in *tough meat.*
3. Difficult to deal with or do, as in *a tough decision.*
4. Able to stand strain or hardship; rugged. *Pioneer women had to be tough.*
5. Stubborn, as in *a tough stain.*
6. Rough or violent, as in *a tough neighborhood.*
7. Unhappy or unlucky, as in *a tough life.*
▷ *adjective* **tougher, toughest**

tou·pee (too-**pay**) *noun* A wig used to cover a man's baldness.

tour (toor) *noun*
1. A trip around a set route, often for sightseeing. ▷ *verb* **tour**
2. When a band, team, or theater group goes **on tour,** it travels to different places to play or perform.

tour·ist (**toor**-ist) *noun* Someone who travels and visits places for pleasure. ▷ *noun* **tourism**

tour·na·ment (**tur**-nuh-muhnt) *noun*
1. A series of contests in which a number of people or teams try to win the championship, as in *a tennis tournament* or *a chess tournament.*
2. In the Middle Ages, **tournaments** were events in which knights jousted against each other. *See* **joust.**

T

tour·ni·quet (tur-nuh-ket) *noun* A bandage or band twisted tightly around a limb to prevent a wound or cut from bleeding too much.

tout (tout) *verb* To praise or publicize in a loud or exaggerated way. *The baseball player was highly touted by the press.* ▷ **touting, touted**

tow (toh) *verb* To pull something behind you, usually with a rope or chain. **Tow** sounds like **toe.** ▷ **towing, towed** ▷ *noun* **tow**

to·ward (tord *or* tuh-**word**) *or* **to·wards** (tordz *or* tuh-**wordz**) *preposition*
1. In the direction of. *Cliff marched toward the door.*
2. With regard to; concerning. *The children showed great respect toward their grandparents.*
3. Just before; near. *It started to snow toward morning.*
4. In order to buy; for. *My parents are saving money toward a new car.*

tow·el (tou-uhl) *noun* A piece of soft cloth or paper that is used for drying or wiping. ▷ *verb* **towel**

tow·er (tou-ur)
1. *noun* A tall structure that is thin in relation to its height. *The picture shows the Leaning Tower of Pisa in Italy.*
2. *verb* To be very tall and dominant. *The skyscraper towered over the other buildings.*
▷ **towering, towered** ▷ *adjective* **towering**

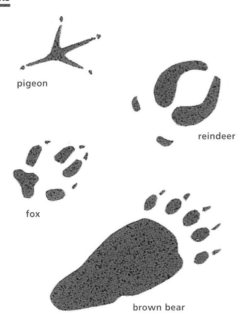

tower

town (toun) *noun* A place that has houses, stores, offices, schools, etc. A town is larger than a village but smaller than a city.

tox·ic (tok-sik) *adjective* Poisonous, as in *toxic waste.* ▷ *noun* **toxin,** *noun* **toxicity** (tok-si-si-tee)

▶ Word History
. . . .
The word **toxic** comes from the Greek word *toxikon,* which referred to the poison in which an arrow was dipped. This word came from the Greek word *toxon,* meaning a bow for shooting arrows. Hunters used poison on the tips of their arrows to make sure their shots killed their prey.

toy (toi)
1. *noun* An object that children play with.
2. *verb* If you **toy** with something, you handle or treat it in a halfhearted, careless way. ▷ **toying, toyed**

trace (trayss)
1. *verb* To follow the trail, path, or course of someone or something; to track. *Marissa traced Paul's footprints and found him playing in the snow.*
2. *verb* To copy a picture or shape by following lines visible through a piece of thin paper. ▷ *noun* **tracing**
3. *verb* To follow, study, or describe the history or development of something. *We traced the history of my family back to Africa.*
4. *noun* A visible mark or sign that something has happened or that someone has been somewhere. *He left without a trace.*
▷ *verb* **tracing, traced**

track (trak)
1. *noun* The marks left behind by a moving animal or person.
2. *noun* A path or a trail.
3. *noun* A prepared path or course for runners or racing animals.
4. *noun* A rail or set of rails for vehicles such as trains and trolleys to run on.
5. *verb* To follow someone or something. *The hunters tracked the bear.* ▷ **tracking, tracked**
▷ *noun* **tracking,** *noun* **tracker**

tracks

pigeon

reindeer

fox

brown bear

track and field *noun* A group of sports events that includes running, jumping, and throwing contests such as the hurdles, pole vault, and shot put. *The picture shows the standard layout of a stadium used for track and field.*

▷ *adjective* **track-and-field**

tract (trakt) *noun*
1. An area or expanse of land. *The farmer worked a tract of land that had been in her family for close to a century.*
2. A group of parts or organs in the body that perform a specific function, as in *the digestive tract.*
3. A booklet or pamphlet, especially one on a religious or political subject.

trac·tion (trak-shuhn) *noun* The friction or gripping power that keeps a moving body from slipping on a surface. *The tires lost traction on the icy roads.*

trac·tor (trak-tur) *noun*
1. A powerful vehicle with either large tires that have deep treads or continuous belts of metal treads. Tractors are often used to pull farm machinery or heavy loads.
2. A truck that has a cab and no body. It is used for pulling a trailer.

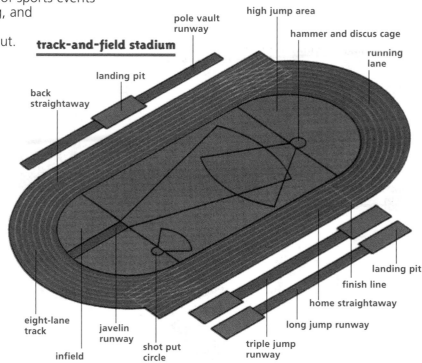

track-and-field stadium

pole vault runway
high jump area
hammer and discus cage
running lane
landing pit
back straightaway
landing pit
finish line
home straightaway
long jump runway
triple jump runway
eight-lane track
javelin runway
shot put circle
infield

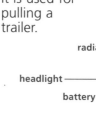

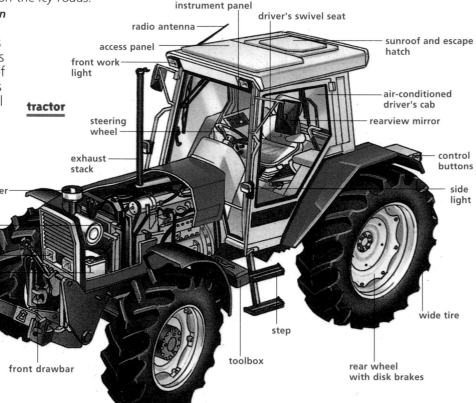

tractor

instrument panel
driver's swivel seat
radio antenna
sunroof and escape hatch
access panel
front work light
air-conditioned driver's cab
steering wheel
rearview mirror
exhaust stack
control buttons
air filter
side light
radiator
headlight
battery
power takeoff (connects tractor to other machinery)
wide tire
front drawbar
step
toolbox
rear wheel with disk brakes

trade (trade)
1. *noun* The business of buying and selling goods; commerce. ▷ *noun* **trader** ▷ *verb* **trade**
2. *noun* A particular job or craft, especially one that requires working with the hands or with machines. *Bob is a carpenter by trade.*
3. *verb* To exchange one thing for another. *We've started a club to trade baseball cards.*
▷ **trading, traded** ▷ *noun* **trade**

trade·mark (trade-*mark*) *noun* A word, picture, or design that shows that a product is made by a particular company. A trademark is usually registered with the government. It can legally be used only by the owner. ▷ *verb* **trademark**

trading post *noun* A store in a wilderness area where people can exchange local products such as furs or hides for food and supplies.

tra·di·tion (truh-dish-uhn) *noun*
1. The handing down of customs, ideas, and beliefs from one generation to the next.
2. A custom, an idea, or a belief that is handed down in this way.
▷ *adjective* **traditional**

traf·fic (traf-ik)
1. *noun* Moving vehicles. *There was heavy traffic in the city.*
2. *verb* To buy and sell goods, especially illegally.
▷ **trafficking, trafficked** ▷ *noun* **trafficking**

traffic light *noun* A set of lights that control traffic. Traffic lights are usually placed where streets intersect.

trag·e·dy (traj-uh-dee) *noun*
1. A serious play with a sad ending.
2. A very sad event.
▷ *noun, plural* **tragedies**

trag·ic (traj-ik) *adjective*
1. To do with or in the style of a tragedy or sad story. *The book had a tragic ending.*
2. Extremely unfortunate, or disastrous, as in *a tragic accident.*
▷ *adverb* **tragically**

trail (trayl)
1. *noun* A track or path for people to follow, especially in the woods.
2. *noun* A mark, scent, or path left behind by an animal or a person. *The dogs were able to pick up the lost hiker's trail.*
3. *noun* Something that follows along behind, as in *a trail of dust.*
4. *verb* To follow the scent or trail of an animal or a person; to track. *The hound kept its nose to the ground as it trailed the squirrel.*
5. *verb* To follow slowly behind others. *Mark was trailing a long way behind.*
▷ *verb* **trailing, trailed**

trail bike *noun* A light, strong motorcycle built for cross-country racing and riding.

trail·er (trayl-ur) *noun*
1. A vehicle that is towed by a car or truck and used to carry things.
2. A mobile home.
3. A short piece of film used to advertise a movie or television program to be shown in the future.

train (trane)
1. *noun* A string of railroad cars powered by steam, diesel fuel, or electricity. *The train shown here is a French TGV Atlantic, a high-speed train that is powered by electricity from overhead wires.*
2. *noun* A group of people, animals, or vehicles traveling in a line, as in *a mule train* or *a wagon train.*
3. *verb* To prepare oneself by practicing, learning, or drilling. *Jocelyn trained as a doctor. Julio trained for the marathon.*
4. *verb* To teach a person or an animal how to do something. *We trained the dog to get the newspaper.*
5. *verb* To bring up children a certain way. *My parents trained me to be polite.*
6. *verb* To make a plant grow in a certain direction or shape.
7. *noun* The long piece of fabric that trails behind a bride's dress.
▷ *noun* **training** ▷ *verb* **training, trained**

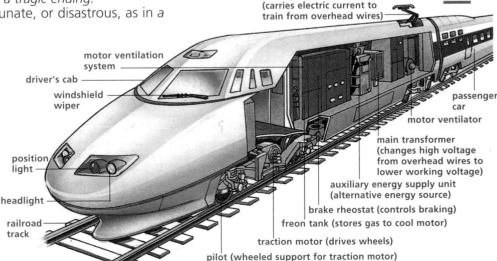

train

pantograph (carries electric current to train from overhead wires)

motor ventilation system

driver's cab

windshield wiper

position light

headlight

railroad track

passenger car

motor ventilator

main transformer (changes high voltage from overhead wires to lower working voltage)

auxiliary energy supply unit (alternative energy source)

brake rheostat (controls braking)

freon tank (stores gas to cool motor)

traction motor (drives wheels)

pilot (wheeled support for traction motor)

T

train·er (tray-nur) *noun*
1. A person who trains circus animals, show animals, or pets.
2. A person who helps athletes get in the best condition to compete in a sports event or exhibition.

traipse (trayps) *verb* To walk or travel about without a plan or purpose. *We traipsed through the woods with our sketchbooks, drawing whatever we found interesting.* ▷ **traipsing, traipsed**

trait (trate) *noun* A quality or characteristic that makes one person or thing different from another. *Loyalty is an important trait for a friend to have.*

trai·tor (tray-tur) *noun*
1. Someone who aids the enemy of his or her country; a person who betrays his or her country or commits treason.
2. Someone who is unfaithful or false to a friend, cause, or trust.

tramp (tramp)
1. *verb* To walk or tread with heavy steps. *We tramped up the hill.*
2. *verb* To go for a long walk or hike. *We tramped through the countryside.* ▷ *noun* **tramp**
3. *noun* Someone who wanders from place to place and does not have a permanent home.
4. *noun* The sound made by heavy steps.
▷ *verb* **tramping, tramped**

tram·ple (tram-puhl) *verb* To damage or crush something by walking heavily all over it.
▷ **trampling, trampled**

tram·po·line (*tram*-puh-**leen** *or* **tram**-puh-*leen*) *noun* A piece of canvas attached to a frame by elastic ropes or springs. Trampolines are used for jumping, either as a sport or for pleasure.

trance (transs) *noun* If you are **in a trance,** you are in a conscious state but not really aware of what is happening around you.

tran·quil (trang-kwuhl) *adjective* Calm and peaceful. ▷ *noun* **tranquillity** *or* **tranquility**

trans·ac·tion (tran-zak-shuhn) *noun* An exchange of goods, services, or money. *At our bank, we can do many transactions via computer.* ▷ *verb* **transact**

trans·at·lan·tic (*tran*-suht-**lan**-tik *or* tran-zuht-**lan**-tik) *adjective*
1. Crossing the Atlantic Ocean. *I made a transatlantic telephone call to my friend in England.*
2. On or from the other side of the Atlantic.

trans·con·ti·nen·tal (*transs*-kon-tuh-**nen**-tuhl) *adjective* Crossing a continent. *We took a transcontinental trip from California to New York.*

trans·fer
1. (transs-**fur** *or* transs-fur) *verb* To move from one person or place to another. *I transferred the ball to my right hand.* ▷ *noun* **transfer** (transs-fur)

2. (transs-fur) *verb* To change from one vehicle or method of transportation to another. *Dustin transferred from the bus to the train.*
3. (transs-fur) *noun* A printed ticket that permits you to change from one vehicle or route to another without paying more money.
4. (transs-fur) *noun* A small picture or design that can be stuck to another surface by rubbing or ironing.
▷ *noun* **transferal** ▷ *verb* **transferring, transferred**

trans·form (transs-form) *verb* To make a great change in something. *Meeting Steve has transformed my life.* ▷ **transforming, transformed** ▷ *noun* **transformation**

trans·form·er (transs-for-mur) *noun* A piece of equipment that changes the voltage of an electric current.

trans·fu·sion (transs-fyoo-zhuhn) *noun* The injection of blood from one person into the body of someone else who is injured or ill.

tran·sient (tran-shuhnt)
1. *adjective* Lasting for only a short time, as in *a transient illness.*
2. *noun* A person without a permanent home who moves from place to place.

tran·sis·tor (tran-ziss-tur) *noun* A small electronic device that controls the flow of electric current in radios, television sets, computers, etc.

tran·sit (tran-sit *or* tran-zit) *noun*
1. A system for carrying people or goods from one place to another on trains, buses, and other vehicles; a public transportation system.
2. If people or goods are **in transit,** they are in the process of going from one place to another.

tran·si·tion (tran-zish-uhn) *noun* A change from one form, condition, or place to another. *Moving from the city to the country was a difficult transition for Hannah.*

tran·si·tive (tran-suh-tiv) *adjective* A **transitive** verb needs an object in order to complete its meaning. The verbs *called* and *visited* are transitive in the sentence: *We called our friends and then visited them.* See **intransitive.**

trans·late (transs-late *or* transs-late) *verb* To express in a different language. *Juanita translated the paragraph from English into Spanish.* ▷ **translating, translated** ▷ *noun* **translation,** *noun* **translator**

trans·lu·cent (transs-loo-suhnt) *adjective* A **translucent** substance is not completely clear like glass but will let some light through. ▷ *noun* **translucence**

trans·mis·sion (transs-mish-uhn) *noun*
1. The act of transmitting or sending something from one person or place to another.

2. Something that is transmitted, such as a telegram.
3. In an automobile, a series of gears that send power from the engine to the wheels.

trans·mit (transs-mit) *verb*
1. To send or pass something from one place or person to another, as in *to transmit a message* or *to transmit a disease.*
2. To send out radio or television signals. *The program will be transmitted next Friday.* ▷ *noun* **transmitter**
3. To cause or allow something such as light, heat, or sound to pass through a material or substance. *Water transmits light.*
▷ *verb* **transmitting, transmitted**

tran·som
(tran-suhm)
noun
1. A small window over a door or another window.
2. If something comes **over the transom,** you did not request it or arrange to receive it. See **building**

door and transom

transom

trans·par·en·cy
(transs-**pair**-uhn-see *or* transs-**pa**-ruhn-see) *noun* Something transparent, especially a photographic slide.
▷ *noun, plural* **transparencies**

trans·par·ent (transs-**pair**-uhnt *or* transs-**pa**-ruhnt) *adjective*
1. A **transparent** substance is clear like glass and lets light through so that objects on the other side can be seen clearly.
2. Obvious or clear, as in *a transparent lie.*

tran·spi·ra·tion (*transs*-puh-ray-shuhn) *noun* The process by which plants give off moisture into the atmosphere. ▷ *verb* **transpire**

trans·plant
1. (transs-**plant**) *verb* To dig up a plant and plant it somewhere else. ▷ **transplanting, transplanted**
▷ *noun* **transplant** (transs-plant)
2. (transs-plant) *noun* A surgical operation in which a diseased organ such as a kidney is replaced by a healthy one. ▷ *verb* **transplant** (transs-**plant**)

trans·port
1. (transs-**port**) *verb* To move people and freight from one place to another. *The truck transported chickens.* ▷ *noun* **transport** (transs-port)

2. (transs-port) *noun* A vehicle that carries people or freight, such as a ship or plane.
3. (transs-**port**) *verb* To fill or overwhelm with strong emotion.
▷ *verb* **transporting, transported**

trans·por·ta·tion (*transs*-pur-**tay**-shuhn) *noun* A means or system for moving people and freight from one place to another. *My bicycle is my main transportation.*

trap (trap)
1. *noun* A device for capturing an animal.
2. *noun* Anything used to trick or catch someone. *The police set a trap at the jewelry store and caught the burglar the next night.*
3. *verb* To capture a person or an animal in a trap. ▷ **trapping, trapped** ▷ *noun* **trapper**

trap·door (trap-dor) *noun* A door in a floor, ceiling, or roof.

tra·peze (tra-**peez** *or* truh-**peez**) *noun* A horizontal bar hanging from two ropes. A trapeze is used by circus performers and gymnasts.

tra·pe·zi·um (truh-**pee**-zee-uhm) *noun* A shape with four sides, none of which is parallel to another. ▷ *noun, plural* **trapeziums** *or* **trapezia** (truh-**pee**-zee-uh)

trap·e·zoid (trap-uh-zoid) *noun* A shape with four sides of which only two are parallel. *See* **shape.**

trap·per (trap-ur) *noun* Someone who makes a living by trapping wild animals, usually for their fur.

trash (trash) *noun*
1. Things that you have thrown away because they are worthless; garbage.
2. Nonsense.

trau·ma (traw-muh *or* trou-muh) *noun*
1. A severe and painful emotional shock.
2. A severe physical wound or injury.

trau·mat·ic (traw-**mat**-ik) *adjective* If something is **traumatic,** it is shocking and very upsetting.

trav·el (trav-uhl) *verb*
1. To go from one place to another; to take a trip. ▷ *noun* **travel** ▷ *adjective* **traveling**
2. To pass or to move; to be transmitted. *Sound travels through water.*
3. In basketball, to move illegally by failing to dribble the ball while walking or running.
▷ *verb* **traveling, traveled**

> **Word History**
> •
> **Travel** comes from the old French word *travailler,* meaning "to suffer; to be troubled; to be worn out." Going from place to place was a difficult experience hundreds of years ago, a fact that no doubt explains the origin of the word.

T

travel agent *noun* A person or company that organizes travel and vacations for its customers. ▷ *noun* **travel agency**

trav·el·er (trav-uh-lur) *noun* Someone who travels. *The traveler looked like he had been away from home for a long, long time.*

trawl·er (traw-lur) *noun* A fishing boat that drags a large net shaped like a bag through the water. ▷ *verb* **trawl**

tray (tray) *noun* A flat, shallow container with a low rim. Trays are used for carrying, holding, or displaying things.

treach·er·ous (trech-ur-uhss) *adjective*
1. Not to be trusted; disloyal, as in *a treacherous spy.* ▷ *noun* **treachery**
2. Dangerous; hazardous. *The icy roads were treacherous.*
▷ *adverb* **treacherously**

tread (tred)
1. *verb* To walk on, over, or along. *We trod the path toward the beach.*
2. *verb* To press or crush with the feet; to trample. *Don't tread on my feet, please.*
3. *noun* The flat, horizontal part of a step.
4. *noun* The ridges on a car tire or the sole of a shoe that help prevent slipping.
5. If you **tread water,** you swim in one place with your body in a vertical position.
▷ *verb* **treading, trod** (trod), **trodden** (trod-in)

tread·mill (tred-*mil*) *noun* A device that is worked by a continuously moving belt or the moving steps of a wheel. Some treadmills are used for exercise.

trea·son (tree-zuhn) *noun* The crime of betraying your country by spying for another country or by helping an enemy during a war.

treas·ure (trezh-ur)
1. *noun* Gold, jewels, money, or other valuable things that have been collected or hidden, as in *buried treasure.*
2. *verb* To love and value very highly something that you have or own. *I treasure my independence.* ▷ **treasuring, treasured** ▷ *noun* **treasure** ▷ *adjective* **treasured**

treas·ur·er (trezh-ur-ur) *noun* The person in charge of the money of a government, company, or club.

treas·ur·y (trezh-ur-ee) *noun*
1. The funds of a government, company, or club.
2. Treasury A government department that is in charge of collecting taxes and managing the public's money.
3. A place where money or treasure is stored. *See* **temple.**
▷ *noun, plural* **treasuries**

treat (treet) *verb*
1. To deal with or act toward people or things in a certain way. *In China, older people are treated with great respect.*
2. To try to cure or heal; to give medical attention to. *The doctor treated the patient's burns.*
3. To process something in order to change it in some way. *Sewage is treated with chemicals to make it harmless.*
4. To give someone a special gift or take someone someplace special. *I'll treat you to dinner on your birthday.* ▷ *noun* **treat**
▷ *verb* **treating, treated** ▷ *noun* **treatment**

trea·ty (tree-tee) *noun* A formal agreement between two or more countries. ▷ *noun, plural* **treaties**

treb·le (treb-uhl)
1. *adjective* Three times as big or three times as many; triple.
2. *adjective* High in pitch, as in *a treble recorder.*
3. *verb* To increase to three times the original amount; to triple. *He expected to treble his original investment by the end of the year.*
▷ **trebling, trebled**
4. *noun* The highest musical part, voice, or instrument.

tree (tree)
1. *noun* A large, woody plant with a long trunk, roots, branches, and leaves. *See* **trunk.**
2. *verb* To pursue and chase up a tree. *Hounds treed the raccoon.* ▷ **treeing, treed**
3. *noun* Something that looks like a tree, such as the branching diagram used to show family relationships or a pole for hanging up clothes.

trek (trek) *verb* To make a slow, difficult journey. *The hikers trekked up the mountain.* ▷ **trekking, trekked** ▷ *noun* **trek**

trel·lis (trel-iss) *noun* A crisscross framework of thin strips of wood. Trellises are used to support growing plants. ▷ *noun, plural* **trellises**

trem·ble (trem-buhl) *verb*
1. To shake, especially from cold, fear, or excitement. *Carla's hands were trembling as she accepted the award.*
2. To vibrate; to quiver or quake. *The earth trembled as the volcano erupted.*
▷ *verb* **trembling, trembled**

tre·men·dous (tri-men-duhss) *adjective*
1. Huge or enormous. *A tremendous explosion shook the house.*
2. Very good or excellent. *We had a tremendous time surfing.*
▷ *adverb* **tremendously**

trem·or (trem-ur) *noun* A shaking or trembling movement. *Earth tremors are very common in places that often have earthquakes.*

trench (trench) *noun* A long, narrow ditch, especially one used to protect soldiers in battle. ▷ *noun, plural* **trenches**

trend (trend) *noun*
1. The general direction in which things are changing. *Recently there has been a trend toward smaller cars.* ▷ *verb* **trend**
2. The latest fashion. *The trend this season is for longer skirts.* ▷ *adjective* **trendy**

tres·pass (tress-puhss *or* tress-pass)
1. *verb* To enter someone's private property without permission. *Victor refused to trespass by walking through his neighbor's property, even though it would save him time.* ▷ **trespasses, trespassing, trespassed** ▷ *noun* **trespasser**
2. *noun* A sin. ▷ *noun, plural* **trespasses** ▷ *verb* **trespass**

tress (tress) *noun*
1. A lock of long hair. ▷ *noun, plural* **tresses**
2. tresses *noun, plural* A woman's or girl's hair, especially when it is worn long and loose.

tres·tle (tress-uhl) *noun* A framework that supports a bridge or railroad track.

▶ **Prefix**
• •

The prefix **tri-** adds the following meaning to a root word: Having or involving three, as in *triangle* (a shape having three angles), *triathlon* (an athletic event having three parts), and *tricycle* (a vehicle having three wheels).

tri·al (trye-uhl) *noun*
1. The examination of evidence in a court of law to decide if a charge or claim is true.
2. The act of trying or testing something; a test.
3. A frustrating or difficult experience that tests a person's faith, strength, or patience. *The first settlers faced a great many trials.*

tri·an·gle (trye-ang-guhl) *noun*
1. A closed shape with three straight sides and three angles. *See* **shape.** ▷ *adjective* **triangular**
2. A triangular percussion instrument made of steel. You play the triangle by striking it with a small metal rod. *See* **percussion.**

tri·ath·lon (trye-ath-lon) *noun* A long-distance race made up of three parts—usually, but not always, swimming, bicycling, and running. ▷ *noun* **triathlete** (trye-ath-leet)

tribe (tribe) *noun* A group of people who share the same ancestors, customs, and laws. ▷ *adjective* **tribal**

trib·u·la·tion (*trib*-yuh-**lay**-shuhn) *noun*
1. Severe distress or suffering.
2. A trying experience.

tri·bu·nal (tri-**byoo**-nuhl *or* trye-**byoo**-nuhl) *noun* A court of law.

trib·u·tar·y (**trib**-yuh-*ter*-ee) *noun* A stream or river that flows into a larger stream or river. *See* **river.** ▷ *noun, plural* **tributaries**

trib·ute (**trib**-yoot) *noun* Something done, given, or said to show thanks or respect. *The president's speech was a tribute to the soldiers who died in the war.*

tri·cer·a·tops (trye-**ser**-uh-*tops*) *noun* A large dinosaur that fed on plants and had three horns and a bony collar in the shape of a fan at the back of its head. *See* **dinosaur.** ▷ *noun, plural* **triceratops** *or* **triceratopses**

trich·i·no·sis (*trik*-uh-**noh**-siss) *noun* A disease caused by tiny worms often found in pork that has not been fully cooked. The symptoms include fever, diarrhea, and painful muscles.

trick (trik)
1. *verb* To fool or cheat someone; to make someone believe something that is not true. *Kevin tricked me into believing that he was related to the governor.* ▷ **tricking, tricked** ▷ *noun* **trick**, *noun* **trickery**
2. *noun* A clever or skillful act, as in *a magic trick.*
3. *noun* A prank or a practical joke.

trick·le (trik-uhl) *verb* To flow very slowly in a thin stream, or to fall in drops. *Water trickled constantly from the faucet.* ▷ **trickling, trickled** ▷ *noun* **trickle**

trick or treat *noun* A Halloween custom in which children go from house to house asking for treats and threatening to play tricks if something is not given. ▷ *verb* **trick-or-treat**

trick·y (trik-ee) *adjective*
1. Likely to use tricks; crafty.
2. Difficult in an unexpected way; requiring careful thought or handling, as in *a tricky question* or *a tricky situation.*
▷ *adjective* **trickier, trickiest**

tri·cy·cle (trye-suh-kuhl *or* trye-sik-uhl) *noun* A children's vehicle that has three wheels.

tri·fle (trye-fuhl)
1. *noun* Something that is not very valuable or important. ▷ *adjective* **trifling**
2. *noun* A small amount; a bit. *Janine was a trifle annoyed because I was late.*
3. *verb* To play with or not take seriously. *Don't trifle with my feelings.* ▷ **trifling, trifled**

trig·ger (trig-ur)
1. *noun* The lever on a gun that you pull to fire it.
2. *verb* To cause something to happen as a reaction. *The man's arrest triggered riots in the streets.* ▷ **triggering, triggered**

tril·o·gy (tril-uh-jee) *noun* A group of three related plays, novels, programs, etc., that together make a series. ▷ *noun, plural* **trilogies**

577

trim (trim)
1. *verb* To cut small pieces off something in order to improve its shape or to get rid of excess. *She trimmed our hair. The butcher trimmed the fat off the roast.*
2. *adjective* Neat, tidy, or in good condition.
▷ **trimmer, trimmest**
3. *verb* To add ornaments or decorations to something, as in *to trim a tree* or *to trim a gown.*
▷ *noun* **trim**
▷ *verb* **trimming, trimmed**

trim·ming (trim-ing)
1. *noun* Something used as a decoration.
2. **trimmings** *noun, plural* The things that are added to or that go with something. *We had roast turkey with all the trimmings.*

tri·o (tree-oh) *noun*
1. A group of three things or people.
2. A piece of music that is played or sung by three people.
▷ *noun, plural* **trios**

trip (trip)
1. *verb* To stumble and/or fall. *He tripped on a banana peel.*
2. *verb* To cause someone to stumble and/or fall.
3. *noun* A journey and/or a visit, as in *a trip to the zoo.*
4. *verb* To make a mistake.
▷ *verb* **tripping, tripped**

tripe (tripe) *noun*
1. The lining of the stomach of an ox or a cow. Tripe is eaten as food.
2. *(informal)* Anything that is useless or worthless.

tri·ple (trip-uhl)
1. *adjective* Three times as big, or three times as many. ▷ *verb* **triple**
2. *adjective* Made up of three parts. *The triple jump involves a hop, a step, and a jump.*
3. *verb* In baseball, to get a hit that allows you to reach third base. ▷ **tripling, tripled** ▷ *noun* **triple**

trip·let (trip-lit) *noun* One of three children born at the same birth.

tri·pod (trye-*pod*) *noun* A stand with three legs that is used to steady a camera or other piece of equipment. *See* **apparatus.**

tri·umph (trye-uhmf) *noun* A great victory, success, or achievement. ▷ *verb* **triumph**
▷ *adjective* **triumphant** (trye-uhm-fuhnt)

triv·i·al (triv-ee-uhl) *adjective* If something is **trivial,** it is not very important. *Don't bother me with such trivial questions.* ▷ *noun, plural* **trivia**

troll (trohl)
1. *verb* To fish by trailing a line with bait from behind a slowly moving boat. ▷ **trolling, trolled**
▷ *noun* **troller**
2. *noun* In fairy tales, a dwarf or giant that lives in a cave, in the hills, or under a bridge.

trol·ley (trol-ee) *noun* An electric streetcar that runs on tracks and gets its power from an overhead wire.

trom·bone (trom-bone) *noun* A brass musical instrument with a long, bent tube that can be slid back and forth to change the pitch of the tones. *See* **brass, orchestra.**

troop (troop)
1. *noun* An organized group of soldiers, scouts, etc.
2. *verb* To move in a group. *Sid and his friends trooped through the house.* ▷ **trooping, trooped**

troop·er (troo-pur) *noun* A state police officer. *The trooper pulled her over for speeding.*

tro·phy (troh-fee) *noun* A prize or an award such as a silver cup or plaque given to a winning athlete or team or to someone who has done something outstanding. ▷ *noun, plural* **trophies**

trop·i·cal (trop-uh-kuhl) *adjective* To do with or living in the hot, rainy area of the tropics.

tropical fish *noun* Any of various small or brightly colored fish that originally come from the tropics. Tropical fish are often kept as pets in aquariums. ▷ *noun, plural* **tropical fish** or **tropical fishes**

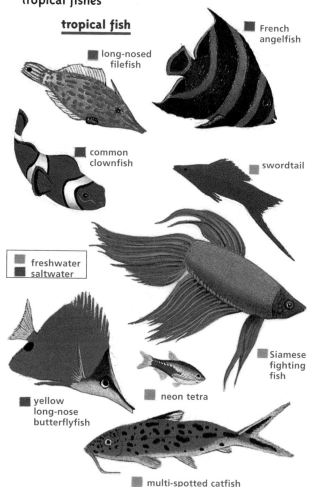

tropical fish

long-nosed filefish

French angelfish

common clownfish

swordtail

freshwater
saltwater

Siamese fighting fish

yellow long-nose butterflyfish

neon tetra

multi-spotted catfish

trop·ics (trop-iks) *noun, plural* The extremely hot area of the earth near the equator. *Many kinds of plants live in the tropics.*

trot (trot) *verb*
1. When a horse **trots,** it moves briskly at a gait between a walk and a canter. ▷ *noun* **trot,** *noun* **trotter**
2. When a person **trots,** he or she runs slowly or jogs. *Each player trotted onto the field as his or her name was called.*
▷ *verb* **trotting, trotted**

trou·ble (truh-buhl)
1. *noun* A difficult, dangerous, or upsetting situation. ▷ *adjective* **troublesome**
2. *verb* To disturb or worry someone. *The letter troubled Peggy.* ▷ *adjective* **troubling,** *adjective* **troubled**
3. *noun* A cause of difficulty, worry, or annoyance. *The trouble with Bob is that he can never be serious.*
4. If you **take the trouble** to do something, you make an extra effort to do it.
5. *verb* To ask someone for help, or to make an extra effort. *Can I trouble you for the time? Joe*

didn't trouble to get up early to say good-bye.
▷ *verb* **troubling, troubled**

trough (trawf) *noun* A long, narrow container from which animals can drink or eat.

trou·sers (trou-zurz) *noun, plural* Another word for **pants.** ▷ *adjective* **trouser**

trout (trout) *noun* An edible freshwater fish that is related to the salmon.

trow·el (trou-uhl) *noun*
1. A hand tool with a flat blade shaped like a diamond. Trowels are used for laying cement, filling holes in plaster, etc.
2. A hand tool with a small, curved blade, used for planting and other light garden work.

tru·ant (troo-uhnt) *noun* A student who stays away from school without permission. ▷ *noun* **truancy** ▷ *adjective* **truant**

truce (trooss) *noun* A temporary agreement to stop fighting.

truck (truhk) *noun* A large motor vehicle used for carrying goods by road. *The picture shows a semitrailer truck, which is made up of a cab and a trailer linked by a flexible joint.*

semitrailer truck

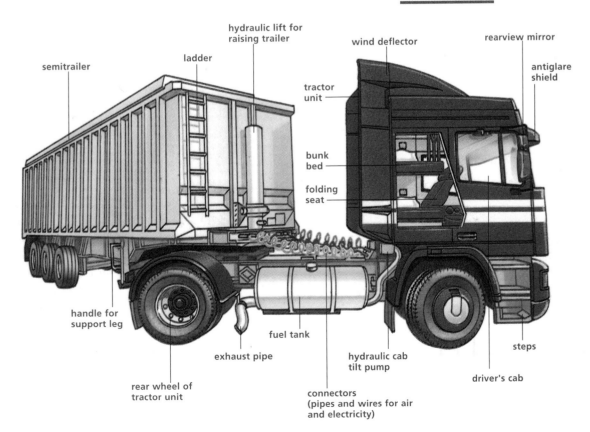

hydraulic lift for raising trailer

ladder

semitrailer

wind deflector

rearview mirror

antiglare shield

tractor unit

bunk bed

folding seat

handle for support leg

rear wheel of tractor unit

exhaust pipe

fuel tank

connectors (pipes and wires for air and electricity)

hydraulic cab tilt pump

driver's cab

steps

trudge (truhj) *verb* To walk slowly and with effort; to plod. *We trudged through the mud in search of the lost calf.* ▷ **trudging, trudged**

true (troo) *adjective*
1. Agreeing with the facts; not false; accurate, as in *a true story.*
2. Loyal or faithful, as in *a true friend.*
3. Real or genuine. *I have finally found true love. The whale is a true but not typical mammal.*
▷ *adjective* **truer, truest** ▷ *adverb* **truly**

trum·pet (truhm-pit) *noun*
1. A brass wind instrument that makes a loud, blaring sound. It has a long, looped tube that flares into a funnel shape and three valves that can be used to change the tones. See **brass, orchestra.**
2. A loud, blaring sound, such as the cry of an elephant. ▷ *verb* **trumpet**

trunk (truhngk) *noun*
1. The main stem of a tree. Tree trunks contain xylem and phloem vessels, which transport fluids up and down the tree. *In this cross section of a tree trunk, you can see the rings of xylem that are created each year.*
2. A large case or box used for storage or for carrying clothes on a long journey.
3. The upper part of your body, not including your head and arms.
4. The long nose of an elephant.
5. An enclosed compartment in a car, usually at the rear, where luggage and a spare tire can be stored.
6. trunks *noun, plural* Shorts worn by men or boys for swimming or boxing.

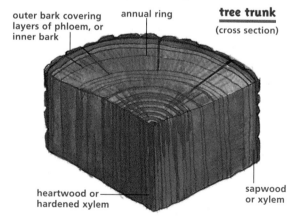

outer bark covering layers of phloem, or inner bark

annual ring

tree trunk
(cross section)

heartwood or hardened xylem

sapwood or xylem

trust (truhst) *verb* If you **trust** someone, you believe that he or she is honest and reliable.
▷ **trusting, trusted** ▷ *noun* **trust** ▷ *adjective* **trusting**

trust·wor·thy (truhst-*wur*-THee) *adjective* Honest, reliable, and able to be trusted, as in *a trustworthy friend.*

trust·y (truhss-tee) *adjective* Capable of being trusted; reliable; dependable. *A trusty friend never lets you down.*

truth (trooth) *noun*
1. The real facts. *Is he telling the truth?*
2. The quality of being true, real, honest, or accurate. *I doubt the truth of this witness's testimony.*
▷ *adjective* **truthful** ▷ *adverb* **truthfully**

try (trye) *verb*
1. To attempt to do something, or to do the best you can. *Try to behave.* ▷ *noun* **try**
2. To examine in a court of law someone accused of a criminal offense. *The person was tried for robbery.*
3. To test the quality, strength, or effect of something. *I decided to try a new chicken recipe.*
4. To put a strain on; to tax, as in *to try someone's patience.*
▷ *verb* **tries, trying, tried**

try·ing (trye-ing) *adjective* If a person is very **trying,** he or she is difficult or annoying.

try·out (trye-out) *noun* A trial or test to see if a person is qualified to do something such as perform a role in a play or play on a team; an audition. ▷ *verb* **try out**

tsar (zar) *See* **czar.**

tsa·ri·na (za-ree-nuh) *See* **czarina.**

T-shirt *or* **tee shirt** (tee-*shurt*) *noun* A light cotton shirt or undershirt with short sleeves and no collar.

tsu·na·mi (tsoo-nah-mee) *noun* A very large, destructive wave caused by an underwater earthquake or volcano.

tub (tuhb) *noun*
1. A bathtub.
2. A round, open container used for packing or storing foods, as in *a tub of ice cream.*
3. A large, wide container used for bathing or for washing clothes.

tu·ba (too-buh) *noun* A large, brass wind instrument with several valves. Tubas have a full, deep tone. See **brass, orchestra.**

tube (toob) *noun*
1. A long, hollow cylinder, especially one used to carry or hold liquids, as in *a test tube.*
2. A long container made of soft metal or plastic with a cap that screws on, as in *a tube of toothpaste.*
3. The hollow rubber ring that is put inside some bicycle tires and filled with air.
4. the tube *(informal)* Television. *Jerry is always watching the tube.*

tu·ber (too-bur) *noun* The thick underground stem of a plant such as a potato.

tu·ber·cu·lo·sis (tu-*bur*-kyuh-**loh**-siss) *noun* A highly contagious bacterial disease that usually affects the lungs.

tu·bu·lar (**too**-byuh-lur) *adjective* Shaped like a tube.

tuck (tuhk)
1. *verb* To fold or push the ends of something into place. *Tuck the sheets in neatly.*
2. *verb* To put to bed and cover snugly. *Mom tucked in the baby.*
3. *verb* To put into a snug or hidden place. *Tuck this away where no one will find it.*
4. *noun* A small fold sewn in material. ▷ *verb* tuck ▷ *verb* tucking, tucked

Tues·day (**tooz**-dee *or* **tooz**-day) *noun* The third day of the week, after Monday and before Wednesday.

Word History

Tuesday was named for Tiw, the old English god of war. The name of the third day of the week was pronounced "Tiw's day," which eventually was spelled Tuesday.

tuft (tuhft) *noun* A bunch of hair, grass, feathers, etc., attached together at the base. ▷ *adjective* tufted

tug (tuhg)
1. *verb* To pull hard. *The little boy tugged on his father's pants in order to get his attention.* ▷ tugging, tugged ▷ *noun* tug
2. *tug or* **tugboat** (**tuhg**-boht) *noun* A small, powerful boat that tows or pushes ships and barges.

tugboat

tug-of-war *noun* A contest between two teams, each holding onto opposite ends of a rope, who try to pull each other over a center line.

tu·i·tion (too-**ish**-uhn) *noun* Money paid to a private school or college in order for a student to receive instruction there.

tu·lip (**too**-lip) *noun* A plant with a tall stem topped with a colorful flower shaped like a cup. Tulips grow from bulbs.

tum·ble (**tuhm**-buhl) *verb*
1. To fall suddenly and helplessly. *Jack and Jill tumbled down the hill.*
2. To do somersaults, handsprings, or other acrobatic feats. ▷ *noun* **tumbler**
3. To roll or toss about. *The sheets and towels tumbled in the clothes dryer.*
4. To move in a hurried, disorderly way. *The puppies tumbled out the door.*
▷ *verb* tumbling, tumbled ▷ *noun* tumble

tum·bler (**tuhm**-blur) *noun* A tall drinking glass with straight sides.

tum·ble·weed (**tum**-buhl-*weed*) *noun* A bushy plant of western North America that dries up in autumn, breaks off from its roots, and blows around in the wind.

tum·my (**tuhm**-ee) *noun* (*informal*) The stomach. ▷ *noun, plural* **tummies**

tu·mor (**too**-mur) *noun* An abnormal lump or mass of tissue in the body.

tu·mult (**too**-muhlt) *noun* Loud noise and confusion. *There was a tumult in the auditorium when the fire bell rang.* ▷ *adjective* **tumultuous** (too-**muhl**-choo-uhss) ▷ *adverb* **tumultuously**

tu·na (**too**-nuh) *noun* A large, edible fish found in warm seas throughout the world. ▷ *noun, plural* **tuna** *or* **tunas**

tun·dra (**tuhn**-druh) *noun* A cold area of northern Europe and Asia where there are no trees and the soil under the surface of the ground is permanently frozen.

tune (toon *or* tyoon)
1. *noun* A series of musical notes arranged in a pattern; a simple melody that is easy to remember. ▷ *adjective* **tuneful**
2. *verb* To adjust the pitch of a musical instrument. *Mr. Nelson tuned our piano.* ▷ *noun* **tuner**
3. *noun* The condition of having the correct musical pitch. *The piano was out of tune.*
4. *noun* Harmony; agreement. *Some of my grandfather's ideas are not in tune with the times.*
5. *verb* If you **tune in** a radio or television program or station, you adjust the dial to receive it.
6. *verb* If you **tune** a car engine **up,** you put it in good working order by adjusting the parts. ▷ *verb* tuning, tuned

tu·nic (**too**-nik *or* **tyoo**-nik) *noun* A loose, sleeveless garment.

tuning fork *noun* A piece of metal with two prongs used for tuning musical instruments. When struck, it vibrates to produce a particular tone.

T

tun·nel (tuhn-uhl) *noun*
1. A passage built beneath the ground or water or through a mountain for use by cars, trains, or other vehicles. *The picture shows cross sections of the Channel Tunnel that runs under the seabed between England and France.*
2. An animal's burrow. ▷ *verb* **tunnel**

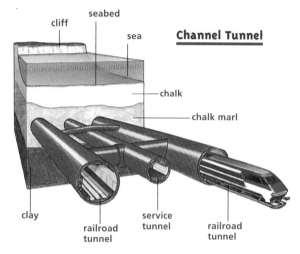

Channel Tunnel

cliff
seabed
sea
chalk
chalk marl
clay
railroad tunnel
service tunnel
railroad tunnel

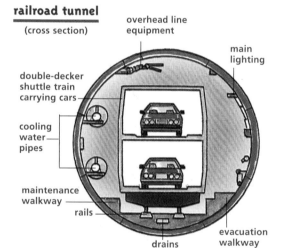

railroad tunnel
(cross section)

overhead line equipment
main lighting
double-decker shuttle train carrying cars
cooling water pipes
maintenance walkway
rails
drains
evacuation walkway

> ## Word History
> ●
>
> The word **tunnel** comes from the older word *tonel,* the name for a net with a wide mouth used for trapping birds. This evolved into *tunnell,* which came to mean any pipe or tube, and then into tunnel, which can be thought of as a long, wide, underground tube.

tunnel vision *noun*
1. The condition in which the eye has no peripheral vision but sees things as if through a tunnel.
2. An extremely narrow outlook on things, without consideration of possible alternatives.

tur·ban (tur-buhn) *noun* A head covering made by winding a long scarf around the head or around a cap. Turbans are worn especially by men in Arab countries and India.

tur·bine (tur-buhn *or* tur-bine) *noun* An engine driven by water, steam, or gas passing through the blades of a wheel and making it revolve. *See* **jet engine.**

tur·bo (tur-boh) *adjective* A **turbo** or **turbo-charged** engine has high-pressure air forced into its cylinders by a turbine, producing extra power.

tur·bo·fan (tur-boh-*fan*) *noun* A type of aircraft engine in which a large fan, driven by a turbine, pushes air into the hot exhaust at the rear of the engine, giving extra power. *See* **jet engine.**

tur·bu·lent (tur-byuh-luhnt) *adjective* Wild, confused, or violent; not calm or smooth, as in *turbulent rapids* or *a turbulent time in history.*

turf (turf) *noun* The surface layer of grass and earth on a lawn or playing field.

tur·key (tur-kee) *noun*
1. A large North American bird with red-brown feathers and a tail that spreads out like a fan.
2. *(slang)* A hopeless or useless person or thing.

wild turkey

> ## Word History
> ●
>
> The **turkey** got its name quite by accident. Native to America, it looks like an African bird that had been brought to Europe from Turkey. When the first European settlers saw this bird in America, they thought it was the African bird, which by then had been named "turkey." By the time the settlers realized the birds were different, everyone was calling the American bird a turkey.

T

tur·moil (tur-moil) *noun* Great confusion. *The city was in turmoil after the blizzard.*

turn (turn)
1. *verb* To change direction. *Turn left at the corner.*
2. *noun* A change in direction or position, or the point where such a change takes place. *He took a turn to the right. Take a left at the next turn.*
3. *verb* To spin or to rotate. *Turn the wheel.*
4. *noun* The act of turning; a rotation, as in *one turn of the wheel.*
5. *verb* To change appearance or state. *The liquid turns into a vapor when heated.*
6. *noun* A change in events or time, as in *a turn for the worse* or *the turn of the century.*
7. *verb* To become. *My skin turns darker in the sun. The milk turned sour.*
8. *verb* To move a switch, faucet, etc., in order to control the supply of something. *Turn down the volume.*
9. *verb* To unsettle, or to make sick. *The strong smell turned my stomach.*
10. *noun* If it is your **turn** to do something, it is your chance or duty to do it. *The pitcher had her turn at bat.*
11. *noun* A **good turn** is a helpful action.
12. *verb* If you **turn** something **down,** you refuse it.
13. *verb* If someone **turns in,** the person goes to bed.
14. *verb* If someone **turns up,** he or she appears.
15. *verb* (*slang*) If something **turns** you **on,** it makes you enthusiastic or excited. ▷ *noun* **turn-on**
▷ *verb* **turning, turned** ▷ *noun* **turn**

tur·nip (tur-nuhp) *noun* A round, white or yellow root vegetable.

turn·out (turn-*out*) *noun* The number of people at a gathering or an event. *We expected a low voter turnout, but many people came to the polls.*

turn·pike (turn-*pike*) *noun* An expressway on which tolls are paid.

turn·stile (turn-*stile*) *noun* A revolving gate or movable bar at an exit or entrance. A turnstile lets people pass through one at a time.

turn·ta·ble (turn-*tay*-buhl) *noun* A circular, revolving surface. A turntable can be used for playing phonograph records.

tur·pen·tine (tur-puhn-tine) *noun* A clear liquid made from the sap of certain pine trees. Turpentine is often used to thin paints.

tur·quoise (tur-koiz *or* tur-kwoiz) *noun*
1. A valuable, blue-green stone used in making jewelry. *See* **mineral.**
2. A blue-green color.
▷ *adjective* **turquoise**

tur·ret (tur-it) *noun*
1. A round tower on a building, usually on a corner. Many castles have turrets.

2. A structure on a tank, warship, or fighter plane that holds one or more guns. It usually rotates so that the gun can be fired in different directions.

tur·tle (tur-tuhl)
noun
A reptile that can pull its head, legs, and tail into its hard shell for protection. Turtles live on land and in water. *The shell of the matamata turtle looks like a dead leaf.*

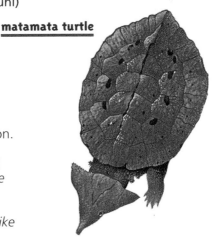

matamata turtle

tur·tle·neck (tur-tuhl-*nek*) *noun*
1. A high collar that turns down and fits snugly around the neck.
2. A sweater or shirt with such a collar.

tusk (tuhsk) *noun* One of the pair of long, curved, pointed teeth of an elephant, a walrus, a wild boar, and some other animals.

tus·sle (tuhss-uhl) *verb* To fight or wrestle vigorously; to scuffle. ▷ **tussling, tussled** ▷ *noun* **tussle**

tu·tor (too-tur) *noun* A teacher who gives private lessons to one student at a time. ▷ *verb* **tutor**

tu·tu (too-too) *noun* A short ballet skirt made of several layers of stiff net.

tux·e·do (tuhk-see-doh) *noun* A man's jacket, usually black with satin lapels, worn with a bow tie for formal occasions. ▷ *noun, plural* **tuxedos**

TV (*tee*-vee) *noun* Short for **television.**

tweed (tweed) *noun* A rough wool cloth woven with yarns of two or more colors.

twee·zers (twee-zurz) *noun, plural* A small pincers used for pulling out hairs or for picking up very small objects.

twelfth (twelfth)
1. *adjective* That which comes after eleventh and before thirteenth. *My mom was the twelfth person chosen for the jury.*
2. *noun* One part of something that has been divided into 12 equal parts, written $\frac{1}{12}$.

twelve (twelv) *noun* The whole number, written 12, that comes after 11 and before 13.
▷ *adjective* **twelve**

twen·ty (twen-tee) *noun* The whole number, written 20, that is equal to 2 times 10.
▷ *adjective* **twenty**

twice (twisse) *adverb* Two times.

twig (twig) *noun* A small, thin branch of a tree or other woody plant.

twi·light (twye-*lite*) *noun* The time of day when the sun has just set and it is beginning to get dark.

twin (twin)
1. *noun* One of two children born at the same birth. ▷ *adjective* **twin**
2. *adjective* Belonging to a pair that are exactly the same, as in *twin beds.* ▷ *noun* **twin**

twine (twine)
1. *noun* A very strong string made of two or more strands twisted together.
2. *verb* To wind or grow in a coil. *Ivy twined around the trellis.* ▷ **twining, twined**

twinge (twinj) *noun* A sudden pain or unpleasant feeling. *Ellen felt a twinge of sadness as she waved good-bye.*

twin·kle (twing-kuhl)
1. *verb* To shine with quick flashes of light; to sparkle. ▷ **twinkling, twinkled**
2. *noun* A flash of light.

twirl (twurl) *verb* To turn or spin around quickly. *Courtney felt dizzy from twirling around the room.* ▷ **twirling, twirled** ▷ *noun* **twirl**

twist (twist) *verb*
1. To turn, wind, or bend. *Andy twisted the top off the jar. The road twisted through the mountains.*
2. To wind two strands of something together.
3. To sprain. *I twisted my ankle.*
4. When you **twist** someone's words, you purposely change the meaning of what he or she said.
▷ *verb* **twisting, twisted** ▷ *noun* **twist**

twis·ter (twiss-tur) *noun* (informal) A tornado.

twitch (twich) *verb* To make small, jerky movements. *The animal's nose twitched.*
▷ **twitches, twitching, twitched** ▷ *noun* **twitch** ▷ *adjective* **twitchy**

twit·ter (twit-ur) *noun*
1. The short, high, chirping sounds that a bird makes. ▷ *verb* **twitter**
2. A state of nervous excitement. *The crowd was in a twitter before the concert started.*

two (too) *noun* The whole number, written 2, that comes after 1 and before 3. **Two** sounds like **to** and **too.** ▷ *adjective* **two**

ty·coon (tye-koon) *noun* A very wealthy, powerful businessperson.

type (tipe)
1. *noun* A kind or a sort. *What type of bike do you have?*
2. *noun* Small pieces of metal with raised letters, numbers, punctuation marks, etc., on their surfaces. Type is used in printing.
3. *verb* To write something with a typewriter or computer. ▷ **typing, typed**
4. *noun* Printed letters and numbers. *The picture shows two styles of type: serif, which has a small line, or serif, at the ends of the main strokes of most letters, and sans serif, which has no serifs.*

styles of type

type
serif

type
sans serif

type·set (tipe-set) *verb* To put a piece of writing into a typed form that can be used in printing. ▷ **typesetting, typeset** ▷ *noun* **typesetter** ▷ *adjective* **typeset**

type·writ·er (tipe-*rye*-tur) *noun* A machine that prints letters, numbers, and punctuation marks when you press keys with your fingers.

> ▶ **Word History**
> ●
>
> The first **typewriter** for use by the general public was invented by Christopher Latham Sholes, an American, in 1868. The machine, which Sholes called a "type-writer," had only capital letters. Still, it was used by a number of famous writers, including Mark Twain, who in 1875 produced the first book ever written on a typewriter, *The Adventures of Tom Sawyer.*

ty·phoid (tye-foid) *noun* A serious infectious disease with symptoms of high fever and diarrhea that sometimes leads to death. It is caused by germs in food or water.

ty·phoon (tye-foon) *noun* A violent tropical storm. Typhoons occur in the western Pacific Ocean.

typ·i·cal (tip-uh-kuhl) *adjective*
1. Having traits or qualities that are normal for a type or class; conforming to a type or class. *My family lives in a typical small town.*
2. If someone does something that is **typical,** the person behaves in his or her usual way. *It's typical of Toby to forget my birthday.*
▷ *adverb* **typically**

typ·ist (tye-pist) *noun* Someone who uses a typewriter or computer to write things.

ty·ran·no·saur (ti-ran-uh-sor) *noun* A huge dinosaur that fed on meat and walked upright on its hind legs.

ty·rant (tye-ruhnt) *noun* Someone who rules other people in a cruel or unjust way. ▷ *noun* **tyranny** (tihr-uh-nee) ▷ *adjective* **tyrannical** (ti-ran-i-kuhl)

T

Uu

About U

Spelling Hint: Words that begin with a *yoo* sound are spelled *u* or *eu*. Examples: ukulele, uranium, utility, eucalyptus, Europe, euthanasia.

ud·der (uhd-ur) *noun* The baglike part of a female cow, sheep, etc., that hangs down near its back legs. The udder contains the glands that produce milk.

UFO (yoo ef oh) *noun* An object that is seen or is thought to be seen flying in the sky, believed by some people to be a spaceship from another planet. UFO is short for *Unidentified Flying Object.*

ug·ly (uhg-lee) *adjective*
1. If someone or something is **ugly,** it is not attractive or pleasant to look at.
2. Disgusting or unpleasant. *I heard an ugly rumor that the top team in our league cheats.*
3. Nasty or mean, as in *an ugly mood.*
▷ *adjective* **uglier, ugliest**

u·ku·le·le (yoo-kuh-lay-lee) *noun* A small, four-stringed guitar originally made popular in Hawaii.

▶ **Word History**

Ukulele is the Hawaiian name for the musical instrument that was first brought to Hawaii by the Portuguese in 1879. In Hawaiian, *uku* means "flea" and *lele* means "jumping." This seemed an appropriate name for the instrument for two reasons. First, a ukulele player's fingers can seem to move around the strings like a jumping flea. Also, "The Flea" was the nickname of an army officer named Edward Purvis who helped make the ukulele popular in Hawaii.

ul·cer (uhl-sur) *noun* An open, painful sore on the skin or on the lining of the stomach.

ul·ti·mate (uhl-tuh-mit) *adjective*
1. Last or final. *Adrienne's ultimate career goal is to become a doctor.*
2. Original or basic. *The sun is the ultimate source of all our energy.*
3. Greatest or best. *This car is the ultimate example of speed and luxury.*
▷ *noun* **ultimate** ▷ *adverb* **ultimately**

ul·ti·ma·tum (uhl-tuh-**may**-tuhm) *noun* A final offer or demand, especially one that carries with it the threat of punishment or the use of force if rejected. *Jeffrey's new boss gave him an ultimatum: Start getting to work on time or find another job.* ▷ *noun, plural* **ultimatums** *or* **ultimata** (uhl-tuh-**may**-tuh)

ul·tra·light (uhl-truh-*lite*) *noun* A very light aircraft, usually for one person, which is powered by a small engine.

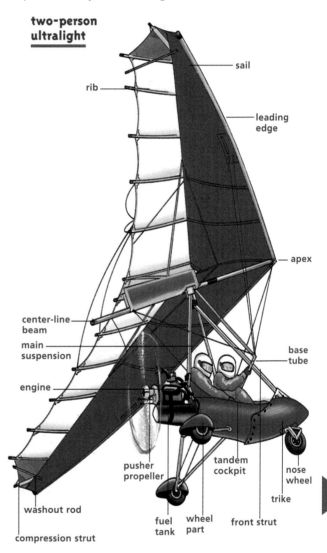

two-person ultralight

sail
rib
leading edge
apex
center-line beam
main suspension
engine
base tube
pusher propeller
tandem cockpit
nose wheel
trike
washout rod
fuel tank
wheel part
front strut
compression strut

ul·tra·sound (uhl-truh-*sound*) *noun* Sound whose frequency is too high for the human ear to hear. Ultrasound waves are used in medical scans.

ul·tra·vi·o·let light (*uhl*-truh-**vye**-uh-lit) *noun* Light that cannot be seen by the human eye. It is given off by the sun and causes the skin to get darker.

um·bil·i·cal cord (uhm-bil-uh-kuhl) *noun* The tube that connects an unborn baby to its mother's body and through which it gets oxygen and food.

um·brel·la (uhm-**brel**-uh) *noun* A folding frame with a circular cloth stretched over it that you hold over your head to protect you from the rain or the sun.

um·pire (**uhm**-pire) *noun* An official who rules on plays in baseball, tennis, and certain other sports. *With his arms spread out, the umpire is showing that the runner is safe.* ▷ *verb* **umpire**

umpire

Prefix

The prefix **un-** adds one of the following meanings to a root word:

1. Not, as in *unemployed* (not employed), *unbelievable* (not believable), and *unavoidable* (not avoidable).

2. The opposite of, as in *unlock* (to do the opposite of lock) and *undress* (to do the opposite of dress).

un·a·ble (uhn-**ay**-buhl) *adjective* If you are **unable** to do something, you cannot do it.

un·ac·cept·a·ble (uhn-uhk-**sep**-tuh-buhl) *adjective* If something is **unacceptable,** it is not good enough to be allowed or accepted. ▷ *adverb* **unacceptably**

un·ac·cus·tomed (uhn-uh-**kuhss**-tuhmd) *adjective* If you are **unaccustomed** to something, you are not used to it.

un·adul·ter·at·ed (uhn-uh-**duhl**-tuh-*ray*-tid) *adjective* If a substance is **unadulterated,** it is pure; it has not had anything extra or artificial added to it.

un·aid·ed (uhn-**ay**-did) *adjective* If you do something **unaided,** you do it on your own without any help.

u·nan·i·mous (yoo-**nan**-uh-muhss) *adjective* Agreed on by everyone, as in *a unanimous decision.* ▷ *adverb* **unanimously**

un·ap·proach·a·ble (*uhn*-uh-**proh**-chuh-buhl) *adjective*
1. Someone who is **unapproachable** is not friendly or easy to get to know.
2. If a place is **unapproachable,** you cannot get to it. *The mountain hut is unapproachable by road.*

un·armed (uhn-**armd**) *adjective* Someone who is **unarmed** is not carrying any weapons.

un·au·tho·rized (uhn-**aw**-thuh-rized) *adjective* If something is **unauthorized,** it is done without official permission.

un·a·void·a·ble (*uhn*-uh-**voi**-duh-buhl) *adjective* If something is **unavoidable,** it is impossible to prevent. ▷ *adverb* **unavoidably**

un·a·ware (*uhn*-uh-**wair**) *adjective* If you are **unaware** of something, you do not know that it exists or is happening.

un·bear·a·ble (uhn-**bair**-uh-buhl) *adjective* If something is **unbearable,** it is so bad or unpleasant that you cannot stand it. ▷ *adverb* **unbearably**

un·be·com·ing (uhn-bi-**kuhm**-ing) *adjective*
1. Not attractive or not flattering, as in *an unbecoming outfit.*
2. Not in good taste; not proper, as in *unbecoming behavior.*

un·be·liev·a·ble (*uhn*-bi-**leev**-uh-buhl) *adjective* If something is **unbelievable,** it is so strange, amazing, surprising, or wonderful that you find it hard to accept that it is true.

un·bend·ing (uhn-**ben**-ding) *adjective* If someone is **unbending,** the person is very firm or stubborn and will not change his or her mind.

un·break·a·ble (uhn-**bray**-kuh-buhl) *adjective* Not able to be broken, or not likely to be broken, as in *unbreakable dishes.*

un·bro·ken (uhn-**broh**-kuhn) *adjective*
1. Not broken; whole. *After the earthquake, we found that only a few of our glasses and dishes were unbroken.*
2. Not interrupted; without a stop or break; continuous. *Looking down from the airplane, I was able to see miles of unbroken forest.*
3. Not tamed or trained for use with a harness. *Only the best rider can manage an unbroken horse.*
4. Not bettered or topped, as in *an unbroken sports record.*

un·bur·den (uhn-**bur**-duhn) *verb* If you **unburden** yourself, you tell another person about your troubles, fears, or worries. *Jerome unburdened himself by confessing what he had done.*
▷ **unburdening, unburdened**

586

un·can·ny (uhn-**kan**-ee) *adjective*
1. Very strange and difficult to explain or understand; mysterious; eerie, as in *uncanny sounds.*
2. Remarkable or extraordinary, as in *an uncanny sense of direction.*
▷ *adverb* **uncannily**

un·cer·tain (uhn-**sur**-tuhn) *adjective*
1. If you are **uncertain** about something, you are not sure about it.
2. If the weather is **uncertain,** it is likely to change.
▷ *noun* **uncertainty**

un·civ·i·lized (uhn-**siv**-uh-lized) *adjective*
1. Not yet civilized or educated, as in *an uncivilized people.*
2. Uncivilized behavior is rude and wild.

un·cle (**uhng**-kuhl) *noun* The brother of your mother or father, or the husband of your aunt.

un·com·fort·a·ble (uhn-**kuhm**-fur-tuh-buhl *or* uhn-**kuhmf**-tuh-buhl) *adjective*
1. If you are **uncomfortable,** you do not feel relaxed in your body or your mind. *Speaking in front of an audience makes Stacy uncomfortable.*
▷ *adverb* **uncomfortably**
2. Something that is **uncomfortable** makes you worry or feel pain, as in *an uncomfortable situation* or *uncomfortable shoes.*

un·com·mon (uhn-**kom**-uhn) *adjective* Rare or unusual; out of the ordinary. *Grizzly bears are uncommon in this area.*

un·com·pli·men·ta·ry (uhn-*kom*-pluh-**men**-tuh-ree) *adjective* If someone says **uncomplimentary** things about you, the words are insulting, rude, or negative.

un·com·pro·mis·ing (uhn-**kom**-pruh-*mye*-zing) *adjective* If you are **uncompromising,** you refuse to give in or change your ideas or accept something that is not exactly what you wanted.
▷ *adverb* **uncompromisingly**

un·con·cerned (*uhn*-kuhn-**surnd**) *adjective*
1. Not interested; indifferent. *Dan is always sure that he is right; he is unconcerned with what other people think.*
2. Not worried, anxious, or upset. *Although the boy had a fever, the doctor remained unconcerned.*

un·con·di·tion·al (*uhn*-kuhn-**dish**-uh-nuhl) *adjective* Not limited by any conditions; without limitations, as in *unconditional surrender.*
▷ *adverb* **unconditionally**

un·con·firmed (*uhn*-kuhn-**furmd**) *adjective* Not yet known to be true, as in *unconfirmed rumors.*

un·con·scious (uhn-**kon**-shuhss) *adjective*
1. Not awake; not able to see, feel, or think. *The woman was knocked unconscious when she fell off the horse.*
2. Unaware of something. *George was unconscious of the fact that the bus was leaving.*
3. Not done on purpose. *It was an unconscious mistake.*

un·con·sti·tu·tion·al (uhn-*kon*-stuh-**too**-shuh-nuhl) *adjective* Not in keeping with the basic principles or laws set forth in the constitution of a state or country, especially the Constitution of the United States. *It is unconstitutional to interfere with someone's right to free speech in this country and many others.*

un·con·trol·la·ble (uhn-kuhn-**troh**-luh-buhl) *adjective* Something that is **uncontrollable** cannot be stopped, held in, or restrained, as in *uncontrollable laughter.* ▷ *adverb* **uncontrollably**

un·co·op·er·a·tive (*uhn*-koh-op-uh-ruh-tiv) *adjective* If you are **uncooperative,** you refuse to help people or do what they ask.

un·couth (uhn-**kooth**) *adjective* Rough and rude. *We were surprised at their uncouth behavior.*

un·cov·er (uhn-**kuhv**-ur) *verb*
1. To take a cover off something. *Uncover the casserole so that it will cool off more quickly.*
2. To reveal something; to make something known. *The investigation uncovered a major fraud.*
▷ *verb* **uncovering, uncovered**

un·daunt·ed (uhn-**dawn**-tid) *adjective* If you are **undaunted,** you are not discouraged or frightened by dangers or difficulties. *We were undaunted by the long drive ahead.*

un·de·cid·ed (*uhn*-di-**sye**-did) *adjective*
1. If you are **undecided** about something, you have not made up your mind about it.
2. Not yet settled. *The result of the election is still undecided.*

un·de·ni·a·ble (*uhn*-di-**nye**-uh-buhl) *adjective* Something that is **undeniable** is clearly true.
▷ *adverb* **undeniably**

un·der (**uhn**-dur) *preposition*
1. Below or beneath. *The key is under the mat.*
▷ *adverb* **under**
2. Less than a number or amount. *Children under 12 will not be admitted.*
3. According to. *Under the rules, she can't reenter the game.*
4. Controlled or bound by, as in *under oath.*

un·der·arm (**uhn**-dur-*arm*)
1. *adverb* Underhand. *Helene pitched underarm.*
2. *noun* The armpit, or the part of the body that is under the arm.
▷ *adjective* **underarm**

un·der·brush (**uhn**-dur-*bruhsh*) *noun* Bushes, shrubs, and other plants that grow beneath the large trees in the forest or woods.

un·der·clothes (**uhn**-dur-*kloze*) *noun, plural* Underwear.

un·der·de·vel·oped (*uhn*-dur-di-**vel**-uhpt) *adjective*
1. Not completely or normally developed, as in *underdeveloped film* or *underdeveloped muscles*.
2. In an **underdeveloped nation,** most people are poor and there is not yet much industry.

un·der·dog (uhn-dur-*dawg*) *noun* A person, team, or group that is expected to be the loser in a game, a race, an election, or other contest.

un·der·es·ti·mate (uhn-dur-**ess**-tuh-*mate*) *verb*
1. To think that something is not as good or as great as it really is. *Never underestimate your opponent's ability.*
2. To make a guess that is too low. *Karen underestimated the amount of food we would need.*
▷ *verb* **underestimating, underestimated** ▷ *noun* **underestimate** (uhn-dur-ess-tuh-muht), *noun* **underestimation**

un·der·foot (*uhn*-der-fut) *adverb*
1. Under your feet; on the ground. *It's slippery underfoot.*
2. In the way. *The kitten was always underfoot.*

un·der·go (*uhn*-dur-goh) *verb* To experience or have to go through something. *After undergoing a serious operation, Heather had to stay in the hospital two weeks.* ▷ **undergoes, undergoing, underwent, undergone**

un·der·ground (uhn-dur-*ground*) *adjective*
1. Below the ground, as in *an underground stream.*
2. Secret or hidden, as in *an underground organization.*
▷ *noun* **underground** ▷ *adverb* **underground** (*uhn*-dur-ground)

Underground Railroad *noun* A network of people who secretly helped slaves from the South escape to free states in the North or to Canada before the American Civil War.

un·der·hand (uhn-dur-*hand*) *adjective* Thrown or pitched with the hand below the shoulder or elbow level. ▷ *adverb* **underhand**

un·der·hand·ed (uhn-dur-*han*-did) *adjective* Sneaky or dishonest; done in secret; unfair. *She used underhanded methods to defeat her opponent in the election.*

un·der·line (uhn-dur-*line*) *verb*
1. To draw a line under a word or sentence. *Marco underlined the word "please" five time in the note he wrote asking his mother's permission to go to the party.*
2. To stress how important something is. *The president underlined the significance of the treaty.*
▷ *verb* **underlining, underlined**

un·der·mine (uhn-dur-mine) *verb* To weaken or destroy something slowly. *His constant criticism*

undermined my confidence. ▷ **undermining, undermined**

un·der·neath (*uhn*-dur-neeth) *preposition* Under or below. *They left their shoes underneath the bed.* ▷ *adverb* **underneath**

un·der·nour·ished (*uhn*-dur-**nur**-isht) *adjective* Someone who is **undernourished** is weak and unhealthy from lack of nutritious food.

un·der·pants (uhn-dur-*pants*) *noun, plural* Short pants worn as underwear.

un·der·pass (uhn-dur-*pass*) *noun* A road or passage that goes underneath another road or a bridge.

un·der·priv·i·leged (*uhn*-dur-**priv**-uh-lijd) *adjective* Someone who is **underprivileged** is usually poor and does not have the advantages or opportunities that richer people have.

un·der·sea (*uhn*-dur-see) *adjective* Located, done, or used below the surface of the ocean, as in *undersea plants* or *undersea exploration.*

un·der·shirt (uhn-dur-*shurt*) *noun* A shirt with short sleeves or no sleeves worn as underwear.

un·der·side (uhn-dur-*side*) *noun* The bottom side or surface of something, as in *the underside of a boat* or *the underside of a rock.*

un·der·stand (*uhn*-dur-stand) *verb*
1. To know what something means or how something works. *I don't understand your question.*
2. To know very well. *Do you understand Spanish?*
3. To have sympathy for someone. *The therapist understands teenagers.*
4. To believe that something is true; to gather from indirect information. *I understand that Jane's family is moving to New Jersey.*
▷ *verb* **understanding, understood** ▷ *noun* **understanding** ▷ *adjective* **understanding**

un·der·stand·a·ble (*uhn*-dur-**stan**-duh-buhl) *adjective* Easy to grasp or understand. *My math teacher makes even the most difficult concepts understandable.* ▷ *adverb* **understandably**

un·der·take (*uhn*-dur-take) *verb*
1. To agree to do a job or task; to accept a responsibility. *Benito undertook the care of the homeless puppy.*
2. To set about; to try or attempt. *We will undertake a long, difficult journey.*
▷ *verb* **undertaking, undertook, undertaken** ▷ *noun* **undertaking**

un·der·tak·er (uhn-dur-*tay*-kur) *noun* Someone whose job is to arrange funerals and prepare dead bodies to be buried or cremated.

un·der·tow (uhn-dur-*toh*) *noun* A strong current below the surface of a body of water that usually flows in a direction opposite to that of the surface current. An undertow can pull swimmers away from the shore.

un·der·wa·ter (uhn-dur-*waw*-tur) *adjective* Located, used, or done under the surface of the water. *The picture shows a submersible and a remote-operated vehicle, both of which are used for underwater exploration.*
▷ *adverb* **underwater**

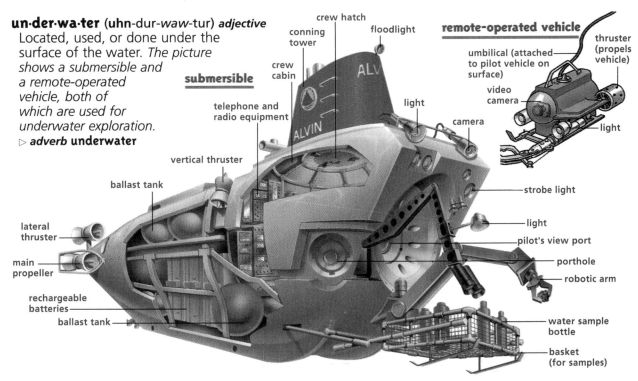

crew hatch
conning tower
floodlight
remote-operated vehicle
thruster (propels vehicle)
umbilical (attached to pilot vehicle on surface)
crew cabin
submersible
ALV
video camera
telephone and radio equipment
light
camera
ALVIN
light
vertical thruster
strobe light
ballast tank
light
lateral thruster
pilot's view port
main propeller
porthole
robotic arm
rechargeable batteries
ballast tank
water sample bottle
basket (for samples)

un·der·wear (uhn-dur-*wair*) *noun* Clothes that you wear next to your skin, under your outer clothes; underclothes.

un·der·weight (*uhn*-dur-**wate**) *adjective* Having less than the normal or required weight; weighing too little.

un·der·world (uhn-dur-*wurld*) *noun*
1. The part of society that is involved in organized crime.
2. In Greek and Roman mythology, the **underworld** is the place under the ground where the spirits of dead people go.

un·de·sir·a·ble (*uhn*-di-**zye**-ruh-buhl) *adjective* Not wanted or not pleasant. *The medicine had no undesirable effects.*

un·dis·turbed (uhn-diss-turbd) *adjective* Not bothered, or not interrupted; peaceful and calm. *The baby slept undisturbed through the loud party.*

un·do (uhn-doo) *verb*
1. To untie, unfasten, or open something.
2. To remove or reverse the effects of something. *I wish I could undo my mistake.*
▷ *verb* **undoes, undoing, undid, undone**

un·done (uhn-duhn) *adjective* Not finished or not completed. *Because I ran out of time, I left the last part of the test undone.*

un·dress (uhn-dress) *verb* To take clothes off. *Martha undressed the baby.* ▷ **undresses, undressing, undressed**

un·dy·ing (uhn-dye-ing) *adjective* Lasting forever. *You have my undying gratitude.*

un·earth (uhn-urth) *verb*
1. To dig something up. *Ted unearthed an arrowhead in his yard.*
2. To find, discover, or uncover something after searching for it. *The detective was hired to unearth the source of the security leak.*
▷ *verb* **unearthing, unearthed**

un·eas·y (uhn-ee-zee) *adjective*
1. Worried, nervous, or anxious. *I always feel uneasy before a test.*
2. Awkward, uncomfortable, or embarrassed, as in *an uneasy silence.*
▷ *noun* **uneasiness** ▷ *adverb* **uneasily**

un·em·ployed (*uhn*-em-ploid) *adjective* Someone who is **unemployed** does not have a job or work of any kind. ▷ *noun* **unemployment**

un·e·qual (uhn-ee-kwuhl) *adjective*
1. Not the same in size, value, or amount, as in *an unequal division of property.*
2. Not well matched or not well balanced. *The teams were unequal because all the good hitters were on the Cardinals.*
▷ *adverb* **unequally**

un·e·ven (uhn-ee-vuhn) *adjective*
1. Not flat, smooth, or straight, as in *uneven ground.*
2. Not regular, or not consistent. *The actor gave an uneven performance.*
3. In mathematics, an **uneven number** is a whole number that does not have two as a factor. *Seven is an uneven number.*
▷ *adverb* **unevenly**

un·e·vent·ful (*uhn*-i-vent-fuhl) *adjective* Not interesting, or not exciting, as in *an uneventful afternoon.* ▷ *adverb* **uneventfully**

un·ex·pect·ed (*uhn*-ek-spek-tid) *adjective* Something that is **unexpected** is surprising because you did not think it would happen. ▷ *adverb* **unexpectedly**

un·fair (uhn-fair) *adjective* Not fair, right, or just. *I know I could have done better, but I think your criticism was harsh and unfair.* ▷ **unfairer, unfairest** ▷ *noun* **unfairness** ▷ *adverb* **unfairly**

un·faith·ful (uhn-fayth-fuhl) *adjective* Not loyal, or not trustworthy. *The spy was unfaithful to his country.* ▷ *adverb* **unfaithfully**

un·fa·mil·iar (*uhn*-fuh-mil-yur) *adjective*
1. Not well known or not easily recognized; strange. *The room was filled with unfamiliar people.*
2. If you are **unfamiliar** with something, you do not know about it, or you do not have any experience using it. *I am unfamiliar with this type of computer.*

un·fas·ten (uhn-fass-uhn) *verb*
1. To release or to detach. *He unfastened the boat from the dock.*
2. To open something that has been fastened. *She unfastened the lock.*
▷ *verb* **unfastening, unfastened**

un·feel·ing (uhn-fee-ling) *adjective* Without kindness or sympathy; cruel. *Only an unfeeling person would ignore this injured dog.*

un·fit (uhn-fit) *adjective*
1. Not suitable, or not good enough. *Polluted water is unfit to drink.*
2. Not healthy, or not strong. *Mary Ellen is unfit from lack of exercise.*

un·fold (uhn-fohld) *verb*
1. To open and spread out something that was folded. *I unfolded the map.*
2. When a story or plan **unfolds,** more of it becomes known.
▷ *verb* **unfolding, unfolded**

un·fore·seen (uhn-for-seen) *adjective* Not expected or not planned. *I was late because of an unforeseen delay.*

un·for·get·ta·ble (*uhn*-fur-get-uh-buhl) *adjective* good, bad, etc., that you will not forget it, as in *unforgettable experience.* ▷ *adverb* **unforgettably**

un·for·giv·a·ble (*uhn*-fur-giv-uh-buhl) *adjective* If someone does something **unforgivable,** he or she does something so bad or mean that you cannot forgive the person. ▷ *adverb* **unforgivably**

un·for·tu·nate (uhn-for-chuh-nit) *adjective* Unlucky, as in *an unfortunate accident.*
▷ *adverb* **unfortunately**
Not wise, proper, or suitable. *Robert was an unfortunate choice for goalie.*

un·friend·ly (uhn-frend-lee) *adjective*
1. Not friendly; feeling or showing dislike.
2. Not pleasant or not favorable. *This jungle has a hot, unfriendly climate.*
▷ *adjective* **unfriendlier, unfriendliest** ▷ *noun* **unfriendliness**

un·grate·ful (uhn-grate-fuhl) *adjective* If you are **ungrateful** for something, you are not thankful for it and do not show or feel appreciation for it. ▷ *adverb* **ungratefully**

un·hap·py (uhn-hap-ee) *adjective*
1. Without joy; sad, as in *an unhappy child.*
2. Not lucky or fortunate, as in *an unhappy incident.*
3. Not suitable, as in *an unhappy choice.*
▷ *adjective* **unhappier, unhappiest** ▷ *noun* **unhappiness** ▷ *adverb* **unhappily**

un·health·y (uhn-hel-thee) *adjective*
1. Not healthy; in poor health; not well.
2. Resulting from poor health. *Her lack of appetite was an unhealthy sign.*
3. Harmful to one's health. *Eating too much junk food is an unhealthy habit.*

un·heard-of (uhn-hurd) *adjective* Not known or done before, as in *an unheard-of artist* or *an unheard-of athletic feat.*

u·ni·corn (yoo-nuh-*korn*) *noun* An imaginary animal that looks like a horse with one straight horn growing from its forehead. *The unicorn shown here is from a series of tapestries called "The Lady and the Unicorn," made in about 1500.*

unicorn

▶ Word History

The term **unicorn** comes from the Latin words *unum,* meaning "one," and *cornu,* meaning "horn." There were legends of these pure white beasts with one horn in many countries in ancient times, including India, China, Europe, and the Islamic nations. You can also find the Latin root *corn* in the English word *cornet,* which is a type of musical horn.

u·ni·cy·cle (yoo-nuh-*sye*-kuhl) *noun* A vehicle that has pedals like a bicycle but only one wheel and no handlebars.

un·i·den·ti·fied (*uhn*-eye-den-tuh-*fide*) *adjective* Not identified; not known or recognized. *The witness saw an unidentified man leaving the scene of the crime.* ▷ *adjective* **unidentifiable**

u·ni·form (yoo-nuh-*form*)
1. *noun* A special set of clothes worn by all the members of a particular group or organization. Nurses, soldiers, police officers, and mail carriers wear uniforms. *The uniforms of firefighters are shown below hanging from their hooks, ready to be worn.* ▷ *adjective* **uniformed**
2. *adjective* Always the same; never changing. *Refrigerators keep foods at a uniform temperature.*
3. *adjective* All alike; not different in any way, as in *a uniform row of houses.*
▷ *noun* **uniformity** ▷ *adverb* **uniformly**

firefighter uniforms

u·ni·fy (yoo-nuh-fye) *verb* To bring or join together into a whole or a unit; to unite.
▷ **unifies, unifying, unified** ▷ *noun* **unification** (*yoo*-nuh-fi-kay-shuhn)

un·im·por·tant (*uhn*-im-port-uhnt) *adjective* Not important; of no special value or interest; minor.

un·in·hab·it·ed (*uhn*-in-hab-uh-tid) *adjective* If a place is **uninhabited,** no one lives there.

un·in·tel·li·gi·ble (*uhn*-in-tel-uh-juh-buhl) *adjective* If something is **unintelligible,** it cannot be understood. ▷ *adverb* **unintelligibly**

un·in·ten·tion·al (*uhn*-in-ten-shuh-nuhl) *adjective* Something that is **unintentional** is done by accident, not on purpose. ▷ *adverb* **unintentionally**

un·in·ter·est·ed (*uhn*-in-truh-stid) *adjective* If you are **uninterested** in something, you do not want to know about it.

un·ion (yoon-yuhn) *noun*
1. An organized group of workers set up to help improve such things as working conditions, wages, and health benefits.

2. The joining together of two or more things or people to form a larger group.
3. the Union The United States of America. *The president gave the State of the Union address.*
4. the Union The states that remained loyal to the federal government during the Civil War; the North.

u·nique (yoo-neek) *adjective* If something is **unique,** it is the only one of its kind. ▷ *adverb* **uniquely**

u·ni·sex (yoo-nuh-*seks*) *adjective* Able to be used by both men and women, as in *unisex clothing.*

u·ni·son (yoo-nuh-suhn) *noun* If people say, sing, or do something **in unison,** they say, sing, or do it together.

u·nit (yoo-nit) *noun*
1. A single person, thing, or group that is part of a larger group or whole, as in *an apartment unit* or *an army unit.*
2. An amount used as a standard of measurement. *An ounce is a unit of weight.*
3. A machine or piece of equipment that has a special purpose, as in *an air conditioning unit.*
4. The number one.

u·nite (yoo-nite) *verb*
1. If people **unite,** they join together or work together to achieve something. *Let's unite to fight poverty.*
2. To put or join together in order to make a whole. *The states united to form a single nation.*
▷ *verb* **uniting, united** ▷ *noun* **unity** ▷ *adjective* **united**

u·ni·ver·sal (*yoo*-nuh-vur-suhl) *adjective*
1. Something that is **universal** is shared by everyone or everything. *This movie has universal appeal.*
2. Something that is **universal** is found everywhere. *Poverty is a universal problem.*
▷ *adverb* **universally**

u·ni·verse (yoo-nuh-vurss) *noun* The earth, the planets, the stars, and all things that exist in space.

u·ni·ver·si·ty (*yoo*-nuh-vur-suh-tee) *noun* A school for higher learning after high school where people can study for degrees, do research, or learn a profession such as law or medicine. A university is usually made up of colleges. ▷ *noun, plural* **universities**

un·just (uhn-juhst) *adjective* Not just, fair, or right, as in *an unjust accusation.* ▷ *adverb* **unjustly**

un·kempt (uhn-kempt) *adjective*
1. Not combed, as in *unkempt hair.*
2. Not tidy or neat in appearance, as in *an unkempt room* or *an unkempt lawn.*

un·kind (uhn-kinde) *adjective* Not kind; harsh or cruel, as in *unkind words.* ▷ **unkinder, unkindest** ▷ *adverb* **unkindly**

un·known (uhn-nohn) *adjective* Not familiar or not known about, as in *unknown territory.*
▷ *noun* **unknown**

U

un·less (uhn-**less**) *conjunction* Except on the condition that. *I can't come unless someone gives me a ride.*

un·like (uhn-**like**)
1. *adjective* Not alike; different. *I was surprised that the twins were so unlike.*
2. *preposition* Different from; not like. *Unlike Tina, I like music.*
3. *preposition* Not typical of. *It's unlike Doug to be late.*
4. *adjective* In a pair of magnets, **unlike** poles attract each other while like poles repel each other.

un·like·ly (uhn-**like**-lee) *adjective*
1. Not probable. *It is unlikely to snow today.*
2. Not likely to succeed, as in *an unlikely plan.*

un·lim·it·ed (uhn-**lim**-uh-tid) *adjective* Having no limits, bounds, or restrictions. *She has unlimited patience. This card gives you unlimited use of the gym for one year.*

un·load (uhn-**lohd**) *verb*
1. To remove things from a container or vehicle.
2. To remove ammunition from a gun.
▷ *verb* **unloading, unloaded**

un·lock (uhn-**lok**) *verb*
1. To open something with a key.
2. To solve, or to provide a key to, as in *to unlock a mystery.*
▷ *verb* **unlocking, unlocked**

un·luck·y (uhn-**luhk**-ee) *adjective*
1. Someone who is **unlucky** is unfortunate, and bad things seem to happen to him or her.
2. Something that is **unlucky** happens by chance and is unfortunate. *He had an unlucky fall and broke his leg.* ▷ *adverb* **unluckily**
3. An **unlucky** number, date, etc., is one that you think will bring you bad luck.
▷ *adjective* **unluckier, unluckiest**

un·mis·tak·a·ble (uhn-muh-**stay**-kuh-buhl) *adjective* Something that is **unmistakable** is very obvious and cannot be confused with anything else. *The resemblance between the twins was unmistakable.* ▷ *adverb* **unmistakably**

un·nat·u·ral (uhn-**nach**-ur-uhl) *adjective*
1. Not usual or not normal; not happening in nature. *It is unnatural for a fish to live on land.*
2. False, or not sincere. *Stan sounded nervous and unnatural.*
▷ *adverb* **unnaturally**

un·nec·es·sar·y (uhn-**ness**-uh-ser-ee) *adjective* If something is **unnecessary,** you do not need to do it or have it. ▷ *adverb* **unnecessarily**

un·ob·served (uhn-uhb-**zurvd**) *adjective* Not seen or not noticed. *They arrived at night unobserved.*

un·oc·cu·pied (uhn-**ok**-yuh-pide) *adjective*
1. Having no occupants; vacant, as in *an unoccupied apartment.*

2. Not held by enemy forces, as in *unoccupied territory.*

un·of·fi·cial (uhn-uh-**fish**-uhl) *adjective*
1. Not approved by someone in authority, as in *an unofficial report.*
2. Informal, as in *an unofficial visit.*
▷ *adverb* **unofficially**

un·pack (uhn-**pak**) *verb* To take objects out of a box, suitcase, trunk, vehicle, or container of any kind. ▷ **unpacking, unpacked**

un·pleas·ant (uhn-**plez**-uhnt) *adjective* Not pleasing; offensive; disagreeable, as in *an unpleasant odor.* ▷ *adverb* **unpleasantly**

un·plug (uhn-**pluhg**) *verb*
1. To remove a plug from an electric socket. *Mom unplugged the toaster.*
2. To remove a stopper or something that blocks an opening. *She unplugged the drain.*
▷ *verb* **unplugging, unplugged**

un·pop·u·lar (uhn-**pop**-yuh-lur) *adjective* Not liked or approved of by many people. *The mayor made an unpopular decision.*

un·prec·e·dent·ed (un-**press**-uh-*den*-tid) *adjective* Not known or done before; without a previous example. *When presidential candidates Nixon and Kennedy debated each other on television in 1960, millions of people watched this unprecedented event.*

un·pre·dict·a·ble (uhn-pri-**dik**-tuh-buhl) *adjective* If someone or something is **unpredictable,** you do not know what the person will do or what will happen next. ▷ *adverb* **unpredictably**

un·pre·pared (uhn-pri-**paird**) *adjective* Not ready for something. *Since he didn't study, Jim felt unprepared for the test.*

un·pro·voked (uhn-pruh-**vohkt**) *adjective* If an action is **unprovoked,** no one has done anything to cause it or encourage it. *Charlotte's tantrum was unprovoked.*

un·rav·el (uhn-**rav**-uhl) *verb*
1. To unwind a tangled mass of string, wool, or strands of any kind.
2. To undo or pull apart a woven or knitted fabric.
3. To search for and discover the truth about a complex situation. *Dana wants to spend her life unraveling the mysteries of science.*
▷ *verb* **unraveling, unraveled**

un·rea·son·a·ble (uhn-**ree**-zuhn-uh-buhl) *adjective*
1. Not showing reason or good sense. *Don't be so unreasonable; you can't always get your way.*
2. Too great; excessive, as in *an unreasonable price.*
▷ *adverb* **unreasonably**

un·rec·og·niz·a·ble (uhn-*rek*-uhg-**nye**-zuh-buhl) *adjective* Something or someone that is **unrecognizable** has totally changed so that you do not immediately know what or who it is.

un·re·li·a·ble (*uhn-ri-lye-uh-buhl*) *adjective* Something or someone that is **unreliable** cannot be depended upon or trusted.

un·rest (uhn-rest) *noun* Disturbance and trouble; a lack of calm; dissatisfaction, as in *political unrest.*

un·re·strict·ed (*uhn-ri-strik-tid*) *adjective* Without rules or limitations. *This unrestricted airline ticket allows you to fly anywhere in the world.*

un·ripe (uhn-**ripe**) *adjective* Not yet ready to be harvested, picked, or eaten, as in *unripe fruit.*

un·ri·valed (uhn-**rye**-vuhld) *adjective* Better than anything else; having no equal. *Leah's skill at chess is unrivaled.*

un·roll (uhn-**role**) *verb* To open or spread out something that is rolled up. *We unrolled our sleeping bags.* ▷ **unrolling, unrolled**

un·ruf·fled (un-ruhf-uhld) *adjective* Completely calm, especially after a disturbing incident. *Ms. Berkson remained unruffled despite the tornado warnings.*

un·rul·y (uhn-**roo**-lee) *adjective* Hard to control or discipline, as in *unruly hair* or *an unruly mob.* ▷ **unrulier, unruliest**

un·sat·is·fac·to·ry (*uhn*-sat-iss-fak-tuh-ree) *adjective* Not good enough to meet a certain need or standard. *My teacher said my oral report was unsatisfactory because I did not speak loudly enough.* ▷ *adverb* **unsatisfactorily**

un·scathed (uhn-skayTHd) *adjective* Not hurt. *The driver survived the crash unscathed.*

un·scru·pu·lous (uhn-skroo-pyuh-luhss) *adjective* **Unscrupulous** people have few principles or scruples and are not concerned whether their actions are right or wrong. ▷ *adverb* **unscrupulously**

un·seen (uhn-**seen**) *adjective* Hidden or not able to be seen. *The far side of the moon remained unseen until 1959.*

un·set·tle (uhn-**set**-uhl) *verb* To upset or to disturb. *The horror movie unsettled me.* ▷ **unsettling, unsettled**

un·set·tled (uhn-**set**-uhld) *adjective*
1. Not calm or not orderly; disturbed, as in *unsettled political conditions.*
2. Not decided or not determined; doubtful, as in *an unsettled question.*
3. Not inhabited. *Many parts of Iceland are still unsettled.*
4. Likely to change; uncertain, as in *unsettled weather.*
5. Not paid, as in *an unsettled bill.*

un·sight·ly (uhn-**site**-lee) *adjective* Ugly and unpleasant to look at, as in *an unsightly scar* or *unsightly litter.*

un·skilled (uhn-**skild**) *adjective* An **unskilled** worker has no particular skill, training, or experience.

un·sound (uhn-**sound**) *adjective*
1. Not strong or not solid; weak; unsafe, as in *an old, unsound bridge.*
2. Not based on good judgment or clear thinking; not sensible, as in *unsound advice.*
3. Not healthy, as in *an unsound mind.*

un·sta·ble (uhn-**stay**-buhl) *adjective*
1. Not firm or not steady; shaky, as in *an unstable ladder.*
2. Likely to change, as in *an unstable government.*
3. An **unstable** person has rapid changes of mood and behavior.

un·stead·y (uhn-**sted**-ee) *adjective* Shaky or wobbly; not firm, as in *an unsteady voice.* ▷ *adverb* **unsteadily**

un·suc·cess·ful (*uhn*-suhk-sess-fuhl) *adjective* If someone is **unsuccessful,** the person does not do well or get what he or she wants. ▷ *adverb* **unsuccessfully**

un·suit·a·ble (*uhn*-soo-tuh-buhl) *adjective* Not right for a particular purpose or occasion. *Heavy clothing is unsuitable for a summer hike.* ▷ *noun* **unsuitability** ▷ *adverb* **unsuitably**

un·sure (uhn-**shoor**) *adjective* Not certain or not definite. *I'm unsure if he will come.*

un·tan·gle (uhn-**tang**-guhl) *verb*
1. To remove knots or tangles, as in *to untangle a necklace.*
2. To clear up or explain, as in *to untangle a mystery.*
▷ *verb* **untangling, untangled**

un·think·a·ble (uhn-**thingk**-uh-buhl) *adjective* If something is **unthinkable,** it is out of the question and cannot be considered.

un·ti·dy (uhn-**tye**-dee) *adjective* Not neat; messy. ▷ *noun* **untidiness** ▷ *adverb* **untidily**

un·tie (uhn-**tye**) *verb*
1. To loosen or undo something that has been tied or fastened. *I untied my shoelaces.*
2. To free from something that ties, fastens, or restrains. *The guard untied the prisoner's hands.*
▷ *verb* **untying, untied**

un·til (uhn-**til**)
1. *preposition* Up to the time of. *Wait until tomorrow before you decide.*
2. *preposition* Before. *I won't be ready until Monday.*
3. *conjunction* Up to the time that. *I was enjoying the book until I got to the scary part.*
4. *conjunction* Before. *You can't watch television until you finish your homework.*
5. *conjunction* To the point, degree, or place that. *They ate until they were full. Drive along Main Street until you reach the park.*

un·to (uhn-too) *preposition* An old word for **to**.

un·told (uhn-tohld) *adjective*
1. Too great to be counted or measured. *The hurricane caused untold damage.*
2. Not told or not revealed. *The true story will remain untold.*

un·touched (uhn-tuhcht) *adjective*
1. Not handled or touched by anyone.
2. Left alone or ignored. *The thieves took the money but left the jewelry untouched.*
3. Not moved or not affected. *I cried at the end of the sad movie, but my friend was untouched.*

un·true (uhn-troo) *adjective*
1. False or incorrect, as in *an untrue story.*
2. Not faithful or not loyal. *You must never be untrue to your friends.*

un·used (uhn-yoozd) *adjective*
1. An **unused** item has never been used.
2. Not accustomed. *I am unused to this cold weather.*

un·u·su·al (uhn-yoo-zhoo-uhl) *adjective* Not usual, common, or ordinary; rare. *She has an unusual name.* ▷ *adverb* **unusually**

un·wel·come (uhn-wel-kuhm) *adjective* If someone or something is **unwelcome,** it is not gladly received or accepted.

un·well (uhn-wel) *adjective* Sick or ill.

un·wield·y (uhn-weel-dee) *adjective* Difficult to hold or hard to manage because of its shape, size, weight, or complexity, as in *an unwieldy package.*

un·will·ing (uhn-wil-ing) *adjective* Reluctant or not eager to do something. *Carl is unwilling to clean his room.* ▷ *adverb* **unwillingly**

un·wind (uhn-winde) *verb*
1. To undo something that has been rolled or wound up. *Unwind the yarn.*
2. To relax and become less worried or tense. *Many people play sports to unwind.*
▷ *verb* **unwinding, unwound**

un·wor·thy (uhn-wur-THee) *adjective*
1. Not deserving. *We felt unworthy of such praise.*
2. Not fitting, proper, or appropriate. *His rude behavior was unworthy of a gentleman.*
▷ *adverb* **unworthily**

un·wrap (uhn-rap) *verb* To take the packaging or outer layer off something. ▷ **unwrapping, unwrapped**

up (uhp)
1. *adverb* From a lower to a higher place. *Kyle climbed up to the top of the stairs.*
2. *adverb* In, at, or to a higher place or position. *I looked up.*
3. *adverb* To a higher point or degree. *Food prices have gone up.*
4. *adverb* On one's feet; in an upright position. *I got up from the chair.*
5. *adverb* Entirely. *I used up all the rice.*
6. *adverb* To a higher volume. *Please turn up the radio.*
7. *adjective* Moving upward. *I took the up escalator to the second level.*
8. *adverb* Out of bed. *Are you up yet?*
9. *adjective* Above the horizon. *The sun is up.*
10. *preposition* From a lower to a higher position or place in or on. *We hiked up the mountain.*
11. *preposition* At or to a farther point in or on. *They walked up the street.*
12. *preposition* Toward the source or inner part of. *We sailed up the river.*
13. **up against** Faced with. *We were up against a tough problem.*
14. If you are **up to** a job, you are capable of performing or dealing with it. *Are you up to helping me hang the curtains?*
15. If something is left **up to** a person, it depends on that person or is his or her responsibility. *Mom left it up to us where we should have dinner tonight.*
16. If you are **up to** something, you are doing it. *Do you know what Bill is up to today?*

up·beat (uhp-beet) *adjective* (informal) Optimistic and cheerful, as in *an upbeat personality.*

up·bring·ing (uhp-bring-ing) *noun* The care and training a person receives while growing up. *Brenda had a strict upbringing.*

up·date (uhp-date) *verb*
1. To give someone the latest information. *Please update us on your plans.* ▷ *noun* **update** (uhp-date)
2. To change something in order to include the latest style or information. *We are updating our catalog for next season.*
▷ *verb* **updating, updated**

up·grade (uhp-grade *or* uhp-grade)
1. *verb* To promote someone to a better or more important job or status. *We were upgraded to first class on our flight.*
2. *verb* To improve something. *The restaurant upgraded its service.*
3. *verb* To replace a computer part or a piece of software with a better, more powerful, or more recently released version. ▷ *noun* **upgrade**
4. *noun* (uhp-grade) The upward slope of a hill or road.
▷ *verb* **upgrading, upgraded**

up·heav·al (uhp-hee-vuhl) *noun*
1. A sudden and violent upset or disturbance, as in *the emotional upheaval caused by war.*
2. A forceful lifting up of part of the earth's crust, especially during an earthquake.

up·hill (uhp-hil)
1. *adjective* Sloping upward. ▷ *adverb* **uphill**
2. If something is an **uphill battle,** it is very tiring or difficult to do.

U

up·hold (*uhp*-hohld) *verb* To support something that you believe to be right. *The jury's verdict in the first trial was upheld by the appeals court.*
▷ **upholding, upheld**

up·hol·ster (uhp-hohl-stur) *verb* To put new upholstery on a piece of furniture.
▷ **upholstering, upholstered** ▷ *noun* **upholsterer**
▷ *adjective* **upholstered**

up·hol·ster·y (uhp-hohl-stur-ee) *noun* The stuffing, springs, cushions, and covering that are put on furniture. ▷ *noun, plural* **upholsteries**

up·keep (uhp-keep) *noun* The work or cost of keeping something in good condition.

up·on (uh-pon) *preposition* On.

up·per (uhp-ur) *adjective* Higher in position or rank, as in *an upper floor* or *the upper house of a legislature.*

up·per·case (uhp-ur-*kayss*) *adjective* Uppercase letters are capital letters. ▷ *noun* **uppercase**
▷ *verb* **uppercase**

upper hand *noun* A position of advantage or control. *Her years of experience gave her the upper hand during the last tense games in the tennis match.*

up·per·most (uhp-ur-*mohst*)
1. *adjective* Highest in place, rank, or importance. *Our apartment is on the uppermost floor of the building.*
2. *adverb* In the highest or most important place or rank. *As a parent, my children's happiness is always uppermost in my mind.*

up·right (uhp-*rite*)
1. *adjective* Standing straight up; vertical. *Fence posts are upright.* ▷ *noun* **upright** ▷ *adverb* **upright**
2. *adjective* Honest and fair; moral. *He is an upright citizen.*
3. *noun* An **upright piano** has strings that are arranged vertically, or up and down.

up·ris·ing (uhp-*rye*-zing) *noun* A rebellion or a revolt.

up·roar (uhp-*ror*) *noun* Shouting, noise, and confusion. *The close game ended in an uproar.*

up·roar·i·ous (uhp-ror-ee-uhss) *adjective*
1. Noisy or confused; full of uproar.
2. Extremely funny, as in *an uproarious joke.*

up·root (uhp-*root*) *verb*
1. To tear or pull out by the roots. *The hurricane uprooted a lot of trees.*
2. To force someone to leave. *The fire uprooted many families from their homes.*
▷ *verb* **uprooting, uprooted**

up·set (uhp-*set*) *verb*
1. To make someone nervous or worried. *The bad news upset us.*
2. To tip, turn, or knock something over. *Matt upset the glass of milk.*

3. To make someone feel ill. *Fried foods always upset my stomach.*
4. To interfere with. *The storm upset our plans.*
5. To defeat unexpectedly. *Our team upset the state champions.*
▷ *verb* **upsetting, upset** ▷ *noun* **upset** (uhp-*set*)
▷ *adjective* **upset** (uhp-set)

up·side down (uhp-*side*) *adverb*
1. With the top at the bottom. *When you turn an hourglass upside down, sand begins to fall from the upper bulb to the lower one.* ▷ *adjective* **upside-down**
2. In a confused or messy condition. *The children turned the place upside down looking for the missing puzzle piece.*

up·stairs (uhp-stairz)
1. *adverb* Up the stairs. *I ran upstairs to get my sweater.*
2. *adverb* To or on a higher floor. *My bedroom is upstairs.*
3. *adjective* On an upper floor. *You'll have more privacy if you use the upstairs phone.*
4. *noun* The upper floor or floors of a building. *I spent all morning cleaning the upstairs of our house.*

up·stream (uhp-streem) *adverb* Toward the source of a stream; against the current. *It's difficult to swim upstream.* ▷ *adjective* **upstream**

up·tight (uhp-tite) *adjective* (slang) Tense, nervous, or anxious. *Doreen was uptight after the accident.*

up-to-date *adjective* If something is **up-to-date,** it contains the most recent information or is in the latest style.

up·ward (uhp-wurd) *or* **up·wards** (uhp-wurdz)
1. *adverb* Toward a higher place or position. *The wind took the balloon steadily upward.*
2. *adjective* Moving or rising toward a higher place or position, as in *an upward slope.*

ur·a·ni·um (yu-ray-nee-uhm) *noun* A silver-white radioactive metal that is the main source of nuclear energy. Uranium is a chemical element.

Ur·a·nus (yur-uh-nuhss *or* yu-ray-nuhss) *noun* The seventh planet in distance from the sun. Uranus is the third-largest planet in our solar system. It has 15 known moons as well as nine rings circling its equator. *See* **planet.**

ur·ban (ur-buhn) *adjective* To do with or living in a city, as in *urban problems* or *the urban population.*

urge (urj)
1. *verb* To encourage or persuade someone strongly. *Joni's father urged her to try harder.*
▷ **urging, urged**
2. *noun* A strong wish or need to do something. *Todd felt a sudden urge to go for a run.*

ur·gent (ur-juhnt) *adjective* If something is **urgent,** it needs very quick or immediate attention. ▷ *noun* **urgency** ▷ *adverb* **urgently**

u·rin·ar·y system (yoor-uh-*nar*-ee) *noun* The organs and body parts that produce, store, and release urine. In humans and other mammals, it includes the kidneys, bladder, and tubes that carry urine.

u·ri·nate (yoor-uh-nate) *verb* To pass urine from the body. ▷ **urinating, urinated** ▷ *noun* **urination**

u·rine (yoor-uhn) *noun* The liquid waste that people and animals pass out of their bodies. Urine consists of water and wastes taken out of the blood by the kidneys. It is stored in the bladder.

urn (urn) *noun*

1. A vase with a base or pedestal. An urn is used as an ornament or a container. *The picture shows an urn made in ancient Greece.*
2. A large metal container with a faucet used for making and serving coffee or tea. **Urn** sounds like **earn.**

urn

us (uhss) *pronoun* The form of **we** that is used after a verb or preposition. *No one saw us. The letter was written to us.*

us·age (yoo-sij *or* yoo-zij) *noun*

1. The way that something is used or treated. *Careless usage will ruin this computer.*
2. The way that a language is usually spoken and written. *That word has changed in usage.*

use

1. (yooz) *verb* To do a job with something. *I used a penknife to cut through the wrapping.*
2. (yooz) *verb* To spend or consume by using. *Use your time wisely. He used up the mustard.*
3. (yooss) *noun* The action of using something. *All the phones were in use.*
4. (yooss) *noun* The right or ability to use something. *My sister has the use of the car today. She lost the use of her right arm.*
5. (yooss) *noun* A purpose for which something can be used. *This tool has several uses.*
6. (yooss) *noun* Advantage or benefit. *There's no use in worrying about it.*
7. (yooss) *noun* The need to use something. *Do you have any use for these empty jars?*
8. (yooz) *verb* If you **use** someone, you take advantage of the person in order to get something that you want.
▷ *noun* **user** ▷ *verb* **using, used**

used

1. (yoozd) *adjective* Already made use of, as in a *used car.*

2. (yoost) *adjective* If you are **used to** something, you know it well.
3. (yoost) *verb* If you **used to do** something, you did it in the past.

use·ful (yooss-fuhl) *adjective* Something that is **useful** is helpful and can be used a lot. ▷ *noun* **usefulness**

use·less (yooss-liss) *adjective*

1. Something that is **useless** has no use or value or is not helpful.
2. Hopeless; not capable of producing any result. *It's useless to ring that broken doorbell.*
3. *(informal)* Not very good. *I'm useless in the kitchen.*

user-friendly *adjective* If something such as a computer is **user-friendly,** it is easy for people without experience to learn and operate.

ush·er (uhsh-ur) *noun* Someone who shows people to their seats in a church, theater, or stadium. ▷ *verb* **usher**

U.S.S.R. (yoo ess ess ar) *noun* Another name for the former **Soviet Union.** The initials U.S.S.R. stand for *Union of Soviet Socialist Republics.*

u·su·al (yoo-zhoo-uhl) *adjective* Normal, common, or expected. ▷ *adverb* **usually**

u·ten·sil (yoo-ten-suhl) *noun* A tool or container, often used in the kitchen, that has a special purpose.

u·ter·us (yoo-tur-uhss) *noun* The hollow organ in women and other female mammals that holds and nourishes a fetus; the womb. ▷ *noun, plural* **uteri** (yoo-ter-eye) *or* **uteruses**

u·til·i·ty (yoo-til-uh-tee) *noun*

1. A basic service supplied to a community, such as telephone, water, gas, or electric.
2. A company that supplies a basic utility.
3. Usefulness. *Tools were invented for their utility.*
4. A **utility program** on a computer is one that performs a specific task that allows the computer to run more efficiently. One kind of utility program, for example, manages computer files.
▷ *noun, plural* **utilities**

ut·most (uht-*mohst*) *noun* The most, or the greatest possible. *The government said it would do its utmost to help the refugees.* ▷ *adjective* **utmost**

ut·ter (uht-ur)

1. *verb* To speak or to make some sort of sound from your mouth. *Ian uttered a few words under his breath.* ▷ **uttering, uttered** ▷ *noun* **utterance**
2. *adjective* Complete or total. *The play was an utter disaster.* ▷ *adverb* **utterly**

U-turn (yoo) *noun*

1. A turn in the shape of a U made by a vehicle in order to go in the opposite direction.
2. A complete reversal of policy or attitude. *The debate caused me to make a U-turn in my thinking.*

va·cant (vay-kuhnt) *adjective*
1. Empty or not occupied, as in *a vacant house*
or *a vacant lot.*
2. Available. *This job is vacant.* ▷ *noun* **vacancy**
3. If someone looks **vacant,** the person has a
blank expression on his or her face.

va·cate (vay-kate) *verb* To leave, or to leave
something empty. *Patrick vacated his seat for the
woman on crutches. Hotel guests should vacate
their rooms by 10 A.M.*
▷ **vacating, vacated**

va·ca·tion (vay-kay-shuhn) *noun* A time of rest
from school, work, and other regular duties;
especially a pleasure trip away from home. *The
photograph shows some tourists on vacation in
Thailand.* ▷ *verb* **vacation**

vacation

vac·ci·nate (vak-suh-nate) *verb* To protect
someone against a disease by giving the person
an injection or a dose of a vaccine. ▷
vaccinating, vaccinated ▷ *noun* **vaccination**

vac·cine (vak-**seen** *or* vak-seen) *noun* A
substance containing dead, weakened, or living
organisms that can be injected or taken orally.
A vaccine causes a person to produce
antibodies that protect him or her from the
disease caused by the organisms.

vac·u·um (vak-yuhm *or* vak-yoom) *noun*
1. A sealed space from which all air or gas has
been emptied.

2. A vacuum cleaner. ▷ *verb* **vacuum**

vacuum cleaner *noun* A machine that picks up
dirt from carpets, furniture, etc. To work, a
vacuum cleaner reduces the air pressure inside
itself. Then dirt is carried into it by outside air
rushing to fill the partial vacuum.

va·gi·na (vuh-**jye**-nuh) *noun* The passage in
women and other female mammals that leads
from the uterus, through which babies are born.

vague (vayg) *adjective* Not clear or not definite.
I have only vague memories of my grandfather.
▷ **vaguer, vaguest**

vain (vayn) *adjective*
1. If you are **vain,** you are conceited or too
proud of yourself, especially of the way you
look.
2. Unsuccessful or futile. *Ben made a vain
attempt to stop the bus.*
Vain sounds like **vane** and **vein.**
▷ *adjective* **vainer, vainest**

val·en·tine (val-uhn-*tine*) *noun*
1. A gift or greeting card sent to a friend,
relative, or loved one on Valentine's Day. *I got a
valentine from a secret admirer.*
2. A sweetheart or loved one chosen on
Valentine's Day. *Be my valentine.*

Valentine's Day *noun* February 14, a day
named in honor of Saint Valentine, a Christian
martyr of the third century A.D. It is celebrated
by sending valentines.

val·iant (val-yuhnt) *adjective* Brave or
courageous, as in *valiant soldiers* or *a valiant
effort.* ▷ *adverb* **valiantly**

val·id (val-id) *adjective*
1. Sensible; based on facts or evidence. *You can
leave early if you have a valid reason.*
2. Acceptable or legal. *To travel on the train, you
need a valid ticket.*
▷ *noun* **validity** ▷ *verb* **validate**

val·ley (val-ee) *noun*
1. An area of low ground between two hills,
usually containing a river.
2. An area of land drained by a river system. *The
Nile Valley was the site of many ancient cities.*

val·or (val-ur) *noun* Great bravery or courage,
especially in battle.

val·u·a·ble (val-yoo-uh-buhl *or* val-yuh-buhl)
1. *adjective* Something that is **valuable** is worth a
lot of money or is very important in some other
way, as in *a valuable jewel* or *valuable
information.*
2. **valuables** *noun, plural* Possessions that are
worth a lot of money. *My mother put her jewelry
and other valuables in the hotel safe.*

val·ue (val-yoo)
1. *noun* What something is worth. *What is the value of this watch?*
2. *verb* To think that something is important. *I value Anna's friendship greatly.*
3. *verb* To assess how much something is worth. *The auctioneer valued the painting at $75.00.*
4. *noun* In mathematics, an assigned or calculated number or quantity. *Find the value of x + 3 if x is 7. (The value is 10.)*
5. *noun, plural* People's **values** are their beliefs and ideas about what is most important in their lives.
▷ *verb* **valuing, valued**

valve (valv) *noun* A movable part that controls the flow of a liquid or gas through a pipe or other channel. *See* **engine, heart.**

vam·pire (vam-pire) *noun*
1. Any of the bats of Central and South America that feed on the blood of birds and mammals, especially livestock.
2. In folktales and horror stories, a **vampire** is a dead person who rises from the grave to feed on the blood of humans.

van (van) *noun*
1. A large, enclosed truck used for moving animals or household goods from place to place.
2. A smaller motor vehicle that is shaped like a box. A van has rear or side doors and side panels that often have windows.

van·dal (van-duhl) *noun* Someone who needlessly damages or destroys other people's property. ▷ *noun* **vandalism** ▷ *verb* **vandalize**

vane (vayn) *noun*
1. A **weather vane** is a pointer that swings around to show the direction of the wind.
2. The flat part of a bird's feather. *See* **feather.**
Vane sounds like **vain** and **vein.**

va·nil·la
(vuh-nil-uh)
noun A flavoring made from the seed pods of a tropical orchid. It is used in ice cream, candies, cookies, and other foods.

vanilla

vanilla orchid

vanilla pods

van·ish (van-ish) *verb*
1. To disappear suddenly. *The submarine vanished under the water.*

2. To cease to exist. *Dinosaurs vanished millions of years ago.*
▷ *verb* **vanishes, vanishing, vanished**

van·i·ty (van-uh-tee) *noun* A feeling of extreme pride and conceit. ▷ *noun, plural* **vanities**

vanity plate *noun* A motor vehicle license plate with letters or numbers selected by the owner. A vanity plate often spells out a clever slogan or the owner's name.

van·quish (vang-kwish) *verb*
1. To defeat or conquer an enemy in battle. *The Americans and the French vanquished the British, ending the Revolutionary War.*
2. To defeat an opponent in a contest or competition.
3. To overcome an emotion or a fear.
▷ *verb* **vanquishes, vanquishing, vanquished**

va·por (vay-pur) *noun*
1. Fine particles of mist, steam, or smoke that can be seen hanging in the air.
2. A gas formed from something that is usually a liquid or solid at normal temperatures. *Clouds are made of condensed water vapor.*

var·i·a·ble (vair-ee-uh-buhl)
1. *adjective* Likely to change, as in *variable weather.* ▷ *noun* **variable**
2. *noun* In mathematics, a **variable** is a symbol, such as *x, y,* or □, that stands for a number.

var·i·a·tion (vair-ee-ay-shuhn) *noun*
1. A change from the usual. *My time in the hospital was boring because there was no variation.*
2. Something that is slightly different from another thing of the same type. *This story is a variation of a familiar fairy tale.*

va·ri·e·ty (vuh-rye-uh-tee) *noun*
1. Difference, or change. *My little brother only eats burgers; there is no variety in his diet.*
2. A selection of different things.
3. A different type of the same thing, as in *a new variety of rose.*
▷ *noun, plural* **varieties**

var·i·ous (vair-ee-uhss) *adjective*
1. Different. *This dress comes in various colors.*
2. Several. *I have various hobbies.*

var·mint (var-muhnt) *noun (informal)*
1. An undesirable animal, such as one that kills a rancher's livestock.
2. A person who is undesirable, obnoxious, or troublesome.

▶ **Word History**
. . . .
Varmint, a word often used in stories and movies about the West, is a variant of the word *vermin* and developed from the Latin word *vermis,* meaning "worm."

V

var·nish (var-nish) *noun* A clear coating that you put on wood to protect it and give it a shiny finish. ▷ *noun, plural* **varnishes** ▷ *verb* **varnish**

var·y (vair-ee) *verb*
1. To change or to be different. *Mimi's handwriting varies, depending on her mood.*
2. If you **vary** something, you make changes in it. *I try to vary my route home from school by taking Main Street on one day and Grove Street the next.*
▷ *verb* **varies, varying, varied** ▷ *noun* **variant**

vase (vayss *or* vayz)
noun An ornamental container often used for flowers. *The picture shows an enameled vase made in the 1930s.*

vase

vas·sal (vass-uhl) *noun* In the Middle Ages, a person who was given land and protection by a lord in return for loyalty and military service.

vast (vast) *adjective* Huge in area or extent. *The Sahara is a vast desert. Paula has a vast collection of comic books.* ▷ **vaster, vastest** ▷ *noun* **vastness** ▷ *adverb* **vastly**

vat (vat) *noun* A large tank or container used for storing liquids. *At the vineyard, we saw wine fermenting in vats.*

vault (vawlt)
1. *verb* To leap over something using your hands or other support. *Jonathan vaulted over the fence to retrieve his baseball from his neighbor's backyard.* ▷ **vaulting, vaulted** ▷ *noun* **vault**
2. *noun* A room or compartment for keeping money and other valuables safe, as in *a bank vault.*
3. *noun* An underground burial chamber.

VCR (vee see ar) *noun* An electronic machine that is connected to a television set. It uses magnetic tape to record or play back movies and television programs. VCR is short for *VideoCassette Recorder.*

VDT (vee dee tee) *See* **video display terminal.**

veal (veel) *noun* The meat from a calf.

vee·jay (vee-*jay*) *noun* An announcer on a television program that features music videos.

veer (vihr) *verb* To change direction or turn suddenly. *The car veered to avoid hitting a dog. The wind veered from east to northeast.*
▷ **veering, veered**

veg·an (vee-guhn *or* vej-uhn) *noun* A vegetarian who does not eat any animal or dairy products.
▷ *noun* **veganism** ▷ *adjective* **vegan**

veg·e·ta·ble (vej-tuh-buhl) *noun* A plant grown to be used as food. Vegetables are usually eaten as side dishes to entrees or in salads. *The picture shows a variety of different vegetables.*

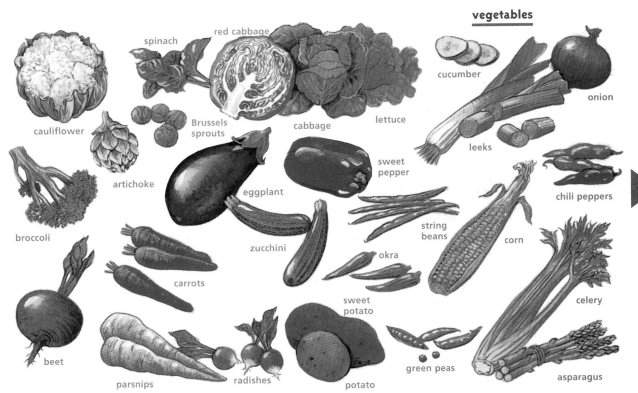

vegetables

cauliflower · spinach · red cabbage · Brussels sprouts · cabbage · lettuce · cucumber · onion · leeks · chili peppers · artichoke · sweet pepper · eggplant · broccoli · zucchini · string beans · corn · okra · carrots · sweet potato · celery · beet · green peas · parsnips · radishes · potato · asparagus

V

599

veg·e·tar·i·an (*vej*-uh-**ter**-ee-uhn) *noun* Someone who eats only plants and plant products and sometimes eggs or dairy products. ▷ *noun* **vegetarianism** ▷ *adjective* **vegetarian**

veg·e·ta·tion (*vej*-uh-**tay**-shuhn) *noun* Plant life or the plants that cover an area. *Jungles have thick vegetation.*

ve·he·ment (**vee**-uh-muhnt) *adjective* If you are **vehement** about something, you express your feelings about it very strongly. ▷ *noun* **vehemence** ▷ *adverb* **vehemently**

ve·hi·cle (**vee**-uh-kuhl) *noun* Something in which people or goods are carried from one place to another. Vehicles can range in size and power from a sled or tricycle to an express train.

veil (vayl) *noun*
1. A piece of material worn by women as a covering for the head or face. *This woman is wearing a wedding veil.*
2. Something that hides like a veil or curtain, as in *a veil of mist* or *a veil of secrecy.*
▷ *verb* **veil**

wedding veil

vein (vayn) *noun*
1. One of the vessels through which blood is carried back to the heart from other parts of the body. *See* **circulation.**
2. One of the stiff, narrow tubes that form the framework of a leaf or an insect's wing.
3. A narrow band of mineral in rock. *A vein of silver ran through the mine.*
Vein sounds like **vain** and **vane.**

Vel·cro (**vel**-kroh) *noun* The trademark for a fastener that consists of two pieces of fabric. One piece is covered with tiny hooks that stick to the tiny loops on the second piece.

vel·lum (**vel**-uhm) *noun*
1. Fine parchment paper made from the skin of a calf, lamb, or baby goat.
2. Very high quality writing paper.

ve·loc·i·ty (vuh-**loss**-uh-tee) *noun* Speed. *The velocity of the rocket is 3,000 mph.* ▷ *noun, plural* **velocities**

vel·vet (**vel**-vit)
1. *noun* A soft, thick fabric made from cotton, silk, or other materials.
2. *adjective* Made of velvet, or covered in velvet.
3. *adjective* Smooth and soft like velvet, as in *velvet fur.*
4. *noun* The soft skin on the growing antlers of a deer. *See* **antler.**

ven·det·ta (ven-**det**-uh) *noun* A long-lasting feud between two families, gangs, etc.

vend·ing machine (**vend**-ing) *noun* A machine in which you insert money to buy food items, beverages, or other products.

ven·dor (**ven**-dur) *noun* A person who sells something, as in *a fruit vendor.*

ve·ne·tian blind (vuh-**nee**-shuhn) *noun* An indoor window covering made from thin strips that can be raised or tilted to vary the amount of light coming in.

ven·geance (**ven**-juhnss) *noun* Action that you take to pay someone back for harm that he or she has done to you or someone you care about. *In the comic book, the superhero took vengeance on the ring of smugglers.*

ven·i·son (**ven**-uh-suhn) *noun* The meat of a deer.

ven·om (**ven**-uhm) *noun*
1. Poison produced by some snakes and spiders. Venom is usually passed into a victim's body through a bite or sting. *This diagram of a snake's jaw shows where its venom is stored.*
2. Ill will; spite or malice. *Elliott responded to the bully's question with venom in his voice.*

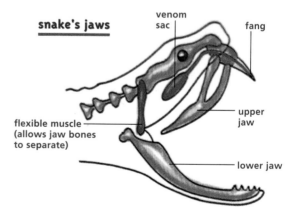

snake's jaws

venom sac

fang

flexible muscle (allows jaw bones to separate)

upper jaw

lower jaw

vent (vent)
1. *noun* An opening through which smoke or fumes can escape.
2. *noun* The shaft of a volcano through which smoke and lava escape. *See* **volcano.**
3. *verb* If you **vent** your feelings, you show them in an obvious way. *Tyrone vented his anger by slamming the door.* ▷ **venting, vented**

ven·ti·late (ven-tuh-*late*) *verb* To allow fresh air into a place and to send stale air out. *We ventilated the hot, musty attic by opening the windows.* ▷ **ventilating, ventilated** ▷ *noun* **ventilation,** *noun* **ventilator**

ven·tri·cle (ven-truh-kuhl) *noun* Either one of the two lower chambers of the heart. The ventricles receive blood from the atria and pump it to the arteries. *See* **heart.**

ven·tril·o·quism (ven-tril-uh-*kwiz*-uhm) *noun* The art of throwing your voice so that your words seem to come from a source other than yourself. ▷ *noun* **ventriloquist**

ven·ture (ven-chur)
1. *noun* A project that is somewhat risky, as in *a business venture.*
2. *verb* To put yourself at risk by doing something daring or dangerous. *The explorers ventured cautiously into the dense jungle.*
▷ **venturing, ventured**

ven·ue (ven-yoo) *noun* A place where an event is held. *The lawyer asked for a change of venue for the trial.*

Ve·nus (vee-nuhss) *noun* The second planet in distance from the sun. Venus is the sixth-largest planet in our solar system and is brighter in our sky than any other heavenly body except the sun and moon. *See* **planet.**

ve·ran·da *or* **ve·ran·dah** (vuh-ran-duh) *noun* An open porch around the outside of a house, often with a roof.

verb (vurb) *noun* A word that expresses an action or a state of being. *Do, run, be, have,* and *think* are verbs.

ver·bal (vur-buhl) *adjective*
1. To do with words, as in *a verbal aptitude test.*
2. Spoken, as in *a verbal agreement.*

ver·dict (vur-dikt) *noun*
1. The decision of a jury on whether an accused person is guilty or not guilty.
2. A decision or an opinion. *What's your verdict on my chicken casserole?*

verge (vurj)
1. If you are **on the verge** of doing something, you will do it soon. *Hector is on the verge of leaving his job.*
2. *verb* To be very near to something. *The man's odd behavior was verging on insanity.* ▷ **verging, verged**

ver·i·fy (ver-uh-fye) *verb*
1. To prove that something is true. *Several witnesses verified Roberta's account of the accident.*
2. To test or check the accuracy of something.

The scientist verified her findings by doing the experiment again.
▷ *verb* **verifies, verifying, verified** ▷ *noun* **verification** ▷ *adjective* **verifiable**

ver·min (vur-min) *noun*
1. Any of various small, common insects or animals that are harmful pests. Fleas, rats, and lice are vermin.
2. A mean or offensive person.
▷ *noun, plural* **vermin**

ver·sa·tile (vur-suh-tuhl) *adjective* Talented or useful in many ways, as in *a versatile entertainer* or *a versatile tool.* ▷ *noun* **versatility**

verse (vurss) *noun*
1. One part of a poem or song. A verse is made up of several lines.
2. Poetry.

ver·sion (vur-zhuhn) *noun*
1. One description or account given from a particular point of view. *If you believe Alexandra's version of the accident, her brother clearly wasn't at fault.*
2. A different or changed form of something such as a book or car. *I liked the movie version of the novel.*

ver·sus (vur-suhss) *preposition* Against. *Today's game is the Baltimore Orioles versus the New York Yankees.* In general, versus is abbreviated *vs.* When referring to court cases, however, it is abbreviated *v.,* as in the 1954 Supreme Court decision *Brown v. Board of Education of Topeka (Kansas).*

> ▶ **Word History**
> •
> **Vertebra** comes from the Latin word *vertere,* meaning "to turn." Having separate vertebrae in the backbone rather than a single, solid bone allows the body to turn and bend easily.

ver·te·bra (vur-tuh-bruh) *noun* One of the small bones that make up the backbone. ▷ *noun, plural* **vertebrae** (vur-tuh-*bree* or vur-tuh-*bray*)

ver·te·brate (vur-tuh-brit *or* vur-tuh-brate) *noun* Any animal that has a backbone. *Fish, amphibians, reptiles, birds, and mammals are all vertebrates.* ▷ *adjective* **vertebrate**

ver·tex (vur-teks) *noun*
1. The highest point of something, as in *the vertex of the mountain.*
2. The point where two lines meet to form an angle.
▷ *noun, plural* **vertices** (vur-tuh-*seez*)

ver·ti·cal (vur-tuh-kuhl) *adjective* Upright, or straight up and down. *Telephone poles and skyscrapers are in a vertical position.* ▷ *adverb* **vertically**

ver·y (ver-ee)
1. *adverb* To a great extent, much, or most. *I am very pleased to see you.*
2. *adjective* Exact. *You're the very person I wanted to see.*

ves·sel (vess-uhl) *noun*
1. A ship or a large boat.
2. A tube in the body that fluids pass through. Arteries and veins are blood vessels.
3. A hollow container for holding liquids, such as a bowl, vase, or jar.

vest (vest)
1. *noun* A short, sleeveless piece of clothing that is worn over a blouse or shirt.
2. *verb* To give power or authority to some person or group. *The Constitution vests the president with the power to veto a bill.* ▷ **vesting, vested**

ves·tige (vess-tij) *noun* A trace or sign of something that no longer exists. *The explorer found vestiges of an enormous dinosaur.*

vet (vet) *noun*
1. (informal) A veterinarian.
2. (informal) A veteran, as in *a Vietnam vet.*

vet·er·an (vet-ur-uhn) *noun*
1. Someone with a lot of experience in a profession, a position, or an activity. *The candidate is a veteran of many political campaigns.*
2. Someone who has served in the armed forces, especially during a war.
▷ *adjective* **veteran**

Veterans Day *noun* November 11, a day honoring men and women who served in the armed services and fought in wars for the United States. Formerly known as *Armistice Day,* this national holiday was first observed to celebrate the armistice, or truce, that ended World War I on November 11, 1918.

vet·er·i·nar·i·an (vet-ur-uh-ner-ee-uhn) *noun* A doctor who is trained to diagnose and treat sick or injured animals. *The veterinarian shown here is checking the dog's heartbeat.*

veterinarian

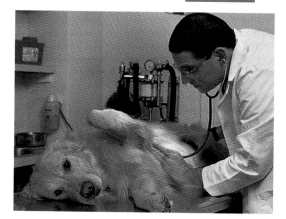

vet·er·i·nar·y (vet-ur-uh-*ner*-ee) *adjective* To do with the treatment of animals, as in *veterinary studies.*

ve·to (vee-toh)
1. *noun* The right or power of a president, a governor, or an official group to reject a bill that has been passed by a legislature and to keep it from becoming a law. ▷ *noun, plural* **vetoes**
2. *verb* To stop a bill from becoming a law.
3. *verb* To forbid, or to refuse to approve. *Mom vetoed my idea of watching a late movie on a school night.*
▷ *verb* **vetoes, vetoing, vetoed**

vex (veks) *verb* To annoy or irritate somebody.
▷ **vexes, vexing, vexed** ▷ *noun* **vexation**
▷ *adjective* **vexatious,** *adjective* **vexed**

vi·a (vye-uh *or* vee-uh) *preposition* By way of. *This train goes to Los Angeles via Denver.*

vi·a·ble (vye-uh-buhl) *adjective* Workable or capable of succeeding, as in *a viable plan.*
▷ *noun* **viability**

vi·a·duct (vye-uh-duhkt) *noun* A large bridge that carries a railroad track, road, or pipeline across a valley or over a city street.

vi·brant (vye-bruhnt) *adjective* Bright or lively, as in *vibrant colors* or *a vibrant personality.* ▷ *noun* **vibrancy** ▷ *adverb* **vibrantly**

vi·brate (vye-brate) *verb* To move back and forth rapidly. *The house vibrated during the earthquake.*
▷ **vibrating, vibrated** ▷ *noun* **vibration**

vice (visse) *noun* Immoral or harmful behavior. *Lying and cheating are vices.* **Vice** sounds like **vise.**

vice president *noun* An officer who ranks second to a president and acts for the president when necessary.

vice ver·sa (visse vur-suh *or* vye-suh vur-suh) *adverb* A Latin phrase meaning "the other way around." *You help me and vice versa.*

vi·cin·i·ty (vuh-sin-uh-tee) *noun* The area near a particular place. *After the robbery, the police sealed off all roads in the vicinity.* ▷ *noun, plural* **vicinities**

vi·cious (vish-uhss) *adjective*
1. Cruel and mean, as in *vicious lies.*
2. Evil or wicked, as in *a vicious crime.*
3. Fierce or dangerous, as in *a vicious dog.*
▷ *noun* **viciousness** ▷ *adverb* **viciously**

vic·tim (vik-tuhm) *noun*
1. A person who is hurt, killed, or made to suffer, as in *an accident victim* or *a murder victim.*
2. A person who is cheated or tricked, as in *a swindler's victim.*

vic·tim·ize (vik-tuh-*mize*) *verb* To pick someone out for unfair treatment. *The gang victimized the new boy.* ▷ **victimizing, victimized** ▷ *noun* **victimization**

V

vic·tor (vik-tur) *noun* The winner in a battle or contest.

vic·to·ry (vik-tuh-ree) *noun* A win in a battle or contest. *This tennis player is holding up her arms to celebrate her victory.* ▷ *noun, plural* **victories** ▷ *adjective* **victorious** (vik-tor-ee-uhss) ▷ *adverb* **victoriously**

victory

vid·e·o (vid-ee-oh)
1. *adjective* To do with the visual part of a television program or with a computer display.
2. *noun* The visual part of television.
3. *noun* A recording of a movie or television show that can be played on a VCR.
4. *noun* A videotaped performance of a song, as in *a rock video.*
▷ *noun, plural* **videos**

vid·e·o·cas·sette (vid-ee-oh-kuh-set) *noun* A plastic case that contains videotape. It can be inserted into a VCR and used to record or play back movies and television programs.

videocassette recorder See **VCR.**

video display terminal *noun* The monitor or display screen of a computer. A video display terminal is also known as a *VDT.* See **computer.**

video game *noun* An electronic or computerized game played by using buttons or levers to move images around on a television or computer screen. Video games often emphasize fast action.

vid·e·o·tape (vid-ee-oh-*tape*) *noun*
1. Magnetic tape on which sound and pictures are recorded.
2. A recording on this kind of tape. ▷ *verb* **videotape**

vie (vye) *verb* To compete. *Jason vied with Eliza for their mother's attention.* ▷ **vying, vied**

view (vyoo)
1. *noun* The act of looking or seeing; sight. *Their first view of the mountains was from an airplane.*
2. *noun* What you can see from a certain place. *The view from my window is lovely.*
3. *noun* The range or field of sight. *The deer disappeared from view.*
4. *noun* What you think about something, or your opinion. *What are your views on gun control?* ▷ *verb* **view**
5. *verb* To look at something. *Many people viewed the dinosaur exhibit.* ▷ **viewing, viewed**

view·point (vyoo-*point*) *noun*
1. The place or position from which a person views a situation, an event, etc.
2. An attitude or a way of thinking. *I tried to understand my sister's viewpoint, even though I didn't agree with her.*

vig·i·lant (vij-uh-luhnt) *adjective* Watchful and alert. *The guard found it hard to stay awake and keep vigilant.* ▷ *noun* **vigilance** ▷ *adverb* **vigilantly**

vig·or (vig-ur) *noun*
1. Great force or energy. *The lawyer defended her client with vigor.*
2. Physical energy or strength. *My puppies are full of vigor.*

vig·or·ous (vig-ur-uhss) *adjective* Energetic, lively, or forceful, as in *vigorous exercise* or *a vigorous protest.* ▷ *noun* **vigor** ▷ *adverb* **vigorously**

Vi·king (vye-king) *noun* A member of one of the Scandinavian peoples who invaded the coasts of Europe between the 8th and 11th centuries. See **longship.**

vile (vile) *adjective*
1. Evil or immoral, as in *a vile crime.*
2. Disgusting or repulsive, as in *vile language.*
▷ *adjective* **viler, vilest** ▷ *noun* **vileness**

vil·la (vil-uh) *noun* A large, luxurious house, especially one in the country.

vil·lage (vil-ij) *noun* A small group of houses that make up a community. A village is usually smaller than a town. ▷ *noun* **villager**

vil·lain (vil-uhn) *noun* A wicked person, often an evil character in a play. ▷ *adjective* **villainous**

vin·dic·tive (vin-dik-tiv) *adjective* Someone who is **vindictive** does not forgive and wants revenge. ▷ *noun* **vindictiveness** ▷ *adverb* **vindictively**

vine (vine) *noun* A plant with a long, twining stem that grows along the ground or climbs on trees, fences, or other supports. Melons, cucumbers, and pumpkins grow on vines.

vin·e·gar (vin-uh-gur) *noun* A sour liquid made from fermented wine, cider, etc., and used to flavor and preserve food.

vine·yard (vin-yurd) *noun* An area of land where grapes are grown.

vin·tage (vin-tij)
1. *noun* The wine produced in a particular year.
2. *adjective* Very good, or the best of its kind. *Cecilia gave a vintage performance.*

vi·nyl (vye-nuhl) *noun* A flexible, waterproof, shiny plastic that is used to make floor coverings, raincoats, and other products.

vi·o·la (vee-oh-luh) *noun* A stringed musical instrument that looks like a violin but is slightly larger and has a deeper tone. *See* **orchestra, strings.**

vi·o·late (vye-uh-*late*) *verb*
1. To break a promise, a rule, or a law. *The driver violated the law by failing to stop at a stop sign.*
2. To treat a person or place with no respect.
3. To disturb rudely or without any right, as in *to violate someone's privacy.*
▷ *verb* **violating, violated** ▷ *noun* **violation,** *noun* **violator**

vi·o·lence (vye-uh-luhnss) *noun*
1. The use of physical force.
2. Great force or strength. *The violence of the hurricane destroyed many homes.*

vi·o·lent (vye-uh-luhnt) *adjective*
1. Showing or caused by great physical force. *The announcer said that a violent storm would hit our area this evening.*
2. Showing or caused by strong feeling or emotion, as in *a violent temper.*

vi·o·let (vye-uh-lit) *noun*
1. A small, low plant with small flowers that are usually purple, yellow, or white. Pansies are a type of violet.
2. A blue-purple color. ▷ *adjective* **violet**

violets

vi·o·lin (vye-uh-lin) *noun* A musical instrument with four strings, played with a bow. *See* **orchestra, strings.** ▷ *noun* **violinist**

VIP (vee eye pee) *noun* The initials **VIP** stand for *Very Important Person.*

vi·per (vye-pur) *noun*
1. Any poisonous snake.
2. An adder. *See* **adder.**

vir·gin (vur-jin) *adjective* Untouched, or in its natural state, as in *virgin snow* or *virgin forests.*

vir·tu·al·ly (vur-choo-uh-lee) *adverb* Nearly or almost. *We have virtually finished.* ▷ *adjective* **virtual**

virtual reality *noun* An environment that looks three-dimensional, created through a computer. Virtual reality seems real to the person who experiences it. *See* **interactive.**

vir·tue (vur-choo) *noun*
1. Moral goodness. ▷ *adjective* **virtuous** ▷ *adverb* **virtuously**
2. An example of moral goodness. *Kindness is a virtue.*
3. Any good quality or trait. *This luggage has the virtue of being lightweight.*

vir·tu·o·so (vur-choo-oh-soh) *noun* A highly skilled performer, especially a musician. ▷ *noun, plural* **virtuosos** or **virtuosi** (vur-choo-oh-see)

vir·u·lent (vihr-yuh-luhnt) *adjective*
1. If a disease is **virulent,** it is very severe or harmful, as in *a virulent virus.*
2. Bitter, spiteful, or full of hate, as in *virulent criticism* or *a virulent speech.*
▷ *noun* **virulence** ▷ *adverb* **virulently**

vi·rus (vye-ruhss) *noun*
1. A very tiny organism that can reproduce and grow only when inside living cells. Viruses are smaller than bacteria. They cause diseases such as polio, measles, the common cold, and AIDS. *See* **AIDS.**
2. The disease caused by a virus.
3. Hidden instructions within a computer program designed to destroy a computer system or damage data.
▷ *noun, plural* **viruses**

vi·sa (vee-zuh) *noun* A document giving permission for someone to enter a foreign country.

vise (visse) *noun* A device with two jaws that open and close with a screw or lever. A vise is used to hold an object firmly in place while it is being worked on. **Vise** sounds like **vice.** *See* **machine.**

vis·i·ble (viz-uh-buhl) *noun* Something that is **visible** is able to be seen. *The island was visible on the horizon.* ▷ *noun* **visibility** ▷ *adverb* **visibly**

vi·sion (vizh-uhn) *noun*
1. The sense of sight. *Eagles have excellent vision.*

2. A lovely or beautiful sight. *In her youth, my grandmother was a vision of loveliness.*
3. The ability to think ahead and plan, as in *a leader of great vision.* ▷ *noun* **visionary**
4. Something that you imagine or dream about. *Malcolm has visions of being a famous author.*

vis·it (viz-it) *verb* To go to see people or places. ▷ **visiting, visited** ▷ *noun* **visit,** *noun* **visitor**

vi·sor (vye-zur) *noun*
1. A brim that sticks out of the front of a cap to shade the eyes from the sun.
2. A movable shade inside a car, above the windshield, that protects the eyes from glare.
3. The movable, see-through shield on the front of a helmet that protects the face.

vis·u·al (vizh-oo-uhl) *adjective*
1. To do with seeing, as in *a visual nerve.* ▷ *adverb* **visually**
2. Designed or able to be seen. *Charts, films, and slides are visual aids used to improve learning.*

vi·su·al·ize (vizh-oo-uh-*lize*) *verb* To picture something or to see something in your mind. *I can't visualize myself driving a motorcycle.* ▷ **visualizing, visualized** ▷ *noun* **visualization**

vi·tal (vye-tuhl) *adjective*
1. Very important or essential. *A good education is vital.* ▷ *adverb* **vitally**
2. To do with life. *The doctor checked the accident victim's breathing, pulse, and other vital signs.*
3. Necessary for life. *The heart and lungs are vital organs.*
4. Full of life or energetic, as in *a vital personality.*

vi·tal·i·ty (vye-tal-uh-tee) *noun* Energy and liveliness. *Puppies are usually full of vitality.*

vi·ta·min (vye-tuh-min) *noun* One of the substances in food that is necessary for good health. *Vitamin C helps protect you against colds.*

vi·va·cious (vye-vay-shuhss *or* vi-vay-shuhss) *adjective* A **vivacious** person has a lively personality. ▷ *noun* **vivacity** (vi-vass-i-tee) ▷ *adverb* **vivaciously**

viv·id (viv-id) *adjective*
1. Bright and strong, as in *vivid colors.*
2. Lively or active, as in *a vivid imagination.*
3. Sharp and clear, as in *vivid memories.* ▷ *noun* **vividness** ▷ *adverb* **vividly**

viv·i·sec·tion (*viv*-uh-sek-shuhn) *noun* The use of live animals for scientific and medical research.

vo·cab·u·lar·y (voh-kab-yuh-ler-ee) *noun* The range of words that a person uses and understands. *Charles impressed his teachers with his large vocabulary.* ▷ *noun, plural* **vocabularies**

vo·cal (voh-kuhl)
1. *adjective* To do with the voice.

2. *adjective* If someone is **vocal,** the person is outspoken and often expresses his or her opinions.
3. *noun, plural* In music, the **vocals** are the parts that are sung. ▷ *adverb* **vocally**

vocal cords *noun, plural* Either of two pairs of bands or folds of membranes in the larynx. When air from the lungs passes through the lower pair, it causes them to vibrate and produce sound.

vo·cal·ist (voh-kuh-list) *noun* A singer.

vo·ca·tion (voh-kay-shuhn) *noun*
1. A job or profession, especially one that needs special training. *Felicia's vocation is medicine.* ▷ *adjective* **vocational**
2. A strong feeling for a particular job, especially a religious career.

vo·cif·er·ous (voh-sif-ur-uhss) *adjective* If someone is **vociferous,** the person is noisy and talkative and insists on being heard. *A vociferous argument broke out between the two neighbors.* ▷ *adverb* **vociferously**

vod·ka (vod-kuh) *noun* A strong alcoholic drink that is clear in color and is made from grain or potatoes.

vogue (vohg) *noun* If something is **in vogue,** it is the current fashion.

voice (voiss)
1. *noun* The power to speak and sing. *Lois has lost her voice.*
2. *noun* The sound produced when you speak or sing. *Martha has a high voice.*
3. *verb* When you **voice** an opinion, you express it. ▷ **voicing, voiced**
4. *noun* The right to express your opinion. *The members of Margaret's team were angry that they had no voice in making the decision.*

voice mail *noun* A system that allows you to leave and play back spoken messages by telephone.

voice·print (voiss-*print*) *noun* A graph that shows the special patterns and characteristics of an individual speaker's voice.

void (void)
1. *noun* An empty space. *Clara felt that there was a void in her life after her best friend moved away.* ▷ *adjective* **void**
2. *adjective* If a result is declared **void,** it does not count anymore. ▷ *verb* **void**

vol·a·tile (vol-uh-tuhl) *adjective*
1. A **volatile** chemical will evaporate very easily or is unstable in some other way. ▷ *noun* **volatility**
2. Someone who is **volatile** has rapid mood changes.

volcano ▶ vulture

vol·ca·no (vol-**kay**-noh) *noun* A mountain with vents through which molten lava, ash, cinders, and gas erupt, sometimes violently. Volcanoes occur along the boundaries of the earth's plates, where molten rock is forced upward from magma reservoirs. *This picture shows an erupting volcano.* ▷ *noun, plural* **volcanoes** or **volcanos**

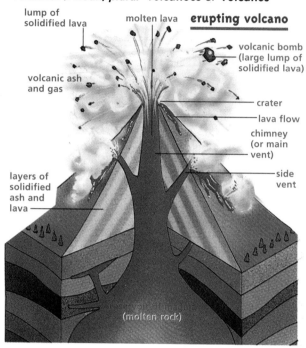

erupting volcano

lump of solidified lava
molten lava
volcanic bomb (large lump of solidified lava)
volcanic ash and gas
crater
lava flow
chimney (or main vent)
side vent
layers of solidified ash and lava
(molten rock)

vol·ley (vol-ee) *noun*
1. A shot in games such as tennis and soccer where the ball is hit or kicked before it can bounce. ▷ *verb* **volley**
2. The firing of a number of bullets, missiles, etc., at the same time.
3. A burst or outburst of many things at the same time, as in *a volley of protests.*

vol·ley·ball (vol-ee-*bawl*) *noun*
1. A game in which team members use their forearms and hands to hit a large ball over a net and try to make the ball hit the ground on their opponent's side. Volleyball can be played on a court or on the beach.
2. The ball used in this game.

volt (vohlt) *noun* A unit for measuring the force of an electrical current or the stored power of a battery. Volts are used to measure **voltage.**

▶ Word History

The word **volt** can be traced back to Count Alessandro Giuseppe Antonio Anastasio Volta (1745–1827). This Italian scientist invented the first electric battery in 1800.

volt·age (vohl-tij) *noun* The force of an electrical current, expressed in volts. *Twelve volts is the voltage of most car batteries.*

vol·ume (vol-yuhm) *noun*
1. A book. *Our library owns thousands of volumes.*
2. One book of a set. *This encyclopedia has 20 volumes.*
3. The amount of space taken up by a three-dimensional shape such as a box or a room. To figure out the volume of a rectangular object, you multiply its length by its height by its width.
4. Loudness. *Please turn down the volume on your radio.*

vol·un·tar·y (vol-uhn-*ter*-ee) *adjective*
1. Willing; not forced, as in *a voluntary decision.*
2. Controlled by the will. *You move your arms and legs with voluntary muscles.*
3. Done on purpose and not by accident, as in *voluntary manslaughter.*

vol·un·teer (*vol*-uhn-tihr)
1. *verb* To offer to do a job, usually without pay. ▷ **volunteering, volunteered** ▷ *noun* **volunteer**
2. *adjective* Formed or made up of volunteers, as in *volunteer firefighters.*

vom·it (vom-it) *verb* When you **vomit,** you bring up food and other substances from your stomach and expel them from your mouth. ▷ **vomiting, vomited** ▷ *noun* **vomit**

vote (voht) *verb* To make a choice in an election or other poll, usually by pulling a lever on a machine, writing on a ballot, or raising your hand. ▷ **voting, voted** ▷ *noun* **vote,** *noun* **voter**

vow (vou) *verb* To make a serious and important promise. ▷ **vowing, vowed** ▷ *noun* **vow**

vow·el (vou-uhl) *noun* A speech sound made with a free flow of air through the mouth. Vowels are represented by the letters *a, e, i, o, u,* and sometimes *y.*

voy·age (voi-ij) *noun* A long journey, as in *the immigrants' ocean voyage to the United States.* ▷ *noun* **voyager** ▷ *verb* **voyage**

vul·gar (vuhl-gur) *adjective* Rude or in bad taste, as in *vulgar language* or *a vulgar joke.* ▷ *noun* **vulgarity** (vuhl-ga-ri-tee)

vul·ner·a·ble (vuhl-nur-uh-buhl) *adjective* If someone or something is **vulnerable,** it is in a weak position and likely to be hurt or damaged in some way. ▷ *noun* **vulnerability** ▷ *adverb* **vulnerably**

vul·ture (vuhl-chur) *noun*
1. A large bird of prey that has dark feathers and a bald head and neck. Vultures are related to hawks, eagles, and falcons. They feed mainly on the meat of dead animals.
2. A greedy or ruthless person who takes advantage of others.

About W

wack·y (wak-ee) *adjective* (slang) Odd or crazy in a silly or amusing way. ▷ **wackier, wackiest** ▷ *noun* **wackiness** ▷ *adverb* **wackily**

wad (wahd)
1. *noun* A small, tightly packed ball or piece of something soft, as in *a wad of cotton* or *a wad of chewing gum.*
2. *noun* A tight, thick roll, as in *a wad of dollar bills.*
3. *verb* To press or roll something into a wad. *Wad up the shirt and throw it in the laundry bag.*
▷ **wadding, wadded**

wad·dle (wahd-uhl) *verb* To walk awkwardly, taking short steps and swaying from side to side. *The geese waddled into the barnyard.*
▷ **waddling, waddled** ▷ *noun* **waddle**

wade (wayd) *verb*
1. To walk through water.
2. To move through something slowly and with difficulty. *Shawn waded through a lot of technical material to get the answer he needed.*
▷ *verb* **wading, waded**

wad·er (way-dur) *noun*
1. A bird such as the crane or heron that wades in shallow water looking for food.
2. **waders** *noun, plural* Thigh-high, waterproof boots used for fishing in deep water.

wa·fer (way-fur) *noun*
1. A thin, light, crisp cookie or cracker.
2. A thin, flat piece of candy.

waf·fle (wahf-uhl)
1. *noun* A type of cake baked in an appliance that presses a crisscross pattern into it.
2. *verb* (informal) To avoid giving a direct answer to a question; to keep changing your mind or position. *The politician waffled on the question of raising taxes.* ▷ **waffling, waffled** ▷ *noun* **waffle,** *noun* **waffler**

waft (wahft) *verb* To float or be carried through the air, as if by a breeze. *As it grew colder, snowflakes started wafting to the ground.*
▷ **wafting, wafted** ▷ *noun* **waft**

wag (wag) *verb* To move something quickly from side to side or up and down. *The dog wagged its tail.* ▷ **wagging, wagged** ▷ *noun* **wag**

wage (waje)
1. **wage** *noun* or **wages** *noun, plural* The money someone is paid for his or her work.
2. *verb* If you **wage** a campaign or a war, you start it and carry on with it. ▷ **waging, waged**

wa·ger (way-jur) *noun* A bet. *The two boys made a wager on who could eat the most hot dogs.*
▷ *verb* **wager**

wag·on (wag-uhn) *noun*
1. A vehicle with four wheels that is used to carry heavy loads and is pulled by a horse or horses.
2. A child's toy vehicle or cart with four wheels and a long handle that is used for pulling.

wagon

wagon train *noun* In frontier times, a line or group of covered wagons that traveled west together for safety.

waif (wafe) *noun*
1. A homeless, lost, or abandoned person, especially a young child.
2. A stray animal.

wail (wale) *verb* To let out a long cry of sadness or distress. *The baby began to wail when her mother left the room.* **Wail** sounds like **whale.**
▷ **wailing, wailed** ▷ *noun* **wail**

waist (wayst) *noun*
1. The middle part of your body between your ribs and your hips.
2. The part of a garment that covers the body around the waist area.
Waist sounds like **waste.**

wait (wate) *verb*
1. To stay in a place or do nothing for a period of time until someone comes or something happens. *We waited an hour for the train.* ▷ *noun* **wait**
2. To look forward to something. *Nilda waited all week for her best friend to return from vacation.*
3. To be delayed or put off. *The picnic will have to wait until the weather clears.*
4. If you **wait on** someone, you serve as the person's waiter, waitress, salesperson, or servant. **Wait** sounds like **weight.**
▷ *verb* **waiting, waited**

wait·er (way-tur) *noun* A man who serves people food and beverages in a restaurant.

607

waiting room *noun* A room or an area where people sit and wait for something such as a train, an airplane, or a doctor's appointment.

wait·ress (way-triss) *noun* A woman who serves people food and beverages in a restaurant.

waive (wayv) *verb*
1. To give up something by choice. *The man waived his right to a lawyer and confessed everything to the police.* ▷ *noun* **waiver**
2. To postpone, or to set aside. *The speaker waived the presentation and instead answered questions from the audience.*
Waive sounds like **wave**.
▷ *verb* **waiving, waived**

wake (wayk)
1. *verb* To become fully conscious after being asleep. *I wake up at 6:00 A.M., when my alarm goes off.*
2. *verb* To rouse someone from his or her sleep. *I will wake you early.*
3. *noun* A watch kept over the body of a dead person before the funeral.
4. *noun* The trail of ripples in the water left by a moving boat.
5. *noun* The trail left by something passing through. *The tornado left destruction in its wake.*
▷ *verb* **waking, woke** (wohk) *or* **waked, waked** *or* **woken** (wohk-in)

walk (wawk)
1. *verb* To move along by placing one foot on the ground before lifting the other. ▷ *noun* **walk**, *noun* **walker**
2. *noun* A journey on foot.
3. *verb* To accompany or to go with. *I'll walk you to school.*
4. *noun* A path or other area that is set apart or designed for walking.
5. *verb* To make or help walk. *It's your turn to walk the dog.*
6. *noun* In baseball, the right of the batter to go to first base after the pitcher has thrown four pitches that are not swung at and are not called strikes by the umpire. ▷ *verb* **walk**
7. *(informal)* If you **walk all over** somebody, you take advantage of the person.
▷ *verb* **walking, walked**

walk·ie-talk·ie (waw-kee taw-kee) *noun* A radio that is held in the hand, powered by batteries, and is used to communicate over short distances.

walk·o·ver (wawk-oh-vur) *noun (informal)* A very easy victory.

walk·way (wawk-way) *noun* A path or passage for walking.

wall (wawl) *noun*
1. A solid structure that separates two areas or supports a roof. ▷ *verb* **wall**

2. Anything that blocks the way, shuts something in, or divides one thing from another; a barrier, as in *a wall of marchers, a wall of fire,* or *a wall of secrecy.*

wal·la·by (wol-uh-bee) *noun* A small marsupial of the kangaroo family. Wallabies are found in Australia, New Zealand, and New Guinea. Many wallabies are about the size of a rabbit.
▷ *noun, plural* **wallabies**

red-necked wallaby

wal·let (wol-it) *noun* A small, flat case for holding money, photographs, and/or cards.

wal·lop (wol-uhp) *verb (informal)* To hit someone or something very hard. *The batter walloped the ball over the fence.* ▷ **walloping, walloped** ▷ *noun* **wallop**

wal·low (wol-oh) *verb*
1. To roll around in mud or water.
2. To enjoy something greatly, or to get completely involved in something. *Dan wallowed in self-pity after he lost the game.*
▷ *verb* **wallowing, wallowed**

wall·pa·per (wawl-pay-pur) *noun* Patterned or colored paper that is pasted in sections to a wall in order to decorate a room. ▷ *verb* **wallpaper**

wal·nut (wawl-nuht) *noun* A sweet nut that grows on a tall tree and has a hard, wrinkled shell. The wood of the walnut tree is often used to make furniture.

wal·rus (wawl-ruhss) *noun* A large sea animal that lives in the Arctic. Walruses have tusks, flippers, tough skin, and a thick layer of blubber. They are related to seals and sea lions.
▷ *noun, plural* **walruses** *or* **walrus**

walruses

▶ **Word History**

Early hunters and explorers often used familiar words to name new and unusual animals that they came across. **Walrus** comes from two Dutch words, *walvis,* meaning "whale," and *ros,* meaning "horse." In Old English, the animal had been called a "horsewhale."

waltz (wawlts) *noun*
1. A smooth, gliding ballroom dance with a regular 1-2-3 beat. ▷ *verb* **waltz** ▷ *noun* **waltzer**
2. A piece of music that accompanies a waltz.
▷ *noun, plural* **waltzes**

wam·pum (wahm-puhm) *noun* Beads made from polished shells strung together or woven to make belts, collars, and necklaces. Wampum was used by some American Indian tribes as money.

▶ **Word History**
• •
▶ **Wampum** is the name that American Indians in New England gave to the strings of polished shells they used as money. It is short for *wampumpeak.* Tribes in other parts of North America called their money by different names. In the Virginia area it was called *roanoke,* and in the northwest part of the United States it was called *hiaqua.*

wand (wond) *noun* A thin rod or stick, especially one used by magicians.

wan·der (won-dur) *verb*
1. To move about without a particular purpose or place to go; to roam; to ramble. ▷ *noun* **wanderer**
2. To get lost; to stray. *The hikers wandered from the trail.*
3. To stray from a particular subject; to become easily distracted. *My mind wandered during the boring lecture.*
▷ *verb* **wandering, wandered**

wane (wayn) *verb*
1. To become less or smaller in size, importance, or strength. *As the job progressed, Jewel's enthusiasm waned.*
2. When the moon **wanes,** it appears to get smaller. *See* **moon.**
▷ *verb* **waning, waned**

wan·gle (wang-guhl) *verb (informal)* To gain something by clever, tricky, or dishonest methods. *I managed to wangle a front-row seat.*
▷ **wangling, wangled**

want (wont)
1. *verb* To feel that you would like to have, do, or get something; to wish for; to desire. *I want an apple. I want to go on vacation.*
2. *verb* To need or require something. *What this story wants is some suspense.*
3. *noun* A lack. *In many poor countries, people are dying for want of food and medicine.*
4. *noun* A need, desire, or requirement. *My wants are few.*
5. *noun* The condition of being very poor or needy; poverty, as in *a family in want.*
▷ *verb* **wanting, wanted**

war (wor) *noun*
1. Fighting between opposing forces.
2. A struggle or fight against something. *We are waging a war against hunger.*
▷ *verb* **war**

war·bler (warb-lur) *noun* Any of several small, lively American songbirds. Many warblers have brightly colored feathers.

ward (word)
1. *noun* A large room or section in a hospital where many patients are taken care of.
2. *noun* A person who is under the care of a guardian or the court. *The orphan was a ward of the state.*
3. *noun* For voting purposes, a district of a town or city.
4. ward off *verb* To prevent something from attacking or hurting you. *I'm trying to ward off a cold by taking a lot of vitamins.* ▷ **warding, warded**

war·den (word-uhn) *noun*
1. Someone in charge of a prison.
2. An official who is responsible for enforcing certain laws, as in *a game warden.*

ward·robe (word-robe) *noun*
1. A collection of clothes, especially all the clothes belonging to one person.
2. A tall piece of furniture or a closet used for storing clothes.

ware (wair) *noun*
1. wares *noun, plural* Things that are for sale; goods. *Many merchants displayed their wares at the fair.*
2. Items of the same general kind, as in *silverware, hardware,* or *software.*
Ware sounds like **wear** and **where.**

ware·house (wair-hous) *noun* A large building used for storing goods or merchandise. ▷ *verb* **warehouse**

war·fare (wor-fair) *noun* The fighting of wars, or armed combat, as in *jungle warfare.*

war·like (wor-like) *adjective* Hostile, aggressive, or likely to start a war, as in *warlike behavior.*

warm (worm)
1. *adjective* A bit hot; not cold.
2. *verb* To increase the temperature of something. *Come in and warm your hands by the fire.*
3. *adjective* Holding in body heat, as in *a warm sweater.*
4. *adjective* Very friendly. *We were given a warm welcome.* ▷ *adverb* **warmly**
5. *verb* If you **warm up** before a sports match or athletic activity, you stretch or exercise gently in preparation. ▷ *noun* **warm-up**
6. *verb* When an engine **warms up,** it starts to run smoothly.
▷ *noun* **warmth** ▷ *verb* **warming, warmed**
▷ *adjective* **warmer, warmest**

warm-blood·ed (bluhd-id) *adjective* **Warm-blooded** animals have a body temperature that remains approximately the same, whatever their surroundings. *Birds and mammals, including humans, are warm-blooded animals.*

warn (worn) *verb*
1. If you **warn** someone, you tell the person about a danger or a bad thing that might happen. *My mother is always warning me that too much candy is bad for my teeth.*
2. To give advice. *The reports warned about the dangers of smoking.*
Warn sounds like **worn.**
▷ *verb* **warning, warned** ▷ *noun* **warning**

warp (worp) *verb* If an object **warps,** it gets twisted, curved, or bent out of shape.
▷ **warping, warped**

war·rant (wor-uhnt)
1. *noun* An official piece of paper that gives permission for something, as in *a search warrant.*
2. *verb* To guarantee. *The manufacturer warrants all its products.* ▷ *noun* **warranty**
3. *verb* To deserve. *Barbara's history report warrants an A.*
▷ *verb* **warranting, warranted**

war·ren (wor-uhn) *noun* A group of underground tunnels where rabbits breed and live.

war·ri·or (wor-ee-ur) *noun* A soldier, or someone who is experienced in fighting battles. *See* **samurai.**

war·ship (wor-ship) *noun* A ship with heavy guns that is used in war. *See* **ship.**

wart (wort) *noun*
1. A small, hard lump on the skin. Warts are caused by a virus.
2. A small lump or bump that grows on a plant.
▷ *adjective* **warty**

war·y (wair-ee) *adjective* Cautious and careful. *Danny is always very wary of dogs.* ▷ **warier, wariest** ▷ *noun* **wariness** ▷ *adverb* **warily**

was (wuhz) *verb* The form of **be** used with *I, he, she,* or *it* or with singular nouns in the past tense. *I was at the restaurant before everyone else.*

wash (wosh)
1. *verb* To clean with water or soap and water.
▷ *noun* **wash,** *noun* **washing**
2. *noun* Clothing that needs to be or has been washed. *Put the wash in the laundry room.*
▷ *noun, plural* **washes**
3. *verb* To wear away by the action of moving water. *Storms washed away most of the beach.*
4. *verb* If the sea **washes** something **up,** it leaves it on the shore.
▷ *verb* **washes, washing, washed**

wash·a·ble (wosh-uh-buhl) *adjective* If a material is **washable,** you can wash it without causing any damage to it.

wash·er (wosh-ur) *noun*
1. A washing machine.
2. A ring that fits between a nut and a bolt to give a tighter fit or prevent a leak.

washing machine *noun* A machine that washes clothes, linens, and similar items.

Wash·ing·ton's Birthday (wosh-ing-tuhnz) *noun* A holiday that honors the birthday of George Washington, the first president of the United States. Originally celebrated on February 22, Washington's actual birthday, this holiday is now observed on the third Monday in February as part of **Presidents' Day.**

was·n't (wuhz-uhnt) *contraction* A short form of *was not. Today's weather wasn't great, but our picnic was fun anyway.*

wasp (wosp) *noun* A flying insect that has a slender body. Female wasps can give a painful sting. *See* **nest.**

waste (wayst)
1. *verb* If you **waste** something, you use or spend it foolishly or carelessly. *Don't waste your time.* ▷ *noun* **waste**
2. *verb* If someone **wastes away,** the person gets thinner and weaker because of illness.
3. *noun* Garbage, or something left over and not needed, as in *chemical waste.*
4. *noun* What the body does not use or need after food has been digested.
Waste sounds like **waist.**
▷ *verb* **wasting, wasted** ▷ *adjective* **waste**

waste·bas·ket (wayst-bass-kit) *noun* A small basket or open container used for scraps of paper or other small items of trash.

waste·ful (wayst-fuhl) *adjective* If you are **wasteful,** you use things up needlessly or carelessly and do not think about saving them.
▷ *noun* **wastefulness** ▷ *adverb* **wastefully**

waste·land (wayst-land) *noun* An area of land that is barren or empty; land where few plants or animals can live.

watch (woch)
1. *noun* A small clock usually worn on the wrist.
2. *verb* To look at something. *Annie was watching the news on TV.*
3. *verb* To be alert or careful about something. *Watch what you're doing with those scissors.*
4. *verb* To keep guard over. *Will you watch my packages while I go get a soda?* ▷ *noun* **watch**
5. *noun* A person or group that guards or protects. *The sailor was on the night watch.*
6. *noun* The time that a guard is on duty. *His watch ends at midnight.*
▷ *noun, plural* **watches** ▷ *verb* **watches, watching, watched**

watch·dog (woch-*dawg*) *noun*
1. A dog trained to guard a house, property, or people.
2. Someone who guards against theft, waste, or illegal practices. *A consumer watchdog protects the public against illegal business practices.*

watch·ful (woch-fuhl) *adjective* Observing carefully; alert. *The dog kept a watchful eye on the door until the family came home.* ▷ *noun* **watchfulness** ▷ *adverb* **watchfully**

wa·ter (waw-tur)
1. *noun* The colorless liquid that falls as rain and fills oceans, rivers, and lakes.
2. waters *noun, plural* The water in an ocean, a river, or a lake.
3. *verb* To pour water on something. *Would you please water the plants?*
4. *verb* If your mouth **waters,** it produces saliva in response to the sight, smell, or thought of food.
5. *verb* If your eyes **water,** tears fill them.
6. *verb* If you **water** something **down,** you make it weaker, usually by adding water.
▷ *verb* **watering, watered**

water buffalo *noun* A black buffalo with long horns that curve upward and outward. Found in Asia, it is often used to pull or carry heavy loads. ▷ *noun, plural* **water buffalo, water buffalos,** *or* **water buffaloes**

wa·ter·col·or (waw-tur-*kuhl*-ur) *noun*
1. Paint that is mixed with water, not oil. *See* **artist.**
2. A picture painted with watercolors. ▷ *noun* **watercolorist**

wa·ter·cress (waw-tur-*kress*) *noun* A plant found in wet soil or running water. It has pungent leaves and is used mostly in salads.

water cycle *noun* The constant movement of the earth's water. Plants give off moisture, and water from rivers and oceans evaporates, making water vapor. This vapor rises, forms clouds, and then falls as rain, hail, or snow.

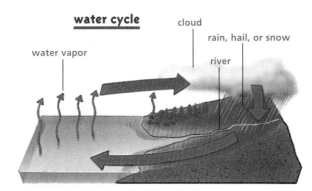

water cycle
cloud
rain, hail, or snow
water vapor
river

wa·ter·fall (waw-tur-*fawl*) *noun* Water from a stream or river that falls from a high place to a lower place.

wa·ter·front (waw-tur-*fruhnt*) *noun* Any land or area of a city or town that is located beside a body of water. *The seafood restaurant is on the waterfront.* ▷ *adjective* **waterfront**

watering can *noun* A metal or plastic container with a handle and a long spout used for watering plants.

water lily *noun* A plant that grows in freshwater ponds and lakes. Its wide, flat leaves float on the water, and it has fragrant, colorful flowers. ▷ *noun, plural* **water lilies**

wa·ter·logged (waw-tur-*logd*) *adjective* If something is **waterlogged,** it is so filled or soaked with water that it becomes heavy or hard to manage. *My shoes became waterlogged from walking in puddles.*

water main *noun* A large, main pipe in a system of pipes that carry water.

wa·ter·mark (waw-tur-*mark*) *noun*
1. A mark or design in paper that you can see when you hold the paper up to the light.
2. A mark on a wall or other surface that shows how high the water in a river, a lake, or an ocean has risen.

wa·ter·mel·on (waw-tur-*mel*-uhn) *noun* A large, juicy fruit that grows on vines. It usually has a thick, green rind, many seeds, and sweet, watery pulp that is pink, red, or yellow.

water moccasin *noun* A poisonous snake that lives near water and in swamps in the southeastern part of the United States. It is also called a cottonmouth.

wa·ter·proof (waw-tur-*proof*) *adjective* If something is **waterproof,** it keeps water out, as in *a waterproof raincoat.* ▷ *verb* **waterproof**

wa·ter·shed (waw-tur-*shed*) *noun*
1. A ridge or area of high land that separates two river basins.
2. The region or land area that drains into a river or lake.
3. An important factor; a turning point. *The Civil War was a watershed in U.S. history.*

water-ski *verb* To travel on skis over water, towed by a boat. ▷ **water-skiing, water-skied** ▷ *noun* **water-skier,** *noun* **waterskiing**

wa·ter·tight (waw-tur-*tite*) *adjective*
1. If something is **watertight,** it is completely sealed so that water cannot enter or leave it. *Make sure that the cover on the jar is watertight.*
2. If an argument is **watertight,** it has no faults and can be clearly understood.

water vapor *noun* The gas produced when water evaporates.

wa·ter·way (waw-tur-*way*) *noun* A river, canal, or other body of water on which ships and boats travel.

wa·ter·wheel (waw-tur-*weel*) *noun* A large wheel that is turned by water flowing over or under it. Waterwheels are used to provide power.

wa·ter·works (waw-tur-*wurks*) *noun, plural* The system that provides water to a community or town, including reservoirs, pipes, machinery, and buildings. Waterworks can be used with a singular or a plural verb.

watt (wot) *noun* A unit for measuring electrical power. ▷ *noun* **wattage**

wat·tle and daub (wot-uhl and daub) *noun* A mixture of woven sticks and mud or clay that people once used to build houses. See **Iron Age.**

wave (wayv)
1. *verb* To move your hand back and forth to get someone's attention or to say hello or good-bye. *Sonja waved at me as she was leaving the basketball game.* ▷ *noun* **wave**
2. *verb* To move or sway back and forth or up and down. *The trees waved in the breeze.*
3. *noun* A moving ridge on the surface of water, especially the ocean. *The waves were crashing onto the beach.*
4. *noun* A curl in your hair. ▷ *verb* **wave**
5. *noun* A vibration of energy that travels through air or water, as in *sound waves* or *radio waves.*
6. *noun* A sudden change or increase, as in *a heat wave* or *a crime wave.*
Wave sounds like **waive.**
   ▷ *verb* **waving, waved** ▷ *adjective* **wavy**

wave·length (wayv-*length*) *noun*
1. The distance between one crest of a wave of light or sound and the next.
2. *(informal)* If you are **on the same wavelength** as someone, you have similar thoughts.

wa·ver (way-vur) *verb*
1. To be uncertain or unsteady. *Nadja never wavered in her determination to win the competition.*
2. To quiver or to tremble. *My voice wavered when I was asked to speak in front of the whole class.*
   ▷ *verb* **wavering, wavered** ▷ *noun* **waver**

wax (waks)
1. *noun* A yellow substance that is secreted by bees and is used for building honeycombs.
2. *noun* A substance made from fats or oils and used to make crayons, polish, and candles.
3. *verb* To put wax or polish on something such as a car or furniture. *When Stephen finished waxing the table, he could see his own reflection in it.*
4. *verb* When the moon **waxes,** it appears to get larger. See **moon.**
5. *verb* To grow, or to become. *They waxed enthusiastic about the party plans.*
   ▷ *verb* **waxes, waxing, waxed** ▷ *adjective* **waxy**

way (way) *noun*
1. A direction. *Which way is north?*
2. A road or a route. *Do you know the way home?*
3. A method or style of doing something. *Is this the right way to spell your name?*
4. A manner or a style. *She smiled in a way that warmed up the whole room.*
5. Distance. *I ran a long way before stopping to catch my breath.*
6. The opportunity to do or get what one wishes. *My bossy sister always tries to get her way.*
7. A point or a detail. *In many ways, you are right.*
8. Space or a path. *Make way for the people coming through.*
9. **ways** *noun, plural* Habits or customs.
Way sounds like **weigh** and **whey.**

we (wee) *pronoun, plural* The people who are speaking or writing. **We** sounds like **wee.**

weak (week) *adjective*
1. Having little strength, force, or power, as in *a weak person, a weak argument,* or *a weak light.* ▷ *adverb* **weakly**
2. Likely to break, fall, or collapse. *The bracelet has a weak link near the clasp.*
3. Lacking flavor. *This is very weak tea.*
4. Lacking in skill or knowledge. *I am weak in spelling.*
5. Your **weak** points are the things that you are not very good at.
Weak sounds like **week.**
   ▷ *adjective* **weaker, weakest** ▷ *noun* **weakness** ▷ *verb* **weaken**

weak·ling (week-ling) *noun* A person without physical or moral strength.

wealth (welth) *noun*
1. A great amount of money, property, or valuable possessions; riches.
2. A great amount of anything, as in *a wealth of ideas* or *a wealth of information.*

wealth·y (wel-thee) *adjective* Someone who is **wealthy** has a lot of money or property.
   ▷ **wealthier, wealthiest**

wean (ween) *verb*
1. When you **wean** babies, you start giving them other food instead of their mothers' milk.
2. If you **wean** someone **from** something, you help him or her give it up gradually.
   ▷ *verb* **weaning, weaned**

weap·on (wep-uhn) *noun*
1. Something that can be used in a fight to attack or defend, such as a sword, gun, knife, or bomb. ▷ *noun* **weaponry**

2. Anything that can be used to win a fight, struggle, or contest. *This football team's best weapon is its quarterback.*

wear (wair)

1. *verb* To be dressed in something, or to carry or have something on your body. *Max wore a red shirt. Rosie wore a butterfly pin.* ▷ *noun* **wearer**

2. *verb* To have, or to show. *She wears her hair short. He wore an angry frown.*

3. *noun* Clothes. *Let's go to the boys' wear department.*

4. *noun* The gradual damage done to something by constant use. *My coat is showing signs of wear.*

5. *verb* To last a long time. *These boots have worn well.*

6. *verb* If an activity **wears** you **out,** it makes you very tired.

7. *verb* If you **wear out** your clothes, you make them ragged and useless.

8. wear away *verb* To destroy something slowly, bit by bit. *Carlos wore away my patience.*

9. wear off *verb* To become less. *Slowly, the effects of the painkiller wore off.*

Wear sounds like **ware** and **where.**

▷ *verb* **wearing, wore** (wor), **worn**

wea·ry (wihr-ee) *adjective*

1. Very tired, or exhausted. *We were weary after the long trip.*

2. Having little patience or interest; bored. *James grew weary of eating the same lunch every day.*

▷ *adjective* **wearier, weariest** ▷ *noun* **weariness**
▷ *adverb* **wearily**

wea·sel (wee-zuhl) *noun* A small animal with a long, slender body; short legs; and soft, thick, reddish brown fur. It feeds on rats, mice, rabbits, small birds, and snakes.

weath·er (weTH-ur)

1. *noun* The condition of the outside air or atmosphere at a particular time and place. Weather can be described as hot or cold, wet or dry, calm or windy, clear or cloudy.

2. *verb* If wood, stone, or another material **weathers,** it changes after being outside for a long time.

3. *verb* If you **weather** a storm or crisis, you get through it.

4. If you are **under the weather,** you aren't feeling very well.

Weather sounds like **whether.**

▷ *verb* **weathering, weathered**

weather-beaten *adjective* Something that is **weather-beaten** is damaged or worn by the weather.

weather forecast *noun* A prediction about the weather for the next day or the next few days.

▷ *noun* **weather forecaster**

weath·er·ize (weTH-uh-rize) *verb* To protect a home or other structure from heat loss by putting in insulation, stripping, and caulking.
▷ **weatherizing, weatherized** ▷ *noun* **weatherization**

weather vane *noun* A device placed on the ground or on the roof of a building that turns freely to show which way the wind is blowing.

weave (weev)

1. *verb* To make cloth, baskets, and other objects by passing threads or strips over and under each other. ▷ *noun* **weaver**

2. *verb* To spin a web or cocoon. *The spider wove a web.*

3. *verb* To move from side to side or in and out in order to get through something. *Tamara wove her way through the crowd.*

4. *noun* A method or pattern of weaving. *That basket has an open weave. This carpet has a tight weave.*

Weave sounds like **we've.**

▷ *verb* **weaving, wove** (wohv) *or* **weaved, woven** (woh-vin) *or* **weaved**

web (web) *noun*

1. A very fine net of sticky threads made by a spider to catch flies and other insects.

2. Anything put together in a careful or complicated way; something that snares or traps, as in *a web of city streets* or *a web of lies.*

3. The fold of skin or tissue that connects the toes of a duck, frog, or other animal that swims.

web-foot·ed (fut-id) *adjective* Having toes that are connected by a web or fold of skin. *Ducks are web-footed.*

wed (wed) *verb*

1. To get married to someone. *Someday I hope to wed my sweetheart.*

2. To perform a marriage ceremony. *The judge wed the happy couple.*

▷ *verb* **wedding, wedded** *or* **wed**

we'd (weed) *contraction* A short form of *we would, we had,* or *we should. We'd like to go to Aunt Ruth's house for the holidays.* **We'd** sounds like **weed.**

wed·ding (wed-ing) *noun* A marriage ceremony.

wedge (wej)

1. *noun* A piece of food, wood, metal, or plastic that is thin at one end and thick at the other. *Christie helped herself to a wedge of cheese.*

2. *verb* To split, force apart, or hold in place with a wedge. *Ramón wedged open the door with a small piece of wood.*

3. *verb* To squeeze or crowd into a limited space. *The six of us wedged ourselves into the tiny car.*

▷ *verb* **wedging, wedged**

Wed·nes·day (wenz-dee *or* wenz-*day*) *noun* The fourth day of the week, after Tuesday and before Thursday.

> ### Word History
> •
>
> In Old English, **Wednesday** was *Wodensdaeg,* or "Woden's day." Woden was the Scandinavian god of agriculture, as well as of war, wisdom, and poetry. In ancient times, Wednesday was often the day when crops were planted.

wee (wee) *adjective* Very small; tiny. **Wee** sounds like **we.**

weed (weed)
  1. *noun* A plant that is seen as useless or harmful and growing where it is not wanted.
  2. *verb* If you **weed** your garden, you pull the weeds out.
  3. *verb* If you **weed** something **out,** you remove it because it is useless or harmful.
  Weed sounds like **we'd.**
  ▷ *verb* **weeding, weeded**

week (week) *noun*
  1. A period of seven days, usually from Sunday to Saturday.
  2. The hours or days that a person works or spends in school each week. *My mother works a 40-hour week. The school week begins on Monday morning.*
  Week sounds like **weak.**

week·day (week-*day*) *noun* Any day of the week except Saturday or Sunday.

week·end (week-*end*) *noun* The period of time from Friday night through Sunday night.

week·ly (week-lee)
  1. *adjective* Done, happening, or appearing once a week or every week, as in *a weekly visit* or *a weekly newspaper.*
  2. *adverb* Once a week, or every week. *We do our grocery shopping weekly.*
  3. *noun* A newspaper or magazine that is published once a week. ▷ *noun, plural* **weeklies**

weep (weep) *verb* To cry because you feel very sad or very emotional. ▷ **weeping, wept (wept)** ▷ *adjective* **weepy**

wee·vil (wee-vuhl) *noun* A beetle with a snout that curves downward. The weevil is a pest to farmers because its larvae eat grain, cotton, fruit, and other plants and crops.

weigh (way) *verb*
  1. To measure how heavy or light someone or something is by using a scale.
  2. To have a particular weight. *He weighs 75 pounds.*

3. To consider something carefully before deciding. *The jury weighed the evidence.*
  4. If you are **weighed down,** you have too much to carry, do, or think about.
  Weigh sounds like **way** and **whey.**
  ▷ *verb* **weighing, weighed**

weight (wate) *noun*
  1. Someone or something's **weight** is the measure of how heavy the person or thing is.
  2. A unit, such as the ounce, pound, or ton, that is used for measuring weight.
  3. A heavy object used to hold things down, as in *a paperweight.*
  4. weights *noun, plural* Heavy objects that people lift as an exercise to make their muscles stronger.
  5. A heavy load or burden; pressure. *The weight of all this work is making me nervous and tense.*
  Weight sounds like **wait.**

weight·less (wate-liss) *adjective*
  1. Having little or no weight. *Snowflakes are weightless.*
  2. Free of the pull of gravity. *Astronauts are weightless in outer space.*
  ▷ *noun* **weightlessness** ▷ *adverb* **weightlessly**

weight lift·er (lift-ur) *noun* A person who lifts weights in competitions or for pleasure. ▷ *noun* **weight lifting**

weird (wihrd) *adjective* Strange or mysterious. ▷ **weirder, weirdest** ▷ *noun* **weirdness** ▷ *adverb* **weirdly**

weird·o (wihr-doh) *noun* (*slang*) A very odd or strange person. ▷ *noun, plural* **weirdos**

wel·come (wel-kuhm)
  1. *verb* If you **welcome** someone, you greet the person in a friendly way. ▷ *interjection* **welcome**
  2. *adjective* If something is **welcome,** you like it or are glad to have it.
  3. *verb* If you **welcome** something, you are glad to have it.
  4. *adjective* "You're **welcome**" is the polite response when someone says, "Thank you."
  ▷ *verb* **welcoming, welcomed** ▷ *noun* **welcome** ▷ *adjective* **welcoming**

weld (weld) *verb*
  1. To join two pieces of metal or plastic by heating them until they are soft enough to be joined together. ▷ *noun* **weld,** *noun* **welder**
  2. To bring together; to unite. *The friends were welded together by their love of acting.*
  ▷ *verb* **welding, welded**

wel·fare (wel-fair) *noun*
  1. Someone's **welfare** is the person's state of health, happiness, and comfort. *For your own welfare, you should try to get more sleep.*
  2. Money or other help given by a government to people who are in need.

W

well (wel)
1. *adverb* If you do something **well,** you do it in a good, skillful, or satisfactory way.
2. *adverb* Thoroughly. *Wash your hands well.*
3. *adverb* Much; to a great extent. *It was well after midnight when the telephone rang.*
4. *adverb* In a close or familiar way. *I know them well.*
5. *adjective* Healthy. *You're looking well.*
6. *noun* A deep hole from which you can draw water, oil, or natural gas from under the ground.
7. *interjection* You say **well** to show surprise or doubt. *Well, look who's here!*

we'll (weel) *contraction* A short form of *we will* or *we shall. We'll have to send Uncle Bill a birthday card.* **We'll** sounds like **wheel.**

well-balanced *adjective*
1. Nicely or evenly balanced. *Eat a well-balanced diet of fruits, vegetables, grains, meats, and dairy products.*
2. Sane or sensible. *A well-balanced person is not easily upset.*

well-behaved *adjective* Acting properly and with good manners, as in *well-behaved students.*

well-being *noun* Health and happiness. *A good diet gives you a sense of well-being.*

well-known *adjective* Known by many people; famous, as in *a well-known actor.*

well-off *adjective*
1. If someone is **well-off,** he or she is wealthy or rich.
2. If someone is **well-off,** everything is going well for him or her.

were (wur) *verb* The form of **be** used with *we, you,* or *they* or with plural nouns in the past tense. *We were thrilled to hear that our class won first prize in the recycling contest.* **Were** sounds like **whir.**

we're (wihr) *contraction* A short form of *we are. We're about to begin a new chapter in our geography books.*

weren't (wurnt *or* wur-uhnt) *contraction* A short form of *were not. Weren't you at the party?*

west (west)
1. *noun* One of the four main points of the compass. West is the direction in which the sun sets. ▷ *adverb* **west**
2. West *noun* Any area or region lying in this direction.
3. the West *noun* In the United States, the region that is west of the Mississippi River.
4. *adjective* To do with or existing in the west, as in *the west side of the street.*
▷ *adverb* **westerly,** *adverb* **westward**

west·ern (wess-turn)
1. *adjective* In, of, toward, or from the west.
2. *adjective* To do with a western region, as in *western Canada.*

3. Western *adjective* To do with the West, as in *Western ranches.*
4. Western *or* **western** *noun* A cowboy movie or television show set in the western part of the United States, especially during the last half of the 19th century.

West In·dies (in-deez) *noun, plural* A string of islands in the western hemisphere that separates the Caribbean Sea from the Atlantic Ocean.

west·ward (west-wurd)
1. westward *or* **westwards** *adverb* To or toward the west. *The sun appears to travel westward during the day.*
2. *adjective* Moving to or toward the west. *Many pioneers wrote diaries about their westward journeys.*

wet (wet)
1. *adjective* Covered with or full of liquid, as in *a wet cloth.*
2. *adjective* Not yet set or dry, as in *wet cement* or *wet paint.*
3. *adjective* Rainy. *This is the wet season.*
4. *verb* To make something wet. *Wet the cloth before you wipe those shelves.* ▷ **wetting, wet** *or* **wetted**
▷ *adjective* **wetter, wettest**

> **Synonyms: wet**
>
> **Wet,** the opposite of *dry,* means covered with or full of a liquid, usually water: *Our dog got the whole kitchen wet when he shook himself after coming in from the rain.*
>
> **Damp** means slightly, and often unpleasantly, wet: *We all got sick after spending the weekend in the damp mountain air.*
>
> **Moist** describes something that is slightly damp or not quite dry: *It helps to use a moist cloth when you wipe off your bicycle.*
>
> **Dank** describes something that is slightly wet and more unpleasant than just damp: *The dank air in Jamie's creepy basement made it just right for telling ghost stories.*
>
> **Soggy** means completely wet and heavy with extra liquid: *The cushions on the lawn chairs are soggy from last night's rain.*
>
> **Humid** describes air that is full of moisture: *It was so humid outside that we knew rain was on the way.*

wet·land (wet-*land or* wet-luhnd) *or* **wet·lands** (wet-*landz or* wet-luhndz) *noun* Marshy land; land where there is much moisture in the soil.

we've (weev) *contraction* A short form of *we have. We've finished the main course; now it's time for dessert.* **We've** sounds like **weave.**

whack (wak) *noun*
1. *(informal)* A hard, sharp hit or slap. ▷ *verb* **whack**
2. *(slang)* An attempt. *I'll take a whack at the math problem.*

whale (wale)
1. *noun* A large sea animal that looks like a fish but is actually a mammal that breathes air. Dolphins and porpoises are members of the whale family.
2. *verb* To hunt for whales.
▷ **whaling, whaled**
Whale sounds like **wail.**

killer whale

dorsal fin

flipper

tail fluke

whal·er (way-lur) *noun*
1. Someone who hunts whales for their meat, oil, and bones. ▷ *noun* **whaling**
2. A boat used to catch whales.

wharf (worf) *noun* A long platform, built along a shore, where boats and ships can load and unload; a dock. ▷ *noun, plural* **wharves** (worvz) *or* **wharfs**

what (wot *or* wuht)
1. *pronoun* The word **what** is used in questions to discover more about something or someone. *What music do you like? What did you say?*
2. *pronoun* The thing or things that. *I heard what you said.*
3. *adjective* The word **what** is used to emphasize how great, small, strange, etc., something or someone is. *What a surprise! What a nut!*
4. *adverb* In which way; how. *What does it matter?*
5. *interjection* The word **what** is used to show surprise or anger. *What! That can't be true!*

what·ev·er (wot-ev-ur *or* wuht-ev-ur)
1. *pronoun* Anything that. *Wear whatever you like.* ▷ *adjective* **whatever**
2. *pronoun* No matter what. *Whatever you do, don't be late.*
3. *pronoun* Which thing or things; what. *Whatever made him think that you would be coming over this afternoon?*
4. *adjective* Any that. *Order whatever food you want.*
5. *adjective* Of any kind or type; at all. *He said nothing whatever about how he liked his gift.*

what's (wots *or* wuhts) *contraction* A short form of *what is* or *what has*. *What's the problem? What's happened to my dress?*

wheat (weet) *noun* A cereal grass whose grain is used for making flour, pasta, and breakfast foods. *See* **grain.**

wheel (weel)
1. *noun* A round frame or object that turns on an axle. Wheels are used to work machinery or move a vehicle.
2. *noun* Anything that uses or is shaped like a wheel, as in *a spinning wheel* or *a steering wheel*.
3. *verb* To push something on wheels. *Wheel your bicycle up the hill.*
4. *verb* To turn. *The deer wheeled and ran away.*
5. wheels *noun, plural* *(slang)* An automobile.
Wheel sounds like **we'll.**
▷ *verb* **wheeling, wheeled**

wheel·bar·row (weel-ba-roh) *noun* A small cart with one wheel at the front, often used to carry things around in yards or gardens.

wheel·chair (weel-chair) *noun* A chair on wheels for people who are ill, injured, or disabled.

wheel·ie (wee-lee) *noun* *(informal)* If you do a **wheelie** on a bicycle or motorcycle, you ride with the front wheel off the ground.

wheeze (weez) *verb* To breathe with difficulty, making a whistling noise in your chest. People sometimes wheeze when they have asthma or a bad cold. ▷ **wheezing, wheezed** ▷ *noun* **wheeziness** ▷ *adjective* **wheezy**

whelk (welk) *noun* A large snail that lives in salt water and has a spiral shell.

when (wen)
1. *adverb* The word **when** is used to ask about the time of an event. *When was Martin Luther King, Jr., born?*
2. *conjunction* At the time that. *I told Jake the news when I saw him yesterday.*
3. *conjunction* At any time; whenever. *When I swim, I get water in my ears.*
4. *conjunction* Although; but. *I went out when I should have been studying.*
5. *conjunction* Considering the fact that. *How can we meet the deadline when we have so much left to do?*

when·ev·er (wen-ev-ur) *conjunction* At any time. *We'll eat whenever you're hungry.*

where (wair)
1. *adverb* The word **where** is used to ask about the place or position of someone or something. *Where is Emma now?*
2. *conjunction* In, at, or to the place that or in which. *I visited the house where my friend lives. I'll go where you go.*
3. *conjunction* In or at which place. *I went home, where I took a nap.*
4. *pronoun* What place. *Where are you from?*
Where sounds like **ware** and **wear.**

where·a·bouts (wair-uh-bouts)
1. *adverb* Roughly where. *Whereabouts in New York did you stay?*

W

2. noun The place where someone or something is. *I'm afraid we don't know Billy's whereabouts.* Whereabouts can be used with a singular or plural verb.

where·as (*wair-az*) *conjunction* On the other hand. *My parents eat meat, whereas I am a vegetarian.*

where·up·on (*wair-uh-pon*) *conjunction* After which; at which time; and then. *The doorbell rang, whereupon the dog barked.*

wher·ev·er (*wair-ev-ur*) *conjunction* In, at, or to any place. *We'll go wherever you suggest.*
▷ *adverb* **wherever**

wheth·er (*weTH-ur*) *conjunction*
1. If. *I wonder whether it will rain.*
2. The word **whether** is used to show a choice between two things. *Have you decided whether you'll go out or stay in?*
Whether sounds like **weather.**

whew (*hyoo*) *interjection* A word used to show relief, discomfort, or surprise. *Whew! Am I glad that my exams are finished.*

whey (*way*) *noun* The watery part of milk that separates when milk sours or when you make cheese. **Whey** sounds like **way** and **weigh.**

which (*wich*)
1. *adjective* The word **which** is used to ask about a choice of things. *Which dress shall I wear?*
2. *pronoun* What one or ones. *Which is yours?*
3. *pronoun* The one or ones that. *I agree on which tastes best.*
4. *conjunction* The one or ones mentioned; that. *Our car, which we bought several years ago, has never given us trouble.*
Which sounds like **witch.**

which·ev·er (*wich-ev-ur*)
1. *pronoun* Any one or ones. *Buy whichever you want.*
2. *pronoun* No matter which. *Whichever you buy is fine with me.*
3. *adjective* Any one or ones. *Read whichever book seems the most fun.*
4. *adjective* No matter which. *Whichever book you read, you'll like it.*

whiff (*wif*) *noun*
1. A light puff of air or smoke.
2. A faint smell in the air.
▷ *verb* **whiff**

while (*wile*)
1. *noun* A period of time. *It was a long while before I spoke to him again.*
2. *conjunction* During the time that. *Can you feed my hamster while I am away?*
3. *conjunction* Although. *While I usually do well in math, I think I failed this test.*
4. *verb* To pass or spend time in a pleasant or

relaxed way. *We whiled away the morning reading the Sunday newspaper.* ▷ **whiling, whiled**

whim (*wim*) *noun* A sudden idea or wish. *I made brownies on a whim.*

whim·per (*wim-pur*) *verb* To make weak, crying noises. *The puppy whimpered when I stopped petting it.* ▷ **whimpering, whimpered** ▷ *noun* **whimper**

whine (*wine*) *verb*
1. To make a shrill, drawn-out sound that is sad or unpleasant. *The wind whined in the chimney.*
2. To complain or moan about something in an annoying way. *Jerry whines when he doesn't get his way.* ▷ *noun* **whiner**
Whine sounds like **wine.**
▷ *verb* **whining, whined**

whin·ny (*win-ee*) *noun* A horse's low, gentle neigh. ▷ *noun, plural* **whinnies** ▷ *verb* **whinny**

whip (*wip*)
1. *noun* A long piece of leather on a handle, used especially for driving horses and cattle.
▷ *verb* **whip**
2. *verb* To move, pull, or take something suddenly. *Pat whipped the present from behind his back.*
3. *verb* (*informal*) To defeat badly. *Our team whipped the Tigers last week.*
4. *verb* To beat something such as eggs or cream into a foam.
▷ *verb* **whipping, whipped**

whip·poor·will (*wip-uhr-wil*) *noun* A plump bird with brown, gray, and black spots on its brown feathers. It is found in eastern North America and feeds and sings at night. Its call sounds very much like its name.

whir (*wur*)
1. *verb* To move, fly, or operate with a buzzing or humming sound. ▷ **whirring, whirred**
2. *noun* A buzzing or humming sound. *We could hear the whir of the helicopter overhead.*

whirl (*wurl*)
1. *verb* If something **whirls,** it moves around quickly in a circle. *Leaves were whirling across the playground.* ▷ **whirling, whirled**
2. *noun* A fast or confused movement. *There was a whirl of activity just before the party.* ▷ *verb* **whirl**
3. (*informal*) If you **give** something **a whirl,** you try it out.

whirl·pool (*wurl-pool*) *noun*
1. A current of water that moves quickly in a circle and pulls floating objects toward its center.
2. A soothing bath in which all or part of the body is covered by whirling currents of hot water. Also called a *whirlpool bath.*

whirl·wind (wurl-*wind*)
1. *noun* A wind like a cyclone that moves in a tall column and goes around and around rapidly and often violently.
2. *adjective* Very quick and sudden. *We went on a whirlwind tour of the city.*

whisk (wisk)
1. *noun* A metal tool that you use for beating eggs or cream. ▷ *verb* **whisk**
2. *verb* To move something quickly or suddenly. *Our plates were whisked away before we finished eating.*
3. *verb* To brush or remove with a quick, sweeping motion. *He whisked the crumbs off the table.*
▷ *verb* **whisking, whisked**

whisk·er (wiss-kur) *noun*
1. whiskers *noun, plural* The hairs that grow on a man's face; a beard.
2. One of the hairs that grows on a man's face, especially on the cheeks and jaw.
3. One of the long, stiff hairs near the mouth of some animals such as cats and rabbits.

whis·key (wiss-kee) *noun* A strong, alcoholic drink made from barley, corn, or rye. ▷ *noun, plural* **whiskeys**

whis·per (wiss-pur)
1. *verb* To talk very quietly or softly. *I whispered a question to the girl in the next row.* ▷ **whispering, whispered** ▷ *noun* **whisper**
2. *noun* A soft, rustling sound, as in *the whisper of leaves in the breeze.* ▷ *verb* **whisper**

whis·tle (wiss-uhl)
1. *noun* An instrument that makes a high, shrill, loud sound when you blow it.
2. *verb* To make a high, shrill sound by blowing air through your lips.
3. *verb* To make a whistling sound. *The kettle will whistle when the water is boiling.*
4. *noun* A whistling sound made by the lips or by a whistle.
5. *verb* To move very fast with a whistling sound. *The train whistled past.*
▷ *verb* **whistling, whistled**

white (wite)
1. *noun* The lightest color; the color of snow or milk. ▷ *adjective* **white**
2. *noun* The **white** of an egg is the part around the yolk. *See* **egg.**
3. *adjective* Light in color, as in *white meat of a chicken.*
4. *adjective* Pale or pallid. *Her face was white with fear.*
5. *adjective* Pale gray or silver. *My grandfather has white hair.*
▷ *adjective* **whiter, whitest**

white blood cell *noun* A colorless blood cell that is part of the body's immune system. It protects the body against infection by destroying diseased cells and germs.

White House *noun*
1. The official home of the president of the United States, located at 1600 Pennsylvania Avenue in Washington, DC.
2. The office or power of the president of the United States. *The White House issued a statement about the President's health.*

white noise *noun*
1. A mixture of sound waves that creates a noise used to mask annoying or distracting sounds.
2. Background noise from appliances such as air conditioners and fans.

white·wash (wite-*wosh*)
1. *noun* A mixture of lime and water used for painting walls and wood fences white. ▷ *noun, plural* **whitewashes** ▷ *verb* **whitewash**
2. *verb* To cover up someone's mistakes, crimes, or wrongdoings. ▷ **whitewashes, whitewashing, whitewashed**

whit·tle (wit-uhl) *verb*
1. To cut or shave small pieces from wood or soap with a knife.
2. To make or carve something by doing this.
3. To reduce bit by bit. *The cost of paying for an extra car every month is whittling away at my parents' savings.*
▷ *verb* **whittling, whittled** ▷ *noun* **whittling**

whiz *or* **whizz** (wiz)
1. *verb* To move very fast, often with a buzzing sound. ▷ **whizzes, whizzing, whizzed**
2. *noun* (*slang*) A person who has great skill or ability in a particular field or activity, as in *a computer whiz.* ▷ *noun, plural* **whizzes**

who (hoo) *pronoun*
1. The word **who** is used to ask questions about people. *Who is that man?*
2. The word **who** is used to show which person you are talking about or to give more information about someone. *The woman who lives next door is our good friend. I visited my grandmother, who wasn't very well.*

whoa (woh) *interjection* A command that means "stop," spoken mainly to a horse.

who'd (hood) *contraction* A short form of *who would* or *who had. Who'd be the first person you would tell if you won a million dollars?*

who·ev·er (hoo-ev-ur) *pronoun*
1. Anyone at all, or no matter who. *Whoever made this mess will have to clean it up.*
2. Who. *Whoever could that be at the door?*

whole (hole)
1. *adjective* Entire or total; all of. *I've eaten a*

W

whole loaf of bread. *The whole class applauded.*
2. *adjective* Complete, with nothing missing. *I have the whole series, all 25 books.*
3. *noun* The entire thing; all the parts of something. *Two halves make a whole.*
Whole sounds like **hole.**

whole number *noun* Any of the set of numbers beginning with 0 and continuing with each number being one more than the number before it. The whole numbers are 0, 1, 2, 3, 4, . . . They go on and on without end. Numbers such as –5, $2\frac{1}{2}$, and 5.3 are not whole numbers.

whole·sale (hole-*sale*) *adverb* When storekeepers buy things **wholesale,** they buy them cheaply in large quantities in order to sell them at a profit.
▷ *noun* **wholesaler** ▷ *adjective* **wholesale**

whole·some (hole-suhm) *adjective*
1. Healthy, or good for you, as in *a wholesome diet.*
2. Suggesting good health, a sound mind, or good or moral behavior.

whole wheat *adjective* Made from the entire kernel of wheat, as in *whole wheat bread.*

who'll (hool) *contraction* A short form of *who will* or *who shall. Who'll go next?*

whol·ly (hoh-lee) *adverb* Completely. *Joshua was found to be wholly responsible for the accident.*
Wholly sounds like **holy.**

whom (hoom) *pronoun* What or which person or people. **Whom** is the form of **who** that functions as the object of a verb or preposition. It is often used in formal speech and writing. *To whom am I speaking? I don't know whom to call. For whom are you buying this gift?*

whom·ev·er (hoom-ev-ur) *pronoun* The form of **whoever** used as the object of a verb or preposition. *Give it to whomever you want.*

whoop (hoop *or* hup *or* wup) *noun* A loud cry or shout. *Kim gave a whoop of joy.* ▷ *verb* **whoop**

whooping cough *noun* An infectious disease that makes children and babies cough violently and breathe noisily.

whooping crane *noun* A large, white crane with black wing tips and a red face. Its call sounds like a trumpet. Whooping cranes live in Canada and the United States, but today there are only about 200 of them in all.

who's (hooz) *contraction* A short form of *who is* or *who has. Who's your favorite sports star?*
Who's sounds like **whose.**

whose (hooz) *pronoun*
1. The word **whose** is used to ask who something belongs to. *Whose skateboard is this?*
2. The word **whose** is used to indicate the person or thing that you are talking about.

That's the girl whose party I've been invited to.
Whose sounds like **who's.**

why (wye)
1. *adverb* The word **why** is used to ask about the reason for something. *Why did you leave?*
2. *conjunction* The reason for which. *That is why I'm mad at him.*
3. *interjection* The word **why** is used to show mild surprise or to show that a person is pausing to think. *Why, I guess you're right.*

wick (wik) *noun* The twisted cord running through a candle, an oil lamp, or a lighter that soaks up the fuel and burns when lit.

wick·ed (wik-id) *adjective* Very bad, cruel, or evil.
▷ *noun* **wickedness** ▷ *adverb* **wickedly**

wick·er (wik-ur) *noun* Thin, flexible twigs or branches, usually from a willow tree, that are woven to make baskets and furniture.
▷ *adjective* **wicker**

wick·et (wik-it) *noun* One of several small wire arches through which balls are hit in croquet.

wide (wide)
1. *adjective* Having a certain distance from one side to the other or from edge to edge. *The room is 14 feet wide.*
2. *adjective* Large from side to side; broad. *We drove through a wide tunnel.* ▷ *verb* **widen**
3. *adjective* Covering a large number of things. *We stock a wide range of magazines.*
4. *adjective* Completely open, as in *wide eyes.*
5. *adverb* Not close to. *The batter swung wide of the ball.*
6. *adverb* Over a large area. *We traveled far and wide.*
7. *adverb* To the full extent. *The dentist told me to open my mouth wide.*
▷ *adjective* **wider, widest** ▷ *adverb* **widely**

wide·spread (wide-*spred*) *adjective*
1. Happening in many places or among many people. *There is widespread concern about global warming.*
2. Fully open. *I greeted my aunt with widespread arms.*

wid·ow (wid-oh) *noun* A woman whose husband has died and who has not married again.
▷ *adjective* **widowed**

wid·ow·er (wid-oh-ur) *noun* A man whose wife has died and who has not married again.
▷ *adjective* **widowed**

width (width) *noun* The distance from one side of something to the other. *What is the width of this carpet?*

wife (wife) *noun* The female partner in a marriage.

wig (wig) *noun* A covering of real or artificial hair made to fit someone's head.

wig·gle (wig-uhl) *verb* To make small movements from side to side or up and down. ▷ **wiggling, wiggled** ▷ *noun* **wiggle,** *noun* **wiggler** ▷ *adjective* **wiggly**

wig·wam (wig-*wahm*) *noun* A hut made of poles and covered with bark or hides. Some American Indian tribes, chiefly in the eastern United States, once lived in wigwams.

wild (wilde)
1. *adjective* Natural and not tamed by humans, as in *wild animals.*
2. *adjective* Not controlled, or not disciplined, as in *wild children.*
3. *adjective* Overcome with an emotion such as grief, anger, or happiness. *My dad went wild when he won the lottery.*
4. *adjective* Crazy, fantastic, or reckless. *He had a wild plan for how to get rich overnight.*
5. *noun* An area that has been left in its natural state; wilderness.
▷ *noun* **wildness** ▷ *adjective* **wilder, wildest**
▷ *adverb* **wildly**

wild·cat (wilde-*kat*) *noun* Any of several wild members of the cat family that are small or medium in size, including the bobcat, ocelot, and lynx. Wildcats are distantly related to the domestic cat.

wil·der·ness (wil-dur-niss) *noun* An area of wild land where no people live, such as a dense forest. ▷ *noun, plural* **wildernesses**

wild·flow·er (wilde-*flou*-ur) *noun* Any flower of a plant that grows in a field, woods, or any wild area without the help of human beings.

wild·life (wilde-*life*) *noun* Wild animals living in their natural environment.

will (wil)
1. *noun* Written instructions stating what should happen to someone's property and money when the person dies.
2. *noun* The power to choose or control what you will and will not do. *Do you have the will to go on a strict diet?* ▷ *verb* **will**
3. *noun* Strong purpose; determination. *Cicely has an amazing will to succeed.*
4. *verb* **Will** is a helping verb used to show that something is going to take place or exist in the future or to show determination. *We will leave tonight. I will help you.* ▷ *verb* **would**

will·ful (wil-fuhl) *adjective*
1. Deliberate, as in *willful damage.* ▷ *adjective* **willfully**
2. Someone who is **willful** is determined to have his or her own way. ▷ *noun* **willfulness**

will·ing (wil-ing) *adjective* Ready and eager to offer help or do what is asked. ▷ *noun* **willingness** ▷ *adverb* **willingly**

wil·low (wil-oh) *noun* A tree with narrow leaves and thin branches that bend easily. Willows are often found near water.

wilt (wilt) *verb*
1. If a plant **wilts,** it begins to droop.
2. If a person **wilts,** he or she becomes tired through lack of energy or food.
▷ *verb* **wilting, wilted**

wimp (wimp) *noun* (informal) A weak or cowardly person. ▷ *adjective* **wimpy**

win (win) *verb*
1. To come in first in a contest. ▷ *noun* **win,** *noun* **winner**
2. To gain or deserve something. *Julius won his brother's respect.*
▷ *verb* **winning, won**

wince (winss) *verb* To flinch or shrink back because you are in pain, embarrassed, or disgusted. *Logan winced when the teacher yelled at him in front of the whole class.* ▷ **wincing, winced** ▷ *noun* **wince**

winch (winch) *noun* A machine that lifts or pulls heavy objects. A winch is made up of cable wound around a rotating drum. A ship's anchor is lifted with a winch. *See* **portcullis, rescue.**
▷ *noun, plural* **winches** ▷ *verb* **winch**

wind
1. (wind) *noun* Moving air. ▷ *adjective* **windy**
2. (wind) *noun* The ability to breathe; breath. *That tackle really knocked the wind out of the quarterback.* ▷ *verb* **wind**
3. (winde) *verb* To wrap something around something else. *Wind this scarf around your neck before you go outside.*
4. (winde) *verb* To twist and turn. *The road winds up the mountain.*
5. (winde) *verb* To turn the key of a clock. *Be sure to wind the clock so that it keeps time correctly.*
6. wind up (winde) *verb* (slang) If you **wind** something **up,** you finish it. ▷ *noun* **windup**
▷ *verb* **winding, wound** (wound)

wind-chill factor *noun* A measurement given in degrees that reports the combined effect of low temperature and wind speed on the human body. Also called the *chill factor* or the *wind-chill index.*

wind·ed (win-did) *adjective* If you are **winded,** you are out of breath because of exercise or a sudden blow to the stomach.

wind·fall (wind-*fawl*) *noun*
1. Fruit that has been blown off a tree.
2. A sudden piece of good news or good luck, usually an unexpected gain of money.

wind instrument *noun* A musical instrument, such as a flute, trumpet, or harmonica, played by blowing. *See* **brass, harmonica, woodwind.**

wind·mill (wind-*mil*) *noun*
A machine operated by wind power that is used to grind grain into flour, pump water, or generate electricity. *The picture shows a 19th-century windmill. Its sails turn the wallower, which is connected by a series of shafts and cogwheels to the greater spur wheel, which turns the millstones to grind grain into flour.*

win·dow (win-doh) *noun*
1. An opening, especially in the wall of a building, that lets in air and light. Windows are usually enclosed by a frame that contains panes of glass or clear plastic. They can usually be opened and shut.
2. A single sheet or pane of glass in a window. *I hit a long fly ball that broke my neighbor's window.*

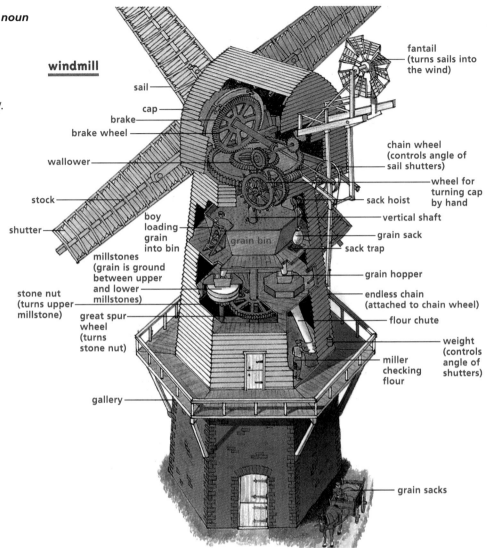

windmill

fantail (turns sails into the wind)

sail

cap

brake

brake wheel

wallower

stock

shutter

boy loading grain into bin

millstones (grain is ground between upper and lower millstones)

stone nut (turns upper millstone)

great spur wheel (turns stone nut)

gallery

chain wheel (controls angle of sail shutters)

wheel for turning cap by hand

sack hoist

vertical shaft

grain sack

sack trap

grain bin

grain hopper

endless chain (attached to chain wheel)

flour chute

weight (controls angle of shutters)

miller checking flour

grain sacks

▶ Word History

· ·

Window is based on two old Norwegian words, *vinde*, meaning "wind," and *auga*, meaning "eye." Appropriately, a window is an "eye on the wind," allowing light and air into a room.

win·dow·pane (win-doh-*pane*) *noun* A single sheet or section of glass in a window.

window-shop *verb* If you **window-shop**, you look at merchandise in store windows but do not buy anything. ▷ **window-shopping, window-shopped**

wind·pipe (wind-*pipe*) *noun* The tube that links the lungs with the throat and carries air for breathing. *See* **respiration.**

wind·shear (wind-*shihr*) *noun* A sudden change in wind speed and direction that is caused by a downward flow of cool air. Windshears occur during thunderstorms. They can cause aircraft to lose altitude quickly.

wind·shield (wind-*sheeld*) *noun* The window of strengthened glass or plastic in the front of a motor vehicle that protects the driver and passengers from the wind. *See* **car.**

wind·surf·ing (wind-*surf*-ing) *noun* The sport of sailing by standing on a board with a flexible mast and a sail and holding onto a curved bar known as a *boom*. ▷ *noun* **windsurfer**

windsurfing

wind·swept (wind-*swept*) *adjective* Exposed to or blown by the wind.

wind turbine *noun* An engine that is driven by propellers and uses energy from the wind to make electricity.

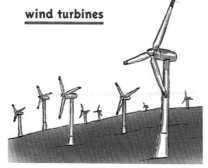

wind turbines

wine (wine) *noun* An alcoholic drink made from the fermented juice of grapes. **Wine** sounds like **whine.**

wing (wing) *noun*
1. One of the feather-covered limbs of a bird that the bird flaps in order to fly. *See* **bird.**
2. A movable part on an insect or a bat that allows it to fly.
3. A winglike structure on an aircraft that makes it able to fly.
4. An outer part or extension of something. *The new wing of the hospital will be opened next month.*
5. wings *noun, plural* The sides of a theater stage that cannot be seen by the audience.

wing·span (wing-*span*) *noun* The distance between the outer tips of the wings of a bird or an aircraft.

wink (wingk)
1. *verb* To close one eye briefly as a signal or a friendly gesture. ▷ **winking, winked** ▷ *noun* **wink**
2. *noun* The time it takes to wink; a very short time; an instant. *I'll be ready in a wink.*

win·ner (win-*ur*) *noun*
1. A person, a team, an animal, or a thing that wins a contest.
2. (*informal*) A person, an idea, or a plan that seems likely to succeed.

win·ning (win-*ing*)
1. *adjective* Successful or victorious. *Our softball team had its first winning season this year.*
2. *adjective* Pleasing, attractive, or charming. *You have a winning smile.*
3. winnings *noun, plural* Something that is won in a game or competition, especially money.

win·ter (win-*tur*) *noun* The season between autumn and spring, when the weather is coldest. ▷ *adjective* **wintry**

win·ter·green (win-*tur-green*) *noun* A low evergreen plant with white flowers and red berries. Its leaves produce a minty oil used in medicines and flavorings. ▷ *adjective* **wintergreen**

wipe (wipe) *verb*
1. To clean or dry by rubbing. *Wipe the table with a sponge. Wipe your feet.*
2. To clear or remove by rubbing. *Wipe the lipstick off your cheek.*
3. wipe out To destroy something totally. *The earthquake wiped out the whole village.*
▷ *verb* **wiping, wiped**

wire (wire)
1. *noun* A long, thin, flexible piece of metal. Wire can be used to pull or support things or to conduct an electrical current.
2. *noun* A telegram. ▷ *verb* **wire**
3. *verb* To fasten things together with a piece of wire.
4. *verb* To install or put in wires for electricity.
▷ *verb* **wiring, wired** ▷ *noun* **wiring**

wir·y (wye-ree) *adjective*
1. Tough and stiff, as in *wiry hair.*
2. A **wiry** person is thin but tough.
▷ *adjective* **wirier, wiriest**

wis·dom (wiz-*duhm*) *noun* Knowledge, experience, and good judgment.

wisdom tooth *noun* Any of the four teeth that come in last, usually after adolescence. ▷ *noun, plural* **wisdom teeth**

wise (wize) *adjective* Having or showing good judgment and intelligence. *A wise old man gave me some excellent advice. You made a wise decision.* ▷ **wiser, wisest** ▷ *adverb* **wisely**

wish (wish)
1. *noun* A strong desire or longing for something. ▷ *noun, plural* **wishes**
2. *verb* To want something very much. *I wish I could go home now.*
3. *verb* To hope for something for somebody else. *I wish you a happy new year!*
▷ *verb* **wishes, wishing, wished**

wish·bone (wish-*bohn*) *noun* A bone shaped like a Y in front of the breastbone of most birds. According to superstition, when two people pull a wishbone apart, the one who gets the longer piece will have a wish granted.

wisp (wisp) *noun* A small and delicate piece, strand, or streak of something, as in *a wisp of hair* or *a wisp of smoke.* ▷ *adjective* **wispy**

wis·te·ri·a (wi-stihr-ee-uh) *noun* A vine plant with woody stems and hanging clusters of blue, white, pink, or purple flowers.

wist·ful (wist-fuhl) *adjective* Sadly wishful; yearning or longing. *As the old woman thought about the happy days of her youth, a wistful smile came to her face.* ▷ *adverb* **wistfully**

wit (wit) *noun*
1. The ability to say clever and funny things. *Alice's wit is known by all.*

2. Someone who can say clever and funny things. *He is a wit.*

3. wits *noun, plural* The ability to think quickly and clearly. *Danny had the wits to find an escape route.*

witch (wich) *noun* A person, especially a woman, believed by some people to have magic powers. **Witch** sounds like **which.** ▷ *noun, plural* **witches**

with (wiTH *or* with) *preposition*
1. In the company or care of. *Come with me. You can leave the package with me.*
2. Having. *I'm looking for someone with a good sense of humor.*
3. In a way that shows. *She dressed with care.*
4. In addition to. *We had chicken with rice.*
5. In the opinion of. *It's okay with me.*
6. By using. *You cut meat with a knife.*
7. In regard to. *Are you happy with your grades?*
8. Against. *Brother fought with brother in the Civil War.*
9. In support of. *Are you with me on this issue?*

with·draw (wiTH-draw *or* with-draw) *verb*
1. To remove or take away something. *Sandra withdrew the cash from her bank. Alex withdrew his support for the project.*
2. To drop out, or to go away. *Lee withdrew from the match because of injury. The soldiers withdrew from the town.*
▷ *verb* **withdrawing, withdrew, withdrawn**
▷ *noun* **withdrawal**

with·drawn (wiTH-drawn *or* with-drawn) *adjective* A **withdrawn** person is very shy and quiet.

with·er (wiTH-ur) *verb* When something **withers,** it shrivels up because it has lost moisture.
▷ **withering, withered**

with·hold (with-hohld *or* wiTH-hold) *verb* To keep something back, or to refuse to give something. *She tried to withhold her anger. My parents withheld their permission for a party.* ▷ **withholding, withheld**

with·in (wiTH-in *or* with-in) *preposition*
1. Inside. *Within the cave was a dragon.* ▷ *adverb* **within**
2. Not beyond the limits of. *I want you back within the next 10 minutes.*

with·out (wiTH-out *or* with-out) *preposition*
1. Not having; lacking. *I completed the project without help.*
2. Not accompanied by. *My parents went on vacation without me.*
3. In a way that avoids. *We ate dinner without speaking.*

with·stand (with-stand *or* wiTH-stand) *verb* To stand strongly against; to resist. *The dock withstood the pounding of the waves.*
▷ **withstanding, withstood**

wit·ness (wit-niss) *noun*
1. A person who has seen or heard something. *I was a witness to the accident.*

2. A person who gives evidence in a court of law.
3. A person who signs an official paper to prove that he or she watched a contract, will, or other legal document being signed.
▷ *noun, plural* **witnesses** ▷ *verb* **witness**

wit·ty (wit-ee) *adjective* Someone who is **witty** says or writes humorous or clever things.
▷ **wittier, wittiest** ▷ *adverb* **wittily**

wiz·ard (wiz-urd) *noun*
1. A person, especially a man, believed to have magic powers; a sorcerer.
2. Someone who is extremely good at something. *My dad is a wizard in the kitchen.*

wob·ble (wob-uhl) *verb* To move unsteadily from side to side. *The cups wobbled on the tray.*
▷ **wobbling, wobbled** ▷ *adjective* **wobbly**

woe (woh) *noun* Great sadness or grief; sorrow; suffering. ▷ *adjective* **woeful** ▷ *adverb* **woefully**

wok (wok) *noun* A pan shaped like a bowl that is used especially for stir-frying food.

wolf (wulf)
1. *noun* A wild mammal that is related to the dog and hunts in a pack for prey. ▷ *noun, plural* **wolves** (wulvz)
2. *verb* To eat quickly and greedily. *The hungry child wolfed down his dinner.*
▷ **wolfing, wolfed**

Asiatic wolf

wol·ver·ine (wul-vuh-reen) *noun* A powerfully built mammal with dark brown fur and a long, bushy tail. Wolverines are found in northern regions. They are related to weasels.

wom·an (wum-uhn) *noun* An adult female human being. ▷ *noun, plural* **women** (wi-min)
▷ *adverb* **womanly**

wom·an·hood (wum-uhn-hud) *noun*
1. The time or state of being a female adult. *My mom says that entering womanhood brings with it many responsibilities.*
2. Women as a group. *I stand before you representing all of American womanhood.*

womb (woom) *noun* The hollow organ in female mammals that holds and nourishes a fetus; the uterus.

wom·bat (wom-bat) *noun* An Australian animal that looks like a small bear. Wombats are marsupials. The female carries her young in a pouch.

wombat

W

won (wuhn) *verb* Past tense and past participle of **win**. *We have won the game.* **Won** sounds like **one.**

won·der (wuhn-dur)
1. *noun* Something so remarkable or impressive that it causes surprise or amazement; a marvel. *The Grand Canyon is one of the natural wonders of the world.*
2. *noun* The feeling caused by something remarkable or impressive; awe. *I listened in wonder as my grandmother told me about the day she met Martin Luther King, Jr.*
3. *verb* To be curious about something; to want to know or learn more. *I wonder why they're late.*
4. *verb* To be amazed and impressed by something. *We wondered at Linda's ability to hit the bull's-eye every time.*
▷ *verb* **wondering, wondered**

won·der·ful (wuhn-dur-fuhl) *adjective*
1. Causing wonder; remarkable, amazing, or impressive. *The porpoise is a wonderful and intelligent creature.*
2. Very good; excellent. *In my opinion, she would be a wonderful governor.*
▷ *adverb* **wonderfully**

▶ Synonyms: wonderful

Wonderful originally described something that caused someone to be filled with awe or wonder. Now it also refers to anything that is unusually good: *That was a wonderful party. Tony is a wonderful human being.*

Interesting describes something that is intriguing or captures someone's attention: *The short story had an interesting plot and unforgettable characters.*

Fascinating describes something so interesting that you want to know more about it: *Delia thinks the idea of space travel is fascinating.*

Delightful means highly pleasing: *My friend Jan has a delightful personality.*

Spectacular means dramatic and sensational: *After the ball game we watched a spectacular fireworks display.*

Astonishing describes something that causes great wonder or surprise: *We received the astonishing news that we won the contest!*

---

won't (wohnt) *contraction* A short form of *will not. You won't be sorry if you vote for Joe for class president.*

wood (wud) *noun*
1. The hard substance that forms the trunk and branches of a tree. ▷ *adjective* **wooden**

2. woods *noun, plural* An area of thickly growing trees; a forest. ▷ *adjective* **wooded**
Wood sounds like **would.**

wood·chuck (wud-*chuhk*) *noun* A North American animal that has a stout body and brown or gray fur. It lives underground and sleeps all winter. The woodchuck is also called a **groundhog.**

wood·land (wud-luhnd) *noun* Land covered mainly by trees; a forest.

wood·peck·er (wud-*pek*-ur) *noun* Any of a number of birds that live in forests throughout the world. Woodpeckers have strong, pointed bills, which they use to drill holes in trees to get insects.

wood·wind (wud-*wind*) *adjective* The **woodwind** section of an orchestra is made up of wind instruments that were originally made of wood, such as the flute, clarinet, and oboe. *The illustration shows a clarinet, with its main parts labeled, and five other instruments from the woodwind section of an orchestra.* ▷ *noun* **woodwind**

great spotted woodpecker

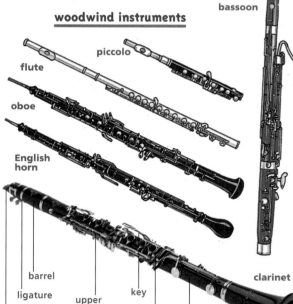

woodwind instruments

piccolo
flute
oboe
English horn
bassoon
barrel
ligature
upper joint
key
ring key
mouthpiece containing reed
lower joint
bell
clarinet

W

wood·work (wud-*wurk*) *noun*
1. Things made out of wood, especially wooden parts inside a house, such as window frames, doors, and moldings.
2. woodworking The art or craft of making things from wood. *The picture shows a range of tools used in woodworking.* ▷ *noun* **woodworker**

woodworking tools

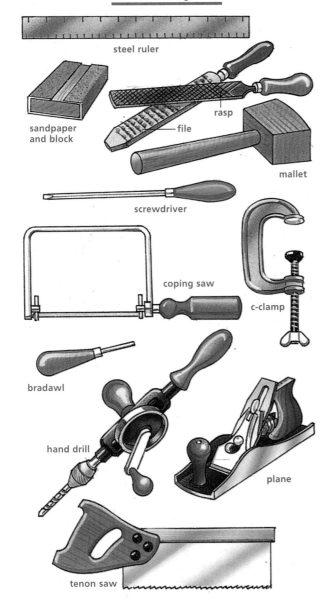

steel ruler

sandpaper and block

rasp

file

mallet

screwdriver

coping saw

c-clamp

bradawl

hand drill

plane

tenon saw

wool (wul) *noun*
1. The soft, thick, curly hair of sheep and certain other animals such as the llama and alpaca. Wool is spun into yarn, which is used to make fabric.
2. Yarn or fabric made of wool.
3. Anything made of a thick mass of fibers, as in *steel wool.*
▷ *adjective* **woolen,** *adjective* **woolly**

word (wurd)
1. *noun* A unit of one or more spoken sounds or written letters that has a meaning in a given language. *There are seven words in this sentence.*
2. *noun* A brief remark or comment. *Let me give you a word of advice.*
3. *noun* A short conversation. *May I have a word with you?*
4. *noun* News, or a message. *Is there any word from your brother in London?*
5. If you **give your word,** you promise you will do something.
6. *verb* To put into words. *Make sure you word your request so that everyone can understand it.*
▷ **wording, worded**

word·ing (wur-ding) *noun* The way in which something is said or written; the choice and arrangement of words. *Ben rewrote the letter several times to get the wording just right.*

word processing *noun* The use of a computer or similar machine to type and print documents. Words are viewed on the screen and can easily be changed, moved, copied, and stored. ▷ *noun* **word processor**

word·y (wur-dee) *adjective* Having or using too many words. *The newspaper article criticized the politician's speech as being too wordy.* ▷ **wordier, wordiest**

work (wurk)
1. *noun* Effort or labor to get something done. *Solving problems is hard work.*
2. *verb* To get something done by using your energy or ability. *Let's work together on the project.*
3. *verb* To function properly. *Does your computer work?*
4. *verb* To have a job. *I work in the advertising department of a newspaper.*
5. *verb* To bring about or to cause. *This medicine worked wonders on my cold.*
6. *noun* A person's job; what someone does to earn a living. *What kind of work do you do?*
7. *noun* A task. *We finished our work on the car today.*
8. *noun* A piece of music, a painting, or a sculpture, as in *a work of art.*
9. works *noun, plural* The moving parts of a watch or machine.
10. *verb* If you **work out** a puzzle, you solve it by thinking hard.
11. *verb* When you **work out** in a gym, you do physical exercise. ▷ *noun* **workout**
▷ *verb* **working, worked**

work·a·ble (wurk-uh-buhl) *adjective* If a plan is **workable,** it can be carried out.

work·a·hol·ic (wur-kuh-**hol**-ik) *noun* Someone who feels driven to work hard. A workaholic puts in long hours and rarely takes time off.

625

work·bench (wurk-*bench*) *noun* A strong table used by someone who works with tools, such as a carpenter or a mechanic.

work·book (wurk-*buk*) *noun* A book with problems and exercises to be done by students.

work·er (wur-kur) *noun*
1. Someone who is employed to do a job.
2. A female bee, ant, termite, or other insect that does all the work for the colony but does not reproduce.

work·man (wurk-*muhn*) *noun* A man who does manual work or who works with machines.
▷ *noun, plural* **workmen**

work·man·ship (wurk-*muhn*-ship) *noun* The skill and care with which something is made, usually by hand.

work·shop (wurk-*shop*) *noun*
1. A room, shed, or other building where things are made or fixed.
2. A group of people who meet to discuss, learn about, or practice a particular skill, as in *a writers' workshop.*

work·sta·tion (wurk-*stay*-shuhn) *noun*
1. An area with the equipment needed to do a specific job. A workstation is usually used by one person.
2. A computer that runs programs and allows people to gain access to a computer network.

world (wurld) *noun*
1. The earth. *We took a trip around the world.*
2. A particular part of the earth, as in *the Western world.*
3. Everyone who lives on earth. *The world is threatened by pollution.*
4. An area of activity, as in *the world of sports.*
5. A large amount; a great deal. *Your advice did me a world of good.*
6. A division of living things, as in *the animal world.*

world-class *adjective* Of the highest rank or level in the world. *Luís is a world-class chess player.*

World War I *noun* A war fought from 1914 to 1918, mainly in Europe. The United States, Great Britain, France, Russia, Italy, Japan, and other allied nations defeated Germany, Austria-Hungary, Turkey, and Bulgaria.

World War II *noun* A war in which the United States, France, Great Britain, the Soviet Union, and other allied nations defeated Germany, Italy, and Japan. World War II started in 1939 when Germany invaded Poland and ended in 1945 with the surrender of Germany and Japan.

world·wide (wurld-wide) *adjective* Extending or spreading throughout the world, as in *worldwide fame* or *worldwide concern.*

worm (wurm)
1. *noun* A small animal that lives in the soil. Worms have long, thin, soft bodies and no backbones or legs.
2. *verb* To move like a worm by wriggling or twisting and turning from side to side. *I wormed my way through the crowd.* ▷ **worming, wormed**

earthworm

ring or segment

light-sensitive slimy skin

clitellum or saddle

head

worn (worn)
1. *verb* Past participle of **wear.**
2. *adjective* Damaged by wear or use. *Worn tires can be very dangerous.*
Worn sounds like **warn.**

worn-out *adjective*
1. No longer useful or in good condition. *I guess I should stop wearing these worn-out jeans.*
2. Very tired; exhausted. *The runner was worn-out after the marathon.*

wor·ry (wur-ee)
1. *verb* To be anxious or uneasy about something. ▷ **worries, worrying, worried**
2. *noun* Anxiety, or nervousness. *Worries about his test kept him awake.*
3. *noun* Something that makes you anxious. *The sick child was a great worry to his parents.*
▷ *noun, plural* **worries** ▷ *noun* **worrier** ▷ *adjective* **worrying** ▷ *adverb* **worriedly**

worse (wurss)
1. *adjective* More inferior; less good. *Your handwriting is worse than mine.*
2. *adjective* More evil or bad. *His next crime will be even worse.*
3. *adjective* More unpleasant, severe, or harmful. *The weather is supposed to be worse tomorrow.*
4. *adjective* More ill. *The patient is worse.*
5. *adverb* In a worse way. *We played worse than ever.*
6. *noun* Something that is worse. *You've heard the bad news, but I have worse to tell you.*

wor·ship (wur-ship)
1. *verb* To express love and devotion to God or a god. ▷ *noun* **worship**
2. *noun* A church service.
3. *verb* If you **worship** someone, you think that the person is wonderful.
▷ *verb* **worshiping** *or* **worshipping, worshiped** *or* **worshipped**

worst (wurst)
1. *adjective* Most inferior, harmful, or

W

unpleasant; worse than any other one. *That was the worst storm this town has had in 10 years.*
2. adverb In the worst way. *She played worst in the final match.*
3. noun Someone or something that is the worst. *Of the three actors, he was the worst.*

worth (wurth)
1. adjective Having a certain value in money. *This painting is worth a fortune.* ▷ **noun worth**
2. adjective Deserving, or good enough for. *It's worth going to the sale for the bargains.*
3. noun The quality that makes someone or something valuable or important. *Do you know the worth of a good education?*

worth·less (wurth-liss) **adjective** If something is **worthless,** it has no value or is useless. ▷ **noun worthlessness**

worth·while (wurth-wile) **adjective** Useful and valuable. *Learning Spanish is a worthwhile activity.*

wor·thy (wur-THee) **adjective**
1. Having value or merit; good or worthwhile. *I'm happy to give money to a worthy cause.*
2. Good enough for; deserving. *This candidate is worthy of our support.*
▷ **adjective worthier, worthiest**

would (wud) **verb**
1. Past tense of the helping verb **will.** *He said he would go.*
2. Would expresses a possibility. *It would snow if it were colder.*
3. Would expresses frequent or habitual action in the past. *I would go to the beach every summer when I was young.*
4. Would expresses a request. *Would you please open the window?*
Would sounds like **wood.**

would·n't (wud-uhnt) **contraction** A short form of *would not. Wouldn't you rather play ball than watch television?*

wound
1. (woond) **noun** An injury in which the skin is cut, usually because of an accident or violence. ▷ **verb wound**
2. (woond) **verb** To hurt someone's feelings. *Your insult wounded me deeply.* ▷ **wounding, wounded** ▷ **noun wound**
3. (wound) **verb** Past tense and past participle of **wind.** *He wound up the clock.*

wran·gle (rang-guhl) **verb**
1. To argue or debate in a noisy or angry way. ▷ **noun wrangle**
2. To herd horses and livestock on the range. ▷ **noun wrangler**
▷ **verb wrangling, wrangled**

wrap (rap)
1. verb To cover something with paper, material,

etc. *Wrap the present. Wrap a sweater around your shoulders.*
2. verb To hide by covering. *The mountain was wrapped in fog.*
3. verb To wind or to clasp. *The baby wrapped her arms around her father's neck.*
4. noun An outer garment such as a coat or shawl.
5. If you are **wrapped up** in something, you are totally involved in it.
Wrap sounds like **rap.**
▷ **verb wrapping, wrapped**

wrap·per (rap-ur) **noun** The protective material in which something is wrapped, as in *a candy wrapper.*

wrath (rath) **noun** Great anger; rage. *I could not hide my wrath after hearing that the factory was closing, leaving 200 people out of work.*

wreak (reek) **verb** To cause or to inflict. *The bull wreaked havoc in the china shop.* **Wreak** sounds like **reek.** ▷ **wreaking, wreaked**

wreath (reeth) **noun** A circle of flowers, leaves, or branches that are twisted together.

wreck (rek)
1. verb To destroy or ruin something. ▷ **wrecking, wrecked**
2. noun The remains of something that has been destroyed or damaged. *The divers were searching for the wreck of an ancient ship.*

wreck·age (rek-ij) **noun** The broken parts or pieces lying around at the site of a crash or an explosion.

wren (ren) **noun** A small songbird with a long, slender bill; brown feathers; and a small tail that sticks up.

wrench (rench)
1. verb To pull something suddenly and forcefully. *Firefighters had to wrench open the car door.*
2. verb To injure yourself by twisting a part of your body. *I wrenched my back.*
3. noun A tool with jaws for tightening and loosening nuts. ▷ **noun, plural wrenches**
▷ **verb wrenches, wrenching, wrenched**

wrest (rest) **verb**
1. To twist, pull, or tear away. *Enrique wrested the ball from his puppy's mouth.*
2. To take by force or violence. *The soldiers wrested control of the town from the rebels.*
Wrest sounds like **rest.**

wres·tle (ress-uhl) **verb**
1. To fight by gripping or holding your opponent and trying to throw the person to the ground.
2. If you **wrestle** with a problem, you try to solve it by thinking very hard.
▷ **verb wrestling, wrestled**

627

wres·tling (ress-ling) *noun* A sport in which two opponents try to throw or force each other to the ground. ▷ *noun* **wrestler**

wretch·ed (rech-id) *adjective*
1. Miserable or unfortunate. *I can't wait till I am over this wretched cold.*
2. Mean or evil. *Everyone in town was afraid of the wretched bank president.*
▷ *noun* **wretch**

wrig·gle (rig-uhl) *verb* To twist and turn. *Sarah wriggled in her seat.* ▷ **wriggling, wriggled**

wring (ring) *verb*
1. To squeeze the moisture from wet material by twisting it with both hands. ▷ *noun* **wringer**
2. To get by using force or threats. *The government agents tried to wring a confession from the spy.*
Wring sounds like **ring.**
▷ *verb* **wringing, wrung** (ruhng)

wrin·kle (ring-kuhl) *noun* A crease or line in skin or in material. ▷ *verb* **wrinkle**

wrist (rist) *noun* The joint that connects your hand and your arm.

wrist·watch (rist-woch) *noun* A watch worn on a strap or band that fits around the wrist.

write (rite) *verb*
1. To put down letters, words, or numbers on paper or another surface, using a pen, pencil, etc. *Please write your name on the paper.*
2. To be the author or composer of stories, poems, articles, or music.
3. To send a letter or word of some kind. *Please write when you're away.*
Write sounds like **right.**
▷ *verb* **writing, wrote** (rote), **written** (rit-in) ▷ *noun* **writer**

writhe (riTHe) *verb* To twist and turn around, as in pain. *Sammy writhed in agony after breaking his ankle.* ▷ **writhing, writhed**

writ·ing (rye-ting) *noun*
1. The act of putting letters on paper. *Writing gives me a chance to organize my thoughts.*
2. A written work such as a story, book, or poem.
3. Written form. *Put your request in writing.*
4. Handwriting.

wrong (rawng *or* rong) *adjective*
1. Not correct or not true, as in *wrong answers.*
2. Bad or immoral. *It is wrong to steal.*
▷ *noun* **wrong** ▷ *adverb* **wrongly**

wrong·do·ing (rawng-doo-ing *or* rong-doo-ing) *noun* Any act or behavior that is wrong, evil, or illegal. *The court cleared him of all charges of wrongdoing.*

Xx

Xe·rox (zee-roks) *noun* Trademark name for a kind of photocopier. ▷ *verb* **Xerox**

X·mas (kriss-muhss *or* eks-muhss) *noun* Christmas.

Word History

The *X* in **Xmas** represents the Greek letter *chi.* X is the first letter of the Greek word for Christ and is often used alone to stand for Christ.

X ray (eks) *noun*
1. An invisible high-energy beam of light that can pass through solid objects. X rays are used to take pictures of teeth, bones, and organs inside the body.
2. A photograph of the inside of a person's body, taken using X rays. *The picture shows an X ray of a human hand.* ▷ *verb* **X-ray** ▷ *adjective* **X-ray**

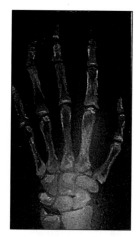

X ray

xy·lo·phone (zye-luh-fone) *noun* A musical instrument with wooden bars of different lengths that are struck to give different notes.

Word History

The word **xylophone** literally means "the sound of wood." It combines two Greek words: *xylon,* meaning "wood," and *phone,* meaning "sound."

About Y ◀

The letter **y** can serve as either a vowel or a consonant. Many words that begin with a consonant *y* can trace their origins back to Old English or Middle English. Examples: yield, yard.

yacht (yot) *noun* A large boat or small ship used for pleasure or for racing. ▷ *noun* **yachting**

yak (yak) *noun*
An ox of Tibet and central Asia that has long, shaggy hair. Yaks are used as work animals.

yaks

ya·ki·to·ri (yah-ki-**tor**-ee) *noun* A Japanese dish made with small pieces of fish, chicken, beef, or vegetables that have been soaked in soy sauce and cooked on skewers.

yam (yam) *noun*
1. The starchy root of a trailing vine that grows in the tropics. It is ground into flour or eaten as a vegetable.
2. A large sweet potato that has reddish flesh.

yank (yangk) *verb* To give a sudden, sharp pull; to jerk. *Joel yanked the ball out of my hands.*
▷ **yanking, yanked** ▷ *noun* **yank**

Yan·kee (yang-kee) *noun*
1. A person born or living in one of the northern states, especially a state in New England.
2. A person who fought for the Union during the Civil War.
3. Any person born or living in the United States.

yap (yap) *verb*
1. To bark repeatedly with short, high sounds.
2. *(slang)* To talk in a noisy, stupid way.
▷ *verb* **yapping, yapped**

yard (yard) *noun*
1. A unit of length equal to 3 feet or 36 inches. A softball bat can be up to 34 inches, just slightly shorter than a yard.
2. An area of ground surrounding or next to a house, school, or other building.
3. An enclosed area used for a certain type of work or business, as in *a navy yard.*
4. An area next to a railroad station where trains are switched, repaired, or stored.

yard·stick (yard-*stik*) *noun*
1. A measuring stick that is one yard long.
2. A standard used to judge or compare things or people. *The yardstick I use to judge comedians is whether or not they make me laugh.*

yar·mul·ke (yah-muh-kuh *or* yar-muhl-kuh) *noun* A small, round cap that Jewish men and boys wear on their heads, especially during religious services.

yarn (yarn) *noun*
1. Fibers such as wool, cotton, silk, or nylon that have been twisted or spun into long strands for use in knitting or weaving.
2. *(informal)* If someone **spins a yarn,** he or she tells a long and exaggerated story.

yawn (yawn) *verb*
1. To open your mouth wide and breathe in deeply, often because you are tired or bored.
▷ *noun* **yawn**
2. To open wide. *The entrance to the huge cave yawned before us.*
▷ *verb* **yawning, yawned**

year (yihr) *noun*
1. The period of time in which the earth makes one complete trip around the sun, about 365 days and 6 hours.
2. On the calendar that we commonly use today, a **year** is a period of 365 days, or 366 in a leap year, divided into 52 weeks or 12 months. The year begins January 1 and ends December 31.
3. Any period of 12 months. *After saving his allowance for a year, Pedro was finally able to afford a computer.*
4. A part of a year spent in a particular activity, as in *the school year.*

yearn (yurn) *verb* To wish or long for something very strongly. *Deirdre yearned to be a doctor.*
▷ **yearning, yearned** ▷ *noun* **yearning**

yeast (yeest) *noun* A yellow fungus used to make bread dough rise and to ferment alcoholic drinks.

yell (yel) *verb* To shout, cry out, or scream loudly.
▷ **yelling, yelled** ▷ *noun* **yell**

yel·low (yel-oh)
1. *noun* One of the three primary colors, along with red and blue. Yellow is the color of lemons and butter.
2. *noun* The yolk of an egg.
3. *verb* To become or make yellow. *The newspaper article about my parents' wedding has yellowed with age.* ▷ **yellowing, yellowed**
▷ *adjective* **yellow**

yellow jacket *noun* A wasp that has black and bright yellow stripes. It usually nests in or near the ground and has a painful sting.

yelp (yelp) *verb* When a dog **yelps,** it makes a sharp, high, crying sound, showing that it is in pain. ▷ **yelping, yelped** ▷ *noun* **yelp**

yen (yen) *noun*
1. The main unit of money in Japan.
2. *(informal)* If you have a **yen** for something, you want it very much.

yes (yess)
1. *adverb* A word used to show that you agree or that something is true. *Yes, I think you are right. Yes, this is a very good book.*
2. *noun* An answer that shows agreement, approval, or acceptance. *Everyone said yes to our invitation.*
3. *noun* A vote or voter in favor of something.
▷ *noun, plural* **yeses** or **yesses**

yes·ter·day (yess-tur-dee *or* yess-tur-*day*)
1. *noun* The day before today. *Today is Tuesday, so yesterday was Monday.*
2. *noun* The recent past. *Many fashions of yesterday look silly today.*
3. *adverb* On the day before today. *I started my report yesterday.*

yet (yet)
1. *adverb* Up to now; so far. *I haven't received an answer yet.*
2. *adverb* At the present time; now. *You're not allowed out yet.*
3. *adverb* In addition; even. *There were yet more surprises in store.*
4. *adverb* At some future time; eventually. *I'll win her heart yet.*
5. *conjunction* But. *Celia studied hard yet didn't pass the exam.*

yew (yoo) *noun* An evergreen tree or shrub with a red-brown bark; poisonous, dark green needles; and red berries. It is grown widely as a decorative plant or hedge. The wood of the yew is often used to make archery bows. **Yew** sounds like **ewe** and **you.**

yield (yeeld) *verb*
1. To produce something. *The field yielded 90 tons of potatoes.* ▷ *noun* **yield**
2. To surrender or to give in. *The troops yielded the town to the enemy.*
▷ *verb* **yielding, yielded**

yo (yoh) *interjection* *(slang)* A word used to get someone's attention, say hello, or acknowledge being called.

yo·del (yoh-duhl) *verb* To sing in a voice that changes rapidly between high and low sounds. ▷ **yodeling, yodeled** ▷ *noun* **yodeler**

yo·ga (yoh-guh) *noun* A system of exercises and meditation that helps people become mentally relaxed and physically fit. Yoga came originally from Hindu teachings.

yo·gurt (yoh-gurt) *noun* A slightly sour food prepared from milk fermented by bacteria. *This photograph shows yogurt with fruit and nuts.*

yogurt

> ### Word History
> The word **yogurt** comes to us from Turkey and has been in our language for over 300 years. Making yogurt was a way of preserving milk before machines for refrigeration were invented.

yoke (yoke) *noun*
1. A wooden frame attached to the necks of oxen or other work animals to link them together for plowing. See **plow.** ▷ *verb* **yoke**
2. The part of a shirt, blouse, or dress that fits around the shoulders and neck.
Yoke sounds like **yolk.**

yolk (yoke) *noun* The yellow part of an egg. If the egg is fertilized, the protein and fat from the yolk nourish the developing embryo. **Yolk** sounds like **yoke.** See **egg.**

Yom Kip·pur (yom kip-ur *or* yohm ki-poor) *noun* A Jewish holiday that falls 10 days after Rosh Hashanah during September or October. On Yom Kippur, Jewish people fast to atone for sins.

yon·der (yon-dur) *adverb* Over there. *We're heading yonder.* ▷ *adjective* **yonder**

you (yoo) *pronoun*
1. The person or people that someone is speaking or writing to. *Maria likes you a lot.*
2. Anyone, or people in general. *You never know.*
You sounds like **ewe** and **yew.**

you'd (yood) *contraction* A short form of *you had* or *you would. You'd be better off stopping home for lunch before going to the store.*

you'll (yool) *contraction* A short form of *you shall* or *you will. You'll be happy to know I got an A on my history report.* **You'll** sounds like **Yule.**

Y

young (yuhng)
 1. *adjective* Someone who is **young** has lived for a short time.
 2. *adjective* Something that is **young** has existed for a short time. *The United States is said to be a young nation.*
 3. *adjective* Having the qualities of a young person; fresh; vigorous. *My grandmother is young for her age.*
 4. *noun* The offspring of an animal. *A mother cat will protect her young.* ▷ *noun, plural* **young**
 ▷ *adjective* **younger, youngest**

young·ster (yuhng-stur) *noun* A young person.

your (yur *or* yor) *adjective* Belonging to or having to do with you. *Your homework is late.*

you're (yur *or* yer) *contraction* A short form of *you are. You're the first person I've spoken to about this problem.*

yours (yurz *or* yorz) *pronoun* The one or ones belonging to or having to do with you. *I like my bike even though yours is newer.*

your·self (yur-self) *pronoun* Your own self. *Help yourself to some food.* ▷ *pronoun, plural* **yourselves**

youth (yooth) *noun*
 1. The time of life when a person is no longer a child but is not yet an adult.
 2. The quality or state of being young. *The rookie player has youth on his side. My grandfather has the energy and fresh ideas of youth.*
 3. A young person, especially a young male between 13 and 18 years of age.
 4. Young people in general. *The future of our nation lies in the hands of the youth of today.*

you've (yoov) *contraction* A short form of *you have. You've got to be kidding!*

yowl (youl) *noun* A long, mournful cry; a howl.
 ▷ *verb* **yowl**

yo-yo (yoh yoh) *noun* A toy consisting of a string wound around a flat reel. You loop the string over your finger and flick the reel up and down on the string.

Yule (yool) *noun* Another word for **Christmas. Yule** sounds like **you'll.**

Yule·tide (yool-*tide*) *noun* The Christmas season.

yup·py (yuhp-ee) *noun* A young person with a well-paid job and an expensive lifestyle. Yuppy comes from the phrase *young urban professional.* ▷ *noun, plural* **yuppies**

Zz

About Z
· · · · · · · · · · · · · · · ·
Most words that begin with **z** can trace their origins back to languages other than Old English. For example, *zenith* and *zeal* come from Greek, and *zany* comes from Italian.

za·ny (zay-nee) *adjective* Humorous in an unusual, crazy way. ▷ **zanier, zaniest** ▷ *adverb* **zanily**

zap (zap) *verb* (slang)
 1. To shoot or destroy with force, as in an electronic game.
 2. To cook with microwaves. *Dinner will be ready as soon as we zap the potatoes.*
 3. To change channels on a television set with a remote control.
 ▷ *verb* **zapping, zapped**

zeal (zeel) *noun* Enthusiasm and eagerness. *Wanda attacked the job with zeal.* ▷ *noun* **zealot** (zel-uht) ▷ *adjective* **zealous** (zel-uhss)

ze·bra (zee-bruh) *noun* A wild animal of southern and eastern Africa. A zebra is similar to a horse except that it is smaller and has black and white stripes on its body. A zebra's stripes help protect it from predators.

zebras

ze·nith (zee-nith) *noun*
 1. The point in the sky directly overhead.
 2. The highest point. *His new hit record puts him at the zenith of his career.*

zep·pe·lin (zep-uh-lin) *noun* An airship, or dirigible, with a rigid frame. A zeppelin is shaped like a cigar. *See* **airship.**

> ### ▶ Word History
>
> Count Ferdinand von Zeppelin of Germany was a soldier and adventurer with a keen interest in flight. After he retired from the German army, Zeppelin devoted his time to designing and building airships. In 1900 he completed his first rigid dirigible, which was named a **zeppelin** in his honor. By the time he died in 1917, the word zeppelin was being used to mean any dirigible.

ze·ro (zihr-oh) *noun*
1. The numeral or figure 0, which indicates the number of objects in an empty set.
2. A point on a thermometer or other scale at which numbering or measurement begins. *It was 10 degrees below zero yesterday.*
3. Nothing. *All their hard work added up to zero when it snowed and the party was canceled.*
▷ *noun, plural* **zeros** *or* **zeroes** ▷ *adjective* **zero**

zest (zest) *noun* Enthusiasm and liveliness, as in *a zest for life.*

zig·zag (zig-zag) *noun* A line or course that moves in short, sharp turns or angles from one side to the other. ▷ *verb* **zigzag**

zilch (zilch) *noun* (*slang*) Absolutely nothing; zero. *I looked for the results of the ball game in the newspaper but found zilch.*

zinc (zingk) *noun* A blue-white metal that is used in some alloys and for coating metals so that they will not rust. Zinc is a chemical element.

zin·ni·a (zin-ee-yuh) *noun* A garden plant with round, brightly colored flowers.

zinnias

zip (zip)
1. *verb* To fasten clothes with a zipper.
2. *noun* A short, hissing sound, as in *the zip of a bullet.* ▷ *verb* **zip**
3. *verb* (*informal*) To move fast. *The car zipped around the corner.*
▷ *verb* **zipping, zipped**

zip code *or* **ZIP code** *noun* A number given by the Postal Service to each delivery area in the United States. Zip codes speed the sorting and delivery of mail. ZIP stands for *Zone Improvement Plan.*

zip·per (zip-ur) *noun* A fastener for clothes or other objects. A zipper consists of two strips of metal or plastic teeth that link up when the strips are pulled together.

> ### ▶ Word History
>
> The **zipper** can trace its roots to Whitman L. Judson, the American who invented it in 1893. Judson named his invention the Universal Fastener, but people kept trying to find a more clever term. An employee of the B. F. Goodrich Company came up with the name zipper after the company decided to use these fasteners on the sides of their new rain boots.

zith·er (zith-ur *or* ziTH-ur) *noun* A musical instrument made up of a flat box with strings stretched across it. Instruments in the zither family can have up to 40 strings, which are plucked with a pick or with the fingers.

zo·di·ac (zoh-dee-ak) *noun* A circular, imaginary belt in the sky that includes the path of the sun, the moon, and the planets. The zodiac is divided into 12 equal parts, each named for a different constellation.

zone (zohn) *noun*
1. An area that is separate from other areas and used for a special purpose, as in *a "No Parking" zone* or *the end zone of a football field.*
2. Any of the five areas of the earth divided according to climate. There are two frigid zones, two temperate zones, and one torrid zone.

zoo (zoo) *noun* A place where animals are kept for people to see or study them.

zo·ol·o·gy (zoh-ol-uh-jee) *noun* The science that deals with the study of animal life. ▷ *noun* **zoologist** ▷ *adjective* **zoological** (zoh-uh-loj-i-kuhl)

zoom (zoom) *verb*
1. To move quickly with a loud, humming sound. *The train zoomed by us.*
2. To increase or rise rapidly and suddenly. *Food prices have zoomed since last year.*
▷ *verb* **zooming, zoomed**

Zu·ni (zoo-nee) *or* **Zu·ñi** (zoo-nyee) *noun* A member of a tribe of American Indians that now lives in western New Mexico. ▷ *noun, plural* **Zuni** *or* **Zunis,** *or* **Zuñi** *or* **Zuñis**

Z

The Braille Alphabet

Louis Braille, a teacher of blind people, developed the Braille system of reading and writing in 1829. Each letter, number, phrase, and punctuation mark in the Braille System consists of a different arrangement of one to six raised dots. A blind person can read the raised letters of a book or magazine printed in Braille through the tips of his or her fingers. He or she can also write in Braille with a Braillewriter, a machine like a typewriter.

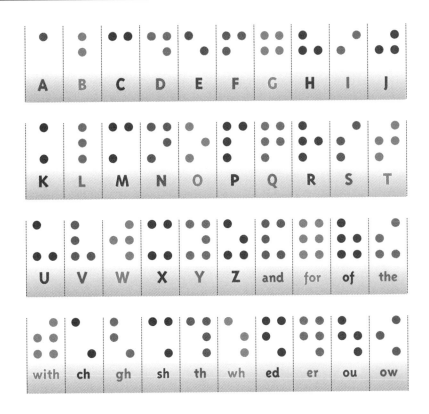

American Sign Language

American Sign Language (ASL) is the language most deaf people in the United States and Canada use. ASL speakers combine hand gestures with facial expressions and larger body movements to communicate. Even though it is based on English, ASL has its own grammar, which differs from English grammar. Most signs represent words or concepts, but signers also use signs for individual letters to spell names and other words that are not frequently used. All of the letter signs are formed with a single hand.

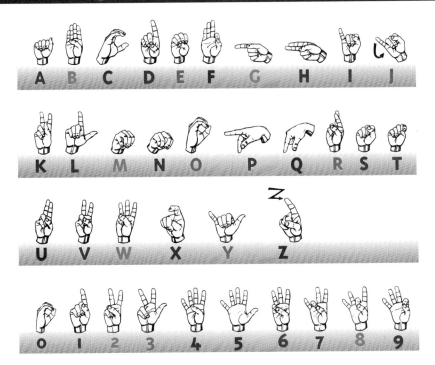

ARCTI

Beaufort
Sea

Baffin
Bay

Greenland
Sea

GREENLAND
(DENMARK)

NORWA

Arctic Circle

ICELAND DENMARK

THE NETHERLANDS

UNITED
KINGDOM

BELGIUM

ALASKA
(U.S.)

Gulf of
Alaska

Hudson
Bay

CANADA

IRELAND

LUXEMBOURG
SWITZERLAND
LIECHTENSTEIN
SLOVENIA
CROATIA
MONACO
ANDORRA

FRANCE

ATLANTIC
OCEAN

SAN
MARINO
VATICAN CI

UNITED STATES OF AMERICA

BOSNIA AND HERZEGOVINA
PORTUGAL

SPAIN

YUGOSLAVIA

DOMINICAN
REPUBLIC

ALBANIA
MACEDONIA

30°N

MEXICO

BAHAMAS

PUERTO RICO (U.S.)

VIRGIN ISLANDS (U.S., U.K.)

St. KITTS AND NEVIS

CANARY
ISLANDS
(SPAIN)

MOROCCO

Gulf of
Mexico

CUBA

HAITI

ANTIGUA AND BARBUDA

WESTERN
SAHARA
(disputed)

ALGERIA

Tropic of Cancer

JAMAICA

DOMINICA

HAWAIIAN
ISLANDS
(U.S.)

BELIZE
GUATEMALA
EL SALVADOR
HONDURAS
NICARAGUA
COSTA RICA
PANAMA

St. LUCIA

CAPE VERDE

MAURITANIA

MALI

N

Caribbean Sea

St. VINCENT
AND THE GRENADINES

PACIFIC
OCEAN

BARBADOS
GRENADA

SENEGAL

BURKINA
FASO

TRINIDAD AND TOBAGO

GAMBIA

GUINEA-BISSAU

VENEZUELA

GUYANA

GUINEA

NIGER

SURINAME
FRENCH
GUIANA
(FRANCE)

SIERRA LEONE

LIBERIA

COLOMBIA

ECUADOR

Equator

CÔTE D'IVOIRE

GHANA
TOGO
BENIN

SÃO TOMÉ
AND PRINCIPE

GABO

TAHITI
(FRANCE)

PERU

BRAZIL

EQUATORIAL
GUINEA

CONG

ANGOL

BOLIVIA

Tropic of Capricorn

PARAGUAY

30°S

CHILE

URUGUAY

Ca
Goo

ARGENTINA

FALKLAND ISLANDS
(U.K.)

60°S

Cape Horn

Antarctic Circle

ANTA

OCEAN

Norwegian Sea

Barents Sea

SWEDEN

FINLAND

ESTONIA
LATVIA
LITHUANIA
BELARUS
CZECH REPUBLIC
AUSTRIA
SLOVAKIA
UKRAINE
HUNGARY
MOLDOVA
ROMANIA
BULGARIA
GREECE
TURKEY
MALTA
CYPRUS
LEBANON
ISRAEL
JORDAN

POLAND
NY
ARMENIA
Black Sea
GEORGIA
ALY
NISIA
LIBYA
EGYPT

Kara Sea

RUSSIA

KAZAKSTAN

AZERBAIJAN

UZBEKISTAN
TURKMENISTAN

Caspian Sea

SYRIA
IRAQ
KUWAIT
BAHRAIN
QATAR
SAUDI ARABIA
OMAN
UNITED ARAB EMIRATES
YEMEN

IRAN

AFGHANISTAN

PAKISTAN

KYRGYZSTAN
TAJIKISTAN

MONGOLIA

CHINA

NEPAL
BHUTAN
BANGLADESH
INDIA
MYANMAR
(BURMA)

Laptev Sea

East Siberian Sea

Sea of Okhotsk

NORTH KOREA

Sea of Japan

JAPAN

SOUTH KOREA

60° N

PACIFIC OCEAN

30° N

LAOS VIETNAM

TAIWAN

HONG KONG
(U.K.)

South China Sea

PHILIPPINES

GUAM (U.S.)

MARSHALL ISLANDS

Bay of Bengal

Arabian Sea

THAILAND
CAMBODIA

BRUNEI
MALAYSIA

PALAU

MICRONESIA

NAURU

KIRIBATI

MALDIVES

SRI LANKA

SEYCHELLES

SINGAPORE

I N D O N E S I A

PAPUA NEW GUINEA

SOLOMON ISLANDS

TUVALU

AMERICAN SAMOA
(U.S.)

WESTERN SAMOA

Mediterranean Sea

CHAD

SUDAN

CENTRAL AFRICAN REPUBLIC

ERITREA

DJIBOUTI

ETHIOPIA

SOMALIA

0°

ROON

UGANDA

RWANDA
BURUNDI
ZAIRE

KENYA

TANZANIA

MALAWI

COMOROS

INDIAN OCEAN

MAURITIUS

Coral Sea

VANUATU

FIJI

NIUE

TONGA

NEW CALEDONIA
(FRANCE)

ZAMBIA

MOZAMBIQUE

AMIBIA

BOTSWANA

MADAGASCAR

ZIMBABWE
SWAZILAND

SOUTH AFRICA

LESOTHO

AUSTRALIA

Tasman Sea

30° S

NEW ZEALAND

60° S

0°S

CTICA

30° E   60° E   90° E   120° E   150° E   180°

AFGHANISTAN

cap: Kabul
pop: 18,400,000
area (sq. mi.): 251,773 sq.
mi.
lang: Dari Persian, Pashtu,
Uzbek
money: afghani

ALBANIA

cap: Tiranë
pop: 3,500,000
area (sq. mi.): 11,100
lang: Albanian, Greek
money: lek

ALGERIA

cap: Algiers
pop: 28,400,000
area (sq. mi.): 918,497
lang: Arabic, Berber, French
money: dinar

ANDORRA

cap: Andorra la Vella
pop: 62,000
area (sq. mi.): 185
lang: Catalan, French,
Spanish
money: franc, peseta

ANGOLA

cap: Luanda
pop: 11,500,000
area (sq. mi.): 481,353
lang: Portuguese, Bantu
money: kwanza

ANTIGUA AND BARBUDA

cap: St. John's
pop: 100,000
area (sq. mi.): 171
lang: English
money: dollar

ARGENTINA

cap: Buenos Aires
pop: 34,600,000
area (sq. mi.): 1,065,189
lang: Spanish, Italian
money: peso

ARMENIA

cap: Yerevan
pop: 3,700,000
area (sq. mi.): 11,306
lang: Armenian
money: dram

AUSTRALIA

cap: Canberra
pop: 18,400,000
area (sq. mi.): 2,966,4200
lang: English, aboriginal
languages
money: dollar

AUSTRIA

cap: Vienna
pop: 8,100,000
area (sq. mi.): 32,377
lang: German
money: schilling

AZERBAIJAN

cap: Baku
pop: 7,300,000
area (sq. mi.): 33,400
lang: Azeri, Russian,
Armenian
money: manat

BAHAMAS

cap: Nassau
pop: 300,000
area (sq. mi.): 5,380
lang: English, Creole
money: dollar

BAHRAIN

cap: Manama
pop: 4,600,000
area (sq. mi.): 268
lang: Arabic, English, Farsi,
Urdu
money: dinar

BANGLADESH

cap: Dhaka
pop: 119,200,000
area (sq. mi.): 55,813
lang: Bengali, Chakma, Bagh
money: taka

BARBADOS

cap: Bridgetown
pop: 300,000
area (sq. mi.): 166
lang: English
money: dollar

BELARUS

cap: Minsk
pop: 10,373,000
area (sq. mi.): 80,134
lang: Byelorussian, Russian
money: ruble

BELGIUM

cap: Brussels
pop: 10,200,000
area (sq. mi.): 11,799
lang: Flemish, French,
German
money: franc

BELIZE

cap: Belmopan
pop: 200,000
area (sq. mi.): 8,867
lang: English, Spanish, Creole
money:dollar

BENIN

cap: Porto-Novo
pop: 5,400,000
area (sq. mi.): 43,483
lang: French, Fon, Yoruba
money: CFA franc

BHUTAN

cap: Thimphu
pop: 800,000
area (sq. mi.): 18,147
lang: Dzongkha, Nepali,
Tibetan
money: ngultrum

BOLIVIA

cap: Sucre
pop: 7,400,000
area (sq. mi.): 424,165
lang: Spanish, Quechua,
Aymara
money: boliviano

BOSNIA & HERZEGOVINA

cap: Sarajevo
pop: 3,500,000
area (sq. mi.): 19,741
lang: Serbo-Croatian
money: dinar

BOTSWANA

cap: Gaborone
pop: 1,500,000
area (sq. mi.): 231,804
lang: English, Setswana
money: pula

BRAZIL

cap: Brasília
pop: 157,800,000
area (sq. mi.): 3,286,470
lang: Portuguese, Spanish,
others
money: real

BRUNEI DARUSSALAM

cap: Bandar Seri Begawan
pop: 300,000
area (sq. mi.): 2,226
lang: Malay, English, Chinese
money: dollar

---

cap = capital; pop = population; area (sq. mi.) = area measured in square miles; lang = language; money = the basic unit of the country's official currency

BULGARIA

cap: Sofia
pop: 8,500,000
area (sq. mi.): 44,365
lang: Bulgarian, Turkish
money: leva

BURKINA FASO

cap: Ouagadougou
pop: 10,100,000
area (sq. mi.): 105,869
lang: French, Sudanic
    languages
money: CFA franc

BURUNDI

cap: Bujumbura
pop: 6,400,000
area (sq. mi.): 10,759
lang: French, Kirundi, Swahili
money: franc

CAMBODIA

cap: Phnom Penh
pop: 10,600,000
area (sq. mi.): 70,238
lang: Khmer, French
money: rie

CAMEROON

cap: Yaoundé
pop: 13,500,000
area (sq. mi.): 179,714
lang: English, French, others
money: CFA franc

CANADA

cap: Ottawa
pop: 29,600,000
area (sq. mi.): 3,849,672
lang: English, French
money: dollar

CAPE VERDE

cap: Praia
pop: 400,000
area (sq. mi.): 1,557
lang: Portuguese, Crioulo
money: escudo

CENTRAL AFRICAN REPUBLIC

cap: Bangui
pop: 3,200,000
area (sq. mi.): 240,534
lang: French, Sangho, others
money: CFA franc

CHAD

cap: N'Djamena
pop: 6,400,000
area (sq. mi.): 495,755
lang: French, Arabic, others
money: CFA franc

CHILE

cap: Santiago
pop: 14,300,000
area (sq. mi.): 302,779
lang: Spanish
money: peso

CHINA, Peoples Rep. of

cap: Beijing
pop: 1,218,800,000
area (sq. mi.): 3,696,100
lang: Mandarin, Yue, others
money: yuan

CHINA, Rep. of (Taiwan)

cap: Taipei
pop: 21,200,000
area (sq. mi.): 13,885
lang: Mandarin, Malay,
    others
money: dollar

COLOMBIA

cap: Bogotá
pop: 37,700,000
area (sq. mi.): 439,735
lang: Spanish
money: peso

COMOROS

cap: Moroni
pop: 500,000
area (sq. mi.): 838
lang: Arabic, French,
    Comoran
money: CFA franc

CONGO

cap: Brazzaville
pop: 2,500,000
area (sq. mi.): 132,046
lang: French, Kongo, Teke
money: CFA franc

COSTA RICA

cap: San José
pop: 3,300,000
area (sq. mi.): 19,652
lang: Spanish, English
money: colones

CÔTE D'IVOIRE
(Ivory Coast)

cap: Yamoussoukro
pop: 14,300,000
area (sq. mi.): 124,503
lang: French, Dioula, others
money: CFA franc

CROATIA

cap: Zagreb
pop: 4,500,000
area (sq. mi.): 21,829
lang: Serbo-Croatian
money: kuna

CUBA

cap: Havana
pop: 11,200,000
area (sq. mi.): 44,218
lang: Spanish
money: peso

CYPRUS

cap: Nicosia
pop: 700,000
area (sq. mi.): 3,572
lang: Greek, Turkish, English
money: pound

CZECH REPUBLIC

cap: Prague
pop: 10,400,000
area (sq. mi.): 30,449
lang: Czech, Slovak
money: koruna

DENMARK

cap: Copenhagen
pop: 5,200,000
area (sq. mi.): 16,633
lang: Danish
money: krone

DJIBOUTI

cap: Djibouti
pop: 600,000
area (sq. mi.): 8,950
lang: French, Arabic, Afar,
    Somali
money: franc

DOMINICA

cap: Roseau
pop: 100,000
area (sq. mi.): 290
lang: English, Creole
money: dollar

DOMINICAN REPUBLIC

cap: Santo Domingo
pop: 7,800,000
area (sq. mi.): 18,704
lang: Spanish
money: peso

ECUADOR

cap: Quito
pop: 11,500,000
area (sq. mi.): 109,483
lang: Spanish, Quechua,
     Jivaroan
money: sucre

EGYPT

cap: Cairo
pop: 61,900,000
area (sq. mi.): 386,650
lang: Arabic, English, French
money: pound

EL SALVADOR

cap: San Salvador
pop: 5,900,000
area (sq. mi.): 8,124
lang: Spanish, Nahuatl
money: colon

EQUATORIAL GUINEA

cap: Malabo
pop: 400,000
area (sq. mi.): 10,832
lang: Spanish, Fang, Bubi
money: CFA franc

ERITREA

cap: Asmara
pop: 3,500,000
area (sq. mi.): 36,170
lang: Tigre, Kunama, others
money: birr

ESTONIA

cap: Tallinn
pop: 1,500,000
area (sq. mi.): 17,413
lang: Estonian, Russian,
     Latvian
money: kroon

ETHIOPIA

cap: Addis Ababa
pop: 56,200,000
area (sq. mi.): 435,606
lang: Amharic, Tigre, Galla
money: birr

FIJI

cap: Suva
pop: 800,000
area (sq. mi.): 7,056
lang: English, Fijian, Hindi
money: dollar

FINLAND

cap: Helsinki
pop: 5,100,000
area (sq. mi.): 130,119
lang: Finnish, Swedish
money: markka

FRANCE

cap: Paris
pop: 58,100,000
area (sq. mi.): 220,668
lang: French
money: franc

GABON

cap: Libreville
pop: 1,300,000
area (sq. mi.): 103,346
lang: French, Fang, others
money: CFA franc

GAMBIA

cap: Banjul
pop: 1,100,000
area (sq. mi.): 4,127
lang: English, Mandinka,
     Wolof
money: dalasi

GEORGIA

cap: Tbilisi
pop: 5,570,000
area (sq. mi.): 26,911
lang: Georgian, Russian,
     Armenian
money: tetri

GERMANY

cap: Berlin
pop: 81,700,000
area (sq. mi.): 137,838
lang: German
money: mark

GHANA

cap: Accra
pop: 17,500,000
area (sq. mi.): 92,098
lang: English, Akan, others
money: cedi

GREECE

cap: Athens
pop: 10,500,000
area (sq. mi.): 51,146
lang: Greek, English, French
money: drachma

GRENADA

cap: St. George's
pop: 100,000
area (sq. mi.): 133
lang: English, French patois
money: dollar

GUATEMALA

cap: Guatemala City
pop: 10,600,000
area (sq. mi.): 42,042
lang: Spanish, Mayan
money: quetzal

GUINEA

cap: Conakry
pop: 6,500,000
area (sq. mi.): 94,964
lang: French, Peul, Mande
money: franc

GUINEA-BISSAU

cap: Bissau
pop: 1,100,000
area (sq. mi.): 13,948
lang: Portuguese, Crioulo,
     others
money: peso

GUYANA

cap: Georgetown
pop: 800,000
area (sq. mi.): 83,000
lang: English, Indian
     languages
money: dollar

HAITI

cap: Port-au-Prince
pop: 7,200,000
area (sq. mi.): 10,579
lang: French, Creole
money: gourde

HONDURAS

cap: Tegucigalpa
pop: 5,500,000
area (sq. mi.): 43,277
lang: Spanish, Indian
     languages
money: lempira

HUNGARY

cap: Budapest
pop: 10,200,000
area (sq. mi.): 35,919
lang: Hungarian
money: forint

ICELAND

cap: Reykjavik
pop: 300,000
area (sq. mi.): 39,769
lang: Icelandic
money: kronur

INDIA

cap: New Delhi
pop: 930,600,000
area (sq. mi.): 1,266,595
lang: Hindi, English, others
money: rupee

INDONESIA

cap: Jakarta
pop: 198,040,000
area (sq. mi.): 735,268
lang: Bahasa Indonesian,
    Javanese, others
money: rupiah

IRAN

cap: Tehran
pop: 61,300,000
area (sq. mi.): 636,293
lang: Farsi, Turkic, Kurdish
money: rial

IRAQ

cap: Baghdad
pop: 20,600,000
area (sq. mi.): 167,924
lang: Arabic, Kurdish
money: dinar

IRELAND

cap: Dublin
pop: 3,600,000
area (sq. mi.): 27,137
lang: English, Gaelic
money: punt

ISRAEL

cap: Jerusalem
pop: 5,500,000
area (sq. mi.): 7,847
lang: Hebrew, Arabic, English
money: new sheqalim

ITALY

cap: Rome
pop: 57,700,000
area (sq. mi.): 116,303
lang: Italian
money: lira

JAMAICA

cap: Kingston
pop: 2,400,000
area (sq. mi.): 4,232
lang: English, Jamaican
    Creole
money: dollar

JAPAN

cap: Tokyo
pop: 125,200,000
area (sq. mi.): 145,856
lang: Japanese
money: yen

JORDAN

cap: Amman
pop: 4,100,000
area (sq. mi.): 37,737
lang: Arabic, English
money: dinar

KAZAKSTAN

cap: Almaty
pop: 16,900,000
area (sq. mi.): 1,049,200
lang: Kazakh, Russian,
    German
money: tenge

KENYA

cap: Nairobi
pop: 28,300,000
area (sq. mi.): 224,960
lang: Swahili, English, others
money: shilling

KIRIBATI

cap: Tarawa
pop: 76,320
area (sq. mi.): 266
lang: English, Gilbertese
money: dollar

KOREA, DEM. PEOPLE'S REP. OF (North Korea)

cap: Pyongyang
pop: 23,500,000
area (sq. mi.): 46,540
lang: Korean
money: won

KOREA, REP. OF (South Korea)

cap: Seoul
pop: 44,900,000
area (sq. mi.): 38,025
lang: Korean
money: won

KUWAIT

cap: Kuwait
pop: 1,500,000
area (sq. mi.): 6,880
lang: Arabic, English
money: dinar

KYRGYZSTAN

cap: Bishkek
pop: 4,400,000
area (sq. mi.): 76,642
lang: Kyrgyz, Russian, Turkic
money: som

LAOS

cap: Vientiane
pop: 4,800,000
area (sq. mi.): 91,428
lang: Lao, French, Sino-
    Tibetan languages
money: new kip

LATVIA

cap: Riga
pop: 2,500,000
area (sq. mi.): 24,900
lang: Latvian, Lithuanian,
    Russian
money: lat

LEBANON

cap: Beirut
pop: 3,700,000
area (sq. mi.): 4,015
lang: Arabic, French, others
money: pound

LESOTHO

cap: Maseru
pop: 2,100,000
area (sq. mi.): 11,716
lang: English, Sesotho, others
money: maloti

LIBERIA

cap: Monrovia
pop: 3,000,000
area (sq. mi.): 38,250
lang: English, Niger-Congo
    languages
money: dollar

LIBYA

cap: Tripoli
pop: 5,200,000
area (sq. mi.): 679,359
lang: Arabic, Italian, English
money: dinar

LIECHTENSTEIN

cap: Vaduz
pop: 30,000
area (sq. mi.): 62
lang: German, Alemannic
    dialect
money: Swiss franc

LITHUANIA

cap: Vilnius
pop: 3,788,000
area (sq. mi.): 25,170
lang: Lithuanian, Polish,
    Russian
money: litas

LUXEMBOURG

cap: Luxembourg
pop: 400,000
area (sq. mi.): 998
lang: French, German, Luxembourgisch
money: franc

MACEDONIA

cap: Skopje
pop: 2,100,000
area (sq. mi.): 9,928
lang: Macedonian, Albanian, others
money: dinar

MADAGASCAR

cap: Antananarivo
pop: 14,800,000
area (sq. mi.): 226,657
lang: French, Malagasy
money: franc

MALAWI

cap: Lilongwe
pop: 9,700,000
area (sq. mi.): 45,747
lang: English, Chichewa, Bantu languages
money: kwacha

MALAYSIA

cap: Kuala Lumpur
pop: 19,900,000
area (sq. mi.): 127,316
lang: Malay, English, others
money: ringgit

MALDIVES

cap: Male
pop: 300,000
area (sq. mi.): 115
lang: Divehi, English
money: rufiyaa

MALI

cap: Bamako
pop: 9,400,000
area (sq. mi.): 478,764
lang: French, Bambara, Senufo
money: franc

MALTA

cap: Valletta
pop: 400,000
area (sq. mi.): 122
lang: Maltese, English
money: lira

MARSHALL ISLANDS

cap: Majuro
pop: 100,000
area (sq. mi.): 70
lang: English, Marshallese, Japanese
money: U.S. dollar

MAURITANIA

cap: Nouakchott
pop: 2,300,000
area (sq. mi.): 419,212
lang: Hassanya Arabic, Wolof, others
money: ouguiya

MAURITIUS

cap: Port Louis
pop: 1,100,000
area (sq. mi.): 720
lang: English, Creole, others
money: rupee

MEXICO

cap: Mexico City
pop: 93,700,000
area (sq. mi.): 761,604
lang: Spanish, Mayan, others
money: peso

MICRONESIA

cap: Palikir
pop: 111,000
area (sq. mi.): 270
lang: English, Trukese, others
money: dollar

MOLDOVA

cap: Chisinau
pop: 4,300,000
area (sq. mi.): 13,012
lang: Moldovan, Russian
money: ruble

MONACO

cap: Monaco
pop: 31,000
area (sq. mi.): 0.6
lang: French, English, Monegasque
money: franc

MONGOLIA

cap: Ulaanbaatar
pop: 2,300,000
area (sq. mi.): 604,247
lang: Mongolian, Turkic, Russian
money: tugrik

MOROCCO

cap: Rabat
pop: 29,200,000
area (sq. mi.): 172,413
lang: Arabic, Berber languages, French
money: dirham

MOZAMBIQUE

cap: Maputo
pop: 17,400,000
area (sq. mi.): 303,769
lang: Portuguese, African languages
money: metica

MYANMAR

cap: Yangon
pop: 44,800,000
area (sq. mi.): 261,789
lang: Burmese, Karen, Shan
money: kyat

NAMIBIA

cap: Windhoek
pop: 1,500,000
area (sq. mi.): 317,818
lang: Afrikaans, English, others
money: dollar

NAURU

cap: Yaren
pop: 9,880
area (sq. mi.): 8
lang: Nauruan, English
money: dollar

NEPAL

cap: Kathmandu
pop: 22,600,000
area (sq. mi.): 56,136
lang: Nepali, others
money: rupee

NETHERLANDS

cap: Amsterdam
pop: 15,500,000
area (sq. mi.): 15,770
lang: Dutch
money: guilder

NEW ZEALAND

cap: Wellington
pop: 3,500,000
area (sq. mi.): 103,736
lang: English, Maori
money: dollar

NICARAGUA

cap: Managua
pop: 4,400,000
area (sq. mi.): 50,193
lang: Spanish, Indian languages
money: cordoba oro

NIGER

cap: Niamey
pop: 9,200,000
area (sq. mi.): 489,189
lang: French, Hausa, Djerma
money: CFA franc

NIGERIA

cap: Abuja
pop: 101,200,000
area (sq. mi.): 356,667
lang: English, Hausa, others
money: naira

NORWAY

cap: Oslo
pop: 4,300,000
area (sq. mi.): 125,181
lang: Norwegian, Lapp, Finnish
money: kroner

OMAN

cap: Muscat
pop: 2,200,000
area (sq. mi.): 82,030
lang: Arabic, Balochi, others
money: rial omani

PAKISTAN

cap: Islamabad
pop: 129,700,000
area (sq. mi.): 310,403
lang: Urdu, English, others
money: rupee

PALAU

cap: Koror
pop: 15,000
area (sq. mi.): 179
lang: English
money: dollar

PANAMA

cap: Panama City
pop: 2,600,000
area (sq. mi.): 29,762
lang: Spanish, English
money: balboa

PAPUA NEW GUINEA

cap: Port Moresby
pop: 4,100,000
area (sq. mi.): 178,260
lang: English, Melanesian, Papuan
money: kina

PARAGUAY

cap: Asunción
pop: 5,000,000
area (sq. mi.): 157,047
lang: Spanish, Guarani
money: guarani

PERU

cap: Lima
pop: 24,000,000
area (sq. mi.): 496,222
lang: Spanish, Quechua, Aymara
money: nuevo sol

PHILIPPINES

cap: Manila
pop: 68,400,000
area (sq. mi.): 115,831
lang: Filipino, English, others
money: peso

POLAND

cap: Warsaw
pop: 38,600,000
area (sq. mi.): 120,727
lang: Polish
money: zloty

PORTUGAL

cap: Lisbon
pop: 9,900,000
area (sq. mi.): 36,390
lang: Portuguese
money: escudo

QATAR

cap: Doha
pop: 500,000
area (sq. mi.): 4,247
lang: Arabic, English
money: riyal

ROMANIA

cap: Bucharest
pop: 22,700,000
area (sq. mi.): 91,699
lang: Romanian, Hungarian, German
money: leu

RUSSIA

cap: Moscow
pop: 147,500,000
area (sq. mi.): 6,592,800
lang: Russian, Ukrainian, others
money: ruble

RWANDA

cap: Kigali
pop: 7,800,000
area (sq. mi.): 10,169
lang: French, Kinyarwanda, Bantu
money: franc

ST. KITTS AND NEVIS

cap: Basseterre
pop: 40,000
area (sq. mi.): 101
lang: English
money: dollar

ST. LUCIA

cap: Castries
pop: 151,000
area (sq. mi.): 238
lang: English, French patois
money: dollar

ST. VINCENT AND THE GRENADINES

cap: Kingstown
pop: 114,000
area (sq. mi.): 150
lang: English, French patois
money: dollar

SAN MARINO

cap: San Marino
pop: 30,000
area (sq. mi.): 24
lang: Italian
money: lira

SÃO TOMÉ AND PRINCIPE

cap: São Tomé
pop: 100,000
area (sq. mi.): 372
lang: Portuguese
money: dobra

SAUDI ARABIA

cap: Riyadh
pop: 18,500,000
area (sq. mi.): 839,996
lang: Arabic
money: riyal

SENEGAL

cap: Dakar
pop: 8,300,000
area (sq. mi.): 75,750
lang: French, Wolof, others
money: CFA franc

SEYCHELLES

cap: Victoria
pop: 100,000
area (sq. mi.): 171
lang: English, French, Creole
money: rupee

SIERRA LEONE

cap: Freetown
pop: 4,500,000
area (sq. mi.): 27,925
lang: English, Krio, others
money: leone

SINGAPORE

cap: Singapore
pop: 3,000,000
area (sq. mi.): 224
lang: Malay, Tamil, Chinese, English
money: dollar

SLOVAKIA

cap: Bratislava
pop: 5,400,000
area (sq. mi.): 18,932
lang: Slovak, Hungarian, others
money: koruna

SLOVENIA

cap: Ljubljana
pop: 2,000,000
area (sq. mi.): 7,819
lang: Slovenian, Serbo-Croatian, others
money: tolar

SOLOMON ISLANDS

cap: Honiara
pop: 400,000
area (sq. mi.): 10,640
lang: English, Papuan, others
money: dollar

SOMALIA

cap: Mogadishu
pop: 9,300,000
area (sq. mi.): 246,300
lang: Somali, Arabic, others
money: shilling

SOUTH AFRICA

cap: Pretoria, Cape Town, and Bloemfontein
pop: 43,500,000
area (sq. mi.): 472,359
lang: Afrikaans, English, Nguni, others
money: rand

SPAIN

cap: Madrid
pop: 39,100,000
area (sq. mi.): 194,896
lang: Spanish, Catalan, others
money: peseta

SRI LANKA

cap: Colombo
pop: 18,200,000
area (sq. mi.): 25,332
lang: Sinhalese, Tamil, English
money: rupee

SUDAN

cap: Khartoum
pop: 28,100,000
area (sq. mi.): 966,757
lang: Arabic, Dinka, others
money: dinar

SURINAME

cap: Paramaribo
pop: 410,000
area (sq. mi.): 63,037
lang: Dutch, Sranan Tonga, English
money: guilder

SWAZILAND

cap: Mbabane
pop: 1,000,000
area (sq. mi.): 6,704
lang: Siswati, English
money: lilangeni

SWEDEN

cap: Stockholm
pop: 8,900,000
area (sq. mi.): 173,731
lang: Swedish, Lapp, Finnish
money: krona

SWITZERLAND

cap: Bern
pop: 7,000,000
area (sq. mi.): 15,941
lang: French, German, Italian
money: franc

SYRIA

cap: Damascus
pop: 14,700,000
area (sq. mi.): 71,498
lang: Arabic, Kurdish, Armenian
money: pound

TAJIKISTAN

cap: Dushanbe
pop: 5,800,000
area (sq. mi.): 54,019
lang: Tadzhik, Russian
money: ruble

TANZANIA

cap: Dar-es-Salaam
pop: 28,500,000
area (sq. mi.): 364,886
lang: Swahili, English, others
money: shilling

THAILAND

cap: Bangkok
pop: 60,200,000
area (sq. mi.): 198,456
lang: Thai, Chinese, others
money: baht

TOGO

cap: Lomé
pop: 4,400,000
area (sq. mi.): 21,622
lang: French, Ewe, others
money: CFA franc

TONGA

cap: Nuku'alofa
pop: 104,000
area (sq. mi.): 270
lang: Tongan, English
money: pa'anga

TRINIDAD AND TOBAGO

cap: Port-of-Spain
pop: 1,300,000
area (sq. mi.): 1,980
lang: English, Hindi, others
money: dollar

TUNISIA

cap: Tunis
pop: 8,900,000
area (sq. mi.): 63,170
lang: Arabic, French
money: dinar

TURKEY

cap: Ankara
pop: 61,400,000
area (sq. mi.): 301,381
lang: Turkish, Kurdish, Arabic
money: lira

TURKMENISTAN

cap: Ashgabad
pop: 4,500,000
area (sq. mi.): 188,417
lang: Turkmen, Russian, others
money: manat

TUVALU

cap: Funafuti
pop: 9,670
area (sq. mi.): 10
lang: Tuvaluan, English
money: dollar

UGANDA

cap: Kampala
pop: 21,300,000
area (sq. mi.): 93,354
lang: English, Luganda, Swahili
money: shilling

UKRAINE

cap: Kyiv
pop: 52,000,000
area (sq. mi.): 23,100
lang: Ukrainian, Russian, others
money: karbovanet

UNITED ARAB EMIRATES

cap: Abu Dhabi
pop: 1,900,000
area (sq. mi.): 32,000
lang: Arabic, Persian, others
money: dirham

UNITED KINGDOM

cap: London
pop: 58,600,800
area (sq. mi.): 94,226
lang: English, Welsh, Scottish Gaelic
money: pound

UNITED STATES

cap: Washington, DC
pop: 263,200,000
area (sq. mi.): 3,618,770
lang: English, Spanish, others
money: dollar

URUGUAY

cap: Montevideo
pop: 3,200,000
area (sq. mi.): 68,037
lang: Spanish
money: new peso

UZBEKISTAN

cap: Tashkent
pop: 22,700,000
area (sq. mi.): 172,700
lang: Uzbek, Russian, others
money: som

VANUATU

cap: Port-Vila
pop: 200,000
area (sq. mi.): 5,700
lang: Bislama, English, French
money: vatu

VATICAN CITY

cap: Vatican City
pop: 800
area (sq. mi.): 0.17
lang: Italian, Latin
money: lira

VENEZUELA

cap: Caracas
pop: 21,800,000
area (sq. mi.): 352,143
lang: Spanish, Indian languages
money: bolivar

VIETNAM

cap: Hanoi
pop: 75,000,000
area (sq. mi.): 127,330
lang: Vietnamese, Chinese, others
money: dong

WESTERN SAMOA

cap: Apia
pop: 200,000
area (sq. mi.): 1,133
lang: Samoan, English
money: tala

YEMEN

cap: Sanaa
pop: 13,200,000
area (sq. mi.): 203,796
lang: Arabic
money: rial

YUGOSLAVIA, FED. REP. OF (Serbia and Montenegro)

cap: Belgrade
pop: 10,500,000
area (sq. mi.): 26,940
lang: Serbo-Croatian, Albanian
money: dinar

ZAIRE

cap: Kinshasa
pop: 44,100,000
area (sq. mi.): 905,563
lang: French, Kongo, others
money: zaire

ZAMBIA

cap: Lusaka
pop: 9,100,000
area (sq. mi.): 290,586
lang: English, Bantu languages
money: kwacha

ZIMBABWE

cap: Harare
pop: 11,300,000
area (sq. mi.): 150,803
lang: English, Shona, others
money: dollar

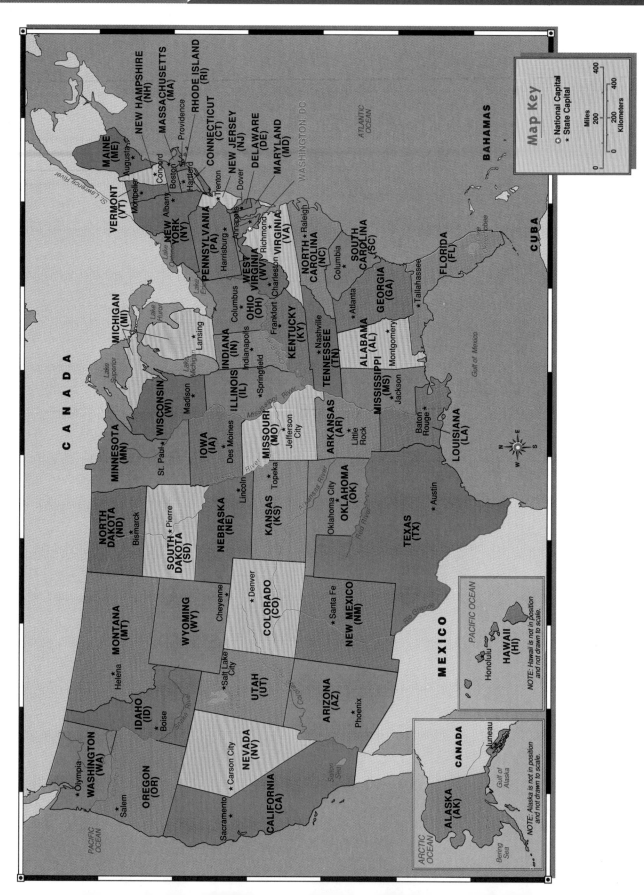

Map Key

○ National Capital
★ State Capital

Miles
0   200   400

Kilometers
0   200   400

ATLANTIC OCEAN

CANADA

St. Lawrence River

NEW HAMPSHIRE (NH)
MASSACHUSETTS (MA)
RHODE ISLAND (RI)
MAINE (ME)
★ Augusta
Montpelier ★
★ Concord
VERMONT (VT)
Boston ★ Providence
Hartford ★
CONNECTICUT (CT)
NEW JERSEY (NJ)
DELAWARE (DE)
MARYLAND (MD)
WASHINGTON, DC
BAHAMAS

NEW YORK (NY)
Albany ★
PENNSYLVANIA (PA)
★ Harrisburg
Trenton ★
Dover ★
Annapolis ★
Richmond ★
VIRGINIA (VA)
WEST VIRGINIA (WV)
Charleston ★
OHIO (OH)
Columbus ★
Frankfort ★
RALEIGH ★
NORTH CAROLINA (NC)
SOUTH CAROLINA (SC)
Columbia ★
CUBA

Lake Ontario
Lake Erie
MICHIGAN (MI)
Lake Huron
Lansing ★
Lake Superior
Lake Michigan

INDIANA (IN)
Indianapolis ★
KENTUCKY (KY)
Nashville ★
TENNESSEE (TN)
Atlanta ★
GEORGIA (GA)
Tallahassee ★
FLORIDA (FL)
Lake Okeechobee

WISCONSIN (WI)
Madison ★
MINNESOTA (MN)
St. Paul ★
IOWA (IA)
Des Moines ★
ILLINOIS (IL)
Springfield ★
Ohio River
Mississippi River

MISSOURI (MO)
Jefferson City ★
ARKANSAS (AR)
Little Rock ★
ALABAMA (AL)
Montgomery ★
MISSISSIPPI (MS)
Jackson ★
Baton Rouge ★
LOUISIANA (LA)
Gulf of Mexico

NORTH DAKOTA (ND)
Bismarck ★
SOUTH DAKOTA (SD)
Pierre ★
NEBRASKA (NE)
Lincoln ★
KANSAS (KS)
Topeka ★
OKLAHOMA (OK)
Oklahoma City ★
Arkansas River
Red River
TEXAS (TX)
Austin ★

N E S W

MONTANA (MT)
Helena ★
WYOMING (WY)
Cheyenne ★
COLORADO (CO)
Denver ★
NEW MEXICO (NM)
Santa Fe ★
Rio Grande
MEXICO

IDAHO (ID)
Boise ★
UTAH (UT)
Salt Lake City ★
Great Salt Lake
Snake River
ARIZONA (AZ)
Phoenix ★
Colorado River

WASHINGTON (WA)
Olympia ★
OREGON (OR)
Salem ★
NEVADA (NV)
Carson City ★
CALIFORNIA (CA)
Sacramento ★
Salton Sea

PACIFIC OCEAN

PACIFIC OCEAN
Honolulu ★
HAWAII (HI)
NOTE: Hawaii is not in position and not drawn to scale.

CANADA
Juneau ★
Gulf of Alaska
ALASKA (AK)
ARCTIC OCEAN
Bering Sea
NOTE: Alaska is not in position and not drawn to scale.

State	Postal Abbreviation	Nickname	Population*	Capital	Year of Admission (Order of Admission)
Alabama	AL	Heart of Dixie; Camellia State	4,135,543	Montgomery	1819 (22)
Alaska	AK	The Last Frontier (unofficial)	586,872	Juneau	1959 (49)
Arizona	AZ	Grand Canyon State	3,832,294	Phoenix	1912 (48)
Arkansas	AR	Land of Opportunity	2,398,767	Little Rock	1836 (25)
California	CA	Golden State	30,866,851	Sacramento	1850 (31)
Colorado	CO	Centennial State	3,470,216	Denver	1876 (38)
Connecticut	CT	Nutmeg State, Constitution State	3,280,959	Hartford	1788 (5)
Delaware	DE	First State, Diamond State	689,214	Dover	1787 (1)
Florida	FL	Sunshine State	13,487,621	Tallahassee	1845 (27)
Georgia	GA	Peach State, Empire State of the South	6,751,404	Atlanta	1788 (4)
Hawaii	HI	Aloha State	1,159,614	Honolulu	1959 (50)
Idaho	ID	Gem State	1,067,250	Boise	1890 (43)
Illinois	IL	Prairie State	11,631,131	Springfield	1818 (21)
Indiana	IN	Hoosier State	5,661,800	Indianapolis	1816 (19)
Iowa	IA	Hawkeye State	2,812,448	Des Moines	1846 (29)
Kansas	KS	Sunflower State	2,522,574	Topeka	1861 (34)
Kentucky	KY	Bluegrass State	3,754,715	Frankfort	1792 (15)
Louisiana	LA	Pelican State	4,287,195	Baton Rouge	1812 (18)
Maine	ME	Pine Tree State	1,235,396	Augusta	1820 (23)
Maryland	MD	Free State, Old Line State	4,908,453	Annapolis	1788 (7)
Massachusetts	MA	Bay State, Old Colony	5,998,375	Boston	1788 (6)
Michigan	MI	Great Lakes State, Wolverine State	9,436,628	Lansing	1837 (26)
Minnesota	MN	Gopher State, North Star State	4,480,034	St. Paul	1858 (32)
Mississippi	MS	Magnolia State	2,614,294	Jackson	1817 (20)
Missouri	MO	Show Me State	5,192,632	Jefferson City	1821 (24)
Montana	MT	Treasure State	823,697	Helena	1889 (41)
Nebraska	NE	Cornhusker State	1,605,603	Lincoln	1867 (37)
Nevada	NV	Silver State, Sagebrush State, Battle Born State	1,327,387	Carson City	1864 (36)
New Hampshire	NH	Granite State	1,110,801	Concord	1788 (9)
New Jersey	NJ	Garden State	7,789,060	Trenton	1787 (3)
New Mexico	NM	Land of Enchantment	1,581,227	Santa Fe	1912 (47)
New York	NY	Empire State	18,119,416	Albany	1788 (11)
North Carolina	NC	Tar Heel State, Old North State	6,842,691	Raleigh	1789 (12)
North Dakota	ND	Peace Garden State	635,927	Bismarck	1889 (39)
Ohio	OH	Buckeye State	11,016,385	Columbus	1803 (17)
Oklahoma	OK	Sooner State	3,212,198	Oklahoma City	1907 (46)
Oregon	OR	Beaver State	2,977,331	Salem	1859 (33)
Pennsylvania	PA	Keystone State	12,009,361	Harrisburg	1787 (2)
Rhode Island	RI	Little Rhody, Ocean State	1,005,091	Providence	1790 (13)
South Carolina	SC	Palmetto State	3,603,227	Columbia	1788 (8)
South Dakota	SD	Coyote State, Mount Rushmore State	711,154	Pierre	1889 (40)
Tennessee	TN	Volunteer State	5,023,990	Nashville	1796 (16)
Texas	TX	Lone Star State	17,655,650	Austin	1845 (28)
Utah	UT	Beehive State	1,690,000	Salt Lake City	1896 (45)
Vermont	VT	Green Mountain State	569,784	Montpelier	1791 (14)
Virginia	VA	Old Dominion	6,377,141	Richmond	1788 (10)
Washington	WA	Evergreen State	5,135,731	Olympia	1889 (42)
West Virginia	WV	Mountain State	1,812,194	Charleston	1863 (35)
Wisconsin	WI	Badger State	5,006,591	Madison	1848 (30)
Wyoming	WY	Equality State	466,185	Cheyenne	1890 (44)

• These population figures were taken from the 1992 (estimate) U.S. Census.

President	Born	Where born	Died	Dates of term(s)	Party
1. George Washington	Feb. 22, 1732	Westmoreland Co., VA	Dec. 14, 1799	April 30, 1789–March 3, 1797	Federalist
2. John Adams	Oct. 30, 1735	Braintree, MA	July 4, 1826	March 4, 1797–March 3, 1801	Federalist
3. Thomas Jefferson	April 13, 1743	Shadwell, VA	July 4, 1826	March 4, 1801–March 3, 1805	Democratic-Republican
				March 4, 1805–March 3, 1809	
4. James Madison	March 16, 1751	Port Conway, VA	June 28, 1836	March 4, 1809–March 3, 1813	Democratic-Republican
				March 4, 1813–March 3, 1817	
5. James Monroe	April 28, 1758	Westmoreland Co., VA	July 4, 1831	March 4, 1817–March 3, 1825	Democratic-Republican
6. John Quincy Adams	July 11, 1767	Quincy, MA	Feb. 23, 1848	March 4, 1825–March 3, 1829	Democratic-Republican
7. Andrew Jackson	March 15, 1767	New Lancaster Co., SC	June 8, 1845	March 4, 1829–March 3, 1833	Democrat
				March 4, 1833–March 3, 1837	
8. Martin Van Buren	Dec. 5, 1782	Kinderhook, NY	July 24, 1862	March 4, 1837–March 3, 1841	Democratic
9. William Henry Harrison	Feb. 9, 1773	Berkeley, VA	April 4, 1841	March 4, 1841–April 4, 1841*	Whig
10. John Tyler	March 29, 1790	Greenway, VA	Jan. 18, 1862	April 6, 1841–March 3, 1845	Whig
11. James Knox Polk	Nov. 2, 1795	Mecklenburg Co., NC	June 15, 1849	March 4, 1845–March 3, 1849	Democratic
12. Zachary Taylor	Nov. 24, 1784	Orange Co., VA	July 9, 1850	March 4, 1849–July 9, 1850*	Whig
13. Millard Fillmore	Jan. 7, 1800	Locke, NY	March 8, 1874	July 10, 1850–March 3, 1853	Whig
14. Franklin Pierce	Nov. 23, 1804	Hillsboro, NH	Oct. 8, 1869	March 4, 1853–March 3, 1857	Democratic
15. James Buchanan	April 23, 1791	Mercersburg, PA	June 1, 1868	March 4, 1857–March 3, 1861	Democratic
16. Abraham Lincoln	Feb. 12, 1809	Hardin Co., KY	April 15, 1865	March 4, 1861–March 3, 1865	Republican
				March 4, 1865–April 15, 1865*	
17. Andrew Johnson	Dec. 29, 1808	Raleigh, NC	July 31, 1875	April 15, 1865–March 3, 1869	National Union
18. Ulysses Simpson Grant	April 27, 1822	Point Pleasant, OH	July 23, 1885	March 4, 1869–March 3, 1873	Republican
				March 4, 1873–March 3, 1877	
19. Rutherford Birchard Hayes	Oct. 4, 1822	Delaware, OH	Jan. 17, 1893	March 4, 1877–March 3, 1881	Republican
20. James Abram Garfield	Nov. 19, 1831	Orange, OH	Sept. 19, 1881	March 4, 1881–Sept. 19, 1881*	Republican
21. Chester Alan Arthur	Oct. 5, 1830	Fairfield, VT	Nov. 18, 1886	Sept. 20, 1881–March 3, 1885	Republican
22. Grover Cleveland	March 18, 1837	Caldwell, NJ	June 24, 1908	March 4, 1885–March 3, 1889	Democratic
23. Benjamin Harrison	Aug. 20, 1833	North Bend, OH	March 13, 1901	March 4, 1889–March 3, 1893	Republican
24. Grover Cleveland	March 18, 1837	Caldwell, NJ	June 24, 1908	March 4, 1893–March 3, 1897	Democratic
25. William McKinley	Jan. 29, 1843	Niles, OH	Sept. 14, 1901	March 4, 1897–March 3, 1901	Republican
				March 4, 1901–Sept. 14, 1901*	
26. Theodore Roosevelt	Oct. 27, 1858	New York, NY	Jan. 6, 1919	Sept. 14, 1901–March 3, 1905	Republican
				March 4, 1905–March 3, 1909	
27. William Howard Taft	Sept. 15, 1857	Cincinnati, OH	March 8, 1930	March 4, 1909–March 3, 1913	Republican
28. Woodrow Wilson	Dec. 28, 1856	Staunton, VA	Feb. 3, 1924	March 4, 1913–March 3, 1917	Democratic
				March 4, 1917–March 3, 1921	
29. Warren Gamaliel Harding	Nov. 2, 1865	Corsica, OH	Aug. 2, 1923	March 4, 1921–Aug. 2, 1923*	Republican
30. Calvin Coolidge	July 4, 1872	Plymouth, VT	Jan. 5, 1933	Aug. 3, 1923–March 3, 1925	Republican
				March 4, 1925–March 3, 1929	
31. Herbert Clark Hoover	Aug. 10, 1874	West Branch, IA	Oct. 20, 1964	March 4, 1929–March 3, 1933	Republican
32. Franklin Delano Roosevelt	Jan. 30, 1882	Hyde Park, NY	April 12, 1945	March 4, 1933–Jan. 20, 1937	Democratic
				Jan. 20, 1937–Jan. 20, 1941	
				Jan. 20, 1941–Jan. 20, 1945	
				Jan. 20, 1945–April 12, 1945*	
33. Harry S. Truman	May 8, 1884	Lamar, MO	Dec. 26, 1972	April 12, 1945–Jan. 20, 1949	Democratic
				Jan. 20, 1949–Jan. 20, 1953	
34. Dwight David Eisenhower	Oct. 14, 1890	Denison, TX	March 28, 1969	Jan. 20, 1953–Jan. 20, 1957	Republican
				Jan. 20, 1957–Jan. 20, 1961	
35. John Fitzgerald Kennedy	May 29, 1917	Brookline, MA	Nov. 22, 1963	Jan. 20, 1961–Nov. 22, 1963*	Democratic
36. Lyndon Baines Johnson	Aug. 27, 1908	near Stonewall, TX	Jan. 22, 1973	Nov. 22, 1963–Jan. 20, 1965	Democratic
				Jan. 20, 1965–Jan. 20, 1969	
37. Richard Milhous Nixon	Jan. 9, 1913	Yorba Linda, CA	April 22, 1994	Jan. 20, 1969–Jan. 20, 1973	Republican
				Jan. 20, 1973–Aug. 9, 1974**	
38. Gerald Rudolph Ford	July 14, 1913	Omaha, NE		Aug. 9, 1974–Jan. 20, 1977	Republican
39. James Earl Carter, Jr.	Oct. 1, 1924	Plains, GA		Jan. 20, 1977–Jan. 20, 1981	Democratic
40. Ronald Wilson Reagan	Feb. 6, 1911	Tampico, IL		Jan 20, 1981–Jan. 20, 1985	Republican
				Jan. 20, 1985–Jan 20, 1989	
41. George Herbert Walker Bush	June 12, 1924	Milton, MA		Jan. 20, 1989–Jan. 20, 1993	Republican
42. William Jefferson Clinton	Aug. 19, 1946	Hope, AR		Jan. 20, 1993–	Democratic

*Died while in office   **Resigned from office

Index of Picture Labels